Make the Grade.
Your Atomic Dog Online Edition.

The Atomic Dog Online Edition includes proven study tools that expand and enhance key concepts in your text. Reinforce and review the information you absolutely 'need to know' with features like:

- **Review Quizzes**
- Key term Assessments
- Interactive Animations and Simulations
- Notes and Information from Your Instructor
- Pop-up Glossary Terms
- A Full Text Search Engine

Ensure that you 'make the grade'. Follow your lectures, complete assignments, and take advantage of all your available study resources like the Atomic Dog Online Edition.

<u>How to Access Your Online Edition</u>

- **If you purchased this text directly from Atomic Dog ....**
  Visit atomicdog.com and enter your email address and password in the login box at the top-right corner of the page.

- **If you purchased this text NEW from another source....**
  Visit our Students' Page on atomicdog.com and enter the **activation key located below** to register and access your Online Edition.

- **If you purchased this text USED from another source....**
  Using the Book Activation key below you can access the Online Edition at a discounted rate. Visit our Students' Page on atomicdog.com and enter the **Book Activation Key in** the field provided to register and gain access to the Online Edition.

Be sure to download our *How to Use Your Online Edition* guide located on atomicdog.com to learn about additional features!

This key activates your online edition. Visit atomicdog.com to enter your Book Activation Key and start accessing your online resources. For more information, give us a call at (800) 310-5661 or send us an email at support@atomicdog.com

my822@yahoo.com
Vick0719

205AS4R36

PKG

CENGAGE
Learning™

*Some online Editions do not contain all features.

Production and Operations Management

Martin K. Starr

Second Edition

CENGAGE
Learning™

Australia • Brazil • Canada • Mexico • Singapore • Spain • United Kingdom • United States

Production and Operations Management,
Second Edition
Martin K. Starr

V.P Product Development: Dreis Van Landuyt

Development Editor: Sarah Blasco

Marketing Manager: Rob Bloom

Custom Production Editor: K.A. Espy

Permissions Specialist: Kalina Ingham Hintz

Manufacturing Manager: Donna M. Brown

Sr. Production Coordinator: Robin Richie

Technology Project Manager: Angela Makowski

Production Service: Rebecca Roby

Cover Designer: Phoenix Creative, LLC.

Cover Image: Getty Images

Compositor: KGL/Cadmus

For product information and technology assistance, contact us at
Cengage Learning Customer & Sales Support, 1-800-354-9706

For permission to use material from this text or product,
submit all requests online at **cengage.com/permissions**
Further permissions questions can be emailed to
permissionrequest@cengage.com

Library of Congress Control Number: 2007940200

ISBN-13: 978-1-426-63705-6
ISBN-10: 1-426-63705-5

PKG ISBN-13: 978-1-426-63057-6
PKG ISBN-10: 1-426-63057-3

Cengage Learning
5191 Natorp Blvd.
Mason, OH 45040
USA

Cengage Learning is a leading provider of customized learning solutions with office locations around the globe, including Singapore, the United Kingdom, Australia, Mexico, Brazil, and Japan. Locate your local office at:
international.cengage.com/region

Cengage Learning products are represented in Canada by Nelson Education, Ltd.

Visit Atomic Dog online at **atomicdog.com**
Visit our corporate website at **cengage.com**

Printed in the United States of America
1 2 3 4 5 6 7 11 10 09 08

Brief Contents

Contents

Chapter 3 Demand Creation and Predictive Planning   71

Chapter 4 Understanding Quality: Its Management and Strategic Importance   103

Chapter 8 Management of Technology (MOT) 281

Chapter 9 Teamwork Planning Requires Job Design 319

Chapter 10 Supply Chain Capacity Planning   365

Chapter Outline   365

Chapter 13 Aggregate Planning to Balance Supply and Demand   509

Chapter 14 Inventory Management for Smooth and Continuous Demand Patterns   551

Chapter 15 Material Requirements Planning (MRP) for Sporadic Demand Patterns 601

Chapter 16   Production Scheduling for Manufacturing and Service Operations   645

Chapter 17   Cycle-Time Management Increases Productivity   691

Special Characteristics

Production and Operations Management, 2nd Edition, is a mid-level textbook that teaches the complete MBA introductory course for the field of P/OM. First, it presents all of the concepts essential to understanding strategies and tactics in the P/OM field. Second, it provides problem solving of the quantitative decision issues that are always associated with P/OM.

This text allows students with a solid P/OM systems-oriented framework to connect P/OM decisions with those of the other functional field managers (e.g., finance, marketing, human resource management, accounting). Interconnectedness is the way that successful business operates. That explains why managers always praise the systems approach. Then, why are most textbooks not written with the systems approach?

The answer is a surprising one, namely, the organization of business schools does not follow the systems approach. In most business-school buildings, marketing, finance, general management, accounting, and P/OM are physically separated. Being on different floors, or different compartments, professors wave to each other in the lobby. Since they seldom talk with each other about business, they cannot plan or teach cross-functional curricula. P/OM may be housed together with quantitative methods or with general management.

Therein lies another interesting aspect of this book. P/OM is not only a cross-functional field, it is also a composite of both organizational behavior and quantitative methods. People, technology, and materials are blended together in the *process* for producing goods and services. It is P/OM's responsibility to make the parts work together in a harmonious composition. The creation of this book is founded on the principle that P/OM education must deal simultaneously with the qualitative aspects of general management of the organization and the quantitative analysis of the best way to make such *processes* operate.

Only from a platform of properly blended qualitative and quantitative concepts, insights, and experiences is it feasible to include cross-functional issues that impact process decisions. The traditional textbook works on the premise that in business schools, functional subjects are taught as separate and individual entities. The quality of business decisions will not be enhanced by that approach. As a result, companies reward career skills that enable cross-talk between functions. Problem solving is improved with cross-fertilization. Profit margins rise. Continuity and sustainability increase. In this age of as much total interconnectedness as possible, P/OM is ascending in the organization to a strong position of leadership. This book is dedicated to that proposition.

Seven Attributes

(1)   This text is online and in paperback.

Production and Operations Management, 2nd Edition, is a multimedia publication of Atomic Dog/Cengage Learning. This Cincinnati-based company is famous for simultaneously providing two forms of publication: (1) online interactive Internet publications and (2) the equivalent book in paperback. Students may purchase access to the online edition as a stand-alone product. The paperback text is optional. Atomic Dog is famous for its production system capabilities, which result in high-quality books at price levels that students can afford.

(2)   **The systems viewpoint prevails throughout.**

The systems viewpoint is how companies actually look at problems. The systems view has a strong applications orientation, which, to use baking as an analogy, means baking real bread instead of talking about the theory of baking bread. As another example, ballgames are not won by talking a good game. When P/OM is taught with the systems perspective, it is like having the master baker or the winning coach as your instructor. The systems perspective champions application over theory and problem solving over philosophical discussions.

(3)   **Global perspective.**

The author's background combines academic pursuits with global consulting assignments that require understanding how P/OM interacts with creating, making, and selling goods and services in a variety of industries and cultures throughout the world. That is what the author calls *global-literacy*. This text strives to incorporate the best practices of the global masters of processes as well as the dynamic state of the global marketplace. The systems approach requires "sticking your nose in everyone's business." There are so many links throughout the book and they lead to sites all over the world. This is new technology that energizes the mandate of global-literacy.

(4)   **Strategy and tactics.**

Strategy requires the exercise of qualitative thinking based on (and even driven by) quantitative tactical knowledge. Quantitative activity starts with numbers such as sales per year, output per day, and labor costs per hour. The numbers can be added, averaged, multiplied, divided, and used for percentages. All of these are quantitative exercises. This text recognizes the importance to management of quantitative analyses related to percent defects, order quantities, discounts, workforce, and production schedules. A proper blend of qualitative issues and quantitative analyses produces *concept-literacy* and *numerical literacy*. A good MBA education requires such complete qualitative (strategic) and quantitative (tactical) coverage. Great managers excel at both forms of literacy.

(5)   **Alternative methods to solve problems.**

Understanding the nature of a problem is the first step in solving a problem. There are often alternative ways to solve problems. For example, problems can be analyzed with logic and common sense, and then solved using good rules of thumb (heuristics). Some problems have inputs (data) and outputs (results) that occur repeatedly and follow classic analyses. These problems (e.g., linear programs) are software-scalable from small-scale to large-scale models. Spreadsheets are very scalable. Once a problem is diagnosed and the solution template developed, the cost of solution is related to the time required to input data and the care required to control input errors.

Production and Operations Management, 2nd Edition, relates to software called QuantMethods Production/Operations Management (QMpom). These are programs that are dedicated to the solution of generic problems, e.g., inventory management, linear programming, forecasting, and queuing. QMpom makes it possible for students to concentrate on having relevant input data for each problem and proper interpretation of solutions. Good business analysis requires knowing what needs to be quantified and what should be treated qualitatively. Understanding how to resolve problems necessitates using appropriate methods to provide optimum cost/benefits.

(6)   **The text has a modular construction.**

This book is designed to be modular. That means various parts of the book can be arranged in different orders. The flexibility of this text, especially with respect to how parts are sequenced, permits the teacher to customize materials to his or her own course preferences. The traditional course moves through the parts in conventional order (1->2->3->4). However, starting with Part 4 followed by Parts 1->2->3 emphasizes the importance of change management. Chapters can be skipped, especially in the tactical sections of Parts 2 and 3. For example, MRP can be saved for a later course on inventory planning methods.

(7) **Text materials emphasize business literacy and current events.**

The *business-literacy* of this text is in step with the fact that production and operations managers must be extremely well-informed about everything that is going on in the world of business. This text emphasizes business literacy in the *current business climate*. Online publication technology used for this text makes possible total timeliness. Being business-literate means that students using this text are exposed to topics that are under discussion in the boardrooms of major global companies—not years later, but in real time. Students appreciate the currency of their learning materials.

Organization of the Book

Prologue

A prologue should be a clarifying announcement before the curtain rises; it is more than an introduction before the serious discussion has begun. All of the wisdom that the author has gained in taking this project from its beginning to its end is shared with the audience here. That is the purpose of the Prologue. It explains the fundamental relationships between the managers in the business. It reveals their involvement with P/OM and with each other. It is like a view from the top of the mountain—and accompanying this view is a dynamic graphic, which is first a 2D and then a 3D map. This is a chart that shows routes and destinations. The problems that will be encountered are what this book is all about.

Structure

Every chapter begins with a comprehensive list of Learning Objectives that are tied to materials provided throughout that chapter. The Learning Objectives contain major points to be mastered in the chapter, and students are advised to start each chapter by reading this list of points. Underlining major points that are not clear, and checking back after reading the chapter can help organize the great amount of new terms and unique concepts that P/OM comprises.

After completing each chapter, if some bullet-points are still vague, four steps are recommended: (1) Consult the key terms at the end of each chapter. (2) Find the text location for the appropriate key term, which is in boldface type with a note in the margin. (3) Read the text in that location to learn about the concept in the bullet list. (4) Consult the glossary.

Each chapter's content starts with a section titled "The Systems Viewpoint." This section illuminates the multifunctional connections that create a community of practice for the topics covered in that chapter. "The Systems Viewpoint" is followed by a section titled "Strategic Thinking." After the systems elements are understood, the strategic implications of this viewpoint are explained. These two sections are meant to elevate chapter contents to the level of thinking that managers value.

Real-World Themes with Spotlights

Two to three Spotlights in each chapter offer anecdotal insights about P/OM. For example, there are stories about business successes and failures, entrepreneurial persistence, ethical challenges, well-known secrets[1] of leadership, and mastery of special decision models that are often used by business but seldom taught in P/OM introductory courses.

Showcasing actual companies and individuals, Spotlights illuminate often hidden subjects with real-world themes such as: Stanford University's AIM providing hundreds of

---

1. A great example of an oxymoron is "well-known secret." In fact, the secrets are available to everyone but only smart managers pay attention.

online plant visits[2] and attention to the success of small- and medium-size companies (e.g., Boutwell, Owens & Company, Global Concepts, Inc., McIlhenny Corp., and Modern Plumbing, Inc.).

There are Spotlights on understanding the nature of innovation; e-shopping, and why every bottle of Tabasco® tastes the same. The Spotlight is turned on Shouldice Hospital, which pioneered flow shop surgery for zero-defects in hernia repair, and on HEC in Montréal, where P/OM strives to improve performance of every hospital function. Efforts are made to answer what makes Chick-fil-A® and Starbucks® so successful, and why Toyota's founders credit Henry Ford as responsible for their company's success. Spotlights hone in on pressing issues of job creation, attitudes of different generations of workers, the use of benchmarking to improve performance, and regulation by the Sarbanes–Oxley (SOX) Act, which impacts P/OM in many ways.

Problems Section

A Problems Section appears in each of the twenty chapters. On average, there are 20 problems per chapter, which results in approximately 400 problems total. These problems are worked out in the Instructor's Manual in Word documents and in the Solutions Manual as PDF files. In addition, Excel spreadsheet solutions are provided for many of the problems. Also, there are numerous references to the QMpom software which is discussed further below.

Enrichment Activities (EA)

There are 20 Enrichment Activities, one for each chapter of the text. These EAs provide additional materials to enhance the discussions found in that P/OM chapter. A set of problem questions, referred to as Enrichment Challenges, accompany each Enrichment Activity to further develop the concepts discussed.

The EA topics are listed below in chronological order. An asterisk is used to denote eight entirely new EA topics as distinguished from the thirteen that had appeared in the first edition as "Supplements."

The first ten EA topics are: (1) Decision Models, (2) Decision Trees, (3) Forecasts Using Exponential Smoothing Methodology, (4) A Scoring Model for Comparing Alternative Gas Station Designs (based on the HOQ), (5) How Purchasing Managers Use Hedging to Control Cost Fluctuations, (6) A Total Productive Maintenance Model, (7) Small Lot Quality Acceptance using Hypergeometric O.C. Curves, (8) Net Present Value (NPV) Modeling, (9) Ergonomics (also known as) Human Factors, (10) The Breakeven Decision Model for Supply Chain Planning.

The second ten EA topics are: (11*) Real and Spurious Correlations using Correlation Coefficients and the Coefficient of Determination, (12*) Scoring Model for Certification of Suppliers, (13*) Aggregate Scheduling using the Transportation Model (TM) with Backorders Allowed, (14*) When Should Just-in-Time (JIT) Be Used by Buyers? (15) Part-Period, Lot-Sizing Policy for MRP, (16*) Increasing Bottleneck Capacity, (17) Simulation of Queuing Models, (18*) PERT/Cost/Time (and Quality), (19*) Ferris Wheel Model for Continuous New Product Development, (20*) The Calculation of Lifetime Value (LTV) Losses.

Online and in Print

Production and Operations Management, 2nd Edition, is available online as well as in print. The online version demonstrates how the interactive media components of the text enhance presentation and understanding. For example,

- Animated illustrations help clarify concepts and bring them to life.
- Clickable glossary terms provide immediate definitions of key concepts.

---

2. Alliance for Innovative Manufacturing (See Spotlight 1-1).

- References and footnotes "pop up" with a click.
- Highlighting capabilities allow students to emphasize main ideas. They can also add personal notes in the margin.
- The search function allows students to quickly locate discussions of specific topics throughout the text.
- An interactive study guide at the end of each chapter provides tools for learning with interactive key-term matching and the ability to review customized content in one place.

Students may choose to use just the online version of the text or both the online and print versions together. This gives them the flexibility to choose which combination of resources works best for them. To assist those who use the online and print version together, the primary heads and subheads in each chapter are numbered the same. For example, the first primary head in Chapter 1 is labeled 1-1, the second primary head in Chapter 1 is labeled 1-2, and so on. The subheads build from the designation of their corresponding primary head: 1-1a, 1-1b, etc. This numbering system is designed to make moving between the online and print versions as seamless as possible.

Finally, next to a number of figures and exhibits in the print version of the text, you will see an icon similar to the one shown below. This icon indicates that this figure or exhibit in the Online Edition is interactive in a way that applies, illustrates, or reinforces the concept.

Ancillary Support

Atomic Dog/Cengage Learning is pleased to offer a robust suite of supplemental materials for instructors using its textbooks. These ancillaries include a Test Bank in ExamViewPro software, PowerPoint® slides, Solutions Manual, and Instructor's Manual.

The Test Bank for this book includes more than 700 carefully constructed questions in a wide range of difficulty levels, including true or false, multiple-choice, short-answer questions, and answers. The Test Bank offers not only the correct answer for each question, but also a rationale or explanation for the correct answer and a reference—the location in the chapter where materials addressing the question content can be found. This Test Bank comes with ExamViewPro software for easily creating customized or multiple versions of a test, and includes the option of editing or adding to the existing question bank.

A full set of PowerPoint slides—approximately 600—is available for this text. This is designed to provide instructors with comprehensive visual aids for each chapter in the book. These slides include outlines of each chapter, highlighting important terms, concepts, and discussion points.

The Solutions Manual presents a solution in PDF format for every problem in the Problems Section of each chapter. Also, in the Solutions Manual, the answers for the Enrichment Challenges are presented in PDF format. Some problems are worked out long-hand; others have suggested solutions using Excel spreadsheets and/or the recommended software, QMpom, for this text. Many problems are solved in more than one way.

The Instructor's Manual provides backup and reinforcement, revisualization, and new imaginative ideas for the materials in the text. Teachers can copy materials from the IM for student handouts in class. Here is what the Instructor's Manual contains:

- Lecture/lesson plans
- Brief but cogent summaries of every section in the text, including glossary definitions for key terms

- Answers to the Spotlight review questions that are provided in the text with each of the 41 Spotlights
- Answers to the Review Questions found in the text
- Answers to the Practice Quiz questions found in the text
- Answers to all items in each chapter's Problems Section.
- Answers to the Enrichment Challenges in each chapter's Enrichment Activity
- Web exercises
- Critical Thinking exercises with suggested answers
- Team exercises
- Essay questions with suggested answers
- A list of additional Resources

Optional Material Provided on the Instructor's Resource CD

Several cases are provided as optional material for this text, including:

TOM's of Maine. Colgate has purchased Tom's of Maine but is committed to allowing the company to run with the same set of high-placed values for environmental protection, eschewing animal testing, and with a great emphasis on helping out in the Maine community that is home. A major P/OM focus is on product quality.

Rosenbluth International, now a fully absorbed part of American Express, provides an historical example of production and operations management excellence in a service environment. A major P/OM focus is on service quality, which was the Rosenbluth International hallmark.

The Saturn Project case presents an important historical story about the development of an incredible new company and its eventual decline. This is a lesson in the annals of the American automobile industry. This case describes the start-up of the Saturn Corporation by the General Motors Corporation. The case tracks the first fourteen years of Saturn's evolution and its impact as an environmental champion with a trendsetting line of autos designed for recycling. What occurred that led to the end of the dream about automobile production at the Saturn plant in Spring Hill, Tennessee? The history of the Saturn Corporation is an invaluable lesson for students of P/OM. A major P/OM focus is on environmental protection and sustainability.

QMpom Software

This text can be supported by unique and powerful optimization software with a browser interface that operates on PCs and MACs, with the familiar Windows format. The software works as well, for those who prefer it, with a UNIX environment. This software will solve problems for most significant P/OM models that are described and used in *Production and Operations Management*, 2nd Edition. For example, problems in forecasting, queuing, and inventory theory are solved quickly and directly online. The data inputs are simple and straightforward. The solution methods for all of these numerical problems do not have to be understood by the student. The interpretation of the output solutions follows in line with the descriptions in the text. The outputs are concise and include graphical charts and tables. There is a Help Manual for all of the models. The software package known as QuantMethods Production/Operations Management (QMpom) is available at http://www.quantmethods.com.

About Atomic Dog

Atomic Dog is faithfully dedicated to meeting the needs of today's faculty and students, offering a unique and clear alternative to the traditional textbook. Breaking down textbooks and study tools into their basic "atomic parts," we then recombine them and utilize rich digital media to create a "new breed" of textbook.

This blend of online content, interactive multimedia, and print creates unprecedented adaptability to meet different educational settings and individual learning styles. As part of Cengage Learning, we offer even greater flexibility and resources in creating a learning solution tailor-fit to your course.

Atomic Dog is loyally dedicated to our customers and our environment, adhering to three key tenets:

Focus on essential and quality content: We are proud to work with our authors to deliver a high-quality textbook at a lower cost. We focus on the essential information and resources students need, and present them in an efficient but student-friendly format.

Value and choice for students: Our products are a great value and provide students with more choices in "what and how" they buy—often at savings of 30 to 40 percent less than traditional textbooks. Students who choose the Online Edition may see even greater savings compared to a print textbook. Faculty play an important and willing role—working with us to keep costs low for their students by evaluating texts and supplementary materials online.

Reducing our environmental "paw-print": Atomic Dog is working to reduce its impact on our environment in several ways. Our textbooks and marketing materials are all printed on recycled paper. We encourage faculty to review text materials online instead of requesting a print review copy. Students who buy the Online Edition do their part by going "paperless" and eliminating the need for additional packaging or shipping. Atomic Dog will continue to explore new ways that we can reduce our "paw-print" in the environment and hope you will join us in these efforts.

Atomic Dog is dedicated to faithfully serving the needs of faculty and students—providing a learning tool that helps make the connection. We hope that after you try our texts, Atomic Dog—like other great dogs—will become your faithful companion.

Acknowledgments

I thank Polly Starr for her solid research contributions. This text would not have been so far-reaching, current, literate, and diverse without Polly's research and writings. She authored the spotlights. They are gourmet fare for those who appreciate history and the joy of insights that her research has revealed. I appreciate the valuable hours of discussion about the cases, basic philosophical issues, and proper pedagogy with her.

I thank my colleagues, Dr. Jim Gilbert and Dr. Henrique Correa (both of the Crummer Graduate School of Business, Rollins College). Jim provided real life contributions as we worked together on various consulting projects that enhanced my perceptions about how things should work if P/OM is properly used. In discussions with Henrique Correa about P/OM at the Resende Plant, I absorbed valuable cross-cultural insights. P/OM in Brazil is not quite the same as P/OM in the United States. There are important differences in viewpoints concerning how to handle problems and decisions. These differences apply directly to what a good P/OM text must have, i.e., cultural breadth, depth and flexibility.

My thanks to Dr. Britt M. Shirley of the University of Tampa for the Instructor's Manual, which adds richness and power to the entire package of teaching methods and concepts. I am grateful to Dr. Marilyn M. Helms of Dalton State College for her incredible team efforts in building thousands of modular exam questions that are found in the ExamView Test Bank, all of which are accessible on the Instructor's Resource CD that is a valued part of Atomic Dog's pedagogical ancillaries.

Some of the greatest lessons about P/OM I have learned from my colleague Dr. Sushil Gupta at Florida International University (FIU). Sushil is a master teacher. Guided by "the big picture" he has created insightful and attractive spreadsheets that help students learn about the nature of P/OM problems. One of my students said that solving problems on Professor Gupta's spreadsheets is like having pancakes with real maple syrup. Run-of-the-mill spreadsheets are like corn syrup. Professor Gupta's spreadsheets are on the IRCD for this text.

Most importantly, I want to acknowledge contributions of the Atomic Dog team. Steve Scoble initiated the POM 1e project. Many organizational changes have occurred since then. Laureen Ranz took over from Steve. She provided great insight, leadership, and solid development work. Then, an organizational change occurred once again and Sarah Blasco assumed the leadership role. Sarah's verve and creativity led the project to an ever-greater (team-driven) successful culmination. I applaud Sarah for her ability to deal with complexity with calm and assurance. On the production floor, where books are made using a host of P/OM skills, Tina Espy, Custom Production Editor, has orchestrated the production of a beautiful structure for *POM* 2e.

Our team has produced a truly high-quality product that is the holy grail of P/OM perfectionists. Great production calls for open minds, strong support, wide-ranging vision, and creative mentalities. These were given in abundance from all of the above and many not mentioned. I acknowledge their contributions with thanks and appreciation.

Martin K. Starr

**Martin K. Starr** is Distinguished Professor Emeritus of Production and Operations Management and Management Science at the Crummer Graduate School of Business, Rollins College, in Winter Park, Florida. Starr is also Professor Emeritus of Operations Research and Management Science at Columbia University's Graduate School of Business, where he established the Production and Operations Management Department with a systems orientation. Professor Starr was Director of the Center for Enterprise Management (CEM) at both Columbia University and Rollins College. CEM's agenda included research, publication, and related consulting.

At Columbia, CEM was known for its studies that tracked and compared the performance of U.S. firms with Japanese firms in America for seven consecutive years. Later, this benchmarking was extended to European firms in America. CEM at Rollins benchmarked supply chain performance in the healthcare system. It developed cost/benefit simulation models to determine optimal mix of nursing services and technology. Other studies involved reengineering plant layout and how companies use computer training and distance learning.

Professor Starr has published 25 books on various subjects including texts on inventory, operations management, systems management, global alliances, executive decisions and product design. Starr has published over 100 articles on such topics as modular product design, rapid and continuous project management, product variety and diversity, systems engineering, knowledge management, intellectual property value, teaching students to be effective consultants, marketing dynamics, and security operations and disaster management.

Starr is past president of TIMS (The Institute of Management Sciences–now part of INFORMS) and past president of POMS (Production and Operations Management Society). He is currently Chair of the Council of POMS Presidents. He was editor-in-chief of the journal *Management Science* for 15 years. In addition to societal activities, Starr has been consultant to many companies including AT&T, ABB, Boston Consulting Group, Bristol-Myers Squibb, Citibank, CNL, Chrysler, DuPont, Eastman Kodak (Rochester and Cape Town), ExxonMobil, Fiat, GE Capital, Hendry Corporation, HP, IBM, Lever Brothers, Merrill Lynch, Phillips Electronics, Yacimientos Petroliferos Fiscales de Argentina (YPF), and Young & Rubicam.

In 2006, the Production and Operations Management Society Board of Directions named the society's highest award in honor of Starr through the establishment of the *Martin K. Starr Excellence in POM Practice (E-POMP) Award* in his name. The award is based on exceptional quality of contribution and innovation made to the field of production and operations management by POM practitioners. It is an international award, open to all POM practitioners from around the world.

Our subject, "production and operations management," is about *making goods* (such as cars, cans of soup, and computers) and, equally, about *providing services* (such as food, transportation, entertainment, education, and health care). Essential and basic to all of these activities is *doing work well* that *transforms something to something more valuable.*

Throughout this text, goods and services are referred to as products. Although a firm may be goods-oriented or service-oriented, successful firms increasingly recognize that they must deal with both the goods they sell and the services they provide. U.S. car companies might be more successful if they saw themselves as providing services to customers who buy their automobiles. Lexus and Acura excel in that commitment to their customers. On the other hand, restaurants do not prosper when their service is shabby, no matter how good their food. Usually, however, excellence in both goods and services occur together. Customers are not pleased when only one or the other is excellent.

To earn revenue, production and operations teams must provide transformations that have *value for customers*. The goods and services must also add value to the assets of *the transforming agent* (which is the company). The revenue earned must have a margin of profit that rewards investors and sustains the business for employees over long periods of time. Although core P/OM methods, materials, technology, and skills change over time, the goals of the P/OM field have not been altered. *Excel* at job performance to *satisfy* the customers and earn a profit to *sustain* the organization.

This book is about excelling, satisfying, and sustaining. Doing the job well means delivering *products* of qualities that match or exceed customer expectations. Companies strive to do this with high productivity. Chapter 2 explains why attainment of high levels of productivity is so critical to success. As a start, eliminating waste raises productivity. Smart work methods have low costs and on-time deliveries. High customer satisfaction promotes an additional benefit. Employees prefer to work for a company that generates and maintains strong customer loyalty. Customers are rarely satisfied when employees are disgruntled. Therefore, company policies that promote worker loyalty are more likely to produce happy customers, too.

The second edition of *Production and Operations Management* (called POM 2e) stresses the importance of strategic partnerships—between P/OM and all functional areas of the company—to *do the job well,* which is essential for success. To define/understand "functional areas," see the glossary of this text and study Figures PRL-1 and PRL-2.

POM 2e explains why the systems approach is necessary to achieve strategic partnerships with all functional domains of the firm. For the moment, the best translation of "the systems approach" is to "see the big picture as a guiding principle." Using a sports example, the average time between taking shots at the hoop for all players is a systems measure. The score of the highest scoring player is not. The systems measure is complex. A high number can be good or bad depending upon points for baskets, turnovers, etc.

The Prologue is new and first appears in this text edition (POM 2e). It has been added to reinforce the building of relationships needed to understand how strategic partnerships work. Getting business functions to work together in strategic partnerships can best be taught in business schools using P/OM as the core, or the hub of a wheel (refer to Figure PRL-1).

The hub position for P/OM is sensible because P/OM is custodian of the supply chain and caretaker of product qualities. This incredible responsibility cannot be assumed by finance, or marketing, etc., even if one of these other functions wanted to do so. It is not suited to the goals and abilities of finance, human resource management, marketing, research and development, engineering, accounting, and the many tangential functions that are suggested by Figure PRL-2.

The systems mission to integrate and coordinate functions must be understood to achieve success in making, selling, and distributing products (goods and services). For

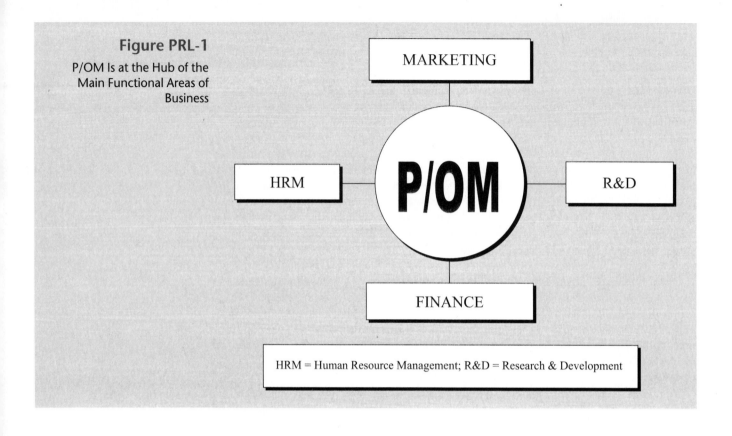

Figure PRL-1

P/OM Is at the Hub of the Main Functional Areas of Business

HRM = Human Resource Management; R&D = Research & Development

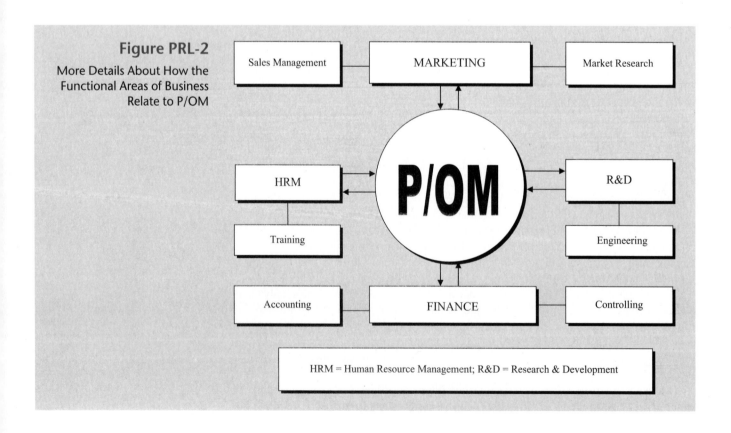

Figure PRL-2

More Details About How the Functional Areas of Business Relate to P/OM

HRM = Human Resource Management; R&D = Research & Development

example, marketing is not the only function focused on getting and keeping customers for the product. Sales may be in the trenches contacting customers but other functions are doing their part behind the scenes. Sales and marketing had to participate in choosing the product line, but this decision is not made by marketing alone. If done correctly, the entire organization participates in strategic thinking about what to make and sell. P/OM needs to be consulted about the feasibility of any strategy. Can the product be made and delivered at an appropriate cost, and with qualities that provide profit opportunities? Cost and price determine profit margin. P/OM process experts must be consulted. P/OM decisions are intrinsic to profit margin goals and achievements.

Strong teamwork supports increased profit margins. Functionally integrated teams are powerful competitors. Such teams consist of production and operations, marketing, finance, accounting, human resource management, research, engineering, and all other business units, which work together to achieve corporate objectives. Put another way, these functional units cooperate as an integrated system in performing activities aimed at achieving the company's goals. They pool knowledge, experience, skills, and abilities.

Although our field of study is P/OM, it is important to note how the other functional fields play their roles. Not only cooperation—but also coordination—is required to pursue and achieve the company's objectives. The way in which coordination is achieved using communication can be best illustrated by two graphics. First, Figure PRL-3 shows seven system stages in a flat world representation. Second, Figure PRL-4 shows the seven system stages in a hierarchical arrangement. The seven system stages, cutting across all business functions, contribute to formulating and carrying out company strategy.

Figure PRL-3 is a beginning guide for explaining the seven rings (or stages) that strongly impact P/OM strategy. Refer to Figure PRL-3 as each ring (or stage) is discussed. This will help to relate the parts to the whole, i.e., to fathom the big picture.

The seven stages have a natural sequence for discussion, which starts with ring 1 (product design—in the center) and goes to ring 7 (sustainability of the business over time—at the outside). Each stage leads logically to the next stage. However, all of the stages interact and all of the seven simultaneously exist. In spite of good planning, reasonable sequences of cause and effect can sometimes produce unsatisfactory results. For example, if it is found that a product design cannot be made at a reasonable price by any process the engineers can devise, then it will be necessary to go back and redesign the product.

When problems occur, they trigger feedback loops—i.e., return to earlier stages (ring numbers) to remove problems, change outcomes, and improve results. Feedback means that outcomes in an outer (larger–later) ring can lead to revision of decisions made earlier. In other words, reconsideration of decisions made in smaller-earlier rings is part of the design process. Thus, *process design* problems (in ring 2) lead to reevaluation and change of *product design* decisions in ring 1. As an example that illustrates the scope of feedback, an environmental problem encountered at stage 7 may require corrections to be made at any (and even all) prior stages, including initial strategic decisions about product design (stage 1).

Part 1 of this text, entitled Strategic Perspectives for Product Line Planning, consists of four chapters. The goal of strategic planning is to achieve organizational objectives. If the current product line does not achieve current organizational objectives, then the product line must be completely reevaluated. The fact that a company is committed to an entire product line (of established items, services, or combinations) does not alter the fact that strategic planning of the product line is best done without shackles and constraints of present commitments. This gives an advantage to newcomers (called greenfield start-ups as compared with brownfield modifications and corrections).

It is useful to strategize in this way—as if no commitment had been made. It is as if no special allegiances existed, no investments or polarized opinions, no history had to be explained and rationalized. Later, what is wished for—and what exists—can be aligned. It is also possible to change objectives when conditions such as the economy or competitive technology are altered. The crucial point is that once objectives are chosen, the guidance

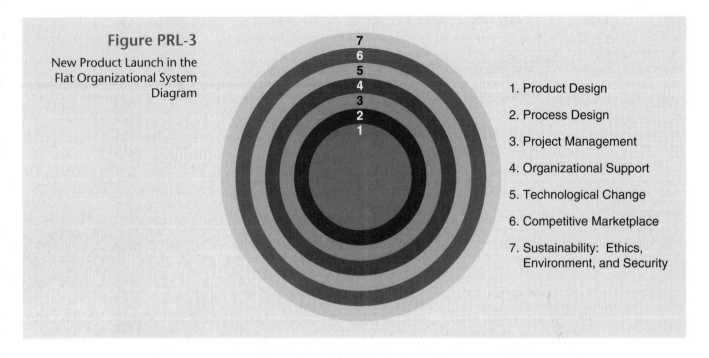

Figure PRL-3

New Product Launch in the
Flat Organizational System
Diagram

1. Product Design

2. Process Design

3. Project Management

4. Organizational Support

5. Technological Change

6. Competitive Marketplace

7. Sustainability: Ethics,
Environment, and Security

of the system is locked onto its own polar star. GPS navigation proceeds toward the same goal, no matter what the route selected, i.e., "quickest, scenic, or no-toll route" options.

Strategic planning involves the specifics elements of Figure PRL-3, moving from the innermost ring to the outermost ring. The rings will be discussed, one-by-one, starting with product design (also product line design). To dart-throwers and archers, ring 1 (the innermost circle in Figure PRL-3) contains the bull's eye. For marketplace competitors, it also contains the bull's eye. If this target is missed, it is impossible to win (successfully compete). This is the beginning of strategic planning. Ring 1 is the primary critical stage called *product design* (*product line design*) For established product lines, ring 1 can eventually lead to redesign, but that comes later on in the planning process.

For consistency, the rings in the figure will be called stages of development from now on, and until Figure PRL-4 is discussed.

Stage 1 includes goods and services—separately, and often together. For example, copy machines are manufactured goods purchased together with service and maintenance contracts. Other examples of goods and services (inherently coupled) include restaurants, supermarkets, hotels, airlines, schools, and hospitals. Quick-service restaurants (QSR) epitomize a critical conjunction of goods and services. The goods (foods) offered are accompanied by services (as important as foods) such as drive-through or in-store counter order and delivery, packaging, bagging, paying, parking, special-order cooking, getting the order right, and restroom cleanup.

Although the breadth of stage 1 strategies is industry dependent, an impressive range of creative ideas can be illustrated. Financial products such as ETF's (exchange-traded funds) have attracted hordes of new investors. Toyota's Prius surprised veterans of the car industry who thought they knew what customers did not want—i.e., hybrids. Stage 1 experts are frequently wrong. Toyota's product line sales of hybrids exceeded one million gas-electric vehicles worldwide in June 2007. Apple's iPod and Nintendo's Wii were unexpectedly successful stage 1 innovations. In every one of the surprise-success cases, the product line design was creative to begin with, but fine-tuning was used to feedback corrections.

Restaging mature products that have been through all of the rings is a tough job that starts with ring 1 again. The problems faced by a coach hired to revamp a losing team that had been world champions are considerable. Efforts to rejuvenate old restaurants often fail. One reason is that all surrounding rings have been affected by failure and have become part of the cause of that failure. Remedies for failure must be systems-wide. In the same vein, having a good product design does not guarantee a systems-wide winner. In addition to ring 1, *there are still six more ring fields to traverse.*

When old products lose their attractiveness in the marketplace, companies try to replace them with alluring alternatives. Sometimes, products can be repositioned by price changes and by advertising and marketing methods. New product success relies on all of the ring variables working together. However, if the product design fails to achieve objectives, then the entire system fails. The first link in the chain is crucially important but the chain consists of six additional links, which must function properly. Planning will now proceed to move outward from the center of Figure PRL-3.

Stage 2 (the second ring) represents *process design* (or later on, *redesign*). Process design applied to an entire product line is a bigger system to contend with than process design on a product-by-product basis. There are interactions to consider. An ideal process for one product may be detrimental for another product. That fact may lead to a process revision for both products. It may also lead to a product line redesign. Strategic thinking requires that the product line now and its evolution into the future be fully considered.

Process rings surround product rings because every product is made and delivered to the customer by a process. Without a producing process, there is no product—nothing to market. Badly designed processes deliver goods and services that are unacceptable to customers and company alike. Costs may be too high and production too slow. If quality is poor or inconsistent, customers will *not* repeat purchases. Returns and word of mouth complaints will take an increasingly heavy toll.

Success of the entire system is dependent upon designing processes that make and deliver products that fulfill or exceed stated quality standards. Accurate deliveries must be on time, without damage. Processes must provide profit margins that conform to plans or are better than planned. In not-for-profit situations, the benefits of services delivered should outweigh the costs.

Cost-benefit analyses are used to justify product and process decisions for both profit and non-profit systems. Since P/OM is the custodian of the process, it is essential that stages 1 and 2 be harmoniously interactive across the product line. In other words, the marketing, production, and engineering managers responsible for stages 1 and 2 need to cooperate. All must recognize it is impossible to design the product line independent of each other and their respective process considerations.

Ring number 3 in Figure PRL-3 represents the *project management stage*. Projects (represented by ring 3) surround stages 1 and 2. The reality is that projects are the method and procedures required to create and bring to fruition product line and process designs. Projects (are a system) composed of many interrelated project modules. These are sets of activities required to design the product line and the processes to make and deliver the goods and services.

Part 4 ("Changing the System") includes Chapter 18, "Project Management for New Products and Processes." Projects are neither strategies nor operational tactics. They are activities guided by strategies and aimed at developing operational tactics. Projects are organized plans for carrying out the wishes of the strategists. That is why "changing the system" is deferred until the last part of the book. At that point, there is sufficient knowledge about P/OM goals and objectives for the projects to be viewed realistically. Nevertheless, it is important to keep in mind that Parts 1, 2, and 3 of this text are brought about by means of projects (Part 1's title is "Strategic Perspectives for Product Line Planning"; Part 2's title is "Designing Processes"; Part 3's title is "Operating the System").

The three rings marked 1, 2, and 3 in Figure PRL-3 show how projects are the activities responsible for creating successful products and processes. Projects are not only the means to achieve new goals. Projects are also the means to change the status quo (by restaging). Fast-moving project completions can be critical. Getting to the marketplace before competitors can be crucial. The goal is to be in time to catch the demand wave that often motivates consumers to try the new product. Often, early-triers become brand loyal. This means that they are resistant to competitors' efforts to capture their loyalty and to switch them to the competitors' product lines.

Stage 4 (ring 4) in Figure PRL-3 represents *organizational support*. P/OM strategy must take into account the fact that projects flounder when organizational support is not broad, deep, and sustained. The fourth ring surrounds the other three rings because the inner-three will fail if the fourth stage is not fully committed to the strategy. When only part of the executive team supports the new product line, and/or believes that processes are well-designed, and/or approves of the project plan, then there is significant probability that the project will fail. On the other hand, with strong management agreement and with board commitment to project success, the odds-makers would raise the ante (the amount risked in a wager).

Stage 5 (ring 5) in Figure PRL-3 represents *technological change*, which is a key factor forcing organizational support for a new product line and consequent development of new processes. When the speed of memory chips goes up while the cost of those chips goes down (Moore's Law), the existing product line design can be outmoded in days. An organization that has not committed to change when confronted with the fact that its product line is technologically out-of-date will have to face the music or leave the theater. Discussions about technological change are provided in Chapter 8, "Management of Technology (MOT)." Some possible visions of technological changes that may be on the horizon are presented in Chapter 20 (see Section 20-5), "Readying Operations Management for Future Conditions."

Stage 6 (ring 6) in Figure PRL-3 represents the *marketplace*. Competition will determine the success of all previous stages. The marketplace decides which technologies (ring 5) survive, which will prosper, and which will be history. Some large automobile manufacturers are betting on ethanol. Others predict success for electric cars, or even hydrogen-based fuel, at a later date. Global mobile phone makers and telecommunication service competitors offer a rich array of plans, features, and prices. iPhones that work exclusively with AT&T's services reflected new expensive technology with an entirely different dialing system. At the introduction, pundits were not convinced that Apple could so radically revise consumer expectations.

Uncertainty about what the market will accept is based partly on price, but also technology and quality. Part 1, exploring P/OM's role in strategic planning, introduces important marketplace mechanisms such as price elasticity, customers' expectations (the customer's voice—House of Quality—Section 4-9a), and demand forecasting in Chapter 3. But even six interactive stages are not enough to explain the big (systems) picture that determines success or failure.

The final stage is number 7 in Figure PRL-3. This seventh ring represents *sustainability within the global social fabric*. Stage 7 includes ethics, environmental stewardship, and security. Stage 7, in an increasingly global world, dominates all of the previous stages. Sustainability has recently been recognized as a profit generator. On the other hand, impaired sustainability is a profit destroyer and a cause for failure. This new major global force must be understood to achieve success in creating the product line and launching new products to change existing product lines.

Stages 6, 5, 4, 3, 2, and 1 are surrounded by stage 7. In the *long run*, sustainability (stage 7) determines success and failure of companies that are competing for customers and employees in the global marketplace. It is increasingly powerful in medium and even in short-run time frames. A seemingly good plan at stages 1 and 2 can run aground when tested against stage 7 criteria.

The next step is to transform the flat circles into the management pyramid shown in Figure PRL-4. Communication linkages between managers are not realistically based on the flat organization of Figure PRL-3. In fact, management decision making emanates from level number 4 (not ring number 4). The idea behind Figure PRL-4 is that managers

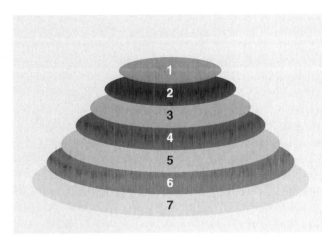

1. Product Design

2. Process Design

3. Project Management

4. Organizational Support

5. Technological Change

6. Competitive Marketplace

7. Sustainability: Ethics, Environment, and Security

Figure PRL-4

Diagram of the New Product Launch Atop the Seven-Level Tower

communicate up and down the *hierarchical* levels of the pyramid in Figure PRL-4. This concept produces a different perspective about the systems orientation and the nature of strategy and tactics.

From here on, the more appropriate terminology will discuss levels instead of stages. Rings are no longer a relevant label.

Top management, residing and operating at level 4, must be aware of what is going on at all levels. Managers communicate both up and down: up to the project managers who, in turn, communicate with the process engineers and new product designers; down to those managers who are doing technology assessments at level 5. At first glance, it may seem that level 5 has nothing to do with the product and process designing functions at levels 1 and 2. In fact, the technology being used at levels 1 and 2 can become passé in the blink of an eye. Level 1 and 2 designers must be aware of possible transitions that occur because of developments at level 5. Top management must decide which technologies pass through its osmotic barrier to become new products and enabling processes.

Figure PRL-4 also shows that management decision making at level 4 must be able to deal with marketplace reactions at level 6. Level 6 uses business intelligence (BI), discussed in Spotlight 12-2, and calls upon market research to guide future decision making.

Level 7 of Figure PRL-4 is the global, social fabric that interweaves ethics and environmental issues. The ethical factors are often culture-driven. There are also security problems that relate to the fact that emergent methods of terrorism provide power and economic reward to those who attempt to disable existing systems. Although level 7 is the newest level that concerns the P/OM field, it is the level that demands increasing amounts of management attention. Management at level 4 must reach far down (and up) to comprehend the environmental issues, problems of ethics, and systems of security that relate to effects of decisions made at level 4 about projects (3) for changing the product line and the enabling processes.

The special relevance of Figure PRL-4 should be evident because the flat world of Figure PRL-3 does not explain the complexity of management needing to look in two different ways. Not only is there a doorway effect with a need to look in two different directions, but there is also the distance that must be traveled to integrate strategies and tactics across all seven levels (see Spotlight 11-2: Don't Separate Strategy and Tactics). Management at level 4 must reach up three levels and down three levels to make certain that tactics are congruent with strategies. This is essential if strategies are to be effective.

Strategic Perspectives for Product Line Planning

Figure PT1-1 Strategic Planning for the New Product Line of Goods and Services

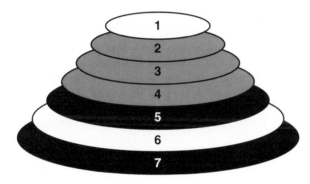

1. Product Design

2. Process Design

3. Project Management

4. Organizational Support

5. Technological Change

6. Competitive Marketplace

7. Sustainability: Ethics, Environment, and Security

Strategic planning begins with clear specifications about the new product line which is composed of both goods and services. This includes who is buying the output; how much is being bought; what prices are being charged; what qualities are promised, what are the delivery schedules, etc. Management must consider the entire system to focus on success. Figure PT1-1 highlights the linkage of levels 1 and 6 with strong connections to levels 2, 3 and 4.

Chapter 1 (Product Line Planning and the Systems Approach) is the entry portal for strategic planning. Strategic planning requires that the product line be designed using the systems approach. An alternate name for the systems approach is "the big picture." Note in Figure PT1-1, level 1 rests on all six levels below it in the pyramid as its foundation.

Chapter 2 (Productivity and Strategic Planning) explains how to measure productivity and how it has strategic importance. High levels of productivity are obtained only when level 1 planning enables level 2 process designs that provide high output rates at low costs with quality standards assured. This epitomizes efficient processes that result from competent application of the systems approach.

Chapter 3 (Demand Creation and Predictive Planning) explains demand forecasting and predictive planning for the product line. Ability to forecast demand is based on being able to predict the results of different prices, product features and their qualities. Product line design is based on proactive thinking, meaning design strategies are fashioned to create demand at a cost and price that will provide good returns on investments. The alternative is to passively design a product line and then try to guess what demand will result. P/OM's responsibility is to create supply levels that match demand levels. Large costs occur if P/OM misses in either direction, i.e., over- or under-supply to match demand.

Chapter 4 (Understanding Quality: Its Strategic Importance) builds an understanding of quality which is critical at all levels. TQM (total quality management) applies to the product and process (levels 1 and 2). At level 4, the organizational support for quality must be total. The marketplace must evaluate the competitive qualities (level 6). Quality is a major component of strategic planning. Consumer demand is driven by value, which is roughly approximated as quality divided by price. Price and quality are both related to costs, and costs are an integral component of productivity. To take all of the elements into account, the systems approach is essential.

Product Line Planning and the Systems Approach

chapter

1

Chapter 1 defines production and operations management (P/OM) and explains how this management field is applicable to both manufacturing and services. It also elaborates on the advantages of the systems perspective, which links production and operations management to all other managerial functions in the organization.

After reading this chapter, you should be able to:

- Define and explain operations management and contrast it with production management.
- Explain categories of the systems approach and why they are important to P/OM.
- Detail the systems approach that is used by P/OM.
- Understand how P/OM—using the systems approach—increases the competitive effectiveness of the organization.
- Understand why this text is titled *Production and Operations Management*.
- Distinguish between the application of P/OM to manufacturing and services.
- Explain how special P/OM capabilities provide competitive advantages.
- Relate information systems to the distinction between production and operations.
- Explain how the input–output (I/O) model defines production and operations.
- Describe the stages of development of companies with respect to OM and P/OM.
- Discuss positions in P/OM that exist in the organization and career success in P/OM as a function of process types.
- Explain the effects of globalization on P/OM careers.

The Systems Viewpoint

Chapter 1 explains production and operations management (P/OM). Chapter 1 also shows how P/OM relates to strategic planning and the systems viewpoint. The systems point of view requires consideration of P/OM dealing with all business functions, such as marketing and finance.

It is easy to say "P/OM," but it takes a long time to say "production and operations management." Differences and similarities will be explained as the text continues. However, if one term is more easily used than the other to stand for both production and operations management, that term is *operations management*. Most production managers will accept the appellation of operations manager but not vice versa. Therefore, *operations management* can be used instead of production and operations management. Also, OM can be used in place of P/OM; however, PM is not a good substitute for P/OM unless only manufacturing is clearly involved.

If the part that operations managers play is to be effective, it should be systems-based. Compare the operations manager to the coach of a sports team. What is the coach's job for a baseball, football, basketball, or soccer team? It is to guide the team to achieve competitive excellence. The coach knows that making the team win requires coordinating the contributions of the individual players. Winning takes teamwork, and the coach tries to develop that cooperative ability. Teamwork skills require a systems viewpoint. The systems viewpoint means that everything that is important to goal achievement is included in the analysis. If the goals cannot be achieved, then the strategies must be changed. Instead of the sports analogy, product line development can be used. The same teamwork requirement applies. (In this paragraph, P/OM applies, so production and operations managers are described as operations managers.)

Strategic Thinking

The systems viewpoint requires strategic planning. Goals and strategies must be congruent and realistic. Assume that the game being coached is called business and that players' positions are known as marketing, finance, operations, etc. The successful coach emphasizes coordination of these functions to pursue a strategy aimed at achieving the objectives. Apply this same statement to football, baseball, basketball, soccer, etc., and it works as well. Managers of all functional areas need to understand P/OM, and P/OM managers need to understand areas that interact with their own. Understanding global competitors requires understanding their strategies within the context of the international character of their operations management systems. That is why this text directs P/OM managers to focus on the use of the systems approach for strategic planning and tactical actions. The need begins with the development of strategies for product line planning.

1-1 Explaining Production and Operations Management (P/OM)

Production and **operations management** is the work function that oversees making goods and providing services. Because it provides what others sell, finance, and account for, it is an indisputable partner in the business. Product line planning is the starting point for strategic planning.

This book will familiarize students with the language and abbreviations used by production and operations managers—such as writing P/OM (or even faster, OM) for operations management. Important P/OM terms are explained in the text and their definitions are also presented.

The OM language describes methods, tools, procedures, goals, and concepts that relate to the management of people, materials, energy, information, and technology. Operations managers learn how to study a process by observing it and mapping its flow; from that platform, its performance can be improved. OM allows the state of a production process to be assessed. P/OM often starts from scratch with a new product line. In that case, what is known from prior experiences must be brought to bear.

Production
Activities used to create (and deliver) goods or furnish (and deliver) services to customers.

Operations management
Managing activities used to produce (and deliver) goods or furnish (and deliver) services to customers.

1-1a Use of Models by P/OM

The Greyhound bus driver is an operations manager assessing highway-driving conditions. The driver knows how rain slows velocity (v), which cuts down miles that can be driven per day (m). The manager in charge of operating the fleet of buses could describe this relationship as follows: $m = vt$, where m is the driver's output in miles driven per 8-hour day; v is the velocity, measured in miles per hour; and $t = 8$ hours.

This method of quantitative description is often used by P/OM to build a model—*a representation of the real situation.* The model permits P/OM to test the effect of different t's and v's. A general quantitative model that describes output is $O = pt$, where O is output per day. O changes as a function of the production rate per hour (p) and the length of time worked (t).

P/OM develops models to describe productivity (p) as a function of scheduling, training, technology, and capacity.

There are various P/OM models used to make equipment selection, workforce and production scheduling, quality control, inventory, distribution, plant location, capacity, maintenance, and transportation decisions, among others. Decision models organize the elements of a problem into actions that can be taken, forecasts of things that can happen that will affect the results, and thereby, the relative likelihood of the various outcomes occurring. Thus, decision models organize all of the vital elements in a systematic way.

1-1b Working Definitions of Production and Operations

The generic or collective definition of operations emphasizes rational design, careful control, and the systematic approach that characterizes the methodology of P/OM. Production/operations is a big umbrella that always includes services and often includes **manufacturing**. Production almost always stands for manufacturing alone.

Defining Operations

Operations are purposeful actions (or activities) methodically done as part of a plan of work (a strategy) by a process that is designed to achieve practical ends (objectives). This definition is applicable for manufacturing without reservation. This definition further justifies the use of the term *operations* for manufacturing.

Defining Operations Management (OM)

Operations management is the systematic planning and control of operations. This definition implies that management is needed to ensure that actions are *purposeful*—designed to achieve practical ends so goals and targets are required. These statements apply equally well to P/OM.

Production and operations management (P/OM) makes sure the work is done *methodically*—that is, characterized by method and order. The fact that a *process* is used suggests the presence of management to install a procedure for working systematically.

Operations management is responsible for a *plan of work*—a thoughtful progression from one step to another. Plans require details for accomplishing work. These details are often called the *tactics of the plan. Practical ends* are not realized without operations management that is able to provide strategies and tactics for public service objectives, which can include the ability to gain market share on a bus route or participation in a recycling plan. Everyone wants to be able to gain market share. There is a need to review why some organizations consider it embarrassing to make a profit.

Operations management uses *methodology* that consists of *procedures*, *rules of thumb*, and *algorithms* for analyzing situations and setting policies. They apply to many different kinds of service and manufacturing processes. In brief, operations management consists of tactics such as scheduling work, assigning resources including people and equipment, managing inventories, assuring quality standards, process-type decisions that include capacity decisions, maintenance policies, equipment selection, worker-training options, and the sequence for making individual items in a product-mix set.

The functions of P/OM overlap and interact. They are driven by demand from the market, where P/OM manages the supply to meet the demand. Strategic planning for the product line requires recognition of the fact that P/OM must be included to assess the feasibility of matching supply and demand.

Manufacturing Applications of P/OM

The operations used by manufacturing can be represented by many different verb and object phrases that describe doing things to various materials, such as pressing and turning metal (on a lathe), cutting paper, sewing clothes, sawing and drilling wood, sandblasting glass, forming plastics, shaping clay, heat-treating materials, soldering contacts, weaving fabric, blending fuels, filling cans, and extruding wires. Similarly, there are a variety of assembly phrases, such as snapping parts, gluing sheets, fitting components, and joining pieces together. This kind of work is done in factories.

Manufacturing
The processes that constitute the transformation function of the I/O model; those processes that produce goods. See Figure 1-5

Operations
Activities that are used to produce (and deliver) goods or furnish (and deliver) services to customers.

Operations used by manufacturing include such diverse activities as shielded metal arc welding (SMAW), which is also called stick welding. This photo shows a U.S. Navy sailor repairing a critical on-board component. He uses a manual process. With high volumes of work, robot welders are used. Similar to this is manual assembly, which is replaced by robot-like automated assembly when the volume of production is large enough. Many services are dedicated to bringing things together. Dating services are a prime example.

Manufacturing Examples Autos, planes, refrigerators, and lightbulbs are made in factories. On the other hand, fast-food chains like McDonald's and Burger King view the assembly of sandwiches from meat, buns, and condiments as a manufacturing application that demands the highest levels of quality for cleanliness and consistency. Also, costs must be kept low enough so that a profit can be made at a price that attracts customers. The price of fast-food products, said to be highly elastic, strongly affects demand volume. The concept of manufacturing sandwiches is a departure from traditional restaurant operations. It provides a P/OM basis for requiring methodical performance to achieve practical goals.

Service Applications of P/OM

Service operations in the office environment are quite familiar, i.e., filing documents, typing input for the word processor, and answering the phone. There are similar lists of verbs and objects that apply to jobs done in banks, hospitals, and schools; grant a loan, take an X-ray, and teach a class, are a few examples. Movies are one of the biggest export products of the United States. Operations management applied to entertainment and sports makes good sense. In the United States, administration of the law is a major industry that requires operations management. Law firms are aware of the importance of productivity management and quality improvement.

Jobs in some service industries are not as well paid as jobs in manufacturing. This is because the smart design of service industry operations is behind that of manufacturing. In the earliest years of manufacturing, many employees were paid small amounts of money. The kinds of operations that each person could do made only minor contributions to the profitability of the enterprise. Successful firms integrated the minor contributions of the many. As manufacturing operations and the technology behind them became better understood and the process was rationalized, fewer people were needed because each could make greater contributions.

The service industries are in the process of rationalizing operations so that individual contributions will become increasingly valuable in the same way that occurred in manufacturing. Consider the labor-intensive environment of check processing in a bank. It is reminiscent of the labor-intensive character of work that dominated manufacturing from the turn of the twentieth century through the mid-twentieth century and still exists in various places in the world.

Service Examples Those who have worked for UPS, Federal Express, or the post office are able to list the various service operations related to delivering mail and packages. Those who have worked for the IRS will have another set of job descriptions to define specific operations that characterize tax collection activities of the federal government. Also, if one has worked for The Gap, Banana Republic, Eddie Bauer, The Limited, Wal-Mart, The Sharper Image, Kmart, Sears, or other retail operators, he or she will be able to define processes that are pertinent to merchandise selection and pricing, outsourcing, distribution logistics, display, and store retailing. The experience will have similarities and differences with supermarkets that must also cope with dated products such as milk and greens that speak for themselves regarding freshness.

Successful mail-order (and Internet) companies like Lands' End, Amazon, L.L.Bean, Victoria's Secret, Norm Thompson, and Barnes & Noble are good examples of entrepreneurial firms that have struggled to master changes in technologies to gain the operational advantages of smart logistics. Distribution, in retail, mail order, and Internet B2C (business-to-consumer web customers), is a production process that lends itself to all of the benefits that excellent **information systems** and new technology can bestow.

The credit card business is another splendid example of a situation that combines many aspects of service functions. MasterCard, VISA, and American Express are totally

© 2008 Jupiterimages Corporation

Spools of thread are made into traditional Welsh bedspreads, tweeds, and traveling rugs in the Trefriw Woolen Mills between Llangollen and Holyhead in North Wales, United Kingdom. Trefriw also makes shoulder bags, sports jackets, and caps. Trefriw invites visitors to their working mill museum. See http://www.t-w-m.co.uk.

Information systems
Good information systems capture all data relevant to P/OM planning and decision making.

dependent upon smart operations management to provide profit margin excellence. The IT component of the credit card business model is almost transparent, but it is still very difficult to do well with consistent performance.

1-1c P/OM Is at the Hub of the Business Model

The product line of goods and services determines the operations needed to match supply and demand. The business model combines marketing forces (including competition), financial investments, and operating costs. This business model had to be thought out in detail during strategic planning.

A product that cannot be made or delivered on time, with quality, and at an acceptable cost must be referred back to marketing and general management. If financial support is insufficient to develop a satisfactory process, that fact must be referred back to finance and marketing. If employee resources are inadequate to operate the processes, that fact must be referred back to HRM, marketing, finance, and general management. These and other issues place P/OM at the hub (core and center) of the business model.

The planning details (of the model), once accepted, have to be adhered to by all of the business functions. When results do not jibe with plans, it is essential that all parties re-examine original assumptions and make adjustments as soon as practicable. As will be recognized from the following discussion, the functional field approach cannot be accepted. Although this is true in general, it is particularly so in a global business environment. The systems approach is essential.

1-2 Production and Operations Management: The Systems Approach

There are only two approaches that P/OM can use:

1 The functional field approach
2 The systems approach

Functional field approach
The functional field approach is widely used; with this approach, operations management is strictly tactical.

With the **functional field approach**, operations management is expected to perform its P/OM function with minimum reference to other parts of the business—such as marketing and finance. The functional field approach concentrates on the specific tasks that must be done to make the product or deliver the service. This approach is tactical, not strategic.

A typical organization chart—but with hierarchical details mainly for P/OM—is shown in Figure 1-1. The P/OM department is headed by a senior vice president of operations, who has the general manager as well as staff heads (for quality, materials, and engineering) reporting to him or her. The chart also shows without details marketing, finance, accounting, R&D, and other functions.

There are no lines connecting people in the other functional areas to people in P/OM. The only connection is at the president's level. Within the P/OM area, there are a limited number of connections, and these are hierarchically structured. The traditional organization chart does not reflect the systems approach wherein anyone can talk to anyone else if they are part of the problem or part of the solution. Teamwork is difficult to achieve with self-contained functions. This is called a "stovepipe" organization because each function operates as if it has its own separate compartment with its own chimney.

Systems approach
The big view that includes everything that might account for what is happening; accents connections and interactions between all functions.

The **systems approach** integrates P/OM decisions with those of all other business functions. This is an integrated and coordinated team-playing model of the organization.

The challenge is to make the firm perform as a team. The systems approach entails having all participants cooperate in solving problems that require mutual involvement. It begins with strategic planning and moves to tactical accomplishments.

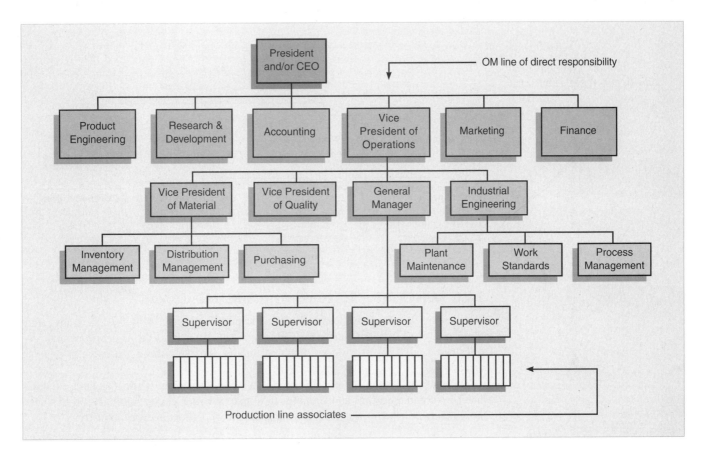

Figure 1-1

Traditional Organization Chart Shows Self-Contained Functional Areas

Heiner Müller-Merbach has provided a useful way of describing the systems approach as a combination of concepts.[1] Figure 1-2 depicts the various meanings that he has associated with the systems approach.

"The systems approach focuses the consideration of wholes and of their relations to their parts. The systems approach is necessarily comprehensive, holistic and interdisciplinary. However, there are several types of systems approaches around, quite different from each other and competing with one another,"[2] Müller-Merbach notes.

1-2a Using the Systematic–Constructive Approach

The **systematic** systems approach is considered the Western tradition whereas the **systemic** systems approach is characteristic of Eastern philosophies. The systems approach this book uses is systematic: analytic, synthetic, and constructive.

The systems approach called *introspection* is based on the **analytic reduction** of systems into their parts, which is characteristic of the sciences.

The systems approach called *extraspection* is characteristic of philosophy and the humanities. It strives to integrate objects and ideas into higher-order systems using synthesis. The field of general systems is closely associated with this effort to develop metasystems of knowledge.

Say that a computer stops working. Following introspection, it is opened up and taken apart. By means of analysis, components are tested to find the cause of the trouble.

Synthesis is required to reassemble the computer. Using extraspection, perhaps a better overall configuration can be found.

Combine analysis and synthesis to obtain the third systems approach, called **construction**. It is "characteristic of the engineering sciences and their creative design of systems for practical purposes."[3]

Creative design that uses both analysis and synthesis is the systems approach described in this book.

Systematic

Analytic, synthetic, and creative systems approach that might be said to work from the inside out.

Systemic

Holistic and contemplative systems approach that might be said to work from the outside in.

Analytic reduction

Break the system down into manageable parts for study.

Construction

Combining analysis and synthesis reflects creative engineering.

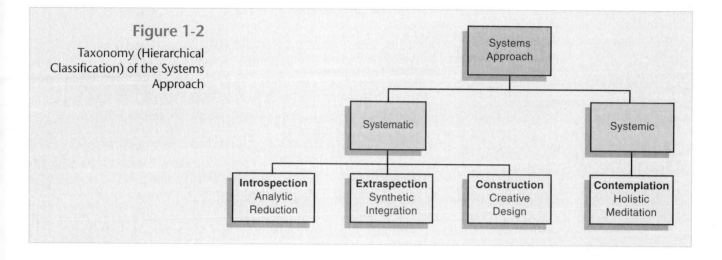

Figure 1-2
Taxonomy (Hierarchical Classification) of the Systems Approach

1-2b Why Is the Systems Approach Required?

The systems approach is needed because it produces better solutions than any other approach—especially the functional field approach. It leads to better decisions and provides better problem-solving for complex situations, enabling those that use it to be more successful.

Think of the systems approach in terms of the sports team. If the players are coordinated by communication and training, they play a better game. Similarly, in business, those using the systems approach are the leading competitors in every industry.

1-2c Defining the System

OM system
Alternative name for the P/OM system; OM is more service-oriented than P/OM.

Elements that qualify to be part of a system are those that have a direct or indirect impact on the problem, or its solution—on the plan or the decision. Thus, a P/OM **system** is everything that affects product line formulation, process planning, capacity decisions, quality standards, inventory levels, and production schedules. A P/OM system incorporates all factors with an effect on the purposes and goals of the organization.

Figure 1-3 is a symbolic picture of a system. The shape (or core) encloses all factors that have a strong effect on the purposes and goals of the system. Weak forces outside of the core may also have to be considered.

Figure 1-4 shows an organization chart with the system's shape mapped as a circle across certain functions. This is meant to reflect the fact that problems and opportunities include various people, departments, etc. The problem map cuts across P/OM as well as certain specific parts of marketing and accounting.

This is meant as a symbolic representation of the fact that people in departments falling inside the shaded area are involved with the problem being considered. Major responsibilities appear to fall within the domain of the general manager, a particular supervisor, and plant maintenance. All other departments have only partial involvement.

The key to understanding the relevant system is to identify all of the main players and elements that interact to create the system in which the real problem resides. Even though the problem solution may be assigned to the operations management team, the resolution requires cooperation of all the organizational participants in the problem.

1-3 Structure of the Systems Approach

The systems approach requires identification of all the elements related to purposes and goals. The question to be answered: What accounts for the attainment of the goals?

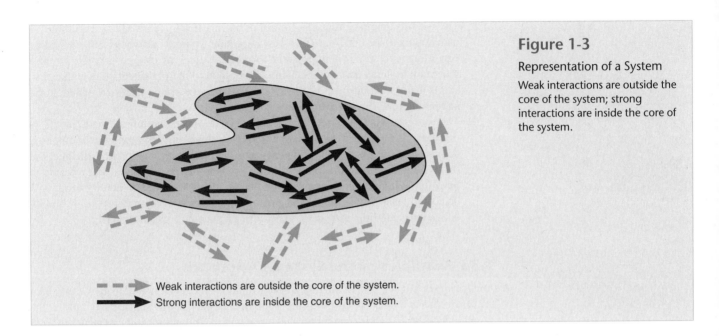

Figure 1-3

Representation of a System

Weak interactions are outside the core of the system; strong interactions are inside the core of the system.

Weak interactions are outside the core of the system.
Strong interactions are inside the core of the system.

1 The visual concept depicted in Figure 1-3 is one way to answer the question.
2 Another way is to use a math model that shows what accounts for the performance of the system and the attainment of its goals. The equation, shown here, is read "The goals y_i are a function of all relevant factors x_j and t_j." That is:

$$\{y_i\} = f\{x_1, x_2, \ldots, x_j; \quad t_1, t_2, \ldots, t_j\} \tag{1-1}$$

Figure 1-4

System's Problems Are Mapped over a Traditional Organization Chart

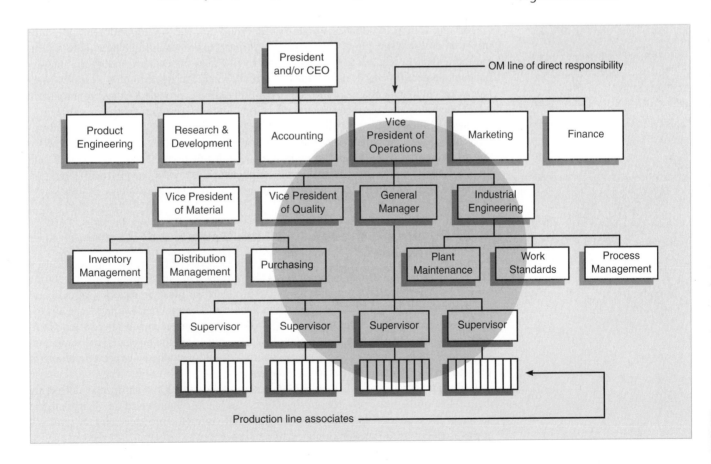

3 The systems approach requires control of timing. It is to be noted that Equation 1-1 includes measures of time (t_j) as an important systems parameter. By recording conditions over time, it is possible to measure rates of change—which are also important systems descriptors. Timing is critical to the performance of orchestras, sports teams, and business organizations. To achieve *synchronization* of functions, and harmony, the systems approach is required.

4 The systems approach requires teamwork. Coordination of all participants is essential. Designing a productive process for making sandwiches or toothpaste, delivering packages, or servicing cars requires cooperation among all members of the system. To operate a process properly, it is necessary for all participants to have the systems' perspective. In particular, the attainment of quality requires a dedicated team effort. A mistake by anyone involved in the attainment of quality is like the weak link of a chain, which causes the whole system to fail.

1-3a Examples of the Systems Approach

As previously pointed out, managing a sports team is an excellent example of a purposeful effort that is enhanced by using the systems approach. Another fine example is the symphony orchestra whose conductor makes certain that all participants are synchronized (on the same timeline). If the violins, woodwinds, and brass treat their participation as if they were separate functional fields, bedlam would result. Everyone looks to the conductor to keep the components of the system related and balanced.

For current purposes, the main example to explore is a generic business model whereby operations managers make products and/or deliver services. Using the systems approach to coordinate the business-unit team is essential to balance supply and demand, meet schedules, minimize costs, guarantee quality-standards fulfillment, maximize productivity, and optimize the use of critical resources.

For fun, a more abstract example that is widely known to both children and adults might be useful at this point. Jigsaw puzzles strike a chord because being able to assemble them smartly requires a systems perspective. Vision is needed to relate the interdependent elements of pieces using clues of various kinds. Puzzle difficulty increases when pieces are cut to look alike and little color differentiation is provided. Edges are important when internal spatial characteristics send no real hints concerning congruent outlines.

Puzzles become geometrically more difficult as the number of pieces increases. Similarly, as a system becomes larger with more complex interactions, it becomes more difficult to fathom its structure and to understand how it functions. Operations management problems are composed of complex subsystems, which require interfunctional communications to uncover *patterns* that relate the subsystems to the whole system.

1-3b Designing the Product Line Using the Systems Approach

The product line (goods and/or services) is the starting point of strategic thinking for the firm. Every factor relevant to success of the product line must be included in deliberations among all functional managers of the business. The product line is tested against marketing assumptions. Market research starts with the concept and later, after prototypes are made, tests them in the marketplace. If services are the products, the same considerations apply. Price points are conceived that should generate an expected volume of demand for the chosen qualities of the products.

If the products test well, then P/OM designs processes for making and delivering them. Most of the time, process improvements can be suggested based on changes in the design of the products. The costs of making and delivering the products, and the qualities of the products, are a function of materials and processes.

The discussion between marketing and P/OM involves finance as well. The kind of processes used will determine investments required by P/OM to be underwritten by the financial managers. All business functions are involved in strategic planning, and this means that the systems approach is essential.

1-4 Differentiating Between Goods and Services

There is less difference than similarity between P/OM in manufacturing and OM in **service** organizations. Manufacturing is the fabrication and assembly of goods, whereas services generate revenues either independently of goods or to help the user of those goods. Banking, transportation, health care, and entertainment are all services. They change the customer's location, financial condition, and sense of well-being. Increasingly, manufacturers recognize the importance of servicing customers, and service systems recognize the value of using manufacturing capabilities.

The methodology of P/OM was first developed by and for manufacturing, but it has now been extended to services with great success.

Service industries involve an increasing percent of the workforce. Thus, more attention needs to be directed toward achieving coherent and efficient operations for services.

Similarities between services and manufacturing can be noted when service operations are based upon repetitive steps in information processing. Almost identical methods apply with respect to production scheduling, job design and design of the workplace, process configurations, and quality achievement. High-volume repetitive operations on physical items (i.e., for fast foods or blood testing) constitute production whether they belong to manufacturing or services. Similar analogies can be made for lower volumes of production and services delivered.

The similarities stop and significant differences occur when the operations involve contact between people. Person-to-person activities that require transfer of information and/or treatments offered by one to another are difficult to schedule; activity times vary more than with machines. Human-to-human interactions involve many more intangibles than interactions between people and machines. The contact aspect of services requires different methods for analysis and synthesis than are needed for manufacturing systems.

At the same time, care should be taken to avoid stereotyping services as being all too human and, therefore, difficult to control for quality and productivity. It does a disservice to services to consider them quixotic or flawed by humanism, while manufacturing is admired for its elegant, efficient technological component. A most respected thinker has written, "Until we think of service in more positive and encompassing terms, until it is enthusiastically viewed as manufacturing in the field, receptive to the same kind of technological approaches that are used in the factory, the results are likely to be . . . costly and idiosyncratic."[4]

The point to make is that services that are currently rendered in an inherently inefficient way often can be transformed into rational repeatable activities that emulate the best of manufacturing environments. However, often is not always. Some services are not amenable to the concept of manufacturing in the field. One might be fearful if the services rendered by a doctor were based on a repetitive manufacturing model. At the same time, many aspects of open-heart surgery are the better for such systematization. The same can be said for blood testing, taking X-rays, and other repetitive aspects of the healthcare business (see Spotlights 5-2 and 10-2). Juxtaposed to this, some products, such as artwork, are epitomized by being custom-made. They lose most of their value if they are manufactured.

Another significant difference between the provision of services and manufacturing occurs because of inventory. It is not considered possible, usually, to stock services. For example, when the machine repairperson is idle there is no way to build up an inventory of repair hours that can be used when two machines go down at the same time. In most service businesses, this is one of the great waste factors.

Service
Includes every form of work except manufacturing of goods.

© 2008 Jupiterimages Corporation

Rush hour traffic on an eight-lane toll highway will be serviced by eight tollbooths, including some that are equipped for e-pass (electronic pay). A significant difference between toll service operations and manufacturing is that when the tollbooth operator is idle, there is no way to build up an inventory of time to be used when the waiting lines are long. However, toy manufacturers prepare inventory in September to satisfy Christmas demand.

On the other hand, many companies use automated systems to provide custom-tailored information such as stock, bond, and mutual fund quotes for anyone knowing the symbols. Phone-call requests for product information are answered by a digitized voice that instructs the caller to use a Touch-Tone phone to input the product of interest and his or her fax number. The appropriate fax is automatically transmitted within a minute. This entire service transaction, without human intervention, is becoming increasingly common and epitomizes automated manufacturing and/or service processes.

Voice recognition technology is getting so good that a new era is about to occur that will likely revolutionize the service function. Contacts by computer have become kindly and comfortable to customers. Machine ability to understand customers' responses has also altered the contact relationship. Logical reasoning by computers for service requests is likely to be far better than what can be supplied by outsourced, call-center employees whose native language and cultural milieu are different from the caller's. This voice recognition advantage of computers using the Internet will alter outsourcing of call-center functions for banks, e-stores, etc.

1-5 Contrasting Production Management and Operations Management

What is the difference between *production* management and *operations* management? Production is an old and venerable term used by engineers, economists, entrepreneurs, and managers to describe physical work both in homes and in factories to produce a material product.

Production management
Managing activities used to produce (and deliver) goods to customers.

Traditionally, **production management** involves planning and decision making for the manufacture of goods such as airplanes, cars, tires, soup, paper, soap, cereal, shoes, shirts, skirts, sweaters, dentifrice, clothing, furniture, and the parts that go into many of these products. Parts and components manufacture is a large portion of finished goods manufacture. Production managers are also responsible for luxuries.

Operations management is a more recent term associated with services performed by organizations such as banks, insurance companies, fast-food servers, and airlines. Government jobs are also in the services. Healthcare providers, including hospitals and schools, belong in the services category. Running the Olympic games is an operations management job. It is not surprising that there has been a rapid growth of service jobs in the U.S. economy. The current ratio of service jobs to manufacturing jobs is nearly four to one, compared to an approximate one-to-one ratio in the 1950s. As a result, the number of people that are now engaged in operations is far larger (and still growing) than the number of people that work in the production departments of manufacturing firms.

Manufacturers have come to view service to the customer as part of the quality of the product line. This includes repairing defective products as well as providing regularly scheduled maintenance. Auto manufacturers learned a great deal from Acura when Honda launched that division with a service mission that eclipsed anything in auto service that preceded it. One of the best automotive service operations before Acura was Honda itself, so there was precedent to follow. Xerox, after losing significant market share, began to establish strict guidelines for the maximum allowable downtimes that would be tolerated for its copying machines. Until the 1990s, IBM provided almost no service to its personal computer customers. After a serious fall from grace, IBM changed its policy and became a full-service company to all of its customers.

Having developed a successful consulting business model, which accounted for most of its profits, IBM sold its personal computer product line to Lenovo, China's leading PC-maker, for $1.75 billion dollars in December 2004. Lenovo completed the purchase of IBM's PC division in May 2005, after receiving clearance from the U.S. Committee on Foreign Investment in March 2005. Lenovo became "the world's third-largest PC maker," according to *The New York Times*, Business Day, p. C5, May 2, 2005. After a rocky transition, earnings swung back to black in the fourth quarter of fiscal 2007.

Lenovo inherited from IBM the right to sponsor the 2008 Beijing Olympics. This includes designing the 2008 Olympic Torch and supplying the digital foundation of the Olympics administration. A year-long test period was designed by Lenovo to check on all aspects of operations. Using 14,000 pieces of computing equipment, Lenovo gathers and stores participants' data, displays scores, and organizes all activities of the BOCOG (Beijing Organizing Committee for the Games of the XXIX Olympiad). This major undertaking dwarfs all operational control systems employed by OM at prior Olympics.

1-5a Information Systems Are Essential for Manufacturing and Services

The growing recognition of the importance of the service function in manufacturing has broadened the situations to which the term *operations* is applied. Manufacturers have become more comfortable with the notion that they must cater to the customer's service requirements. Information systems provide the necessary data about customer needs so that operations management can supply the required services.

Both services and manufacturing are increasingly responsive to—and controlled by— information systems. Therefore, knowledge of computers, computer programming, networking, and telecommunications is essential in both the manufacturing and service environment.

Schools of business include both goods and services under the term *operations*, whereas industrial engineering departments are still inclined to teach "production" courses. Nevertheless, there is inevitable convergence of both to an information-dominated workplace. *Operations is the familiar management term for an information systems environment*, so the word "operations" fits nicely.

Programming and maintenance (both service functions) have become increasingly important to manufacturing. Further, the relevance of service to customers increasingly is viewed as a part of the total package that the manufacturer must deliver. Manufacturing joins such distinguished service industries as transportation, banking, entertainment, education, and health care. In that regard, note the following trends for manufacturing:

1. The labor component (the input of blue-collar workers) has been decreasing as a percent of the cost of goods at an accelerating rate for over 50 years.

2. The technological component as a percent of the cost of goods has been increasing for many years. In the past 20 years, this effect has become multiplicative, with computers controlling sophisticated and costly equipment across vast distances via satellites and networks.

3. As information systems play a larger part in manufacturing, highly-trained computer programmers (sometimes called *gold-collar workers*) and white-collar supervisors add to growing sales and administrative (**overhead**) costs, which have to be partitioned into the cost of goods. These costs are an increasing percent of the cost of goods. Traditional methods for assigning these costs can lead to detrimental OM decisions. New accounting methods, called activity-based costing (ABC), should be used to improve overhead accounting. Operations managers need to discuss these issues with their colleagues from accounting.

4. The systems approach requires communication between functions and the sharing of what used to be (and still are, in many traditional firms) mutually exclusive databases. The databases of marketing and sales, OM, R&D, engineering, and finance are cross-linked when advantageous. That sharing is crucial to enabling the systems approach to work. There are many examples of both manufacturing and service industries where shared databases have been installed and utilized successfully.

Overhead
Costs that do not directly generate revenues but are essential to operate the business, e.g., heating and AC.

5 The technology of the twentieth century is moving rapidly into retirement along with a lot of executives who grew up with its characteristics. It's a new ball game with new players who feel free to deal with the distinction between services and manufacturing as well as between operations and production in their own way.

Practitioners now have stepped into the twenty-first century, but they have yet to get accustomed to it. It is a good bet that the taxonomy of the twenty-first century will categorize production as a subheading under operations, and services will be an integral part of manufacturing.

When a discussion applies equally well to both manufacturing and services, it is often referred to as P/OM. As explained earlier, it is increasingly common to call it OM. In this text, OM will be used to describe both manufacturing and services. P/OM will be used in situations where the manufacturing component is relevant and conclusions are likely to be different from those applicable to service systems alone.

1-6 Basic P/OM Transformation Model: Input–Output System

Transformation

One of the most important parts of the P/OM system. It is the transformation process capability to cut metal, polish brass, take temperatures, build cars, and so forth.

All operations management and production systems involve **transformation**. Alteration of materials and components adds value and changes them into goods that customers want to own. The raw materials and components before transformation could not be used—and therefore had no utility—for the customer. Service conversions have customer utility even though no transfer of goods takes place. The conversion may be a change of location or related to the customer's state of well-being (e.g., visiting the doctor or the repairperson fixes the machine).

The manufacturing transformation of raw materials into finished goods is successful if customers are willing to pay more for the goods than it costs to make them. Consider what has to be done to make a product. The raw materials for glass, steel, food, and paper have no utility without technological transformations. New processes are constantly being invented for improving the transformations and the products that can be obtained from them.

The same transformation rules apply to services. The conversion is successful if customers are willing to pay more for the services than it costs to provide them. To illustrate a service transformation, consider an information system in a bank. A check that is issued results in the electronic transfer of funds (ETF) from the paying account to the paid account, clearly an input–output transformation.

Another information transformation is to take raw data and turn it into averages and standard deviations. The latter is characteristic of the operations aspect of market research. As another service example, consider the transformation that is at the heart of the airline business—moving people from one place (input) to another (output) for profit. Other inputs are fuel, food, and the attention of the flight attendants.

Figure 1-5 represents a generalized input–output transformation model. Generalized means that it is a standard form that could be applied to any system where conversions are taking place. Inputs are fed into the transformation box—representing the process. The "process" often includes many subprocesses. If the process is to make a burger sandwich, then important subprocesses include cooking the hamburger and toasting the buns.

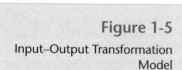

Figure 1-5
Input–Output Transformation Model

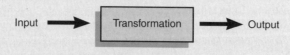

Input–output is the basic P/OM model.

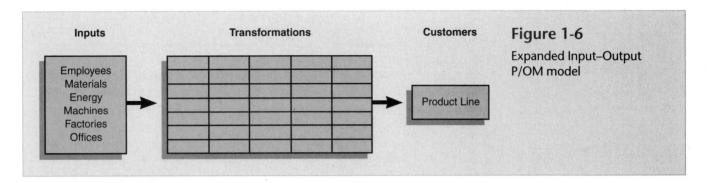

Figure 1-6

Expanded Input–Output
P/OM model

The inputs are combined by the process, resulting in the production of units of goods or the creation of types of services. The transformed units emerge from the facility (factory, office, etc.) at a given rate. Time needed to carry out the transformation determines the production rate. The transformed inputs emerge as outputs to be sold or used beneficially. The transformation model depicts work being done. This work involves the use of resources made up of people, materials, energy, and machines to achieve transformations.

Figure 1-6 illustrates an expanded version of the input–output transformation model. There are many boxes now within the transformation grid. Each box represents operations that generate the product line, which can be goods or services. Productive P/OM systems have well-designed transformations.

Transformations are being accomplished when people are served chili at Wendy's or when they give blood to the Red Cross, have their teeth cleaned by the dentist, or visit Disney World to be entertained. A travel agency will have secured the necessary reservations and tickets for the customer's flight to Orlando, Florida, and for the hotel. The travel agent designs the trip and fits it to the customer's specifications concerning dates and costs using reservation and other information systems to complete all necessary transactions. When the desired outputs are fully specified, the transformations can be planned, along with the inputs, and the plan can be carried through to completion. The culmination of the transformation process constitutes the desired output—a visit with Mickey Mouse.

1-6a Costs and Revenues Associated with Input–Output Models (I/Os)

Cost management is a key function associated with all aspects of P/OM. A major portion of the cost of goods or services originates with operations. Figure 1-7 is meant to illustrate how costs are related to I/O models. Controlling costs is of prime concern to all managers.

For the most part, **costs** are readily categorized into **variable costs** and **fixed costs**. Generally, costs are considered to be easily measured, although the treatment of overhead costs is subject to debate. Also, a variety of accounting methodologies exist. The differences between them are not trivial because they can impact P/OM decisions in significantly disparate ways. P/OM and accounting coexist in the same system, and they are interdependent when the measurement of costs interacts with P/OM decision making. Quality, another key criteria associated with all aspects of P/OM, interacts with costs in a variety of ways, as do productivity, timeliness of delivery, and styles and sizes of products and services.

Variable costs
See **Direct costs**.

Fixed costs
See **Indirect costs**.

Inputs Associated with Variable (or Direct) Costs

The input components of the transformation model that apply to an airline transportation process include fuel, food, crew pay, and other costs. Variable operating costs increase as there are more flights flown and more people flying. Variable costs are also called *direct costs* because they can be applied directly, without ambiguity, to each unit that is processed.

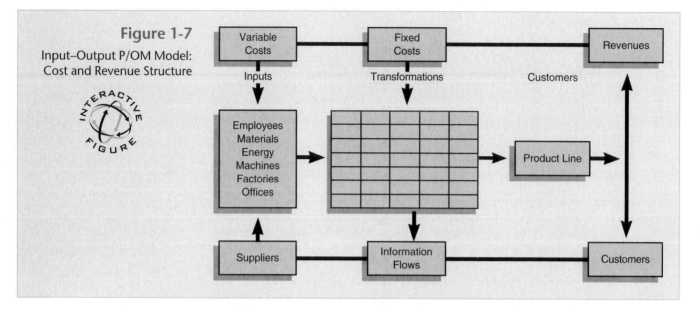

Figure 1-7

Input–Output P/OM Model:
Cost and Revenue Structure

The same reasoning applies to a manufacturing example. The variable costs for the inputs include labor, energy, and all of the materials purchased from suppliers and used to make the product. Materials include raw materials, subassemblies, semifinished materials, and components. The more finished the purchased materials, the less work that has to be done by the purchaser (i.e., less value can be added by the purchaser).

Transformations Associated with Fixed (or Indirect) Costs

Depreciation
Dividing the total cost of an asset to reflect how much of that cost applies to each period of its useful life.

© 2008 Jupiterimages Corporation

Decisions about fixed costs (also called *indirect costs*) are not easily reversible. Bundles of money, of all denominations, are analogous to measuring how much overhead is incurred. Finance with P/OM's assistance must control how much overhead has to be paid even when no positive cash flow (revenue) is coming into the company.

When Delta or American Airlines buys aircraft from Boeing or Airbus Industries, the airline increases its already substantial fixed cost investment in planes. Fixed costs are also called *indirect costs* because they are part of overhead and must be allocated to units of output by some formula.

Often the charge per year—called **depreciation**—is calculated by dividing the cost of the investment by the number of years in the estimated lifetime of the investment. For example, a $30 million aircraft with a 15-year lifetime would generate $2 million of depreciation per year. This is called *straight-line depreciation* because the amount per year does not change. There still remains the question of how to allocate a portion of the $2 million as an applicable charge for a particular passenger flying from Milan to New York on that aircraft. Determining the appropriate fixed costs to be charged to each job, unit made, or passenger mile flown is a joint responsibility of P/OM and accounting.

An alternative approach for adding capacity without increasing investment is to lease instead of buy aircraft. This shifts the financial burden of buying capacity to the variable input cost mode. The same distinction applies when a manufacturer analyzes the net long-term economic value of renting a factory building instead of either building or buying a facility. Leasing a facility shifts the fixed costs of building acquisition to the variable costs associated with inputs.

Delta and American also have investments in maintenance facilities, airport terminals, and training and education systems, as well as in their workers and management. The payments that airlines make to support the operations of airports generally are fixed and not variable costs. Airports—like factories—are major fixed-cost facilities; treat them as fixed costs because the same expenses must be met no matter how many flights depart or arrive there. However, if part of the airport charges is based on the number of flights an airline makes, then both fixed and variable (input) costs must be considered. As for investments in training and management, companies use consultants as a way to keep down their fixed costs. For similar reasons, they often lease transportation.

Outputs Associated with Revenues and Profits

Passengers pay the airline for transportation. The number of passengers (units) that are transported (processed) by the airline is the output (sometimes called *throughput* to emphasize the output rate) of the system. It usually is measured by passenger miles flown system wide (or between two points) in a period of time. Throughput is managed to balance supply (capacity) and demand. The demand level for transportation between any two points is related to marketing factors, not the least of which is the price for a round-trip ticket.

All of the airlines do not charge the same amount for a roundtrip ticket. By adjusting price, airlines often can affect the percent occupancy of their flights. Such *marketing decisions* are part of the total system that affects operations. They typify the need for systems coordination to relate P/OM with the other functional areas within the framework of the transformation model. Southwest Airlines has used efficient operations to maintain low costs. This allows them to charge low prices. This business model has made Southwest Airlines uniquely profitable.

The manufacturer can measure output in terms of the number of units of each kind of product it produces. Because there may be many varieties such as sizes and flavors, it is usual P/OM practice to aggregate the output into some common unit, such as standard units of toothpaste produced. Both forms of information would reflect the variability of demand, but the aggregate measure much less so than the detailed product reports. Depending upon the demand levels, the marketing department could stimulate sales by dropping prices or raising prices to slow demand that is exceeding supply capabilities.

If lower prices are effective in generating new business, then the demand is said to be elastic to price. When there is price elasticity, operations must keep costs down so that the advantage of low prices can be obtained. Marketing ultimately controls the volume of business that production must process. Financial planning has determined the operating capacity for peak demand. This, in turn, translates back to the amount of inputs that need to be purchased to meet demand.

The systems perspective is required to make sure that all participants are connected directly to the revenue-generating capacity of the I/O system. The information system helps to foster the process of keeping connected. Many kinds of data are regularly transmitted between participants. For example, information about what is selling—and what is in stock—leads to production scheduling decisions. It also leads to initiatives by the sales department. The levels of inventory are perpetually examined to make sure that no stock outages occur, and care is taken to keep track of what is in the finished goods inventory.

1-7 P/OM Input–Output Profit Model

The purpose of this section is to link the equation for profit—which is critical for people in business—to the input–output transformation model.

The **I/O profit model** is derived from the costs and revenues shown in Figure 1-7. The model assigns the costs and revenues of the traditional equation of profit to the inputs, the outputs, and the transformation process—all based on a specific period of time (*t*).

In Equation 1-2, total costs, *TC*, are subtracted from revenue, *R*, yielding profit, *P*.

$$P = R - TC \qquad (1\text{-}2)$$

In Equation 1-3, total costs, *TC*, equal the sum of total fixed costs, *FC*, and total variable costs, *vc(V)*. The latter is the variable costs per unit (*vc*) multiplied by (*V*), which is volume in production units for the time period (*t*).

$$TC = FC + vc(V) \qquad (1\text{-}3)$$

Equation 1-4 represents the calculation of revenue where price per unit, *p*, is multiplied by *V*, sold in (*t*). *p(V)* equals revenue.

I/O profit model

The input–output model captures all costs and revenues so profit can be determined.

$$R = p(V) \qquad (1\text{-}4)$$

Equation 1-5 is the statement of how the factors of profit (P) come together. It is useful in other ways as well. Setting profit equal to zero and solving for demand volume provides the breakeven volume. Questions surface about how demand volume changes according to the prices charged. Another interesting issue is the relationship of FC on vc.

$$P = R - TC = p(V) - FC - vc(V) = (p - vc)V - FC \qquad (1\text{-}5)$$

1-7a How Has the Profit Model Changed over Time?

Nothing in the structure of the profit model has changed over time; the equations are the same. What has changed is the technology that the fixed costs can buy, and in turn, that investment affects the variable costs. In addition, there have been major changes in the knowledge base about the productivity of processes and the quality they can deliver. Knowledge has been developed that affects the volume of output that the fixed costs can deliver.

It is the production system (or the system of operations) embedded in the profit model that has changed a great deal. The performance of the input–output transformation system has been altered, resulting in increased productivity of the system. The architecture of the operating system has been changing for many years, but recently at an accelerated rate.

1-8 The Stages of P/OM Development

The profit model operates differently according to the stage of development of the company's input–output operating system. This strategic issue must be understood by the functional area managers and addressed in a coordinated fashion. The stage reflects the degree to which a company's activities have been coordinated and carried out. Thus, stage determines company effectiveness (ability to do the right thing) and efficiency (ability to do the thing right). As a company improves its stage of operations, it is expected that its profitability will increase. However, it is necessary to relate the company's stage of development to that of its competitors.

Input–output model

The basic production systems model, which assumes transformation in between inputs and outputs.

Each company's input–output profit model indirectly and directly reflects the impact of the competitors' **input–output model**s. The cost structures, prices, volumes, and profit margins reflect the influence and extent of the competition. If the competitors all are at the same stage and one of them starts to move to a higher stage, the expected result is that the advancing company will gain market share, while the remaining companies experience a decrease in share and volume. This then gets translated into higher variable costs and lower profit margins. P/OMs must be involved in competitive analysis, which means that the company's planning participants fully understand the stages of development of all competing companies.

How a company manages its profit model provides insight into the role that P/OM can play in a company. Decisions concerning capacity and the resulting economies of scale capture only a portion of the story; the extent to which new technology is utilized to offset high variable labor costs also plays a part. The development stage relates as well to the management of the throughput rate, quality attainment, and variety achievement.

Stage I companies operate on the premise that there is no competitive advantage to be gained by changing the production process. Therefore, the process usually is relatively unrefined and often out-of-date. Management, seeing no leverage in processes, pays minimal attention to production and operations. Stage I firms squeak by on quality. Because the competitors are not much better, everyone appears indifferent. In such firms, management and its resources are insufficient to do more than keep up with demand. Survival occurs only when and if the competition is in the same boat. Marginal firms do not survive long in a market that is dominated by higher-stage companies. Figure 1-8 provides a

	Internally	**Externally**
Neutral	Stage I	Stage II
Supportive	Stage III	Stage IV

Figure 1-8

Stages of P/OM Development

simple matrix for categorizing stages of a company's P/OM development. This is applicable to manufacturing and service product lines.

1-8a Special P/OM Capabilities

At the other end of the spectrum, there are companies that use operations to gain unique basic advantages through the development of special capabilities. The concept of competing on capabilities is clearly formulated by Stalk, Evans, and Shulman.[5] The advantages gained can vary from speeding up distribution to tactical superiority in managing inventories, or product preeminence obtained from effective product development and total quality management (TQM).

Stage IV companies practice *continuous improvement (CI)*, which means that they persistently remove waste. They aggressively seek to innovate in their unswerving pursuit of quality. Stage IV companies have a high level of basic advantages that are unique to them, whereas Stage I companies have virtually none. Stages II and III fall in-between on various scales of performance.

This approach is based on work done by Wheelwright and Hayes (W&H), cited in their article in the *Harvard Business Review*.[6] They have created a framework applicable to manufacturing firms (P of P/OM). This approach also utilizes work by Chase and Hayes (C&H) detailed in their article in the *Sloan Management Review*.[7] Their framework is applicable to service firms (OM of P/OM). This article puts together the concept of stages of development for both manufacturing and service firms.

1   A Stage I company is centered on meeting shipment quotas and providing service when requested. C&H call it "available for service" and cite, as an example, a government agency. A Stage I company has no planning horizon and is predisposed to be indifferent to P/OM goals. It is reactive to orders and has no quality agenda. Worker control is stressed. The company is not conscious of special capabilities for itself or for its competitors. W&H describe such firms as being internally neutral, which means that top management does not consider P/OM as being able to promote competitive advantage and, therefore, P/OM is kept in neutral gear.

2   A Stage II company manages traditional P/OM processes and has a relatively short-term planning horizon. It makes efforts to secure orders and to meet customers' service desires. The primary goal of Stage II companies is to control costs. Quality tends to be defined as products or services that are not worse than some standard. These companies consider the most important advantages to be derived from economies of scale, which means that as output volume increases, costs go down. W&H describe such firms as being externally neutral; they strive to have parity in P/OM matters with the competition.

3   A Stage III company installs and manages manufacturing and service processes that are equivalent to those used by the leading companies. C&H describe this as "distinctive service competence." A Stage III company makes efforts to emulate the special capabilities of the best companies. Quality and productivity improvement programs are utilized in an effort to be as good as the best. Stage III

Stage IV companies aggressively seek to innovate product design and development while assisting environmental improvements. For example, Wal-Mart, teamed with GE, announced (August 2006) that in the next 12 months the plan was to sell 100 million compact fluorescent lamps (CFL). The idea is to replace incandescent bulbs on a broad basis. In the wings are other new developments. Potentially, LED lamps will replace CFLs in the next wave of innovation. Market replacements, on this scale, are a great deal of hard work for P/OM and others. Thomas Edison, inventor of the incandescent bulb, said that "Genius is 1 percent inspiration, 99 percent perspiration." Stage IV companies do not shirk the hard work.

Project management
Managing project activities in a way that is both professional and effective.

firms have a relatively long-term planning horizon supported by a detailed P/OM strategy. W&H describe such firms as being internally supportive, meaning that P/OM activities support the Stage III company's competitive position.

4 A Stage IV company is a P/OM innovator. It has short- and long-term planning horizons that are integrated. Long-term P/OM planning requires excellence in **project management** to bring about changes needed to adapt to new environments. Short-term P/OM involves meeting standards by controlling the production process. Both short and long are crucial elements in the success of the firm. Both demand that P/OM be a part of the top management strategy team because the production processes are held to be a source of unique advantage gained through special capabilities, as are product and service design.

Project management is a P/OM responsibility that offers significant advantage to those in OM who know how to use project management methods to innovate quickly and successfully for competitive advantage. W&H describe such firms as externally supportive, which means that competitive strategy "rests to a significant degree on the firm's manufacturing capability." C&H conclude that Stage IV firms offer services that "raise customer expectations." Stage IV firms use the systems approach to integrate service and manufacturing activities.

Reengineering (REE)
Term used to signify that the current processes are to be completely redone.

It takes a lot of work to progress through successive stages. It is unlikely that an existing P/OM organization can skip a stage. Only with total reorganization is it possible for a Stage I company to become a Stage III or IV. **Reengineering (REE)**, which is defined as starting from scratch to redesign a system, is an appealing way to circumvent bureaucratic arthritis and jump stages. However, it is costly and, if not done right, has a high risk of failure. Mastery of this P/OM text will lower that risk.

1-9 Organizational Positions and Career Opportunities in P/OM

To qualify for an operations management job, there are several reasons it helps to have an undergraduate degree in business or an MBA. First, P/OM is at the hub of the business model. This requires an understanding of the various functional business partners to achieve successful strategic planning. Second, there are many concepts to learn and a special P/OM language to master.

A single, introductory course in P/OM will not suffice. The system's perspective is instrumental for success. This requires knowledge about the various business functions including marketing, finance, accounting, and human resources management. Vice versa, a marketing career is enhanced by an understanding of P/OM. The same applies to careers in all other functional areas.

1-9a Career Success and Types of Processes

It is essential when talking about careers in P/OM to recognize that *one of the major differences in P/OM jobs relates to the kinds of processes* that are involved in the transformation of inputs into outputs. This means such things as the continuity of processing, the number of units processed at one time, the volume of throughput between setups, and the degree of repetition of the operations.

It can be seen from the historical development of P/OM that manufacturing started with custom work, which in many ways resembles an artist at work. For example, the shoemaker who fits and makes the entire shoe for each customer is an artist in leather. Most often, the left and right shoes differ. However, for store-bought shoes, customized attention to fitting the customer is not possible.

Services often are of the custom variety. The medical doctor sees one patient at a time and treats that patient as warranted. Service processes can prosper by making them more like manufacturing. In time, manufacturing learned how to process small batches efficiently. Some service systems, like elevators, lend themselves to batch processes.

Continuous flow processes were developed by a variety of industries, including chemical processors, refineries, and auto assembly manufacturers. Fast-food chains try to emulate this kind of process to handle a continuous flow of information and to assemble sandwiches.

Until the late 1970s, there were basically three different ways to get work done. A fourth (flexible processes) was added when computers began to change the way processes were designed. The four categories are:

- *Project*. Each project is a unique process, done once, like launching a new product, building a plant, or writing a book. Both service providers and manufacturers need to know how to plan and complete projects that are associated with the evolving goals of "temporary" organizations. Projects appeal to people who prefer nonrepetitive, constantly evolving, creative challenges. Projects do not attract people who opt for a stable environment and the security of fixed goals—associated with the flow shop. There is a unique profile of people who prefer the project environment to other process types and who excel in that milieu.

- *Batch processing*. Facilities are set up, and n units are made or processed at a time. Then the facility is reset for another job. *When $n = 1$, or a very few, it is called custom work*, and it is done in a custom shop. When n is more than a few, and the work is done in batches, it is called a *job shop*. The average batch size in job shops is 50. The work arrangement ceases to be a job shop when the work is done in serial flow shop fashion. With the job shop, many different kinds of goods and/or services can be processed. As the batch size gets larger for manufacturing or services, more effort is warranted to make the process efficient and to convert it to a serialized production system. Job shops, with their batch production systems, appeal to people who prefer repetitive assignments within a relatively hectic environment. The job shop generally involves a lot of people interactions and negotiations. The tempo of batch production is related to the number of setups, cleanups, and changeovers.

- *Flow shop processing*. As the batch size increases so that production can be serialized, either continuously or intermittently, it is rational for both manufacturing and services to pre-engineer the system. This means that balanced flow is designed for the process before it is ever run. It is expected that variable costs will decrease as the fixed-cost investments increase. Continuous process systems require a great deal of planning and investment. Flow shops run the gamut from crude setups arranged to run for short periods of times (such as days or weeks) to continuous process systems that have been carefully designed and pre-engineered for automation. The more automated processes appeal to people who like a controlled, stable, and well-planned system. The lower costs of flow shop production are related to *economies of scale*.

- *Flexible (programmable) processing systems*. As far back as the 1980s, a new process category began to emerge that continues to grow faster than any other P/OM segment. Flexibility is derived from the combination of computers controlling machines, making this option the high-tech career choice. People who enjoy working with computers prefer these technologically-based environments. There are two aspects to this attraction. First is the application of the technology to do the work, and second is the programming of the computers to instruct and control the equipment that does the work. Associated with the adoption of the new technology is much experimentation. Openness to learning is essential because the systems are continuously changing and need high levels of adaptability. People who like to work with high technology are attracted to this process configuration.

An assessment has found that this category continues to grow, but the extent of its application has narrowed. Flexibility has been stymied by design constraints and higher costs than had been expected. Each product design decision removes degrees of freedom for further design opportunities. The second crankshaft is easier to make than the seventh one. While progress has been slowed, there is belief that *mastery* of flexible technology will continue to be improved. Investments in FMS are conditioned by the payoffs resulting from being able to increase variety without incurring large setup costs for each new product design made on the same production line (called *economies of scope*).

Many people prefer working with a specific type of process. There are also people who prefer to work in either manufacturing or services; these issues usually are more important than type of industry preferences. For an example of the first kind, autos, airplanes, and computers are associated with assembly-oriented industries. Real advantages often accrue to companies that hire employees from similar but not the same industries. For example, in September 2006, Alan Mulally, head of commercial airlines for Boeing and a force behind the Dreamliner (787), was hired by Bill Ford to become CEO of Ford Motor Co.

Hiring across service industry types is also popular. A person having expertise in the hotel business is likely to be courted for employment by resorts, theme parks, and restaurants. The Ritz Carlton Corporation has made some remarkable competitive strides with respect to the quality of hotel service that can be applied broadly to the entire hospitality class of service. Club Med, which represents one of the best of the resort industry, has a very strong—transferable—P/OM orientation.[8] Club Med, Cirque du Soleil, and Four Seasons Hotels and Resorts are operations management cases in the Harvard Business School series. Media and entertainment are two other service areas with a strong draw on career selection.

Certain industries and services have intense regionality, i.e., Florida, Hawaii, Mexico, and the Caribbean represent a cross-section for the resort business. Thailand was building a reputation for an exotic holiday destination until the tsunami destruction (December 26–27, 2004). It has since rebuilt its beaches, hotels, restaurants, and reputation.

Michigan, Ohio, and within the last 30 years, many Southeastern states of the United States are beehives of automotive activities. At one time, only Detroit was known as the center of the carmaker's world. Then Toyota, Honda, Subaru, Hyundai, Mercedes, and BMW found new locations far away from Detroit.

New York City, a leader in financial markets, is also a prominent location for product lines in publishing and entertainment; Amsterdam and New York City are preeminent sources for diamond cutting and sales, respectively. Starbucks is growing in Japan, and tourists walk past Starbuck's Café in Beijing's Forbidden City in China. Global locations compound the complexity of career decisions in operations.

1-9b Operations Management Career Paths

There are many different kinds of P/OM careers. No one can describe all of them because the scenarios of opportunity are always changing. Consider the *actual* pattern of developments that started with Y2K (the year 2000). The Y2K fear was that computers would be unreliable when the calendar shifted from 1XXX to 2XXX. Computers, with fixes for changing 2-digit dates into 4-digit dates, worked well. However, as the year 2000 took effect, it was people who became irrational. Technology hardly failed at all.

Events have helped to shape the character of P/OM jobs. The Enron failure led to Sarbanes-Oxley revitalizing the importance of operations-oriented accounting to identify real costs and revenues. The World Trade Center disaster of September 11, 2001, completely altered the management of security operations at airports in scope and importance.

Career paths differ according to whether line or staff positions are chosen. *Line* position means responsibility for producing products or services. The term comes from working on the production line. *Staff* positions by definition are not on the production line, but supportive of the line. Staff positions provide information, guidance, and advice on topics such as cost, quality, suppliers, inventories, and work schedules. Titles for both line and staff positions vary in different companies, and specific details of responsibilities would differ for each position. However, the generalities regarding accountability remain the same.

Knowing about career paths provides a useful perspective for a person starting the study of P/OM. It should be noted, however, that the field is dynamic and changing. It is involved in organizational experimentation with teamwork and the systems approach. The use of multifunctional teams is increasing and likely to spawn new kinds of positions and career opportunities.

1-9c Global Aspects of Career Paths

Among the vast possibilities of exciting new careers are managers of global P/OM support networks, which need to connect and synchronize factories and service systems located all over the world. P/OM is an international endeavor. With the North American Free Trade Agreement (NAFTA) accepted, the General Agreement on Tariffs and Trade (GATT) being implemented, and the Doha Development Round continuing but stalled,[9] the European Union (EU) has become a giant market for goods and services as well as a new environment for manufacturing and service operations. The Pacific Rim has come alive with manufacturing, and great new markets are opening up in Southeast Asia. The off-and-on again agreement to create a free trade zone for the Americas stretching from Alaska to Argentina (34 countries including the United States) is yet another potential indicator of the internationalization of operations management. Suppliers from everywhere will be competing in the global market. A career in P/OM will involve much travel and an equally large amount of global communication. P/OM careers will require ability to coordinate and synchronize systems on a global scale.

In the following list, twelve traditional career paths are provided that highlight differences between line and staff positions. Manufacturing jobs are followed by a list of service professions. Both include line and staff positions. Titles only approximate the progression from top through middle management to first-level management. For services there is an even greater problem to get titles that fairly represent progression through the management hierarchy.

P/OM Careers in Manufacturing—Line

1. Corporate Vice President of Manufacturing
2. Divisional Manager of Production
3. Plant Manager
4. Vice President of Materials Management
5. Project Manager of Transitions
6. Department Foreman or Forelady, Department Supervisor

P/OM Careers in Manufacturing—Staff

7. Director of Quality
8. Inventory Manager, Materials Manager, or Purchasing Agent
9. Production Schedule Controller
10. Project Manager/Consultant (Internal or External)
11. Performance Improvement Manager
12. Methods Analyst

P/OM Careers in Services—Line

1. Corporate Vice President of Operations
2. Divisional Manager of Operations
3. Administrative Head

  4. Department Manager or Supervisor
  5. Facilities Manager
  6. Branch Manager or Store Manager

P/OM Careers in Services—Staff

  7. Quality Supervisor
  8. Materials Manager or Purchasing Agent
  9. Project Manager/Consultant (Internal or External)
  10. Staff Schedule Controller
  11. Performance Improvement Manager
  12. Systems or Methods Analyst

By explaining a few of these titles in more detail, it is possible to provide quick insight into various aspects of the P/OM field. Also, it further clarifies differences between manufacturing and service systems.

1-9d Manager of Production or Operations: Manufacturing or Services

The manager of operations in services and the production manager in a manufacturing plant are in line positions, meaning that they are responsible for the inputs, the outputs, and the transformation process. These managers oversee the people and technology doing the job, which could be preparing and serving food; taking blood and giving shots; or making DVDs and programming robots on the line. As a rule, they report to a corporate vice president, who has multifunctional responsibilities, or they report directly to the president of the company. Middle managers and selected staff functions report to the manager of production or operations.

For example, department supervisors report to the manager of production and operations. The supervisor's position is a line job. In manufacturing, the supervisor, who is often called foreman or forelady, oversees some part of the production process. In service operations, the supervisor title describes the person responsible for some specific function such as reservations or insurance premium collection.

This is a high-level position, but the character of the job depends upon the stage of the company. In Stage IV firms, this person will regularly be invited to lunch in the boardroom because of top management's keen interest in operations.

1-9e Inventory Manager or Materials Manager

The inventory or materials manager holds a staff position that is accountable for controlling the flow of input materials to the line. The function of this job is to determine when and how much to order, and how much stock to keep on hand. There are myriad titles associated with these jobs. Many manufacturing and some service firms have vice presidents of materials management because the cost of materials as a percent of the total cost of goods sold is high. In service firms like Starbucks and JetBlue Airways, materials are similarly important. Service firms tend to have a larger labor cost component, and the airlines have high fixed costs. Nevertheless, the cost of coffee has been rising, and fuel costs have been volatile and very high. The inventory managers might consider hedging when purchasing coffee and kerosene (see Enrichment Activity 13).

1-9f Director of Quality

There are a great number of jobs in the quality assurance area and even more titles. Most of these jobs are staff positions that range from auditing quality levels to doing statistical analyses for control charts. The director of quality or quality manager (who could be a vice president) is in charge of the various quality activities that are going on in the firm.

In some companies, line workers have been given quality responsibilities, so it is possible to find supervisors with quality team assignments. Quality adjustments to inputs, including vendors, and to the transformation process are common. Quality positions usually focus on improving the quality of outputs by inspecting for defects, preventing them from happening, and correcting their causes. Quality management is just as important in service firms as it is in firms manufacturing goods, but it is more elusive to measure what customers consider quality and, therefore, more challenging to deal with service quality.

1-9g Project Manager/Consultant (Internal or External)

There are important P/OM jobs relating to projects. These can include the development of new products and services as well as the processes to make and deliver them. Constructing a refinery, putting the space station into orbit, writing this online and paper textbook—are all projects. Consultants, both internal and external, are usually engaged in project management. External consultants are employees of a consulting firm. P/OM is an excellent entree for a consulting career. Internal consulting applies only to the company for which the employee works (e.g., GE, UPS, FedEx, and Amgen are companies that have very successful records using their own internal employees as project consultants).

During volatile business times, transition management is used with various scenarios such as downsizing, turnarounds, and business process redesign. Companies have created positions that indicate responsibility for some form of transition in the job title. For example, a project manager of transitions is in charge of downsizing or rightsizing the company, turnarounds (restoring a company that is in trouble to good financial health), and reengineering (starting from scratch to redesign the firm). Various new job titles have appeared such as outsourcing manager and the transformational CEO, which indicates that the management of change is taking place.

Spotlight 1-1 Alliance for Innovative Manufacturing (AIM)
Take an Online Plant Tour at Home with AIM: How Everyday Things Are Made

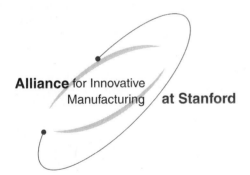

Stanford University, through a cooperative venture with industry partners in the Alliance for Innovative Manufacturing (AIM), takes students on plant visits and guided tours of many kinds (see http://manufacturing.stanford.edu).

The material is exceptionally well-designed and informative. Over 40 different products and processes with almost 4 hours of video are available to build an understanding of how things are made. For example, there is a 13-minute video on how to make glass bottles. Some other "how they are made" products include motorcycles and their engines, cars, chocolate, and clothes. Knowledgeable guides talk the viewer through the stages and steps of processes as well as products.

An interactive section called *Test Your Knowledge* provides a quick self-evaluation with clear directions about what videos to watch to correct misperceptions about how to make jelly beans, plastic bottles, and glass, or how many parts go into a Boeing 777.

There are 12-minute clips on casting, 20-minute clips on molding plastics, 17-minute clips on forming and shaping, 5-minute clips on machining, and 4-minute clips of video on assembly operations. Video controls are furnished for pause, slow down, etc. Exercises take the form of "what did you learn," "think about it," and FAQs. There is about an hour of video discussing careers in manufacturing. Dr. Mark Martin hosts many other experts from industry in this enlightening excursion.

Don't miss this chance to learn what successful P/OM students need to understand about both manufacturing and services. P/OM practitioners have to be conversant with every process detail. Otherwise, the car will not move, the cake will not bake, the cost per unit will not be competitive.

Spotlight 1-1 (Continued)

The combined knowledge at the AIM website represents a storehouse of information that has taken a long time for many smart people to figure out.

The AIM website references books that are of the same genre. A very significant series is available that describes *How Products Are Made*. These are published by Gale of Cengage Learning. The seventh volume was published in March 2002. The first volume is dated December 1993. About 250 firms are listed sponsors and supporters of these not inexpensive reference books, which explain in detail (but not for engineers) how silver, paper currency, pianos, and hundreds of other products are made. "The set includes everything from artificial turf to the artificial heart valve" [*American Reference Books Annual* (*ARBA*), January 2003].

At the same website, AIM references *Watch It Made in the U.S.A.: A Visitor's Guide to the Companies That Make Your Favorite Products*, 3d ed., by Karen Axelrod and Bruce Brumberg. The publisher is Avalon Travel Publishing, and this edition was published in September 2002. This book describes more than 300 companies that are open for actual plant visits. There is information about hours and fees (90 percent are free) for factories, visitor centers, and company museums across the country. There is additional information at http://www.factorytour.com.

AIM references another publication of interest. The PCN (Pennsylvania Cable Networks) describes guided journeys of 28 popular plants including those making pianos, pretzels, and helicopters.

Dr. Richard Reis is executive director of the Alliance for Innovative Manufacturing (AIM) at Stanford University. He and the AIM organization deserve much credit for the educational achievement described here. AIM is referred to as a continuous learning community composed of industry practitioners and academics (both students and faculty qualify), which means that many people are contributing to the library and its upkeep. As of July 8, 2007, there had been more than a million hits at the AIM website. To learn more about AIM, visit http://www.stanford.edu/group/AIM.

Review Questions

1 What is an online plant tour, and why should we be interested in taking one?
2 How do assembly plant tours relate to preparing a mailing of many thousands of pieces?
3 What causes a faint seam along the side of glass bottles? If you never asked yourself this question, what big lesson can you learn from this simple exercise?
4 There are interesting blogs related to "How Everyday Things Are Made." What method would you use to locate such blogs, and how would you rate the blogs you find?
5 Are there other sites that provide plant tours, or is the Stanford-AIM URL unique?

Sources: Correspondence with AIM, April and July 2007; *The Stanford Magazine*, "Everyday Things, Start to Finish," January/February 2005; *The Mercury News*, "Explaining How Things Are Made," August 10, 2003; *The New York Times, Circuits*, September 11, 2003. Also, see http://manufacturing.stanford.edu; http://www.stanford.edu/group/AIM; and http://www.stanford.edu/group/AIM/AIMPrograms/AIMCertificate/AIMCert.html.

Spotlight 1-2 Atomic Dog/Cengage Learning—A Better Way

Cincinnati, Ohio
www.atomicdog.com

Founded in March 2000, Atomic Dog Publishing is a next-generation publisher that specializes in developing web-based print and interactive textbooks. Atomic Dog's textbooks blend online content delivery, interactive multimedia components, and print to form a unique learning and teaching environment.

From the outset, the company's publications are designed to be immediate (evergreen content), interactive, and affordable (25 to 40 percent less than competitive titles).

In April 2006, Atomic Dog became part of Cengage Learning Custom Solutions, which further validated and recognized Atomic Dog's effective business model. This beneficial partnership collaboration between leaders in new publishing media produced an even more powerful organization for the development of text materials of excellence.

Traditional Publishing Model

The traditional textbook publishing process is linear—a textbook project begins at a certain point and proceeds systematically through a series of steps. It is one-way—the end-user of the textbook has very little input or influence on the process.

Traditional Process

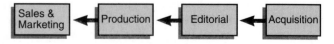

For higher education publishers looking to move their textbooks online, breaking down decades' worth of content, in some cases, and managing those digital assets once completed compose just one part of the challenge. A second, even more daunting, part is developing a textbook delivery platform. The integration of traditional print content with multimedia technologies is yet another. Instead of addressing the problem in a holistic way, most publishers have chosen to tackle the content problem and find partners in order to cobble together a delivery solution.

However, if a publishing company is truly serious about building interactive, digital textbooks, then it must change the entire publishing model, from author acquisition to sales and marketing. The rich media capabilities, dynamic interaction, immediate delivery, and demand for timeliness that the web represents require a complete rethinking of "What is a textbook?"

Atomic Dog Model

Atomic Dog's publishing model is a continuous process, with feedback across all levels, and one where end-users (students and instructors) play an integral role. Atomic Dog/Thomson Custom Solutions has three functional groups that do not exist within a traditional publishing company—Interactive Media, Engineering, and Quality Assurance (QA)/Customer Support.

Interactive Media works with authors and editors to develop a storyboard calling for key animations and interactive learning objects. Static charts, figures, tables, and references to external material take on new meaning in a digital textbook. Authors have to break free from traditional thinking and embrace the pedagogical possibilities of a digital textbook.

In addition to technology development, Engineering is concerned with the conversion of content (manuscript) source files into XML and bringing the content into Atomic Dog's proprietary learning environment.

Quality Assurance has two key roles—(1) enforcing strict quality standards across all functional groups (as shown in the illustration that follows) and (2) interacting with and supporting the end-users, both students and instructors. During the production process, Interactive Media and Engineering work with the production team to produce equivalent online and print versions of the textbook.

When work is completed by Production and Engineering, the textbook is handed over to QA for final testing and sign-off before being "released." After adoption by an instructor, QA/Customer Support interacts with students and instructors to answer registration and usage questions, as well as collect feedback on problems and new feature

requests. The process then feeds back into itself, resulting in a continuously evolving textbook—analogous to a software revision process.

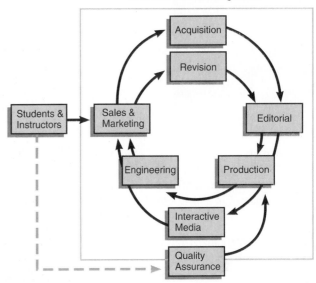

New Breed Publishing Model

The power of the Atomic Dog Model is that it is continuous, nonlinear, highly interactive, and designed to get its products to market faster and at lower cost than traditional publishers. Since inception, Atomic Dog sales have grown an average of 50 percent each year.

Atomic Dog is truly an environmentally friendly publisher. This is not lip service or public relations. Atomic Dog's product line is green. Textbooks and marketing materials are printed on recycled paper. Students buying online editions study without consuming paper. They also spare trees by eliminating the need for packaging and shipping. Atomic Dog is justifiably proud of its reduced "pawprint" on the environment.

Review Questions

1 How does Atomic Dog qualify as a production and operations management (P/OM) system?
2 Is Atomic Dog a typical textbook producer or is it unique in some way? If you think it is unique, explain how you think it is different.
3 Traditional textbook publishing is called a linear model. Why is this so?
4 What is a textbook delivery platform?
5 What is the role of QA/Customer Support?

Source: Atomic Dog/Cengage Learning, 2008.

chapter

1

Taxonomy
Methods of classification and categorization of phenomena usually arranged in a hierarchical structure.

Stages of P/OM development
Four stages that loosely characterize how much management counts on P/OM for success.

Summary

Chapter 1 begins with an explanation of production and operations management (P/OM). It presents the role of P/OM in strategic planning for the product line and subsequently for the processes that are required to make, fashion, and deliver the products. It explains why the systems approach is essential for successful strategic planning of the business model using coordination of all functions of the business.

Next, the systems approach is defined as systematic and constructive methodology using systems **taxonomy**. The implementation of the systems approach employed by P/OM is detailed and explored with examples applied to manufacturing of goods and to services. In that context, production management is compared to operations management. Chapter 1 explains how information systems play a vital role in both manufacturing and services. Also, the basic model of P/OM—the input–output transformation model—is developed, along with the costs and revenue that are associated with its use. This leads to a discussion of the input–output profit model and how it has changed over time.

Stages of P/OM development are introduced with attention paid to special capabilities (strategic and tactical) derived from P/OM that allow a company to reach highly competitive stages of development. This leads to deliberation about the kind of P/OM positions that might be encountered by other functional managers in the organization, as well as the type of careers that P/OM offers.

Two Spotlight feature boxes conclude this chapter. The first opens a doorway to how things are made, and the second provides a powerful example of how strategic planning produced a nontraditional set of operations for the publishing industry. See Spotlight 1-1: Alliance for Innovative Manufacturing (AIM) and Spotlight 1-2: Atomic Dog/Cengage Learning.

Key Terms

Analytic reduction (p. 9)	Production (p. 5)
Construction (p. 9)	Production management (p. 14)
Depreciation (p. 18)	Project management (p. 22)
Fixed costs (p. 17)	Reengineering (REE) (p. 22)
Functional field approach (p. 8)	Service (p. 13)
Information systems (p. 7)	Stages of P/OM development (p. 30)
Input–output model (p. 20)	Systematic (p. 9)
I/O profit model (p. 19)	Systemic (p. 9)
Manufacturing (p. 6)	Systems approach (p. 8)
OM system (p. 10)	Taxonomy (p. 30)
Operations (p. 6)	Transformation (p. 16)
Operations management (p. 5)	Variable costs (p. 17)
Overhead (p. 15)	

Review Questions

1 What is operations management? Define OM. Compare it to P/OM. Distinguish between production and operations management.

2 What are the differentiating characteristics of services as compared to those of manufacturing? Illustrate the distinctive aspects of each by naming industries and citing specific companies that represent each.

3 To what category of P/OM does hotel management belong? What fixed and variable costs are appropriate for this industry?

4 To what category of P/OM does agricultural management belong? What fixed and variable costs are appropriate for this industry?

5 How do information systems relate to operations management?

6   Why is the systems approach essential to assure real participation of OM in a firm? What does the systems approach have to do with company strategy?

7   What types of costs are usually associated with inputs? Give specific examples from the education field.

8   What costs are identified with the equipment that provides transformations? Give specific examples from the fields of manufacturing and transportation.

9   How do outputs convert into dollars of revenue? How are these dollars related to fixed and variable costs as described in Questions 7 and 8?

10   Explain the stages of P/OM development and try to identify some companies that might be representative of each stage.

11   What changes have occurred over time in the following profit model?

$$P = (p - vc)V - FC$$

12   Describe career paths of P/OM for both manufacturing and service systems.

Problems Section

Note: This section has various problems that can be formulated and solved using QuantMethods Production/Operations Management software (QMpom). The appropriate model categories are indicated for each problem.

1   Develop the transformation process to

a. make wine.

b. produce wooden lead pencils (consult http://science.howstuffworks.com/question465.htm).

c. bake bread.

2   Draw the input–output model that could be used to run a successful restaurant. Label the variable costs for labor and materials, and detail those costs. What fixed costs apply to this model?

3   What are the headings for the columns and the titles for the rows? The stages refer to the development level of the P/OM function.

Stage I   Stage III
Stage II   Stage IV

4   Draw an input–output model for a Starbucks store. Label as many of the specific and detailed inputs and outputs as you can. (Figure 1-7 is a model of categories to include.) What transformations link inputs with outputs? (It is helpful to visit a Starbucks store. Observe operations. If possible talk to a manager about how drinks are assembled.)

5   Repeat what you have done in Problem 4 for a Dunkin' Donuts store. Make a detailed comparison between Starbucks and Dunkin' Donuts.

6   A manufacturing plant and equipment cost $150 million and are estimated to have a lifetime of 25 years. Straight-line depreciation is to be used. Additional fixed costs per year are $4 million. Variable costs are $1.25 and price is set at $3.25. State annual profit when annual volume, in million units, is

a. 10.

b. 2.5.

c. 5.

d. 8.

e. What is the breakeven volume in millions of units? (Using the QMpom module called Capacity Management Models (Breakeven) will facilitate solving this situation.)

7   A call center and its equipment cost $120 million and are estimated to have a lifetime of 30 years. Straight-line depreciation is to be used. Additional fixed costs per year are $6 million. Variable costs are $2.50; price is set at $3.75. State annual profit if annual volume in millions of units is

a. 10.

b. 8.

c. What is breakeven cost? (Using the QMpom module called Capacity Management Models (Breakeven) will facilitate solving this situation.)

8   A manufacturing plant and equipment cost $200 million and are estimated to have a lifetime of 20 years. Straight-line depreciation is to be used. Additional fixed costs per year are $5.5 million. Variable costs are $1.50 and price is set at $2.50. What will annual profit be if the annual volume is 10 million units?

Using the QMpom module called Capacity Management Models (Breakeven) will facilitate solving Problem 8.

9   A service center has installed a new computer system with local area networking at a cost of $1.6 million. The system is expected to serve for 8 years, and straight-line depreciation is acceptable. There are additional fixed costs of $300,000 per year. This service repair center charges each customer a flat fee of $30. The variable costs are $20. What will profit be if the annual volume is

a. 50,000 units?

b. 25,000 units?

c. 75,000 units?

d. What is the breakeven point and what is the breakeven cost? (Using the QMpom module called Capacity Management Models (Breakeven) will facilitate solving this situation.)

10   Four companies are described as follows. Characterize each in terms of the stage of P/OM development that seems appropriate as described in Section 1-8. Classify each situation and explain the reason for the classification used.

a. This manufacturer pays little attention to the quality of the product. The owner is convinced that customers are plentiful but not loyal. Hard sell is stressed.

b. This service organization tries to keep up with its competitors by copying everything they do as soon as possible. The president believes that development costs are saved and that being a fast imitator results in a competitive advantage.

c. This manufacturer is constantly working at being as good as the best of the competitors. They have improved quality repeatedly while holding costs constant. The production manager participates in strategy formulation.

d. This service organization aims at global leadership based on the finest operations in the world. The service is constantly being improved, which gives the organization a proactive leadership role in its industry.

Practice Quiz

1   Production and operations management is symbolized by P/OM because

a.   production management is more important than operations management.

b.   production and operations management are identical and of equal importance.

c.   production and operations management are similar in many important ways.

d.   production management is less important than operations management.

e.   the International Standards Association in Geneva chose that designation.

2   The distinction between production and operations is best described as

a.   production makes goods; operations delivers services.

b.   production is automobile manufacturing; operations is everything else.

c.   production is heavy manufacturing; operations are light manufacturing.

d.   operations are associated with banks, airlines, insurance companies, and restaurants only; production is everything else.

e.   Shakespeare in *A Midsummer Night's Dream* (while thou dost operate; yet not produce a single product).

3   The Greyhound Bus driver's productivity (miles driven per day) is measured by m where $m = vt$, where v is velocity and t is time driven per day (see Section 1-1a). If the company was to increase the length of a driver's shift from $t = 8$ to $t = 10$ hours, how would driver productivity change?

a.   The equation $m = 10v$ reflects a productivity increase of 50% over $m = 8v$.

b.   The equation $m = 10v$ reflects a productivity increase of 25% over $m = 8v$.

c.   The equation $m = 10v$ reflects a productivity increase of 15% over $m = 8v$.

d.   The equation is irrelevant because the driver's performance will be affected by traffic.

e.   The driver's performance is tracked by computer using GPS, and management will penalize drivers for unscheduled stops.

4   The distinction between strategies and tactics is best described by which of the following statements?

a.   Good strategies overpower poor tactics.

b.   Strategies are plans; tactics are objectives; they work together.

c.   The strategy is *make 1,000 SUVs per shift*; the tactic is *never on Sundays*.

d.   The strategy is *no work on Sundays*; the tactic is *make 982 SUVs per shift*.

e.   Good strategies are not "good" if the best tactics are not good enough.

5   The functional field approach to P/OM is

a.   primarily tactical in its perspective.
b.   essentially strategic in its point of view.
c.   not well-represented by a traditional organization chart.
d.   connected, coordinated, and interrelated with marketing.
e.   connected, coordinated, and interrelated with finance.

6   The systems approach to P/OM is

a.   primarily tactical in its perspective.
b.   essentially strategic in its point of view.
c.   not well-represented by a traditional organization chart.
d.   independent of marketing and finance goals.
e.   based on success in achieving teamwork.

7   The systems approach is based on a powerful philosophy. Which of the following statements is most accurate?

a.   There is one systems approach but two different schools of thought.
b.   The systemic approach is typical of the analytical Western-world approach.
c.   The systematic approach is typical of the holistic Eastern-world philosophy.
d.   The joint contributions of introspection and extraspection are not systematic.
e.   The constructive approach is neither systemic nor systematic.

8   The input–output model (I-T-O) defines production and operations. Managing the model is what P/OM does because

a.   engineering is required to manage transformations.
b.   economic theory is required to manage input rates.
c.   marketing management is required to manage output rates.
d.   the input–output model operates with random transformations (T).
e.   I-T-O captures all the costs and revenues of the system.

9   Stages of P/OM development are beneficial for benchmarking the status of a firm.

a.   Stage I characterizes SMB (SMB = small and medium-size businesses).
b.   Stage IV firms are large-size business organizations.
c.   Stages are useful to assess the firm's prospects for future development.
d.   Transitions from Stage I to Stage III are common because only internal issues are involved.
e.   Transitions from Stage III to Stage IV require changing a neutral stance to a supportive stance.

10   Career opportunities of many kinds exist in the P/OM field. Before seeking specific careers, it is important to sort out the truth from fiction. One of the following statements is false. Which one is it?

a.   Jobs requirements and expectations differ according to the type of P/OM process.
b.   Flow shop processing fits well with managers who enjoy stabilizing and controlling systems.
c.   Managers who like to work with many people in hectic environments do well in the batch production environments, which include many service systems.
d.   Global firms require that their managers speak many languages.
e.   The profile of managers who do well with projects is well-known and unique.

Additional Readings

Abernathy, William J., K. B. Clark, and A. M. Kantrow. *Industrial Renaissance.* New York: Basic Books, 1983.

Ackoff, R. L., J. Magidson, and H. J. Addison. *Idealized Design.* Upper Saddle River, NJ: Wharton School Publishing, 2006.

Chase, Richard B., and Robert H. Hayes. "Beefing-Up Operations in Service Firms." *Sloan Management Review* (Fall 1991): 17–28.

Horovitz, Jacques. *Winning Ways: Achieving Zero-Defect Service.* Productivity Press, 1990.

Karol, R., and B. Nelson. *New Product Development for Dummies.* Hoboken, NJ: Wiley Publishing, Inc., 2007.

Levitt, Theodore. "Production-Line Approach to Service." *Harvard Business Review* (September–October 1972).

Müller-Merbach, Heiner. "A System of Systems Approaches." *Interfaces,* vol. 24, no. 4 (July–August 1994): 16–25.

Parkinson, C. Northcote. *Parkinson's Law.* Boston: Houghton Mifflin Company, 1957.

Peters, Tom, and R. H. Waterman, Jr. *In Search of Excellence.* New York: Basic Books, 1983.

Stalk, George, Philip Evans, and Lawrence E. Shulman. "Competing on Capabilities: The New Rules of Corporate Strategy." *Harvard Business Review* (March–April 1992): 57–69.

Tihamér von Ghyczy, "The Fruitful Flaws of Strategy Metaphors." *Harvard Business Review* (September 2003): 86–94.

Wheelwright, Steven C., and Robert H. Hayes. "Competing Through Manufacturing." *Harvard Business Review* (January–February 1985): 99–109.

Notes

1. Heiner Müller-Merbach. "A System of Systems Approaches." *Interfaces*, vol. 24, no. 4 (July–August 1994): 16–25.
2. Ibid., 16–17.
3. Ibid., 17.
4. Theodore Levitt. "Production-Line Approach to Service." *Harvard Business Review* (September–October 1972). Although this article is old, it is still totally relevant. It is considered a classic. Our interpretation of "idiosyncratic" is eccentric and erratic.
5. George Stalk, Philip Evans, and Lawrence E. Shulman. "Competing on Capabilities: The New Rules of Corporate Strategy." *Harvard Business Review* (March–April 1992): 57–69.
6. Steven C. Wheelwright and Robert H. Hayes. "Competing Through Manufacturing." *Harvard Business Review* (January–February 1985): 99–109.
7. Richard B. Chase and Robert H. Hayes. "Beefing-Up Operations in Service Firms." *Sloan Management Review* (Fall 1991): 17–28.
8. Jacques Horovitz. *Winning Ways: Achieving Zero-Defect Service.* Productivity Press, 1990.
9. "View Partnerships Through Trade" at http://wwwustr.gov. Enter "Doha" in the search window for information about the Doha Development Round.

Enrichment Activity 1: Decision Models
A Distribution Problem: How to Ship—Plane or Train?

A decision matrix arranges outcome data into rows and columns. The following matrix presents a decision problem where the rows are shipping "strategies" (plane or train) and the columns are "states of nature"—so called because they are events not under the decision maker's control. In this case, the states of nature are weather conditions.

Outcomes are the entries in the cells of the matrix. They will reflect the fact that planes will be delayed if there is fog, while trains are not affected by the weather. The buyer has promised the shipper a bonus if the delivery can be early. Conversely, the buyer sets a penalty if the delivery is delayed. The decision problem is organized by the matrix as follows:

Probabilities	Low	High
States of Nature	Fog (*F*)	Clear (*C*)
Strategy 1: Plane	Delayed	Early
Strategy 2: Train	On time	On time

Before putting numbers in this matrix, look at the symbolic representation of the following decision matrix. It shows outcomes as $O(i,j)$, where i represents different strategies (rows), and j represents different states of nature (columns). Also, the probabilities of the states of nature—obtained by some forecasting method—are represented by $p(j)$'s, $j = either\ F\ or\ C$.

Probabilities	$p(F)$	$p(C)$
States of Nature	Fog	Clear
Strategy 1: Plane	$O(P,F)$	$O(P,C)$
Strategy 2: Train	$O(T,F)$	$O(T,C)$

Calculating the Numerical Outcomes or Payoffs

Assume the following set of values describes the profit that the shipper gets if the delivery is early, late, or on time. Weather permitting, the flight arrives on time and the company makes $4,500. If the flight is delayed, the firm can still earn $1,500.

Train delivery will earn $3,000 either way because the train arrival time will not be subject to weather. In addition, shipment by plane costs $800 and by train $300. These costs will be subtracted from the profits. Often, the payoff portion of the matrix is calculated by formulas or observations. The payoff matrix for each outcome is shown with probabilities of 0.1 and 0.9 obtained from weather forecasts. (Note: The sum of the probabilities must always be equal to one.)

Probabilities		0.1	0.9
States of Nature	Cost	Fog	Clear
Strategy 1: Plane	−$800	+$1,500	+$4,500
Strategy 2: Train	−$300	+$3,000	+$3,000

After subtraction:

Probabilities	0.1	0.9
States of Nature	Fog (F)	Clear (C)
Strategy 1: Plane	+$700	+$3,700
Strategy 2: Train	+$2,700	+$2,700

Calculating the Expected Values (*EV*)

An expected value is a measure of the average outcome. There is an expected value for each strategy. It is obtained by multiplying the probabilities for each state of nature by the outcome in that column and adding the products across all of the columns. The computing formulas are shown here:

$$EV(Plane) = p(F) \times O(P, F) + p(C) \times O(P, C)$$
$$EV(Train) = p(F) \times O(T, F) + p(C) \times O(T, C)$$

Now using numbers:

$$EV(Plane) = 0.1 \times 700 + 0.9 \times 3700 = 3,400^*$$
$$EV(Train) = 0.1 \times 2700 + 0.9 \times 2700 = 2,700$$

The decision—noted by an asterisk—is to ship by plane because that strategy has an expected value of $3,400 whereas the expected value for shipping by train is lower, i.e., *EV*(Train)$2,700.

Enrichment Challenges 1

1 The forecast of 0.1 and 0.9 is based on last year's weather. When the past 5 years of weather data is consulted, the following results are obtained.

Year	1	2	3	4	5
P(Fog)	0.1	0.2	0.3	0.2	0.5

Determine the best strategy for each year. Then decide how to use all of the weather data to reach the best possible decision.

Productivity and Strategic Planning

Chapter Outline

Chapter 2 illustrates the existing competitive edge organizations gain by using P/OM planning and decision making. P/OM is the only function responsible for creating and running highly productive systems. If P/OM is not included in strategic planning, the odds are that productivity will be lower than it could be and lower than that of the most serious competitors. Less than best productivity is a severe handicap.

If P/OM knowledge and experience is included in strategic planning, productivity will be factored into all considerations. That kind of systems thinking is essential for maximum productivity. The history of operations management has been to continually invent methods that raise productivity.

Chapter 2 explains why all four chapters in Part 1 represent strategic planning using the systems approach.

After reading this chapter, you should be able to:

- Understand the strategic importance of productivity to an organization.
- Evaluate the applicability of various measures of productivity.
- Explain what contributes to good productivity.
- Discuss how to improve productivity.
- Explain why productivity is a systems issue.
- Relate productivity and price.
- Explain demand elasticity as a systems link between P/OM and marketing.
- Describe the effects of quality on elasticity.
- Explain why quality elasticity is critical to P/OM.
- Apply the concepts of economies of scale and division of labor to the management of operations.
- Relate productivity and CAD/CAM.
- Relate productivity and FPS/FMS.
- Explain mass customization and relate that capability to productivity.
- Explain how the history of P/OM shows continual improvement in the P/OM input–output transformation model with resultant increases in productivity.

The Systems Viewpoint

Attainment of productivity that is higher than, or at least equal to, the best that the competitors can achieve is essential to success of strategic plans. Put another way, inferior productivity is a disadvantage that must be overcome if a business is to be sustainable. The measurement of productivity creates quandaries because it can be defined in many different ways. For adequate comparison, a firm may need to measure productivity in several ways. One thing is common to all definitions of productivity. Namely, **productivity** is always a measure of outputs over inputs. It is, therefore, a measure of the efficiency with which resources are utilized to create revenue and profit.

Productivity

Various measures of the ratio of outputs to inputs.

Productivity gets good grades when a high rate of output is obtained at low cost. This is the case even when outputs are hard to measure, as in some service operations. Although P/OM is custodian of the production I/O process, and responsible for achieving high productivity, all employees at every level of the company are involved in attaining excellence in productivity. Everyone has the ability to increase or decrease the organization's productivity. Those managers who have cultivated the systems point of view recognize that good productivity is contagious; so is poor productivity. Employees sense whether the company culture promotes high or low productivity, and they respond in accordance with the cultural norm. This makes the productivity condition a contagion factor with systems-wide implications.

Another strong systems-type interaction relates to price—**demand elasticity**, which links the price charged to the volume that can be sold. Competitive pressures to reduce prices lead to demands that P/OM improve productivity to decrease costs. Also, business lost because of price competition decreases volume, which reduces capacity utilization, leading to larger overhead charges per unit. Reductions in discounts that are based on volume increase variable costs per unit. Productivity measures reveal the integration of all factors that are operating in the business system.

From a broader point of view, P/OM history shows that the overall trend in global economies is to increase productivity. Productivity growth has reflected the impact of a continuous stream of developments in technology and operations management methodology.

Demand elasticity
Extra amounts of product sold when a unit price decrease occurs. The reverse applies: When there is a price increase, lesser amounts are sold.

Strategic Thinking

A highly productive manufacturer of buggy whips in 1926 would be no better off today than an inefficient and lackadaisical one. The most productive maker of engineering slide rules during the 1950s was Keuffel & Esser. Although this company had the largest market share then, it is no longer in existence. K&E did not have a strategy to cope with the advent of electronic calculators and then computers. Outmoded products would not still be available if the production process to make them had been highly productive. High productivity is necessary but not sufficient to assure competitiveness.

Adaptability is critical when product design technology (or style) changes. For example, the most efficient supplier of iceboxes had no advantage when refrigerators replaced the older technology. Additionally, some companies were really good at making vinyl records (collector's items now) but that did not help them survive rapid changes as the music industry moved from 8-track tapes to 8 mm audiocassettes to CDs and now to DVDs. Regarding videotape formats, the Betamax system by Sony was the first successful commercial product. Matsushita aggressively pursued the VHS format, which replaced Betamax, but that is of little consequence now since DVDs are outmoding any tape system. Five-and-a-quarter floppy disks have disappeared, and 3.5-inch floppy disks have been largely superseded by memory cards, flash sticks, etc.

The lesson to learn from all of these cases is that productivity excellence is useless without market acceptance. P/OM strategic thinking is "find the best product line for the marketplace, and then make them at the lowest cost, highest quality, and overall at max productivity levels." As Peter Drucker is quoted to have said, "Do the right thing, and then do the thing right." Strategy planning for operations is directly concerned with "Do the right thing."

Later on, there will be attention paid to the strategies of choosing the "right" processes. *Product design* and *product development* lead to *process design* and *process development*. Product and process are both components of the strategic imperatives for P/OM. Output as inventory that cannot be sold is unproductive and cannot be counted in measuring productivity.

2-1 Productivity—A Major P/OM Issue

Productivity is a critical business variable that directly impacts the "bottom line"; improved productivity raises net profits. P/OM is responsible for the productivity of the process. This is such a critical factor in a company's overall productivity that excellence in productivity achievement is a major P/OM issue.

Productivity is a system property that interacts with other system properties such as reliability and consistency, as well as customers' perceptions of quality. Productivity interacts with the variable costs of goods and services, as well as with the fixed costs of facilities, training, and technology. Productivity interacts with the presence and the availability of management as a resource. It is often found that output rates and qualities are better on regular work shifts as compared to "graveyard" shifts because managers are scarce resources for the latter.

2-1a The Measurement of Productivity

Productivity measures the performance of the organization's processes for doing work. The American Production and Inventory Control Society (APICS) definition follows, but other definitions also will be given. Productivity is an important way of grading how well P/OM and the rest of the system are doing. Productivity is a score like RBIs (runs batted in) or ROI (return on investment).

Productivity is defined as "an overall measure of the ability to produce a good or a service. It is the actual output of production compared to the actual input of resources. Productivity is a relative measure across time or against common entities. In the production literature, attempts have been made to define **total productivity** where the effects of labor and capital are combined and divided into the output."[1]

The APICS Dictionary definition of productivity can be converted into the terms of this text by recognizing that productivity is the ratio measure of output (O) divided by input (I). This is the I/O model depicted in Figures 1-5, 1-6, and 1-7.

Operations management views the measurement of productivity as essential for assessing the performance of an organization's productive capacity over a specific time period and in comparison to the competition. When outputs are high and inputs are low, the system is said to be efficient and productive.

$$\text{productivity} = \frac{\text{outputs}}{\text{inputs}} = \text{measure of production efficiency} \qquad (2\text{-}1)$$

This productivity measure compares the quantity of goods or services produced in a period of time (t) and the quantity of resources employed in turning out these goods or services in the same period of time (t).[2]

Equation 2-1 is relatively easy to measure for physical goods. It is more difficult to find appropriate measures for some services outputs such as units of education or health care. Creative knowledge workers provide other instances of intangible outputs that are highly valued, but elusive to calculate. The effort has to be made to appraise the value of these outputs in a standardized way to provide a **benchmark** (or standard) for measurement. Productivity measures are benchmarks for comparing how well the system is doing compared to other systems, or over time.

Sales perceives productivity as high customer sales volume (called an *effective marketing system*) accompanied by low producer costs (called an *efficient producer system*). Thus:

$$\text{productivity} = \frac{\text{effectiveness}}{\text{efficiency}} = \frac{\text{high customer sales volume}}{\text{low producer expenses}} \qquad (2\text{-}2)$$

From a systems point of view, the inclusion of sales provides a correct measure of output for productivity measurement. It is hardly productive to make a lot of product that is not sold, even if the cost of making it is low.

At the same time, P/OM employs productivity measures to assess how well the production system is functioning. The kinds of questions that are being addressed are: how many units of resources are consumed to produce the output, and how many units of output can be made with a fixed amount of capacity?

Total productivity
See **Multifactor productivity**.

© 2008 Jupiterimages Corporation

Productivity measures can be common-sense ratios, like the number of meals served from noon until 1 P.M. by a quick-service restaurant or the number of people that each cashier processes during that same period of time.

Benchmark
The comparison between two measures of performance where one is considered to be the standard against which the other is compared.

Both ways of viewing productivity have benefits. They stem from different interests that need to be shared. The best interests of the company are served by merging what is learned about P/OM's efficiency and sales/marketing effectiveness.

Labor efficiency is an often-used measure of productivity where productivity is a ratio of output units produced to input labor resources expended per unit of time (t). Equations 2-4 and 2-5 show productivity measured as units of output per dollar of labor in a period of time. That would provide a measure of **labor productivity**.

First, however, note that the dimensions for output and input are shown in Equation 2-3.

Labor productivity
Partial accounting for productivity that is due to the use of human labor to do the job.

$$\text{output} \frac{\text{units}}{\text{hour}}, \text{ and input} = \frac{\text{dollars}}{\text{hour}} = \text{hourly wages} \qquad (2\text{-}3)$$

Then, Equation 2-4 measures labor productivity over a specific period of time, t.

$$\text{productivity}(t) = \frac{\text{output}(t)}{\text{input}(t)} = \frac{\text{units of output}(t)}{\text{dollars of labor}(t)} \qquad (2\text{-}4)$$

This relationship measures how many dollars of labor resources are required in period (t) to achieve the output rate (t), and indicates how much output is being obtained for each dollar spent.

Converting Output into Dollars for Labor and Multifactor Productivity

Another way of stating the measure of productivity is to put a dollar value on the output volume per unit of time. The input cost is already stated in dollars per hour. The advantage of this method is that it can deal with the productivity of the system across different kinds of units; for example, the productivity of a paint company that puts paints of many colors in cans of many sizes could be measured. This approach is used for national accounting of productivity where there are many different kinds of units to be included (i.e., furniture, clothing, energy, and food). Dollars can standardize the output measure across diverse categories.

Labor productivity, often measured as the ratio of sales dollars to labor cost dollars, is called a *partial measure of productivity*. It is partial because it only looks at labor and does not include capital. Equation 2-5 presents this measure with only actual revenue-generating sales included in the numerator. Later, other measures are shown, which include finished goods not-yet-sold and/or work-in-process (WIP), which is not-yet-completed.

$$\text{labor productivity}(t) = \frac{\text{output}(t)}{\text{input}(t)} = \frac{\text{sales in dollars}(t)}{\text{dollars of labor}(t)} \qquad (2\text{-}5)$$

Multifactor productivity (MFP) can be measured in different ways. As shown in Equation 2-6, sales and finished goods are considered as outputs, but work-in-process is not. Also, labor costs and capital expenditures (amortized) are treated as inputs. Multifactor productivity (as shown in Equation 2-6) is measured as the ratio of dollars earned to dollars spent. Total factor productivity is another name associated with inclusion of more factors than labor. Multifactor (and total factor) productivity is measured on a regular basis to determine how well the U.S. industrial base is doing and whether it is improving its competitive position in the world.

Multifactor productivity (MFP)
Also called **total productivity**; reflects the joint effects of many factors including labor and capital.

$$\text{multifactor productivity}(t) = \frac{\text{all outputs of goods and services}(t, \$)}{\text{total input resources expended}(t, \$)} \qquad (2\text{-}6)$$

	Years	Multifactor Productivity
Table 2-1 Average Annual Percent Changes in Multifactor Productivity	1948–1973	2.2
	1973–1990	0.5
	1990–1995	0.5
	1995–2000	1.3
	2000–2006	1.7
	1948–2006	1.4

Note: U.S. Bureau of Labor Statistics (2000); Office of Productivity and Technology (May 24, 2007).

"A change in multifactor productivity reflects the difference between the change in output (production of goods and services) and the change in labor and capital inputs engaged in the production of the output. Multifactor productivity does not measure the specific contributions of labor, capital, or any other factor of production. Instead, it reflects the joint effects of many factors, including new technology, economies of scale, managerial skill, and change in the organization of production."[3]

If it seems useful to include work-in-process in the numerator because WIP is certain to be sold, then that should be done. Similarly, it may be important to include all costs and expenses in the denominator (i.e., energy, material, and miscellaneous costs). This is called *total productivity* as distinguished from *total factor productivity*.

Trends in Multifactor (MFP) Productivity

Table 2-1 shows the average annual percent changes in multifactor productivity for the United States over different periods of time.[4]

U.S. productivity averaged just slightly above 2 percent per year from 1948 through 1973. That was considered to be healthy, though not robust, growth. Then came "the shrinking era," which lasted for 22 years from 1973 through 1995. These were tough years for U.S. manufacturing firms. The U.S. auto industry observed that new Japanese plants in America (transplants in Tennessee, Ohio) in the 1970s were twice as productive as traditional U.S. auto plants in Detroit.

There began a long learning process on the part of U.S. auto manufacturers to increase their productivity. It took a dozen years, but it worked. U.S. auto making reflects more productive processes. The improvement applies to more than automobiles. After many years of declining growth rates, and even some years of negative growth, U.S. productivity has accelerated to levels equivalent to the post–World War II years.

The renewal of U.S. productivity growth is not surprising. Great efforts have been made in the manufacturing sectors to improve efficiency. Subjects such as total quality management (TQM), reengineering, and turnarounds, discussed in the general press, are not fads. They herald solid accomplishments. Adoption of new technology promises more developments yet to come.

However, it is important to separate the manufacturing component of the total productivity measure from the service component. Measures of service productivity are much lower than those of manufacturing and have not been posting notable improvements around the world. There have been substantial investments in computers and telecommunications within the service sectors, but only recently are there real signs of improvement. At last, broad-based changes in productivity can be reported. This will accelerate as P/OM managers learn how to apply the new technologies to service systems. This productivity differential constitutes a significant difference that currently exists between services and manufacturing.

Capital productivity
Partial accounting for productivity that is due to invested capital.

Capital Productivity

There are further ways to measure productivity in line with other purposes. Equations 2-7 and 2-8 measure **capital productivity** in two different ways. Capital productivity is a partial accounting for productivity. It is productivity due to invested capital in technology. First, there is the number of units of output per dollar of invested capital.

$$\text{capital productivity}(t) = \frac{\text{output}(t)}{\text{input}(t)} = \frac{\text{units of output}(t)}{\text{dollars of capital}(t)} \qquad (2\text{-}7)$$

The second measure of capital productivity is a pure ratio based on dollars of output per dollar of invested capital.

$$\text{capital productivity}(t) = \frac{\text{dollar value of output units}(t, \$)}{\text{dollars for capital resources}(t, \$)} \qquad (2\text{-}8)$$

Such measures of capital productivity might help organizations in the service sectors to address the value of returns on investments in computers and telecommunications. By extending this reasoning, it is possible to develop other partial measures of productivity with respect to areas such as energy expended, space utilized, and materials consumed. In Figure 1-7 this would translate into energy consumed for the transformation of inputs into outputs. It would have to include the energy consumed by suppliers as well as the energy required to deliver goods and services to customers.

Students and practitioners of business know that productivity improvements translate into more profits and greater profitability for organizations and improve the state of the economy. In the same vein, economists believe that productivity improvements translate into higher standards of living and greater prosperity. Productivity measures get factored into inflation calculations as well as other economic scenarios. Increases in productivity are generally regarded as a means of checking inflationary trends. Table 2-1 is well correlated with national prosperity.

This is because by working smarter—not harder—profit margins increase. There is more money available to invest in other business opportunities. The shortage of capital drives interest rates up. However, if there are more jobs available than people to fill them, labor becomes scarce, and rising salaries begin to fuel the expansion of inflation. High productivity is a counterforce to inflation. Fewer people are needed to produce more work. The cost of goods and services moves down with productivity improvements. The contribution of P/OM to the well-being of the national economy is widely recognized.

Relative productivity compares the performance of competitive processes for which P/OM is accountable. This means that if two processes are under consideration for a new product, the productivity measures associated with each product should be derived. When quality problems exist, adjustments downward must be made to productivity. For example, the value of sales plus finished goods plus WIP must be reduced by the cost of defectives. Final decisions about the two processes will not be made on productivity advantages alone, but relative productivity will play a major part in planning.

Relative productivity
Measure of comparison between similar processes.

2-1b Operational Measures of the Organization's Productivity

Productivity measures can be common-sense ratios such as the value of pieces made in a factory divided by the cost of making them, or the number of documents produced by the typing pool divided by the number of people doing word processing. Such operational measures of productivity are valuable benchmarks to companies that are focused on continuous improvement. Relative productivity is such a benchmark.

A productivity measure used by restaurants is the daily dollars generated per table. Many fast-food restaurants use dollars generated per square foot. Airlines measure plane occupancy per flight and average occupancy per route, as well as for all routes flown. Department stores use sales dollars per square foot of space. Mail-order companies measure sales dollars for categories (i.e., fashion, toys, and luggage) by type of illustration (i.e., color and size) on a percent of page basis. Trends in same-store sales can be followed as a benchmarking guide to retail productivity. Many companies measure the productivity of their complaint departments by the ratio of the number of complaints dealt with per day divided by the number of complaint handlers.

Productivity measures should be chosen to reflect strategic goals. For example, some schools can maximize instructor productivity by having large classrooms. The relevant input–output model is apparent. The total of student-in-class hours per instructor increases with large classrooms but personal contact with the instructor per student is reduced. With large class sizes, instructors must be entertaining to get good ratings. Student ratings of instructors may not be a satisfactory measure of educational productivity. Teachers' grading of students is especially difficult in large-size classes. Appropriate benchmarks for educational productivity exemplify the difficulties of measuring what counts.

Formulating appropriate productivity measures to capture the effectiveness of operations is always a P/OM benchmarking challenge. It takes insight and creativity to measure what matters in performance and what truly can be controlled and corrected.

2-1c Productivity Is a Systems Measure

Every function in the company that has some measurable accomplishment can be evaluated with respect to productivity. The productivity of the company is the composite of the contributions of the individual productivity functions.

Volume of output sold is a measure of the productivity of the sales department. Cost of goods sold is a measure of the productivity of the process designers, the R&D department, and the operations managers. It also is a measure of the purchasing department's ability to find the best materials obtained at the lowest possible costs and highest qualities.

Output delivered to the customer is a measure of the ability of the distribution system to be on time with undamaged delivery. Output delivered is subject to warranties. Does the company listen to the "voice of the customers" with respect to difficulties in repairing or returning defectives for the entire product line? If not, future sales productivity can be impaired. Many companies lose track of the fact that warranties exercised represent productivity decreases.

Productivity issues are woven into all parts of the supplier-producer-customer value chain and the input–output transformation process. This further explains why productivity is a strategic systems issue. The supplier-producer-customer value chain, by definition, adds value at every step, which illustrates strategic impact operating on a global scale. The next section explores the relevance of international factors on productivity.

Productivity Is a Global Systems Measure

Although much knowledge exists about production systems and operations management, there have been and continue to be serious productivity problems in the world. These problems have afflicted many developing countries where capital to invest in new technology is scarce, and technical knowledge and training are lacking. There also have been productivity problems in industrialized countries where productivity growth has been cyclical.

Japan's phenomenal productivity growth rates of the 1980s could not be maintained. Nevertheless, Japanese productivity in a variety of industries continues to be formidable. Thus, with respect to auto parts, "On average, the plants in Japan were 18 percent more productive than ones in the United States, and 35 percent more productive than ones in Europe."[5] Further, "Japanese parts makers surveyed increased their productivity by almost 38 percent from 1992 to 1994; the American companies made gains only in the mid-20s."[6] In 2008, Toyota was well on its way to overtaking GM as the leading auto producer in the world. Toyota has developed an astonishing ability to launch new products desired by the marketplace. Speed to market is phenomenal. The hybrid Prius and the inexpensive (at least, at first) Scion are two good examples. Scion, according to Forbes.com (July 26, 2007) "could be the new millennium version of the original Volkswagen Beetle." If this reference is not clear, look up Volkswagen Beetle in Wikipedia.

Toyota's productivity for all of its processes is outstanding. The Toyota production system (called TPS) is referenced continually by businesses all over the world. TPS is P/OM-hub-centric, connecting all other business functions (see Figures PRL-1 and PRL-2 in the Prologue).

Other spectacular global P/OM performers—from product development to process productivity—include Nintendo with its successful Wii and DS, and Apple's iPhone with sales of 525,000 units on the first weekend that the phone was available (Saturday, June 30, 2007, through Sunday, July 1, 2007).

Productivity improvements can be registered by companies that reduce the number of direct employees, increase the use of part-time help, rely more on subcontracting of parts, and employ outside maintenance companies, among other things. In this regard, it is to be noted that Japanese firms typically rely heavily on their suppliers and part-time help. Other aspects of Japanese manufacturing methods logically account for world-class productivity accomplishments. Nevertheless, the phenomenal Japanese productivity records have diminished substantially in recent years.

Other leading industrial nations have experienced productivity declines. Many hypotheses have been offered to explain the inability to sustain stable productivity growth in a turbulent era of new technological development. One suggestion is that the productivity of industrial nations is converging to a global mean.[7] Another is that old technology gets used up, and it is difficult to switch to the new technologies and make them profitable.[8] It also takes smarter management. In spite of this, the U.S. economy shows many signs of increased productivity while reducing the manufacturing labor force and increasing the service sector labor force.

The outsourcing of services has become familiar. Outsourced call centers provide an excellent example of a global phenomenon. Calls originating in Bellevue, Iowa, may be answered by English-speaking operators in Bangalore, India. When outsourcing is used in a proper way, productivity does go up. Usually, input costs are reduced more than output rates. In other words, output volume is decreased for many reasons, including removal of defectives. What is lost in the simple ratio measure is the damage to long-term loyalty.

Competitors keep jockeying and leapfrogging each other with the adoption of new technologies that initially reduce productivity. There are various causes for the reduction. The new technology is imposed on old processes by employees who lack training and experience with the new technology. Product life is short. This allows little time to enjoy the advantages of new technology applied to evanescent and even obsolescent product lines. Quality deterioration is an almost hidden enemy of productivity when defectives are created global distances away from the managers who are responsible for carrying out strategic plans. Speed to remedy weaknesses is also impaired.

Increasingly, companies buy from suppliers located around the world and sell in markets that are equally dispersed. Production facilities, including fabrication, assembly, chemical and drug processes, and service facilities (e.g., call centers), are located globally. In the big picture, productivity performance is the result of international interactions. If productivity is being measured in dollars, or local currencies, exchange rate problems can distort the picture. On the other hand, exchange rate imbalances cause gains and losses that relate to the productivity of investments, which are reflected in ROI (return on investment) measures. It takes an astute management to sort this all out.

2-1d Bureaucracy Inhibits Flexibility and Productivity

A major factor that accounts for poor productivity is bureaucracy—the great inhibitor of flexibility. Bureaucratic systems are rampant worldwide. North America and Europe have more than their share, and they are equally prevalent in Asia, Latin America, and Africa. The definition of the term that is being used here is bureaucracy as institutionalized officialism, which has layers of red tape to cut through in order to conclude activities and operations. Bureaucracy spreads its reach as it proliferates through an organization placing controls over controls in the quest for low risk. It should be emphasized that all systems have an inherent risk aversion that results in their developing methods to protect the status quo.

The positive side to bureaucracy should not be overlooked. In the late nineteenth century, Max Weber was an advocate for *legal domination* (law administered by the state).[9] Weber viewed bureaucracy as a force to counteract the Kafka-like (unpredictable intimidation and lack of civil rights) effects of traditional domination (feudal rules determined by monarchs and patriarchs).

In regard to positive aspects of bureaucracy, it can be noted that bureaucracy plays an important stabilizing role in organizations that are undisciplined and prone to accidents. Routines known to be safe are insurance against risk of catastrophic damage. The downside of bureaucracy is that the pendulum always swings too far. Once bureaucracy gains control, it strives to remove corrective counterswings and maintain existing conditions. The status quo often impedes progress and supports rigidity.

Flexibility is related to productivity in a number of ways. Conditions change and the ability to adapt to new situations is measured by flexibility. New technology and the need to be global are among the most important changes in conditions that require flexibility. Product life is shorter and the need to modify product designs requires flexibility. The productivity advantages associated with producing large volumes of identical units is being replaced by mass customization methods that permit small volumes having greater variety to be produced. Design variations are being used for different countries and even for various regions of the same country. Carrying out strategic plans requires flexibility.

Bureaucratic organizations are dedicated to resisting change. What P/OM must deal with in fulfilling strategic plans is how to circumvent bureaucracy, which is, by intent, the protector and champion of the status quo. Bureaucracy is the opponent of operational change. When bureaucratic constraints are removed, often by decentralization, and more recently by reengineering, afflicted organizations regain some ability to rebound.

Japanese organizations that exhibited great resilience when they first started their major export drives also began to succumb to the problems of age and success. Age is correlated with circulatory insufficiencies in human beings and a lack of communication in organizations. This lack also is associated with zero empowerment of employees to do what makes sense instead of what the bureaucratic rule book dictates.

Success leads to complacency and arrogance—even though it does not have to do so. Bureaucratic organizations are very successful at inhibiting innovation and change. It remains to be seen how successful organizations worldwide will be in learning to counter these inhibitors.

Size of Firms and Flexibility

It is worth noting that small- and medium-sized firms, and new businesses as well, tend to exhibit greater flexibility and adaptability to change than large, centralized organizations. That is why, under stress, AT&T, Dell, Disney, Ford, GM, IBM, Sony, Sears, and other giant corporations used different forms of decentralization to improve their chances of recovering market preeminence. Organizational awareness of the need for flexibility has surfaced, but solutions for big bureaucratic companies have been elusive. The Iacocca Institute at Lehigh University in the United States now supports its "Global Village" as well as the Global Village on the Move." Both focus on leadership[10]

Small- and medium-sized firms are organizations with about 300 people. That number has been suggested by various managers, and there also is a great deal of unanimity that the upper limit should be no more than 500.[11] Given the usual proportions of administrative personnel and those of other functions, this suggests that a sensible limit for the size of an efficient production system is in the neighborhood of 100 to 200 people. By using divisional structures, it is reasonable to assume that a number of relatively autonomous divisions of sensible size can be related within the firm.

Research and Development (R&D)

The characterization of age and size also applies to the productivity of R&D departments. Some of the largest expenditures for R&D amounting to billions of dollars have been highly unproductive. GM spent multiple billions of dollars over many years while its fortunes declined.

There is ample evidence that small research budgets produce the most impressive results. The employees of a small start-up company are in constant communication. Large research units have all of the problems previously mentioned in connection with bureaucracy. Smaller dynamic organizations utilize the systems approach without having to consciously decide to do so. Everyone knows everyone else and they talk regularly. In many cases, the employees achieve a high degree of interfunctional coordination.

The productivity of R&D efforts is a legitimate concern of P/OM. Applied research and development fosters the next wave of new products and services. P/OM must be part of the team that carries the ball from start to finish for actual new product development and implementation. The way in which this is done is the concern of P/OM. Poor R&D productivity yields inferior processes, difficult operations, poor quality, high costs, and low profit margins. The rules for achieving high levels of productivity in research and development are similar to those that apply to good project management, which is a P/OM responsibility.

2-2 Productivity and Price–Demand Elasticity

Almost every company in the global market competes on price. It is one of the key decision factors for customers. Quality is another key factor but it is often hidden. One of the purposes of Chapter 4 is to clear up confusion on that matter.

When a company is competing on price, it means that it will lose some sales when a competitor offers a lower price that it cannot match. Everyone in the company looks to P/OM at this point. The CEO requests increased productivity to lower costs. That usually translates into attaining greater output volume. It is assumed that quality will remain unchanged.

To ask for increased productivity is a special way of asking for lower costs. Unions often take it to mean work faster for the same pay, which makes them reluctant to participate in productivity improvement. Speeding up production can compromise quality. Operations management should try to avoid supporting productivity increases gained in this way; the improvement is temporary, at best. Other ways of obtaining lower costs include the use of cheaper components and raw materials that lowers quality.

The CEO had something else in mind. When requesting increased productivity, the CEO meant using technology and good P/OM methods to improve the process, not lower the quality. The CEO's call for increased productivity is in response to competitive bids.

Decreasing quality to match lower prices is not a way to keep customers. Improved productivity, if it is to translate into greater customer satisfaction and loyalty, must come from working smarter, not harder. This means improving productivity by means other than asking people to work faster, which usually degrades quality.

This highlights the strong functional interaction between marketing and P/OM. The managers of these areas are associates working together to manage the effects of price–demand **elasticity** on production costs and on meeting quality standards.

Price–demand elasticity is another example of a crucial relationship between systems partners (marketing and P/OM) required for successful strategic planning.

2-2a Elasticity Relationship

Elasticity is a rate-of-change measure that expresses the degree to which demand grows or shrinks in response to a price change. In Equation 2-9, elasticity is expressed as a

Elasticity
Degree to which demand grows or contracts in response to price decreases or increases.

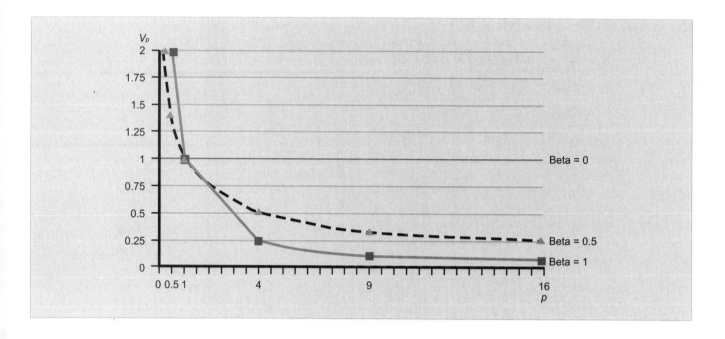

Figure 2-1

Price Elasticity for Beta = 0.0, 0.5, and 1.0, with $k = 1$

function that relates changes in price (p) with changes in demand volume (V_p). Thus, demand levels (or volumes, V) are a function (f) of price—in line with the degree of elasticity represented by beta (β).

$$V_p = f(p, \beta) \quad 1 \geq \beta \geq 0 \qquad (2\text{-}9)$$

Equation 2-10 spells this out in more detail. V_p is the demand volume associated with price p, and the elasticity coefficient, β. The degree of elasticity increases as beta moves to one (1). This is called high elasticity. Demand is described as completely *inelastic* when beta equals zero (0).

$$V_p = kp^{-\beta} \qquad (2\text{-}10)$$

A product with high elasticity experiences large decreases in demand as price increases, whereas, a product with low elasticity experiences small decreases in demand with the same degree of price increases. Low elasticity, called *inelasticity*, means that demand levels are relatively insensitive to price changes.

Price elasticity
See **Demand elasticity**.

Marketing managers frequently ask market researchers to study the **price elasticity** of products or services to determine how fast demand falls off as price is increased. Figure 2-1 shows a highly elastic situation ($\beta = 1$) where the demand volume changes greatly with price changes. In the same figure, an inelastic case is shown ($\beta = 0$) where demand volume does not change at all with price changes. The midway case ($\beta = 0.5$) falls between the other two. Equation 2-10 was used as the basis for these lines.

Note: k in Equation 2-10 is a constant equal to the demand volume level when beta is zero. $V_p = kp^{-\beta} = kp^{-0} = k$, since $p^0 = 1$. When beta is 1, $V_p = k/p$.

Perfect inelasticity—when demand does not change, no matter what the price—is an accurate description of the situation when an industrial customer is dependent on one supplier for special materials. Most customers try to get out of such a constraining situation for obvious reasons.

Elasticity is a complex relationship. The rate of change between price and demand is not always smooth and regular. There can be kinks in the line or curve. These occur, for example, when an increase in price causes demand to increase, which might happen when price becomes high enough to have "snob appeal," which opens a new market. Despite difficulties, it is important to measure elasticity, thereby relating price and volume.

The elasticity–productivity tie between operations management and marketing is:

1 Demand volume falls as price rises, but this is also relative to what prices competitors charge. When a competitor lowers prices, it is equivalent to a price increase for the customer who stays with a supplier who does not lower prices.

2 To be competitive, it is often necessary to find ways to match price decreases offered by competitors. This is a price–demand volume elasticity issue that assumes quality is unchanged.

3 If marketing lowers the price (p), then the profit margin will decrease in accordance with the formula $(p - vc)V$, where V is demand volume, $(p)V$ is revenue, and $(vc)V$ is total variable cost.

4 P/OM is always trying to find a way to decrease total variable cost without degrading quality. For example, if a new material is developed that is as good as the old material but costs less, then P/OM shifts to the new material.

5 The only way to achieve number 4 is to work smarter, and this is facilitated by means of technology-based or methodology-based productivity improvements.

6 Marketing tries to control demand volume through pricing. If competition drops the price, based on an improved process, emulation of the improvement is needed.

7 P/OM tries to match supply to demand through production scheduling and capacity planning. Marketing and P/OM must work together, combining their interactions by using the systems approach.

© 2008 Jupiterimages Corporation

Technology, such as laptops with a wireless connection to the Internet, allows employees to work virtually anywhere, on many subjects, without geographical restriction. This raises productivity.

Quality
Production defines it as conformance to standards whereas marketing rates the customer's satisfaction.

2-2b Elasticity of Quality

The *demand volume* of goods or services sold as a function of *price* is the traditional focus of elasticity analysis. Years ago that simple model may have sufficed, but it no longer is valid. For strategic planning, it is vital that marketing determine how **quality** levels of the product line affect competitive status (demand volume at a given price). In turn, P/OM must ascertain the unit costs for various process configurations operating at appropriate production volume levels. This subject brings together so many systems factors that are of mutual concern to P/OM, marketing, and finance.

   Customers in the marketplace take both price and quality into account. Customers' quality expectations often override price considerations. This applies to commercial and industrial customers as well as retail consumers of goods and services.

   A product or service that has special qualities is said to have uniqueness, which means that other competitive products lacking those special qualities have a lower degree of substitutability. For example, a product with special features (such as the iPhone), or service rendered by a well-liked person (favorite waitress), has a competitive advantage. Competitive analysis will show when two products are competing head-on, as if they were identical products, being perfect substitutes for one another. Perceived highest quality renders a product less vulnerable to substitution. That means the product is less quality elastic.

   How can the effects of quality on demand levels be determined? This is equivalent to asking how to determine the quality–demand volume elasticity. There are ways in which market research can approach this issue that are similar to the way price–demand volume elasticity is determined. Essentially, it is necessary to establish how much extra money customers would be willing to pay for superior quality or for an added quality feature.

   By noting the distribution of the additional amounts of money that people would pay for superior quality or an added feature, it is possible to quantify the effects of quality and price on demand elasticity. In effect, two price elasticity studies are conducted. The first study is done without the added quality. The second study is done with it. Throughout this discussion, it should be kept in mind that *the achievement of quality standards is a direct responsibility of P/OM.*

Table 2-2	Study	Quality	Beta Values	Demand Elasticity
Comparing Elasticities and Betas with Higher or Lower Quality Levels	1	Lower	Closer to 1	More elastic
	2	Higher	Closer to 0	Less elastic

Table 2-2 indicates that the demand elasticity of the second product (market research study 2) will be less than that of the first product. This is because the added quality of the second product makes the first items or services less substitutable.

Although this is a book about P/OM and not market research, these functions are highly interdependent. Market research enables P/OM to determine the kind of connections that link quality, price, and demand elasticity in the customer's mind.

These factors relate design and process decisions with the financial choices that are available to the firm. The system interaction includes the fact that quality varies with the kind of equipment that is used and the amount of training that the employees receive.

2-3 Economies of Scale and the Division of Labor

Economies of scale

Reductions in variable costs directly related to increasing volumes of production output.

There are three principles that P/OM must be schooled in to take advantage of productive opportunities. They are **economies of scale**, the division of labor, and economies of scope. The third principle will be considered later.

Economies of scale are reductions in variable costs directly related to increasing volumes of production output. Economies of scale are driven by increases in volume (V). Scale, as used here, is a surrogate for increasing volume. Equation 2-11 illustrates that total variable costs is both a P/OM and marketing responsibility. Since costs decrease with an increasing volume of production, this is also a matter of concern for finance. If a financial decision is made to use high-volume technology with greater fixed costs, the trade-off is lower vc.

$$\text{Total variable costs} = vc(V) \qquad (2\text{-}11)$$

V is a function of the total market size that exists, the number of competitors and their shares, and the controllable variables of the organization's price and quality. Although marketing and P/OM work together on the consequences of V, P/OM is working on the reduction of vc—which is also a function of V—with no loss in quality.

Materials and labor are an important component of the variable per unit cost, vc. The design of the product or service determines what materials are needed. It is common knowledge that greater purchase volumes generally are rewarded with discounts. That is only one of the interactions of vc and V. The machines that can be used for high-volume outputs are significantly faster than machines that are economic for low-volume outputs. High volumes can sustain pre-engineering and improvement studies of the interactions between the design of jobs and the processes used, while low volumes cannot. High volumes generate learning about how to do the job better; low volumes do not.

The design of jobs determines the amount of labor and the skill levels required. The responsibility for low, unit variable costs leads P/OM to want high volumes so that it can take advantage of the resulting economies of scale.

For many reasons, including the material discounts previously discussed and a general learning effect, variable costs per unit decrease as volume increases. This result, called the *economies of scale*, is quite similar to the Boston Consulting Group's (BCG) "Experience Curve," which yields a 20 to 30 percent decrease in per unit costs with each doubling of the volume.[12] It is reasonable to consider the "doubling of volume" as a surrogate for the "doubling of experience," as in BCG terminology.

An approximation of this relationship is shown in Figure 2-2.

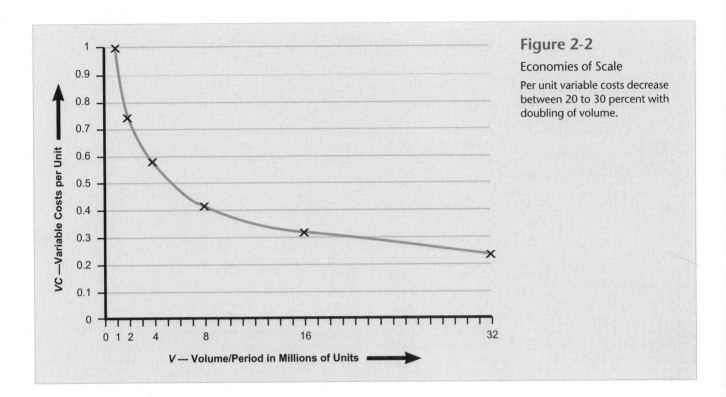

Figure 2-2

Economies of Scale

Per unit variable costs decrease between 20 to 30 percent with doubling of volume.

A coincident concept, proposed by Adam Smith (a Scottish economist) in the 1700s, was for the division of labor.[13] Labor was to be divided into specialized activities that could be honed to ever-greater skill levels. This notion follows from the theory that "practice makes perfect." To make division of labor worthwhile, the volume of production must be sufficient. Adam Smith said, "The division of labor depends on the extent of the market." With a large enough volume, activities could be segmented, and serialized process flows could be developed. Workers would be specialists in their assignments. Note that division of labor appears in the history section, which follows.

2-4 History of Improvements of P/OM Transformations

Literacy in P/OM requires an understanding of how the P/OM field has developed with respect to the transformation process and, thereby, productivity, quality, volume, and variety. The stages of history have moved production and operations capabilities from low-volume custom work through high-volume rapid and continuous output systems.

Attention shifts from custom crafts, which are art-based, to the theory of production, which has evolved over time. This theory consists of six established steps and a potential seventh one. There is emphasis on manufacturing because the theory evolved from the production of goods, but the theory has now transcended manufacturing and is applicable to service operations.

Figure 2-3 depicts P/OM history in a timeline chart. Dates mentioned are approximate (but satisfactory). It is not possible to pinpoint exactly when each contribution was made.

2-5 Discussion of the History of P/OM

The capability of P/OM processes to deliver goods and services has changed in steps or stages over time. The study of the history of P/OM production transformation processes

© 2008 Jupiterimages Corporation

The flexibility concept (Step 6 in Figure 2-3) permits computers to control equipment in the bank, plant or plane. This revises the traditional way that machines operate. It also allows mass customization. See 2-5g.

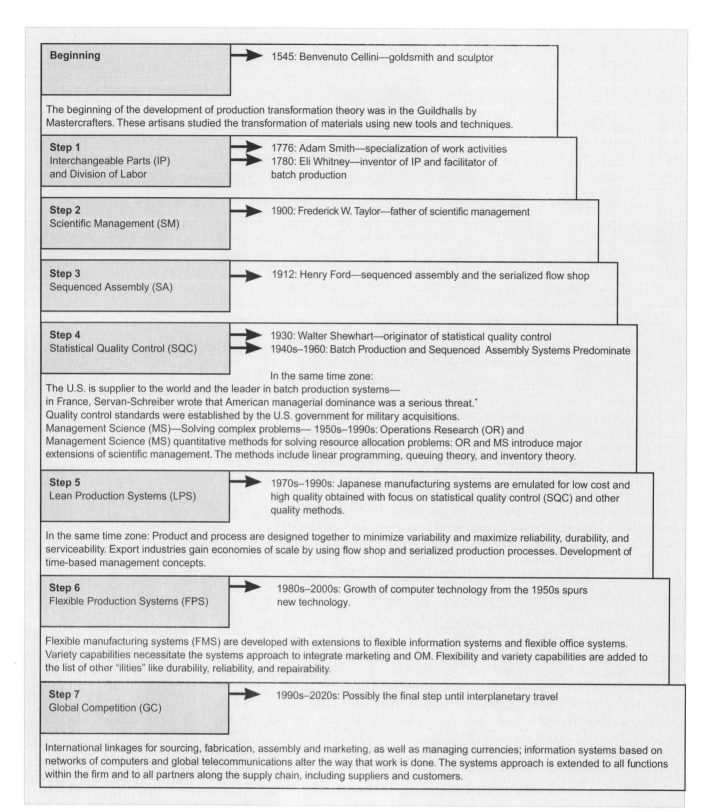

| Beginning | → | 1545: Benvenuto Cellini—goldsmith and sculptor |

The beginning of the development of production transformation theory was in the Guildhalls by Mastercrafters. These artisans studied the transformation of materials using new tools and techniques.

| **Step 1** Interchangeable Parts (IP) and Division of Labor | → | 1776: Adam Smith—specialization of work activities |
| | → | 1780: Eli Whitney—inventor of IP and facilitator of batch production |

| **Step 2** Scientific Management (SM) | → | 1900: Frederick W. Taylor—father of scientific management |

| **Step 3** Sequenced Assembly (SA) | → | 1912: Henry Ford—sequenced assembly and the serialized flow shop |

| **Step 4** Statistical Quality Control (SQC) | → | 1930: Walter Shewhart—originator of statistical quality control |
| | → | 1940s–1960: Batch Production and Sequenced Assembly Systems Predominate |

In the same time zone:
The U.S. is supplier to the world and the leader in batch production systems—
in France, Servan-Schreiber wrote that American managerial dominance was a serious threat.*
Quality control standards were established by the U.S. government for military acquisitions.
Management Science (MS)—Solving complex problems— 1950s–1990s: Operations Research (OR) and Management Science (MS) quantitative methods for solving resource allocation problems: OR and MS introduce major extensions of scientific management. The methods include linear programming, queuing theory, and inventory theory.

| **Step 5** Lean Production Systems (LPS) | → | 1970s–1990s: Japanese manufacturing systems are emulated for low cost and high quality obtained with focus on statistical quality control (SQC) and other quality methods. |

In the same time zone: Product and process are designed together to minimize variability and maximize reliability, durability, and serviceability. Export industries gain economies of scale by using flow shop and serialized production processes. Development of time-based management concepts.

| **Step 6** Flexible Production Systems (FPS) | → | 1980s–2000s: Growth of computer technology from the 1950s spurs new technology. |

Flexible manufacturing systems (FMS) are developed with extensions to flexible information systems and flexible office systems. Variety capabilities necessitate the systems approach to integrate marketing and OM. Flexibility and variety capabilities are added to the list of other "ilities" like durability, reliability, and repairability.

| **Step 7** Global Competition (GC) | → | 1990s–2020s: Possibly the final step until interplanetary travel |

International linkages for sourcing, fabrication, assembly and marketing, as well as managing currencies; information systems based on networks of computers and global telecommunications alter the way that work is done. The systems approach is extended to all functions within the firm and to all partners along the supply chain, including suppliers and customers.

Figure 2-3

The Histo-Map: A Timeline of P/OM Developments

allows us to determine which events triggered these stages of production theory. The ultimate goal is to learn the theory, understand it, and possess the advantages that accrue to literate managers.

2-5a Artisans, Apprentices, and Trainees—The Beginning

The Renaissance period (1300s–1600s) signaled a surge of intellectual and productive vitality in Europe. That surge swept away the dark ages and fostered accomplishments in the arts and sciences centered on artisans, apprentices, and craft guilds. Production transformations were by hand. Output volumes were very small.

Before the Industrial Revolution began (around 1770), craft guilds emphasized pride of workmanship and training for basic manual operations with appropriate hand tools. The shoemakers' children learned from their fathers and mothers. Process techniques were manual skills handed down from generation to generation.

From a transformation point of view, this was good management of the labor inputs. The use of apprentices improved productivity in the artisans' shops because the less skilled (and lower paid) apprentices did much of the preliminary work. This freed the master craftsmen to devote their time to the activities requiring higher skills. On-the-job training produced a continuous stream of greater skills.

Apprenticeship still has significance for many service functions. Great chefs almost always are the pupils of great chefs. The formula would seem to reside in the balance of art and science. When the important knowledge resides in the minds and hands of skilled workers, then the percent of art is high and the percent of science is low. Over time, this percentage has shifted in manufacturing so that engineering, technology, and computer programming play an increasing role.

The art element in manufacturing is disappearing. Computer know-how is replacing people know-how. It use to be that the tool and die department was crucial to the success of metal-working companies, and the best die makers were considered artists. (Tools and dies are the shape formers in the metal-working businesses.)

Now, **computer-aided design (CAD)** and **computer-aided manufacturing (CAM)** are primarily science, and the old industrial arts are giving way to the new programming arts. This also is happening in service industries and is an effect that can be expected to accelerate in the future.

2-5b Interchangeable Parts (IP)—P/OM's First Step

Eli Whitney invented the concept of **interchangeable parts** for the fabrication of rifles around 1780, which coincides with the dates usually given for the beginning of the Industrial Revolution. The notion of interchangeable parts was the catalyst around which new methods for production transformation began to develop. These methods spawned and supported the Industrial Revolution.

Whitney was not the sole inventor of interchangeable parts. In France, Nicolas LeBlanc had invented the same P/OM concept. Neither Whitney nor LeBlanc knew about each other's ideas. Whitney obtained a U.S. government contract for "ten thousand stand of arms." The contract was awarded because of his newly developed production capabilities.

The concept of interchangeable parts is defined as follows: It allows batches of parts to be made, any one of which will fit into the assembled product. For example, headlights, fenders, tires, and windshield wiper blades are not specially made for each car. One 60-watt bulb is like another and does not have to be fitted to each socket. The reason that the parts are interchangeable is that each one falls within the **design tolerances**. Designers are responsible for stating acceptable ranges, which are the design tolerances.

Machines that could produce parts to conform to the designer's tolerances were the keystone. Hand labor, better suited to custom work, began to be replaced by machinery. The effects of this change hastened the Industrial Revolution. Within a short time, IP was

Computer-aided design (CAD)
Software that creates design drawings for any product.

Computer-aided manufacturing (CAM)
Software that communicates design specifications to the CAM software, which translates the specs into instructions for the production machinery.

Interchangeable parts
Manufacturing concept that makes batches of parts, any one of which will fit into the assembled products.

Design tolerances
Minimum and maximum dimensions for parts that fit together for proper performance.

an accepted part of the production transformation process being applied to the manufacture of rifles, sewing machines, clocks, and other products.

In 1776, Adam Smith saw that the use of the division of labor as a means of increasing productivity was market volume dependent. The pin factory that he studied had sufficient production volume to warrant specialization. The production transformation process was revolutionized—combining worker specialization with interchangeable parts changed all of the productivity standards. Expectations were raised to new levels.

2-5c Scientific Management (SM)—P/OM's Second Step

Scientific management
Systematic approach to doing work well.

Frederick Winslow Taylor (1856–1915) introduced **scientific management**, the numerical measurement and analysis of the way work should be done. One of his landmark studies dealt with the speed and feed rates of tools and materials for metal cutting. Other studies focused on how to lay bricks and how to move iron castings. Taylor's testimony at hearings concerning the setting of rational railroad fees for shipments in interstate commerce brought national prominence to his analytic methodology.

This step in production theory added the idea that the transformation processes could be improved by studying and simplifying operations. This view required rationalizing the job, the workplace, and the workers. Strangely, it had been overlooked until the turn of the twentieth century. Finding economies of motion and putting materials near at hand were the kinds of improvements that Taylor addressed. In this step, the workplace and the design of the job were enhanced to improve the productivity of the transformation process. These industrial engineering ideas, often called *methods engineering*, have proved to be as useful for service applications as for manufacturing.

Called the father of "scientific management," Taylor was one of the key progenitors of industrial engineering (IE). There were others as well. Associated with this era are Henry L. Gantt, Frank and Lillian Gilbreth, and other individuals who were attempting to develop a theory of managing workers and technology in the United States. Henri Fayol was developing similar management theories in France.

Taylor started the process of systematizing all of the elements that are part of the manufacturing system. The same industrial engineering techniques developed by Taylor are still used by banks, insurance companies, and investment houses as well as by truckers, airlines, and manufacturers. They are well-suited for repetitive operations such as those that characterize fast-food chains and information processing systems. Industrial engineering methods are recognizable as the forerunners of techniques that are currently applied in the search for continuous improvement.

Taylor and his associates developed principles and practices that led to a present-day backlash. He and other contributors to scientific management have been accused of dehumanizing the worker in pursuit of efficiency. Today, the accusation might hold, but it did not when judged by the value system of the early 1900s.

The criticism does not damage the case for benefits that can be derived from using the industrial engineering approach, which grew out of scientific management. Work simplification and methods engineering are both IE techniques for making jobs better for workers.

2-5d Sequenced Assembly (SA)—P/OM's Third Step

Sequenced assembly
Continuous flow assembly line.

In 1912, Henry Ford developed **sequenced assembly**, which allows assembly to be a continuous flow shop process. Timing must be perfect so that what is needed for assembly arrives on time. Ford developed the sequenced assembly process as a continuous flow production line for automobiles, changing the pace from batch to continuous sequenced assembly.

The serialized flow shop was born. The key was learning to achieve synchronization and control of the process flows. The moving assembly line required a high level of component interchangeability. Ford succeeded in achieving complete synchronization of the process flows.

By means of the principles of interchangeability, division of labor, and flow synchronization, Ford altered the production transformation process. He changed the perception of productivity standards and goals in a conclusive way. In so doing, he built an industrial empire that helped the United States become the world leader in productivity. The United States continues to maintain its lead, although other nations—especially those once considered to be less developed countries (such as China and India)—have been improving their productivity consistently.

Ford's contribution to production theory and to the revision of the transformation process had a major impact on the Japanese automobile industry. It also affected other industries of many kinds all over the world. There was a new rhythm to the transformation process.

Contrast U.S. and Japanese production processes in the 1980s. The major portion of production and operations activities in the United States utilized batch processes. Batch work with small lots does not lend itself to the kind of synchronization that applies to the automobile industry or the continuous flows of chemical processes.

When the Japanese export industry began to compete aggressively in global markets, they chose to shun batch-type production systems. Instead they elected to specialize in high-volume, serialized flow shops, which extended the concept and application of assembly synchronization to manufacturing and assembly systems.

2-5e Statistical Quality Control (SQC)—P/OM's Fourth Step

Interchangeable parts required manufacturing methods that made batches of parts conforming to tolerance limits. Shewhart developed the theory of **statistical quality control (SQC)** that enabled manufacturing to design and control processes that could achieve these objectives. SQC was focused on the producer's ability to control the variability of the process that was making the parts that had to fit within the specified tolerance limits. For the first time, the output of the transformation process could be stabilized and controlled. This was a major contribution to production theory.

Statistical quality control (SQC)
Methodology to stabilize and control a system.

Walter Shewhart's major work, which was published in 1930, described his concepts about why SQC works and how to apply it.[14] Deming and Juran also participated in the development of SQC theory and later on played a crucial role in its implementation and dissemination.[15]

The United States was the first country that consistently used SQC, which it did through the 1940s and the early 1950s, but by 1960 the majority of SQC users were in Japan. U.S. organizations reported that they had dropped SQC to make cost reductions. Quality was considered good enough to replace costly staff departments with inspectors at the end of the production line. By the 1980s, however, under great competitive pressure from quality-driven Japanese organizations, many U.S. companies restored SQC and enhanced it with broader concepts into total quality management (TQM) activities.

Organizations like Motorola, Toyota, and GE are considered to be pioneers leading the development of TQM (and Six Sigma—see Spotlight 7-2) within the framework of the systems approach. The total quality management approach applied to the production transformation system integrates the goals of productivity and quality. It represents a major step forward in the theory of production and an organizational feat to have gained broad acceptance at all levels. Six-Sigma[SM], a registered service mark of Motorola—which developed it—is a culmination of TQM. Motorola reported more than US$17 billion in savings from Six Sigma as of 2006 (see Six Sigma—Wikipedia).

The next three steps are in formative stages, and their impact on productivity cannot be fully evaluated at this time.

2-5f Lean Production Systems (LPS)—P/OM's Fifth Step

During the 1970s–1990s, Japanese organizations spearheaded by Toyota developed a new kind of production methodology called **lean production systems** (also called the

Lean production systems
Processes that have been designed to minimize their inherent wastes—of time, materials, and money.

Toyota Production System). These systems combine a deep understanding of quality with a desire to be fast (if not the fastest) and a fanatical distaste for all kinds of waste. Lean production systems methodology is now a worldwide endeavor.

Time wasted is singled out. Every effort is made to use pre-engineering of products and process design to maximize quality achievements, minimize variability, and do it all as rapidly as possible. Part of being lean is being fast—in production. Many Japanese organizations were not fast in reaching decisions. Toyota substituted persistence for perfection and over time began to innovate at astounding speeds. Advocates of "lean" became lean producers with high-output volume targets, minimum cycle times, and rapid new product development.

By introducing time management and goals for short cycle times and rapid project development, other new factors were introduced into the production transformation system. The timing of transformations rose to a new level of importance, and, secondly, rapid project management began to mean that the transformation process could be changed from doing one thing to another very quickly.

The Japanese auto industry has been leading in the development of lean and fast production systems. Toyota's production planners, who were architects of the revised production system, stated that Toyota's ideas were a continuation of the concepts that Henry Ford had been developing.[16] In Europe, the notion of leanness was directly associated with speeding up cycle times and project development times. Half-time systems were advanced by Saab. The goal was to cut in half the time currently required to do any operation.

Many U.S. organizations have adopted at least some aspects of lean and rapid manufacturing methods. Six Sigma when properly conceived and executed is a means to lean production systems. Motorola's management originally set itself the goal of reducing defectives to less than four defects per million parts.[17] Having demonstrated that near-zero defect rates are attainable, Motorola now has set another radical target, which is to reduce existing cycle times by 90 percent. This means that a part that currently takes 10 minutes to produce eventually will be made in 1 minute instead of 5 minutes. Note the Saab half-time objective mentioned earlier. Highlighting reduced cycle-time objectives brings new features to the production transformation process.

2-5g Mass Customization with CAD, CAM, and FPS— P/OM's Sixth Step

Computer-aided design that is able to program flexible production machinery represents powerful new technological capabilities. When design and programming are combined, opportunities develop for computers to instruct and control machines instead of needing hands-on command by human operators. The purpose of using such equipment is different from the goal of "mass production" where one item is made in extremely high volume. The one color (black) Model T Ford epitomizes "mass production." However, with flexibility, the purpose is **mass customization**, where high-levels of variety can be produced in great volume because the production line can be adjusted without incurring significant setup times and costs. For example, many different colors and models can be made on the same production line at almost no additional cost as compared to traditional "mass production."

Computer-aided design (CAD) abilities alter traditional relationships of strategic planning. CAD and computer-aided manufacturing (CAM) work hand-in-hand. CAM is dovetailed and synchronized with CAD. Software for CAD is able to calculate strength of materials in specific configurations, which also ties-in with manufacturability. As a result of P/OM's responsibility for processes, P/OM must participate in strategizing for the product line design. CAM and **flexible production systems (FPS)** are not the same, but they are related. Flexible processes are capable of switching production from one product to another with almost no time delay. CAD and CAM when used with flexible technology provide the ideal components for "mass customization."

Mass customization
Flow shop efficiencies without traditional constraints on variety.

Flexible production systems (FPS)
Computer programming enables process changes to be accomplished quickly and without delaying throughput.

The initial thrust was in manufacturing. **Flexible manufacturing systems (FMS) are** designed to produce a high variety of outputs at low cost. Computer-controlled change-over is engineered into the system. Instead of human hands changing machine settings, electronics and mechanics provide the interface between the computer and machinery. Flexible technologies allow fast and inexpensive changeovers. The equipment can be programmed to move from one product setup to another product setup in an instant.

Using FMS, design and machine software talk to each other. CAD software creates new design drawings. It runs tests on all important reliability and durability characteristics, such as fatigue strength. CAD communicates design specifications to software that translates, instructs, and controls the production machinery; i.e., CAM. CAD and CAM work together to determine the feasibility of manufacturing the new design and suggest improved design alternatives.

CAD/CAM-type technology is used to design and manufacture many different products such as semiconductors, automobile grills, and aircraft parts. John Deere has invested millions of dollars in the creation of CAD/CAM systems for the manufacture of tractors. Boeing used CAD/CAM (specifically, CATIA V5 from Dassault Systèmes) to design all of the parts of its 787 Dreamliner. CATIA facilitated real-time meeting between design teams located all over the world with sophisticated audiovisual capabilities. Design at Boeing has moved from the draftsman's table to the computer.

Coordination problems can arise that are entirely new to airline designers. Airbus megajet A380 fell two years behind schedule when preassembled cabin wiring bundles made in Germany did not fit the plane being assembled in France. This global coordination problem (acknowledged by CEO of EADS, Christian Streiff, in October 2007) was caused by incompatible versions of CATIA software in Germany and France.

The flexibility concept joins computers and equipment of many other kinds, including assembly-line processes and office machines. It also is possible and often desirable to include human beings in the network. Flexibility can be applied to information systems—flexible information systems (FIS) and to flexible office systems (FOS) as well as to FMS.

Mass customization capabilities to produce small numbers of many varieties include extensive application of systems thinking to integrate marketing needs and P/OM scheduling abilities. Using marketing forecasts, P/OM managers decide what to make, but the decisions are constrained by the FMS menu, which was predetermined at the initial planning stage.

The need to produce increased variety is market-driven. The transformation process has to be able to change over from making one thing to another, quickly and inexpensively. A great deal of effort goes into altering the transformation process so it can deal with the goal of increased variety. Technology and methodology must enable nearly instant setups and changeovers from one model to another to satisfy market demands. The payoff will be increased productivity of the joint production–marketing system, as exemplified by customized jeans.

Levi Strauss has put the customer directly in touch with the factory. "Sales clerks at an original Levi's store can use a personal computer and the customer's vital statistics to create what amounts to a digital blue jeans blueprint. When transmitted electronically to a Levi's factory in Tennessee, this computer file instructs a robotic tailor to cut a bolt of denim precisely to the customer's measurements."[18] Ten years after this reference, Levi Strauss' "personal pair service," which manufactures and delivers made-to-measure denims, was recognized as an aspect of "mass customization." Hellriegel et. al. wrote, "Perhaps the most significant contribution of advanced manufacturing technologies is that of mass customization—that is the ability to produce a wide variety of a product by using the same basic design and production equipment but making certain modifications to the demand of a broader market. For example, Levi Strauss has successfully used computer-assisted design systems to help design customized leather outfits and jeans for customers."[19]

There is a dedicated strategic effort to achieve competitiveness through flexibility in America. It combines the goals of leanness (speed) and flexibility and is known by

Flexible manufacturing systems (FMS)
Designed to produce a variety of outputs at low cost.

© 2008 Jupiterimages Corporation

CAD (computer-aided design) terminals communicate design specifications for the construction of planes and ships to an integrated computer-aided manufacturing (CAM) network that reaches throughout the manufacturing system, allowing complex system designs such as the cockpit shown here.

various names including "agile enterprise, agile business architecture, and agile project management"[20] These names are meant to emphasize the ability to react quickly and with flexibility. The agile organization is supposed to be alert and nimble, keen and lithe. Bureaucratic organizations (as we currently know them) cannot qualify.

2-5h Global Competition: Year 2010 Plus—P/OM's Seventh Step

It is conjectured that in the future the transformation process will continue increasing in complexity and productivity. On a worldwide scale, a broad range of goods and services should be within the spending capabilities of many people living in developing countries. More management will be needed to plan and control such systems. A greater number of operations managers will be required with far fewer workers on the production line. The global village will be sharing services—such as education and health care—that are mutually rewarding. Onerous service tasks will be relegated to service robots. Hopefully, people will have time to spend their money as they wish.

The input–output production transformation model will be internationalized. There will be global competition at every link in the supply chain. International sourcing, fabrication, assembly, distribution, and marketing will prevail. The costs of the inputs and the values of the outputs will be affected by dozens, if not hundreds, of different currencies. Managing currencies will be part of the transformation process. The euro has simplified currency management and provides a good model for other regional currencies.

Information systems will be based on international networks of computers. Global telecommunication systems will transmit conversations that are spoken in 80 different languages. Translation will be accomplished by language-capable computers with voice–language recognition. Voice response in the appropriate language will be expected.

The systems approach will extend to all functions within the organization and all partners along the supply chain, including suppliers and customers. Production and operations will develop transformation processes that require great management skills while decreasing burdensome labor components. Substantial productivity increases will be obtained. There have been many unexpected turns in the road, and there will be more as 2010 gets nearer.

IBM provides a good case in point. Mr. Palmisano (CEO, Chairman of the Board) sees the globalization of services as the next big shift in the business landscape. IBM and others are building networks for delivering technological services that are similar to the interdependent manufacturing networks that have evolved. For example, the 451 parts of the iPod are made by companies all over the world, but not by Apple.

Spotlight 2-1 Boutwell, Owens & Co., Inc.

A "Total Package Service" Provider That Takes Packaging from the Drawing Board to the Loading Dock—An Example of Excellence in Entrepreneuring.

Boutwell, Owens & Co., Inc., is a small family-owned manufacturer of paperboard cartons, inserts, "skin" packaging, and retail display cards in Fitchburg, Massachusetts. The company succeeds in a somewhat stagnant market because of its emphasis on quality and service. Boutwell, Owens sees itself not as a printer of product packages, but as a "total package service" provider that takes packaging from the "drawing board to the loading dock."

Boutwell, Owens provides different levels of service to companies depending on their size. For small companies, "we get them into the marketplace with a sharp-looking package," said Ward McLaughlin, Boutwell, Owens' president. For large companies, Boutwell, Owens not only designs their packaging, but manages their inventories as well. Customers include such familiar names as Radio Shack, Weyth, Polaroid, Oral B, Milton Bradley, Garrity Industries, Hewlett-Packard, and Honeywell.

Today's market demands bring on a whole new dimension of salespeople. Successful salespeople are trained and educated to interact at all levels with the customer base (called *depth selling*). Selling a package that will sell the customer's product is the goal, rather than on the basis of the lowest price. A good understanding of a target cost point needs to be established. The salesperson should be well versed in art and structures to help direct the customer with the building of files as well as directing the customer to the proper stock on which to print art. Selling goes beyond just marketing and purchasing. A true professional will work with the customers' manufacturing, planning logistics, and equipment to ensure that the product flows through their plant quickly and smoothly.

Boutwell, Owens is successful because, according to vice president of operations Larry Kelley, "We're a job shop. We do whatever the customer needs done. We'll take on the jobs that no one else will do. Our consistency and commitment to improvements truly make our company stand out in front of the competition. We put a lot of emphasis toward training and educating our teams on procedures and policies. This type of commitment has made a big difference. We are a company that takes a big interest in our customers' needs and works toward filling those needs."

President Ward McLaughlin points out that "a company comes to us mainly because of our ability to ... get them out of trouble, and when they find out that our quality and service stay equal to what we first initiated, they stay" with Boutwell, Owens.

The company runs three shifts to meet demand. Its workforce has grown from 60 to 170 employees since 1985. Boutwell, Owens is proud of its ability to set up machines fast and meet tight deadlines. Fast turnover of orders is critical when dealing with large retailers. "The Wal-Marts, the Kmarts, the big retailers are pretty relentless," said Brian Jansson, vice president of finance. "Orders will be canceled automatically if you're late." Boutwell, Owens has been growing through acquisitions and purchasing new equipment to provide an expanding array of services for its customers. Quality improvement is a continual goal. The company received three awards in the 19th Annual Gold Ink Awards Competition in August 2006. Winners were chosen from nearly 1,600 entries submitted within 46 different categories. Winning required surpassing competitors on print quality, technical difficulty, quality of color separations, and overall visual effect. As a foundation for quality, Boutwell, Owens certified for ISO 9001 registration. View the company's certificate at http://www.boutwellowens.com/pdf/ISO9001.pdf.

Customer loyalty is highly correlated with employee job satisfaction. Boutwell, Owens achieved national recognition for its human relations in the sixth annual "Best Workplace in America (BWA)" program sponsored November 2006 by the Master Printers of America and Printing Industries of America, Inc. This award is a major accomplishment, having great significance for excellence in service since employee loyalty is a key component of the service profit chain (see the following chart).

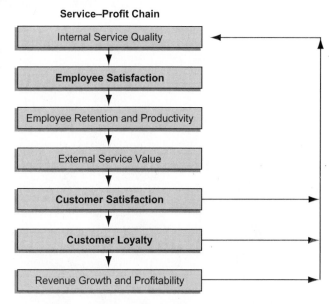

Service–Profit Chain

The chart is a simplification of a figure in "Putting the Service–Profit Chain to Work," James L. Heskett, Thomas O. Jones, Gary Loveman, W. Earl Sasser, Jr., and Leonard A. Schlesinger. *Harvard University Review* (rev.), July 2000. Also see *The Value Profit Chain*, James L. Heskett, W. Earl Sasser, Jr., and Leonard A. Schlesinger, The Free Press, 2003.

Review Questions

1. What products does Boutwell, Owens & Co., Inc., sell?
2. What is meant by the statement that Boutwell, Owens & Co., Inc., supplies different service levels to its clients according to the client's size?
3. Boutwell, Owens & Co., Inc., is a true master of P/OM. How can you justify this claim?
4. President Ward McLaughlin points out that "a company comes to us mainly because of our ability to ... get them out of trouble." What is the nature of this business model?
5. What is the company's URL, and when you go to its website, what stands out about the material that you find there?

Sources: Communications with Brian Jansson; assistance from Ward McLaughlin, April 2007; Original contact: Bruce Phillips. "Building Packages That Move the Product." *Fitchburg-Leominster Sentinel and Enterprise* (June 27, 1994). More recent articles: Neil Brett. "The Total Package: Boutwell, Owens & Co. Can Be Anything to Its Clients." *Paperboard Packaging* (April 2002), and "Boutwell, Owens Co., Fitchburg, Massachusetts, Installs the First U.S. Model of the Mitsubishi Tandem Perfector." *Paperboard Packaging* (December 2004).

Spotlight 2-2 Lars Kolind: Transformation of Ideas into Sustainable Businesses

A Discussion with Lars Kolind, Chairman, PreVenture A/S

Lars Kolind is famous for his major organizational changes at Oticon Holding S/A. He reorganized Oticon by cutting away hierarchies and fostering new patterns of communication, which catalyzed project creation in new product development. It was essential for Oticon to break with the past because the company had lost its leadership role to new technologies in the hearing-aid markets of the world. Kolind's plan was to go to a flat, project-oriented organization (labeled "the spaghetti organization"). That plan successfully returned the company to technological and market preeminence.

When Lars Kolind left Oticon in 1998, he founded an early-stage business development firm called PreVenture A/S. In 2007, the firm is no longer an active venture investor. Now, it "harvests" investments already made in an outsourcing arrangement with BankInvest. Lars Kolind is on the board of directors of this large venture capital operator (see http://www.biventure.dk/default.aspx).

Because of its success as an incubator for start-ups, PreVenture A/S is likely to be studied by academic researchers as a further development of similar principles applied to Oticon. The idea behind Danish-based PreVenture A/S was to make "transformation of ideas into sustainable businesses (that are) systematic, knowledge-based, efficient and fun." As stated by Kolind, "We work in five phases in the life of a start-up business:

1 Business Conception: From idea to business plan
2 Business Discovery: From business plan to market introduction
3 Business Launch: From market introduction to documented user acceptance
4 Business Expansion: From documented user acceptance to breakeven in first market
5 Business Transition: Introduction to mass market and adjustment of owner structure"

Companies that partnered with PreVenture had to agree to use (and, if possible, improve) the growth model developed by Lars Kolind and his team. That model structured and disciplined the operations of the start-ups in accord with the five phases listed here.

The original PreVenture partners included Isabella Smith A/S, a trading company with products related to TV host Isabella Smith; Retail Internet A/S, running a permission-based e-mail marketing service called Jatak.com; YellowTel A/S, providing access to information about products and services in both Poland and Sweden; KeepFocus A/S, offering a system that helps reduce electricity, water, and heat usage; MusicShop AG, with a system for legal and secure distribution of digital music on the Internet; and Homelinc, distributing digital media from Internet and PC to A/V equipment in the home.

Typical of Lars Kolind's broad systems thinking, PreVenture A/S developed a model for venture capitalists to emulate. The model creates value for various constituencies. Entrepreneurs increase their probability of success using this growth model. Shareholders and investors do well because adherence to the model provides architecture and structure for learning to improve continually. PreVenture held shares in its partner companies, which remains a good formula for mutual success. Employees of the firms enjoy stability of employment and potential financial gains. Overall, this systematic process provides sustainability from which everyone gains.

When asked about his business philosophy, Mr. Kolind said, "I realized that what I learned about large organizations during my 10 years as CEO of Oticon holds also for small and young businesses. There should be no such thing as an employee, only associates. Everyone should be given maximum freedom to choose what he or she wants to do, and everyone should be urged to utilize the broadest possible set of competencies in their work. I continue not to believe in hierarchies—let teams do the work.

"I am convinced that complete transparency is the only effective basis for communication and knowledge sharing. I have no intention of managing an organization through carefully thought out plans and budgets. Success is about vision and values. I am surprised how many companies still maintain hierarchical organizations and information systems. They remind me more about the 1920s than of the 21st century. We know today what it takes to create organizations, which are uniquely competitive and innovative, yet also sustainable." In April 2007, Lars Kolind stated that the significant point to take away from this discussion is the PreVenture succeeded because it "sells *efficient early stage business development* as its product."

Review Questions

1 What products did the Danish company PreVenture S/A sell, and how well did it do in this business?
2 What business model was used by PreVenture S/A?
3 Lars Kolind is famous as the organizational innovator who made a small Danish hearing-aid company into an industry leader with shares on a par with Siemens and Sony. What was that company, and what is the story?
4 What are the five phases in the life of a start-up business?
5 Google "venture capital model" and "venture capital growth model." Do you find that the growth model described by Lars Kolind is widely used? Discuss.

Source: Lars Kolind, from personal correspondence with Mr. Kolind (February 18–28, 2003, and April 9–14, 2007). In correspondence dated April 10, 2007, Lars Kolind stated, "The good news is that at least three out of six original investments will turn out to be successful, which is much better than industry average: Retail Internet was sold in November 2006 at a price which pays back the entire fund, ... Isabella Smith is progressing very well and the same goes for KeepFocus. That's a 50% success rate, which no doubt comes from the systematic approach—the Growth Model. ... We expect Isabella and KeepFocus to have new owners within the next two years ... keeping well within the ten-year horizon we had in 2000." He also wrote, "You never know how much value you have created in venture business before the last company is sold. But the fact that the first exit has paid back the entire fund after 6 years indicates that we have created substantial value. ... Other venture funds that were established (around 2000) have lost roughly 50% of their value in the same period."

chapter 2

Summary

Productivity is a critical business systems variable because it strongly impacts the bottom line and it involves strategic planning among all of the business functions. Ultimately, productivity is a major P/OM responsibility. There are many ways to measure productivity, including those used to describe the national economy. Measures can be made in terms of labor productivity, capital productivity, or both. For business units, the measures relate more directly to the kinds of activities the company does. These are the operational measures of productivity used by an organization. Productivity measures should be adjusted to capture the relevant system. This challenge must be met by using the systems approach.

Bureaucracy inhibits flexibility and, therefore, constrains productivity improvement. Small firms are less bureaucratic than large ones and, therefore, are more flexible and able to pursue initiatives for greater productivity. Research and development (R&D) organizations are related to P/OM and should be studied in terms of their productivity, which is usually better for smaller organizations. These are strategic issues to consider.

Productivity and price–demand elasticity are interdependent. The importance to P/OM and marketing of the elasticity relationship for both price and quality are explained. Then, economies of scale and the division of labor are linked to productivity. The chapter concludes with the history of the improvement of P/OM input–output transformations and resultant productivity increases is presented in seven steps.

There are two Spotlight feature boxes in this chapter. These boxes illustrate real applications of the materials in the chapter. See Spotlight 2-1. Boutwell, Owens & Co., Inc., must constantly be creating new products for its customers, with high productivity being essential. Spotlight 2-2: Transformation of Ideas into Sustainable Businesses has the great advantage of a discussion with one of the ablest strategic-thinking venture capitalist of the global scene, namely, Lars Kolind, Chairman, PreVenture A/S.

Key Terms

Benchmark (p. 40)
Capital productivity (p. 42)
Computer-aided design (CAD) (p. 53)
Computer-aided manufacturing (CAM) (p. 53)
Demand elasticity (p. 39)
Design tolerances (p. 53)
Economies of scale (p. 50)
Elasticity (p. 47)
Flexible manufacturing systems (FMS) (p. 57)
Flexible production systems (FPS) (p. 56)
Interchangeable parts (p. 53)
Labor productivity (p. 41)
Lean production systems (p. 55)
Mass customization (p. 56)
Multifactor productivity (MFP) (p. 41)
Price elasticity (p. 48)
Productivity (p. 38)
Quality (p. 49)
Relative Productivity (p. 43)
Scientific Management (p. 54)
Sequenced assembly (p. 54)
Statistical quality control (SQC) (p. 55)
Total productivity (p. 40)

Review Questions

1 Why is productivity a crucial element of strategic planning?
2 Why is productivity measurement vital to P/OM?
3 Why is productivity measurement vital to national government economists?
4 What is the importance of productivity measurement to marketing management?
5 What role does the systems approach play with respect to productivity measurement?
6 What is good and bad about bureaucracy with respect to productivity? One hundred years ago, it was considered a major organizational advance over what preceded it. Why is it now considered an impediment?
7 How does the division of labor concept help a market research firm put together a report for a client?

8   What is the value of knowing about the six historical steps in the development of production theory? Is the suggested seventh step likely to have an impact on the future of operations management?

9   How does the concept of interchangeable parts apply to

   a. vacuum cleaners?
   b. jigsaw puzzles?
   c. flashlights?

10   What is meant by lean (or agile) production systems?
11   How does business going global create new problems or opportunities for P/OM?
12   What relationship connects productivity and price–demand elasticity?
13   What relationship connects productivity and quality–demand elasticity? Is price implicitly included?
14   What are economies of scale? How do they relate to productivity and the systems approach?

Problems Section

Note: This section has various problems that can be formulated and solved using QuantMethods Production/Operations Management software (QMpom). The appropriate model categories are indicated for each problem.

Data for Problems 1–6: In a 1-year period, the Productive Components Corporation (known as PCCorp) has shipped units worth $1,200,000 to its customers. It produced units worth $250,000 for finished goods (*FG*) inventory. PCCorp has $50,000 of work-in-process (*WIP*) units. During the same 1-year period of time, PCCorp had a labor bill of $140,000. Its capital expenses for the year are calculated to be $430,000. Materials were purchased costing $530,000. Energy expenses were $225,000, and miscellaneous expenses were estimated to be $75,000.

   Using the QMpom module called Capacity Management Models (Breakeven) will facilitate solving the six (6) problems that are numbered 1 through 6. A transformation of terms is required as described in each problem.

1   Calculate the labor productivity for PCCorp with respect to units shipped.
   In place of fixed cost, use sales; set variable cost to zero; in place of selling price, use labor cost. Breakeven volume in solution is equivalent to labor productivity.

2   Calculate the multifactor productivity composed of labor and capital for units shipped plus finished goods for PCCorp.
   In place of fixed cost use (sales + finished goods); set variable cost to zero; in place of selling price use (labor cost + capital expenses). Breakeven volume in solution is equal to multifactor productivity.

3   What is PCCorp's total productivity?
   Abbreviating, in place of FC use (sales + *FG* + *WIP*); *VC* = 0; in place of *SP*, use total of all costs. *BEV* in solution is equal to total productivity.

4   What is PCCorp's capital productivity?
   For *FC*, use (sales + *FG* + *WIP*); *VC* = 0; *SP* = capital expenses. *BEV* is capital productivity.

5   The value of the units shipped must be reduced because $350,000 worth of them have been returned as defective. Of the finished goods units (*FG*), $150,000 worth have been found to be defective. All work-in-process (*WIP*) units are within tolerances. Rework on the defective units reduces their value by 70 percent. What is the cost of the quality problem that has surfaced? Discuss what this means in terms of total productivity.
   Use QMpom, noting Problem 3, to show that total productivity has dropped to 0.82.

6   Calculate the multifactor productivity composed of capital, materials, and energy consumed for the total reworked output, which consists of units shipped plus *FG* plus *WIP*.
   Use QMpom, noting Problem 2, noting that labor costs have been by-passed in this calculation.

7   Productivity measures the ratio output values to the cost of inputs. Good productivity is shown by high ratio values; improved productivity is shown by higher ratio values over time.
   Does the following equation capture the meaning of productivity?

$$Productivity = pV/(vc)V$$

   where pV = price per unit x volume sold per year
   and $vc(V)$ = the variable cost per unit x volume made per year

8   Because *V* is in both the numerator and the denominator of the productivity equation,

$$Productivity = pV/(vc)V$$

Reduce the equation: **Productivity** $= p / (vc)$ and interpret the results.
Is productivity well described by the ratio of price per unit to variable cost per unit?

9 Elasticity describes how V (sales volume) changes as a function of p.

a. Does the following equation capture the meaning of elasticity?

$$V_p = kp^{-\beta}$$

As in the text, elasticity of demand volume V_p is a function of a price, p. The coefficient of elasticity is beta, which ranges from zero to one, and k is a constant.

b. Explain the following statement: If beta equals zero—indicating perfect and complete inelasticity—the constant, k, has a value equal to the demand volume for the product or service for all prices (p).

c. Why is it critical for P/OM to make every effort to continually raise quality standards and expectations for the product described in Problem 9(b)?

d. Fill in the following table for the elasticity equation:

$$V_p = kp^{-\beta}$$

letting $k = 5,000$ and $\beta = 0, 1, 0.5,$ and 0.25.

p	V_p ($\beta = 0$)	V_p ($\beta = 0.25$)	V_p ($\beta = 0.5$)	V_p ($\beta = 1.0$)
1.00				
1.50				
2.00				
2.50				

10 Link productivity, elasticity, and profit (P) using the typical profit equation:

$$P = (p - vc)V - FC$$

where $p = \$1.00$, $vc = \$0.50$, fixed costs ($FC$) $= \$10,000$, and $V =$ sales volume
Also, $k = 100,000$ units per year when $\beta = 1.0$ and $p = \$1.00$.
Using the QMpom module called Capacity Management Models (Breakeven) will facilitate solving Problem 10; use of spreadsheets will expedite solving Equation 2-10.

a. Using Equation 2-10, describe what occurs if the price is raised to $2.00.

b. Assume that increasing investments in technology improve productivity, such that by increasing FC to $15,000, vc is reduced to $0.40. Does this investment make sense? Do the necessary calculations and explain the results.

11 For Problem 10, assume that the equation for the economies of scale is

$$vc_v = KV^{-\alpha}$$

letting $\alpha = 0.5$ and $K = 160$
Also, vc_v is the per unit variable cost for volume V, K is a constant, and alpha (α) is the coefficient for economies of scale. As in Problem 10, solve for Part a. Why is Part b not applicable?
Using the QMpom module called Capacity Management Models (Breakeven) will facilitate solving Problem 11; use of spreadsheets will expedite solving Equation 2-10.

12 Explain how the application of the division of labor into specialized workstations might increase the size of the alpha coefficient in Problem 11. How might this affect the profit equation?

Practice Quiz

1 The measurement, by a firm, of its productivity improvement is most analogous to which one of the following measures?

a. tracking an auto's miles per gallon
b. logging pounds of fertilizer applied
c. daily measure of dieter's weight
d. on-wall charting of Junior's height
e. amount of frequent flier miles

2 The traditional measure of productivity is

a. cost per calorie of work.
b. output per unit of input.

    c.   input per unit of cost.

    d.   efficiency per dollar.

    e.   efficiency of the sales force.

3   The productivity of a sales force is properly measured by

    a.   the number of sales representatives working for the firm.

    b.   the dollar sales of the best sales rep divided by the worst.

    c.   the average sales per sales representative.

    d.   the effectiveness multiplied by the efficiency.

    e.   the measure of labor productivity.

4   Multifactor productivity measurement is used by the U.S. government because

    a.   it combines in one overall cost all input factors that create the total output of goods and services. This is the best way to measure national productivity.

    b.   it is the tradition of many governments to combine the labor and capital factors. This is the best way to measure GDP.

    c.   correlations can be performed on the multiple factors to indicate the degree of independence of the factors from each other.

    d.   the years 1973 through 1979 had an average multifactor productivity measure of 0.3. This was followed by even worse years, which provided strong evidence that government action would be needed to correct the situation.

    e.   the American auto industry finds it useful to employ multifactor analyses when they lobby the U.S. Congress. It is not likely that measurable change can occur as a result.

5   Productivity issues are woven into all aspects of the supplier-producer-customer value chain. It follows, then, that productivity is a systems measure. With this agreed upon, which of the following statements is false?

    a.   Capital productivity is of interest in the broad context of the systems measure.

    b.   Japanese productivity in automobile manufacturing is still extremely high although Japan has suffered national deterioration of productivity over many years.

    c.   Poor European productivity has affected U.S. productivity in some ways.

    d.   Worldwide, old technologies have been used up and new technologies are difficult to assimilate, but that is taking place gradually.

    e.   Bureaucracy is one of the organizational factors at the heart of the productivity slowdown in many industries. That situation is being solved by bankruptcies and closures.

6   Measures of the elasticity of demand as a function of price have always been thought to be the exclusive domain of marketing managers. P/OM has shown that this is not the case and, in this regard, which of the following statements is false?

    a.   Rational product prices (goods or services) reflect the cost of making and delivering the products.

    b.   Product prices and quality are tied together; quality is driven by P/OM costs.

    c.   Marketing managers believe that the elasticity effect is derived from psychological factors, and P/OM dismisses these statements as being irrational.

    d.   So-called demand–price elasticity overlooks the true relationship, which is demand–price and quality elasticity.

    e.   The volume of production (V) affects production unit costs; the price of the product affects the demand volume (D); there is a need to align V and D.

7   What are the relationships among product quality, productivity, and price elasticity? Identify which one of the following choices is wrong.

    a.   As productivity increases, the price–elasticity relationship becomes more elastic, which means that a change in price drives a more significant change in demand (+ or –).

    b.   Perceived product quality is related to consistency of performance, utility, reliability, durability, as well as intangible qualities, e.g., appearance. Consumers will pay more for better levels of tangible qualities. Price–elasticity curves reflect this relationship.

    c.   As processes become more productive, greater amounts of cash flow (funds) can be directed to improving perceived product quality.

    d.   Price elasticity can be affected by advertising, the expenditure for which is facilitated by productivity improvements that decrease waste and increase free cash flow.

e. Economies of scale improve productivity, but the change in production volume could lead to new methods that decrease product qualities such as reliability of the product and consistency of performance between different products coming off the same line.

8 What do economies of scale and the division of labor do to the P/OM system? Which one of the following choices is incorrect?

a. Breaking the job into parts and assigning individuals or teams to each part allows more repetitive practice, which provides learning to do the job better.

b. Doing the job better frequently saves money and improves quality of outputs.

c. Saved money can be used to lower prices, increase quality, and advertise more.

d. Increased quality can decrease price elasticity, which permits prices to be raised without decreasing demand, which generates more revenues.

e. Better revenues mean higher profits, which allow redesigning jobs to have more team members using less technology and thereby further increase the division of labor.

9 The history of P/OM improvement of the transformation function of the input–output model is a clear set of steps in both theory and application. Which of the following statements is incorrect?

a. Apprenticeship was one of the first stages of learning to do operations efficiently. Even so, it remains a major component of success, especially in service operations.

b. Without interchangeable parts, manufacturing would be costly. For example, each Saturn Vue would have to be handmade from start to finish.

c. The service sector has found some similarities to interchangeable parts manufacture. For example, the Shouldice Hospital in Toronto, Canada, treats hernia operations as iPods or computers along an assembly line. This improves quality of operations and lowers the cost.

d. Statistical quality control is used to monitor product dimensions at the process level. Since the development of SQC, firms have the ability to achieve near-zero defects from any production system.

e. Scientific management produced better ways to cut metals and improved bricklaying. This translates into less costly stock transactions, better flight schedules, and quick-service restaurant efficiencies.

10 Lean production systems are also considered to be agile and fast-moving. Which of the following methods and attributes do "agile" systems not employ? (Note: If there are some unfamiliar terms, search for them on the Internet before choosing an answer.)

a. design of parts to be interchangeable, modular, and group technology-based

b. parts that can be assembled with efficiencies of sequenced assembly methods

c. inspection procedures to weed out defectives in the pursuit of zero-defects

d. flexible programming to allow fast setups and changeovers

e. globally-connected systems that permit immediate communications between partners along the supply chain

Additional Readings

Anupindi, Ravi, Sunil Chopra, Sudhakar D. Deshmukh, Jan A. Van Meighem, and Eitan Zemel. *Managing Business Process Flows*. Upper Saddle River, NJ: Prentice Hall, 1999.

Baumol, William J., Sue Anne Blackman, and Edward N. Wolff. *Productivity and American Leadership: The Long View*. Cambridge: MIT Press, 1991.

Britton, Andrew. Economic Commission for Europe Discussion Papers. *Economic Growth in the Market Economies 1950–2000*, vol. 1, no. 1, 1991. New York: United Nations (GE.91-23315).

Deming, W. E. *Out of the Crisis*. MIT Center for Advanced Engineering Study, 1986.

Fabricant, Soloman. *A Primer on Productivity*. New York: Random House, 1969.

Forrester, Jay W. "Changing Economic Patterns." *Technology Review* (August/September 1978).

Hellriegel, D., S. E. Jackson, and J. W. Slocum Jr., *Management: A Competency-Based Approach*, 10e. Cincinnati, OH: Thomson South-Western, 2005.

Juran, J. M., and F. M. Gryna Jr., *Quality Planning and Analysis*, 2e. New York: McGraw-Hill, 1980.

Moser, Klaus. *Mass Customization Strategies—Development of a Competence-Based Framework for Identifying Different Mass Customization Strategies*. Lulu.com, January 2007.

Ohno, Taiichi. *Toyota Production System: Beyond Management of Large-Scale Production*. Japan: Diamond Publishing Co. Ltd., 1978.

Servan-Schreiber, Jean-Jacques. *The American Challenge*. New York: Atheneum, 1968.

Shewhart, W. A. *Statistical Method from the Viewpoint of Quality Control*. Washington, DC: The Department of Agriculture, 1939.

Smith, Adam. *An Enquiry into the Nature and Causes of the Wealth of Nations*, 1776.

Notes

1. John H. Blackstone and James F. Cox. *APICS Dictionary*, 11e. APICS Educational and Research Foundation, 2004.

2. Soloman Fabricant. *A Primer on Productivity*. New York: Random House, 1969, p. 3. This definition adds "in a period of time (*t*)" to Fabricant's definition. He is considered to be the "father of productivity measurement."

3. The U.S. Department of Labor, Bureau of Labor Statistics, *News*. USDL 94-327 (July 7, 1994). The Bureau of Labor Statistics public database, LABSTAT, is available on the Internet.

4. The U.S. Department of Labor, Bureau of Labor Statistics, Press release. (February 1995). Available at http://data.bls.gov/servlet/SurveyOutputServlet; June 2003.

5. *The New York Times* (November 5, 1994): D19.

6. Ibid., but this quote is attributed to Donald P. Wingard, managing partner for Andersen's Americas Automotive Practice.

7. William J. Baumol, Sue Anne Blackman, and Edward N. Wolff. *Productivity and American Leadership: The Long View*. Cambridge: MIT Press, 1991.

8. Jay W. Forrester. "Changing Economic Patterns." *Technology Review* (August/September, 1978).

9. Weber considered legal domination as an ideal form of bureaucracy as compared to alternative organizational forms such as charismatic and traditional domination, which related to societal control by monarchies and religious institutions.

10. The "Global Village" and the "Global Village on the Move" have created uniquely interesting programs to develop future leaders for business and industry. See http://www.iacocca-lehigh.org.

11. Cited by the study "Foreign-Affiliated Firms in America," conducted by the Center for the Study of Operations at Columbia University, 1991.

12. Boston Consulting Group. *On Experience* was published as part of the *Perspectives* series by the BCG company in 1968, with a third printing and preface by Bruce Henderson, then president of BCG, in 1972.

13. Adam Smith. *An Enquiry into the Nature and Causes of the Wealth of Nations*, 1776 (a five-volume treatise).

14. W. A. Shewhart. *Statistical Method from the Viewpoint of Quality Control*. Washington, DC: The Department of Agriculture, 1939. This is a classic in the OM field.

15. W. E. Deming. *Out of the Crisis*. MIT Center for Advanced Engineering Study, 1986. Also, a valuable reference is J. M. Juran and F. M. Gryna Jr., *Quality Planning and Analysis*, 2e. New York: McGraw-Hill, 1980.

16. T. Ohno. *Toyota Production System: Beyond Management of Large-Scale Production*. Japan: Diamond Publishing Co. Ltd., 1978.

17. Called the six-sigma program, the goal is to strive for 3.4 defects per million parts.

18. *The New York Times* (November 8, 1994).

19. D. Hellriegel, S. E. Jackson, and J. W. Slocum Jr., Management: *A Competency-Based Approach* 10e. Cincinnati, OH: Thomson South-Western Publishing Co., 2005

20. See the Agile Alliance and the Agile 2008 Conference in Toronto with emphasis on agile software development and agile project management.

Enrichment Activity 2: Decision Trees

Decision trees (DTs) provide another important method for representing decision problems. There are certain kinds of problems that DTs can organize that are very cumbersome in matrix form. Sometimes, it is a toss-up as to which is preferred. At other times, only DTs can be used.

The decision problem presented in Enrichment Activity 1 (in Chapter 1) was matrix-modeled. This problem can also be modeled with decision trees. Later on, a productivity decision example will be given where decision trees are much preferred to matrices, and by extension, where they must be used.

First, the decision tree is drawn in Figure EA2-1 to represent the shipper's situation.

Following are the rules for using decision trees. It is helpful to observe how the given problem is translated from decision-matrix form into a decision tree.

Start with the various strategies emanating from the first decision box. Some trees have many decision boxes, although this tree has only one. Also, there can be many lines that fan out from any decision box. This tree has only two.

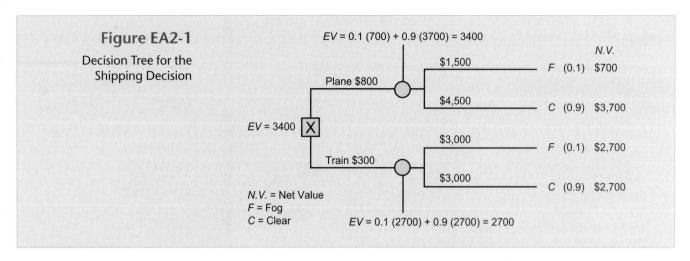

Figure EA2-1

Decision Tree for the Shipping Decision

$EV = 0.1 (700) + 0.9 (3700) = 3400$

Plane $800

$EV = 3400$ X

Train $300

$1,500

$4,500

$3,000

$3,000

N.V.

F (0.1) $700

C (0.9) $3,700

F (0.1) $2,700

C (0.9) $2,700

N.V. = Net Value
F = Fog
C = Clear

$EV = 0.1 (2700) + 0.9 (2700) = 2700$

Label the strategies with their costs. At the end of each strategy line, there is a chance-event circle. From that circle emanate the states of nature that can occur. There is a line for every state of nature, and each is labeled with the appropriate probability and revenue. By tracing out the costs and revenues encountered along each branch of the tree, a unique endpoint for profits is derived. Label the net value (*N.V.*) of each endpoint.

Work backwards through the tree. Wherever two or more states of nature merge at a chance-event circle, obtain the expected value for profit at that circle and mark it.

Continue working backwards through the tree. Whenever two or more strategies (such as by plane or by train) merge at a decision-point box, carry the largest expected value to that box. For this tree, the choice is between 3400 and 2700. Because the former is larger, and this tree is profit oriented, label the decision-point box with $EV = 3400$. If the decision problem is not in terms of profits, then use net costs and expected costs.

When the decision tree has a sequence of strategies (see the next example), then, working backwards, follow that sequence of strategies that accounts for the largest EV for profit. This is the EV that has been carried to the first decision-point box of the network. For the preceding tree, the strategy ship by plane, which is the top branch of the tree, is the winner.

Decision Sequences of Greater Length—A Game of Chance

Decision problems that involve a sequence of alternative strategic choices are particularly well-suited to decision tree organization for solution. When there are many sequences of the type "if this, then that," the decision tree is the only sensible way to represent such complexity.

Start with a simple example. Assume the following game of chance:

If X chooses to play the first game, called A, and wins, then X can play the second game, called B. X does not have to play B or A.

To play A or B costs $50.

If X wins A, X receives $50. There is an 80 percent probability of winning A. If X wins the second game, B, X receives $200. There is a 60 percent probability of X winning B. What should X do?

Figure EA2-2 shows that the expected value for trying to play both games is $46. There is a 20 percent chance that X will lose the first game and be out the $50. However, there is an 80 percent chance that X will win the first game, which means that X just breaks even. X must go on to play the second game.

Decision-Matrix Equivalent

When the tree in Figure EA2-2 is converted into its decision-matrix form (see Table EA2-1), it is possible to appreciate the economy of representation of the tree approach for large, multistage decision problems.

In the following problems, a productivity decision problem is posed that is best resolved by the decision-tree method.

Enrichment Challenges 2

1 The Pin Factory can buy a new machine—called M1—that costs $40,000. There is an 80 percent chance that sales will get an order for which this machine can be used with significant productivity advantages. If that order does not

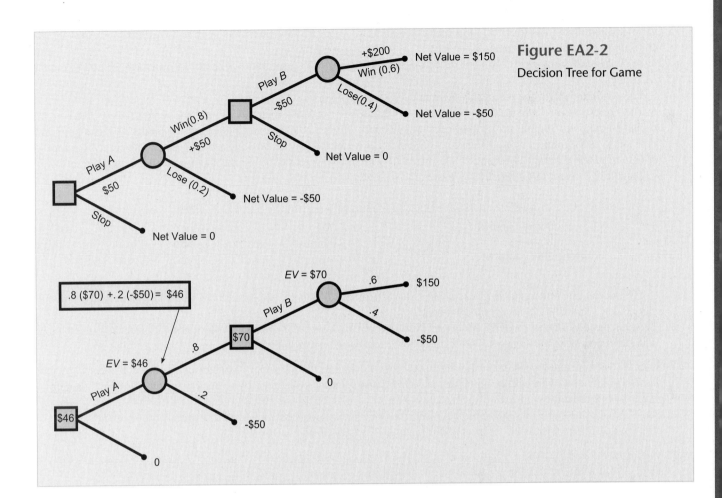

Figure EA2-2

Decision Tree for Game

	Probabilities				
	0.48	**0.32**	**0.20**		
	Win A	**Win A**	**Lose A**		
	Win B	**Lose B**	**Stop**	**EV**	
Play A	0	0	–$50	–$10	
Play A and B	$150	–$50	–$50	$ 46	
Do not play	0	0	0	0	

Table EA2-1

Decision Matrix for Two-Stage Problem

materialize, then the machine will not be used for the foreseeable future. Normally, one would wait to see if the order was received, but that cannot be done in this case because the M1 has a 3-month lead time. If M1 is purchased today, it will be online just in time.

If the order is received and the machine is online, then the Pin Factory will earn $50,000. It also will be given the opportunity to bid on a much bigger job. The bigger job requires buying four more M1 machines, which will be delivered in time to be online for the new job, if the Pin Factory wins the bid. The management team estimates that the probability of winning the bid is 60 percent. The revenue from getting the new order will be $300,000. Should the Pin Factory decide to try for these orders?

2 American Auto Supply (AAS) has been given an opportunity to become a certified supplier by one of the major auto companies in Detroit. They have been offered the following proposition:

Stage 1: Submit engine-mount parts from a sample mold. If they pass, there will be an order for 100,000 engine-mount parts, and a chance to:

Stage 2: Submit samples for shock-absorber assemblies. If these pass lab tests, there will be an order for 100,000 shock-absorber assemblies, and a chance to:

Stage 3: Submit samples for bumper assemblies. If these pass the tests, there will be an order for 100,000 bumper assemblies.

The deadline is tight for accomplishment of each stage.

The conditions are that AAS pays for the molds and all costs associated with making sample parts. There is no reimbursement for tooling-up for parts that fail to pass the test. Further, engineering has stated that these parts are difficult to make to meet the specifications. The chances of success by the deadline are estimated to be 50 percent for the engine-mount and bumper assemblies. There is a 40 percent chance of failure for the shock-absorbers assemblies.

Total direct costs (*TDC*) for 100 samples are as follows:

Parts	TDC	ppu
Engine mounts	$ 8,000	($0.20)
Bumpers	$16,000	($0.40)
Shock absorbers	$10,000	($0.20)

The profits per unit (*ppu*) *if awarded* the contract for 100,000 units are listed next to the total direct costs within parentheses. Should AAS accept the challenge?

3 Because the deadline is so tight, American Auto Supply has asked for changes in the proposition to give them more latitude in preparing the samples. The changes being requested appear in rewritten Stages 2 and 3, as follows:

Stage 2: Submit samples for either the shock-absorber assemblies or the bumper assemblies, not both. If the second part passes the lab tests, there will be an order for 100,000 units. Then AAS can go on to qualify for the third part. Therefore, Stage 3 would become:

Stage 3: Submit samples for the third part, which is either the bumper assembly or the shock-absorber assembly. If these pass the tests, there will be an order for 100,000 units of that assembly.

Demand Creation and Predictive Planning

Chapter Outline

Cycles
Repetitive patterns of sequenced values, which generally return to the same, or to a proportionately equivalent, starting point.

Chapter 3 explores strategic planning for new and existing products (goods and services). Referred to as "life cycle planning," this involves understanding the strategic interactions of P/OM with marketing. Life **cycles** start with the introduction of new products and the early growth of market share. The next life cycle stage is the stabilization of market share (often termed a mature brand). The stable period has been getting shorter because of the rapid advance of technology and the increased effectiveness of marketing communication and advertising. The next life cycle stage is the decline of share, which may be followed by redesign or by withdrawal of the product from the market.

Methods to evaluate consumer demand are necessary. Chapter 3 explains demand forecasting. Forecasting models can estimate demand in terms of sales volume and market share over a given period of time. It is necessary to be able to predict the sales generated by different prices, product features, and product qualities. Forecasting ability is dependent upon access to market research data. Plans based on good predictions are essential to the formulation of successful operational strategies. This, in turn, leads to tactical decisions to carry out the strategic plans. Discussion of tactical factors begins in Part 2 and continues in Part 3. Change is inevitable, and Part 4 deals with the strategic perspectives of sustainability.

After reading this chapter, you should be able to:

- Clarify the distinction between strategy and tactics.
- Detail how P/OM can contribute to the strategy planning team.
- Discuss disruptive innovation and explain its effect on existing strategies.
- Explain what "Best Practice" means to P/OM.
- Define life cycle stages and explain why they are important.
- Forecast relevant information for new product development.
- Forecast relevant demand data for production scheduling.
- Teach others about choosing forecasting techniques.
- Contrast various forecasting methods.
- Know when and how to apply linear regression analysis.
- Show how to evaluate forecast errors.
- Explain the benefit of learning from mistakes.
- Explain why it is important to maintain forecasting history.

The Systems Viewpoint

Organizations that base their plans on where they have been rather than on what appears to be happening in their future are like drivers who steer by looking through the rearview mirror. That is dangerous and counterproductive. The systems viewpoint integrates the past, present, and future. Forecasts are necessary to describe the future. These forecasts must coordinate demands for products and services with supplies of resources that are required to meet the demands. Forecasts for market demands set the agenda for how the entire company will use its people, commit its resources, call on outside suppliers, and plan its work schedules. As such, the forecast is the platform for strategic planning. Good strategy is aimed at modifying the forecast to influence what the future might bring rather than just accepting the forecast as an inevitable truth. In this way, management earns its

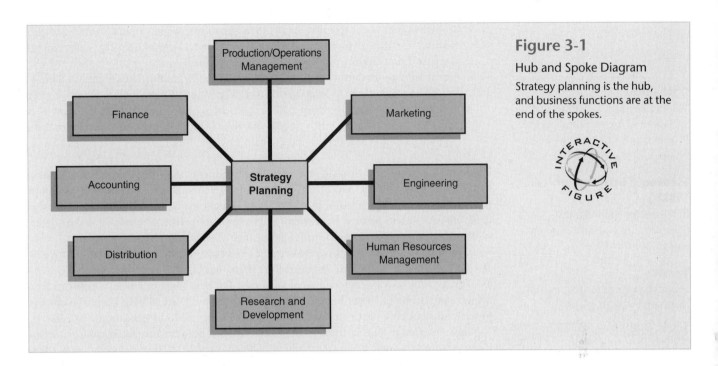

Figure 3-1

Hub and Spoke Diagram
Strategy planning is the hub, and business functions are at the end of the spokes.

rewards by better fitting production capabilities (short- and long-term) to marketing possibilities. This systems point of view, which starts with strategic planning and progresses to tactical details, has the best chance of maximizing profits.

Strategic Thinking

Strategic thinking (planning) to realize objectives involves teamwork of all functions. P/OM is part of that team. Recall the hub and spoke diagram from the Prologue. Here it is called Figure 3-1 and it puts strategy planning at the center of the system and all of the business functions at the end of the spokes. This is how the CEO visualizes the situation. The coordinating function is management. The coordinating system's mechanism is strategy. After there is agreement about strategies to be followed, the P/OM function decides on the tactics to be used to pull together the various functions. Given an agreed-upon strategy, P/OM moves into the hub position from its own point of view. Marketing and finance see themselves at the center of the universe from their own points of view.

3-1 Production and Operations Management Strategies for Survival and Success

Strategy is the comprehensive big-picture plan for the organization's future. It has to be product-oriented and marketing-aware to take customers and competition into account. It has to be process-oriented and P/OM-oriented to deliver the product that customers want. It needs to be systems-oriented to coordinate finance, marketing, and P/OM. This entails broad-based, cooperative goal setting followed by planning to achieve four goals:

Strategy
Comprehensive and overall planning for the organization's future.

1 Survival of the organization under the stress of technological change as well as economic and political factors. Hurricanes, earthquakes, etc., are just as real.
2 Adaptation to a global business environment. This must include adjusting to the effect of different values—such as more importance placed on sustainability, environmental protection, and global warming.

3 Conversion from a reactive mode to a proactive mode, which means not just waiting for things to happen. Proactive means taking actions to make things happen. This certainly applies to entrepreneurial behavior.

4 Eventually go for profit maximization, but in the beginning, make certain there is sufficient **cash flow** to keep the business running. Cash flow is actual money received minus actual money that is spent in a given period of time. If more is received than spent, the cash flow is positive. If more is spent than received, there is money owed. Cash flow is then negative.

Many companies are divided into **strategic business units (SBUs)** in order to help them define clear, strong, and effective strategies. Each strategic business unit develops plans centered on its own set of products, and each can be compared to similar business units with respect to process performance. The systems perspective is essential to determine what accounts for the competitive advantage of successful SBUs.

Illustrating the distinction between strategies and **tactics** helps to further define strategy: Do the right "thing" (strategic choice) before doing the "thing" right (tactical choice)! As an example, consider the company that tried to make better buggy whips in order to fend off the competition of Henry Ford's Model T. That company would have been well advised to work on an electric starter because the Model T engine had to be hand-cranked to start it.

Another analogy that is used to help differentiate between strategies and tactics is: Know where you want to go (the strategic choice—a goal) before deciding on the best way to get there (the tactical choice—the means to an end). This is equivalent to stating that the goals set by strategies are like destinations. The decision to fly, drive, or take a train is a tactical decision that cannot be made until the origin and destination are known.

Either strategies or tactics can provide "**disruptive innovation**" which is the name that Clayton Christensen[1,2] has given to events, discoveries, inventions, and the like that overturn the existing, dominant technology or methodology. Good examples are vinyl phonograph records replaced by CDs and digital imaging replacing traditional film-based photography. **Disruptive technology** is the catalyst bringing about fundamental changes in the business model. Disruptive innovation causes old strategies to become moribund.

3-2 Participants in Planning Strategies

Because strategies are the future plans for the company, strategies must be created by those who know enough about the business to do such planning. Usually, therefore, strategies will be formulated by those at the top of the organization, aided by those with special knowledge who may be located anywhere inside or outside the company. The cast of characters involved in strategic planning usually is composed of a top management group, line and staff managers, and various specialists in relevant fields. The participants change as conditions are altered.

Strategy development is a continuous and ongoing process, because strategies must be revised as conditions change. It is a matter of survival through adaptation. A new competitive product entry, an improvement in the competitor's delivery system, a change in the law or in economic conditions, or a new technological development that enhances the competitor's process often will call for modification of prior strategies. Therefore, the nature of the changes that are occurring will determine which specialists may be consulted. Those responsible for strategic planning must know enough to seek out the appropriate specialists as conditions warrant.

3-2a P/OM's Role in Developing Strategies

From the systems point of view, only in small companies can one person know enough about the business to do strategic planning without teammates. As firms get larger, no one person can handle all of the activities that need to be done.

Cash flow

The net amount of cash received and spent in a given time period. Positive cash flow means "money is in the bank."

Strategic business units (SBUs)

Independent subdivisions considered to be profit-making entities for the company.

Tactics

Detailed procedures required to carry out strategic plans.

Disruptive innovation

See **Disruptive technology**.

Disruptive technology

A disruptive technology (or innovation) is one that overturns the existing dominant product and/or process. It disrupts the status quo.

© 2008 Jupiterimages Corporation

Because of pollution concerns, factories in many countries have employed technology to monitor and control harmful emissions. Auto companies are developing hybrid, hydrogen, and electric cars. P/OM has a unique strategic role in employing technology to improve the environment.

In larger firms, the systems perspective dictates that representatives of all of the functional departments that define "knowing enough about the business" play a part in strategy development. Figure 3-1 illustrates the need for coordination since no one person holds all the cards.

There are some additional differences between organizations with respect to who participates in planning the strategies for products and processes. If the technology used for the process is recent and complex (new and high-tech), then operations managers are more likely to be part of the strategic planning team. Such proactive participation applies to both manufacturing and service industries. Participation applies to banking, insurance, investment brokers, transportation, health care, hospitality, and outsourcing, too.

If P/OM know-how is not properly represented, then strategic planning is operating at a limited level. The same is true if other functional areas are not represented. The benefits of the systems approach are missing, and the organization is operating at a disadvantage with respect to survival under technological stress, adaptation to a global environment, and conversion from reactive to proactive competitive positions.

3-2b Who Carries Out the Strategies?

Operations managers are always involved in carrying out strategic plans, even when they are not part of the strategic planning team. Operation centers are where the work is done that creates the products that customers buy. This applies to the operations room of banks and airlines and the production floor of the manufacturer.

Independent of who formulates company strategies, decisions that stem from those strategies are carried into action by tactics. Tactics are the procedures used by the line managers of the organization to carry out the strategic plans. Tactical applications are the normal operating mode of line managers of the organization and include production scheduling, materials planning, and quality control.

The terms *strategy* and *tactics* have military origins. Strategy is directed at winning the "war" while tactics are designed to win the "battles." Generals and admirals decide what battles have to be fought, when, where, and in what way. Line officers carry out the mission, determining the specific "hows."

Use of the terms *strategy* and *tactics* is common in companies where line management is recognized as being the responsibility of P/OM. Overseeing production workers who are on the line, making goods and delivering services, is only part of the job. Line managers must be aware of the company's productivity goals and quality objectives to be an effective part of the strategy team.

Strategic planners determine the what, when, and where of new products. P/OM is then responsible for how to make and deliver these new products. New product decisions require planning future capabilities and capacities. Strategies also are concerned with the production and replacement of existing products at given costs and levels of investment. Regardless of whether P/OM participates in the development of such strategic plans, these plans are administered by operations managers.

In organizations that are strongly integrated, operations managers participate in planning the evolution of both new and existing products. That evolution over time is called the **product life cycles**. Plans for the life cycles—called **life cycle strategies**—set in motion the designing of the input-transformation-output systems that are the basis of production. Life cycle strategies will be further defined later in this chapter.

Synergy is an action of separate agents that produces a greater effect than the sum of their individual actions, i.e., one plus one makes three. **Syzygy**, besides being the only word in the English language that has no vowels and three y's, comes from a Greek word for "conjunction." It is the point when maximum tidal pull is exerted because the planets and moon have lined up to support each other's gravitational forces.

Stage IV organizations capitalize on synergy and syzygy by encouraging broad communication about all matters relating to strategic planning. Stage IV organizations

Product life cycles
See **Life cycle strategies**.

Life cycle strategies
The systems approach is essential to preplan successfully start-ups through re-staging and replacement of withdrawals for the entire product line.

Synergy
Agents producing a greater effect when acting together than the sum of their separate effects.

Syzygy
Point when maximum tidal pull is exerted because the planets and the moon have lined up.

achieve the teamwork ideals of the systems approach, whereas Stage I organizations do not have what it takes for all of its functions to pull together.

Companies tend to move to higher stages if and when their organizations come to realize that important strategic leverage is gained through the participation of P/OM. It is an exciting time for operations managers because in almost every organization P/OM is being integrated into the corporate planning fabric. Successful new competitors, often from abroad, have fully coordinated strategic planning teams.

3-2c Adopting "Best Practice"

Being "in the know" prevents P/OMs from inadvertently working against the company's success. Yet, what is to be done if the stage of the organization, or the politics of the organization, or the chemistry of the managers causes policies to be followed that do not place the production and operations managers onto the strategy teams?

By working actively (as compared to working passively) in the realm of

1 new product development and
2 quality enhancement practices,

P/OM can get involved with the strategic domain, without ever having been appointed to a strategic planning committee.

Passive participation of P/OM is characterized by doing just what is asked and nothing more. Active participation involves learning about what is being done elsewhere and then trying to get Best Practice adopted whenever possible. P/OM must play an instrumental role at both the strategic and tactical levels to determine what Best Practice is regionally, especially with competitors and, ultimately, anywhere in the world.

Both new product development and quality enhancement practices are gateways to the strategic domain. Total quality management (TQM) is susceptible to either continuous improvement or to the marked departure from prior procedures (starting out with a clean piece of paper) that reengineering requires. New products, whether goods or services, provide opportunities for reinventing, or reengineering, process flows. The constant effort to improve products and process flows provides a transition between strategies and tactics for operating the system.

3-2d The Management Component of P/OM Is a Scarce Resource

Strategies for the introduction of new products and for replacement of existing products must be formulated with the fact in mind that operations managers' time and talents are limited resources. Managerial capabilities must be spread over both new product start-ups and ongoing output responsibilities.

Because production managers and operations managers are a scarce resource, its personnel should be used wisely. This means bringing P/OM knowledge to bear as early as possible—in the strategy formulation process. By doing so, it is possible to avoid squandering limited P/OM time and talent on remedial "fire fighting" and efforts to play "catch-up" at a later time.

3-3 Understanding Life Cycle Stages: Crucial for P/OM Action

Throughout the company, the planning function marches to the drumbeat of life cycle stages. Operations managers need to be aware of the timing and stages that drive the project management schedules of new products, as well as the production and delivery schedules of the company's mature products.

Cycles are composed of four stages that appear in a regular way over time. All products and services go through the following stages:

1 Introduction to the market.
2 Growth of volume and share.
3 Maturity is the phase when growth ceases. Volume and share of market are stable and in equilibrium.
4 Decline or decay occurs when deteriorating sales leads to restaging the product or withdrawing it from the marketplace.

These life cycle periods are discrete stages in each product's life that need to be understood in order to manage that product. Marketing is responsible for using different pricing, advertising, and promotion activities during appropriate stages. P/OM is responsible for intelligent management of the production transformation process, which changes in various ways according to the life cycle stage. The changes or transitions between stages require knowing how to adjust the production system's capabilities.

3-3a Introduction and Growth of the New Product (Goods and Services)

There are two main phases of life cycle stages. The first consists of the introduction and growth of the product. The "idea" for the product and its development precedes the introduction. The entire team works on ascertaining the marketing feasibility of the idea, as well as the feasibility of making it and delivering it. R&D may have made sample product so that market research can test its customer acceptability. When it is approved, P/OM and engineering swing into action to create the production system that can make and/or assemble it. During this process of bringing the idea to reality, there are many "make or buy" analyses.

None of this is easy. It takes a lot of effort and attention to detail. There is much time and talent needed to conceptualize the product, design its specifics, organize the process for making it, cost it out, pilot test it, and so forth.

When the product is accepted, it is released for production and marketing. Timing and coordination are critical. The product must be ready for delivery to customers on promised due dates. As Lodish et. al say, "To properly plan and execute a product launch, it is imperative that marketing confirm the product availability date. Development and marketing must be in lock-step to ensure an effective launch."[3]

All of this takes place in the introductory stage.

3-3b Maturity of the New Product (Goods and Services) and Eventual Decline

When the new product or service stops growing, it is considered mature. This means that its volume is stabilized at the saturation level for that brand. The competitors have divided the market, and only extraordinary events, such as a strike at a competitor's plant, are able to shift shares and volumes.

Previously P/OM had to deal with producing larger and larger quantities of product. Now the input–output relationship reaches equilibrium. Marketing takes specific actions during this phase to maintain the product's share of the market. Prices often are lowered. Coordination between P/OM and sales is essential to meet delivery schedules on time. Finally, the product begins to lose share, volume drops, and, depending on the strategy, the product is either restaged or terminated.

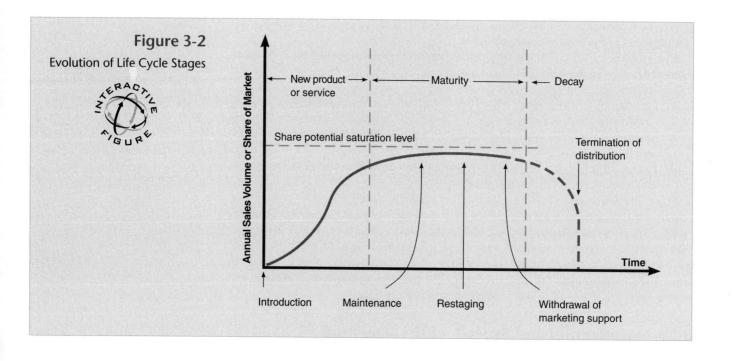

Figure 3-2

Evolution of Life Cycle Stages

It is generally expected that a replacement product will have been developed, tested, and be ready to be introduced. It is the substitute for the decaying product. It will have been assigned the capacity of the product that has been replaced. The cycle of the new product is similar to that of the one that is replaced in that it goes through introduction, growth, maturation, and decline. Figure 3-2 illustrates the evolutionary path followed by a new product or service. It shows the three main life cycle stages.

Consider the revenue-generating lifetime of the new product. (This consideration is applicable to goods and/or services—so product should be read as either or both.) During the introduction, expenditures usually are high to bring the new product to the distributors, retailers, and customers. The cash flow is negative (more money is spent than is received).

More is being spent on the introduction of the product and promotion of growth than the product revenue returns. Later, when the customer base has been established, net revenue increases, and expenditure decreases. During the stable period of product maturity, if the product enjoys a loyal following, promotions of any kind may be unnecessary. Eventually, competitive moves are likely to lead to price cuts and the withdrawal of the product from the market. The extent of the stable interval has been decreasing in many categories because of technological changes as well as aggressive competitive behaviors.

Product life cycles have been speeding up, which means that growth has to occur faster. The product does not stay in the mature stage as long and has to be replaced more often. More new product introductions are required to replace waning products. The challenge for P/OM is the rapidity of adjustment to all of the life cycle stage changes and to go through them frequently.

P/OM thinking is crucial to each of the four stages. The new design that is about to enter production has been finalized. There still are many questions to be answered. How much product must be made for distribution at start-up? How much product will be needed to keep the supply lines filled to meet the demand during growth? How much capacity is to be used at each of the stages? How much training will the evolving work configurations require? Make or buy decisions can change. What should be bought at first, at the lower volumes, might be better made in the plant, at the higher volumes that are associated with maturity.

3-3c Protecting Established (Mature) Products (Goods and Services)

Organizations that have been successful with their new product introductions can bank on having established products or services that generate positive cash flow (more money is received than is spent). The "bank" is not as good as it used to be, though, because the competitive rate of new product introductions has increased markedly in recent years. P/OM requires the cash to pay labor and buy materials from suppliers. Generally, P/OM spends more cash than any other department in the company. These cash accounts for operating expenses may total 70 percent of all cash spent by the company.

Because of global organizations, there are more competitors in the game, and because there are more competitors, each organization competes harder. Increased competition has led to higher levels of market volatility. Nevertheless, for most product categories, there is still plenty of opportunity to benefit from the mature product life cycle stage. P/OM benefits from the security of established products because they have stable material and labor skill requirements. They also provide the opportunity to improve the productivity of these processes.

3-4 Forecasting Life Cycle Stages for P/OM Action

Life cycle stages provide a classification for understanding the kinds of trends that can be expected in demand. During new product introductions, demand is led by the need to "fill the pipeline." This means getting product into the distribution centers, warehouses, and stores from which customers can be supplied.

When growth starts to occur, there is a trend line of increasing sales. The trick is to estimate how fast demand will increase over time, and for how long a period growth will continue. There are good methods used by market research to find out what is happening. This information is fed back through sales to P/OM for purposes of capacity planning and production scheduling.

3-4a Perspectives on Forecasting

An umbrella manufacturer is preparing production and distribution schedules. There is a sign on the wall: "Where will it rain next week?" When it rains, umbrella sales pick up. Meteorological models have improved in recent years so that fairly good weather forecasts can be made. Many businesses, especially when scheduling outdoor events, hire weather forecasters who have a good track record.

Forecasting is not the term generally used to talk about the composition of a random draw of cards or how a roulette wheel performs. Those are statistical phenomena for which probabilities are known. Las Vegas and Atlantic City have built their gambling casino profits on the laws of probability—but customers still have to come and play. Customer attendance is not a known probability. The casinos try to forecast attendance.

Forecasting is used to foretell sales demand volume even though the probabilities have never been formally studied. Businesspeople often use their sense of what is happening to reach decisions that might be better made if someone had kept a record of what had taken place already. There is often some empirical basis for estimating what is likely to happen in the future.

Marketing models for predicting sales (lacking a contract) deal with levels of uncertainty that make forecasts of demand volumes, market shares, and revenues difficult, but not irrational. One of the best sources of information about the future is the past. For new products, there is no past, and so other methods can be tried. For example, what is most similar? Lacking that, market research will find out what people think they will buy.

To compete in the global market, companies must deal with different time zones around the world. For example, banks use state-of-the-art technologies to process transactions that occur when their front office is closed. The backroom of the bank is operating 24/7. Airlines and computer software firms (like Oracle and SAP) must support their systems with operations around the clock. This calls for constant online forecasting.

Forecasting
Describing future events and their probabilities of occurrence.

If possible, use existing data to develop forecasts. The Rivet Factory has to forecast sales of products to order materials and to develop production schedules. The Mail Order Company has to forecast demand in order to have the right number of trained agents and operators in place. Ford Motor Company has to forecast car sales so that dealer stocks are of reasonable size for every model.

In every sales forecasting situation, the volatility of demand will determine how likely it is that a good forecast can be made. Stable patterns that persist for a long period of time make company forecasters confident that a credible job of forecasting can be done. Shaky estimates make company forecasters uneasy, so they search for new factors to correlate with the demand system.

Sales patterns are becoming less stable with increasing competition and information. Food sales that once were stable now are affected by medical reports about the food's effect on health. Auto and home sales are among many products that are strongly influenced by interest rates, which fluctuate more in a global environment. Exports and imports are sales that move around the globe in response to currency fluctuations that are increasingly unstable. Consequently, better forecasting methods need to be used by the companies that are affected by increased volatility.

How well can one forecast the future? The answer will depend on the stability of the pattern of the **time series** for the events being studied. The underlying pattern can be hard to find, but not impossible. Even if a pattern is found, the question remains, how long will it persist? When will it change? Those willing to forecast accept the challenge.

3-4b Extrapolation of Cycles, Trend Lines, and Step Functions

Extrapolation is the process of moving from observed data (past and present) to the unknown values of future points. Extrapolation of time series is a fundamental method. Figure 3-3 extrapolates past values to provide predictions of sales in the future.

A time series is a stream of data that represents past measurements. Each event is time-tagged so that it is known where it is located in the series of data. Figure 3-3 shows a linear trend for sales volume. It is extrapolated by extending a line drawn between the last two observations. P/OM must decide if the new point (Δ_t) is credible for planning future production supply volumes.

Figure 3-4 shows an erratic pattern of peaks and valleys for sales volume. This random cyclical pattern of monthly sales can be extrapolated if the cyclical patterns can be

Time series

Stream of numbers that represents different values over time.

Extrapolation

Process of moving from observed data to the projected values of future points.

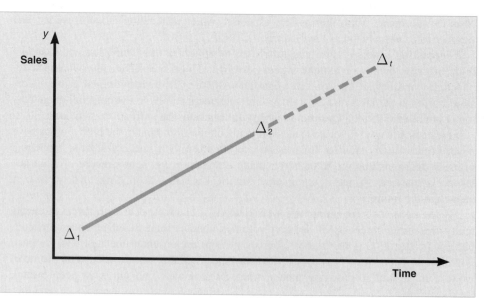

Figure 3-3

Extrapolation of Trend Line Is Used to Predict Future Sales

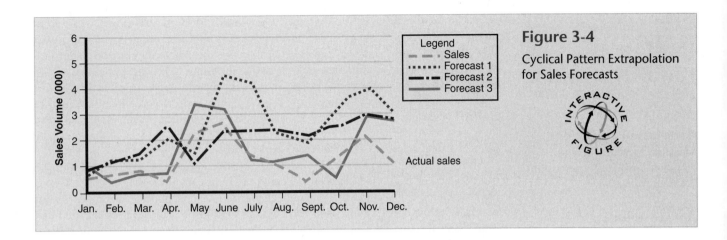

Figure 3-4

Cyclical Pattern Extrapolation for Sales Forecasts

assumed to reoccur. In Figure 3-4, three forecasts had been made for future sales by extrapolating the cyclical patterns of prior months' sales.

Extrapolations of time series can be based on

1 Cyclical wave patterns
2 Trend lines
3 Step functions
4 Combinations of any or all of these patterns

Step functions look like stairs—going up or going down. It is hoped that the forecast can predict when the next step will occur and how far up or down it goes. Short-term cycles can be piggybacked on long-term cycles. All kinds of combinations are possible. The key point is that cycles, trends, and steps are the basic pallet for the development of forecasting models based on time series.

Time series data also can reflect regular or erratic bursts called pulses. If these spikes appear from time to time and some pattern can be associated with them, they could be added to the list of what can be extrapolated or projected into the future.

3-4c Time Series Analysis

It is always useful to try to find causal links between well-known cycles—such as the seasons—and demand patterns that are being tracked. Thus, there are seasons for resort hotels and home heating oil. Cycles are one form of time series that is often used by business to forecast other events related to that time series. There are other categories of time series that are useful to know about. **Time series analysis** deals with using knowledge about cycles, trends, and averages to forecast future events.

The *term time series analysis* deserves explanation. Time series analysis is "analysis of any variable classified by time, in which the values of the variable are functions of the time periods."[4]

The time series consists of data recorded at different time periods such as weekly or daily for the variable, which could be units produced or demands received. Forecasters attempt to predict the next value or set of values that will occur at a future time. In time series analysis, external causes are not brought into the picture. The pattern of the series is considered to be time-dependent. That is why APICS' definition states "the values of the variable are functions of the time periods."

Using symbols, a forecast is to be made from some series of numbers $x_1, x_2, \ldots x_n$. The numbers might be monthly sales for the past year. The question is: Can these numbers be used to indicate monthly sales for next year? How will the time series be used to make a forecast? Production schedules will be drawn up to satisfy demand. Orders will

Time series analysis
Analysis of a stream of numbers in a time series.

be placed for inventory to be purchased. Workers will be hired and trained, or let go as the production crew is downsized. Rented space will be increased, decreased, or it will stay the same. Many decisions require believable forecasts before they can be made.

Time series analysis uses statistical methods, including trend and cycle analysis, to predict future values based on the history of sales or whatever the time series describes.

If the time series shows a linear trend, as in Figure 3-3, there is a constant rate of change (increasing size) of the numbers. Linear decreases also can occur. Nonlinear trend lines arise where the rate of change is geometric. In such cases, the rate of change can be calculated, and projections can be made mathematically.

Similar reasoning applies to step functions. If they occur regularly, a good estimate can be made of the period between steps and the timing of future steps. Step functions are characteristic of systems that can only change in given quantities. Thus, if sales must be made in lots of 100 units, then each change in demand will occur in hundred-unit steps. Sales for January could be 400, 500, or 600. It could step up or down, or stay the same as December sales, which were 500.

3-4d Correlation

When a series of *x* numbers (such as the monthly sales of razors over a period of years) is causally connected with the series of *y* numbers (the monthly sales of razor blades), then it is beneficial to collect the information about *x* in order to forecast *y*. In this case, the direction of causality is from *x* to *y* because razors sold create demand for razor blades. Thus:

$$y = f(x)$$

To forecast the *y* series of numbers $y_1, y_2, \ldots y_n$, collect the *x* series of numbers and modify each element of *x* to produce the equivalent value of *y*. Thus:

$$y_i = f(x_i)$$

This relationship is not perfect. Therefore, *y* is said to be correlated with *x*. A **correlation coefficient** (*r*) can be calculated to measure the extent of correlation of *x* with *y*, where *r* can take on values from −1 to +1. At $r = -1$, *x* and *y* are perfectly correlated—in opposite directions. As *x* gets large, *y* gets small, and vice versa. When $r = 0$, no correlation exists. When $r = +1$, *x* and *y* are perfectly correlated moving in the same direction. Note that for the historical forecast, if each month of the time series is identical with the one 12 months before, then the autocorrelation coefficient would be equal to 1. **Autocorrelation** is the term applied to correlation of one part of a time series with another part of the time series. The equation for correlation coefficients is given with the material on **linear regression**.

3-4e Historical Forecasting with a Seasonal Cycle

The historical forecast is based on the assumption that what happened last year (or last month, etc.) will happen again. The pattern is expected to repeat itself within the time period. This method works if a stable pattern (which is often seasonal) exists. The hotel and resort business is typically involved with historical forecasts, as is the agriculture business. In each case, special circumstances can arise that lead to the desire to modify the historical forecast. In the case of hotels and resorts, the state of the economy can modify the ups-and-downs of occupancy rates. Agricultural pursuits are modified by rainfalls and temperature fluctuations (see modifications to the historical forecast in the sections that follow).

When last year's monthly sales values are used to predict the next year's monthly sales values, the method is based on using past history to forecast. The same concept applies to weekly or daily sales, which can be forecast on a semiannual, quarterly, or monthly basis. Table 3-1 shows the historical forecast technique applied to data that exhibit a seasonal cycle. No modification has been made for an overall change in annual sales, which is the basis of the historical forecast.

Correlation coefficient
Measures the strength and direction of a linear relationship between two variables.

Autocorrelation
Measures how well a time-shifted variable correlates with itself. For example, summer temps are well correlated year after year.

Linear regression
Statistical technique for determining the best straight line that can be fitted to a set of data.

© 2008 Jupiterimages Corporation

Historical cycles can become apparent by studying the calendar. In the case of P/OM, there are regularities and patterns that lend themselves to capacity planning, production scheduling, and purchasing decisions for both manufacturers and service systems.

Month	Actual Sales 2007	Forecast of Sales 2008
January	1,500	1,500
February	1,600	1,600
March	1,800	1,800
April	2,000	2,000
May	2,300	2,300
June	2,500	2,500
July	2,350	2,350
August	2,100	2,100
September	1,850	1,850
October	1,650	1,650
November	1,550	1,550
December	1,400*	1,400

*Note: The December estimate of 1,400 units is based on the prior year's sales.

Table 3-1

Historical Forecast with Seasonal Data

The method for making a modified historical forecast is also presented. It should be pointed out that in practice the greatest percent of all forecasts are made by using the nonmodified historical method.

When stable, cycles can provide insights that are very important for P/OM tactical planning. When they work, historical cycles allow P/OM to excel at capacity planning and production scheduling for mature manufactured products and services. The historical forecast is not appropriate for a new product introduction unless there is similarity to some other product that is already on the market.

3-5 Forecasting Methods

This text discusses the following eight forecasting methods:

(a) Base series modification of historical forecasts
(b) Moving averages for short-term trends
(c) Weighted moving averages
(d) Regression analysis and correlation (Calculating correlation coefficients and coefficients of determination are treated as advanced methods in Enrichment Activity 11.)
(e) Use of multiple forecasting methods
(f) The Delphi method
(g) Means of comparing forecasts using forecasting errors (Section 3-6)
(h) Exponential smoothing (This advanced technique is described in Enrichment Activity 3.)

Mathematical equations are used for various kinds of forecasting. It is important to stress that equations do not make forecasts "the truth." They are methods attempting to ascertain "the truth." Also, a great deal of good forecasting can be done without mathematics. Further, with or without mathematics, no forecast is ever guaranteed.

3-5a Base Series Modification of Historical Forecasts

If the time series pattern remains fixed, but the demand level has increased overall, then a base series modification can be used. Assume that in 2007 quarterly demands were

10, 30, 20, 40, adding up to annual demand of 100 units. Further, assume that in 2008 the annual demand is expected to increase to 120 units. Adjust quarterly forecasts as follows:

$$120 (10/100) = 12$$
$$120 (30/100) = 36$$
$$120 (20/100) = 24$$
$$120 (40/100) = 48$$

Adjusted quarterly demands total to 120 units. Note how the cyclical patterns are matched. Next year, assuming the pattern continues and the base level increases to 150, the time series would be 15, 45, 30, 60, with the sum of 150.

3-5b Moving Averages for Short-Term Trends

Moving averages can be used to extrapolate to next events if the following conditions occur:

1 There is no discernible cyclical pattern,
2 The system appears to be generating a series of values such that the last set of values provides the best estimate of what will be the next value, and
3 There is **forecasting momentum** in the time series' movements.

A decision must be made concerning how many readings should be included in the moving average set (N). Is it better to use two, three, four, or more periods? The quest is to find the optimal number of prior periods to include in the moving average series. How far back to go depends on the speed with which the series changes and the recency of events that tend to determine the future. "Very recent" means few values; "not so recent" means more values. That is a workable rule of thumb.

When the magnitude of the trend is great, and the trend pattern is consistent, then the fewer the number of periods in the set, the better. If the trend is gradual (up or down), and if fluctuations around the average are common, then having more periods of time in the set is better than having too few.

A moving average supplies a forecast of future values based on recent past history. The most appropriate (often the last, and latest) N consecutive values, which are observations of actual events such as daily demand, are recorded. These data must be updated to maintain the most recent N values. Then, using the last, and the latest, N values:

$$\hat{x}_t = the\ forecast\ value\ of\ x\ in\ period\ t$$

(The hat sitting on top of x signifies it is the forecast.)

$$x_t = the\ actual\ value\ of\ x\ observed\ in\ period\ t$$

The computing equations are

$$\hat{x}_{t+1} = \frac{(x_t + x_{t-1} + \ldots + x_{t-N+1})}{N} \qquad (3\text{-}1)$$

and

$$\hat{x}_{t+2} = \hat{x}_{t+1} + \frac{x_{t+1} - x_{t-N+1}}{N} \qquad (3\text{-}2)$$

Each next period's forecast is updated from the last period's forecast by dropping the value of the oldest period of the series x_{t-N+1} and adding the latest observation, x_{t+1}.

This yields Equation 3-2 for the forecast of the second period ($\hat{x}_{t+2}$). In this way, new trends are taken into account, and old information is removed from the system. The moving average method applies to any time period: hours, days, weeks, months, or years.

As an example, consider a 4-period monthly moving average in Table 3-2.

Forecasting momentum
Time series being forecast is observed to follow a course or direction that appears to be the result of an inherent force (momentum).

Month (t)	Actual (x_t)	Forecast ($\hat{x}_t$)	Error ($x_t - \hat{x}_t$)
1	10		
2	30		
3	40		
4	40		
5	50	30	+20
6	60	40	+20
7		47.5	

Table 3-2

4-Period Monthly Moving Average Forecast

Four values of x_t are required before a forecast $\hat{x}_t$ can be made and before the error can be calculated. The first forecasted value is 30. It is derived as follows:

$$(40 + 40 + 30 + 10)/4 = 30$$

When the actual demand occurs, it turns out to be 50. The error of the forecast is +20. This means that the forecast has fallen short by 20 units.

The sixth period forecast using Equation 3-2 is

$$30 + (50 - 10)/4 = 40$$

It also could be calculated using Equation 3-1:

$$(50 + 40 + 40 + 30)/4 = 40$$

From Table 3-2, the forecast of 40 is incorrect. The actual result is 60. Then the following period forecast is

$$(60 + 50 + 40 + 40)/4 = 47.5$$

The moving average is slowly increasing with the trend in the actual values of x. Being slow is acceptable if there is a gradual trend with some variability in successive values. In this case, the P/OMs might wish for a faster response in order to schedule production closer to actual. Also, if there is a turn in the trend line, this averaging method will follow the turn, but too slowly. Something can be done to speed things up.

One approach is to decrease the number of observations N in the moving average. This will make the forecasts more responsive to recent events. Try it out with $N = 2$ and see for yourself that the seventh week forecast will be 55 instead of 47.5 as in the previous example. Another approach is to use weighted moving averages.

3-5c Weighted Moving Averages (WMA)

A way to make forecasts more responsive to the most recent actual occurrences is to use weighted moving averages. The new forecast equation is

$$\hat{x}_{t+1} = (w_t)x_t + (w_{t-1})x_{t-1} + \ldots + (w_{t-N+1})x_{t-N+1} \qquad (3\text{-}3)$$

w_t = weights for periods t

Let the sum of the weights w_t be 1; thus,

$$\sum_{t-N+1}^{t} w_t = 1$$

Note that when all weights are equal, the weighted moving average is the same as the moving average. Thus, Equations 3-4 and 3-5 are equivalent to Equation 3-1.

$$w_t = w_{t-1} = \ldots = w_{t-N+1} = \frac{1}{N} \forall_t \quad (\forall_t = \text{for all } t) \qquad (3\text{-}4)$$

$$\hat{x}_{t+1} = \frac{1}{N}x_t + \frac{1}{N}x_{t-1} + \ldots + \frac{1}{N}x_{t-N+1} \qquad (3\text{-}5)$$

Choosing weights that allow the most recent period to have the greatest impact, and later periods decreasing importance, a sample equation might look like this:

$$\hat{x}_{t+1} = 0.4x_t + 0.3x_{t-1} + 0.2x_{t-2} + 0.1x_{t-3}$$

The four weights 0.4, 0.3, 0.2, and 0.1, sum to one.

The biggest weights are assigned to the most recent events when there seems to be a continuing trend (or momentum). This would not be applicable where the values cycle. Thus, Thursday's sales are not the best predictors of Friday's sales—when sales on Fridays are more like sales on other Fridays than any other day.

In a rapidly changing system, w_t may be much greater (>>>) than w_{t-1} and w_t >>> w_{t-1} >>> w_{t-2} ... etc. This is equivalent to reducing the size of N, which was discussed in the section on moving averages.

As has been noted, with the previous method of moving averages, all the w_t were treated as being equal. Then, use Table 3-2 for $t = 5$, to get a forecast for $t + 1 = 6$:

$$\hat{x}_{t+1} = \hat{x}_6 = 0.25(50) + 0.25(40) + 0.25(40) + 0.25(30) = 40$$

Using the weights (.4, .3, .2, .1) and the numbers from the previous example of Table 3-2, the result is obtained:

$$\hat{x}_{t+1} = 0.4(50) + 0.3(40) + 0.2(40) + 0.1(30) = 20 + 12 + 8 + 3 = 43$$

The weighted system is responding more rapidly to the possible trend. It has raised the forecast to 43 as compared to the unweighted moving average of 40. The same effect is seen for the next period. Introducing the sixth period's actual value of 60, the new forecast for the seventh period has a better reaction rate, rising to 51 from 47.5.

$$\hat{x}_7 = 0.4(60) + 0.3(50) + 0.2(40) + 0.1(40) = 24 + 15 + 8 + 4 = 51$$

Thus, weighted moving averages can track strong trends more accurately than unweighted moving averages. It should be noted that the procedures can easily be programmed for computers. Enrichment Activity 3 describes exponential smoothing, which requires specification of an alpha factor. Alpha is made larger to capture momentum. Using the QuantMethods Software for forecasting with exponential smoothing, an alpha of 0.6 delivers a forecast of 44.85 for period $t = 6$. This is even better than the 43 obtained with weighted moving averaging above. When alpha $= 0.95$, the forecast moves to 49.5. The largest forecast will be 50 when alpha $= 1$.

3-5d Use of Linear Regression Analysis

Another valuable method that assists forecasting is regression analysis. This method is useful when trying to establish a relationship between two sets of time series numbers. The simplest assumption that is generally made first is that the relationship between the correlate pairs is linear. It is the easiest assumption to check. However, if nonlinear relations are suspected, there are strong, but more complex methods for doing nonlinear regression analyses.

The numbers can be simultaneous so that $x(t = 1)$ and $y(t = 1)$ are considered correlate pairs. In more general terms, these pairs would be $x(t = k)$ and $y(t = k)$. Or, alternatively, one time series can lead to another period that is later or earlier.

Thus, when $x(t = k)$ and $y(t = k + r)$ are paired, the time series y is ahead of the time series x by r periods. Also, the time series x lags the time series y by r periods. For example, if the x value for January is to be correlated with the y value for April, $r = 3$. Whichever way it is stated, it means that future values of y can be predicted on the basis of actual observations of the values of x—which are made r time units before the forecast date.

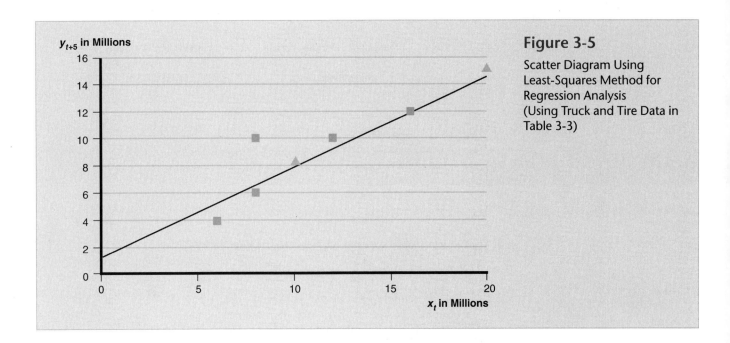

Figure 3-5

Scatter Diagram Using
Least-Squares Method for
Regression Analysis
(Using Truck and Tire Data in
Table 3-3)

When outcomes are to be forecast, the knowledge that one time series leads another is valuable information. In Figure 3-5, the pairs of points x_t, y_{t+5} are plotted. A regression line is calculated and drawn. Based on this line, if x is known for 2007, then y can be predicted for 2012.

Sales of after-market tires—replacement tires, not tires that come with a brand new car—are related to new car sales as well as to used cars that are on the road. Assume that the sale of light truck replacement tires is strongly correlated with the sales of new light trucks five years earlier.

Realistically, used truck tires must be considered. They would have different lead times depending upon their age. The number of trucks on the road of various ages having different tire sizes would be part of the picture. For clarity, this illustration is kept simple.

Regression analysis makes use of the **least-squares method** to estimate the value of future outcomes, y_{t+k}, if a leading factor x_t can be found. Causality between y_{t+k} and x_t is not assumed. A causal factor that is common to both x and y and which operates as an unknown link may be responsible for whatever relationship is found. Least-squares analysis is based on minimizing the sum of the squared deviations of each of the points that do not lie directly on the regression line. See the off-line points in Figure 3-5.

Using the data in Table 3-3, tire sales are to be forecast from a time series of light truck sales.

It is assumed that the strongest relationship between light truck sales and light truck tire sales in the aftermarket is when the two time series are five years apart. This can be tested by studying the fit of regression lines for time series that are k years apart.

It is explained next how to fit a least-squares line to these data. This line will be an estimate of the way in which truck sales affect tire sales five years later. For this example, a linear trend is assumed. More complex equations can be used for nonlinear trends. Once the line is determined, it can be used to extrapolate future tire sales.

This least-squares line model uses (what are called) *normal equations* to determine a linear relationship between x_t and y_{t+5}. The least-squares line minimizes the total variance of the distances of the observed points from the theoretical line. Normal Equations 3-6 and 3-7 achieve this objective.

$$\sum_{t=1}^{t=N} y_{t+5} = aN + b \sum_{t=1}^{t=N} x_t \qquad (3\text{-}6)$$

Least-squares method
Statistical method that finds a line fits a linear relationship between two variables which minimizes the sum of the differences between predicted and observed values.

Table 3-3	Year t	Light Truck Sales x_t (in Year t) (in millions)	Year t+5	Light Truck Tire Sales y_{t+5} (in Year t + 5) (in millions)
Forecasting Light Truck Tire Sales Five Years After the Light Truck Sales	1	6	6	4
	2	8	7	6
	3	12	8	10
	4	8	9	10
	5	16	10	12

$Y = aN + bX$ (*simplified*—see the last row of Table 3-4 for X)

$$\sum_{t=1}^{t=N} x_t y_{t+5} = a \sum_{t=1}^{t=N} x_t + b \sum_{t=1}^{t=N} x_t^2 \qquad (3\text{-}7)$$

$XY = aX + bX^2$ (*simplified*—see the last row of Table 3-4 for Y, Y^2, X^2 and XY)
For our example, $N = 5$, which is the total number of pairs of x_t and y_{t+5}. Table 3-4 presents the data needed for this analysis.

The equations with numbers derived from Table 3-4 are

$$42 = a(5) + b(50) \text{ (using Equation 3-6) and}$$
$$464 = a(50) + b(564) \text{ (using Equation 3-7)}$$

Solving for *a* and *b*, obtain: $a = 61/40 = 1.5250$; $b = 11/16 = 0.68750$.

These values are introduced in the least-squares line:

$$y_{t+5} = a + bx_t = \frac{61}{40} + \frac{11}{16} x_t \qquad (3\text{-}8)$$

which simplifies to

$$y_{t+5} = a + bx_t = 1.53 + 0.69 x_t \qquad (3\text{-}9)$$

This least-squares line and the actual scatter of values around it are shown in Figure 3-5.

To show how to use this line, suppose that the sixth year observation has been made, i.e., for: $t = 6$, $x_t = 10$. The regression line indicates that in year 11, $y_{t+5} = 8.40$, which means that 8,400,000 tires would be the sales forecast.

Next, assume the seventh year observation has been made and that when $t = 7$, $x_t = 20$. The regression line indicates that $y_{t+5} = y_{12} = 15,280,000$ tires should be the sales forecast for year 12. This line would be used for forecasting only if the observed data appear to fit it well.

Table 3-4	Data from Table 3-3 and calculations to parameterize the normal equations.				
Truck and Tire Linear Regression	T	x_t	y_{t+5}	$x_t(y_{t+5})$	x_t^2	$y_{(t+5)}^2$

T	x_t	y_{t+5}	$x_t(y_{t+5})$	x_t^2	$y_{(t+5)}^2$
1	6	4	24	36	16
2	8	6	48	64	36
3	12	10	120	144	100
4	8	10	80	64	100
5	16	12	192	256	144
Sums	50	42	464	564	396
	$X = 50$	$Y = 42$	$XY = 464$	$X^2 = 564$	$Y^2 = 396$

Correlation Coefficient and the Coefficient of Determination

These data do fit well. A correlation coefficient (r) is a measure of how well the line fits the data. Specifically, r shows the strength and direction of the linear relationship between two variables (e.g., trucks and tire sales). QMpom (forecasting—linear regression) calculates the value of r at 0.8368. This is high but less than perfect correlation which has a coefficient of 1.00. Also, there is visual confirmation of a good fit in Figure 3-5.

The equations for the correlation coefficient r and the coefficient of determination (r^2) are presented in Enrichment Activity 11. Also, discussed in Enrichment Activity 11 is the fact that r goes from –1 through 0 to +1. The value of $r = +1$ signifies that the two variables move in the same direction, i.e., as one gets larger so does the other, and all points fall on the line which has a positive slope. The value of $r = -1$ signifies that the two variables move in opposite directions, i.e., as one gets larger the other gets smaller, and all points fall on the line which has a negative slope.

The coefficient of determination (r^2) is the square of the correlation coefficient. r^2 values lie between 0 and 1. There are no negative values and it is a measure of the proportion of variation that is explained by the line.

3-5e Pooling Information and Multiple Forecasts

Methods for pooling information from various sources to provide better forecasts should be explored. It is critical that all parties share their forecasts as much as possible and try to find ways to combine them. Usually, stronger forecasts can be obtained if both data and experience are pooled.

One of the keys to success in combining forecasts is trial and error. What seems to work is retained and what fails is discarded. As an example of pooling, the results of the regression analysis just completed could be augmented by a Delphi-type estimation of light truck tire sales for the next year. The Delphi participants might be the regional sales managers.

Formal methods can be used to evaluate how well different forecasting techniques are doing. At each period, the method that did best the last time is chosen for the forecast that will be followed. Forecasts are still derived from the alternative methods, but they are recorded and not followed. When the actual demand results are known, the various forecasting methods are evaluated again, and the one that is most successful is chosen to make the prediction for the next period.

Averaging of forecast results also is used. The results of taking forecasts from more than one method and averaging these results to predict demand has been successful in circumstances where choosing the best method (as described earlier) produces frequent alteration of the chosen method.

3-5f The Delphi Method

Delphi is a forecasting method that relies on expert estimation of future events. In one of its forms, the experts submit their opinions to a single individual (the facilitator) who is the only one that knows who the participants are and what they have to say. The person who is the Delphi facilitator combines the opinions into a report, which, while protecting anonymity, is then disseminated to all participants. The participants are asked whether they wish to reevaluate and alter their previous opinions in the face of the body of opinion of their colleagues. Gradually, the group is supposed to move toward consensus. If it does not, at the least, a set of different possibilities can be presented to management.[5]

Survey results could be shown (individually to preserve anonymity) to the Delphi panel of experts with the following question: "Do you think sales will be higher, lower, or the same?" Consensus might lead to modification of the managers' targets. Why not let these "experts" talk to each other and discuss their opinions? If one of the experts is the CEO, or a Nobel laureate, the dialogue might not be unbiased. People with greater debating capabilities are not necessarily people with more insight. The Delphi method is meant to put all participants on an equal footing with respect to getting their ideas heard.

Delphi has been used for technological forecasting, energy policy planning, drug abuse reduction, and political strategizing. It has many adherents and as many detractors.

3-6 Comparative Forecasting Errors

All forecasting errors $x_t - \hat{x}_t = \in_t$ are based on comparing, the actual demand for time period t, with $\hat{x}_t$, the forecast demand for that same period. Two kinds of forecasting errors can occur.

First, actual demand is greater than the forecast. This is a forecasting underestimate. By convention, when actual demand is greater than forecast demand, the error term $\in_t$ is positive. Second, actual demand is less than the forecast. This is a forecasting overestimate, and in this case, $\in_t$ is negative.

To choose a forecasting method, it is necessary to be able to compare the errors that each method generates for particular circumstances. There are five major measures of error that are used. The choice is dependent upon the situation and what kind of comparison is wanted. Thus, absolute measures are used to count all errors conservatively.

Absolute measures are signified by open brackets $|\in_t|$, which mean that positive and negative errors are treated the same way. The reason for doing this is to prevent positive and negative errors from canceling each other out.

The most common measure of error is called *mean absolute deviation (MAD)*. To calculate MAD, take the sum of the absolute measures of the errors and divide that sum by the number of observations.

$$\sum_t |\in_t| \div n$$

Also, quite common is the mean squared error (MSE) measure. It is calculated by squaring all of the error terms and adding them together. Then, this sum is divided by the number of observations. Because squares of both positive and negative errors become positive numbers, MSE does not allow the two kinds of errors (+ and −) to cancel out each other. However, the squares of large errors become significantly larger than the squares of small errors. Therefore, MSE magnifies large errors. MAD treats all errors linearly and is a more conservative measure.

Cumulative forecast error (CFE) is simply the sum of all the error terms and is useful when overestimation errors do cancel out underestimation errors. As an example, if the error term represented inventory shortages when actual demand is greater than forecast demand, i.e., $x_t > \hat{x}_t$, and if it stood for stock on-hand when $x_t < \hat{x}_t$ assuming that stock on-hand could be used to fulfill shortages, the CFE would represent the net inventory situation.

Sometimes the standard deviation of the error distribution, $\sigma_\in$, is used. It is the square root of the MSE. Another method for comparing errors is called *mean absolute percent error (MAPE)*. It is the result of dividing each absolute error term by its respective actual demand term. This gives a fraction that describes how large the error is as compared to the demand. Multiply the fraction by 100 to convert to percentages. Then, all of the terms are summed and divided by the number of observations, as shown in Table 3-5. This table examines one forecasting method with observations taken over $n = 4$ weeks. All are row sums—taken across columns.

Each of the forecast error measures is presented in the following equations:
MAPE (Mean Absolute Error):

$$\sum_{t-1}^{t-N} (|\in_t|/x_t)100 \div n = 244.3/4 = 61.08 \qquad (3\text{-}10)$$

MAPE reveals poor forecasts. Note that for week one, the absolute percent error was 100, and the next two weeks are large percentages as well. Because the fourth week was reduced to 14.3, perhaps the system is stabilizing.

					Sum	
Week number, t	1	2	3	4		
Actual demand, x_t	3	8	5	7		
Forecast, $\hat{x}_t$	6	4	9	6		
Error, $x_t - \hat{x}_t = \epsilon_t$	–3	+4	–4	+1	–2 = CFE	
Error squared, $\lvert \epsilon_t^2 \rvert$	9	16	16	1	42	
Absolute error, $\lvert \epsilon_t \rvert$	3	4	4	1	12	
Absolute percent error, $(\lvert \epsilon_t \rvert / x_t)\,100$	100	50	80	14.3	244.3	

Table 3-5

Table of Computations for Comparing Forecast Errors

CFE (Cumulative Forecast Error):

$$\sum\nolimits_{t-1}^{t-N} \epsilon_t = -2 \qquad (3\text{-}11)$$

as shown in the sum column of Table 3-5. This minus CFE measure may reveal a bias toward overestimation. The sample is too small to tell.

MAD (Mean Absolute Deviation):

$$\sum\nolimits_{t-1}^{t-N} \lvert \epsilon_t \rvert \div n = 12/4 = 3.0 \qquad (3\text{-}12)$$

This is the most conservative estimate of error. Without knowing the size of demand, these 3 units of error might seem very small. They are not, and the MAD measure of 3 is significant because the average demand is $23/4 = 5.75$. MAD is more than 50 percent of the average demand.

MSE (Mean Squared Error):

$$\sum\nolimits_{t-1}^{t-N} \epsilon_t^2 \div n = 42/4 = 10.5 \qquad (3\text{-}13)$$

As expected, the MSE measure of 10.5 units is large. It is more than three times MAD and 1.8 times the average demand of 5.75.

MSE was magnified by the fact that the error values of 3, 4, and 4 became 9, 16, and 16.

Standard Deviation: $[\sqrt{MSE}]$

$$\sigma_\epsilon = \sqrt{MSE} = \sqrt{\sum\nolimits_{t=1}^{t=N} \frac{\epsilon_t^2}{n}} = \sqrt{10.5} = 3.24 \qquad (3\text{-}14)$$

The standard deviation of the error distribution is closely approximated by MAD. That is because the square root of the MSE removes the magnification of error that is inherent in MSE. It should be noted that MSE is a preferred measure when larger errors have disproportionate penalty as compared to small errors. This would be the case when the penalties are proportional to the square of the errors.

New measures can be devised when special circumstances exist. Thus, if underestimation results in stock outages that lead to severe penalties whereas overstock carries a small charge, it is necessary to adjust the comparative measures that are used to evaluate forecasting systems.

3-6a Keep a Record of Past Errors

Managers change forecasts that are derived by numerical methods because they know about other factors that are not included in the calculations. This results in modifications of forecasts that can be called predictions and estimates.

It is, therefore, wise to maintain a *history of all forecasting errors*, i.e., a history of: $x_t - \hat{x}_t = \epsilon_t$. This should be done for all methods that are used and for all personnel that

© 2008 Jupiterimages Corporation

Online B2C catalog companies need to forecast demand levels by time of day and day of week to have the right number of trained agents and operators in place at the call center. B2C is e-business nomenclature for business selling to consumers.

are making the forecasts, predictions, and estimates. Some people are good at forecasting and others are not. Also, some people are good at forecasting under certain circumstances and not good in others.

Companies gain major advantages by finding out who can make good estimates under what circumstances. Further, there are situations where people can learn to make better forecasts, predictions, and estimates as a result of feedback about how well they have done in the past. When a record is not kept, all such advantage potentials are lost.

Spotlight 3-1 Sophisticated Forecasting for Decision Making Without Sophisticated Math

The capacity to anticipate future business conditions and events with as much accuracy as possible is a key characteristic of companies that dominate their markets. Our understanding of the forces that affect business outcomes has become increasingly complex, and, at the same time, the mathematical techniques required for sound forecasting have grown increasingly sophisticated and—for the person who would apply them—demanding.

Fortunately, it is not necessary to perform the math yourself in order to use these mathematical forecasting techniques. There are now a number of good software packages available to help you shortcut the computational process. Three of the most convenient tools for simulating future scenarios are add-ins to Microsoft Excel developed by Palisade Corporation—@RISK for risk analysis and simulation, RISKOptimizer® for optimizing simulated decisions, and PrecisionTree.®

@RISK uses a technique known as "Monte Carlo simulation" to answer what-if questions. It allows planners and decision makers to take into account all possible outcomes of any particular course of action. For any uncertain value in your spreadsheet, you simply insert a probability function. The software then calculates and recalculates outcomes, each time using a set of random values from the probability functions you inserted. Depending on the number of uncertainties and the range of their possible outcomes, a Monte Carlo simulation can involves thousands of recalculations before arriving at its results. These are in the form of distributions of possible outcomes. A simple example is illustrated in Section 17-8, "Monte Carlo Simulation of a Queuing Situation."

Sometimes scenarios and outcomes involve a complex tangle of what-if questions. To resolve problems such as resource allocation, product mix, and scheduling, a decision maker needs to account for a number of scenarios at once. RISKOptimizer has been designed to help resolve this kind of dilemma. It simultaneously answers the question "what if?" and the question "what's best?" To do this, it combines Monte Carlo simulation with a general set of rules for calculating the best strategies to use. The function of the software is to rank and combine solutions to the various components of the decision.

PrecisionTree allows you to structure future business processes graphically and analyze the process right in your spreadsheet. It uses influence diagrams (cause and effect diagrams) to quickly define the structure of a decision and decision trees to define the formal structure in which key decision points and chance events are linked. When you use the software to examine a decision, the result you produce is a graphical tree, and you can add the probabilities of events or payoffs at each branch in this tree.

Procter & Gamble (P&G) is one of many *Fortune* 500 companies that rely on Palisade tools, and on @RISK and PrecisionTree in particular. The company has used @RISK since 1993, when it confronted a number of decisions about where to locate plants in situations that involved more than one country. These decisions involved not only cost and capital allocation but currency fluctuation, as well. The company now uses the software throughout the enterprise to simulate the entire range of its investment decisions—new products, extending product line, geographical expansion, and manufacturing savings projects.

More recently P&G added PrecisionTree to its arsenal of quantitative tools. The attraction of this tool is its capacity to model and assign value in complex forecasts that involve multiple, sequential decision steps. P&G finds it particularly valuable for evaluating "real options" in terms of each potential investment's impact on shareholder value. Decision trees are really the only tool that can help the user understand the risks and opportunities that accompany each phase in a course of action, and because its output is graphical, the results are easily shared by staff at all levels.

The number of P&G staff that has been trained on the Palisade software testifies to the tools' user-friendliness and broad applicability in business. More than a thousand employees throughout all P&G divisions can testify to the fact that you don't need to be a mathematician to create quantitatively sound, data-driven forecasts.

Source: Courtesy of the Palisade Corporation, 798 Cascadilla Street, Ithaca, NY 14850; telephone 800-432-7475; sales@palisade.com, http://palisade.com. March 17, 2005; updated April 11, 2007.

Review Questions

1 Why is it important to understand the following statement: "The capacity to anticipate future business conditions and events with as much accuracy as possible is a key characteristic of companies that dominate their markets"?

2 Why is it not necessary for all organizations to have trained staff members to perform math computations needed to forecast future sales of goods and services? How can any company plan its resource allocations and production schedules without such forecasts?

3 The forecasting system, @RISK (product of the Palisade Corporation) uses Monte Carlo simulation methods. What is the Monte Carlo method?

4 Procter & Gamble (P&G) is one of many *Fortune* 500 companies that use tools from the Palisade Corporation. What need does a company like P&G have for forecasting software?

5 What kind of forecasting model is PrecisionTree®?

Source: Courtesy of Palisade Corporation. Palisade Corporation is a leader in risk analysis, decision analysis, data analysis, and optimization software. For more information about Palisade software products, books, and training and consulting services, visit http://www.palisade.com. Academic and student versions are available.

Spotlight 3-2 Planning Tree of Management Options

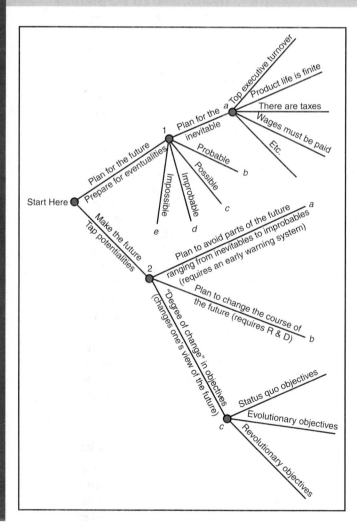

"It's kind of fun to do the impossible." Walt Disney

The Socratic Method teaches by asking the right questions. Learning occurs when doors are opened to permit searching in new and different places. The planning tree starts with the question, "Should managers prepare for eventualities (passively accept the forecast) or should managers make the future happen?" The best answer might reside in what Walt Disney said.

In business modeling terms, this is the difference between (a) having supply to meet demand (the forecast sales) or (b) setting the sales target. Answering the question, "which do you prefer, (a) or (b)?" with "both" or with "it depends" will raise additional questions.

Summary

Strategic planning requires teamwork. P/OM should be part of the team. Chapter 3 discusses P/OM's role in helping to develop strategies and its assignment to carry them out. P/OM is responsible for seeking out and adopting "Best Practice." Life cycle stages are developed. This includes introduction and growth of new products, followed by their maturation and decline. P/OM is expected to protect established products. The challenge is difficult when competitors introduce disruptive innovations. Recognition of problems and fast action to deal with disruptions are needed.

Forecasting is essential for proper management of life cycle stages. Extrapolation and correlation can be used with time series analysis. Other important forecasting methods that are covered include moving averages, weighted moving averages, regression analysis, correlation coefficients, coefficients of determination, multiple forecasts, and the Delphi method. Also, the means for evaluating the different forecasting methods by comparing the kinds of errors they generate is explained. An Enrichment Activity on the exponential smoothing method is provided.

Two Spotlight feature boxes conclude this chapter. These boxes illustrate real applications of the materials in the chapter. See Spotlight 3-1: Sophisticated Forecasting for Decision Making Without Sophisticated Math and Spotlight 3-2: Planning Tree of Management Options.

Key Terms

Autocorrelation (p. 82)　　　　　　　　Life cycle strategies (p. 75)
Cash flow (p. 74)　　　　　　　　　　　Linear regression (p. 82)
Correlation coefficient (p. 82)　　　　　Product life cycles (p. 75)
Cycles (p. 72)　　　　　　　　　　　　Strategic business units (SBUs) (p. 74)
Disruptive innovation (p. 74)　　　　　Strategy (p. 73)
Disruptive technology (p. 74)　　　　　Synergy (p. 75)
Extrapolation (p. 80)　　　　　　　　　Syzygy (p. 75)
Forecasting (p. 79)　　　　　　　　　　Tactics (p. 74)
Forecasting momentum (p. 84)　　　　Time series (p. 80)
Least-squares method (p. 87)　　　　　Time series analysis (p. 81)

Review Questions

1 Contrast strategies and tactics from a P/OM perspective.

2 What is the effect of disruptive innovation?

3 How does disruptive technology differ from disruptive innovation?

4 What is suboptimization and why is it a concern of P/OM?

5 What is meant by the statement "P/OM is a scarce resource"?

6 What is a time series? How would it be used to make predictions about emerging technological developments?

7 Is there a basis for predicting periods of prosperity and of economic slowdowns on the basis of cycles?

8 What are life cycle stages? Why does the concept of life cycle stages unite P/OM with other members of the organization in using the systems approach?

9 Detail the life cycle stages and explain them.

10 What is extrapolation and how is it used?

11 What is correlation? What is autocorrelation? Distinguish between them.

12 What is an historical forecast? When is it used?

13 Why are long life cycle stages considered desirable? Does this apply to start-up and growth as well as the mature stage?

14 How does the hub and spoke diagram for a large company differ from that of a small company? Draw the contrast with the classic organization chart. Relate both of these types of diagrams to organizational structure and infrastructure.

15 What is Best Practice when applied to a business system?

16 When are multiple forecasts desirable?

Problems Section

Note: This section has various problems that can be formulated and solved using QuantMethods Production/Operations Management software (QMpom). The appropriate model categories are indicated for each problem.

1 If a series of numbers is {14, 23, 28, 34} what is the best estimate for the next value? What method can be used? Compare the QMpom module called Forecasting Models (Averaging) with knowledge-based reasoning. Also, compare 2 periods with weights spread evenly with an exponential smoothing alpha of 0.20. This is a trick question since the answer is based on subway stops in New York City.

2 A time series for actual sales figures is given in the following table.

Using the QMpom module called Forecasting Models (Averaging) will facilitate solving Problem 2. Let the alpha value stay at the default setting since the problem does not request exponential smoothing. From the results, develop the table of errors. For part b. use the weights with the QMpom Averaging model.

Month	Actual x_t	Forecast $\hat{x}_t$	Error $x_t - \hat{x}_t = \in_t$
1	10		
2	30		
3	40		
4	40		
5	50		
6	60		
7	50		
8	40		
9			

a. Use the moving average method with $N = 3$ to develop forecasts for months four through nine. Calculate the error terms, $x_t - \hat{x}_t = \in_t$.

b. Employ weights of 0.5, 0.3, and 0.2 to obtain weighted moving average forecasts for the same time period. Calculate the error terms $x_t - \hat{x}_t = \in_t$. Compare the results in parts 2(a) and 2(b).

3 It has been stated that sales for 2009 will be 50 percent greater than 2008, but the historical pattern will continue to hold. Complete the 2009 forecast.

Month	Actual Sales 2008	Forecast of Sales 2009
January	1,500	
February	1,600	
March	1,800	
April	2,000	
May	2,300	
June	2,500	
July	2,350	
August	2,100	
September	1,850	
October	1,650	
November	1,550	
December	1,400	

Note: July through December sales estimates are based on the prior year's sales.

4   The Highway Department is considering using a 6-month moving average to forecast crew hours needed to repair roads month by month for the coming year. To test whether this method is accurate, use last year's data (shown in the following table) to predict the last six months' crew hours to compare with the observed values. Start with the average of January through June to compare with the actual value of 200 for July and so on through December. Remember that the prediction for the next month is the average of the actual values of the previous six, not the predicted values!

   Using the QMpom module called Forecasting Models (Averaging) will facilitate solving Problem 4. Let the alpha value stay at the default setting since the problem does not request exponential smoothing.

Month	Crew Hours
January	110
February	120
March	140
April	180
May	250
June	200
July	200
August	220
September	280
October	120
November	100
December	80

5   Referring to Problem 4, prepare an analysis of the errors in using the 6-month moving average as a predictor.

6   Referring to Problems 4 and 5, use a 3-period moving average to forecast the last six months and compare directly to the 6-month forecast developed there. Here, the first forecast is the average of April, May, and June to compare with the actual value of 200 for July and so on through December. Using the QMpom module called Forecasting Models (Averaging) will facilitate solving Problem 6. Let the alpha value stay at the default setting since the problem does not request exponential smoothing.

7   Referring to Problems 4, 5, and 6, use a 6-period *weighted* moving average to forecast the last six months and compare directly to the unweighted forecasts for 6-month and 3-month periods. Use the weights 0.1, 0.1, 0.1, 0.2, .0.2, and 0.3 with the 0.3 weighting the most recent datum point. Using the QMpom module called Forecasting Models (Averaging [with weights]) will facilitate solving Problem 7. Let the alpha value stay at the default setting.

8   The following table presents data concerning the sales of minivans for 10 years. It is believed that the demand for minivan replacement tires is highly correlated with the sales figures three years earlier.

Year t	Minivan Sales x_t in Year t (in millions)	Minivan Tire Sales y_t in Year t (in millions)
1	10	4
2	12	6
3	11	7
4	9	5
5	10	8
6	12	7
7	10	5
8	9	7
9	8	8
10	7	6

   Do an analysis of x_t and y_{t+k}, where $k = 3$ years, using the least-squares method and linear regression. Note that seven years of data will be used to prepare the regression line. The forecast for tires will go from year 11 through year 13. Using the QMpom module called Forecasting Models (Linear Regression) will facilitate solving Problem 8. That program allows determination of the correlation coefficient and the coefficient of determination (see Enrichment Activity 11). Discuss the significance of your results. QMpom also allows calculation of the MAD error and the standard error.

9   Using the information given in Problem 8, it is now stated that there is another person in the company who feels that $k = 4$ should be tried. Use it and compare the results. Note that six years of data will be available to prepare the regression line. The forecast for tires will go from year 11 through year 14. Using the QMpom module called Forecasting Models (Linear Regression) will facilitate solving Problem 9. That program allows determination of the correlation coefficient and the coefficient of determination (see Enrichment Activity 11). Discuss the significance of your results. QMpom also allows calculation of the MAD error and the standard error.

10 What does autocorrelation have to do with the methodology used in Problem 8?

11 This table presents the results of forecasting using moving averages. Comparison is made of actual demand and the forecast for a period of seven days.

Day number, t	1	2	3	4	5	6	7
Actual demand, x_t	4	5	2	3	1	3	4
Forecast demand, $\hat{x}_t$	3	6	2	4	3	1	3
Error, $x_t - \hat{x}_t = \in_t$							
Error squared, $\in_t^2$							
Absolute error, $\|\in_t\|$							
Absolute percent error, $(\|\in_t\| / x_t)\,100$							

Complete this table and work out each of the forecast error evaluation methods explained in Section 3-6: MAPE, CFE, MAD, MSE, and $\sigma_\in$.

Discuss the results comparing the various evaluation methods.

12 The time series for $\in_t$ is as follows:

$$\{+600, -300, +500, +100, -50, +60, -40, +30, -50, +20\}$$

Measure MAD, MSE, CFE, and σ_ε.

13 The time series for $\in_t$ is as follows:

$$\{+600, -300, +500, +100, -50, +60, -40, +30, -50, +20\}$$

Analyze this time series in such a way as to shed additional light on what seems to be happening.

14 It should be noted that MSE is preferred to MAD for error measurement when larger errors have disproportionate penalties as compared to smaller errors. This would be the case when the penalties are proportional to the square of the errors.

Two forecasting methods are used. The first method gives the time series for $\in_t$ as follows:

$$\{+600, -300, +500, +300, -500\}$$

The second method gives the time series for $\in_t$ as follows:

$$\{+100, -200, +800, +100, -100\}$$

Compare the two time series of errors obtained using the two different forecasting methods. Discuss the results in light of the statement concerning penalties.

Practice Quiz

1   The difference between tactics and strategies is best described by which of the following statements?

   a.   Strategies are what CEOs create; tactics bubble up from the plant floor.
   b.   Strategies lead to forecasts; tactics are based on predictions.
   c.   Strategies are long-range plans; tactics are short-range plans.
   d.   Strategies require adaptation but not conversion to a proactive stance.
   e.   Strategies are concerned with profit maximization, not with cash flow sufficiency.

2   P/OM's role in developing strategies is to

   a.   bring technological knowledge to the table.
   b.   serve as the hub of the system, pulling together the other functional inputs.
   c.   be the coordinator between marketing and finance.
   d.   keep a record of past errors in the forecasting capacity.
   e.   establish production capacity to match supply with forecasted demand.

3   Life cycle stages are not properly described by one of the following multiple choices. Which is the incorrect choice?

   a.   Forecasting is not related to life cycle stage analysis.
   b.   Synergy can account for faster than expected growth of market share during start-up.
   c.   New products of Stage IV organizations move up faster and stay put longer.
   d.   Life cycles are getting shorter as technology developments accelerate.
   e.   An efficient sales force can alter the time period of various life cycle stages.

4   Forecasting is one of the most powerful generic methodologies that can help P/OM planners. The best forecasts can be obtained by

   a.   ignoring short-term cycles.
   b.   concentrating only on long-term cycles.
   c.   removing trend lines from the data.
   d.   looking for patterns that can be extrapolated.
   e.   using time series analysis software.

5   Correlation is a statistical measure of similarity or dissimilarity. Which of the following options is incorrect?

   a.   With correlation of one, the two variables are tracking each other perfectly.
   b.   If correlation is two, a calculation error has been made.
   c.   If correlation is minus one, the two variables move in perfectly opposite directions.
   d.   Life cycle growth of market share has a correlation of one with profitability.
   e.   Life cycle market share and sales volume are well-correlated if market size is steady.

6   Historical forecasting is based on the assumption that

   a.   moving averages are seldom useful for capturing trends.
   b.   the past will repeat itself.
   c.   base series modification will be necessary.
   d.   weighted moving averages capture more information than unweighted moving averages.
   e.   use of multiple forecasting methods will improve the prediction.

7   What does base series modification of historical forecasts of demand level accomplish?

   a.   Base series modification treats demand level as a constant but changes the pattern of variation in line with expectations.
   b.   Base series modification changes either the demand level or the pattern of variation as deemed necessary.
   c.   Base series modification keeps the pattern of variation between time periods fixed but changes the demand level of the time series.
   d.   Base series modification is equivalent to utilizing the moving average methodology.
   e.   Base series modification requires regression analysis to provide the coefficients of correlation.

8   In forecasting, when are weighted moving averages preferred to (plain) moving averages?

   a.   when the manager prefers to make the forecast equally responsive to the last three or four actual occurrences
   b.   when the manager believes that successive values in the time series are random
   c.   when there is enough computing power to go through the extra calculations involved
   d.   when the manager prefers to make the forecast more responsive to the most recent actual occurrences
   e.   when it is known that the competition is using WMA

9   What best describes the Delphi method for forecasting?

   a.   Oracle software is used to organize information and provide a prediction.
   b.   A poll is taken by a licensed pollster to determine, for example, who will win the next presidential election.
   c.   Forecasts are chosen that produce the least forecasting error in a benchmark study.
   d.   Forecasts are based on price elasticity and the average price charged per unit.
   e.   Experts' estimations of future events are used to converge on a consensus forecast.

10   Which of the following statements about comparative forecasting errors is incorrect?

   a.   The most common measure of forecast error is MAD (mean absolute deviation). It prevents positive and negative errors from canceling each other.
   b.   Mean squared error (MSE) also prevents positive and negative errors from canceling each other, but the squares of large numbers overpower those of smaller numbers.

c. Standard deviation ($\sigma_\in$) is the square root of MSE. It does not prevent positive and negative errors from canceling each other. However, for $\sigma_\in$ the squares of large numbers as compared to the squares of small numbers is not as overpowering.

d. Cumulative forecast error (CFE) is useful when overestimation errors do cancel out the effects of underestimation errors.

e. Mean absolute percent error (MAPE) provides a ratio that describes how large the error is as compared to the value of the variable (say, demand).

Additional Readings

Armstrong, J. Scott. *Principles of Forecasting.* Dordrecht, Netherlands: Kluwer Academic Publishing (paperback version—April 2001).

Box, G. E. P., and G. M. Jenkins. *Time Series Analysis: Forecasting and Control.* San Francisco: Holden-Day, 1970.

DeLurgio, S. A., and C. D. Bhame. *Forecasting Systems for Operations Management.* Burr Ridge, IL: Irwin, 1991.

Drucker, P. *Managing in Turbulent Times.* London: Pan Books, 1981.

Linstone, Harold, and Murray Turoff (eds). *The Delphi Method: Techniques and Applications.* (free download at Wikipedia—Delphi method), 2002.

Lodish, Leonard M., Howard L. Morgan, and Shellye Archambeau. *Marketing That Works: How Entrepreneurial Marketing Can Add Sustainable Value to Any Sized Company.* Upper Saddle River, NJ: Wharton School Publishing, 2007.

Magaziner, I., and R. Reich. *Minding America's Business.* New York: Vintage Books, 1982.

Makridakis, S., S. C. Wheelwright, and V. E. McGee. *Forecasting: Methods and Applications.* New York: John Wiley & Sons, 1983.

Notes

1. Clayton M. Christensen. *The Innovator's Dilemma: The Revolutionary Book That Will Change the Way You Do Business.* Boston, MA: Harvard Business School Press, 1997, 2003.

2. Clayton M. Christensen. *The Innovator's Solution: Creating and Sustaining Successful Growth.* Boston, MA: Harvard Business School Publishing Corp., 2003.

3. Leonard M. Lodish, Howard L. Morgan, and Shellye Archambeau. *Marketing That Works: How Entrepreneurial Marketing Can Add Sustainable Value to Any Sized Company.* Upper Saddle River, NJ: Wharton School Publishing, 2007.

4. The definition of time series analysis is given by John H. Blackstone and James F. Cox, in the *APICS Dictionary*, 11e. APICS Educational and Research Foundation, 2004.

5. See Murray Turoff and Starr Roxanne Hiltz, http://eies.njit.edu/turoff/Papers/delphi3.html. A version of this paper appeared as a chapter in *Gazing into the Oracle: The Delphi Method and Its Application to Social Policy and Public Health.* Michael Adler and Erio Ziglio (eds.). Kingsley Publishers, January 1996.

Enrichment Activity 3: Forecasts Using Exponential Smoothing Methodology

Often, the use of the exponential smoothing method for forecasting is preferred to the weighted moving average method. Like the weighted moving average (WMA) method, exponential smoothing calculates an average demand—usually giving more weight to recent actual demand values than to the older ones.

Exponential smoothing is a simpler method, requiring fewer calculations than WMA, which needs *N* weights and *N* periods of data for each forecast estimate. Exponential smoothing needs only three pieces of data. Also, it can be more effective because only one weight, alpha (α)—called the smoothing constant—has to be chosen. This makes it easier to experiment with past data to see which value of alpha provides the least forecast error.

Exponential smoothing has been found to be more effective in a variety of situations. Many forecasting and control systems employ exponential smoothing because it works better than the older methods of moving averages and WMA. It has proved effective for diverse applications. Fighter aircraft use exponential smoothing to aim their guns at moving targets. In effect, they forecast the location of enemy jets during flying missions. This application shows how fast the exponential smoothing method can track a consistent, but dynamically changing pattern.

Table EA3-1	$\alpha x_t + (1 - \alpha)\hat{x}_t = \hat{x}_{t+1}$	α
Exponential Smoothing with a Range of Alphas	$0.000(60) + 1.000(40) = 40$	0.000
	$0.100(60) + 0.900(40) = 42$	0.100
	$0.200(60) + 0.800(40) = 44$	0.200
	$0.300(60) + 0.700(40) = 46$	0.300
	$0.375(60) + 0.625(40) = 47.5$	0.375 moving average result
	$0.400(60) + 0.600(40) = 40$	0.400
	$0.500(60) + 0.500(40) = 50$	0.500
	$0.550(60) + 0.450(40) = 51$	0.550 weighted moving average result
	$0.600(60) + 0.400(40) = 52$	0.600
	$0.700(60) + 0.300(40) = 54$	0.700 <– this result is discussed below
	$0.800(60) + 0.200(40) = 56$	0.800
	$0.900(60) + 0.100(40) = 58$	0.900
	$1.000(60) + 0.000(40) = 60$	1.000

Manufacturers use exponential smoothing to forecast demand levels, which experience the same kind of nonrandom but volatile shifts from time to time. In such cases, the situation is dynamically changing, but the recent past has the most information about the near future. Exponential smoothing can catch these shifts and make rapid adjustments to inventory levels. Other manufacturers use it because it requires less computational work and is readily understood.

Exponential smoothing methodology remembers the last estimate of the average value of demand and combines it with the most recent observed, actual value to form a new estimated average. As in prior materials, hats over the x's stand for forecast values of demand; t is now; and $t + 1$ is the next period for which the forecast is to be made.

$\hat{x}_t$ is the last forecast made—it was for period t, which is today, meaning the present time. The new forecast of demand to be made for period $t + 1$ is $\hat{x}_{t+1}$. The actual result observed for the period t, which is the present time is x_t. All x_t values—no hats—are recorded values of actual demand.

Equation EA3-1 forecasts demand in period $t + 1$ as an alpha-based average of the actual demand in the last period t, and the demand that had been forecasted for that period, t.

$$\hat{x}_{t+1} = \alpha x_t + (1 - \alpha)\hat{x}_t \qquad (EA3\text{-}1)$$

The preceding period's forecasting equation would then have been:

$$\hat{x}_t = \alpha x_{t-1} + (1 - \alpha)\hat{x}_{t-1} \qquad (EA3\text{-}2)$$

The period before t, i.e., $t - 1$, would be described by Equation EA3-3.

$$\hat{x}_{t-1} = \alpha x_{t-2} + (1 - \alpha)\hat{x}_{t-2} \qquad (EA3\text{-}3)$$

Replacing $\hat{x}_t$ in Equation EA3-1 with the right-hand side of Equation EA3-2 yields Equation EA3-4:

$$\hat{x}_{t+1} = \alpha x_t + (1 - \alpha)[\alpha x_{t-1} + (1 - \alpha)\hat{x}_{t-1}] \qquad (EA3\text{-}4)$$

Combining terms leads to the simplified version in Equation EA3-5:

$$\hat{x}_{t+1} = \alpha x_t + \alpha(1 - \alpha)x_{t-1} + (1 - \alpha)^2 \hat{x}_{t-1} \qquad (EA3\text{-}5)$$

Substituting the right-hand side of Equation EA3-3 into Equation EA3-5, and continuing in this fashion, yields Equation EA3-6—which is the generalized form for the exponential smoothing forecast of demand for period $t + 1$:

$$\hat{x}_{t+1} = \alpha x_t + \alpha(1 - \alpha)x_{t-1} + \alpha(1 - \alpha)^2 x_{t-2} + \alpha(1 - \alpha)^3 x_{t-3} \ldots + \qquad (EA3\text{-}6)$$

The response rate of the exponential smoothing model is a function of the alpha value that is used. When alpha is large, the actual demand in the prior period is given great weight in the forecast for the next period. If alpha is one, the forecast for the next period is the actual value of the prior period. The forecast results are markedly affected by the alpha that is used, as is shown in Table EA3-1.

Table EA3-1 employs the same numbers that were used for the moving average and weighted moving average calculations for $t = 7$ in Table 3-2. Table EA3-1 shows the effect of α on the forecast for the seventh period when $t = 6$; $t + 1 = 7$, and $\hat{x}_{t+1} = \hat{x}_7$.

The exponential smoothing updating system requires only one operation. For example, if $\alpha = 0.700$, and the sixth period actual result was found to be $x_6 = 60$, and the forecast for the sixth period was for 40, then the seventh period forecast is $\hat{x}_{t+1=7} = 54$.

$$\hat{x}_{t+1=7} = 0.700(60) + 0.300(40) = 54 \text{ (read subscript as } t+1 = 7)$$

Small values of alpha are used for stable systems where there is, at most, a minimum amount of random fluctuation. Large values of alpha are used for changing and evolving systems where much reliance is placed on the last observation. New products, as they move through their life cycle stages, start with a large alpha value, which gradually diminishes as the product enters its mature stage. For most production scheduling systems in both the job shop and the flow shop, alpha is kept small, in the neighborhood of 0.050 to 0.150, to decrease the system's response to random fluctuations.

Enrichment Challenges 3

1 Using the data in Problem 2 in the Problems Section, apply exponential smoothing to develop a forecast comparable to what is asked for in parts a and b. Note that exponential smoothing goes back to the first prediction, so assume that the forecast for $t = 1$ is 10 and sequentially calculate all forecasts through $t = 8$. Analyze the errors for $t = 4, \ldots, 8$ for direct comparison with the $N = 3$-period moving averages calculated in parts a and b of Problem 2 in the Problems Section. Run for alpha of 0.3 and 0.7 and discuss the benefits of each kind of approach. You can use the QMpom forecasting model for exponential smoothing. Try both alpha values, 0.3 and 0.7.

2 Simulate the effect of using $\alpha = 0.05$ on the following set of very seasonal data:

Month	Sales
1	500
2	800
3	1,200
4	2,000
5	4,000
6	8,000
7	10,000
8	7,000
9	6,000
10	1,000
11	500
12	300

Now, choose $\alpha = 0.85$ and compare the results.

To initiate the calculations, assume that the forecast for $t = 1$ is 600.

You can use the QMpom module called Forecasting Models for exponential smoothing. Try both alpha values, 0.05 and 0.85.

Understanding Quality: Its Management and Strategic Importance

4

Strategic planning that does not include complete understanding of the role of quality as part of the strategy is flawed and vulnerable to failure at any time. Chapter 4 constructs the understanding of quality and the conceptual foundation of quality management.

This foundation must allow two viewpoints to coexist and cooperate. Producers (manufacturers or service providers) view quality as a set of standards and specifications that must be met (called *conformance*). On the other hand, customers view quality as attributes that please them.

Finally, there are organizational measures of quality that combine the two views in various ways. These include global ISO quality standards, the Malcolm Baldrige National Quality Award system, and other competitions for prizes.

Mastery of Chapter 4 provides a portal to Chapter 7, which is the quantitative (statistical) platform for tracking and correcting processes that drift from the specified quality levels.

After reading this chapter, you should be able to:

- Explain why quality is a fundamental factor in strategic planning.
- Distinguish between producers' and consumers' quality concepts.
- Define and analyze quality in terms of its many dimensions.
- Explain how both tangible and intangible quality dimensions are measured.
- Detail the things to consider when developing a rational warranty policy.
- Discuss ISO 9000 standards in an international context.
- Apply the costs of quality to determine rational product strategies.
- Describe the control monitor feedback model.
- Discuss quality mapping.
- Explain why quality competitions and prizes are given worldwide.

The Systems Viewpoint

Everyone in the company contributes to the quality of the established product line. In recognition of this fact, excellent companies train everyone in quality achievement, which applies to all aspects of manufacturing and services. Manufacturers must include services (repair, maintenance, and training) for the product line. Services require administrative support and office management.

Planning for change in product quality is an integral part of new product development. Often, the change is a product quality upgrade. This may or may not act as a disruption of the traditional system. The systems viewpoint is inherent in the definition of good quality for both goods and services because it links what customers want to the production transformation process that makes and delivers the goods and services.

Quality goals are determined by the voice of the customer, and P/OM tries to keep on target. The P/OM approach is to look into each activity where quality could be improved. The process may begin with analysis of the easiest improvements (called *low-hanging fruit*). P/OM is responsible for orchestrating and synchronizing the system to produce quality products (goods and services).

Strategic Thinking

The perception of quality is in the eyes of the customer. Marketing has the ears to hear the voice of the customer. Then, communication between market researchers and P/OM is crucial to determine what the company will deliver to the customer. Sometimes, qualities delivered at the budgeted costs is not what all of the customers want.

The product has to satisfy a variety of customer types (called *market segments*). Before it is possible to measure how good a job is being done, a set of standards needs to be drawn up and agreed upon. There can be so many dimensions for product qualities that strategic thinking about quality will be a formidable task. For example, qualities that are associated with a great vacation or a restaurant of choice differ between market segments.

Costs associated with achieving the right quality level for each quality dimension must be factored into the selling price and what the competition provides. The decisions and compromises involved are what strategic thinking for this chapter is all about. Since September 11, 2001, safety and security have joined the list of qualities that cannot be taken for granted. Quality of life is a growing concern as urban populations grow and global warming heats up.

4-1 Why Is Better Quality Strategically Important?

While the consumer's perception of "good" quality is important, the perception of poor or terrible quality is a disaster. The lack of perceived quality is the portal to strategic failure. Absence of perceived quality is a critical variable in the business system. When it comes to gaining competitive advantage, better quality has leverage with new and old customers.

Products having better quality have a marketplace advantage. Because customers prefer to buy products they perceive to be of better quality, often they are willing to pay more for the superior qualities. Products perceived to be of lower quality are less likely to be substituted for products of better quality. Lower quality results in higher elasticity. This means that price increases cause demand to drop faster than with products having higher quality (and lower elasticity). Better quality translates into greater protection against competitors.

Better producer's quality saves money for the company by decreasing defectives that must be scrapped or reworked. This can be a very big savings because much money and time have been used to add value to the product, which then fails inspection and has to be scrapped. With so much value added, rework is required. Rework expenses often are considerable. Further, the company with a better product can afford to offer a superior warranty, which has marketing attraction for customers. Even with the superior warranty policy, the better product leads to less frequent rework and replacement.

Better quality increases customer loyalty. An investment in quality can be called an expense for improved *customer holding*. The greatest part of marketing expenditures is to attract new customers, called the *switching expense*. Retaining current customers makes sense. Trade-offs between the cost of getting new customers and the additional price paid for better quality to hold onto existing customers favor the investment in quality.

Alienating existing customers with product weaknesses and failures has a host of other side effects, which are undesirable. Word spreads quickly about product failures. There are a growing number of consumer protection publications. Government agencies pursue other aspects of consumer protection using various means to remove defective products from stores. Large-scale auto, food, and battery callbacks are given prime-time coverage on TV. A quality program decreases the probability of callback situations.

Better product quality obtained at a reasonable price generally goes hand-in-glove with growth in market shares and increases in revenues. Sometimes quality improvements result in decreases in court costs for claims of harm caused by malfunctions and other types of liability. Another advantage of better quality is that people who work in companies that really have better quality enjoy an environment of higher morale. See The Service-Profit Chain in Spotlight 2-1 which describes Boutwell, Owens & Co., Inc.'s high customer loyalty as being highly correlated with employee job satisfaction.

4-2 Why Is Total Quality Management Important to Achieve Better Quality?

Total quality management (TQM)

Applying systems vision to every aspect of quality in the organization.

Total quality management (TQM) is called *the prime directive* in this book. What is meant by this? The "prime directive" denotes the critically important and overriding rule that cannot be compromised. *If quality management is to achieve continuously better results, then TQM is the procedure of choice.* Translating this into quality-specific terms, the prime directive for TQM is that the systems approach to quality must be used company-wide. Thus, as an unequivocal rule:

TQM must always be inherent in management strategy. TQM, by definition, requires a company-wide systems approach to quality. Everyone and everything plays a role.

The attainment of TQM is the critical precursor of excellence in quality. To begin with, it is an organizational matter. Everyone in the organization has one or more roles that are related to the attainment of quality. People must be able to communicate with each other in the common pursuit of quality for TQM to operate. The achievement of TQM requires that the entire system be seen in perspective (i.e., view of things in their true relationship or importance). Strategic planners must set the right quality goals. P/OM must use the right strategies and tactics to attain the quality goals that have been set.

TQM is the application of the systems concept of quality that cuts across functional areas. Everyone in the company must know the goals. They must share the same quality objectives. Like the orchestra that needs to play in synchronization to achieve quality sounds, the company needs to synchronize its players to achieve company-wide quality. Ignore or discard any one of the elements and the quality chain is as weak as the weakest link. That is the basic philosophy of TQM.

Some people do not like the name "TQM," and they think that name has been bandied about and overused. However, everyone agrees that what TQM stands for is correct. It is, therefore, necessary to examine the concept of TQM carefully to see what makes it so important.

Those who practice the systems approach know that this is a sound foundation for the attainment of superior quality. If the practice of TQM is done right, it can put a faltering company back on track. If done badly, TQM can alienate those who put themselves on the line to support it. The label "TQM" assures no one of anything. It is essential to read the ingredients on the label of this system of practice. All TQMs are not alike.

4-3 Two Definitions of Quality

Before the sound approach to TQM can be developed, it is necessary to define quality. The word *quality* is used in two different ways.

1   *The producer's view*—Qualities are properties of things without distinction about being good or bad. Thus, the product conforms in all regards to the company's quality specifications.

2 *The consumer's view*—Qualities relate to the "degree of excellence" of things. Thus, consumers have come to expect and believe they deserve a quality product.

The two definitions of quality are held and exercised by different interests. One person can have both points of view, depending on what hat they are wearing at the time. Everyone has an intrinsic sense of what quality means to them as a consumer. They want the best that can be had, so they are always judging the "degree of excellence."

As a producer, it is often necessary to compromise and set quality standards that are not the best in their class. If the level of quality that is set by management is viewed as unacceptable by the market, then the strategic planners have failed. Inexpensive automobiles do not have the same set of qualities as expensive ones. There are different markets for SUVs and compacts. It is the producer's problem to choose appropriate quality standards so that the market judges them to be fitting for that price class.

Producers strive to balance the market forces for high quality with consumers' cost preferences and the company's production capabilities. Figure 4-1 illustrates a common economic concept of the optimal quality level.

There are valid exceptions to the relationships that Figure 4-1 depicts. The cost of quality does not necessarily rise as the quality level increases. The fact that many times quality can be improved without spending money will be discussed at a later point. There also is the issue of how improved quality is obtained, allowing that money is spent. Is it on training, technology, or both?

Figure 4-1 depicts a limit to how much quality can be improved. This concept can be faulted as not taking scientific possibilities and the ingenuity of creative people into account. There also is a question about the dollar volume of sales approaching saturation no matter how much better the quality level is made. Given such issues, it is difficult to

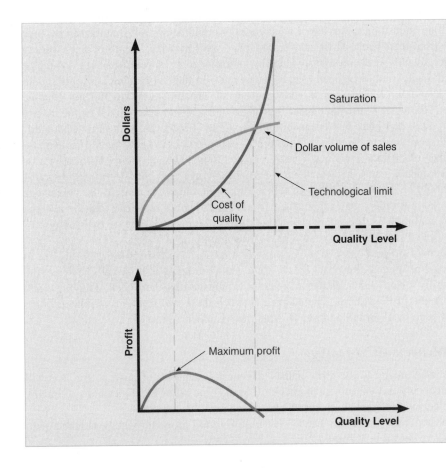

Figure 4-1

Cost of Quality and Dollar Volume of Sales—Yield Maximum Profit as a Function of the Quality Level

know where the quality level of maximum profit occurs. Nevertheless, quality level standards should be set in accord with the notion of maximum profit.

Some producers may be endowed with an innate sense of how to set quality standards so as to best balance costs and benefits. Most producers have to learn how to deal with such issues. This is an essential part of what P/OM does since process design determines what can be gained from the application of TQM.

4-4 The Dimensions of Quality

Dimensions of quality

No form of quality can be achieved until that form is defined.

The **dimensions of quality** are the descriptors that must be examined to determine the quality of a product. The wine business is an enormous industry on a global scale. How do the presidents of wine companies characterize the quality of their products? They measure their production output by bouquet, color, and taste plus chemical analyses. Cars are evaluated within categories of cost, by their power, safety features, capacities, fuel efficiencies, and style, among other things. Appearance and style dimensions, so often important, are difficult to rate. Experts at ladies' fashion shows are at no loss for words. Yet this billion-dollar industry is only able to explain successes and failures after the fact.

When rating the quality of cities to live in, the authors of such research base their studies on dimensions that define quality of life. The complex set of demographically sensitive criteria includes amount of crime, cost of living, job availability, transportation, winter mildness, and the quality of schools for families with children.[1]

The starting point for managing quality is to define the relevant set of quality dimensions, recognizing the special needs of market niches and segments. Not everyone will agree about what should be on the list or about the importance of the dimensions that are on the list. Individuality accounts for different perceptions about "what counts."

A sample of customers was asked what qualities could be improved in the service they received from their bank. Their answers included the following: length of time waiting for tellers should be decreased; availability of officers for special services should be increased; banks should be open longer hours; rates on interest-bearing accounts should be raised; and service charges should be dropped. The list was long and not everone agreed on all points. At the same bank, a group of officers was asked to define the quality of the services their bank offered or should offer. The officers' answers show what a different perspective prevails between customers and producers. They wanted to increase the number of different products that the bank offers (CDs, checking accounts, passbooks, mortgages, loans, investment services); the average time spent by tellers per transaction should be small; variability of tellers' times should be decreased; the percentage of times that customers wait longer than five minutes should be small; and the average length of waiting lines for tellers should be about three people. Waiting lines of zero or one signify that something is wrong with staffing assignments.

What could bring these two groups closer together? Customers describe quality in terms of personal ideals. The bankers describe quality in terms of how well they meet the economically sound standards that have been established by their bank. They also talk about changing the standards. The balance between these two positions is related to the costs and benefits of providing more of what the customer wants.

4-4a Models of Quality

Start to model quality in the form of lists of generic categories of quality. The lists will enable producers and consumers to check off and define all of the dimensions of quality that each deems applicable to the products.

Eight categories, derived by David Garvin, a Harvard professor who researched quality issues, are shown in Table 4-1.[2]

1. Performance	2. Features	**Table 4-1**
3. Reliability	4. Conformance	Eight Primary Quality
5. Durability	6. Serviceability	Dimensions Recommended
7. Aesthetics	8. Perceived quality	by David Garvin

The quality dimensions shown in Table 4-1 are discussed here. The automobile is used as one example. A resort hotel is used as a service example. Describing qualities provides excellent practice in taking the first steps necessary to install a quality program.

The *performance dimension* relates to the quality of the fundamental purpose for which the product is purchased. How well does the car do what it is supposed to do? Are the rooms quiet and the beds comfortable?

The *features dimension* refers to product capabilities not considered to be part of normal performance expectations. These might be GPS and satellite radio for the car, or a spa and wireless Internet for the resort.

The *reliability dimension* relates to performance that can be depended upon with a high level of assurance. The car starts, drives, and does not break down. If the windshield wipers do not work, there is a reliability problem. For the resort, if the room key does not work all of the time, there is a reliability problem.

The *conformance dimension* alludes to the degree to which the measured production qualities correspond to the design quality standards that have been specified. Windshield wipers are not supposed to fail (say) for the first five years and the room key is expected to work for a normal stay. Conformance is definitely the producer's responsibility (auto and resort management). P/OM is charged with meeting the conformance dimensions of quality. They are the specified quality standards.

The *durability dimension* deals with how well the product endures in the face of use and stress. Some cars are roadworthy after being driven more than 100,000 miles. Some room phones fail within a few weeks. Rooms get quite shabby with constant use in a few years.

The *serviceability dimension* is related to how often, how difficult, and how costly it is to service and repair the product. Serviceability for both cars and resort rooms involves the combination of preventive and remedial maintenance.

The *aesthetics dimension* refers to the appearance of the product. For both autos and resorts, design styling counts initially, and maintenance is crucial.

Industrial designers and operations managers form a powerful team to apply the systems approach to all of the linked factors that relate to the eight quality dimensions.

The *perceived quality dimension* relates to the customers' perceptions of the product's quality and value received for monies paid. This dimension integrates the prior seven dimensions with the customers' sense of value for them. Market research is one of the most important means for determining the customers' perceptions.

Table 4-2 presents a more detailed categorization of quality dimensions. It emphasizes the difference between tangible and intangible attributes. Because it is more detailed, it shows the weakness of attributing quality to one or two dimensions. Quality resides in the totality—which is inherent for the systems approach.

For different individuals, certain dimensions are more important than others. Overall, it should be evident that quality definition is enhanced by requiring and enabling a systems perspective.

Frequently, there are regional differences in quality perceptions. Hard water areas have their own special quality dimensions for soap. Snow tires have no impact in the South. Such effects are amplified in the international marketplace. P/OM may have to set different standards for region A as compared to region B.

Quality definition is not simple. The measurement of how well a product or service performs its conforming functions is essential if standards are to be determined. There

Table 4-2
 	
An Extended Taxonomy
of Quality Dimensions
	I. Functional Qualities (the "ilities")
	 1 Utility of main purpose or performance
	 2 Dependability of function
	   a. Conformance to standards from day one, and on, over time
	   b. Reliability: Does it function properly over time?
	   c. Durability: How long does it function with heavy use?
	     (i) How much wear (stress) can it take?
	     (ii) Does functional deterioration occur with use or time?
	
	   d. Failure characteristics and expected lifetime probabilities
	   e. Maintainability—Serviceability I
	     (i) Cost of preventive maintenance (PM)
	     (ii) Frequency and time required for PM
	     (iii) Cost of predictive maintenance (PREDM)
	
	   f. Repairability—Serviceability II
	     (i) Quality—as good as new?
	     (ii) Cost and time for remedial maintenance (RM)
	
	   g. Guarantees and warranties
	 3 Human factors using the product capabilities
	   a. Safety and security—Can be tested partially
	   b. Comfort—Market researchable
	   c. Convenience—Market researchable
	II. Conceptual (Nonfunctional) Qualities
	 1 Aesthetics
	 2 Style
	 3 Appearance
	 4 Image
	   a. Self-image of user: Related to price
	   b. Self-image of user: Related to prestige
	 5 Timeliness of design
	 6 Demography of ownership
	 7 Variety
	   a. Degree of choice
	   b. Rapidity of new models and selection obsolescence

is no point in measuring the wrong things. When the standards are established to everyone's satisfaction, then P/OM can make the right products, test them, and improve the process.

Assumptions must be made about the way in which the measurable, physical factors relate to the consumers' evaluations of the "ilities" of the product. The "ilities" include utility, dependability, reliability, durability, serviceability, maintainability, repairability, and warrantability. Manufacturability, which includes assembly, is a producer's concern although it has its affects on the consumers' "ilities."

Drift-decay quality phenomena

Decay of product performance can occur as a result of usage or age.

A factor underlying a number of the "ilities" is the **drift-decay quality phenomenon** in which performance of a product gradually diminishes over time. Decay is characteristic of a great many functional attributes of mechanical, chemical, and electrical products. Lightbulbs, when first used, will generate some given number of lumens. A typical 75-watt bulb starts its life with about 1,170 lumens of light. It ages as a function of both hours of use and the number of times that it is turned on and off. It may also be true of the quality of service contacts which have been said to deteriorate when "familiarity breeds contempt." It is uncommon to hear that "familiarity breeds admiration" although that does regularly occur in the classroom.

	Measurements	
Quality Dimensions	**Tangible**	**Intangible**
Conformance to specifications	SQC/TQC Zero defects	Arbitrary critiques by experts
Consumer perceptions	Market research	Market research
Management evaluations	Competitive comparisons	Competitive comparisons

Table 4-3 presents a chart that describes how the measurements for all of the dimensions in the quality tables can be obtained. The distinction between manufacturing and services need not be drawn because products of both types of producers have many tangible and intangible elements.

Table 4-3

How Quality Is Defined and Measured

Definition of Failure—Critical to Quality Evaluation

Failure occurs when a product ceases to perform in an acceptable fashion. Sometimes it is in the mind of the customer. Almost everyone has had a favorite restaurant that has fallen from grace. With respect to physical failure, there are engineering as well as logical conventions that define it. The car does not start. The fish is raw. The lightbulb is burned out. The room is not made up. If the light source is considered "failed" after its output falls below a certain threshold, then P/OM needs to consider that aspect of quality standards.

A certain percent of lightbulbs fail at start-up. Failure probabilities follow a U-shaped curve, which is known as the Weibull distribution. Customers who buy a new bulb, insert it, and see it fail are unlikely to write a letter of complaint. There is no time to complain about small failings. Manufacturers and distributors do not get good feedback about a spoiled piece of fruit, hotel rooms that are not perfectly clean, or where a light bulb is burnt out.

P/OM needs to address the questions: Why do early failures occur? Is there something in the process that could be changed? Marketing needs to develop a policy for learning about early failures. P/OM and marketing working together might be able to remove the stigma.

With globally-outsourced producers, problems are compounded. A rash of quality problems with products made in China and exported to the United States have made apparent the difficulty of controlling the quality of non-domestic production. Tainted pet food, toys made with leaded paints, contaminated food products, and unsafe tires are examples of what has been called "The Quality Fade."[3] Among the questions to be raised is "Why was there no overseeing function for P/OM at the outsourcing site?"

P/OM should be fully aware of how they can influence the failure rates and characteristics of the products that they are producing. They also should be working closely with R&D and engineering design to develop new production capabilities that can increase the product's expected lifetime or **mean time between failures (MTBF)**. The measure MTBF is often used to depict reliability. A competitive benchmark of expected lifetime is a useful guide. However customers' willingness to put up with failures is the ultimate standard for acceptability.

In the case of lightbulbs, MTBF is often as low as 750 hours, which can require changing bulbs every month. *In a 31-day month, there are 744 hours.* In comparison, the MTBD for CFLs (compact flourescent lamps) is about 8,000 hours or roughly ten times greater. Marketing managers should be fully aware of their products' MTBF rates and the failure characteristics of competitors' products. They should also know from their P/OM colleagues what it would cost to improve the MTBF by (even) 1 percent as well as how much could be saved on warranties, cost of replacing failed units, etc.

Mean time between failures (MTBF)

Product's expected lifetime of satisfactory utility in normal application.

There are many reasons why failure and reliability, as definitions of quality, play an extremely important role. Some types of failure are life threatening. This consideration plays an important part in the costs of protection through insurance and litigation. Every effort must be made to ensure safety and to document that this effort has been honest. The courts of law expect such ethical behavior.

Some types of failure do not permit repair. The definition and specification of quality also should be concerned with the ease of maintenance and the cost of replacement parts. These factors affect the consumer's judgment of quality.

Warranty Policies

A product warranty is a guarantee by the producer to protect the customer from various forms of product failure. The specifics are spelled out in contractual fashion. Thus, it is typical to state for how long a time, and for how much use, the product is covered. The conditions of use are generally stated.

What is the basis for a sensible warranty policy? First, there are the competitive marketing requirements. If Hyundai has a 10 year/100,000 mile guarantee for its used vehicles, what should Ford and GM offer for their new cars? Does it make sense to offer a warranty policy that costs more than it gains? Warranties involve interactions between products and promises made by production and marketing. The systems approach is essential to make certain that costs and gains are balanced.

Second, the operational reliability of the product is critical. How many cars, phones, etc., will fail, in what ways, after how much time? Given the schedule of failures by time and type, it is possible to figure out how much a blanket, or partial, warranty will cost the company. It is feasible to determine how many customers will be left without company support. These customers will not be repeat purchasers of that brand of auto in the future. Policies of partial warranties to cover different components under varying circumstances also can be formulated in terms of costs and ultimate customer dissatisfaction. P/OM will be instrumental in helping to determine rational warranty policies. There is also an issue about warranties for service functions such as health care, transportation, and education. In various ways, some guarantees exist, but they are vague and ambiguous in comparison with the guarantees for goods.

Management must know the reliability of its products and services to come up with a rational specification of guarantees and warranty periods. An important systems dialogue must take place to set the terms of warranty coverage and period. The essence of this thinking should be founded on the knowledge of the product and the process. That is the responsibility of P/OM's quality control functions within the organization.

The Service Function—Repairability

Repairability (and/or maintainability) are quality dimensions that require a fully functional service capability. Speed of service is an important auxiliary attribute. A service policy is an agreement between the company and its customers that spells out how much service will be rendered, how fast that service will be provided, what service steps will be taken, and what charges will be borne by the customer (warranty contract).

Nikon has a service policy of repairing the entire camera and not just the parts that are responsible for the immediate cause of failure. Their service policy includes furnishing an estimate by mail or phone before beginning work. Service policies are taken very seriously by customers who require service. Organizations distinguish themselves from one another by the care that they show and the fairness of their service policy.

Another service issue is the use of preventive versus remedial service. The preventive maintenance advantage from a P/OM perspective is that it can be scheduled. It also reduces the severity, frequency, and cost of unexpected failures.

Setting up the service policy requires an understanding of the product to determine the preventive maintenance service interval and the charges for that service, as well as the cost of repair parts. In some instances, the service function is a profit center. On the other side of the coin, breakdowns result in calls for nonscheduled maintenance. They jeopardize customer loyalty and usually involve higher costs for the same procedures as preventive maintenance. A broken down car must be towed. From this point of view, the service function is a cost center with opportunities to reduce costs through careful planning.

How should the optimal maintenance function be designed? Should it be a profit center, a cost center, or can it be allowed to function on a reactive basis? P/OM is the only business function that can propose reasonable alternatives and cost each out in a reasonably precise fashion. These alternatives are not likely to include the optimal service policy, but using iteration, successive service scenarios can be tested and then implemented to achieve gradual improvement over time.

4-4b Functional Human Factors—Quality Dimensions

Quality management must focus on the importance of human factors such as safety, security, comfort, and convenience. The human factors area (also called *ergonomics*) relates equally well to office or factory conditions. It concerns dangers from products in use and services provided such as plane trips and taxi rides.

Many human factor qualities are overlooked until they exceed reasonable limits and are then rejected. For example, the comfort of a chair in a restaurant might be considered acceptable until it passes a threshold, and then it becomes a factor for evaluation of the restaurant. Using market segmentation according to body types, only some customers may find the restaurant chair uncomfortable.

Many safety factors cannot be seen. Starting in 1996, Firestone ATX tires got a reputation for tread separation causing SUV rollovers. In 2006, Bridgestone Firestone Corp. was still trying to reach the 5 percent of original tire owners for replacement. Word of mouth in such situations has a large negative effect. Proper P/OM heads off the existence of such issues. Food safety is another invisible factor. Customers rely on food companies to take proper measures to ensure that salmonella is not present. Contaminant control is a P/OM responsibility.

The health quality of foods related to processing and ingredients such as trans-fatty acids and partially hydrogenated oils is a quality issue. Nutritionists decry the use of too much fat, too many calories, too much sodium, etc. P/OM makes the product that uses these ingredients. However, the recipes are part of the product design, which relates to management strategy, marketing planning, and market research information. Because the underlying properties of food are invisible to the consumer, labeling has taken on importance that is proportional to the consumer's ability to use that kind of knowledge. Problems can be traced to inadequate and incompetent strategic planning.

4-4c Nonfunctional Quality Factors—Aesthetics and Timing

Nonfunctional qualities play a major role in the consumer's judgment of quality. Appearance and style are intangibles, and customer satisfaction with aesthetics is difficult to measure. There can be high variability in what constitutes preferred designs, and there are ambiguous design criteria for what works. Because appearance, style, and other nonfunctional qualities are intangibles, expert opinion and market research are the only ways to measure satisfaction. Nevertheless, these dimensions are as important to the definition of product quality as any that are found in the functional categories of quality.

Market research often attempts to determine the image that consumers conjure up of themselves to justify the purchase of items. Self-image is significant for high-ticket items such as Rolls Royces or Mercedes. Self-image applies to a broad range of acquisitions such as healthclub memberships, art purchases, top-of-the-line cameras, maid service, and trips into space on Russian satellites.

How consumers interpret intangible qualities involves sociological and psychological dimensions of quality. Thinking along these lines is not easily associated with P/OM, which strives to meet the standards that are specified. That is why industrial designers play a major role in product design decisions. There is broad systems responsibility to achieve effective nonfunctional attributes for a product. Ultimately, P/OM is charged with making exactly what designers fashion.

Timeliness is another elusive nonfunctional quality dimension. It is most evident in the fashions and styles of clothing, athletic footwear, iTune downloads, and the latest fad of youthful school-age market segments. The extent to which styles go in and out of fashion is never overlooked by those who are in the seller's chair. If vibrant laptop colors have real lasting power, the inventory of drab computers will have to be sold at a loss. Otherwise, there will be a glut of colored laptop cases. Managing inventories of home furnishings products requires an understanding of the dynamics of style shifts. For example, the furniture suit business (e.g., Thomasville) requires being on top of inventory shifts of types and colors of wood.

The Variety Dimension

Variety

The number of product alternatives (in a given product class) that are made available to the customer.

Marketing can assist strategic planners in their evaluation of the importance of **variety** of choice. Variety is defined as the number of product alternatives (in a given product class) that are made available to the customer. Variety can include different quality dimensions at different prices. The key to defining variety is that customers see the various choices as substitutable alternatives.

The number of flavors that Jello offers is an illustration of variety as a quality. Does the customer want to buy green or red Jello? If green, will it be lime- or kiwi-flavored? In Brazil, it might be avocado-flavored. Having set down what the customer seems to want, what does P/OM have to do to switch the production line from green to red? How much does that cost? Will it be less expensive to switch from red to green? Answers to such questions are based on operational considerations.

Variety often increases a brand's market share because people like to switch flavors from time to time. They might switch away from their favored brand to get a different flavor occasionally. Variety of the product line is dependent upon process capabilities to shift inexpensively from one color, flavor, or size to another. Can different prices be charged for choices among varieties? If it costs a lot to add another variant, customers must be willing to pay for the additional choice, and that is a matter of price elasticity.

Customized product is the apex of variety. Suits made to fit a special customer are one of a kind. Suits off-the-rack and then altered to fit are still customized but at a lower level. Industrial consumers can also choose between altered to fit or tailor-made equipment. The highest variety levels fall within that range of customization. P/OM produces the level of variety determined by marketing strategy. Because variety entails additional production costs, marketing has to factor these expenses into the equation. P/OM is in charge of the knowledge base in the business unit that can inform marketing about the costs of variety. Together, marketing and P/OM examine the trade-offs between higher costs and greater sales.

At the same time, variety develops loyal customers in special market niches. Some customers prefer regular cola. Others prefer diet drinks. Some like vanilla or cherry added to the drink. Others like more caffeine. Some choose bottles and others choose cans. Choice is a quality that is a competitive factor. It must be understood by marketing and P/OM alike.

4-5 Setting International Producer Standards

There are quality standards in the United States. There are similar but not identical quality standards in many countries around the world. Standards are global because suppliers exist throughout the world. The International Organization for Standardization (ISO) is supported by 140 countries. ISO is constantly engaged in setting standards for products, processes, information systems, and the environment with respect to every type of organization and activity. The organization makes a point of declaring that ISO is not an acronym of its name but is derived from the Greek prefix meaning "equal" (as in *isobars*). The English acronym would be IOS, and in French it would be OIN (standing for Organisation Internationale de Normalisation). This information underscores the true international character of the ISO 9000 and ISO 14000 families of standards, which are known as "generic management system standards." ISO 9000 and ISO 14000 are discussed in this text.

4-5a U.S. Quality Standards

The U.S. military established standards in the 1940s, during World War II, which related inspection sample sizes and observed sample values of averages and variability to the probable true values of the entire production batch.[4]

Practically speaking, almost every purchase made by the military was subject to these standards. This introduced quality standards to a broad range of private businesses in the United States.

The American National Standards Institute (ANSI) and the American Society for Quality Control (ASQC) have jointly published a series of quality specifications—called the Q90 series—which reflect the standards of the International Standards Organization. In fact, Q90 through Q94 are Americanized versions of the international standards ISO 9000 through ISO 9004.

4-5b Origin of the International Organization for Standardization (ISO) and Explanation of the ISO 9000 Quality Standards

The organization, ISO, provides certification of conformance to quality standards that is known as ISO 9000. ISO officially began operation on February 23, 1947. Because "International Organization for Standardization" would have different abbreviations in different languages ("IOS" in English, "OIN" in French for Organisation internationale de normalisation), it was decided at the outset to use a word derived from the Greek isos, meaning "equal."

ISO nongovernmental organizations form a network of the national standards institutes, currently numbering 156 countries, on the basis of one member per country. The Central Secretariat of ISO, which coordinates the entire systems, is located in Geneva, Switzerland. ISO is the world's largest developer of standards whose United States representative is the American National Standards Institute (ANSI). ISO has developed a comprehensive system for certifying that companies in any part of the world have voluntarily met the standards and qualify as ISO certified. The most well known ISO standards are the ISO 9000 (quality series) and the ISO 14000 (environmental series). There is much to be learned by going to http://www.iso.org and clicking on various items. Start, however, with the annual report under "About ISO" in the top navigational pane.

Scope of ISO 9001

ISO 9001 are quality management systems that define customer requirements and explore how to improve customer satisfaction. This includes but is not limited to the following considerations:

- Management Commitment and Responsibility
- Documentation Requirements
- Planning

- Resources
- Sales and Marketing
- Purchasing
- Product Realization
- Design and Development
- Monitoring, Measurement, and Analysis of Data
- Customer Satisfaction and Continuous Improvement

Why Is ISO 9001 Important to Customers?

Customer satisfaction is one of the primary objectives of the ISO 9001 quality system. There must be continual improvement as shown in the quality objectives that support the quality policy. This is accomplished by the adoption of process approaches that can be checked and improved. Minimizing defects lowers costs. It also improves meeting regulatory requirements and satisfying customer expectations.

Why Do We Need International Standards?

Between 1947 and the present day, ISO published more than 16,455 International Standards. ISO's work program ranges from standards for traditional activities, such as agriculture and construction, through mechanical engineering, to medical devices, to the newest information technology developments.

Standardization of screw threads helps keep chairs, children's bicycles, and aircraft together with minimum wasted time. Try to solve the repair and maintenance problems that would be caused by a lack of standardization. Standards establish common parts and international consensus on terminology, which makes technology transfer easier.

Without the standardized dimensions of freight containers, international trade would be slower and more expensive. Without the standardization of telephone and banking cards, life would be more complicated and more expensive. A lack of standardization may even affect the quality of life itself: for the disabled, for example, when they are barred access to consumer products—public transportation and buildings—because the dimensions of wheelchairs and entrances are not standardized.

Standardized traffic symbols provide danger warnings no matter what the spoken language. Consensus on grades of various materials give a common reference for suppliers and clients in business dealings.

Agreement on a sufficient number of variations of a product to meet most current applications allows economies of scale with cost benefits for both producers and consumers. An example of failure is the lack of standardization of paper sizes. ISO 216 defines A and B paper series. ISO 269 defines a C paper series, and there is more. This is not a happy situation for printers and faxes being interchangeable around the globe. This failure is costing almost every user a lot of money that is wasted.

Standardization of performance or safety requirements of diverse equipment makes sure that users' needs are met while allowing individual manufacturers the freedom to design their own solution on how to meet those needs.

Standardized protocols allow computers from different vendors to "talk" to each other. Standardized documents speed up the transit of goods, or identify sensitive or dangerous cargoes that may be handled by people speaking different languages. Standardization of connections and interfaces of all types ensures the compatibility of equipment of diverse origins and the interoperability of different technologies.

Agreement on test methods allows meaningful comparisons of products, or plays an important part in controlling pollution—whether by noise, vibration, or emissions. Safety standards for machinery protect people at work, at play, at sea . . . and at the dentist. Without the international agreement contained in ISO standards on quantities and units, shopping and trade would be haphazard, science would be—unscientific—and technological development would be handicapped.

Standards contribute to making the development, manufacturing, and supply of products and services more efficient, safer, and cleaner. ISO generic management standards can deal with quality (ISO 9000) and the environment (ISO 14000) though the vast majority are highly specific to a particular product, material, or process.

Standards enhance global competitiveness of businesses and quality of life by promoting and facilitating voluntary consensus standards and conformity assessment systems. The existence of divergent national or regional standards can create barriers to trade. International standards are the technical means by which political trade agreements can be put into practice.

Initially these standards are voluntary but may become market requirements if adopted by regulatory or governments.

The original ISO materials were written in great detail with guideline books that contain policies, rules, and principles. They applied to both manufactured and service products. Being familiar with the statements of these standards in their original 9000 to 9004 form is helpful in understanding the transformation and growth of global-based quality requirements.

> *ISO 9000:* Provides overall guidance for prospective users of the ISO standards. It explains the ISO system, in general, and gives directions for using the other components of the **ISO 9000 series** as described in the following standards.
>
> *ISO 9001:* Applies to firms that are engaged in the pre-market stages including design and development, and also in the in-market stages including production, installation, and servicing.
>
> *ISO 9002:* Applies to firms that are only engaged in the in-market stages of production, installation, and servicing and not engaged in the pre-market stages of design and development.
>
> *ISO 9003:* Applies to firms that deal with testing and inspection of products when they are acting as an inspection agent or as a distributor.
>
> *ISO 9004:* Describes the accepted quality management system and serves as a guide to the application of that system to production systems for goods and services.

ISO 9000 series
Generic ISO management of systems standards for quality.

Many U.S. companies require their suppliers to adhere to ISO 9000 standards or the ANSI/ASQC equivalent standards Q90–Q94. In the same sense, U.S. companies wanting to do business in Europe and in Asia are committing resources to the considerable work that needs to be done for certification. Environmental standards ISO14000 are being globally adopted in growing numbers.

4-5c Japanese and Chinese Quality Standards

Japanese companies adhere to ISO 9000 when it is useful to do so in order to participate in European and U.S. markets. At the same time, over a long period of time, the Japanese have published their own, often quite stringent, quality standards for products as diverse as fiber-optic cable, cellular telephones, high-definition television, and rice.

For many years, they also have utilized systems of quality standards, such as the **Japanese Industrial Standard Z8101**. These specifications resemble those developed in the United States.

Japanese Industrial Standard Z8101
Set of Japanese standards equivalent to the EURO/U.S.–ISO standards.

The Japanese government has been yielding to pressure to open their markets, which are still blocked by excessively rigorous standards that favor domestic producers. Because this will be happening, P/OM must be alert to follow continuous changes in Japanese standards over time. Some of these will permit the entry of American products into markets that are not currently available. This is another illustration of the degree to which P/OM must be in the network to receive the latest information about international standards and specifications.

China has significant quality problems and only recently is trying to establish some vague standards. This must and will change. There is a great opportunity for P/OM input in the Chinese outsourcing system, which has not been recognized by U.S. companies. The reason is that outsourcing has been an exclusively financial decision. No communication with P/OM has taken place. That is changing. P/OM is learning to deal with these challenges.

4-5d Database of Quality Standards

Collecting and maintaining a worldwide database of prices and qualities for potential global-based suppliers—and of actual and possible customers as well—provide a real competitive advantage. In business environments where every factor has been carefully studied, it has become essential to know what quality standards can be realized for given prices. Even commodities (say, grains or oils) have different purities, cleanliness, and ingredients. Such a database can be made to reflect changes in prevailing suppliers' prices for various conditions of supply and demand. The demand for the best quality potatoes (say, McDonald's and Frito-Lay) will be chasing diminished supply in those parts of the world where growth is diminished by drought. A well-fashioned database can alert the purchasing agents to changing conditions that might significantly impact the company.

Some companies offer a database with prices, qualities, and delivery dates. This allows buyers and suppliers to connect. Oracle's E-Business Suite (Internet Procurement) provides integration with numerous ERP and supply chain programs. Onvia DemandStar connects business and government to online opportunities. In the United Kingdom, but globally by Internet, Digital Trading advises its supply chain customers that "mass customization is a reality" and "your supply chain automatically innovates tomorrow's products" (http://www.digitaltrading.co.uk). Some other leaders in electronic databases that allow online collaboration are IBM, Microsoft, SAP, Oracle, and Covisint (a subsidiary of Compuware) working in automotive, healthcare, identity management, and the public sector (see http://www.covisint.com).

Business-to-business (B2B) e-commerce is growing at hundreds of trading sites. Quality and price are main factors in this growing arena. The **costs of quality** are crucial determinants of price.

Costs of quality
Costs of preventing defects, of appraisal, and of failures.

4-6 The Costs of Quality

A good approach to understanding quality is to analyze the costs associated with achieving, or failing to achieve, it. There are many shapes that cost curves can take. Therefore, nothing should be taken for granted in a specific case. However, it is useful to state some generalizations about the costs of quality. First, there are three basic costs of quality. These include the costs of prevention, appraisal, and failure.

4-6a The Cost of Prevention

Prevention involves the use of conscious strategies to reduce the production of defective product, which by definition does not conform to agreed-upon quality standards. The entire system must be designed, coordinated, and controlled to prevent defectives. This includes the materials and equipment used, appropriate skills, and the correct process to deliver product conforming to standards. Presumably by spending more, the percent of defectives can be reduced. Figure 4-2 shows this kind of relationship, although the real shape of the curve would have to be determined for a specific situation.

If some mistake causes defectives to occur, and the problem is noticed and corrected, then it is fair to say that quality improvement was free. Defectives have been prevented from occurring by remedying a wrong. In service organizations, as in manufacturing,

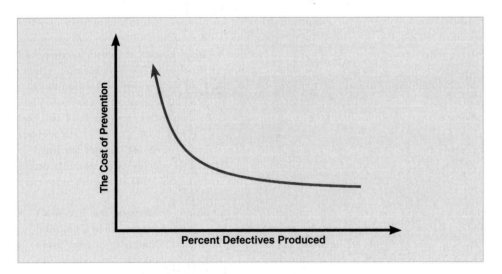

Figure 4-2

It Becomes Increasingly Expensive to Decrease the Percent Defectives Produced

As spending for preventive maintenance increases, the percent defective decreases. These costs are process investments made before production. Examples of dedicated preventive maintenance spending are described in Spotlight 4-2 (the Japanese poka-yoke system). The percent defective decreases with increased investment in prevention as shown by the arrow that points upward and to the left.

there are many examples of cost-free quality improvements. Philip Crosby wrote a book about quality being free[5] and established a quality school for executives that emphasized this focus as part of its curriculum.

The cost of prevention goes up when quality standards are raised. *It is a reasonable policy to raise the quality standards whenever the prior standards are being consistently met.* The costs involved in achieving these ever more stringent specifications will increase, gradually at first, and then markedly as the technological limitations of the materials and the process are approached. This is shown in Figure 4-3.

In manufacturing, the **tolerance limits** define the range of acceptable product. As an example, the lead that fits into a mechanical pencil might be specified as 0.5mm. This describes the diameter of the lead. No one supposes that each piece of lead that comes in a container marked 0.5mm will be exactly 0.5mm. The tolerance limit sets the standard.

For example, it could be specified that each piece of lead must fall within the range of 0.5mm plus or minus one twentieth of a millimeter (0.5 ± 0.05). This means that the lead diameter could be as wide as 0.55mm and as thin as 0.45mm. In comparison, if the stated tolerance limit allowed a range of 0.51 to 0.49, that would be much tighter and more costly to achieve.

Figure 4-3 illustrates the exponential increase in costs as the accepted tolerance range is tightened and approaches the technological limits of the process. When the tolerance range becomes tighter (i.e., 0.005 is tighter than 0.05), the cost of getting all of the units produced to fall within that range becomes greater. When designers narrow the defined acceptable range, then existing equipment may not be able to do the job. A greater percentage of output will not conform to the new standard. Everything that falls outside the tolerance range limit is called defective. These defectives must either be scrapped or reworked. Both are considered part of the cost of failure.

Another example of prevention is related to Taguchi's methods. These are aimed at designing products that can be manufactured with minimum defectives. Statisticians often talk about the design of experiments that permit testing various alternatives to determine which produce the least variance. That idea is applied by **Taguchi methods** to design products that conform to specifications with the least variability.

It is said that the United States and Europe use goalpost standards for quality. When a product is accepted by a go, no-go gauge, that is equivalent to having the football go anywhere between the goalposts. It counts as one point after touchdown or as a three-point field goal. Quality control chart limits are just like goalposts, too. Taguchi proposes an optimal quality point and deviations from that as loss function measures.

Tolerance limits

The plus and minus parts of tolerance limits (e.g., 6.00 ± 0.05) are like the goalposts described in the entry for Taguchi methods. The normal inspection process accepts products that measure within the upper and lower values of the tolerance limits. Statistical quality control (SQC) charts have equivalent upper and lower control limits. When the set of sequential sample means falls inside those "posts," the process is assumed to be stable. This is the most often used method for SQC.

Taguchi methods

Optimal quality point and a loss function to describe deviations from that optimal.

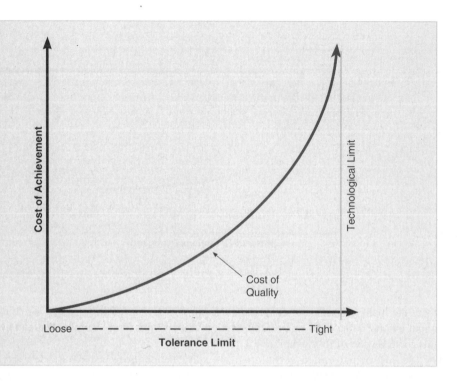

Figure 4-3

As the Specified Tolerance Limit Moves from Loose (Easily Achieved with Normal Skills and Equipment) to Tight (Difficult to Achieve Even with Special Skills and Equipment), the Cost of Achieving That Limit Rises Geometrically

Investments to decrease defectives increase exponentially when the tolerance limits are tighter than the existing process equipment can deliver. Redesign of the product and the process can help find a way around the barriers to improvement.

Six-sigma

Product design and production processes that deliver near-zero defects (six-sigma is 3.4 defects per million parts).

Extreme quality achievement

Conformance to standards must be as near to perfect as possible.

Acceptance sampling methods

Set the inspection parameters for drawing a sample from a production lot.

Detailing

Involves removing all defectives from the rejected lot so that every item remaining conforms to specifications.

Alternatively, move the goalposts close together so that most field goals would miss the mark and not qualify for points. Motorola has done just that with the six-sigma system. **Six-sigma** is a very stringent quality standard allowing only 3.4 defectives per one million parts (see Spotlight 7-2). Goal-seeking with stringent quality requirements is assisted by many techniques, including the Taguchi methods. Six-sigma is a powerful advocate of preventing quality failures. However, it also teaches defect detection and correction when prevention fails. It is akin to requiring very-near-zero defects, which is an **extreme quality achievement**.

4-6b The Cost of Appraisal (Inspection)

When product is examined to see if it conforms to the agreed-upon standards, it is undergoing inspection and appraisal. Both terms are used interchangeably and have to do with the evaluation of whether or not the product conforms to the standards. Product that is not judged to conform because it fails to fall within the tolerance limits is sorted out. There must be a policy regarding what to do with product that does not conform, for each way that it may not meet specifications. Some types of defectives have to be scrapped; others can be reworked and sold for scrap or at a discount.

The usual way to sort out the items that do not fall within the tolerance limits is to inspect all of the items. It is possible to use **acceptance sampling methods**, which, as the name indicates, consist of inspecting a sample of the production lot. If the sample fails to pass, then the entire lot is inspected and detailed. **Detailing** means removing the defectives so that every item in the lot conforms to the specifications. Therefore, when detailing, the inspector separates the bad from the good.

Figure 4-4 shows the three basic costs of quality. One is the cost of prevention of defects (previously seen in Figure 4-2). Second is the cost of inspection, which increases as the percent defective in the production lots increases. The reasons for the cost increase are that more inspectors are needed and an increased amount of detailing is necessary. If sampling is used, more samples of greater size will be taken. All other things being equal, the increase in inspection costs would be almost linear, and not too steep, as a function of increasing percent defectives. The inspection cost line is shown in Figure 4-4.

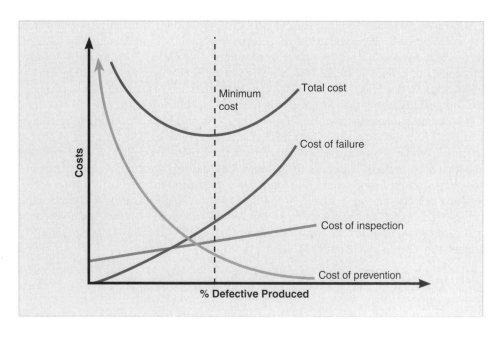

% Defective Produced

Figure 4-4

When the Three Basic Costs of Quality Are Added Together, They Sum to a Total Cost Curve That Has a Minimum Cost Point

For the cost of prevention, the *y*-axis represents spending to reduce defectives. The arrow points up and to the left. Inspection costs and failure costs occur after the process delivers the output. Inspection costs rise with greater percent defective since items require special handling. They must be analyzed, documented, and in some cases repaired or detailed. The costs of failures are directly proportional to the number of defectives that consumers will experience. Total cost is minimized at a specific level of percent defective.

Costs of failures
Can comprise costs stemming from replacement warranties, legal actions, customer aliena-tion, and employee loss of pride in company and product line.

Lifetime value (LTV) of customers
Stream of revenue spent by each loyal customer over the lifetime of his/her relationship with a store (or brand).

Product callbacks
Costs that include labor and material rework, decreased customer loyalty, and litigation losses.

Figure 4-4 puts together Figures 4-2 and 4-3. It also shows the cost of failure, which tends to increase exponentially as the percent defectives produced (and not caught by inspection) increases. The fourth curve in Figure 4-4 is the total cost of quality, which is the sum of the other three curves.

4-6c The Cost of Failure

In Figure 4-4, the cost of failure rises linearly, at first, and then accelerates as the per-centage of defectives increases. This might reflect a replacement cost for failed items that are under warranty. Then, as the percent of defectives continues to rise, product fail-ure costs can be far more severe. The curve starts to move up geometrically. Severe **costs of failures** occur when customers begin to defect to competitors as a result of product failures.

This lost revenue stream, often called the *lost* **lifetime value (LTV) of customers**, has to be taken into account as a significant cost of failure. An estimate of the average lifetime value of a customer is an important guide for deciding how much to spend to prevent failures that damage customer loyalty. LTV can be a large amount of revenue. For example, it can be thousands of dollars lost if a regular pizza customer of a partic-ular fast-food take-out service defects to another one because of dissatisfaction. Lost revenue streams are markedly greater when a business traveler permanently shifts hotel chains.

Further, serious failures could involve liability of very large sums of money. The expense of litigation in court trials, as well as the accompanying bad publicity, has costs that are difficult to estimate. Additional costs of failures are related to **product callbacks**, which require rework involving labor and material costs. Product callbacks often carry other penalties beyond the cost of repairing or replacing failed product. These include possible legal damage claims, bad publicity, and the loss of customers. Curves that chart the cost of failure are likely to have steeply ascending, exponential, or geometric shapes.

4-6d The Total Cost of Quality

The three kinds of costs in Figure 4-4 permit derivation of a *total cost curve*. This curve is U-shaped. Total costs are minimized at some level of percent defectives.

However, there can be disagreement with this proposition. Situations exist in which, for small increases in prevention costs, percent defectives will be dramatically reduced. Also, there are conditions when the cost of failure does not rise exponentially because the impact of failure is trivial (the pencil point broke) or because inspection catches 100 percent of the defectives. With effective inspection, the percent defectives produced are substantially higher than the percent defectives shipped.

On the other hand, if the cost of failure rises very fast, then the indicated minimum cost point is pushed toward the zero level of percent defectives. The total cost of quality increases geometrically as the percentage defectives rises. Six-sigma assumes that this situation of serious consequences for failure exists (the airplane control system does not recognize that the course setting is heading into a mountain.)[6]

Zero defects was the goal set by Phillip Crosby of Philip Crosby Associates. The curves for the costs of quality are logical in certain circumstances; they are conjectural and plain wrong in others. However, modeling quality costs remains an important effort and worthwhile endeavor for P/OM.

Zero defects

When zero defects is not the standard, then some level of defects is expected.

4-7 Quality and the Input–Output Model

To achieve specified output quality, two basic components of the input–output model must have satisfactory input quality.

First: The quality of input components (all materials received from suppliers) must be maintained at designated levels. Also, work skills must meet standards. Often, because of employee turnover, new workers must be trained before they participate in the transformation process. Other inputs, including energy and cash flow, must conform to designated levels.

Second: The transformation process needs to be capable and controlled to deliver the desired output quality. Often, transformations involve internal transfers made between departments as well as external transfers between suppliers and the firm.

4-7a Controlling Output Quality

The fundamental control model for quality is based on feedback and correction. This is the basic process by which P/OM adjusts the production system to conform to specifications for the product.

Figure 4-5 shows the information linkages of this system. The monitor (M) checks actual output measures against conformance standards. Deviations from standards are

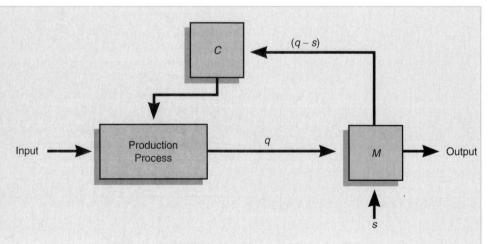

Figure 4-5

Quality Control Feedback Model: Monitor (M) Notifies Controller (C) of Quality Deviations $(q - s)$ Where (q) Is Output Quality and (s) Is the Quality Standard

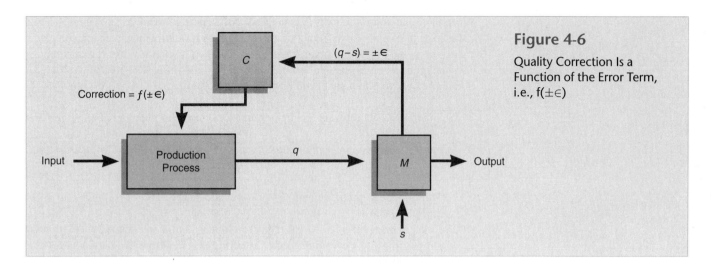

Figure 4-6

Quality Correction Is a Function of the Error Term, i.e., $f(\pm \in)$

sent to the controller (C), which has been instructed to reduce the variation. After the controller has made its corrections, the monitor should pick up the fact that standards are being met again.

The monitor (M) measures $(q - s)$ where q is the output quality and s is the conformance standard. M sends information about deviations to the controller (C). A model that carries out this concept should be developed for each quality dimension that counts. Most quality standards can be monitored by automated quality control equipment.

How should this job be organized? If it is done automatically, there is a lot of control equipment to maintain. Assume that 30 dimensions are being monitored and controlled. The cost of this control effort might be larger than the benefits. Perhaps less than 30 dimensions should be monitored continuously. The use of sampling as explained in Chapter 7 should be considered.

Figure 4-6 shows the difference $(q - s) = (\pm \in)$. This $(\pm)$ measure of epsilon is the error term that the controller (C) has been programmed to correct. The controller adjusts the production process in line with its instructions.

Say the product is paint and that color hue and brightness are being monitored. The controller adds white, black, and colored pigments to the mixture in accord with instructions concerning specific patterns of deviations from the standards.

4-8 TQM Is Systems Management of Quality

TQM might better have been called SMQ—standing for *systems management of quality*. Because it was not, every time that TQM appears, it is necessary to translate that name into systems terms. This means that partial quality concepts are not acceptable. Instead, it must be understood that TQM requires complete organizational involvement. In Sections 4-2 and 4-9b (on Quality Function Deployment) it is called *company-wide* pursuit of quality. This total systems scope means that everything and everyone that has anything to do with quality achievement (directly and indirectly) must be included in planning, designing, and then in controlling the production processes.

Because total quality management requires using the systems approach to quality, all of the people, functions, factors, and elements that play a relevant part in determining quality must be included in setting standards, monitoring observations, and controlling for deviations of the process. The role of every component, ingredient, and person that participates in the process, and thereby in the quality of its product, must be understood and taken into account. This is done in planning and designing the standards for products, processes, and control systems. The control system cannot otherwise correct deviations from standards.

When the input–output process is connected to the control model, as in Figures 4-5 and 4-6, a major part of the systems structure required for total quality management is in place. The part that is missing is the organizational arrangement that allows for the interchange of information between the people who plan for quality and make decisions about it.

Summarizing five points that have been made:

1 Standards for all relevant quality dimensions must be clear, unambiguous, and jointly held.

2 People, machines, or combinations must serve as monitors. This entails their comparing the outputs of processes to the agreed-upon standards.

3 Process managers must strive constantly to meet the standards that have been set for all products. Achievement of process standards requires suppliers to meet specified standards.

4 Process managers must be sure that monitors and controllers are in regular communication to deal with process exceptions (deviations from standards) that trigger controller action.

5 Procedures to handle deviations from quality standards must be predetermined. Controllers must know that they are empowered by process managers to correct unacceptable deviations in pre-programmed scenarios.

4-9 Mapping Quality Systems

The systems approach to quality requires mapping the relationships between customers and those that supply them. Although all functions of business should be thinking about customers, marketing is assigned the responsibility to represent them. In the same way, P/OM and engineering are accountable for supplying product to customers. This permits mapping the mutual concerns of sales and marketing with operations and engineering.

4-9a House of Quality (HOQ)

House of Quality (HOQ)
Mapping and tracking system for all relevant quality dimensions for a real product.

The **House of Quality (HOQ)**[7] is an example of a mapping procedure designed to organize the relationship between what customers want and what the company's product delivers. The basic structure is a matrix with customers' needs listed in rows (What's wanted) and product design features listed in columns (How needs are satisfied). The HOQ emphasizes the importance of "listening to the voice of the customer."

At the intersections of each row and column is a numerical estimate of how well the company's product satisfies customers' needs. Customers' needs are not all the same. Accordingly, special rows are created for each market segment. Additional walls can be added to show how well customers' needs are met by competitors' design features.

Other aspects of this method include analysis of design feature interactions. For example, sealing and insulating a car door to protect against weather and noise will affect the ease of opening and closing that door. There is a design feature trade-off since customers want good insulation, minimum noise, and ease of opening and closing doors.

Enrichment Activity 4 provides an example of a one-wall house used to compare total quality of various service station designs. A scoring system totals the numbers in the matrices.

4-9b Quality Function Deployment (QFD)

HOQ was also seen as a cascade of linked houses, which carry customer needs and wants (the *voice of the customer*) from design specifications to production planning and supply chain management. This permits P/OM to connect what is going on in operations, on the floor of the plant to be linked with customer perceptions of quality.

A fully-linked structure typifies the ideal realization of **quality function deployment (QFD)**.[8] QFD promotes group planning and decision making. It also conveys the idea of moving from strategies to tactics. The direct impact of tactics on strategies is revealed. If FedEx sorting machines jam frequently, the strategy for speedy delivery of packages is not achievable. Customer needs and wants will not be realized until the quality of package processing is consistently excellent by this linkage.

Quality function deployment (QFD)
Extending quality throughout the firm's activities.

Listening to the voice of the customer is a major step in new product development and innovation. It is not enough, however, because customers do not always know what will please them. For example, customers could not envision air-conditioning units for the home before they were a reality. The iPhone was not created because customers asked for it to be designed. There is a risk in committing to a new product that does not exist because of the belief that customers will want it. See Spotlight 17-2 on innovation.

The systems approach requires listening to what customers say and watching what they do. In addition encouraging customer complaints often elicits visions of opportunities that otherwise are not imagined by customers or producers alike.

The name associated with mapping quality system throughout the organization is quality function deployment. QFD is a comprehensive program with a complete agenda for extending quality throughout the firm's activities.[9] The QFD approach originated in Mitsubishi's Kobe shipyard in 1972. Toyota and its suppliers further developed the methods and their application. Many U.S. companies, both in services and manufacturing, have employed its use. The list of applications includes automakers, banks, electronic firms, retailers, schools, and stockbrokers. The Ford Motor Company played a leading role in the early application of QFD concepts in the United States.

It is necessary to assign responsibility for each of the quality dimensions within and throughout the entire organization, as well as outside it. Each organization must determine the best deployment system, including the extension to suppliers. It is evident that when the customer is included in the deployment pattern, there is an even greater opportunity to achieve excellence in quality. Questions to consider: Who are the players? What training have they received? What means exist for enhancing communication? How does the Internet tie in?

Competitive systems undergo incessant change. Quality issues and dimensions must be reevaluated. This results in the need to constantly update the way in which the quality function is deployed. Changes in the environment and in competitors' products require modifying the system's approach by constantly improving quality function deployment.

The procedures used in constructing the HOQ can help determine where accountability for quality resides. That is why the HOQ can affect organizational design as well as the quality of products. The basic idea is that cross-functional mapping of all elements that participate in the attainment of quality goals is a process in its own right.

Anything that affects quality must be included within the boundaries of the quality system. This is another way of saying that the map must include all factors that affect any of the quality dimensions. To be sure all relevant factors are included, it is necessary to name all of the participants that plan, design, and control quality. These participants can then identify additional contacts that they make on an informal basis.

It is a good idea to develop an *organization chart* to reflect the deployment of the quality function. This then can be studied to determine whether there are bureaucratic forces within the organization that inhibit instead of encourage and foster quality. Even as a technique, it should be noted that the HOQ provides discipline and procedure, but its regimentation can inhibit discussion and creative thinking.

In this regard, it is important to make QFD as user-friendly as possible. This will encourage cross-functional communication. Different approaches exist for promoting interfunctional problem solving. **Action learning** is a technique for rotating people through various jobs in pursuit of broader understanding. Communication enhancements between engineers, designers, marketers, and P/OM are worth promoting.

Action learning
Training technique that rotates employees through a variety of jobs.

Another aspect of QFD is the extent of the deployment. In Japan, there are tens of thousands of firms that are said to have total dissemination, called *company-wide total quality control* or *CWTQC*. A distinction should be drawn between CWTQC and QFD. QFD pinpoints those in the organization who have responsibility for quality. CWTQC postulates that everyone in the organization plays a part in quality attainment.

4-9c Teamwork for Quality

Quality circles (QCs)
Groups with teamwork assignments for quality achievement.

CWTQC is often identified with groups of workers who meet regularly in what are sometimes called **quality circles (QCs)**. These groups are organized around products. Membership in a circle belongs to anyone that influences the quality of the specific products. The circle concept has been called by different names and has met with varying degrees of success.

Teamwork for productivity is enhanced when the quality perspective is brought to light. Absenteeism and turnover diminish because the team's morale is high when there is a concerted effort to produce quality products, which endear customers. Pride in the job done and in the quality of the product is not a convenient fiction of human resources managers. It is a real force and a source of energy for continuing excellence.

The negatives also must be addressed. When the team is not well-designed, if the support of top–down management is not sincere, the quality circle effort will backfire. Backfire means that the situation after failure is worse than it was before the effort was made. Training is important, but it must be targeted with clear goals in mind to be successful. Without training, or with poor training, the backfire is also plainly heard.

Technology interacts with quality in a variety of ways. New processes are better able to control tolerances at reasonable cost. Materials with new properties appear regularly. Control systems based on new technologies are able to function with increasing precision. Optical scanners and other kinds of technological sensory systems improve the inspection function. They can collect information on many dimensions and in greater detail than human inspectors. Computers using data-mining analysis can spot trends and problems faster than ever before allowing quick feedback and correction.

4-10 Industry Recognition of Quality

General MacArthur's effort to put Japanese industry back on its feet after World War II was incredibly successful. There are many people, both Japanese and American, who played a part in that effort. One whose name stands out is Dr. W. Edwards Deming.

Deming espoused the notion that firms with outstanding quality products could capture markets that otherwise would not be available to them. Such firms would be able to stay in business and create new jobs. He also believed that improvements in quality benefited consumers, workers, and producers alike.

Deming's 14 points, in Table 4-4, are representative of the broad systems view that he held, in which every aspect of business played a part in quality achievement.

The MacArthur Commission, which had been set up to deal with Japanese industry, called on Deming to help Japanese firms after World War II. The Japanese managers found Deming's ideas and his 14 points appealing. They listened to him, further developed many of his ideas, and consulted with him for years.

4-10a The Deming Prize

Deming Prize
Awarded since 1951 by JUSE (Japanese Union of Scientists and Engineers).

Since 1951, the Japanese Union of Scientists and Engineers (JUSE) has awarded the **Deming Prize** to companies (from any country) that have achieved outstanding quality performance. Deming, as an American statistician, advised Japanese manufacturers about various principles of quality including his work with Dr. Shewhart on statistical process

1 Create constancy of purpose toward improvement of product and service, with the aim to become competitive, stay in business, and provide jobs. **2** Adopt the new philosophy. We are in a new economic age. Live no longer with defective materials and poor workmanship. **3** Cease dependence on inspection. Require statistical evidence of process control from suppliers. **4** End the practice of awarding business on the basis of price. Reduce the number of suppliers. **5** Improve constantly and forever. Use statistical methods to detect the sources of problems. **6** Institute modern aids for training on the job. **7** Institute leadership. Improve supervision. **8** Drive out the fear to express ideas and report problems. **9** Break down barriers between departments. **10** Eliminate production quotas, slogans, and exhortations. **11** Create work standards that account for quality. **12** Institute a training program in statistical methods. **13** Institute a program for retraining people in new skills. **14** Put everybody in the company to work to accomplish the transformation. The transformation is everybody's job. Emphasize the previous 13 points every day.	**Table 4-4** Deming's 14 Points for Quality Achievement[10]

control (SPC). The Japanese felt that Deming's influence was so great that they named the prize for him.

The scope of this highly regarded prize is twofold. It emphasizes success with both SPC and QFD. This encompasses organizational efforts and participation of many employees in such activities as quality circles. In addition, the prize rewards companies with high standards and low defective rates.

Deming himself made a point of acknowledging the fact that service companies have won the award. "Service organizations have won the Deming Prize in Japan; for example, Takenaka Komuten, an architectural and construction firm, won the Deming Prize in 1979. They studied the needs of users (in offices, hospitals, factories, hotels, trains, subways)." He listed three other service firms that won the Deming Prize in successive years (1982, 1983, and 1984). Deming considered quality methodology essential for such diverse services as care of the aged and "perhaps even the U.S. mail."[11]

American companies that have won the Deming Prize are Florida Power and Light (FPL) and a Texas Instruments division located in Japan. Although FPL won the prize in 1989, the company's quality effort was restructured in 1990 because the initiative to win and the promotional celebration thereafter had created a bureaucracy, which was moving the company off the track of its real business.

4-10b The Malcolm Baldrige National Quality Award

During the 1980s, U.S. companies felt the power that Japanese competitors exercised because of their devotion to quality. A variety of government initiatives were undertaken in the United States to spur improvement of the quality of American products. The Malcolm Baldrige National Quality Award was conceived as a program to promote competitiveness based on high standards of quality management among U.S. companies.

One of the governmental initiatives was the passage of Public Law 100-107. This was the Malcolm Baldrige[12] National Quality Improvement Act, and it was signed into law on August 20, 1987. Thereby, the U.S. Congress established the **Baldrige Award** for those companies that lead in quality accomplishments.

Baldrige Award
Quality improvement act signed into law on August 20, 1987.

Year	Company	Location	Product or Service*
1988	Globe Metallurgical, Inc.	Cleveland, OH	(M) iron-based metal products
1988	Motorola, Inc.	Shaumburg, IL	(M) electronic equipment
1988	Westinghouse Commercial Nuclear Fuel Division	Pittsburgh, PA	(M) nuclear fuel
1989	Milliken and Co.	Spartanburg, SC	(M) textiles
1989	Xerox Corp.	Stamford, CT	(M) business products and systems
1990	Cadillac Motor Car Co.	Detroit, MI	(M) luxury automobiles
1990	Federal Express Corp.	Memphis, TN	(S) express delivery service
1990	IBM-Rochester	Rochester, MN	(M) computer systems and hard disk storage devices
1990	Wallace Co., Inc.	Houston, TX	(D) industrial pipe, valves, and fittings
1991	Marlow Industries, Inc.	Dallas, TX	(M) thermoelectric cooling devices
1991	Solectron Corp.	San Jose, CA	(M) printed circuit boards, systems assembly, and testing
1991	Zytec Corp.	Eden Prairie, MN	(M) computer power supplies; repair facility
1992	AT&T Transmission Systems	Morristown, NJ	(M) telecommunication transmission equipment
1992	AT&T Universal Card Services	Jacksonville, FL	(S) credit and long-distance calling card services
1992	Graniterock Co.	Watsonville, CA	(M) concrete and road treatments; also retail building materials
1992	Texas Instruments Defense Systems	Dallas, TX	(M) defense electronics equipment & Electronics Group
1992	The Ritz-Carlton Hotel Co.	Atlanta, GA	(S) hotel management
1993	Ames Rubber Corp.	Atlanta, GA	(M) rubber rollers for copiers
1993	Eastman Chemical Co.	Kingsport, TN	(M) chemicals, fibers, plastics
1994	AT&T Consumer Communications	Basking Ridge, NJ	(S) long-distance services (domestic and international)
1994	GTE Directories Corp.	Dallas, TX	(S) publishing and selling advertising for telephone directories
1994	Wainwright Industries, Inc.	St. Peters, MO	(M) stamped and machined metal products

* *M* = manufacturer, *S* = service provider, *D* = distributor
Source: Malcolm Baldrige National Quality Award—Profiles of Winners, 1988–1994.

Table 4-5

Malcolm Baldrige Award-Winning Companies (1988–1994)

The funding for the Baldrige Award comes in part from the Foundation for the Malcolm Baldrige National Quality Award. Donor organizations from private enterprise have succeeded in raising funds to permanently endow the award program. The National Institute of Standards and Technology (NIST), which is part of the U.S. Department of Commerce, manages the award program. The American Society for Quality Control (ASQC) assists in that management under contract to NIST.

In the first seven years (1988–1994), there were 22 Baldrige Awards (for an average of 3.14 per year). Six awards (27 percent) were given to service organizations (and one distributor). The award winners range in size. These 22 companies are listed in Table 4-5. There is a special small business category; the other two categories are manufacturers and service companies. There is a maximum of two winners per category, and only companies located in the United States can win. Judging is done by the Board of Examiners, which consists of leading experts from U.S. businesses and education, health care, and nonprofit organizations. For 2007, the board consists of about 540 members. Of these, 12 serve as Judges, approximately 100 serve as Senior Examiners, and the rest are Examiners.

The criteria for the Baldrige Award are representative of TQM. It is vital to recognize that TQM epitomizes a systems-oriented framework. The Baldrige Award criteria are

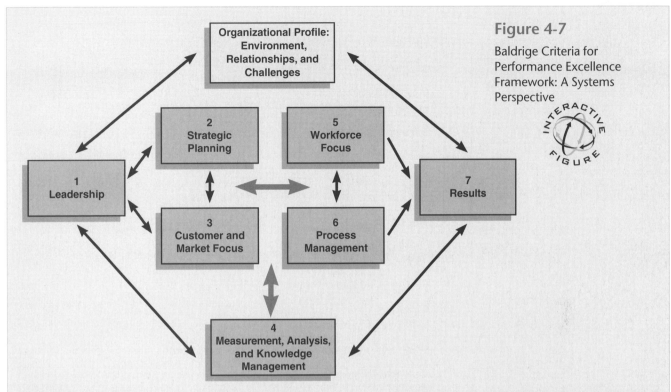

Source: Criteria for Performance Excellence 2007 (Harry S. Hertz, Director, Baldrige National Quality Program), National Institute of Standards and Technology, Technology Administration, Department of Commerce.

Figure 4-7

Baldrige Criteria for Performance Excellence Framework: A Systems Perspective

characterized by dynamic relationships, as shown in Figure 4-7. Seven core components span all aspects of quality and performance. They add up to the total score of 1,000 points, as shown in Figure 4-8.

In the next 12 years (1995–2006) there were 49 Baldrige Awards (for an average 4.1 per year). Ritz Carlton Hotels received a second Baldrige Award. A number of school systems received awards, as did healthcare-provider organizations. Growth in the average number of awards is evidence of increased interest in the process on the part of small and medium-size organizations. All award winners from 1995 through 2006 are listed in Table 4-6.

Award criteria change slightly from year to year, but the process is still representative of TQM. The change noted is that the criteria framework is increasingly systems-oriented.

Even a relatively cursory analysis of the point allocations indicates the breadth of perspective of the Baldrige approach. Note that results (outcomes) are 45 percent of the score. The emphasis is on management of quality, which is different from the Deming Prize, which highlights the process.

Applications for the Baldrige Award continue to increase. There were 49 applications in 2002, 60 in 2004, and 86 in 2006, which is a 15 percent growth rate per year from 2002 to 2006.

Source: http://www.quality.nist.gov.

The 2006 Malcolm Baldrige National Quality Award recipients are Premier, Inc., San Diego, California, for services; MESA Products, Inc., Tulsa, Oklahoma, for small businesses; and North Mississippi Medical Center, Tupelo, Mississippi, for health care.

Figure 4-8

2007 Criteria for Performance Excellence (for the Malcolm Baldrige Award)

2007 CRITERIA FOR PERFORMANCE EXCELLENCE—ITEM LISTING

Preface: Organizational Profile

P.1   Organizational Description
P.2   Organizational Challenges

2007 Categories and Items	Point Values
1.0 Leadership	**(120 pts.)**
1.1 Senior Leadership	(70 pts.)
1.2 Governance and Social Responsibilities	(50 pts.)
2.0 Strategic Planning	**(85 pts.)**
2.1 Strategy Development	(40 pts.)
2.2 Strategy Deployment	(45 pts.)
3.0 Customer and Market Focus	**(85 pts.)**
3.1 Customer and Market Knowledge	(40 pts.)
3.2 Customer Relationships and Satisfaction	(45 pts.)
4.0 Measurement, Analysis, and Knowledge Management	**(90 pts.)**
4.1 Measurement, Analysis, and Improvement of Organizational Performance	(45 pts.)
4.2 Management of Information, Information Technology, and Knowledge	(45 pts.)
5.0 Workforce Focus	**(85 pts.)**
5.1 Workforce Engagement	(45 pts.)
5.2 Workforce Environment	(40 pts.)
6.0 Process Management	**(85 pts.)**
6.1 Work Systems Design	(35 pts.)
6.2 Work Process Management and Improvement	(50 pts.)
7.0 Results	**(450 pts.)**
7.1 Product and Service Outcomes	(100 pts.)
7.2 Customer-Focused Outcomes	(70 pts.)
7.3 Financial and Market Outcomes	(70 pts.)
7.4 Workforce-Focused Outcomes	(70 pts.)
7.5 Process Effectiveness Outcomes	(70 pts.)
7.6 Leadership Outcomes	(70 pts.)
TOTAL POINTS	**(1,000 pts.)**

Source: Criteria for Performance Excellence 2007 (Harry S. Hertz, Director, Baldrige National Quality Program), National Institute of Standards and Technology, Technology Administration, Department of Commerce.

Year	Company	Location	Product or Service*
1995	Armstrong World Industries, Inc.	Lancaster, PA	(M) building products (home and commercial interiors)
1995	Corning, Inc.	Corning, NY	(M) telecommunications products (fiber optics)
1996	ADAC Laboratories	Milpitas, CA	(M) high-technology healthcare products
1996	Custom Research Inc.	Minneapolis, MN	(S) smart market research
1996	Dana Commercial Credit Corp.	Toledo, OH	(S) leasing and financial services
1996	Trident Precision Mfg. Inc.	Webster, NY	(M) sheet metal and electromechanical components (small business)
1997	3M Dental Products Div.	St. Paul, MN	(M) crown and bridge materials and adhesive
1997	Merrill Lynch Credit Corp.	Jacksonville, FL	(S) diverse line of credit products
1997	Solectron Corp., Inc.	Milpitas, CA	(M) electronics and supply chain consulting
1997	Xerox Business Services	Rochester, NY	(S) document outsourcing and consulting
1998	Boeing Airlift and Tanker Programs	St. Louis, MO	(M) C-17 Globemaster 111 airlifter
1998	Solar Turbines Inc.	San Diego, CA	(M) midrange industrial gas turbine systems
1998	Texas Nameplate Company, Inc.	Dallas, TX	(SB) info labels affixed to refrigerators, trucks
1999	STMicroelectronics, Inc., Region Americas	Carrollton, TX	(M) integrated circuits for consumer electronics, etc.
1999	BI	Minneapolis, MN	(S) performance improvement programs (small business)
1999	The Ritz-Carlton Hotel Company, LLC	Atlanta, GA	(S) luxury hotels worldwide
1999	Sunny Fresh Foods	Monticello, MN	(SB, M) further-processed egg products
2000	Dana Corporation—Spicer Driveshaft Division	Toledo, OH	(M) automotive drive shafts to global customer base; now Torque Traction Technologies
2000	KARLEE Company, Inc.	Garland, TX	(M) precision sheet metal and machined components
2000	Operations Management, Inc. (OMI, Inc.)	Greenwood Village, CO	(S) operation/maintenance of municipal water/wastewater systems
2000	Los Alamos National Bank	Los Alamos, NM	(SB) independent, full-service community banking
2001	Clarke American Checks, Inc.	San Antonio, TX	(M) digital printing; check reorder express
2001	Pal's Sudden Service	Kingsport, TN	(SB) quick-service restaurant (QSR); leadership in quality
2001	Chugach School District	Anchorage, AL	(E) school district is 22,000 square miles; 214 students, accessible only by aircraft
2001	Pearl River School District	Rockland Co., NY	(E) excellence in k–12 grade public school program
2001	University of Wisconsin–Stout	Menomonie, WI	(E) 27 undergraduate and 16 graduate degree programs
2002	SSM Health Care	St. Louis, MO	(HC) healthcare provider with automated information system
2002	Branch-Smith Printing Division	Fort Worth, TX	(SB) designing, printing, binding, and mailing
2002	Motorola Commercial, Government & Industrial	Schaumburg, IL	(M) two-way radio systems for fire, police, and public service Solutions Sector organizations
2003	Saint Luke's Hospital of Kansas City	Kansas City, MO	(HC) comprehensive teaching and referral; extreme cases
2003	Baptist Hospital, Inc.	Pensacola, FL	(HC) comprehensive health care system in FL Panhandle
2003	Community Consolidated School District 15	Palatine, IL	(E) K–8; 12,390 students; 35% above national average
2003	Stoner, Inc.	Quarryville, PA	(SB) specialized cleaners, lubricants and coatings

Table 4-6

Malcolm Baldrige Award-Winning Companies (1995–2006)

Year	Company	Location	Product or Service*
2003	Caterpillar Financial Services Corporation	Nashville, TN	(S) second largest captive-equipment lender in United States
2003	Boeing Logistics Support Systems	St. Louis, MO	(S) aircraft maintenance, cost reduction; aircrew training (was Aerospace Support)
2003	Medrad, Inc.	Indianola, PA	(M) develops, manufactures, and services medical devices
2004	Robert Wood Johnson Univ. Hosp. Hamilton	Hamilton, NY	(HC) acute care; services 350,000 residents of Hamilton
2004	Kenneth W. Monfort College of Business,	Greely, Co	(E) 1of 5 AACSB accredited undergraduate business degree Univ. of Northern CO programs in the United States
2004	Texas Nameplate Company, Inc.	Dallas, TX	(SB) custom nameplates to ID equipment; see also 1998
2004	The Bama Companies	Tulsa, OK	(M) develops, manufactures, frozen products served by QSRs, e.g., McDonalds
2005	Bronson Methodist Hospital	Kalamazoo, MI	(HC) inpatient/outpatient care in cardiology, orthopedics, surgery, oncology, etc.
2005	Richland College (RLC)	Dallas, TX	(E) two-year community college; continuing education to more than 20,000 students
2005	Jenks Public Schools (JPS)	Jenks, OK	(E) K–12; 9,000 students; top Academic Performance Index
2005	Park Place Lexus	Plano, TX, Grapevine, TX	(SB) sells/services Lexus with high CSI (client satisf. index)
2005	DynMcDermott Petroleum	New Orleans, LA	(S) manages/operates DOE's Strategic Petroleum Reserve Operations Co. (U.S. emergency oil stockpile)
2005	Sunny Fresh Foods, Inc. (SFF)–Cargill	Monticello, MN	(SB, M) further-processed egg products, see also 1999 subsidiary
2006	Premier, Inc.	San Diego, CA	(S) health care strategic alliance
2006	MESA Products, Inc.	Tulsa, OK	(SB) cathodic protection systems
2006	North Mississippi Medical Center	Tupelo, MS	(HC) largest rural hospital in the United States
2007	PRO-TEC Coating Co.	Leipsic, Ohio	(SB) coated sheet steel
2007	Mercy Health System	Janesville, Wisc.	(HC) three hospitals plus clinics
2007	Sharp HealthCare	San Diego, Calif.	(HC) four acute care and three specialty hospitals
2007	City of Coral Springs	Coral Springs, Fla.	(NP) nonprofit municipal corporation
2007	U.S. Army Armament Research, Development and Engineering Center (ARDEC)	Picatinny Arsenal, N.J.	(NP) nonprofit military R&D

* M = manufacturer, S = service provider, SB = small business, E = education, HC = health care, D = distributor
Source: Http://www.quality.nist.gov; see Web Exercise 2.

Table 4-6
(Continued)

Spotlight 4-1 Curt Reimann: Strengthening the Connection Between Operations Management and Organizational Performance via Baldrige Quality Award Criteria

An Interview and Discussion with Dr. Curt W. Reimann, Director (1987 – 1995,) Malcolm Baldrige National Quality Award, National Institute of Standards and Technology (NIST)

Dr. Reimann emphasizes that the Malcolm Baldrige National Quality Award has three basic purposes: to promote quality awareness; to recognize quality achievement; and to publicize successful quality strategies. "In simplest terms," he says, "the Award is intended to strengthen national competitiveness via improved business performance. Improvement occurs by way of creating and spreading a body of knowledge about quality and performance that helps connect processes and results." Originally open only to for-profit U.S. businesses, eligibility has been extended to not-for-profit organizations, including those in health care and education.

Reimann played an instrumental part in developing and annually revising the Award criteria. He points out that "the criteria seek to operationalize the basic concepts of quality and overall performance management and to make performance more assessable.

"Use of the criteria helps organizations to focus on key requirements for competitiveness and societal success. Product and service quality are critical but are by no means the only requirements. Other requirements that need to be integrated into an organization's response to the criteria include productivity, speed, innovation, human resource management, information systems, customer knowledge and relationships, business ethics, safety, and enviromental sustainability. These key requirements must be translated into specific operational terms and appropriate metrics."

Although the core purposes of the Award as well as its national competitiveness goal are the same as when the Award was created in 1987, the criteria continue to evolve toward integrated performance management. In today's global business environment, there is increasing focus on innovation, including innovation processes and practices. Reimann emphasizes that "the Award is about national learning; but learning about performance requirements and practices is pursuit of a moving target," he says, "so the criteria themselves are a key vehicle to capture such learning." In addition to criteria, conferences and case studies provide important avenues for sharing lessons learned. Also, many U.S. states and other nations, including Japan, have established awards based on the Baldrige model, further enhancing the learning and sharing.

Dr. Reimann believes that there should be more use of the Baldrige Award concepts in business schools. The concepts, he says, "are particularly important to operations management, which is now more significant, interesting, and challenging than ever before in business planning and decision making. The Award criteria can help students of operations management understand the larger strategic context for operations design and management, and to become familiar with emerging practices in performance measurement and assessment. Award criteria and case studies can help students bridge across business school disciplines and provide integrative capstone experiences."

A chemist by training, Dr. Reimann received his Ph.D. from the University of Michigan. Prior to becoming Baldrige Award Director, he was a scientific researcher and science manager at NIST* for 25 years. Since 1996, he has been a chaired professor at Tennessee Technological University, College of Business. He also provides services to NIST's Manufacturing Extension Partnership program and Goodwill Industries International.

Review Questions

1   What does the subtitle "Strengthening the Connection Between Operations Management and Organizational Performance via Baldrige Quality Award Criteria" mean?

2   What "body of knowledge" exists, and how does P/OM use it to promote improved business performance and strengthened national competitiveness?

3   Dr. Curt Reimann was Director of the Baldrige Quality Award from its inception (1987) until 1995. Dr. Reimann says "the (Baldrige Award) criteria continue to evolve toward integrated performance management." Let us call this IPM and answer the question, "What constitutes IPM?"

4   Present Director Dr. Harry Hertz says that the Baldrige Award criteria "help organizations respond to current challenges; (provide) openess and transparency in governance and ethics; (satisfy) the need to create value for customers and the business." Explain how so many good things can result from one award.

Spotlight 4-1 (Continued)

5 The Balanced Scorecard (BSC) is often mentioned as a parallel in criteria to the Baldrige Award. Read Spotlight 18-2 (Balanced Scorecards: Benchmarking the Strategy-Focused Organization) and go to http://www.balancedscorecard.org. Read the webpage "What is the Balanced Scorecard?" Then, answer the question, "In what way is the BSC similar to the Baldrige Award?"

*NIST (the National Institute of Standards and Technology) was founded in 1901. It is a nonregulatory federal agency within the U.S. Department of Commerce, Technology Administration, located in both Gaithersburg, Maryland, and Boulder, Colorado. NIST's mission is to develop and promote measurement, standards, and technology to enhance productivity, facilitate trade, and improve the quality of life. NIST carries out its mission using four programs: (1) the Baldrige National Quality Program (promotes performance excellence); (2) the NIST Laboratories (conducting research that advances the U.S. technology infrastructure); (3) Hollings Manufacturing Extension Partnership (a nationwide network of local centers offering technical and business assistance to smaller manufacturers); and (4) the Advanced Technology Program (accelerates the development of innovative technologies by cofunding R&D partnerships with the private sector). See http://www.nist.gov/public_affairs/general2.htm.

Sources: Discussions and correspondence with Dr. Curt W. Reimann, July 3, 2003, February 6, 2005, and April 15, 2007. Also, see "Quality and Performance Management in the 21st Century," Dr. Curt W. Reimann, *Mayberry Newsletter, Tennessee Technological University*, 1999.

Spotlight 4-2　Fail-Safe and Fault-Proof: The Poka-Yoke System

Poka-yoke is the Japanese name for technology specifically designed to prevent defectives from occurring. It is proactive technology used to stop accidents that cause quality problems with resultant costs and waste. This is in contrast to SPC (statistical process control), which is reactive, allowing control charts to indicate that something has gone awry. Poka-yoke aims at prohibiting the possibility of certain specific kinds of predicaments.

Shigeo Shingo developed the Poka-yoke system for problem-prevention. These Japanese words mean "mistake-proofing," which can be considered in the same vein as weatherproofing. In the case of weatherproofing, steps are taken to prevent wind, rain, cold and/or heat from entering the building. Such proofing systems are not perfect but they help. In the same way, Poka-yoke systems are neither perfectly fail-safe nor totally fault-proof.

A Poka-yoke system mechanically or electronically can carry out an early-warning inspection. When abnormalities arise with the process, information is fed back to people and/or machines trained and/or programmed to take immediate corrective action. Instantaneous feedback is a critical function because it allows corrections to be made before trouble develops.

Mistake-proofing technology follows mistake-eliminating methodology. This means that process design steps are taken to prevent problems from arising in the normal course of using the process. The process is designed to prevent errors such as mixing the wrong ingredients using the wrong amounts of materials, inserting a part the wrong way (see Figure 4-9), or even getting a hand smashed by putting it in the wrong place. Knock-aways function by pushing hands, arms, and feet out-of-the-way before a large punch press slams shut on whatever happens to be in its way.

Timing is of the essence. Poka-yoke systems may not be perfect at circumventing defectives created by equipment failures or human error, but they are the result of scenarios and simulations designed to examine everything that could go wrong. If a preventive means is in place, and an accident occurs, it is vital to redesign the Poka-yoke to handle the situation so that there is no possibility of repeating the error. Learning from mistakes is inherent to Poka-yoke. The goal of quality improvement is zero defects.

One option is for machines to be designed to shut down automatically in the presence of a problem. Sensors can often determine machine abnormalities faster than product variability. Technology allows machines that are acting erratically to shut themselves down. Many kinds of operations can be brought to a halt before defective product is produced. A sensor determines that temperature is too high. NASA space launches are replete with Poka-yoke technology to prevent liftoff-failures of any kind. Equipment is monitoring many components as well as launch performance.

Put in terms of SQC (statistical quality control) the goal of Poka-yoke is to take action before assignable causes are detected by a control chart. It requires inventiveness to configure a "mistake-proofing" system. In a case where defectives cannot be prevented, technology can mark the location

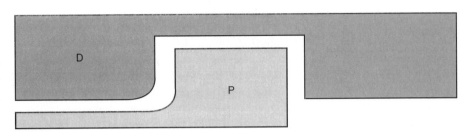

Figure 4-9

Piece P must be inserted into the die D with the curve to the left as shown. A defective is produced if the curve is to the right.

of defects so they can be repaired quickly. This might prevent having to shut down a machine before its regular maintenance time. Poka-yoke includes various warning systems like lights that flash and buzzers that sound when abnormalities or imbalances are detected.

Mechanical and electronic devices are not the only source of sensors. People are often able to sense process abnormalities. Training and technology combined with a sixth sense about anomalies can provide early warnings that something is not right.

Noting the condition of machines is not part of normal quality control practice. Technology awareness makes mistake prevention an area of opportunity for P/OM and process managers. Sensing devices, switches, and motion detectors are among the arsenal of mechanisms that are mentioned by Shingo in his book, which cites scores of examples of Poka-yoke.[13]

An example of a Poka-yoke device will help to highlight how defect-prevention works. Consider the curved piece of metal (P) in Figure 4-9

This curved metal piece is called a "blank" (i.e., an unstamped piece of metal). It is inserted in a fixture (D), which holds the piece while it is being stamped. There is a die in the press that will emboss the softer metal with an I.D. number when the press is closed. It is imperative that the embossing take place on the proper face of the metal piece.

Defectives are made whenever the piece (P) is inserted upside down. When correctly inserted, the curve on the left side of piece (P) matches the curve on the left side of the fixture (D), as shown in Figure 4-9. If incorrectly inserted, the curves do not match. Training is ineffective because the people who do this job are from a constantly shifting group of part-time workers.

Q. What technology has been used to prevent this defective from occurring?

A. Fixture D has been designed so that the curve of piece P matches the curve of figure D only when the embossing configuration is correct.

Review Questions

1 What is the Poka-yoke concept, and from what are these words derived?

2 How did Poka-yoke come about?

3 How is Poka-yoke accomplished?

4 What is the difference between Poka-yoke and accident prevention?

5 How does Poka-yoke differ from the fail-safe concept?

Sources: Wikipedia entry for Poka-yoke; also, Nikkan Kogyo Shimbun, Ltd. *Poka-Yoke: Improving Product Quality By Preventing Defects.* Productivity Press, 1987 (Japanese) 1988 (English); also: *Zero Quality Control: Source Inspection in the Poka-Yoke System* by Shigeo Shingo. English translation © 1986 by Productivity Press, Inc., P.O. Box 13390, Portland, OR.

Summary

The reason that better quality is strategically important is explained. TQM—the systems management approach to quality—is the way to obtain better quality. Chapter 4 states the case that before better quality is obtained, quality has to be defined. There is a difference in the way that consumers and producers think about quality. Various dimensions of quality are explored. One of many is the warranty policies that companies offer. Another is the kind of services that is given. How international standards are set is discussed, including U.S., international ISO 9000, Japanese, and other quality standards. The costs of quality are explored, including the costs of prevention, appraisal, and failure. Control of output quality is not possible without a feedback system, which is explained. Mapping to understand quality is demonstrated by describing how the House of Quality (HOC) and quality function deployment (QFD) are related. Pros and cons of quality circles are examined. Prizes and awards for best quality are detailed.

Two Spotlight feature boxes conclude this chapter. These boxes illustrate important applications of the material in the chapter. Spotlight 4-1 shows the connection between quality management excellence and the way an organization performs. Dr. Curt W. Reimann builds a bridge between what industry does and what business schools teach. This spotlight delivers an important and complex message.

Spotlight 4-2: Fail-Safe and Fault-Proof: The Poka-Yoke System is a revelation of what can be done to improve process performance in a myriad of circumstances that include manufacturing, health care, education, transportation, and entertainment. Poka-yoke principles decrease unnecessary mistakes without violating any ethical rules.

Key Terms

Acceptance sampling methods (p. 120)	Japanese Industrial Standard Z8101 (p. 117)
Action learning (p. 125)	Lifetime value (LTV) of customers (p. 121)
Baldrige Award (p. 127)	Mean time between failures (MTBF) (p. 111)
Costs of failures (p. 121)	Product callbacks (p. 121)
Costs of quality (p. 118)	Quality circles (QCs) (p. 126)
Deming prize (p. 126)	Quality function deployment (QFD) (p. 125)
Detailing (p. 120)	Six-sigma (p. 120)
Dimensions of quality (p. 108)	Taguchi methods (p. 119)
Drift-decay quality phenomenon (p. 110)	Tolerance limits (p. 119)
Extreme quality achievement (p. 120)	Total quality management (TQM) (p. 106)
House of Quality (HOQ) (p. 124)	Variety (p. 114)
ISO 9000 series (p. 117)	Zero defects (p. 122)

Review Questions

1 What is the role of quality in strategic planning?
2 What is the competitive role of quality and why is it important?
3 What is TQM and why is it important for attaining better quality?
4 What are the differences between consumer and producer definitions for quality?
5 How does the systems approach apply to the following statement: *Quality—like a chain—is betrayed by its weakest link.*
6 Discuss the statement *Although the name TQM may be viewed by some as faddish, the fundamental concept is not.*
7 What quality dimensions apply to the software industry?
8 Set down appropriate quality dimensions for a hybrid automobile.
9 What problem exists because quality standards can age?
10 Explain P/OM's relationship with market research.
11 Explain how consistency of conformity translates into low reject rates.

12   Discuss the strengths and weaknesses of quality circles. Are they similar to student cohort work groups?
13   What are the ways to reduce the cost of detailing?
14   Explain what the House of Quality does and how it works.
15   Describe how QFD functions.
16   What prize competitions exist for quality and why are these prizes given?

Problems Section

Note: This section has various problems that can be formulated and solved using QuantMethods Production/Operations Management software (QMpom). The appropriate model categories are indicated for each problem.

1   The costs of quality are given by the following equations:

$$C_a = 100D + 1500$$
$$C_p = -50D + 6300$$
$$C_f = De^{0.5D}$$

where:

C_a is the cost of appraisal,
C_p is the cost of prevention, and
C_f is the cost of failure.

Note that D is the percent defectives and $0 \leq D \leq 100$.
Determine the total cost of quality when there are no defectives. $D = 0$ and product quality is perfect.

2   Given the information in Problem 1, determine the total cost of quality when $D = 90$. No company could stay in business with $D = 90$, as will be apparent from the calculations.

3   Given the information in Problem 1, determine the total cost of quality when $D = 0$, 10, and 15. Plot all of the points.

4   Using the information in Problem 1, comment on the shape and position of these cost of quality curves.

5   Using the information in Problem 1, is there a minimum total cost? What is it?

6   Assume that the cost of appraisal is the same no matter what the value of D.
Can this situation be explained in a rational way?
Calculate the minimum total cost of quality with appraisal costs removed.

7   Make a list of the variables that should be included in a model for a rational warranty policy for each of these four products. Develop a specific warranty policy.
  Using the QMpom module called Quality Control Models (Pareto Analysis, Histograms, and Fishbone) will facilitate solving the following five situations.

  a. Automobile (specify the type and cost)
  b. Four-pack of regular lightbulbs (specify the type and cost)
  c. Four-pack of CFL (compact flourescent lamps)
  d. Something that breaks easily
  e. Something that is highly unlikely to break down

8   How should responsibility for quality be positioned within and throughout the U.S. government? Should there be a Department of Quality? Relate this discussion to both products and services. Then, relate this discussion to the quality of safety and security.

9   Develop an HOQ-type matrix for the Computer Laptop Company, which manufactures and markets laptops for the mid- to low-price range market such as students in college. Label the rows with the customers' needs and label the columns with the properties of the product. Consider customer service to be an important requirement.
  Using the QMpom module called Quality Control Models (Pareto Analysis, Histograms, and Fishbone) will facilitate solving the customer service goal.

10 The tolerance limits for the lead in the mechanical pencil are (0.5 ± 0.05). What tolerance limits should be specified for the tube in the pencil into which the lead is inserted? Discuss the quality problems that are related to this issue. Does it make sense to go back to the operations managers of the company that makes the lead to ask them what it would take to get tighter tolerances?

11 The quality feedback system informs the controller about the error term: $(q - s) = \pm \in$. The controller takes corrective action based on $(\pm \in)$. When the system is in equilibrium, $(q - s) = 0$ and no corrective action is warranted. Assume that the standard is s = 2. The controller's correction of q is $\partial(\pm \in_t) = \theta \in_t = -(0.5) \in_t$. In the following case, the value of q, which is regularly 2, has just jumped to 3. Show how the quality controller corrects the production process. Note: The table provides early guidance and suggests a way to organize calculations.

T	q	s	$\in_t$	$-(0.5)\in_t$	$q - (0.5)\in_t$
1	2.0	2.0	0	0	2
2	3.0	2.0	1	−0.5	3 − (0.5)
3	2.5				

Note: Corrective action is taken on the last value of q in column 2. This produces changes to q as shown by $q - (0.5) \in_t$ in column 6.

   Fill out the table to $t = 5$. Explain what is happening. How would a θ-value of –0.3 behave? How would a θ-value of –0.7 behave? Discuss.

12 Given the information in Problem 11, assume that the standard is s = 2. Also, the correction made by the controller is $-(1/2)(\pm \in)$. The value of q, which is regularly 2, has just fallen to 1. Show how the quality controller corrects the production process.

T	q	s	$\in_t$	$-(0.5)\in_t$	$q - (0.5)\in_t$
1	2.0	2.0	0	0	2
2	1.0	2.0	−1	0.5	1 + (0.5)
3	1.5				

Fill out the table to $t = 5$. Explain what is happening. How does this situation differ from that in Problem 11? How would $\theta = -0.3$ behave? What about $\theta = -0.7$? Discuss.

Practice Quiz

1 The difference between producers' and consumers' quality concepts is best described by which of the following statements?

   a. Consumers like products that they perceive have high quality at low prices, which translates into good value. Producers like products with high margins, which may result from high prices and low costs.
   b. Producers believe that by conforming to blueprint specifications (which provide consistency of product qualities), consumers award top quality ratings to such products.
   c. Consumers define quality by choosing products that please them. Producers define quality in terms of conformance, which means consistently meeting their own product specifications.
   d. Consumers are not all alike, which means that quality is a variable that depends on the market segment. Producers select the quality of their products to appeal to the largest market segments.
   e. There is no difference between producers' and consumers' quality concepts.

2 P/OM's most important role in developing TQM (total quality management) is to

   a. bring process knowledge to the table.
   b. show everyone how each person in the company impacts quality and what each of them can do to improve quality.
   c. provide leadership company-wide for constant improvement.
   d. keep records of all defectives that occur and their causes.
   e. reengineer the system as soon as competitors bring out a new product.

3 Listed among quality dimensions are the "ilities." These include

   a. possibilities.
   b. probabilities.
   c. facilities.
   d. reliabilities.
   e. impossibilities.

4 Human factors are important quality dimensions. These include consideration of

   a. safety and comfort.
   b. the ergonomics of variety.

    c.   effects of irrationalities.

    d.   nonfunctional quality factors.

    e.   aesthetics and timing.

5   Which of the following statements is incorrect?

    a.   ISO 9000 explains the ISO system.

    b.   ISO 9001 applies to firms that are involved with production.

    c.   ISO 9002 applies to firms that act as inspection agents.

    d.   ISO 9004 serves as a guide to the Japanese Industrial Standard Z8101.

    e.   ANSI/ASQC standards Q90–Q94 are equivalent to ISO 9000 standards.

6   The method of the costs of quality provided an economic business model that could permit a company to allocate its quality budget in an optimal way. Assume you own a seafood restaurant and want to apply the cost model to your business. Which allocation would you choose?

    a.   prevention, 10%; inspection, 15%; failure, 75%

    b.   prevention, 10%; inspection, 40%; failure, 50%

    c.   prevention, 20%; inspection, 25%; failure, 55%

    d.   prevention, 30%; inspection, 40%; failure, 30%

    e.   prevention, 40%; inspection, 50%; failure, 10%

7   What does the quality control (input–output) feedback model signify? Which of the following statements is incorrect?

    a.   The (input–output) electronic control system consists of a monitor and a control unit. The latter can adjust the production process to conform to specific standards.

    b.   The quality control feedback system can operate on at least one dimension of production output. Control systems can be applied to more than one variable.

    c.   Mapping models (such as the House of Quality model) provide standards for many quality dimensions that can serve as benchmarks for the monitor-control feedback system.

    d.   Feedback models provide powerful means for mapping quality systems. Therefore, it pays to create a feedback model before building appropriate mapping models (such as the House of Quality mappings).

    e.   Quality function deployment allows everyone (in the HOQ) to be consulted about where it pays to install a feedback control system.

8   Industry recognition of quality takes on many forms, including prizes and awards. Which of the following statements is incorrect?

    a.   The Deming Prize has been given by JUSE (Japanese Union of Scientists and Engineers) since 1951 to companies from any country that has an outstanding record of quality performance.

    b.   The Malcolm Baldrige National Quality Award was established in 1987 by the U.S. Congress for recognition of outstanding quality achievement. It is awarded to many categories of companies, but they must all be located in the United States.

    c.   The Sterling Award (see http://www.floridasterling.com) has been given to 52 organizations from 1992 through 2007 by the governor of the state of Florida. It is awarded for significant improvement and achievement of performance excellence. The Sterling criteria are based on the Baldrige Award criteria.

    d.   EFQM has been awarding the European Quality Awards (EQA) since 1992 to high-performing organizations in Europe. Award assessors come from a pool of senior managers and top academics in Europe. "The European Quality Award sits at the pinnacle of dozens of regional and national quality awards." In 2001, the committee wrote that they were shocked to find that no big company qualified for the prize. This was a wakeup call because their prize standards are based on the Baldrige Award and the Deming Prize in Japan. Since that date many prize winners have been recognized. See http://www.efqm.org.

    e.   In the United States, the National Institute of Standards and Technology (NIST) and the American Society for Quality Control (ASQC); in Europe, EFQM; and in Japan, the JUSE, provide prizes and awards to encourage companies from abroad to relocate to their own region of the world. They have been very successful in doing this.

9   The scoring models used by the Baldrige Award Committees are

    a.   first benchmarked against a House of Quality model.

    b.   based on pure numbers derived from ratios where the quality dimensions such as innovation and leadership cancel out.

    c.   regularly updated by the U.S. Department of Commerce to reflect new knowledge.

d. combinations of numbers using the products of the powers.

e. reflections of the personal opinions of the Baldrige Board of Examiners.

10 Dr. W. Edwards Deming was influential in helping Japanese industry reestablish itself after the destruction of World War II. Deming helped Japanese industry become the benchmark leader for quality practices. Deming's 14 points capture the essence of his principles for quality achievement. Which one of the following principles is not part of the 14 points?

a. Reduce the number of suppliers.

b. Improve supervision and institute leadership.

c. Start training in statistical methods.

d. Use instinct to detect problems.

e. Cease dependence on inspection.

Additional Readings

Arthur, Jay. *Lean Six Sigma Demystefied: A Self-Teaching Guide*. McGraw-Hill Book Co., 2007.

Bounds, G., L. Yorks, M. Adams, and G. Ranney. *Beyond Total Quality Management*. McGraw-Hill, Inc., 1994.

Crosby, Philip B. *Quality Is Free (The Art of Making Quality Certain)*. McGraw-Hill, 1979. Also by Philip Crosby, *Zero Defects: Myth and Reality*. 2001 (available from the bookstore at http://www.philipcrosby.com).

Deming, W. Edwards. *Out of the Crisis*. MIT Center for Advanced Engineering Study, 1986.

Deming, W. Edwards. *The New Economics for Industry, Government, Education*. MIT Center for Advanced Engineering Study, 1993.

Dodge, Harold F., and Harry G. Romig. *Sampling Inspection Tables*, 2e. John Wiley & Sons, Inc., 1944.

Gygi, Craig, Neil DeCarlo, Bruce Williams, and Foreward by Stephan R. Covey. *Six Sigma for Dummies*. Hoboken, NJ: Wiley Publishing, 2005.

Hauser, John R., and Don Clausing. "House of Quality." *Harvard Business Review* (May–June 1988): 63–67.

King, Bob. *Better Designs in Half the Time*. Methuen, MA: Goal/QPC, 1989.

Marsh, S., J. W. Moran, S. Nakui, and G. Hoffherr. *Facilitating and Training in QFD*. Methuen, MA: Goal/QPC, 1991.

Pande, Peter S., and Lawrence Holpp. *What Is Six Sigma?* McGraw-Hill, 2001.

Pande, Peter S., Robert P. Neuman, and Roland R. Cavanagh. *The Six Sigma Way: How GE, Motorola, and Other Top Companies Are Honing Their Performance*. McGraw-Hill, 2000.

Notes

1. See, for example, D. Savageau. *Places Rated Almanac*. IDG Books Worldwide, Inc., 2000.

2. *Harvard Business Review* (November–December 1987).

3. "'Quality Fade': China's Great Business Challenge." *Knowledge @ Wharton*, July 25–August 7, 2007. See knowledge@wharton.upenn.edu.

4. Harold F. Dodge and Harry G. Romig. *Sampling Inspection Tables*, 2e. John Wiley & Sons, Inc., 1959. These tables specified the parameters for efficient sampling plans that could be used to accept or reject production lots.

5. Philip B. Crosby. *Quality Is Free* (The Art of Making Quality Certain). McGraw-Hill, 1979.

6. American Airlines Flight 965 was the worst air disaster of 1995. This preventable accident resulted from a systems failure. The navigation computer locked on "R" but that designation of a guidance beacon had been changed from Cali to Bogata without sufficient notification. See the Wikipedia entry for American Airlines Flight 965.

7. Successful popularization of the HOQ method resulted from the article by John R. Hauser and Don Clausing, which appeared in the *Harvard Business Review* (May–June 1988): 63–73. Also, a book about the HOQ was written by Bob King. *Better Designs in Half the Time*. Methuen, MA: Goal/QPC, 1989.

8. International TechneGroup Incorporated of Milford, Ohio, has software called *QFD/Capture*, which permits participants from all contributing functions to enter data and analyze its impact on quality.

9. QFD was developed in Japan in the late 1960s by Professors Shigeru Mizuno and Yoji Akao. With the help of Professor Akao, the QFD Institute was founded in 1993. It is located in Ann Arbor, MI. See http://www.qfdi.org.

10. Dr. Deming continuously fine-tuned his 14 points. As a result, there are many variations of them. Table 4-4 was one of his final versions. It had been prepared for Dr. Deming's Quality Seminars, which were given at Columbia University's Graduate School of Business in the mid-1990s.

11. W. Edwards Deming. *The New Economics for Industry, Government, Education*. MIT Center for Advanced Engineering Study, 1993.

12. See http://www.quality.nist.gov.

13. Shingo, Shigeo. *Zero Quality Control: Source Inspection in the Poka-Yoke System*. English translation © 1986 by Productivity Press, Inc., Norwalk, CT.

Enrichment Activity 4: A Scoring Model for Comparing Alternative Gas Station Designs (Based on the HOQ)

Two scoring matrices based on the HOQ are shown in Figures EA4-1A and EA4-1B. Each matrix rates the qualities of two different business models for a gas service station.

Business Model	Fast Service	Limited Personnel				
A	Importance Weights	Transaction Speed	Speedpass RFID at Pump	No Food	Little Merchandise	TOTAL
Fast Service	6	9	6	0	1	96
Easy Payment	4	1	6	0	2	36
Personal Service	5	1	1	0	1	15
Merchandise	2	1	2	0	2	10
Food	3	0	0	0	0	0
TOTAL	20	65	69	0	23	157

Figure EA4-1A

Matrix A: Rating the Customer Satisfaction Qualities of a Gas Station Designed for Speed of Service

Customer wants (rows) are assigned a measure for their relative importance (see column labeled Importance Weights). Columns reflect the design of the service station. Station A emphasizes speed and has an RFID (Speedpass type) reader but no food and few items for sale in the store. Station B emphasizes service. It has hot and cold food and a variety of types of merchandise. The weights are the same for both kinds of stores because

Business Model	All Service	Helpful Personnel				
B	Importance Weights	Transaction Speed	Credit Card Reader Pump & Store	Hot/Cold Food	Ample Merchandise	TOTAL
Fast Service	6	3	3	2	2	60
Easy Payment	4	1	3	4	3	44
Personal Service	5	1	6	7	8	110
Merchandise	2	1	7	3	8	38
Food	3	0	8	9	2	57
TOTAL	20	29	98	96	86	309

Figure EA4-1B

Matrix B: Rating the Customer Satisfaction Qualities of a Gas Station Designed for High-Level Personal Attention (Service with a Smile), Having Hot and Cold Food and Ample Merchandise

they were derived by market research to reflect what customers consider to be important at the gas station.

At each intersection there is a number that reflects how well the design of the gas station (column) delivers what the customer wants in that row. Put another way, each cell reflects how well that aspect of station design satisfies customer needs.

Supplier X						
	Importance of Need	**Own Delivery Trucks**	**Inspected Before Delivery**	**Factory Stage**	**Percent of the Business**	**TOTAL**
Quality	5	4	7	3	6	
Delivery	3	9	2	3	2	
Prices	4	3	5	5	7	
TOTAL						

Supplier Y						
	Importance of Need	**Own Delivery Trucks**	**Inspected Before Delivery**	**Factory Stage**	**Percent of the Business**	**TOTAL**
Quality	5	2	6	7	1	
Delivery	3	1	3	6	1	
Prices	4	5	2	5	8	
TOTAL						193

Figure EA4-2

Comparing the Qualities of Suppliers X and Y

Two matrices permit comparison of the total satisfaction delivered by the alternative designs. For all numbers, the larger they are, the more important they are considered to be. Row values are multiplied by the column weights.

There is always concern about additive scoring models. If apples and oranges are treated as if they were the same, it is because *fruit* is the common measure of interest.

The first column of Matrix A in Figure EA4-A has a sum value of 65, which indicates that transaction speed (fast pumping) is an appreciated quality of this station. Customers also like the use of an RFID (fast) credit card reader. It lets customers make payments without waiting for station personnel. That column gets a 69. No food provides zero quality and little merchandise totals to 23.

Fast service (weight of 6) contributes 96 points or 61 percent of the total of 157. In Matrix B's station design, the credit card reader at the pump and in the store contributes 98 points to the quality total of 309. Hot and cold food provides another 96 points. B is favored by almost two to one (309:157).

A different scoring model is introduced in Chapter 11, Section 11-8. It uses only multiplication and is therefore immune to the problem of adding apples and oranges. It requires much more computation and is still subject to the criticism of "where did those weights come from?"

Enrichment Challenges 4

The Pin Company has a supplier rating system, which is based on mapping the company needs for quality, fast and reliable delivery, and low prices against the capability of the suppliers to satisfy these needs.

The two matrices in Figure EA4-2 present the data that have been collected for Suppliers X and Y. Make a comparison of X and Y and choose the preferred supplier. Explain the choice.

Note: The buyer's wants have been given Importance of Need weights in the first column. The properties of Suppliers X and Y are:

1 *Own delivery trucks*—Relates to how many trucks each supplier leases or owns.
2 *Inspected before delivery*—Relates to the procedures used by the supplier to check the quality of outgoing shipments.
3 *Factory stage*—Relates to the kind of equipment that the supplier uses to make the products where state-of-the-art or ahead of it gets the highest rating.
4 *Percent of the business*—Refers to how many other customers each supplier has and what percentage of the supplier's total business the Pin Company represents. The best percentage is considered to be about 10 percent.

Designing Processes

Figure PT2-1 Process Capabilities Are Critical; Management Uses
Projects to Create Them

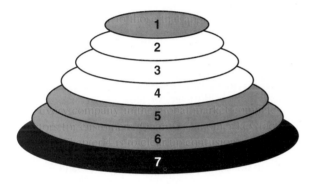

1. Product Design

2. Process Design

3. Project Management

4. Organizational Support

5. Technological Change

6. Competitive Marketplace

7. Sustainability: Ethics,
   Environment, and Security

Part 2 is a bridge that connects the strategic planning of Part 1 with the tactical planning of Part 3. There is a great deal of back and forth between levels 1 and 2. At the same time, at level 3, product line and process projects are ongoing. Product and process designing require project management. Figure PT2-1 shows the strong linkage of levels 2 and 3 with 4.

Chapter 5 (Process Configuration Strategies) emphasizes understanding the characteristics of various process configurations. Processes are classified by types, e.g., *job shop* and *flow shop*. Differences by type convey important strategic meaning. For example, a high-volume process will differ from a custom process in many ways that must be understood by both strategists and tacticians.

Chapter 6 (Process Analysis and Redesign) explains flow-charting methods to organize information. Using these methods enables process designers to analyze and improve the configuration. Application of these methods is part of the project.

Chapter 7 (Quality Assurance) examines various quality improvement methods that apply to both human skills and technology. The operations of every process have two kinds of variability—that gets in the way of perfect consistency. It is crucial to know how to deal with causes of variation. Chapter 7 is a *must* for process designers.

Chapter 8 (Management of Technology (MOT)) explores the technological components of a process. Chapter 9 (Teamwork Planning Requires Job Design) investigates the human skill inputs to a process. Organizing and managing technological and human requirements demands understanding the way that they are interrelated. Management of technology (MOT) and Human Resource Management (HRM) are entire course topics in their own right. However, good process design requires attention to such matters.

Chapter 9 is discussed together with Chapter 8 in the paragraph above.

Chapter 10 (Supply Chain Capacity Planning) tackles the linkage connecting many processes. Goods and services move between suppliers and from producers to distributors to retailers and ultimate customers. The complex network is called the supply chain, but it is really a demand chain that pays its suppliers for fast delivery of what it needs. Design issues for this process include how much capacity to install and what to do about bottlenecks.

Chapter 11 (Facilities Planning: Location and Layout) decides what kind of building is needed. Where to locate is constrained by rent or buy or build considerations. Facilities require more planning than might be immediately obvious. Facility decisions affect process designs in many ways.

There is a strong connection between levels 2, 3 and 4 with levels 1, 5 and 6.

Process Configuration Strategies

5

c h a p t e r

Chapter 5 concentrates on the nature of three major process configuration strategies. These are the custom shop, the job shop, and the flow shop. Other process configurations including flexible process systems and intermittent flow shops are explained. Projects are unique work configurations treated in Part 4, which deals with "Changing the System."

Processes are differentiated with respect to assembly (synthetic), disassembly (analytic), and combinations of putting things together and taking them apart. By understanding the type of process, managers can do a better job. Thus, work configurations and process types are classified in a useful way for operational purposes (design, analysis, and improvement).

After reading this chapter, you should be able to:

- Distinguish between processes and work configurations.
- Explain the three major kinds of work configuration.
- Discuss why maintenance of equipment is a process.
- Explain how simulation can be used to improve a process.
- Distinguish between synthetic and analytic processes.
- Reveal why it is essential to chart every process step.
- Compare custom shops, job shops, batch work, and flow shops.
- Define cycle time and use it to design a flow shop.
- Explain flexible process systems.
- Relate all of the work configurations with respect to volume and variety.

The Systems Viewpoint

Strategies are more likely to be successful if they have been formulated using the systems approach. An equivalent statement is that strategies are more likely to be successful if they have been formulated using all of the factors that are relevant to their success. The systems approach allows the process choice to be based upon what the competition is doing, the state of technology, what the customer will like, the costs of production, the control of quality, and the ability to schedule delivery. Note the systems implications of sourcing, which are detailed in this chapter. First, however, focus on processes.

The process is composed of subprocesses. Each is like an input–output system that is connected to another input–output system. Each is a link of the means–end chain, and a process in its own right. The connected links form a chain of conversions. The chain is the total process.

Although the parts of the process can be studied individually, the systems approach ultimately always focuses on the whole. The systems approach often uncovers relationships in one part of the chain that affect relationships in other parts of the chain.

Before an appropriate process design can be fashioned, it is essential to have a common understanding of what a process is, and be able to define the term.

Strategic Thinking

Interrelated systems components are driven by strategic issues that underlie the purpose of the process. The strategic drivers for the process are the rationales for the transformations. The sequences of linked, input–output systems form process chains to make the product and deliver services. Strategic decisions must translate cost, quality, and delivery requirements into specific methods used to realize the objectives. That is why process configurations link strategy with tactics.

5-1 What Is a Process?

A **process** is a series of activities or steps that are goal-oriented. The *APICS Dictionary* defines **process steps** as: "The operations or stages within the manufacturing cycle required to transform components into intermediates or finished goods."[1]

There is no reason to limit this definition to manufacturing. It applies equally well to service functions. The steps of the process are specific and concrete. They tell how to make things like air conditioners, or cars; how to fill things like cans with beans or tubes with toothpaste; or how to provide medical or travel services.

Process steps often require the use of science and technology. Chemistry may be required to make the product. Instructions for what steps to take are varied; they may be recipes for making bread or blueprints for making the breadbox. Processes are named for what they make, like cheese, auto assembly, and research reports.

5-1a Work Configurations Defined

It is important to distinguish between processes, which are the steps and activities required to make the product, and work configurations that help accomplish production. There are many kinds of processes, but only a few basic types of **work configuration**. The work configuration is the physical setup used to make the product. It is the arrangement of people and equipment and the way materials and work in process flow from place to place in the plant, or in the office.

As noted, the type of activity flow used for the process is called the work configuration. There are six fundamental kinds of work configuration:

- Custom shops—for "one of a kind" items
- Job shops—for batch processing
- Flow shops—for serialized processing
- Flexible manufacturing systems—for rapid model changeovers
- Continuous flow processing—for nonstop systems
- Projects—for developing new structures and systems

Projects are a type of work configuration that is used for start-up purposes, such as for major new undertakings like building a bridge. The focus of this chapter is on processes for production systems that are up and running, so projects will be treated in Part 4 (Changing the System). Continuous flow processing will be discussed, but because it is very specialized and highly engineered, it will not receive the kind of attention the other five categories receive.

The kind of work configuration that is used is a function of volume and variety. Large volumes of identical items are not treated in the same way as small volumes of many different kinds of items. Work configurations constitute a main theme of this chapter.

The process steps must be fully specified. This means that the technology of the process is explicit and the work configuration for carrying out the process is explained in detail. This level of specification is absolutely essential for process design and control. No technicalities can be ignored.

The maintenance program for jet engines is a process. Inadvertently, an O-ring was left out of a jet engine on a 727 that plunged 20,000 feet before the pilot could shut down that engine and safely level out. Tragedy was averted and the same lesson was learned

Process
Series of activities or steps required to transform materials and deliver services.

Process steps
Stages of the *process*.

Work configuration
Type of production process.

Project
Work configuration that is used for start-up purposes with major new undertakings.

© 2008 Jupiterimages Corporation

Nuclear power plants require total process control, which necessitates that P/OM inputs be included at every level of their management. As of 2007, France produced 78.1 percent of its total electricity needs by nuclear generation. Statistics for Lithuania, Belgium, Sweden, the United States, and the United Kingdom (photo) were 72.3, 54.4, 48.0, 19.4, and 18 percent, respectively. Because of design improvements and better oversight by competent P/OM process experts, U.S. numbers are likely to increase significantly in the future. Reluctance to go nuclear has been based on trouble at the Three Mile Island nuclear reactors in Pennsylvania and Chernobyl in Russia. (See http://www.pbs.org/wgbh/amex/three and http://www.uic.com.au/nip22.htm.)

Simulations

Pretend runs of various product and process design options.

again: In a process, each part has a place and each step of the process must be taken correctly every time the process is used. In this case, the lives of many people depended upon rigorous adherence to process specifications.

Note that the concept of "inadvertent behavior" is totally unacceptable for proper process management. There can be no surprises. Accidents are inadmissible. Haphazard performance must be designed out of the process. Extensive use of checklists or other means of achieving conformance are mandatory. Further, the pilot's training included situations of this kind so that disaster could be averted. The maintenance process had failed, but the flying process was able to handle the contingency.

The concept of "normal accidents," as explained in Charles Perrow's 1984 book *Normal Accidents: Living with High-Risk Technologies* (reissued in 1999 by Princeton University Press) is not reasonable within the framework of the operations management mandate. The belief that technological complexity renders accidents inevitable overlooks the notion that "nothing is left to chance" and the quality objective (e.g., Phil Crosby) to achieve zero defects. This topic became popular in the press during the Y2K era of anxiety as the millennium year 2000 approached. ("Is Complexity Interlinked with Disaster? Ask on Jan.1," *The New York Times*, December 11, 1999.) The answer on January 1, 2002, was that Y2K had come and gone without problems. On the other hand, movies had anticipated September 11, 2001, but they were not believed to be a real possibility. In retrospect, operations management could have helped to prevent 9/11. P/OM has now been enlisted to prevent future incidents of similar destructive scope.

5-1b Process Simulations

Simulations are "pretend" runs of what might occur using models of processes. For example, pilot training uses simulations of contingencies to eliminate the serious repercussions of unintentional errors. Process simulations are imitation processes that mimic the real-world process. Contingency planning requires first identifying *things that might happen* before addressing *what might be done* to avoid damage and disaster.

The board game Monopoly® is a simulation of real estate transactions. People buy and sell real estate. Some make money while others lose it. Except for the latter fact, Monopoly is not a very accurate simulation of real estate dealings. Another example of a simulation is "rotisserie (or fantasy) baseball," where the performance of real players is used to simulate the behavior of fictitious teams on which the betting is fierce.[2]

Simulations are successfully used for training, testing, and analyzing. Factory processes and production schedules can be created and improved. Under controlled conditions, contingencies artificially arise that allow individuals to practice remedial actions. This learning takes place without being involved in actual crises.

Computer simulations have been used to test the design of the Boeing 787. In this way, the plane has been flown before it is built. It is subjected to engine failures and turbulence beyond anything that will ever be experienced in actual flight. Simulation modeling also is used for production scheduling and inventory control. It is a powerful means of studying the performance of the system as a whole—which is in keeping with the systems approach. Simulation is one of the best methods available for designing good processes. It is a methodology that embodies the systems approach, and it is especially effective where nothing should be left to chance.

The process for flying an airplane is detailed. The manuals for procedures are filled with information. All of the controls have to be coordinated. Each procedure for taking off and landing must be precisely stated and checked. Maintenance processing is intricate. Every wire, chip, and instrument in the Boeing 787 must do its job correctly. Onboard instrumentation must call attention to problems and flaws. Designing the planes and then building them are two more processes. Four processes are mentioned in this paragraph, and all of them use simulation to improve the performance of that process.

5-2 Classifying the Process

The definition of a process must be able to encompass the great diversity of processes such as Disney theme parks, the Houston chain of restaurants, cable television services, power generation systems, automated teller machines (ATMs), newspapers produced and delivered every day, healthcare centers, and academic centers that use pedagogical processes for educational purposes. With such enormous diversity, it is imperative that a strong classification system be developed for process types.

5-2a Charting the Process

1 It also is critical to be able to chart in total detail every step of the process. To get an idea of what is required, try to specify in detail the program that would enable a robot to dress itself. It is hard to separate the methods used from the technology required.

2 The program required to just tie shoelaces poses enough of a problem to make the point. There is difficulty in setting down the appropriate detail to enable machines to do things that people do by intuition.

5-2b Choosing the Process Technology

It is necessary to be able to deal with the question of how to choose a process technology. In choosing the process, work configuration should not be chosen by default. It must first be decided: Should the process excel when volumes of a few varieties are large or should it excel when volumes are low for each of a high number of varieties? Excel means that the process has some winning combination of higher quality, lower costs, and shorter delivery times than the processes used by competitors.

Consider again, what is a process? It is a detailed description of the input–output transformation sequence. Different kinds of equipment can be used to make the same things. The choice will depend upon what work configurations are best-suited for the expected volumes and varieties of product outputs.

5-2c Means and Ends

The study of P/OM requires understanding what is needed to achieve the desired ends: Technology and training are essential at all levels within the organization, and in the suppliers' organizations, to achieve the strategic objectives of the company. From a systems point of view, it is important to note that the ends of one part of the process are often the means of the next part of the process.

A means–end model connects strategies with tactics. **Ends** are strategic objectives; *means* are tactical process components designed to achieve *ends*. Starting with ends, the means are derived. Somewhere between ends and means, strategies start morphing to tactics. If the results of the tactics are not considered satisfactory, it is necessary to revisit strategic planning. Reformulation of strategies is not a failure; it is expected by strategic planners.

Raw material transformations are the means for making components. Components are converted into parts. Parts are assembled into products. Products are grouped together into boxes. Cartons of boxes are delivered to carriers. Carriers move cartons to distributors, and they in turn make deliveries to retailers who sell the products to customers. This **supply chain** is a specific example of a generic means–end chain.

The means–end supply chain does not stop with delivery. Customers who buy and use the products initiate the chain of payment. Customers return money to the retailers who pay the wholesalers who pay the distribution centers, which remunerate the producers. The goal was to create the means for obtaining revenue. That objective started the entire systems process. Thus, when that customer's money enters the bank, there is a short-term

Ends
Final part of the means–end chain, until another system is defined.

Supply chain
All of the elements that make up the products and services delivered to customers.

conclusion to the process. In the long-term, other factors also must be considered to assure that customers remain loyal. The payment process and the marketing process are critical parts of the means–end chain.

5-2d Strategic Aspects of Processes

Managers choose the components of a means–end chain to go from where they see the firm is to where they want the firm to go. That choice is driven by strategies to achieve the selected goals. The strategic drivers are designed to achieve the purpose of the process. Another way of viewing the strategic drivers for the means–end chain is by identifying the process as an interconnected set of transformations of linked, input–output systems. Strategic decisions about processes translate cost, quality, and delivery requirements into specific methods used to realize objectives. The choice of *process configurations is the critical link between strategies and tactics.*

5-3 Types of Process Flows

There are many ways of categorizing process flows. One of the best ways is to note the difference between analytic and synthetic processes. Combinations of the two basic types of processes are common, but all processes tend to be more like one than the other.

It makes sense to broadly define analytic and synthetic processes at this time so that the comparison can be kept in mind. Synthetic processes combine things, usually putting many parts together to make one or a few products. Analytic processes take things apart, creating many products from a few.

5-3a Synthetic Processes

Synthetic process

Combines the various materials, components, subassemblies, etc., into a single, basic product (sbp) or into several similar products.

A **synthetic process** is a process in which a variety of components come together, ultimately to form a single product. Progressive assembly, which follows the instructions of how to build sequentially the subassemblies and final assemblies, is an example of the synthetic function. Instructions for construction emphasize the correct order for putting things together.

Any sequential process can be delineated by an assembly diagram such as the one drawn in Figure 5-1. This kind of schematic is used by process designers to make sure that all the nuts and bolts are assembled in the right order. The sequence of assembly goes from twigs to branches (which are subassemblies) to the trunk (which is the final assembly). If the trunk started to spread out again at the roots, the process would be starting to be analytic. Processes that combine assembly (synthetic) and disassembly (analytic) are more common than pure processes of either kind.

Synthetic processes employ synthesis that is defined as many inputs combining to form a whole. The purest example of synthesis is many to one, but in reality this is often tempered by a relatively synthetic process, which combines the many to form a few.

Synthesis characterizes the automobile assembly plant, where many components are brought together to form a few car models. A Closer Look 5-1 illustrates an automobile assembly process, showing what goes into making an automobile and in what order these components are introduced to the assembly process.

Another typical synthetic process is that required to bring a number of different kinds of information together with the purpose of analyzing the data and then writing the final report. This is the main function of a market research shop, which should be as much a master of the synthetic process as the automobile assembly plant.

A prime objective for every kind of synthetic process is to have a smooth flow of the items being processed. As these items flow along, they become more and more complete. The stage of completion could be specified by the percent of the total processing time that has been consumed up to that point.

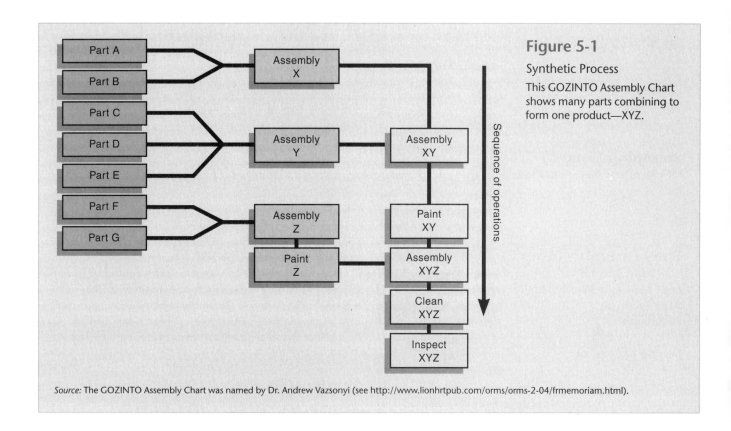

Figure 5-1

Synthetic Process

This GOZINTO Assembly Chart shows many parts combining to form one product—XYZ.

Source: The GOZINTO Assembly Chart was named by Dr. Andrew Vazsonyi (see http://www.lionhrtpub.com/orms/orms-2-04/frmemoriam.html).

For the auto assembly process, a total processing time of 32 hours is not unusual; the engine might join the chassis at the point where more than 70 percent of total assembly time has passed. The first completion of data analysis for the market research report might occur when less than 30 percent of the total report writing process is completed.

To keep the process from being interrupted, it is necessary to have an ample supply of the right components (parts or information) on hand at the places where they are needed. They could be brought to where they are needed, as they are needed, which is called **just-in-time**. Alternatively, they could be brought to where they are to be used long before they are needed to avoid any slip-ups in the timing of the deliveries. That kind of protection is called **just-in-case**.

This issue of storage of components and timing of their delivery is directly related to the rate at which the process is working. Three important questions need to be answered:

1 How many units come off the line every hour? Say that there are ten. This means that every six minutes a unit is complete

2 How long does it take to make a unit? The fact that a unit is complete every six minutes does not always mean that it took six minutes to complete it.

3 How many lines are operating and have to be fed with components or information?

Assume that the information assembly process to write a report is initially poorly balanced. This means that the process would be erratic, stopping and starting. Because it did not flow smoothly, there would be times when data was backed up waiting to be processed. At other times, idle people and idle computers would be sitting around waiting for data to process.

The operations manager can smooth the flow by creating workstations at which specific tasks would be done. The tasks would follow the logical progression of the assembly

Just-in-time

Inventory delivery principle associated with a lean-and-mean company philosophy.

Just-in-case

Inventory delivery principle associated with a play-it-safe production philosophy.

A Closer Look 5-1 Synthetic Process—How an Automobile Is Assembled (Many Parts to One)

The following six steps are brief generic descriptions of the synthetic process that is used to assemble a vehicle.

Stamping (Step 1)

The Stamping Department produces major body panels such as roofs, side panels, and fenders. Employees stack stamped panels for delivery to the Body Assembly Department.

Body Assembly (Step 2)

The Body Assembly Department uses automated operations such as robotic welding to reduce labor intensivity. After assembly, white bodies are sent to the Paint Department.

Paint (Step 3)

Before primer and topcoat applications, coatings are applied to each vehicle for corrosion protection, prevention of water leaks, wind noise, and paint chipping. Then, painting robots apply topcoat and perform some sealer and undercoating operations.

Trim & Final (Step 4)

Vehicle personality becomes evident at Step 4—"our car" starts to look like "your car." The Trim & Final Department uses innovative technology such as the tilt line, which allows employees to work comfortably to install underbody components such as fuel tanks and wire harnesses. Installation of front and rear windshields is an automated operation, as is engine and transmission installation.

Quality Control (Step 5)

To ensure that all quality standards and engineering specifications are met, each employee inspects his/her own work. Quality Control Department employees give each vehicle a rigorous inspection. These activities occur throughout the manufacturing process and before shipping to customers.

Shipping (Step 6)

Vehicles ready for delivery are transferred to the company's Shipping Yards.

---

chart. Some things cannot be done before others. The time to complete tasks at each workstation would be made about equal, creating what is called a balanced line.

In this chapter, perfectly balanced lines are assumed. Later chapters treat the real-world complication of lines that are not perfectly balanced. This occurs when the amount of work at stations is unequal. Stations have different amounts of idle time. Perfect balance also assumes that there is no rest time at any station. Perfect balance assumptions are difficult and sometimes impossible to achieve when people dominate the activities at workstations. Perfect balance can be approached using machine assistance for people at workstations. One can most easily visualize perfect line balance as resulting from a totally mechanized and robotic assembly system where the entire synthetic process is synchronized.

For this case, assume that a paced conveyor belt is used. It is stopped at each station for C minutes. The *cycle time* of C minutes is the pace that is set for the conveyor belt. That means that a finished unit comes off the production line every C minutes.

5-3b Analytic Processes

Analytic process

Turns a single, basic ingredient into several or (even) many products.

An **analytic process** is characterized by *progressive disassembly*. It is the reverse of the synthetic process as it breaks up one thing into many things. Going backwards on the assembly chart, the treeing process is reversed. It starts with the trunk and moves out to the branches and then to the twigs. A variety of products can be obtained from the "source." This type of process is illustrated in Figure 5-2.

The name "analytic" process is derived from the fact that analysis is involved. Analysis is defined as breaking up a whole into its parts to find out their nature. An analytic process breaks up the whole in order to use the parts for various reasons. See A Closer Look 5-2 for an example of the analytic process as it pertains to chocolate products.

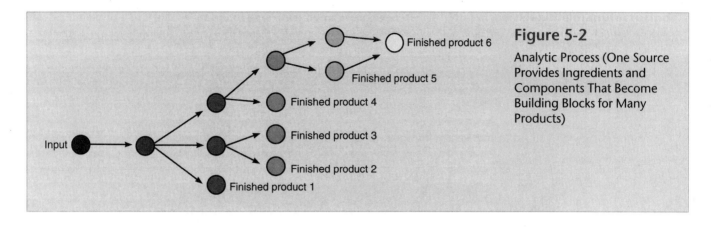

Figure 5-2

Analytic Process (One Source Provides Ingredients and Components That Become Building Blocks for Many Products)

The purest example of an analytic process would be where one thing is converted into many derivatives without having to add anything else. Most analytic processes have one main, basic ingredient that is converted into a number of derivative products often with the help of additional materials.

Chocolate requires an analytic process to convert the main raw material—cacao beans cut from (9-inch) pods that grow year round on the cacao trees—into many different products such as cocoa powder, unsweetened, bittersweet, semisweet, sweet, milk, and white chocolate, in various forms such as chocolate bars, chips, and syrup. Other derivatives are chocolate chips, bakers' chocolate, and cocoa butter. Sugar is an additive for many of the products. Milk chocolate requires the addition of milk solids and sugar. Less expensive chocolates substitute fats and emulsifiers for cocoa butter.

The analytic process also applies to information systems. Previously, it was used to describe a synthetic process where data from a variety of sources were combined to create a report. The analysis of data, used by laboratories, functions in the opposite way. A blood sample is drawn and tested, yielding data on blood sugar, cholesterol, and red cell count, among other things. The final report decomposes the blood sample into many end categories. These are used by doctors to evaluate health and to diagnose symptoms of health problems.

5-4 Sourcing for Synthetic Processes

The flowcharts for synthetic processes show how various materials, components, and parts are fed into the main stream, where they are joined together to form the product that marketing will sell. Purchasing the materials, components, and parts (or data) from different sources requires dealing with many different suppliers.

Typically, the operations manager is not responsible for the sourcing decisions. Because these decisions impact strongly on the performance of operations, there is a need for coordination. The systems approach is essential to make certain that purchasing and P/OM are playing on the same team.

There are prices, qualities, and delivery reliabilities to compare. These include on-time delivery of the correct amount with the agreed-upon quality and cost. Acquisition strategies for synthetic processes are significantly different from those needed for analytic processes, though both require comprehension of the mechanisms that apply to their particular kind of supply chain.

Synthetic processes usually involve many parts and one or more suppliers for each of them. All of these parts cost the company consequential amounts of money. The cost of materials for synthetic processes has been a large percent of the cost of goods sold (COGS). It can be as high as 80 percent. It is, on average, around 40 to 50 percent, and it is increasing for many firms.

A Closer Look 5-2 Analytic Process—Chocolate Products

- The basic process is composed of cleaning, grinding, conching, and mixing ingredients of various kinds in different amounts.
- Micronizing is a preroasting thermal (or heat) treatment needed to obtain a clean separation from the husks (shells).
- Winnowing is shelling the beans.

- Cleaning at various stages is essential before grinding (milling) because various kinds of impurities that damage quality must be removed.
- Grinding (milling) precedes liquification.
- To produce a powdery product from high-fat cocoa mass, it must be partially defatted so cocoa butter is extracted by pressing, which leaves a solid material known as cocoa press cake.

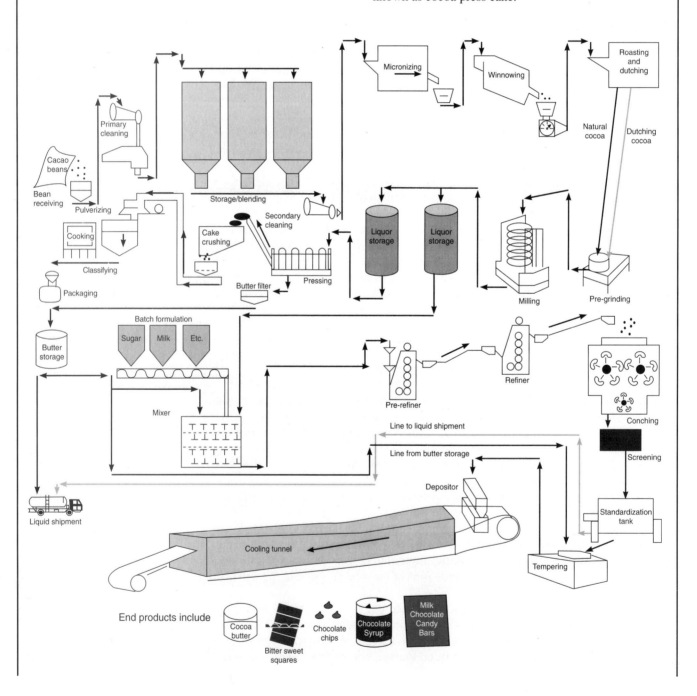

A Closer Look 5-2 (Continued)

- Pulverizing cocoa press cake produces cocoa powder, which is used in many ways by food industries and by final consumers.
- Cocoa butter is refined in several stages before conching.
- Dutching is the alkalization (adding alkalies) of powder and liquor to modify the flavor and color of chocolate, called dutched cocoa and chocolate.
- Conching is a high-energy mixing to distribute cocoa butter and flavoring.

- Tempering is a heating and cooling process to set up the correct crystal structure in the fat.
- Differences in the quality of chocolate are due not only to beans and recipes used; they are dependent on the production process used.
- End products include cocoa powder, chocolate flavored syrups, chocolate chips, dark chocolate, milk chocolate candy bars, and cocoa butter.

Being the low-cost producer is a major goal of most firms. Even Rolls Royce, with its very high price tags, has redesigned its operations to reduce costs significantly. Because of the impact of purchase prices on total costs, most synthetic process industries are very strict with their suppliers. As a result of the impact of supplier costs on the bottom line, outsourcing has been used increasingly, with China taking a commanding lead in exports of low labor cost items. Concomitantly, there have been quality problems, termed the "quality fade."[3]

Increasingly, a rational cost structure for purchased products from all suppliers has become the objective of companies with synthetic processes. To achieve this, it is necessary to have suppliers that are the low-cost producers for all of the parts and components the company purchases. This creates the potential for cost advantages from savings that are made on all of the parts and components that are purchased. If the savings that can be made are not taken, they are called *opportunity losses*. Those firms that are on top of the situation, thereby avoiding opportunity losses and realizing the potential savings, achieve significant competitive advantages. Companies using synthetic processes are particularly vulnerable if they are ignorant of this fact.

The cost of materials component of the COGS is normally understated for synthetic processes. This means that the COGS is also understated. The costs are understated because the costs of purchased materials do not include all of the costs of quality.

In particular the costs of failures, as measured by losses of customer loyalty, are totally missed. Also the cost of rework due to suppliers' defectives is not usually associated with the cost of purchases. Missing these factors understates the costs. Further, the cost of designing and installing supplier certification programs has been growing as competitors pay increasing attention to the triad of critical dimensions: price, quality, and speed of delivery. The cost of materials should reflect the cost of the supplier certification program.

Suppliers that do not deliver on time delay production and that, in turn, holds up deliveries to customers. Delivery on time is a critical quality dimension in its own right. Delivery delays can have a substantial impact on customer loyalty. With this in mind, the choice and management of suppliers to ensure that the highest delivery standards are set and met is becoming another competitive requirement for synthetic processes.

5-5 Sourcing for Analytic Processes

Typically, analytic processes begin with the purchase of the single commodity, which the process transforms into many derivative products—such as cacao beans into chocolates, sweet crudes into various fuels, corn into breads, sugars, fuel additives, and grapes into wine and vinegar. For analytical processes, purchasing agents choose worldwide sources for the basic input component. The price, quality, and delivery of the core purchasing ingredient are subject to the kinds of fluctuations that characterize that particular commodity market.

Commodities are considered generic materials. Within any one commodity class, the materials are treated as being relatively indistinguishable from each other. "Relatively" is used because operations managers of analytic processes know that qualities of commodities vary, which greatly affects the quality of their finished products.

The sourcing decisions have a major impact on how well the process functions. Because it is seldom P/OM that reaches these sourcing decisions, a systems approach is essential to coordinate the operations and procurement of materials. It also is important to note that the systems approach focuses on many different issues according to whether the materials will be subject to synthetic or analytic processing.

Analytic processes, by their definition, have a totally different supplier situation than that which applies to synthetic processes. There are many suppliers of the same few commodities. Frequently, price is the main factor that drives the acquisition of the input materials. Yet, as was stated earlier, it is always subject to quality considerations, which P/OM and the agency doing the sourcing coordinate within the framework of the systems approach.

Prices are established by the specific commodity exchange that trades in that commodity. The Chicago Board of Trade and the New York Mercantile Exchange are well-known commodity trading exchanges in the United States for many of the raw material ingredients that require analytic processes. Most countries have equivalent exchanges.

Sourcing in the commodity markets requires a variety of special skills. Purchasing strategies play a major role in determining the average price paid for a commodity. The average is taken of the price paid across many transactions. This can include both buying and selling the commodity. Some contracts are made at present prices; others involve commodity prices at future dates. The operation of futures markets is discussed in courses and books on financial trading. There are different traditions and techniques required to successfully buy corn, coffee, salt, rice, gold, platinum, copper and other metals, cattle, hogs and other livestock, as well as fuels and oils from plants and flowers such as sunflowers and peanuts. There are different ways of bidding for commodities and establishing contracts in the futures markets.

Factors such as weather can affect crop prices for commodities such as oranges and grains. The prices of metals, including gold, copper, and platinum, will vary according to local and world events. The average prices that are affected by such extraneous factors get translated into the eventual prices of the derivative products. A freeze in Florida drives the price of oranges up, and a crisis in Russia causes the price of gold to jump. When many farmers have abundant crops that they bring to the market, the excess of bumper crops drops the prices.

Money is made and lost by managers of analytic processes who trade in their commodities as another necessary side to their business. The advantage that can be realized by astute maneuvering in the commodity markets is one of the features of dealing in analytic processes. It is hard to overlook the fact that some very large coffee companies have made more money trading in green coffee bean futures than in selling bags and cans of their brand of coffee. The same kind of parallel exists for other commodities where the trading required for purchasing provides a business opportunity in its own right.

5-6 Marketing Differences

The marketing approach for analytic products is different from that of synthetic products. When a company is making and selling both, there is a decision required as to how to specialize or generalize the selling function as well as the producing function.

5-6a Marketing Products of Synthetic Processes

For synthetic processes, it is important to be very focused and sharp about marketing and selling the basically one product to be sold. At the same time, one product permits concentration on the marketing plan. There is only one sales force, and it does not have to divide marketing resources among several different product lines. At the end of the supply chain, marketing is specialized. Upstream, at the beginning of the chain, purchasing deals with an array of suppliers. It is production dealing with suppliers and processes that has an array of differences to master.

5-6b Marketing Products of Analytic Processes

For analytic processes, there are often quite disparate end products. Each addresses a different market constituency. Each requires different marketing techniques. Gasoline for autos is an entirely different market from industrial fuels, and both contrast with kerosene for jets. A variety of marketing plans are needed, and separate sales forces are required. The marketing budget must be allocated to diverse end products. Downstream, at the end of the supply chain, marketing is diversified. Upstream, where the supply chain begins, purchasing is focused.

A commodity is often defined as a group of items that are indistinguishable from each other. There is reason to take exception to this characterization. The qualities of commodities are not homogeneous within any category. Differences are often *overlooked or dismissed* by the commodity purchasing process. The end-user, however, recognizes the difference.

First, consider the statement (heard increasingly) that the computer has become a commodity. To begin with, that means that the brand is irrelevant. It also means that one does not care who made the components. *Intel Inside* and *Core™ 2 Duo Inside* are attempts to counter this trend by means of labeling. The question "Does that work?" is answered by the fact that Intel keeps doing that. However, the production process to make a computer is increasingly a combination of synthetic processes (all leading to essentially the same thing) and analytic processes (being customized and leading to many variations of significance).

A major strategic advantage is available to those who capitalize on the differentiation of commodity qualities. They can buy on terms of quality as well as by price. The quality advantage can be utilized to advantage at the downstream end of the analytic process in each of the markets of the derivative products. Intel has additional marketing plans for *Core 2 Quad* and *Core 2 Extreme*. Creative opportunity for branding strong products always exists.

There are many types of wheat grains. Varieties of corn are so numerous that only experts can catalog them. Some soybean products are cleaner than others. Some crops just barely qualify with respect to nutritional standards for cattle feeds; others are considered to be superior. The standards apply to quality requirements that range from minerals to vitamins.

Cranberries are graded by the cooperatives that sort and package them. Wet harvesting is less expensive and inferior to dry harvesting. Wet cranberries need to be dried and then sorted according to their color and bounciness, a surrogate for firmness. Within the grading categories for cranberries there exists a great deal of product quality variability.

Many commodities are shipped in bulk using railroad boxcars, large trucks, and the cargo holds of ships. The method of transportation and the care with which the shipment is arranged will affect the quality of the merchandise when it is received. The logistics of transport are very important in this regard for quality as well as with respect to the timeliness of delivery.

Educating the consumer about quality differentials for various commodities is not usual. Utilizing the differences for creating consumer preferences and price differentials has been done successfully for wine grapes. There is a complex mystique about vintages. Prices can range from under $5 to $500. To a somewhat lesser degree, the same marketing approach using quality differentiation has been applied effectively to coffee beans.

The choice of quality grades for commodity inputs to the analytic processes will have major impact on the quality of the derivative products. Instead of talking about *GIGO* (garbage-in, garbage-out), the time has come to talk about *QUIQUO*, which emphasizes the more positive aspect of process management (quality-in, quality-out).

It is better to see the glass as being half filled than to see it as being half empty. Those who say that quality should play a larger part in determining purchasing decisions for analytic processes are on-target. Price alone cannot continue to be the key to sourcing and purchasing for analytic processes.

Chocolate fanciers know that all cacao beans are not alike. Most chocolate comes from forastero trees, which grow in West Africa and Brazil. Scarcer and more flavorful beans come from criollo and trinitario trees, which are found in Central America. Having the best beans is essential for preparing the best chocolates.

5-7 Best Practice (Benchmarking: Process)

Best practice

Process standard based on identifying those who perform the process in the best way.

Benchmarking

Method for comparing two or more processes with one that is considered to be the best.

Best practice is a process standard that has strong roots in the systems approach. The idea is to identify those who perform the entire process in the best ways yet known. Striving to make one's own process the best in the "class" is like aiming to win the gold at Olympic events; the prior year's records of gold medal winners are the standards for best practice in that event. The procedure of comparing one's own process against the best is called **benchmarking**. It is used to compare various activities in P/OM, such as service ratings, product excellence, quality attainment, sales effectiveness, purchasing performance, and also to compare production processes.

Best process requires a combination of systems factors. Best ingredients are a necessary but not sufficient condition for product excellence. Best process (BP) must be combined with best ingredients (BI) to bring out the best product (BPR). The factors in the equation are multiplicative:

$$(BP)(BI) = (BPR)$$

If either (BP) or (BI) = 0, meaning low quality, then (BPR) = 0. Thus, for example, in A Closer Look 5-2, for the highest quality chocolate product, the conching step must knead the mixture until it is totally smooth. This process step can continue for as long as three or four days to achieve best process (BP) results. Combined with the best cacao beans (BI), the best product (BPR) can be attained.

The resulting differentiation raises commodity products above the customary concept of being indistinguishable and homogeneous and places them into special niches—like Godiva chocolates. This increases profit margins of the derivative products of analytic processes. It also provides an opportunity for developing competitive advantage in terms of the quality of commodities, which is often overlooked.

5-8 Mixed Analytic and Synthetic Processes

Many processes are combinations of synthetic and analytic processes. For example, maple syrup from the maple tree is a commodity that gets converted into maple sugar, pancake syrup, candies, and cakes. To produce each end product requires that other commodities be added to the mixture.

Generally, one type of process predominates, that is, the process is primarily either synthetic or analytic. In the case of maple syrup, the process is predominately analytic even though additives are needed to produce the final set of products.

The assembly of digital cameras is a synthetic process. Also, the computer chips inside the cameras are constructed and assembled by a synthetic process. Yet, many of the computer chips—sourced from all over the world—are treated as if they are commodities. To counter the concept that all chips are alike, Intel and Advanced Micro Devices spend freely to make claims of unique advantages. As described later, cameras, MP3 players, cell phones, etc., are mixtures of analytic (V) and synthetic (A) processes. So too are cars, books, clothing, and cans of food.

5-8a The OPT System and the Theory of Constraints (TOC)

OPT is a production scheduling system developed by Dr. Eliyahu Goldratt in the period 1978–1986. In the mid-1980s, it was renamed by him (and for good reason) as the **Theory of Constraints (TOC)**. This method deserves consideration whenever efforts to schedule production are seriously constrained by finite (having bounds) capacity limits.

OPT stands for "optimized production technology." An alternative (from Britain) says that T stands for "Timetables." OPT and TOC are adjustive to the existence of bottlenecks. Spotlight 16-2 features an interview with Dr. Goldratt.

OPT and TOC are the same methods. They are methods of finite scheduling of production—which means lot-by-lot scheduling. The methods of OPT belong in the context of tactical scheduling activities.

The concepts of OPT and TOC were initiated by Goldratt's professional consulting company.[4] His principles of *synchronized production scheduling* have had major impact on production methodology applicable to job shops, batch production, and project management.

5-8b OPT, TOC, and V-A-T

OPT classifies processes by means of the acronym *VAT*. A V-process is analytic, starting with a single commodity at the bottom and branching out into refined products at the top. An A-process is synthetic, starting at the bottom with several inputs, which are combined to yield a single marketable product.[5] The combination is named by OPT as a T-process. The charts in this text have been guided by these conventions.

OPT focuses attention on the fact that each type of process (V, A, and T) has unique production scheduling aspects. Also, each type of process has characteristics that work best with specific types of work process configurations. Proper matching of work process configurations with the synthetic components and the analytic components of process flows can provide significant advantages.

5-9 Work Process Configuration Types

There are fundamental differences in the way that both synthetic and analytic processes can be designed or configured. A primary factor for classification is the number of units produced at one time. That number is often referred to as the lot size, N. Lot size applies to discrete production runs as compared to continuous production output systems, which include flow shops (assembly lines) and continuous (liquid) flow systems.

Another classification factor is the variety level. It is customary to find that, as the lot size goes up, the variety level diminishes. In part, this is a statement that reflects old technology where setup time was inversely related to time and cost per part. New *flexible process systems (FPS)* technology has altered this formula to a degree.

5-9a The Custom Shop

The **custom shop** is the work configuration in which products or services are "made-to-order." Custom work is like tailoring a suit of clothes to fit one specific individual. This kind of work process is usually associated with a lot size of one, i.e., $N = 1$.

OPT
Also known as the theory of constraints.

Theory of Constraints (TOC)
Production scheduling system that optimizes overall performance (throughput) by recognizing constraints.

Custom shop
Work configuration used for products or services that are made-to-order, and actually one of a kind.

Many custom shops, like machine shops and cabinetmakers, use synthetic processes, doing one custom job after another. As for analytic processes, laboratories might be viewed as custom shops where a specific ingredient (such as blood) is broken down into its components for detailed analysis.

What does the custom shop look like? Not too much space is required to house the limited materials needed for the jobs at hand. There is **general-purpose equipment (GPE)**, needed by relatively few people with craft skills who turn out the product. Often, the workers are owners and entrepreneurs operating in a small workshop housed in a store or garage.

The information equivalent is a small office, often working online from home, just large enough to allow for computers and printers, some files, and telephones. If a walking service is offered, such as hairstyling, or cooking and language lessons, there must be space for clients. See, for example, http://www.momsnetwork.com and note 2008 Picks Work at Home Directory for MOMS.

5-9b The Job Shop

The job shop is not a custom shop or a flow shop that operates a serialized production line. The **job shop (JS)** is a work configuration for processing work in *batches or lots*. N, the lot size, can vary within these guidelines. The job shop produces N units at a time for shipment, for stock, or a combination.

There are over 100,000 job shops in the United States and a larger number in Europe. Job shops account for over 70 percent of all manufactured parts in the Western world. Both in the United States and in Europe, the typical lot size is 50 units. Because these numbers are consistent over time, there is continued need for purchasing managers to order inventory in small quantities.

The work configuration of the job shop has equipment at various locations, and batches of work queue up waiting for processing at each location in accordance with what needs to be done. The equipment is of the general-purpose type so it can be used to do many different jobs.

For most job shops, the variety of the work that can be accomplished is substantial. This is in keeping with the large array of process equipment, the broad range of skills of the operators, and the kind of demands that are the basis of the job shop business. The demands received by job shops arise from industrial firms that place orders for the great variety of parts, often in substantial numbers, but not enough to warrant using the serialized production configuration of the flow shop. The same description applies to service systems, which are almost entirely batch work oriented.

The job shop is able to produce the entire line of products, which any combination of general-purpose machine tools can create. The capabilities of the job shop are extensive, and it can turn out a lot of different items. For example, a drill press will make holes of different sizes in various materials. A lathe is used to turn the outside diameters of cylindrical parts. Reports can be of any size, and catering services are valued for their flexibility in menu choices and size of the catered group.

Job shops have some **special-purpose equipment (SPE)** for larger batch sizes. Instead of using a turret lathe, an automatic screw machine can turn out many more cylindrical parts once it is set up. In general, for higher volumes of output, the job shop has intermediate-level equipment that falls between GPE and SPE.

Figure 5-3 illustrates an operations or routing sheet for a part manufactured in a job shop. The sequential steps for die-casting and machining are listed on the operations sheet. It furnishes information about where the equipment to be used is located.

The bill of materials, which often is found on blueprints, spells out instructions about materials and tools. Thus, together, the routing sheet, the bill of materials, and the blueprints provide all the information needed to do the job.

Information processing equipment is general purpose most of the time. Computers are wonderful general-purpose machines, which when loaded with software can become

---

General-purpose equipment (GPE)
Flexible machinery that can do many different kinds of jobs.

Job shop (JS)
Used when there are many varieties of products to process in small quantities

Special-purpose equipment (SPE)
Efficient in repetitive production of the same unit.

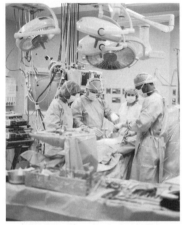

©2008 Jupiterimages Corporation

The OR (operating room) is a crucial part of the healthcare system. Most operating rooms are job shops in which the variety of work that can be accomplished is substantial. However, there are superb examples of flow shop operating rooms. For example, Shouldice Hospital in Toronto has an enviable performance record for successful hernia operations (see Spotlight 5-2). At the Texas Heart Institute in Houston, Dr. Denton Cooley and his associates have performed over 100,000 open-heart operations with flow shop methods.

Figure 5-3

The Bill of Materials and the Operations Sheet Used by a Job Shop for Batch Production

Bill of Materials

Item Motor switch MS60

Drawings 95.6—95.8

Sheet No. 1 of 1

Assembly 3 HP motor X22

Part No.	Part Name	No./Item	Material	Quantity/Item	Cost/Item	Operations
P14	Casing	1	Zn	0.2 lbs	$5.15	Cast, trim
P21	Spring	2	Sprg. St.	—	1.64	Buy
•	•	•	•	•	•	•
•	•	•	•	•	•	•
•	•	•	•	•	•	•
P7	Clips	4	AL15	—	0.25	Buy

Operations Sheet

Part No. P14

Part Name Casing

Blueprint No. 95.7

Economic Lot Size 750

Process Time/Lot 6hrs

Setup Time See below

Use for   Motor Switch MS60

Motor Switch MS61

Subcontract Hamilton

Quantity per 1

1

500/order

Material Zn

% Scrap 10

Supplier Vaun

Weight 0.2lb/

Cost $1.65/

Operation No.	Operation	Location/Machine	Std. Time in Minutes Operations	Setup
1	Change die	F5	—	30
2	Injection molding	F5	3	—
3	Remove	F5	5	—
4	Deflash	F4	7	—
5	Tumble	F7	20	10
6	Plate	G3	10	12

highly specialized. In banks, dedicated, special-purpose equipment (SPE) is required to handle checks. The high volumes of transactions in check handling are treated with both job shop and flow shop configurations, according to the processing transactions. Over time, banking equipment is moving toward total flow shop configurations. Many word processing applications are job shops.

What does the job shop look like? The space is much larger than for the custom shop. It has to be big enough to contain the materials, general-purpose equipment (GPE), and people with skills. Most job shops are labor-intensive. Employees have crossover skill sets since running many jobs at the same time is characteristic of the job shop.

5-9c The Flow Shop

Flow shops (FS) are serialized work configurations where one unit of work is at various stages of completion at sequential workstations located along the production line. They

Flow shops (FS)
Serialized work configurations.

© 2008 Jupiterimages Corporation

In typical flow shop configurations, conveyors are used to transfer work from station to station. Beverage factories transfer empty bottles to filling equipment, and then to labeling, capping, packaging, and shipping operations. Procedures are highly automated at rates that yield a minimum number of defectives while maintaining high productivity.

Continuous processes

Produce one product continuously or fan out derivative products as part of continuous stream.

Logistics

Science and operations of procurement and supply.

are dedicated production facilities, which, like auto assembly lines, can be kept running day-after-day. Demand is sufficient to warrant a sequential production process that moves work from one station to the next. Usually, a paced conveyor carries the work from station to station, stopping for a carefully chosen period of time at each station. The length of time that it is stopped is called the *cycle time*. A great deal of effort goes into balancing the line. The cycle time includes some time for rest, which reduces the output rate.

The flow shop also is often described as being a serialized production process, which means sequentially in order, regular and continuous. To contrast the operating characteristics of the job shop with those of the flow shop, see Figure 5-4.

Usually, the supply capabilities of the flow shop are equal to or greater than the average demand. For those intervals when demand exceeds supply, the flow shop might be replicated in parallel. This often is the case when the labor component of the flow shop is high and the capital investment component is low. Sometimes the rate of throughput can be increased by using more powerful technology.

As an alternative method of increasing the supply, the flow shop can be changed from a one-shift basis to a multishift basis. This can include overtime operations or a temporary shift to a two- or three-shift basis. When demand is seasonal, flow shops are configured to provide multishift operations to match peak load demands with a single-shift basis for off-peak times.

Flow shops are dedicated processes where materials and components from suppliers merge and join the production line in an uninterrupted sequence. It is more difficult to configure analytic processes, from start to finish, as a flow shop. Once the ingredients for the derivatives have been obtained, it is possible to run with the flow shop configuration.

A flow shop for chocolate-making can be initiated after the conching of the blended mixture of liquor and cocoa butter (see A Closer Look 5-2). At that point, a synthetic process can be used to make chocolate bars, chocolate kisses, and so forth. To feed the flow shop, there always must be a supply of chocolate blend.

Some analytic processes can be designed to permit the fanning out of the derivative products as part of a continuous flow process stream. These are called **continuous processes**, the work configuration where the product flows through pipes continuously as it is being treated and processed. Good examples of such continuous processes come from the chemical and petrochemical industries. They may be used for making plastics and synthetics such as nylon thread. Also, petroleum-refining and beer-making typify continuous process flow shops, designed to be high-volume, cost-effective systems.

An excellent example of efforts to approximate a continuous flow for analytic processes is found in the area of distribution. Related to rationalization of the distribution process is the field called **logistics**. Logistics concerns the use of methods for obtaining effective procurement, storage, and movement of materials. Logistics processes operate the distribution systems, which move finished goods downstream in the supply chain.

Distribution of product is a fanning-out process. Shipments of goods go from the producers' sources to warehouses, and from there to regional distribution centers that move the goods to retailers. The retailers distribute the product to the ultimate consumers. Meanwhile, cash flow moves up the chain from the customers to the producer.

The *supply chain* epitomizes analytic processes. Great efforts are being made to keep product moving throughout the supply chain in quantities that are related to actual needs at various nodes in the network. Thus, value adding is maximized by the proper procurement schedule that minimizes storage at every stage. When material arrives as needed, the process is characterized as being *just-in-time*.

Henry Ford's sequenced assembly line received so much publicity that flow shops came to be identified with synthetic processes by terms such as "mass production." Analytic processes deserve as much attention. When there is sufficient demand, job shop assignments for batches of work that relate to analytical processes can be converted into the much more economic flow shops that disassemble the basic commodities into a set of

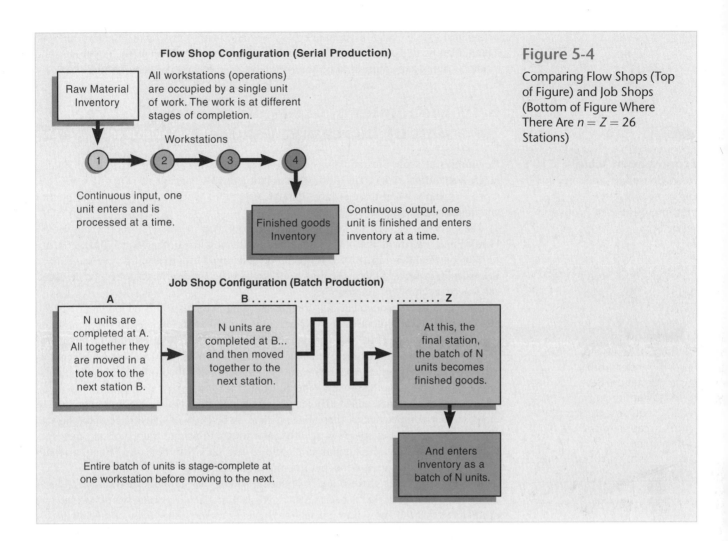

Figure 5-4

Comparing Flow Shops (Top of Figure) and Job Shops (Bottom of Figure Where There Are $n = Z = 26$ Stations)

final products. These often entail the transfer of liquids. They are continuous flow-through processes such as encountered in refining petroleum, but they are also used for milk and its by-products.

Combinations of analytical and synthetic flow shops abound in extracting and blending by vintners and beer makers. Telephone switching centers continuously connect and disconnect lines with each other, using process techniques that bring things together and disassemble them in great numbers and with incredible speed. The operations within computers that allow them to perform in this way follow the same mixture of analytics and synthetics.

The Benefits and Constraints of Flow Shops

The advantages of converting both analytic and synthetic processes into flow shop form are three-fold:

1 Cost per unit will be significantly reduced.
2 Qualities of the product can be raised to higher standards.
3 Consistency of the qualities can be increased.

Flow shops must be justified by volume. The fixed costs required to design and equip the process are high. The increased fixed costs needed to equip the system must be traded off against the decrease in variable costs associated with a less labor-intensive process. The marketing department and the sales force must be able to generate enough demand to allow capital expenditures to be amortized over a reasonable period of time.

5-10 Economies of Scale—Decreasing Cost Per Unit by Increasing Volume

Economies of scale

Reductions in cost per unit that can be obtained by producing greater quantities of goods and services.

Economies of scale are reductions in costs per unit achieved as a result of producing larger volumes of work. The flow shop epitomizes this concept of being able to work more efficiently when there is large enough volume of work to support process studies and investments in process equipment.

The theory dates back to Adam Smith. The flow shop in practice was first applied by Henry Ford, who made it work for the entire production line of the Model T Ford. Henry Ford recognized that repetitive tasks could be done more efficiently if people specialized in particular aspects of the sequential work process. He successfully applied the theory to sequenced assembly of automobiles.

There had to be enough call for doing each of the repetitive jobs on a regular basis to allow for the development of specialized workstations where people did the same thing over and over again. Thus, one person is assigned the exclusive use of the hammer, and another person is assigned the exclusive use of the screwdriver. They become the hammer and screw-driving experts, respectively. Adam Smith called this method of organizing people working on the process "the division of labor."

In present-day terms, added efficiencies are gained from being able to train people to increase their competence as specialists. If there is no body of knowledge about how to use a hammer so that everyone is equally good whether they are trained or not, then specialization in the use of hammers is pointless. The same can be said if training would improve the way the job is done, but training is not used.

In many companies, there is a lack of understanding that training can improve any and every activity. In part, this is because there is a lack of know-how and, worse yet, no one even knows that the know-how exists. For whatever reason, if the body of knowledge for training is not available, then one of the main reasons for specialization is missing. Yet, there are additional reasons for flow shop type specialization.

Economies of scale can be gained from the use of special-purpose equipment. SPE often requires different work routines and leads to training by the supplier of the equipment. Even if that training is not offered, the worker learns to use the new equipment and a form of self-training occurs. The hammer specialist is given a pneumatic hammer and gradually develops new skills in hammering. Repetitive tasks can become boring, but alternatively, even without SPE, learning and self-training can reward the repetitive job assignment.

Further economies of scale become possible because of volume production. These include expanded levels of coordinated promotional, advertising, and marketing activities. High-volume purchasing should earn well-deserved discounts. Work in process can be minimized in a well-designed flow shop process. In a related advantage, value adding can be maximized. There is focus of purpose because of concentration on doing the same things over and over. This can be turned to advantage.

When sufficient demand exists, the flow shop is the preferred process. It is the simplest and most efficient production configuration. Economies of scale make it worthwhile to try to aggregate enough volume to justify using it.

When sufficient demand does not exist, the use of the flow shop provides one of the best strategies for getting the demand level to be sufficient. The flow shop tends to support itself by lowering costs. This allows for decreases in price and/or increases in marketing support. The superior quality of flow shop product (if the flow process is properly designed) enhances customer preference and supports increased demand volume.

The negative press that the flow shop gets because repetitious work is boring and mind-numbing can be overcome with proper job design and the rotation of jobs. These subjects are addressed in discussions about human resources management.

The contrast between job shop and flow shop production is worth examining. Lacking specialization, working with batches is a less efficient production configuration. Being a greater producer of product variety is the direct cause of increased complexity. The traffic of batches of work moving around in tote boxes generates patterns of interference. Controlling traffic requires extra planning to avoid tie-ups and blockages. Job shop batches interact with each other, waiting for their turn, competing for facilities and floor space. The mix of jobs is seldom the same. Since patterns are changing, repeated planning is required and costly. Correctness of each plan will vary. Sometimes the plan will be perfect and more often somewhat off-the-mark. Consequently, the precision, scope, and timing of each day's job shop plan will be less on-target than for the flow shop.

5-10a Economies of Scope

Interesting alternatives came into being with the technological development of computer-enabled flexible systems. Their downside is cost. Flexible manufacturing systems (FMS) and flexible process systems (FPS) are discussed under the generic terminology of FMS. It should be noted that flexibility is associated with the term **economies of scope**. This entails a uniquely different rule of economics than economies of scale.

Economies of scope are realized when setup cost reductions allow more frequent setups and, thereby, smaller lot sizes can be run. If it costs nothing to change production from green socks to red socks, then greater variety can be achieved without losing time or money. The value of variety will then determine how much a firm might be willing to invest in equipment and training that would allow the green to red and back to green shift.

The technologies required to allow economies of scope are computer systems connected to mechanical devices that turn out the product. In the beginning, there must be product designs that take into account what the manufacturing devices can do and how the computers can control them. For example, it might be possible to go from white to tan to light green to black without expenditures for cleaning up between colors. At going back to white, the equipment would be cleaned up and started again on the cycle. In this case, the costs of adding color in this way have to be balanced against the benefits.

5-11 The Intermittent Flow Shop

An alternative work configuration that has many flow shop benefits is called the *intermittent flow shop*. It can be used when demand volume is not sufficient to justify a full-scale flow shop. The design of an **intermittent flow shop (IFS)** allows it to be set up and run for an interval of time, then shut off.

IFSs are not as efficient as permanent flow shops because they need to be turned on and off as required. This means that the same complete engineering of the process will not pay. Also, to have a large flow shop investment not running for long periods of time is counterproductive. Nevertheless, the IFS can be viewed as a step in the *transition* of a company process as it moves from being a job shop to a flow shop.

IFSs are turned on when high output volumes are needed in short periods of time. They can be used to build up stock when the savings of flow shop speed counterbalance the cost of carrying stock. Sometimes a special order is received that requires larger volumes of product than are normally made. The intermittent flow shop is a possible solution.

Economies of scope
Realized when setup cost reductions allow more frequent changeovers without increasing the cost per unit of output.

Intermittent flow shop (IFS)
Run for an interval of time and then shut down until required again.

Many different computer motherboards can be produced by the same equipment in response to programming the specifications of orders on hand. This is because the process is a flexible process system (FPS), which in manufacturing terms is called a flexible manufacturing system (FMS). Very little human operator intervention is required in a well-designed system.

The ability to use serialized production for work that formerly or also had been done in batches requires planning and investment. Once it is planned and the facilities are available, it gets called into being by need, but requires both setup times and learning times to get the line running. As with pure flow shops, the intermittent form can be used for both synthetic and analytic processes. The criteria for establishing optimal runs apply.

A flow shop that can be shut down and dismantled does not have the same high level of special-purpose equipment as a full-time dedicated flow shop. It will not be as cost efficient, but it still makes use of the principles of flow shops.

These principles relate the total time required to make a complete unit of product, requiring $i = 10$ operations. There are n workstations (see bottom of Figure 5-4). C is called the cycle time. The relationship *with no idle time* at any station is specified by Equation 5-1:

$$nC = \sum_{i=1}^{i=10} t_i \tag{5-1}$$

This example assumed that the job consists of ten steps but the number is defined by the actual problem. If the sum of operation times is 30 minutes and the entire job (all ten steps) is done at one station, then $n = 1$ and the cycle time, $C = 30$ minutes. The output rate is $60/30 = $ two units per hour.

Assume that the same job will be done with two stations. Then, $n = 2$, and $C = 15$. Cycle time has been cut in half. The output rate is doubled since $60/15 = 4$. Cost/benefits must be tested. Weigh the cost of the extra station against the doubling of the output rate.

Determination of when to use the IFS form of flow shop is guided by the principle that flow shop production is more costly to set up than batch production, but thereafter per unit costs are lower. It is necessary to calculate the demand level at which the total costs are about the same for batch production or the intermittent flow shop. This is the *point of indifference* as to which work configuration is used. It also is referred to as the point where the two kinds of processes break even with respect to total costs.

5-12 Flexible Process Systems

The alternative to the classic flow shop is the **flexible process system (FPS)**. For manufacturing it is called the **flexible manufacturing system (FMS)**. Applied to services, it is called FPS or **FOS** for **flexible office system**.

Flexible systems may be used as if they were flow shops even though they produce higher variety. Computer-driven equipment is able to change setups in seconds. The economics of these systems facilitate increasing physical variety (called *diversity* to distinguish it from marketing variety). The effect of rapid, low- or no-cost setup changes (referenced as economies of scope) is startling and yet, underdeveloped. Robotics development will be the driving force in the future.

Each station is capable of doing a set of different things and switching from one member of the set to another in an instant. Table 5-1 is a simple illustration of the principle. Station 1 shifts instantly between the operations a, b, c, and d. Station 2 shifts between e, f, g, and h. Station 3 shifts between i, j, k, and l.

Assume one product that this FMS can make is aei. Other products are bfj, cgk, and dhl. *If only the columns are products*, then four different products could be made with flow shop speeds and costs. *If all possible combinations* (using output from all three stations) were products, then there would be $4 \times 4 \times 4 = 64$ different products that could be made with the workstation advantages of flow shop processes. (See modular production in Chapter 10, Section 10-11.)

If the three stations are connected and coordinated to work together, they constitute a cellular manufacturing system. This requires programming so that each station can do its

Flexible process system (FPS)

Encompasses flexible manufacturing systems (FMS) as well as flexible information systems.

Flexible manufacturing system (FMS)

They produce throughput like flow shops and can shift from one product set-up to another very quickly which promotes variety.

Flexible office systems (FOS)

They can shift from one office assignment to another very quickly which epitomizes multi-tasking on a computer.

Product	1	2	3	4	Table 5-1
Station x	a	b	c	d	Flexible Process System with Three Workstations (x, y, and z) and Four Products (1, 2, 3, and 4)
Station y	e	f	g	h	
Station z	i	j	k	l	

work, and methods of conveyance can move the work from one station to another. The components of the cell are programmed to coordinate activities on a number of items having somewhat different designs.

Although they are different, as a general rule, jobs of similar family characteristics will be assigned to particular manufacturing cells. In that way, variants of the programming can be economically developed. The efficient production of families of parts is a concept that is known as *group technology*. Consequently, this application of FMS is classified as **group technology cellular manufacturing systems**.[6]

High-technology systems are converting paper trails into digital form. Processes that expedite paperless offices provide a great amount of flexibility. Freedom from paper requires radically new forms of processes. Slow adoption of what seems so logical and economical stems in part from the need to shoehorn old habits into new-tech systems.

There is ample evidence that the use of optical scanning methods and voice-activated request systems has decreased reliance on old-style record keeping. Companies in all industries are employing data-based technologies to revamp the accustomed information systems approach for recording, storing, and informing transactions.

Home shopping networks use advanced information processing. Figure 5-5 depicts a possible flowchart for the home shopping process.

With the Internet, customers are able to browse through catalogs and interact directly with the computer system. These are representative of flexible service systems.

Group technology cellular manufacturing systems
Workstations linked together on common sets of projects and families of parts.

Figure 5-5

Home Shopping Online Processing Flowchart

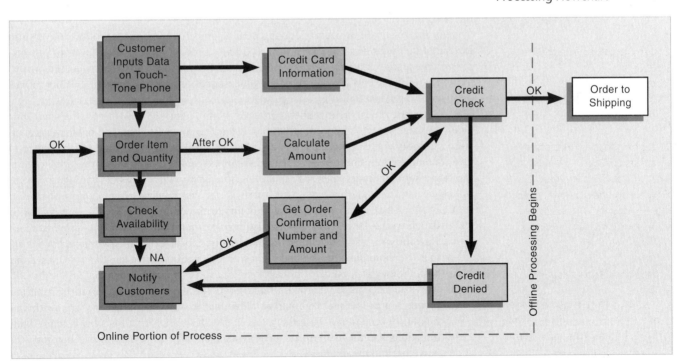

	Product Structure–Product Life Cycle Stage			
	I	II	III	IV
Process Life Cycle Stage	Low Volume–Low Standardization One of a Kind	Multiple Products Low Volume	Few Major Products Higher Volume	High Volume–High Standardization Commodity Products
Job shop	Commercial printer			
Batch production		Heavy equipment		
Flow shop			Automobile assembly	
Continuous flow				Sugar refinery
	Economies of Scale ⟶ Lower Unit Costs ⟶			

Batch = larger lots than JS

Source: Adapted from the *Harvard Business Review*; an exhibit from "Link Manufacturing Process and Product Life Cycles: Focusing on the Process Gives a New Dimension to Strategy," by Robert H. Hayes and Steven C. Wheelwright, January–February 1979, pp. 133–140.

Table 5-2

Matrix of Product Life Cycle Stages (Columns) versus Process Life Cycle Stages (Rows)

5-13 Shifting Work Configuration Types

Hayes and Wheelwright[7] developed the matrix shown in Table 5-2. It captures an important aspect of the relationship between product life cycle stages and process life cycle stages.

The product life cycle stages are labeled "product structure" by the authors. This terminology is translatable to categories of volume and variety.

Process life cycle stages are labeled "process structure" by the authors. This terminology is equivalent to type of work configuration.

The relationship depicted by the matrix indicates that as products move from low volume and high variety (left) to high volume and commodity products with no variety (right), the process type moves from the job shop (top) to the continuous flow system (bottom). The diagonal, moving downward and from left to right, delineates the progression. Also, the authors distinguish between smaller job shops and larger ones by calling the latter batch work.

This matrix takes an operations-oriented approach to defining product life cycles instead of the focus that marketing uses. It defines product life cycles in terms of increasing volume and decreasing variety. This matrix shows the connection between the growth in demand volume and the nature of the process that can deliver enough product to balance supply and demand.

It is possible to use a flow shop for lower-volume and higher-variety products. This would be like moving heavy equipment in Table 5-2 down one box and off the diagonal. Auto assembly could be raised one row and made a batch process. Such off-the-diagonal positions are permissible, special, and difficult to sustain. The following admonitions should be kept in mind:

1 If the actual company process falls above the diagonal, it is not well suited to handling the larger volume that the market demands, and it can provide more flexibility for variety than the market requires. Both of these deviations have costs that exert pressure on the company to move back to the diagonal to be on a par with its competitors.

2 If the actual company process falls below the diagonal, it is geared to handling higher volumes than the market demands, and is less able to cope with the flexibility needed for the variety levels that the market requires. Once again, both directions for the deviations have costs that exert pressure on the company to move back to the diagonal.

As the authors of the matrix state, "A company that allows itself to drift from the diagonal without understanding the likely implications of such a shift is asking for trouble."[8]

5-13a Expanded Matrix of Process Types

Six classes for work configurations were mentioned at the start of this chapter. Projects were dropped from that list because they apply to start-ups and not online production systems. Projects are treated in Part 4. That leaves five to consider here. Because the matrix in Table 5-2 illustrates only four process types, a new matrix has been constructed to reflect the positioning of the five process types. The custom shop has been added to the matrix.

This makes it clear that an FMS process can act like a custom shop, a job shop, or even a flow shop. It makes no sense to emulate a flow shop because it is more expensive to develop than a nonflexible flow shop, and has higher maintenance costs. When variety is sought by marketing, emulation of the custom or job shops may be warranted. Also, the fourth stage, which represents continuous production of commodity products, is possible for FMS but not economical.

5-14 The Extended Diagonal

Expanding the matrix in Table 5-2 extends the diagonal as seen in Table 5-3. The custom shop is now shown producing one unit at a time. If the custom shop manager decides to make two units on a customized basis, then that would move the X one box to the right of the diagonal. To do this, perhaps some process steps would need to be modified to facilitate making two units more efficiently than one at a time. Off-diagonal positions are viewed as requiring special process descriptions. There is a need to explain and justify off-diagonal activities.

5-14a Adding the Custom Shop

The smooth progression along the diagonal is not disrupted by the addition of the customized shop. Customized process abilities are associated with the highest level of variety and the most unique products. The custom shop is akin to a small project shop where the size of projects is on a different scale than launching a new product.

The custom shop creates a new northwest corner, expanding the matrix so that it can produce one-of-a-kind variety far more economically than the job shop.

This places the job shop second in position on the matrix, where it fulfills the mission of producing lot sizes in batches of 50 units on average. True assembly line flow shops turn out thousands of units for very few product varieties. Continuous flow systems are better served by dedicated equipment than by flexible systems.

	One at a Time	Medium Volume	High Volume	Highest
Custom shop	X			
Job shop		X		
Flow shop			X	
Continuous flow shop				X
Flexible systems	X	X	X	

Table 5-3

Matrix of Product Life Cycle Stages (Output Volume) Versus Process Life Cycle Stages (Type of Work Configuration)

Table 5-4

Matrix (For Services): Product Life Cycle Stages (Columns) Versus Process Life Cycle Stages (Rows)

Output Volume Increases Moving Right				
Job shop	Offices			
Batch		Textbooks		
Flow shop			Fast foods	
Continuous flow				Newspapers
Economies of Scale ⟶ Lower-Unit Costs ⟶				

Legend: Batch = larger lots than JS

Source: Adapted from the Harvard Business Review; an exhibit from "Link Manufacturing Process and Product Life Cycles: Focusing on the Process Gives a New Dimension to Strategy," by Robert H. Hayes & Steven C. Wheelwright, Jan.–Feb. 1979, pp. 133–140. Copyright © 1978 by the President and Fellows of Harvard College; all rights reserved.

5-14b The Role of FMS

It is noteworthy that the addition of flexible systems to the matrix in Table 5-3 stops the diagonal progression and bends the variety level back to the highest level that can be obtained with a flow shop. The volume also circles back to one or a few at a time, like the custom shop. Because of the ability to achieve nearly instantaneous changeovers from one job to another, the flexible process acts as if it were a flow shop.

Flexible systems make a distinct break with the past. This is the first time that production technology permits hybrid results. The hybrid in this case combines the variety of the job shop with the economies of scale advantages of the flow shop. Flexible technology opened processing vistas not conceived of before advanced computer developments.

5-14c Applied to Services

It is also convenient to extend the basic matrix (Table 5-2, which applied to manufacturing) so that it can reflect the same set of considerations when applied to services. This results in Table 5-4.

The systems view of relationships between service products and processes is similar to the relationships for manufacturing. The fact is that processes tend to develop from higher variety to lower variety as market success moves demand volume from low to high. Supply, in order to match demand, requires alterations of the process type. Off-diagonal positions must be justified.

5-15 Aggregating Demand

Demand is affected by variety, price, and the quality of the product. By controlling these variables, it is possible to aggregate demand. The accumulation of volume is done to move toward process configurations designed for higher-volume levels. One of the most used controls is lowering the price. Usually (but not always) lower price increases demand in line with normal price-elasticity relationships. Increasing item variety (say 2 colors instead of 1) is another means of increasing aggregate demand.

The elasticity relationship of product quality and price with demand volume is not the classic model where only price elasticity is taken into account. When customers cannot find substitutes for unique qualities of products, they will pay more to get what they like. This makes those product qualities into forces for less elasticity. Figure 5-6 relates supply capabilities, product variety, product quality, and price to demand.

All of the boxes are interrelated. Variety and quality (box 3) and price and delivery (box 4) drive demand (box 1). The degree of change in demand reflects the particular

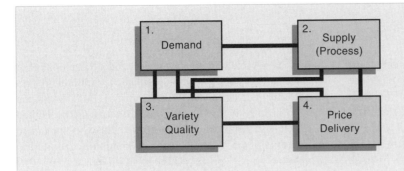

Figure 5-6

Variables That Affect Aggregation of Demand (All Links Flow Two Ways)

relative elasticity of each market segment. Not to be overlooked is the effect of work process configurations on supply (box 2). Supply feeds demand. How supply and demand match determines the economic feasibility of the system. A box representing the product design is always present. A change in product design can alter the parameters for demand aggregation. This is closely associated with quality in box 3.

Flexible manufacturing systems are outstanding potential sources of control over the factors shown in the Figure 5-6. If the FMS process costs are at a minimum—paralleling flow shop economies of scale—it is possible to gain market share and aggregate volume by lowering prices. The same reasoning applies to the advantages of high variety, which is a reason for FMS. Superior quality of FMS products is derived from the excellence of equipment that can be programmed. Flexible systems use enhanced control features to provide tight tolerance excellence.

Using an FMS permits a company to aggregate volume of new products that can then be assigned to conventional flow shop processes. In other words, flexible manufacturing systems can help facilitate the transformation of batch-type processes to dedicated flow shop facilities. In essence it is the process that facilitates the growth in demand that can then sustain flow shop configurations.

Spotlight 5-1 The Ford Motor Company: Henry Ford—A Process Genius

Summary: The history of leadership in the Ford Motor Company reveals that the systems approach is vital if P/OM, marketing, and finance are to be on a winning team. When the Ford functions are each marching to their own drummer, Ford's performance deteriorates so rapidly that extreme measures are required to sustain the company. Once again that scenario is being played out.

Henry Ford changed America a century ago, a time when auto manufacturers were rushing into business and usually disappearing nearly as quickly. What made Henry Ford's company a success was his idea of designing a car the average man could afford. His idea was to keep lowering manufacturing costs in order to continually reduce the price and enlarge the market. This business plan, which focused on the highly efficient sequenced assembly process, earned Henry Ford a major fortune.

Before Ford's Model T was introduced on October 1, 1908, most Americans had no choice but to watch and yearn as automobiles grew bigger, faster, and so expensive that only the rich could afford them. In 1906, *The North American Review* printed an article titled "An Appeal to Our Millionaires." It warned, "Unfortunately, our millionaires, and especially their idle and degenerate children, have been flaunting their money in the faces of the poor as if actually wishing to provoke them." This anti-auto feeling

Spotlight 5-1 (Continued)

in the United States prior to the Model T's debut was summed up by Woodrow Wilson, then president of Princeton University. In 1906, he described drivers of horseless carriages as "a picture of arrogance and wealth, with all its independence and carelessness." At the time, it was estimated that more Americans died in car accidents in the first six months of 1906 than had been killed in the Spanish-American War.

The Model T's price just before World War I was $360. Billboards advertised "Even You Can Afford a Ford." Farmers loved the Model T. By attaching a belt to the crankshaft or rear axle, a farmer gained a power source and labor-saving device for hundreds of uses on the farm. Custom Model Ts became taxis, buses, trucks, fire engines, delivery vans, and police cars. Model Ts accounted for two-thirds of all automobiles in America.

In 1914, the first traffic light in the United States went up in Cleveland, Ohio. Four years later, Woodrow Wilson, who had become president of the United States, owned his own Model T. A farmer's wife summed up the feelings of the country in a letter to Ford in 1918. She wrote, "You brought joy into our lives." The car had opened the American landscape, altered the outlook of consumers everywhere, and changed the way automobiles would be manufactured and sold.

Henry Ford was a great mechanic and manufacturing innovator. Of all the automotive pioneers in Detroit at the time, none knew more about cars than Henry Ford. After several situations turned into disastrous failures, Ford was quoted as maintaining that, "failure is the opportunity to begin again, more intelligently." With all his talents and uncanny understanding of auto mechanics, his genius did not lie in working with his hands or reading blueprints. He was called a cut-and-try mechanic, unable to visualize things and put them on paper. With his deep understanding of the whole system, his genius seemed to work by adding a sense of simplicity and completeness to the Model T. He knew his customers were mechanically unschooled and therefore the automobile had to be easy to operate or they would not buy it in the numbers he envisioned. His success in accomplishing this goal depended on how much he could get other people to work for his interests, from financial backing to choosing his engineers and associates.

With the belief that the Model T could not be improved but the process of making it could, Ford opened his new River Rouge plant in Dearborn, Michigan, where he was able to control the entire process of automobile manufacturing. Raw materials were brought in on the company's own fleet of ships and were methodically transformed into vehicles. The plant was dedicated to saving time and money. New tools and ideas were introduced each day. For instance, a new tool allowed a drill press operator to drill 10 holes at once (instead of one at a time). Ford developed one of the leading time-study departments in the United States. It was comprised of about 80 men who canvassed the factories, recording the number of minutes required to complete each new process. In only seven years, from 1919 to 1926, River Rouge grew to include 93 buildings, 75,000 employees, and output of 4,000 cars per day.

As Henry Ford grew older, he failed to accept that cars should be styled and have more than one color. He had created one of the world's major fortunes with his business plan, and he flatly refused to change it. Because the Ford family owned 100 percent of the stock, no one could tell him what to do, including his only son, Edsel, who had been made president of the company in 1919. Even after the market forced him to abandon the Model T in 1927, Ford clung to the past and constantly interfered with his son's attempts to make Ford into a modern corporation like General Motors.

By 1945, Ford Motor executives had lost track of the company's operations. Concern from the War Production Board led the Secretary of the Navy to release Henry Ford's grandson (one of Edsel's four children) from service so that he could take over the company. The elder Henry, failing in health, reluctantly agreed to make his grandson, Henry Ford II, president. Two years later, Henry Ford died.

Henry Ford II turned out to be a gifted executive who made considerable progress in saving the Ford Motor Company. He was 28 years old and not experienced when he took control of the company. He recruited Ernest Breech from GM to reorganize the company. An immediate change was the accounting system. That was followed by decentralization of management. Henry Ford II had read Peter Drucker's 1946 book, *Concept of the Corporation*. Its tenet: No institution can exist under one-man rule.

Henry II faced a myriad of challenges including the overseas development of operations in 78 countries. The new International Division netted $48 million in 1949. The Thunderbird (1955) gave Ford a 2-seater of its own. Ford's F-Series truck line came to maturity in the 1960s. These were good years. The Mustang, introduced in 1964, was a great success. Automotive safety efforts intensified in the late 1960s. By 1970, these efforts helped to reduce the death toll on U.S. highways for the first time since 1958, even though Americans drove 5 percent more miles. Ford ranked fifth in size among U.S. corporations.

From 1970 to 1978, Lee Iacocca came aboard as president of Ford Motor Company under Chairman Henry Ford II. The two men were profoundly different in outlook.

High on Iacocca's priority list was styling. A car's outer appearance was "frozen" by Iacocca before engineers could design the inner mechanics. Whether this design handicap accounted for the Pinto disaster is not clear. Litigation over the Pinto's fuel tank resulted in the recall of 1.5 million cars. The company culture had become fixated on cost, profit, and short-term results. Henry II quietly began taking power away from Lee Iacocca, firing him in 1978 before retiring in 1980.

Philip Caldwell became CEO in the same year that Hewlett-Packard announced the release of its first personal computer in 1980. Ford Motor Company certainly needed new leadership to compete with Japan and to change public perceptions of the inferior quality of Ford products. In the years from 1973 to 1980, the world had suffered the worst energy crisis in modern times. OPEC had implemented an oil embargo that crippled the United States. In 1973, gas station lines were sometimes miles long and energy shortages caused many brownouts throughout the country. The government decided to initiate new fuel economy measures and issued safety and emission control regulations as well.

Caldwell arrived at his leadership position after coming up through the ranks at Ford with no shortcuts. He and his executive vice presidents were hailed in *The Wall Street Journal* as a new breed of manager, the kind of men who ran the company "before it was overrun by flamboyant marketing managers." Under Caldwell's team of managers, the company made a great effort to ameliorate the downsizing of 60,000 employees by communicating to UAW officials that quality had to improve. Plants that achieved this objective would remain open. The company admitted publicly that the difference between Ford and its Japanese competitors was not the quality of workers but Ford's inferior management policy which did not emphasize continuous improvement in product quality. It was this admission that eased labor tensions and enabled a satisfactory agreement in 1982 between the company and its union. Philip Caldwell conveyed the mission statement to all Ford workers: "Quality is Job 1." This was the cornerstone of Japanese manufacturing as preached by the guru of quality, W. Edwards Deming, who was a consultant to Ford Motor.

Modular assembly was introduced in 1985 (subassemblies produced on automated ancillary lines that feed the main assembly line). The Aerostar was the first vehicle produced with this method. Don Petersen, the new chairman and CEO in February 1985, following Caldwell's retirement, approved a $3.5 billion budget for the Taurus/Sable. Within that billion-dollar budget, Ford engineers tore apart hundreds of cars sold by competitors, a process called *reverse engineering*, to learn best practices of other companies.

Starting in 1987, Ford bought several car companies. It was rumored that Ford's executives could thus drive Jaguars without guilt. In 1992, Ford bought 33 percent of Mazda. Land Rover and Volvo were added. As market demand moved from sedans to sport utility vehicles, the Bronco and Bronco II, Ford's early SUVs, were replaced by the Ford Explorer that debuted in 1991 and rode a huge wave of popularity. By 1998 Ford had sold 3 million Explorers.

William Clay Ford, Jr. (Bill Jr.), as Chairman, and Jacques Nasser, as CEO and President, became the new leaders of Ford in 1999. The two men did not agree on how to run the company. However, under their leadership, the company entered a new marketplace, the virtual world of the Internet. Several websites were linked and a new company, Covisint, was formed in 2000, backed by an automotive consortium of Ford, Daimler-Chrysler, and GM. Covisint, a B2B (business to business) global organization, became the virtual marketplace for the automobile industry and their suppliers.

Today, Covisint is owned by Compuware. It continues to improve automakers' supply chain efficiency. A Covisint unit provides the Ford Supplier Portal, a secure virtual network that is continually enhancing the system of collaborative business processes with suppliers in seven different languages across the global network.

The years 2000 and 2001 brought recalls and replacements of all Ford Explorer Firestone Wilderness AT tires—almost 20 million tires in all. With 100 Firestone-related lawsuits, and a $5.5 billion loss from the Firestone recall, it was clear that Ford Motor was going in the wrong direction. In October of 2001, Ford's Board of Directors removed Nasser and put operating responsibility in the hands of a Ford for the first time in 22 years.

Bill Jr., great-grandson of Henry Ford and now Chairman and CEO of Ford Motor Company, was faced with a company losing billions of dollars, demoralized employees, and questionable quality of its cars and trucks.

In remaking the company into a flagship of sustainable flexible manufacturing, Ford's goal is to recycle almost all parts of its cars and trucks. Ford was the first auto company to certify its plants around the world under ISO 14001, a series of environmental standards. (See Chapter 20, Section 20-6)

In 2007, he continues to work as an environmentalist/industrialist with an eventual goal of transforming Ford Motor Company into a new model of clean, eco-efficient products (hybrids, ethanol, hydrogen, etc.) and sustainable manufacturing.

A day after Ford Motor announced a 5.8 billion quarterly loss in October 2006, Bill Jr. relinquished his job of CEO and president of the company to make room for a new Chief Executive and President, Alan Mulally. As former head of Boeing's commercial jet-building division, Mulally (reputed father of Boeing's Dreamliner) was chosen with deliberate care by Bill Jr., who continues as Chairman. Most of Mulally's compensation will be based on performance. Both men agree on what they call "The Way Forward" plan. In an interview available on Forbes.com, Mullally states that the first step is to match capacity to demand. (By that, he means closing down unproductive plants and dismissing unnecessary salaried and hourly employees.) The next step

Spotlight 5-1 (Continued)

is to improve quality and response to customer needs. A changeover to flexible manufacturing is necessary to be competitive. At present, there is a separate line for every vehicle. Mulally states, "We want to get to the place where we use those assets to produce two or three or four or five models on the same line. That will be the long-term plan to create a viable Ford."

The Toyota system may be the benchmark that Ford must now surpass if it is to survive. Ironically, Henry Ford's system was the benchmark that gave birth to the Toyota Production System (TPS).*

Review Questions

1 Henry Ford changed America and the world with a production process and a business plan that were unlike anything that had ever been tried before. What was unique about this production process?

2 What can we learn about P/OM from the history of the Ford Motor Company?

3 During the late 1960s, American automobile companies engaged with the U.S government in efforts to improve safety on the highways. Why was that effort necessary? Was that effort effective? Examine data through 2007.

4 Lee Iacocca was president of the Ford Motor Company from 1970 to 1978. It is interesting that Lee Iacocca, like Edsel Ford, was primarily interested in styling. He would design for appearance before designing for functional characteristics (how does it drive) and before process design issues (how is it made) had been resolved. Why would designing for appearance before functional and process decisions had been made cause serious problems for P/OM departments?

5 What are Ford Motor Company's plans with respect to hybrid, electric, and hydrogen vehicles? Research this question by using websearch: "Ford Motor and Alternative Fuels."

*Taiichi Ohno credited Henry Ford for the TPS. He was inspired after reading Ford's 1926: Ford, Henry. *Today and Tomorrow.* Originally published in 1926; Commemorative edition issued by Productivity Press. University Park, IL, 1988; http://www.covisint.com/about; http://www.biz.yahoo.com/ic/101/101123.html (Information on Covisint); http://www.forbes.com/2006/10/24/ford-ceo-mulally-biz-cx_jf_1024ford_print.html; http://en.wikipedia.org/wiki/Ford_Family_Tree.

Sources: Douglas, Brinkley. *Wheels for the World: Henry Ford, His Company, and a Century of Progress.* Viking, 2003; Gordon, John Steele. The Greatest Comeback. *American Heritage*, July 2003; Hakim, Danny. "A Family's 100-Year Car Trip." *The New York Times* (June 15, 2003); Bodek, Norman. *Kaikaku: The Power and Magic of Lean: A Study in Knowledge Transfer.* PCS Press, 2004; Banham, Russ. *The Ford Century: Ford Motor Company and the Innovations That Shaped the World.* New York: Artisan (a division of Workman Publishing Company), 2002.

Spotlight 5-2 Shouldice Surgery
The Focused Factory in Health Care

Dr. Edward Earle Shouldice, 1890–1965, a major in the Canadian army during World War II, discovered that many young men were denied enlistment because of untreated hernias. Because of world crisis (1940), doctors and hospital resources were scarce, especially for surgical repair of hernias, which were non-emergency procedures that took approximately 3 weeks of hospitalization.

Shouldice took on the challenge. He operated on 70 of these men, contributing his services at no cost and using an innovative method that hastened their recovery. His patients were delighted with the success, and news of the surgery spread the word about the Shouldice method of treatment. After the war, hundreds of patients contacted Dr. Shouldice to request surgery. Because of a scarcity of hospital beds, Shouldice opened his own hospital in Toronto, Canada.

In 1945, with a cook, secretary, and nurse, he was repairing two hernias per day in a single operating room. In 1953, he purchased a large country estate in Thornhill, Ontario, and converted it to the current facility, which sits on 20 acres of landscaped grounds including a putting green. The hospital is an 89-bed facility with 5 operating theaters and a team of 10 surgeons that serves a worldwide clientele. Visitors are likely to pass groups of patients who stroll about in lounging robes because they have had their hernias repaired on the previous day. Shouldice uniquely combines a non-hospital ambience with 60 years of accumulated experience with hernias.

Shouldice surgical teams perform only hernia operations. They have repaired more than 300,000 hernias with a greater than 99 percent success rate. The average chance of hernia recurrence after a Shouldice repair is less than 1 percent, compared to the North American average of over 10 percent. These performance measures explain why Shouldice is often referred to as a model for benchmarking. Harvard professor Regina Herzlinger selected the Shouldice model in her book, *Market Driven Health Care*, and has since released a second book, *Consumer Driven Health Care*, in which there is a chapter written by Daryl Urquhart and Alan O'Dell, defining details of the focused model of healthcare delivery, as practiced in the Shouldice Hospital model.

Patients receive local anesthesia, contributing to the exceptional safety of the operation. A sedative (sleeping pill) is provided the night before surgery. The average operation takes 45 minutes. A Shouldice patient's postoperative recovery begins as he or she walks out of the operating room. The following morning there is an exercise program with fellow patients. Confidence builds quickly in the hernia repair. Comparing notes and discussing concerns with other patients is an excellent way to dispel anxieties. The average hospital stay is 3 days. Patients return to work in an average of 8 days after their hernia repair.

Shouldice Hospital performs 32 operations per day on average, 242 days per year. This results in about 7,600 happy people per year. The hospital surgeons do not work on weekends. Because these doctors have exclusively devoted all their time and resources to the practice of hernia surgery, they have developed a valuable sixth sense in the recognition and handling of all the problems that surround hernia pathology.

A hernia is the protrusion of an organ through a weakness in the abdominal wall. This weakness can be congenital, acquired (from heavy lifting), or created following abdominal operations. Hernias do not go away—they only get bigger. Women get hernias, too. (Every week there is an average of 10 women at Shouldice for surgery.) There are no stereotypes for hernias. At Shouldice, patients have ranged from 4 months to 100 years of age.

To understand the method of repair, one must know that the muscles of the groin portion of the abdominal wall have 3 distinct layers. The Shouldice method repairs each layer in turn by overlapping its margins as the edges of a coat overlap when buttoned. The end result reinforces the muscular wall of the abdomen. No foreign bodies such as synthetic screens or meshes are used, except in extreme cases where there is tissue damage. The Shouldice method is called pure tissue repair.

Claims by other institutions that they use the "Shouldice technique" or the "Canadian method" do not take into account that the "formula," though not a secret, extends beyond surgery to the total care package. Operating rooms are designed for efficient flow shop surgery, and participants are practiced in synchronized activities. The teams are aware of anomalies and prepared for contingencies in a way that is the hallmark of focused factories, which were first introduced to the P/OM field by Wick Skinner in 1974. Focused factories comprise specialized groupings (cells) of core competencies. They concentrate on practice to perfection of one clearly defined process. Specialization occurs as a result of high volumes of similar work.

In 1947, a few patients suggested an annual reunion, which grew to include an average of 1,000 patients per event. The reunion included dinner, entertainment, camaraderie, and a medical checkup and became so popular amongst Shouldice alumni that the hospital had to temporarily discontinue the event in order to redesign it to a more manageable size and format. Following up on all patients every year after they leave is an integral part of Shouldice research efforts.

This is a rare instance of medical care matching best practices in production. Shouldice Hospital provides business students with the chance to learn the considerable benefits occurring with reorganization of traditional thinking. Working in such an environment empowers everyone to continue this practice. The 2007 Shouldice site on the Internet is a marvel in conveying information to potential candidates for surgery. The site uses a simplified web-based method of completing medical questionnaires so that a surgeon can review the information and the Shouldice staff can arrange a booking date in a timely manner. An 18-minute video, "Understanding Hernias," is available on request from the http://www.shouldice.com website.

An independent study on patient satisfaction at Shouldice Hospital was conducted by Concordia University's Molson School of Business. The survey included over 400 patients, chosen randomly and questioned 3 times: at admission, 3 days into their stay, and 1 month post op. The results are as follows: On a scale measuring degrees of satisfaction from 1 to 10 with 5 indicating "Satisfied," the total was 9.1, indicating "Delighted." In a measurement of overall service quality where "Good Quality" was 5, the overall rating was 9.2, indicating "Extremely Good Quality."

On February 11, 2005, Shouldice Hospital participated in a live video teleconference with the American Hernia Society, in which a classic Shouldice inguinal hernia repair was performed at Shouldice and viewed simultaneously on a

Spotlight 5-2 (Continued)

giant screen by hundreds of surgeons attending an AHS conference in San Diego. Two-way audio and visual communications were available to receive and respond to questions from the San Diego audience. Upon completion of the operation, the patient walked out of the operating room as part of the standard Shouldice routine. It was a perfect example of what can be accomplished by a unique medical "focused factory." Dr. Edward Shouldice would be pleased with the performance.

Review Questions

1 Why is it said that Shouldice Hospital is like a focused factory?
2 What is the focus of Shouldice Hospital?

3 Why is it that imitating the Shouldice surgical procedure does not result in equivalent quality?
4 Are there other industries (services included) where the focused factory is evident and successful?
5 What can be learned from the Shouldice follow-up on all patients?
6 What is the rationale for the annual reunion of Shouldice alumni?

Sources: Courtesy of Shouldice Hospital, April 24, 2007. http://www.shouldice.com. Herzlinger, Regina. *Market Driven Health Care.* Boston, MA: Addison Wesley, 1999; Skinner, C. Wickham. *The Focused Factory. Harvard Business Review* (May 1974): 113–121; Correspondence with Daryl Urquhart, Director of Business Development, Shouldice Hospital, Ltd., April 2007.

Summary

One important differentiating characteristic of processes is whether they are synthetic or analytic. Synthetic processes assemble; analytic processes disassemble. It is noted that the theory of production constraints (TOC, also referred to as the OPT system) makes this structural distinction before attempting to synchronize schedules for finite production capacity.

Process configuration strategies are explained. There are basically six different ways to do work, and five of these are appropriate for online production systems. The five types of work systems are custom shops for one-of-a-kind output, job shop and batch production, serialized one-after-another output of the flow shop, small lots with high variety from flexible process systems, and continuous output flows from refinery-type systems. These work configurations are significant for strategic planning and for tactical execution. Cycle time of the flow shop will be encountered again in Chapter 17, where cycle-time management of the flow shop is shown to be a vital P/OM responsibility.

Two Spotlight feature boxes conclude this chapter. Spotlight 5-1 shows the genius of Henry Ford and the problems of the Ford Motor Company when management loses track of the big system. Spotlight 5-2 illuminates one of the great process achievements of all time. Shouldice Hospital has shown that surgery can reap the benefits of focused factories.

Key Terms

Analytic process (p. 152)
Benchmarking (p. 158)
Best practice (p. 158)
Continuous processes (p. 162)
Custom shop (p. 159)
Economies of scale (p. 164)
Economies of scope (p. 165)
Ends (p. 149)
Flexible manufacturing system (FMS) (p. 166)
Flexible office system (p. 166)
Flexible process system (FPS) (p. 166)
Flow shops (FS) (p. 161)
General-purpose equipment (GPE) (p. 160)
Group technology cellular manufacturing systems (p. 167)

Intermittent flow shop (IFS) (p. 165)
Job shop (JS) (p. 160)
Just-in-case (p. 151)
Just-in-time (p.151)
Logistics (p. 162)
OPT (p. 159)
Process (p. 147)
Process steps (p. 147)
Projects (p. 147)
Simulations (p. 148)
Special-purpose equipment (SPE) (p. 160)
Supply chain (p. 149)
Synthetic process (p. 150)
Theory of Constraints (p. 159)
Work configuration (p. 147)

Review Questions

1 The management of supply is related to the management of demand. What does this statement mean?

2 It is said that the existence of the demand for a product leads to the creation of the industry that can supply products to satisfy that (need) demand. If need drives supply, then what accounts for the sales of DVDs, CDs, MP3 players, digital cameras, the iPhone, and air conditioners? Consumers did not ask for these products until after they were made available. Producers took the risk of tooling up for high volumes of production in order to obtain low enough prices so that consumers would buy these items.

3 Is it true that the drivers of demand are price, quality, and variety? Are there other drivers?

4 What is a process?

    a. Does a process differ from a procedure? How?

    b. Does a process differ from a method? How? Hint: Use the dictionary to look up "procedure" and "method." Then, relate process to technology and note the relationship between process and product technology.

5 What is a custom shop? Why is the custom shop a natural start for an entrepreneur?

6 What rules apply for managing a successful custom shop?

7 In 1999, Au Bon Pain Co., a fast-food franchise, renamed itself Panera Bread Company (PNRA—Nasdaq) and sold its Au Bon Pain division to private equity groups. Both companies stress high-quality coffee, buns, sandwiches, and soups. There are four to five times more PNRAs than ABPs, which means greater familiarity with PNRA operations. Which are more applicable for Panera: rules for running a good custom shop or those for a good job shop?

8 Describe a job shop. What prescriptions apply for managing a successful job shop?

9 Would most entrepreneurs prefer to run a job shop or a custom shop?

10 Contrast analytic processes with synthetic processes and give examples of both kinds of systems. Can simulation be used to study these processes?

11 Discuss the advantages and disadvantages of moving from one work configuration stage to another. Refer to Tables 5-2, 5-3, and 5-4. What are the pros and the cons of moving down the diagonal to higher volumes or up the diagonal to higher variety? Can simulation be used to evaluate the benefits of employing each work configuration?

12 What are economies of scope? Do they eliminate economies of scale or can these two kinds of process economies work together?

13 What kind of a business process is exemplified by a supermarket? Deal with the entire process of ordering, stocking the shelves, customers shopping, checkout counters, etc.

14 What kind of business process and work configuration is used by the post office? Discuss the process. Can you estimate how many transactions are handled per minute by your own local post office?

Problems Section

Note: This section has various problems that can be formulated and solved using QuantMethods Production/Operations Management software (QMpom). The appropriate model categories are indicated for each problem.

1 Much used by the automobile industry for the assembly process is a paced conveyor to move the chassis from station to station. This is usually cited as an example of a pure synthetic process.

    a. Is this true?

    b. If the assembly process of an older auto assembly plant in New Jersey takes 32 hours, and there are 1,000 workstations along the conveyor path, what is the length of time that the conveyor is stopped at each station?

2 A new auto assembly plant has been built in Kentucky. It has an assembly process that takes 22 hours, and there are 800 workstations along the conveyor path. What is the length of time that the conveyor is stopped at each station?

3 With reference to Problems 1 and 2, what is the cycle time for each auto assembly plant? Comment on the comparison of the New Jersey plant with the Kentucky plant.

4 With reference to Problems 1, 2 and 3, what is the hourly production output rate at each plant? Assuming two 8-hour shifts, six days a week, compare the weekly output of the New Jersey plant and the Kentucky plant.

5 The average annual investment cost of a workstation in New Jersey has been calculated to be $100,000. It has been calculated to be $150,000 in Kentucky. The hourly cost at a workstation is $60 in New Jersey and $40 in Kentucky. How do the two plants compare with respect to the cost of labor for making a car? For each location, what is the breakeven volume and what is the total cost at breakeven? Using the QMpom module called Capacity Management Models (Cost-Volume and Breakeven) will facilitate solving Problem 5.

6 An interesting comparison can be drawn between the Volvo method of building autos in Sweden and that of U.S. auto companies. Specifically, the Volvo Company has pioneered a team approach for assembling an auto. The Volvo team builds the car on a platform. Even the engine is put together by the same team and mounted on the chassis. This means that the workers come to the work instead of the work coming to the workers.

    a. If it takes Volvo workers 40 hours to assemble a car in this way, what is the cycle time?

    b. How many stations are there?

    c. Analyze the pros and cons of the Volvo assembly system.

)

d. Does the Volvo system constitute a synthetic flow shop?

e. Volvo does not use this team assembly method for its U.S. plant. Why is that so?

7 The highest volume item in a job shop is made in lots of 1,000 units once every week. Demand is 52,000 units per year or 200 units per 8-hour day. As an alternative, it has been suggested that an intermittent flow shop (IFS) should be set up twice a year to satisfy the same demand. Use the following data to compare the costs of each production strategy.

IFS setup costs = $3,700.00 per setup
LT for setup is 1 day, which is small enough to be ignored.
Cost per unit with IFS = $5.00
Time per unit with IFS = 0.1 minute per unit
Regular batch setup costs = $1,000 per setup
Cost per unit with regular batch production = $8.00
Time per unit with regular batch production = 1.0 minutes
Carrying cost is 1 percent per month

Using the QMpom module called Inventory and Production Models (Economic Production Lot Size) will facilitate solving Problem 7.

8 Applying the information given in Problem 7, consider the following:

Since an IFS has been suggested, why not analyze, at the same time, the use of a programmable FMS. This particular product lends itself to membership in a family of parts that could be made with a group technology cellular manufacturing system. The investment for the manufacturing cell would be shared with other members of the family. An estimate has been made that its share of the annual investment would be $200,000 per year. The cost per unit would be $2.00 and the time per unit is 0.50 minute.

Do you recommend this option? Explain and discuss.

Using the QMpom module called Inventory and Production Models (Economic Production Lot Size) will facilitate solving Problem 8.

9 Define and compare the six basically different ways of doing work in terms of the seven factors listed here. Each kind of process system (i.e., one of the six types of work configurations) is best suited to a particular set of conditions. These conditions arise from factors such as the following:

a. How complex is the character of the product line

b. Equipment associated with the process

c. Nature of the market

d. Financial situation of the firm

e. How many units are to be made or serviced

f. How profitable is the venture

g. What is the competition like

10 The approach to evaluating alternative work configurations can be modeled to provide more structure. To exemplify, a model is constructed to evaluate under what conditions the intermittent flow shop (IFS) will be selected in preference to the batch production of a job shop (JS).

For the IFS, setup, takedown and changeover costs have to be amortized over the lot size that is run. The IFS produces N units at a cost of c dollars per unit with a fixed setup cost of S dollars.

Compare that cost with the cost of setup for the job shop production process, S'. The lot size is the same but the cost per unit, $c' > c$. The cost comparison is shown here with some hypothetical numbers for costs and a lot size of $N = 100$.

$$IFS : (cN + S)/N = (3 \times 100 + 500)/100 = \$8.00 \text{ per unit made}$$

$$JS : (c'N + S')/N = (4 \times 100 + 300)/100 = \$7.00 \text{ per unit made}$$

So, choose to use the job shop to make the 100 units.

Next, assume that the lot size is 500 units.

$$IFS : (cN + S)/N = (3 \times 500 + 500)/500 = \$4.00 \text{ per unit made}$$

$$JS : (c'N + S')/N = (4 \times 500 + 300)/500 = \$4.60 \text{ per unit made}$$

So, choose the IFS.

Now, assume that both setup costs are double.

a. What is the choice when the lot size is $N = 100$?
b. What is the choice when the lot size is $N = 500$?

11 If the total time to make a wireless presenter mouse is 24 minutes and it is made at four workstations, how long is the cycle time?

12 Create a board game to simulate the workflow through the four workstations in Problem 11. Describe and discuss the procedures.

Practice Quiz

1 The difference between processes and work configurations is best summed up by which answer?

a. Maintenance programs for jet engines are examples of work configurations. Building the jet engine is a process.
b. Simulations are processes. Board games are used to structure work configurations.
c. Work configurations can be charted and improved. Process improvement is specified by technology with few degrees of freedom.
d. Work configurations apply to manufacturing. Delivery of services is a process.
e. Processes are composed of activities required to make a product or deliver a service, e.g., how to make and present a cheese soufflè. Work configurations are physical arrangements used to make the product, e.g., flow shop or in batches.

2 What are the differences between synthetic and analytic processes?

a. Analytic processes make synthetic materials that are close imitations of the real thing. Synthetic leather is used for autos and attaché cases.
b. Synthetic processes combine components to make unique end products. Analytic processes are reversals of the synthetic process.
c. Synthetic processes separate the whole into its parts, which are then used to make various end products. Analytic processes are reversals of the synthetic process.
d. Synthesis is a chemical process. Analysis is scientific method.
e. Analytic process is progressive assembly. Synthetic process is the reverse.

3 Process timing includes the rate at which supplies are delivered to the workstations. Which one of the supply options listed here is not sensible?

a. Delivery of *just enough* is a method that suggests efficiency. There is no need for extra storage space to contain the "more than enough" inventory; also, the carrying costs are kept to a minimum.
b. Using the *just-in-case* method provides enough safety stock to take care of those situations where a problem arises such as when the delivery truck has a flat tire.
c. *Just-in-time* is very efficient. It minimizes storage space and makes the supplier a partner to the process.
d. *Play it safe* is a method that provides backup for risky factors in the supply chain. For example, if demand is volatile and the process might have to make more items to fill orders generated by the sale force, it pays to carry more materials and supplies.
e. *Patience is a virtue* stresses going with the flow. If materials are short, slow the line, and if orders are greater than expected, fill them on backorder.

4 Which of the following statements about processes is incorrect?

a. For synthetic processes, it is important to use very focused marketing because there is little room for error. The old saying *you win some, you lose some* does not apply.
b. Analytic processes tend to produce commodities.
c. Marketing of commodities derived from analytic processes is based on lowest price because unique qualities are not associated with commodities.
d. Inputs to analytic processes are themselves commodities, which if carefully chosen for quality can play a role in the quality of the output commodities.
e. Purchasing for synthetic processes is upstream, and quality requirements are stringent at that point because they strongly impact the product quality downstream.

5 Which of the following statements is incorrect?

  a. Use of special purpose equipment (SPE) is crucial to economic well-being for batch work in the job shop.

  b. Custom shop work is not only "made-to-order" but also only small quantities are made with one-of-a-kind being the essence of customization.

  c. Job shops process work in batches or lots. The average lot size of 50 units has been fairly constant over a long period of time for the United States and Europe.

  d. If supply is less than demand in a company using flow shop process design, a possible solution is to employ two or three shifts.

  e. Economies of scale are not as substantial with intermittent flow shops as they are with full-fledged flow shops.

6 Economies of scale are related to changes that occur in costs per unit made as the volume of production goes up or down. Economies of scope are related to the costs of changing over from one item to another on the same production line. Scope refers to variety of types of outputs and scale refers to volume of units produced. Which of the following statements is likely to be wrong?

  a. Three corn-growing farms merge in the belief that economies of scale will help their bottom line.

  b. Three firms merge combining egg and milk production, cheese manufacture, and farming corn, in the belief that product variety will operate as economies of scope and help their bottom line.

  c. Product life cycle stages and process life cycle stages are related by the cost and benefits of economies of scale (volumes of production) and economies of scope (variety of the product line). The variety of output of a commercial printer would be suitable for a job shop configuration.

  d. The demand for earth-moving equipment is segmented into heavy, medium, and light capacities. This multiple line of low-volume products is suitable for a batch work in job shops of substantial size. This industry has cycles, and during an expansion period, the batch configuration could be transformed into an intermittent flow shop.

  e. The diagonal of the matrix of process types matches volumes of production required and variety of products demanded. If conditions shift, it is possible to move vertically or horizontally, leaving the diagonal. For example, a quick service restaurant utilizes a flow shop for certain items (burgers) and batch processes for others (salads).

7 Flexible manufacturing systems (FMS) are a subcategory of flexible processing systems (FPS). This is a work configuration category that developed after 1950. Which of the following statements is incorrect?

  a. Flexible work systems (FWS) permit a modicum of variety levels in the product line. With FWS, lot sizes can be as small as one.

  b. FMS are based on the marriage of computer controls and robotic tools. Also required are programmable means of moving work between stations.

  c. Flexible processing is the foundation for economies of scale. These apply to both the manufacture of goods and service deliveries.

  d. Computer software for word processing, spreadsheets, presentations, etc., represents some of the capabilities required for flexible office systems (FOS). The ability to move from one task to another with very little job-changeover time is the key.

  e. Group technology is a scheme for designing a quick-shift ability to produce members of a family of products, such as gears with different diameters and number of teeth.

8 Which one of the following statements is incorrect?

  a. Without computer-driven flexibility, there can be no economies of scope.

  b. For the most part, office environments are job shops.

  c. Publishers of paper textbooks can use home publishing software to complete one-at-a-time customized books. However, in general, publishers run batches of thousands of books through the print shop.

  d. Continuous production flow systems differ from discrete flow shop systems because the product is actually flowing on a continuous basis, as with chemical manufacturing, electrical production, and newspaper printing.

  e. Quick service restaurants are usually categorized as flow shops even though some are more efficient flow shops than others. To make the flow effective, the customer is made part of the workforce.

9 The owner of a job shop for printing pamphlets and catalogs wants to aggregate the volume of certain products to be able to install a flow shop factory within the job shop factory. This is akin to establishing a cellular manufacturing capability. Which of the following statements is incorrect?

  a. Lowering price aggregates demand—in most cases. However, there are situations where the price-elasticity curve is "kinked." That means it moves in the reverse direction. For example, prestige gifts lose credibility if price is dropped in such a way that the recipient of the gift will be aware that it was purchased by the gift-giver at a discount.

b.   Increasing variety without having to stop production for more than a few minutes is a way to aggregate volume without incurring large costs. For example, changing the flavor of toothpaste can be done quickly.

c.   Better quality is a guarantee that demand will increase, especially if there is no price increase. More demand is the same as aggregating volume.

d.   Speeding deliveries to customers is known to be an effective way to aggregate demand. However, there are no certainties so some market research might be in order.

e.   Dropping price, increasing variety, and cutting delivery times can be effective means of increasing demand for goods or services. However, the introduction of interesting new technology can have a dramatic effect. The size of computer memory and the speed of the system have been two examples of drivers for aggregating volume. New technology is classified as a quality improvement.

10   The assembly process of a remodeled automobile plant in New Jersey requires 32 hours to build a car at 1,000 workstations. A greenfield plant in Tennessee builds a comparable car in 24 hours at 1,200 workstations. How many cars are completed in an 8-hour shift for each plant? What is the cycle time for each plant? Which row in the table below contains the correct answers?

Row Option	Cars Completed New Jersey (in 8-hr. shift)	Cars Completed Tennessee (in 8-hr. shift)	Cycle Time New Jersey	Cycle Time Tennessee
a.	250	320	1.92 min.	1.50 min.
b.	240	400	2.00 min.	1.20 min.
c.	400	250	1.20 min.	1.92 min.
d.	250	400	1.92 min.	1.20 min.
e.	240	320	2.00 min.	1.50 min.

Additional Readings

Abernathy, William J., K.B. Clark, and A.M. Kantrow. *Industrial Renaissance.* NY: Basic Books, 1983.

Arnold, Horace Lucien, and Fay Leone Faurote. *Ford Methods and the Ford Shops.* NY: The Engineering Magazine Company, 1915.

Goldratt, Eliyahu M., and J. Cox. *The Goal*, 2e rev. ed. North River Press, 1992.

Goldratt, Eliyahu M., and R. Fox. *The Race*. North River Press, 1986.

Hayes, Robert H., and Steven C. Wheelwright. "Link Manufacturing Process and Product Life Cycles: Focusing on the Process Gives a New Dimension to Strategy." *Harvard Business Review* (January–February 1979): 133–140.

Hill, Terry. *Manufacturing Strategy: Text and Cases*, 2e. Homewood, IL: Irwin, 1994.

Madison, Dan. *Process Mapping, Process Improvement and Process Management.* Paton Press, 2005.

Normann, R. *Service Management: Strategy and Leadership in Service Business*, 2e. Wiley, 1991.

Sharp, Alec, and Patrick McDermott. *Workflow Modeling: Tools for Process Improvement and Application Development.* Artech House, February 2001.

Smith, Howard, and Peter Fingar. *Business Process Management (BPM): The Third Wave.* Meghan-Kiffer Press, December 2002.

Vollmann, Thomas E., William L. Berry, and D. Clay Whybark. *Manufacturing, Planning and Control Systems*, 3e. Homewood, IL: Irwin, 1992.

Notes

1. John H. Blackstone and James F. Cox. *APICS Dictionary*, 11e. APICS Educational and Research Foundation, 2004.

2. "In Virtual Mudville, the Outlook Is Joyless as Rotisseries Halt," *The Wall Street Journal* (August 11, 1994): 1. This was the day before professional baseball went on strike. See http://baseball.fantasysports.yahoo.com/b1 showing registration for the 2007 season and results to date. Also, note fantasy football, golf, and auto racing.

3. Paul Midler. *Dealing with China's "Quality Fade."* Knowledge @ Wharton, reported in Forbes.com, July 26, 2007.

4. Eliyahu M. Goldratt created OPT and renamed it TOC. The theory is explained in novel form: *The Goal*, 2e rev. ed., by E. M. Goldratt and J. Cox. North River Press, 1992. Also, see *The Race*, E. M. Goldratt and R. E. Fox, North River Press, 1986. See Spotlight 16-2, which is the author's interview with Dr. Goldratt, titled "The Fallacy of Pursuing Local Optimums." Dr. Goldratt's work exemplifies the best systems thinking.

5. It should be noted that, contrary to rules of alliteration, *A* does not stand for analytic in the *VAT* system of nomenclature. Visually, however, *A* starts with "the many" at the base and becomes a single point at the top, which graphs the synthetic concept. *V* starts at the base with one and becomes "the many."

6. See Chapter 10, Section 10-11 on Modular Production and Group Technology and 10-11b on Group Technology.

7. Robert H. Hayes and Steven C. Wheelwright. "Link Manufacturing Process and Product Life Cycles: Focusing on the Process Gives a New Dimension to Strategy." *Harvard Business Review* (January–February 1979): 133–140. Specific reference is to Exhibit 1 on p. 135.

8. Ibid., 135.

Enrichment Activity 5: How Purchasing Managers Use Hedging to Control Cost Fluctuations

The price of aircraft fuel rose dramatically after 2005. Many airlines found themselves unable to absorb the extra costs. Southwest Airlines was not among them because LUV's purchasing managers had seen signs of escalating prices. They had hedged the increase by purchasing future deliveries at of kerosene at prices before the steep increases occurred. (LUV is the stock symbol for Southwest Airlines on the NYSE.)

Process managers are responsible for input prices. Accordingly, they should take into account purchasing strategies when the costs of materials are volatile. Price fluctuations result from such things as increasing demand (oil), weather (oranges), and gold (world tension). Hedging can help protect the production process from sudden exorbitant price increases in basic materials that are used.

Hedging is a purchasing strategy utilizing a futures contract to protect against price fluctuations. Money is neither made nor lost because the buyer is locked into a fixed price, as follows:

1 A futures contract is agreed upon between a buyer (purchasing manager) and a seller. The buyer pays the seller to ship the amount purchased—on a future date—at today's price—called x dollars.

2 At a later time, when production needs material, a cash purchase is made by the buyer for immediate delivery. The cost to the buyer at this later time is y dollars.

3 Simultaneously, the buyer sells the material purchased in step 1. The revenue from that sale is y dollars.

If $x < y$, the price has risen. P/OM must pay more to buy the materials. However, the buyer is protected with a net cost of x for materials. This is because of the profit $(y - x)$ made from buying and selling futures in Steps 1 and 3.

If $x > y$, the price has fallen. P/OM pays less in Step 2 but will not gain that advantage having net costs of x because of the loss $(x - y)$ from buying at x and selling at y in Steps 1 and 3.

With hedging, the buyer always nets out paying x. The company will neither make nor lose money. The advantage of hedging is stability. It insulates the production system from significant price fluctuations.

Enrichment Challenges 5

1 In July, the price of the material used by the process was $0.58 per pound. The purchasing agent expected the price to rise by December and therefore bought a futures contract for 1,000 pounds to be delivered in December. In September, the company needed this material. The price of the material had risen to $0.68 per pound.

   What course of action should the purchasing agent take? What amounts of money will be involved? Show the financial transactions that take place. Include the sums of money for costs and any revenues, if there are any.

2 Now, treat an alternative scenario: In July, the price of the material used by the process was $0.58 per pound. The purchasing agent expected the price to rise by December and therefore bought a futures contract for 1,000 pounds to be delivered in December. In September, the company needed this material. The price of the material had fallen to $0.48 per pound.

   What course of action should the purchasing agent take? What amount of money will be involved? Show the financial transactions that take place. Include the sums of money for costs and any revenues, if there are any.

Process Analysis and Redesign

6

Chapter 6 describes process analysis that leads to process changes aimed at improving performance. Flow-charting the process is the key procedure for developing efficient processes. Each chart shows the various activities that are necessary to make the items or deliver the services. Concurrent with the sequence of activities are the times required to do the work. Charting usually starts with the present process. Ideas for improvement lead to charts for proposed processes. It should be noted that improvements can be made continuously by fine-tuning various activities. On the other hand, the entire process can be redesigned, which allows many constraints in the form of equipment, training, and even ideas and habits, to be bypassed in favor of radical shifts.

After reading this chapter, you should be able to:

- Explain why process analysis and redesign are valued P/OM capabilities.
- Chart any process that needs to be studied using conventional symbols or those of your own choosing.
- Explain which activities should be included in process flowcharts.
- Determine the aspects of time required for process flowcharts.
- Delineate when more detailed symbols should be used on a process chart as compared to less detailed symbols.
- Explain the use of process flow layout charts.
- Discuss the choice of continual improvement of processes as compared to their total redesign.
- Apply process improvement concepts to information systems.
- Describe the impact of setup times and costs on processes.
- Explain SMED and utilize SMED methods for reducing setup times and costs.
- Differentiate between internal and external setup costs.
- Discuss the benefits of a total productive maintenance (TPM) program.
- Explain the steps TPM advocates, and under what circumstances.
- Distinguish between preventive, predictive and remedial maintenance strategies.
- Explain why new developments like computer-aided process planning are important to process managers.
- Describe the use of machine-operator charts.

The Systems Viewpoint

The systems approach is being used when process analysis for the job shop is focused on the total flow. This entails spanning the process from the first operation—including all the purchased supplies—to the last operation, which includes shipping, and contacting the customer to find out if the product was satisfactory and the delivery made on time. Because it is encompassing, the systems approach to improvement often entails altering the process technology internally and externally, at the suppliers' plants and at all points of distribution and contact with customers. Charting operations for process analysis and redesign should include all of the process transformations that affect customer satisfaction. Systems analysis and redesign always involve "the big picture," which is another name for the systems level of process change. Thus, total productive maintenance (TPM) is a systems approach to prevent failure that would slow or stop the process. Single-minute exchange of dies (SMED) is a systems approach to reduce setup times.

TPM includes preventive, remedial, and predictive maintenance. The last of these three requires a systems understanding of the evolution of properties over time. For example, the probability of a bridge collapsing is related to design of the bridge, materials used, age of materials, volume of usage, existence of fatigue cracks in critical locations, etc. Remedial maintenance is not an option if the probabilities are greater than (say) two percent in the next year.

Strategic Thinking

Strategic thinking for P/OM is related to altering the competitive situation by means of operating plans and decisions. Assume that the strategic decision has been made to increase the variety of the product line. The process for doing this starts with the designers and engineers of the product line working in conjunction with the marketing department's evaluation of sales with and without the enhanced variety levels from production. A factor that often enables greater variety of output from production without increasing total costs and thereby decreasing profit margins is the use of equipment that can rapidly change from making one item to another. In manufacturing these are changes of the dies and fixtures, which can be very time-consuming and costly. However, using the SMED approach that is mentioned in "The Systems Viewpoint" section, it is possible to find equipment that can run one job while workers are changing the setup to run a different job. Such equipment allows shifting between jobs with minor penalties (single-minute stoppage). Then, increased variety is obtained with small production penalties. Marketing power is increased when production flexibility is enhanced by a one-time fixed cost increase in the facility expenses.

6-1 Process Improvement and Adaptation

Continuous improvement (CI) of processes is an excellent goal for, and a valued function of, P/OM. An existing process represents an investment in equipment and training, which can be analyzed and redesigned to be as efficient as possible. Costs can be reduced without impairing (and perhaps increasing) reliability, which means only scheduled preventive maintenance. Output is often raised by productivity improvement studies (PIPS) without lowering quality, and sometimes raising it.

Citibank recognized the potential opportunities for continuously analyzing their customers' needs. Every branch bank is evaluated and adapted to the needs of its local customer markets. Changes in customer contact processes include tellers and platform officers and services. Years before the UNUM Group made the Paul Revere Insurance Company part of UNUM, this insurance company pioneered the analysis of internal processes with emphasis on the fact that employees who work together are each other's customers. If every employee listens to the voice of their internal customers, the service experiences of external customers can be greatly enhanced (see the Service-Profit Chain in the Boutwell, Owens & Company Spotlight 2-1). Airlines that empower their attendants to solve customers' problems and train them to do so are noticeably superior in customer ratings. This is hardly a surprise to those airlines that do it. In each case, it took conviction, analysis, and forthright action to improve the process.

The methods for analyzing processes are worthy of study. They are effective and capable of making substantial savings and other improvements that permit the firm to experience greater profit margins, market share, and cash flow. The methods are aimed at achieving best practice in processes.

Continuous process improvement includes streamlining operations, introducing new equipment, and improving the way the job is done and the training for it. Process innovations can occur through the work of R&D, or by means of copying the best.

Continuous improvement (CI)

Incremental improvements are based on keeping the basic system intact and finding ways to eliminate waste and increase quality. Japanese call it *kaizen* (change for the better).

© 2008 Jupiterimages Corporation

Goals must be unambiguous. Target achievements must be consistent. Continuous improvement stems from understanding the job, constant practice, and importing new technology. Often, ingenuity also helps. For example, in automobile assembly, the "doors off" system opens the work space so that technical assemblers can proceed unimpeded.

Process charts

Graphics for doing process analysis.

The method of finding the best, called *benchmarking*, is based on comparative measures that identify leaders in specific kinds of processes. Benchmarking must identify external candidates for best processes, and then, by measuring, comparing, and analyzing, select those processes that will be used as a standard to be achieved. McNair and Leibfried stress continuous improvement using benchmarks as a guide, with the ultimate goal of being "better than the best."[1] They credit Xerox as having developed benchmarking in its current form, starting in the 1970s, and as a result of competitive pressure from Japanese copy manufacturers.

Benchmarked companies do not have to be in the same industry, at least for certain processes. Thus, Lands' End has been benchmarked by computer companies that are trying to become effective with mail order. Disney has been benchmarked by manufacturers that provide service to their customers. The Paul Revere Insurance Company (acquired by the Provident Companies in 1997) has been benchmarked by banks for their team quality programs—modeled on the Olympics—which award bronze, silver, and gold pins.

Good process innovations also can occur because of external forces that impose safety restrictions, pollution regulations, and other governmental controls for the first time. Process adaptation also becomes essential when competitive process advantages occur that leave the others at a disadvantage.

6-2 Process Flowcharts

The use of process charts or process flowcharts is critical to understanding what is going on in the system, how the product is being made, or delivered as a service. **Process charts** are maps of the specific operations, transports, quality checks, storages, and delays that are used by either the present or the proposed system. There is a solid benefit for every organization to chart the processes that it uses to obtain revenues. Wasteful steps that can be removed or remodeled significantly decrease costs and cut time.

Figure 6-1 shows a process chart for making electrical panel boxes. The process chart uses triangles for storage, circles for operations, and squares for inspections. These are some of the conventional symbols. Other symbols will be discussed later. The person doing the process charting has discretion concerning what amount of detail is needed for a particular purpose.

The chart shows that sheet metal is taken from storage for blanking operations on two different machines (M_1 and M_2), which cut out the correct shapes. Two other machines (M_3 and M_4) do cold forming on the blanks for the boxes and covers in batches. Boxes and covers are painted and dried separately in batches. The chart does not point out that a label with the company's name, logo, and the model number of the panel box assembly is applied to the cover. Then, covers and boxes are inspected and assembled with purchased hinges and rivets. The assembled unit is inspected for appearance and cover operation. Satisfactory product is stored in the warehouse.

It is to be noted that much information is not included in this process chart. Times required for operations, lot sizes, and distances that batches have to be transported are all missing. Some process charts have all this information. Also, operations can be broken down into smaller segments. For example, cold forming takes place in three steps that are bundled together for the purposes of this chart. There are many options in drawing up process charts. Simple charts, such as Figure 6-1, are meant to provide an overview of the process at a glance.

6-3 Background for Using Process Analysis

Process analysis

Detailed study of activities required to make the product or deliver the service.

Charting an existing process is a starting point for analysis of that process to see if it can be done in a better way. Process analysis must also be used for a process that has never been done before. **Process analysis** examines the purposes (goals) of the process and tries to find the best possible way to achieve those goals.

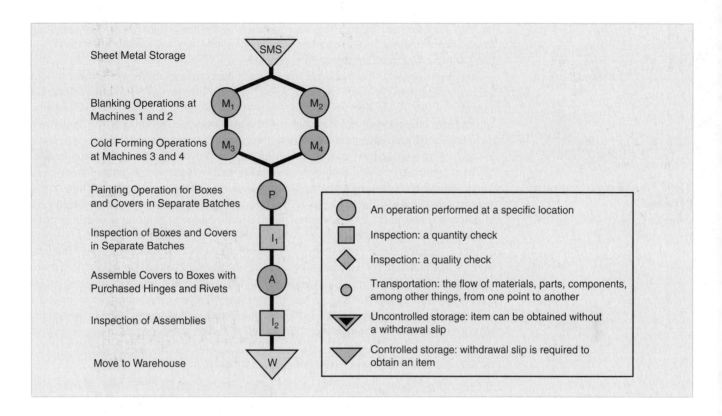

Figure 6-1

Process Chart for Making Electrical Panel Boxes

Setup(s)

Start of the changeover cycle.

Process analysis is an important ongoing activity for job shops. When a job that has never been done before enters the shop, P/OM is responsible for setting up the process, often basing **setup** on similar jobs that have been completed. Therefore, P/OM's experience with prior processes is valuable. Old process charts can be used as guides for planning new processes. Frequently, similar product blueprints have similar process characteristics.

The new job offers an opportunity for modification and improvement of the old process. Using process analysis to adapt one system to fit another is a way of achieving improvement through redesign. Questions to be answered include which machines are to be run, when and where, by which operators, having what training? When orders are repeated, analysis and redesign of these processes makes sense.

For the flow shop, much time and attention needs to be paid to the design of the process sequence. It is more suitable to treat the flow shop as an engineering and capacity planning problem. Complete analysis is critical because the job runs continuously and even pennies that can be saved add up to big amounts. Most job shop processes do not have the volume to justify major pre-engineering with the use of simulation. The process charting described in this chapter applies to job shops.

Process charts for job shops trace the patterns of movement of all materials that come into and go out of the shop. From the receiving docks or the mail-in box to the shipping docks or the mail-out box, tracking by process charts should be done. Typically, the mix of orders in the job shop is so dynamic that it is necessary to improve old processes and invent new ones.

6-3a Process Management Is a Line Function

Process managers are responsible for the production line. That is why they are called line managers. They are getting out or servicing the product. Filling orders is their prime job, but they must take the time to plan the processes for the production line; proper planning saves time in the long run. With good systems in place, they can make routine the function of developing and improving process charts.

There are competitive advantages, including enhanced profitability, for those in P/OM who consistently avoid waste and disruption by improving process flows. A remarkable example of this is the hub and spoke process flow designed by the FedEx Company, which picks up packages at all locations and transports them by air to Memphis, where they are sorted and transported by air to their final destinations. Using bar codes, the location of any package is quickly determined. The process flows are fast and secure. FedEx is a splendid model of what excellence in process design can achieve.

Time-based management (TBM)

Attention paid to reducing time requirements.

Although FedEx is in direct competition with UPS, it remains a leader in **time-based management (TBM)**. For package delivery operations, this means continuous reduction of delivery times. In the logistics area, time is a key performance measure of competitive advantage. The relationship between cost and time cannot be overlooked.

In the broadest sense, there are great opportunities to gain increased profit margins from proper planning for job shop work. As the job shop and batch work take on characteristics of flow shops and continuous flow industries, profit margins increase as do returns on investments. To achieve the gains entails allocating planning time for process management. This means assigning the task of creating new process charts to operations managers who have the appropriate training and skills.

6-3b Demand Is Greater Than Supply

Successful job shops are generally backlogged. In other words, demand is greater than supply. Work must wait before it can be done, and there is pressure to make deliveries on time. This fact needs to be considered in reaching good process management decisions.

In a good job shop, there is concentrated effort on minimizing waste and disruption from machine breakdowns, worker errors, bad materials, and process distortions that cause defectives. Process managers jump to right the wrongs, which is called "putting out fires." The single, most important goal is keeping the orders moving out the door to customers. Therefore, it is an exciting challenge to prevent problems instead of correcting problems after they occur.

With a systems perspective at work, P/OM and marketing can determine which kinds of job orders fit existing capabilities of the shop better than others. Process charts provide the kind of information that enables such determinations to be made.

Marketing can work at selling the optimal mix of orders for the existing machine capacities, worker skills, and management competencies. Specific classes of new orders are complementary to the existing system while others do not fit as well. If the sales force is coordinated with P/OM, better focus for sales and marketing results in total systems improvement.

In a similar sense, some customers are prized for their steady, repeat business while others are occasional buyers who provide less profit for the company. P/OM and marketing need to be coordinated with respect to priorities for customers. Capacity changes can be made to fit the profile for profitable customers and eliminate resource drains for unprofitable customers.

Further coordination is required to recognize that certain new customers may have great potential for growing into the class of "most important" customers. This fact should be taken into account because when drawing up process charts, more attention is likely to be paid to streamlining the production process for prized customers. The effect of putting priorities on customers' orders is always encountered in materials dealing with scheduling.

6-3c Seven Points to Consider for Process Flow Design

1 Alternative process flow designs are always possible. It is useful, therefore, to understand what reasons account for the process flow designs that are being used.

2 Scheduling decisions interact with the designs for process flows that have been developed. Customers are usually very sensitive to delivery lead times, ergo to process features.

3 Product quality is a direct function of process flow design.

4 Product cost and productivity are direct functions of the process flow design.

5 Customers prefer to choose products that maximize value, where:

$$\text{Value} = f\{\text{Quality Worthiness/Total Price Paid}\}$$

6 Because process charting increases quality and decreases costs, it is a means of raising customer satisfaction.

7 Achieving the **best in class** value includes satisfactory delivery dates and service excellence, both of which are components of quality worthiness. These are P/OM process management responsibilities that relate to competent process charting.

Best in class
Top choice for setting the benchmarking standard.

6-3d The Purpose of Process Charts

Process charts make visible and accountable the appointment of people to machines, spaces, and places. The charts make assignments of product orders to work stations, and of materials to machines and stock rooms. Only when charts exist can processing plans be evaluated and improved. Charts assist intelligence and creativity but they are not substitutes for either of them.

Without the assistance of charts, assignments tend to be made in terms of managerial perceptions of existing situations and not in terms of planned-for conditions. The process flow designs are reactive to circumstances and not proactive to opportunities. Updating plans for processes grants a degree of control over circumstances that are dynamically changing. Charts are information support systems that provide concrete means for analysis and improvement.

Orders that produce learning about a new process (routing, equipment, skills, and training) can help the company develop competitive advantages. Embodying new technology in a process chart is equivalent to gaining competitive leverage.

Less dramatic, but of great importance to individual firms, are discoveries that lead to the conversion of a batch-type process into an intermittent flow shop. Discoveries that permit a firm to set up jobs in minutes that used to take hours, and ways to bring new products to market in months instead of years, are exciting opportunities for P/OM. All such major improvements stem from having a deep insight into the present processes, which enable the invention of a much better process.

If it turns out that several managers have differing views as to which orders, customers, and processes are important, the discrepancies should be addressed. There are methods for resolving the differences between multiple decision makers. One of the most used is a policy statement from the CEO or the president.

Distinguishing between orders, knowing which orders are more important than others, and why they are more important is vital to achieving optimal process management. If, as is generally believed, important orders should go before less important orders, then agreement must exist as to what is important to the process managers and to other managers of the firm. Because they have different objectives, sales and process managers often do not see eye-to-eye on what is important. The systems viewpoint can help resolve this quandary.

A particular customer's order might be given top priority and assigned a preferred sequence by marketing. Process managers bristle at the notion that an order already in progress should be stopped and bumped. Major dislocations can arise that require two setups for one order. Difficult cleanups can occur when a new order is pushed in front of other orders that are waiting. The sequence of setups can increase costs greatly.

There usually will be agreement that orders that have large revenues are important. Often such orders will involve large unit volumes. Big orders are likely to be more important than orders that have small volumes. On the other hand, products that have high price tags and ample margins are likely to be more important than products that have low-profit value.

Total profit per order will not suffice as a measure of either order or customer importance. Major customers can place occasional orders for low-profit items. Most job shops associate the value of the customer with the importance of the order. The expected **lifetime value of customers (LTV)** would be a better measure of order importance, if it can be estimated. The investment in process analysis and improvement is justified when it lowers costs and improves quality for valuable customers.

6-3e The Use of Process Charts for Improvements

Process charts can be used to achieve an optimal layout for the factory floor, warehouse, office, restaurant, hotel, or theme park. They permit measures of the effects of switching equipment and people to alternative locations. A common objective is to minimize total transport—the sum of the number of units moved between adjacent workstations, multiplied by the transport distances—for frequently run jobs. If the weight or size is important, that can be factored in as total pounds or cubic feet moved. The right measure can determine when it would be sensible to alter the process by relocating workstations.

Shigeo Shingo, founder of Japanese manufacturing methods, stated, "The prosperity of a resource-poor country like Japan rests solely on the high quality of its labor. Therefore, wasting labor on non-value-added work like transportation must be rejected. In fact, transportation should be seen as a grievous sin."[2]

In addition to transportation, there is a need to consider other important process functions and characteristics. These include the work configuration and the technology of the process being used, the inspection methodology, quality procedures, and delays that occur as a result of the interaction between supply (process) and demand (orders).

Process charts bring up the possibility of replacing older, larger, and slower machines with newer, smaller ones having faster processing rates. If the proper machines are chosen to be replaced, this could decrease the size of the waiting lines, also called *queues* or *work in process (WIP)*. The WIP that forms between any two processing locations is likely to be a profit drain. Decreasing queue length results in space saving, which can be important for reasons other than just the freed-up space.

In all respects, process improvement is a project that moves from present design usage to proposed configurations. Changes are only made after verification that the result of changing provides a net benefit that large enough to warrant the transition. It is smart to postpone changing until other possibilities have been considered that might provide even better results. It is very important to include good estimates of the cost of dislocation in the calculation of net benefit.

6-3f New Orders

Process flowcharts for job shops should be drawn up for new orders, parts that have not been made in the shop before. Job shops vary with respect to the percent of orders regularly repeated. Most experience a high level of new orders. For small new jobs, the process charting is informal, even casual, whereas for large jobs greater care is taken in determining the routing and other particulars.

The custom shop does not experience the conflict of orders waiting for facilities and skills. There are only a few orders in the shop at any one time. Work is one-of-a-kind, so process repetitions are minimal. Therefore, process planning does not provide economic benefits. Further, reorders are nearly zero. This does not mean that it would not be helpful for a custom shop to develop process flowcharts. Such charts can help if the entrepreneurs of the custom shop wish to move toward a job shop, eventually processing large batches of work.

Many process flowcharts will be found on file in the job shop. This is a reflection of the fact that repeat orders are common, and the mainstay of the business consists of a

Lifetime value of customers
The sum of expenditures by the average customer over the total period of time that the customer will purchase.

catalog of parts that can be reordered. Most new work eventually joins the catalog of existing products. Bids on new jobs can be prepared from past history. However, changes in costs, both up and down, need to be factored into the mix. Process charts used for setting the bid help assure that actual costs coincide with bids so that money is not lost.

New batch work interacts with the process flows of existing products. Scheduling conflicts between the newly received orders and older orders that already are on the shop floor must be avoided. Learning curves for new products include start-up problems with fixtures, jigs, software, and other tools that are used for the first time. Start-up problems are time drains. Preplanning by use of process charts can help avoid blocking the use of equipment for which other jobs are waiting.

Overall, the use of process charts can improve operations in the job shop. They provide economic benefits by helping prioritize orders, eliminate conflicts, decrease waiting times, reduce traffic blockages, avoid bottlenecks, and minimize waste for repetitive activities.

6-4 Process Charts with Sequenced Activity Symbols

The American National Standard symbols for Process Charts (ANSI Y15.3M-1979) published by the American Society of Mechanical Engineers (ASME) were withdrawn in 1994 by the ASME. Although first set over 60 years ago, these symbols are no longer regulated because of the growth in types of processes, the need to encourage flexibility, and the impact of computerization of process analysis and redesign. See Figure 6-1 for the six traditional ASME symbols for process charting.

Figure 6-2 shows the "original" process chart for air conditioner chassis that move through a series of uncontrolled storages and transports until assembly. All of the symbols from Figure 6-1 are displayed on each line of the chart. Only one symbol can be chosen for each line.

As shown by the process charts in Figures 6-2 and 6-4, the path used to transport air conditioner chassis from the press shop storage to the assembly area is long and circuitous. The distance that must be traveled between the press shop and the assembly building is about one football field in length. The chassis are moved to weekly storage, then to daily storage. From the daily storage they are moved to assembly every hour. This closely approximates just-in-time arrivals at assembly, but there are a lot of stops in between.

The process starts with uncontrolled storage and by means of transport moves to another storage, and so forth. A line connects the correct activity symbol for each row of the "original" process where "original" means that it is the existing process.

Various measures in the summary box describe the sequential list of activities along the connected pathway. There is the sum of the number of activities (eight). The total transport distance is 300 feet. The length of time required for each unit of the order to go from the start of the process to its finish would be calculated and shown. This is the cycle time, C, which is an important process parameter. Figure 6-2 can be redrawn to include times of each activity and cycle time.

The existing (original) process is analyzed and then redesigned as an improved process. Figure 6-3 represents the "improved" process. Steps 2 through 6 are removed by eliminating both the weekly and the daily storage bank. Instead, a new step 2 is added, as shown in Figure 6-3.

This "proposed" process chart eliminates interim storage and moves the chassis directly to assembly. A heavy-duty, all-weather, covered conveyor is built between the two buildings to do this. A new opening is needed in the solid wall of the assembly building.

Press shop operations now can be synchronized to match assembly timing. The new distance that the conveyor will travel is about 80 feet. Transport distance is decreased by about 73 percent. The small trucks and forklift trucks are eliminated. Instead of eight

Figure 6-2

"Original" Process Chart

Process Chart	Original Analysis		
Job Name	Air Conditioner	Date Charted	10/24/07
Part Name	Chassis	Part Number	CH20
Charted by	PS		

	○	◇	▢	○	▽	▽	Total	Distance
Original	1	1	0	3	3	0	8	300′
Improved								
Difference								

Quantity	Distance	Process Symbols	Explanation
		○ ◇ ▢ ○ ▽ ▽	Press shop storage
	150 feet	○ ◇ ▢ ○ ▽ ▽	Truck moves chassis*
		○ ◇ ▢ ○ ▽ ▽	Weekly buffer
	75 feet	○ ◇ ▢ ○ ▽ ▽	Truck moves chassis**
		○ ◇ ▢ ○ ▽ ▽	Daily bin
	75 feet	○ ◇ ▢ ○ ▽ ▽	Forklift truck***
		○ ◇ ▢ ○ ▽ ▽	Assembled every hour
		○ ◇ ▢ ○ ▽ ▽	Inspected every hour

* 4 times per week to the weekly buffer
** Once a day from weekly buffer to daily bin
*** Hourly to assembly from the daily bin

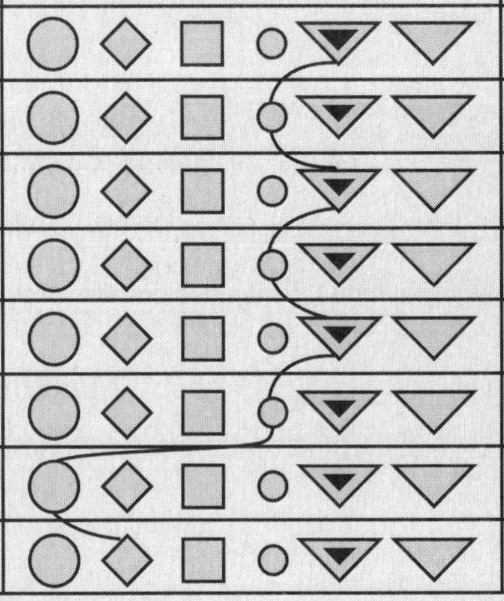

activities, there are only four. Space is freed up. With continuous improvement, there may be even better numbers to report in the future.

6-4a Computer-Aided Process Planning (CAPP)

The ASME no longer sets the standard for the symbols. Process charting has become less regulated and more computerized. Many companies prefer to select symbols that suit their own purposes. There is increased use of process charts to get an overview, which can be accomplished better by using fewer symbols. In Figure 6-1, the chart form is simpler. Only three of the six ASME symbols are used to provide the kind of useful information that can be captured in computer form for **computer-aided process planning (CAPP)**.

For medium- and large-sized job shops, in such industries as auto parts and paints, software is available to assist in process planning.[3] There also are factory simulations available from various software companies that examine the effects of using various process plans. These kinds of software will create process charts that permit analysis and

Computer-aided process planning (CAPP)

Application of computer software to evaluate the performance of a process.

	○	◇	■	○	▼	▽	Total	Distance
Original	1	1	0	3	3	0	8	300'
Improved	1	1	0	1	1	0	4	80'
Difference	0	0	0	−2	−2	0	−4	−220'

Process Chart Proposed Analysis
Job Name Air Conditioner
Part Name Chassis
Charted by PS
Date Charted 10/30/07
Part Number CH20

Quantity	Distance	Process Symbols	Explanation
		○ ◇ ■ ○ ▼ ▽	Press shop storage
	80 feet	○ ◇ ■ ○ ▼ ▽	Conveyor moves chassis*
		○ ◇ ■ ○ ▼ ▽	Assembled every hour
		○ ◇ ■ ○ ▼ ▽	Inspected every hour

* Transfer rate to assembly is 1 chassis every 2 minutes

Figure 6-3
"Proposed" Process Chart

redesign that take into account many processes moving simultaneously through the plant. Queues, bottlenecks, and other interferences can be altered by changing the timing of processes as well as by redesigning equipment assignments.

CAPP and factory floor simulations allow alternatives to be tested in pursuit of continual improvement, an unceasing goal of process planning. Benchmarking better processes, in other companies or divisions of the same company, should be brought into play if possible. Anheuser-Busch compares the process performance of its breweries on a regular basis. This is part of an ongoing process of continual improvement (CI).

6-4b Creating Process Charts

The various process charts should explicitly reflect everything that the process has to do with the cost of goods sold, cash flow, profit margins, productivity, and value-adding transformations. This requires:[4]

1 Stating the exact materials to be used and in the precise amounts that will be consumed. Inventory records indicate purchasing sources. This step provides supply chain information, which links the producer's process with its suppliers. New materials provide an opportunity to improve the process.
2 Noting the times required at every process step including storage and delays, transit, operations, quality control, and inspections. Productivity measures are available from this step; bottlenecks can be identified and methods improved.
3 Indicating the explicit spatial movement patterns of each part as it is transported from place to place within the plant or the office. Plant layout determines the flow patterns. Traffic problems are related to layout. Transport time and cost are to be minimized subject to plant design constraints.

4   Specifying technological transformations that are the fundamental steps of the process. Materials are transformed; information is converted; people and cargo are transported. New technology offers an opportunity to improve the process.

5   Defining the conformance standards for acceptance or rejection of work in process and finished goods is part of process management. Inspection and quality control protocols are indicated on the process charts.

6   Being able to access process charts for each of the various part numbers and products that have been made in the shop. Frequently run products should be kept up-to-date and receive continuous improvement efforts. Less frequently run products are worth cataloging. A new order can be received that uses a process similar to one that was previously charted. This step advocates creating an encyclopedia of all the processes that have ever been done and that might need to be repeated. It reflects the extent of the product line. Process charts can be drawn up for products, parts, and services that constitute potentials for future work. This can be an important systems link between operations and marketing.

7   Knowing how to assign or ship finished product that conforms to quality standards. This step provides supply chain data that links the producer's process with those of its customers.

8   Understanding that process flow-charting is equally applicable for manufacturing and service applications. In the latter case, it can be used to systematize service processes. The symbols need to be changed to conform to the service. For example, computer programmers use their own special set of symbols to characterize information processes.

6-4c Reengineering (REE): Starting from Scratch to Redesign Work Processes

Process redesign can take place in two ways. There is the method of continuous incremental improvements, which the Japanese call "kaizen" and apply to quality enhancement.[5] An alternative is **reengineering**—starting with a clean sheet of paper to radically redesign the process.[6]

Reengineering (REE)

Starting from scratch to redesign the process.

Starting from scratch (zero-based planning) is not necessarily a requirement when new orders are received. Many organizations look for similarities with past orders for which process charts, tools and software, quality conformance standards, and experience with the process flows already exist.

There is a trade-off between zero-based planning and incremental improvement planning. Starting from scratch delays new order processing. It demands the use of the scarce time of process managers for planning instead of for turning out the product and shipping it to the customer. On the other hand, trying to adapt an old process for a new product usually creates suboptimal processes.

This is not always the case. If the degree of similarity between the old order and the new one is high, then there is an opportunity to use the existing process and improve upon it for the adaptation. Some analysis is needed before making that decision.

Although these are two different methods—continual improvement versus starting from scratch—when properly done, they both result in a new process flowchart. The decision about which way is best depends upon management's willingness to use short-term instead of long-term goals.

In some shops, there is a knee-jerk reaction where orders for new products automatically raise the question, "What is most like this?" If there are strong similarities with prior work, the process charts from the close parallel are used to create the new process charts. Often, exact copies are made.

Why reinvent the wheel? This is a misleading rationale. The wheel is constantly being reinvented. Hard rubber tires replaced wooden wheels. R.W. Thomson invented the pneumatic tire. J. B. Dunlop developed the tire industry. Vulcanization (heating rubber with sulfur in a mold) gave rubber the required physical properties, but synthetic rubber tires were a later development. Radial-ply tires replaced the older bias-ply design with better wear and reduced blowouts. Invention of the wheel has not stopped; the design of new wheels is continuous. What did not need to be reinvented was the idea of a circular wheel used for cars, airplanes, and trucks; what needed to be reinvented was how that wheel was to be made.

The idea of starting with a clean sheet of paper is appealing because it allows process managers to create improvements based on changes in technology. New people may have come on board with ideas for innovations that had occurred to no one previously. Different suppliers might contribute insights that had not been previously sought.

Changes in materials can significantly alter processes. Some interesting substitutions have taken place in different industries. A quick sampling includes steel in radial tires, vinyl in windshields, plastics in auto parts, composites in planes and flash memory drives in place of diskettes.

Companies that are doing well have the time and money to take the longer view and go for major redesign. Companies under the gun do not feel that they have the necessary resources. Even if a firm must opt for the short-term approach, awareness of its options is better. After all, decisions based on instinct are better than decisions by default.

6-5 Process Layout Charts

The office or factory floor plan is often used to decide where to locate the various machines, conveyors, storage, and computers. The floor plan shows the size and configuration of the work space and additional details such as the locations of doors, windows, elevators, and closets. Three-dimensional drawings are used when the height of ceilings is important.

Among the reasons for detailing spatial dimensions are to:

1 Calculate the distances that parts will be transported.
2 Choose the best means for transporting parts—by hand, truck, or conveyor.
3 Be certain that there is clearance for large parts.
4 Understand the kind of space the process requires, including space for machines and people as well as tools and work-in-process storage space.
5 Understand the spatial aspects of what can be done to improve the process.

Especially with regard to the largest repetitive batch jobs, it is usual to trace out the paths on the floor plan. It then is possible to improve the process layout. This links the use of *process flow layout diagrams* (Figures 6-4 and 6-5) with the process flow charts for analysis already introduced in Figures 6-2 and 6-3.

Figure 6-4 is the physical description and layout of the "original" method for moving air conditioner chassis from press shop storage to the assembly building.

Figure 6-5 illustrates the new arrangement in the "proposed" process flow layout chart.

The reduction in physical distance is immediately evident by comparing the process flow layout charts in Figures 6-4 and 6-5. The comparison illustrates how layout diagrams can assist in making flow process improvements. The cost of the structural modifications to allow the conveyor's entry into the assembly building must be taken into account.

A wall has been broken through that yields direct conveyor access to the assembly function. The altered process flow is presented in Figure 6-5. As was known from the flow process chart analyses, transport distance is decreased markedly, and space is freed up at the cost of structural change. The revised process is much closer to deliveries as needed or just-in-time systems.

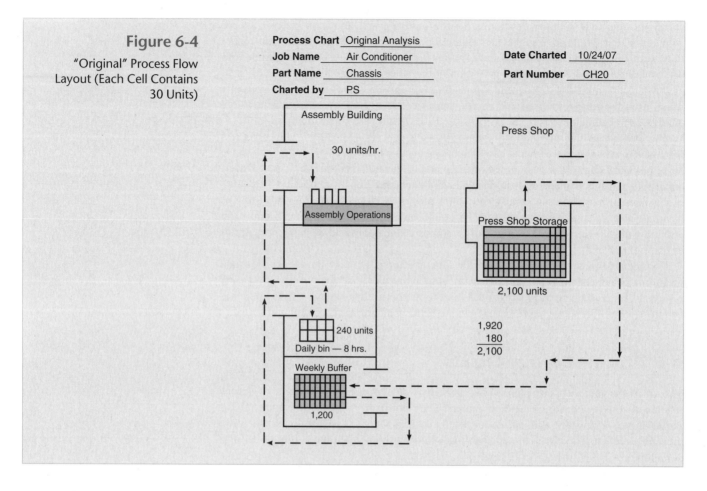

Figure 6-4

"Original" Process Flow Layout (Each Cell Contains 30 Units)

Process Chart _Original Analysis_
Job Name _Air Conditioner_
Part Name _Chassis_
Charted by _PS_
Date Charted _10/24/07_
Part Number _CH20_

Assembly Building

30 units/hr.

Assembly Operations

Press Shop

Press Shop Storage

2,100 units

240 units
Daily bin — 8 hrs.

Weekly Buffer

1,200

1,920
180
2,100

6-6 Analysis of Operations

The process can be viewed as a total flow system. The activities that make up the flow are called the *operations*. Step by step, from start to finish, the term *operations* is generically employed to describe all operations on materials in the factory, the office, the bank, etc.

The term *operations* often is applied to every kind of activity done in a process, but it is always applied to production transformations, which are the circles in Figure 6-1. People who provide services to other people often are called *operators*. Inspections for both quality and quantity are referred to as *operations*. So is the action of storing raw materials and work in process in a warehouse or bin. Similarly, the term is used to describe the transportation of batches between workstations, or cargo between marine terminals, and people between airports.

Operations can be decomposed into detailed elements such as searching for a part, reaching for it, grasping and turning it. This level of detail is generally reserved for discussion about time studies and human resources management. When changes are made to one or a few operations, then continuous improvement is the method being used. This is the operations level of process change as compared to the systems level.

Most process analyses start by looking at the operations level and noting that certain operations embedded in the processes are more likely than others to provide a basis for improvement. There also are typical transports and inspections that can be eliminated without losing delivery advantages and quality.

Improvements that are made to the individual operations of the flow process chart usually start with physical operations (the circles in Figure 6-1). Each of these operations

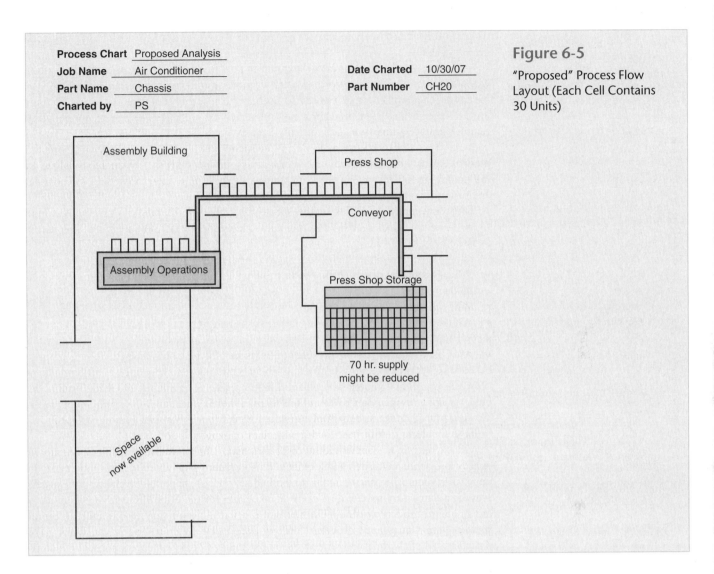

Process Chart Proposed Analysis
Job Name Air Conditioner
Part Name Chassis
Charted by PS

Date Charted 10/30/07
Part Number CH20

Figure 6-5

"Proposed" Process Flow Layout (Each Cell Contains 30 Units)

Assembly Building

Press Shop

Conveyor

Assembly Operations

Press Shop Storage

70 hr. supply might be reduced

Space now available

can be analyzed separately for improvement. A new computer program might be written that decreases cycle time or improves quality.

6-6a Value Analysis for Purchased Parts or Services

Value analysis (VA) is a systematic approach to investigating the functions served by purchased parts, their value to the final product, and whether they are being sourced at the best possible price and quality. It makes sense that high-dollar volume purchased parts receive attention, but often relatively unimportant parts shed light on great potentials for improvement. For value analysis, purchased parts and services are equally applicable.

Assume that a rivet is being used to fasten two units together. VA asks its primary questions: Is this rivet necessary? and What value does it add? After discussion, it became clear that if the two units being joined could be cast as one unit; it would be stronger and less expensive to make. Thus, questioning the need for the inexpensive rivet led to an improved product at a lower cost.

Value analysis also queries if there are other sources for parts. It encourages reexamining make versus buy options. It studies the use of alternative materials that could provide equal or better properties at equal or lower costs. Too tight tolerances can be relaxed, and process steps, such as an inspection, can be eliminated by making it right the first time.

Value analysis (VA)

Systematic investigation of purchased parts decisions.

As part of the VA procedure, employees and suppliers are asked for their suggestions for improvement.

Value analysis has been used by companies and governmental agencies to lower costs without impairing quality. World War II wartime shortages of materials led to VA and the quest for alternative materials to be used as substitutes for scarce materials. Technological change has been producing new materials as well. Awareness of applicability requires searching in places not normally accessed by designers and purchasing agents.

In the late 1940s, a large number of new materials began to appear, such as special plastics, composites, ceramics, and metal alloys. Value analysis was perfectly suited to the determination of whether the substitution of these new materials could lower costs and/or improve the performance of specific products.

There are many examples of the successful use of value analysis procedures. Performed under various names, VA is readily identified by the persistent use of a set of questions:

- What functions are served that justify the use of the present materials and what value do they have?
- What alternative materials might be used?
- What are the disadvantages of the alternative materials?
- What advantages (values) accrue by switching to an alternative?
- After reevaluation, are the present materials still the best ones to use?

When questions cannot be answered, appropriate assignments are made within the value analysis team. After researching the unanswered questions, the group meets again and goes through the same set of questions, making comparisons between present and proposed materials. All qualities and costs are compared.

Value analysis is part of the systems approach, enabling cross-boundary queries in quest of superior materials and services. It is apparent that many factors play a part in material choices. To illustrate, the marketing advantages of dent-free plastic door panels played an important part in the design of materials for the Saturn. Crash tests for safety are an integral part of material choices for autos, so the testing laboratories must be represented. Major savings in headlight design were made by Ford and in the front grille design by Buick. Hybrid engine designs by Toyota involved new components and materials. The U.S. Navy recorded many success stories, which led to its early support for the use of VA on all kinds of Navy equipment.

Value analysis comparisons between present and proposed materials are facilitated by using flow process chart analyses. The analysis of materials often has side benefits of improving specific operations. A furniture manufacturer replaced some wood parts with plastic. This produced major cost savings and quality improvement in the woodworking process, which traditionally does not consider plastic alternatives. Value analysis provided a nontraditional approach. In the same way, the elimination of paper trails in factories and offices, and the replacement with bar codes, optical scanners, and RFID, has changed fundamental process procedures resulting in great improvements in quality, inventory, and production scheduling.

6-6b Other Process Activities: Inspection (Quantity and Quality), Transport, and Storage

A process chart can be used to compare the present method for a quantity check (a square in Figure 6-1) with a revised method of inspection. Inspection operations for quantity checks are often related to withdrawing materials from the storeroom, assuring that an order is properly filled, and paying on a piecework basis. The proposal might be to replace a person with a scanner. Alternatively, the proposal might be to postpone the quantity check until a later stage in the process.

An inspection that provides a quality check (a diamond in Figure 6-1) can be postponed or eliminated. The process chart provides both visual and quantitative data that summarizes the pros and cons of making the change. Recent best practice assigns responsibility for inspections to the worker making the part or providing the service. Quantity and quality checks can often be made together.

Improvements can be made to transport operations (a little circle in Figure 6-1). The recorded savings in Figure 6-3 were due to a creative idea about cutting unnecessary transportation. It is noteworthy that, in this case, the transport function was singled out of the overall process flow for attention.

Improvements can be made to storage operations. The air conditioner press shop to assembly example works well here, too. Storage was eliminated in the proposed process flow layout charts (Figures 6-4 and 6-5). These were uncontrolled storages (a little dark triangle inside a bigger triangle—both with apex down—in Figure 6-1). This example also illustrates a case in which storage functions have been plucked out of the overall flow process to receive special attention.

With controlled storage (a triangle with apex down as shown in Figure 6-1), a withdrawal slip is required to obtain an item. The control feature is used to protect against pilferage and to ensure that a known level of inventory exists. However, controlled storage is more expensive to administer than uncontrolled storage, where an item can be obtained without a stock request form. The loss of inventory control in the uncontrolled case can increase the out-of-stock, order, and carrying costs. These additional costs must be compared with the savings obtained by removing administration of the storage.

6-7 Information Processing

Information systems are the lifeblood and circulatory system of organizations worldwide. Their necessity to organizational well-being does not mean that their program applications and data storage systems function flawlessly. Applications can produce results that are not well-aligned to the strategic purposes of the company. Tactical errors can arise from incorrect data collection as well as improper data-mining and analysis.

There is an information flow that parallels and mimics the materials that are moving though the input-transformation-output process. That data explains the locations of all materials and the degree of transformation that has been accomplished. Bar codes and RFID are popular ways of identifying this information. The way that this information is used by P/OM is related to the programs abilities for status reporting and analysis by such functions as inventory control, quality assurance, production scheduling, and maintenance requirements.

Production schedules may call for additional production time to meet due dates. New orders may require more frequent setups with smaller lot-size runs. Capacity reports may reveal problems that suppliers encounter as well as bottlenecks caused by equipment failures. Computer breakdowns can halt service for telephone systems or prohibit flying aircraft until air traffic control's computer system is restored.

There is an affinity and relationship between the information technology (IT) department and P/OM, which is varied, intense, and continuous. The interdependence is related to personnel skills, technological abilities, and information requirements. P/OM depends on IT and vice versa. The convergence of interests is in the strategic and tactical aspects of process design, analysis and redesign.

6-8 Process Changeovers (Setups)

Changeovers are the steps that need to be taken to alter a process; to revise its output; to prepare equipment and people to do a new job. The term *setup* is usually applied to

Changeovers
Steps that need to be taken to prepare equipment and people to do a new job.

Put-away
End step before the next setup, make-ready cycle.

starting-up a new job, which means cleaning-up from the old one. For process analysis, it is best to separate these two steps and deal with setup and **put-away** (cleanup) as two distinct activities.

Of critical importance to job shop processes are the changeover costs and times. These are often treated as being synonymous so that mention of cost implies time and vice versa. Thus, the generic term *setup* is often used to include time and cost and everything that has to be done to change the process from one product to another.

Setup costs are often proportional to setup times. However, the relationship breaks down when a lot of technology is devoted to allowing very rapid setups. Then there is a cost of not using this technology for the purposes for which it was intended, namely, short runs of many designs that fit within the family of parts (technology group) that can be made on this equipment. Further, when the setup can take place off-line, it can take longer and still cost much less than when it must interrupt the production process.

Machines in the office and on the plant floor have to undergo cleanup from prior jobs and then be reset. People have to shift jobs, often moving from one location to another. The learning curve comes into play every time operators bring a new order online, which also is part of the changeover process.

Changeovers are a challenging form of activity. They occur because it is necessary to shift gears to convert the process from doing one thing to doing another thing. Imagine having to take the gearbox apart each time before shifting gears. Imagine the impact on driving if this was required to shift the gears of a car. Further, the analogy requires that many different cars be involved. Thus, a manual for changing over the gearboxes is needed for hundreds or even thousands of different car models. Each of the changeovers can pose a spectrum of difficulties that range from inconsequential to monumental.

Transferring this analogy to the job shop environment, envision the following script. A "good" customer orders four units of an item, which takes a couple of minutes to make, but the setup time is half a day. Here are some numbers to consider:

Cost per unit = $0.80
Setup cost = $800
Order size = 4 units
Lot size = number of units to be determined

Assume that the setup cost includes the cost of labor of two people working four hours each and the cost of lost production related to four hours of downtime of two machines.

To make this item costs less than a dollar if the setup cost is ignored, but if the setup cost is amortized over the four items, they each cost $200.80. One additional assumption is that this item is reordered, from time to time, by various customers. What options are open to the process manager as he or she goes about preparing the production schedule?

The most apparent option is to run a larger number of items than four. If 40 items are produced, then the cost per item is reduced to $20.80, which is still far from providing a reason to celebrate. Running a lot size of 400 provides a cost per unit of $2.80, which might be reasonable from the customer's point of view.

6-8a Single-Minute Exchange of Dies (SMED)

Another option is the one that Taiichi Ohno of Toyota Motor Manufacturing U.S.A., Inc. took. He asked his process managers for a revolutionary reduction of setup times. They redesigned the process so that hours for setup were reduced to single digit minutes.

Before describing the character of that revolution, it is interesting to note the historical events that triggered the modification. Taiichi Ohno asked Shigeo Shingo, who was at that time with the JMA,[7] to cut setup times for a particular operation from four hours to three minutes. Shingo, who was an advocate of cutting all setup times to less than ten minutes, was shocked by Ohno's "utterly unreasonable directive"[8] into totally rethinking the anatomy of changeovers.

"In developing the idea of the **single-minute exchange of die (SMED)** setup, I blasted a tunnel through the mountain, so to speak, dramatically shortening the time it took to move between processes or operations. Cutting 4-hour setup changeovers to three minutes simply blasted out of existence the band-aid approach of economic lot sizes," Shingo wrote.[9]

The SMED system for cutting changeover times is based on the recognition that there are setup steps that can be done without shutting the machine down. Examples of SMED setups can be found in the activities of the pit crew, which changes the racing car's tires without shutting the car off. Changeover time in the pit is an important measure of the racing team's capability and performance.

Watch setup teams do their work. See if some steps could have been done before turning off the machine. These setups while running online are referred to as *external* setups. By redesigning processes and their setup procedures, it is possible to increase the number of external setup steps. With this in mind, here are six steps that lead to cost (and time) reductions for setups:

1 Recognize those setup tasks that can be done while the machine is running. Setup tasks (with external elements) can be set up while the machine is working on another order.

2 Study those setup tasks that can only be done when the machine is shut down. These are called internal setup elements.

3 Redesign and convert as many internal setup tasks as possible into external category tasks.

4 Each and every setup element for an operation should be scrupulously analyzed and examined in search of continuous improvement.

5 Find creative ways to utilize idle time of setup crews. For example, partial setup preparations, parallel machine systems, automatic *put-aways* (see Figures 6-6, 6-7, and 6-8).

6 Consider the use of flexible processing systems and robot assistants.

It used to be that setup times were larger for machines that worked faster. The trade-off for paying more for setting up was the lower per unit costs of the outputs. Although this relationship still generally holds, the application of SMED concepts reduces the downtime of high-volume equipment by doing much of the setup while the machine is working on another order or the new order.

Was Shingo's insight a special moment in history or inevitable? The same question can be asked about Henry Ford's development of sequenced assembly and Eli Whitney's invention of interchangeable parts. These are all significant manufacturing inventions with major consequences for operations in general.

Perhaps the "time was right." Alternatively, maybe eventually the inevitable would have occurred. Such speculation does not diminish the contribution or the credit that these inventors deserve.

Further, flexible manufacturing systems can provide rapid built-in changeovers for a specific menu of production items. The SMED concept is substantially assisted by the development of programmable setups, which are enabled by computer-driven mechanical equipment. Robots are a type of programmable setup system that is gaining use globally.

Robots are ideal for rapid-changeover systems. The sound engineering concepts of SMED combine with the programmable capabilities of robotics to bring about a revolution in the engineering mind-set. The old engineering truism that changeover times and costs must increase with the use of volume-efficient equipment is disappearing.

The fact that SMED is having such a major impact on manufacturing makes it easy to overlook the fact that SMED concepts are not limited to manufacturing. The ability to move from one order to another with minimum changeover delay is applicable to many

Single-minute exchange of dies (SMED)
Setups that take less than a minute.

© 2008 Jupiterimages Corporation

For racing cars, the activities of the pit crew must be perfectly meshed. Every step is clockwork. What may seem to be minor errors often turn out to lose races. An example of SMED setups and changeovers is the functioning of the pit crew, which changes a racing car's tires without shutting down the engine.

In each race there are four or five pit stops; each lasts 15 to 18 seconds, which means the pit crew works 1.5 minutes per week. In addition, the pit crew practices a lot and rebuilds the cars from the ground up with new parts made by them. See http://en.wikipedia.org/wiki/Pit_stop.

service systems. The restaurant business is filled with changeover costs. Cooking is setup intensive, and dishwashing exemplifies the takedowns and cleanups.

In education, consider the setup times required for each class. Every exam requires someone to write it. Many students must take it, at least enough to pay for the setup costs. Ask a professor about the agony of writing a make-up exam for one or two students who failed to take the scheduled exam. Someone must grade that exam. In travel, think about the setup times to get a cruise ship underway. Finally, consider the question: Are there setup times required to operate a computer? Because the setup times can be substantial, every business that relies on computers can gain advantages by decreasing setup times.

In summary, setup times are vital process parameters. The reduction of changeover times can dramatically improve the competitive advantages of a company. Consequently, this is one of the most promising methods for process improvement in the present operations environment. As setup times are reduced to minutes and then seconds, the economies of scope come into being. This means that variety can be achieved without a penalty. With increased variety, marketing, operations, and distribution have to coordinate their activities. A real systems effort is called for because increased variety adds more opportunity and complexity to challenge management.

6-8b Machine-Operator Charts: Process Synchronization

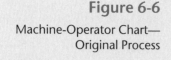

Machine-operator chart (MOC)

Means for visualizing the way in which workers (can) tend machines over time.

Another process chart that deserves attention is the **machine-operator chart (MOC)**. The MOC provides a means for visualizing the way in which workers can tend machines over time. It encourages visual analysis of the interaction of operators with the machines they operate. It permits evaluation of the efficiency of the relationship. The MOC permits intelligent assignments of operators to machines and allows for synchronization of operations (and operators) because time-matching is inherent in the charting.

The time that operators spend tending machines often includes setup times, which interrupt production. Product output is stopped while tool alignments are made and fixtures and jigs are adjusted. Replacing the paper for the fax or the inkjet cartridge for the printer are other illustrations of machine-operator interactions that stop production. The cleanup activity is such a major fact of life for many processes that there is irony in the fact that setup has come to mean the whole changeover process including cleanup.

Figure 6-6 shows a machine-operator chart in which all of the *make readys* and *put-aways* are designed to be internal setup elements. The machine and the operator are both

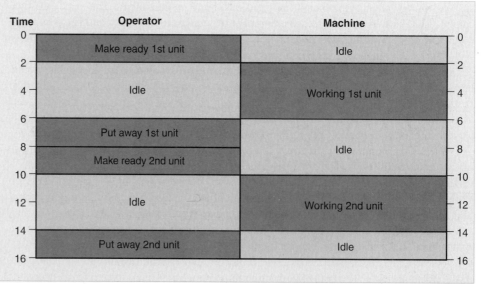

Figure 6-6

Machine-Operator Chart—
Original Process

Time	Operator	Machine	
0	Make ready 1st unit	Idle	0
2	Idle	Working 1st unit	2
4			4
6	Put away 1st unit	Idle	6
8	Make ready 2nd unit		8
10	Idle	Working 2nd unit	10
12			12
14	Put away 2nd unit	Idle	14
16			16

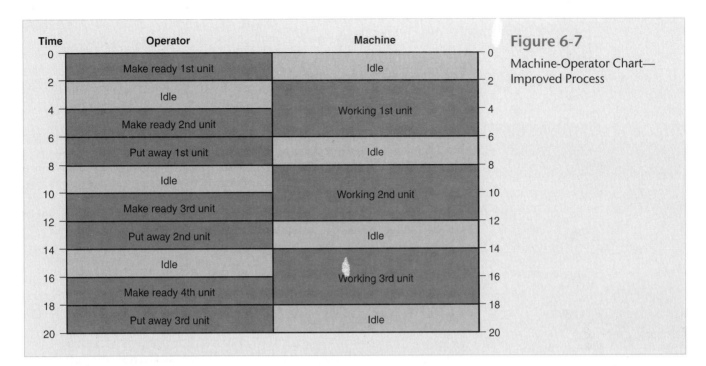

Figure 6-7

Machine-Operator Chart—
Improved Process

idle 50 percent of the time. In 16 time units, the operator is idle $4 + 4 = 8$, and the machine is idle $2 + 4 + 2 = 8$. Operator and machine are badly coordinated.

As an example, a part to be painted is mounted in the painting cabinet while the paint nozzles are shut off. The spray-paint nozzles are activated and then shut off so the part can be removed and a new one mounted.

In Figure 6-7, process designers have found a way to mount the next part while the prior one is being removed. The operator makes ready the next part to be painted while the prior part is being painted. The one exception is the first unit, which is loaded before the start-up of the paint cabinet.

The operator has externalized the make-ready element but is still constrained by the internal setup characteristics of the put-aways, which means that the machine must be turned off to remove the part. This partial SMED-like improvement has decreased the operator's idle time from 50 percent to 33.33 percent. The same decrease (50 percent to 33.33 percent) applies to the machine's idle time. This ignores the two periods of idle time that are required for the first part to be painted. Continuing with the spray paint example, the part to be painted is loaded onto a fixture while another part is being painted. When the spray unit is shut off to remove the part, the fixture with the next part drops into place in the paint cabinet.

Figure 6-8 depicts a successful application of SMED. Both *make ready* and *put-away* have been converted into external setup capabilities. Once the system is up-and-running, both the operator and the machine are 100 percent utilized.

A continuous circular conveyor enters the painting booth at the front. The part is spray painted as it moves along, leaving the spray booth from the rear. The conveyor circles back to the station outside the paint booth where the operator loads parts onto the conveyor and removes painted parts from it.

6-9 Total Productive Maintenance (TPM)

Total productive maintenance (TPM) is a systematic program to prevent process breakdowns, failures, and stoppages. Process disruptions can be caused by many factors such as poor materials, tool breakage, power failures, and absenteeism.

Total productive maintenance (TPM)
Rational blend of maintenance alternatives.

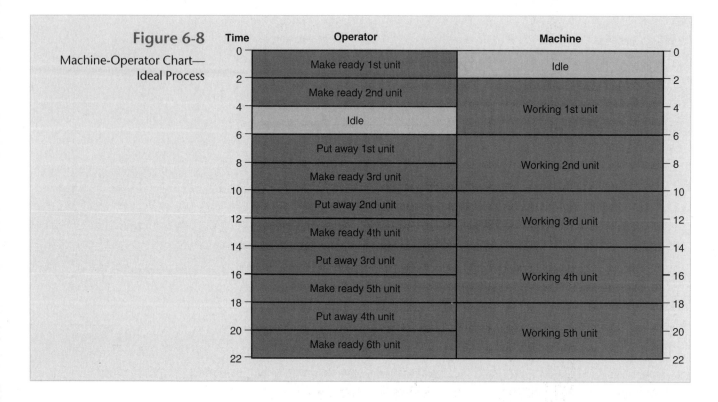

Figure 6-8

Machine-Operator Chart—
Ideal Process

Remedial maintenance (RM)

Maintenance after failure.

Preventive maintenance (PM)

Maintenance performed before failure.

Predictive maintenance (PDM)

Maintenance based on knowledge of signs and symptoms that something is likely to go awry in the future.

One important cause of disruption is machine breakdowns, including computer failures. Machine breakdowns can stop an entire process with large penalties to be paid. TPM is a systems approach to preventing such failures. TPM encompasses preventive, remedial, partially preventive, and predictive maintenance strategies.

Remedial maintenance (RM) repairs equipment and replaces parts only when failure occurs. **Preventive maintenance (PM)** services equipment (repair and replacement) at regularly scheduled intervals. The intervals are chosen to make it unlikely that more than a given number of failures will occur before PM takes place. Partial-preventive maintenance (PPM) is incomplete servicing scheduled at regular intervals to decrease the probability of failure and the need for remedial maintenance. Only those components are serviced which have high failure probabilities and those components that lead to a systems-wide failure. Dependencies between component failures must be known.

Predictive maintenance (PDM) is based on knowledge of signs and symptoms that something is likely to go awry in the future. A monitor is used for all of the variables that are apt to be tell-tales. For example, if a machine is vibrating more than usual, that may signal that a worn gear needs replacement. For service applications, if a customer has not returned to the supermarket within his or her accustomed purchase interval, that might signify that an unregistered complaint has led the person to shop elsewhere. Predictive maintenance is also sensitive to failure dependencies and strives to avoid permitting the domino effect prevail

Predictive maintenance can be costly and should be justified by the cost/benefit analysis that indicates repair is possible to avoid high penalties. A variety of P/OM systems are well-suited to this application. Control charts provide management by exception for important quality variables that could readily include maintenance dimensions. *Poka-yoke* (see Spotlight 4-2) is a Japanese method aimed at preventing production line failures. Control systems that monitor status are broadly applied in both early-stage and aging equipment failures associated with the Weibull (bathtub-type) failure distributions.

Total productive maintenance is a program that addresses all factors that slow down or stop a productive process. If the computer goes down as the bank is about to transfer substantial funds overseas at the end of the day, the interest that would not be earned might well be in the millions. Because of the risk exposure, backup systems would be part of the failure prevention system. This is because computer failures can be costly. TPM programs are absolutely essential when failure and/or process stoppage is life threatening. Backing up equipment and using redundant systems do not constitute preventive maintenance, but they are strategies to lower probabilities derived by predictive maintenance. Reinforcement to increase fail-safe properties is part of sound TPM strategies.

Three questions can help determine how large an expenditure for TPM is reasonable:

1 Is the specific process vulnerable to a breakdown that will slow or stop production output? Accidents on a roadway that stop traffic meet this definition.

2 Do conditions exist for a domino effect and/or failure contagion?

3 Is any production disruption costly? Is complete systems failure a disaster?

If the answer to any one of the three questions is "yes," TPM is indicated. If "yes" is the answer to more than one of these questions, TPM is critical. There are plenty of cases where the answer is "no" to all three question.

Job shop machine breakdowns are serious, but they can be finessed in several ways. First, the equipment is general purpose and, therefore, similar machines are available on the same plant floor. Second, the order being processed at the time of breakdown is one of many orders that are being worked on in the shop, so the extent of the disruption is limited.

A worst-case scenario can occur for the job shop where the order is already delayed, the customer is important and annoyed, and the breakdown occurs on the only machine that is well-suited for the particular order. The job shop will still survive but the financial conditions may take a hit.

An example of a serious case is stoppage of the flow shop. The flow shop investment is high and the effect on large customers is not acceptable. TPM is probably in the cards.

When the costs of disruption are extreme, including life threatening, the vulnerability is often addressed by **redundancy**. That is, two pieces of equipment are used, one for the process and the other as backup. This is a TPM strategy calling for the redesign of the system. The cost of redundancy can be assessed as an alternative to the cost of failure. Used widely by banks, the design of "nonstop computers" (remember Tandem, which became part of Compaq, now part of HP) was based on duplication of functions, backup of components, and redundancy of circuits. Commercial jets can fly on one engine, but at least two must be provided.

It is useful to note that redesign can mean changing the process methods, that is, the systems being used. It can mean changing the process technology, including substituting other equipment, and/or by using redundant equipment for fail-safe performance.

Consider a ceramic fixture used to hold a unit of work in a heat-treating chamber. Suppose that this fixture shatters every now and then. Because the fixture cannot be replaced with something more durable, and because it is not too costly, the redundancy level that the process manager suggests is six fixtures.

Why did the process manager select six instead of two or three? The answer lies with other factors that determine redundancy levels, including the **lead time (LT)** or amount of time needed to secure a replacement. Lead time starts with recognizing the need for the placement of an order and ends with the receipt of that order. The minimum order size might be six. In this case, assume that the LT is three to four weeks and the supplier is reluctant to produce only one fixture at a time because the setup costs are too high to run one at a time.

For many machines, redesign is costly, redundancy is affordable, and lead time is short. In these cases, the goals of TPM are achievable by keeping one or more backups in stock and keeping contact with the supplier to make certain that lead times and availability have not changed.

© 2008 Jupiterimages Corporation

Total productive maintenance (TPM) can head off troubles by using proper diagnostic systems. The illustration shows an off-shore petroleum platform that is extremely vulnerable to corrosion necessitating care and maintenance. Storms (especially hurricanes) will reveal any weakness that maintenance has not addressed. Good maintenance will minimize damage. As another example, air traffic control equipment must be serviced with a zero breakdown policy to ensure safe landings.

Redundancy
Duplication and repetition to provide a safety margin against systems failures. Used when failure carries large penalties.

Lead time (LT)
Interval that elapses between seeing the need for placing an order and receiving the goods or services.

Redesign is used when the cost of failure is high, the probability of a breakdown is too great, and it cannot be lowered by preventive maintenance or better practice. That is another example of total productive maintenance (TPM) having a broader agenda than even the most dedicated preventive maintenance program.

It is useful to note that the cost of failure (c_f) and the probability of it occurring (p_f) lead to an expected cost of failure:

$$\bar{c}_f = p_f c_f$$

Redesign is essential when the size of $\bar{c}_f$ is large. The expected cost of failure can be a large number, even though p_f is small, if c_f is large. In this regard, it is often stated that $c_f =$ infinity when the cost of life is involved. The expected cost of failure is too large for everyone to judge although jury awards refute this statement. In any case, loss of life warrants redesign. Similar concepts and terminology are used to determine optimal levels of preventive maintenance when the expected costs of failure are not excessive.

Total productive maintenance (TPM) is a complete plan to prevent failures of various kinds. It is an across-the-board attack on machine and systems breakdowns. It includes shifting to new technology, which is more reliable. It employs statistical quality control methodology and, based on results, leads to the redesign of systems with planned redundancy. TPM and Six-sigma should be strongly related (see Spotlight 7-2).

When TPM is not required, remedial and preventive maintenance are the remaining options. There are many different levels of preventive precautions that can be taken. The alternative is to wait for a failure and then use remedial maintenance (RM) to repair the problem. The zero-level of preventive maintenance is RM alone.

RM addresses two kinds of failures:

1 The first and worst kind of failure stops the process. Remedial maintenance is called for immediately. The lights are out in New York City. What is Con Ed going to do about this critical failure?

2 The second kind of failure leads to degradation of the system's performance. Repairs are made, but this kind of problem is not critical and tends to reoccur. The total cost of remedial maintenance becomes a large enough figure to command attention. During the stormy season, light failures occur at least twice a week. The local power company does pretty well in repairing the problem within an hour or so.

The cost-effective scenario for each kind of failure is different. In both cases, it often turns out that some level of preventive maintenance is warranted.

There is willingness to spend a great deal to prevent a failure if the cost of that particular kind of failure is high. Analysis of alternative strategies for failure prevention include the degree to which failure probabilities can be reduced and the cost of achieving that reduction versus the penalty cost of that failure. The conditions for a relevant trade-off analysis exist.

Figure 6-9 illustrates the relationship between the probability of failure (p_f) and the cost of prevention (c_p). It is seen that as partial preventive maintenance (PPM) moves from remedial maintenance (no preventive maintenance) toward maximum TPM, the probability of failure decreases quickly at first, and then slows down, even though proportionately greater amounts of money are being spent. When warranted, predictive maintenance (PDM) could be factored into the partial preventive maintenance plan. It would provide early-diagnostic remedial steps based on symptoms of failure in place of actual failure.

A power failure in a plant or office constitutes a breakdown of the first kind. Without the backup of a redundant power supply, the ongoing systems will be forced to shut down. To avoid power failure, the processes of the power plant are examined in detail. The intent is to pinpoint the causes and the preconditions of power failures. The techniques that apply are identical to those used for prevention of defective products with TQM and when applying statistical methods of process analysis.

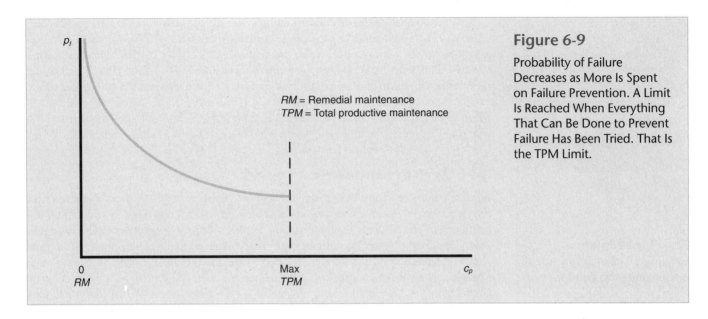

Figure 6-9

Probability of Failure Decreases as More Is Spent on Failure Prevention. A Limit Is Reached When Everything That Can Be Done to Prevent Failure Has Been Tried. That Is the TPM Limit.

Every potential cause is studied. A maintenance agenda is set up to remedy problems and reduce the probability of failure. Aircraft maintenance programs have been worked out with care and provide an excellent model to copy.

The second type of failure is epitomized by lightbulbs burning out. This kind of failure is seldom critical. There are usually several bulbs to light the space, and as soon as one burnout occurs, remedial maintenance can be employed.

A plan can be developed for decreasing the number of lightbulbs that need to be replaced at one time, which costs a great deal because each replacement requires a new setup for correction of the fault. The use of one setup to replace all bulbs at the same time, whether or not they have burned out, is worthy of consideration. Families of bulbs belonging to different age groups can be used if markings differentiate to which family each bulb belongs.

One setup to replace all bulbs, burnt out or not, is a good example of the importance of setup theory for process management. The example also underscores the fact that TPM is part of process analysis. Should lightbulbs be replaced as they burn out, or in family groups, or should all bulbs be replaced at a proper interval?

It is generally less expensive to use preventive maintenance than corrective maintenance. A trade-off model should be employed as discussed in the following sections.

6-9a The Preventive Maintenance Strategy

There are 1,000 lightbulbs at risk for failure with rates described as follows. The TPM policy is to replace, all at once, the 1,000 light bulbs 6.5 times a year (every eight weeks). Each replacement entails a cost of $5.00 per bulb and a setup cost of $1,000. For this TPM policy, the total annual cost would be 6.5 (1,000 × $5 + $1,000) = $39,000.

Burned out bulbs are only replaced during the TPM sweep. This could mean that workplace light is not always sufficient. To avoid having insufficient light, there might be a basis for having some extra bulbs installed. The cost of such redundancy is not included in this sample analysis, but it readily could be added.

6-9b The Remedial Maintenance Strategy

The alternative strategy is to replace each bulb as it burns out. That costs $10 per lightbulb. The bulbs are rated as having an expected lifetime of 900 hours. The plant operates two 8-hour shifts seven days per week for a total of 112 hours per week (900 ÷ 112 = 8.0).

This means that on average, every eight weeks all of the lightbulbs will be replaced. Thus, each light bulb must be replaced 6.5 times per year ($8 \times 6.5 = 52$ weeks). On average, 6,500 bulbs burn out each year, and that means the total cost of replacement on a one-by-one basis is $65,000. For this situation, since $65,000 − $39,000 = $26,000, the preventive maintenance strategy has a distinct advantage over remedial maintenance.

If a special (and costly) bulb could be designed to beep two hours before it burned out, a policy of PDM could be used. This knowledge would not save money, so who would buy the costly bulb? Management would buy it if safety factors applied.

6-9c Zero Breakdowns

Just like quality programs designed to achieve zero defectives, TPM can set down goals for zero machine, equipment, and total systems breakdowns. A breakdown, by definition, is a malfunction. The failure was supposed to be headed off by the preventive maintenance program. A policy of **zero breakdowns** specifies that everything possible will be done to eliminate malfunctions and failures. Air Force One, the President's plane, is serviced with a zero breakdown policy. Most people balance their checkbook with a zero defects goal. On the other hand, baseball scoring assumes that defects will occur. A strikeout is a hitter's defect. On the other hand, a ground ball missed by the shortstop is a defensive error. Runs, hits, and errors are not about to be rewritten by a zero defect policy.

Zero breakdowns

Requires eliminating any and all malfunctions and failures.

When a failure occurs, it compromises the process, and further analysis is warranted. This includes the possibility that shorter intervals between servicing could head off unscheduled repairs. The extra cost of replacing parts more frequently also can be examined. Preplanning is essential to achieve zero breakdowns as is the case with zero defects.

Cost trade-off models may be constructed if the cost of an unscheduled repair can be calculated. One factor that needs to be included is the cost of process disruption. Usually this is a large cost, which explains why aggressive total productive maintenance (TPM) programs are viewed with favor by companies that try them out.

There are many aspects about TPM that could be applied to security at airports and to other national vulnerabilities. Spot the anomalies and take corrective action epitomizes the predictive maintenance component of TPM.

6-9d TPM for the Flow Shop

For the flow shop process, the worst-case scenario is when the breakdown stops the line. This occurs when a station along the path of the conveyor ceases being able to function. Unless the prior stations on the line are immediately notified to stop producing, WIP begins to accumulate, forming queues in front of the nonfunctioning machine. To avoid severe congestion and eliminate safety hazards, it usually is necessary to shut down the prior workstations.

This scenario has many costs associated with it. There is the cost of repairing the equipment (remedial maintenance) at the station. The cost of lost production can be considerable. Another cost that often is overlooked is the cost of line start-up, which might require relearning and the production of defectives.

Another kind of flow shop breakdown is when all the equipment stops because of a power failure. The same kind of effect is produced by a failure of the paced conveyor unless the work is suitable for hand carrying or moving by forklift between stations. In addition, some automobile companies empower workers to stop the line when serious problems develop with systems-wide implications. The kind of problems that are systems wide include passing defectives to downstream stations, which wastes their work, complicates repair, and hides the defect.

The severe costs of flow shop stoppages generally guide the choice of an effective complete program of preventive maintenance. This is done after the shift ends or on a weekend when there will be no interference with the maintenance team. These maintenance procedures require similar considerations regarding what is done online and off-line as those that applied to SMED changeover and setup situations. Predictive maintenance is worth consideration if PDM can be installed with a beneficial trade-off of costs and benefits.

The production line is gone over thoroughly, cleaned up, and prepared to run without further maintenance until the next scheduled overhaul. Aircraft receive major preventive maintenance at longer intervals than the more frequently scheduled minor preventive maintenance. The same applies to automobile servicing.

Equipment failure always is an important consideration for process designers. Interdependent serialized production systems that are prone to breakdowns cannot be tolerated. A breakdown anywhere in the chain halts the entire system. If redundant systems with immediate switchovers are not feasible for protection, then it is essential to use TPM, including PDM, to bring the process as near to zero-breakdown levels as possible.

Spotlight 6-1 Occupation Outsourcing
Where Have All Those Jobs Gone?

A tipping point (TP) occurs when a growth process such as increasing sales per week, or an epidemic of flu cases reported per day, stops accelerating and begins to decelerate—or vise versa. Malcolm Gladwell, in his book *The Tipping Point* (Little, Brown and Company, 2000), cites decreasing crimes as another example. Looking at the following table provides some good examples of tipping points in percent distributions of the workforce.

relate to farming and not to food processing, which has grown to keep pace with average population increase. Agricultural output in the United States has increased dramatically, although there are fewer farms (of larger size) and the total farm workforce has declined precipitously.

The percent of the total workforce engaged in manufacturing in the United States was increasing dramatically until about the 1920s when a reduction began that was reversed

Percent Distribution of Workforce in Agriculture, Manufacturing, and Services from 1760 to 2010*

Date	1760	1790	1820	1850	1880	1910	1940	1970	2000	2010**
Agriculture	0.96	0.93	0.84	0.73	0.53	0.32	0.20	0.12	0.07	0.05
Manufacturing	0.01	0.04	0.11	0.20	0.38	0.54	0.52	0.40	0.20	0.10
Services	0.03	0.03	0.05	0.07	0.09	0.14	0.28	0.48	0.73	0.85
	1.00	1.00	1.00	1.00	1.00	1.00	1.00	1.00	1.00	1.00

*Services include information, education, health care, transportation, and hospitality
**Data for 2010 are based on extrapolating trends from 1970 to 2000.

Source: Based on data from Public Policy Forecasting, Inc. (Starr, Martin. *Global Corporate Alliances and the Competitive Edge.* Quorum, Westport, CT, 1991.

Shifting from Labor-Intensive to Capital-Intensive Systems

Agriculture is an operations-intensive series of processes that tend to be overlooked by traditional P/OM studies although agribusiness accounts for billions of global trade dollars. Farm products require inputs of labor, technology, and a great deal of energy, which are P/OM responsibilities. Managing the transformation process (growing, harvesting, processing, etc.) and handling the outputs (distribution) are crucial P/OM roles.

The percent of the total workforce engaged in farming in the United States changed dramatically from 1760 (more than 95 percent) to 2010 (about 5 percent). These numbers

temporarily during World War II. After the war, the decrease gained momentum as new technology was introduced and productivity rose markedly.

High-skill jobs in manufacturing have been increasing in the United States. The mid- and low-skill jobs have been disappearing. Low-skill jobs have been outsourced, first to Mexico and more recently to China and Southeast Asia. Service jobs, such as call centers and help desks, have also been outsourced to many countries and especially India.

By 2003, the manufacturing workforce in the United States was less than 20 percent of the total workforce. As was the case with farming, manufacturing output increased in spite of the workforce percent reduction because of various

Spotlight 6-1 (Continued)

factors. First, the total population had increased so that a diminishing workforce percent did not signify an absolute reduction of the same magnitude. Also, automation and "off-shore" manufacturing accounted for replacements of U.S. workers.

The Mexican cross-border outsourcing effect has been diminishing since the 1990s. Factories on the Mexican side of the U.S. border are called maquiladores. In colonial Mexico, millers charged a "maquila" to process customers' grains. At one time over one million Mexican workers were employed by 3,000 plants from the United States, Canada, Europe, Japan, Taiwan, etc. The attraction was lower labor prices than in the United States and the benefits of the North American Free Trade Agreement (NAFTA, January 1994). These labor cost imbalances have been modified and the emergence of China as the lowest cost supplier changed the equation.

As of August 2004, China's share of the U.S. import market "had grown to 16.3 percent, surpassing Mexico as the largest exporter to the US." This quote is from the World of Garment-Textile-Fashion website, found at http://www.fibre2fashion.com. In 2005, the textile quota system ended, and the percentage of imports from China iincreased further. The increase since 2004 is estimated to be between 30 and 40 percent, which results in a share betweeb 21.2 and 22.8 of the U.S. import market.

The agricultural shift in work configurations provides insights about what is currently happening in manufacturing as well as in service industries and IT occupations. Agriculture has been moving from laborious custom-type farm jobs to high-speed technology employed for land preparation, crop planting, watering, fertilizing, pest control, and harvesting. Although the shift is enormous, there remain itinerant laborers such as grape pickers from South America to generate disputes about their status. Still, change is inevitable. The advantage is shifting from direct labor costs to indirect technology investments as the process of farming continuously improves with new technology. There has been growth of small organic farms. As with traditional farms, the small are assimilated by the largest agricultural companies which have begun to market organic products.

In manufacturing, the shift-point (or tipping point) is being reached where, in spite of cheap labor abroad, new technology has the economic edge. The total cost of using automation at home is becoming significantly lower than using trained labor abroad. Breakeven points for preferring automation are approaching in one industry after another.

The cost advantages of increased domestic productivity, and the superior quality of products made at home, become apparent. Net present value calculations do not tend to reflect

such rewards and thereby penalize technology investments to replace low-labor costs. Quality problems from abroad have grown significantly and will impact decisions in all industries concerning decisions to off-shore manufacturing jobs. Shifting patterns do not make a clear impression until the tipping point is reached. There is no easy way to know when that will occur—and if it will occur,

Further, off-shore manufacturing adds transportation costs that are usually considered to be so small in comparison to labor cost savings that they are overshadowed. Transport became efficient when it gained the technological benefits of large container ships and advanced materials handling. Nevertheless, added transportation and other logistics costs will become relevant as automation costs drop. Transportation costs have also increased because of security considerations which make it essential that an information record be available at all times for item that is part of a cargo. The entire system of factors will again play a role in reaching sensible location decisions for manufacturing.

Fewer limitations apply to entrepreneurs in manufacturing because they are willing to forgo immediate profit to start up a business. For larger companies, when the tipping point in manufacturing is recognized, capital spending budgets will rise, but this will not restore former employment levels in manufacturing. With lower percentages of the total workforce in both agriculture and manufacturing, where will all the new jobs go? Note in the table that service jobs are growing at a substantial rate. It is often thought that service jobs are low paying and the image is that of working at the counter for McDonald's. However, new P/OM service jobs include ways to promote safety and security, reduction of supply chain waste, and revenue maximization.

Joseph Carson, director of global economic research at Alliance Capital Management LP, says that factory employment is declining globally because new technology has made factories more efficient, permitting higher output with "far fewer workers." In spite of declining manufacturing employment, says Mr. Carson, "global industrial output rose more than 30 percent." [John Hilsenrath and Rebecca Buckman. "Factory Employment Is Falling WorldWide." *The Wall Street Journal* (October 20, 2003): A2, A8.]

Review Questions

1 The percentage of the total workforce engaged in farming in the United States changed markedly from 1790 to 2008. What are those percentages, and what explains the change?

2 The percentage of the total workforce engaged in manufacturing in the United States follows quite a

different pattern. The manufacturing percentage of the total workforce reached a peak during the 1920s. What was the percentage and does that pattern make sense?

3 Off-shoring and outsourcing are ways of reducing the labor-intensive component of the manufacturing cost of goods sold. Is this selling out on the nation's ability to manufacture?

4 Explain the following statement: "In manufacturing, the shift-point (or tipping point) is being reached where, in spite of cheap labor abroad, new technology has the economic edge."

5 Will the agricultural model of shifting from high-level labor-intensive workforce engagement to low-level labor engagement apply to manufacturing?

Sources: Malcolm Gladwell. *The Tipping Point: How Little Things Can Make a Big Difference.* NY: Little, Brown and Company, 2000; World of Garment-Textile-Fashion website: http://www.fibre2fashion.com; John Hilsenrath and Rebecca Buckman. "Factory Employment Is Falling WorldWide." *The Wall Street Journal* (October 20, 2003): A2, A8.

Spotlight 6-2 Call Centers and E-Shopping
Successes and Failures of B2C (Business to Consumers Means Selling to Customers on the Internet)

Since the advent of the web, many Internet-based retailers have not obtained satisfactory financial results. During the same period, leading in-store retailers have been relatively profitable using traditional modes for selling and delivering goods to customers. Direct-mail call center–based retailers have continued success when their organizations have been founded on efficient production and operations management methods. All success stories have at least two characteristics. The first is customer-centric thinking that is attuned to the voice of the customer. The second is a passionate devotion to operations management applied to all aspects of the business (i.e., call centers, online-Internet order systems) and warehouse distribution systems (receiving and shipping).

Start with an illustration of failure. Webvan.com opened for business in 1998 and declared bankruptcy in 2001. Webvan remains the biggest e-tailing dollar failure that has ever occurred. Applying classic in-store retailing standards, Webvan's inability to reach breakeven within a reasonable period of time would not have been tolerated. Yet, the high fixed and variable costs of Webvan's operations might have been controlled if P/OM had been party to Webvan's top management decisions.

Accomplished operations managers would have seen that the volume of business required to recover fixed costs was not going to be attained within an acceptable planning horizon. If and when invited to the table, P/OM sits as a watchdog over matters such as cost recovery and sufficient cash flow to pay workers and suppliers. P/OM is responsible for the cost of goods sold, which consists of materials, labor, energy, etc. It is traditionally accountable for quality, productivity, delivery, and operating costs. With finance, it is able to evaluate the payback period of investments and the likelihood of reaching breakeven points in a reasonable time, which is known as *breakeven time.*

One can only speculate about what blinded Webvan's highly talented executive team. A fair guess is—if venture capitalists do not demand a reasonable payback period, neither does management. The impact of investments on the bottom line was overlooked because venture capitalists of the bubble era aggressively pursued capacity growth rates rather than demand volume and adequate profits. Journalists of that period supported the proposition that the Internet had brought a technological revolution to standard business practice.

Uncertainty existed in 1999 about the survival of traditional retailers. In-store retail was labeled pejoratively the "old economy." Internet retailing, labeled the "new economy," was accompanied by astonishing price earnings ratios for dot.com stock prices. In this environment, management concentrated on raising increasing amounts of money—to buy more technology to take control of markets that did not yet exist.

Around March 2000, the "new economy" bubble burst. On Tuesday, July 10, 2001, *The New York Times* front-page headline read, "An Ambitious Internet Grocer Is Out of Both Cash and Ideas." The article stated that Internet-grocer Webvan had spent $1.2 billion of investors' money before declaring bankruptcy. Suddenly, opinions about Internet retailers were as negative as they had previously been positive. Business media now described dot.coms as a transient phenomenon that would never replace traditional modes of selling goods. The business model for retail dot.coms was said to be inherently flawed.

The *flawed-Internet* surmise was as baseless as the *invincible-Internet* proposition. Both opinions were formed without benefit of operations management knowledge and a systems point of view. Gradually, after the bubble burst, recognition grew that ignorance, not the Internet, was the culprit. Ideas began to surface about how defects in the business model could be corrected.

Spotlight 6-2 (Continued)

Here is how some of Webvan's problems might have been avoided. The firm should not have rushed to invest in technology aimed at serving markets not-yet-existent. Capacity planning needed to be synchronized with revenue growth. Webvan should have preserved cash rather than spend prematurely to erect barriers against competitive entry. The burn rate (of investor cash) was excessive needing controls.

Webvan's problems may have stemmed from erroneous forecasts of market growth timing. This produced an extraordinarily high breakeven point. Perhaps, in the time of Webvan, venture capitalists considered breakeven concepts to be anachronistic. Webvan set up distribution centers across more geography than it could handle over a short time. Its product line was too ambitious. Probably, Webvan's most significant error was to believe that customers would never desire alternative shopping opportunities once their home delivery system was in place. Webvan took risks based on the belief that a shopping revolution would occur because of Webvan's existence.

Another element contributing to failure was that Webvan's managers had no previous experience with the grocery business and supermarket operations. Webvan's managerial expertise was in technology and not inventory. The logistics of their supply chains (requiring P/OM expertise) were out of kilter. Carrying costs were too high. Low inventory turns created aging merchandise. Webvan's technologists were an asset, but team experience with groceries was essential for mastery of supermarket competitions.

As 2001 began, Webvan's market strategy and budget were not creating enough demand to match the warehouse capacities that had been created. It was clear that the cost of switching customers from conventional, in-store shopping to Internet shopping was much higher than had been imagined.

Amazon.com provides a real contrast. Amazon's management slowed company expansion when the breakeven point increased relative to actual demand. Warehouse costs were slashed and operations were honed to stark efficiency. Marketing took aim at increasing volumes. As a major move, shipping became free for orders above $25. That rule worked and it has remained in place. Amazon developed its own unique method for listening to the voice of the customer. Every inquiry and order goes to building a customer profile, which is compared to other customers of similar propensities. Amazon successfully prompts customers about what they might like to buy.

Even so, Amazon stock (AMZN–NYSE) tells a story of ups and downs since going public in May 1997. In Q4 of 1999, AMZN was at $120. Hopes had been dashed when, in Q3 of 2002, AMZN was under $10. The next run-up occurred in Q4 of 2003 when AMZN rebounded to $60.

The stock fell back to around $35 in Q1 of 2005. In July 2007, AMZN reached a high of $88.90. Although Amazon no longer enjoyed the extravagant optimism that it once had, it is now considered a survivor and leader in the B2C marketplace.

Amazon formed partnerships, at various times, with Target, Circuit City, Borders, Petco, Toy-R-Us, and other firms to increase their base and spread the risk. These partnerships provided customers with combinations (in varying degrees) of online, call center, and in-store buying, as well as in-store pick-ups and returns. Even though difficulties ended some of these partnerships, in general, they represented a successful new retailing model that combined "clicks and bricks." Carrie Johnson of Forrester Research told the *E-Commerce Times* (November 17, 2003) that "the undisputed king of online partnerships, at least so far, is Amazon.com. The e-tailer has used its own success to convince brick-and-mortar companies ranging from Borders to Target to link arms with it."*

Items purchased at Target.com can be returned to Target stores. The same applies to purchases made at Costco.com and Walmart.com. They can be returned to Costco stores and Wal-Mart stores respectively. These are examples of successful applications of mixed-mode shopping by established retailers. There is an immediate connection made at the webpages of Walmart.com, where "Find A Store" (by Zip code) leads to "Ship Free to Your Store." This is (1) order online; (2) Wal-Mart delivers to the most convenient store; (3) an e-mail is sent to the customer to alert for pickup. Surveys have made it clear that interchangeability of online transactions with in-store activities is valued by customers. Lands' End at Sears stores fulfills its commitment to the mixed-mode of "clicks and bricks and phones" by permitting customers to talk with live operators and allowing them to return merchandise to the Sears stores.

Webvan might be around today if it had forsaken its pure-Internet strategy in favor of mixed-mode partnerships with call centers and stores. The mixed-mode transactions must reflect P/OM devotion to costs, delivery, and quality.

Review Questions

1 Spotlight 6-2 is about B2C. To understand B2C, it helps to find out about B2B and contrast the two. What is the difference between B2C and B2B? For those who are unfamiliar with B2B, see http://www.bahamasb2b.com/e-commerce/b2c_basics.htm. Click on B2B Basics.

2 How does P/OM have improve the profitability of business-to-consumer (B2C)? Could P/OM

applications have changed B2C bubble-companies into solid businesses?

3 Turning from the past to the present, what is the existing situation with respect to call centers and e-shopping (B2C)? What is the future likely to bring?

4 What advantages do small- and medium-sized enterprises (SMEs) have when competing with large companies online in the retail industry? Are advantages well-known to entrepreneurs?

5 What disadvantages do small- and medium-sized enterprises (SMEs) have when competing with large companies online in the retail industry? Are there any strategies for the SMEs to use to overcome their disadvantages?

Keith Regan. "Building E-Commerce Partnerships That Work." E-Commerce Times (November 17, 2003), http://ecommerce times.com/story/32139.html.

Sources: Martin K. Starr. "Application of P/OM to E-Business: B2C E-Shopping." *International Journal of Operations & Production Management*, vol. 23, no. 1 (2003): 105–124. At Lands' End Live phone or chat is available. At http://www.Sear s.com, note websites for Kmart, Lands' End, etc. At Costco.com, note LOCATIONA in the upper-right corner. Use left-hand navigation pane to FAQs and go to "How do I return an item?" At Walmart.com, go to Site to Store in the left-hand navigation pane. At Target.com, go to Help and click on Return an item.

chapter 6

Summary

How to analyze and redesign existing processes is the subject of this chapter. It provides information about how to create process charts and process flow layout charts. Process charts trace the present sequence of activity symbols. Process flow layout charts trace the paths of parts on the floor plan. Each can be analyzed leading to process improvements. Then each can show the proposed process side-by-side with the present one. The growing impact of computer-aided process planning is discussed. The use of reengineering (REE), process planning with a clean sheet of paper, is contrasted with continuous improvement. An example of information process analysis is given.

The chapter also includes discussion of SMED (single-minute exchange of dies) methods for decreasing the costs and times required to change over from one process to another. This has become increasingly important as companies strive to offer their customers greater product variety. Machine-operator charts allow synchronization of operator setups with machines. When setup constraints are reduced, major improvements can be made in productivity. Total productive maintenance (TPM) is explained with respect to preventive, predictive, and remedial maintenance strategies. All of these topics add up to a strong competitive ability with respect to the analysis and redesign of processes.

Two Spotlight feature boxes conclude this chapter. These boxes illustrate real applications of the materials in the chapter. Spotlight 6-1: Occupation Outsourcing leads to an important discussion about where processes are located. The trend to move certain kinds of processes abroad may be decelerating. Spotlight 6-2: Call Centers and E-Shopping highlights two major changes that have occurred in the retail business. It is shown that P/OM must play a part in strategic and tactical planning for Internet-based businesses.

Key Terms

Best in class (p. 191)

Changeovers (p. 201)

Computer-aided process planning (CAPP) (p. 194)

Continuous improvement (CI) (p. 187)

Lead time (LT) (p. 207)

Lifetime value of customers (LTV) (p. 192)

Machine-operator chart (MOC) (p. 204)

Predictive maintenance (PDM) (p. 206)

Preventive maintenance (PM) (p. 206)

Process analysis (p. 188)

Process charts (p. 188)

Put-away (p. 202)

Redundancy (p. 207)

Reengineering (p. 196)

Remedial maintenance (RM) (p. 206)

Setup (p. 189)

Single-minute exchange of dies (SMED) (p. 203)

Time-based management (TBM) (p. 190)

Total productive maintenance (TPM) (p. 205)

Value analysis (VA) (p. 199)

Zero breakdowns (p. 210)

Review Questions

1 What are the conventional symbols used for process charting? What has happened to these conventional symbols? Are there any other activities that make up processes that are not covered by the conventional symbols?

2 What are the distinctions between process flow charts and process flow layout charts? When should one or the other be chosen?

3 How does process charting apply to job shops? How does it apply to intermittent (short-run) flow shops? How does it apply to long-term, continuous flow shops?

4 What is CAPP? Is it important?

5 How do process charts show the receipt of materials from suppliers as part of the process? How do they show shipments of finished goods to distributors?

6 Why should process charts be drawn up by process managers who are responsible for everything that happens on the production line?

7 Explain the following statement:

It is unfortunate if process managers are so busy taking care of existing customers that they do not feel they have time to plan for new jobs. Time should be allocated to setting up the systems to routinize the function of developing and improving process charts.

8 Is it sensible and justified that "prized customers" get more time and attention for process charting than others?

9 What are the purposes served by machine-operator charts?

10 How does process analysis aid in the discovery of new ideas?

11 What setup times are required to operate a computer? Describe them. Address the issue of reducing them.

12 TPM programs are absolutely essential when process stoppage is life threatening. Give examples and explain.

Problems Section

Note: This section has various problems that can be formulated and solved using QuantMethods Production/Operations Management software (QMpom). The appropriate model categories are indicated for each problem.

Problems Concerned with Process Analysis and Charting

The idea is to create process flowcharts that are serious attempts to capture the actual process that is taking place. Some environments in which this can be done include service-oriented, fast-food chains. Note: If possible, visit a fast-food restaurant at off-peak hours and talk to the manager about this assignment. Explain that it requires your understanding the process and how it is managed.

Using the QMpom module called Quality Control Models will facilitate solving the seven (7) problems that are numbered 1 through 7.

1 Analyze the way burgers are cooked and served at McDonald's. Then draw a process chart for the steps that are required. Draw a process flow layout chart for the McDonald's store that is being studied.

2 Analyze the way french fries are made and served at Burger King. Then draw a process chart for the steps that are required. Draw a process flow layout chart for the Burger King being studied.

3 Analyze the way chili is made and served at Wendy's. Then, draw a process chart for the steps required to make and serve it. Draw a process flow layout chart for the Wendy's restaurant being studied.

There are many processes with which most people have some experience, such as changing a tire (a service) or baking a cake (a product). These are presented here along with some other processes that can be charted.

4 Analyze the servicing process that takes place at a gasoline station. Then draw a process chart that compares self-service at the gasoline station with full-service for a fill-up and oil check. It is said that full-service was the standard before 1980. Is that correct? Draw the process flow layout chart for the station.

5 Analyze the service process of making travel arrangements. Then draw a process chart for a travel agent setting up the itineraries and reservations for a business trip to be taken by two company executives who are traveling by air from Chicago to Los Angeles. Draw a process flow layout chart for the agent and the agency. Compare this to booking on the Internet.

6 Analyze the service process for putting a spare tire onto a car after having a flat. Then draw a process chart appropriate for changing the tire. Draw a process flow layout chart that shows where all the materials are kept and how they are moved around. Is a flat tire an anachronism?

7 Analyze the process for baking a cake. Then, draw a process chart for baking a cake. Draw a process flow layout chart as well.

Problems Concerned with Creating a Production Process

Before it is possible to create a production process, it is necessary to know how the product, such as cheese or concrete, is made. Similarly, for services, it is necessary to know what steps are required to deliver the service, such as servicing copy machines or writing a research report. There are many sources of information about how to make and do things.[10]

Using the QMpom module called Quality Control Models will facilitate solving the seven (7) problems that are numbered 8 through 14.

8 Research the process for making cheese. Create a process chart for producing wheels of cheese in volume as a business venture. What work configuration (job shop or flow shop) do you recommend?

9 Research the process for making concrete. Create a process chart for mixing cement to make concrete in volume as a business venture. What work configuration (job shop or flow shop) do you recommend?

10   Research how to make a jar of jam. Create a process chart for producing jars of jam in volume as a business venture. What work configuration (job shop or flow shop) do you recommend?

11   Research the process for making vinegar. Create a process chart for producing 16- and 32-oz. bottles of vinegar to be sold in supermarkets. What work configuration (job shop or flow shop) do you recommend?

12   Research how to service copy machines. Create a process chart for providing this service on a business-like basis. What work configuration do you recommend?

13   Analyze how to write a research report. Create a process chart for providing this service on a business-like basis.

14   With respect to Problem 13, a market research consulting firm has considered using virtual offices, meaning that some percent of their report writers work at home on personal computers. How might this concept change the process chart? How might it change the process flow layout chart?

15   Draw the machine-operator chart for the following situation:

- There are two operators and one machine.
- Make ready takes two time periods.
- Machine processing time requires four periods.
- Put-away takes two time periods.

There has been no attempt to employ SMED concepts so both make ready and put-away have to be done as internal activities with the machine turned off.

Figure 6-6, entitled "Machine-Operator Chart—Original Process," showed what occurs when this situation exists with one operator.

a. What can be done with two operators?

b. How does this compare with the 50 percent idle times associated with one operator in the original process?

16   Using the information in Problem 15, what can be done if SMED methods permit make ready for unit (n) while unit ($n - 1$) is working on the machine?

The Preventive Maintenance Strategy Problem

In the subway system of Metropolis, there are 100,000 lightbulbs that are at risk for failure with rates described as follows. The complete preventive maintenance policy is to replace all of the bulbs at once, four times per year. These lightbulbs are long-life lightbulbs, which cost more than regular ones.

Each of these bulbs has an expected average life of 3,000 hours and cost $7.00. The setup cost for each subway station is $5,000 and there are 50 stations.

In the subway, each lightbulb remains lit, day and night, all year long, which is a total of 8,760 hours. Burned out and broken bulbs are only replaced during the TPM sweep. This could mean that station platform light is not always sufficient. At an extra cost, remedial replacement could be used. The total sweep would still take place, replacing all lightbulbs, whether or not they were newly replaced.

17   For this problem, ignore remedial replacement and its extra cost.

a. Is a total replacement sweep four times per year likely to be sufficient? Note: The distribution is such that many lightbulbs burn out long before the expected lifetime is reached, and many last considerably longer than 3,000 hours.

b. What is the total cost for following this TPM policy?

The Remedial and Predictive Maintenance Strategy Problem

The alternative strategy (using the information in Problem 17) is to replace each bulb as it burns out. Replacement costs $5 per lightbulb in addition to the $7 purchase cost per bulb. As noted in the previous problem, the bulbs have an expected lifetime of 3,000 hours. Each lightbulb in the subway remains lit, day and night, all year long, a total of 8,760 hours. The expected number of times each bulb will burn out per year is 2.9. For ease of calculation, round this off to 3 times per year that each lightbulb must be changed.

18   For this problem:

a. What is the total cost of following the remedial maintenance policy?

b. Which is preferred, TPM or RM?

c. If the purchasing agent is able to buy the bulbs for $6.00, will it make a difference?

d. How can this problem be addressed as an application of predictive maintenance strategy?

19 How does the service (setup and changeover) procedure used for racing cars differ from that of regular auto servicing? Is there anything that can be learned from the difference? What does this query have to do with SMED?

20 Paint stores avoid having to carry thousands of different cans of paint for each of the colors customers want. The customer picks out the color that is wanted from color-coded chips or strips of paper. The code number is entered into the computer, which then generates the formula for that particular color. The machine that has the basic color ingredients is set to input six drops of this and four drops of that into a basic flat or semi-glossy or glossy white. For example, to make a lemon white the recipe is two drops of *y*, one drop of *gy* and two drops of *oy*. Note that the colors are added to only three basic types of white paint.

Draw the process diagram for this method of producing variety needed by the customer. Compare it to the situation where the paint company is obliged to make all of the different colors in the factory and ship them to each retailer.

Using the QMpom module called Quality Control Models will facilitate solving Problem 20.

21 The cost of controlled storage (CST), where a withdrawal slip is required to obtain an item, is $70 per item so controlled per month. The cost of uncontrolled storage (UCST), where an item can be obtained without a stock request form, is $10 per item so stored per month. An uncontrolled item that costs $30 is known to suffer pilferage losses of three items a month. There are 100 of these items in storage. Which is preferred, CST or UCST?

Practice Quiz

1 Benchmarking is an important P/OM method intended to accomplish specific goals. Which of the following choices is incorrect?

a. Benchmarking can be used to compare "best" performance against "existing" performance where "best" is identified as the performance of the leader in a specific activity.

b. Benchmarking can be used to compare "today's" performance against "yesterday's" performance. The time interval can be adjusted to the circumstances. For example, a useful measure might be "this month (or year)" against "last month (or year)."

c. Benchmarking can be used to compare various suppliers. For example, delivery time consistency might be of measured.

d. Benchmarking cannot be used for process improvement because charting methods have been developed that are standard procedures.

e. "Personal Best" is a benchmark used by sporting enthusiasts.

2 Lead time (LT) is a generic term for a production phenomenon. Which of the following statements is incorrect?

a. Lead time occurs only in production and operations management systems (P/OM). Note: Logistics costs are generally part of P/OM accounting.

b. Excessive lead time is the reason that synthetic materials are used instead of nonimitation materials. For example, faux leather is often used for autos and attaché cases because lead time to obtain real leather is excessive.

c. Because long lead time is costly, every effort should be made to shorten lead time.

d. The costs of lead time include the costs of the delivery system and the costs of waiting for deliveries to be made or having too much stock on hand.

e. Lead time is a production phenomenon because production scheduling must account for any delays in supplies from outside sourcing as well as from bottlenecks within the system.

3 How do process flowcharts differ for custom work, job shops with batch production, flow shops as well as intermittent flow shops, and projects? Which of the following choices is wrong? Note: Answer e. is correct. This material is not discussed in this chapter, but because the comparison is relevant and useful it is offered at this time.

a. An order for a new job of substantial batch size has been obtained. The item has not been made by this job shop before. Check to see if the product is similar to any other products that have been made previously. If feasible modify existing process charts. If not, draw up a new process flowchart to include the sequence and timing of all activities required.

b. Intermittent flow shops do not require process flow-charting because they are temporary systems. Intermittent flow shop workers are much like artists whose procedures are discovered as they work. Because intermittent flow shops are never more than single shift, the investment in time and money is not significant.

c. For the shop doing custom work, draw generic process flowcharts to capture the majority of the kind of work that is done. Usually, it does not pay to detail a new process chart for each custom job that is accepted. Also, custom workers are often much like artists whose procedures are discovered as they work.

    d.   Flow shops are commitments to dedicated technology (special-purpose equipment) and well-trained employees at assigned workstations. The engineering required to assure smooth flows with good balance requires process flow charts that are detailed and worked over until costs of unnecessary idle time and bottlenecks are minimized.

    e.   Projects have specialized flowcharts that are detailed with respect to the sequence and timing of all activities. Projects are similar to custom work in the sense that they are not repeated in batches (job shop) or made continuously (flow shop). What differentiates the two is that projects involve major commitments with big investments and large penalties for delays.

4   Which two of the following statements about process changeovers are incorrect?

    a.   Single-minute exchange of dies (SMED) is a theory of production that explains when to switch from batch production to a flow shop system.

    b.   Changeovers are an aspect of operations management where it has always been taken for granted that the greater the existing volume of production—the more costly it is to shift from one job to another. For example, a basic lathe (least expensive form) is used to make a wood post. When design of that post changes, it will take time to set up for the new version of the post. However, when the posts are made in batches of 10, the basic lathe is not recommended. Instead, a turret lathe is chosen because it is faster to shift tooling from one design to another.

    c.   The learning curve comes into play every time operators bring a new order on line.

    d.   Changeover costs are often proportional to changeover times. If computers can decrease changeover times, then product variety can be increased without penalties.

    e.   Setup costs are proportional to take down and cleanup times.

5   Quick-changeover ability is a major P/OM objective. Which of the following choices is incorrect?

    a.   Setup (and take-down) tasks that can be done while the system is doing another job are called external setup elements. Another way of saying this is setup tasks that can be done when the machine is running are more efficient than those requiring the machine to be shut down, as in b.

    b.   Setup (and take-down) tasks that can only be done with the system shut down are called internal setup elements.

    c.   Determine which setup tasks can be done with the machine running and which cannot be done with the machine running. Minimize total setup time with preference shown for reducing internal setup times.

    d.   Hire creative operations-oriented people who can find ways to convert internal setup elements into external setup elements.

    e.   The concepts of internal and external setup times do not apply to servicing (repair and maintain) aircraft in flight.

6   Total productive maintenance (TPM) is an important P/OM objective. Breakdowns are costly and disruptive. Inoperability and slowdowns can severely damage the bottom line. On a more personal note, consider what is the best choice given the options of taking the car in for regular servicing or breaking down on the expressway. But, there are no guarantees that servicing will prevent a breakdown. There are, however, changes in the probabilities of unanticipated failures. With these thoughts in mind, two of the following statements about smart maintenance are wrong. Which two of the following options are incorrect?

    a.   Remedial maintenance (RM) must be justified by an analysis that shows that fixing something before it breaks is warranted economically.

    b.   Slowdowns (meaning the equipment works at less than the customary rated speeds) cannot be avoided by using preventive maintenance (PM) methods. PM is designed to limit failures and will not effect degradation of performance.

    c.   Fail-safe designs are applied to systems where failure can be at least damaging and possibly catastrophic. In the catastrophic case, the need for preventive maintenance of fail-safe backups is essential.

    d.   Redundant components are a design method used to provide failure prevention. However, failure prevention through redundancy adds to the cost of quality. Savings can be made in TPM because remedial maintenance can be used for an equipment failure; a duplicate (or backup) system is still functioning.

    e.   Predictive maintenance (PDM) is based on science and not art. It is associated with predicting the need for remedial maintenance rather than preventive maintenance.

7   Which of the following statements is incorrect?

    a.   Reengineering (called *REE*, which means *starting from scratch*) is a sound concept for revamping a system that is in need of thorough change. Downsizing firms has been called reengineering by those who wanted to participate in the REE fad. This is an unfortunate mislabeling of REE. Cost reduction does not start with a clean piece of paper.

b. Determining the optimal size for a workforce to achieve clearly stated objectives is neither the method nor the language associated with reengineering.

c. An alternative method for improving the performance of a system is continuous improvement (CI). The Japanese call this "kaizen" and have demonstrated that it works best when everyone in the company plays a part.

d. Continuous improvement (CI) is practiced in the United States and Western Europe with great success. However, organizational issues arise when management changes because old habits tend to reappear when the champions of the new (CI) approaches are no longer present to oversee their accomplishments.

e. Reengineering went through a period of being lauded as a cure for most business problems. REE was oversold when it became a journalistic sensation with the advent of the trade book, *Reengineering the Corporation* by Hammer and Champy in 1993. The book has been revised (June 2001). Business process reengineering (BPR) is another name for the same concept, which remains a viable approach to achieving major business improvement.

8 Which of the following statements is incorrect?

a. Process charts are simple to use and powerful in application because the graphics provide an alternative mind-set that promotes another way of thinking.

b. Sorting through details in rows and columns of numbers can be difficult. An equivalent process chart with flow-through rates allows insights concerning problems such as bottlenecks.

c. A recommended use of process charts is to determine where in the process time studies should be located for setting company-wide standards and piece rates.

d. Process charts are effective means of achieving an optimal layout for the factory floor, office, or warehouse.

e. Traditionally, an isosceles triangle with vertex down appearing on process chart with sequenced activity symbols stands for a controlled storage, i.e., a withdrawal slip is required to obtain an item from this storage.

9 There are many ways to design symbols for process charts. The IT (information technology) industry has adopted symbols that are unique to computer programming. For the job shop, the ASME (American Society of Mechanical Engineers) no longer regulates the symbols to be used. Nevertheless, the old traditional symbols are well-known. The following statements adhere to the original ASME symbols. However, two of the statements are incorrect. Which answers are wrong?

a. A small isosceles triangle within a larger isosceles triangle where both are drawn with their vertex down, appearing on a process chart with sequenced activity symbols, stands for an uncontrolled storage, i.e., no withdrawal slip is required to obtain an item from this storage.

b. Eighth-of-an-inch circles stand for operations performed at specific locations on the job shop floor.

c. Diamonds are inspections for qualities. For example, an empty toothpaste box is blown off the conveyor leading to shrinkwrap. That is an automatic quality inspection check and it would be so listed on the process chart.

d. Quarter-inch circles stand for transports of materials, components, and other parts, from one location to another. Conveyors move toothpaste boxes to shrinkwrap.

e. Quarter-inch square boxes stand for inspections of quantities. For example, six packs of shrinkwrapped toothpaste boxes are loaded by the operator into the master shipping case. Inspecting for 36 units in each box could be done by weight.

10 The office building has 2,500 lightbulbs. Compare PM and RM maintenance policies. The preventive maintenance (PM) policy is to replace all bulbs at once 6.5 times a year. Each replacement costs $5 for the bulb and the work. There is a setup cost of $1,000. The remedial maintenance policy is to replace each bulb as it burns out. Each replacement costs $10 for the bulb and the work. There is no setup cost. Bulbs have an expected lifetime of 900 hours. The plant operates two 8-hour shifts, 7 days per week.

Which row in the following table contains the correct answers for the comparison?

Row Option	Preventive Maintenance	Remedial Maintenance
a.	$93,000	$56,000
b.	$78,000	$130,000
c.	$97,500	$162,500
d.	$117,500	$195,000
e.	$39,000	$65,000

Additional Readings

Brumberg, B., and K. Axelrod. *Watch It Made in the USA: A Visitor's Guide to the Companies That Make Your Favorite Products*, 3e. Avalon Travel Publishing, October 2002.

Hammer, Michael. *Beyond Reengineering*. New York: Harper Collins, 1995.

Hammer, Michael. *The Agenda*. New York: Crown Business, 2001.

Hammer, Michael, and James Champy. *Reengineering the Corporation*. New York: Harper Collins, 1993.

Imai, M. Kaizen, *The Key to Japan's Competitive Success*. New York: Random House Business Division, 1986.

Ishiwata, Junichi. *IE for the Shop Floor: Productivity Through Process Analysis*. Connecticut: Productivity Press, 1991.

Madison, Dan. *Process Mapping, Process Improvement and Process Management*. Paton Press, 2005.

McNair, C. J., and Kathleen H. J. Leibfried. *Benchmarking: A Tool for Continuous Improvement*. Harper Business, 1992.

Nakajima, Seiichi. *TPM Development Program: Total Productive Maintenance*. Connecticut: Productivity Press, 1989.

Ohno, Taiichi. *Workplace Management*. Connecticut: Productivity Press, 1988.

Robinson, Alan. *Continuous Improvement in Operations: A Systematic Approach to Waste Reduction*. Connecticut: Productivity Press, 1991.

Shingo, Shigeo. *A Revolution in Manufacturing: The SMED System*. Connecticut: Productivity Press, 1985.

Shingo, Shigeo. *The Shingo Production Management System, Improving Process Functions*. Connecticut: Productivity Press, 1992.

Notes

1. C. J. McNair and Kathleen H. J. Leibfried. *Benchmarking: A Tool for Continuous Improvement*. John Wiley & Sons, Inc., with arrangement from Harper Business, 1995.

2. Shigeo Shingo. *The Shingo Production Management System, Improving Process Functions*. Connecticut: Productivity Press, 1992.

3. Visiprise is based in Alpharetta, Georgia. Go to http://www.visiprise.com. Click Solutions; Visiprise Manufacturing Planning; Visiprise Computer-Aided Process Planning (CAPP). As an alternative, check out http://www.solumina.com

4. Shingo lists four process functions that should be under constant surveillance for improvement. These are processing, inspection, transportation, and delays.

5. M. Imai. Kaizen. *The Key to Japan's Competitive Success*. New York: Random House Business Division, 1986.

6. Michael Hammer and James Champy. *Reengineering the Corporation*. New York: Harper Collins, 1993; Michael Hammer. *Beyond Reengineering*. New York: Harper Collins, 1995. Michael Hammer. *The Agenda*. New York: Crown Business, 2001. Chapter 4 is titled, "Put Process First."

7. JMA is the Japan Management Association.

8. Ibid. footnote 1, 150.

9. Ibid. 147, 149.

10. For learning about processes that are actually used for making things, see the 27 volumes of *The Science and Invention Encyclopedia*. Westport, CT: H.S. Stuttman, Inc. Another good book to consult about real processes is the *Science Encyclopedia*. New York: Dorling Kindersley, Inc., 1993. Also see Enrichment Activity 1.

Enrichment Activity 6: A Total Productive Maintenance Model to Determine the Appropriate Level of Preventive Maintenance to Be Used

The policies of TPM are employed to choose the optimal level of preventive maintenance to use, including the option of zero preventive maintenance.

A simple equation is written for the expected total cost of following three alternative strategies, called $x = 1, 2, 3$:

> $(x = 1)$ No preventive maintenance, called remedial maintenance(RM)
>
> $(x = 2)$ Partial preventive maintenance, called PPM
>
> $(x = 3)$ Complete preventive maintenance, called CPM

x	Strategy	p_f	c_f	c_p	$\overline{TC}(x)$	Table EA6-1
1	RM	0.50	$10,000	—	$5,000	Data Needed to Compare Maintenance Strategies
2	PPM	0.30	$10,000	1,000	$4,000	
3	TPM	0.10	$10,000	$2,000	$3,000	

Using numbers based on the type of curve shown in Figure 6-9 allows a comparison between the expected total costs of the three maintenance strategies, $x = 1, 2, 3$.

$$p_f c_f + (1 - p_f)c_{nf} + c_p = \overline{TC}(x) \qquad (6\text{-}1)$$

$p_f = $ the probability of failure associated with the cost of prevention, c_p, and time period t

$c_p = $ the cost of failure

$c_{nf} = $ the cost of no failure, which is equal to zero $\left(\text{i.e., } c_{nf} = 0\right)$

$\overline{TC}(x) = $ the expected total cost of maintenance strategy x

Table EA6-1 provides relevant data and the expected total cost for each maintenance strategy.

The TPM strategy is indicated. It has the lowest expected cost of $3,000. It is useful to note again that a superior TPM strategy (call it TPM+) might be developed that reduces the probability of failure to less than 0.1.

Enrichment Challenges 6

1 Would a TPM + strategy be warranted if by spending $2,500 for the cost of prevention, the probability of failure could be reduced to 0.08?

2 What level of probability reduction would make the TPM and TPM + strategies equivalent? This value of p is called a breakeven point because, at least as far as the numbers are concerned, there is indifference between the choices of these two strategies.

3 What other factors might tip the balance in favor of TPM+ or TPM in spite of being tied with respect to $\overline{TC}(x)$?

Quality Assurance

Chapter 7 presents methods for providing quality assurance (QA). Why talk about quality assurance instead of quality achievement, quality control, etc. The answer is that QA is comprised of a set of systems-wide activities aimed at establishing confidence that quality goals will be achieved. The role of quality in strategies and tactics must be clear and guaranteed (i.e., without doubt). Chapter 7 provides the seven (7) classical methods for ensuring the achievement and control of quality. These methods are well-known and widely practiced quality achievement methods. The TQM approach discussed in Chapter 4 must be understood before mastery of the seven methods can pay off. QA is responsible for ensuring that TQM prevails.

Quality starts with a zero-error mind-set. A good model stems from the ideals of the Olympic perspective—an attitude required for quality achievement. The entire supply chain system must pass muster. Suppliers' goods are checked for adherence to quality standards using acceptance sampling (AS). AS involves trade-offs that balance the cost of sampling against the risk of accepting more defectives than permissible. This leads to negotiations between suppliers and buyers based on the size of Type I and Type II errors. Type I errors occur when an innocent person is found guilty by a jury of peers (or when a medical test falsely proclaims illness in a healthy patient). Type II errors occur when a guilty person is found innocent by a jury of peers (or when a medical test erroneously declares an ill person to be healthy). Type I errors occur when work is rejected on false premises. Type II errors occur when work is accepted that should be rejected (according to mutually agreed upon standards).

Six-sigma

A quality standard that strives for no more than 3.4 defectives in one million parts by using many different methods to reduce defectives produced.

After reading this chapter, you should be able to:

- Explain what defines quality and why quality is important to company success.
- Explain the role of quality assurance and relate it to TQM.
- Determine how many pieces to make to fill an order when the probabilities of producing defectives are known.
- Describe the seven classical process quality control methods.
- Show how to collect and use data to create check sheets, bar charts, histograms, and Pareto charts.
- Discuss the use of cause and effect (Ishikawa/fishbone) diagrams.
- Explain the difference between measuring variables and counting attributes.
- Construct control charts for variables and attributes.
- Explain the difference between assignable causes and chance causes.
- Explain how to interpret control chart signals for $\bar{x}$-charts, *R*-charts, *p*-charts, and *c*-charts, including upper and lower control limits (*UCL* and *LCL*).
- Understand the meaning of "runs" on a control chart and know how to use them as early warning systems.
- Discuss the use of inspection with and without control charts.
- Describe acceptance sampling and explain when it is used.
- Detail the basis of the negotiation between suppliers and buyers with respect to risks of accepting defective work (Type II error) and rejecting acceptable work (Type I error).
- Explain the use of the average outgoing quality limits.
- Pull together the systems-oriented picture of quality as a major competitive factor.
- Explain the importance of **six-sigma** to Quality Assurance.

The Systems Viewpoint

In achieving effective team effort for gold medal quality, not all competitors strive to be the best in the world. Some are happy to be silver or bronze. Others consider being at the Olympics a sufficient reward. Companies have similar goal differences. It is important to realize that not all companies strive to be the best.

Nevertheless, because quality failures are widely recognized to have negative impact on long-term performance, all companies consider quality improvement to be a common goal. Striving for quality unites all of the components and constituencies of the system. That does not mean that everyone strives with equal vigor and equivalent knowledge.

All of the parts that go into an assembly are multiplicatively interrelated so that the probability of failure gets increasingly worse and the number of extra parts that must be made increases geometrically. This is an example of the effect of systems interdependencies. When dependencies exist, the appropriate mind-set for achieving quality is to analyze and understand the entire system.

It is typical of dependent systems that suppliers and buyers are sharing risks. Without 100 percent inspection of the shipment, and using a test sample from the shipment, the buyer risks accepting more defects than an agreed-upon percentage (p). The seller (supplier) risks having the buyer reject the shipment based on a test, although with 100 percent inspection it would be found that the shipment conforms to an agreed-upon limit of no more than a specific p. Statisticians call seller's risk a Type I error and buyer's risk a Type II error.

These two types of errors are interdependent. Generally, as one gets larger the other gets smaller. At the cost of larger sample sizes, both error types are reduced. It is useful to be conscious of these errors as they affect general management decision making—as well as when negotiating quality sampling plans between buyers and sellers.

In a continuing effort to improve quality, the standards by which quality is measured are raised and the criteria are tightened. With very high standards and the desire to have zero defects, a six-sigma program may be warranted (see Spotlight 7-2).

Strategic Thinking

Type I and Type II errors are significant measures of the strategic decision performance of P/OM. To view this situation in more general terms, Type I errors occur when a truly innocent person is found guilty by a judge or a jury. Type I errors also occur when a medical test falsely proclaims cancer in a healthy patient. When a supplier's shipment has been rejected by a test sample, that supplier may call for a 100 percent inspection. Defectives can be removed from the shipment by a procedure called detailing. Type I errors are called errors of commission because an action follows the test result. The innocent person goes to jail or even worse things can happen. The cancer prognosis will lead to further testing and treatment. The shipment can be detailed.

Type II errors occur when a guilty person is found innocent by a judge or jury of peers. The person goes free. The medical test erroneously declares an ill person to be healthy. There is no treatment and the true state of affairs may be learned at a later point. The shipment is accepted and the buyer may or may not discover that the percent defectives (p) were above the contract specification. These Type II errors are called errors of omission. How does one discover that he or she did not marry the person best suited to be a lifelong companion? The effects of Type I and Type II errors can be tactical or immensely significant strategies for competitive success. In this regard, balancing errors of commission and omission requires strategic thinking that unites all of the components and constituencies of the system. All of the parts that go into an assembly are multiplicatively interrelated. Information about supply and demand is seldom based on complete knowledge and is therefore sample data. Tests leading to strategic decisions may not be formal but they remain tests. It is not wise to set goals based on thinking about only one type of error.

Quality control charts are central to the methods for controlling quality that are discussed in this chapter. When a sample point falls above the chart's upper-control limit or below the lower-control limit, that signals a possible change in the process. The outlier could be a real signal of trouble or it could be a Type I error that commissions a search for unwarranted causes. The other side of the coin is often overlooked. If the control limits are set wide apart (say, three-sigma) instead of closer (say, two-sigma), then signals of problems that are developing may not be given soon enough. This Type II error overlooks the opportunity to remedy a situation before it develops a more serious character. Setting control limits brings the production manager face-to-face with interacting error systems.

7-1 The Attitude and Mind-Set for Quality Achievement

The most important goals for process analysis are higher quality, improved productivity, and lower costs. Quality is so important to the well-being of the firm that it is the key focus of this chapter. For quality methods to be successful, all participants in the organization must have their collective minds set on quality achievement. This is done by reducing the probability of failure (p_f) to meet a variety of standards for all components. If at the same time that (p_f) is being reduced, the standards are being raised, then the mind-set for being the best in quality achievement and competitive capability is functioning.

7-1a The Zero-Error Mind-Set and Six-Sigma

Zero-error mind-set
Abhorrence of defectives and determination to prevent them from occurring.

The appropriate **zero-error mind-set** is to abhor defectives and do as much as feasible to prevent them from occurring. When they occur, learn what caused them and correct the situation. Meanwhile, raise the goals and improve the standards. Tougher hurdles are part of the quality framework, which seeks continuous improvement. Do it right the first time is the motto of the approach that champions zero errors.

Zed defects (ZD)
Policy that requires eliminating any and all causes of defects.

This is often termed, in an almost military manner, **zed defects**. The last letter of the English alphabet is called "zee" or "zed." Quality guru Philip Crosby (see Additional Readings) popularized the zed term, which he used as a cornerstone of his quality goals.

Those who say that no defects are permissible are at odds with those who say that a few defects are to be expected. The latter group goes on to say that one should learn from mistakes and take the necessary measures to prevent them from recurring. The safest position is to be flexible.

Good advice is to go for a "no defects" policy. If and when it fails to work, switch to a "learn from mistakes" policy. After corrective action has been taken to correct the mistakes, switch back to the zero-errors goal.

7-1b The Olympic Perspective

Olympic perspective
The Olympic credo of striving to be better is readily translated into dynamic goals of continuous improvement for management.

The **Olympic perspective** calls for team play with everyone striving to achieve the company's personal best. To the managers of the firm, "going for the gold" is no less a meaningful objective than for Olympic teams. The plan calls for breaking process quality records with continued and marked improvements.

7-1c Compensating for Defectives

Compensating for defectives
Because of start-up defectives, to ship the ordered quantity, produce more than the order size.

For job shops, the first items made, during and right after setup, are likely to be defective. If the order size calls for 70 units and the expected percent defective to get the job right is p, then prepare to make 73.7 or, rounding up, 74 pieces. This is called "**compensating for defectives**" and the methodology and concepts apply to batch production.

$$\text{Batch size} = \frac{\text{Order Quantity}}{(1-p)} = \frac{70}{(1-0.05)} = 73.7 \qquad (7\text{-}1)$$

Expand this concept to an assembled unit (like a computer) that consists of n electronic components, each of which has a known probability p_i of being defective ($i = 1, 2, 3, \ldots, n$). Assuming that component failures are independent of each other, and that the components cannot be tested separately but only after assembly, then the number of electronic assemblies to make would be

$$\text{Batch size} = \frac{\text{Order Quantity}}{\prod\limits_{i=1}^{n}(1-p_i)} \qquad (7\text{-}2)$$

Say the order quantity is 100 units and there are five components to be assembled, each of which has a 10 percent probability of being defective. How many units should be made in the batch?

$$\text{Batch size} = \frac{100}{(1-0.1)^5} = \frac{100}{0.59} = 169.5 \qquad (7\text{-}3)$$

With rounding, the decision is to make 170 units. The interesting effect of the multiplicative probabilities of five units is to increase the number of units that must be made to fill the order by 70 percent.

If there had been only one component (with $p = 0.10$) that could lead to defective performance, then the correct number to make to fill the order would be $100/0.9 = 111$.

With such examples of systems interdependencies, the correct attitude for quality achievement requires wanting to understand the entire system. It is unrealistic to set goals for only one cause of failure. The effort must be made to perceive all of the causes of defectives in order to measure the interactive probability of failure (p_j) or the probability of proper performance, which is ($1 - p_j$).

7-2 Quality Control (QC) Methodology

The body of knowledge that relates to quality attainment starts with the detection of problems. This is followed by diagnosis based on the analysis of the causes of the problems. Next comes prescription of corrective actions to treat the diagnosed causes. This is followed up through observations and evaluations to see how well the treatment works. The entire set of steps is called **quality control (QC)**.

Figure 7-1 presents one version of the quality control model, which is related to the fundamental cycle of scientific method.

Quality control (QC)
The process of quality attainment starts with detection of problems, followed by diagnosis of cause of problem, prescription of corrective actions to take, and finally followed up through observation and evaluation.

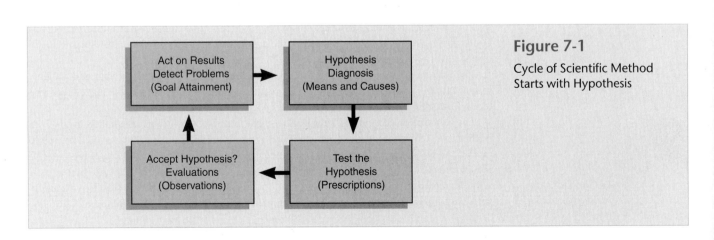

Figure 7-1

Cycle of Scientific Method Starts with Hypothesis

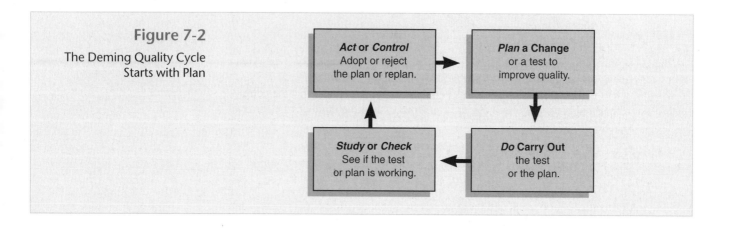

Figure 7-2

The Deming Quality Cycle
Starts with Plan

Deming
Dr. W. Edwards Deming
became a leader in the American
quality revolution after 1980.

Deming applied the model of the scientific method to quality control. He used four steps (Plan-Do-Study-Act),[1] as shown in Figure 7-2. Shingo[2] felt that control of quality was missing from the Deming cycle. Deming included quality control as an action. To avoid confusion on this matter, the control function is shown alongside of Act in the top-left hand box of Figure 7-2.

Often, the person doing the work does the checking and exercises the control. Sometimes, checking and controlling are done by a member of the quality control department. There are many instances where both are used. There are some instances where neither is used.

Quality originates with a thorough understanding of the process. If management does not have a complete understanding of all processes used by their businesses, the models for quality attainment in Figures 7-1 and 7-2 will not work. P/OM is involved in getting everyone in the company motivated to know all about the processes being used and changes under consideration.

7-3 The Seven Classic Process Quality Control Methods

Process quality control methods are used to analyze and improve process quality. There are seven time-honored and well-established methods, as shown in Table 7-1. These are data check sheets, bar charts, histograms, Pareto analysis, cause and effect charts, statistical quality control charts, and run charts.

Method 6 covers the preparation and employment of statistical quality control charts. It is the most elaborate and powerful approach of all the methods. Although Method 7 is commonly listed as a separate procedure, it is based on the use of the statistical control charts developed in Method 6.

The time period from which these methods are derived goes back to Shewhart.[3] Few modifications have been made, but all methods have been affected by computers and technology that can capture, analyze, and chart necessary data.

The amount of computing required to track multiple measures of quality used to be prohibitive. Consequently, simple methods were developed during the period from 1930 through 1950. Data collection was straightforward. Uncomplicated charts were used to present results. These graphical techniques are so powerful that they are being used with increasing frequency born of great success. They can be understood by workers who are only briefly trained in quality control methodology, yet another advantage.

1 ***Data check sheets (DCSs)*** organize the data. They are ledgers to count defectives by types. They can be spreadsheets which arrange data in matrix form when pairs of variables are being tracked. Sometimes, like spreadsheets they are called check sheets.

2 ***Bar charts*** represent data graphically. For example, the number of pieces in five lots can be graphically differentiated by bars of appropriate lengths. Often data is converted from check sheets to bar charts and histograms.

3 ***Histograms*** are frequency distributions. When data can be put into useful categories, the relative frequencies of occurrence of these categories can be informative.

4 ***Pareto analysis*** seeks to identify the most frequently occurring categories; for example, what defect is the most frequent cause of product rejections, next to most, etc. This facilitates identification of the major problems associated with process qualities. It rank orders the problems so that the most important causes can be addressed. It is a simple but powerful method that is the outgrowth of Methods 1, 2, and 3.

5 ***Cause and effect charts*** organize and depict the results of analyses concerning the determination of the causes of quality problems. The fishbone (or Ishikawa) chart is based on listing variables that are known to effect quality. **Scatter diagrams** help determine causality.

6 ***Statistical quality control (SQC) charts***—of which there are several main types—are used for detecting quality problems, much as *early warning detection systems* (EWDS). SQC charts also can help discern the causes of process quality problems.

7 ***Run charts*** can help spot the occurrence of an impending problem. Thus, run analysis is another EWDS. It can be a great help in diagnosing the causes of problems.

Table 7-1

The Seven QC Methods are discussed in the five Sections 7-3 through 7-8

Computer power has been used intelligently by P/OM to extend the reach of quality analysis to a wide range of measures, without complicating the analysis. The seven methods can be utilized across a great spectrum of quality dimensions without creating unnecessary analytic complications. There is every good reason to avoid unnecessarily complex analyses in favor of simple methods that are easy to use and straightforward to understand.

7-3a Method 1—Data Check Sheets (DCSs)

The first method to consider is the use of **data check sheets**. These are used for recording and keeping track of data regarding the frequency of events that are considered to be essential for some critical aspect of quality.

For a particular product, there may be several data points required to keep track of different qualities that are being measured. It is useful to keep these in the same time frame and general format so that correlations might be developed between simultaneous events for the different qualities.

A data check sheet, such as shown in Figure 7-3, could record the frequency of power failures in a town on Long Island in New York State. The data check sheet shows when and how often the power failures occur. The DCS is a collection of information that has been organized in various ways, one of which is usually chronologically.

Data check sheets (DCSs)

Spreadsheets can be used to count and record defectives by types and times of occurrence.

Figure 7-3

Data Check Sheet—Type of Power Failures (A through F)

Date	A	B	C	D	E	F	Comments	Location
12/6/06	X						Crew delay	P21
1/2/07			X				6 hr. service	P3
2/15/07				X			3 hr. service	P22
3/7/07				X			Snowstorm	P21
4/29/07			X				3 hr. service	P3
5/15/07						X	Flooding	R40
6/7/07				X			Crew delay	P5
7/29/07		X					R40/no service	P21–R40
8/21/07			X				Road delays	B2
9/30/07			X				Crew delay	R40
11/2/07					X		Partial crew	P3
12/14/07		X					Flat tire	P5
Total	1	2	4	3	1	1		

The information about when power failures have occurred can be used in various ways. First, it provides a record of how frequently power failures arise. Second, it shows where the failures occur. Third, it can reveal how quickly power is restored. Fourth, it can show how long each failure has to wait before receiving attention, usually because work crews are busy on other power failures. None of these measures explain the causes, however.

After the data check sheet is completed, problem identification follows. Then causal analysis can begin. The data check sheet can now be called the data spreadsheet to conform to the computer era. Data capture is more efficient now that it is operating with software on the computer. Organized collection of data is essential for good process management.

7-3b Method 2—Bar Charts

An often-used graphical method for presenting statistics captured by data check sheets is a **bar chart**. It is simple to construct and understand. People who are turned off by tables of numerical data often are willing to study a bar chart. Figure 7-4 shows a bar chart for the recorded number of power failures that were listed on the data check sheet (Figure 7-3).

The six types of failures listed as A through F on the data check sheet are represented with separate bars in Figure 7-4. The number of incidents is shown by the *y*-axis. Bar graphs compare the number of single-event types (e.g., types of complaints). A separate

Bar chart

Graphical method that uses bars of different lengths to present numerical and/or statistical data.

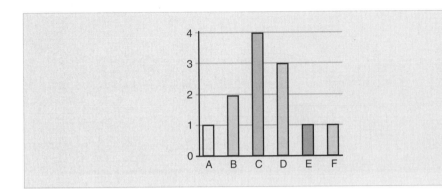

Figure 7-4

Bar Chart for the Type of Power Failure

bar is used for each data set. The types should be chosen to be operationally useful, i.e., something can be done to reduce the number of incidents.

7-3c Method 3—Histograms

Histograms are bar charts that measure the frequencies (f_i) of a set of k outcomes ($i = 1$, $2, \ldots, k$). The purpose of the histogram is to reflect the distribution of the set of data. Therefore, histograms are drawn to show the frequency with which each outcome (of all possible outcomes) occurs divided by the total number events. The result is a bar chart representation of the distribution of relative frequencies. This is equivalent to a discrete probability distribution. When the sample size is n:

$$\sum_{i=1}^{k} f_i = n \ (i = 1, \ldots, k) \tag{7-4}$$

Frequencies are converted to probabilities (or relative frequencies) when (f_i) is divided by n:

$$p_1 = \frac{f_1}{n}, \ p_2 = \frac{f_2}{n}, \ldots, \ p_k = \frac{f_k}{n} \tag{7-5}$$

and these p_i sum to one:

$$\sum_{i=1}^{k} p_i = 1 \tag{7-6}$$

Note that in Figure 7-5, the x-axis describes the number of paint defects ($i = 0, 1, 2, \ldots, 8$) that have been found per hour during an inspection of autos coming off the production line. The y-axis records the observed frequency f_i for each number of paint defects. The sample size is normalized so that $\Sigma f_i = 100$ and f_i goes from zero to greater than eight.

Auto Finishes—Quality on the Line

In this sample of $\Sigma f_i = 100$, the relative frequency for the number of times that no paint defects are found is 15 out of 100. This is quite low and needs an explanation. In many auto companies, the standards for paint and finish are so high that few cars are found faultless. The definition of a defect is often set by such stringent standards that a customer would not be able to detect the imperfection.

Figure 7-5 shows that one defect is found 20 percent of the time. More than one defect occurs 65 percent of the time. There is a notable decrease in the number of paint defects, yet more than 8 paint defects occur nine times. Even with rigorous standards, this chart should not please the P/OM in charge of quality.

Histograms

Bar charts that illustrate the relative frequencies of a set of outcomes as a discrete probability distribution.

© Jupiterimages Corporation

Highway driving takes a toll on automotive finishes. New car buyers are not willing to accept a product with any imperfections of the finish. Perfect finishes in automobile painting take a great amount of technology and manufacturing care.

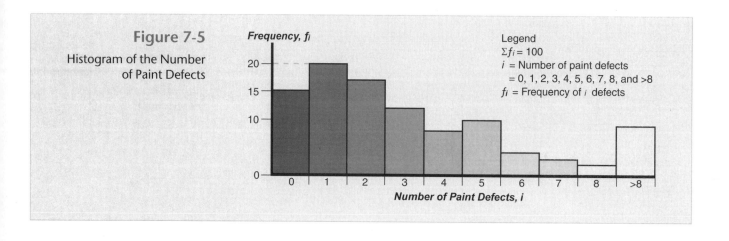

Figure 7-5

Histogram of the Number of Paint Defects

In addition to customer's demands for a perfect and long-lasting auto finish, government rules about paints and workers (OSHA–Occupational and Safety Health Administration) have become tougher and regulations about pollution have imposed additional burdens on auto companies. The systems perspective, in this regard, is essential. It links P/OM, marketing, finance, and human resource management with governmental bureaucracy.

All auto companies operating with the United States have been developing new processes that decrease the pollution associated with conventional petroleum solvents used for the clearcoat, top-layer finishes. New powder-paint process have delivered more durable finishes with fewer defects and less pollution.

7-3d Method 4—Pareto Analysis

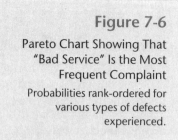

Pareto analysis

Determines the most frequent types of defects and puts them in rank order.

One goal of **Pareto analysis** is to determine which problems occur the most frequently. The problems can then be arranged in the rank order of their relative frequency of occurrence. Figure 7-6 shows how a Pareto chart can be used to analyze a restaurant's most frequent quality problems.

"Bad service" is the number one complaint. Among all five complaints, it occurs 54 percent of the time. "Cold food" is the second most frequent criticism with 22 percent of the objections. The third grievance is about ambiance—"Noisy" (12 percent). The fourth criticism is that the restaurant is "too expensive" (8 percent). Excessively salty food is the fifth complaint (4 percent).

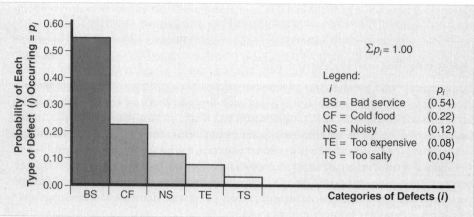

Figure 7-6

Pareto Chart Showing That "Bad Service" Is the Most Frequent Complaint

Probabilities rank-ordered for various types of defects experienced.

The rank order of the hierarchy of defect causes is evident in Figure 7-6. The probabilities reflect a high degree of skew (exaggeration) for the top two sources of complaints. This kind of skew is typical of Pareto frequencies that are found in actual situations. The first two causes of defects account for 76 percent of the complaints.

The 20:80 Rule

Pareto analysis is designed to separate the most frequent quality problems and complaints from less frequent ones. Often, 20 percent of the total number of problems and complaints occur 80 percent of the time. This is called the **20:80 rule**. Some things occur far more frequently than others. In the restaurant case, 2 out of 5 quality problems account for 76 percent of the complaints.

What is important about these numbers is the need to be sensitive to the real issues of "what counts." If the most frequent complaint is trivial (such as "too popular"), then, P/OM moves on to complaints that matter and where something can be done to improve the situation. Pareto charts do not separate the critical few from the unimportant many.

Pareto Procedures

The procedure to get Pareto-type information can take many forms. First, it helps to develop a comprehensive list of all the problems that can be expected to occur. To do this, many people should be consulted both inside and outside the company. Surveys, telephone interviews, and focus groups can be used to find out what problems people say they have experienced.

Complaints are a valuable source of information. Accurate records can be maintained using computerized data checklists. Organized efforts to secure serious feedback about complaints is a marketing responsibility. Complaints are so vital to P/OMs that they should encourage marketing to keep Pareto data on complaints. They should monitor changes in complaints both by type and frequency. Clusters of complaints at certain times provide important diagnostic information for process managers. Problems mentioned in the text range from power failures, to scratches on an auto's finish, to complaints about restaurant service.

Some problems arise during **inspection** of the product while it is on or leaving the production line. These are internally measurable problems. Other problems must wait for customer experiences. They are learned about through complaints from customers who write or call toll-free numbers set up by the company to provide information and receive complaints. Surveys also pick up complaints or they become apparent when customers seek redress within the warranty period. Retailers, wholesalers, and distributors know a lot and can communicate what they hear from their customers.

7-3e Method 5—Cause and Effect Charts (Ishikawa aka the Fishbone)

To determine the cause of a quality problem, start by listing everything in the process that might be responsible for the problem. A reasonable approach is to determine the factors that cause good (or bad) quality. These potential causes are grouped into categories and subcategories, as is done for the following example, which lists many of the factors responsible for the quality of a cup of coffee.

After the list a chart will be drawn. **Cause and effect charts** show at a glance what factors affect quality and thereby what may be the causes of quality problems. These charts are organized with the quality goal at the right.

The processes used to grow coffee beans, harvest, roast, store, and ship the coffee would be included in this cause and effect diagram if there was control over these factors. This coffee-making process begins with making a cup of coffee. All participating processes are part of the causal system.

20:80 rule
Twenty percent of the total number of problems (complaints) that have been checked off (on the data check sheet) are likely to occur 80 percent of the time.

Inspection
Inspectors can reduce defectives shipped but not defectives made.

Cause and effect charts
All factors that impinge on quality are listed in a hierarchy of categories and subcategories. These are illustrated by fishbone diagrams. See Figure 7-7.

Process charts play a crucial role in causal analysis. They map everything that is happening in the process and are often listed as an eighth process quality control method.

Causal Analysis

The quality of a cup of coffee is a big business with growth opportunities, challenges, and concerns. Chains of coffee shops have opened thousands of stores all over the United States, Europe, and Asia. Starbuck's (http://www.starbucks.com) and Dunkin' Donuts (http://www.dunkindonuts.com) have enormous numbers of stores all over the world.

With billions of dollars at stake, companies find it worthwhile to scrutinize various business models each with its own concept of how consumers perceive quality.

Table 7-2 captures many of the multidimensional factors that determine the quality of coffee. Specifically, Table 7-2 presents a list of causal factors that should be considered by all participants in the system that affects coffee quality. After making the list, these variables can be charted using the fishbone construction method developed by Ishikawa.[4]

There are nine main variables and different numbers of subcategory variables. The latter are shown in Figure 7-7 as fins radiating from the nine lines of the main variables, connected to what looks like the spine of a fish. The subcategories are listed in Table 7-2 under the nine main variables.

The diagram is conducive to systems-wide discussion, involving everyone, concerning the completeness of the diagram. Have all the important factors been listed? When the fishbone diagram is considered complete, then follows the determination of what variations should be tested. Market research is used to connect the process variations tested to consumer reactions.

Returning to the power failure situation, consider some of the many causes of power failures that exist. The household consumer of electricity is unlikely to know which cause is responsible for any failure.

The electric utility, on the other hand, can do the necessary detective work to determine what has caused each failure. Method 4 (using Pareto charts) can provide a useful approach to identify the most frequent types of power failures, probably by region and extent. Method 5 (using Ishikawa diagrams) now helps with the search for causes of these problems. To sum up, Ishikawa diagrams enumerate and organize the potential causes of various kinds of quality failures.

Scatter Diagrams

Scatter diagrams

Figures composed of data points that are thought to be associated with each other, as calories consumed (x) and weight (y).

Scatter diagrams are composed of data points that are associated with each other, such as height and weight. The pairs of data are plotted as points on the chart. The idea is that if data are related—that is, if x is related to y—this fact will show up in the graph. The graph for height and weight could be expected to indicate that as height increases so does weight.

Because even strong relationships are far from exact, the plots of points will be scattered around an imaginary line that could be drawn to capture the relationship. If a relationship exists, it might be seen. It also can be measured by statistical means. Spurious relationships can show up. There are no guarantees with scatter diagram methods; they are, at best, a way to probe for relationships.

Let x be one of many factors that the fishbone diagram indicates as a possible cause of the quality problem, y. If that is true, then y is a function of x.

$$y = f(x)$$

A scatter diagram is created for various values of x and y that have been obtained by experimentation, observation, or survey. Two results are shown in Figures 7-8 and 7-9. First, consider Figure 7-8.

The various (x,y) points are tightly grouped around the line: Although a relationship appears to exist, there is not sufficient information to assume that x and y are causally

Table 7-2

Variables for the Quality of a Cup of Coffee

Coffee Beans—Type Purchased
Source of beans (locations in Sumatra, Colombia, Jamaica, Costa Rica, Hawaii, etc.)
Grade of beans
Size and age of beans
How stored and packed (how long stored before grinding)
Roasting Process
Kind of roaster
Temperatures used
Length of roasting
Grinding Process
Type of grinder
Condition of grinder
Speed and feed used
Fineness of grind setting
Length of grinding
Quantity of beans ground
Stored for how long before use
Coffee Maker
Drip type or other; exact specs for coffee maker
Size and condition of machine (how many prior uses)
Method of cleaning (vinegar, hot water, detergents)
How often cleaned
Number of pounds of coffee used
Water
Amount of water used
Type of water used (chemical composition)
Storage history before use
Temperature water is heated to
Filter
Type of filter used
(material: paper (and type), gold mesh, other metals)
Size of filter
How often used
How often replaced
Coffee Server
Type of container
Size of container
How often cleaned
How long is coffee stored
Coffee Cup
Type of cup
Size of cup
Cleaned how (temperature of water, detergent)
Cleaned how often
Spoon in Cup—Sweetener—Milk or Cream
Type of spoon (material/how often cleaned and how)
Type of sweetener used
Type of milk: 1 percent, 2 percent, half and half, skim, light cream, heavy cream, etc.

related. Further testing is in order and a logical framework for causality must be built. Still *x* and *y* appear to have something to do with each other instead of appearing to have no relationship.

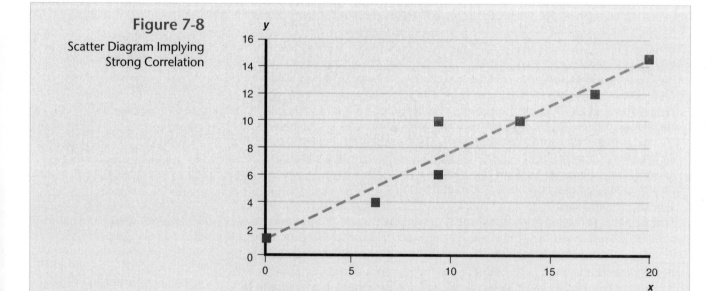

Figure 7-7

Ishikawa Diagram aka a Fishbone Diagram—What Creates (Causes) a Good Cup of Coffee?

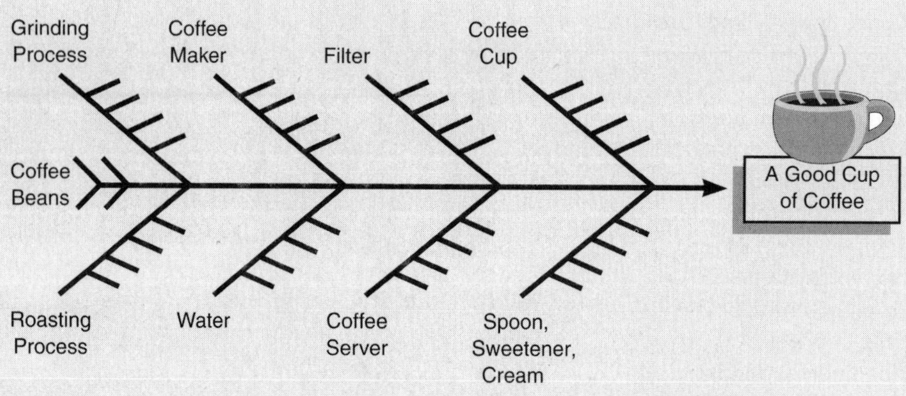

Grinding Process   Coffee Maker   Filter   Coffee Cup

Coffee Beans

Roasting Process   Water   Coffee Server   Spoon, Sweetener, Cream

A Good Cup of Coffee

In Figure 7-9 the various (x,y) points are far more widely scattered. This indicates that no strong relationship exists between x and y. The pattern is best described as a random assortment of points.

Although the scatter diagram does not give a statistical measure of the correlation between x and y, it graphically suggests that such does exist. It is reasonable to use statistical methodology to confirm strong correlations so that prescriptions can be made to reduce and/or remove quality problems. The regression analysis that was introduced in Chapter 3, Section 3-5d is perfectly suited to fit a best (least-squares) line to these data. After calculating the regression line, the next step is to obtain the correlation coefficient (see Enrichment Activity 11). Figure 7-8 will have a high value of r and Figure 7-9 will have a low value of r.

Revisiting the power failure case, for diagnostic and prescriptive purposes, the cause of each power failure should be tracked down and noted: Lines are knocked down by cars and trucks as well as by wind storms; transformers fail more often under peak demands; and fires result from overloaded power generation equipment correlated with summer heat spells. Time of day, day of the week, date of the year may all be useful data for patterns to be found. The computer makes it easy to enter a lot of information and analyze the data for patterns.

Figure 7-8

Scatter Diagram Implying Strong Correlation

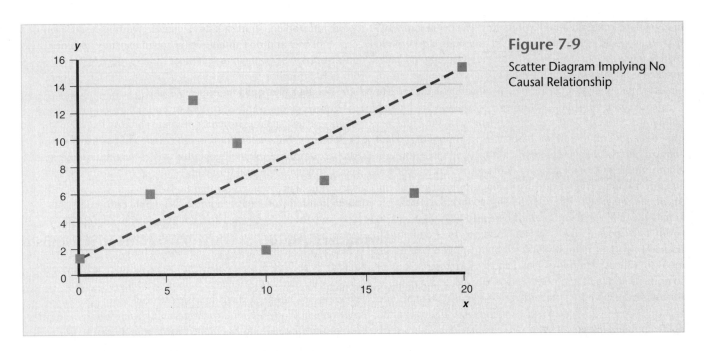

Figure 7-9

Scatter Diagram Implying No Causal Relationship

Knowing the most frequently occurring types of failures might lead to solutions that could reduce their frequency. Overhead wires in certain locations could be buried at a cost that might be much lower than the expensive remedial actions taken after storm-caused failures. Power-grid sharing could be initiated before overloads occur. Strong correlations provide information that connects types of failures with the times and places that they occur, which may facilitate problem solving.

7-4 Method 6—Control Charts for Statistical Process Control

The prior five methods are significant as means to understand the nature of the process. Method 6, on the other hand, is a powerhouse for monitoring conditions of the process and for stabilizing processes. Method 6 includes a variety of control charting systems. Each variety is so significant a category that it deserves a new section in its own right.

Output from a process is measured with respect to qualities that are considered to be important. For quality to be consistent, it must come from a process that is stable, i.e., one with fixed parameters. This means that its average m and its standard deviation s are not shifting. To understand the concept of stability, it is necessary to develop the statistical theory of stable distributions.

A stable distribution is described as being stationary. This means that its parameters are not moving. **Statistical process control (SPC)** can provide methods for determining if a process is stable. **Statistical quality control (SQC)** encompasses SPC as well as other statistical methods, including **acceptance sampling**, covered later in this chapter. In common usage, SPC and SQC both describe the application of control charts as a means to warn about unstable systems.

It is important to note that in real production situations, enough data are obtained to create reliable control charts. Then, more data are collected to examine whether the process is stable. Evidence of temporary instability often is thrown out as being associated with start-up conditions. The process is reexamined to see if it has stabilized after the start-up. The initial sample size is often 25 to 30 sets of data, followed by another 25 to 30 sets of data. Typically, a data set would consist of two to ten successive observations from which a mean and standard deviation would be determined.

Statistical process control (SPC)

The control charting aspect of statistical quality control (SQC).

Statistical quality control (SQC)

Encompasses statistical process control (SPC) as well as other statistical methods, including acceptance sampling.

Acceptance sampling

Inspecting acceptability of suppliers' shipments by using sampling of required qualities instead of 100 percent inspection.

Once the process is considered stable, then regular observations are made at scheduled intervals. If the process is not stable, and that often occurs when starting up a new system, then Steps 1, 2, 3, and 4 apply:

Control Chart Steps (View the process in Figure 7-2)

1 Diagnose the causes of process instability. (Study)
2 Remove the causes of process instability. (Act)
3 Check results. (Plan)
4 Go back through Steps 1–3 until stability is achieved. (Do)

7-4a Chance Causes are Inherent Systems Causes

Chance causes
See **Assignable causes**.

Variability exists in all systems. Two seemingly identical manufactured parts have their own signatures, like fingerprints, when measured to whatever degree of fineness is required. Systems with less variability may differ with respect to measurements in thousandths of an inch whereas systems with more variability may be noticeably different in terms of hundredths of an inch. The degree of fineness has to do with the kind of fit that is needed between parts, and this requirement is reflected by the tolerance limits the designers have set.

There are two basically different kinds of variability. The first kind is an inherent (intrinsic and innate) property of the system. It is the variability of a stable system that is functioning properly. That variability is said to be caused by **chance causes** (also called simple causes). These causes cannot be removed from the system, which is why they are called inherent systems causes. They are also called chance causes because they are predictable and stable in statistical terms, as are the number of heads from an honest coin throw.

A process that experiences only chance causes, no matter what its level of variability, is called a stable process. The variability that it experiences is called random variation.

7-4b Assignable Causes are Identifiable Systems Causes

Assignable causes
Identifiable causes of process problems that create variability. They are traceable and can be removed.

The second kind of variability has traceable and removable causes, which are called assignable or special causes. Unlike chance causes, these causes are not background noise. They produce a distinct trademark, which can be identified and traced to its origins. They are called assignable because these causes can be designated as to type and source, and removed.

The process manager identifies the sources of quality disturbances—a tool that has shifted, a gear tooth that is chipped, an operator who is missing the mark, an ingredient that is too acidic—and does what is required to correct the situation. Thus, tool, die, and gear wear is correctable. Broken conveyor drives can be replaced. Vibrating loose parts can be tightened. Human errors in machine setups can be remedied. These are examples of **assignable causes** that can be detected by the methods of statistical process control (SPC).

An alternative name that might be preferred to assignable causes is identifiable systems causes. Quality control charts are the means for spotting identifiable systems causes. Once identified, knowledge of the process leads to the cause, which is then removed so that the process can return to its basic, inherent causes of variability. The ability to do this enhances quality attainment to such a degree that Method 6 is widely acknowledged as powerful and necessary.

A process that is operating without any assignable causes of variation is stable by definition, although its variability can be large. Stability does not refer to the degree of variability of a process. Instability reflects the invasion of assignable causes of variation, which create quality problems.

Classifications by variables
Variables such as weight can be measured on a continuous scale.

There are different kinds of control charts. First, there is **classification by variables** where numbered measurements are continuous, as with a ruler for measuring inches or with a scale for measuring pounds. The variables can have dimensions of weight, temperature, area, strength, variability, electrical resistance, loyalty, satisfaction, defects, typing errors, complaints, accidents, readership, and TV viewer ratings. The fineness of the units of measure is related to the quality specifications for the outputs.

Second, there is **classification by attributes**. Output units are classified as accepted or rejected, usually, by some form of inspection device that only distinguishes between a "go" or a "no go" situation. Rejects result from measurements falling out of the range of acceptable values that are pre-set by design. Rejects are defective product units. Under the attribute system of classification, process quality is judged by the number of defective units discovered by the pass-fail test. It is charted as the percentage of defects discovered in each sample, and is called a **p-chart**. Also under the attribute system of measurement is the **c-chart**, which counts the number of nonconformities of a part. For example, in the eye of the specialist, a particular diamond can be categorized as having various imperfections, which are counted. Distributions of the number (c) of imperfections is the basis of the c-chart.

7-5 Method 6—Control Charts for Means (Variables)—$\bar{x}$-Charts

The $\bar{x}$-chart uses classification by variables. A sample of product is taken at intervals. Each unit in the sample is measured along the appropriate scale for the qualities being analyzed. The **control chart** is a graphic means of plotting points, which should fall within specific upper- and lower-bound limits if the process is stable.

Table 7-3 illustrates a sequence of quality measures, called x_i (i = output number) where x_i can be measured on a continuous scale that permits classification by variables. The sample subgroup size, n, is 3 in Table 7-3, and the sample subgroups are labeled with Roman numerals I, II, III, and so on.

There are two subgroup samples of 3. The output interval between them is 4. Subgroup sample sizes between 2 and 10 are common. The interval between subgroups varies widely, depending on the output rate and the stability of quality for the product. Relatively stable processes and those that do not carry severe penalties for undetected assignable causes can support larger intervals between samples than unstable or high penalty systems.

The sample mean for each subgroup $\bar{x}_j$ is obtained.

$$\bar{x}_\mathrm{I} = \frac{x_1 + x_2 + x_3}{3}, \ \bar{x}_\mathrm{II} = \frac{x_1 + x_2 + x_3}{3}, \text{etc.} \tag{7-7}$$

In general

$$\bar{x}_j = \frac{\sum x_i}{n} \tag{7-8}$$

The grand mean, $\bar{\bar{x}}$, is the average of the sample means, that is:

$$\bar{\bar{x}} = \frac{\bar{x}_\mathrm{I} + \bar{x}_\mathrm{II} + \ldots + \bar{x}_\mathrm{N}}{N} \tag{7-9}$$

where N is the number of sample subgroups being used.

Classification by attributes
Units are classified as accepted or rejected, e.g., it is too heavy for the delivery system.

p-chart
Plots successive sample measures of the percent defective for specific quality attributes.

c-chart
Control chart for multiple numbers of defectives in a single unit.

$\bar{x}$-chart
Basic quality control chart designed for variables measured on a continuous scale such as tire pressure and particle emissions.

Control chart
Chart is based on the process average for percent defectives, with upper- and lower-control limits and plotted points of successive sample means.

		Table 7-3
Subgroup Sample I	$x_1 \ x_2 \ x_3$	
Interval Between Samples I and II	$x_4 \ x_5 \ x_6 \ x_7$	Subgroup Sample Size Is 3;
Subgroup Sample II	$x_8 \ x_9 \ x_{10}$	Interval Between Samples Is 4
Interval Between Samples II and III	$x_{11} \ x_{12} \ x_{13} \ x_{14}$	

7-5a The Belgian Chocolate Truffle Factory (BCTF)

Data have been collected by the P/OM department for the famous truffle bonbons made by the Belgian Chocolate Truffle Factory. They are marketed all over the world as being hand-dipped with best ingredients. Even though the company claims customization as an advantage, complaints are received that the candies are uneven in size and weight.

This is an ideal opportunity to use an *x*-chart to find out if the chocolate-making process is stable or erratic. Hand-dipping chocolates may lead to high variability in size and weight of product without creating an unstable production process.

The standard weight per piece set by BCTF is 30 grams of the finest chocolate. A perfect pound box would contain 16 chocolates, each weighing 28.35 grams. Company policy, based on principles of ethical practice, is to err on the side of giving more, rather than less, by targeting 1.65 extra grams per piece. However, extra chocolate is expensive. Worse yet, if weight and size are inconsistent, the larger pieces create dissatisfaction with the truffles that meet the standard. Also, consistency of size is used by customers to judge the quality of the product. Weight is easier to measure than size and is considered to be a good surrogate for it.

The company wants to test for consistency of product over a production day. Samples were taken over the course of one day of production at 10:00 A.M. and 11:00 A.M., and at 1:00 P.M., 3:00 P.M., and 4:00 P.M. The hours chosen are just before the line is stopped for tea break and/or for cleanup. The sample subgroup size is of four consecutive days with the observations made at the specific time. This yielded 20 measures and five sample subgroup means.

For instructional purposes, this sample is about the right size. For real results, all five days of production for a typical week should be examined. Except as an example, a 1-day sample is too small. There is a rule of thumb widely used: *Practitioners consider 20 to 25 subgroup means as appropriate for a start-up or diagnostic study.*

Table 7-4 offers 5 sample subgroup sets of data as the columns (*j*) with one for each time period. Measurements are in grams. There is a range measure R_j in this chart that will be used later. It is the difference between the largest and the smallest number in the column.

where

$$\bar{x}_j = \frac{\sum x_i}{n}; i = 1, 2, \ldots, 4 \qquad (7\text{-}10)$$

The grand mean value is $(151.50)/5 = 30.30$, which indicates that, on average, these chocolate truffles are 1 percent heavier than the standard. This average value seems well suited to the ethical considerations of the firm because it is above, but not too far above, the target value of 30.00 grams. BCTF's policy is ethical but expensive. Customers get more than a pound of chocolates on a regular basis.

In Table 7-4, individual sampled values fall below the 30-gram target five times, even though in all cases they are well above 28. The lowest value sampled was 29.50. The

Table 7-4	Subgroup *j*	I	II	III	IV	V	
Weight of Belgian Chocolate Truffles (in Grams)	Time:	10 A.M.	11 A.M.	1 P.M.	3 P.M.	4 P.M.	Sum
	$x_i = 1$	30.50	30.30	30.15	30.60	30.15	
	$x_i = 2$	29.75	31.00	29.50	32.00	30.25	
	$x_i = 3$	29.90	30.20	29.75	31.00	30.50	
	$x_i = 4$	30.25	30.50	30.00	30.00	29.70	
	Sum	120.40	122.00	119.40	123.60	120.60	
	$\bar{x}_j$	30.10	30.50	29.85	30.90	30.15	151.50
	R_j	0.75	0.80	0.65	2.00	0.80	5.00

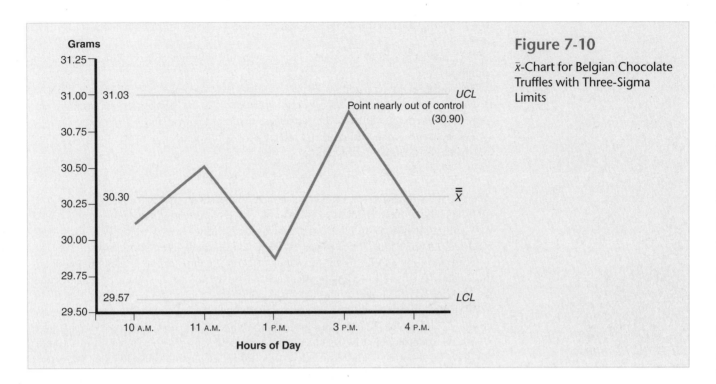

Figure 7-10

$\bar{x}$-Chart for Belgian Chocolate Truffles with Three-Sigma Limits

highest value is 32. The three highest values all appear at 3:00 P.M., which also has the largest sample mean value and the largest R value.

7-5b Upper- and Lower-Control Limits (*UCL* and *LCL*)

Control limits are thresholds designed statistically to signal that a process is not stable. Control limits will now be derived for the $\bar{x}$-chart. Before doing that, study Figure 7-10 to identify what these control limits look like. Note that the 3:00 P.M. sample is identified on the chart as being nearly out of control.

This $\bar{x}$-chart with *UCL* and *LCL* has no points outside the limits, and therefore no points are specifically out of control. Nevertheless, the 3:00 P.M. sample, when it is backed up by a lot more data, is the kind of visual warning that usually warrants attention.

Perhaps, the 3:00 P.M. sample is taken during the afternoon tea break, during which the chocolate mixture becomes thicker and the molding machine tends to make heavier pieces. The cleanup comes after 3:00 P.M. Tracking and discovering such causes will lead to the elimination of the problems. Although the process is stable, it appears to have too much variability (32.00–29.50). It may need to be redesigned. The chocolate mold-filling machines might need replacement or rebuilding. Workers using the filling machines might need additional training. From the previous comment on variability, it becomes apparent that there is a need to study the range measure. That will be done shortly.

The control chart drawn in Figure 7-10 is based on plotting the sample means $\bar{x}_j$ from Table 7-4. It is important to note that the underlying distribution is that of the sample means. It is necessary to estimate the variability of this distribution of the sample means in order to construct control limits around the grand mean of a process. The upper-control limit (*UCL*) and the lower-control limit (*LCL*), shown in Figure 7-10, could have been determined by calculating the standard deviation for the sample means $\bar{x}_j$ given in Table 7-4.

An easier calculation of variability uses the range, *R*. It is well suited for repetitive computations that control charts entail. Column values of *R* for BCTF are given in Table 7-4. The range within each subgroup, is defined as:

$$R = x_{MAX} - x_{MIN}$$

Control limits

Upper-control limits (*UCL*) and lower-control limits (*LCL*) are developed in different ways depending upon the type of chart being used.

The largest x value in the 10:00 A.M. sample subgroup is 30.50 and the smallest is 29.75, so $R = 0.75$.

UCL and LCL will be computed shortly using the average value of R for the subgroup samples.

Statistical quality control works because the variation observed within each subgroup ($R_I, R_{II}, \ldots,$ etc.) can be statistically related to the variation between the subgroup means. Only if the process is stable will the two different measures of variability be commensurable.

The between-group variability is related to the differences between the grand mean and successive sample means. Thus:

$$(\bar{x}_I - \bar{\bar{x}}), (\bar{x}_{II} - \bar{\bar{x}}), \ldots, (\bar{x}_N - \bar{\bar{x}}) \qquad (7\text{-}11)$$

whereas, the within-group variability is related to the values ($R_I, R_{II}, \ldots,$ etc.). If the process is stable, the plotted points of the sample means—reflecting between-group variability—will fall within control limits that are based on within-group variability. If the process is unstable, some of the plotted points are likely to fall outside the control limits.

This reasoning applies to various kinds of control charts. Present discussion concerns the $\bar{x}$-chart. This is followed by application of control limits to the chart for ranges, called the R-chart, and, then, the p-chart for attributes and the c-chart for defects per part.

When the process is not stable because of the existence of assignable causes, between-group variability exceeds within-group variability. Note that the observations taken within the subgroup are always taken as close together as possible, whereas in the interval between subgroups, allow sufficient time for an assignable cause to enter the system. The subgroup size is kept small. That way, a high degree of homogeneity should exist for the observations within each subgroup. In a stable system, the same homogeneous condition will apply to all the samples, no matter when they were taken.

To construct the control chart:

1 Individual samples are taken from the parent population in groups of size n.
2 $\bar{x}$ and R measures are calculated for each sample subgroup.
3 The control limits *UCL* and *LCL* are computed.

The sample means $\bar{x}_I$, $\bar{x}_{II}$, $\bar{x}_{III}$, etc., are distributed in accordance with the size of n. Figure 7-11 is meant to illustrate how the distribution of the sample means is narrower

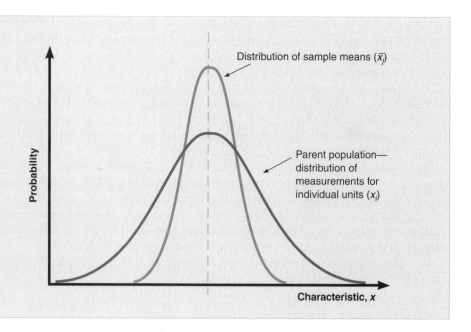

Figure 7-11

Distribution of the Sample Means Is Narrower Than the Distribution of the Parent Population

than the distribution of the parent population. The distribution of the sample means is used for the control chart construction because it has less variability.

The relationship between the variability of a stable parent distribution and that of the distribution of the sample means is known as the central limit theorem. This is described by Equation 7-12.

$$\sigma_{\bar{x}}^2 = \sigma_x^2 \div n \tag{7-12}$$

The left-hand side ($\sigma_{\bar{x}}^2$) is the variance of the distribution of sample means ($\bar{x}$ values).

The right-hand side of Equation 7-12 is the variance of the parent population distribution divided by n.

Translating the equation into words, sigma square of the sample means (x-bar) on the left side equals sigma square of the population values (x) divided by n on the right side.

Equation 7-13 is the equivalent relationship for the standard deviation parameter, which is the square root of the variance. This is called the standard error of the mean.

$$\sigma_{\bar{x}} = \sigma_x \div \sqrt{n} \tag{7-13}$$

Translating into words again, sigma of the sample means (x-bar) on the left side equals sigma of the population values (x) divided by the square root of n on the right side.

If the subgroup size is equal to one, $n = 1$, then $\sqrt{1} = 1$, and the two standard deviations (sigmas) of the distributions are identical. A subgroup size of one defeats the purpose of measuring within and between subgroup variability. It would not be used, but it proves the logic of the equation.

A subgroup size of $n = 2$ is the smallest feasible size for SPC (statistical process control).

If n is a large number, then the $\sqrt{n}$ is also a large number and the standard deviation of the sample means ($\sigma_{\bar{x}}$) gets small, eventually approaching zero. The distribution of sample means takes on the appearance of a vertical line. This, too, is an extreme case, mainly useful to test the sense of the equation.

Continuing with the fundamental equations that underlie control chart theory, it should be noted that $\sigma_{\bar{x}}$), which is the standard deviation of the distribution of the sample means, is calculated as follows:

$$\sigma_{\bar{x}} = \sqrt{\frac{\sum_{j=1}^{N} \left(\bar{x}_j - \bar{\bar{x}} \right)^2}{N}} \tag{7-14}$$

($j = 1, 2, \ldots, N$) where N = the number of subgroup sample means that are calculated. For small samples, the denominator of Equation 7-14 is often $N - 1$.

Meanwhile, to make certain that the relationship between the sample means parameter and that of the parent population is clear, review: σ_x = the standard deviation of the parent population, calculated by Equation 7-15:

$$\sigma_x = \sqrt{\frac{\sum_{i=1}^{nN} \left(x_j - \bar{\bar{x}} \right)^2}{nN}} \tag{7-15}$$

($i = 1, 2, \ldots, nN$) where (nN) = the total number of observations. nN is the total sample size. (n) is the sample subgroup size. It is multiplied by the number of sample subgroups taken (N). For small values of nN, the denominator is often $nN - 1$.

Rather than going through the laborious calculations for sigma, the range R is the preferred measure. R will be employed for the control charts used in this chapter.

The grand mean used for the control chart can be measured in different ways, thus:

$$\bar{\bar{x}} = \frac{\sum_{j=1}^{nN} x_i}{nN} = \frac{\sum_{j=1}^{N} \bar{x}_j}{N} = \frac{606}{4(5)} = \frac{151.50}{5} = 30.30, \tag{7-16}$$

Table 7-5	Subgroup Size (n)	A_2	D_3	D_4
Conversion Factors for $\bar{x}$- and R-Charts	2	1.88	0	3.27
	3	1.02	0	2.57
	4	0.73	0	2.28
	5	0.58	0	2.11
	6	0.48	0	2.00
	7	0.42	0.08	1.92
	8	0.37	0.14	1.86
	9	0.34	0.18	1.82
	10	0.31	0.22	1.78
	12	0.27	0.28	1.72
	15	0.22	0.35	1.65
	20	0.18	0.41	1.59

and the average range is

$$\bar{R} = \sum \frac{R_j}{N} = \frac{5}{5} = 1.00 \tag{7-17}$$

The data used for $\bar{\bar{x}}$ and $\bar{R}$ come from Table 7-4.

The $\bar{R}$ measure must now be converted to represent the sample standard deviation. The conversion factors relating the range to the sample standard deviation have been tabled and are widely available. The conversion factor for upper and lower three-sigma limits is A_2. It is given in Table 7-5.

A_2 is used for *UCL* and *LCL* for the $\bar{x}$-chart.
D_3 is used for the *LCL* for the *R*-chart.
D_4 is used for the *UCL* for the *R*-chart.

The meaning of A_2 multiplied by $\bar{R}$ is shown in Equation 7-18:

$$A_2\bar{R} = k\sigma_{\bar{x}} = 3\sigma_{\bar{x}} = 3\frac{\sigma_x}{\sqrt{n}} \tag{7-18}$$

The calculations for the upper-control limit $UCL_{\bar{x}}$ and $LCL_{\bar{x}}$ for the lower using three standard deviations ($\pm 3\sigma$) are as follows:

$$UCL_{\bar{x}} = \bar{\bar{x}} + A_2\bar{R} \text{ and } LCL_{\bar{x}} = \bar{\bar{x}} - A_2\bar{R} \tag{7-19}$$

The calculations for the Belgian Chocolate Truffle Factory are given by Equation 7-20:

$$UCL_{\bar{x}} = 30.30 + (0.73)(1.00) = 31.03$$
$$LCL_{\bar{x}} = 30.30 - (0.73)(1.00) = 29.57 \tag{7-20}$$

7-5c How to Interpret Control Limits

The limits used in Figure 7-10 resulted from the previous calculations. The 3:00 P.M. point would have been outside the control limits if two standard deviations had been used instead of three. The 3:00 P.M. point was 30.90, and the $UCL_{\bar{x}}$ for two-sigma would have been 30.79. This outlier could trigger a costly process evaluation, which might not be justified. The x-bar value of 29.85 for the third subgroup is uncomfortably close to the $UCL_{\bar{x}}$ value of 29.81. Another possible costly trigger. For this process, 3-sigma seems more satisfactory than 2-sigma.

Using Equation 7.18: $\sigma(x\text{-bar}) = \sigma_{\bar{x}} = 0.2433, \quad 2\sigma(x\text{-bar}) = 2\sigma_{\bar{x}} = 0.4866 = 0.49$

Then, from Equation 7-20:

$$UCL_{\bar{x}} = 30.30 + 0.49 = 30.79$$
$$LCL_{\bar{x}} = 30.30 - 0.49 = 29.81$$

The number of standard deviations used will control the sensitivity of the warning system. Three-sigma charts remain silent when two-sigma charts sound alarms. Alarms can signal out-of-control as well as false alarms.

Understanding how to set the control limits is related to balancing the costs of false alarms against the dangers of missing real ones. One-sigma limits will sound more alarms than two-sigma ones. The judicious choice of k for $\pm k\sigma$ is an operations management responsibility in conjunction with other participants to assess the two costs stated earlier. There must be an evaluation of what happens if the detection of a real problem is delayed. The systems-wide solution is the best one to use.

The probability of a subgroup mean falling above or below three-sigma limits by chance rather than by cause is 0.0028, which is pretty small, but still real. For two-sigma, it would be 0.0456, which is not small. In some systems, two successive points must go out of control for action to be taken. There are fire departments that require two fire alarms before responding because of the high frequency of false alarms. When a response is made to out-of-control signals, knowledge of the process is the crucial ingredient for remedying the problem.

7-6 Method 6—Control Charts for Ranges (Variables)—*R*-Charts

The $\bar{x}$-chart is accompanied by another kind of control chart for variables. Called an **R-chart**, it monitors the stability of the range. In comparison, the $\bar{x}$-chart checks for the stationarity of the process mean, i.e., checks that the mean of the distribution does not shift about—while the R-chart checks that the spread of the distribution around the mean stays constant. In other words, R-charts control for shifts in the process standard deviation.

The $\bar{x}$- and R-charts are best used together because sometimes an assignable cause creates no shift in the process average, or in the average value of the standard deviation (or $\bar{R}$) but a change occurs in the distribution of R values. For example, if the variability measured for each subgroup is either very large or very small, the average variability would be the same as if all subgroup R values were constant. Remembering that the sampling procedure is aimed at discovering the true condition of the parent population, the use of $\bar{x}$- and R-charts provides a powerful combination of analytic tools.

R-chart
Control Limits are applied to the range (R) chart, which usually is a companion to the $\bar{x}$-chart. Together the two charts supply powerful diagnostics for process behavior.

The equations for the control limits for the R-chart are

$$UCL_R = D_4 R \quad \text{and} \quad LCL_R = D_3 R$$

The Belgian Chocolate Truffle Factory data from Table 7-4 can be used to illustrate the control chart procedures. Continuing to use k = three-sigma limits and the conversion factors given in Table 7-5, the R-chart control parameters are obtained.

$$D_4(\text{for } n = 4) = 2.28, D_3(for\ n = 4) = 0, \text{ and } \bar{R} = \frac{5.00}{5} = 1.00 \quad (7\text{-}21)$$

These are used to derive the control limits.

$$UCLR = (2.28)(1.00) = 2.28 \quad \text{and} \quad LCLR = (0.00)(1.00) = 0.00$$

Figure 7-12 shows that the R-chart has no points outside the control limits. The same pattern prevails as with the $\bar{x}$-chart. The 3:00 P.M. point is close to the upper limit. This further confirms the fact that the process is stable and is unlikely to do much better. However, the sample is small, and good chart use would throw out the 3:00 P.M. sample and take about 25 more samples before making any decision.

Figure 7-12

The *R*-Chart: Three-Sigma Limits

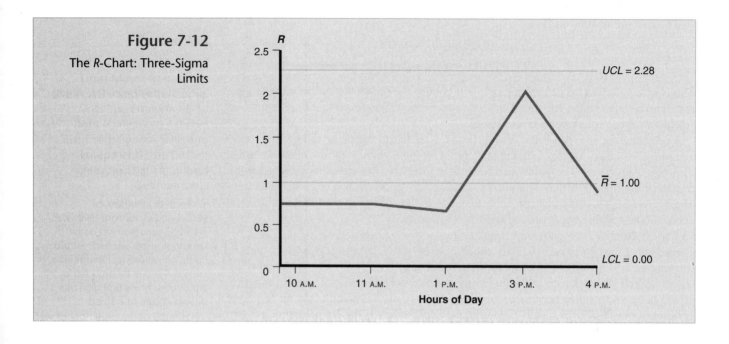

7-7 Method 6—Control Charts for Attributes—*p*-Charts

The *p*-chart shows the percent defective in successive samples. It has upper- and lower-control limits similar to those found in the $\bar{x}$- and *R*-charts. Compare what is measured for the *p*-chart to what is measured for the $\bar{x}$-chart. The attribute used is good (accepted) or bad (rejected).

Monitoring by variables is more expensive than by attributes. The inspection by variables requires reading a scale and recording many numbers correctly (for example, successive measurements of the weight of cans of peanuts that must be at least 16 ounces). Measurement error must be avoided. A reading of 15.99 is unacceptable whereas 16.01 is acceptable. Numbers have to be read arithmetically. Their significance must be understood to allow proper actions to be taken.

In comparison, the attributes used by the *p*-chart (from a go/no-go gauge) are simpler. Go/no-go is an unequivocal pass-fail exam. Many times it can be performed by a visual check—good or bad? Attribute measurement methods build in the acceptable and unacceptable ranges. Monitoring by attributes can often be automated. The engineering of the inspection process is an investment in simplifying the task. When error prevention is critical, assessment by attributes often is safer.

Only one chart is needed for the attribute, *p*, which is the percent defective. The *p*-chart replaces the two charts $\bar{x}$ and *R*. Also, only the upper-control limit really matters. The lower-control limit is always better as it gets closer to zero defectives.

The value of *p* is defined as follows:

$$p = \frac{\text{number rejected}}{\text{number inspected}} \tag{7-22}$$

Assume that the Belgian Chocolate Truffle Factory can buy a new molding machine that has less variability than the current one. BCTF's operations managers in cooperation with the marketing managers and others have agreed to redefine acceptable standards so that profits can be raised while increasing customer satisfaction. Also, it was decided to use a *p*-chart as the simplest way to demonstrate the importance of the acquisition of the new molding machine.

Subgroup j	I	II	III	IV	V	
Time:	10 A.M.	11 A.M.	1 P.M.	3 P.M.	4 P.M.	Sum
x_i						
1	30.50R	30.30	30.15	30.60R	30.15	
2	29.75	31.00R	29.50R	32.00R	30.25	
3	29.90	30.20	29.75	31.00R	30.50R	
4	30.25	30.50R	30.00	30.00	29.70	
NR	1	2	1	3	1	8
p	0.25	0.50	0.25	0.75	0.25	

Table 7-6

Weight of Chocolate Truffles (in Grams) (R = Rejects Due to Excessive Weight)

NR equals the number of rejects in each subgroup.

Previously, a defective product was defined as a box of truffles that weighed less than a pound. What was in the box was allowed to vary, as long as the pound constraint was met. Now the idea is to control defectives on each piece's weight.

The new definition of a reject is as follows: A defective occurs when $x_i < 29.60$ grams or $x_i > 30.40$ grams. This standard set on pieces is more stringent than the earlier one set on box weight. The new standards will always satisfy BCTF's criteria to deliver nothing less than a pound box of chocolate.

It has been suggested that the data of Table 7-4 be tested against the p-chart criteria. Rejects are marked with an R on the table. The number of rejects (NR) is counted, and p is calculated for each subgroup in Table 7-6.

Table 7-7 summarizes the results found in Table 7-6. It shows that the p values are too high. BCTF either has to go back to the old standard or get the new machine. This analysis might provide the motivation for changing machines. The p-chart parameters are calculated as follows: first, compute

$\bar{p}$ = average percent defective, which is defined by:

$$\bar{p} = \sum \frac{\text{number rejected}}{\text{number inspected}} = \frac{8}{20} = 0.40 \qquad (7\text{-}23)$$

Companies that subscribe to the concepts of TQM are committed to obtaining defective rates that are less than 1 percent, and this is 40 percent. It is evident that the new criteria and the present process are incompatible. Constructing the p-chart confirms this evaluation.

The control chart for single attributes, known as the p-chart (there is a c-chart for multiple defects), requires the calculation of the standard deviation (s_p). For the p-chart computations, the binomial description of variability is used:

$$s_p = \sqrt{\frac{\bar{p}(1 - \bar{p})}{n}} = \sqrt{\frac{(0.40)(0.60)}{4}} = \sqrt{0.06} = 0.245 \qquad (7\text{-}24)$$

Shifting to more conservative 1.96 sigma limits means that 95 percent of all subgroups will have a p value that falls within the control limits,[5] which are determined as follows:

$$UCL_p = \bar{p} + 1.96 s_p = 0.40 + 1.96(0.245) = 0.40 + 0.48 = 0.88$$

Subgroup No.	NR	n	p
I	1	4	0.25
II	2	4	0.50
III	1	4	0.25
IV	3	4	0.75
V	1	4	0.25
Sum	8	20	
Average			**0.40**

Table 7-7

Summary of the Findings (NR = Number of Rejects)

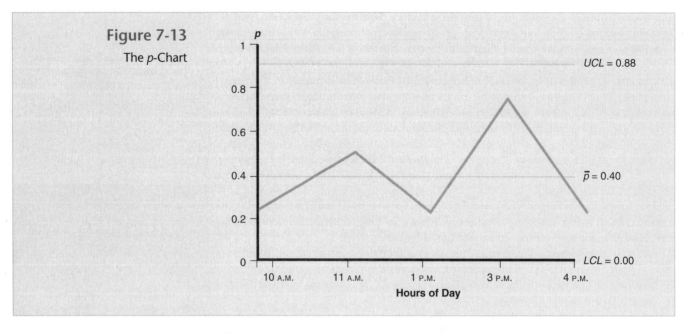

Figure 7-13

The *p*-Chart

and

$$LCL_p = \bar{p} - 1.96s_p = 0.40 - 0.48 = -0.08 < 0.000 = 0.00$$

The LCL_p cannot be less than zero, so it is set at zero.

Note that UCL_p and LCL_p are functions of s_p that can vary with the sample size n. Thus, if the 11:00 A.M. sample had nine measured values, instead of four, then

$$s_p = \sqrt{\frac{\bar{p}(1-\bar{p})}{n}} = \sqrt{\frac{(0.40)(0.60)}{9}} = \sqrt{0.027} = 0.163 \qquad (7\text{-}25)$$

s_p has decreased, and this would reduce the spread between the limits, just for the 11:00 A.M. portion of the chart. The control limits can step up and down according to the sample size, which is another degree of flexibility associated with the *p*-chart.

The appropriate control chart for percent defectives for the data given in Table 7-6 for the Belgian Chocolate Truffle Factory is shown in Figure 7-13.

There are no points outside the *UCL*, although the 3:00 P.M. value of 0.75 is close to the upper limit's value of 0.88. The same reasoning applies, namely the process is stable, but the 3:00 P.M. sample should be eliminated from the calculations and 25 more samples of four should be taken.

7-7a *c*-Charts for Attributes: The Number of Defects per Part

The *c*-chart shows the number of defectives in successive samples. It has upper- and lower-control limits similar to those found in the $\bar{x}$-, *R*-, and *p*-charts.

The finish of an automobile or the glass for the windshield is typical of products that can have multiple defects. It is common to count the number of imperfections for paint finish and for glass bubbles and marks. The expected number of defects per part is $\bar{c}$. The statistical count *c* of the number of defects per part lends itself to control by attributes, which is similar to *p*, the number of defectives in a sample.

It is reasonable to assume that *c* is Poisson distributed because the Poisson distribution describes relatively rare events. (It was originally developed from observations of the number of Prussian soldiers kicked by horses.) There is an insignificant likelihood that a defect will occur in any one place on the product unless there is an assignable cause. That is what the *c*-chart is intended to find out.

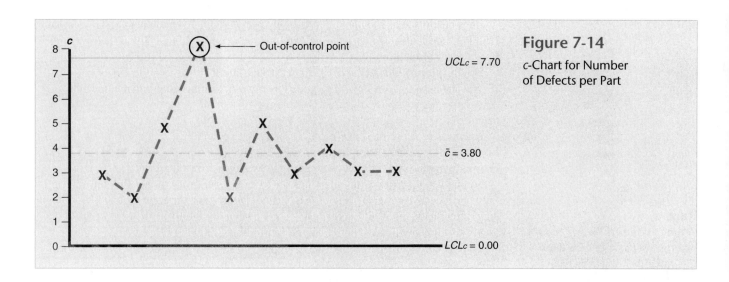

Figure 7-14

c-Chart for Number of Defects per Part

The standard deviation of the Poisson distribution is the square root of $\bar{c}$. Thus:

$$UCL_c = \bar{c} + k\sigma_c = \bar{c} + k\sqrt{\bar{c}} \qquad (7\text{-}26)$$

and

$$LCL_c = \bar{c} - k\sigma_c = \bar{c} + k\sqrt{\bar{c}} \qquad (7\text{-}27)$$

The best explanation is achieved by means of an example with data from Table 7-8 charted in Figure 7-14.

The number of defects are counted per unit sample and have been recorded in Table 7-8. Two-sigma control limits are calculated for $\bar{c} = 3.8$ and $\sqrt{\bar{c}} = \sqrt{3.8} = 1.95$. Hence:

$$ULC_c = 3.8 + 2\sigma_c = 3.8 + 2(1.95) = 7.70 \text{ and}$$
$$LCL_c = 3.8 - 2\sigma_c = 3.8 - 2(1.95) = -0.10 = 0$$

A negative *LCL* is interpreted as zero and the *UCL* is breached by the fourth sample as shown in Figure 7-14. This violation seems to indicate that all is not well with this process. It is possible to throw out the fourth sample and recalculate the charts. In reality, larger samples would be taken to establish the initial charts, and then further samples would determine the stability of the process.

7-8 Method 7—Analysis of Statistical Runs

A run of numbers on a control chart is successive values that all fall either above or below the mean line.

Sample No.	Number of Defects	Sample No.	Number of Defects
1	3	6	5
2	2	7	3
3	5	8	4
4	8	9	3
5	2	10	3

Legend: Total number of defects = 38; Total number of samples = 10; Average number of defects per sample = 3.8

Table 7-8

Database for a *c*-Chart

Consider this scenario. For months, the control chart has indicated a stable system. However, the latest sample mean falls outside the control limits. The following conjectures should be made:

Has the process changed or is this a statistical fluke?

Was the out-of-control event preceded by a run of sample subgroup mean values?

A run is a group of consecutive sample means that all occur on one side of the grand mean.

If there was a run of six or more, assume that something is changing in the process. Look for the problem. Sample the process again, as soon as possible. Make the interval between samples smaller than usual until the quandary is resolved.

Sometimes a separate run chart is kept to call attention to points that are falling on only one side of the mean value of the chart. Separate charts are not required if the regular control charts are watched for **runs**. The charting decision is dependent upon the likelihood that runs will play a major role in controlling quality.

The $\bar{x}$-chart in Figure 7-10 shows no runs. The R-chart in Figure 7-12 shows a run of three consecutive points below the grand mean. The p-chart in Figure 7-13 shows no runs. Charts often show short runs of two, three or four, because short runs are statistically very likely to occur.

Runs can appear on either side of the grand mean, $\bar{\bar{x}}$.

The probability of two consecutive $\bar{x}$'s falling above $\bar{\bar{x}}$ is $1/2 \times 1/2 = 1/4$.

The probability of two consecutive $\bar{x}$'s falling below $\bar{\bar{x}}$ is $1/2 \times 1/2 = 1/4$.

The probability that there is a run of two, either above or below $\bar{\bar{x}}$ is $1/4 + 1/4 = 2/4 = 1/2$.

The probability of a run of three above is $(1/2)^3 = 1/8$, and a run of three below is the same.

The probability of a run of three being either above or below is $(1/8 + 1/8) = 2/8 = 1/4$.

To generalize, the probability of a run of r above the grand mean is $(1/2)^r$, and the same below, so above and below is

$$p(r) = (2)(1/2)^r = (1/2)^{r-1} = \frac{1}{2^{(r-1)}} \qquad (7\text{-}28)$$

Then, the probability of a run of six ($r = 6$) is

$$p(r = 6) = \frac{1}{2^{(6-1)}} = \frac{1}{2^5} = \frac{1}{32} = 0.03125 \qquad (7\text{-}29)$$

Note that a run of 6 having a probability of $1/32 = 0.03125$ has about the same probability that a sample mean has of being above the UCL with 1.86σ limits. Thus, a run of six adds serious weight to the proposition that something has gone awry.

The run chart also shows whether the sample means keep moving monotonically, either up or down. Monotonically means always moving higher or moving lower and never reversing direction.

The run of three in Figure 7-12 is not monotonic. A monotonic run signals even greater urgency to consider the likelihood that an assignable cause has changed the process's behavior. Statistical run measures do not take monotonicity into account. Further, they do not factor in the slope of the run. Steep slopes send more urgent signals of change. The analyst must consider monotonicity and slope.

7-8a Start-Ups in General

Many, if not most, processes, when they are first implemented, moving from design to practice, are found to be out of control by SPC models. Process managers working with the SPC charts and 25 initial samples can remove assignable causes and stabilize the process. The continuity of the process that is required is characteristic of flow shop type configurations. Nevertheless, the p-chart has been used with orders that are regularly repeated in the job shop.

Runs

A run of numbers on any control chart is a succession of values that fall either above or below the mean line.

7-9 The Inspection Alternative

Some firms have practiced inspecting out defectives instead of going through the laborious process of classifying problems, identifying causes, and prescribing solutions. This approach to process management is considered bad practice. Inspection, in conjunction with SPC, plays an important role by providing sample means, allowing workers to check their own output quality, and inspecting the acceptability of the suppliers' shipments (called *acceptance sampling*).

Inspections and inspectors reduce defectives shipped. They do not reduce defectives made.

7-9a One Hundred Percent Inspection (100%)— or Sampling?

An option for monitoring a process is using 100 percent (100%) inspection of the output. There are times when 100% inspection is the best procedure. When human checking is involved, it may be neither cost-efficient nor operationally effective. Automated inspection capabilities are changing this.

The use of 100% inspection makes sense for parachutists and for products where failure is life-threatening. Inspections that are related to life-and-death dependencies deserve at least 100% and, perhaps, even 1,000% inspection. For parachute inspections and surgical cases, a second opinion is a good idea. It is human nature that it is easier to spot defects in the works of others than in one's own work.

NASA continuously monitors many quality factors at space launchings. Aircraft takeoff rules are a series of checks that constitute 100% inspection of certain features of the plane. There are no serious suggestions about doing away with these forms of 100% inspection. There have been occasions when pilots forgot to do a checking procedure with dire consequences.

An economic reason to shun 100% inspection is that it is often labor intensive. This means it is likely to be more expensive than sampling the output. Sampling inspection is the other alternative. The few are held to represent the many. The body of statistical knowledge about sample sizes and conditions is sound and is treated shortly.

A common criticism of 100% inspection is that it is not fail-safe because it is human to err. Inspectors' boredom makes them very human in this regard. Sampling puts less of a burden on inspectors.

Inspection procedures performed by people are less reliable and have lower accuracy when the volume of throughput is high. Imagine the burden of trying to inspect every pill that goes into a pharmaceutical bottle. If the throughput rate is one unit per second and it takes two seconds to inspect a unit, then two inspectors are going to be needed and neither of them will have any time to go to the bathroom. With present scanner technology, the dimensions of the problem are changed.

In such a situation, sampling inspection is a logical alternative. If destructive testing is required (as with firecrackers), sampling is the only alternative. Otherwise, the firecracker manufacturer will have no product to sell. Destructive testing is used in a variety of applications such as for protective packaging and for flammability. The sampling alternative is a boon to those manufacturers.

7-9b Technological and Organizational Alternatives

The situation for inspection is changing in several ways, with important consequences for process management and quality control.

As automated inspection has become more technologically powerful, less expensive, and more reliable than sampling, the balance shifts to 100% technology-based inspection.

Robotic welding has improved the quality of product while removing difficult and hazardous work from human welders. Robot programming allows many different tasks to be performed in sequence; robots move from one weld point to another. However, care must be taken to prevent robots from getting into each other's way.

This is a new trend that promises consumers a step function improvement in the quality of the products they buy.

Robot inspectors have vision capabilities that transcend that of humans, including infrared and ultraviolet sight. They have optical-scanning capabilities with speeds and memories that surpass humans. Additionally, they have the ability to handle and move both heavy and delicate items as well as dangerous chemicals and toxic substances.

There are other changes occurring with respect to who does inspections. In many firms, each worker is responsible for the quality control of what he or she has done. This is proving effective, but the job must be such that the operator is in a position to judge the quality, which is not always the case. For those situations, alternative quality controls are developed and supported by teamwork.

Teamwork originated with Japanese manufacturing practice, but it has spread so widely that it cannot be associated with any one country's style. Rather, it should be identified with the type of organization that accepts empowerment of all employees. The employees are often called associates.

Many organizations now champion the practice of having associates inspect their own work. No other inspectors are used. Quality auditors are gone. There may be a quality department, but it is there to back up the associates with consulting advice. This variant of traditional 100% inspection has been winning adherents in high places in big companies all over the world.

7-10 Acceptance Sampling (AS)

Acceptance sampling is the process of using samples at both the inputs and the outputs of the traditional input–output model. Acceptance sampling uses statistical sampling theory to determine if the supplier's outputs shipped to the producer meet standards. Then, in turn, AS is used to determine if the producer's outputs meet the producer's standards for the customers. Acceptance sampling checks conformance to agreed-upon standards. It should be noted that SPC is used during the production process. Also, AS operates with the assumption that the production process is stable.

In the 1920s at Western Electric Company, the manufacturing division of AT&T, statistical theory was used to develop sampling plans that could be employed as substitutes for 100% inspection. Usually, the purchased materials are shipped in lot sizes, at intervals over time. The buyer has set standards for the materials and inspects a sample to make certain that the shipment conforms. Sometimes the supplier delivers the sample for approval before sending the complete shipment.

Military purchasing agencies were some of the first organizations to require the use of acceptance sampling plans for purchasing. There were published military standards such as U.S. MIL STDS-105 D, and more recently ANSI/ASQC Z1.4-1981.

Similar standards applied in Canada and other countries as well. Sampling plans are often part of the buyer–supplier contract.

Acceptance sampling is particularly well suited to exported items. Before the products are shipped to the buyer, they are inspected at the exporting plant. Only if they pass are they shipped. The same reasoning makes sense for shipments that move large distances, even within the same country.

There are companies that specialize in acting as an inspection agent for the buyer. The inspectors sample the items in the suppliers' plants with their full cooperation. Suppliers that have a trust relationship with their customers sample their own output for acceptability to ship.

However, in early 2007, it began to be noticeable that outsourced quality from China was deteriorating. Serious quality problems began to emerge that dealt with health and safety. The problems applied to a wide range of products. Indications are that importers are not inspecting what is being shipped into the United States. The difficulties may well be even more serious than that. Standards for acceptability may not have been stated or enforced.

When done properly, acceptance sampling is always used in conjunction with statistical quality control (SQC). It is assumed that when the lot was made the process was stable with a known average for defectives $\bar{p}$, which is used for either the average percent or average decimal fraction of defective parts. The sample should have that same percent defectives.

How much variability can be tolerated in the sample? A sampling plan sets limits for the amount of variability that is acceptable. The reasons that the limits might be exceeded include:

1 The number of defectives found in the sample exceeded the limits even though the process was stable with a process average of $\bar{p}$. There is a limit as to how much variability will be allowed before this assumption (1) and the lot are rejected.

2 With three-sigma limits, there is the expectation that 27 out of 10,000 sample mean points will fall outside of the control limits and 13.5 out of 10,000 will be above the upper-control limit.

3 The statistical variability exceeded the limits because the process was out of control (not stable) during the time that the lot was being made. For example, 35 out of 10,000 sample mean points fall outside of the three-sigma limits.

When the sample has too many defectives, the lot will be rejected and returned to the manufacturer—or it can be detailed. Detailing means using 100% inspection of rejected lots to remove defectives. If inspection was done at the supplier's plant, there is no need to pay to transport defectives in order to return them. Also, there is a warning. The defective lot has been rejected. This may alter production schedules and lead to expediting the next lot.

7-10a Acceptance Sampling Terminology

The basic elements of sampling plans are

1 N = the lot size. This is the total number of items produced within a homogeneous-production run. Homogeneity means that the system remained unchanged. Often, conditions for a homogeneous run are satisfied only for the specific shipment. Large shipments can entail several days of production. Each time the process is shut down, or a new shift takes over, there is the potential for changes impacting the process. SQC can be used to check if the process remains stable.

   Every time there is a change of conditions, such as a new start-up (new learning for the learning curve), the stability of the process has to be checked. Each time one worker relieves another, it should be assumed that a new lot has begun. There may be a new start-up after a coffee break or the lunch hour.

   It is assumed that the sample is representative of the lot. It also is assumed that the average percent defectives ($\bar{p}$) produced by the process does not change from the beginning to the end of the run. If $\bar{p}$ does change, the sample should pick up that fact because there will be too many or too few defectives in the sample. The "too few" condition is not usually a cause for concern but it should be a warning of statistical distortions.

2 n = the sample size. The items to be inspected should be a representative sample drawn at random from the lot. Inspectors know better than to let suppliers choose the sample.

3 c = the acceptance number.

4 The sampling criterion is defined as follows: n items are drawn from a lot of size N, k items are found to be defective,

if $k > c$, reject the entire lot,

if $k = c$, accept the lot,

if $k < c$, accept the lot.

Example: Five items ($n = 5$) are drawn from a lot size of 20 ($N = 20$). The acceptance number is set at $c = 2$. Then if three items are found to be defective ($k = 3$), reject the entire lot because $k > c$. If two or fewer items are found to be defective, k is either equal to or less than c; therefore, accept the lot. It makes sense to remove the defectives from the lot. This means that ($n - 2$) units are returned to the lot. The defectives may be able to be repaired or require scrapping.

When the acceptance number is $c = 0$, one defective rejects the lot.

7-11 O.C. Curves and Proportional Sampling

Operating characteristic curves (O.C. curves)

Graphics that show what happens to the probability of accepting a lot as the actual percent defective in the lot goes from zero to 100.

Operating characteristic curves (O.C. curves) show what happens to the probability of accepting a lot (P_A) as the actual percent defective in the lot (p) goes from zero to one. Each O.C. curve is a unique sampling plan. The construction of O.C. curves is the subject of the material that follows. However, becoming familiar with reading O.C. curves is the first requisite.

A good way to start is to examine why the use of proportional sampling does not result in the same O.C. curve for any lot size. Proportional sampling is equivalent to taking a fixed percent (PRC) of any size lot (N) for the sample (n). Thus:

$$PRC = 100\left(\frac{n}{N}\right) \tag{7-30}$$

and

$$n = \frac{PRC(N)}{100} \tag{7-31}$$

Set PRC at (say) 20 percent. Then if the lot size is $N = 100$, the sample size $n = 20$. If $N = 50$, $n = 10$; if $N = 20$, $n = 4$. Figure 7-15 shows three O.C. curves that apply where $c = 0$.

Figure 7-15

O.C. Curves for Three Proportional Sampling Plans Where the Critical Difference Is the Sample Size *n*. (The Acceptance Number *c* = 0 for All Three Plans)

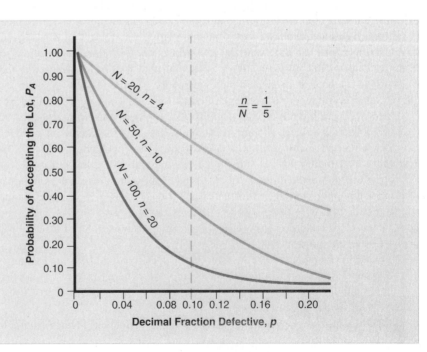

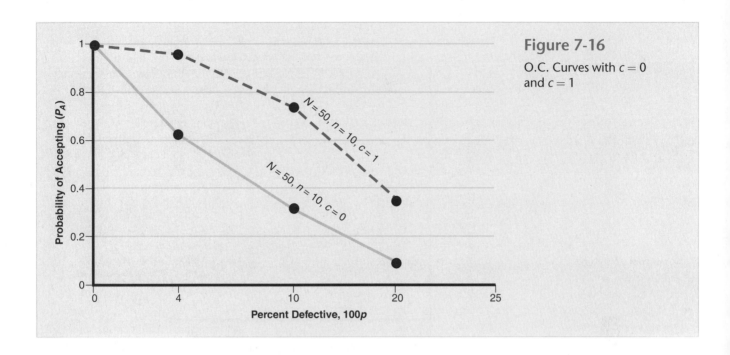

Figure 7-16

O.C. Curves with $c = 0$ and $c = 1$

The three O.C. curves show that *proportional sampling* plans will not deliver equal risk. The $n = 4$ plan is least discriminating. Its probability of accepting lots with 10 percent defectives is about 60 percent.

The $n = 10$ plan has a P_A around 35 percent and the $N = 20$ plan has a P_A about 10 percent. Each plan produces significantly different P_A's.

It has been established that O.C. curves with the same sampling proportion (n/N ratio) do not provide the same probability of acceptance. They are not even similar O.C. curves.

Also, the acceptance number c has a big effect on the probability of acceptance. This can be seen by studying the O.C. curves in Figure 7-16.

When c is increased from 0 to 1 for $n = 10$ and $N = 50$, there is a marked decrease in the discriminating ability of the sampling plan. This is because the probability of accepting a lot with a given value of p rises significantly when the acceptance number (c) increases from zero to one. Consequently, c provides control over the robustness of the sampling test. $c = 0$ is always a tougher plan than $c > 0$.

The other controlling parameter is n. Return to Figure 7-15 and notice that as n goes from 20 to 10 to 4, the probability of acceptance increases. The larger the value of n, the more discriminating is the sampling plan. The sample size n drives the value of P_A, whereas the effect of N is not great, except when it is quite small. The curves in Figure 7-15 would not differ much from those that would apply there if all of the sampling plans had the same $N = 50$.

Designing a sampling plan requires determining what the values of P_A should be for different levels of p. This is to provide the kind of protection that both the supplier and the buyer agree upon. Then, the O.C. curve can be constructed by choosing appropriate values for n and c. Note that an agreement is required. The design is not the unilateral decision of the buyer alone. The situation calls for compromise and negotiation between the supplier and the buyer. Figure 7-17 shows what is involved.

7-11a Negotiation Between Supplier and Buyer

Two shaded areas are marked alpha and beta (α and β) in Figure 7-17. The α area is called the supplier's risk. Alpha gives the probability that acceptable lots will be rejected

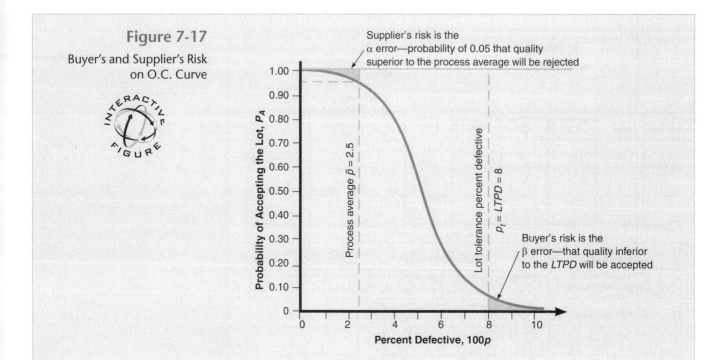

Figure 7-17

Buyer's and Supplier's Risk on O.C. Curve

INTERACTIVE FIGURE

Supplier's risk is the α error—probability of 0.05 that quality superior to the process average will be rejected

Process average $\bar{p} = 2.5$

Lot tolerance percent defective

$p_t = LTPD = 8$

Buyer's risk is the β error—that quality inferior to the *LTPD* will be accepted

Probability of Accepting the Lot, P_A

1.00
0.90
0.80
0.70
0.60
0.50
0.40
0.30
0.20
0.10
0

0   2   4   6   8   10

Percent Defective, 100p

by the sampling plan, which the O.C. curve represents. Acceptable lots are those that have a fraction defective $\bar{p}$ that is equal to or less than the process average $\bar{p}$, which operates as the limit for α.

The $\bar{p}$ threshold for alpha is also called the *average quality limit (AQL)*. It makes sense that the supplier does not want lots rejected that are right on the mark or better (with a lower value) than the process average. A sensible buyer–supplier relationship must be based on the buyer's knowledge of the process average $\bar{p}$.

The beta area represents the probability that undesirable levels of defectives will be accepted by the O.C. curve of the sampling plan. Beta is called the *buyer's risk*. The limiting value for beta, defined by the buyer, is called the lot tolerance percent defective, *LTPD*, or p_t. If decimal fraction defective is used instead of percent defective, the limit is called *lot tolerance fraction defective (LTFD)*. It is also known as the *reject quality limit (RQL)*.

LTPD (or *LTFD* or *RQL*) sets the limit that describes the poorest quality the buyer is willing to tolerate in a sampled lot. The buyer wants to reject lots with values of p that fall to the right of this limit on the *x*-axis of Figure 7-17. The use of sampling methods makes it impossible to be certain. There is a probability that the sample will falsely indicate that the percent defective is less than the limiting percent defective p_t. This is the probability of accepting quality that is inferior to the *LTPD*. The buyer compromises by agreeing that the quality level p_t be accepted by the sampling procedure no more than beta percent of the time.

7-11b Type I and Type II Errors

Decision theory has contrasted the two kinds of errors with which the alpha and beta risks of error correspond. Type I errors are false rejections of good lots. It typifies the product that might have become a great success had it been launched, but it was bypassed because the test rejected it. Type I error is known as alpha. It is identified as an error of omission.

Type II errors, known as β errors, are the probability of incorrectly accepting bad lots. This is equivalent to the mistake of launching a new product that fails because the test incorrectly accepted it as a winner. Type II errors are identified as errors of commission.

One must know the costs of making each kind of error in specific circumstances to decide which is preferable. It is important to note that these two errors are related. As one of them decreases the other increases.

7-11c The Cost of Inspection

Given the process average, $\bar{p}$, the α-level, the consumer's specification of p_t, and β, then a sampling plan can be found that minimizes the cost of inspection. This cost includes the charge for detailing, which entails inspecting 100 percent of the items in all rejected lots to remove defective pieces.

Such a sampling plan imputes a dollar value to the probability (α) of falsely rejecting lots of acceptable quality. The supplier can decrease the α-type risk by improving quality and thereby reducing the process average. Real improvements of $\bar{p}$ might be costly. It is hoped that the buyer would be willing to accept part of this increased cost in the form of higher prices. In one way or another, the supplier and the buyer will share the cost of inspection. Therefore, it is logical to agree that the rational procedure to be followed is to minimize inspection costs as they negotiate about the values for *LTPD* and β.

The sampling plan will deliver the specified α and β risks for given levels of $\bar{p}$ and p_t. If the process average $\bar{p}$ is the true state of affairs, then α percent of the time, $N - n$ pieces will be detailed. This means that the average number of pieces inspected per lot will be $n + (N - n)(\alpha)$. This number is called the *average sample number (ASN)*.

7-12 Average Outgoing Quality Limits (AOQL)

An important acceptance sampling criterion is average outgoing quality (AOQ). AOQ measures the average percentage of defective items the supplier will ship to the buyer, under different conditions of actual percent defectives in the lot.

In each lot, the sample of n units will be inspected. The remaining $(N - n)$ units will only be inspected if the lot is rejected. The expected number of defectives in the unsampled portion of the lot is $\bar{p}(N - n)$. Out of every 100 samples, P_A will be the percent of samples passed without further inspection. The defective units in the samples passed will not be replaced (detailed).

On the other hand, $1 - P_A$ of the 100 samples will be rejected and fully detailed identifying all defectives. Thus: $(P_A)(\bar{p})(N - n)$ is the average or expected number of defectives that will be passed without having been identified for every N units in a lot.

The average outgoing quality (AOQ) changes value as $\bar{p}$ goes from zero to one. See Equation 7-32.

$$AOQ = P_A \bar{p}\left(\frac{N - n}{N}\right) \tag{7-32}$$

Note that P_A changes with $\bar{p}$ in accordance with the specifics of the sampling plan, which is based on the values of n and c that are chosen. Thus, AOQ is a function of all the elements of a sampling plan. It is, therefore, a useful means of evaluating a sampling plan. Specifically, for each value of p, an AOQ measure is derived. It is the expected value of the fraction defectives that would be passed without detection if the process was operating at value p. The AOQ measure reaches a maximum level—called the *average outgoing quality limit (AOQL)*—for some particular value of p. This is shown in Figure 7-18.

Table 7-9 presents the AOQ computations, which are based on Equation 7-32.

AOQL value occurs when $\bar{p} = 0.5$. This particular sampling plan ($P_A = f(p)$) is developed by the hypergeometric method described in Enrichment Activity 7.

The maximum value of AOQ, the AOQL, has been calculated as 12/64. This average outgoing quality limit (AOQL) describes the worst case of fraction defectives that can be

Figure 7-18

Average Outgoing Quality
as a Function of the Process
Fraction Defective, p

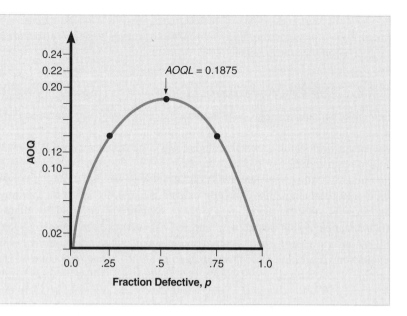

shipped, if it is assumed that the defectives of rejected lots are replaced with acceptable product and that all lots are thoroughly mixed so that shipments have homogeneous quality.

7-13 Multiple-Sampling Plans

Multiple-sampling plans are utilized when the cost of inspection required by the single-sampling plan is too great. Single-sampling plans require that the decision to accept or reject the lot must be made on the basis of the first sample drawn. With double sampling, a second sample is drawn if needed. Double sampling is used when it can lower inspection costs.

Double-sampling plans
Require two acceptance numbers ($c_2 > c_1$) so that a second sample is only required if the first sample is neither accepted nor rejected by the test, i.e., $c_1 < k_1 \leq c_2$ where k_1 is the number of defectives in the first sample.

The **double-sampling plan** requires two acceptance numbers c_1 and c_2 such that $c_2 > c_1$. Then, if the observed number of defectives in the first sample of size n_1 is k_1: Accept the lot if $k_1 \leq c_1$.

Reject the lot if $k_1 > c_2$.

If $c_1 < k_1 \leq c_2$, then draw an additional sample of size n_2.

The total sample is now of size $n_1 + n_2$.

The total number of defectives from the double sample is now $k_1 + k_2$. Then:

Accept the lot if $(k_1 + k_2) \leq c_2$.

Reject the lot if $(k_1 + k_2) > c_2$.

Double sampling saves money by *hedging*. The first sample, which is small, is tested by a strict criterion of acceptability. Only if it fails are the additional samples taken. Double-sampling costs have to be balanced against the costs of the single large sample.

Table 7-9

Computing Average
Outgoing Quality Limit
($N = 4, n = 1, c = 0$)

$\bar{p}$	P_A	$(N - n)/N$	AOQ
0	1	3/4	0
1/4	3/4	3/4	9/64
1/2	1/2	3/4	12/64 (AOQL)
3/4	1/4	3/4	9/64
1	0	3/4	0

Multiple sampling plans follows the same procedures as double sampling where more than two samples can be taken, if indicated by the rule: $c_j < k_j \leq c_{(j+1)}$. As with double sampling, the sample sizes are specified with upper and lower acceptance numbers, which get larger for additional samples. When the cumulative number of defects exceeds the highest acceptance number c_n the lot is rejected. Thus, reject the lot if:

$$(k_1 + k_2 + \ldots + k_j + \ldots + k_n) > c_n$$

In the same sense, the costs of multiple-sampling plans can be compared to single or double sampling. Sequential sampling may be cost-effective where many samples of large size have to be taken regularly. The sequential sampling procedure is to take successive samples with rules concerning when to continue and when to stop. In effect, it determines the spacing shown in Table 7-3.

Tables exist for single- and double-sampling plans that make the choice of a plan and the design of that plan much simpler.[6]

Multiple-sampling plans
Extend double sampling concepts to permit more than two samples to be taken. Another variant is sequential sampling with rules concerning when to continue and when to stop.

7-14 Binomial Distribution

For the binomial distribution to apply, the sample size should be small as compared to the lot size. The criterion is given after Equation 7-33, which is the binomial distribution.

$$P_A = Prob(j, n, p) = \frac{n!}{j!(n-j)!}\left(p^j\right)\left(q^{n-j}\right) \qquad (7\text{-}33)$$

n = sample size; p = the decimal fraction defective and $q = 1 - p$.

P_A is the probability of acceptance as previously used in the chapter. The lot size N is assumed to be infinite so it does not appear in Equation 7-33. The assumption of large enough N is considered to be met when $n/N \leq 0.05$.

When $j = 0$, the probabilities are calculated for the sampling plan with $c = 0$. Just to be sure that the factorial is known, it is $n! = n(n-1)(n-2)\ldots(1)$ and $0! = 1! = 1$.

The O.C. curve for $n = 100$, $c = 0$, is calculated from computing Equation 7-34 for sample size $n = 100$, and the acceptance number $c = 0$. With this sample size, it is expected that the lot is 2,000 or larger. Also, this sample size has been chosen to enable a later comparison with the use of the Poisson distribution for creating O.C. curves and because most tables for the binomial distribution[7] do not go up to $n = 100$.

$$Prob(0; 100, p) = \frac{100!}{0!(100-0)!}\left(p^0\right)\left(q^{100}\right) = q^{100} = (1-p)^{100} \qquad (7\text{-}34)$$

Note that 100! is divided by 100! and that equals one. Hence $p^0 = 1$. Table 7-10 is derived by using this binomial computing formula with the beginning of the entire range of possible values of fraction defectives. Figure 7-19 shows the plot of this O.C. curve.

For the acceptance number $c = 1$, it is necessary to derive the binomial for $j = 0$ and $j = 1$. Add these results together. Thus: $Prob(0; 100, p) + Prob(1; 100, p)$ will be used to derive the O.C. curve for $n = 100$ and $c = 1$. The computations follow in Equation 7-35.

Fraction Defective (p)	1 −p	$P_A = (1-p)^{100}$	Table 7-10
0.00	1.00	1.000	Binomial Derivation of O.C. Curve with $j = 0$
0.01	0.99	0.366	
0.02	0.98	0.133	
0.04	0.96	0.017	
0.05	0.95	0.006	
.	.	.	
.	.	.	
1.00	0.00	0.000	

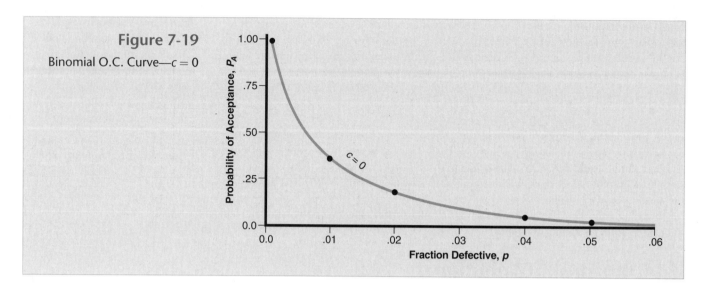

Figure 7-19

Binomial O.C. Curve—$c = 0$

$$\text{Prob}(1; 100, p) = \frac{100!}{1!(100 - 1)!}\left(p^{1}\right)\left(q^{99}\right) = 100p(1 - p)^{99} \qquad (7\text{-}35)$$

In this case 100! is divided by 99!, which leaves 100 as a remainder. The result can be used for computing Table 7-11 with the beginning of the entire range of possible values of fraction defectives, p.

Calculation of $P_0 = 100p(1 - p)^{99}$ when $q = 0.99, 0.98$, and so on, is done readily with a spreadsheet on the computer. However, for those who want a computing method without electronic aids, use logarithms and antilogs, remembering that decimals have negative characteristics.

To calculate the $c = 1$ plan, add the P_A values for each row of Tables 7-10 and 7-11, deriving Table 7-12.

Figure 7-20 combines the plot of this O.C. curve with $c = 1$ and that of Figure 7-19 with $c = 0$ so that a comparison can be made.

As expected, the O.C. curve for $c = 0$ is far more stringent than for $c = 1$.

7-15 Poisson Distribution

An even easier method for creating O.C. curves uses the Poisson distribution[8] to approximate the binomial distribution when p is small (viz., when $p < 0.05$). The mean of this distribution is $m = np$ with n the sample size and p the fraction defective. A sample size of $n \geq 20$ is customary. Like the binomial, sampling with replacement is assumed. That

Table 7-11

Binomial Derivation of O.C. Curve with $j = 1$

Fraction Defective (p)	$q = 1 - p$	$P_A = 100p(1 - p)^{99}$
0.00	1.00	0.000
0.01	0.99	0.370
0.02	0.98	0.271
0.04	0.96	0.070
0.05	0.95	0.031
.	.	.
.	.	.
.	.	.
1.00	0.00	0.000

Fraction Defective (p)	P_A (c = 0) P_A (j = 0)	P_A (j = 1)	P_A (c = 1) Sum P_A (j = 0 and j = 1)
0.00	1.000	0.000	1.000
0.01	0.366	0.370	0.736
0.02	0.133	0.271	0.404
0.04	0.017	0.070	0.087
0.05	0.006	0.031	0.037
.	.	.	.
.	.	.	.
1.00	0.000	0.000	0.000

Table 7-12

Binomial Derivation of O.C. Curve with c = 1

means that N is large enough to be treated as not being statistically affected (diminished) by sampling.

The fundamental equation for the Poisson distribution is Equation 7-36:

$$P_A = Prob(j; m) = \frac{m^j e^{-m}}{j!} \tag{7-36}$$

Let $j = 0$, which is equivalent to $c = 0$, and let $n = 100$. Then, because $m = np$, the mean $m = 100p$. Thus,

$Prob(0; m) = e^{-100p}$. It is simplest, however, to use the mean value in the center column of Table 7-13 to calculate the values of the probability of acceptance (P_A) in Table 7-13.

Observe that this result is essentially the same as that obtained by using the binomial distribution. As with the binomial, a sampling plan where $c = 1$ requires computations of P_A for $j = 0$, and $j = 1$.

The computing equation is

$$P_A = Prob(1; m) = \frac{m^1 e^{-m}}{1!} = me^{-m} \tag{7-37}$$

Again, it is easier to use m in the middle column of Table 7-14 to calculate the amount that $j = 1$ increases the probability of acceptance, P_A.

Summing the third column contributions to P_A, row by row, from Tables 7-13 and 7-14 derives Table 7-15.

The Poisson approximation of the binomial is good for small values of p. Compare the binomial tables with the Poisson tables through the range of $p = 0.00$ to 0.05. These O.C.

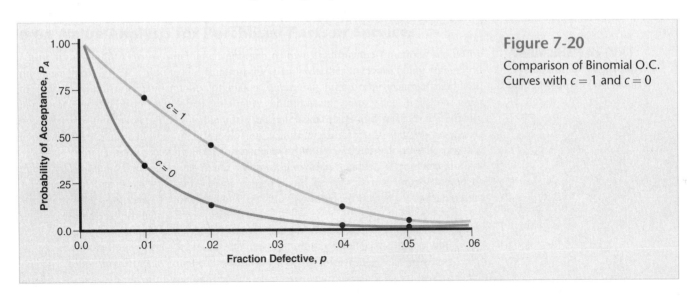

Figure 7-20

Comparison of Binomial O.C. Curves with c = 1 and c = 0

Table 7-13	Fraction Defective(p)	100p = m	$P_A = e^{-m}$
	0.00	0	1.000
Poisson Derivation of O.C.	0.01	1	0.368
Curve with $j = 0$	0.02	2	0.135
	0.04	4	0.018
	0.05	5	0.007
	.	.	.
	1.00	100	0.000

curves are sufficiently similar that either approach can be used. However, at 0.05 the error rises above 10 percent. Previously, it was stated that the Poisson should be used with $p < 0.05$, or 5 percent. Because the binomial is always more accurate, if there is doubt about using the Poisson, the binomial is not a difficult alternative.

It will be instructive to compare one larger value (for $c = 0$ and $p = 0.10$). The binomial result is

$$P_A = (1 - 0.10)^{100} = 0.000027$$

The Poisson result is

$$P_A = e^{-100(0.10)} = 0.000045$$

The Poisson approximation yields an error of 2/3 or 67 percent when $p = 0.10$, which is substantial. That is $(45 - 27)/27 = 2/3 = 0.67$.

Table 7-14	Fraction Defective(p)	100p = m	$P_A = me^{-m}$
	0.00	0	1.000
Poisson Calculations for O.C.	0.01	1	0.368
Curve with $j = 1$	0.02	2	0.271
	0.04	4	0.073
	0.05	5	0.034
	.	.	.
	1.00	100	0.000

Table 7-15	Fraction Defective (p)	$P_A (c = 0)$ $P_A (j = 0)$	$(j = 1)$	$P_A (c = 1)$ Sum $P_A (j = 0$ and $j = 1)$
Poisson Distribution for O.C. Curve with $c = 1$	0.00	1.000	0.000	1.000
	0.01	0.368	0.368	0.736
	0.02	0.135	0.271	0.406
	0.04	0.018	0.073	0.091
	0.05	0.007	0.034	0.041
	.	.	.	.
	1.00	0.000	0.000	0.000

Spotlight 7-1 McIlhenny Company
Manufacturing Tabasco to the Highest Quality Standards

The finished product: Hundreds of bottles of Tabasco® pepper sauce sit on a conveyor belt in the Avery Island factory.

On Avery Island, about 100 miles west of New Orleans, McIlhenny Company makes a line of products whose brand name is known around the world. The diamond logo of Tabasco® brand pepper sauce is one of the most recognized symbols of dependable quality by its customers. One of the reasons for its familiarity is the consistently high quality of the unique taste of the Tabasco® sauce. Process masters are essential to achieve such constancy of high-quality production. Product quality begins with planting and growing the ideal kind of peppers. Avery Island provides just the right kind of environment, as do Central and South American countries such as Brazil, Ecuador, Venezuela, Nicaragua, and Panama, where tabasco peppers are also grown. It is interesting to note that in 1870, Edmund McIlhenny received *letters patent* for his unique formula for processing peppers into a fiery red sauce. The same process is in use today. Avery Island remains headquarters for the worldwide Company, which is still owned and operated by direct descendents of the founder.

The tabasco peppers (a variety known botanically as *Capsicum frutescens v. tabasco*) must be picked when they are the perfect shade of red. Pickers use the *petit bâton rouge* (little red stick) as their color guide. The process for turning the peppers into the famous sauce is long and exact. To counter natural variations in the heat level of peppers due to weather conditions, steps are taken during the manufacturing process to minimize variation in the heat level of the final product. The peppers are mashed and mixed with a touch of salt and aged for three years.

The factory is the production sweetspot—where productivity is highest and (logically) quality problems are minimized. The factory currently produces in excess of 600,000 bottles of its high-quality pepper product a day and are shipped all over the world. The warehouses at the Avery Island plant are gigantic adjacent spaces separated into domestic and international destinations. They are filled with products of all sizes (2-, 5-, and 12-ounce bottles plus the 1/8-ounce miniatures).

McIlhenny Company, a master of quality control, is also a supplier of country store products and lots of interesting information. Visit the Company's webpage at http://www.TABASCO.com.

Review Questions

1. Anyone with a tolerance for spicy tastes will have tried the Tabasco® brand of pepper sauce. When you talk about Tabasco® with someone who uses it a lot in cooking or for their personal food preparation, a frequent question is "How do they keep the taste so consistent from bottle to bottle over time?" Is it pure luck, or do peppers have such low variability?

2. What are the steps in the production process?

3. During a visit, the production manager revealed the production sweetspot. What does *sweetspot* mean? Is it unique to production of Tabasco®? What is the sweetspot number?

4. The warehouses at the Avery Island plant of the McIlhenny Company are huge and separated into domestic and international destinations. The product line has been expanding into a variety of foods and sauces. Describe this product line after visiting the Tabasco® Country Store at http://www.tabasco.com. The entire product line can be obtained by going to the Product Locator. What P/OM problems often arise as a result of expanding the variety of the product line? How do you think the McIlhenny Company handles these?

5. The drive from New Orleans to New Iberia along U.S. 10 is over bayou and bay. At times the highway

Spotlight 7-1 (Continued)

seems like a long ribbon floating on water. This trip to the Avery Island plant permits a visit to the original Tabasco® Country Store (now one of three). If time is short, you can shop at the Tabasco® Country Store website (see 4). Running three stores and a B2C (business to customer) website puts the company into additional business operations where good P/OM practice is essential. What pattern characterizes the locations of these three retail stores? What goals do the Tabasco® Country Stores (including the website) seem to have?

Sources: Visit with Mr. Stephen C. Romero, Vice President of International Sales, McIlhenny Company, April 2000; Conversations with McIlhenny personnel, April 2001; Shane K. Bernard, Ph.D., Historian and Curator, McIlhenny Company, August 2001; Troy Romero, Director of Manufacturing, email correspondence (Lotus Notes), August 2001. Correspondence with the McIlhenny Company, 2007.

The Tabasco® marks, bottle, and label designs are registered trademarks and servicemarks exclusively of McIlhenny Company, Avery Island, LA 70513. Correspondence with the McIlhenny Company, 2007.

Spotlight 7-2 Six-Sigma Is a Management System
Can We Afford Six-Sigma Quality?

The answer to this question requires analysis of the situation. How effective is the present TQM program? Alternatively, what kinds of quality problems exist? Would a six-sigma quality improvement program cost more than the benefits derived? What would a six-sigma program cost? What is the value of potential benefits? If present lack of quality is costly, or a threat to health and life, then a six-sigma program should be considered.

The following table shows estimates of how many defects occur in various circumstances. The range of levels of defectives starts with more than ten in a hundred (more than 10 percent), which is intolerable quality for most situations. The bottom row, airline fatality goal, is listed as less than one in a billion. This is six-sigma in the usual quality control chart calculation. Six-sigma (next to the bottom row), as created by Motorola, is normally measured in terms of a chain of failure probabilities that would apply to an electronic system with many interdependent components. This procedure results in different values than derived by the usual k-sigma control limit calculations of statistical quality control charts. Specifically, it is defined as 3.4 defects in one million events. The result of the six-sigma stretch (as used by Motorola) takes into consideration values that drift from the mean. This measure is less protective than that of the standard method of calculation.

Before the benefits of a six-sigma program are accepted, management must define what it is calling "defective." For example, when is the coffee not hot enough, the delivery too slow, the finish too blemished, the movie too long, etc.? The discussions in Chapter 4 are essential for knowing how to define quality. Once defined, product qualities for both goods and services, often fall into what management calls an acceptable range. On the other hand, a zero defects goal may be realized because everything falls in the acceptable range. If management can find a way to do this, and still stay solvent, the competition is asleep at the switch. There is no call for six-sigma quality goals.

If, however, variability, which is inherent in the production of every "physical good" and "measurable service," causes products to fall outside acceptable limits, then some reduction in defective level will be warranted—if the cost does not exceed the benefits.

Motorola started the six-sigma crusade. Perhaps the reason stems from the fact that old attitudes about acceptable levels of defectives were no longer feasible in the era of integrated circuit boards. Motorola's Communications Sector operations manager summed it up. "We were using all the other popular quality-control ideas that everyone else uses. We had so many defects we couldn't even measure them. We have some large data-communications systems with tens of thousands of parts, so you can see how reckless it is to operate at three-sigma."

The questions that we began with were answered at Motorola. Before six-sigma, quality was bad at Motorola. Incremental gains in defect reduction could be obtained by studying the systems and improving procedures. These steps to study and improve were warranted by the net benefits obtained—but they weren't enough. Extreme measures could be justified to improve the reliability of Motorola's systems because they were composed of tens of thousands of parts. The six-sigma program was readily justified and became the new culture at Motorola.

Application	Level of Defectives	Span of Standard Deviations
Government tax advice by phone	More than 10 in 100	$1.27\sigma = 10.2$ in 100
Doctors' prescription clarity	About 1 in 100	$2.30\sigma = 1.07$ in 100
Restaurant bill accuracy	Less than 1 in 100	$2.50\sigma = 0.62$ in 100
Payroll processing	About 1 in a 1,000	$3.05\sigma = 1.15$ in 1,000
Japanese auto defect goal	Less than 1 in a 1,000	$3.10\sigma = 0.97$ in 1,000
Good airline baggage handling	Less than 1 in 10,000	$4.00\sigma = 0.32$ in 10,000
Television set manufacturers	Less than 1 in 100,000	$4.50\sigma = 0.34$ in 100,000
Computer manufacturers	Less than 1 in 1,000,000	$5.00\sigma = 0.29$ in 1,000,000
Six-sigma—Motorola's goal	3.4 in one million	$6.00\sigma = 3.40$ in 1,000,000*
Airline fatality goal	Less than 1 in a billion	$6.00\sigma = 0.99$ in 1,000,000,000**

*Six-sigma calculation by Motorola shifts the mean, which reduces the expected protection level.

**Normal distribution calculation of 6.00σ.

As Motorola set out to rewire its quality attitudes, their rigorous new quality process had a major contagious effect on other companies like GE, Allied Signal, Hewlett-Packard, Xerox, Ford, Bank of America, Sears, Home Depot, and Lockheed Martin Corporation. That does not mean that everyone caught the wave. It is doubtful that government tax advisors are going to embark on a six-sigma crusade. It might help the callers, but would taxpayers and the government want to pay for added qualities of advice? Note, in the table below, the poor level of protection that the taxpayer will receive correct information from the IRS.

What are the six-sigma methods? The best answer is that they are everything that is necessary to bring about both continuous, incremental improvement and radical, starting from scratch reengineering. The goal is 3.4 defectives per million output events. The means is to change the inputs and the transformation system. In other words, the systems concept is to change product line designs and/or all processes being used to transform the inputs into the desired outputs.

Six-sigma can best be viewed as an attack on variability. That is a war that can always be fought but it must be worth winning to embark on a six-sigma campaign. All of the statistical tools and the human motivation methods that are available can be used to reduce variability. Sometimes, there is the so-called "low-hanging fruit," which means that with little time and effort, significant reductions in defectives can be achieved. However, it should be kept in mind that relaxing quality standards will lower the percent defectives that are reported, but it will not dent variability. Therefore, implicit in the use of six-sigma is that quality standards are either kept the same or raised.

Many six-sigma companies have their own teaching units. Motorola University (MU) trains people from a variety of companies. MU and a host of consulting firms have open enrollment for black belt and green belt certifications. For differentiation, yellow belts are starters (about 20 hours of class training); green belts are intermediate (about 80 hours); black belts are near the top (about 125 hours of training); master black belts can train the trainers.

Review Questions

1 What is sacrosanct about six-sigma? Why not use nine-sigma?

2 Do the levels of defectives for the ten applications in the table in this Spotlight seem reasonable? For example, do errors in resstaurant checks occur about one in a hundred times? Discuss all ten applications from this point of view.

3 Six-sigma programs require a total systems approach. Why is this so?

4 Philip Crosby (a quality guru in his time) was not enthusiastic about six-sigma because he advocated zero defects. How many sigma would zero defects require? What must be made clear to discuss six-sigma and zero defects in the same conversation?

5 *Low hanging fruit* is a favorite starting point for quality improvement programs. Explain what this means and relate it to six-sigma quality programs.

Sources: McCarty, T., Lorraine Daniels, Michael Bremer, and Praveen Gupta. *The Six Sigma Black Belt Handbook.* New York: McGraw, 2005. El-Haik, Basem, and David M. Roy. *Service Design for Six-Sigma: A Roadmap for Excellence.* Hoboken, NJ: John Wiley & Sons, 2005. Stuart Gill, Mark. "Stalking Six-Sigma," *Business Month* (January 1990). See http://mu.Motorola.com (2007–2008 schedules).

chapter 7

Summary

The conceptual basis of quality assurance is large and profound. The methodology of quality management is extensive. This chapter presents views of the major approaches used, including data check sheets, histograms, scatter diagrams, Pareto charts, and Ishikawa/fishbone diagrams. Then the very important statistical control charts (x-, R-, p- and c-charts) are explained—how they work and why they work. Average outgoing quality limits and multiple sampling are part of the treatment of acceptance sampling methods used for buyer–supplier quality relations.

Two Spotlight boxes conclude this chapter. These boxes illustrate real applications of the material in the chapters. See Spotlight 7-1: McIlhenny Company, which produces a product that exhibits great consistency in spite of the fact that natural forces of variability are inherent in the process. Spotlight 7-2: Six-Sigma Is a Management System is another way of formulating the TQM approach.

Key Terms

Acceptance sampling (p. 239)
Assignable causes (p. 240)
Bar chart (p. 232)
c-chart (p. 241)
Cause and effect charts (p. 235)
Chance causes (p. 240)
Classification by attributes (p. 241)
Classification by variables (p. 240)
Compensating for defectives (p. 228)
Control chart (p. 241)
Control limits (p. 243)
Data check sheets (DCSs) (p. 231)
Deming (p. 230)
Double-sampling plan (p. 260)
Histograms (p. 232)
Inspection (p. 235)
Multiple sampling plans (p. 261)

Olympic perspective (p. 228)
Operating characteristic curves (O.C. curves) (p. 256)
p-chart (p. 241)
Pareto analysis (p. 234)
Quality control (QC) (p. 229)
R-chart (p. 247)
Runs (p. 252)
Scatter diagrams (p. 236)
Six-sigma (p. 226)
Statistical process control (SPC) (p. 239)
Statistical quality control (SQC) (p. 239)
20:80 rule (p. 235)
$\bar{x}$-chart (p. 241)
Zed defects (p. 228)
Zero-error mind-set (p. 228)

Review Questions

1   Develop a data check sheet for:
   a. Basketball scores
   b. Top-ten players for runs batted in (RBIs)
   c. Football statistics (provide some options)
   d. Top box office winners
   e. Leading recording artists

2   Develop a data check sheet for setup times for:
   a. Service time in a sit-down restaurant
   b. Service time in a fast-food restaurant

   Note: First define service time explicitly.

3   Draw a fishbone diagram for the causes of poor grades on reports in school.
4   An airline has requested a consultant to analyze its telephone reservation system. As the consultant, draw a fishbone diagram for the causes of inadequate telephone service.
5   Prepare a cause and effect analysis for the qualities of a fine cup of tea.
6   How do run charts provide early warning signals that a system may be going out of control?

7   What purposes are served by control charts?

8   What would the blueprint look like for 2.54 centimeter (cm) nails to be tested by a go/no-go gauge that has (acceptable) tolerances of ±0.04 cm? Sketch this blueprint.

9   Explain why service systems are said to have higher levels of variability from chance causes than manufacturing systems.

10 A job shop that never produces lot sizes greater than 20 units cannot employ the *x*-bar and *R*-charts of SQC. Why is this so? What kind of quality management can be used?

11 Stylish Packaging is a flow shop with a high-volume, serial-production line making cardboard boxes. An important quality is impact resistance, which requires destructive testing. Can SQC methods be used with destructive testing? What quality control method(s) are recommended? Discuss.

12 Can the consumer tell when an organization employs SQC? Can the consumer tell when it does not employ SQC?

13 Differentiate between assignable and chance causes of variation. What other names are used for each type of cause? Give some examples of each kind of variation. How can one tell when an assignable cause of variation has arisen in a system?

14 Define a stable system. Why is the condition of stability relevant to P/OM activities?

15 Why is the use of statistical quality control by drug and food manufacturers imperative? Would you recommend two-sigma or three-sigma control limits for food and drug applications of SQC? Explain.

16 One of the major reasons statistical quality control is such a powerful method is its use of sequenced inspection. Explain why this is so.

17 How should the subgroup size and the interval between samples be chosen? Is the answer applicable to both high-volume, short-cycle time products (interval between start and finish) and low-volume, long-cycle time products?

18 Differentiate between the construction of the $\bar{x}$ -, *R*-, *p*- and *c*-charts. Also distinguish between the applications of these charts. Are the charts applicable to both high-volume, short-cycle time products (interval between start and finish) and low-volume, long-cycle time products?

19 What is meant by "between-group" and "within-group" variability? Explain how these two types of variability constitute the fundamental basis of SQC.

20 Use the concepts of "within-group" variability and "between-group" variability to answer the following questions:

   a. Are the designer's specifications realistic?

   b. Is the production process stable?

   c. Is the process able to deliver the required conformance specifications?

Problems Section

Note: This section has various problems that can be formulated and solved using QuantMethods Production/Operations Management software (QMpom). The appropriate model categories are indicated for each problem.

1   Draw a scatter diagram for the following data where it is suggested that *df* (defective fraction) is a function of temperature *T*. Note the following definition of *T*.

Sample No.	T	df
1	120	80
2	110	75
3	105	65
4	112	73
5	118	78

   T is the temperature of the plating tank and *df* is the measure of defective parts per thousand, after plating. Does there seem to be a special relationship (correlation) between *T* and *df*?

   Using the QMpom module called Forecasting Models (Linear Regression) will facilitate solving Problem 1. Include the correlation coefficient in the discussion.

2   After setup in the job shop, the first items made are likely to be defectives. If the order size calls for 125 units, and the expected percent defective for start-up is 7 percent, how many units should be made?

3   A subassembly of electronic components, called M1, consists of 5 parts that can fail. Three parts have failure probabilities of 0.03. The other two parts have failure probabilities of 0.02. Each M1 can only be tested after assembly into the parent VCR. It takes a week to get M1 units (the lead time is one week), and the company has orders for the next five days of 32, 44, 36, 54, and 41. How many M1 units should be on hand right now so that all orders can be filled?

4 Use SPC with the following table of data to advise this airline about its on-time arrival and departure performance. These are service qualities highly valued by their customers. The average total number of flights flown by this airline is 660 per day. This represents three weeks of data. It is suggested that a late flight be considered as a defective. Draw up a *p*-chart and analyze the results. Discuss the approach.

The Number of Late Flights (NLF) Each Day

Day	NLF	Day	NLF	Day	NLF
1	31	8	43	15	22
2	56	9	39	16	34
3	65	10	41	17	29
4	49	11	37	18	31
5	52	12	48	19	35
6	38	13	45	20	44
7	47	14	33	21	37

Assuming that days 1, 8, and 15 are Mondays; 2, 9, and 16 are Tuesdays, etc., use QMpom to determine if there is any correlation between day of the week and the number of late flights. Using the QMpom module called Forecasting Models (Linear Regression) will facilitate solving Problem 4. Also, use of the QMpom module called Quality Control Models (Statistical Quality Control [SQC]) will help create the *p*-chart.

5 New data have been collected for the BCTF. It is given in the following table. Start your analysis by creating an $\bar{x}$- chart and then create the *R*-chart. Provide interpretation of the results.

Weight of Chocolate Truffles (in Grams)

Subgroup *j*	I	II	III	IV	V	
Time x_i	10 A.M.	11 A.M.	1 P.M.	3 P.M.	4 P.M.	Sum
1	30.00	30.25	29.75	29.90	30.05	
2	30.50	31.05	29.80	29.00	29.60	
3	29.95	30.00	30.05	29.95	29.90	
4	30.60	29.70	29.80	29.65	29.85	

Using the QMpom module called Forecasting Models (Linear Regression), analyze the effect of the time of day on the truffle weights of samples. Also, use of the QMpom module called Quality Control Models (Statistical Quality Control [SQC]) will help create the $\bar{x}$- chart and the *R*-chart.

6 For the data in Table 7-4, throw out the 3:00 P.M. data and substitute instead the following four values of x_i: (30.15), (29.95), (29.80), and (30.05).

   Recalculate the parameters for the $\bar{x}$- chart and draw the revised chart. Discuss the results.

   Using the QMpom module called Forecasting Models (Linear Regression), analyze the effect of the time of day on the revised truffle weights of samples. Also, use of QMpom module called Quality Control Models (Statistical Quality Control [SQC]) will help revise the $\bar{x}$- chart.

7 Recalculate the *R*-chart parameters without 3:00 P.M. data and using the new data supplied in Problem 6 for Table 7-4. Discuss the results.

   Use of QMpom module called Quality Control Models (Statistical Quality Control [SQC]) will help revise the $\bar{x}$- chart.

8 What is the probability of a run of eight points all above the mean? What is the probability of a run of 10 points above or below the mean?

9 For the following tabulated data, draw the *p*-chart. Compare these results with those based on Table 7-7. (*NR* = number of rejects; *n* = sample size).

Subgroup No.	NR	n	p
1 - Monday	1	9	–
2 - Tuesday	2	9	–
3 - Wednesday	1	9	–
4 - Thursday	3	16	–
5 - Friday	1	9	–
	SUM	SUM	

Using the QMpom module called Forecasting Models (Linear Regression), analyze the effect of the day on the number of rejects in each sample. Also, use of the QMpom module called Quality Control Models (Statistical Quality Control [SQC]) will help create the *p*-chart.

10 A food processor specified that the contents of a jar of salsa should weigh 14 ± 0.10 ounces net. A statistical quality control operation is set up, and the following data are obtained for one week:

		Sample No.		
1 – Mon.	14.10	14.06	14.25	14.06
2 – Tues.	13.90	13.85	13.80	14.00
3 – Wed.	14.40	14.30	14.10	14.20
4 – Thurs.	13.95	14.10	14.00	14.15
5 – Fri.	14.05	13.90	13.95	14.60

Using the QMpom module called Forecasting Models (Linear Regression), analyze the effect of the day on the sample means for the weight of the contents of the salsa jars.

a. Construct an $\bar{x}$- chart based on these 5 samples.

b. Construct an *R*-chart based on these 5 samples.

c. What points, if any, have gone out of control?

d. Discuss the results.

Also, use of the QMpom module called Quality Control Models (Statistical Quality Control [SQC]) will help create the $\bar{x}$- chart and the *R*-chart.

11 Use a data check sheet to track the Dow Jones average, regularly reported on the financial pages of most newspapers. Record the Dow Jones closing index value on a data check sheet every day for one week. Do an Ishikawa analysis, trying to develop hypotheses concerning what causes the Dow Jones index to move the way it does. Draw scatter diagrams to see if the hypothesized causal factors are related to the Dow Jones.

Using the QMpom module called Quality Control Models (all models in this section) will help in the analysis.

12 A method for determining the number of subgroups that will be sampled each day will be developed. Apply it to the situation where the total number of units produced each day is 1,000. The subgroup sample size is 30 units, and the interval between subgroups is 200 units.

a. How many subgroups will be sampled each day?

b. How many units will be sampled each day?

c. What should be done if the sampling method damages one out of three units?

Method: Dividing the production rate per day by the subgroup sample size plus the interval between samples (given in units) determines the number of samples to be taken per day. If the subgroup sample size is $n = 3$ units, and the interval between sample subgroups is $t = 4$ units, and the total number of units produced each day is $P = 210$, then the calculation to determine the number of subgroups sampled each day, called *NS*, is as follows:

$$NS = P/(n + t) = 210/(3 + 4) = 30$$

The total number of units that are sampled and tested for quality is $n(NS) = 90$. This means that 90 units would be withdrawn from the production line and tested. If the quality-testing procedure damages the product in any way, the sample interval would be increased and the sample size might be reduced to two.

Practice Quiz

1 Embarking on a quest for better quality is an important P/OM quality assurance objective. Which of the following answers is incorrect?

a. Use Pareto analysis to create a chart of customer complaint frequencies. Starting with the most frequent complaint, analyze what can be done to rectify the situation. Proceed to the next most frequent complaint. Continue in this way to address all complaints.

b. The use of a control chart to determine if price-marking errors are stable could be beneficial in evaluating the price-marking process.

c. A fishbone analysis and chart might help management understand the causes of damaged packaging on the shelves. This work could even reduce the number of damaged packages.

d. Draw an Ishikawa diagram to note all classes and subclasses of the causes of broken eggs inside of egg cartons. Take action as possible to remove the causes.

e. Employ scatter diagrams to study sales levels on different days of the week. This will help with scheduling checkout personnel and could lead to incentives for shoppers on days that have low turnout.

2 Which one of the following statements is incorrect about compensating for defectives?

a. Job shops are vulnerable to producing defectives at start-up. However, if the batch sizes are large (say in the hundreds of units) this problem is not as serious.

b. Flow shops may require some compensation for defectives produced when coffee breaks occur for workers on the line.

c. Flow shops may require some compensation for defectives produced when plant visits occur in which visitors speak to workers on the line.

d. Custom shops are not afflicted by defectives, so compensating for defectives is a non-problem.

e. Workers with small batches (say 50 units) are more likely to require compensation for defectives when no instrumentation is used to calibrate the settings.

3 A data check sheet has been created in spreadsheet form to reflect the output rate of a small direct mail agency. The number of envelopes completed in 10-minute intervals is observed five times a day for two weeks (10 days). The acceptable production rate runs from 33 to 39. Under 33 is not considered to be economic use of fixed cost resources. Above 39 creates bottlenecks in the mailroom and entails overtime pay, both of which are undesirable. Mailing rates that are less than 33 and more than 39 are labeled defectives. The analysis has been completed and reported in points a. through e., but there is one mistake. Locate the one answer that is incorrect.

Day/Sample #	1	2	3	4	5
1	31	36	43	41	26
2	36	38	42	40	35
3	36	35	37	38	34
4	32	33	35	37	38
5	30	32	33	34	36
6	31	38	37	37	36
7	36	36	32	30	32
8	43	42	37	35	33
9	26	38	35	32	34
10	32	33	35	34	36

a. In the 10 samples of $n = 5$ there are 18 "defective" production rates. That translates into an average percent defective of 36.0 percent, which is a larger number than most business managers will tolerate. Perhaps the specifications of 33–39 are too tight for the kind of work variability that is encountered. Especially suspect is the idea that high production rates (above 39) should be treated as defectives.

b. There are 12 instances of processing rates that are too low and six instances of rates that are too high. The average output rate (including too highs and too lows) is 35.16 pieces ready for mailing per 10-minute interval. This is 0.84 lower than 36.00, which is in the middle of the tolerance range of 33 through 39. Perhaps this indicates that the problem of lows is more severe than the problem of highs (see a.).

c. Thirty-nine percent (of all "defective" production output rates) occurs in the first sample that is taken each day of the 2-week period. This is too high a percentage to occur by chance. Perhaps there is a setup (daily start-up) problem for the people working in the shop that could be corrected.

d. Weekly demand for the product is 12,000 pieces sealed and mailed. That is easily achieved with one shift working 8 hours per day for five days per week (8/5).

e. The patterns of underproducing and overproducing are accentuated during the first two days of sampling. Six of the 18 defectives (33.3 percent) occur within the first two days of sampling. Perhaps a setup problem arose for the people taking the samples as they began to measure output. Alternatively, there may have been an interaction between the observers and the observed.

4 Based on the sampled information collected by the small, direct mail agency in Problem 3, the company president raised some questions, which her operations manager answered. Which answers do you fault?

a. Q. Why does the structure of this study use the assumptions of a *p*-chart? Was it necessary to work with attributes based on pass or fail conclusions instead of measured variables?

   A. It is true that the *x*-bar and *R*-charts provide more powerful analysis. However, they require more work. As an example, the length of time to complete each package for mailing could have been used as the variable under study. Such measurement is premature at this stage when the problem is that production output often falls outside of the 33–39 range.

b. Q. Would the company benefit from using Pareto analysis? Can that type of charting be applied to this production output rate situation?

   A. Pareto analysis fits the bill. This Pareto chart has two bars. The first is 67 percent in height. It represents 12 undersupply situations that occur more often than the oversupply situation. The second bar representing oversupply is 33 percent in height. If the error of undersupply costs more than the error of oversupply, there is every reason to focus first on reducing the problems creating undersupply.

c. Q. What is the upper-control limit (*UCL*) for the *p*-chart? For these data, does the chart show a process that is satisfactory, stable, and in control?

   A. The $UCL_p = 0.773$. This is obtained as follows: $UCL_p = .352 + 1.96(.215) = 0.773$. The choice of $k = 1.96$ is related to a 95 percent probability that all subgroups will have a *p* value that falls within these control limits. All values of *p* fall below this limit. Therefore, there is nothing wrong.

d. Q. What is the lower-control limit (*LCL*) for the *p*-chart? For these data, does the chart show a process that is satisfactory, stable, and in control?

   A. The $LCL_p = .352 - 1.96(.215) < 0.00$, so zero is the best lower limit. The choice of $k = 1.96$ is related to a 95 percent probability that all subgroups will have a *p* value that falls within these control limits. All values of *p* fall above the zero lower limit. Therefore, there is nothing wrong.

e. Q. What role does the standard deviation play in the structure of the fishbone (Ishikawa) analysis? Can the company profit from the use of this charting method?

   A. Fishbone diagrams identify causes of variability. They do not assess the amount of variability that is assignable to each cause. It would be beneficial to color code the vertebrae of the fish bones. For example, strong positive causal effects would be red with a plus sign. Strong negative causal effects would be red with a minus sign. Medium effects would be in blue, etc.

5 The operations manager has retabulated the sampled information collected by the small, direct mail agency in Problem 3. He has increased the acceptable production rate range from 31 to 41. He explains that fixed mailing costs can be decreased by substituting less expensive labor when production rates are lower. When output rates are higher, he proposes removing some mailroom bottlenecks by automating certain functions. Now, mailing rates that are less than 31 and more than 41 are labeled defectives. His staff has completed the analysis and prepared a report, but there is one mistake. Locate the one answer that is incorrect.

a. In the 10 samples of *n* = 5 there are 8 "defective" production rates. That translates into an average percent defective of 16.0 percent, which is much better than the prior value of 36 percent. However, it is still too large. This shows that the range is not the culprit. The problem is the variability of how long it takes to do the job. That aspect of the situation should be studied.

b. There are four instances of processing rates that are too low and four instances of rates that are too high. Changing the acceptable range has not altered the average output rate, which is 35.16 pieces ready to mail per 10-minute interval. Underproduction remains more of a problem than overproduction.

c. The percent of all defectives that occurs in the first sample is 37.5, which is not much better than the 38.9 associated with the previous tolerance range. This is still too high a percentage to occur by chance. It is necessary to consider that a setup (daily start-up) problem exists for the people working in the shop and it should be corrected.

d. From the first sampled value on every one of the 10 days, observe that there is a run of numbers that are at or below the center point target of the tolerance range (36). There is only one instance of a number being greater (43) than the target value in the 10 observations.

e. The patterns of underproducing and overproducing are no longer accentuated during the first two days of sampling. Previously, there may have been an interaction between the observers and the observed, but that is no longer the case.

6 Statements about the achievement of quality are often technical, but their implications are so important that they need to be understood by managers who are neither engineers nor technically trained experts in SQC. Five such statements are now made, and two of them are considered to be "iffy." Spot the observations that need further discussion.

a. Spelling errors in letters answering complaints are considered grievous quality failures. Every hour a sample of four letters is taken and scrutinized for typos. On the wall is a p-chart that shows that defective letters are 2 percent of the total sample (average value). The manager explains that the company wants to catch a situation where error production jumps. This can happen because one of the letter writers is tired or not feeling well. The manager thinks that the control system keeps everyone on their toes and is well worth the expense.

b. Continuing with the system for answering complaints, the control limits are set at a one-sigma distance from the mean line $\bar{p} = 0.02$). Because the standard deviation is 0.07, this means that the upper-control limit is set at 0.09 and the lower-control limit is zero. The manager feels a sense of comfort with this conservative one-sigma warning of impending trouble. Two-sigma would warn less frequently. The cost of investigating false alarms must be weighed against the cost of missing real problems.

c. A three-sigma upper limit for the complaint response system would be set at 0.23. Because one defective letter out of four represents a p-value of 0.25, that would signal a warning. Because of the sample size ($n = 4$), three-sigma and one-sigma are going to be warning at the same time. Perhaps, it would pay to change the sample size to 10. Then, one defective letter would have $p = 0.10$, and this would make the one-sigma upper limit more sensitive than the three-sigma limit.

d. In a different application, applying quality control charts to swimming pool maintenance, a run occurs starting on Monday and continues through Friday. (A run is a group of successive sample means all occurring on one side of the process grand mean.) The run of seven sample means above the grand mean are measures of the pH level of the water in the pool. The probability of this run occurring by chance is 1.5 in a hundred. The pool manager decides to wait for the readings from the next two days, stating that if both are above the mean, then corrective action will be taken.

e. The pool manager is delaying action until two more samples are taken. If Saturday's pH measure adds another sample mean to the run, then the odds of a run of seven occurring by chance is about 8 in a thousand. If Sunday's pH measure adds an eighth number to the run, then the odds will be about 4 in a thousand.

7　Four of the five statements that follow are correct. Which of the following statements is incorrect?

a. There are now inspection alternatives that have important consequences for process management and quality control. For a long time, 100% inspection was considered a trap. It sounded good but in reality was fraught with problems such as inspector weariness, lack of consistency and accuracy, and inability to match fast production rates. Automated and robotic inspection overcomes many of these problems. It can surpass human inspectors by being able to inspect things in hostile environments (such as searching for water on Mars). Robotic devices can be more accurate in chemistry, physics, and memory. However, 100% inspection will still fail when destructive testing is required.

b. Acceptance sampling is beneficial in many applications. For example, when the purchaser is across the ocean from the seller, it is possible to use AS before the shipments are loaded in the cargo holds. If the lots do not pass the test, they can be detailed (100 percent inspected) to remove all of the defectives before shipping.

c. The elements of acceptance sampling include lot size (N), sample size (n), the acceptance number (c), the number of defectives found (k), and the rule if $k > c$, reject the entire lot. These elements are fundamental parts of operating characteristic curves (O.C.curves). A weakness of ordinary O.C. curves is that they do not reflect buyer's and supplier's risks.

d. Nonstatisticians tend to believe that a sampling plan should maintain proportionality of the sample size to the lot size, i.e., (n/N) = constant. For example, let the sample size be 10 percent of the lot size. This approach will produce different acceptance plans, which means that proportionality is not an acceptable criterion for choosing sample sizes.

e. Each acceptance sampling plan can be examined to determine the imputed buyer's risk (beta error known as Type II) and the imputed supplier's risk (alpha error known as Type I). It is desirable that the creator of the sampling plan build in the alpha and beta that are in line with management's objectives and the negotiations between the buyer and the supplier. Otherwise, alpha and beta are default values determined after the fact.

8　Which of the following statements is incorrect?

a. Average outgoing quality (AOQ) is the average percentage of defective items the supplier will ship to the buyer— under different conditions of actual percent defectives (p) in the lot (N).

b. The average outgoing quality changes value as p goes from zero to one in this equation $AOQ = (P_A) p(N - n)/N$. It should be noted that P_A changes with p in accordance with the specifics of the sampling plan.

c. The AOQ curve resembles an upside-down catenary curve (or half of an ellipse) that reaches a maximum level called the average outgoing quality limit ($AOQL$) at some particular value of p. The $AOQL$ describes the worst case of fraction defectives that can be shipped subject to two conditions. First, all defectives of rejected lots are replaced with acceptable product. Second, all lots have homogeneous quality.

d. Multiple-sampling plans are recommended when they cost less than single-sampling plans. Double sampling is only used when it can lower inspection costs by hedging. First, a sample size that is smaller than would be required for single sampling is taken. If it fails to accept the lot, then a second sample is drawn. It is useful to obtain the costs for both procedures when single sampling seems expensive. This notion extends to multiple sampling, which consists of more than two successive samples.

e. O.C. curves can be derived by using either the binomial or the Poisson distributions. The Poisson approximation of the binomial saves computational time, but it is only good for large values of p.

9 The foundation of statistical quality control (SQC) is based on several fundamental factors. Which one of the following is not correct?

a. The statistical structure of control charts compares "within-group" variability with "between-group" variability. They do not match when a change has occurred over time between groups; within-group variability remains the same. The mismatch signals that the system has gone out of control.

b. For starting up a control chart on a new process, it is desirable to have 20 successive samples. It is not unusual for initial sample means to be outside the control limits. Throw the outliers away and collect additional sample means. Also, analyze causes of other outages and remove the source of these assignable causes.

c. SQC charts are equally applicable to batch production in the job shop and continuous production in the flow shop. The p-chart might be more easily used with the job shop. The $\bar{x}$- and R-charts might apply more readily to the flow shop.

d. The best subgroup size and interval between samples is determined by the stability of the production process, the cycle time for a completed product, the cost of tracking problems, and the cost of ignoring problems. There are a lot of factors to take into account, but in general, intervals between samples should be small if process change can occur at any time, cycle time is short, cost of missing a process change is high, and sampling cost is reasonable. Similarly, use large samples if setup costs are high for each new sample, product cycle time is long, or "within-group" data is homogeneous. Use small samples when the process is likely to shift values during the sampling interval and when the cost of each observation within a sample is high.

10 Six-sigma as practiced by Motorola, General Electric, and Lockheed-Martin is TQM (total quality management). In business literature, the TQM emphasis is on the ample list of appetizers. However, TQM is a full-service menu, which includes the hardcore, statistical entrees that are not the subject of popular trade books. A good P/OM text must be fair and balanced in this regard. Statements a. through e. are intended to set an educational agenda for organizations that seek to achieve mastery of quality. One of the items is not feasible. Which is the incorrect answer?

a. Everyone in the firm should be familiar with the seven fundamental methods that must be exercised to achieve highest levels of quality. In particular, all employees should be able to create data check sheets and spreadsheets that allow tabulation and calculation of patterns and parameters applying to their own work. See Table 7-1, The Seven QC Methods.

b. Only those people involved with the production process can apply root cause analysis (RCA). The application of RCA (another name for fishbone and Ishikawa diagrams) must be performed by those who understand what makes the process tick.

c. A group of people within the organization should be trained in the statistical aspects of control chart construction and six-sigma derivations. If someone really understands six-sigma they should also be able to discuss the pros and cons of using five-sigma or seven-sigma as alternatives. To do this requires understanding fundamentals that underlie the cost structure of generic k-sigma plans (k is to be chosen as the optimal protection plan for each particular application).

d. Big companies may find it useful to train some of their employees as Master Black Belts and have other employees working their way up from "Yellow Belts," "Green Belts," and "Black Belts." Six-sigma is explored in Spotlight 7-2. Also, see the application by GE at http://www.ge.com/railservices/about/sixsigma.html.

d. And visit "six sigma" at Wikipedia. Scroll down to "Implementation roles." Note the definitions of all belts. Small and medium-size companies (SMEs) may not be able to justify spending to train any color Belts at all.

e. On an individual note, golfers and tennis players have a good chance of improving the game that they play and advancing their game to a higher plateau by using the seven methods for quality achievement shown in Table 7-1. Individual dedication may not be sufficient to include control chart methods (6.), but the other methods will go a long way to increasing "personal bests." The same applies to devoted chefs.

Additional Readings

Bounds, G., L. Yorks, M. Adams, and G. Ranney. *Beyond Total Quality Management*. New York: McGraw-Hill Book Co., Inc., 1994.

Crosby, P. E. *Quality Is Free*. New York: McGraw-Hill Book Co., Inc., 1979.

———. *Quality Is Still Free*. New York: McGraw-Hill Book Co., Inc., 1995.

Crowden, D. J. *Statistical Methods in Quality Control*. Englewood Cliffs, NJ: Prentice-Hall, Inc., 1957.

Deming, W. E. *Out of the Crisis*. Boston: MIT—Center for Advanced Engineering Studies, 1986.

Dodge, Harold F., and Harry G. Romig. *Sampling Inspection Tables, Single and Double Sampling*, 2e. New York: Wiley, 1959.

Feigenbaum, A.V. *Total Quality Control*, 3e. New York: McGraw-Hill Book Co., Inc., 1991.

George, Michael. *Lean Six-Sigma for Service: How to Use Lean Speed and Six-Sigma Quality to Improve Services and Transactions*. McGraw-Hill Trade, Spiral Edition, June 2003.

Grant, Eugene L., and Richard S. Leavenworth. *Statistical Quality Control*, 6e. New York: McGraw-Hill Book Co., Inc., 1988.

Greene, Richard Tabor. *Global Quality: A Synthesis of the World's Best Management Methods*. Burr Ridge, IL: Irwin, 1993.

Ishikawa, K. *What Is Total Quality Control? The Japanese Way*. Englewood Cliffs, NJ: Prentice-Hall, Inc., 1985.

Juran, J. M. *Quality Control Handbook*, 4e. New York: McGraw-Hill Book Co., Inc., 1988.

Littauer, S. B. "Technological Stability in Industrial Operations." *Transactions of the New York Academy of Sciences*, Series II, vol. 13, no. 2 (December 1950), 67–72.

Main, Jeremy. *Quality Wars: The Triumphs and Defeats of American Business*. A Juran Institute Report. New York: The Free Press, 1994.

McCarty, T., Lorraine Daniels, Michael Bremer, and Praveen Gupta. *The Six-Sigma Black Belt Handbook*. New York: McGraw, 2005.

Pande, Peter, and Lawrence Holpp. *What Is Six-Sigma?* McGraw-Hill Trade, 2001 (also an e-book).

Rath and Strong. *Rath and Strong's Six-Sigma Pocket Guide*. McGraw-Hill Trade, Spiral Edition, March 2003.

Scholtes, P. R., et al. *The Team Handbook*. Joiner Associates (608-8134). Madison, WI, 1989.

Shewhart, W. A. *Economic Control of Quality of Manufactured Product*. Princeton: D. Van Nostrand Co., Inc., 1931.

Shingo, Shigeo. *Zero Quality Control*. Connecticut: Productivity Press, 1986.

Wadsworth, H., K. Stephens, and A. Godfrey. *Modern Methods for Quality Control and Improvement*. New York: Wiley, 1986.

Notes

1. W. E. Deming. *The New Economics for Industry, Government, Education*. Cambridge: MIT Center for Advanced Engineering Studies, 1993, 135. (Deming used *study*, not *check*, for his Quality Cycle analysis; see Figure 7-2.)
2. Shigeo Shingo. *Zero Quality Control*. Connecticut: Productivity Press, 1986, 32.
3. Walter A. Shewhart. *Economic Control of Quality of Manufactured Product*. Princeton: D. Van Nostrand, 1931. Walter Shewhart's seminal work dates back to the research time he spent with the U.S. Department of Agriculture in the late 1920s.
4. K. Ishikawa. *What Is Total Quality Control? The Japanese Way*. Englewood Cliffs, NJ: Prentice-Hall, 1987.
5. It is useful to note the effect of the value of k on the probability $(p_{\bar{x}})$ that a sample mean falls within the control limits $\pm k\sigma$. The following table shows the effect of k.

k	$(p_{\bar{x}})$
1.00	68.26%
1.64+	90.00%
1.96	95.00%
2.00	95.44%
3.00	99.73%
4.00	99.99%

6. Harold F. Dodge and Harry G. Romig. *Sampling Inspection Tables, Single and Double Sampling*, 2e. New York: Wiley, 1959.
7. A classic collection of mathematical tables is in *The Handbook of Mathematical Functions with Formulas, Graphs, and Mathematical Tables*. U.S. Department of Commerce, National Bureau of Standards, Applied Mathematics, Series 55. June 1964.
8. Poisson tables can be used to determine the probabilities of c or less defects where c and j are equivalent.

Enrichment Activity 7: Hypergeometric O.C. Curves

Enrichment Activity 7 provides the third method for designing O.C. curves for single sampling. Why bother with this third method when the binomial and the Poisson have been shown to create reasonably accurate O.C. curves for their specific conditions? The reason for choosing one method instead of another is based on the relationship of the sample size n to the lot size N. In this case, termed the hypergeometric, the small size of N makes it necessary to do sampling without replacement.

This means that if there is a lot size of $N = 4$, and it is known that there is one defective in that lot, then for the first sample there is a one in four chance of drawing the defective part. If the defective is not found in this first sample, then the second sample has a one out of three chance of being the defective. The probability goes from 25 to 33.3 to 50 percent. The hypergeometric distribution takes this effect of diminishing N into account, whereas the binomial and the Poisson do not.

The hypergeometric distribution is used when the lot size N is small and successive sampling affects the results. Each next sample reduces the number of unsampled units remaining in the lot. The sample is first drawn from N units, then from $N - 1$, $N - 2, \ldots$ units, etc.

If items are replaced to keep N of constant size, there is a significant chance that the same item would be sampled more than once. Also, with destructive testing, sampled items cannot be replaced because they have to be destroyed to be tested.

The hypergeometric distribution given in Equation EA7-1 applies to a sampling plan with acceptance number, $c = 0$. [Repeated note: The factorial of any number is written $m!$ and is calculated by $(m)(m-1)(m-2)\ldots(1)$.]

$$P_A = \frac{(N - x)!(N - n)!}{(N - x - n)!N!} \qquad (EA7\text{-}1)$$

x = the possible number of defectives in the lot and
$x/N = p$ is the possible fraction defective of the lot.
As x is varied from 0 to N, the appropriate values of P_A are determined. This allows a plot of P_A versus p (or $100\,p$, the percent defective). Then, in the case where $N = 4$, $n = 1$, and $c = 0$, Equation EA7-2 for P_A is:

$$P_A = \frac{(4 - x)!(3)!}{(3 - x)!4!} = \frac{(4 - x)}{4(3 - x)} = \frac{4 - x}{4} = 1 - p \qquad (EA7\text{-}2)$$

p is the symbol for fraction defective. The right-most term of Equation EA7-2 is $(1 - p)$. It is obtained by substituting $x = Np = 4p$ into the next to the right-most term of the equation.

Varying p to derive P_A results in Table EA7-1. This is the same distribution that was used to derive the values of AOQ and $AOQL$ in this chapter.

The hypergeometric formula when $c > 0$ has the same additive requirements for the probability of acceptance with $j = 0$ and $j = 1$ that were shown for the binomial and Poisson distributions. Equation EA7-3 gives the general hypergeometric equation.

$$P_j = \frac{C_{n-j}^{N-x} C_j^x}{C_n^N} = \frac{(N - x)!x!n!(N - n)!}{(n - j)!(N - x - n + j)!j!(x - j)!N!} \qquad (EA7\text{-}3)$$

The example first derives the hypergeometric O.C. curve for $c = 0$ with $j = 0$, and then, using addition, for $j = 1$ and finally for $c = 1$. For this example, the lot size is $N = 50$ and the sample size is $n = 10$. All calculations for Table EA7-2 are based on Equation EA7-3.

The next step is to determine additions to the probability of acceptance when $j = 1$. Calculations for Table EA7-3 are based on Equation EA7-3.

Table EA7-4 adds the respective rows of Tables EA7-2 and EA7-3.

This $c = 1$ plan is a nonrigorous acceptance plan because it has such high probabilities of accepting 10 percent and even 20 percent defectives.

x	$x/N = p$	P_A	Table EA7-1
0	0.00	1.00	Hypergeometric Distribution for Equation EA7-2 Where $c = 0$
1	0.25	0.75	
2	0.50	0.50	
3	0.75	0.25	
4	1.00	0.00	

Table EA7-2	x	$p = x/N$	P_A
Hypergeometric for O.C. Curve with $j = 0$ and $c = 0$	0	0.00	$\dfrac{50!10!40!}{10!40!50!} = 1.000$
	2	0.04	$\dfrac{48!2!10!40!}{10!38!2!50!} = 0.637$
	5	0.10	$\dfrac{45!5!10!40!}{10!35!5!50!} = 0.311$
	10	0.20	$\dfrac{40!10!10!40!}{10!30!10!50!} = 0.083$

Table EA7-3	x	$p = x/N$	P_A+
Hypergeometric Distribution for O.C. Curve with $j = 1$	0	0.0	There are no defectives in the lot; therefore, the additional probability of acceptance with the relaxed acceptance criterion of $j = 1$ is zero. $P_A +$ signifies that this is measuring the additional probability of acceptance.
	2	0.04	$\dfrac{48!2!10!40!}{9!39!50!} = 0.326$
	5	0.10	$\dfrac{45!5!10!40!}{9!36!4!50!} = 0.432$
	10	0.20	$\dfrac{40!10!10!40!}{9!31!9!50!} = 0.268$

Table EA7-4			$c = 0$		P_A
The $c = 1$ Hypergeometric Distribution	x	p	$j = 0$	$j = 1$	$c = 1$
	0	0.00	1.000	0.000	1.000
	2	0.04	0.637	0.326	0.963
	5	0.10	0.311	0.432	0.743
	10	0.20	0.083	0.268	0.351

Enrichment Challenges 7

1 Develop the hypergeometric for $N = 5$, $n = 2$, and $c = 0$.

    a. Write out the table for P_A.

    b. Draw the O.C. curve.

2 Develop the hypergeometric for $N = 5$, $n = 2$, and $c = 1$.

    a. Write out the table for P_A.

    b. Draw the O.C. curve.

3 Develop the hypergeometric for $N = 50$, $n = 2$, and $c = 0$.

    a. Construct the table for P_A.

    b. Draw the O.C. curve.

    c. Compare this result to the hypergeometric distribution that was developed in the Enrichment Activity 7 for $N = 50$, $n = 10$, and $c = 0$.

4 Develop the hypergeometric for $N = 50$, $n = 2$, and $c = 1$.

    a. Write out the table for P_A.

    b. Draw the O.C. curve.

    c. Compare this to the hypergeometric distribution that was developed in the Enrichment Activity 7 for $N = 50$, $n = 10$, and $c = 1$.

5 The situations in Problems 3 and 4 meet the binomial requirement that $n/N < 0.05$.

    a. Use the binomial distribution to create the table for P_A.

    b. Draw the O.C. curve.

    c. Compare the results of the hypergeometric in this case with those of the binomial distribution.

6 Comment on the use of the Poisson distribution for the situations given in Problems 3 and 4.

Management of Technology (MOT)

Chapter Outline

VARs

Value-added resellers represent a powerful marketing channel that is not widely known (except in the business). VARs add features such as professional services to existing products that increase the value of the product to the company.

Chapter 8 relates the management of technology to P/OM responsibility for the transformation process. As technology changes, there is competitive pressure to adopt the new technology. It comes from the outside interfaces of the organization. This includes sales, marketing, **VARs** (value added resellers) as well as shareholders and the investment community. Meanwhile, internal to the organization, there is resistance to change. Protection of the status quo arises in spite of the fact that the new technology is likely to improve productivity, quality, etc. VARs play an important role in industries such as electronics and information technology (IT). It is worthwhile using Google to find the Wikipedia explanation for VARs.

Two schools of thought emerge. First, it is widely believed that necessity is the mother of invention. If so, everyone should view adoption of new technologies as mothered by necessity. The second school of thought does not accept the fact that need drives invention. It is believed that customers cannot even dream of the consequences of new technology. Entrepreneurs, greenfield firms and those new to the market have an advantage. For them, invention (new technology) is the mother of necessity. Only after seeing an iPhone is demand created to own one. P/OM must believe that both schools are right some of the time.

After reading this chapter, you should be able to:

- Explain the role of technological transformation as it relates to P/OM.
- Explain how technology transformation capabilities relate to information technology (IT) management.
- Discuss the specifics of technology management, relating it to the management of skills.
- Specify a ratio percent that reflects the mixture of skills and technology used over time.
- Explain the problem of applying new technology to old systems—why is this a technology trap?
- Explain technology timing.
- For glass windshields or tires, what is the difference between OEM and a replacement parts manufacturer?
- Explain the relationship between an OEM and a value added reseller (VAR).
- Discuss the role of new technology in such applications as search engines used in health care and education.
- Explain the interaction of process technology with the supply chain to deliver the product.
- Differentiate between the management of technology (MOT) for the original product market (OEMs = original equipment manufacturers) and the replacement product market.
- Explain P/OM's role in the management of the technology of storage, warehousing, and distribution.
- Explain P/OM's role in the management of the technology of packaging and delivery systems.
- Discuss the reason for including the technology of testing (product qualities) as part of P/OM's responsibility.
- Explain how the management of testing technology relates to P/OM's awareness of legal statutes and governmental rules.
- Reveal why design for manufacturing (DFM) and design for assembly (DFA) are vitally important to P/OM.
- Explain why design for manufacturing and design for assembly are treated as a management of technology challenge.
- Discuss procedures for evaluating and selecting designs based on DFM and DFA criteria.
- Illustrate P/OM's technology management responsibilities for changeover capabilities.
- Describe some new technologies that P/OM will be managing in the future, including expert systems, cyborgs and robots, and miniaturization.

The Systems Viewpoint

The management of technology is a shared (*systems*) responsibility with powerful leverage for company success and failure. Correct timing for the acquisition of new technology is more successful when it is a team effort because these decisions are best made with the involvement of all relevant forms of expertise. Timing issues increase the dimensional scope of the system that must be considered. Including relevant participants enlarges the playing field. Who can best provide estimates of when competitors will change technology? Competitive technology timetables are significant decision drivers. Who should lead and who should follow? Ultimately, how many customers really care. P/OM evaluations of the effects of technology changes on productivity, unit costs, and quality will underlie proper P/OM strategies. The text explains why the management of technology must be considered for:

1 Manufacturing and Service Delivery,
2 Storage and Warehousing, and
3 Information Systems and the Supply Chain.

These broad categories break down into such basic operations as process equipment, packaging, testing, telecommunications, and the delivery of products and services.

However, buying new technology at the right time is necessary but not sufficient to win the cup. As technology changes, there is pressure to adapt new technology so that it conforms to old systems and methods. This tendency sells new technology short. Old technology makes new technology subservient. It should be the other way around. This situation is described in Chapter 8 as the "technology trap." Systems thinking about new technology must also consider the points raised in the section that follows.

Strategic Thinking

At the technology interface, systems viewpoints and strategic thinking blend into each other. Judgments about the costs of adopting new technologies and their effects on customers' satisfaction (in both short- and long-term cases) will be crucial. Strategic planning is dependent upon forecasts of technology shifts and their rates of change. Financial advice concerning the best timing of major expenditures involves the market's sensitivity to the dynamics of how work is done at present and how that could change if the new technologies are adopted. Also involved is executive consideration of the availability of management as a resource that can deal with the changing technology. Measuring concepts that go along with the strategic systems approach to managing technology timing include computation of the payback period, breakeven point, breakeven time, and the length of the cost recovery period. For example, if replacing old equipment with new equipment in the office, or on the plant floor, has a payback period, or cost recovery period, of 3 months, that would be attractive and hard to ignore, whereas a period of 3 years might not be acceptable.

Because it is able to manipulate this payback period, human nature takes over. When new-tech is developed, one response is to adopt it and force it to fit the existing system for doing things. This was called the "technology trap." Another approach is to "show" that it will never pay off. Existing bureaucracies are accustomed to doing things in a particular way. Changing to accommodate new technology can be considered to be costly and potentially debilitating. Methods are easily found to disprove the case for advantages gained. One of the most impressive methods has the "seal of approval" of many in management. It is a revered financial approach known as the net present value (NPV) calculation. Enrichment Activity 8 presents this methodology and points out it pros and cons.

8-1 Technology Component of Transformation

Technology

Equipment employed to accomplish the transformation that is basic to the fundamental P/OM input–output model.

Technology plays a commanding role in accomplishing the input–output transformation that is P/OM's main concern. From the P/OM perspective, **technology** consists of equipment employed in a manner—defined by scientific knowledge about the conditions necessary—to bring about specific transformations. The equipment includes computers, machinery, tools, and communication systems. Combined with people's skills, materials are transformed and services are provided. Technology components of transformation also can be categorized by types of processes, such as physically transforming glass for auto windshield applications, rubber for tires for trucks and bicycles, or steel for bridges, tunnels, and buildings; assembling parts to make toasters, airplanes, or computer chips; transferring information; and providing services.

Information technology transformations have undergone the most rapid evolution of any of the production and operations systems mentioned earlier. There are two reasons that this is the case. First, information systems are part of the planning and decision fabric for doing work of any kind. Therefore, IT is embedded in manufacturing, healthcare, education, hospitality, and any other operations. Second, IT has zoomed ahead on the basis of electronic and digital technology developments related to computers, networks, and the Internet. Technological developments cannot be discussed without including the joint participation of P/OM and IT.

8-1a Management of the Technology Component

Management of technology (MOT)

Requires knowing what technologies exist, their state of development, and when to shift from one format to another.

Management of the technology component of input–output systems transformations is often called **management of technology (MOT)** when it is taught as a subject in business schools. Management of technology operates at three distinct levels.

1   At the personal and societal levels, management of technology (MOT) for products and processes includes meeting or exceeding governmental regulations controlling technology for health and safety purposes. This is quality assurance for customers and workers. Also governmental, patent jurisprudence operates to stimulate invention of new technological input and transformation systems by protecting inventors against dishonest competition for lengthy periods of time. Illegal copying of an invention and profiting thereby is called *infringement*. The legal definition of *infringement* and the courts' punishment for this crime are continually undergoing revision, with resulting stricter laws and harsher punishments for infringement. The protection of intellectual property is a personal and societal issue that requires constant vigilance.

2   At the company level, management of technology is focused on satisfying customers and gaining competitive advantage. Some firms invest in the development of new technology to gain an advantage, which might be protected by patents. Another option is to copy the new technology of competitors. This imitative strategy is neither illegal nor immoral if it does not violate agreements including those of patents. It is not acceptable when it leads to successful charges of infringement. To avoid litigation, many firms pay competitors for the use of their new technology by licensing the rights.

3   Management of technology at the international level involves all of the areas of levels 1 and 2. However, various countries have different rules and policies. There are many international agreements, which are constantly being altered by new trade agreements. A challenge to those managing technology is to keep up with the international scope of changes regarding the safety of the workplace and the protection of customers. Applicability of patents, the courts' rulings on infringement, and the regulation of license agreements are international subjects that require systems cooperation between all of the legal and operations

management participants in the worldwide marketplaces. To have international P/OM capability requires extensive knowledge and constant updating. Companies cannot do business on a global scale without this expertise.

The three levels interact. The outsourcing of technology to firms that operate abroad under different laws and controls, under varying ethical standards and concepts, raises critical issues in levels 1 and 2 about quality assurance, protection of intellectual property, and the sustainability of companies in a rapidly evolving technological environment. Outsourcing is a major cause of reduction of technological abilities.

There are many outsourcing offshore models including BOT (build, operate, and transfer). BOT is considered to be least vulnerable to criticisms of loss of control and technological reduction. This is because the company moving operations offshore has the right to maintain some supervision over the process design and its operation. The T of BOT is crucial control. The company can retake control of the offshore processes and transfer them back home. BOT is found in India but not in China, where ownership of production assets is ill-defined if not illusory.

Companies that decide to go offshore without some degree of BOT are doing so for the sake of tomorrow's balance sheet. They are jeopardizing long-term survivability based on core competences in developing technologies.

8-2 The Technology Trap

Technological changes occur in clusters or droves. The *discontinuity* of major waves of new technology *can create a trap*, called the **technology trap**. Consider this headline: "Companies have spent vast sums on technology. Now they have to figure out what to do with it all."[1] This *Wall Street Journal* feature refers to information technology (IT). The fact is that, with 15 years of history to go on, the international economy did very well with new technology but some companies (such as Digital Equipment, Data General, Enron, WorldCom) failed to survive. In general, new companies did better than old ones.

The trap is wanting to own new technology, but not knowing how to use it to reshape old systems. The key to the problem is recognizing that information systems have been in place for decades. Generally, it is the legacy information systems (the old way of doing things) that resist change and make new technology conform to tradition.

Traditional ways of doing things are hard to change; thus, new technology has been made subservient to the old systems. In other words, old systems are frozen into place, and the new technology has not been able to thaw out the old procedures in order to establish new ones.

The tendency to use new technology to mimic old systems is likely to be detrimental. Companies that have started out with a reengineering point of view and a reinvent business processes mind-set have succeeded in gaining technological advantages. Dr. Zuboff of the Harvard Business School has shown that those companies that have rethought the systems they use for doing work have profited from introducing computer technology. Those that computerized without altering the existing systems did not do well.[2] To be successful, companies must not only continually change their equipment, but also their processes, and most importantly, the mind-set of their management and employees.

This subject is ideally placed in the near-midpoint of this text because the use of new technology in old ways is a tactical blunder that would not have occurred if the strategic objectives had been properly formulated. Old technology looks to the past whereas new technology looks to the future. Better to wait for adoption of new technology to time it for bringing about systems-wide change.

Technology trap
To avoid this trap, systems studies should upgrade the way that work is done in keeping with the capabilities of new technology.

8-3 Technology Timing

Management of technology involves knowing when to shift from one form of technology to another. Should the old computer technology be replaced by the latest available, or should the organization wait for future developments? What does waiting cost? It entails continuing use of an older technology that might be slower or more expensive. Newer technology might produce a higher quality product. On the other hand, new technology often entails costs of learning and *shakedown risks* of unexpected bugs and glitches. Shakedown and break-in are both concerned with start-up problems.

The timing of shifts in technology involves assessment of the costs and savings made by changing now as compared to the costs and savings from deferring the acquisition. These should include the advantage, particularly with industrial customers, of having the reputation of being a technology leader instead of a follower.

Postponement and deferral of new technology development may be a sound MOT strategy when:

1   Development costs are high.
2   Shakedown problems can alienate customers.
3   Infringement cannot be substantiated.
4   The benefits of new technology are likely to require more years of development.

8-3a Innovate or Imitate

If the benefits of being a leader in technological development are not significant, then copying technology without infringing across the global boundaries that apply can prove advantageous. Being second (or even third) can be a successful technology timing strategy.

Payback period
Defined as the period of time required for an investment to produce revenues that pay back the debt.

Usually, investments are made in developing new technology when the payback period is relatively short compared to the expected lifetime that the development will be generating profits and savings. **Payback period** is the estimated number of years that will be required to produce enough profits or savings to offset the expenditures completely. Some companies prefer to talk about *breakeven time*, essentially the same concept at work. *Cost recovery period* also is used. It is the time required to accumulate profits that fully offset the expenses entailed in replacing old technology with new technology. All of these measure the time required to pay off alternative investments. It is a favored way to evaluate choices in technologies.

Different criteria will apply according to the specifics of the situation. However, as a rule of thumb, in stable markets that are estimated to last about 10 years, a 3-year payback period was often considered to be the allowable upper limit. In the days of rapidly evolving technology, much shorter time periods have to be set.

An example illustrates how important patent protection can be in determining whether to be an innovator or an imitator.

First case: Assume that the innovator will spend one billion dollars $(10)^9$ developing the new product/process which then has a yearly return of 200 million $2(10)^8$ dollars per year. Without considering the diminishing value of money over a long time horizon (net present value) it will take five years for the investment to be recovered (paid back). This assumes that patents protect the innovator against competition. Net present value is briefly examined in the following discussion and then in Enrichment Activity 8 at the conclusion of this chapter.

Second case: Everything is the same except that the innovator does not receive any patent protection. As a result, competitors copy the product/process and start to earn 10 percent of the innovator's return, which reduces net to 180 million dollars per year. It takes the innovator 5.55 years to recover the original investment. Meanwhile, the competitors are dividing up revenues of 20 million per year. Before the innovator breaks even, competitors have made over 100 million in revenues.

An alternative for evaluating technology changes is **net present value (NPV)**, which discounts future earnings according to the expected interest rates that prevail. With a 6 percent interest rate, earnings at the end of one year would be divided by 1.06. Earnings that apply only to the second year would be divided by $(1.06)^2 = 1.12$. Earnings that apply only to the nth year would be divided by $(1.06)^n$. With NPV, it will take the innovator longer than 5.55 years to achieve breakeven. NPV calculations are explained in the Enrichment Activity for this chapter.

NPV is a financial management tool. The fact that P/OM and finance must use it together to manage technological decision making is illustrative of the need for using the systems approach for MOT.

Net present value (NPV)
Method for discounting the cost of future expenditures and the value of future savings.

8-3b Make It or Buy It

The P/OM decision to "make" or "buy" components is often related to technological expertise and to the cost of leading or following in technology. "Buy" avoids having to invest in and learn the new technology that "make" entails. The decision to buy uses someone else's expertise, which makes sense during times of technological volatility. It makes less sense during periods of technological stability, which have been called "the quiet times" by a creative colleague.

To keep abreast of technological developments, it may be essential to make certain components. Making also can provide opportunities to achieve best quality and gain competitive advantages. Evaluation of the make or buy decision is a constant challenge to P/OM. Chapter 14 provides models for attaining quantitative decisions about "make or buy."

Many companies have appointed people to the job of technology assessment and management. This job requires being able to evaluate the present status of technology and future state probabilities. It is part of the job to coordinate P/OM, finance, and marketing to determine as a team how to manage technological timing. Among the technology timing issues to be considered are

1 Assessing technology plans of competitors and the importance of matching them. Can customers tell the difference?
2 Knowing the cost and/or benefits of the current technological level of the firm.
3 Understanding the costs of transition and the payback period.
4 Knowing when to move up the technological ladder. Periods of volatility are to be avoided, whereas periods of relative stability are preferred.
5 Involving technological forecasting, which requires knowing that part of technology development is in the laboratory and the other part is on the factory or service process floor. It may also be out in the field with the service crews.

8-3c Alone or with a Partner

Risk sharing is possible when an appropriate partner can be found. The innovator with a partner can gain insights, share financial exposure, and partner on managing the many aspects of the innovation. Some of the advantages that can be gained from a partnership arrangement are as follows.

1 Greater knowledge about the product line and the marketplace.
2 Experience with the process for making the product or delivering the service. For example, building a new hotel with an innovative hospitality strategy is easier when the partner has experience in the hospitality industry.

3 Teamwork always has advantages if the partners are truly on the same team with the same goals.

4 Financial risk is shared, which means that great success is apportioned but so are serious losses.

5 Management time is often a scarce resource that each partner contributes to the whole system.

8-4 The Art and Science of Technology

The nature of work blends people and machinery together to form the technology of processes. What often is missed is the interplay of equipment capabilities and human skills. Both play a role in determining how specific forms of technology create processes for making and doing things. Technology is a synthesis of these two factors. Managing technology requires managing the combination of people skills with computers, robotics, and other equipment.

Before 1950, definitions of technology placed more stress on the "arts" part of the interactions that occur between people's skills using tools and machines than on the materials and machines themselves. This makes sense because skills with machines used to constitute a larger part of the technologies responsible for all kinds of products. Such skills included the ability to measure and test using calipers, micrometers, and all kinds of laboratory equipment, including microscopes, to assess the chemistry of products. At one time, rulers and scales were high-powered technological developments.

In their early interactions, machines did less and people did more. Go back to the seventeenth century, before the torrent of inventions associated with the Industrial Revolution. Look at how the percent contribution made by skills (as compared to the percent contribution made by machines) goes down over time.

Figure 8-1 shows the decline in the percent participation of human skills—as a generalized shape for an average process—over a period of 400 years.

Recently, engineering and science have made people increasingly peripheral to operations. The art skills are built into the equipment. The further back one goes in time, the more reliance on people's skillful contributions, the smaller the contributions of machine technology, and the more that materials used were closer to basic commodities and less specialized. Now, there is more value added by advanced technology and less by people's skills.

The decrease is slow for many years and then speeds up. Recent usage accelerates the decrease of the arts and skills portion relative to technology and science. The mixture

Figure 8-1

Participation of Skills as a Percent of Total Labor Plus Machine Inputs—Estimates from 1600 to 2000

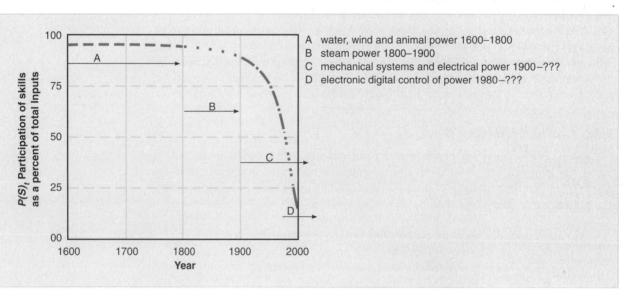

A water, wind and animal power 1600–1800
B steam power 1800–1900
C mechanical systems and electrical power 1900–???
D electronic digital control of power 1980–???

within technology has shifted markedly. In the first half of the twentieth century, machines developed capabilities for moving and lifting power. They were acclaimed for their sheer strength and endurance, not for their smartness and adeptness, which had to be derived from the human operator.

Starting in the 1950s, machine intelligence began to be developed. At first, the speed of doing simple calculations and the size and persistence of memory seemed to spell out the basic advantages of machine calculations. Yet, it was believed that machine intelligence had serious limitations that would never approach human capabilities. These beliefs are disappearing. Computers working together with machines now can perform an array of functions that surpass what humans alone can do in all forms of arts and skills.

Geometrically increasing numbers of applications can be cited where industry places greater reliance on machines than people for physical skills, performance learning abilities, and fast decision making with large databases. The technological replacements apply to making things and providing services. They apply to the skills and equipment required to inspect and test results. Machines are winning at chess.

On the other hand, the expanding role of technology has increased the amount of knowledge work required by industry. Such creative knowledge work, essential for planning, designing, and programming, is predominantly done by people with special training who are aided by computers. It has been said that the P/OM workforce has been replacing blue collars with scholars.

Thus, the increasing role of technology has changed the way operations must be managed in a number of ways. P/OM people must understand more about the technology of the process and the computers that are used to control the process. Skilled machinists, tool and die makers, and artisans with tools are disappearing. In their place are programs such as CAD-CAE-CAM (computer-aided design, computer-aided engineering, and computer-aided manufacturing). Knowledge work has grown with greater technology, and managing such creative efforts has become part of the P/OM responsibility.

© 2008 Jupiterimages Corporation

The person in this illustration could be playing "fantasy football" but the odds are that she is a professional engaged in reviewing the appearance of a new product design, the menus for catering a great party, or inventory levels in the wine cellar. She might even be deciding on the best PowerPoint presentation to use with a potential new client. Computer abilities have brought a diverse set of talents into the P/OM domain.

8-5 The Development of Industrial Processing Technologies

There are many different materials that could be used to illustrate the shift from art-based skills to technology-based processes; steel, rubber, paper, and glass are among them. Each provides wonderful examples of processes that increasingly make use of intelligent machines and a wealth of scientific knowledge about the properties of materials.

P/OM manages technology of products that are so taken for granted that few stop to wonder how this is done in a factory or a restaurant. What skills and technologies must be managed to make windshields? What skills and technologies must be managed to prepare hundreds of dinners served at theme parks, hospitals, and schools? Food preparation skills involve an assortment of materials that are unique because they differ by quality and availability.

8-5a Manufacturing and Services

Processes for manufacturing and services are quite different in some ways and very similar in others. Consider windshields, on the one hand, and food, one the other. The supply chain for glass starts in the mines with sand and sandstone. The supply chain for food starts in the fields with plants and trees, and on the farm for corn, milk, eggs, and meats. Both involve processes that serve multibillion-dollar markets on a global scale. The respective technologies involved have long and glorious histories, which must be continually updated because of new developments.

The story about the management of technology in the glass industry begins with recognition that float glass is the starting component for automotive glass. Automotive glass requires the use of much higher levels of technology than household glass. Safety glass is mandated for automobile windshields in the United States and many other countries because it will not shatter under impact. Managing the technology of glass windshields requires knowledge of the glass-making process, the windshield forming process, the windshield insertion process, and many other processes too. There is no chance of winging it.

Supply chains for services in food and beverages originate in many locales. Satisfying the requirements of restaurants and supermarkets involves more sources than are needed by manufacturers of windshields. Quality assurance is more difficult in these service areas and management is distributed thinly. As a result, technology for checking quality is a major management problem. Chemical and biological tests have to be run to assure the safety of imported ingredients. Managing the technology of food processes requires knowledge about growing it, harvesting and caring for it (see storage in the next section), and of animal husbandry. There are many preparation processes for freezing, canning, bottling, etc., and all of this in anticipation of further processes by the chefs and consumers of supermarket products. No chance exists for doing this successfully without preparation, forethought, and sufficient information and experience.

8-5b Storage and Warehousing

OEM

Original equipment manufacturer refers to the company that makes the product, which is then incorporated by others as a component. Computers, cars, and phones are filled with components made by OEMs that have nothing to do with the brand that customers buy. iPhones are a perfect example.

There are very many models of cars and each of these has year by year changes. The result is that **OEM** (original equipment manufacturer) windshield glass is made in great volume for the annual model of every make and model of automobile. On the other hand, replacement windshield manufacturers must have all of the important stock-keeping units (SKUs) in their inventories. That means SKUs for new models as well as SKUs for past car models.

The technology for the supply chain that deals with automotive replacement glass is different from the technology that is the foundation for the original glass market. Some replacement glass is produced as an added amount of product with original production runs. It is sent in small batches to the distributors dealing with the service outlets that include glass retailers, collision and body shops, and dealer service stations. This unique supply chain system exists in stores and on the web (e.g., http://89glass.com or http://www.windshieldstogo.com).

The demand for replacement auto glass in the United States is large. Windshield replacement alone is in excess of 8 million units per year in the United States plus a million in Canada.[3] This demand is generated by thousands of different kinds of vehicles on the road. "There are over 15 thousand automotive glass SKUs . . . in North America, and this number is growing exponentially."[4]

The supply chain that is feeding the car manufacturers with OEM glass is an entirely different kind of process than that which applies to replacement glass firms. Inventories of the most popular cars that are still on the road in each market must be available to supply the auto glass replacement companies with the windshields upon demand. Cross shipping between warehouses can reduce the size of the inventory that must be carried. Information technology is at the heart of knowing where everything is so that orders that are received can be swiftly filled before losing customers.

Managers that deal with OEM are often unaware of the repair and replacement marketplace. Obsolescence is a two-edged sword. That which has become obsolete can become passé, live too much in the present. They overlook likely, and even highly probable, developments in the future.

Smart warehouse technology includes RFID (radio frequency identification) for the location of specific models of windshields. Bar codes are being used with less frequency because their technology is more labor intensive and less reliable. Asset identification has become a major contribution of RFID.

Storage of food is a different matter. The shelf life of food is almost always a point of concern. There is no time to cross-ship for most food items and so storage is maintained at points that are closer to the supermarkets or distributors of food to restaurants. Canned foods have the longest shelf life. Frozen foods require expensive temperature-controlled storage, which must be monitored to be certain that the food temperatures do not go below a fixed standard. With fish and other similar foods where spoilage can be deadly, there is in place the HACCP (Hazard Analysis Critical Control Point) system. The HACCP rules are monitored 24/7/365 by the FDA. This is explained in Section 20-4d. The use of IT (information technology) is essential. The rigorous management of technology with respect to food distribution systems is not a "maybe"—it is a "must."

8-5c Information Technology and the Supply Chain

Manufacturers' outputs move from the plant to the warehouse and then with the best possible distribution logistics to the customers. Windshields are bulky, easily broken or scratched, and difficult to store. Automobile manufacturers will avoid large inventories. Their preference is to have almost just-in-time delivery but to avoid disastrous situations of the line stopped and waiting for windshields, a reasonable number are kept in stock. A process decision must be made. Should the line be stopped or should cars be completed without their windshields in place. Technology management is at the crux of the decision. Can windshields be inserted in a satisfactory manner—after the car is completed? The answer is "no." To do so requires redesign of the product and process. This is a management of technology issue.

Information technology must connect windshield suppliers with carmakers online in real time. The alternative to stopping the line (a crucial P/OM process decision) is to complete the car and repair it at the end of the line. No one will be surprised to learn that the quality of windshield installation after car completion are never accomplished with the same quality as windshields being installed at the proper design point in the process.

Management of technology for food and beverage products moving through myriad supply chain channels is an IT challenge. The dates "use by" are equivalent to marking a product as obsolete and perhaps dangerous—as of a given date. Discounts apply for food that is growing old but is acceptable. There are still "day old bread stores." There are no "day old windshields." In fact, some windshields of bygone eras have become very valuable as collectors' items.

Information technology has the power to monitor materials flowing through supply chains worldwide. IT also keeps track of cash flow, over- and undersupply of raw materials, WIP, and finished goods. Smart benchmark tracking includes measures of competitive advantage and disadvantage. Also important, IT must stay abreast of new technology and assist management in reaching decisions about when to shift from one technological level to a higher one. Adequate management of the supply chain is totally dependent on complete information about all participants in the system. Communication on an immediate basis between participants is a technological imperative, which is made increasingly complicated by the large number of different telecommunication systems and their networks.

An important part of the technology of supply chains is the means by which the various players (suppliers, producers, and customers) are able to know where things are located. This includes the trucks, trains, and planes used to carry the goods. Customers want to know when they can expect delivery of the various products they have ordered from suppliers.

The Association of American Railroads (AAR) has an information system that keeps track of where all railroad boxcars, tank cars, and hopper cars are in the country. Using this information, individual companies monitor their rolling stock. Security issues have dictated restricted access to railcar location data. An operations center links the railroads

© 2008 Jupiterimages Corporation

Reflection of the sky in the glass windows of an airline terminal is a part of the story. Is that glass darkening as the sun gets brighter? Does that glass cut the glare? How does it compare to windshield glass? Greenhouse glass has improved markedly. It used to fail on average every 5 years. Now, it is guaranteed for more than 30 years.

with national intelligence organizations (24/7). Security systems are enhanced by real time monitoring and capability for surveillance of designated trains.

UPS and FedEx use the combination of optical scanners, network telecommunications, and computer-database management to track package movements for their customers. Bar-code readers continuously send information to the tracking computer to trace package movements for their customers. Similar bar-coded information technology and RFID systems are used within factories to track the status of products and components.

Everyone that is part of the supply chain has something they are shipping or something they are receiving, or both. That consideration applies to adjacent stations within factories, banks, investment brokers, hotels, and restaurants. It is worth noting that the supply chain concept applies equally well to external and internal suppliers, producers, and customers; the systems point of view always encompasses the trio.

8-6 Technology of Packaging and Delivery

Glass windshields can shatter and chip if not properly handled. Transport, handling, and packaging technologies differ according to whether the market that is being served is for original transparencies (high-volume shipments) or for individual windshields that are shipped from the distribution center when requested by the auto service for specific customers.

Most products need some kind of protection during shipping. The production process can have near-zero defectives as a result of excellent quality management. Unfortunately, the damage done during delivery of the product can zoom the real defective rate—as seen by the customer—to outrageous levels. The manufacturer may not know about this situation for a long time. Complaints are not made on products not purchased. Feedback from warehouses, truckers, and retailers can take a long time. Awareness of such problems dawns slowly.

A consumer package goods company experienced a downturn in sales of its bar soap in a specific sales region. As part of the investigation for the causes of the problem, it was found that the product on the shelves of the supermarkets had damaged boxes. This condition was attributed to a change in handling procedures in the distribution center, which had started using a forklift truck to move the product. The forklift truck operator had previously worked in a scrap metal business. The problem was remedied by training.

A firm that manufactures dinnerware of medium-grade porcelain china discovered that full sets of dishes and cups were being delivered with three out of every ten pieces broken. They also found the company was infrequently called by customers to ask for replacements. More often, customers accepted the loss because it was not fine china, but they never ordered from this company again. Further, when the company was called to ask for replacements, the person representing the company had no interest at all in tracing the shipment to learn what caused the damage.

P/OM was on top of the issue of production defectives. The production process was stable and in control. Production had low-defective rates for this china product. The shipment-defective rates completely altered the "delivered rate of defectives." Package design, actual packing, and handling methods were the sources of trouble. From the systems point of view, the defective rate was unacceptable and more than one system had to be changed to remedy this situation.

The quality of the delivered product is part of TQM accountability. The packaging technology and handling methods are part of that accountability. The chinaware company must question every aspect of the systems that caused the breakage, and then it must determine what should be done to correct the problems to prevent any breakage from happening.

8-6a Systems Analysis

P/OM is responsible for delivering a quality product under all circumstances. P/OM must undertake a systems analysis of the delivery process where packaging is the technology. The systems analysis entails getting answers to three lines of inquiry.

1   What product-protection parameters have been specified for the packaging? What has the designer done to achieve these specifications? Typical questions would be:

- From what height can the package be dropped without breakage?
- Has the package been designed to withstand travel-specific stresses and strains (air, boxcar, truck, etc.)?
- How much vibration can the packaged product tolerate?
- What compression force will the package support?
- What happens if liquids are spilled on the packaging?
- Does humidity affect the performance of the package in terms of any of these quality dimensions?
- What are the temperature extremes the package can withstand?
- Finally, has the package design been adequately tested?

2   Did the actual handling of the package that resulted in broken product fall outside of the designer's specifications?

- If it did, in what ways did the actual treatment exceed the limits for which this product was protected?
- If it did not, can the packaging system be redesigned?

3   Has something permanently changed in the delivery system's way of handling the package?

- If so, can the packaging technology be upgraded, or can a new delivery system be found?
- If a new delivery system is feasible, will the current packaging technology suffice?
- If nothing has permanently changed in the delivery system, is the current package design satisfactory?

The systems approach focuses on getting to the root of the problem. Was the package designed correctly? Was the package tested correctly? If it was designed correctly, then what caused the breakage? If it was not designed correctly, how should the package be designed and tested?

The china had been packed in a fiberboard box, which was placed inside a corrugated box. There were no styrofoam inserts, which strengthen the box and protect its contents (called *unitized packaging*). Plastic "popcorn" was used.

Packages can be made of cardboard, plastics, wood, and combinations of materials. Inserts and fill offer even more options. There are too many kinds of packaging materials and systems of packaging to try to do more than present the basic scope of this subject.

8-7 Technology of Testing

Each kind of packing material has its own unique characteristics. Various tests have been developed to determine strengths and weaknesses. Corrugated boxes are marked with a figure to indicate the number of impact pounds the box can withstand before bursting. For example, "100 test" indicates less strength than "200 test" or "300 test."

Packaging experts have expressed concern that too few and too simple tests should not be interpreted as more than vaguely indicative of package integrity. The bursting-strength test reflects just one type of resistance on which a package must be rated. Even this one rating for impact is suspect for a variety of reasons. Humidity can affect the strength of cardboard and will not be reflected by the test measure. What passes a bursting-strength test in Maine may fall short in Florida. In short, correct measurement of package strength is dependent on a thorough understanding of packaging technology.

In general, testing technology is conditional upon a complete comprehension of the process being tested. The ramifications of testing technology apply to a great range of applications, which include designing products to have minimum variability in manufacturing.

8-7a Testing by Simulation

Empirical testing

Well-known as a check against poor design performance that might be hidden otherwise.

Simulation

The imitative representation of the functioning of a system or process by means of the functioning of a surrogate system or process.

An important testing alternative is **empirical testing**, simulating the worst cases of the kind of handling the package design can be expected to undergo. With this kind of experimental testing, it also is possible to examine alternative package designs.

It is best to combine structural knowledge of packing materials—package engineering—with testing by **simulation**, which is a pragmatic procedure. Simulation for package testing means dropping, kicking, gouging, vibrating, pouring liquids onto, heating up, and cooling down, among other things. It is not easy to simulate all of these conditions. Still, it may be easier to use simulation methodology than engineering knowledge of the complex processes.

Simulation testing technology plays a most important part in designing windows for homes and office buildings. High floors of the latter do experience severe winds. The testing method should consider both broken panes and blown-in window frames. In addition, it must consider leakage. How high a wind should these windows protect against? Hurricanes are classified as winds above 75 miles per hour, and window designers need to provide protection for occasions above that level in hurricane zones.

P/OM working together with product designers and R&D can test the output of the process and reconfigure the way the product is designed and made. Testing technology is part of the P/OM kit of tools. Excessive auto recalls can be avoided by pretesting for contingencies. The silent interior of the car is a function of the way car doors are sealed. Models can be tested before the production system is finalized. Wind tunnels, which are used for testing airplane performance, also are used for testing the performance of windows.

Legal statutes and governmental rules are the concern of P/OM. Building to specifications requires knowing what the changing specifications are and what must be done to meet expectations. Knowing the law is part of the system's knowledge. Fulfilling the law is a matter of process. Testing is needed to determine if the requirements are being met.

Thus, after Hurricane Andrew the building codes for southern Florida, devastated by that storm, were changed so that roofs would not blow off and windows would not implode. The California highway system adopted more stringent building codes following the collapse of sections of highway during the 1994 earthquake.

8-8 Quality Assurance Technology

One of the most important aspects of total quality management (TQM) is inspection and testing technology. Such quality testing technology is at the heart of quality control. The technology of testing has been advancing at a rapid rate. As in other aspects of technological development, increasing amounts of the art of quality achievement and control are being built into the machines by using science.

Inspection is epitomized by visual abilities, although there are many other senses for gathering information. Using vision, inspectors can check quality (unacceptable finish) or quantity (too many air bubbles in a piece of glass). The quantity of product is readily determined by optical scanners, which can count bar codes with more reliability than human inspectors.

Optical scanners at checkout counters reading universal product codes (UPC) that are printed on all packages reflect applications of bar-code technology. Now commonplace in supermarkets, they are being used in factories and banks to determine the status of transactions. They are used increasingly because their capabilities are improving. They have a great deal of information redundancy, which means that even damaged packages can be read as well as bar codes on round and odd-shaped surfaces.

The multiple functions of adding up the bill and deducting the item from inventory are readily programmed into the supermarket's computer system, with which the optical scanner communicates. The same technology working with a filling machine can determine how many pills to put into a bottle or when the fill level is reached for a bottle of juice.

For quality control applications, scanners must be able to perceive and differentiate along each of the critical quality dimensions. The criteria for product acceptability can be programmed precisely by computer software and translated into the language of the scanner so the inspection process can distinguish between acceptable and defective products. Inspection technology continues to develop along both quantitative and qualitative lines.

For perfumes, a good nose is a requirement. Are there machines that have a better analytic smelling capability? To judge wines, taste, vision and smell are essential. Are machines in the wings to take over these tasks? For now, these sensory skills are best supported by machines, not replaced by them. At the same time, there has been continuous development of machine inspection abilities. These include sensing systems for temperature, pressure, and weight. Visual sensors deal well with shape and size.

Sensory capabilities used to be only people skills; now technology has been developed to replace people in some areas. The complete replacement of human inspectors by machine inspectors is still far from being accomplished. Nevertheless, P/OM is experiencing a major "change" in inspection technology that is targeted right at the heart of operations.

New technology permits automation of the statistical quality control process. SQC monitoring equipment inputs data directly into a database. The statistical characteristics of the processes being monitored are continuously calculated. Appropriate quality control charts can be drawn automatically and submitted on a regular basis to QC inspectors for their interpretation. Symptoms and signs of systems being out of control can be incorporated in the programs.

Computer software is programmed to increase the frequency with which samples are taken as well as their sizes when the defective rate increases. When runs are detected and/or out of control, points are noted and the size and frequency of samples are adjusted. Under specific circumstances, the appropriate employee is notified about the situation so that interventions by workers can occur. The application of these methods to employee drug testing is an interesting extension of the same kinds of methodology and technology.

Testing procedures are the technology that quality control relies upon. Optical scanning is among machine sensory systems that are more sensitive than human ones, and are preferred. Computer programming of the SQC function is one of the most important technological developments at this time.

© 2008 Jupiterimages Corporation

The total food system involves an incredible number of processes to sow and harvest, produce and package, prepare, plate, and serve. Throughout all of these processes, technology plays an immense role and that technology has been evolving over thousands of years.

8-9 Systems Design of Technology (Product Plus Process)

It used to be that designers only considered the needs of end-users when designing the product. P/OM was not consulted about how best to fabricate and assemble the product. Later, designs that were not feasible to manufacture would have to be redesigned, which compromised other aspects of the product. The manufacturing process was jerry-rigged as a measure of last resort to make the product.

8-9a Design for Manufacturing (DFM) and Design for Assembly (DFA)

Design for manufacturing (DFM) and **design for assembly (DFA)** start with the goal of feasible fabrication and assembly. They then move on to higher-order quality objectives. It is now acknowledged to be good practice to have the design team include P/OM consultation from the start of the project to achieve feasibility and sensibility.

Because fabrication is distinctly different from assembly, it is useful to maintain separate agendas for DFM and DFA. On the other hand, often, but not always, the

Design for manufacturing (DFM)

Changes are made in both design specifications and fabrication procedures to simplify manufacturing operations.

Design for assembly (DFA)

Changes are made in both design specifications and assembly procedures to simplify the assembly activity.

manufacture of parts leads to their assembly, so that both functions are complimentary. They should be dovetailed and designed to work well together. When a producer combines components from different suppliers, DFA must be coordinated by the assembler. Windshields and restaurant meals epitomize DFM and DFA combinations.

Even when it may not seem as if assembly is part of the product manufacturing cycle, it should be considered relevant. Pouring vinegar into a bottle is a kind of assembly of the product with its package. Packaging engineers and process managers for soft drink and beer companies view their technologies as an advanced form of serialized flow shop production. Packaging is often the ultimate stage of the manufacturing process, as in canning foods and boxing toothpaste. Consequently, the product and packaging should be designed and planned together.

The second order objective of DFM and DFA is to design parts that can be made with minimum variability. This may require testing the design by running pilot studies to produce sample product using the kind of equipment and technology that will be used for full-scale fabrication. Pilot studies are reduced-scale simulations of full-scale production processes. Simulations make it possible to approximate the dimensional variability that will occur during manufacturing. This can lead to redesign of the product and the process. Simulation is a strong method for design modification where the objective is minimal variation.

Table 8-1 shows the dimensional fit or **tolerance matching** for three (key-fits-in-cylinder) lock designs. T_i is the thickness of the key and W_i is the width of the slot into which the key fits. If the key is exactly 0.5 in thickness and the slot is 0.6 in width, then, the key can always slide into the cylinder. Exact dimensions do not occur in nature. Assume that 98 percent of the time the key is 0.5 ± 0.05 and the slot is 0.6 ± 0.04. The range for the key is 0.45 to 0.55 and the range for the slot is 0.56 to 0.64. If the key is 0.45 and the slot is 0.64, the key will fit but quite loosely. The lock designers must determine if the key will it be able to engage the pins and turn the cylinder. At the other extreme, the key will be 0.55 and the slot will be 0.56. The key's fit in the slot may be too tight. Again, designers will have to decide which of the three designs in the table is preferred.

The fabrication variances of Design 3 are lowest, but the key will not fit the cylinder slot a large percentage of the time. It is likely that Design 2 will be preferred because it is less loose and not as tight as Design 1. The considerations that are illustrated by Table 8-1 are relevant or planning DFA products and processes.

In searching for the optimal, product design and process design technology are being modified by using a feedback system similar to that of quality control. The comparable cycle of improvement is the one used in quality control, which is plan-do-study-act or plan-do-check-act.

The difference from the quality control application in this case is that design of the product has not yet been completed and accepted. Further, the process for making the product has not yet been finalized, and the product has not been released for manufacture. There is time to experiment with pilot plant-type production.

The idea is similar to the package-testing example previously discussed in this chapter. The design is pilot tested in a manufacturing setting or assembly environment that comes as close as possible to the real-world, full-scale situation. Simulation of manufacture and/or assembly is the appropriate way to describe these experiments.

Tolerance matching
Quality products must have parts that fit together properly.

Table 8-1	i	T_i	W_i	Loose	Tight
Tolerance Matching for Key of Thickness T_i in Slot of Width W_i for Designs $i = 1, 2, 3$	Design 1	0.5 ± 0.05	0.6 ± 0.04	0.19	0.01
	Design 2	0.5 ± 0.02	0.6 ± 0.04	0.16	0.04
	Design 3	0.6 ± 0.01	0.6 ± 0.04	0.05	-0.05

It may be best to start with two designs, both of which are considered feasible alternatives. The two variants are fabricated with a process that captures as much of the actual production process as possible, with as large a sample size as possible.

The guiding principle of diminishing returns has been discussed earlier, but for those who are more comfortable with a number, 50 is used as an acceptable minimum and several hundred is a good target, if it can be achieved economically. The realities of the situation will determine what can and cannot be done in assembling a sample of sufficient size to use for DFM and DFA comparisons. Further, if it is feasible to produce a large sample, and if it is reasonable to employ statistical design methods, such as the analysis of variance, the power of the DFM/DFA study is enhanced.

The system must be stable by the criteria of SQC. The best quick check on this is to plot the values of the sample in a histogram to see if a unimodal distribution emerges. Bimodality is a clear indication that the system has to be stabilized. Other techniques should be used if possible to assure stability or to help stabilize the system.

Given a stable system, the comparison between the variances of the two designs can be made. The design alternative with the lowest variance in addition to the best tolerance match may give direction to the search for another design alternative. It is best that a P/OM group consisting of designers, process managers, marketing managers, R&D scientists, and development engineers interpret the data and plan for the next set of designs to be produced.

8-9b Changeover Technologies

The technology used for setups and model changeovers is a major process driver. That technology determines the flexibility of the line. If the technology permits, a great number of models can be run in small batches with the cost efficiency of the flow shop, but the variety output of a job shop. DFM can play a crucial role. It allows the choice of a design with excellent setup characteristics instead of accepting a changeover situation by default.

Changeover technologies have been substantially decreasing the time it takes to shift what is being produced from one model to another. The engineering of changeovers, almost always dependent on the creation of new technology, has undergone a major revolution as envisioned by Shingo when he introduced his single-minute exchange of dies (SMED) philosophy.[5] The new setup methods often increase productivity and improve quality at the same time.

Flexible process systems (Section 5-12) epitomize technological flexibility but at a cost which introduces economic and financial rigidity. The key is to find ways to increase the breadth and scope of investments in computerized flexibility. Multi-purpose robots having flexible movement and transfer paths hold promise of achieving economically viable blends of mechanical forces and electronic programming (see Section 8-10).

8-10 New Technologies—Cybernetics

For P/OM to effectively manage technology, it is necessary to distinguish between old technologies and new ones that promise to alter the landscape significantly. Some of the new technologies have been the subject of study for a long time, but recent developments indicate they needed 20 or 30 years to reach the point of practical application. Some new technologies have not yet reached that point.

Cybernetics[6] is the study of similarities between human brains and electronic systems, including sensory devices, computers, and robotic analogs for doing work. It compares the way electronic signals are generated by information in the computer system with the human use of light and sound, among other things. In the human, signals are

Cybernetics
Study of similarities between human attributes and electronic systems.

transmitted between adjacent nerve cells called *neurons*, across a boundary called a *synapse*. The state of the synapse determines whether or not a signal can pass across the boundary. This description has many similarities to electronic systems.

The interdependence of human systems and computer networks provides a new definition for management of technology. The terminology includes the development of:

1 Machines that permit flexible manufacturing and flexible processes
2 *Adaptive systems* that emulate and surpass many human abilities
3 *Neural networks* for creating *artificial intelligence* as well as *learning organizations* and *expert systems*. (**Neural networks** involve computer programs modeled like human synaptic neuron networks.)

8-10a Flexibility—FMS, FOS, FSS, and FPS

Flexible manufacturing systems (FMS) are individual machines and/or groups of machines (called *cells*) that can be programmed to produce a menu of different products. The one thing the products on the menu have in common is the fact that the machine or cell can make all of them when supplied with appropriate tooling.

The changeover times for these computer-controlled systems are negligible, meaning that very small batches (typical of the job shop) can be produced with the economic advantages of serialized flow shops. Theoretically, the batch size can be one. **Flexible office systems (FOS)** and **flexible service systems (FSS)** are also an outgrowth of the new technological capabilities. **Flexible process systems (FPS)** is a generic name for the same technological capability when it is applied to any work situation that utilizes the flexibility concept in a manufacturing or nonmanufacturing environment.

Flexible warehouses are a good example. Areas of the warehouse are not dedicated to particular classes of items. Instead, products can be stored wherever space allows. The computer remembers where the items are by storing the product SKU code, the space code, and the number of units at that location.

With technological flexibility, questions arise concerning how many different products can be produced on the same flexible system. How big is the menu? That seems to depend on the culture of the FPS users. For FMS, American companies use fewer menu options than Japanese firms, which use fewer options than German companies. The numbers are not precise, but they are sufficiently different to override statistical differences. Table 8-2 provides some approximate numbers.[7]

Adaptive capabilities bring flexibility to automated systems. The outputs of these systems are known by the term *mass customization*. This is in contrast to traditional *fixed automation*, which has high changeover costs if changeover is even possible. Fixed systems deliver high-output volumes with good quality, but no variety. Fixed systems are in trouble when demand falls off for the high-volume product they produce.

Fixed-automation does not even permit changeovers at high cost because they have been dedicated to one thing, such as a V8 engine. Ford Motor Company had built such a plant, but could not use it when the petroleum crisis in the 1970s killed the possibility of selling V8 engines.

Neural networks
Models (artificial intelligence) of interconnected decision nodes paralleling the human brain and nervous system.

Flexible manufacturing systems (FMS)
Programmed to produce a menu of different capabilities. Changeover time to move from one menu item to another is negligible because of the computer.

Flexible office systems (FOS)
Office processes are in many ways similar to manufacturing with both job shop batch production and flow shop (or intermittent flow shop) work configurations. When computer controlled, FOS can be designed to change over from one job to another with negligible setup times.

Flexible service systems (FSS)
In quick-service restaurants, theme parks, the U.S. Post Office, FedEx, and UPS, there are ample examples of flexible service systems.

Flexible process systems (FPS)
Generic name for all kinds of computer-controlled robotic and machine systems that can change over to offer a menu of capabilities.

Table 8-2	Germany	Japan	United States
Comparison by Countries: Number of Varieties Produced by the Average FMS	80	50	7

8-10b Expert Systems

Expert systems are *computerized sequences* or strings of intelligent inquiries and answers that are copies of what the "experts" do to solve problems or to accomplish specific kinds of tasks. These smart procedures are developed by copying the way the experts go about solving the problems. The problems are complex so it is necessary to have a means of catching all the details. It is not always clear why experts do what they do. The simplest procedure is to ask.

Ultimately, all of the expert responses will have been obtained and emulated. For complex problems, it can take a long time to piece together the necessary conditions to be able to emulate the expert. The expert system may be dedicated to few or many variants. Different external factors can be encountered. Once completed, expert programs must be tested and debugged.

Consider an insurance expert in marine underwriting. This is a specialized insurance policy writer for ships who knows what questions to ask in order to determine the appropriate premium to charge. The expert system is built to conform to the questions and decisions made by this expert, incorporating experiences with many kinds of ships of different ages and other relevant data.

Figure 8-2 illustrates decision-tree representation of the marine underwriting expert system. Figure 8-2 is a simplified version of the questions that must be asked. After these questions have been answered, the policy situation is identified as one out of 15,552 different possibilities. Real marine underwriters have written policies for each of these situations and determine the appropriate premium in each case. The expert system is therefore able to identify the type of policy and premium that applies.

A list of questions associated with the decision-tree nodes, stages, and phases follows:

0 α—Start when?
1 What type of policy is wanted—*a*, *b*, *c*, or *d*?

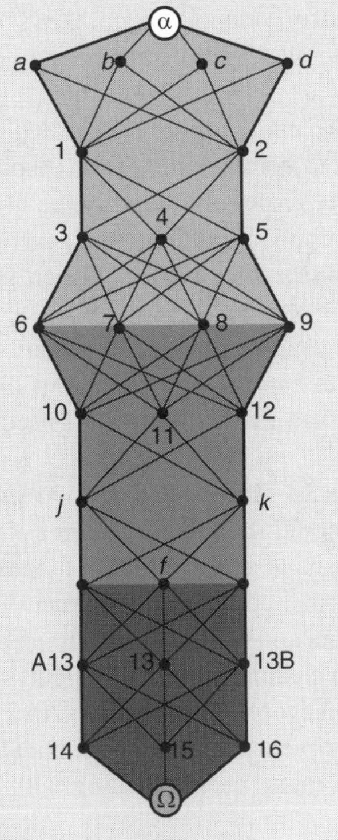

Expert systems
Computerized sequences or strings of intelligent inquiries with answers that are modeled on what "experts" would do to solve specific problems or to accomplish given tasks.

Figure 8-2

Expert System Decision Tree for a Marine Underwriting Application

Subplan Phase 1
First–stage choices

Second–stage choices

Third–stage choices

Subplan Phase 2
First–stage choices

Second–stage choices

Third–stage choices

Subplan Phase 3
First–stage choices

Second–stage choices

Third–stage choices

2 Inboard or outboard engine—1 or 2?
3 What type of ship is it—3, 4, or 5?
4 Where is the ship berthed—6, 7, 8, or 9?
5 What kind of maintenance policy—10, 11, or 12?
6 Fire protection, built-in or portable—*j* or *k*?
7 Type of policy allowed—*e*, *f*, or *g*?
8 Specify computer and GPS optionals—A13, 13, or 13B?
9 Crew training—14, 15, or 16?
10 Are you ready to choose the policy Ω and determine premium?
11 Select Ω and reset system!

This requires obtaining all the necessary information an expert marine underwriter should have to draw up an appropriate maritime insurance policy for vessels of given sizes and characteristics. The variety (in details) of ships to be insured is enormous. Classes of situations must be created to establish coverage and rates to be charged.

Questions are followed by appropriate answers. Once the expert program is written, all of the vessel's specifications can be input to the computer. The program will follow the inquiry to response strings. If successful, it will fill out the policy form and determine the coverage options and premiums to be charged.

These decision trees branch over and over, with many conditional paths leading to highly complex networks. If two more 3-part questions were added to the simple tree shown in Figure 8-2, it would be comprised of 139,968 unique policy situations.

Adding to the complexity are the various paths of best practice for the many kinds of situations that can arise. The networks are converted into computer programs that copy the best practice of experts. They have the advantage of being able to copy more than one expert and then combine all the best results. Expert systems can combine experts of one kind with experts of another kind. Also, an expert system's capabilities can learn and improve with experience.

It is noted that when an expert is confronted with a choice previously made, say *A*, sometimes the expert opinion has changed, or there can be recognition that this time *A* is accompanied by *M* whereas the previous time there was no *M* to consider. The expert now chooses *B*. The database must be amended, and *M* may have to be added as another consideration.

Why are expert systems used? There are many reasons, including the fact that experts are in short supply. Also, expert systems can combine the expertise of more than one person, which results in a meta-expert system. Expert systems can be used to reduce bottlenecks when demand is greater than the supply. Applications to complex manufacturing processes are warranted where there is a shortage of experts. Expert systems augment the selection process.

The fallibility of humans, even experts, can be alleviated. Expert systems can help to eliminate mistakes. Also, an expert system can provide a solution that can be reviewed by a human expert in much shorter time than that expert would need to derive the solution in the first place.

Imagine an expert system that provides an airline pilot with a recommendation about whether or not to land in bad weather. It could save lives. Expert systems can be used to monitor, in moments, complex multidimensional quality control; it could save lives. Expert systems can be used to monitor, in moments, complex multidimensional quality control systems readings that would take many hours and/or days for a human judge to evaluate.

Expert systems can guide ships through channels that are difficult to navigate; monitor and shut down NASA space launches when everything does not check out; provide safety checks (and shutdowns) for nuclear power plants. Expert systems can replace outmoded and archaic organizations that rely on too many people dealing with too much information that needs to be rapidly integrated.

Air traffic control (ATC) is an excellent candidate for expert systems. ATC is a network of people responsible for the position of planes in their sectors, which then get handed over to people in adjacent sectors. Expert systems provide instantaneous and seamless communications, just what is needed to assist the human controllers who at present are too fragmented.

Expert systems can read many controls at the same time and integrate the systems data. The applications of these ideas promise changes in the management of technology that are going to alter substantially the way things are done.

Discussion about expert systems should draw the distinction between them and **artificial intelligence (AI)**. Expert systems are based on copying the procedures of the experts. AI is based on copying the nervous system of humans to develop mechanisms that have the capability of sensing and learning; there are strong analogies to the structure of the brain and the way the brain works.

Mechanisms that are analogous to human nervous systems are called *neural networks*. Neural networks are being designed to enable computers to read handwriting and to emulate the kinds of functions associated with intelligence in human beings. A machine with artificial intelligence should seem intelligent to an intelligent human being.

Part of the mystique of AI is defining a test that will conclusively indicate an intelligent machine. The search for the test is philosophical, and the field has attracted many who are more interested in the means to the end than the end. Still, though there are claims of success, artificial intelligence remains a research area of uncertain value. That does not preclude the fact that there will be increasing applications of intelligent machines in the smart factory and office.

Artificial intelligence (AI)
Based on copying the nervous system of human beings to develop mechanisms that have the capability of sensing and learning.

8-10c Cyborgs and Robots

Cyborg is a coined word that combines the *cyb* of *cyb*ernetics with *org* from *org*anisms. Cybernetic organisms are a form of technology that links people and machines to achieve results neither could otherwise obtain. Someone wearing a pair of reading glasses is a cyborg. Higher-linkage cyborgs occur when the glasses adapt to the amount of light or change focus depending on whether the subject is near or far. Strong cyborg interactions result in greater adaptive behavior on the part of both the person and the machine.

Heroic measures to keep a person alive combine machine technology with the human body as a cybernetic organism. Anyone with a pacemaker is a grateful cyborg. The same principles apply to scuba diving. Air tanks strapped to the diver's back and a breathing device with a regulator that adjusts to depths are crucial to life in an underwater environment.

Jacques Cousteau advanced the technology that permits people to stay underwater for long periods of time. "Cousteau was engaged in an extended stay program in Conshelf III, an 18-foot diameter sphere in which his team of six aquanauts spent 27 days at 328 feet (100 m), followed by a 3-day decompression."[8] Although the predecessors of humanity were likely to have been water breathers, it is not a matter of skill to stay underwater for any length of time. Technology alone makes it possible.

Cousteau and others have pursued the idea that people could be given breathing implants similar to the gills of a fish (tissue capable of absorbing oxygen from water and releasing carbon dioxide from the blood stream). If that ever is done, a better example of a cyborg will be hard to find. Some practical reasons for wanting to be able to live underwater include the ability to mine for minerals and extract oil on the sea floor. Such cyborgs would provide a technological breakthrough.

It is easy to extrapolate to sustaining life in the space lab, on space trips, and in communities on the moon and Mars. Some practical reasons for wanting to be able to live in outer space include the ability to use gravity-free factories to produce products to much

Cyborg
A coined word combining "cyb" from *cybernetics* with "org" from *organism.*

Robots
Evolving from mechanical devices that perform complex, repetitive tasks into computer-controlled systems with broad sensory abilities, discernment, and forms of intelligence.

finer tolerances (i.e., ball bearings). Certain chemicals are dangerous to handle in the Earth's atmosphere, which would be stable on the moon. Various medical conditions would be advantaged by low-gravity treatment centers. Process management will never be the same, given the significant technological changes that will occur.

At the other end of the spectrum are the **robots** that do many jobs in the factory. The painting robots and the welding robots take careful programming to enable them to do the job right for each of the various car models that come down the line. They can change over from the positions required for one model to that of another in nanoseconds. Robots are excellent changeover devices. Consequently, when model flexibility is desired, the construction of robots is warranted.

Still to come (as more than the Roomba® vacuum cleaner of iRobot Corporation) are home-cleaning robots and gardener robots that combine the motor skills of a human with the strength of a machine and the intelligence that a programmer can instill. Already in existence is the healthcare orderly robot (see Section 20-5d).

8-10d The Technology of Computer–User Interfaces

Programming is another illustration of the way technology necessitates bringing together machines interacting with operator skills. Instead of using their hands to set the machines and make them do their work, programmers write the code for the computers that interface with the machines. Because programming is done by people to tell machines what to do, they must both speak the same language.

The technology of computers is hidden from users. Programmers instruct machines by using special languages. When a user clicks a mouse, hundreds or even thousands of lines of code can be the internal response of the system, which is translated into the configuration on the screen.

Even computer-literate users do not understand "machine language." Instead, their literacy is bounded by understanding the software they use. There are enough problems dealing with relatively user-friendly software such as Word, Excel, PowerPoint, WordPerfect, and Lotus. The use of operating systems other than Windows, particularly Unix and Linux, is growing rapidly. There will be continual challenges to the fundamentals of computer literacy.

Programming technology is required for the regulation of factories and offices. It also is critical to make correct machine settings, for control over setups and changeovers, to schedule production, to maintain inventory control, and to schedule maintenance activities. Programming languages needed for these activities are not user friendly.

Individuals take for granted that someone else does the programming and that they can neither change it nor understand all of the assumptions that were made. They have become accustomed to user-friendly desktop publishing, graphics, word processing, spreadsheet calculations, database management, indexing, outlining, and spell checking. Scientists can work at home on simulations, scientific model building and analysis, and myriad other applications of methods so advanced they were once considered feasible only on mainframes.

This form of technology, if it is to be effectively used, requires higher levels of training than the kinds of technology that preceded it. Gone are the skills of tool and die masters who worked the materials by hand. They are replaced by the considerable knowledge required of those who must write machine instructions for CAD/CAM/CAE software for designers. The programs for computer-aided design must be congruent with the programs for computer-aided manufacture because CAM programs convert CAD instructions into directions for factory machinery.

There is every reason to believe that this is just the beginning of powerful wireless office and home network systems. The technology keeps on advancing. Also, coming soon are voice-activated systems that will gradually do away with "archaic" keyboards and mouse controllers.

8-10e   Other New Technology Developments—Materials and Miniaturization

When reference is made to new technology, this usually is taken to mean that an industrial science improvement has occurred in equipment and machinery. For example, Intel and Motorola have continuously increased the power of their computer chips. Usually, new technology replaces existing technology, which results in old technology. Gone are the ancient bulky and weighty calculating machines that were slow and costly.

New technology also relates to stronger and better materials that have been developed. The weight of a typical computer monitor or TV set has been cut by more than 80 percent since practical LED screens emerged. Automotive and aircraft designers have reduced the weight cars and planes markedly. To do this, glass, plastics, aluminum, and laminates have been used extensively.

Miniaturization was originally pioneered by Sony for its own product line. It caught on and every product was reduced in size and weight. To make small products requires processes that can fabricate and assemble miniaturized parts. This has led to new process equipment. Yet, a new wave of miniaturization is on the horizon. The field of applied science that deals with nano-sized particles (smaller than 1 micrometer) is known as **nanotechnology**.

Nanotechnology is very diverse in what it contains. Applications include health care, fabric treatments, computer chips, cosmetics, and suntan lotions. Google nanotechnology to read the Wikipedia entry. It describes the origin of the field, its fundamental concepts, as well as the long-term assessment regarding the future of this technology.

Improvements in management qualify as new industrial arts.[9] Technologies and methodologies blend into each other providing improvements in quality and productivity. Accordingly, TQM, MRP, JIT, and SMED are all replete with technological inventions. Some of these acronyms are yet to come in the readings ahead.

Nanotechnology
The incipient science of very small particles leading to processes that provide surface modification, drug delivery, internal medical probes, and other dramatically new products.

Spotlight 8-1   An Entrepreneur's Story

In enormous numbers, career seekers are turning their backs on the so-called security of corporate life. Opting to be their own bosses, U.S. citizens from all backgrounds have chosen a riskier path: entrepreneurship. Over 672,000 new companies with employees were started in 2005 and the trend is increasing. As Phaedra Hise writes in *Fortune Small Business* (FSB) dated February 1, 2007, "Everyone is partaking of this surge—women, minorities, immigrants, teenagers, and corporate refugees alike." She believes that no nation compares to the United States in terms of its willingness to accept risk-takers in society.

Small businesses are the engine of our national economy. They hire a larger percentage of employees and contribute a greater percentage of tax revenue to our government than any other business grouping. The current entrepreneurial boom is more diverse than the mid-1990's surge of technology start-ups. However, the risks are still high. According

to the U.S. Small Business Administration, over 540,000 small businesses closed in 2005. This Spotlight tells the story of one man who chose to build his own plumbing firm and succeeded in establishing a profitable and well-founded small business.

Frank John Bracco was born in the Sheepshead Bay neighborhood of Brooklyn, New York. His hard-working parents provided a loving and caring life for the family, but there was nothing in the family budget for Frank and his four siblings in terms of higher education. In 1960, his family relocated to New Jersey. Until he was 14, Frank delivered newspapers, painted houses, worked for a moving company, and did landscaping jobs. The rule in the Bracco home was simple. Half of the money earned goes into the family budget.

After graduating from high school in 1969 and a short stint as a truck driver, Frank chose plumbing as a career direction. His first job as helper brought him $2.00 per hour. As an apprentice for a contractor from the U. S. General Service Administration, Frank was a fast learner. He endured the harsh winters of New York, working on many

Spotlight 8-1 (Continued)

commercial jobs including a project at the Statue of Liberty. Frank's perseverance and his increasing skills and abilities led to a journeyman position which enables the title-bearer to take full responsibility of a skilled craftsman.

As the door was opening for him to move up to master craftsman and contractor, Frank Bracco looked at his options. Already it was evident that his salary would not be enough to raise a family. The days of post–World War II America had come and gone and the entire country was changing demographically. America's middle class was more like "Friends," with single status becoming a larger percentage of the population. Unlike his coworkers, Frank gambled on his vision of a better future. Leaving friends and family behind, he moved to Central Florida in October 1972.

Before leaving, Frank knew there was one important relationship that needed his attention. Frank and Sherril had met in high school. He had never forgotten her. Frank set out to do whatever he could to persuade her to join him in Florida. They married in 1975. One day after their marriage, Sherril said to Frank, "We're here. Now what are we going to do?" He replied, "We are going to build a business." Modern Plumbing was founded by Frank Bracco out of the back of their car with a commitment to deliver a quality product.

In the days, months, and years that followed, Frank and Sherril were busy. Word-of-mouth from satisfied customers served as advertising. The company incorporated in 1979, becoming Modern Plumbing and Irrigation, Inc., with approximately 10 employees including office and staff. Knowing that his reputation for quality work was the basis for his success, he followed his father's advice: "I gave you two things, your name and your credit. Don't mess them up!" The business grew steadily.

In the early 1980's, Modern Plumbing and Irrigation increased to nearly 70 employees to cover production of 600 residential homes per year. New equipment and site development were added to meet the demand of residential communities. U.S. Homes became one of their customers by 1980. In 1983, interest rates skyrocketed to 18 percent, and the demand for residential homes fell. The number of employees plummeted to six. A few years later, the company added fire protection to their line. By 1985, the number of company employees had increased to 20.

There was no one to caution Frank about the sheer effort it would take to adapt to changing business conditions. With two divisions to manage plus site development, his work had become a constant marathon. There were 16-hour workdays, some without profit. Many projects required more attention than expected. Twice the new company came close to bankruptcy. Entrepreneurial pressures finally took their toll. In 1987 Frank had a triple bypass heart operation.

In the hospital, Frank had time to reassess his priorities. He decided that three business divisions were deflecting energy away from the company's core competency. He closed the irrigation, site development, and fire protection lines in 1989. In 1990 he gave the company a new name: Modern Plumbing Industries, Inc. The company implemented profit-sharing as a means of sharing the company's success with the employees who made it possible. Focusing exclusively on plumbing and piping in the commercial, institutional, and custom-built residential home market, business prospered.

In 1995, Frank was faced with a difficult decision. Should he accept a contract for a huge project that would use all his men and resources for a long and indeterminate time? He had learned the hard way that growth is good but has to be controlled with certain other factors such as continued service to current customers and avoidance of overcommitting his employees and resources. Balancing these factors, he turned down the tempting offer.

When his company began, there was no one to ask for advice. As Modern Plumbing became a well-known and respected enterprise, friendships with contractors and owners led to conversations about new methods in the industry. Trade associations offered opportunities to learn from peer groups and invited members to think "outside the box" to better manage their businesses. Topics discussed in these meetings were employee management, training, profitability, insurance management, contract language, and job cost management. What was learned from these contacts saved time spent reinventing the wheel. Since good business decisions rely on accurate cost and time estimates for projects, Frank made sure that his estimators were the best in the business. He kept his accounting simple and did his own payroll.

Sherril's support and belief in Frank never wavered during the years of entrepreneurship. A son was born, followed by a daughter and then a son. All siblings are college graduates. Tracey, their daughter, is now a lawyer. Their two sons have joined their father's business. Charles, who had worked in his father's company since he was 15, is now responsible for the office. Anthony focuses on education and learning construction. Both Charles and Anthony have contributed their own unique abilities to the management team. They both practice their father's leadership philosophy.

A spirit of cooperation exists between father and sons (no prima donna behavior in the Bracco family). Although disagreements are welcome in private, family rules prevail. Communication is on two levels, personal and business.

Never discuss personal matters in front of employees. Keep your word. Maintain trust. In Frank Bracco's philosophy, family, employees, and community are all related. Simple rules produce the best results.

In 2005 a new program called Helper Training was created. It enables current helpers to get on the same page and new helpers to get up to speed on basics. The first module of training is the history of plumbing as well as the history of the company. The rest of the 6-module course introduces helpers to materials and their application to various plumbing systems.

By 2007, Modern Plumbing Industries, Inc., had 110 employees working on large commercial or major renovation projects, and the company had added some residential custom homes as well. The business had earned many safety awards along with an excellent workers' compensation rating modifier. Modern Plumbing's field technicians and office staff enjoy high quality benefits equaling the best of large corporations. Among the many benefit listings: 100% medical insurance, life insurance, short-term disability, matching 401(k) program, bonuses, and a generous number of annual paid days off including vacation with a carry-over provision. Profits continue to be equally divided between employees, shareholders, and retained earnings. The company makes regular donations to local charities. Most important is Frank's relationship with his employees. As a mentor, he encourages them to use every opportunity for education and advancement.

Over the years, Frank Bracco has become a successful entrepreneur. With support from his family and the respect and loyalty of company employees, Frank Bracco's company has provided satisfaction to his customers and the community he serves. Based on a commitment to quality and a few simple rules, the Bracco philosophy can be applied by anyone who is contemplating his or her own business.

To all of us who take our plumbing, heating, cooling, and refrigeration for granted, a bit of history will remind us of the importance of these industries in maintaining our quality of life. Without water, there is no life. Contaminated drinking water has always been a major worldwide problem. In 312 BC, the ancient Romans began building aqueducts to provide citizens with fresh water 1,500 years before the use of electricity and gas heat. The craft and

science of plumbing has supported our civilization and health for countless years.

It was in the 1880s that a transition from outhouses to indoor plumbing moved rapidly in the United States. Specialized plumbing skills developed and evolved into one of our most important and essential industries. These skills protect the health of our country. Today, with declining numbers of trainees entering the field along with an aging workforce, the Carl D. Perkins Career and Technical Education Improvement Act of 2006 was passed almost unanimously by the U.S. House and Senate. The act encourages young people to consider a craftsman's career as a well-paid and valuable occupation.

One of the goals of the Perkins Act was to provide individuals with opportunities throughout their lifetimes to develop, in conjunction with other education and training programs, the knowledge and skills needed to keep the United States competitive.

Reflecting on the success of Frank Bracco's leadership provides a great start in achieving these goals.

Review Questions

1 Why is entrepreneurship described as "riskier" than working as a salaried employee for an existing business?

2 If estimators do not make accurate projections of costs and times for plumbing jobs, what are the consequences? There is a 30-day trial at http://www.phccweb.org for the PHCC Labor Calculator. What does that imply regarding this question?

3 Explain how generational differences might affect Modern Plumbing, Inc.

4 What kinds of training are available for the plumbing industry?

5 What makes a successful entrepreneur? Use Frank Bracco as a model.

6 The number of business start-up failures in 2007 was large. Why was this so?

Sources: Carl D. Perkins Career and Technical Education Act: http://www.acteonline.org; Conversations with Frank, Charles, Anthony, Sherril, and Tracey Bracco, April 2007; History Channel DVD, "Modern Marvels—Plumbing: The Arteries of Civilization, Cat No. AAE-76477.

Spotlight 8-2 The Race for Next-Generation Technology

By congressional mandate issued in 2001, one-third of all ground combat vehicles must be able to operate unassisted by 2015. DARPA, the Defense Advanced Research Projects Agency, is the central research and development organization for the U.S. Department of Defense. DARPA has handed out millions of dollars to contractors for new designs for robotic land vehicles with little to show for it. Because no military contractor was able to meet the challenge, the Defense Department placed a $1 million dollar bet that someone outside the military establishment could produce an autonomous ground vehicle that navigates and drives entirely on its own with no human driver and no remote control. If successful, it would be the vehicle of choice for the U.S. Army and, at the same time, open the gates of opportunity for civilian use undreamed of at this moment.

The first Grand Challenge for Autonomous Ground Vehicles was designed as a field test for mobile robotic contestants to travel a route chosen by DARPA within a 10-hour time limit over rugged desert-like terrain. Such vehicles could assist and save the lives of U.S. armed forces on the battlefield.

On March 13, 2004, the first contest was scheduled. It pitted 15 challengers against one another in a race for the 7-figure bounty. Most applicants were sponsored by universities, large corporations, or small investor groups. Some were private hobbyists using their own funds. Their unmanned vehicles were required to perform general route selection and navigation as they followed the Challenge route over the rough terrain of the Mojave Desert from Barstow, California, to Las Vegas. Speed was the deciding factor, and the 10-hour time limit was designed to push vehicle speeds far beyond current technologies.

The 2004 route covered 200 miles. A series of waypoints would define a corridor within which the vehicles had to remain. The corridor width varied from miles to small passageways of 10 feet and was designed to test the robot vehicles across open terrain, winding trails, and paved roads. Ashlee Vance, in the October 9, 2003, edition of *The New York Times*, described what DARPA expected from the competition. A robotic vehicle must be able to "sense" its environment, instantly perceiving terrain features, ground conditions, obstacles, and other vehicles. It must see, steer, accelerate, brake, and navigate on its own, with guidance only from a series of global positioning system (GPS) coordinates. The coordinates would be given to the competing teams by DARPA two hours before the race. Immediately, each team would enter the data into computers on its vehicle and then turn over the vehicle to DARPA.

As scheduled on the morning of March 13, 2004, the robotic vehicles started with 20 yards between them, each governed by an on–off system. They had to guide themselves from one GPS point to the next, passing around or over ditches, water, rocks, barbed wire, and other vehicles. To meet DARPA requirements, the machines were required to average at least 20 miles an hour over all, while avoiding houses and other buildings.

Of the challengers in the 2004 race, one relatively low-cost approach was taken by two partners calling themselves Team Phantasm. One partner was a calibrator of electrical instruments and (as a hobby) created robots for the Battle-Bots competition, where machines fight each other to destruction. The other was a semi-retired programmer and network administrator who liked to write software. Using gear donated by Kawasaki Motors, the two men built their all-terrain vehicle with a dome made of bulletproof material that opened up like flower petals, with the capability of righting itself if it tipped over. Their budget was $50,000.

The Carnegie Mellon group, known as the Red Team, had millions of dollars and a long list of corporate sponsors. William "Red" Whittaker, a professor at Carnegie Mellon's Robotic Institute, was known for his pioneering in building unmanned machines. Some of his work included building robots to investigate hazardous waste sites and building systems for planetary exploration. More than 30 fellow faculty members and students worked with him to outfit a 1986 Hummer with the latest autonomous technology for the Grand Challenge.

Despite the enthusiasm and competitive spirit of the 15 teams that participated in the 2004 race, there were no winners. None could complete the route. Most of the teams generally wished they had more money, like Team Arctic Tortoise from Alaska. Some hoped to start businesses as a result of their work. Before the race, Professor Whittaker was quoted as saying, "I don't know whether there will be a winner, but there aren't going to be any losers."

Future Grand Challenge events were scheduled every 18 months until a team won or there were no more funds or contestants. All vehicles were to be developed without government funding. It was agreed that DARPA would retain "right of first access" to winning technology, but teams would retain ownership of their intellectual property. For the next race, DARPA made the course harder and doubled the former prize, offering $2 million to the team whose autonomous vehicle could successfully complete the route faster than its rivals within a 10-hour period.

The second Grand Challenge was scheduled for October 8, 2005, with applicants representing 36 states and 4 foreign countries. DARPA was delighted with the large number of contestants. Out of 195 applicants, 43 semifinalists were invited to compete in a National Qualification Event (NQE) held at the California Speedway in Fontana, California, in September of 2005. The NQE eliminated all but 23 finalists. A site near Primm, Nevada, was chosen as the starting point for the difficult circuitous 132-mile route through the Mojave Desert.

At 6:30 A.M. PDT on Saturday, October 8, 2005, the Grand Challenge race began with the distribution of CDs containing the GPS route coordinates for each vehicle's computer system. Spectators, participants, and well-wishers watched with excitement as they gathered to witness an event that many believed was equivalent to the Wright brothers' first flight. The roads chosen were deliberately rough and dangerous, with three tunnels that challenged the vehicles' global positioning systems and devices. Autonomous computer control systems on board used the latest sensing devices, lasers, cameras, and radar to enable the robots to make intelligent decisions as each vehicle navigated paths with dangerous boulders. Would the robotic controller sense the difference between a rock and a tumbleweed? Could it calculate whether a crevice was too deep to cross?

Vehicles that failed to finish the 132-mile route either veered off-route or crashed into an obstacle, despite a safety feature that allowed them to stop the 10-hour clock without penalty. Some lost their sensor devices during one jolt too many. One failed in less than 10 minutes. Someone had neglected to activate the machine's stabilizing system before the start signal.

"The impossible has been achieved," Sebastian Thrun shouted, as Stanley, his team's autonomous Volkswagen Touareg R5, crossed the finish line on October 8, 2005, clocking an average of 19.1 miles per hour. The Stanley Racing Team, composed of faculty and students from Stanford's School of Engineering, cheered the victory, having seen failure 18 months earlier. At that time, no vehicle had been able to complete more than 7.4 miles. In this race, five vehicles crossed the finish line; four made it within 10 hours, while the fifth valiantly returned the next day to finish the route in 12 hours, 51 minutes.

Professor Thrun, director of the Stanford Artificial Intelligence Laboratory and leader of the Stanley Racing Team, had watched on his computer as his winner maneuvered 132 miles in 6 hours and 54 minutes, finishing the course and taking first place among the four contestants that completed the chosen route within the required time.

Thrun, 38, is well-qualified as a pioneer in the field of probabilistic robotics. He programs his machines to adjust their responses to incoming data based on the probability that the data are correct. In 1998, as he was programming a tour-guide robot to navigate a crowded museum, he realized that true intelligence is knowledge of one's own ignorance. Like humans, robots will always make mistakes in an inherently unpredictable world.

Model-based robots can't simulate real-world complexity. Reactive robots lack the ability to plan ahead. Thrun began to program his machines to adjust their responses according to the degree of probability that the incoming data were correct. Even though Stanley was outfitted with radar, cameras, and GPS, there was a moment when the robot's sensors misinterpreted incoming data as the vehicle approached the edge of a cliff. Thrun's road-finding and obstacle-recognition software judged the data to have a significant probability of error and the vehicle responded instead to its separate laser readings, successfully avoiding disaster.

"Before, it was a question if we would ever be able to create cars that drive themselves," said Thrun after the race. "Now it's a question of when."

Sandstorm took second place, crossing the finish line in 7 hours, 5 minutes. Built by Carnegie-Mellon University's Red Team, Sandstorm was the 1986 Hummer veteran of the previous Grand Challenge. Red Team had given Sandstorm a new engine and suspension, as well as a special platform that protected delicate sensors from jolts and bumps.

Ten minutes after Sandstorm crossed the line, Carnegie-Mellon's second entry placed third at 7 hours, 15 minutes. Rebuilt by Red Team Too using a 1999 Hummer, this vehicle was equipped with a fast networking capability called CANbus with multiple microcontrollers communicating with one another. On both vehicles, sensors fused laser and radar data into a composite model of surrounding terrain, identifying less navigable areas. Also, an array of moving sensors probed hard-to-find areas that might have been missed by fixed sensors.

Both CMU teams were again under the leadership of robotics professor William Whittaker. Players included a project manager, Michele Gittleman, and more than 50 CMU undergrad and graduate students. Boeing, Caterpillar, and Intel sponsored the effort, which gave the teams an unofficially reported several-million-dollar budget. Professor Whittaker, known for his military-style rigor, is quoted as saying, "The question isn't just 'Can you do it?' It's 'Can you do it on any given day, in any circumstances, under any conditions, on any route?'"

Sponsored by the Gray Insurance Company, the popular finisher Gray Bot took fourth place with a 2005 Ford Escape hybrid built by the Kat-5 Gray team from the New Orleans suburb of Metairie. Despite the upheavals of Hurricane Katrina and the fact that some team members' homes had been damaged by the storm, the Kat-5 vehicle finished in 7 hours, 30 minutes.

The Grand Challenge program manager, Ron Kurjanowicz, was quoted at the end of the contest as saying, "The camaraderie and competitiveness that have been the hallmark of the Grand Challenge since its inception demonstrates America's heritage of resourcefulness. It is a truly powerful

Spotlight 8-2 (Continued)

mix of American ingenuity, team spirit, competitiveness, entrepreneurship, engineering, and computer science."

Ron Kurjanowicz emphasized his conviction that the Grand Challenge has stimulated the creation of a new community of innovators—inventors, mechanics, computer scientists, students, and engineers—who typically have not been involved with DARPA's activities.

DARPA's director Dr. Tony Tether congratulated all the teams for their dedication and hard work. He said, "You have made history. Your work could change the face of human transportation forever."

Many of the participants commented on the fact that reliable driverless vehicles could also have multiple civilian applications. Sebastian Thrun declared that self-driven cars could save up to 43,000 lives lost on U.S. roads each year. In a statement to the press, he said, "Self-driven cars will be much safer as they will not be subject to human error as they are now." Dr. Thrun hopes to design a car capable of driving from San Francisco to Los Angeles in real traffic within a few years.

On November 3, 2007, DARPA's third Grand Challenge competition was held. It was called the Urban Grand Challenge, featuring autonomous ground vehicles conducting simulated military supply missions in a mock urban environment. The winning vehicle, named Boss, was sponsored by an alliance called Tartan Racing. The team was led by Dr. William "Red" Whitaker from Carnegie-Mellon who accepted the $2 million prize. To see videos and documents of the 2007 race go to http://www.grandchallenge.org. In summary, a safer future of transportation is in the making through competition and cooperation.

Review Questions

1 Governmental organizations are calling upon private citizens, small companies, and academia to take a crack at solving problems that large military-industrial companies do not seem able to solve. From repair and replacement of our infrastructure to space travel, what are the main impediments that block initiative for funding and accomplishing timely projects? Is bureaucracy an impediment? Explain your answer.

2 Why would anyone prefer to compete in a DARPA-like competition rather than play the lottery to win $2 million dollars? Are the odds better to successfully design a robotic vehicle to guide itself at a decent speed across obstacle-laden, rough desert terrain than to win at roulette?

3 Can you describe a different example of next-generation technology development by private sources that has received major press attention? Note Review Question 1.

4 What were the conceptual and technical problems associated with winning the DARPA award?

5 Relate DARPA-type product development and project management.

6 What does the DARPA competition have to do with transition management?

Sources: Ashlee Vance. "Robotic Road Trip on a Military Mission." *The New York Times* (October 9, 2003); http://www.darpa.mil/grandchallenge; http://www.darpa.mil/grandchallenge/index.asp. To see videos of the 2005 race, go to http://www.grandchallenge.org and click "Downloads." Then click "Stanley Video" and others from a list of videos and documents. If you have Windows Media Player, you can view the action on your screen as the robotic machines make their way across bridges and rough terrain. WebCasts of the race can be found at the same site. http://www.stanfordracing.org; Report to Congress: DARPA Prize Authority, March 2006. For the 2007 competition, go to http://www.grandchallenge.org or http://www.darpa.mil/grandchallenge/Teams/TartanRacing.asp.

Summary

Chapter 8 explains why P/OM must understand how to manage technology. Technology is one of two crucial components of the input–output transformation model. The two components are people with production skills and technology with engineering capabilities to improve upon what people can do. Managing the combination is an awesome P/OM responsibility.

There is a technology trap. New technology is often applied to the management of old (legacy) systems without changing the legacy methods. The results range from wasteful to unfavorable. Technological upgrading requires excellence in timing. Holding on to the status quo results in using sophisticated means for killing the adoption of new technology when it should be adopted—and adapted.

Illustrations of new technology are applied to various industries including food preparations and windshields. Levels of technological sophistication are explored for the replacement versus the original market (OEM) requirements and the supply chain technology appropriate to each. The technology of packaging and delivery is included, as is the technology of testing and quality assurance technology. The technologies of design for manufacturing (DFM) and design for assembly (DFA) are explored, including a tolerance matching example for evaluating and selecting the preferred design.

Discussion of managing technology could not be complete without mention of changeover technologies and description of the technologies including cybernetics, flexible processing systems, expert systems, cyborgs, robots, and nanotechnology.

Spotlight 8-1 describes technology that we take for granted even though it is continuously developing and is critical for the well-being of society. This spotlight is about an entrepreneur who built his own plumbing firm into a profitable and successful small business. Spotlight 8-2 points out that technology development can be accelerated by proper governmental incentives without intervention in the invention process. This technology for driverless cars can have a profound effect on road safety.

Key Terms

Artificial intelligence (AI) (p. 301)
Cybernetics (p. 297)
Cyborg (p. 301)
Design for assembly (DFA) (p. 295)
Design for manufacturing (DFM) (p. 295)
Empirical testing (p. 294)
Expert systems (p. 299)
Flexible manufacturing systems (FMS) (p. 298)
Flexible office systems (FOS) (p. 298)
Flexible process systems (FPS) (p. 298)
Flexible service systems (FSS) (p. 298)

Management of technology (MOT) (p. 284)
Nanotechnology (p. 303)
Net present value (NPV) (p. 287)
Neural networks (p. 298)
OEM (p. 290)
Payback period (p. 286)
Robots (p. 302)
Simulation (p. 294)
Technology (p. 284)
Technology trap (p. 285)
Tolerance matching (p. 296)
VARs (p. 282)

Review Questions

1 What are the effects of rapid technological change?
2 How is technology a component of the I/O transformation?
3 Explain the management of technology in three ways: a. personal and societal, b. company, and c. international levels.
4 What is the technology trap?
5 What are the basic elements of good packaging and how do they relate to the management of technology?
6 What are shakedown risks?
7 How does packaging relate to the supply chain and what is supply chain technology?

8   What is the technology status of a glass blower?
9   When is the advantage of having a reputation for being a technology leader likely to pay off?
10   What is good technology timing?
11   Why is P/OM concerned about the licensing of technology? Relate the answer to an example.
12   How is NPV used to kill a new technology project?
13   Why is NPV used and can it be misused?
14   Relate P/OM's management of technology to R&D.
15   Compare the effects of replacement and original market demands on MOT.
16   What should be done about delivery processes that increase defective rates?
17   Discuss P/OM's responsibilities with respect to testing technology.
18   What steps need to be taken to achieve DFM and DFA?
19   What are pilot studies?
20   Describe some new technologies.
21   How do expert systems work? Does P/OM have any use for them?
22   What methods are available for assessing the technology plans of competitors?
23   What is the difference between payback period, breakeven time, and the cost recovery period?
24   Explain why it is considered better to change technologies when the development cycles enter a period of relative stability instead of during periods of volatility.

Problems Section

Note: This section has various problems that can be formulated and solved using QuantMethods Production/Operations Management software (QMpom). The appropriate model categories are indicated for each problem.

1   Bursting strength and product support (within the container) are measured for two different package designs called A and B. The container will be used to ship printers by air.

	Bursting Strength (BS)	Product Support (PS)
Box A	100 test	8
Box B	200 test	6

a. Assume that the computed value of the package design V is modeled as follows: $V = (BS)(PS)^2$ and the biggest number is the best. What does the scoring model value of each package indicate? Which box is best?

b. It has been stated that the product support number (6) for Box B should be reduced to (5) if the shipment is made by sea. Recent strategy calls for sending 70 percent of these printers by sea and 30 percent by air. (Using the QMpom module called Decision Theory Models (Decision Analysis) will facilitate solving this situation.)

2   Using the same questions as in Problem 1, answer parts a and b for the following table:

	Bursting Strength (BS)	Product Support (PS)
Box A	100 test	10
Box B	200 test	6

In this case, the product support number (10) for Box A is cut in half and the number (6) for Box B is reduced to (5) as in Problem 1. Also, the strategy calls for sending 80 percent of the printers by sea and 20 percent by air.
As in Problem 1, using the QMpom module called Decision Theory Models (Decision Analysis) will facilitate solving Problem 2.

3

a. Compare technologies as follows: Turn on various computers and note the time it takes each to boot up. The distribution of times will represent a range of setup times for the computer. How variable are these setup times? Explain the meaning of this exercise to the management of technology by P/OM.

b. Is it reasonable to compare word processors (as technology) by the following method? Test how long it takes each word processor—on the same computer—to do the same task, such as repositioning from the first page to the fiftieth page of a 100-page document.

4   Use a multiplicative scoring model ($V_{D_i} = L_i^2 T_i^3$) to evaluate alternative designs with respect to excellence for DFM and DFA. Table 8-3 presents the Loose (L) and Tight (T) categories for tolerance matching with three different designs. Assume that ideal looseness is 0.10 and ideal tightness is 0.03. The importance weights are given in the equation for Looseness (L) and Tightness (T).

    The preference is for small numbers overall.

i	T_i	W_i	Loose	Tight	**Table 8-3**
Design 1	0.5 ± 0.05	0.6 ± 0.04	0.19	0.01	Tolerance Matching for Key of Thickness T_i in Slot of Width W_i for Designs $i = 1, 2, 3$
Design 2	0.5 ± 0.02	0.6 ± 0.04	0.16	0.04	
Design 3	0.6 ± 0.01	0.6 ± 0.04	0.05	−0.05	

5   Calculate the payback period for a technology expense of $1 million if the new technology immediately starts to earn revenues of $100,000 per month. Operating costs plus depreciated fixed costs are estimated to be $30,000 per month. How does this payback period differ from the cost recovery period?

    Using the QMpom model called Capacity Management Models (Breakeven and/or Cost-Volume) will facilitate solving Problem 5.

6   Create an expert system for determining an optimal diet for anyone interested. Build a decision tree such as the one shown in Figure 8-2.

7   Show how Figure 8-2, which designs an expert system for marine underwriting, leads to 15,552 uniquely different situations.

8   With respect to the material in Problem 7, explain the statement that two more 3-part questions would lead to 139,968 uniquely different situations.

9   With respect to the material in Problem 8, how many uniquely different situations would three more 3-part questions yield?

10   Why is air traffic control (ATC) an excellent candidate for expert system support?

Practice Quiz

1   The management of technology (MOT) is an important P/OM responsibility. What forms does this responsibility take? All but one of the answers below is correct. Which answer is incorrect?

   a. Skills and technology blend together. Management must determine the right balance to use for job accomplishment, and this changes over time.

   b. Society depends on management knowledge about the employment of technology for health, safety, and security. Services include transportation, health care, and education. Management of intellectual capital (in the form of patents) is another instance of social requirements.

   c. Management of technology within the firm is often the crucial factor in determining competitive advantage or disadvantage. When to adopt the next generation technology is paramount in every manager's mind.

   d. Management of technology for P/OM at the firm level does not involve patents. There are lawyers to take care of the legal questions and accountants to determine the value of intellectual capital.

   e. Management of technology at the international level is broadened by the fact that countries outside the United States provide patent protection to their own nationals, and the laws of these countries may not align perfectly with those of the United States. In addition, appropriate technology for manufacturing may differ according to the blend of skills and technology that exists in different parts of the world. Manufacturing plants in China have quite different technology levels than those in the United States.

2   Technology management is challenging. Some of the problems associated with the management of technology are listed in a. through e. Which one statement is incorrect?

   a. Technology changes tend to occur in clusters. This is because opportunities to get into a new field bring many entrepreneurs to the marketplace where they innovate. This leads to improvements upon improvements. The market decides what it likes.

b.   Tomorrow's technology can make obsolete what was brand new today. This discontinuity can be a pitfall for those who invest in everything that is new. Picking correctly is a P/OM responsibility.

c.   The hypothesis about disruptive technologies includes the fact that customers may not immediately embrace the fruits of new technology. This sends a signal to companies that they should maintain course with what their customers like. A company that listens to the voice of the customer may be out of the running when the tune that voice is singing suddenly changes. Google "disruptive technologies."

d.   The technology trap is a common phenomenon in which new equipment is put to work running old systems and procedures without studying the opportunities to change the systems and procedures in line with capabilities of the new technology.

e.   Postponement of new technology investments is often reasonable when learning can be achieved with minimum costs and disruption, and it is clear that infringement is not a possible competitor's complaint.

3   When is being second in the application of new technology on behalf of the company's customers a reasonable management of technology strategy? Which answer below is wrong?

a.   Development costs are high and patent protection is not likely to shelter the first to market with a new product design or product derived from a new process.

b.   Shakedown is testing a system being used for the first time (as a shakedown cruise for a new aircraft carrier). It is also testing an existing system to which new features have been added. The test is intended to uncover faults and defects. Shakedown is also used for training in new technology. All aspects of shakedown are hard on the first customers. The penalties can be reduced significantly by being second in line.

c.   If the expected lifetime of use is much longer than the payback period, it is often reasonable to avoid the burden of being first.

d.   If company A is first and companies B, C, etc., can easily imitate what company A has done without paying consequences such as infringement penalties, then there is reason for company A to question being the first to develop the new technology. Other factors must be present to make any one company decide to be first. That reason could be related to indirect benefits. Support for the supersonic Concorde by Britain and France (long ago) established the company that makes the Airbus now. There is no doubt that the reputation of Airbus was enhanced in a major way by the Concorde because Boeing never developed a supersonic plane. The Concorde, which first flew in 1976, was built by a European consortium led by the British Aircraft Corporation and the French Sud Aviation.

e.   If many years are required for the development of new technology, there must be government support (as was the case for Concorde). When Bell Labs developed the transistor, it was recognized that decades would be required for one firm to develop that technology. As a result, AT&T's Bell Labs invited interested companies to a conference at which this new technology was given to all companies that wanted to participate in developing transistors.

4   A comparison between two alternative technologies is being made. Which one statement about such comparisons is incorrect?

a.   Comparing savings using net present value (NPV), the investment cost would be in present dollars, and the savings stream would be the sum of continually decreasing amounts of money as savings are realized month after month in the future. Also, it is necessary to subtract maintenance (and other) costs. They should be discounted to the same degree as the savings in each specific future time period. The technology to select is the alternative that has greater savings.

b.   Payback periods can be compared. Using this method, the amount to be paid back would be in present dollars. The savings stream is summed without discounting for the expected lifetime of the new technology and its savings. Also, it is necessary to subtract maintenance (and other) costs from the savings that are being summed. The technology selected will have the shortest period of time to pay back the investment.

c.   Total cost recovery periods can be compared. The same computations that were used with payback periods apply because savings minus maintenance (and other) costs are identical to the payback amounts. Choose the alternative that promises the shortest time interval to achieve total cost recovery of the investment in technology.

d.   Comparisons of savings (whether they are discounted or not) are suspect because a variety of factors like the costs of materials, energy, and labor are not locked in over time. This warning is especially noteworthy if the savings are estimated to continue over a long time period (say, more than 20 years). The only way to make these calculations believable is to pinpoint the sources of savings and to estimate how they will change over the savings horizon.

e.   Interest rates play a major part in net present value calculations, so it is necessary to estimate how interest rates will change over time. Forecasting interest rates is so challenging that some analysts prefer to use sensitivity analysis to bracket the most probable range of interest rates. Then, upper- and lower-bound NPVs can be used to compare alternative technologies.

5 There are many different materials that illustrate the shift from art-based skills to technology-based processes. Among these are steel, rubber, paper, and glass. The developments in glass making are as dramatic as can be found because at the skill level, glass work is highly regarded as artistry. On the other hand, advanced technology for automotive windshield glass illustrates a mastery over materials for commercial use. With respect to these issues, only one of the following statements about materials technology is wrong. Which option is incorrect?

a. Dale Chihuly is a world-renowned glass artist with custom-made creations that are magnificent. His Seattle studio is famous for apprenticeship training and its output, which demonstrates total mastery of glass skills. See http://www.chihuly.com.

b. In 1959, the British firm of Pilkington introduced entirely new glass technology called the float process for making flat glass. The continuous ribbon of glass (melted sand) floated on a bath of melted tin. The new process became the primary method for making flat glass worldwide, replacing casting, rolling, and polishing glass, a process with many imperfections. A major decline in the skill to technology ratio occurred.

c. To fabricate large glass windshields requires a mixture of high levels of labor skills with corresponding levels of technology. Production for original use and replacement markets use highly mechanized, mass-production flow shops.

d. Using advanced technology, some windshields are made without human labor in entirely automated systems. These applications have the further advantage of not requiring car and windshield designers to consult with manufacturers, which saves the expense of designing for manufacturing (DFM).

e. Float glass (house windows) is the starting component for automotive glass, which requires higher levels of technology than household glass. Safety glass is required in the United States. It is a sandwich of two pieces of float glass (called lites) that are annealed and then cooled for strength. Placed between the inboard and outboard lites is a polyvinyl butyryl laminate. The sandwich is bonded by heat and pressure.

6 OEM (original equipment manufacturer) describes a company that produces hardware to be installed and sold under a different company name. Computers like Dell, IBM, HP, and Compaq are filled with such parts. Sometimes the part is marketed under the name of the purchaser from the OEM. See, for example, http://www.cnet.com/Resources/Info/Glossary/Terms/oem.html.

Windshields are bought from many large glass manufacturers and installed by GM, Ford, Toyota, etc. On the other hand, the replacement market for glass windshields is less high volume with hundreds of models. Similarities exist with the tire market. For both tires and windshields, distribution requires many different dealerships. The characteristics of the replacement market are described in the following choices, but one of the statements is inaccurate. Which statement is faulty?

a. It is essential to be able to forecast with some accuracy the demand for each year and model of car. Windshields are not standardized items. Further, demands will differ by region of the country because brands and their models have varying appeal in different locations. For example, convertibles have larger market shares where the average temperatures are higher. Therefore, it really pays a replacement goods firm to study forecasting and test various methods to adopt the strongest protocol.

b. Stock levels should be ample to cover (uncertain) demands. The loss of many sales because the right stock was not available is a serious drain. Because dealers may not want to carry large stocks, it is a good idea for the glass companies to have their own warehouses as filled as possible with every possible variety of windshields.

c. Distribute the windshields so that the right models are in the correct places to fill customer requirements. Tie distribution policy tightly to the forecasting information.

d. Keeping track of forecasting success and failures by region is important. Constant tracking permits learning that enables the forecasting system to react more quickly to changing conditions. For example, there has been more rain than usual, or a shift in shopping patterns is emerging since the large, new mall opened.

e. Set up the production system so that fast changeovers can be accomplished. Smart investment in changeover technology permits the production system to quickly react to changing demands of the marketplace. Every year brings many new models, and the process must be able to start producing these models although, at first, demand will be low. As the car models age, the demand for new windshield models will grow. At the same time, old cars stop rolling and must be de-listed when demand ceases to be profitable.

7 Four of the following five statements are correct. Which statement is incorrect?

a. Consumer package goods are not appetizing to customers when their shelf display packaging seems old or damaged. Thus, part of the P/OM assignment is to work with designers to achieve durable and attractive packaging.

Packaging processes are production lines with elaborate technology. Sometimes, it is necessary to stop the packaging line to change labels even though the same containers are being used. Understanding the technology for raising and moving items is necessary to ensure that distributors handle merchandise without harming overall product quality.

b.   The technology of testing is related to every aspect of quality control: ingredients, packaging, delivery time, and delivery condition. A significant change has occurred in testing technology that permits accurate inspection of 100 percent of the items using automated sensing systems with computers. This alters the cost of quality in favor of inspecting out defectives instead of prohibiting failures under all circumstances.

c.   Products have various qualities that can change as a function of time. Freshness dating is an example of the dynamics of product qualities. After the date, cheese, milk, and bread can be expected to deteriorate in an obvious fashion. Reading freshness dates is not uniformly simple. Chemical methods of maintaining freshness and increasing shelf life include partial hydrogenation, which is likely to become a subject of discussion in the future. Radiation technology is used to maintain the freshness of military food packs. Package damage is a function of shipping methods and amount of handling. Technology of shipping by containers in palletized form has changed the scenario of distribution and had a significant impact.

d.   Optical scanners at checkout counters reading the universal product codes (UPC) have transformed the checkout operation at supermarkets. The same bar code use in plants and warehouses provides immediate registration of item locations and the quantities stored. Algorithms are programmed at smart warehouses to optimize the placement of input to and output from the warehouse.

e.   Design for assembly (DFA) is dependent upon tolerance matching so that parts can be put together easily. At the same time, tolerance matching can be programmed in the computer to provide just the right amount of clearance and play when parts are being assembled. The technology can be related to CAD (computer-aided design) software.

8   Which one of the following statements is incorrect?

a.   Cybernetics is the study of similarities between human brains and electronic systems. The parallels include sensory systems (for seeing, hearing, etc.), motor systems, memory, and computational abilities.

b.   The outgrowth of cybernetic studies has been development of new technology that permits flexible manufacturing. Also, neural networks have been developed for studying artificial intelligence.

c.   Automated systems are dedicated to making one specific item (e.g., 4-door red Ford Mustangs) whereas flexible systems are capable of making a number of items (e.g., 2-door and 4-door red, blue, and white Ford Mustangs).

d.   Expert systems could be designed to optimize the level of variety that an FMS can produce. Expert systems capture the methods of those with experience in planning for flexibility. Expert systems in conjunction with the human experts can lead to more creative solutions than either of the players can produce alone.

e.   Miniaturization is another major factor in the development of new technology. The advantage of smaller chips that are faster and more powerful is apparent to any student of the history of computers. In the 1950s, large rooms were filled with systems that were significantly less powerful than many children's toys today. The effects on military operations and health care are remarkable. Any one of these may be part of the next industrial revolution: Education based on interactive Internet access, Google owning the Library of Congress on a chip, nanosecond search engines directed by voice only, and vaccines with nano-sized particles for killing cancer cells.

9   Which one of the following statements is incorrect?

a.   Expert systems lend themselves to applications such as marine underwriting.

b.   Air traffic control is an excellent candidate for expert systems.

c.   The value of stock market portfolios could be enhanced by expert systems.

d.   Amazon uses highly developed expert systems based on artificial intelligence to offer its customers additional book choices.

e.   Zagat's uses survey data to provide information about restaurant choices.

10   Which of the following statements is incorrect?

a.   The proper timing of investments in new technology is not a matter of luck. Change is occurring all of the time and there is a best time to get on or off the train.

b.   During the dot.com bubble, high-level investments were made without the kind of analysis that management of technology considers essential. This resulted in enormous loses that might have been avoided by using MOT.

c.   Disruptive technologies are of major concern to top management. However, only those versed in P/OM and management of technologies are able to use the compass that tells which way to turn. See http://www.disruptivetechnologies.com.

d. Technology assessment involves learning the plans of competitors. If this is done with tact, there will be no ethical questions to answer.

e. Whoever needs role models for judging technology contests should take a look at Glasstech, Inc. This company epitomizes great technological creativity. It states on its webpage (http://www.glasstech.com/about_us.htm) that it is the world's leading manufacturer of glass bending and tempering equipment for the automotive and architectural markets.

Additional Readings

Ashby, W. Ross. *An Introduction to Cybernetics.* New York: Wiley, 1956.

Beer, Stafford. *Decision and Control: The Meaning of Operational Research and Management Cybernetics.* New York: Wiley, 1994.

Evans, Alan, Kendall Martin, and Mary Anne Poatsy. *Technology in Action.* Englewood Cliffs, NJ: Prentice Hall, 2007.

Hessel, M. P., M. Mooney, and M. Zeleny. "Integrated Process Management: A Management Technology for the New Competitive Era." *Global Competitiveness: Getting the U.S. Back on Track.* (ed.) M. K. Starr. Norton for the American Assembly, 1988.

Hofstadter, Douglas, and the Fluid Analogies Research Group. *Computer Models of the Fundamental Mechanisms of Thought.* New York: Basic Books, 1995.

Jones, Billy Mac. *Magic with Sand: A History of AFG Industries, Inc.* Wichita State University Business Heritage Series, Center for Entrepreneurship, College of Business Administration, WSU, Wichita, KS, 1984.

Keen, Jack M., and Bonnie Digrius. *Making Technology Investments Profitable.* New York, John Wiley & Sons, November 2002.

Laube, David R. *Business Driven Information Technology.* Palo Alto, CA, Stanford University Press, September 2003.

McGrath, Michael E. *Product Strategy for High-Technology Companies*, 2e. McGraw-Hill Trade, October 2002.

———. *Product Strategy for High-Technology Companies: How to Achieve Growth, Competitive Advantage, and Increased Profits.* Burr Ridge, IL: Irwin, 1995.

Pollack, Michael G. "The AGR Channel-to-Market." *US Glass* (February 1994): 59 . (AGR is auto replacement glass.)

Roberts, Edward B. (ed.). *Generating Technological Innovation.* Sloan Management Review, Executive Bookshelf. New York: Oxford University Press, 1987.

Shingo, Shigeo. *A Revolution in Manufacturing: The SMED System.* University Park, IL: Productivity Press, 1985.

Tooley, F. V. (ed.). *Handbook of Glass Manufacture* (2 volumes). New York: Ashlee Publishing Co., Inc., 1985.

U.S. Congress Joint Economic Committee, "The U.S. Trade Position in High Technology: 1980–1986." 1987.

Zuboff, Shoshana. *In the Age of the Smart Machine, the Future of Work and Power.* New York: Basic Books, 1988.

Notes

1. From the "Technology Report" section of *The Wall Street Journal,* June 24, 1994. Also, see: http://partnerships.typepad.com/civic/2004/09/technology_trap.html.
2. Shoshana Zuboff. *In the Age of the Smart Machine, the Future of Work and Power.* New York: Basic Books, 1988.
3. Canadian Broadcasting Corporation synopsis dated 1996: http://www.glasslinks.com/newsinfo/cbcstory.htm
4. Michael G. Pollack. "The AGR Channel-to-Market." *US Glass* (February 1994): 59. (AGR is auto glass replacement.)
5. Shingo, Shigeo. *A Revolution in Manufacturing: The SMED System.* University Park, IL Productivity Press, 1985.
6. Stafford Beer. *Decision and Control: The Meaning of Operational Research and Management Cybernetics.* New York: Wiley, 1994. Also, Google Wikipedia for "cybernetics" and go to http://www.smc2007.org.
7. Studies from the Columbia Business School Center for the Study of Operations found results similar to those reported by Jay Jakumar of the Harvard Business School in *Technology Review* (July 1985): 78–79.
8. *The New Illustrated Science and Invention Encyclopedia.* Westport, CT: H.S. Stuttman, Inc., 1987, p. 2972.
9. M. P. Hessel, M. Mooney, and M. Zeleny. "Integrated Process Management: A Management Technology for the New Competitive Era." *Global Competitiveness: Getting the U. S. Back on Track.* (ed.). M. K. Starr. Norton for the American Assembly, 1988, pp. 121–158.

Enrichment Activity 8: Net Present Value Model (NPV) Tends to Discourage Investments in Innovative Technology

The net present value model recognizes that analysis of cash flow over time places a higher value on money that is in one's hand as compared to money to be received at a later time. A dollar today is worth more than a dollar next year. The reason is that a dollar owned now can be invested today. It can be put to work. For example, it can earn interest annually to be paid upon withdrawal in one year. Specifically, $0.9434 (94.34 cents) if invested for one year at 6 percent will yield one dollar at the end of that year. Therefore, the present value of a dollar paid a year from now is $0.9434.

Table EA8-1 shows present value calculations for three different interest rates, namely, 3 percent, 6 percent and 10 percent. X (%) values represent the net present value of a dollar paid at the end of n years.* For example, at 10 percent a dollar is worth 62 cents if paid at the end of five years. Y(%) values are the cumulative sum of the X(%) payments based on the fact that the income stream is paid each year and accumulates in value. At the end of $n = 5$ years, the total amount of revenue received by the 10 percent investor has a present value of $3.79.

Examining Table EA8-1 in more detail:

Column X(3%) of Table EA8-1 shows the present values of a dollar paid after $n = 1$ year, after $n = 2$ years, etc., up to $n = 5$ years later, based on a 3 percent interest rate.
Column Y(3%) of Table EA8-1 shows the cumulative sum of payments made up to n years later based on a 3 percent interest rate. The result is $4.57971 or $4.58.
Column X(6%) of Table EA8-1 shows the present values of a dollar paid after $n = 1$ year, after $n = 2$ years, etc., up to $n = 5$ years later, based on a 6 percent interest rate.
Column Y(6%) of Table EA8-1 shows the cumulative sum of payments made up to n years later based on a 6 percent interest rate. The result is $4.21236 or $4.21.
Column X(10%) of Table EA8-1 shows the present values of a dollar paid after $n = 1$ year, after $n = 2$ years, etc., up to $n = 5$ years later, based on a 10 percent interest rate.
Column Y(10%) of Table EA8-1 shows the cumulative sum of payments made up to n years later based on a 10 percent interest rate. The result is $3.79079 or $3.79.

Table EA8-1 — Present Values for Single Payments X and Cumulative Payments Y at Interest Rates Shown in Brackets Compounded Annually over a Period of n Years						
n	X(3%)	Y(3%)	X(6%)	Y(6%)	X(10%)	Y(10%)
1	0.97087	0.97087	0.94340	0.94340	0.90909	0.90909
2	0.94260	1.91347	0.89000	1.83339	0.82645	1.73554
3	0.91514	2.82861	0.83962	2.67301	0.75131	2.48685
4	0.88849	3.71710	0.79209	3.46511	0.68301	3.16987
5	0.86261	4.57971	0.74726	4.21236	0.62092	3.79079

Without discounting, five annual payments of one dollar (at the end of each year) would be worth $5.00. An investment of $5.00 dollars now would have a payback period of five years.

With a 3 percent interest rate, the year-after-year annual payments for five years is worth 42 cents less than $5.00, i.e., 5.00 – 4.58 = $0.42. The payback period with discounting at 3 percent increases to about five and a half years.

With a 6 percent interest rate, the year-after-year annual payments for five years is worth 79 cents less than $5, i.e., 5.00 – 4.21 = $0.79. The payback period with discounting at 6 percent increases to a little more than six years.

With a 10 percent interest rate, the year-after-year annual payments for five years is worth $1.21 cents less than $5, i.e., 5.00 – 3.79 = $1.21. The payback period with discounting at 10 percent increases to over seven years and three months.

Two points are evident. First, the use of present value increases the payback period and makes investments in new technology less attractive. Second, managers who are risk averse and who want to avoid being labeled as proponents of new technology investments use high interest rates with present value analysis to make it very difficult to justify new capital expenditures.

High carrying cost estimates have regularly been used by management to block new product and advanced technology investments. The hurdle rate, which is the minimum return on investment that will be accepted by management, is set higher than for other expenditures (such as normal inventory). This Spotlight has shown how application of net present value with high carrying cost (interest) rates can be used to block projects that are not favored.

In spite of this fact, the net present value model does a real service to decision makers and planners by providing an honest assessment of the value of deferred revenues. Reasonable hurdle rates can be set when all functional areas of the firm including P/OM participate in the discussion.

Enrichment Challenges 8

1 What is net present value (NPV)?

2 Who uses NPV?

3 Why do companies use NPV?

4 When should NPV calculations be disregarded?

5 The NPV of $1,000 paid at the end of each year for 3 years with interest of 6 percent is $2,673. Is the NPV more or less if the interest rate is 3 percent? Explain your answer.

Sources: Tables of net present value can be downloaded from http://www.toolkit.cch.com/tools/npvtab_m.asp. This includes both X (%) and Y (%) tabulations.

**There are other choices (for example, http://www.finaid.org/loans/npv.phtml). The date of tables is not important because information they contain does not change with time. Also, use a spreadsheet with the equation $NPV(n) = (1 + r)^{-n}$ where r is the interest rate.

Notes

*If payments start at the beginning of the period, the first payment would be one dollar. In other words, the first period payment will be equal to 1.00 in Table 8-4. All other payment amounts will be dropped to the $(n + 1)$ row.

**For example, "Table of Present Values of an Annuity." R. S. Burington. *Handbook of Mathematical Tables and Formulas*, 5e. McGraw-Hill, New York: 1973. (Current reprint available.)

Teamwork Planning Requires Job Design

9

Chapter Outline

Chapter 9 explores the importance of human contributions as part of process design. The same need for inclusion applies to planning teamwork and consequent job design. How long it takes to do a job is a detail that has major implications for production rates, costs of doing work, quality of outputs, and continuity. In this sense, it is essential to understand how to set time standards for production jobs. Time standards are based on *job observation studies*. Also, *work sampling* provides another method for gaining useful observations about job characteristics in order to improve the way teams function. Managing the work system includes job design, job evaluation, job improvement, work simplification, and job enrichment. Underlying the effectiveness of process is the commitment to training, which interacts with job design and team achievements.

After reading this chapter, you should be able to:

- Explain why, during times of technological volatility, training people in teamwork is increasingly important for successful P/OM.
- Describe traditional (older) training methods.
- Describe advanced (newer) training methods.
- Discuss teamwork problems of performance evaluation.
- Explain why activity-based costing systems are increasingly vital for proper job design and for effective P/OM planning and decision making.
- Describe how to perform job observations (or time studies) to determine standard output rates and costs.
- Explain leveling and normal time.
- Describe the method for determining adequate sample size for the time study.
- Explain how work sampling is used to improve job design.
- Describe the method for determining adequate sample size for the work-sampling study.
- Explain how job observation can improve job design.
- Detail the nature and applicability of synthetic time standards.
- Describe job design, improvement, and enrichment.
- Discuss issues of wage determination.

The Systems Viewpoint

P/OM, with its process orientation, manages both technology and human resources (HR). P/OM success is facilitated by strong systems identification with the department of human resource management (HRM). P/OM depends on the assistance of HRM for hiring and training that enhances teamwork for the mutual benefit of all personnel in pursuit of company goals. One difficulty of making the systems approach work is that people from different departments have various perspectives and unique orientations. The systems approach requires a dedicated effort to get finance, marketing, P/OM, and other functions to work as a team. HRM holds many of the cards for achieving teamwork.

Strategic Thinking

The common thread is a comprehensive strategy clearly understood by all participants in the organization. Where is this vision and mission statement best developed, stored, and explained? It is at the interface of operations and human resource management. Given a bond of shared commonality, people recognize the strengths that come from their individual differences. Teamwork becomes more effective. Staying within the bounds of each department is equivalent to asking the same person who packed your parachute to inspect it. It is safer to have diverse perspectives. Always have other people than the packer inspect the packing of the parachute.

Creative insights have a higher probability of occurring when there are more independent minds cooperating. However, there has to be shared strategic commitment. HRM and P/OM work well together when they share knowledge of the company strategy and commitment to the systems approach, which fosters coordination between the functional departments. Training for teamwork is a systems-wide concern where success is based on having a focused common strategy. Coordinated mutuality is the foundation for an enriching workplace producing quality products. For the systems approach to work, job designs must interact and facilitate teamwork based on focused commonality of strategy. Generalists sharing their knowledge about each other's areas of expertise should be rewarded for enriching the common purpose.

9-1 Training and Teamwork

These are times of technological volatility. The result is that personnel are dealing with rapid shifts in what they are doing and how they are doing it. Operations managers must teach themselves first, and then others, how to adapt to extreme and sudden changes. Training in new process technologies is enhanced by teamwork that starts with a cooperative relationship between the operations management department and the human resource management (HRM) department.

In many companies, most of the people hired are interviewed by HRM. In general, the staffing of jobs in the company is influenced by the HRM department. HRM personnel play a major role in matching people and jobs. Many companies now screen for team players. These are people who enjoy cooperating with fellow workers instead of competing with them. Japanese companies in the United States regularly use this approach to hire workers. They have endeavored to steer clear of unions. However, when this has not been possible, efforts have been made for management to team up with the unions, as is the case with Toyota and GM's joint venture, New United Manufacturing Motors Inc. (NUMMI).

GM had closed the NUMMI plant in the early 1980s because it was the worst GM assembly plant in North America. This Fremont, California, plant was reopened as an experimental joint venture of GM and Toyota in 1985. The first Corollas came off the NUMMI line in September 1986. By 2002, NUMMI was rated as one of the best auto assembly plants in North America. Every manager in Detroit's Big 3 companies (now called the Big 2.8) was advised to visit the NUMMI plant to learn "how it's done."

As of July 2007, NUMMI produced per year 250,000 cars (Toyota Corolla and Pontiac Vibe) and 170,000 trucks (Toyota Tacoma). There are 5,440 "team members" and 4,550 of them are UAW (United Auto Workers) union members. This makes NUMMI the only Toyota plant using UAW labor *and* one of the highest-labor-cost manufacturing facilities in the entire American automotive industry.[1] There is speculation that Toyota will pull out when the UAW contract expires in August 2009. Only major moves by the UAW could forestall the end of an era, heralded as an example of Toyota's ability to excel in a union-based HRM environment. It will be worthwhile to follow events as they occur in this case.

HRM plays a key role in hiring. HRM is also the department that organizes training programs throughout the company. Training can foster the teamwork that P/OM's success requires. In addition, P/OM works closely with HRM to inform those who train and hire about requirements as operational needs are modified by competitive and technological changes. Training and teamwork are foundations for quality products and processes. Teamwork is a function of morale, which HRM influences through administration of payment and pension plans and in a variety of other ways as well. Close coordination of P/OM with HRM helps P/OM keep in touch with the state of employee morale. Note the Service-Profit Chain applied to Boutwell, Owens & Co., Inc., in Spotlight 2-1.

9-2 Training and Technology

All P/OM systems are dependent upon the participation of people. The human factor always plays a part and teamwork counts. Even for entirely automated systems, people make plans, build plants, and maintain and change them. Generally, semiautomated combinations of people and machines provide greatest flexibility. Managers and engineers use adaptive systems to guide the achievement of flexible automation.

The basic equation relating people and equipment shown here has been used for many years:

$$\text{Workers} + \text{Machines} = \text{Process Capabilities}$$

What is lacking in this equation is the fact that people need training and teamwork to use technology effectively. Training provides skills, and skills with machines translate into quality and productivity. The systems approach provides recognition of the fact that a machine focus is too narrow. Equipment is confined and isolated in the picture of what makes a process work. Technology is a better word because it includes product design, materials used, process methods, and flows of information that reflect underlying systems and software. Therefore, the preferred equation is

$$\text{Teamwork} + \text{Training} + \text{Technology} = \text{Process Capabilities}$$

For each dollar spent on technology, companies can spend two or three dollars training people to use that technology in a skilled and efficient manner. The goal is to determine the best blend of technology and training. Some guidelines for deciding what to do are as follows:

- Plan the process capabilities and keep the plan simple.
- Count on people for quality outputs, strong productivity, and good ideas.
- Provide sufficient training to make *both* old and new technology work.
- Avoid the technology trap (Section 8-2).
- Avoid going beyond the limits of technological expertise.

It had been widely written that GM expected Toyota to employ robotics and complex equipment at their joint venture, NUMMI. Instead, intense training was used with simple technology to produce a high-quality car in the old substandard GM Freemont, California, plant.

This exemplifies preference for workers skillful with general-purpose equipment over automated operations using robotics and other special-purpose equipment. However, as in the NUMMI case, the costs of labor rise along with healthcare and other appealing options begin to surface such as robotics and outsourcing. The decision to invest in technology to replace workers has to be carefully compared with the decision to train workers in place of technology.

Technology and training can be traded off, but not completely. A glass blower's job description is heavy on training and light on technology. Auto windshield glass tips the scales in the other direction. The chef of a great Italian restaurant eschews a microwave but revels in an expensive espresso machine.

9-3 Operations Managers and Workers

The daunting problem that P/OM has faced since it began to be studied by organizational theorists and industrial engineers has been how managers and workers should relate to each other. How employees best work together is a continuous topic of concern. Production and operations managers need to know how to foster competence, how to obtain commitment, how to develop and maintain motivation, and how to secure the loyalty of people who work in the system. All of this can be summed up as P/OM seeking to develop successful teamwork.

The past decade has seen such turbulence in downsizing of companies that concepts of loyalty to the firm by both workers on the floor and management are stretched thin. There also are numerous examples of adversarial relationships between management and workers, with or without union involvement.

The manufacturing workforce in the United States continues to shrink in size. But, at the same time, manufacturing employees play a more important part than ever in achieving competitive performance. The service workforce expands vigorously, but low productivity is frequent. Good relationships between managers and workers characterize globally successful competitors. In most prosperous domestic firms, management and workers are a team. Some firms use participative management, where workers help management reach decisions and share decision-making responsibilities.

Close harmony with workers has been evident in such plants as Toyota, Saturn, Honda, and Nissan. The HRM component is increasingly recognized as a part of successful competitive strategies, with emphasis on selection, training, motivation, and commitment to excellence. HRM also must forge new relationships with unions that bring out the best of P/OM practice.

The U.S. steel industry has returned to profitability after years of hard times. Two factors that are usually cited are

1 The change of technology to continuous casting, processing the metal while red hot into final products, constituting a flow shop. The older traditional methods were labor-intensive, job shop operations. First the metal was poured into molds; then it was cooled. Next the mold was stripped; then the metal was reheated for processing into the final product. The change saved energy and labor costs.

2 The changing relationships of the companies and their unions, which were traditionally highly adversarial, as they learned to become cooperative. Since the "hard times," the United Steel Workers and the companies they have organized have agreed on flexibility in assignments and cooperation, allowing for job rotation and job **cross-training**. Unions have been given more say. Often, the unions are given one or more seats on the board of directors.

In the steel industry, unions and management have learned to work together, using technology and training to survive and prosper. Similar accommodations have been made in aerospace, machine tools, and the chemical industries. New connections between technology and human resources management are not as evident in the Detroit-based automotive industries.

© 2008 Jupiterimages Corporation

Good relationships between managers and workers characterize globally successful competitors. In most prosperous firms, managers and workers are a team. Increasingly, multimedia, interactive on-the-floor training programs are being employed as part of the teamwork exercises.

Cross-training

Permits workers to enjoy job rotation between stations of the flow shop and also between areas of specialization in the job shop.

9-4 Present Training Methods

Traditional training methods that are widely used include on-the-job training, classroom instruction, audiovisual methods, workshops and seminars, case methods, games and simulations, role-playing, and self-instruction. These traditional training methods have long been in place, and everyone who has held a job and gone to school has been exposed

	Objectives	Methods
Table 9-1	Information transfer	Lectures and discussion
Relating Training Objectives	Learning skills	Demonstration, practice, and group exercises
and Methods	Positive attitude	Experiential (on-the-job) learning
	Individual behavior	Disciplined practice, consistent feedback, and experiential memory
	Organizational behavior	Team building with management reinforcement

to some if not all of them. However, the technology that delivers training programs is undergoing constant upgrading.

Training program effectiveness is determined by four basic elements:

1 Objectives of training (what is needed)
2 Curriculum design of the training programs
3 Delivery methods of the training program
4 Measurement of training program effectiveness

Table 9-1 shows present methods for achieving traditional objectives.

For any of the methods, support and reinforcement of training in the actual work environment are critical if behavioral change objectives are to be met. Unfortunately, reinforcement is often bypassed for practical reasons like lack of time and money.

Current training trends show utilization of both traditional and innovative methods for a variety of applications, including organizational development, management and supervisory development, and technical skill development.

9-5 New Training Methods

The repertoire of training techniques has been expanding to include more experimentation and new technology. They now include cross-training, called *action learning*; team learning; computer-based training (CBT); and distance learning. All of these use various levels of interactive video and multimedia systems in conjunction with computers. Leading global companies expect P/OM involvement in the development of advanced training methods. The list of companies to which this applies includes AT&T, Darden, Disney, Dell, FedEx, GM, HP, Honda, IBM, Intel, Motorola, Texas Instruments, and Toyota.

9-5a Action Learning

Action learning, trading jobs for a period of time, is effective. It encourages systems thinking by allowing people to stand in each other's shoes and play each other's roles. Action learning encourages team building and leads to the cooperative environment needed for team learning.

9-5b Team Learning

Team learning adds to personal learning by emphasizing the interdependencies that exist between people working toward a common goal. It also is called *cooperative learning*. An example is teaching the baseball team to play together as a coordinated group instead of teaching each player how to be individually better at their assigned positions.

Team learning follows **team building**, which involves training groups of people to have a common focus. Often referred to as obtaining a personal commitment to the company "family," this approach is intended to remove adversarial relations. The

© 2008 Jupiterimages Corporation

Classroom instruction and discussion are widely used traditional training methods. The classroom can be augmented with new technology capable of asynchronous (off-line, not-in-class, flexible timing) participation. Classroom exercises require synchronous (online, real-time, in-class, on time) participation.

Action learning
Trading jobs for a period of time allows one to stand in the other's shoes and encourages systems-wide thinking.

Team learning
Also called *cooperative learning*; applies to group effort to achieve excellence with a specific process.

Team building
Trust-building training is enhanced by a common set of goals.

belief is that when internal competition is replaced with cooperation, then learning can begin.[2]

Although team-building methods are well understood, they are treated as experimental by many organizations. "Not finance. Not strategy. Not technology. It is teamwork that remains the ultimate competitive advantage, both because it is so powerful and so rare."[3]

Team learning requires applying the systems approach. In every organization, there are people who, like a pitcher, catcher, or batter, can make greater contributions to winnings by being team players than by being individual stars. For business, team learning targets cooperation instead of what has come to be known as "personal best."

Honda of America has utilized team learning for its P/OM managers to enable them to shift easily across a broad spectrum of jobs. At Honda, the job description at any moment in time is related to what needs to be done. Honda P/OM "associates" are not interchangeable, but they can play all the positions as needed. GE has stated its desire to be a **learning organization (LO)**, which is another way of referring to team learning. In correspondence with John F. Welch, Jr. (then Chairman and CEO of GE), A. M. de Lange observed that GE may have LO cells but the entire organization is not committed to being an LO.[4]

9-5c Computer-Based Training (CBT)

Scenarios and simulations that imitate real life can be run on the computer. The advantages of such instruction are that time can be compressed. Many things can be made to happen that would take years to occur in the real world. Extremes in demand and breakdowns in supply can be experienced by the student, enabling him or her to see how well a course of action works. There is a supply chain game (known as the beer game—see Section 10-5b), which epitomizes this valuable kind of learning.

CBT is like training with a flight simulator. Horrible events—such as losing an engine while encountering hurricane-force winds—can be dealt with over and over again using a simulator *before* they are actually experienced while flying a real plane. Computer-based training offers the advantages of repeating a situation as needed and avoiding the risks of real losses if the wrong things are done. Such failures are simply part of the computer record.

There are several disadvantages. One is the cost of creating computer programs that capture all of the necessary elements of reality. Another disadvantage is that it may not be possible to make a computer behave like the real world. The full system of interconnected factors may not be known (or knowable) *a priori* to the simulation-model builder and the simulation programmer. In this case, every effort is made to keep on improving the reality content of the CBT. On the whole, CBT is best used to deal with situations where training on the computer can be said to parallel reality. A reality check is always necessary. It must be explicit and convincing to the trainers and trainees.

9-5d Distance Learning (DL)

Distance-learning training can be delivered through the use of all-known media including online video, videotapes, computer screens, and printed manuals, as well as teleconferencing or videoconferencing, DL can travel (and often does) via satellites, to reach trainees in multiple physical locations individually and sometimes simultaneously. Networked computer-based training simulation methods are widely employed, and there are many other forms that it takes.

One of these is interactive video, which represents a range of options using TV and two-way communication. At its simplest, the camera is located in only one location, but the ability to communicate is two-way. Often, the camera follows the teacher, charts, and diagrams. Students can be located miles away, as is the case with the British Open

Learning organization (LO)

Observes, responds, and adapts to changes that alter conditions for successfully carrying out its mission and it learns from its mistakes as well as its successes.

© 2007 Jupiterimages Corporation

Computer-based training has proven highly effective when the programmed instruction has been carefully worked out in detail and tested with actual trainees. Interactive video and computer-based training can be used at the student's discretion and time availability.

University, which has successfully educated many thousands of students, every year, from all over the United Kingdom.

Within companies, there can be cameras at two locations so that production and operations managers can converse and see each other. This also is called videoconferencing. It can be used in two ways: teams can train each other in respective skills, and they can transfer knowledge in a more effective way than by telephone alone.

Distance learning is like a three-legged stool where the three legs are labeled "anywhere," "anytime," and "anyone." Self-paced learning (anytime) has enormous appeal to very busy people having different schedules. The quality of the education is always at issue. Experts must check out what is being taught and certify that it is what is done in the classroom.

"Anytime" is often referred to as *asynchronous learning*. The classroom epitomizes synchronous education. Distance learning does not preclude in-class instruction. They can share the learning system as long as students are able to spend some time in a designated classroom. DL allows the learning to take place "anywhere." As far as "anyone," some students prefer one or the other method of learning. Most students prefer each one under specific circumstances. The future of education and training in the decade ahead will find both approaches live and well. Expect continued improvements in both modalities of educational delivery systems.

9-6 Performance Evaluation (PE)

Evaluation of individual performance (PE) is commonly used but can be counterproductive because the people who are measured distrust it. There is resentment based on the feeling that PE is not accurate, yet workers are permanently categorized by it. It should be noted that management performance evaluation may be less tangible than worker **performance evaluation**. In many organizations, both tangible and intangible factors are used.

As a counterpoint to negative reactions about PE, many companies claim that its use is essential to remove poor performers as quickly as possible, to provide incentives for excellent performance, and to provide feedback to people so they can improve their performance. PE is part of standard management practice all over the world.

Therefore, it is necessary to understand that a person's real contribution to the group may not be captured by the PE measures that are used. Most performance comparisons are made by determining **average performance**. Then, measures are grouped as being above and below the average. By definition, half of the people measured will be below the average. This immediately punishes part of the group, as always happens when the average is used, even if everyone in the below average group outperforms everyone else in the world.

Because the dimensions of the measures may miss some important contributions that individuals make to the system's performance, one must conclude that there are dangers in this approach. The measurement of team or group performance is not subject to most of these criticisms. Because performance measures are widely used for reasons that are logical, it may be possible to temper them with group performance measures.

Evaluation of worker performance begins with the measurement of output. Then, a standard is required to compare with the actual output. Process managers can define expected outputs for machines, but find definitions of expectations elusive for people.[5]

Why is the question of performance evaluation so important? The reason is that the human resources component of the total cost of goods and service is sizable. It is larger in the service sector than in manufacturing, and it has been growing at a fast rate. The supply chain, of which manufacturing is just a part, has a great deal of direct labor in it. Warehousing, delivery, and retailing tend to be labor-intensive services in the supply chain that the producer cannot do without.

Performance evaluation
Lauded for feedback, PE allows employees *at all levels* to improve their performance. Criticized for being inaccurate and subjective, there is mistrust on the part of those who are below average.

Average performance
Many observations are taken to obtain average performance (or average time), which is then adjusted to obtain productivity standards.

It reaches into the suppliers' organizations as well. Suppliers have varying levels of labor in their products and then these too must be delivered to the manufacturers. Human resources plays a significant role in management and staff functions. Many of these costs show up as overhead costs instead of labor. In short, there are many places where people play a part and the human resources costs are hidden.

Some industries are more labor intensive than others. The level of direct impact on factory costs is usually related to the efforts made to measure and control labor costs. In the banking industry, check processing remains labor intensive and performance evaluation is an ongoing activity. Major efforts are made to measure and control labor costs.

The problem of measuring on-the-line labor costs will continue to interest many companies. Measuring workers' performance remains critical wherever management wants to understand the company's costs and people play more than a trivial part in the cost structure of the system. The service sector can expect continuous growth in the performance evaluation area and in cost control of its labor component.

9-7 Using Lean Production and Accounting Cost Standards

Production standards are criteria specifying the amount of work to be accomplished in a given period of time. Standards are statements of expected output from which costs can be estimated. Production standards are widely used by manufacturing and service industries in this way.

Standards are needed to enable management to compute the real costs of production. Measurement of costs provides estimates of the cost of goods and services.

How standards are set will be discussed later. How standards are used will be examined now. Winning companies use standards as *targets to beat and not as goals to meet*. Just meeting goals can put a lid on accomplishments, whereas beating goals can motivate continuous improvement.

Here are a few P/OM situations that require good production standards:

How much to charge for a new product or service is dependent on what the real costs are. These costs are to be recovered, and then a profit is added on top of them.

Fixed and variable costs are used for breakeven analysis. This provides a capacity goal for the company. It cannot make money until it generates the breakeven volume. Direct labor is part of the variable cost component. Indirect labor, administration, and R&D are part of the fixed cost component.

Lean production is focused on eliminating waste. Performance measurements are aimed directly at eliminating non-value-adding activities. Productive throughput that has value-added is sometimes called the value stream. The assumption of stable production systems that meet the quality assurance rules associated with control charts (see Sections 7-4 through 7-8) is critical. Lean production is a point of view. Along with its drive to improve processes is the language and methodology of **lean accounting**. In various ways, Section 9-7a on activity-based accounting captures the essence of lean accounting, which is directed to measuring only those activities which contribute to profitability and profit margins. Target costing is used. This is based on determining what an item, activity, or service can be allowed to cost. Then the process including labor and materials are redesigned to fulfill the cost expectations. This drives the system to change itself in order to match value stream costs to customer values.[6]

Plant selection needs estimates of labor costs for different areas of the country. With proper use of labor, lean labor costs are derived. Production scheduling allocates jobs, thereby assigning labor costs. Inventories of work-in-process and finished goods are storing labor costs on the shelves and in storage bins. Traditional labor costs overstate these inventories as compared to lean accounting labor costs.

Production standards
Statements of the expected output rates from which the costs of the product can be estimated.

Lean production
Gleaned from the Toyota Production System (TPS) it is a generic process to reduce the seven wastes which include defects, overproduction, waiting, excess: (transport, inventory, motion, and processing).

Lean accounting
Uses value stream mapping to reflect elimination of waste and continuous improvement (Kaizen). Note that value stream mapping captures information about the actual flow of materials and services required to bring the product to the customer.

© 2008 Jupiterimages Corporation

This gas plant worker is redirecting pipe flows. His job has been carefully studied for safety and efficiency. Job design is an implicit part of the training program. During training, workers may come up with suggestions for improvements. These should be fed back to the job designers and trainers.

It is important to eliminate waste by determining and producing optimal product mixes. The calculation is dependent on being able to estimate profit per piece—based on cost per piece—for each product that could be in the mix. The product mix based on traditional cost accounting will reflect labor that is poorly used, and even not used but waiting and wasted. The product mix based on lean accounting will maximize returns on investment and profit margins.

The same kind of reasoning applies to the selection of technology used in place of labor. Proper calculation requires knowing what the labor costs are now and what they are likely to be in the future. If labor costs are rising and the costs of technology are decreasing, when will it be reasonable to shift from labor to technology? Companies that bid for jobs with municipalities, or bid as suppliers to companies, must know their labor costs. Otherwise they could lose money by winning contracts. Capacity planning requires estimates of variable costs for different work configurations. Traditional accounting numbers will mislead the decision makers in all of these cases.

Especially with respect to services, the variability of labor expenses adds more uncertainty than most other costs to the organization's competitiveness. It is simple to predetermine the costs of materials, energy, space, insurance, and equipment. The quandary of estimating how much labor will be used to set up a job, and then produce a batch of given size, is complicated by behavioral factors. In this regard, the service estimate is more uncertain than the manufacturing estimate. While it is more difficult to apply lean accounting in such cases, it can be done by trying to visualize the services as a flow shop process. Labor estimation for the flow shop is easier than for the job and batch shop. This is another reason the flow shop is a preferred work configuration. Reduction of variability is a favorite reason P/OM tends to choose machines in place of people.

Even with the flow shop in place, there has been growth in the wage rates of indirect labor such as administrative, sales, promotional, clerical, and research personnel. It was anticipated that the growing number of computers would decrease such overhead charges. The reverse is true as, on average, they have continued to increase. It is, therefore, important to examine the basis for assigning indirect and overhead costs.

9-7a Activity-Based Costing (ABC) Systems and Job Design

The method of assigning overhead costs to products based on direct labor dollars associated with specific job designs has been traditional. Many times the mix of resources required to make a product is badly reflected by volume-driven measures such as direct labor. In such cases, **activity-based costing (ABC) systems** should replace the traditional cost-accounting methods. Under such circumstances, actual expenses (*AE*) for resources including charges for materials, energy, and direct, short-term labor and overtime are subtracted from revenues (*R*) to yield the short-term contribution margin (*STCM*). Thus

$$STCM = R - AE$$

The other portion of operating expenses are assigned to resources that were acquired prior to actual use. These general expenses (*GE*) cover resources committed for purchasing, machine time, engineering, and administration. Permanent direct labor is a part of these expenses, which are divided into used general expenses (*UGE*) and unused general expenses (*UNGE*). How much of the cost of purchasing should be added to this particular job? How much inventory remained unused? These costs are subtracted separately from the short-term contribution margin to yield operating profit (*OP*). Thus

$$STCM - UGE - UNGE = OP$$

Activity-based costing (ABC) systems

Replaces traditional, volume-driven cost accounting methods with expenses only for resources actually used by the production system.

Example:

$$\text{Materials of } \$5 + \text{Energy of } \$3 + \text{Direct Labor of } \$4 = AE \text{ of } \$12$$

$$STCM = \text{Revenue of } \$18 - AE \text{ of } \$12 = \$6$$

Assume that all costs are multiplied by 10^4 and apply to one job and one week.

The overhead to be allocated is measured by the company for one week and applied in normal fashion to this job. However, it will be broken into two parts as follows:

Assume that:

$$GE = \$ 3 \text{ with } UGE = \$1 \text{ and } UNGE = \$2; \text{ Then,}$$

$$STCM \text{ of } \$6 - UGE \text{ of } \$1 - UNGE \text{ of } \$2 = OP \text{ of } \$3$$

The approach makes evident that overhead charges of $2 are labor costs that would have occurred whether the job was done or not.

It should be emphasized that ABC systems make clear the labor costs that would not have been incurred if the job had not been done. ABC also makes evident the labor costs that would have occurred anyway, and divides these into used and unused portions. This facilitates evaluation of job and process design. This is similar to lean accounting described in Section 9-7.

Traditional costing systems lump (and therefore hide) the charges for resources that have been paid for—whether or not they are utilized. The equation used by the leading proponents and creators of ABC to explain the subject[7] is (in units or dollars):

$$\text{Activity Available} = \text{Activity Usage} + \text{Unused Capacity}$$

$$GE = UGE + UNGE$$

It may be easier to understand what is being suggested by converting the previous equation into a cost equation as follows:

$$[\text{Costs Assignable for Products Made (Activity Usage, } UGE)$$

$$= \text{(equals) Costs of Resources Available (Activity Available, } GE)$$

$$- \text{(minus) Costs of Resources Unused (Unused Capacity, } UNGE)]$$

The costs of resources that are used are considered to be real costs that can and should be assigned to costs of goods sold. The costs of unused resources are cause for concern. Too much capacity may have been put into place. If that is the case, and there is repeated evidence of unused capacity, it should be reduced or alternative uses for that capacity should be found in the longer term. Unused capacity of all kinds, including labor, materials, energy, and technology, should be tracked.

ABC is the accounting system that accomplishes that goal. P/OM needs that information to reach intelligent decisions.

The subject of activity-based costing (ABC) is usually explored in accounting texts. More recently, P/OM has included ABC accounting methods when discussing the increasing irrelevance of using labor charges as the guide for allocation of overhead charges, or when discussing capacity planning. These are the two places where a discussion of activity-based costing (ABC) seems most appropriate.

Without ABC, the decision to buy new technology can be negatively impacted. Traditional net present value (NPV) accounting penalizes long-term planning where large positive income streams will not begin until far in the future (see Enrichment Activity 8). Meanwhile, labor-intensive situations that could be relieved by technology are penalized with significant overhead charges. Job design is negatively impacted. As a result, the company tends to avoid these kinds of activities and loses out on potential opportunities to be a leader in the area.

As an illustration of how the problem of assigning overhead costs to output has relevance for P/OM, consider the old Yale & Towne lock manufacturing company, which because of incorrect allocation of overhead caused the spring-making department to be closed. Thereafter, springs were purchased, which led to an increase in real costs and a loss of control over quality. The traditional accounting system had done a real disservice to P/OM. ABC or lean accounting would not have permitted closing the spring department. In the same vein (no surprise) the process managers fought the decision to shut down the spring-making department.

ABC (and lean accounting) can be credited with raising awareness of misleading information that traditional accounting methods can provide. The approach ties in with results that were obtained employing linear programming to optimize the use of limited resources years before ABC was developed.

When linear programming (LP) is used to determine an optimal product mix, it is frequently the case that full capacity utilization results in lower profits than properly configured partial capacity utilization. LP depends on good measures of labor productivity, availability of capacity, utilized capacity, and unused capacity. The labor productivity is a function of the design of jobs.

9-8 Setting Time Standards—Job Observation

Get a group of people together and compare their golf or tennis scores. Big differences exist. Check how many push-ups each person can do and how fast they can input data at a computer terminal. Variability in the time it takes different people to do the same job description can be reduced by training, but it can never be eliminated. In many cases, companies use so little training that the distribution of times is larger than one might reasonably expect to be the case.

Some people might be good golfers, but poor typists. Variances in "time to accomplish" exist among people within jobs and different jobs require different skills. To find a common ground for setting standards and evaluating the efforts and outputs of workers, it is necessary to build a sound structure and begin the analysis on a simple level.

Diagnostic production studies, where the worker is observed constantly over a long period, go back in time to the early 1900s. The approach can be compared to 100 percent inspection. Both the job and the worker are examined in great detail. This method has shortcomings so it is seldom used. Its primary weaknesses are high costs, unreliable results, worker confusion, and hostility. However, when diagnostic studies lead to improvement of job design they are focusing on the right target.

One hundred percent observations gave way to sampling procedures, which were identified by the name time and motion studies. Time study and work-sampling methods also were derived from statistical developments that date back to the 1920s. It is now politically correct for P/OM to eliminate references to *time and motion studies*, stopwatches, and time studies. That does not mean that the functions are eliminated, just the references. The functions are being done, often in other ways as described ahead. However, the distinction should be made at this point between the study of how long it takes to do specific operations, which is a **time study**, and the study of the motions of which the job is comprised, a **time and motion study**.

Instead of tracking the worker continuously, time and motion studies were based on obtaining a sample of observations sufficient to answer such questions as how long does it take to do each of the component tasks. The main or core process steps are called basic elements. Support steps are called *extraneous elements*. From this information, the expected daily output of workers can be determined.

9-8a Cycle-Time Reduction

The job observation analyst studies the overall job with the purpose of breaking the job down into basic and extraneous elements. These basic elements, when added together,

Time study

The study of how long it takes to do specific operations.

Time and motion study

Sampling and recording what workers do to make, finish, or pack a product. Can be used for service operations.

form the *job cycle*. This job cycle will be the shortest cycle of basic elements required to make the product. It is the repetitive core of the job. Short cycles constitute the main portion of the job. Having a short-cycle time is equivalent to gaining high output rates. Essentially the same considerations apply to process studies leading to *cycle-time analysis* and reduction.

In many instances, the spotlight shifts from the individual to groups of individuals or to the combination of people and technology. The fundamental idea is to time all elements that make up the cycle. This is another aspect of process analysis with emphasis on the basic elements and on the times required to perform them. These are often referred to as *diagnostic observations* instead of *time studies*, a term that carries some negative connotations.

Diagnostic observational methods are not well suited for long-cycle jobs, which do not have short-cycle repetitive basic elements following each other in sequence. Work sampling, used for long-cycle studies, is discussed ahead. The strength of job observational methods lies in their ability to deal with repetitious basic elements.

Job observational methods can be used to set standards or to study how work is done with the purpose of improving the job. The use of time studies for analyzing the performance of individuals has declined as technology has come to play a larger role and labor a smaller one. Decrease in piecework pay, and/or hourly pay, in favor of pay by the day, and/or salaried pay, also has lessened the need for standards that set the expected number of pieces per hour.

The need has also decreased as emphasis is placed on the contribution of group performance to the reduction of cycle time. It is said, if there is only so much time and money to be spent on organizing and improving the process, then process cycle-time reduction and benchmarking are areas of study that are likely to have greater impact on performance than classical kinds of time or job studies.

9-8b Computers Substitute for Stopwatches: Digital Versus Mechanical Clocks

The reasons for job observation include

1 Improving the job
2 Simplifying work
3 Determining expected output rates
4 Calculating each individual's real output rate

All four are applicable to service and manufacturing. The fourth reason is often prompted by need to determine if individuals are performing well, and for payment purposes. Check processing in the bank has a room filled with people doing the same things. Job performance evaluation is ongoing for each one of them. These same labor-intensive conditions that applied to most manufacturing operations circa 1940 still are used in many banks, insurance companies, and travel agencies in various places worldwide.

Although the names "time studies" and "time and motion studies" are out, old-fashioned, and unloved, similar procedures are still widely used. They are called by other names including *process analysis* and *cycle-reduction studies*. They are done in other ways. The difference may be that *cycle-time analysis places more stress on the group*. Perhaps there is less focus on minutia and unnecessary detail. It is beneficial when detail is replaced by the bigger systems picture.

Although there is general agreement with this statement, nevertheless, standards continue to be set and used everywhere. They are still based on logic, measurement, and analysis. The new methods relying on computers and programming may be even more detailed than the old-fashioned time study.

Figure 9-1 is the job observation study sheet that is used by the Jay-Ray DVD Corporation. The job observation sheet is being used to study the packaging of 10 blank DVDs.

Two basic and four extraneous elements comprise the packing process. The two basic elements set the tempo for the complete short-cycle job. The four extraneous elements support the two main components of the packing process.

Stopwatches, once the mark of a time study observer, now are rarely seen in the United States. This is because technology has developed machines that can be set to pace the worker; computers (PCs and notebooks, as well as computers adapted to timing) are used to time workers with more accuracy than stopwatches offered. Computer databases have been developed that are timing workers, and computer databases contain synthetic time standards.

In a real sense, stopwatches with external observers changed. They underwent a metamorphosis becoming internalized computer timers that were part of the process equipment. As such, they could observe a great deal more without being as intrusive. When computers time workers, they are capturing the moments when the worker feeds the next unit (say a check to the optical reader). They can record every time a worker types the letter "q" or stops feeding data to the machine for any interval that is greater than 5 seconds. Computers using GPS determine when truck drivers stop and how many miles they log between stops. Customer relation (call) centers have total monitor feedback for every one of the answering personnel reporting number of calls, length of calls, number of orders filled, etc.

Computers determine and calculate the intervals between successive steps in the process just as if a stopwatch were at work in the hands of the old-fashioned time study observer. Surveillance has not disappeared. It has become more obscure and hidden. Labor, and especially unions, distrusted stopwatch time studies. It was visible and could be antagonistic. The surveyor is now an unseen machine and, in many organizations, employees do not know what part of their performance is being scanned and tabulated.

Company computers count the number of entry data errors made as a check on clerical quality. Computers observe how long mail-order or airline reservation people spend on the phone. These are just a few more examples of a growing use of time studies without human observers, often done under the name of diagnostic observations.

Because of the parallel between computer and stopwatch as simple timers, it remains useful to consider how stopwatch methods are applied to time both the basic and extraneous elements of the cycle. Various kinds of stopwatches and stopwatch methods were available for different applications as well as to satisfy personal preferences. The major distinction was between *continuous and snap-back use of stopwatches.*

The snap-back approach was used to time each work element. When an element was completed, the watch hand returned to zero to begin timing the next element. Continuous readings are cumulative and require subtraction to determine element times. The computer notebook can be programmed to record in either mode. Subsequent calculations follow the same routines as with the stopwatch, but faster.

"Continuous" is the method shown in Figure 9-1. That can be verified by studying the columns headed 1, 2, A, B, C, and D. The snap-back system saved having to do repeated subtractions, but it was more demanding on the job observation analyst and needed a larger sample for the same precision that could be obtained from the continuous method. The computer as an observation tool can do a 100 percent study without error or intrusion.

The stopwatch is attached to a time study clipboard, which holds the job observation or time study sheet. Jay-Ray DVD's completed time sheet for 30 cycles is shown in Figure 9-1. There is partial information about each basic element and how long it takes. More complete information is available on the left-hand, right-hand operation charts. In addition, there is information about the operation, the operator, the observer, the date, the equipment being used, the setup, materials used, and the speed and feed rates of the equipment.

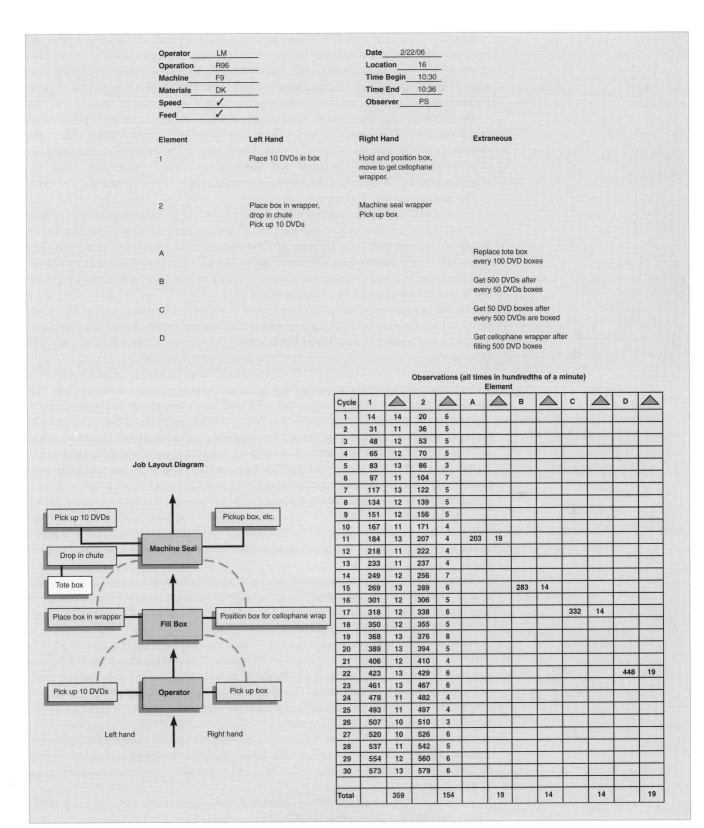

Figure 9-1

Jay-Ray DVD's Job
Observation Sheet

Figure 9-1 also provides a left-hand, right-hand activity analysis sheet that gives the basic elements and their sequence. It explains the extraneous elements and gives the point at which they enter the work sequence. Job observation by computer can pick up the tasks done by each hand, if that seems useful. Jay-Ray DVD's job layout diagram for packing DVDs is shown.

Enough data must be taken to capture all conditions under which the particular job might be done. This could include (for example) different plant settings where the domestic plant is older than the one abroad. Standards may be different in each location. Special methods, materials, locations, and other factors can produce different results. The effects of special factors must be taken into account when costing, pricing, and measuring productivity for delivery schedules.

Job observation studies should not be conducted for poorly designed jobs. They should be made only when it is agreed that the best design has been developed. Design the job before setting any standards. Because of variability, it makes sense to check on a study by replicating the results a sufficient number of times. When job observation results are contested, the variability of study conditions and/or their variance with actual conditions are frequently introduced to win the argument.

The job design (tasks, activities, operations) in Figure 9-1 has been broken down into six elements, but only two elements dominate the process. In this simple case, activities of an operator's left and right hands are described for each basic element. The other elements are long cycle ones used to support the short-element cycles.

The short-cycle job is putting 10 DVD blanks in a box, wrapping and sealing the box with clear plastic, and then dropping the box into the shipping chute. The long-cycle jobs are to refill the bins with DVD boxes that hold 10 DVDs, clear plastic wrapping material, and sealers.

Basic element 1 dictates that the left hand should be placing 10 DVD blanks, which are loose but grouped in tens, into a box while the right hand holds and positions the box so that the DVD blanks can be put into the box. The left- and right-hand operations are coordinated through job design and training.

Basic element 2 consists of the left hand holding the box for the right hand, which seals the box with a clear plastic wrapper. Then the left hand releases the box over a conveyor, which carries it away to a tote box at the end of the conveyor. Each box gently slides into the tote box, which can hold up to 105 of the boxes containing 10 DVD blanks.

Enter in the first column the time it takes to complete element 1 in the first cycle. The time it takes to complete element 2 in the first cycle is recorded next. The stopwatch is continuous, so the first value is 14 and the second is 20, meaning that element 2 required $20 - 14 = 6$ hundredths of a minute.

Next, cycle 2 is observed with values of 31 and 36, which entails $31 - 20 = 11$ and $36 - 31 = 5$, all in hundredths of a minute. The time unit is chosen because it fits the job and can be read on the stopwatch. The stopwatch is a decimal-minute type, which reads directly in hundredths of a minute. The translation of these terms into computer capabilities is straightforward. Specific actions trigger the computer to note the time just as if a stopwatch had been built into the system.

The sample size is 30 cycles, as listed on the sheet. Thirty is chosen as a convenient start-up number that fits the size of the single sheet on the clipboard. Later, it will be determined if a larger sample is needed. The computer has no such restraints or limitations.

When the observations have been completed, the computations start. The sum of the times of the two core elements constitutes the job-cycle time. Cycle 1 required 0.20 min. Element 1 needed 0.14 min. and element 2 consumed the remaining 0.06 min. The second cycle ends at 0.36 min. This means that the second cycle consumed $0.36 - 0.20 = 0.16$ min. In this second cycle, element 1 needed 0.11 min. and element 2 used the remaining 0.05 min. Cycles 3 to 30 are obtained in the same way.

The extraneous elements listed on the time sheet are operations that must be done once for every *n* times that the core cycle is repeated. They support the basic elements of the core process. The right- and left-hand activity chart lists the extraneous element A as the requirement that after 100 DVD blank boxes have been packed and shunted along the conveyor, the tote box they fall into at the end of the conveyor must be taken away and replaced with another one. This occurs once for every 1,000 DVDs that are boxed and removed.

Extraneous element B requires the worker to interrupt the basic work cycle once for every 50 DVD boxes completed. This means stopping after 500 DVD blanks have been packed to get a new supply of the DVD blanks. *Better job design* would allow A and B to occur at the same time, i.e., resupply DVD disks in lots of 1,000. Apply the same thinking to extraneous element C, which resupplies the DVD boxes in 50-unit lots. This could be increased to 100. Combining A, B, and C might be feasible. Extraneous element D obtains clear plastic or cellophane wrappers for 500 boxes.

Extraneous elements break into the short-cycle system regularly. Therefore, when they are included, the total job-cycle time is of much longer duration than the basic elements-cycle time. They disrupt the process and set back the learning curve. It is not unusual for a worker to slow down for awhile on the basic elements after an extraneous element occurs. Also, the worker might meet a friend while going to the storeroom and decide to chat a bit. That would not occur during the job observation study, but would occur in reality. The company would realize less production than the job observation study indicated.

9-8c Shortest Common-Cycle Time

For extraneous element D, the worker replaces the used-up role of plastic (cellophane) with a new one in the plastic wrapping machine. This takes place every 500 DVD boxes, or once every 5,000 DVDs. Because D has the longest extraneous cycle it constitutes *the shortest common-cycle time* necessary to encompass all element cycles that are part of the process.

This is something like finding the lowest common denominator to determine the value of a series of fractions. In this case, it means that 500 cycles of the basic elements are required to include one cycle of the longest extraneous element. A totally proper job observation study would include at least two occurrences of the longest extraneous cycle (D).

To observe 500 cycles imposes such a great observational burden that it may be decided to ignore perfection and include only one of these longest-term cycles. If the time to perform element D is variable, then it could be simulated several times to get a reasonable average value. The same applies to other extraneous elements that have low frequencies of occurrence in the sample. Effects of extraneous elements on the basic element times is another matter that can be simulated if the standard times (the ultimate goal of the study) appear to be sensitive to such effects.

Almost always, even the shortest-cycle, repetitive jobs include long-cycle, extraneous elements. The job observer must be aware of all of the longer-cycle elements so that they are included in the study. The same requirement concerning extraneous cycles applies to computers programmed to make job observations.

The layout chart could have added distances traveled to the picture on the time sheet. How far does the operator have to go to get DVDs, boxes, and clear plastic sheets? The more information the better when trying to reproduce the job observation study results at a later date. It may not be possible to recover finer points about the extraneous elements unless the necessary documentation exists. The computer (as observer) must be programmed to capture the way in which the basic and extraneous elements interact with the layout. Layout design considerations are treated in Section 11-10 through 11-12).

9-8d Productivity Standards

Productivity or production standards are measures of the expected output rate. They can be developed for short-cycle jobs using time study data. How much effort should be spent on developing standards depends to a great extent on the kind of work configuration being used. Enough product must be run in the job shop to warrant developing **productivity standards**. The flow shop qualifies, but in many cases the standards will have been predetermined by engineering design.

Productivity standards
Average performance adjusted by an allowance for rest and delay.

The 10-DVD box packer is part of a flow shop assembly operation for the company known as Jay-Ray DVD. Several workers do the same operations at the same time. Jay-Ray DVD workers are cross-trained, which means they are able to shift operations. Some make DVDs, others format them, label them, and still others pack them. This example takes focus on packing one kind of DVD. The company will have to consider the pack time characteristics of other kinds of DVDs. Each variant has its own individuality, output standards, and costs.

The productivity standard is used to calculate expected output. It is adjusted average performance with an allowance for *rest* and *delay*. The productivity standard enables the process manager to determine how many workers are required to meet expected demand. Labor costs can be estimated for the total job.

Table 9-2 summarizes and operates on the information collected for Jay-Ray DVD. Basic and extraneous elements 1, 2, A, B, C, and D are listed. Total times, as column sums on the time study sheet of Figure 9-1, are carried into the first row of Table 9-2. The total time for element 1 is 359; for element 2 it is 154. Then, for the extraneous elements A, B, C, and D, total times are 19, 14, 14, and 19, respectively.

The third row of the summary sheet lists the number of occurrences that can be expected for each observation of the basic elements. This is 1 for the basic elements of the core cycle and the appropriate fraction for the extraneous elements.

The first row is divided by the second row, yielding the average time for each element. This quotient is multiplied by the third row, yielding an average time per core cycle for each element. The results are shown in the fourth row as average time (also called *selected time*) per core cycle. To illustrate, average time for element 1: $359/30 = 11.96666$; $11.97 \times 1 = 11.97$. This is in hundredths of a minute or 0.1197 minutes. The average time for element 2 = 0.0513 minutes; for element A = 0.0019, and so forth.

Element	1	2	A	B	C	D	Total
TTO	359	154	19	14	14	19	
NO	30	30	1	1	1	1	
ECPO	1	1	1/100	1/50	1/50	1/500	
AT or ST	11.97	5.13	0.19	0.28	0.28	0.04	
LF or AL	0.95	1.00	1.00	1.00	1.00	1.00	
NT or AT	11.37	5.13	0.19	0.28	0.28	0.04	
CF(r&d)	110%	110%	110%	110%	110%	110%	
ST	12.51	5.64	0.21	0.31	0.31	0.04	19.02

Table 9-2

Jay-Ray DVD's Job Observation Summary: Pack 10 DVDs in a Plastic Wrapped Box

TTO = Total time observed
NO = Number of observations
ECPO = Expected cycles per observation
AT or ST = Average time or selected time (in 0.01 minutes)
LF or AL = Leveling factors or allowances
NT or AT = Normal time or adjusted time
CF(r&d) = Correction for rest and delay (r&d)
ST = Standard time (in 0.01 minutes)

9-8e Training Job Observers

The first step to master is the use of the observing tools (e.g., stopwatch or timer). The second step is to master leveling. If the observed worker is "believed to be" faster or slower than average, it is necessary to adjust such performance to what is considered normal. **Leveling factors** are used to convert average time to adjusted or **normal time**. When the computer is used to record times, it captures all workers and the leveling problem is eliminated. This is another advantage of computer time studies. However, it is too easy to overlook the crucial importance of designing good jobs. The computer can mask what the creative time study operator is likely to see, namely, an awkward job with poor layout.

Process managers used to say that the toughest job in the time study procedure was picking an allowance or leveling factor. It is historically interesting that training for leveling was widely practiced. One of the oldest training methods used "movies" made by motion picture cameras. A movie was made of a normal worker doing the job. The picture was shown using projectors with variable speed controls. By adjusting the speed controls, it was possible to make a normal worker seem to work faster or slower. This illustrates another interaction between time studies and time and motion studies. Trained observers need to evaluate job designs as well as people's performance on the job.

The point to emphasize is that all of the time study raters within the company had to agree with each other on what constitutes normal performance speeds for a well-designed job. High degree of conformity meant there would be consistency of ratings by job design for all employees in the same company.

9-8f Setting Wages Based on Normal Time

Normal time is adjusted average time. Pay scales can be set so that normal time workers are being paid wages similar to those being paid by other companies in the region for the same kind of jobs. This removes pay scale inequities between employees in the same company and among workers in other companies. Such parity is particularly desirable for workers within the same industry. Synthetic time standards provide benchmarks for stabilizing what is normal time in similar jobs across companies and industries. Jobs are broken down into components that are common to all work. Each standard component takes an expected (or average) amount of time to perform. Jobs can be constructed of synthetic components just as they can be broken down.

9-8g What Is Normal Time?

Before making a job observation study, workers should be told the full story. The purpose of the study is to develop standards that permit the company to anticipate costs and meet demand requirements. These standards are not meant to exceed what is reasonable. They are intended to prevent overworking operators. Good time standards remove unreasonable expectations, which entrap both management and employees. Workers should also be asked if the job layout is satisfactory or if it can be improved before developing standards. See the discussion about the technology trap in Section 8-2.

An average worker should be selected for the study. The observer tries to make sure that the subject is operating under standard conditions, using routine methods. When the subject of the study seems to work at a normal rate, the leveling factor is determined. For each element, the average time (row 4) and the leveling factor (row 5) are multiplied, which yields the normal time (row 6).

Assume that the observed worker is faster than normal. The observer estimates that this worker is producing 10 percent more output than an average worker. The observer assigns the worker a leveling factor of 110 percent. The normal time will be greater than the average time, meaning that the normal (slower) worker can be expected to take longer than the observed study time.

Leveling factors
Used in time studies of work to convert average time of the person being observed (average performance) to normal time.

Normal time
The output rate of an average worker is the expected production rate of the process.

Examine element 1 in Table 9-2. The operator is working at 95 percent of normal in the judgment of the observer. Multiplication produces a normal time of 0.1137 minutes, which is less than the average time of 0.1197 minutes. Less time to complete an element means that the normal operator works faster and will be able to produce more units than the observed worker.

When the leveling factor is 100 percent, as it is for the remaining five elements in Table 9-2, average time and normal time are equal. This leaves the remaining numbers equal in rows 4 and 6. Many studies require a leveling factor that is not equal to 1. This is because operator skills differ in a variety of ways that are dependent on their motor skills, body size, and experiences.

9-9 Learning Curve Effects

The observer must allow time for learning to take place so that work time stabilizes. Repetition improves performance. Start-up (even for the *n*th time) requires getting back in practice. Learning always takes place, which increases capacity to produce. This raises productivity and lowers the number of defectives produced. Learning is a subject that belongs in discussions of capacity management. Specific discussion of learning curve models will be found in Section 10-12 and in this chapter's Problems Section.

Learning curve
Repetition improves performance with eventual stabilization of output rates.

Even with the most familiar, repetitive work, start-up is slower. With repetition, as the job is being relearned, the operator is said to start moving up the **learning curve**. The effect is substantial when the job is done for the first time. Nevertheless, learning takes place every time that the operator comes on to start a new shift. Job design and job layout are important factors underlying learning speeds.

Computer monitoring picks up the learning curve phenomenon. It provides a great deal of useful information about the learning curves of workers. It is valuable to study these records to determine how to help people move up their respective learning curves faster.

9-9a Job Observation Corrections

Leveling estimates introduce one kind of measurement correction. Time study errors also can occur when the stopwatch is misread or the reading is entered incorrectly. Statistical quality control (SQC) concepts apply. Look at the distribution of element time readings. Extreme numbers that do not seem to belong to the distribution are outlying values that can be thrown out of the sample. If however, outliers are taken seriously, then increased sampling may be warranted.

Subtraction errors can occur when the stopwatch provides continuous readings. They can best be corrected by using several analysts. It is more difficult for one person to redo the calculations. Snap-back readings are more demanding mechanically than continuous readings. Errors can be made in hesitating to snap back or forgetting to do so. Two observers, working together, can be used when breaking in a new observer.

There is another correction to be made. Called the *rest and delay correction factor (r&d)*, it is shown in row 7 of Table 9-2. Some say that (r&d) is the "mother" of all corrections because its requirements are so vague. Nevertheless, the estimation of appropriate (r&d) factors is required for both operator and computer observation systems.

Generally, the number chosen for (r&d) results from negotiations with unions or with workers and their representative groups. The agreed-upon numerical factor is often affected by who is the best negotiator, union or management. After all the finessing with exact observational methods and leveling, it comes as a shock that assigned values for (r&d) commonly range from 5 to 15 percent, depending upon the character of the job, the degree of personal needs, union–management negotiations, and so on.

The point to keep in mind is that without the (r&d) factor, workers might never have a moment to stop. In this case, the left and right hands would constantly be moving packing the DVDs. There would be no time to rest and no time to use the rest room. The best way to set the (r&d) factor is to enlarge the extraneous elements to include a given amount of time to use the rest facilities. A proper scenario should be developed and examined with an appropriate simulation.

Normal time is multiplied by the rest and delay factor, which is always more than 100 percent, yielding standard time. Thus, an (r&d) correction of 110 percent is to be applied to all of the elements as shown in Table 9-2. If some elements are particularly onerous, they might be given a larger (r&d) buffer. Also, it is reasonable, and simpler to calculate (r&d) assigned only to the basic elements.

Total standard time is the basis for calculating production output standards. The sum of the standard times for all the elements is the total standard time of the operation. For the Jay-Ray DVD example, total standard time is 0.1902 minutes.

9-9b Expected Productivity and Cost of the Well-Designed Job

Again, it is worth emphasizing that before measuring productivity and getting a cost for the job, it is essential to evaluate the job design and improve it as much as possible. One method that is used is called *work simplification*. It removes unnecessary steps and streamlines work flows based on common sense, experience, and knowledge (about new technology, etc.).

Assuming that the job is fine, how many boxes of 10 DVDs will the normal Jay-Ray DVD worker produce per hour?

$$POS = 60\frac{\text{min}}{\text{hour}} \div 0.1902\frac{\text{min}}{\text{box}} = 315.46\frac{\text{boxes}}{\text{hour}} \qquad (9\text{-}1)$$

where, POS = Productivity output standard

(Note how the dimensions result in minutes canceling minutes and yielding boxes per hour.)

If 60 minutes per hour had not been used, then 1 divided by 0.1902 = 5.2576 boxes per minute. Multiplying 5.2576 by 60 yields 315.46 boxes per hour. For simplicity, round this output rate to 315 boxes per hour and call it the *expected output rate* for the job.

Assume that the wage rate for this job classification is $6 per hour. (Minimum wage for Summer 2007 is $5.85.) Then the labor cost for packing each box of 10 DVDs would be $6/315 = $0.01905. The expected cost of the operation is a little less than 2 cents apiece. (Problem 18 in the Problems Section assumes a wage rate of $10.)

The major weaknesses of this form of study are defining a normal worker, applying the leveling factor, choosing values for the rest and delay correction, and overlooking influential extraneous elements. Defenders of time study methods claim that satisfactory solutions have been found for all of these problems.

Job observation is a skill, not a science. The use of the stopwatch and leveling both require training and practice. Time study practitioners seldom break down elements into less than 0.04 minutes because smaller intervals are difficult to observe. Another fact worth considering is that the worker's performance may not be stable in the sense of the equilibrium defined by Walter Shewhart for stable control charts. Equilibrium can be especially elusive because of "learning." Time studies should not begin until workers' learning ceases and performance has stabilized.

There remains the issue of determining an adequate sample size for the job observation or time study. How many cycles should be observed? Using automated (100 percent) computer observation eliminates this issue.

9-10 Job Observation Sample Size

Especially for service operations where 100 percent computer monitoring systems are not feasible, observations of performance may need to be made on a sampling basis. This is done to understand the nature of the job, to improve it, to establish pay scales, and to set productivity expectation levels. When this is the case, the need is to set appropriate sample sizes.

Job observation studies are based on sampling n basic cycles of a job. Accordingly, a statistical issue arises about how large a sample (n_j) should be taken for each element, called j. Various formulations can be used depending upon the assumptions made.

Equation 9-3 controls statistical measurement error in terms of sample size for each element j.

Equation 9-3 answers the question: How large a sample (n_j) is needed (how many cycles should be observed) to obtain 95 percent confidence that the true element time (t_j) lies within the range:

$$t_j = \pm 0.05 \bar{t}_j \tag{9-2}$$

The right-hand side of Equation 9-2 states that the range is ± 5 percent of the observed average time.

This is the value 0.05 that appears in the denominator of Equation 9-3.

$$n_j = \left(\frac{1.96 \cdot s_j}{0.05 \cdot \bar{t}_j} \right) \tag{9-3}$$

As for the 1.96 that appears in the numerator of the equation, note that 1.96 sigma defines two tails of a normal distribution each of which has an area of 0.025. This provides the confidence interval within which the true element falls 95 percent of the time.

Assume that $i = 5$ cycles have been observed and that these are the first five cycles in Figure 9-1.

The average times, $\bar{t}_j$ are given in Equation 9-4.

$$\bar{t}_j = \sum_{i=1}^{i=n} t_{ij} \div n = \sum_{i=1}^{i=5} t_{ij} \div 5 \tag{9-4}$$

The average times of the first and second elements for $n = 5$ will be found to be $\bar{t}_1 = 12.4$ and $\bar{t}_2 = 4.8$ from the tabled data in Figure 9-1.

These are now used to compute the sample standard deviation as shown in Equation 9-5.

$$s_j = \sqrt{\frac{\sum_{i=1}^{i=n} (t_{ij} - \bar{t}_j)^2}{n - 1}} \tag{9-5}$$

Obtain s_j for the first five cycles of elements 1 and 2, as follows:

$$s_j = \sqrt{\frac{5.20}{(n-1)}} = \sqrt{\frac{5.20}{(4)}} = \sqrt{1.3} = 1.140 \tag{9-6}$$

$$s_j = \sqrt{\frac{4.80}{(n-1)}} = \sqrt{\frac{4.80}{(4)}} = \sqrt{1.2} = 1.095 \tag{9-7}$$

Now, put these values of $\bar{t}_j$ and s_j into Equation 9-3. This creates Equations 9-8 and 9-9.

For element 1:

$$n'_1 = \left(\frac{1.96 \cdot 1.140}{0.05 \cdot 12.4}\right)^2 = (3.60)^2 = 12.96 \approx 13 \qquad (9\text{-}8)$$

For element 2:

$$n'_2 = \left(\frac{1.96 \cdot 1.095}{0.05 \cdot 4.8}\right)^2 = (8.94)^2 = 79.9 \approx 80 \qquad (9\text{-}9)$$

Whereas $n = 5$ is the number of cycles observed up to this point, n' (used in Equations 9-8 and 9-9) is the number of cycles that *should be* observed. Specifically n' is the required number of cycles to be observed so that there can be 95 percent confidence that the true element time lies within the range shown in Equation 9-2. As previously described, this is ± 5 percent of the observed average time.

The required sample sizes are observations of 13 basic cycles for element 1 and 80 basic cycles for element 2. One element dominates the sample size decision. It is the element that requires the largest value of n'. The largest n', derived in Equation 9-9, is 80. Element 1, with an indicated study sample size of 13, is dominated by element 2 with $n' = 80$. The present sample size is 5. Therefore, 75 additional observations should be made to satisfy the statistical criterion just developed.

Extraneous elements should have no effect on the sample size for core elements. In this case, $s_j = 0$ for all of them because only one value was observed. If a larger sample indicated high variability, then it would be fitting to study extraneous elements apart from the overall core study. It would be unusual to base the study sample size on extraneous elements.

Because the largest value for n', which was 80, is much larger than the actual n, which is 5, some additional observations will be taken. The procedure for sample size evaluation is repeated until the largest value of n'_j is equal to or less than the actual number of observations made, that is, max $n'_j \leq n$.

Good procedure, given the sample of 5 and the indicated need for 75 more observations to get to 80, is to take another 5 or 10 readings and then test again. Problem 2 in the Problems Section requests computations for the first 10 cycles.

These job observation procedures are suitable for short-cycle operations. They provide reasonable cost and output information. For long-cycle, nonrepetitive operations, work sampling is used. Synthetic time standards are used to make estimates for jobs that are being designed and do not yet exist. Both of these methods will be explained ahead.

9-11 Work Sampling and Job Design

Work sampling is applicable to both manufacturing and services. It is singularly well suited to services that do not lend themselves to time studies of the type previously discussed for manufacturers.

Service operations tend to be less repetitive than manufacturing operations. They have longer cycles and they are less routinized. They can be categorized in broad terms, as in the following illustrative case.

Workers often cannot account for the way in which they spend their time. This applies, in particular, to creative and knowledge workers, office and research personnel, and middle and top managers. Their work does not tend to be repetitive like manufacturing and assembly, where time studies can define jobs and rates of output.

Recognition of the opportunity to design jobs that foster teamwork has led P/OM to employ **work sampling**, also called *operations sampling*. This method can determine with reasonable accuracy the percentage of time workers are engaged in different tasks before and after job design.

Work sampling
Provides information about the percentage of time that various activities are being done during the day.

Table 9-3	Activity (*i*)	Number of Observations (*n_i*)	Fraction of Total (*p_i*)
Work Sampling Study in Office	On Phone	100	0.20
	Filing	50	0.10
	Online computer	305	0.61
	Talking in hall	45	0.09
	Total	**500**	**1.00**

In the 1930s, the English statistician, L.H.C. Tippett, reported on his experiments with work sampling in Great Britain's textile factories.[8] Unlike most procedures for sampling the quality of materials, observations of workers' activities are best made randomly over time. As with any sampling system, observations should be of sufficient number to paint an accurate picture of what the workers are doing.

Work sampling methods have to take into account the fact that employees who know they are going to be observed may act differently than if they do not think they are being observed. This means that the best sample is one that has not been anticipated by either the observer or the worker.

Work sampling often is used to determine what fraction of the time workers are idle and how they spend their time when engaged. For office workers, a general classification might include phoning, filing, keying at the computer terminal, and talking with others. It may be difficult to use the computer to track these kinds of jobs. An observer randomly sampled what was happening in the office to develop the data shown in Table 9-3.

When a sufficient sample has been taken, ratios can be formed as descriptive measures of what goes on in the system. In Table 9-3, there are 500 observations of what four people are doing at randomly chosen moments over 5 days. This captures 125 observations of each person. There are 25 observations per day, about three per hour in an 8-hour day. Assume that each observation captures what is going on in a given minute; this is about a 5 percent sample per day because $3/60 = 1/20 = 0.05$.

From Table 9-3, computer use (0.61) is six times as likely as talking (0.09) and filing (0.10) and three times as likely as phoning (0.20). Perhaps it seems to the manager that there is too much phoning. Greater controls over personal calls may be in order. For effective job design, it might be wise to expand the study to do a content analysis of transactions that are taking place over the phone.

P/OM's use of work sampling is not designed to catch workers off-guard. It is intended to map out the way they spend their time leading to teamwork improvements and better job design. Most people are not aware of their allocation of time to activities. This method can help employees utilize their time more fully. Therefore, instead of just observing whether workers are idle or busy, the expanded analysis notes specific allocations of time to functions. This type of study is more appropriately called *operations sampling* than work sampling.

9-11a Work Sample Size

How large a sample is needed? This is the same question asked previously with respect to time studies. The method employed is similar. The equation for *n* is

$$n_i = \left(\frac{1.96}{0.30}\right)^2 \left(\frac{1 - p_i}{p_i}\right) \tag{9-10}$$

n_i = The number of observations to be taken to provide a sufficient sample for the *i*th activity.

p_i = The *i*th operation's activity level observed as a fraction of total observations that an operation occurs. When using this formula, the dominating activity for determining *n* will be the one with the smallest *p*.

$k =$ The number of normal standard deviations required to give a specified probability for the confidence interval. In Equation 9-10, k has been selected to be 1.96 ($k = 1.96$) so that the probability is 95 percent that the true value of p_i falls in the range $p_i \pm (0.30)p_i$.

$0.30 =$ The accuracy range specified by management such that the true value of p_i falls within the range $p_i \pm (0.30) p_i$.

The values of 1.96 and 0.30 were chosen to make the illustration easy to follow. They can be altered to suit particular situations. Selecting "Talking" with the smallest $p_i = 0.09$. This means that $p_i \pm (0.30) p_i$ spans the range for talking from 0.063 to 0.117. That seems a reasonable range for the fraction associated with talking to people in the office.

Using Equation 9-10:

$$n = \left(\frac{1.96}{0.30}\right)^2 \left(\frac{1 - 0.09}{0.09}\right) = (42.6844)(10.1111) = 431.59 \qquad (9\text{-}11)$$

The sample size n can be rounded to 432. Because the actual sample taken was 500 observations, no more sampling is required.

9-12 Time and Motion Studies—Synthetic Time Standards

A solution to problems associated with setting standards for new products, or where people are opposed to being studied on the job, is provided by **synthetic or predetermined time standards**. These standards are created from a subset of elements common to all jobs. The nature of any job can be described by the way in which the common alphabet of work elements is arranged.

Frank Gilbreth was the management pioneer who created the first such alphabet of job elements or modules more than 85 years ago. He called these modules *therbligs* and named 17 of them.[9] Too much detail will not benefit this discussion. Instead of enumerating all of the symbols, a representative group of four provides the picture.

Grasp begins when a hand touches an object. It consists of gaining control of an object, and ends when control is gained.

Position begins when a hand causes the part to line up or locate, and ends when the part changes position.

Assemble begins when the hand causes parts to begin to go together; it consists of actual assembly of parts, and ends when the parts go together.

Hold begins when movement of the part or object, which the hand has under control, ceases; it consists of holding an object in a fixed position and location, and ends with any movement.

Once the standard work elements were identified, it became feasible to study all kinds of jobs, real and imagined. The predetermined times were based on the study of thousands of different operations in which each of these elements appeared. Motion pictures were made of many different kinds of jobs. These were analyzed to determine the appropriate statistical distribution of element times. Expected standard times were obtained from these distributions.

Tables of standard times for a representative set of work elements ("reach," "move," "grasp," and "position") are shown in Table 9-4. They are part of the total system of synthetic standards known as MTM-1, the methods-time-measurement system. In addition to the four work elements previously listed, the total set of predetermined standards includes move, turn, apply pressure, release, disengage, eye travel and eye focus, body, leg and foot motions, and simultaneous coordination of all of these. Using these (as with Table 9-4), a standard time for any usual job can be derived.

Synthetic or predetermined time standards
Used to make estimates for jobs that do not yet exist from a subset of common elements.

TABLE I — REACH — R

Distance Moved Inches	Time TMU				Hand in Motion		CASE AND DESCRIPTION
	A	B	C or D	E	A	B	
3/4 or less	2.0	2.0	2.0	2.0	1.6	1.6	**A** Reach to object in fixed location, or to object in other hand or on which other hand rests.
1	2.5	2.5	3.6	2.4	2.3	2.3	
2	4.0	4.0	5.9	3.8	3.5	2.7	
3	5.3	5.3	7.3	5.3	4.5	3.6	**B** Reach to single object in location which may vary slightly from cycle to cycle.
4	6.1	6.4	8.4	6.8	4.9	4.3	
5	6.5	7.8	9.4	7.4	5.3	5.0	
6	7.0	8.6	10.1	8.0	5.7	5.7	
7	7.4	9.3	10.8	8.7	6.1	6.5	**C** Reach to object jumbled with other objects in a group so that search and select occur.
8	7.9	10.1	11.5	9.3	6.5	7.2	
9	8.3	10.8	12.2	9.9	6.9	7.9	
10	8.7	11.5	12.9	10.5	7.3	8.6	
12	9.6	12.9	14.2	11.8	8.1	10.1	
14	10.5	14.4	15.6	13.0	8.9	11.5	**D** Reach to a very small object or where accurate grasp is required.
16	11.4	15.8	17.0	14.2	9.7	12.9	
18	12.3	17.2	18.4	15.5	10.5	14.4	
20	13.1	18.6	19.8	16.7	11.3	15.8	
22	14.0	20.1	21.2	18.0	12.1	17.3	**E** Reach to indefinite location to get hand in position for body balance or next motion or out of way.
24	14.9	21.5	22.5	19.2	12.9	18.8	
26	15.8	22.9	23.9	20.4	13.7	20.2	
28	16.7	24.4	25.3	21.7	14.5	21.7	
30	17.5	25.8	26.7	22.9	15.3	23.2	
Additional	0.4	0.7	0.7	0.6			TMU per inch over 30 inches

TABLE II — MOVE — M

Distance Moved Inches	Time TMU			Hand In Motion B	Wt. Allowance			CASE AND DESCRIPTION
	A	B	C		Wt. (lb.) Up to	Dynamic Factor	Static Constant TMU	
3/4 or less	2.0	2.0	2.0	1.7				
1	2.5	2.9	3.4	2.3	2.5	1.00	0	
2	3.6	4.6	5.2	2.9				**A** Move object to other hand or against stop.
3	4.9	5.7	6.7	3.6	7.5	1.06	2.2	
4	6.1	6.9	8.0	4.3				
5	7.3	8.0	9.2	5.0	12.5	1.11	3.9	
6	8.1	8.9	10.3	5.7				
7	8.9	9.7	11.1	6.5	17.5	1.17	5.6	
8	9.7	10.6	11.8	7.2				
9	10.5	11.5	12.7	7.9	22.5	1.22	7.4	**B** Move object to approximate or indefinite location.
10	11.3	12.2	13.5	8.6				
12	12.9	13.4	15.2	10.0	27.5	1.28	9.1	
14	14.4	14.6	16.9	11.4				
16	16.0	15.8	18.7	12.8	32.5	1.33	10.8	
18	17.6	17.0	20.4	14.2				
20	19.2	18.2	22.1	15.6	37.5	1.39	12.5	
22	20.8	19.4	23.8	17.0				
24	22.4	20.6	25.5	18.4	42.5	1.44	14.3	**C** Move object to exact location.
26	24.0	21.8	27.3	19.8				
28	25.5	23.1	29.0	21.2	47.5	1.50	16.0	
30	27.1	24.3	30.7	22.7				
Additional	0.8	0.6	0.85					TMU per inch over 30 inches

1 TMU	= .00001	hour	1 hour	= 100,000.0 TMU
	= .0006	minute	1 minute	= 1,666.7 TMU
	= .036	seconds	1 second	= 27.8 TMU

TABLE III A — TURN — T

Weight	Time TMU for Degrees Turned											
	30°	45°	60°	75°	90°	105°	120°	135°	150°	165°	180°
Small — 0 to 2 Pounds	2.8	3.5	4.1	4.8	5.4	6.1	6.8	7.4	8.1	8.7	9.4
Medium — 2.1 to 10 Pounds	4.4	5.5	6.5	7.5	8.5	9.6	10.6	11.6	12.7	13.7	14.8
Large — 10.1 to 35 Pounds	8.4	10.5	12.3	14.4	16.2	18.3	20.4	22.2	24.3	26.1	28.2

TABLE III B — APPLY PRESSURE — AP

FULL CYCLE			COMPONENTS		
SYMBOL	TMU	DESCRIPTION	SYMBOL	TMU	DESCRIPTION
APA	10.6	AF + DM + RLF	AF	3.4	Apply Force
APB	16.2	APA + G2	DM	4.2	Dwell, Minimum
			RLF	3.0	Release Force

TABLE IV — GRASP — G

TYPE OF GRASP	Case	Time TMU	DESCRIPTION	
PICK-UP	1A	2.0	Any size object by itself, easily grasped	
	1B	3.5	Object very small or lying close against a flat surface	
	1C1	7.3	Diameter larger than 1/2"	Interference with Grasp on bottom and one side of nearly cylindrical object.
	1C2	8.7	Diameter 1/4" to 1/2"	
	1C3	10.8	Diameter less than 1/4"	
REGRASP	2	5.6	Change grasp without relinquishing control	
TRANSFER	3	5.6	Control transferred from one hand to the other.	
SELECT	4A	7.3	Larger than 1" x 1" x 1"	Object jumbled with other objects so that search and select occur.
	4B	9.1	1/4" x 1/4" x 1/8" to 1" x 1" x 1"	
	4C	12.9	Smaller than 1/4" x 1/4" x 1/8"	
CONTACT	5	0	Contact, Sliding, or Hook Grasp.	

EFFECTIVE NET WEIGHT			
Effective Net Weight (ENW)	No. of Hands	Spatial	Sliding
	1	W	W x Fc
	2	W/2	W/2 x Fc

W = Weight in pounds
Fc = Coefficient of Friction

Do not attempt to use this chart or apply Methods-Time Measurement in any way unless you understand the proper application of the data. This statement is included as a word of caution to prevent difficulties resulting from mis-application of the data.

Source: MTM Association for Standards and Research.

Table 9-4

Synthetic Time Values for Various Classifications of Motions

The time measurement units (TMU) are given in terms of 0.00001 hour. This means that 1 hour is composed of 105 time measurement units (TMUs). Equivalently, 1 hour = 100,000 TMU.

The procedure for using the synthetic time standards is

1 Describe the job design in detail and identify the work elements.
2 Determine the appropriate times for each work element.
3 Add the element times together. This requires that individual work elements be independent of each other. If not, interactions need to be taken into account. The sum must reflect the true total time for the job.

The MTM Association for Standards and Research has developed computer systems for combining synthetic elements and deriving work standards. MTM-1® is the basic module.[10] Another system, called 4M®, is designed for computer applications. MTM-UAS (Universal Analyzing System) resulted from a collaborative effort with German, Swiss, and Austrian MTM Association groups. It is designed to create standards for batch production. See http://www.mtm.org for more information.

9-12a Evaluation of Applicability

Some advantages of synthetic time standards, as compared to those derived from conventional study methods, are as follows:

1 The leveling factor problem is eliminated. Synthetic time standards average out rating differences across many operators.
2 Synthetic production standards are founded upon element times derived from very large samples of observations. This provides increased reliability of the derived standard time.
3 The speed of preparing cost estimates, as well as their reliability, for new jobs is improved. Production schedules can be quickly determined and modified.

Synthetic time standards are in flux. Their technology changes as conversions are made from tables and charts to computerization. Using an international perspective, predetermined time standards provide a common base for work being done at multiple global locations.

Synthetic time standards are likely to be adopted by companies in parts of the world where labor costs are low. They describe the way that people work and not robots. Timing for robots is determined by engineering requirements.

Transnational and multinational corporations will continue to shift labor-intensive work to areas of the world where there are low costs. Companies will outsource those parts that require labor-intensive inputs. Control over costs requires standards; synthetic time standards will find increasing use for control over outsourced products.

The approach used by synthetic time standards is, in modified form, applicable to the standardization of programming work. Thus, in the United States, systems for developing standards that apply to the cost of writing lines of code have been studied for many years by a variety of companies. The synthetic time standards also have applicability to information processing and other services that conform to the manufacturing orientation.

Labor-intensive service operations in airports, hospitals, banks, and schools can be studied and systematized by the application of the synthetic approach. Service operations have many characteristics that lend themselves to better organization using predetermined time standards. The potential application for service operations is significant, e.g., MTM – HC® for healthcare and MTM – C® for Clerical Activities.

9-13 Managing the Work System

What is the status of the people part of P/OM systems? Are people working smarter, not harder? Is there a common goal to produce a quality product? Are managers viewed as consultants helping workers instead of as judges grading students?

9-13a Job Design, Evaluation, and Improvement

The answer seems to depend on where and when one looks. Many companies have adopted new approaches in dealing with employees. When times get rough, some of them revert to the old ways. Other firms seem to have permanently embraced the integrated empowering approach to employee relations. There is evidence that work system improvements can pay off handsomely. Companies worldwide that follow job design improvement principles that enhance teamwork and workers' sense of security outperform competitors.

There is benefit to be gained by viewing the entire set of jobs in a company as a system involving all employees, workers, and managers. Striving together as a team, their outputs are the revenue earners. Job improvement will result in a blend of effects, including lower costs, increased output rates, better deliveries, greater variety, and above all else, better quality.

Job evaluation
Evaluation of existing jobs permits job enrichment and improvement, and work simplification.

Job evaluation is a term often used to describe the analysis of a job and its improvement. It is more valuable to consider *job evaluation as system evaluation*, in which sets of interrelated jobs are analyzed and improved as an entire network of *linked efforts*. Traditional job evaluation looked upon each job as a separate and independent part of the workplace. This view is not as powerful as the system view.

9-13b Wage Determination

Wage determination
Based on normal time, a reasonable piecework wage can be determined by management.

Wage determination for P/OM employees is based upon the following:

1 Difficulty of jobs performed
2 Amount of training required
3 Amount of skill required
4 Value of these jobs to the company

There are problems defining an unambiguous basis for establishing wages. For example, the difficulty of a job and its value to the company may not be correlated. Skill required and value to the company may even be inversely related. There is a logical flaw in the old approach to wage determination that cannot be remedied by reasoning. This is apparent in reading about legal efforts to prove wage discrimination—say, between women and men.

The traditional approaches to wage determination are still practiced by many organizations, but they are changing. There is no redeeming benefit to studying the old ways. The newer approaches are to set acceptable costs for labor and target those costs as goals. In addition to target costing and the use of activity-based costing (ABC) and lean accounting methods, wage levels are set by market forces for certain skills and experience.

Note that ABC-type thinking results in the attempt to determine what each job contributes to the profitability of the firm. Efforts to define the value of jobs to the company pay off not only in helping develop rational pay scales, but also by putting emphasis on the design of jobs to maximize contribution.

At the experimental end of the spectrum, groups of workers participate in deciding who gets raises and who does not get them. This is *wage self-determination* done by the group for themselves and the people with whom they work. There are many other kinds of arrangements for self-participation in setting wage rates and making joint decisions that improve **conflict resolution** and employee morale.

Conflict resolution
Before wage determination by teams is used, conflict resolution skills must be developed by management.

Old ways of determining wages are being replaced by a systems approach in world-class organizations. The systems approach is based on a common pay rate for team members working together. To the extent that the group is successful in generating profit for the company, they are rewarded as a group by bonuses.

In many companies now there is cross-training, so that many people do different jobs at different times. The old system would have trouble sorting out what each person should be getting paid. Accounting is far easier with the new approach. Everyone in the group receives the same pay, and all work for the same system. Some companies call the bonus system *gain-sharing*. An increasing number of unions are allowing cross-training. There is more emphasis on training, including the use of quality circles, quality of work life groups, and participation groups.

9-13c Work Simplification and Job Design

Work simplification should be used first to develop as good a job as possible. This takes into account the systems view of each job as a service to the next worker in the sequence. When this thinking has been applied, the application of time studies and job observations, including realistic productivity measures, can lead to significant improvements.

The success of **suggestion systems** in companies, where employees are not driven by work standards and where there is little fear of losing one's job, indicates the extent to which improvement can be continuous. Good suggestions are rare in companies where the suggestion might result in someone being fired because a job no longer is necessary. Continuous job design improvement programs work when there is worker security; they work best when there is worker empowerment in a teamwork environment.

In recent years, there has been de-emphasis on work simplification in various industries. This occurs if job shop lot sizes decrease in size. Line changeovers to new and modified outputs are becoming more frequent. Computer-integrated flexible manufacturing systems and adaptive automation require intense preplanning that obviates the need for ongoing improvement of operations. Also, strong methodologies of operations research and management science, such as simulation, are increasingly being used to improve the performance of systems. When these methods compete for investment study dollars with the older methods, the new methods win. Individual job design improvement will disappear as systems design improvement redefines the nature of jobs by doing whatever it takes to foster teamwork.

9-13d Job Design and Enrichment

As technology changes, operators tend to communicate with the computers that run the machines rather than with the machines themselves. This changes the pattern of communication in the factory and in the office. There is more time and opportunity for people to speak to each other. L- and U-shaped workstations have become commonplace in systems of interrelated jobs designed to facilitate communication between workers. Groups of people get together more often to discuss the system of work and how it can be improved. When the ideas of people are taken seriously, and when people know what happens to their work down the line, each job is enriched.

There is ample research evidence that whether the work is in Mexico, China, or the United States, some workers prefer simple, highly repetitive tasks, and others do not. Some like to switch roles. Others prefer to stay at the same tasks. When groups of employees are offered job enrichment opportunities, the group splits into those that want them and those that reject them. Consequently, there is an opportunity for management to explore preferences with each worker. Work assignments can be made according to worker preference in many work systems, because both types of work exist.

The flow shop can be particularly tedious for workers who like variety. As more stations are added, productivity rises. However, cycle time gets shorter, placing an increasing burden on station workers, who have shorter jobs to do with greater frequency. The quality of work can deteriorate under such circumstances. Worker dissatisfaction can increase. In the 1970s, the Vega plant of General Motors at Lordstown, Ohio, suffered a long and difficult strike shortly after it was built because of worker dissatisfaction with the flow shop pace. Job dissatisfaction, in the Vega case, was very costly to GM.

During the 1970s, organizations started to redesign their production lines so workers would be required to do many different jobs. Volvo of Sweden began experimenting with teams that built an entire car. Other organizations decreased the level of specialization in their line-balanced systems. This increased the size of each workstation and the work content per employee.

A group of GM employees on a trip sponsored by the United Auto Workers was sent to Volvo in Sweden for six months. Less than half preferred the Volvo system. All but a few returned to the United States and resumed their old way of working with GM.

Suggestion system
Employee contributions are a great source of ideas for improvement. If no one reads the suggestions, the system is a sham.

Overall, with cross-training and employee involvement in quality, the work content per employee continues to increase. Most of the complaints center around the paced-conveyor flow shop as well as its intermittent forms instead of the job shop, but there are tedious aspects of the job shop as well. The project is usually immune to such complaints. If there is any criticism on the part of project workers, it is the continual crises that afflict the non-routine aspects of their workdays. There may be complaints about flexible processing systems (FPS) because human support teams often perform dull tasks to service their computer masters.

Cross-training for job rotation (where workers exchange jobs) has become increasingly acceptable. Job enlargement (with its larger work content) also has taken hold. Greater worker participation in decision making has been endorsed by both public and private organizations. The ultimate criterion is where the objectives of the organization can be met with less specialization and with less authority over workers.

9-13e The Motivation Factor

A remarkable case history was documented in the 1930s by a study group from Harvard at the Hawthorne Works of the Western Electric Company in Chicago. The study concerned levels of illumination and their affect on productivity. It was discovered that whether the illumination was raised or lowered, productivity was improved. The key finding (known as the *Hawthorne effect*)[11] was that employees responded positively to management's interest and attention. This response level overrode the functional affects of the illumination level. Such complex behavior differentiates people and machines.

Critics of the Hawthorne study claim that the result was a self-fulfilling prophecy. The workers gave the researchers what they wanted. Even if this is true, it still appears reasonable to expect positive reactions from workers to care and attention.

Motivation can be both positive and negative. The latter is associated with poor employee morale. When discussing incentives and motivation, the major difficulty is the measurement problem. Nevertheless, accepting the lack of precision involved, incentives are a real causal factor that can affect worker behavior. Incentives include wages, job title, office size and floor, organizational importance, ability to participate in decisions, vacations, leisure time, and variety of tasks assigned. For the most part, these categories represent intangible qualities that escape definition and measurement.

In summary, P/OM is a people-oriented function. P/OM deals with workers and suppliers. To make the process work, P/OM must be able to understand the changing role of people in the process. This has become even more true as P/OM moves onto an international stage. People throughout the global network are indispensable.

Spotlight 9-1 Lee Cockerell: You Can Create Disney Magic Too
Leadership Lessons from Lee Cockerell

Lee Cockerell

There are important lessons waiting for those who aspire to be great leaders in the Production and Operations Management field. These lessons come in the form of a book titled *You Can Create Disney Magic Too*. It is authored by Lee Cockerell, the retired Executive Vice President of Operations at Walt Disney World. What he learned in his 41 years in the hospitality industry and why he wants you to know what he learned will become clear as the story unfolds. His leadership principles apply to everyone: highly paid executives, MBAs, professionals, and workers earning $7 an hour. Practicing great leadership makes the right things happen by bringing out the best in others. Lee Cockerell tells his own story honestly and clearly. His message is unforgettable and its impact could make you decide to practice Disney magic, too.

It seems unlikely that a boy growing up on a farm in Oklahoma would choose a career path that resulted in a job managing 40,000 Disney employees. On second thought, a farm environment includes everyone in a successful enterprise. Learning how to milk a cow at an early age, Lee's first income came from neighbors who paid 50 cents for a gallon of fresh milk. Already he was learning the importance of pleasing customers.

His mother's values regarding honesty and clarity in communication were certainly positive factors in Lee's early years. Many after-school and summer jobs supplied him with a diversity of experiences. Lee quickly learned that all jobs have what he calls perks and anti-perks. Examples of anti-perks: bosses who yell at employees and long commutes.

Dropping out of Oklahoma State University in his second year, Lee joined the Army in 1964 and served as an Army cook. He learned quickly and took second place in his training program. After leaving the Army, the first-place cook invited Lee to go with him to start their civilian careers at the Washington DC Hilton Hotel. (Lesson learned: associate with top performers.)

Lee's Hilton job was working as a banquet server. He was 20 years old and it was the first time he was exposed to linen table napkins and an array of silverware that went beyond a simple knife, fork, and spoon. After hundreds of weddings and serving a few kings and queens as well as a number of Congressional members at banquets held at the Hilton, he had learned the value of excellent service. When customers don't receive that service, trouble follows.

Years later when Lee was General Manager of a hotel in Springfield, Massachusetts, an irate guest came to his office. The night before, the guest and his wife had ordered a lobster dinner with an expensive bottle of chardonnay to celebrate their 25th wedding anniversary. Waiters were expected to go to the restaurant manager, who was the only one empowered to have a key to the wine cellar. That evening the manager had to leave temporarily, taking the key with him. The waiter searched for the manager in vain as the couple waited impatiently. They had already finished their dinner before they could toast their anniversary. Lee did his best to make up for their bad experience.

From such encounters, Lee learned to improve processes and eliminate hassles on all levels. Businesses are run by processes. He learned that good processes enable employees to do routine things smoothly and consistently, leaving time to do the extra things that make a good business great. He wants you to think about every bad experience as an opportunity to improve operating procedures. Instead of blaming a person, improve the process.

After the banquet server position, Lee took a job as Food and Beverage Control Office Clerk at the Hilton. After 8 months at the new job, he was selected as a management trainee. He learned accounting and inventory management from practical experience, which, for Lee, was the best way to learn.

His office was located in the center of the kitchen since the job was food and beverage control. The advantage of being close to the action was an important discovery. Lee became friendly with all the cooks, dishwashers and employees. People knowing him and seeing him frequently helped to get his work done. In all future jobs, Lee decided to make sure his office was always in the center of action. He didn't realize then that there was another lesson to be learned about using his own authority and it would be a costly learning experience.

Spotlight 9-1 (Continued)

Meanwhile, his job was going well. The chef was an excellent manager, planning carefully organized banquets for 3,000 people. He was a great leader—tough but fair. Lee watched how he led and taught his team. The chef respected everyone at every level. When Lee ordered Crenshaw melons instead of Honeydew, the chef said to him, "Lee, you can be a fool once or a fool all your life. When you don't know something, ask questions—then you will know, and that way you will be a fool only once."

It seems to be a secret that people respect colleagues who ask questions. No one respects someone who thinks or even acts like they know everything. Being humble is a big deal. Many leaders have not learned this. Lee's former boss at Disney, Al Weiss, was never afraid to say, "I don't understand that. Please explain that to me again because I don't get it." That is undoubtedly why Al Weiss was promoted to president of worldwide operations for Walt Disney Park and Resorts.

Back at his Hilton job, Lee ordered 1,500 avocados for a special banquet. They arrived hard as rocks. This was soon after the melon incident and Lee knew he had to find a way to ripen the avocados or risk getting fired. He spread them out on the pool deck. Covering them with blankets in the sun, they ripened just in time. To this day, according to Lee, he can't pick up an avocado without thinking about how important it is to know what you are doing.

The biggest perk of Lee's life happened during the time he worked for Hilton. He met Priscilla, his future bride. It took time and perseverance on Lee's part to convince her to marry him, but eventually the happy newly-weds moved to Chicago together after Lee was promoted to work for the 2,000-room Conrad Hilton Hotel as Food and Beverage Controller. They had a son, Daniel, while in Chicago and Lee was introduced to the complexities and joys of fatherhood.

As a new guy on the block, Lee had quickly come up with a plan to improve the hotel's existing operating system. Letting a little success go to his head, he had forgotten how important it is to make friends and allow people to know him before using his authority to make changes. The chef ordered him out of the kitchen.

Salvaging his performance with difficulty, he learned that you can't get things done by intimidating people. Authority doesn't work without good working relationship skills. Technical expertise is useless when there is silent or open resistance. Nothing gets done. Lee believes that managing under the influence of one's own high self-opinion is as dangerous to a career as drinking and driving. You get things done through relationships with people. That is where great leadership starts.

Lee Cockerell continued to practice his early lessons. He rose through management and executive ranks, first at Hilton and then at Marriott, There were many career moves. In 1992 Disney was in the planning/design stage of a theme park in France. Lee was offered the Directorship of Food and Beverages for the new French theme park. He spoke no French. Fortunately, Priscilla could speak the language well enough to get by and served as translator until Lee could fend for himself.

The Disney theme park was 20 miles east of Paris. It gave Lee all the perks he ever imagined. It was a plunge into learning another culture and a new set of values. The lesson on asking questions served him well. While on a tour of a French wine cellar, Lee asked the guide what vintage was best for a certain wine. He remembered her answer later when all eyes were on him at a wine tasting. With an American's reputation for knowledge of wines at stake, he was asked to identify a wine he knew must be very special to his host. He said, "1974 . . . no, I think it is 1976." The host and his own family looked at him with disbelief. It was the correct answer.

During their experience with French culture, the Cockerell family prospered. If Lee had not accepted this career move, their son, Daniel, would never have met his French bride, Valerie. Lee and Priscilla were promoted to grandparents in 1995, 1998, and 2001.

With Euro Disney up and running, the family moved to Florida. Lee Cockerell concentrated on leadership training and time management. (Lee calls it life management.) His responsibility was to help create an environment for cast excellence and world-class guest satisfaction that would lead to great business results. His leadership lessons formed the basis of the world-famous Disney Great Leader Strategies, which shape the current culture at Disney World in Orlando and influence hundreds of thousands of people through Disney Institute training programs.

Disney's operations managers were soon to be tested. On Tuesday, September 11, 2001, the New York World Trade Center twin towers that had commanded the New York City southern skyline for 30 years were both destroyed by terrorists. Lee and three other Disney executives were faced with a monumental national crisis. They assembled in Disney's Emergency Operation Center (EOC) and in 30 minutes made eight key decisions:

1 Mobilize all buses.
2 Evacuate all 50,000 people from the parks.
3 Offer free hotel rooms to those who require them.
4 Provide cash and food vouchers as needed by all.
5 Offer free phone service to anywhere in the world for all guests and staff.
6 Send costumed entertainers to soothe and calm frightened children.

7 Re-open all parks next day with free tickets to all 9/11 guests.

8 No Disney employees will be laid off—that means none.

The terrorist crisis and all its contingencies were met with common sense decisions that were inclusive and consistent in the treatment of all groups. Caring for everyone and dealing with myriad problems was the hallmark of leadership faced with adversity. By Christmas of that year, millions had been spent. Word-of-mouth spread favorably and so did gratitude from staff, guests, and the community. Disney's emergency actions had resulted in increased loyalty and trust, leading to the return of guests to the parks.

When Lee retired in July 2006, he was the team leader of 40,000 cast members and was responsible for the operations of 20 resort hotels, 4 theme parks, 2 water parks, a shopping and entertainment village, and a sports and recreation complex. He is now dedicating his time to public speaking and authoring his book, *You Can Create Disney Magic Too*, publication date, October 14, 2008. Lee's purpose is to offer powerful strategies to leaders at every level of organizational life. He learned the hard way the crucial difference between managing and leading. Managerial skills are essential for getting things done but excellence requires leaders who not only get things done but get them done the right way and bring out the best in everyone around them. The real magic of great leadership works when no one feels left out.

This Spotlight opens the door to understanding leadership. Lee Cockerell's book will not disappoint its readers. Enjoy the magic!

Review Questions

1 What is the most important key to excellence in leadership?

2 Some people learn from their mistakes while others do not. Why is that so?

3 Is life on a farm good preparation for a business career? Explain the answer.

4 How does an excellent leader use his/her authority?

5 What does Disney magic have to do with business process management?

Source: Pre-publication draft of *You Can Create Disney Magic Too* by Lee Cockerell. Conversations with Lee and Priscilla Cockerell during 2007. See the webpage: http://www.leecockerell.com.

Spotlight 9-2 Dave Crowell and Charlotte Bentley: The Language of Change

Perspectives from Dave Crowell, CEO, and Charlotte Bentley, President, WorldSource One, Inc.

"People engaged in multinational commerce tend to use two languages. The first is English, and the second is the language of performance improvement." Dave Crowell should know. He and business partner Charlotte Bentley have delivered ISO 9000, quality management, and Baldrige-based training to businesspeople from dozens of countries.

When Dave and Charlotte started WorldSource One, Inc., their idea was to provide training and consulting services to multinational corporations and to the far-flung operations of Uncle Sam. Their clients include Goldman-Sachs, Johnson & Johnson, and federal government organizations like the Army, Navy, Coast Guard, and the IRS.

Language was a huge business training concern 20 years ago, but has proved to be a minor issue today. Most of the management-level employees of multinational organizations speak, write, and understand English—at least well enough so that English is clearly the business language of choice around the world. "I was training European managers for NCR Corporation in Belgium, and when it was coffee time, their beverage preferences ranged from *very strong coffee* to *tea with milk*, but their choice of language did not vary—it was English all the way!"

"We've had more trouble with the conceptual side than the language side," explains Dave. "While training Johnson & Johnson employees in Kuala Lumpur, Malaysia, we discovered that a few of the Malcolm Baldrige National Quality Award concepts were not getting through to participants from Japan, Korea, China, and several other countries. For example, one difficult concept was the Baldrige concept of *promoting diversity* in the workplace. After a prolonged discussion, we realized that many Asian companies have a very homogeneous workforce, and becoming *more diverse* is a completely unfamiliar concept in their environment."

Charlotte reports similar conceptual problems working with U.S. Army local national employees in Germany and other European countries. "One Army client that manages

Spotlight 9-2 (Continued)

real estate—housing, offices, ranges and such—has employees from over 60 countries. This organization is well-versed in *diversity*, but has trouble with the concept of *empowerment*. In many parts of Europe, the boss is still the boss, and hierarchical structures are still firmly in place. Empowerment, which is alive and prospering in North America and Japan, is still an emerging concept in many parts of Europe."

Dave, a former quality management executive with IBM, NCR, and EG&G, and Charlotte, a university vice president, have completed dozens of workshops and seminars for people who use English as their second or business language. Charlotte points out that simultaneously covering a subject in several ways (with lectures, visuals, demonstrations, hands-on interactive workshops, and classroom projects, for example) pays huge dividends in terms of increasing understanding. Dave adds his observation that letting go of jargon and adopting standard English terminology also makes a big difference in improved comprehension. "As experts in a subject like the Baldrige Criteria or ISO 9000, we often forget that we've slipped into a vocabulary of special meanings for dozens of otherwise normal English words." Business jargon is deadly to a foreign audience.

There are other quality management training issues, and most of these relate to factors other than language. Thanks to Dr. Deming, Dr. Juran, and countless others who promoted the principles of quality management for several decades, managers around the world have a reasonably good understanding of the basics. It's the barriers to change that slow their progress.

Based on their Baldrige and ISO 9000 training experience, Dave and Charlotte have identified five specific barriers to change that must be considered by all students of quality and performance improvement.

First, many people still think that *higher levels of quality or performance excellence cost more or take more time.* They are reluctant to listen to any arguments to the contrary, and persist on doing things the hard way—*do it, do it over again, and eventually get it right, most of the time.*

Second, there is a *silver bullet crowd*—those who firmly believe that a single tool, method, or practice *will* solve *all*

of the problems within an organization. Unfortunately, they try something for a while, discard it, and go on to another method. Soon, their organizations are scattered with the bones of all those programs that weren't allowed to mature.

The third barrier is *a lack of systems thinking.* Many American managers, and their European and Asian cousins as well, are notoriously deficient in terms of *systems thinking—the "big picture" interaction of people, processes, technology, and feedback.* According to Charlotte, "You simply cannot benefit from the Baldrige Criteria or from ISO 9000 until you understand what systems are and how they work. It's fundamental knowledge!"

Speaking of knowledge, that's the fourth barrier. Dave is convinced that business and other organizations have a long way to go in terms of *knowledge management.* "I'm not talking about portals, servers, and complex technological concepts. Most organizations need better methods of keeping track of what works and what does not, and of finding and institutionalizing the best practices found in their own organizations. Companies are losing generations of knowledge and know-how when they downsize, resize, or reorganize."

The fifth barrier is actually a "set" of *industry-specific barriers* that have become deeply embedded over time. There are many cases that we could cite, but homebuilders are a familiar example. Many of them are so enamored with the *punch list* concept that they are largely incapable of even thinking about *preventing errors and defects.* Most claim that it's easier, more expedient, and even cheaper to do "it" over again, sometimes even twice, than to organize a preventive approach. That's not true, of course, but it is widely *believed* and that's all that really counts.

Time goes on, however, and World Source One training and consulting programs continue to impact clients around the world. They are conducted in English, free of jargon, and resolutely targeted at the five barriers.

Source: Communication with World Source One executives, Dave Crowell (CEO) and Charlotte Bentley (President), January–February 2005 and April 2007.

Summary

Chapter 9 makes it clear that planning teamwork is the mutual goal of P/OM and HRM. There is discussion about traditional and then newer methods of training. The reason that performance evaluation is a controversial topic is explained. Chapter 9 develops the ideas behind designing jobs for production and cost standards. This is followed by the study of time standards. Traditional time study methods are compared with the use of computers to determine how many pieces (or service steps) to expect per hour, i.e., the production standard. The next logical study is that of time and motion for operations. This includes job design improvement and the use of synthetic time standards to set production standards. Work sampling is covered. Chapter 9 concludes with discussion of how to manage the design of larger work systems, including job improvement, evaluation, enrichment, and wage determination.

Two Spotlight feature boxes come at the conclusion of this material. Spotlight 9-1 presents leadership lessons from Lee Cockerell, a master of operations who helped provide the Disney magic. Spotlight 9-2 is an interview with Dave Crowell and Charlotte Bentley about the language of change. It really is all about how to make training effective. Their company, World Source One, Inc., has a history of accumulated experience that must not be missed.

Key Terms

Action learning (p. 324)
Activity-based costing (ABC) systems (p. 328)
Average performance (p. 326)
Conflict resolution (p. 346)
Cross-training (p. 323)
Ergonomics (p. 362)
Job evaluation (p. 346)
Lean accounting (p. 327)
Lean production (p. 327)
Learning curve (p. 338)
Learning organization (LO) (p. 325)
Leveling factors (p. 337)

Normal time (p. 337)
Performance evaluation (p. 326)
Production standards (p. 327)
Productivity standards (p. 336)
Suggestion systems (p. 347)
Synthetic or predetermined time standards (p. 343)
Team building (p. 324)
Team learning (p. 324)
Time and motion study (p. 330)
Time study (p. 330)
Wage determination (p. 346)
Work sampling (p. 341)

Review Questions

1 Why is training for teamwork a concern of P/OM?
2 What is action-learning training?
3 What is computer-based training?
4 Explain why good estimates of labor costs are needed to determine how much to charge for a new product or service.
5 Explain why good estimates of labor costs are needed to determine fixed and variable costs to be used for breakeven analysis.
6 Explain why good estimates of labor costs are needed to determine plant location and selection.
7 Explain why good estimates of labor costs are needed to develop excellent production schedules.
8 Explain why good estimates of labor costs are needed to determine an optimal product mix.
9 Explain why good estimates of labor costs are needed to determine when a technology upgrade should be made.

10   Explain why good estimates of labor costs are needed to make intelligent bids for jobs with federal or local municipalities, or with companies.

11   Frederick W. Taylor thought the relationship between the well-designed job, the best worker, and the reasonable wage scale could be determined by logical analysis and intelligent experimentation. The concept of the well-designed (specialized and efficient) job has been attacked. The same is true of the notion of best workers and worst workers. Taylor has been accused of treating people like machines.

   A guaranteed wage and pay not related to individual productivity have been suggested as a reasonable wage scale. Discuss these issues from the systems point of view.

12   What is meant by the statement "Observations of productivity can be used for purposes of estimation and bidding, but they are unacceptable as a means of setting work standards for the amount of output each employee is expected to produce"?

13   Why is leveling no longer as major a concern for job observation as once upon a time?

14   For the work sampling study (Section 9-11), what should be done about the manager's belief that there is too much phoning?

15   For the work sampling study (Section 9-11), the manager believes too much time is spent filing. What can be done about that?

16   What is meant by the statement "The design of industrial jobs is being replaced by systems design of interrelated jobs"?

Problems Section

Note: This section has various problems that can be formulated and solved using Production/Operations Management software (QMpom). The appropriate model categories are indicated for each problem.

1   Show all computations in tabled form needed to determine the largest value of n' for the first 5 cycles of elements 1 and 2 in the table of Figure 9-1.

2   Show all computations in tabled form needed to determine the largest value of n' for the first 10 cycles of elements 1 and 2 in the table of Figure 9-1.

3   Package Design International (PDI) is a medium-sized company. Typically, because of overload, its executives work 10- to 12-hour days. The president calls for reduction of the average period from order-entry date to delivery date.

   The P/OM department suggests building a supply chain simulator. The simulation would capture all factors that affect order to delivery times. Training and a problem-solving device are estimated to cost $25,000. The operations manager believes it will take 40 hours for each executive to learn how to use this simulator. There are five executives that would be expected to work with the simulator.

   The operations manager has told the president that the simulator would result in $250,000 of additional profit for PDI in the next year. Should the contract for the simulator be given?

   Using the QMpom module called Capacity Management Models (Breakeven), assume FC = $25,000, vc = $ 125 per hour (for five executives) and Selling Price (or revenue) = $250 per hour. Solve for the number of hours to yield savings of $250,000 per year.

4   Finding the shortest common-cycle time for time studies is like finding the lowest-common denominator for describing a series of fractions.

Cycle Number	Core Element 1	Core Element 2	Extraneous Elements			
			A	B	C	D
1	5	4	-	-	-	-
2	3	2	-	-	-	-
3	4	3	-	-	-	-
*	*	*	*	*	*	*
*	*	*	*	*	*	*
100	3	4	20	20	25	30

What is the shortest common-cycle time for the time sheet shown here?

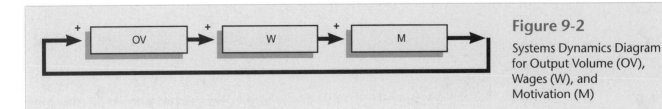

Figure 9-2

Systems Dynamics Diagram for Output Volume (OV), Wages (W), and Motivation (M)

5   As output volume (OV) rises, so do wages (W). This is shown by a plus sign at the end of the arrow connecting OV and W. As W increases, so does worker motivation (M). This is shown by a plus sign at the end of the arrow connecting W and M. Continuing in this way, increasing motivation conditions worker performance to raise output volume. Figure 9-2 illustrates this feedback relationship. However, other factors might be considered in this systems dynamics diagram.[12] Thus, additional inputs (arrows) can be added to the figure to indicate that other factors also affect output volume, wages, and worker motivation, such as quality (Q). Create the diagram and do the analysis for quality (Q).

6   It has been decided to study the activities of a market research company using work sampling. First, however, it has been concluded that any office can be used as a pilot operation where the methods can be developed and tested. Using Table 9-3 as a guide, choose any office and drop in 5 to 10 times, noting each time what every person who works in that office is doing. Then, develop the kind of information that is shown in Table 9-3. Even though the sample is small, analyze this data. How big a sample will be needed?

7   For the market research company study described in Problem 6, what categories of activities might apply? How often should observations be made? Would you recommend using random sampling or taking observations at set times that are known to the employees of this company?

8   A Spanish company packs green olives that have been soaked in brine into 1-pound jars. The olives are first divided into 1-pound-plus batches using a digital scale. On average, there are 32 olives to the pound.

   The olives are inserted in a jar and brine is added. Then the jar is sealed with a twist cap and put on a conveyor. The left-hand, right-hand chart is shown here:

	Left Hand	Right Hand
Element 1	Get olives. Put on scale. Measure 1 lb+.	Get jar.
Element 2	Put olives in jar.	Clamp jar. Get brine.
Element 3	Get screw cap.	Add brine.
Element 4	Screw on cap.	Unclamp jar.
Element 5	Move toward olives.	Put jar on conveyor.

   a. Sketch the process flow and layout.
   b. The time estimates are given in Table 9-5.
   c. Develop a sequence of work elements.
   d. Prepare a job observation or time sheet.

9   Use the information in Problem 8 to determine the standard time for the job.

10 Can predetermined time standards be used for the Spanish olive packing company? Develop the appropriate report.

11 A new set of data has been collected by Jay-Ray DVD using operations sampling instead of time study–job observation.

Activity	Description	Number of Times Observed
1	Place 10 DVDs in box.	212
2	Seal box, etc.	90
A	Put away 100 boxes.	10
B	Get 500 DVDs.	8
C	Get 50 boxes.	7
D	Get cellophane every 500 boxes.	12

   How do these results compare with those derived by the time study in Figure 9-1?

Table 9-5	Element		1	2	3	4	5
Olive Packing Times (in Hundredths of a Minute)	Cycle	1	15	8	7	10	10
		2	13	8	8	11	10
		3	15	7	8	12	10
		4	17	9	9	11	11
		5	12	9	6	10	10
		6	14	7	7	10	9
		7	14	8	6	9	9
		8	13	8	6	9	10
		9	15	7	8	9	11
		10	16	9	7	10	9
	Total time		144	80	72	101	99
	Number of observations		10	10	10	10	10
	Expected cycles		1	1	1	1	1
	Average time		14.4	8.0	7.2	10.1	9.9
	Allowance		1	1	1	1	1
	Normal time		14.4	8.0	7.2	10.1	9.9
	R&D correction		1	1	1	1	1
	Standard time		14.4	8.0	7.2	10.1	9.9

12 With respect to job observation sample size and Equations 9-8 and 9-9, do the calculations for the following data and determine whether it is OK to stop taking additional sample observations.

Cycle Number	$t1$	$t2$
1	13	5.0
2	13	5.0
3	13	5.0
4	13	5.0
5	13	5.0
6	13	5.0
7	13	5.0
8	13	5.0
9	13	5.0
10	13	5.0
Totals	130	50.0

$$\bar{t}_1 = 130/10 = 13.0$$
$$\bar{t}_2 = 50/10 = 5.00$$

$$\text{Data and Computations for } \bar{t}_j = \sum_{j=1}^{10} \frac{t_j}{n}$$

How could this result have occurred?

13 Use activity-based costing to show how much overhead is not applicable to Job X. Assume that all costs are multiplied by 10^4 and apply only to Job X for a 1-week period.

Materials costs = $7;   Energy costs = $3;   Direct labor costs = $5;   Revenue = $22.

What is the short-term contribution margin?

14 Using the information in Problem 13, continue with the following additional data: The overhead to be allocated is measured for one week.

$$GE = \$4, \text{ with } UGE = \$2, \text{ and } UNGE = \$2.$$

What is the operating profit?

15 Using the information in Problems 13 and 14, what is the unused portion of overhead that should not be associated with the profitability of the job?

16 Using the information in Problems 13, 14, and 15, what is the used portion of overhead expenses that should be associated with the profitability of the job?

17 For a learning curve application of the QMpom software, the symbols will match those used by the QMpom module called Learning Curve Models (Learning Curves). Click on Help in the left-hand navigation pane. Let $m = 1$ so $K(m = 1)$ is the cost of producing the first unit. Note that "units" can be specified in costs or time to produce that unit. Let $b = -\lambda$. The Learning Rate $= \lambda$. The Reduction Percent $= 1 - \lambda$. Test $\lambda = 1.0, 0.8, 0.5, 0.2,$ and 0.0, when $K(m = 1) = 1$ minute for n = 1 − 5. The QMpom equation becomes: $K(n) = K(m)(n)^{(-\lambda)}$. If $K(m = 1) = 5$ minutes, then, find the average time to produce the $n = $ 10th unit.

18 Use the format of Table 9-2 and the structure of Equation 9-1 to determine the labor cost for packing each Jay-Ray box of ten DVDs. Assume that the wage rate for this job classification has been raised to $10 per hour.

Practice Quiz

1 Training and technology are competitors for budgetary allotments. There have been swings in allocations as computers, robots, and telecommunications have appeared to provide competitive advantage. At the same time, there have been numerous examples of where investments in training have provided more competitive advantage than the latest model of software or hardware. All but one of the following answers is correct. Which answer is incorrect?

  a. For each dollar expended on technology, there are companies that have spent three dollars on training to employ the new technology with effectiveness and efficiency.

  b. Expenditure on technology should push the envelope beyond the limits of current expertise to gain a competitive advantage.

  c. Team evaluations of training required to use new equipment are better guidelines than manufacturer's recommendations.

  d. For production workers, the use of general-purpose equipment requires greater investment in training than special purpose equipment.

  e. Unions are generally opposed to investments in technology that replace workers, but they are in favor of technology that requires skills and training to be used correctly.

2 Jay-Ray DVD, a high-tech company, now needs to determine the training budget. Choices must be made between traditional training methods and advanced training methods. Selection will be based on evaluations of training program effectiveness. A variety of statements about training programs are listed here. Which statement do you think is incorrect?

  a. Training program effectiveness is determined by aligning training objectives with company needs and justifying the methods and delivery adopted for training.

  b. A training objective might be to instruct accountants in the use of spreadsheets, and an effective delivery method would be computer-based training.

  c. Measurement of training program effectiveness should be accomplished after the program is completed so as to avoid disturbing the instructors and biasing the data.

  d. Action learning is a training program that is high on the risk-return scale. This means that high uncertainty is accepted about events that may occur for each participant who is trading places. At the same time, the breadth and depth of experience for each participant will exceed anything that the classroom can deliver. Finance classes justify high risk–high return under certain circumstances. It is a good idea for human resource managers to learn about this kind of investment.

  e. Team learning as a training option is organizationally challenging. If team learning is greatly rewarding that might alter the options previously determined regarding how much new technology should be used with appropriate training.

3 The repertoire of new training methods does not include one of the following techniques. Which one does not qualify?

a. Team building involves training groups of people to have a common focus.

b. Team learning emphasizes the interdependence between people working toward a common goal.

c. Team performance evaluation requires each team member to rate all the others.

d. Distance learning occurs when training is delivered (usually to multiple locations) through networked computers, teleconferencing, videoconferencing, etc.

e. Computer-based training is like training with a flight simulator.

4 Good production standards are required for a variety of applications. Listed are some of the ways in which the production standards are utilized. Which of the following answers is incorrect?

a. Determining how many workers are needed requires determination of the production standard (expected output in pieces per worker per hour).

b. Supply is calculated by multiplying the production standard by the number of workers per hour. If supply is less than demand, more workers need to be added.

c. Assume that the time to make a unit does not change with production volume but the cost of making a unit does change. Then, the production standard changes as a function of cost. Production standards are used to compute the real costs of product output.

d. Capacity planning requires understanding the complex relationship between variable costs and the volume of production. The production standard has already been factored into this relationship.

e. If the time to make a unit decreases with increasing production volume (learning curve effect) then the production standard must be studied as a dynamic factor.

5 Revenue from a batch of 5,500 machine shop parts made to order and sold to an established customer is $22,000. The actual costs that apply to this job have been calculated from the point of view of activity-based cost analysis (ABC). Which statement is incorrect?

1	Revenue	$22,000
2	Actual materials cost	$6,000
3	Actual energy cost	$2,000
4	Actual direct short-term labor	$4,000
5	Short-term contribution margin	$22,000 - $12,000 = $8,000
6	Permanent direct labor—Used	$1,000
7	Permanent direct labor—Unused	$3,000
8	General expenses	$1,000 + $3,000 = $4,000
9	Operating profit	$8,000 - $1,000 - $3,000 = $4,000

a. Operating profit shown in line 9 of the table is calculated as the short-term contribution margin (5) minus the permanent direct labor *used* for the batch and minus the *unused* portion of that expense. In this way, necessary and unnecessary overhead can be revealed. Steps can be taken to decrease unused expenses.

b. Revenue minus actual expenses to create the product equals the short-term margin contribution. Accounting for the actual expenses requires monitoring the job and all of its components. For example, how much time was expended by labor on the job and at what labor rates? Determining work in the back room by permanent labor on this job leads to general expense statements.

c. Activity-based cost systems raises awareness of how overhead is calculated and applied to specific jobs. Traditionally, overhead allocation is proportional to labor hours, which is inaccurate and misleading.

d. The price per part is $4.50 and the unused portion of the permanent direct labor is about 45 cents.

e. The used (assigned) portion of the permanent direct labor is 18 cents. This means that general expenses are 73 cents.

6 Industrial engineers pioneered the development of methods to determine how long a job should take if it is done properly. Frederick W. Taylor, the father of scientific management, spearheaded the efforts to develop methods engineering and time and motion studies. This occurred at the end of the nineteenth century and the beginning of the twentieth century. Although efficiency experts were the subject of jokes, business took them seriously. Now, more than one hundred years later, nothing fundamental has changed. What has been altered is how the tasks of efficiency experts are now done without Charlie Chaplin's white-frocked doctors of mass production. When a stopwatch and clipboard are not in evidence, there is fair likelihood that the computer is capturing information and calculating expectations out of sight, but not out of mind. Listed are some issues concerning time standards, job observation, time and motion studies, cycle time reduction, and productivity standards. Which answer is incorrect?

a. Job observation is a systematic approach to auditing what is being done in the production system. The audit includes time required to complete the job. From audit information, it is possible to determine how many workers are needed to meet demand and how much it will cost to fill the orders.

b. In line with price-elasticity theory, demand volume could increase or decrease. This leads to consideration of alternative work configurations. Time studies need to be done to determine output rates and costs for the various process options that are being considered. To consider strategic alternatives, it is essential to have time study information available. Using synthetic (predetermined) time standards can help to resolve problems and hasten decision making to optimize company strategy.

c. Any job being studied can be broken down into basic and extraneous elements. The basic elements, when added together, form the (basic) job cycle time. This job cycle will be the shortest period of time required to make the product. This is where effort to increase productivity should be focused.

d. Reasons for job observation include improving and simplifying the way the job is done; calculating expected output rates; and evaluating every individual's real output rate. All are applicable to both service systems and manufacturing.

e. The *shortest common cycle time* includes the longest extraneous cycle time. The *total standard time* spans the entire shortest common cycle time so that all extraneous cycle times are taken into account. Total standard time is the key to productive output, and it must include both the basic elements required to make the product and the extraneous elements. For example, Boston Market provides sides of mashed potatoes, cream of spinach, cranberries, etc., with requests for chicken, meatloaf, or turkey. Assume that the small containers in the hot table run out of stock every 20 orders. This triggers a request for replenishment while the customer may be waiting to be served. Eventually, from the back of the store, new containers are brought out to replenish whichever side dishes are required. In this example, the basic elements are the cycle times required for the servers to fill the customers' orders from the hot table. The extraneous elements are the time to refill the hot table inventories.

7 The job observation summary table for Major's QSR (quick-service restaurant) is shown here with all calculations completed. Management has furnished comments and interpretations of these data. Which comment shows a lack of understanding about the purpose of this information?

Element	1	2	3	A	B	C	Total
TTO	620	360	200	10	50	30	
NO	40	40	40	1	1	1	
ECPO	1	1	1	1/20	1/50	1/15	
AVT/SLT	15.50	9.00	5.00	0.50	1.00	2.00	
LF/AL	0.92	1.00	1.10	1.00	1.00	1.00	
NT/ADT	14.26	9.00	5.50	0.50	1.00	2.00	
C(r&d)	100%	100%	110%	110%	110%	110%	
SDT	14.26	9.00	6.05	0.55	1.10	2.20	
							33.16

Legend: TTO = Total time observed; NO = Number of observations; ECPO = Expected cycles per observation; AVT/SLT = Average time or selected time (in 0.01 minutes); LF or AL = Leveling factors or allowances; NT or ADT = Normal time or adjusted time; C(r&d) = Correction for rest & delay; SDT = Standard time (in 0.01 minutes)

a. The basic job cycle time is 0.2931 minutes per person, paid and meal served. This is equivalent to 204.71 people served at the counter per hour or 3.41 people served per minute. However, these calculations just reflect the core elements of the work. The numbers to look at need to include the extraneous elements. That is, unless someone can be clever about not having extraneous elements interrupt the core work.

b. The total cycle time is 0.3316 minutes per person, paid and meal served. This is equivalent to 180.9 or 181 people served at the counter per hour or 3.02 people served per minute. If the process people can come up with a clever idea about not having extraneous elements interrupt the core work, it would be possible to serve 24 more people per hour.

c. The shortest common cycle time, which is like the lowest common denominator for a series of fractions, is 50 units. Upon completing 50 units, the QSR must restock certain items (extraneous element called B). It takes 0.5 minutes to do this. That has the effect of adding only 0.011 minutes to the total standard time.

d.   The worst offender is extraneous element C. It adds 0.022 minutes to the total standard time of 0.3316. The percent increase is (0.3316 – 0.3096)/0.3096 = 7 percent. That is not insignificant.

e.   No correction has been made for r&d for the core elements whereas there is a correction of 10 percent for the extraneous elements. This may be because leveling factors were used for the core elements but not for the extraneous elements.

8   Points a. through e. reflect on various considerations about what is being done in relatively undisciplined work situations. For example, in the office, people are free to move about and choose what activities they consider timely. Work sampling (also called *operations sampling*) is designed to ascertain work patterns in such nonrepetitive environments. All but one statement is acceptable. Which of the following statements is incorrect?

a.   Observations of workers' activities are best made randomly over time. The reason for this is that when people know that they are going to be observed at a specific time, they will be ready. Some will have gone to the mirror to adjust their hair. Others will be filing because they think that filing is what the boss expects them to be doing.

b.   Work sampling is often aimed at determining how much idle time workers have. The problem of identifying people engaged in "being idle" is difficult because thinking about the best way to do something may be indistinguishable from not thinking about a thing.

c.   Talking is another activity that is difficult to assess. Idle chatter is entirely different from teamwork members problem-solving. The simple request for information, such as "what were you talking about?" may not be the solution. Personal phone conversations are difficult to sort out from business calls. Again, asking for details may not be rewarding.

d.   P/OM's sampling of workers is not designed to catch workers off-guard. It is best, therefore, to ask workers, beforehand, if they can account for the way that they spend their time. When they cannot, it seems sensible to offer work sampling as a method to help in this regard.

e.   There are formulas for sample size that are related to establishing confidence intervals. Such intervals reflect the variability of the data. If it turns out that all employees are on the telephone 96 percent of the time, then there is low variability in activity profiles, and the sample size does not have to be large to believe that the data are accurate.

9   Synthetic time standards can be used to estimate output rates and costs for jobs that have not yet been created or run as a pilot plant. (Pilot plants are less than full-scale production run simulations.) There is a long history in the use of basic work modules for predetermined time standards. The statements in a. through e. examine some aspects of this methodology. One statement is not acceptable. Which statement is incorrect?

a.   Frank B. Gilbreth (author of *Cheaper by the Dozen*, and he did have 12 children) was the management pioneer who created the first set of job elements about 100 years ago. He called the modules *therbligs*, which was almost an inversion (palindrome) of his name. The 17 therbligs are also called an *alphabet* because they can be strung together like letters in a word.

b.   *Grasp, position*, and *assemble* are three basic work modules. Many jobs are combinations of these elements. *Hold*, on the other hand, is not a fundamental part of any job.

c.   A well-known set of work standards is called the MTM – 1Ⓡ. A second generation of synthesized data was called MTM – UASⓇ. From these basic elements, even higher-order systems have emerged. For further information see http://www.mtm.org.

d.   Transnational and multinational corporations continue to shift labor-intensive work to areas of the world where direct labor is relatively inexpensive. Also, firms will outsource parts that require labor-intensive inputs. Control over costs requires standards. Synthetic standards will be increasingly important until automation replaces the labor-intensive component of both manufacturing and services.

e.   Predetermined time systems do not require leveling because workers are not performing jobs that have to be corrected as being done at faster, slower, or average rates. This is an advantage of the predetermined systems.

10   General statements about managing work systems are given in parts a. through e. Which statement is not acceptable?

a.   System-wide evaluations (of a set of interdependent jobs) is less valuable to the organization than individual job evaluations (done one job at a time).

b.   Wage determination is a comparative matter. If the company across the street has similar jobs, it is important to note the wages being paid by that company. For comparison purposes, jobs can be classified by difficulty, training, skills required, and the value of the job to the company.

c.   *Target costing* is a philosophy that some Japanese companies pioneered. It is now used by lean production advocates everywhere. The idea is to set an amount that can be spent for a component. For example, given the wage rate, the specification states that the amount of labor that can be used to make the part is constrained to be no more than *x*. The designers are asked to produce practical specifications that meet the labor constraints. It may be decided to make the part in China at a lower wage rate so that the amount of labor allowed can be raised.

d. *Job enrichment* has as its foundation the motivation of workers to do a good job. It is theorized that in some cultures, but not all cases, pride in workmanship can be elevated by increasing the work content per employee. Volvo, the Swedish automaker, was known for small teams building an entire car. The concept was extreme. A group of workers from GM (Detroit) visited Volvo and worked in the Uddevalla plant. Most of this group, when the experiment ended, rejected the Volvo enrichment plan for themselves in the United States.

e. Human Factors International has a business psychological orientation to human resource management. The company, based in the UK has a website at http://www.humanfactors.co.uk. At this website, clicking on "Article" brings up a menu of topics and industries about which members of this company have written. This is a unique and useful way to get acquainted with a particular aspect of the teamwork and training fields.

Additional Readings

Barnes, Ralph M. *Motion and Time Study: Design and Measurement of Work*, 7e. Hoboken, NJ: John Wiley & Sons, July 1980.

Briscoe, Dennis R. *International Human Resource Management*. Englewood Cliffs, NJ: Prentice-Hall, 1995.

Certo, Sam. *Human Relations Today: Concepts and Skills*. Richard Irwin. Burr Ridge, IL: Irwin, 1995.

———. *Supervision: Concepts and Skill-Building*, 6e. New York: McGraw-Hill/Irwin, January 2007.

Cooper, Robin, and Robert S. Kaplan. "Activity-Based Systems: Measuring the Costs of Resource Usage." *Accounting Horizons* (September 1992).

Forrester, J. W. *Industrial Dynamics*. New York: Wiley, 1961.

Gilbreth, F. B. *Primer of Scientific Management*. New York: D. Van Nostrand, 1914.

Joy, Louis W., III, and Jo A. Joy. *Frontline Teamwork*. Burr Ridge, IL: Irwin, 1993.

Kaplan, Robert S., and David P. Norton. *The Balanced Scorecard: Translating Strategy into Action*. Cambridge, MA: Harvard Business School Press, September 1996.

Katzenbach, Jon R., and Douglas K. Smith. *The Wisdom of Teams: Creating the High-Performance Organization*. Harper Business, 1994.

Maskell, Brian H. *Performance Measurement for World Class Manufacturing*. Cambridge, MA: Productivity Press, 1991.

Meyers, Fred E. and Jim R. Stewart. *Motion and Time Study for Lean Manufacturing*, 3e. Englewood Cliffs, NJ: Prentice-Hall, May 2001.

Neal, James E., Jr. *Effective Phrases for Performance Analysis: A Guide to Successful Evaluations. Neal Publications*, 10e. Englewood Cliffs, NJ: Prentice-Hall, January 2003.

Niven, Paul R. *Balanced Scorecard Step-by-Step: Maximizing Performance and Maintaining Results*. Hoboken, NY: John Wiley & Sons, March 2002.

Roethlisberger, F. J., and W. J. Dickson. *Management and the Worker*. Cambridge, MA: Harvard University Press, 1939.

Rogelberg, Steven G. *Encyclopedia of Industrial and Organizational Psychology* (2 volumes). Thousand Oaks, CA: Sage Publications, August 2006 .

Rothwell, R., Prescott, R., Gibson, C., Herrera, J. *Encyclopedia of Human Resource Management*, Vols I–III . New York: Jossey Bass/Wiley. Publish date June 2008.

Scholtes, P. R., et al. *The Team Handbook*. Madison, WI Joiner Associates (608-238-8134), 1989.

Shenkar, Oded (ed). *Global Perspectives of Human Resource Management*. Englewood Cliffs, NJ: Prentice-Hall, 1995.

Tilley, A. R. *The Measure of Man and Woman: Human Factors in Design*. New York: Henry Dreyfuss Associates. From The Whitney Library of Design, imprint of Watson-Guptill Publications, 1993.

Tippett, L. H. C. "Statistical Methods in Textile Research." *Journal of the Textile Institute Transactions*, vol. 26 (February 1935).

Notes

1. Frank Williams. "NUMMI RIP? Toyota Considers Dumping UAW Plant." Http://www.thetruthaboutcars.com/?p=4045 (July 3, 2007).
2. Jon R. Katzenbach and Douglas K. Smith. *The Wisdom of Teams: Creating the High-Performance Organization*. Harper Business, 1994.

3. Patrick M. Lencioni. "The Five Dysfunctions of a Team: A Leadership Fable." San Francisco: Jossey-Bass, A Wiley Company, 2002. From the introduction. See also, *Team Assessment Addendum,* Pfeiffer, 2007.

4. See http://www.learning-org.com/03.01/0065.html (January 14, 2003).

5. Brian H. Maskell. *Performance Measurement for World Class Manufacturing.* Cambridge, MA: Productivity Press, 1991.

6. Brian H. Maskell and Bruce Baggaley. *Practical Lean Accounting: A Proven System for Measuring and Managing the Lean Enterprise.* University Park, IL: Productivity Press, 2003.

7. Robin Cooper and Robert S. Kaplan. "Activity-Based Systems: Measuring the Costs of Resource Usage." *Accounting Horizons* (September, 1992).

8. L. H. C. Tippett. "Statistical Methods in Textile Research." *Journal of the Textile Institute Transactions,* vol. 26 (February, 1935): 51–55.

9. F. B. Gilbreth. *Primer of Scientific Management.* New York: D. Van Nostrand, 1914.

10. See http://www.mtm.org for information about the various MTM Systems.

11. F. J. Roethlisberger and W. J. Dickson. *Management and the Worker.* Cambridge, MA: Harvard University Press, 1939.

12. J. W. Forrester. *Industrial Dynamics.* New York: Wiley, 1961. This book develops the methods of systems dynamics.

Enrichment Activity 9: Ergonomics (also known as) Human Factors

The traditional part of managing human resources from the point of view of P/OM is taking care of all employees with a special concern for production employees. Doing that well must be extended to taking care of customers. They depend on P/OM to treat them as a valued human resource that needs to be taken care of with respect to safety, security, overall well-being, and comfort.

P/OM must also take care of people making deliveries, manning the checkout counters, and those who work in the suppliers' organizations. P/OM may even be held responsible for providing for the well-being of everyone coming in contact with the company in any way. P/OM knowledge about ergonomics could deflect a lawsuit brought by someone walking on the sidewalk who trips and breaks a leg. How is this possible? First, having considered and documented the possibility provides a legal advantage. Second, having taken steps to prevent broken legs based on knowledge of mistakes people make and putting up barriers to prevent those mistakes is a legal coup. This is where ergonomics enters.

Ergonomics

The systematic study of how people physically interact with their environment, equipment, facilities, machines, and products.

Ergonomics, a British term that is now accepted globally, is the systematic study of how people physically interact with their working environment, including their equipment, facilities, products, and other people. Ergonomic systems design is complex. It promises to try to deliver everything that needs to be done to assure safety, security, overall well-being, and comfort. Equivalent promises are made by identical fields with different names including *human factors, human engineering, and biomechanics.*

The prime rule of ergonomics is safety first for workers at their jobs and consumers using products produced by the company. In the United States, workplace safety is monitored by OSHA, the Occupational Safety and Health Administration created in 1970. There also is a Consumer Product Safety Commission to deal with the safety of products as diverse as children's toys and automobiles.

Acceptable levels of safety are difficult to specify. The ideal situation is "perfect" safety, but like zero defects, perfect safety is an unobtainable state. So-called "*safety factors*" are designed into bridges, ships, and planes. This is done to raise safety to as near-perfect levels as possible. Such safety levels are called *fail-safe systems.* This is supposed to mean that the system is immune to failure. Interpret this as follows: The probabilities of such occurrences are so small they can be ignored. According to Borel, these might be events associated with probabilities in the neighborhood of one in one in a million (0.000001).*

This is interesting because the probability of winning most lotteries is about one in fourteen million. Borel was brilliant but lived in a different era. There were one fourth as many people in the world.

The design of facilities and the working environment is a form of industrial architecture. In many ways, it represents the same kinds of approaches and the same set of human factors objectives as those of industrial designers. Industrial design is the profession that assumes responsibility for the architecture of products, machines, and living spaces, among other things.** Industrial designers are responsible for achieving safety, comfort, and aesthetically pleasing design results.

The human factors area treats both the physiological and psychological characteristics of people. It attempts to provide high levels of safety and comfort. It is concerned with the appearances of things, and the way they affect efficiency. All the senses and interrelationships of the senses to both motor and mental responses are part of the fabric of these factors, which describe the interactions of the worker and the workplace, the plant, and the office as well as the customer and the product. The systems point of view is essential to capture the interactions between the workforce and the workplace.

Not just sight, illumination, and color concern the designer; hearing, noise, taste, smells, temperature changes, and body orientation are other factors that condition the attitudes, performance, safety, and comfort of the system's workforce.

What is not immediately apparent is the flaw in logic of an individual using himself/herself as a physical model of what other people need or want. Self is not a sufficient design guide for the consumer product design or for employee workplace considerations. The requirements of a representative distribution of people can be determined. A design based on statistical knowledge regarding these dimensions would satisfy the minimum requirements for a majority of potential users.

Individual preferences vary with respect to the amount of light that is both comfortable and satisfactory for accomplishing a given job. Many studies have been conducted to determine superior designs for controls such as dials, gauges, and tracking devices on airplanes, cars, and industrial machines. The sense of hearing has been studied with equal fervor. Many production operations are quiet, but others produce extremely high noise levels with effects on workers and potential damage to hearing.

Ergonomics is one of the most important competitive issues in new product and process design.

Enrichment Challenges 9

1 What is the derivation of the word "ergonomics"?

2 It has been said that OSHA has more claims for repetitive stress or overuse syndrome (such as carpal tunnel) than any other occupational illness or injury. How can the design of the environment be put to work to alleviate this serious situation?

3 Because repetitive stress syndrome is the result of continuous repetition of certain motions, what sort of statistical studies might be undertaken to improve the design of the job?

4 What is meant by a fail-safe system?

5 Certain workers have a history of numerous accidents, whereas most workers have few accidents. What can be done for those who are accident prone?

6 Industrial designers have an orientation to the systems approach, which is critical for their success. Why is this so?

*Emile Borel. "Valeur Pratique et Philosophie des Probabilities." *Traite du Cacul des Probabilities et de ses Applications*, tome IV, fascicule 3. (Ed.) Emile Borel (Gautier-Villars Paris: Henry Dreyfuss Associates, 1950).

**A. R. Tilley. *The Measure of Man and Woman: Human Factors in Design.* Henry Dreyfuss Associates New York: Henry Dreyfuss Associates. From The Whitney Library of Design, imprint of Watson-Guptill Publications, 1993, p. 66.

Supply Chain Capacity Planning

10

Chapter 10 defines supply chain capacity management in various ways and relates decisions about supply chain capacity to peak and off-peak demand. Modular design of parts (and service activities can be viewed in the same way) is a means for increasing supply chain capacity. Group technology production methods (applicable to service activities, too) are presented as another method for augmenting supply chain capacity. Breakeven models are at the crux of capacity decisions. For this reason, breakeven analysis is developed as a means of choosing the best among a set of alternative supply chain capacity configurations. Also, linear programming is shown to be a preferred method for determination of how best to design and use supply chain production systems capacities. The relevance of the learning curve model (and thereby, investments in training) to increase supply chain capacity utilization is explained.

After reading this chapter, you should be able to:

- Define supply chain capacity and explain how it is measured.
- Discuss how efficiency and utilization relate to actual measured supply chain capacity.
- Explain why the goal of 100 percent utilization is an outdated objective that can be counterproductive.
- Discuss planning supply chain capacity to deal with peak and off-peak demand.
- Explain how bottlenecks affect supply chain capacity; discuss what to do about them.
- Describe the effects of delay on the capacity to make and deliver products and services throughout the supply chain.
- Set up the beer game to help team members visualize the effects of delay on out-of-stocks and overstocks in the supply chain.
- Explain the application of breakeven as a percent of maximum capacity to determine work configuration preferences.
- Describe why breakeven analysis is called a quintessential systems model.
- Explain how linear programming relates supply chain productive capacity and optimal product mix determination.
- Describe how linear programming depends upon systems-wide inputs.
- Use Solver to calculate the optimal product mix with LP
- Explain how modular production and group technology are approaches that increase realizable supply chain capacity.
- Describe what the learning curve reflects and explain how learning increases actual supply chain capacity.

The Systems Viewpoint

Capacity management relates to how the existing system is used. The systems viewpoint broadens the scope of inquiry to include questions about the existing arrangement and whether alternative configurations might not provide superior alternatives. The discussion of options cannot be pursued without consultations between marketing, finance, R&D, and OM. Capacity is always limited by the supply chain bottleneck. The viewpoint must be systems-wide to scan across facilities with excess capacity in order to spot the overloaded resources that are struggling to keep up with the rest of the system. Delays are another source of capacity problems that are often caused by factors that are outside the organization's boundaries. Thus, suppliers must be viewed as part of the system to understand swings in demand caused by delays that create above peak and below normal requirements throughout the entire supply chain.

Strategic Thinking

Anyone who has ever played the beer model game is permanently converted to strategic systems thinking. As another option, the breakeven model (BEM) deserves an award for being the quintessential strategic systems model of the organization. In spite of the fact that a breakeven model relates every function, it has been taught for years as a capital budgeting function and nothing more. Next, consider linear programming. It is another model that demands systems thinking even though it can be taught as a means of modeling resource management, or simply as "the blending problem." LP is a way of looking at capacity management through the eyes of all participants in the big system. Modularity of parts (design) and group technology (for production of families of parts) are powerful strategic concepts that increase an organization's capacity to competitive proportions. The learning curve is another example of a systems concept that relates the learning individual and the learning organization to higher capacity achievement without spending. In this case, "capacity is free."

10-1 Definitions of Supply Chain Capacity

Actual capacity of the supply chain is the greatest throughput rate that can be achieved with the existing configuration of resources and the accepted product or service mix plans. Altering the product or service mix can (and usually will) change actual realizable capacity. Modifying the existing configuration of resources, equipment, and people in the **supply chain** workforce alters real capacity. The systems point of view includes cash as part of the resources because cash can be converted into new machines, which alter real deliverable throughput capacity. The systems viewpoint includes good ideas, which can increase supply chain **capacity** with minimum expenditures.

The formula for actual measured capacity of the supply chain is

$$C = T \times E \times U$$

C = actual measured capacity (in units converted to standard hours)
T = real time available
E = efficiency
U = utilization

10-1a Standard Hours

T is determined by calculating the amount of *time* that is available when fully utilizing the resources that are already in place to make and deliver product throughput. Doubling the number of machines, trucks, etc., doubles the amount of available time, T.

E is the *efficiency* with which time T can be utilized to make and deliver different kinds of product. Then, $T \times E$ is equivalent to standard hours available to make and deliver the products.

U is how much of the available throughput capacity can be (or is) *utilized*. Lack of orders or breakdowns of productive systems diminish U. When T and E and U are multiplied, the product is C, the actual supply chain capacity that is being (or has been) utilized.

Table 10-1 illustrates the calculations.

Actual capacity
Realistic maximum amount of storage space or output rate that can be achieved with the existing configuration of resources and the accepted product or service mix plans.

Supply chain
The linkage between raw materials and finished products (goods and services) delivered into the hands of the customers.

Capacity
There are two basic types of capacity. One is storage space and the other is throughput flow rates.

Table 10-1	Standard Hours of Product Throughput for the Supply Chain				
Capacity Utilized (C) in Standard Hours of PT	**Part**	**Monday**	**Tuesday**	**Wednesday**	**Thursday**	**Friday**
	T101	25	20	65	18	30
	T102	65	10	25	40	0
	MW11	40	90	50	70	80
	TOTAL	130	120	140	128	110

Note: PT is product throughput

Assume that the supply chain is rated with a *maximum capacity* of 150 standard hours of throughput. It never achieves the maximum, but comes closest to doing so on Wednesday. There are a variety of reasons why the system does not achieve maximum throughput. Two factors embodied in E and U are explained later. Another reason could be that the system has bottlenecks and flow disruptions.

E, the efficiency, is a proportional factor used to convert units of throughput to standard times. Systems of machines and people that work slower have lower efficiency than those that have a higher productive output. Often, the best in the class is given an efficiency of one. It is to be expected that variations in efficiency will occur. Sometimes the source of the variation can be traced. If it is significant variation, then it should be corrected. Unexplained fluctuations in capacity are unpleasant and unprofitable.

If a supply chain is operating at 90 percent of the standard time because a supplier (somewhere along the supply chain line) has delivered defective product, remedial action must be taken with supplies on hand and the problem must be corrected with future deliveries.

U, the utilization, is applied as a proportional correction to standard time when there are supply chain disruptions. Even when everything is running as planned, the value of U is usually less than 100 percent. If the system is operating even faster, the value of U can exceed 100 percent. There are pros and cons related to running supply chains above maximum rated capacity. How long maximum capacity is exceeded also counts.

U is a measure to be wary of when it becomes an objective of management to keep it as close to 100 percent as possible. There are sound economic reasons not to operate supply chains above capacity. For example, stop production when the planned output quota has been met and safety stock is sufficient. Shutting down the production system for 2 hours of an 8-hour day means that the U measure goes to 75 percent. Actual measured supply chain capacity is going to be reduced by a fourth.

Management must establish the fact that supply chains are composed of complex subsystems some of which cannot function above capacity for very long. The costs of unsold throughput must be analyzed. How long will stored output remain as inventory? Are there fluctuations in demand that they will buffer or is the buffer in place already? The costs of arbitrary utilization of supply chain capacity to eliminate less than one hundred percent utilization should be recognized for what it is—waste of time and money due to fear of seeming to waste (unutilized) capacity. An appropriate **decision model** can be constructed to set proper supply chain throughput.

Decision model

Strategies, states of nature, probabilities of states of nature (forecasts for these probabilities), expected values for outcomes, and strategies chosen for delivering outcomes in time with goals and objectives.

As an example, assume that U is 0.963. This is likely to be viewed as a more reasonable utilization factor than 0.750. P/OM, in general, will not tolerate a permanent situation where utilization factors are below 0.900. Still, the target numbers will be dependent on the situation. For example, in service organizations, a value of U might be accepted to keep queues short. Cyclical supply chain demand systems can be expected to cycle between utilization factors in the 0.700 range and then up to more than 100 percent capacity. Cyclical industry companies prefer having excess capacity in reserve and expect to operate effectively below the misleading ideal of 100 percent utilization.

Using data in Table 10-1, the value of 130 actual standard hours of throughput, might have been obtained as follows:

$$C = T \times E \times U = 150 \times 0.9 \times 0.963 = 130 \text{ actual standard hours}$$

The ratio of actual standard hours to maximum standard hours is equal to $130/150 = 0.87$ or 87 percent.

10-1b Maximum Rated Supply Chain Capacities

A critical supply chain definition of capacity is related to containment. In fact, maximum capacity may be directly related to what can be maximally stored or contained somewhere along the supply chain route. Containment capacity takes many forms (i.e., the auditorium has a seating capacity of 360, the gas tank will hold 16 gallons, the restaurant freezer can store up to 40 meals in standard units).

Maximum supply chain capacity can also be defined as maximum sustained throughput of goods or services. Both meanings are regularly used by P/OM. The capacity to contain or store inventory is a well-received measure of capacity. Operations capacity describes how many units can be supplied per unit of time. For services, a bank might compare the maximum number of people the bank teller can process per hour with the maximum number of people the ATM can process per hour. This is a supply chain service capacity comparison.

For a manufacturing supply chain example, compare the maximum number of hot dogs Oscar Meyer can make and ship per hour with the maximum number of hot dogs Hebrew National can make and ship per hour. In this supply chain the ingredients required to make the products have a flow through rate that must match the producers' rates.

This comparison is one that both companies would like to make to compare their PMCs (productivities at maximum capacity). PMC makes an excellent benchmarking measure. In supply chain terms, benchmarking is a systematic comparison of fundamental measures with those of contestants performing similar supply chain functions.

Consider using maximum containments within the supply chain as a benchmarking measure. Generally, the larger the storage facility, the more material sitting around without having value added, and the poorer the performance measure. However, if a company built substantial petroleum storage facilities early in 1973, it would have been in the catbird seat when the oil embargo in the fall of 1973 created severe petroleum shortages. The harsh effects of the oil crisis lasted through the end of March 1974.

The utilization of supply chain containment capacity is an important factor for P/OM to consider. Having extra capacity would not have been a boon to Mobil Oil unless the tanks were filled with crudes and fuels. On the other hand, high utilization of containment capacity runs counter to the desire for low inventory levels, just-in-time deliveries, and constant value adding.

These two kinds of capacity situations have a trade-off relationship. Extracapacity and undercapacity within the supply chain are shown in Figure 10-1. When market **demand** falls below maximum supply capacity ($MD < MSC$), the production system can feed storage and build up inventories. When market demand exceeds maximum supply capacity ($MD > MSC$), the inventory can be used to help meet that demand.

The diagonal line in Figure 10-1 represents the maximum capacity to supply product. It is a rate of throughput that at the end of period T has the capability of producing S units. Realistically, the curved line is sometimes below the diagonal and sometimes above it. For convenience, the market demand rate over the entire period T accumulates total demand of S.

Difficult to Store Service Capacity

The concept developed here and shown in Figure 10-1 does not apply to services as readily as to goods being manufactured. This is because most services cannot be stored. The extracapacity on the left side of Figure 10-1 is wasted idle time for service personnel. For

Demand

Units of product (goods and/or services) requested for delivery within a period of time constitute demand.

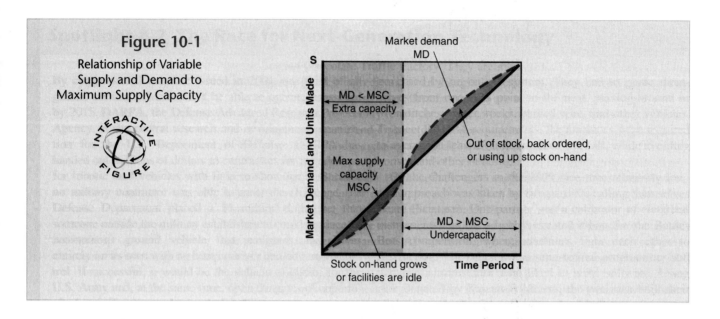

Figure 10-1

Relationship of Variable Supply and Demand to Maximum Supply Capacity

goods it can represent building stock on-hand that can be drawn down when the under-capacity, right side of Figure 10-1, occurs.

Backordering Augments Service Capacity

If the customer is willing, backorders can be used to satisfy demand when there is no inventory available. This applies to services that cannot be stored. It applies as well to the manufacturer who is out of stock. The overloaded system does not have to turn away orders if the customer agrees to wait until other customers' jobs are finished.

10-2 Peak and Off-Peak Supply Chain Demand

Another question about planning supply chain capacity is: "Should the maximum output capacity be great enough to handle peak load?" This is equivalent to providing enough electrical generating power to supply all needs for air-conditioning demand on extremely hot business days. Alternatively, should telephone companies have enough capacity to take care of all phone calls without any delays for Valentine's Day and Mother's Day? These holidays are known as the heaviest traffic days for phone companies.

The rule for putting peak versus nonpeak capacity into place is

Buy peak capacity when: $C_p < C_{np}$

C_p is the extra investment required to assure peak capacity. In other words, it is the investment for peak capacity less that required to meet average demand, depreciated over the life of the system. Say it takes an extra \$5,000,000 to increase capacity from average to peak. This amount is spread out over 10 years, or \$500,000 per year.

C_{np} is the cost of not having capacity to meet demands that are greater than the average demand. It is determined by the costs of such events as brownouts, power failures, loss of goodwill in the community, and there are lost revenues as well. Say that the total cost averages \$30,000 per incident.

Figure 10-2 provides an illustration of the difference between peak and off-peak average demand, as well as the level of normal supply, which is above off-peak average in this case.

To illustrate with a case, assume that the probability that actual supply chain demand exceeds average demand is estimated to be 5 percent of the year or roughly 18 summer days. Total cost associated with C_{np} is

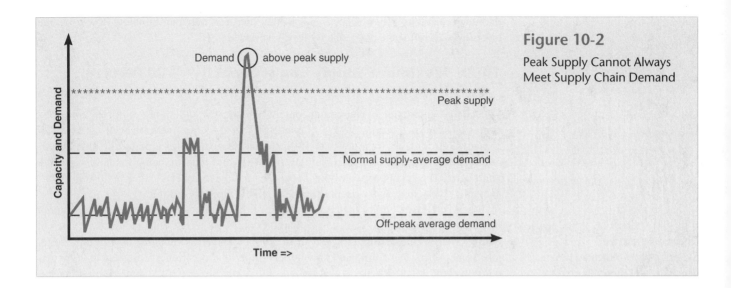

Figure 10-2

Peak Supply Cannot Always
Meet Supply Chain Demand

$$365 \times 0.05 \times \$30,000 = \$547,500$$

This is more than the investment to prevent any brownouts, so the best advice, based on these figures, is to buy the equipment to generate sufficient power to meet peak demands.

10-2a Qualitative Aspects of Supply Chain Capacity

"As is our confidence, so is our capacity."

—William Hazlitt[1]

If our confidence is high, so is our capacity. But this is a different definition of the word. Usually, when capacity is treated in a P/OM context, the quantitative point of view prevails. There are, however, qualitative aspects that are important to cite.

It is not unusual to hear "he or she has the capacity to be a fine ballplayer, chef, manager, . . . , etc." This invokes mental ability or physical skills. Organizations have capacities to deal with problems and opportunities. It is like an inventory of capabilities. Oftentimes, only when tested does the capacity to outperform the normal emerge.

Motorola developed the capacity to meet quality standards that are far superior to most other companies. Robert Galvin, former chairman of Motorola, challenged the company to develop peak capability for quality production.

The company had been embarrassed by the Japanese company Quasar's purchase of its TV division, which had a history of severe defectives—reporting between 150 and 180 defects per 100 sets. Within three years, traditional Japanese quality had asserted itself. The defect rate had dropped to 3 or 4 per 100 sets. Service calls dropped from $22 million to less than $4 million. In-plant repair staff went from 120 to 15. Quality people liked to tell the story. Galvin did not like to hear the story and threw down the gauntlet.

Motorola has since become a world leader in the production of quality products. Motorola set for itself a difficult quality goal of 3.4 defects per million parts. This is associated with (modified) six-sigma limits as compared to three-sigma limits in quality control (see Spotlight 7-2). Motorola was the first company to win the Baldrige Award for quality ability.

Skillful management can increase the level of capacity that is achieved. Managing installed physical capacity properly means obtaining the maximum available capacity. This goal is particularly relevant when dealing with management of peak demand. If the maximum capacity of the process is less than the peak demand, knowing how to assign priorities will influence real capacity levels achieved.

10-2b Maximum Supply Chain Capacity—100 Percent Rating

Capacity as measured by maximum output volume per unit time, or throughput rate, comes closest to capturing the P/OM concept. That does not make it easy to measure. It is possible to produce at more than 100 percent of capacity for a period of time. Maximum capacity depends on who is doing the work and what is being made or serviced. Although 100 percent and maximum capacity are illusive concepts, they are useful standards to go by as long as the users are aware of their arbitrary nature.

When people are part of the process, some of the qualitative aspects of capacity cannot be ignored. Some people work faster than others. Most people fluctuate in their rates of output. There is a **learning curve** at work. People learn from practice how to do a better job. Some people can learn faster than others. Individuality allows some people to do certain jobs better than others. In this regard, all people are not alike. Ambiguity, opportunity, and challenge abound in this arena.

Machines work at different speeds. NASCAR drivers illustrate that point. Different velocities are best for optimal fuel consumption, minimum tire wear, and life of the car. Machines can be set for certain speeds that engineers would say are equivalent to 100 percent of their capacities. Ask the engineer what will happen if the machine is set to work faster. A typical answer will be that the machine will wear out sooner.

Figure 10-3 shows two patterns that are typical of wear-out life and failure as a function of accumulated usage and age. Pattern A illustrates the diminishing output lumens of a lightbulb before final failure. Pattern B shows a Weibull-type distribution, which reflects the high initial mortality of certain products (such as lightbulbs). Then there is a period of low product mortality until it reaches the expected time of failure. Time-of-failure distributions must be understood if capacity is to be managed properly.

Learning curve
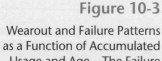
Describes how repeated practice decreases the time required to do a job.

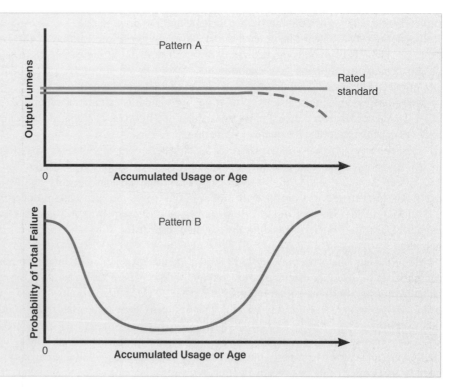

Figure 10-3

Wearout and Failure Patterns as a Function of Accumulated Usage and Age—The Failure Distribution (Pattern B) Is the Weibull Distribution

Setting standards for maximum output capacity creates an interesting comparison between what people and machines can do. For highly repetitive jobs, most machines can be set to work faster than people. For heavy and difficult work, especially in environments that are very hot, noisy, and even life threatening, machines win without question. Thus, robots are the best choice for nuclear experimentation. Also affecting the determination of capacity is the fact that machines can break down and people can be absent. Maximum capacity is usually determined with all the systems on go.

On the other hand, automated voice mail systems are tedious, although improving. They can require listening to endless options. It is not unusual to have to listen to seven or eight alternatives before getting to the one that applies. It is generally faster, and more gratifying, for the customer to speak to an operator but it is more costly.

Capabilities and capacities of automated systems are improving. The bank teller can perform transactions that ATMs cannot handle but for routine requests ATMs are faster and cost less. Especially with services, capacity measures are a function of the kinds of demands on the systems. Excess demand tends to deteriorate the performance of service systems. Requirements for special services that are common in many systems such as health care and education also make it difficult to establish maximum capacity figures.

Capricious Demand

Capacity planning is one of the most important business activities. It is filled with opportunity to manage to advantage and fraught with difficulties. This is especially true if demand is capricious and tough to forecast correctly. Capacity planning is done to reach optimal supply decisions that, it is hoped, will match future demand patterns. This means that capacity planning does not have to be a single frozen value but can be a dynamic trajectory with fluctuations and oscillations. Hackers enjoy swamping server capacity and succeed in bringing systems down. Innocently, the first weekend that the iPhone was sold resulted in so many requests for service that Skype was out of service for many hours.

10-2c Capacity Requirements Planning (CRP)

There are two aspects to **capacity requirements planning (CRP)**. The strategic issues related to long-term planning including **breakeven** concepts and breakeven points and optimal allocation of resources are being treated in this chapter. The shorter-term, tactical issues are operating issues that properly belong to a discussion of material requirements planning. The ability to alter supply chain capacity in steps or stages, as shown in Figure 10-4, is valuable for strategic plans to meet a longer-term goal.

Capacity requirements planning (CRP)
Strategic issues of CRP relate to long-term planning for capacity including breakeven points and optimal allocation of resources.

Breakeven
Breakeven connotes the fact that enough units of product were sold to offset the costs and begin to make a profit.

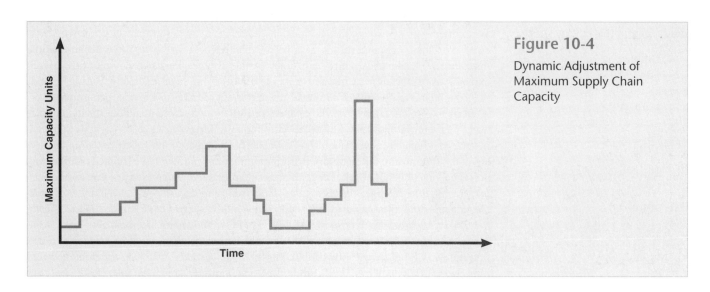

Figure 10-4

Dynamic Adjustment of Maximum Supply Chain Capacity

It takes planning to keep as flexible as possible with respect to supply chain capacity. Combinations of negotiations (as in a power grid) and technology can be brought to bear on a temporary basis. Consider the use of leases and rentals:

Part-time employees are a familiar means for making capacity adjustments, up or down. They do not require either severance pay or fringe benefits. Part-time employees relieve the firm of many other obligations associated with full-time employees. Rentals are an equivalent method for making capacity adjustments with equipment and space without taking on long-term commitments that lock the company into higher capacity than it is likely to need over the long term.

Coproducers and *copackers* are firms used to increase supply by subcontracting with them on a short-, medium-, or long-term basis. For example, a company that sells margarine might make enough to supply 60 percent of its market. The rest of its market demand is supplied by the output of a coproducer that has excess capacity. The product of the coproducer is packed in the subcontracting company's familiar package.

10-3 Upscaling and Downsizing Supply Chain Capacity

Capacity planning for important elements within the total supply chain is often constrained to an optimal size by the engineering requirements of the process. Many chemical processes must be designed and built to a specific size in order to operate properly. Glass windshields require production steps requiring exact amounts of time.

Serialized flow shop processes also are constrained by engineering factors, although to a lesser extent than continuous chemical flow process. Job shop and batch processes are far more flexible with regard to optimal production volume sizes.

To increase maximum capacities, processes can sometimes be operated above their rated capacities by using overtime and faster conveyor speeds. There are quality repercussions and the equipment is seldom designed for sustained overloads.

To meet greater demand, it may be advisable to subcontract with coproducers until such time that additional demand warrants building another plant. Coprocessing does not have the flexibility of batch shops, which can be expanded and contracted within limits.

As the labor component of the process changes, the capacity adjustment reflects this fact, allowing an increase or decrease in the workforce. Because many services are notable for their labor percentage of the cost of goods sold, the capacity adjustment in services often involves people. The increase in service jobs continues to dominate the growth of jobs for the workforce in the United States.

Capacity planning involves not only machinery and labor, but also management. When demand slackens, the notion of reducing managerial capacity (downsizing) emerges. This is particularly the case where management size has grown because of the bureaucratic tendency to hire assistants for assistants. Parkinson's rule that "work expands to fill the time available for its completion"[2] is seen repeatedly during periods of strong markets. Parkinson's rule is carried one step further in the next paragraph.

In many organizations, "work expands until there is no time available for its completion." This means that new information is requested, new tasks are assigned, there are never enough people; everyone is busy. Capacity is increased until there are so many levels in the organizational hierarchy that communications almost never make it all the way up. The management at each level becomes self-protective and an outside consulting firm is often hired to downsize the company. This usually means slicing out the bulge of middle management. After considerable corporate malfeasance at the highest levels during the 2002 recession, compensation of CEOs, CFOs, and other top managers were reassessed and the Sarbanes–Oxley (SOX) act put new constraints on their capacity to act. Spotlight 20-1 raises questions about the possibility that SOX has overachieved and inhibited P/OM creativity. The result seems to be more flexible legal interpretations.

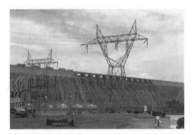

© 2008 Jupiterimages Corporation

Capacity decisions concern how to meet peak demand and yet not have too much in reserve for off-peak times. The capacity of the dam and the transmission lines carried by the towers all play a part in this energy supply chain.

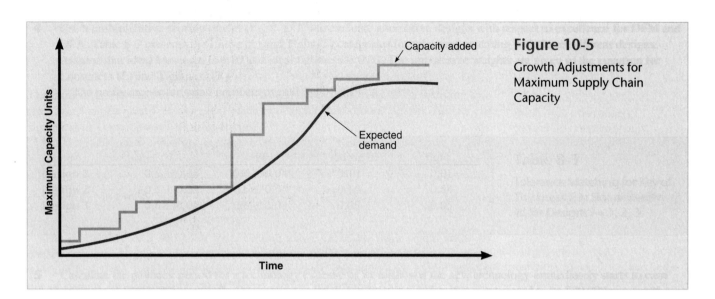

Figure 10-5

Growth Adjustments for Maximum Supply Chain Capacity

For growth operations, excluding continuous processes such as the chemical plants described earlier, there is a need to adjust capacity to match increases in demand. Typically adjustments lead or lag, depending on the industry. Figure 10-5 shows an industry capacity-adding pattern that tries to stay ahead of the curve. This is the situation for electric utilities.

Ideally, adjustments can be accomplished in an ascending staircase of steps. The timing and the size of the increments need to be carefully considered. The issue of whether there are natural increments of added capacity needs to be addressed. These natural increments are like buckets of supply that have minimum cost per unit of added capacity. If not, it may be necessary to reengineer the present supply chain system. Scrap the current one and introduce a new one.

10-4 Bottlenecks and Supply Chain Capacity

Another major issue in determining maximum capacity is the effect of bottlenecks, which limit throughput rates of parts of the supply chain. Real capacity can be much lower than the apparent capacity of individual components of the supply chain. The system's point of view requires that the subject of bottlenecks be thoroughly addressed when dealing with the design and measurement of supply chain capacity.

Toward this end, the effects of finite scheduling and synchronized manufacturing should be considered when dealing with capacity. A review of the **V-A-T** categories for classifying processes is in order. V-A-T was developed by Eli Goldratt's organization, which initially marketed it as **OPT** (Optimal Production Technique). Later, in line with Goldratt's writings it became widely known as **TOC** (Theory of Constraints),[3] See Spotlight 16-2, and Additional Readings (at end of chapter).

V-processes are analytical. They start with a single commodity at the bottom and then branch out into refined by-products at the top. A-processes are synthetic, starting at the bottom with several inputs. These are then combined to yield a single marketable product. The classification would also apply to a few products instead of a single one.

The Theory of Constraints identified combinations of A and V processes as a T-process. Although bottlenecks can and do appear in A and V processes, they are most likely to occur in the T-process. This is because conflicting patterns occur when synthesis and analysis are simultaneously present. It may help to point out that synthesis is also known as *aggregation* (or *assembly*) and analysis is known as *disaggregation* (or *disassembly*). Synthesis is also the act of combining, and analysis is the act of partitioning.

© 2008 Jupiterimages Corporation

Bottlenecks constrain process flows, but it is useful to recall that the name refers to the physical constriction that prevents liquids from spilling when they are poured into a glass. The photo shows seven bottlenecks, which might occur in a complex process.

V-A-T

Categorization for classifying processes. V-processes are analytic. A-processes are synthetic. T-processes are combinations of V and A.

OPT

Original name for a finite production scheduling technique. The lots are of finite size. Now called *Theory of Constraints (TOC)*.

TOC

Theory of Constraints is now the preferred name for finite production scheduling rules.

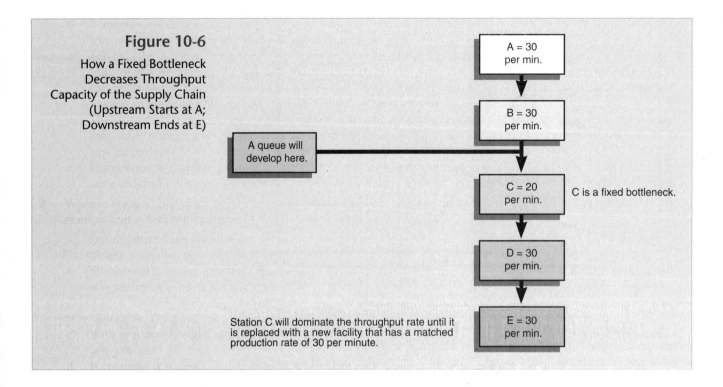

Figure 10-6

How a Fixed Bottleneck Decreases Throughput Capacity of the Supply Chain (Upstream Starts at A; Downstream Ends at E)

A = 30 per min.

B = 30 per min.

A queue will develop here.

C = 20 per min.

C is a fixed bottleneck.

D = 30 per min.

E = 30 per min.

Station C will dominate the throughput rate until it is replaced with a new facility that has a matched production rate of 30 per minute.

Line balancing the flow shop is an important P/OM topic discussed in Chapter 17, "Cycle-Time Management Increases Productivity." This topic is focused on serialized production systems, which are primarily synthetic. When a flow shop is changed over to make different models, analytic characteristics begin to appear.

When determining capacity, it is essential to consider two kinds of bottlenecks. The *first* is a fixed bottleneck in an unbalanced line of a flow shop. Recall that the flow shop is an A-type system. Figure 10-6 illustrates a fixed bottleneck in such a system.

Note that Station C has a maximum throughput rate of 20 per minute. All the other stations are rated 30 per minute. Station C will continue to dominate the throughput rate until it is replaced with a new facility that has a matched production rate of 30 per minute.

The line is unbalanced by Station C. A queue, also called a *waiting line*, will develop upstream from Station C. Flow starts upstream and moves downstream as shown. As the queue grows, upstream stations will cut their output rate to 20 per minute.

They will do so because they see that the queue is growing and may even be impinging on their own workspace. It is also possible that Station C will refuse to accept any more deliveries. The stations downstream from C have no options. They receive 20 units per minute. Maximum capacity is determined by the bottleneck. TOC/OPT principles call for feeding the bottleneck for the reason that C sets the production pace. If it fails to have work, the production rate falls below 20 per minute.

The *second* type of bottleneck can float from station to station in a job or batch shop identified with V-type systems. These temporary bottlenecks are associated with orders that have large lot sizes. The large lot ties up each of the machines on the order's routing schedule. Floating bottlenecks can make the determination of maximum capacity extremely difficult.

One approach is to select some typical order schedules from past records. By simulating the performance of the batch shop under the condition of efficient scheduling, it is possible to determine the maximum capacity of the system.

It also is possible to note where the bottlenecks are most commonly found. By altering the number and types of general-purpose equipment (GPEs), bottlenecks can be shifted and capacity can be increased.

A few additional points:

1 In some batch shops, the degree of repetition is sufficiently high to allow the scheduling for an average or typical day of orders (called an *average order-schedule day*) to be used as the basis for maximum capacity determination. Better scheduling practices might push the upper limit higher.

2 The V-A-T classification associated with TOC/OPT reflects different possible definitions of maximum capacity. The V and T classes are producing mixed models, and some standard such as standard hours is required. In addition to A and V there is the T-type classification, a combination of A and V.

3 Finite scheduling is what it sounds like. Specific lot sizes are finite, bounded, and restricted. They are not unbounded, as is the potential output from a continuous production system or a flow shop. The lots are scheduled on a finite set of machines in such a way as to maximize throughput and speed deliveries.

4 Synchronized manufacturing occurs when finite scheduling succeeds in fitting jobs to machines so that flows are continuous, stations are balanced, and bottlenecks are fed without queues forming. This is another definition of maximum capacity for a given configuration of equipment.

5 Because equipment and jobs interact to create multiple bottlenecks as well as temporary and floating bottlenecks, the achievement of maximum capacity is a function of the jobs the sales department obtains as well as the facilities P/OM has selected. The mix is dynamic and can change rapidly. Measures of maximum capacity may have to be estimates of averages.

6 Permanent bottlenecks, when they can be identified, are true determinants of capacity. They are easiest to spot and deal with in the flow shop, but can exist in the batch system. A good illustration of this is when the tool crib has a long queue in front of it. Every worker must go to the tool crib to requisition tools for the next job. The bottleneck at the tool crib lengthens the setup and changeover times.

7 Ingenuity is required to deal with measuring actual capacity utilization and defining a meaningful rating of real maximum capacity. Further resourcefulness is needed to spot and remove bottlenecks to increase both measures of capacity.

Queues are waiting lines that result from bottlenecks caused by unbalanced capacities in the supply chain. Discussion of queues is appropriate in this chapter on supply chain capacity, but the equations for queuing are tactical methods for designing the waiting lines. That makes queuing equations tangential to the essential elements of strategic planning for supply chain capacity. See Section 17-6 for equational details.

10-5 Delay Deteriorates Performance in the Supply Chain

Any one of the components in the supply chain can be a bottleneck. The capacity of a supplier can be a bottleneck, for instance. Such a bottleneck will cause the producer to cut production runs. Simultaneously, the producer will notify all other suppliers to ship only a proportion of the regular order. Meanwhile, the manufacturer's warehouse will receive reduced shipments of the finished goods.

The distributor also will be shortchanged. Because the distributor does not have a sufficient inventory to meet all of the demands, retailers' orders will be cut. Finally, customers in the stores will be informed that they have to wait until more goods arrive. This situation, if not quickly remedied, can get progressively worse. Competitors, if they can, will surely take advantage of the failure to "hear the customer's voice."

In the previous scenario, every supply chain player is suffering because of the problems of one supplier. The systems approach deals with such interconnectedness of the supply chain. It focuses on finding ways to reveal what kinds of problems each participant can visit on the others, and on how to remedy failures to meet demand with quality products.

10-5a Contingency Planning for Supply Chain Capacity Crises

The producer may look around for a new supplier, or at least one that can make up the shortfall. A potential backup, even though more costly while the emergency exists, should have been known on a contingency basis. Before the supplier failed to deliver, were there any prewarnings? Did the supplier provide all necessary information about the pending problem? Could the supplier and the producer have worked together to eliminate or reduce the severity of the problem? After-the-fact is too late. Contingency planning for supply chain capacity crises deserves to be done beforehand.

At the same time, the other suppliers will be looking for new customers. Their contingency planning should have taken into account the fact that, through no fault of their own, this crisis has arisen for each of them. When these suppliers find other customers, they may have reduced ability to supply the producer. The distributor may start stocking a competing brand, with serious long-term consequences for the producer's market share. This is a good example of the need to use a broad systems perspective to connect all of the critical functions participating in the supply chain.

Retailers may find that the new competing brand is a hit with their customers. The loss of loyal customers is a serious blow stemming from this supply problem. One supplier's failure can destabilize an entire system, causing reduction in profit and losses in competitive leverage that will be hard to regain. Parts of the process linkages are shown in the systems dynamics chart of Figure 10-7.

10-5b A Supply Chain System—The Better Beer Company Game

Why Use a Game?

A game is a powerful teaching method. The game simulates the situation in such a way that the players recognize the factors that are important. If the game is properly designed, it should lead to players improving their "real world" performance. That results when players understand the drivers of outcomes and throughput.

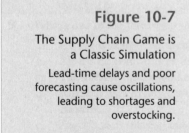

Figure 10-7

The Supply Chain Game is a Classic Simulation

Lead-time delays and poor forecasting cause oscillations, leading to shortages and overstocking.

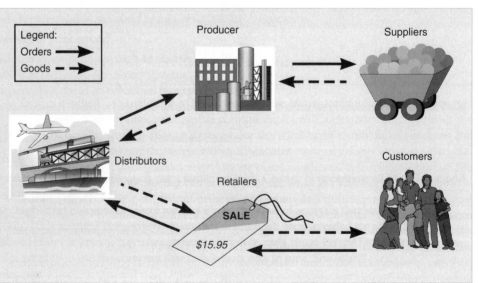

What Can Be Learned from Playing This Game?

Retailers, distributors, and manufacturers can order too much (beer) or too little (beer) when information about actual demand for the brand is delayed along the linkages of a supply chain. The effects of ordering too much or too little as a result of information delays can be costly. The resulting imbalance of demand with existing capacity is important to understand. The game shows how the performance of a linked system is tied to the adequacy of forecasts about future demand. There are measures that can be taken to improve communications and reduce information delays. There are methods for improving forecasts as well. For example, it may not be possible to improve the national estimates of demand unless they are looked at as the sum of regional demands. Once improvement has been made in timeliness of information and better forecasts, the game players can achieve decreased costs.

Professor Jay Forrester used simulation to demonstrate many of these effects in 1961 with his seminal work on systems dynamics.[4] This was at the Sloan School at M.I.T., where the "beer game" was developed in the 1960s. It is a supply chain simulation game[5] that seems to be more than ever entirely applicable and used for instructive purposes.

The "beer game" takes a long time to play. Figures 10-8 and 10-9 replace the game with some charts of simulations that reflect the effects of delays on supply chain decisions made by producers, wholesalers, retailers, suppliers, and customers. These simulations are identified with the *Better Beer Company* whose product, called *Woodstock*, is at the heart of the simulation.

© 2008 Jupiterimages Corporation

Supply chain decisions are often risky, but they are seldom like games of chance where no logic exists to drive the decisions, and they are often aimed at reducing variability rather than gambling because of it.

Week	Begin SOH	Supply	Net SOH	Demand	End SOH	Order Quantity	Delivery Week
1	12	4	16	−4	12	4	5
2	12	4	16	−8	8	8	6
3	8	4	12	−8	4	16	7
4	4	4	8	−8	0	12	8
5	0	4	4	−7	−3	12	9
6	−3	8	5	−6	−1	8	10
7	−1	16	15	−5	10	4	11
8	10	12	22	−8	14	4	12
9	14	12	26	−6	20	0	13
10	20	8	28	−4	24	0	14
11	24	4	28	−4	24	0	15
12	24	4	28	−4	24	0	16
13	24	0	24	−4	20	0	17
14	20	0	20	−6	14	4	18
15	14	0	14	−8	6	8	19
16	6	0	6	−8	−2	10	20
17	−2	0	−2	−4	−6	4	21
18	−6	4	−2	−4	−6	4	22
19	−6	8	2	−4	−2	4	23
20	−2	10	8	−4	4	4	24

Figure 10-8

Supply Chain Simulation of Retailers Ordering from Distributors

Begin week 1 with 12 cases of stock on-hand (SOH). Supply at the start of the week is 4 cases, so net SOH is 16 cases. As expected, the demand is for 4 cases, so end of week 1 SOH is 12 cases. The retailer orders 4 cases and since lead time is 3 weeks, the 4 cases will be delivered at the beginning of week 5. Continue to read Figure 10-8 in this fashion. Note that in weeks 10, 11, and 12, the end SOH rose to 24 cases, double the normal amount.

Figure 10-9

Supply Chain Simulation of Distributors Ordering from Producers (Manufacturers)

To read the chart, follow the same procedure as with Figure 10-8. Thus, week 1 begins with 64 cases of beer at the distributor and end SOH is 64. Lead time is 4 weeks, so the order placed at the end of week 1 is received at the beginning of week 6.

Week	Begin SOH	Supply	Net SOH	Demand	End SOH	Order Quantity	Delivery Week
1	64	16	80	−16	64	16	6
2	64	16	80	−32	48	32	7
3	48	16	64	−32	32	64	8
4	32	16	48	−32	16	64	9
5	16	16	32	−28	4	48	10
6	4	16	20	−24	−4	32	11
7	−4	32	28	−20	8	16	12
8	8	64	72	−16	56	16	13
9	56	64	120	−16	104	0	14
10	104	48	152	−16	136	0	15
11	136	32	168	−16	152	0	16
12	152	16	168	−16	152	0	17
13	152	16	168	−16	152	0	18
14	152	0	152	−24	128	16	19
15	128	0	128	−32	96	32	20
16	96	0	96	−32	64	48	21
17	64	0	64	−64	0	80	18*
18	0	80	80	−94	−16	128	23
19	−16	16	0	−64	−64	80	24
20	−64	32	−32	−32	−64	16	25

*FedEx delivery

*Note that the order for 80 cases made in week 17 is expedited via FedEx at extra cost to be delivered at the beginning of week 18.

In Figure 10-9, the next link in the supply chain connects the producer (manufacturer) and the distributor.

These charts show how the retailer, spotting what seems like a major increase in demand, orders substantially more stock to avoid outages. The retailer's order for more product takes three weeks lead time between placing the order and receiving the shipment. If the increase was just a random pulse in demand, then other retailers might counterbalance the effect by ordering less, because, by chance, they had less than normal demand. The distributor would hardly notice such effects, which tend to cancel each other. The retailer would gradually correct for the extra stock on-hand that resulted.

On the other hand, if there is a common cause for many retailers to experience increased demand, they would all increase their order sizes, perhaps even overreacting with an extra large order to avoid going out of stock. The escalation in order sizes from many retailers would be a red flag to the distributor, who would greatly increase orders placed with the producer.

The 4-week lead time that the producer takes to fill the distributor's orders adds to the delay and increases the chances of large oscillations occurring for all supply chain participants. The producer experiencing such a surge in demand would be best advised to try to meet it with overtime.

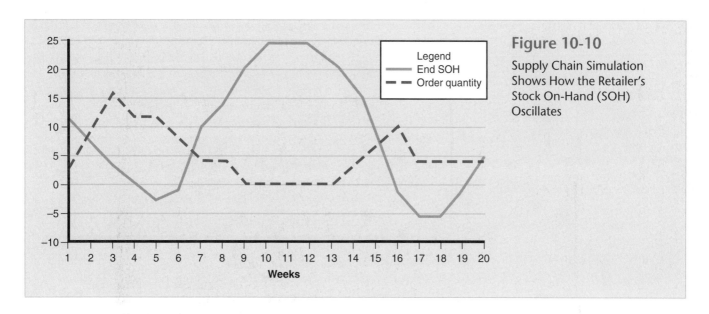

Figure 10-10

Supply Chain Simulation Shows How the Retailer's Stock On-Hand (SOH) Oscillates

Figures 10-10 and 10-11 show the stock on-hand (SOH) and orders placed by the retailer and distributor. It is evident that large oscillations are costing all participants a great deal. This is in spite of the fact that a review of the orders made by both the retailer and the distributor leads to the conclusion that the ordering policies followed were sensible.

Figure 10-12 compares the end stock on-hand (SOH) results for the retailer and the distributor. The effect had seemed enormous to the retailer. However, when the comparison is made with the distributor, the retailer's swings were gentle. The effect is going to be even worse at the producer's level.

If the increased demand seems to be sustained over a reasonable period of time, the producer might invest in more capacity (equipment and people) for what seems like a reasonable change in demand levels. Patient evaluation of the permanency of common causes is easy to counsel, but hard to realize in the face of possible stock outages and unhappy customers, retailers, and distributors. The producer could not resist and invested in more capacity.

The final episode in this scenario is that the cause of the increased demand at the retail level was temporary. It was a common cause, such as might be created by a sensational

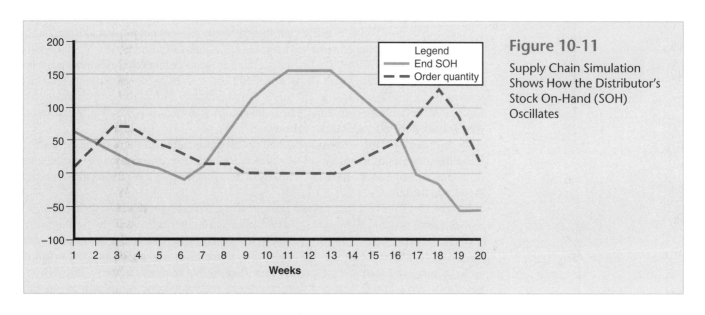

Figure 10-11

Supply Chain Simulation Shows How the Distributor's Stock On-Hand (SOH) Oscillates

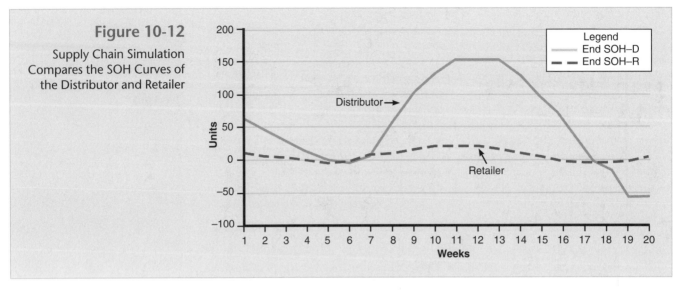

Figure 10-12

Supply Chain Simulation Compares the SOH Curves of the Distributor and Retailer

TV program or a published newspaper article about the product. In reality, the glamour and appeal were gradually forgotten, and the special selling effects eventually disappeared. Remember, this is a game, and the scenario plus what follows are part of role-playing. They are not reality.

The producer now has more capacity than is likely to be used for a long time, if ever. The producer drops the price to be able to sell everything that its new capacity enables it to make. The distributor orders more to take advantage of the probable increase in demand that follows a drop in price. The retailer also is working on lower margins and prefers to push the competitive products.

The product can be beer or soft drinks, cosmetics or food. Supply chains can be extended to industrial products for original equipment manufacturers (OEM). The basic idea of linked supply and demand is valid as long as the relevant supply chain has been identified.

10-5c Cost Drivers for Supply Chain Capacity Planning

Activity-based costing (ABC) systems and lean accounting (LA) methods always help in capacity decisions because they separate costs into those that are associated with resource capacities used and those that are unused. The producer, by monitoring production performance in terms of what is really contributing to the costs of output, would have identified the cost drivers, the costs of the main resource capacities being used. They literally drive costs and profitability. Traditional accounting systems lump many of these costs together and call them *overhead* or *burden*. ABC and LA assign overhead in as correct a way as possible. This is true to the spirit of the purpose. The purpose is to make each product or service reflect its true cost to the company so that it is possible to determine its true contribution to company profits.

In this way, specific costs are obtained for all equipment and facilities being used to make the products of the product line. Each product can be differentiated by the amount of resources that it actually uses. This leads to knowing the real profitability of each product in the line.

Before the TV event that caused sales to jump, Woodstock beer was being charged with the same percent of overhead costs for sales as all other beers made by the company. This charge under conventional accounting hid the fact that Woodstock did not use sales force time to the same extent as the other beers. In fact, sales did almost nothing to sell it.

Sales force and selling expenses are important to this product category. The activity-based cost driver might well be sales force hours required. Various products in this line could be differentiated by the sales force cost driver. Knowing the real costs and profitability of Woodstock might make a big difference in the decision to add new capacity.

Woodstock literally sold itself to a special market segment that found the name appealing. It was unlikely that segment could continue to grow. Even permanent growth was not likely. It was believed that the brand franchise would continue to get smaller as the Woodstock generation disappeared. This logic should drive the capacity decisions for Woodstock. The advantages of ABC and LA occur when capacity decisions are based on fundamental information about costs and profit margins.

ABC and LA are used in other ways for capacity-related decisions. They provide process cost information to product designers. This helps designers control manufacturing costs. Such cost information is related to volume and capacity. If cost drivers are related to capacity, as well they might be, with respect to particular systems, and often to the cost of setups, then designers for DFM and supply chain capacity decision makers need ABC and LA.

10-6 Forecasting Demand and Supply Chain Capacity Planning

When forecasting can be done with a reasonable degree of accuracy, reactive supply chain capacity decisions can be made. If next summer is expected to average 10 degrees hotter than usual, and the air-conditioner maker has a chart like the one shown in Figure 10-13, then production schedules can be set with some degree of confidence.

Figure 10-13 plots AC (air-conditioner) sales versus average weekly summer temperatures. A band is drawn above and below the line. Within that band, 90 percent of sales results have occurred. The band defines a confidence range. The forecast of weather has been correct within ± 3 degrees. Putting it all together, there is a reliable forecast and a strong correlation between that forecast and sales.

Does the process possess the capacity to supply the demand? If it has more capacity than needed, the ABC/LA issue arises of adjusting downward the resource availability by selling it off or by finding alternative products to utilize the capacity. If the process has insufficient capacity to supply the demand, then either sales will be lost or more capacity will be developed by using extra shifts and overtime, new equipment, and coproducers.

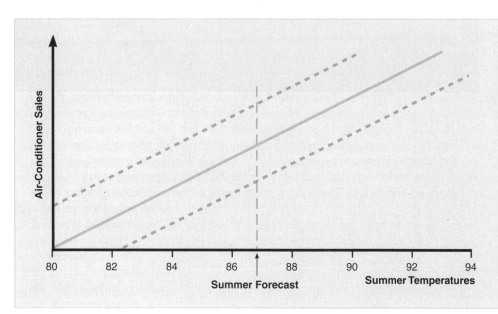

Figure 10-13

Air-Conditioner Sales Versus Average Weekly Summer Temperatures

Note that the summer 2009 forecast is for an average temperature of 87 degrees.

10-7 Supply Chain Capacity and Breakeven Costs and Revenues

Breakeven models are one of the most significant methods for making intelligent capacity decisions. To use breakeven, it is important to review *direct* and *indirect* costs. The breakeven model uses the same costs and revenues as the input–output model that was developed in Chapter 1. This is not a review of costs, however, because the breakeven discussion of costs requires points be made in addition to those that applied to the efficiency of the input–output transformation process.

Variable costs per unit

Variable costs are charges attributable to each unit of product that is made and/or delivered.

Variable costs per unit $= vc$ are the inputs that tend to be fully chargeable and directly attributable to the product in the ABC accounting sense. They also are called *direct costs* because they are paid out on a per-unit of output basis. Direct costs for labor and materials are typical. Variable costs can often be decreased by improving the way that jobs are done.

Material costs can sometimes be reduced using value analysis to improve material usage or find better materials at lower costs. Changing order sizes can increase discounts, and grouping purchases can result in lower transportation costs for full carloads. Lower cost suppliers directly decrease the variable cost of inventory being held and stored. P/OM has many avenues to pursue as it strives to continuously improve quality while reducing variable costs.

There are some classification problems for variable costs. Differentiating between direct and indirect labor costs provides an example. Office work is indirect because such costs usually cannot be attributed to a particular unit of output on a cost per piece or cost per service-rendered basis. If a direct link can be made so that overhead costs can be assigned directly, then such costs should not be equally shared in the overhead pool with other products.

Total variable costs $=$ $TVC = (vc)V$

The result of multiplying the variable cost per unit (vc) by the number of units or volume (V) produced.

Total variable costs $= TVC = (vc)V$ are the result of multiplying the variable costs per unit (vc) by the number of units or volume (V). These are also total direct costs.

Fixed costs $= FC$ have to be paid, whether one unit is made or thousands. For this reason, administrative and supervisory costs are usually treated as fixed charges. Together with purchasing and sales, they are all bundled together as overhead costs. Salaries and bonuses paid to the CEO and to every other manager are overhead because they cannot be assigned to specific products and services.

Fixed costs (FC)

Like rent, they have to be paid whether or not any units are sold. Like an insurance policy, they apply to a specific period of time. FCs are greater for flow shops than for job shops, and greatest for flexible manufacturing systems.

It is possible, with activity-based costing, and/or lean accounting, to more carefully assign fixed charges to each specific product. This is important because breakeven analysis is done for each product in the supply chain and not for a product mix. Incorrect assignment of overhead to the fixed costs will affect the breakeven value. It is generally believed that the basic proportions are evident and that roughly the right numbers are used. ABC can help confirm this and/or correct deviations from the fundamental rule that states, if they do not vary with volume, then they are fixed.

ABC may also help move some charges from the fixed to the variable category. This is possible when the cost per unit made or serviced can be identified by the accounting system and moved to the variable category.

Total costs $=$ $TC = FC + TVC$

TC are the sum of fixed costs and total variable costs.

Total costs $= TC = FC + TVC$ are the sum of the fixed and the total variable costs.

Total revenue $=$ $TR = (p)V$

Total revenue is price per unit (p) multiplied by the volume (V) sold (not just made) in a period of time. TR applies to the same period of time, T.

Total revenue $= TR = (p)V$ is the volume V multiplied by the price per unit p. When goods and services are sold in the marketplace, they generate revenue. This breakeven model treats revenue as a linear function similar to variable costs. Each unit sold generates the same amount of revenue equal to the price (p). Cumulative or total revenue (TR) is equal to the number of units sold to date (V) times the price (p), i.e., $TR = (p)V$. Total revenue equals zero when $V = 0$ because no units are sold. An assumption of breakeven analysis is that all units made and stored are delivered and sold.

The breakeven analysis question is: How many units of throughput need to be sold in order to recover costs and breakeven? The results change over time as factors vary. Fixed costs often grow, prices change, and variable costs per unit decrease with proper P/OM attention.

Marketing is responsible for setting prices to create the required demand volume while still generating a fair profit. The way the demand volume changes as a function of the price set is described by the "price elasticity" of the product or service. Price elasticity is affected by customer quality expectations and the degree to which competitive products are substitutable. Advertising and promotion strategies are costs usually assigned to overhead. All such market drivers are crucial to the P/OM domain because they determine output volumes, and thereby affect supply chain capacity plans.

10-7a Interfunctional Breakeven Capacity Planning

Every functional manager should be involved in breakeven capacity planning. This was the case with input–output process analysis too. There is something for every functional manager to be concerned about with the breakeven model. Without true interfunctional planning, all relevant information cannot be secured. Successful coordination of process activities is not likely to be achieved without the systems approach.

How much supply chain capacity as well as what kind of supply chain capacity needs to be addressed. What work configurations are to be used? Where should the capacity be located? Price will play a part in the revenue line. Technology employed affects fixed and variable costs. Method of depreciation is another accounting issue that interacts with the finance-P/OM decision concerning technological investments to be made. The P/OM tie-in with marketing and finance is inescapable.

The domains of cost concerns are

1   P/OM is accountable for variable cost per unit, a function of the technology employed. Throughput volume and technology used are strongly correlated. P/OM should participate in decisions about both. These responsibilities determine $TVC = (vc)V$.

2   P/OM and finance are mutually involved in major determinants of fixed cost, FC. At the root of this relationship are the technology options and their affect on work configurations that can be used. Work configurations affect the variable costs and quality that can be achieved.

3   P/OM and marketing have to work out the price per unit (p) that customers are to be charged and the demand volume (V) that should result. These decisions lead to estimates of total revenue (TR), total profit (PR), and margin contribution, which is $(p - vc)V$.

10-8 Breakeven Chart Construction for Supply Chain Participants

From raw materials suppliers to producers, distributors, retailers, and delivery systems to ultimate consumers, supply chain capacity decisions must be made. Participants must have matched input–output and throughput capacities along the way. Breakeven charts can be constructed for each participant in the system.

Breakeven charts were developed in the 1930s by Walter Rautenstrauch, a Professor of Industrial Engineering at Columbia University.[6] Breakeven analysis (BEA) has become an influential models of P/OM, providing important information for capacity decisions. Figure 10-14 illustrates the basic chart for one product in the supply chain. It can be a good or a service that is being sold. It must relate to a specific period of time.

Breakeven analysis can be done in either mathematical terms or in graphical form. To understand the breakeven approach to capacity planning for the supply chain, it is easier to start with the graphical approach. Later, an equivalent mathematical formulation will be developed.

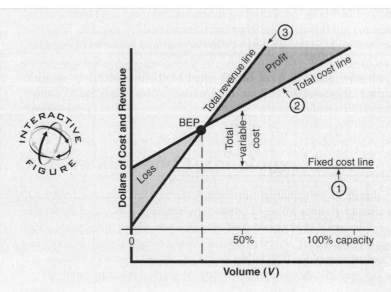

Figure 10-14

Linear Breakeven Chart

The ordinate (*y*-axis) is dimensioned in dollars of fixed cost for line (1), total costs for line (2), and dollars of revenue for line (3). The abscissa (*x*-axis) of the chart represents supply chain volume in units or the percent of capacity utilized for a given period of time. The *x*-axis terminates at 100 percent of capacity. This can be translated into whatever volume of units is equivalent at 100 percent for the given period of time.

10-8a Three Breakeven Lines

Line 1's fixed costs (*FC*) are derived in terms of a specific period of time such as a week, month, or year, which is consistent with the amount of capacity expressed by the *x*-axis. Fixed charges do not change as a function of increased volume or increased capacity utilization. They do change as a function of the time period. Depreciation is greater for three months than for one month, but it may not be three times as great because it depends on the method of depreciation that is used. Straight-line depreciation would be three times greater. Choice among depreciation methods often reflects tax regulations. It should also reflect the amount of resource that is "used up" and, in that regard, capacity decision makers need to consider applying activity-based costing (ABC).

Line 2 in Figure 10-14 is the total cost line where total cost ($TC = FC + TVC$) is the sum of fixed and total variable costs. *TC* increases linearly as throughput volume gets larger. Total variable costs do not begin at the zero level. They are added to fixed costs, which are usually assumed to be the same at all volumes, even at zero production level. Vertical distances in the triangular area lying between the fixed cost line and the total cost line measure the variable costs (*vc*'s).

If overtime is needed, then the total cost line starts to curve up faster. This is illustrated in Figure 10-15, which serves to show that breakeven models can be designed for nonlinear systems.

Depreciation (normally treated as a fixed cost) should be added to the total variable cost, $TVC = (vc)V$, if it can be calculated as a function of equipment utilization. Reduction in equipment life is directly attributable to having made or stored another item. Taxes levied on the basis of units moving through the supply chain or revenues obtained also would be appropriate to add to the variable cost.

Line 3 in Figure 10-14 is the total revenue line, $TR = (p)V$. It is a linear function that increases with greater throughput volume when operating at a low enough share of the total market that free competition can adequately describe the situation. Companies with large market shares often experience diminishing effectiveness with advertising and promotions.

The saturation effect may lead to price discounts and decelerating revenues with increasing volume. This effect is illustrated in Figure 10-15, which demonstrates that breakeven models can be employed for analysis of nonlinear systems.

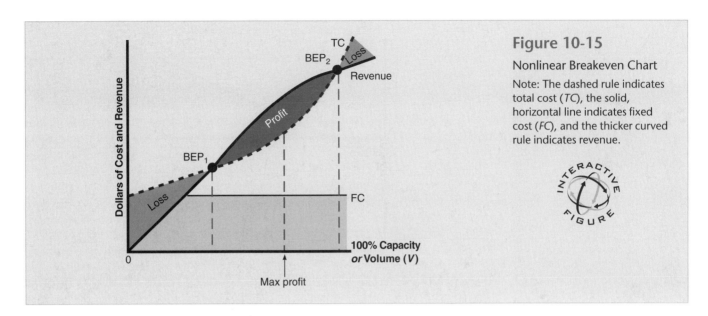

Figure 10-15

Nonlinear Breakeven Chart

Note: The dashed rule indicates total cost (*TC*), the solid, horizontal line indicates fixed cost (*FC*), and the thicker curved rule indicates revenue.

10-8b Profit, Loss, and Breakeven

In Figure 10-14, both profit and loss are shown. The lower-shaded area between the total cost line (2) and the total revenue line (3) represents loss to the company. Loss occurs to the left of the **breakeven point (BEP)**. The upper-shaded area between the same lines represents profit to the company. Profit occurs to the right of the breakeven point. Because it is a linear system, maximum loss begins at the left side of the diagram. With growth of output volume, the loss decreases until it reaches zero at the *BEP*. Then profit starts and it increases linearly throughout the range of positive profits until maximum profit is achieved at 100 percent of capacity.

Breakeven point (BEP)
The sales volume point at which total costs exactly equal revenues. Profit is zero. Then, as sales volume increases, profit > 0.

Figure 10-15 shows a nonlinear breakeven chart where there are two breakeven points. Operating at capacities that lie between the two BEPs is profitable. Operating at capacities to the left of *BEP*$_1$ or to the right of *BEP*$_2$ results in losses. Also noteworthy is the indicated capacity that produces max profit. This graphic model can be used to determine the optimal capacity if the real shapes of the cost and revenue curves can be determined.

The definition of the BEP is that volume (or percent of capacity) at which there is no profit and no loss. Literally, it is the point at which the total costs of doing business exactly balance the revenues, leading to the name "breakeven." This is

$$TR - TC = 0 = \text{profit}$$

The amount of loss is decreasing and cost recovery is improving as volume increases up to the breakeven point. At breakeven, cost recovery is completed. The BEP occurs at a specific volume of production (in units) or a given percent utilization of supply chain (e.g., plant) capacity. The values of BEP are critical for the diagnosis of healthy supply chain systems. The concept is equally applicable to manufacturing and services, and it always applies to a specific period of time.

10-9 Analysis of the Linear Breakeven Model

Figure 10-14 has been redrawn in Figure 10-16 so that the *y*-axis becomes profit and loss. This is accomplished by rotating the total cost line to be parallel with the *x*-axis.

Slope
Slope of the profit line before and after breakeven determines how fast loss and gain occur when demand falls below or rises above the BEP.

The **slope** of the line in Figure 10-16 reflects the rate at which profit increases as additional units of capacity are sold. Above breakeven, it means making profit faster but below breakeven it means creating losses faster. Because companies expect to operate above breakeven, the larger slope is preferred. During the years 2001 and 2002 there

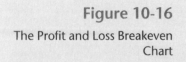

Figure 10-16

The Profit and Loss Breakeven Chart

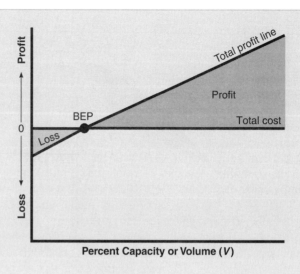

were many dot.com (Internet) firms that failed. These companies could not generate revenues to get them above their breakeven points. They spent money on facilities and equipment. Their *burn rate* of investors' money was too fast. Customer acquisition occurs over a long planning horizon.

Consider the position of the BEP in Figure 10-16. If it moves to the right because of changes in the costs and revenues, then the supply chain must operate at a higher level of capacity before it starts to make a profit. Conversely, by reducing the breakeven point, profit can be made at lower volumes. Companies want to operate above breakeven so lower BEPs are preferred.

Figure 10-17 shows two profit-loss lines marked A and B where A and B are labels associated with specific (and unique) supply chain process alternatives.

Alternative A has a lower BEP than alternative B. This makes A more desirable than B with respect to the position of the BEP. On the other hand, B generates more profit once the point V* has been reached.

At the demand volume represented by point V*, both alternatives yield equal profit. V* is the point of equivalent profit for alternatives A and B. If greater demand than V*

Figure 10-17

Profit and Loss as a Function of Throughput Volume (*or Percent of Supply Chain Capacity Used*); Profit and Loss for A and B Reflect Alternative Supply Chain Systems

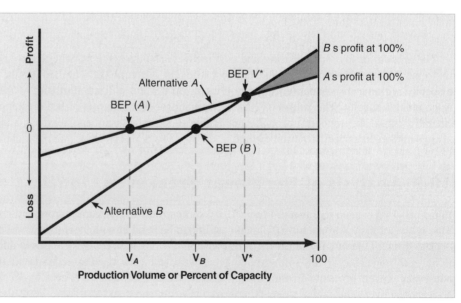

		Breakeven Point	
		High	**Low**
Profit Rate (slope)	**High**	Use forecast	Accept alternative
	Low	Reject alternative	Use forecast

* Within a given time frame.

Figure 10-18

Four Possible Results* with Respect to BEP and Profit-Rate (Slope) in the Choice Between Alternatives A and B. Two Results Require Additional Information from Forecasts

can be generated, alternative B is preferred. If V^* cannot be achieved, then choose alternative A. Figure 10-18 represents the four different situations that can arise in a two-by-two matrix.

Two of the cells lead to clear-cut decisions. An alternative that has a lower BEP and higher profit-rate slope is the clear winner. An alternative that has a higher BEP and a lower profit-rate slope is unequivocally rejected. The two other cells are ambiguous situations requiring a forecast of the expected demand volume.

If the volume forecast is above the breakeven point (BEP) of the two alternatives (see V^* in Figure 10-17), then choose alternative B, which has the highest slope-profit rate. If the volume forecast is below $BEP = V^*$ (in Figure 10-17), then choose alternative A. Below $BEP = V^*$ alternative A returns the greatest profit and also, as the volume drops further, A produces the least loss because it has the smallest slope.

Other combinations can occur. The forecast can span the volumes that fall above and below $BEP = V^*$. Then, the procedure is to determine the expected profit by combining the profit and loss function with the probability distribution of demand using a decision matrix. This decision matrix approach to breakeven analysis is shown in the Enrichment Activity 10.

10-9a Linear Breakeven Equations

The math equivalent for the graphic breakeven chart provides an alternative approach. The symbols of the equations have been presented in Section 10-8. They are repeated here for equations written in terms of output volume (V), or percent of capacity used. This percentage is measured by

$$\% \text{ Capacity} = (100) * \frac{V_{actual}}{V_{maximum}} \qquad (10\text{-}1)$$

Percent of capacity is used with flow shop dominated supply chains because they are designed with known maximum capacity rating. Capital-intensive industries also relate their performance to the percent of capacity used. On the other hand, labor-intensive industries (such as check processing and warehouse operations) are more likely to use measures of throughput volume than percent of capacity.

TR = total revenue per time period T
p = price per unit
V = number of units made and sold in time period T
FC = fixed costs per period T
vc = variable costs per unit of production
TVC = total variable costs = $(vc)V$
TC = total costs per period $T = FC + TVC$
TPR = total profit per period T
Total revenue for period T is
$TR = (p)V$

Total cost for period T is

$TC = FC + (vc)V$

Total profit for the interval T is (in terms of volume):

$$TPR = TR - TC = (p)V - FC - (vc)V = (p - vc)V - FC \qquad (10\text{-}2)$$

Breakeven point (V_{BEP}) is calculated by setting profit equal to zero, thus: $TPR = 0$. Then, Equation 10-2 becomes

$$(p - vc)V_{BEP} = FC \qquad (10\text{-}3)$$

and

$$V_{BEP} = \frac{FC}{p - vc} \qquad (10\text{-}4)$$

10-9b Breakeven Supply Chain Capacity Related to Work Configurations

The fixed costs and capacities of flow shops are much higher than the fixed costs and capacities of job shops. General-purpose equipment (GPE) used in job shops is designed for high variety in low-capacity volumes. Special-purpose equipment (SPE) characteristic of the flow shop is designed for low variety in high-capacity volumes. Even the movement of materials between equipment is mechanized for the flow shop, whereas it is done mostly by hand in job shops.

In trade for the higher fixed costs of the flow shop, P/OM expects to obtain lower variable costs. On the other hand, the manager of the job shop does whatever is possible to keep high-variable costs under control. If there is sufficient stable demand to warrant investment in flow shop capacity, and if technology exists to deliver low-variable costs at the required quality levels, production and operations managers will select parts of the process for flow shop design.

Dialogue should be initiated by P/OM with marketing to investigate the possibility of accumulating sufficient stable demand for the supply chain if it does not currently exist. Modular production abilities allow P/OM to assist in achieving the demand levels that are appropriate for flow shop capacities. See Section 10-12.

Flexible-purpose equipment (FPE) is the third category of process capacity to consider. The fixed costs of flexible manufacturing systems (FMS), flexible processing systems (FPS), and flexible office systems (FOS) are even higher than those of the flow shop. Because flexible, or adaptive, automation can be operated remotely 24/7 with time out for maintenance, the high fixed costs can be amortized across a broad product line.

It is necessary to have planned well ahead for the proper use of FPSs. The high fixed costs require that multishift production be used to increase the volumetric capacity of the system. This allows the *BEP* as a percent of capacity to occur at a reasonably low point, whereas single-shift production will underutilize the FPS equipment, and that can prove costly and ineffective.

With limited use of flexible technology, meaning that it plays a small role in supply chain processes, then the problem of underutilization is minimal. However, when the overall technology of the process is FPE, what is required is careful predesign of the use of the potential capacity to produce a broad mix of products that have strong market appeal. Large investments in flexibility demand great capacity planning.

10-9c Supply Chain Capacity and Margin Contribution

Breakeven analysis provides important parameters for evaluating supply chain capacity decisions. The critical rate of return on capacity is based on the slope of the profit line.

© 2008 Jupiterimages Corporation

Safety and security are crucial P/OM responsibilities. Signage requiring "hard hats and safety boots" may not provide sufficient protection. Fences must be secure (especially from climbing children) and alarms to signal forced entry may be necessary. Dangerous roads must be blocked to traffic. In general, where there is danger in the environment, machines are better exposed to it than people.

The equally critical BEP is determined by the ratio of fixed costs to the per unit margin contribution which is equal to $(p - vc)$.

That is

$$(p - vc)V_{BEP} = FC$$

which means that total margin contribution at breakeven completely recovers the fixed costs and no more. In general, total margin contribution is equal to $(p - vc)V_{actual}$.

Japanese industry specialized in flow shop capacity following the MacArthur initiative to rebuild the Japanese economy after World War II. This concentration on flow shops challenged the Japanese export industries to amass the necessary demand levels to support the cost advantages gained from great production capacities. They met the challenge, at first by specializing in products with low prices and high reliability. Later, having penetrated the markets, they went upscale, still mastering new approaches to high-capacity production. Similar approaches have worked for Korean products and are now being tested by Chinese products.

10-10 Supply Chain Capacity and Linear Programming

Job shop capacity can be mismanaged. The mixture of jobs on different machines can block access by other jobs that would enhance margin contribution. The same applies to mixtures of service jobs. **Linear programming (LP)** is a modeling technique used by P/OM to achieve optimal use of resources. LP shows that it is often not optimal to allow low margin products to block capacity that could be used by higher margin products. Sometimes, the optimal product mix does not fully utilize capacity because of this effect.

It is useful to demonstrate the point LP makes about unused supply chain capacity with a producer-oriented example. This example will be based upon spreadsheet calculations. Table 10-2 shows the production output capabilities of two departments (D1 and D2). Each can make different amounts of two products, V and W.

If Department 1 makes 10 units of product V, or twenty units of product W, either production schedule uses up 100 percent of Department 1's available daily capacity. If Department 2 makes 12 units of V, or 12.5 units of W, either production schedule uses up 100 percent of Department 2's available daily capacity. These statements lead directly to Table 10-3 where profit per unit for each product is given. Note how the fraction of daily capacity in Table 10-3 ties in with the maximum output capacities shown in Table 10-2. For example, making one W unit consumes 0.08 of Department 2's daily capacity. This was derived by dividing 100 percent by 12.5 units per day $(100/12.5 = 0.08)$. Similar steps lead to the computations shown in Table 10-3.

Table 10-4 shows various combinations of products V and W that can be made under the constraints of Tables 10-2 and 10-3. Each combination is called a plan. Table 10-4 also shows the total profit for the day based on the computing formula $2V + 3W$. Unused departmental capacity—called **slack**—is shown for each department. Each plan except 4 has some slack in one of the departments.

Linear programming (LP)
Mathematical modeling technique employed by P/OM to achieve optimal use of resources.

Slack
Unused departmental capacity.

Products	$V_{max\ capacity}$	$W_{max\ capacity}$	Capacity
Department 1—Forge	10.0 units per day	20.0 units per day	100 percent
Department 2—Heat treat	12.0 units per day	12.5 units per day	100 percent

Table 10-2

Maximum Output Capacities (per Day) of Two Departments for Products V and W

Table 10-3	Products	V	W	Daily Capacity
Fraction of Daily Capacity (of Departments 1 and 2) Used to Make Products *V* and *W*, and Profit per Unit for Each Product	Department 1—Forge	0.10	0.05	1.00
	Department 2—Heat treat	0.08333	0.08	1.00
	Profit	$2 per unit	$3 per unit	

Slack is calculated—for each department—as follows for Plan 1:

Department 1 capacity used $= V/V_{max\ capacity} + W/W_{maxcapacity} = 5/10 + 5/20 = {}^3/_4 = 75\%$. Therefore unused capacity (slack) in Department 1 $= 1 - {}^3/_4 = 25\%$
Department 2 Capacity used $= V/V_{max\ capacity} + W/W_{maxcapacity} = 5/12.0 + 5/12.5 = 0.4167 + 0.40 = 0.8167 = 81.67\%$. Therefore unused capacity in Department 2 $= 1 - 0.8167 = 0.1833 = 18.33\%$

As another example, without using the equations, consider Plan 2 where $V = 6$ and $W = 5$. Production of $V = 6$ uses up 60 percent of Department 1's daily capacity and 50 percent of Department 2's daily capacity. Output of $W = 5$ uses up 25 percent of Department 1's daily capacity and 40 percent of Department 2's daily capacity. Next, add up the figures for capacity used. Department 1 has used up $60 + 25 = 85$ percent of its max daily capacity. Department 2 has used up $50 + 40 = 90$ percent of its max daily capacity. Slack (unused capacity) is 15 percent for Department 1 and 10 percent for Department 2. Profit for Plan 2 is $2 \times 6 + 3 \times 5 = \$27.00$. Add comfort by deriving some other plan values, using the numbers in the cells of Table 10-4.

The optimal solution is the combination of V and W units of production that will satisfy the constraints and maximize profit. The best way to find the optimal solution is to use Solver in Excel. The steps for doing this are detailed, but straightforward: Call up Excel in Microsoft Office. Click tools and then click Solver. If you do not have Solver, you will have to install it. Click on Add-Ins, and install Solver.

Table 10-5 shows the matrix values used as input to Solver. Note that columns A, B, and C represent the initial data set as shown in Table 10-2. Columns E, F, and G represent the converted data as shown in Table 10-3 where conversion to fraction of daily

Table 10-4	Plan	V	W	D1 Slack	D2 Slack	Profit
Trial and Error Computation for Seven LP Solutions	1	5	5	25.00%	18.33%	$25.00
	2	6	5	15.00%	10.00%	$27.00
	3	7	5	5.00%	1.67%	$29.00
	4	7.83	4.35	0.00%	0.00%	$32.20
	5	5	7	15.00%	0.58%	$31.00
	6	0	12.5	37.50%	0.00%	$37.50
	7	8	4	0.00%	1.33%	$28.00

Table 10-5		A	B	C	D	E	F	G
Starting Values for Solver	1				0	0		
	2	2	3		2	3	0	
	3	10	20	1.00	0.10	0.05	0	1.00
	4	12	12.5	1.00	0.08333	0.08	0	1.00

capacity had been calculated. Table 10-3 also shows per unit profit rates. In Table 10-5, and thereafter, the departments will be designated as D1 and D2 for the sake of economy.

Following is the Solver procedure, step-by-step, after setting up Table 10-5 on the Excel spreadsheet:

1 Start Excel Solver: click Tools, and click Solver.

2 This brings up the dialog box labeled "Solver Parameters."

3 Consider the variable cell D1 as the amount of *V*—see step 5

4 Consider the variable cell E1 as the amount of *W*—see step 5.

5 Steps 3 and 4 are accomplished in the "By Changing Cells" Window. Click and drag to get $D$1:$E$1 in the BCC Window (The $-sign in front of the column and row means that this entry will be constant when it is copied to another location for various computations. This is called *absolute referencing*. Without the $-sign, relative referencing is used and D1 might become E2.)

6 D2 is the profit per unit for *V;* E2 is the profit per unit for *W*.

7 "Set Target Cell" F2 (click TC window, click F2 cell) and select "Equal to" Max.

8 Write the equation for the target cell as = (D2*D1) + (E2*E1). This is in the spreadsheet and not the Solver window. The same applies to equations for F3 and F4.

9 F3 is defined as the amount of D1's capacity that is used, viz.,
F3 = (D3*D1) + (E3*E1); write this equation for F3.
F3 will be constrained < = 1 in the "Subject to the Constraints" window.
Enter 1.00 in cell G3.

10 F4 is defined as the amount of D2's capacity that is used, viz.,
F4 = (D4*D1) + (E4*E1), write this equation for F4.
F4 will be constrained < = 1 in the "Subject to the Constraints" window.
Enter 1.00 in cell G4.

11 Next, fill in the "Subject to the Constraints" box by clicking "Add."

12 The "Add Constraint" box has three windows. See Table 10-6.

13 Click on "Options" in the "Solver Parameters" dialog box and check "Assume Non-Negative" in the "Solver Options" window.

14 Click "OK" to return to the "Solver Parameters" dialog box.

15 Click "Solve" and the LP problem is solved. See Table 10-7.

16 Note that the answer in Table 10-7 is the same as Plan 6 in Table 10-4.

17 Cells that have changed are D1, E1, F2, F3, and F4. Compare Tables 10-5 and 10-7.

18 Cell D1 remains equal to zero. This means *V* = 0 units.

19 Cell E1 equals 12.5. This means W = 12.5 units.

20 Cell F2 (Target Cell) equals $37.50. This is the maximum profit that can be achieved.

LHS	Constraint	RHS
$F$3	< =	$G$3
$F$4	< =	$G$4
LHS = Left-hand side constraint; RHS = Right-hand side constraint		

Table 10-6

The Constraint Box Has Three Windows

	A	B	C	D	E	F	G
1				0	12.5		
2	2	3		2	3	37.5	
3	10	20	1.00	0.10	0.05	0.625	1.00
4	12	12.5	1.00	0.08333	0.08	1.00	1.00

Table 10-7

Optimal Solution Values Obtained by Solver

21 Cell F3 equals 0.625 which means 62.5 percent of Department 1's capacity is used up. Slack for Department 1 is $1.000 - 0.625 = 0.375 = 37.5$ percent.

22 Cell F4 equals 1.00. This means that 100 percent of Department 2's capacity is used up. Slack for Department 2 is zero.

23 QMpom software for LP is a direct substitute for Solver and entails fewer steps.

Linear programming finds the optimal solution by a strong search method that is much faster than trial and error. The underlying algorithmic method is based on learning about which way improvement lies—and then moving in that direction. The trial and error approach gives a hint about how this works.

An important conclusion is that the maximum profit in Tables 10-4 and 10-7 is achieved with some unused capacity for Department 1. This is Plan 6, which makes zero units of *V*, puts all of its capacity into the higher margin product, *W*. All of Department 2's capacity is used up, which means that nothing else can be made. Slack in D1 is 37.5 so rules about "waste not" need to be viewed with a systems perspective.

Plan 4 has no waste except $5.30 of foregone profit. In other words, Plan 4 has used up all of the capacities of both D1 and D2, but its profit is $32.20, which is $5.30 less than Plan 6 profit. This is 16 percent less profit and all capacity has been depleted. Using Plan 6 means that 37.5 percent of D1's capacity is still available to be employed by the *V* and *W* company in other ways or sold off to a coproducer. Thus, LP aligns with ABC and lean accounting methods to secure great benefits when supply chain capacity planning uses a systems perspective.

For really big problems with massive data sets, linear programming will find optimal solutions which trial and error methods cannot deal with even though trial and error is neither aimless nor random. LP solutions obtained using Microsoft's Solver are widely used by small and medium-sized business organizations. More powerful commercial methods exist for the truly gigantic problems that are found in petroleum blending and other product mix problems

10-11 Modular Production (MP) and Group Technology (GT) Impact on Supply Chains

Modular production (MP)
The principle of modularity is to design and produce the minimum number of parts that can be combined in the maximum number of ways to offer the greatest number of different products or services.

Group technology (GT)
Processes that specialize in *families* of similar parts and/ or activities.

Goods and services with large markets lend themselves to flow shop production and supply chains capable of moving, storing, and delivering great volumes of similar (mass produced) items. Small markets are not good candidates for flow shop systems. Flow shop capacities are too large for items that should be handled in finite lots. With creativity, there are times when a conversion can be made from job shop operations to intermittent and even permanent flow shop status. The transition can take place gradually. Both **modular production (MP)** and **group technology (GT)** provide opportunities to design for high volume capacities, or simply put, design for capacity (DFC).

It is easier to design high-capacity processes when starting from scratch than when attempting to change an existing system. Reengineering is the approach to use when wanting to bring about dramatic, instead of continuous, gradual change of an ongoing system. When starting up a new system, without the clear goal of achieving a flow shop, it is more likely that a job shop will result. There are, at least, six good reasons for this:

1 Investments in job shops carry significantly lower risk levels than flow shops.

2 There is a strong job shop tradition in the United States and Europe. It is based upon technology that preceded computer-controlled equipment and upon typical entrepreneurial endeavors of small- and medium-sized businesses.

3 Markets that characterized the 1950s and 1960s were regional markets of much smaller size than national and even international markets today. These markets did not generate demand volumes of sufficient size to support high-volume processes.

4   It is easier to settle for a job shop that offers good profits than to persevere for a flow shop that has potential for even more profits, but with much more investment and risk management.

5   Some goods and many services cannot be produced by a flow shop. Artists' work is created in the freedom of the custom shop. Services require attention to details that, without creative breakthroughs, defy flow shop capacities.

6   Supply chains that encompass job shops are job-shop–oriented. This means that material flows are generally in batches with comparable cash/information flows.

In spite of these six points, opportunities can exist that permit aggregation of demand to flow shop proportions even though the markets of the products are relatively small. Modular product and process design presents one such opportunity.

Modularity entails specialization in the production of particular parts, or in specific sequences of activities for services (such as programming strings of code, which can then be included as components of more than one program). Modular parts can be combined in a variety of ways to produce many different products or services. The roots of such efforts exist in the well-developed concept of standard parts. Consider the chaos if screw threads were arbitrary and lightbulbs could have hundreds of different sockets. As it is, there are too many varieties of both.

10-11a Modular Production (MP)

The reason for wanting to achieve high-level interchangeability through commonality of parts sharing universal standards is that a part, operation, instruction, or activity, if used in or with several products or services, can accumulate sufficient demand volume to warrant investing in flow shop capacities. This changes the dynamics and economics of the supply chain when the modular part volume is aggregated across many products.

The **principle of modularity** is to design, develop, and produce a minimum number of parts (or operations) that can be combined in a maximum number of ways to offer the greatest number of products or services to customers.

Principle of modularity
See **Modular production (MP)**.

Table 10-8 illustrates the modularity of N parts designated as (PA_i), $i = 1, 2, \ldots, N$.

These N parts are used in M products named (PR_j), $j = 1, 2, \ldots, M$.

As shown in the j-column of the matrix, the product j assembly requires one unit of part 3, two units of part i, and one unit of part N. The sequence of assembly is not indicated.

PA_N denotes the last part listed in Table 10-8.

PR_M denotes the last product name listed in Table 10-8. It is a product using one unit of part PA_N.

Table 10-8

Specification of N Parts Used in M Products

	Variety of Parts (PA_i)					Variety of Products (PR_j)			
	PR_1	PR_2	PR_3	PR_4	...	PR_j	...	PR_M
PA_1	1	0	1	1	...	0	...	0
PA_2	0	1	1	2	...	0	...	0
PA_3	0	0	0	0	...	1	...	0
PA_4	0	1	1	0	...	0	...	0
					...	.	...	.
					...	.	...	.
PA_i	0	0	1	0	...	2	...	0
.	.	.	.	.	...	.	...	.
.	.	.	.	.	...	.	...	.
PA_N	0	0	0	1	...	1	...	1

Legend: PA_i denotes the part identified by the stock number i. PR_j denotes the name or stock keeping number of the product. All $_j$ varieties are listed in the finished goods catalog.

With N different kinds of parts, a total of M different product configurations can be offered to customers. Some of these products require several units of a single part. For instance, PR_4 requires two units of PA_2, and PR_j requires two units of PA_i.

The maximum possible variety, which is the maximum value of M that can be obtained with N different parts, may be very large. This is especially so when there are different possible combinations of the parts and varying numbers of them in combination.

The general objective is to have M as large as possible and N as small as possible.

This is equivalent to saying that the general objective is to have as many products as possible made with the smallest possible number of parts. A useful measure of the effective degree of modular design might be the ratio of the number of products (columns) that can be generated from a given number of parts (rows); that is, the objective: *MAX (M/N)*. Many of the possible combinations cannot exist and would have no appeal as a product choice for customers. It is up to the team to find the right parts for modular specialization.

Computers epitomize the modular concept. Customers can specify many different computers that are made of components that mix and match with ease. There is no other product that has offered customers the right to design their purchase in so many ways. Imagine ordering a TV or a car, or a mobile phone with thousands of options available.

Companies specialize in a relatively few computer parts that make a relatively large number of computer products. The parts are made by flow shops with enormous capacities. Parts orientation accounts for the ever lower price of computers.

Modularity applies to services and projects. When certain activities are used repeatedly in some service function, the steps can be standardized and the process to deal with them can be serialized for the flow shop or even automation. The ATMs used by banks provide a fine illustration of a service that has been designed to provide high-capacity, lower-cost equivalents of teller service.

Long ago it was recognized that parts of computer programs appear over and over. They were standardized and are regularly inserted as modules into computer programs by information systems programmers. Rewriting lines of code is like reinventing the wheel. Modular constructed housing can produce many versions of homes using the same basic parts. Furniture designers are masters of modular sections. Project managers have developed modular techniques to cut the costs of portions of what otherwise is a unique venture. Building developers thrive on separating what is unique about each structure from what is a repetitive activity.

Successful modular design increases demand, promoting increased capacity, allowing flow shop economies to be utilized. The kind of matrix shown in Table 10-8 must have been in the minds of the inventors of Lego and the earlier Erector sets. Modularity helps to assemble the flow shop by creating production systems that specialize in parts instead of products.

Parts-oriented supply chains will not operate in the same way as product-oriented supply chains. Why is that so? Parts have different customers than products. Parts do not reach the ultimate consumer until they have been assembled into products. Economics of scale and scope need to be scrutinized. This leads to defining the role of group technology.

10-11b Group Technology (GT Families)

Group technology deals with processes that specialize in families of similar parts and/or activities in the supply chain. It is technologically feasible to develop efficient flow shops that can make gears of similar design, but different size. The same applies to cams, springs, and so on. The changeover routines to go from one size gear to another are fast and inexpensive. As with modularity, GT has positive impact on the dynamics and economics of the supply chain.

GT parts have similar design, and essentially the same production operations can be used to make them. There is a functional similarity to FMS but the variety level is more straightforward if the family characteristics of the "group" are well-defined. Group technology must assure that minimum transition costs occur as the production line shifts from one variant to another—in the same family of parts. The key is that GT is focused on parts and not on products.

A company using group technology to improve the profit margin of its line of products or services might become so efficient in this specialized family of operations that it could gradually shift its emphasis from products to parts. Eventually, it would become a parts subcontractor to industry and supply institutions with the output of its most efficient operations. The marketing of parts is substantially different from that of products. There is a lot to be learned and much to be earned from developing the potential capabilities of modularity, GT and their focus on parts.

10-12 Learning Increases Supply Chain Capacity

Economic theory indicates that product can be delivered throughout the supply chain at lower unit costs when the throughput volume increases. This effect is well-known by the phrase "economies of scale." The Boston Consulting Group (BCG) confirmed this effect with many empirical studies of a wide variety of industries.[7]

Figure 10-19 shows some general shapes for this function where the decrease varies between 20 and 30 percent with each doubling of volume being processes through the supply chain.

BCG calls this the **experience curve**. The rate of decrease in per unit costs is about 25 percent for each doubling of volume. Volume is a surrogate for experience and consequent learning. After doubling of volume has occurred several times, most of the payoff from learning will have been obtained. Reductions in average unit costs have to get smaller and smaller. Thus, price reduction potentials disappear as the market matures.

As throughput volume gets larger, many factors operate to make the process more efficient. Workers learn to do their jobs better while taking less time. More work gets turned out in a period of time, which is one of the main factors for the decrease in costs. This is equivalent to increasing C, the actual measured capacity. As a reminder:

$$C = T \times E \times U$$

where T = time available, E = efficiency, and U = utilization. There are two ways of accounting for the increase in C.

Experience curve

Rate of decrease in per unit costs is between 20 and 30 percent for each doubling of production output volume.

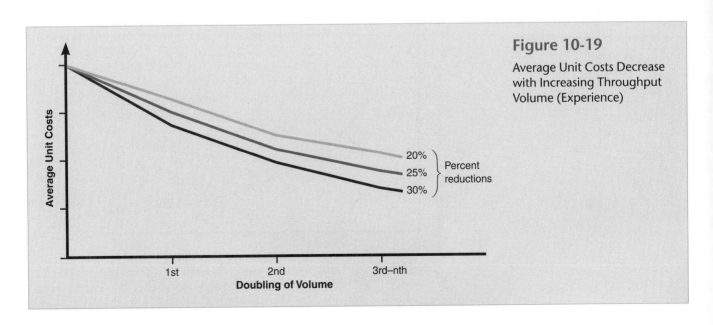

Figure 10-19

Average Unit Costs Decrease with Increasing Throughput Volume (Experience)

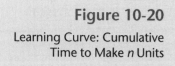

Figure 10-20

Learning Curve: Cumulative
Time to Make *n* Units

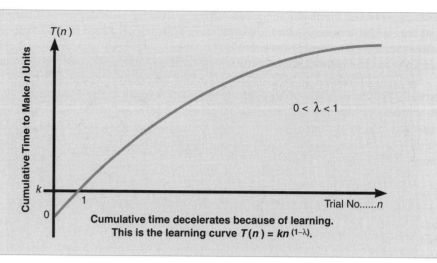

T becomes a larger number of available hours. In other words, because work takes less time, more work can be done. Alternatively, both *E* and *U* can become greater, even greater than 100 percent.

10-12a The Learning Curve

The learning curve is a model for both individuals and teams or groups. It describes how repeated practice decreases the time required to do the job. Thus, the learning curve captures the benefit of repetition and experience in quantitative terms for employees or teams and groups doing the same job routinely.

Two related learning curves are shown in Figures 10-20 and 10-21 with their respective quantitative models.

The equation $T(n) = kn^{(1-\lambda)}$ is read as follows:

$T(n) =$ cumulative time to make *n* consecutive units
$k =$ time required to make the first unit (designated by $n = 1$); *k* is a constant characteristic of the product

Figure 10-21

Learning Curve: Average
Time to Make the *n*th Unit

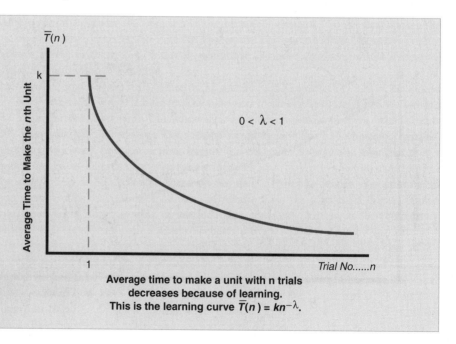

n = the number of units to be made

λ = the learning coefficient, $0 < \lambda < 1$

When $\lambda = 0$, the cumulative time $T(n) = kn^1 = kn$. Thus, $T(n)$ increases linearly at the rate (kn), and there is no learning effect because each unit requires the same amount of production time, which is k.

When $\lambda = 1$, $T(n) = kn^0 = k$, which means that the job has been learned so well that after the first time, the rest of the units are made (literally) in no time at all. $\lambda = 1$, is unrealistic and a goal never to be achieved.

As $\lambda \to 1$, successive units take less time. The curve of Figure 10-20 shows decelerating improvement in learning. The cumulative time to make a unit never approaches a limit (as an asymptote). The value of λ reflects the learning coefficient. The larger that lambda is, the greater the learning rate.

When λ is large, the reduction in work time with each succeeding unit is greatest. Other systems use a reverse nomenclature where the larger the Learning Rate (R)[8] the smaller the reduction in average time to complete the next unit. This is equivalent to $1 - \lambda$ which can be called the reduction rate. QMpom software's learning module uses the R factor.

Another useful form of the learning model is shown in Figure 10-21 where the average time to make a unit (after n repetitions) is calculated by dividing the cumulative time $T(n)$ by n.

$$\overline{T}(n) = \frac{T(n)}{n} = kn^{-\lambda} \tag{10-5}$$

k, n, and λ are the same as before.

When $\lambda = 0$, $\overline{T}(n) = T(n)/n = k$, which is the condition where no learning takes place. Every time the job is done, it takes the same k time units.

When $\lambda = 1$, an unrealistic limit is reached whereby the average time (k/n) is reduced geometrically with each trial. Values of λ between 0 and 1 can yield reasonable decreases in the average time to do a job. For example, with $\lambda = 0.5$, $\overline{T}(n)$ is decreasing as $\frac{1}{\sqrt{n}}$.

With continued practice, learning reaches a plateau where the output rate is relatively constant. When the employee takes a break, there may be some relearning needed. Often it is minimal. The effect becomes greater when the time between stopping and starting is longer. Therefore, for lunch breaks it might not be noticeable. After returning from a lengthy vacation, it is apt to be strongest.

The learning curve has been around a long time.[9] It has not proved directly useful, but it has provided indirect, conceptual insight into problems associated with people doing small lots of different kinds of work. More time is spent learning and getting up to speed than producing effectively. Learning time can significantly diminish productive capacity in the job shop-oriented supply chain. Good process managers, aware of the cumulative penalties of continuous learning and relearning, can control the situation by systematizing the learning function, modularizing learning elements, and by using SMED concepts (Section 6-8a).

Learning benefits for workers in flow shops are pronounced because of the high degree of repetition. There is a perverse, reverse effect when productive throughput declines because of monotony. The learning curve effect on production line start-up times, and the reverse effect, should be considered when designs for manufacturing and assembly (DFM and DFA; Section 8-10) are prepared. New flexible technology provides opportunity for better productivity and quality for small lots.

Costing new products should take learning into account by pricing jobs at the average productivity rate for a reasonably large number n. Time observations for work standards do not begin until after workers' times stabilize at some plateau level.

10-12b Service Learning

In labor-intensive situations, learning curve concepts can be put to good use. How many repetitions does it take to learn a job? How do people differ in catching on? Does a master teacher help? How do the trainees of different trainers perform? What aspects of training make a difference in how quickly and how well experience is converted into improved performance? Who says there is only one plateau? There are better learning theories that allow for multiple plateaus or a succession of plateaus,[10] where learning starts again after a stable interval of continued practice on a lower plateau.

The learning curve's relationship to providing quality services efficiently should be emphasized. Productivity of service jobs has been a recognized problem that is often associated with the lower salaries that characterize services. In the same sense, there is an opportunity to systematize the learning function for the attainment of excellence in service quality.

The idea would be to raise the quality standards after a job has successfully plateaud at a lesser quality standard. Thus, learning curve plateaus could relate productivity with levels of quality improvement. They also apply to the time-based management system of stair-step reductions in process times, which was effectively employed by Japanese automotive manufacturers to lower costs. These kinds of efforts must be fully supported by employees or else they are doomed to failure. On the other hand, there would be great support for learning to improve excellence if it was accompanied by financial bonuses and other kinds of recognition. These kinds of ideas about learning and work standards are particularly applicable to services where they have been consistently underutilized in spite of the voice of the customer.

10-13 Supply Chain Capacity and the Systems Approach

Supply chain capacity decisions are among the most crucial P/OM responsibilities. They set in motion scenarios for start-up and growth that are difficult to alter, unless they have been planned to pursue a dynamic course of change to improve. Following rather than leading means forecasting diligently and always playing catch-up. This is characteristic of the way some companies invest in the introduction of new products. The policy to lead and not follow requires that P/OM work with marketing to create specific demand levels. The capacity to satisfy demand has then been designed and built-in ahead of time. This is characteristic of companies that prefer to accept risk so as to be the market share leader.

Unused capacity is to be avoided in excess, but some of it may be inevitable, and even profitable. It is not possible to forecast perfectly. It is not feasible to plan perfectly. Teamwork is no guarantee of being able to create exactly the demand for which capacity has been prepared. The cost of being undercapacitated is often greater than the cost of storing capacity. Diligence on this point is worthwhile before capacity decisions are finalized.

Capacity can be installed all at once, or it can be gradually increased. The incremental approach entails low risk, but it can foul up meeting market demands, produce higher unit costs, and worst of all, lead to poor and inconsistent quality of product. The capacity decision must have financial support, market rationalization, and P/OM knowledge of how to convert the strategic plan into production-transformation capacity to be installed.

The resulting too much or too little of this or that leads to downsizing, which is demoralizing and costly. Alternatively, the last-minute realization of the need for greater capacity is fraught with difficulties and buys the additional volume at a higher price than would have been incurred from original planning stages. Strategic plans shared by finance, marketing, and P/OM are the foundation for better capacity decisions, which with team learning can get better all the time.

Spotlight 10-1 Where the Race Is Won–An Interview with Don Stuart

An Interview with Don Stuart, President and CEO,
Global Concepts, Inc.

"Demand throughout the supply chain is best managed and satisfied through policies and processes that pull material to the point of use at an accelerated velocity."

"Our pit stops are distribution centers . . . where the race is won. If we can double the speed, we can halve the inventory while improving customer service."

—Don E. Stuart, President and CEO, Global Concepts, Inc.

Don Stuart's statements epitomize the goals of his company. *Everyone looks up to those goals.*

After 16 years of serving as AT&T's corporate general manager in Baskin Ridge, New Jersey, and being responsible for supply chain problems, Stuart formed Global Concepts, Inc. (GCI). He had honed cutting-edge precepts for "full-stream" logistics management and reengineering worldwide supply chains, and Global Concepts was the organization that could bring them to clients.

GCI is a privately held company specializing in delivering high return on investment solutions to their customers. This is accomplished by first re-engineering the processes to meet or exceed best-in-class benchmarks. Next, they apply the proper blend of advanced technology and resources to achieve an economical and competitive advantage to their clients. Included in their arsenal of tools is a state-of-the-art suite of "Decision Support" software applications that design, execute, and continuously measure the results of their improved manufacturing and distribution solutions.

The real-time visibility and "statistical process control" techniques provide both a means to proactively correct problems before they happen and the ability to do "root cause" problem analysis on historical data ensuring a continuous improvement environment for years. GCI's suite of logistics tools is designed to reduce supply chain costs on an accelerated basis. Being fast is very important because

badly run transportation and warehousing or poor material handling and inventory management not only cost more money than they should, but they also put their companies at risk by reducing shareholder value.

Global's logistics tools are generic, meaning that they can be easily configured to a multitude of customized solutions. Typical clients include large-scale retailers, manufacturers, oil companies, and government clients such as the FAA and the DoD, whose supply chains include not only retail locations or point-of-use delivery, but also a complex network from raw material extraction, manufacturing, distribution centers, service centers, vendors, and often internal manufacturing in order to feed international pipelines to major market segments. Rapid applications have been obtained by assembling a world-class team of logistics experts including both practitioners and academics to research problems and propose solutions providing the next world-class logistics practices. These are embodied in the company's core software products. Instead of having to reinvent the wheel for each client, the company configures its applications to meet specific customer needs to achieve a competitive advantage. The result, Don Stuart says, is faster implementation and greater returns on investment for the "virtual warehouse" concept.

Global Concepts, Inc., is a logistics solutions company whose product line of software carries interesting names such as Flow Planner, Logistics Engine, ICE, and Metrics Advantage. Much of the research and development was done in conjunction with NSF's Industry University Cooperative Research Centers (IUCRC) and the auto parts giant, AutoZone. Home base for Global Concepts is Little Rock, Arkansas, and the company also has operations in Atlanta, Georgia; Houston, Texas; and Memphis, Tennessee.

Don points out that targeting consistency in performance of the supply chain (or the demand chain, as he likes to call it) reduces safety-stock inventory caused by demand and lead-time variability. GCI's cost optimization models reduce process variability and operating expenses while improving customer service with less inventory and capital assets.

Stuart earned a mechanical engineering degree from the University of Arkansas. He has said that, as the years progressed, he accidentally became an expert in logistics. It may have been a coincidence that he was at the right place at the right time, but it was no accident; he knew he was there and he knew what had to be done. AT&T consolidated

Spotlight 10-1 (Continued)

most of its manufacturing and distribution operations in the early to mid-1990s, prior to the Lucent spin-off, and Stuart had to bring order out of chaos. As an efficiency expert at AT&T, Stuart helped reengineer multiple business units, saving the company over $800 million in just one of many projects in his last year 1995.

Don has served over the last 15 years as either the Industry Director at The Logistics Institute (TLI), based at Georgia Tech in Atlanta, or as Chairman for the Industrial Advisory Board, NSF's Center for Engineering Logistics and Distribution. There are also university partnerships with experts from Universities of Arkansas, Florida, and Nebraska, as well as Oklahoma University, Ohio State University, Louisville, Virginia Tech, and even Nanyang University in Singapore. In this capacity, he has collaborated on research with Wal-Mart, Tyson's, ConAgra, USPS, UPS, FAA, IBM, Sun Microsystems, the U.S. Department of Defense, Riceland, Shell Oil, and transportation agencies, as a partial listing.

Review Questions

1 What is the business of Global Concepts, Inc. (GCI)?
2 Why does Don Stuart say, "Demand throughout the supply chain is best managed and satisfied through policies and processes that *pull* material to its point of use?"
3 What is the product line available from Global Concepts, Inc.?
4 Why is the president and CEO of GCI talking about "pit stops?" Don Stuart says, "Our pit stops are distribution centers ... where the race is won."
5 How does consistency in performance of the demand chain reduce safety stock?

Sources: Conversations and correspondence with Don Stuart and his staff, August 2007; Wood, Jeffrey. "Global Going National with Software Rollout." *Arkansas Business* (April 21, 2003). See also: http://www.gclogistics.com.

Spotlight 10-2 Sylvain Landry: Healthcare Logistics
Recognizing the Special Character of the Hospital Link in the Healthcare Supply Chain

The healthcare supply chain is composed of many participants that can be grouped into three major categories, namely, (1) manufacturers who ship to (2) distributors, who in turn deliver the broad diversity of healthcare inventories to (3) hospitals, HMOs and health clinics.

Over the past 20 years, stakeholders in the American healthcare sector have proposed a number of different supply chain integration strategies. Stockless materials management and just-in-time are two such strategies favoured by medical supply distributors. Despite what their names might suggest, stockless materials management refers to vendor-managed inventory (VMI) systems, wherein a hospital outsources to a third party all or part of the distribution of supplies to its patient care units. Just-in-time is a vendor scheduling approach aimed at delivering high volume items as they are needed. However, these practices have placed enormous financial pressure on distributors, who have had to conserve large quantities of stock to meet their promised service levels, while their relationships with manufacturers have not kept the same pace. These experiences have demonstrated the need for more comprehensive action.

In the early 1980s, analysts began to study the relationships between distributors and healthcare institutions from a system-based perspective. Slowly, this vision was expanded to include the manufacturer's contribution. Publication, in 1996, of the Efficient Healthcare Consumer Response report (EHCR) became a major milestone in the process, for the study offered a global vision of healthcare supply chain management. The vision in turn allowed the chain's shortcomings to be recognized: duplication of activities, multiple storage locations, ruptures in the information flow, delays and lower service levels. The EHCR study led to the creation of multiple committees and task forces and the prospect that considerable changes could be made in the strategies deployed by logistics stakeholders. However, once a blueprint had been established, corporate imperatives led many decision makers to take individual action.

But healthcare institutions are not just another link in the supply chain, and some of these initiatives have encountered problems. In fact, three logistics factors have hindered the chain's integration. (1) Hospitals are the convergence point for a wide variety of products that support healthcare directly (e.g., medical supplies and pharmaceutical products) and indirectly (e.g., linens, food, stationery, maintenance products). (2) The diverse supply flows bring with them a variety of players within the institution who are involved in the logistical management of these many products. Often these players, most notably the nursing staff, have neither the expertise nor resources to effectively and efficiently manage logistics activities. (3) Before a product reaches the end user (nursing staff or patient), it generally must travel through the institution's internal supply chain, which includes receiving, storage and replenishment, and which, for certain products, can also include production activities (cooking, washing, sterilization, etc.). As a result, it is estimated that up to 46 percent of a hospital's total operating budget is spent on logistics related activities (Chow and Heaver, 1994). On top of supplies and equipment costs, a staggering number of people are conducting logistics activities, and unfortunately, often the wrong people are involved with logistic decisions. For example, it is estimated that nursing staff will spend (on average) 10 percent of their time performing logistics tasks instead of taking care of patients.

This has more than cost and care implications. In countries where there is a shortage of healthcare professionals, the time spent on logistics activities can have an even greater impact on healthcare professionals, as it can become the proverbial straw that breaks the camel's back, resulting in overwork, absenteeism, and sick leave. Despite these sobering results, logistics challenges rarely make it onto senior management meeting agendas in healthcare institutions. Nevertheless, more efficient hospital logistics can provide opportunities for institutions to balance the objectives of healthcare networks, namely, quality of care, accessibility, and cost control (Landry and Philippe, 2002).

For 10 years, the research team of Professor Sylvain Landry at HEC Montréal has conducted a wide range of studies focusing on hospital logistics management. This work, most of which has been carried out as part of HEC Montréal's CHAINE Research Group, has resulted in the documentation of diverse management practices. This diversity has taken the Group to institutions in North America, Europe and Asia to study local contexts and has led to the development of an international network of contacts in the field. The diversity has also applied to the different flows within the healthcare institution: medical supplies, pharmaceutical products, linens, and surgical instruments.

From these various research projects a number of beneficial new practices have been identified. For example, the two-bin system (explained in Chapter 14) can be used as an effective nursing ward replenishment method. The *two-bin system* (also called empty-full or no-count) is an alternative to more popular periodic review systems, such as exchange carts or par level systems, where the quantities consumed are replaced at certain intervals through a central stores-driven replenishment system.

In the two-bin system, the quota of each item is evenly distributed into two compartments or bins. Supplies are then taken from the "active" compartment. When one compartment is empty, the nurses use the second or "backup" compartment. This system is more efficient, as only empty compartments (or their bar-coded labels placed on a board) are scanned by materiel management personnel at predetermined intervals. There is no count of inventory taken at the ward level. The empty condition triggers the replenishment process.

Two conditions must occur to trigger the call for replenishment. A bin must be empty and scanning must be scheduled. This means that scanning must take place within a predetermined replenishment cycle. Landry and Beaulieu's research shows that this system generates substantial savings in terms of product ordering activities. This approach also brings the additional benefit of stock rotation generated by the utilization of two containers, thus reducing the costs related to the common problem of product wastage due to expired items. In addition, product handling is reduced, thus increasing event-related sterility (infection control). Use of the two-bin system also increases the quality of the information on actual consumption at the point of use, which is an essential element of supply chain integration. It is important to emphasize that overall supply chain integration requires the external chain (supplying materials) to be synchronized with the demands of the hospital's internal chain (requiring materials).

Given the scope of the resources deployed and the critical nature of its activities, the operating room (the OR) merits particular attention. To this end, implementation of a *material requirements planning* (MRP) approach is an avenue that should be explored for the proper management of many medical supplies. Experiments conducted with this approach have produced considerable gains. The methodology for solution requires an updated list of preference cards detailing needs for each procedure (and sometimes for each surgeon); an interface between the material requirements planning and the operating room (OR) schedule; and a process to manage changes within a specific time frame (as is present with all MRP systems).

Although these practices can have pronounced technological components, they can also incorporate organizational aspects, such as structures that feature logistics activities or the reassignment of tasks to relieve nursing staff of administrative duties. As other studies have borne out, the objective of this work has been to serve as a pool of knowledge for managers implementing new logistics processes.

Spotlight 10-2 (Continued)

Given this diversity, we believe that a huge potential remains for research work. The study of logistics issues for healthcare institutions offers numerous benefits. Logistics activities within healthcare institutions provide significant cost savings, while more efficient management of these activities can generate productivity gains and allow the nursing staff to re-focus on its primary mission: patient care.

HEC MONTRÉAL

Review Questions

1 What are the three main components of the healthcare supply chain?

2 Efforts to integrate the supply chain are legion. What does this mean, and what forms have these efforts taken?

3 What is the difference between stockless materials management and just-in-time inventory delivery? What are the weaknesses of these two systems?

4 Why is the two-bin system more efficient than exchange carts (replenishment method wherein the mobile nursing unit cart from which items are consumed is replaced with a second identical full cart according to an established schedule) or par level systems (replenishment method wherein the nursing unit inventory is replenished in small quantities according to a predetermined schedule)?

5 Is the two-bin system also a periodic review system?

6 What would be the impacts on the two-bin system of introducing RFID tags instead of using bar-coded labels?

7 What are the key challenges of using MRP logic in the operating room (OR)?

8 Why do Dr. Sylvain Landry and Martin Beaulieu (HEC Montréal) say, "The hospital is a special link in the healthcare supply chain?"

9 Explain what is meant by the statement "a huge potential remains for research work."

Sources: Sylvain Landry, Ph.D., CFPIM, Professor and Director, International Projects, HEC Montréal, and affiliated professor at Bordeaux Business School; Martin Beaulieu, Researcher, HEC Montréal, April 2007. See also: http://www.hec.ca/en and http://www.hec.ca/pages/sylvain.landry/en.

References

Arthur Andersen. *Stockless Materials Management, How It Fits into the Healthcare Cost Puzzle.* HIDA Educational Foundation, 1990.

Chow, G., and T. D. Heaver. "Logistics in the Canadian Health Care Industry." *Canadian Logistics Journal,* vol. 1, no. 1 (1994): 29–73.

CSC Consulting. *EHCR, Efficient Healthcare Consumer Response, Improving the Efficiency of the Healthcare Supply Chain* (1996): 118.

Henning, W. H. "Utilizing Suppliers to the Hospital's Best Interests." *Hospital Materiel Management Quarterly,* vol. 1, no 3 (1980): 39–47.

Landry, S., and R. Philippe. "How Logistics Can Service Healthcare." *Supply Chain Forum,* vol. 5, no. 2 (2004): 24–30.

Rovard-Royer, H. S. Landry, and M. Beaulieu. "Hybrid Stockless—A Case Study: Lessons for Healthcare Supply Chain Integration." *International Journal of Operations and Production Management,* vol. 22, no. 4, (2002): 412–424.

Spear, S., and H. K. Bowen. "Decoding the DNA of the Toyota Production System," *Harvard Business Review,* vol. 77, no 5 (1999): 96–106.

Summary

Chapter 10 begins with definitions of supply chain capacity. Determination of supply chain capacity is one of the most important P/OM responsibilities. Capacity must be set to deal with peak and off-peak loads. Storage of capacity is equally important. Services are especially affected by the difficulties of storing service capacity. It is necessary to understand how backordering augments service and manufacturing supply chain capacity.

Capacity requirements planning (CRP) is introduced. Adding and subtracting capacity through upscaling and downsizing supply chain systems is explained. Bottlenecks are serious constraints on supply capacity. Understanding how to manage bottlenecks is a P/OM necessity. As an additional important factor, delay creates oscillations of supply, which can significantly deteriorate productive performance in the supply chain. This leads to discussion of contingency planning for capacity crises and the use of a supply chain game—the manual simulation called the Better Beer Company.

In turn, cost drivers and forecasting for supply chain capacity planning are introduced. A powerful supply chain method described as the breakeven model for capacity planning is introduced. Breakeven analysis is a valuable planning tool that epitomizes the systems viewpoint by requiring interfunctional cooperation. Breakeven capacity of supply chains is related to work configurations, margin contribution, and profitability.

Another major interfunctional capacity planning model that is introduced is linear programming (usually called by its acronym, LP). Solutions of LP problems using Solver in Microsoft Excel is detailed. LP has critical significance in supply chain planning.

Modular production (MP) and group technology (GT) both represent a focus on commonality of parts within product groups. Both approaches must be backed up by datasets that describe the variables of commonality. This permits the firm to add capacity creatively through design concepts. This proactive effort for design coherence and the efficient use of facilities can be called design for capacity (DFC).

The chapter concludes with a discussion of how learning increases capacity. The learning curve is introduced and applied to service learning. The relationship of capacity planning to systems thinking is reiterated. The chapter supplement combines forecasting, decision making, and breakeven analysis.

Two Spotlight feature boxes conclude this chapter. These boxes illustrate real applications of the material in the chapter. Spotlight 10-1: Where the Race Is Won, an illuminating interview with CEO Don Stuart, hits all the critical buttons for excellence in supply chain planning. In Spotlight 10-2, Dr. Sylvain Landry shows the way in which managing the healthcare supply chain can make a major contribution to reducing healthcare costs.

Key Terms

Actual capacity (p. 367)
Breakeven (p. 373)
Breakeven point (BEP) (p. 387)
Capacity (p. 367)
Capacity requirements planning (CRP) (p. 373)
Decision model (p. 368)
Demand (p. 369)
Experience curve (p. 397)
Fixed costs (p. 384)
Group technology (GT) (p. 394)
Learning curve (p. 372)
Linear programming (LP) (p. 391)

Modular production (MP) (p. 394)
OPT (p. 375)
Principle of modularity (p. 395)
Slack (p. 391)
Slope (p. 387)
Supply chain (p. 367)
TOC (p. 375)
Total costs $= TC = FC + TVC$ (p. 384)
Total revenue $= TR = (p)V$ (p. 384)
Total variable costs $= TVC = (vc)V$ (p. 384)
Variable costs per unit $= vc$ (p. 384)
V-A-T (p. 375)

Review Questions

1   Define capacity. Explain how supply chain capacity is measured. Why is it important?

2   Explain what is meant by the statement that maximum containment is a type of supply chain capacity measure that can have special meaning for services.

3   What motivated a company to build excessive petroleum storage facilities early in 1973? If events had worked out differently, would the storage facilities have been excessive in that supply chain?

4   Explain why maximum throughput is only one measure of supply chain capacity.

5   What is the relationship of maximum output to peak demand?

6   Give an example of a situation where what some might call excessive inventories in the supply chain turned out to be a blessing in disguise.

7   Give an example of constraints in supply chain capacity proving to be a blessing in disguise.

8   Should an airline have enough operators and trunk lines to prevent any calling customers from having to wait when they are responding to a 1-day offer of half-fare travel rates? What do operators and trunk lines have to do with supply chains?

9   List six types of variable costs found in supply chains.

10   List six types of fixed costs found in supply chains.

11   To what extent are accounting data likely to be available in manufacturing organizations with respect to fixed and variable costs that are used in breakeven analysis?

12   To what extent are accounting data likely to be available in service organizations with respect to fixed and variable costs that are used in breakeven analysis?

13   To what extent are accounting data likely to be available in government organizations with respect to fixed and variable costs that are used in breakeven analysis?

14   What do FC and $TVC = vc(V)$ and $TC = FC + TVC$ have to do with the employment of breakeven analysis?

15   What is the role of overhead costs (or burden) in the supply chain?

16   How should overhead be treated for breakeven analysis (BEA)?

17   Relate activity-based cost (ABC) and lean accounting systems to BEA.

18   Regarding airline capacity, air shuttles provide continuous, as-filled capacity, instead of scheduled flights. How does this concept increase capacity by innovative use of equipment?

19   What is capacity requirements planning (CRP)?

20   How do bottlenecks affect capacity of supply chains? What can be done about them?

21   What is modular production (MP) and how is it a form of design for capacity (DFC)?

22   What is group technology (GT) and how is it a form of design for capacity (DFC)?

23   How do MP and GT relate to supply chain capacities?

24   What method is appropriate for determining the optimal product mix? What data are needed to accomplish this goal?

25   How does Microsoft's Excel Solver provide a powerful computational method for supply chain management?

26   Supply chain capacity planning problems require good estimates of variable costs for different work configurations and different volumes of supply. Explain.

27   What form of capacity control is downsizing? What are its goals and disadvantages?

28   Delay in the supply chain wreaks havoc. Why is this true?

29   Discuss the following observation: Breakeven charts can represent only one product in the supply chain at a time, whereas most companies produce a product mix that consists of a number of different items or services that must share resources, including capital and management time. This violates the systems approach to problem solving.

30   Describe supply chain situations in which nonlinear analysis might be required for the breakeven chart analysis.

Problems Section

Note: This section has various problems that can be formulated and solved using QuantMethods Production/Operations Management software (QMpom). The appropriate model categories are indicated for each problem.

1   The peak load for Swimsuits, Inc. (SWIM), a manufacturer of bathing suits, occurs in March and April when the cutters and sewers occupy every square foot in the plant. This determines the maximum output capacity of the company, which is 250 suits per hour. SWIM works a 10-hour day, six days a week. Adding shift time is considered impossible. Therefore, it has been suggested that floor space be expanded by renting an adjoining loft for $1,200 per week. This would increase maximum output capacity by 12 percent. The sales manager believes that SWIM could sell 18,000 bathing suits per week during the 10-week season, at a profit of $1.00 per suit based on existing costs of materials and labor. During the summer, the SWIM plant is less than 50 percent utilized.

Explain why the loft should or should not be rented. Are there any other capacity-based observations to be considered?

Using the QMpom module called Capacity Management Models (Breakeven) with FC = $1200, vc = $15 and R = $16, determine the BEP.

2 The new manager of the electric utility notes that recent summers have been warmer than average. Consequently, for next year she revises upward the probability that actual demand will exceed average demand; this is estimated to occur 8 percent of the year or roughly 29 summer days. She estimates that each power incident can cost far less than her predecessor had spent. Using different management techniques to deal with brownouts, she hopes to reduce the cost per incident to $10,000. Because the previous manager had not invested in additional capacity to cover maximum peak-load requirements, that option is still available. She faces the prospect that it will cost an extra $3,000,000 to increase capacity from average to peak. This amount is spread out over 10 years, or $300,000 per year.

Should peak-load capacity be installed?

3 The classical formula for actual measured capacity is

$$C = T \times E \times U$$

where

C = actual measured capacity (standard hours)
T = time available (actual hours)
E = efficiency
U = utilization

If $T = 240$ standard hours, how can the actual capacity be more than that, say 280 standard hours?

4 In Alba, Italy, many famous restaurants rely on having enough truffles for the culinary delights, which customers travel miles to enjoy. Although customers pay a hefty price for the truffle dishes, the export market for truffles has much larger margins. Truffles are found by using pigs that can smell the strong aroma, and then digging under the ground to get them. Weather conditions have caused the truffle hunters to stay at home, so a truffle shortage is arising at the distributors' level. There are several regional distributors to whom the truffle hunters sell their findings. What are the constraints on capacity?

Hint: It would help to draw the supply chain that characterizes this product. Make certain to indicate that the supply chain starts with a scarce resource that has to be found in the woods. It cannot be farmed. Also, at the end of the supply chain there are two competing sources of demand, one domestic and the other international.

Note how currency fluctuations might affect the shipments of truffles at home and abroad.

5 Company capacity is 1 million units per year for a new food product. The sales force can sell 5 million units over a 5-year period, but only 100,000 in the first year. The breakeven volume is $V_{BEP} = 50,000$ units with $p = 3$, $vc = 2$, and $FC = 50,000$. What is the situation? What recommendations do you support?

Using the QMpom module called Capacity Management Models (Breakeven) will facilitate solving the three (3) problems that are numbered 5 through 7.

6 The Global Company has engaged a management consultant to analyze and improve its operations. His major recommendation is to "conveyorize" the production floor. This would represent a sizable investment for Global.

In order to determine whether or not the idea is feasible, a breakeven analysis will be utilized.

The situation is as follows: The cost of the conveyor will be $200,000 to be depreciated on a straight-line basis over 10 years. The conveyor will reduce operating costs by $0.25 per unit. Each unit sells for $2.00. The sales manager estimates that, on the basis of previous years, Global can expect a sales volume of 100,000 units. This represents 100 percent utilization of capacity. Current yearly contribution to fixed costs is $100,000. Current *vc* rate is $0.50 per unit.

Should Global install this conveyor?

7 Zeta Corporation is considering the advantages of automating a part of its production line. The company's financial statement follows:

Zeta Corporation

Total sales	$40,000,000	
Direct labor		$12,000,000
Indirect labor		$ 2,000,000
Direct materials		$ 8,000,000
Depreciation		$ 1,000,000
Taxes		$ 500,000
Insurance		$ 400,000
Sales costs		$ 1,500,000
Total expenses	$25,400,000	
Net profit	$14,600,000	

The report is based on the production and sale of 100,000 units. The operations manager believes that an additional investment of $5 million can reduce the variable costs by 30 percent. The same output quantity and qualities would be maintained. Using 5-year straight-line depreciation of $1,000,000 per year, construct a breakeven chart. Based on the breakeven analysis, should Zeta introduce the automation?

8 Referring to the linear programming problem discussed in the text of this chapter, show the calculations required to determine D1 and D2 slack for Plans 2 through 7, which appear in Table 10-3.

Using the QMpom module called Mathematical Programming Models (Linear Programming and Product Mix) will facilitate solving Problem 8.

9 A product is currently moved on pallets by a forklift truck. Should a conveyor belt be installed to replace the forklifts? The capacity would remain the same, but the cost structure differs. The Zeta Corporation uses a 1-year time period for comparison.

	Option 1 Forklift Truck	Option 2 Install Conveyor
V_{max}	18,000 units per year	18,000 units per year
FC	$10,000 per year	$12,000 per year
VC	$0.50 per unit	$0.45 per unit
p	$2.00 per unit	$2.00 per unit

Using the QMpom module called Capacity Management Models (Cost-Volume) will facilitate solving Problem 9.

10 Machine 1 is being challenged by Machine 2, which has greater capacity, lower variable costs, and higher fixed costs, but Machine 2 requires a much larger investment. Should the organization buy Machine 1 or Machine 2? The sales department states that demand is larger than supply and that, if they matched demand, they could deliver 6,000 units per quarter. The organization uses a 3-month time period ($T = 3$) for its breakeven analysis.

It could also be $T = 1$ quarter.

	Option 1 Machine 1	Option 2 Machine 2
V_{max}	5,000 units per quarter	10,000 units per quarter
FC	$2,500.00 per quarter	$6,500.00 per quarter
VC	$0.50 per unit	$0.10 per unit
p	$2.00 per unit	$2.00 per unit

Using the QMpom module called Capacity Management Models (Breakeven and Cost-Volume) will facilitate solving Problem 10.

11 The learning equation
$T(n) = kn^{(1-\lambda)}$ is said to apply to a particular job with the following values:
$k = 3$ minutes to make the first unit, $n = 1$
$n = 25$ units, which is the number of units to be made
$\lambda = 0.5 =$ the learning coefficient
Plot $T(n)$, which equals the cumulative time to make n consecutive units, from 1 to 25.

Using the QMpom module called Learning Curve Models (Learning Curve) will facilitate solving the two (2) problems that are numbered 11 through 12.

12   Using the information in Problem 11, plot

$$\overline{T}(n) = \frac{T(n)}{n} = kn^{-\lambda}$$

from $n = 1$ to $n = 25$. k and λ are the same as in Problem 11.

Practice Quiz

1   Capacity planning for the supply chain as well as utilization of existing capacity are P/OM responsibilities. To save page flipping, "the classical formula for actual measured capacity is $C = T \times E \times U$," where C is actual measured capacity in standard hours and T is real-time theoretical capacity available in standard hours. In addition, $E =$ efficiency and $U =$ utilization. All but one statement in a. through e. provide appropriate and useful insights about capacity. Which answer is out of line?

   a.   Realistic measures of capacity equal theoretical measures of *maximum* capacity, (i.e., $C = T$) when efficiency, E, is equal to 100 percent and utilization, U, is equal to 100 percent.
   b.   Utilization, U, is less than 100 percent when demand falls below the theoretical supply capacity, T.
   c.   Utilization, U, is less than 100 percent when equipment breakdowns diminish the theoretical supply capacity, T.
   d.   Efficiency, E, is less than 100 percent when process components are slowed down by lack of training, defective materials, setups, and changeovers.
   e.   For actual measured capacity (i.e., $C = T \times E \times U$) to be greater than T, utilization, U, must be greater than 100 percent, which is not possible.

2   Capacity in the supply chain to produce units of product (throughput) and capacity to store units of product (containment) are related in many important ways for P/OM decision makers. The discussion in parts a. through e. provides many insights. Which of these statements is incorrect?

   a.   Market demand can be highly variable, reaching extreme levels at certain times. For example, production processes cannot make enough toys starting in September for Christmas. One solution is to manufacture the toys year round, storing the inventory in warehouses until needed. The capacity of the warehouses must be large enough to hold inventory from January through August.
   b.   Warehouses that store the toys will be empty after Christmas. Then, they will begin to fill up again. There will be significant carrying charges for storing inventories of toys.
   c.   The inventory carrying costs include the cost of storage space. These costs can be compared with the costs of developing and running a process that can make enough toys starting in September. The output would be shipped to customers starting in September, which could be in line with normal delivery practice.
   d.   Service organizations deliver products that are difficult (sometimes impossible) to store. For example, secretarial, educational, and healthcare services cannot be put into inventory. The capacity for throughput in these services must be utilized when they are created. Therefore, overcapacity in service operations is discouraged by the cost factors.
   e.   Undercapacity in manufacturing results in lost sales or backorders unless inventory exists to ship to demand. Undercapacity in service systems always results in lost orders because services cannot be backordered.

3   Numerous issues relate to capacity planning for the supply chain. These include familiar references to corporate downsizing (e.g., following the implosion of dot.com businesses), the stock market declines, and recessions. Capacity reduction can take on many forms (e.g., workforce reductions). With resurgence of business, and stock market upturns, another capacity issue emerges which is upsizing (or upscaling) capacity. Return to higher production capacities will not necessarily be accompanied by a growth in workforce size that is symmetrical to earlier reductions. *Dynamic resizing* (downturn–upturn cycles) can be taken as opportunities to replace worker skills with new technology. The discussion found in a. through e. continues this dialogue. Which one point of discussion is inappropriate?

   a.   *The Wall Street Journal* headline states that Alpha Company plans downsizing. It intends to eliminate N people over the next 6 months. The accompanying article does not state that the firm's processes will be downscaled to lower capacity. It is assumed that existing equipment will be maintained but run at lower volumes. After downsizing the workforce, it is not unusual for management to raise capacity by replacing personnel (as possible) with high-productivity equipment.
   b.   All resources are part of supply chain capacity. That means that people, space, inventory, equipment, parking lots, cafeterias, computer memory, etc., are part of the capacity to produce different things. Capacity changes affect supply to meet demand for products, meals to feed workers, paperwork to support accounts receivable, etc.

c. There is need to balance capacity of supply chains across all product lines and staff supportive functions when changes in demand require alteration of supply. The balancing problem exists whether the move is upscale from downsizing or vice versa.

d. An issue that arises with dynamic resizing is the fact that flow-through capacity may not be evenly distributed. There can be too much capacity in one part of the supply chain system and too little capacity in another.

e. There are two types of bottlenecks associated with production processes. These are fixed and floating bottlenecks. Fixed types constrain capacity of the supply chain and must be removed to increase capacity. The floating type is temporary and not relevant to capacity issues of process resizing.

4 Supply chains are the lifeblood of the organization. Supply chains connect the downstream (raw material sources) with the upstream (fabrication or service facility). Further upstream are consumers fed by retailers who are supplied by distributors. Along the entire chain, every element can become a bottleneck. A truck gets a flat tire and suddenly becomes the system's bottleneck. Four out of five of the answers below are correct. Which is the incorrect assertion?

a. Bottlenecks cause delays that can substantially deteriorate the performance of the supply chain. Delays throw off the timing of supply chain ordering which results in overstocking and understocking. Both can severely penalize the firm, its suppliers, and its customers.

b. The beer game is a simulation of "purchasing difficulties" that can arise when a company experiences a temporary, capricious (erratic, unpredictable, whimsical) demand. That can happen as a result of a competitor's workforce going on strike, a hurricane closing a plant, the decision of the food channel to feature the brand, or a TV personality saying that brand is his or her favorite. Retailers nationally or regionally experience a sudden demand shift. Purchasing decisions try to cope with the question of how temporary is the change in demand levels. The beer game illustrates how hard it is to deal with such effects.

c. Simulations of supply chain behaviors can only be done with fast computers that have substantial memories. Simulation players develop strategies and input their numbers for order sizes based on computer selection of prior period demands. The scale effect is significant. Small-scale models do not operate in the same way that real-scale systems operate. That is why realistic databases are required to understand the behavior of these delay-sensitive systems.

d. Lead-time effects are nontrivial in creating large swings in stock on-hand. As the lead time decreases, it is possible to rectify problems faster by placing an order for quick delivery. That accounts for the growth in services of FedEx, UPS, and the U.S. Postal Service's Priority and Express mail.

e. If retailers can communicate quickly with their distributors, and the distributors with their manufacturers, about increases and decreases in demand that they are experiencing, then rapid adjustments all along the supply chain can be made to compensate for changes. The large-scale fluctuations can be reduced.

5 For linear breakeven analysis, use the data in the table. It has all been verified to be correct. However, one of the conclusions in points a. through e. is incorrect. Which one is wrong? Use the QMpom module called Capacity Management Models (Breakeven).

1	Maximum total volume for the year	(V_{max})	1,000 units
2	Fixed costs per year	(FC)	$ 6, 000
3	Variable costs per unit	(vc)	$ 6.00
4	Selling price per unit	(p)	$ 22.00
5	Expected operating volume (supply = demand)		650 units
6	Total costs at expected demand		
7	Margin contribution	($p - vc$)	
8	Breakeven point volume	(V_{BEP})	
9	Profit at maximum total volume		

a. Maximum total annual revenue is $22,000. The total variable costs at the expected annual demand of 650 units are $3,900.

b. The total costs at the expected demand of 650 units are $9,900.

c. The total profit at the expected demand of 650 units is $4,000.

d. The breakeven volume is 375 units, which is below the expected demand of 650 units, and this supports the fact that profit will be made.

e. If the company could operate at 100 percent capacity, the total annual profit would be $10,000.

6 A correction has been made by the forecasting team based on product design revisions. Quality has been changed. This includes the item and its service warranties. The price has been raised to $24 per unit. There is an increase in the variable

costs to $14 per unit and a decrease in the fixed costs to $5,000. Expected demand is 500 units. Conclusions based on linear breakeven analysis about the product design revision are listed in points a. through e. One conclusion is incorrect. Which one is wrong? Use the QMpom module called Capacity Management Models (Breakeven).

1	Maximum total volume for the year	(V_{max})	1,000 units
2	Fixed costs per year	(FC)	$ 5, 000
3	Variable costs per unit	(vc)	$ 14.00
4	Selling price per unit	(p)	$ 24.00
5	Expected operating volume (supply = demand)		500 units
6	Total costs at expected demand		
7	Margin contribution	$(p - vc)$	
8	Breakeven point volume	(V_{BEP})	
9	Profit at maximum total volume		

a. Maximum total annual revenue is $24,000. The total variable costs at the expected annual demand of 500 units are $7,000.

b. The total costs at the expected demand of 500 units are $12,000.

c. The total profit at the expected demand of 500 units is zero.

d. The breakeven volume is 500 units, which is at the expected demand of 500 units. No profit will be made.

e. If the company could operate at 100 percent capacity, the total annual profit would be zero.

7 The table summarizes data presented in Problems 10-5 and 10-6 for the original design and the revised design. The third column presents data for the new design (Problem 10-7). Examine the commentaries to these three problems in statements a. through e. One of them is off base. Which one is not acceptable? Use the QMpom module called Capacity Management Models (Breakeven).

	Original Design	Revised Design	New Design
Max total annual volume	1,000	1,000	1,000
Price (p)	$22/unit	$24/unit	$22/unit
Fixed costs (FC)	$6,000	$5,000	$4,000
Variable costs (vc)	$6/unit	$14/unit	$10/unit
Margin contribution $(p - vc)$	$16/unit	$10/unit	$12/unit
Max total variable costs	$6,000	$14,000	$10,000
Total annual costs	$12,000	$19,000	$14,000
(V_{BEP})	375 units	500 units	333 units
Maximum annual profit	$10,000	$5,000	$8,000
Slope	$16/unit	$10/unit	$12/unit

a. Compare the original design and the revised design (Problems 10-5 and 10-6) with respect to breakeven points (BEP) and slopes. The original design (Problem 10-5) possesses revenue and cost attributes that produce a lower BEP (375 versus 500 units) and a better profitability slope ($16 versus $10 per unit of profit per each additional unit sold). Therefore, keep the original design.

b. Compare the original design and the new design (Problems 10-5 and 10-7) with respect to breakeven points (BEP) and slopes. The new design (Problem 10-7) possesses revenue and cost attributes that produce a lower BEP (333 versus 375 units) but the original design has a better profitability slope ($16 versus $12 per unit of profit per each additional unit sold). There is a quandary. To solve this dilemma, it is necessary to determine whether the probabilities of operating above the BEP are greater than the probabilities of operating below the BEP.

c. The application of a decision model is essential when there is a quandary because one alternative has a better breakeven point and the other alternative has a greater profit-loss slope.

d. Compare the revised design and the new design (Problems 10-6 and 10-7) with respect to breakeven points (BEP) and slopes. The new design (Problem 10-7) possesses revenue and cost attributes that produce a lower BEP (333 versus 500 units) and the new design has a better profitability slope ($12 versus $10 per unit of profit per each additional unit sold). There is no quandary. Choose the new design if faced with this choice.

e. To solve the dilemma of choosing between the original design and the new design (Problems 10-5 and 10-7), the market manager is asked for the demand forecast for the next year. The results reported by the market forecasters show a strong likelihood that the annual demand will be 400 units. Therefore, it is decided to stay with the original design.

	Demand Volume 400 units	Demand Volume 500 units	Demand Volume 600 units
Original Design			
Total revenue	$ 8,800	$ 11,000	$ 13,200
Total costs	$ 8,400	$ 9,000	$ 9,600
Total profit	$ 400	$ 2,000	$ 3,600
New Design			
Total revenue	$ 8,800	$ 11,000	$ 13,200
Total costs	$ 8,000	$ 9,000	$ 10,000
Total profit	$ 800	$ 2,000	$ 3,200

e. It is useful to note that margin contribution $(p - vc)$ measures the slope of the profit-loss line. Slope and margin contribution are one and the same. The power of the decision model lies in how it combines the breakeven point, the margin contribution rate, and the probability of operating at each level of volume that the company's capacity permits. See Section 10-10 and Enrichment Activity 10.

8 Gamma Company has applied linear programming to resolve a production capacity problem. The company has two departments: paint and polish. The option exists to use this capacity on different production combinations of the original design (OD) and the new design (ND). Management has furnished comments and interpretations of these data in a. to e. Which one comment is inappropriate? Use of the QMpom module called Mathematical Programming Models (Linear Programming) can provide insights.

Table A

Department Capacities	Original Design (OD)	New Design (ND)
Paint Department	400 units per day	200 units per day
Polish Department	250 units per day	400 units per day
Profit	$10.00 per unit	$12.50 per unit

Table B

Plan	Original Design	New Design	Paint Slack	Polish Slack	Total Profit
1	400 units	0 units	0	NF	NF
2	250 units	0 units	37.5%	0	$2,500
3	0 units	200 units	0	50%	$2,500
4	100 units	100 units	25%	35%	$2,250
5	150 units	100 units	12.5%	15%	$2,750
6	160 units	105 units	92.5%	90.25%	$2,912.50
7	175 units	107 units	97.25%	96.75%	$3,087.50
8	181.8	109.1	0	0	$3,181.75

a. Linear programming is a mathematical method that can find the optimal product mix. Computer programs are able to do this for very large databases. The basic input data for a small problem is shown in Table A. It consists of the capacity of the paint department and the polish department to produce finished product.

b. The profit per unit for each product alternative design is given in Table A. It is essential to know the profit per unit because the product mix will be determined by the production schedule that maximizes profit. Row 1 of Table B states that 400 units of the original design use up all available capacity in the paint department, i.e., slack is zero. Row 1 also states that 400 units of the original design are not feasible (slack = NF) because there is insufficient capacity to turn out 400 units in the polish department.

c. Table B is based on cut-and-try efforts. It can be shown that row 8 is the product mix that will maximize profit at $3181.75. Row 8 indicates that with 181.8 units per day of the original design and 109.1 units per day of the new design, that the slack (available capacity) is zero in both the paint department and the polish department. This means that all available capacity is used up for the max profit solution.

   d. The maximum profit solution will always use up all available capacity. There is no waste and all resources are directed toward making money.

   e. Rows 4, 5, 6, and 7 in Table B show how the optimal solution is being gradually approached. The number of units to be made is increasing as the slack in both departments is decreasing and the total daily profit is increasing.

9 Gamma Company's competitor, Omicron, is introducing modular production (MP) as a means of improving the company's use of its supply chain production capacities. Points a. through e. are management's reflections on how modular production can improve performance. One of these reflections is not correct. Which one of the statements is not correct?

   a. Modular production and group technology (GT) are both examples of designing for capacity (DFC). Group technology should be included in Omicron's initiative to expand capacity by creative product and process design.

   b. One of the advantages of modular production is that the same module (or a GT family member) can be used in two or more products. This is equivalent to raising the demand level for that part. Higher demand moves production toward flow shop work configurations with cost reductions and quality improvements.

   c. In a shop where many different products are made, if each uses different sizes of screws, nuts, and bolts, the inventory problem is more complicated than if these types of fasteners are standardized as much as possible. This illustrates in a simple form the principle behind MP.

   d. The principle of modularity is design, develop, and produce the minimum number of parts (or operations) that can be combined in the maximum number of ways to offer the greatest number of products or services. The principle embodies market wisdom, process ingenuity, and design specialization advantages.

   e. Methods of group technology are not related to part names or part numbering systems. The same observation applies to modular production parts. Principles of modularity and group technology are based on theories of production that transcend naming and numbering schemes used for identification.

10 Learning how to do a better job can include improvements in productivity. This could mean more units in a period of time and at a lower per unit cost. Learning can provide greater quality without a cost increase. Learning has resulted in innovations so that new types of units become available. Marketing relishes the opportunity to expand product variety without increasing costs or decreasing productivity. Learning theory does not directly address this breadth of opportunities. Instead, it concentrates on productivity. The management discussion from a. to e. runs through some of the applications of learning theory to operational efficiency. All but one of the observed points is appropriate. Identify the inappropriate commentary.

   a. Pilot plants are used for learning how to produce a new physical product. Focus groups in market research are also learning environments. The point is to know as much as possible about the system so simulations are used for discovery.

   b. Classical learning curve theory indicates that the average time to do a job can decrease exponentially with job repetitions. The acceleration rate is embodied in the learning coefficient, l. When $l = 0$, there is no learning. Each unit requires the same amount of time.

   c. The Boston Consulting Group postulated the "experience curve" that describes economies of scale. As the volume (scale) of output increases, the costs per unit decrease. Change is a reduction in per unit cost of between 20 and 30 percent with each doubling of volume. There are many logical factors for the reduction such as sourcing discounts and improvements, technology thresholds that need volume for justification, and the benefits of repetition on human cognitive power.

   d. Sports performance requires practice. Success with a musical instrument is also based on practice. Service mastery is different because it is based on personality and cannot be learned. Learning to play well in golf, tennis, chess, etc., is known to make step functions of capability known as plateaus of accomplishment. The trainee can remain for some time at a plateau before making another step function of improvement. Such plateaus do not apply to service capabilities.

   e. Learning to improve at any job is handicapped by assignments to remedy problems. "Putting out fires" does not provide the environment or motivation for continuous improvement (kaizen).

Additional Readings

Almeida, Virgilio A. F., and Daniel A. Menasce. *Capacity Planning for Web Services*, 2e. Englewood Cliffs, NJ: Prentice-Hall PTR, September 2001.

Anderson, David M. *Design for Manufacturability & Concurrent Engineering: How to Design for Low Cost, Design in High Quality, Design for Lean Manufacture, and Design Quickly for Fast Production.* Cambria, CA: CIM Press, 2003.

Baloff, N. "Estimating the Parameters of the Startup Model—An Empirical Approach." *The Journal of Industrial Engineering*, 18, 4 (April 1967): 248–253.

Blackstone, J. H. *Capacity Management.* APICS South-Western Series in Production and Operations Management, 1989.

Boston Consulting Group, Inc. *Perspectives on Experience.* BCG, 1972.

Christopher, Martin. *Logistics and Supply Chain Management.* Burr Ridge, IL: Irwin, 1994.

Cockcroft, Adrian, and Bill Walker. *Capacity Planning for Web Services*, 2e. Englewood Cliffs, NJ: Prentice-Hall PTR, September 2001.

Forrester, J. W. *Industrial Dynamics.* Wiley, 1961.

Goldratt, Eliyahu M. *Theory of Constraints.* Great Barrington, MA: North River Press, 1999; *The Goal*, 3e. Great Barrington, MA: North River Press, 2004.

Gopal Christopher, and Gerry Cahill. *Logistics in Manufacturing.* Burr Ridge, IL: Irwin, 1992.

Leonard, George. *Mastery.* New York: Plume, Penguin Group, 1992.

Parkinson, C. Northcote. *Parkinson's Law.* London: John Murray, 1958.

Rautenstrauch, W., and R. Villers. *The Economics of Industrial Management.* New York: Funk & Wagnalls Co., 1949.

Senge, Peter M. *The Fifth Discipline.* Doubleday/Currency, 1990.

Susman, Gerald I. (Editor). *Integrating Design and Manufacturing for Competitive Advantage.* Oxford, UK: Oxford University Press, April 1992.

Visit http://www.ambcbenchmarking.org for the Agile Manufacturing Benchmarking Consortium™ whose objective is to conduct benchmarking studies of business processes.

Vogel, Harold L. *Entertainment Industry Economics: A Guide for Financial Analysis*, 5e. (breakeven point volumes in the entertainment industry). Cambridge, UK: Cambridge University Press, May 2001.

———. *Travel Industry Economics: A Guide for Financial Analysis* (breakeven point volumes in the travel industry). Cambridge, UK: Cambridge University Press, January 2001.

Yu-Lee, Reginald Tomas. *Essentials of Capacity Management*, Chichester, UK: Wiley Europe, Ltd., April 2002.

Notes

1. This 1823 quotation can be found in *Characteristics*, page 89. William Hazlitt. *Characteristics*. London, England Publisher unknown, 1823.

2. C. Northcote Parkinson. *Parkinson's Law*. London: John Murray, 1958.

3. Eliyahu M. Goldratt. *Theory of Constraints*. Great Barrington, MA: North River Press, 1999.

4. Sprague Electric Company played an important role in this research, which was published as follows: J.W. Forrester. *Industrial Dynamics.* Wiley, 1961.

5. Peter M. Senge. *The Fifth Discipline*. Doubleday/Currency, 1990, 27–54.

6. W. Rautenstrauch and R. Villers. *The Economics of Industrial Management*. New York: Funk & Wagnalls Co., 1949.

7. Boston Consulting Group, Inc. *Perspectives on Experience*. A collection of articles published by BCG, 1972. An article by Bruce D. Hendersen describes the experience curve. See http://www.valuebasedmanagement.net/methods_experience_curve_effects.html.

    Also, note: Experience Curves for Energy Technology Policy (OECD/IEA, 2000) at http://iea.org/textbase/nppdf/free/2000/curve2000.pdf.

8. Learning Rate (R) as defined by QMpom: The ratio of the time or cost to produce the nth unit divided by the time or cost to produce the $\left(\frac{n}{2}\right)th$ unit.

    The percent reduction in time or cost due to the Learning Effect (the percent drop in time or cost that is experienced with each doubling of the cumulative number of units produced) is the complement of the Learning Rate. For example, if the time to produce the 8th unit is 20 percent less than the time to produce the 4th unit, the Learning Rate is 100% – 20%, or 80%.

    In most production situations that have been studied, the Learning Rates fall in the 70% to 90% range (time or cost reductions on the order of 10% to 30% for each doubling of the cumulative output).

9. There was real interest during the 1960s and a belief that productivity could be improved substantially by observing the learning curve phenomenon. See, for example, Nicholas Baloff. "Estimating the Parameters of the Startup Model—An Empirical Approach." *The Journal of Industrial Engineering*, 18, 4 (April 1967): 248–253.

10. The text reference is *Mastery of Self*, a book about multiple plateaus for learning tennis and other sports. George Leonard. *Mastery*. New York: Plume, Penguin Group, 1992.

Enrichment Activity 10: The Breakeven Decision Model for Supply Chain Planning

Breakeven analysis and decision making are interrelated. When demand is uncertain, it must be forecast for the purpose of using breakeven analysis to do capacity planning. Capacity planning, given uncertain demand, will require a forecast. The issue being treated now is how to put BEA and capacity planning together in a decision format.

It is easier to describe this combined model using an example that could be from either a manufacturing or a service industry. The choice was made to use an unspecified generic industry called *ANY Industry*.

The company is comparing present technology with advanced technology. The problem involves capacity planning, cost analysis, and demand analysis. The latter is based on prices charged and qualities perceived by the company's customers. The problem is that there is no clear-cut answer about what to do. One choice has a better *BEP*; the other choice has a better rate of return slope and demand is uncertain. This is a challenging P/OM problem.

The P/OM department at ANY has drawn up breakeven charts for the alternatives. (These are requested in the problem section for this supplement.) They have calculated the breakeven point and the rate of return of profit for both the present technology and the advanced technology.

Table EA10-1 presents the data to calculate the *BEP* and the profit rate. Assume the time period is one year.

The breakeven point is 6,667 units or 66.7 percent of total capacity for the present technology. The breakeven point for the advanced technology is 6,857 units or 68.6 percent of full-capacity utilization.

These may seem to be relatively high breakeven points, but they are not unusual for many industries. Although it would be nice to have breakeven percentages ranging from 30 to 45 percent, capital intensive industries, such as farm equipment and auto production, have high breakeven points. In this case, the advanced technology option is worse than the present technology option. At such a high breakeven point, there is an immediate preference for the lower *BEP*. ANY Industry prefers a lower *BEP*, but this preference gets stronger when the choice is between already high values.

However, before any decision can be made, it is necessary to examine the relative profits of the two plans at greater than breakeven percentages of capacity. The easiest comparison is at 100 percent of the supply chain's capacity.

Profit at 100 percent of capacity:

Present Technology	Advanced Technology
+$500,000	+$550,000

There is a 10 percent advantage for the advanced technology.

It also will be useful to examine the relative losses of the two plans at less than breakeven percentages of capacity. An easy comparison is at 50 percent of capacity, well below breakeven.

Profit at 50 percent of capacity:

Present Technology	Advanced Technology
−$500,000	−$550,000

There is a 30 percent advantage for the present technology.

In summary, the present technology has a small *BEP* advantage (66.7 percent versus 68.6 percent). It also has an advantage when demand falls below the *BEP*. Advanced technology has the advantage above the *BEP*.

	Present Technology	Advanced Technology	**Table EA10-1**
Fixed costs*	$1,000,000.00	$1,200,000.00	Breakeven Data for ANY
Per unit variable costs ($)	50.00	25.00	
Per unit revenue ($)	200.00	200.00	
Annual capacity	10,000 units	10,000 units	
* Fixed costs are depreciated on an annual basis.			

Table EA10-2	Demand Level *D*	Probability of Demand Level
Forecast of Demand for ANY	40% of capacity	0.05
	50% of capacity	0.10
	60% of capacity	0.15
	70% of capacity	0.20
	80% of capacity	0.25
	90% of capacity	0.20
	100% of capacity	0.05
		1.00

Which should be chosen, the lower BEP with its lower rate of profit and lower rate of loss, or the higher *BEP* with its higher rate of return and higher rate of loss? This question can only be answered by ANY if it has a believable forecast to use with the appropriate decision model.

ANY's forecast of annual customer demand is given in Table EA10-2. The derivation of Table EA10-2 should be stated in an actual situation. That permits evaluation of its believability.

A specific amount of profit is associated with each level of demand. The total amount of profit (*TPR*) can be read from the breakeven charts or calculated directly using the following equations. $TPR = (p - vc)V - FC$ which becomes

For present technology: $TPR = 150V - 1,000,000$
For advanced technology: $TPR = 175V - 1,200,000$
For present technology, at 0 percent demand, there is a loss of $1 million. At 100 percent capacity (equivalent to 10,000 units) there is profit of $500,000.

Relate the probability distribution to the profit at each demand level *D*. Multiply profit at *D* by the *probability of D*. Add up these products for all demand levels to obtain the average (or expected) profit for the given strategy.

As derived in Table EA10-3, ANY's expected profit for present technology is

$$\text{Expected Profit} = \sum_{V=0}^{V=100\%} (P_V)(TPR_V) = \$95,000 \qquad (EA10\text{-}1)$$

The *BEP* for present technology is 66.7 percent. Multiplying columns (3) and (1) of Table EA10-3 determines the expected demand, which is 73 percent:

$$0.05(40\%) + 0.10(50\%) + 0.15(60\%) + 0.20(70\%) + 0.25(80\%) + 0.20(90\%) + 0.05(100\%) = 73 \text{ percent}$$

Table EA10-3	(1) Demand (*D*) as a % of Max Capacity	(2) *TPR_v* Profit @ *D*	(3) *P_v* Probability of *D*	Columns (3)(2) (*P_v*)(*TPR_v*)
ANY's Expected Profit for Present Technology	0%	−1,000	0	0
	10	−850	0	0
	20	−700	0	0
	30	−550	0	0
	40	−400	0.05	−20
	50	−250	0.10	−25
	60	−100	0.15	−15
	70	+50	0.20	+10
	80	+200	0.25	+50
	90	+350	0.20	+70
	100	+500	0.05	+25
			1.00	+95

Expected Profit = $95,000 (Profits in Table EA10-3 in 000s)

(1) Demand (D) as a % of Max Capacity	(2) TPR_v Profit @ D	(3) P_v Probability of D	Columns (3)(2) $(P_v)(TPR_v)$	Table EA10-4
0%	−1,200	0	0	ANY's Expected Profit for Advanced Technology
10	−1.025	0	0	
20	−850	0	0	
30	−675	0	0	
40	−500	0.05	−25	
50	−325	0.10	−32.5	
60	−150	0.15	−22.5	
70	+25	0.20	+5	
80	+200	0.25	+50	
90	+375	0.20	+75	
100	+550	0.05	+27.5	
		1.00	+77.5	

Expected Profit = $77,500 (Profits in Table EA10-4 in 000s)

The same kinds of calculations are now done for advanced technology. The expected demand is unchanged because the same demand distribution applies. Determine the profit at 73 percent capacity utilization. It is $77,500. That is the benefit of knowing the expected demand. Expected profit is calculated the long way in Table EA10-4, where profits are expressed in 000s.

$$\text{Expected Profit} = \sum_{V=0}^{V=100\%} (P_v)(TPR_v) = \$77,500 \tag{EA10-2}$$

Following this analysis, it is recommended that ANY Industry retain its present technology. The advanced technology will lower expected profits.

Management should note a few cautions. First, the competition may be shifting in the direction of the new technology, which could be evolving. It might be advisable for the company to invest minimally at this time in order to learn the new technology and be better able to assess it as time passes. Later, both the fixed costs and variable operating costs of the advanced technology may decrease. Further, ANY may be able to increase capacity, currently limited to 10,000 units per year. Quality issues and long-term application of TQM perspectives also should be considered.

If the advanced technology in any way affects the probability distribution, that must be taken into account. Perhaps the new equipment will permit faster delivery and/or more reliable tolerances or delivery schedules. The decision regarding technological choices might be sensitive to shifts in the distribution of the probability of demand.

With the addition of forecasting, the breakeven model has become a unifying systems-wide decision model. All of the functions should be playing a part in preparing the forecast and estimating the costs and revenues.

The decision model with forecasting overrides the problem of what to do when one strategy has a better BEP, but a poorer marginal rate of return, than another strategy. The forecast changes the approach from what is traditional breakeven analysis, where the *BEP* number is derived and all decision makers have in mind an estimate of the likelihood that the company will operate above or below that point. Without this estimate, the breakeven point is meaningless. The decision model has merged the *BEP* and the marginal rate of return into a single problem.

Enrichment Challenges 10

Note: Enrichment Activity 10 has discussion and problems that can be formulated and solved using QuantMethods Production/Operations Management software (QMpom). The appropriate model category is Capacity Management Models (Breakeven).

1 Draw the breakeven chart for ANY's present technology situation. Indicate the breakeven point and the rate of return of profit.

2 Draw the breakeven chart for ANY's advanced technology alternative. Indicate the breakeven point and the rate of return of profit.

3 Table EA10-5 presents a shift in the forecast. What is the effect of the change in the forecast? Will it alter the recommendations?

Table EA10-5

ANY's Expected Profit for Advanced Technology with Revised Demand Forecast (Profit in 000s)

(1) Demand (D)	(2) Profit @ D	(3) Probability of D	(3)(2)	(3)(1)
0%	−1,200	0		
10	−1,025	0		
20	−850	0		
30	−675	0		
40	−500	0		
50	−325	0.10		
60	−150	0.15		
70	+25	0.20		
80	+200	0.25		
90	+375	0.20		
100	+550	0.10		
		1.00		

Facilities Planning: Location and Layout

Chapter Outline

Chapter 11 discusses the four major components of facilities planning. First: where to locate the plant, or the branch, or the warehouse. This is a regional determination. The second issue is to find the specific structure and site to use. The third factor comes before moving in and it is to design the layout. The fourth is to select furniture, lighting, decorative features, and equipment for doing the job. In fact, these four components interact, and no one of them can be considered exclusive of the others.

After reading this chapter, you should be able to:

- Explain the four distinct parts of facilities planning.
- Discuss who is responsible for doing facilities planning.
- Describe the nature of facilities planning models.
- Explain why planning for the design of facilities requires the systems approach.
- Describe the application of the transportation model for location decisions.
- Apply the transportation model to solve location decision problems.
- Determine the relative advantages of renting, buying, or building.
- Show how to use scoring models for facility selection decisions.
- Explain how to deal with the effect of multiple decision makers regarding the choice of locations, sites, and building decisions.
- Describe factors to be taken into account for equipment selection.
- Explain why facilities planning is said to be interactive. *Hint:* Interactive in this case means that consideration goes back and forth between decisions concerning facility location, facility selection, equipment selection, and facility layout.
- Describe what the job of facility layout entails.
- Explain how job design and workplace layout interact.
- Evaluate the use of quantitative layout rules (algorithms).
- Discuss the use of heuristics to improve layouts of plants and offices.

The Systems Viewpoint

Regional facilities planning calls upon a wealth of knowledge and great skills. However, facilities planning on a nationwide level requires expertise from so many areas that it is folly to think that one person alone can do it successfully. International facilities planning takes global team efforts with country specialists. A greater amount of expertise and management ability is required for global supply chain facilities planning.

In all cases, a better job is done by broad-based visionaries and generalists who know how to work together as a team. When generalists and specialists combine their efforts, pooling their viewpoints and knowledge, it is likely that a systems approach to P/OM is essential.

Strategic Thinking

For facilities planning regarding location and layout, strategic thinking is essential to avoid suboptimization. The easiest way to define suboptimization is that it is less good than optimization. It is a result, or series of results, that strays from achieving the objectives that drive strategies. For example, say that a theme park assigns the manager of each of its attractions the goal of minimizing waiting time of customers. That objective for each ride will produce different effects than a single strategic objective to minimize the total waiting time of customers over the course of many rides and an entire day of being in the park. The sum of suboptimization results will not add up to an optimal solution. The sequence of rides taken, the timing of starts and completions, the encouragement of choosing certain intervals to eat and use the restrooms reflect the larger strategic framework.

When the real problem is too big to grasp because there are very many options, the systems approach is indicated. Dividing the (facilities) problem into regional subproblems to make it workable can jeopardize the quality of the solution. It is likely to yield a suboptimal (less than best) solution. Location, site, and building decisions are major components of the larger facilities planning problem. Strategies that yield suboptimal results can damage competitive capabilities. Thus, layout and job design are partners in the achievement of a good flow shop. They need to be considered together. In the job shop, production scheduling, shop-floor layout, and job design are interdependent and best approached as a system. The same kind of reasoning applies to the optimal facility design for a project. In all such situations, facilities planning is a multidimensional systems problem. The appropriate strategy must encompass all relevant elements of the minimum coherent system.

11-1 Facilities Planning

Facilities are the plant and the office within which P/OM does its work. In addition to the buildings and the spaces that are built, bought, or rented, facilities also include equipment used in the plant and the office. There are four main components of **facilities planning** and they strongly interact with each other. These four are

Facilities planning
Four main components are geographic location, structure and specific site, equipment choice, and layout.

1   *Location of facilities.* Where, in the geographic sense, should the various operations be located? Location can apply to only one facility but more generally includes a number of locations for doing different things. Thus, "where is it best to ..." fabricate and assemble each product, locate the service center, situate the sales offices, and position the administration? These decisions impact the supply chain in many ways. Each facility location decision (and there are many decisions for normal supply chain systems) determines a set of times, costs, and risks that remain long after the data used for the decision have been discarded and the name or names of the decision makers can no longer be remembered. It is a good idea to keep a permanent file for all location decisions. In that way, pertinent history can be reconstructed and questions about reengineering the decision can be explored.

Many location factors have to be dealt with in a qualitative fashion. Common sense prevails. Qualitative factors such as being near supplies of raw materials and/or sources of skilled labor vie with being close to customers. Seldom can all desires be satisfied. The options may be to choose one over the other or to compromise with an in-between location. There are similar problems for distributors who want to be located close by all kinds of transportation facilities (road, rail, airports, and marine docks).

Other location factors are better dealt with in a quantitative fashion because common sense does not work. The reason is that some real problems are too big to grasp all of the possible options. Because of this, optimal location assignments are often counterintuitive. For example, if a transportation analysis is made manageable by dividing the problem into regional subproblems, the solution may

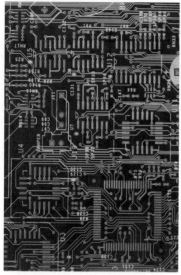

© 2008 Jupiterimages Corporation

Circuit board layout is detailed and precise. The same level of consideration should be carried to the design of the office and the plant. The layout of a customer service center facility should address seating arrangements, computer and telecommunication locations, and enhancements for information retrieval that will speed up the service to customers.

Layout

Plan for the arrangement of the working environment of the company's facilities.

be seriously suboptimal (far from being the best that is possible). The systems approach, which endeavors to include all relevant factors, is needed in this case.

At the same time, there are strategic issues concerning centralization or decentralization of facilities. Should there be a factory in each country? Would a central warehouse be more desirable than regional warehouses or can they both be used to an advantage? Such decisions might be best reached with a combination of qualitative and quantitative considerations.

2 *Structure and specific site selection.* In what kind of facility should the process be located? How should the building or space be chosen? Is it best for the company to build the facility, buy, or rent it? Choice of a specific building is often decided after the location is chosen. However, there are circumstances where the location, site, and structure should be considered together. This makes structure and site decisions complex problems best resolved by using the systems approach.

3 *Equipment choice.* What kind of process technology is to be used? This decision often dominates structure and site options. In turn, there may be environmental factors that limit the choice of locations. Equipment choice can include transport systems and available routes. Interesting systems problems arise that combine all three aspects of facilities planning.

4 *Layout of the facility.* Where should machines and people be placed in the plant or office? There is interaction of equipment choice with layout, structure, site, and location. The size of the facility is determined by both current needs and future projections to allow for growth. Once the location, site, and structure are determined, layout details can be decided.

What path do conveyors, AGVs (automatic guidance vehicles), and other transport systems take? AGVs are computer controlled along prescribed transport paths. Other transport systems include manual systems (like wheelbarrows) and forklift trucks, among others. **Layout** is an interior design problem that strongly interacts with structure and specific site selection and equipment choice.

Change in technology and even in purpose should lead to reexamination of layout decisions, which, in turn, may lead to site and structure considerations. Relocation necessities (caused by political and economic factors) may trigger an entire change sequence. Since decisions about facilities are key factors in supply chain systems planning, openness to dynamic forces of technology and systems status is vital.

Usually, location is addressed first because its consequences may dominate other decisions. This is particularly true when transportation costs are a large part of the cost of goods sold. Location also may be crucial because of labor being available only in certain places. Closeness to market can affect demand. Closeness to suppliers can affect prices and the ability to deliver just in time. Tax considerations might play a part.

Once the location is known, a search for appropriate building structures can be done. However, when several locations are considered suitable and when buildings have been identified that qualify, then the various packages of locations and structures have to be considered together.

11-1a Who Does Facilities Planning?

The treatment of all four of the facilities planning issues is classic P/OM. Their importance is not in question, but the way that these four issues are done and the role of P/OM in the planning process have been changing. In the global world of international production systems, international markets, and rapid technological transfers, facilities planning requires a team effort. It is no longer the sole responsibility of P/OM.

Team effort is required to deal with the issues properly. They deserve consideration by the entire strategic planning team of which P/OM is one important member. Beside the fact that all functional areas should be participants in location decisions, there are additional considerations.

Governmental regulations—from international to national to municipalities—have to be addressed. Legal issues need to be resolved. Lawyers from many countries often are consulted. There are negotiations with communities regarding such matters as financial incentives and tax breaks.

To **rent**, **buy**, or **build** requires specialists who know domestic and international real-estate markets. Trade rules and tariffs are special for trading blocks and their partners. They are constantly changing for GATT, NAFTA, EU, and other trade groups.

Currency conditions and banking restrictions must be interpreted by specialists. The list of special complications to consider is long and particular to each situation.

11-2 Models for Facility Decisions

P/OM's role and its contributions to facilities management are primarily of two kinds. First, P/OM's experience, with what succeeds and what fails for facilities planning, adds valuable insights to the planning team. Second, P/OM knows how to use facilities planning **models** developed by operations researchers, management scientists, and location analysts.

Location decision models can use measures of costs and preferences to reach location decisions. **Transportation models** use costs, and scoring models use preferences. Other models—such as breakeven analysis—can help to select a facility and to choose equipment. Plant, equipment, and tooling decisions need close consultation between engineering, P/OM, and finance. These issues need to be guided and coordinated with top management.

Supermarket and department store locations are often chosen to be at the center of dense population zones. A center of gravity model can be used to find the population center, or the sales volume center—instead of the center of mass—which an engineer finds for structures or ships. Columbus, Ohio, is a popular distribution center because a circle around it within a 500-mile radius encloses a large percentage of U.S. retail sales.

Plant layout models for flow shops require detailed engineering in cooperation with P/OM process requirements. The technical aspects of the process are vitally important in determining layout for a flow shop. Layout for the job shop may be one of the few areas where P/OM is expected to do the job on its own. In actuality, good layout decisions may be based more on models that assist visualization than on models that measure layout-flow parameters.

Nevertheless, there is a need to know that there are layout models for minimizing material transport distances. This is the measured path that work in process must travel in the plant. These models are interesting for special applications, as well as for their quantitative properties. Although their use tends to be limited, they are discussed in this chapter.

How models are used is what counts. Some applications can be criticized as overriding complex issues with simple metrics. The study of P/OM provides the basis for exercising good judgment about choosing models and methods. Layout goals now encourage communication and teamwork instead of imitation of machine performance, which lends itself to precise measurement.

11-3 Location Decisions—Qualitative Factors

Best location is related to the function of the facility and the characteristics of its products and services. Also, location decisions always are made relative to what other alternatives exist—just as building decisions are made relative to what else is available. When

Rent
Payments made regularly by a tenant to a landlord.

Buy
Do a rent or buy analysis.

Build
Alternatives to "build a new facility" would be either "rent" or "buy" a building.

Models
Attempts to image the real thing can be physical, like a plant layout model.

Transportation models
Minimize shipping costs or maximize profits where production facility location and market (shipped to) differentials exist.

Best location
Specially tailored to the particulars of the situation, e.g., close to the market, near suppliers, able to draw on highly-skilled work pools, facilitates joining about 12,000 other maquiladoras (U.S. (and others)-owned and operated assembly factories located along the 2,100-mile border that separates Mexico and the United States, employing over 1 million workers).

© 2007 Jupiterimages Corporation

Location factors play a major role in the economics of timber shipments. The source of the wood and its nearness to timber mills is the first link. Then, mill to shipping port is link two. The third link is from receiving port to lumberyard. Wood is heavy and the transport is costly so it may pay to do as much work as possible within the first link. Location factors play a major role in the hotel and resort business. What are the analogies and/or differences to transporting timber?

© 2007 Jupiterimages Corporation

Blackpool Grand Theatre in Lancashire, England, U.K. (box office telephone: 01253 290190) is an historical Victorian theatre. It is the location for production of theatrical events that take enormous P/OM skills to produce. The raw materials (including audience) must be brought to the theatre in batches for transformation. What is that transformation? The cost of the product is in euros. If you want to book seats, the program can be found at http://www.blackpoolgrand.co.uk.

the building location decision is taken jointly, it is possible to decide to wait for another alternative to appear. This enlarges the scope of the problem and provides another example of the need for a systems-oriented perspective to resolve some location issues.

11-3a Location to Enhance Service Contact

Service industries locate close to their customers to achieve the kind of contact that characterizes good service. Bank tellers and ATMs (automated teller machines) are such contact points. No one wants to travel many miles to make deposits or withdrawals. The closer bank will get the business.

Branch banks, gas stations, fast-food outlets, and public phones are scattered all around town, because distance traveled is one of the main choice criteria used by customers. Shopping malls are located so that many people find it convenient to drive to them. For retail business, best location is decided by the ability to generate high customer contact frequency.

An interesting exception to the advantage of proximity for contact are the services rendered to vacationers. Traveling many miles for sun and surf, or for snow and skiing, the service starts with the airline providing transportation. Then the hotel or resort offers food, shelter, sports, and entertainment.

Facilities planning and management are crucial to success in the hotel and resort business. Location may be at the top of the list. Services, in general, are strongly affected by location, structure, site, equipment, and layout because they all participate in making contact with customers successful.

Government institutions locate services close to the citizens who need them. Municipal governments provide police and fire protection to those who live within the municipality and pay the taxes. Effective federal service requires regional offices.

11-3b Just-in-Time Orientation

Extractors like to be close to their raw materials. On average, gold mining reduces a ton of ore to 4.5 grams of gold. The reduction process has to be near to the mines. Fabricators like to be close to their raw materials and customers. A balanced choice has to be made, which will depend on the specific product. Assembly plants like their component suppliers to be close. They encourage suppliers to deliver on a just-in-time basis. The advantage to the supplier is that enough volume of business must be given by the producer to justify the location. Services usually profit by being close to the customer. Creative solutions are a goal.

The decision to be a nearby just-in-time supplier requires a mutual interchange of trust and loyalty. Just-in-time suppliers benefit from the proximity by being a single source (or one of very few sources) to their customer. Communication can be face-to-face and frequent. Customers benefit from reduction of inventory. Suppliers benefit from stability and continuity.

11-4 Location Factors

Six factors that can affect location decisions are

1   *Process inputs.* Closeness to sources is often important. The transportation costs of bringing materials and components to the process from distant locations can harm profit margins.
2   *Process outputs.* Being close to customers can provide competitive advantages. Among these are lower transport costs for shipping finished goods and the ability to satisfy customers' needs and respond rapidly to competitive pricing—which can provide market advantages.

3 *Process requirements.* There can be needs for special resources that are not available in all locations (i.e., water, energy, and labor skills).

4 *Personal preferences.* Location decision makers, including top management, have biases for being in certain locations that can override economic advantages of other alternatives.

5 *Governmental issues.* Tax, tariff, trade, and legal factors usually matter. Trade agreements and country laws are increasingly important in reaching global location decisions.

6 *Site and plant availabilities.* The interaction between the location and the available facilities makes location and structure-site decisions interdependent.

Shipping costs are the primary concern for the first factor, viz., process inputs. These may be a function of shipping distances. However, there are more likely to be price advantages for specific materials in certain regions and countries.

For the second factor, viz., process outputs, being close to the customer has a variety of advantages including shipping distance for delivery and nearness for direct contact to remedy complaints and to consult on product changes. Being close to the customer facilitates design discussions and suggestions applicable to all phases of the supply chain channel linking producers and customers.

To minimize the total distance between a central warehouse and a number of retail shops, the location of the warehouse is determined by using the mean value of the x and y distances of each location from an arbitrary origin. The normal (0,0) origin works well. The procedure is described as the **centroid location method**. As an example, retail shop A is at ($x = 2$, $y = 1$), retail shop B is at ($x = 1$, $y = 2$), and retail shop C is at ($x = 3$, $y = 3$), and these retailers carry equal weights of importance. Then, for x, the total weights are 3, the sum of x values is six, the mean is 2, i.e., $(2 + 1 + 3)/3 = 2$. The same result is obtained for y. So, locate the central warehouse at $x = 2$, $y = 2$. To utilize this method, look at the QMpom module called Facilities Planning Models (Site Location) as noted in the Problems Section with problems 13, 14, and 15.

Factor three has alternatives such as processing bulk materials at the mining site to reduce their mass, and then further refining at a location close to the customer. In this case, process and transportation costs interact. For special medical procedures people have been known to travel far from home. For a great vacation, Hawaii and Tahiti beckon.

The fourth factor is individual, intangible, and often encountered. For the fifth factor, taxes and tariffs can add costs to either the production or the marketing elements. Legal factors are difficult to estimate and can be substantial. The sixth factor can require the decision to defer making a decision.

Centroid location method
Finds the equivalent of a center of demand (gravity) in a two-dimensional mapping plane. Helps to find the best location for a new gas station or supermarket.

11-5 Location Decisions Using the Transportation Model (TM)

Transportation costs are a primary concern for a new start-up company or division. This also applies to an existing company that intends to relocate. Finally, it should be common practice to reevaluate the current location of an ongoing business so that the impact of changing conditions and new opportunities is not overlooked. Relocating and moving costs can be added to the transportation model (TM).

When shipping costs are critical for the location decision, the TM can determine minimum cost or maximum profit solutions that specify optimal shipping patterns between many locations. Transportation costs include the combined costs of moving raw materials to the plant and of transporting finished goods from the plant to one or more warehouses.

It is easier to explain the TM with the following numerical example than with abstract math equations. A doll manufacturer has decided to build a factory in the center of the

United States. Two cities have been chosen as candidates. These are St. Louis, Missouri, and Columbus, Ohio. Several sites in the two regions have been identified. Real-estate costs are about equal in both.

11-5a Suppliers to Factory—Shipping Costs

The average cost of shipping the components that the company uses to the Columbus, Ohio, location is $6 per production unit. Shipping costs average only $3 per unit to St. Louis, Missouri. In TM terminology, shippers (suppliers, in this case) are called sources or origins. Those receiving shipments (producers, in this case) are called sinks or destinations.

11-5b Factory to Customers—Shipping Costs

The average cost of shipping from the Columbus, Ohio, location to the distributor's warehouse is $2 per unit. The average cost of shipping from St. Louis, Missouri, to the distributor's warehouse is $4 per unit. The same terminology applies. The shipper is the producer (source or origin) and the receivers are the distributors or customers (destinations or sinks). The origins and destinations are shown in Figure 11-1.

Total transportation costs to and from the Columbus, Ohio, plant are $6 + $2 = $8 per unit; for St. Louis, Missouri, they are $3 + $4 = $7. Other things being equal, the company should choose St. Louis, Missouri. However, the real world is not as simple as this.

The complication appears as soon as there are a number of origins competing for shipments to a number of destinations. Another complication is when the supply chain involves what is called transshipment, where destinations become origins. The Columbus factory was a destination for and an origin for shipments of finished goods to the market. Where the supply chain has many linkages, the transportation model is structured to reflect the transshipment alternatives. Two plants and two markets are shown with one source of components in Figure 11-2.

With these multiple facilities, the TM comes closer to capturing the character of real distribution problems. The issue is: Which plants should ship how much product to which distributors? If it turns out that the solution indicates that one plant should ship no units at all, that is equivalent to eliminating that plant and selecting the other one.

The data for the problem are only partially represented by the costs of transportation that are shown on the arrows in Figure 11-2. In addition, supply and demand figures are

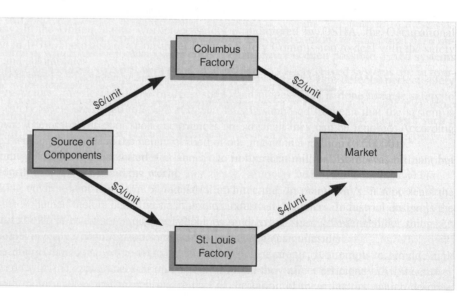

Figure 11-1

Plant Location Decision with One Origin (Supplier), Two Factories, and One Destination (Market)

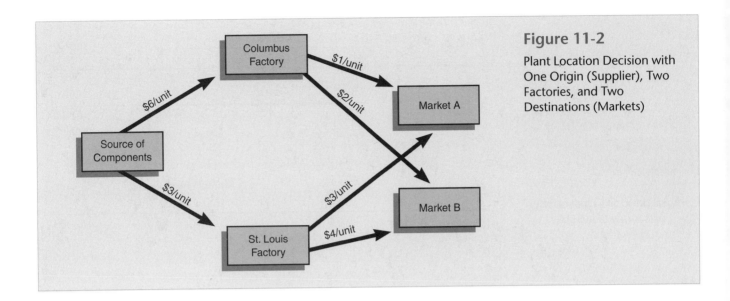

Figure 11-2

Plant Location Decision with One Origin (Supplier), Two Factories, and Two Destinations (Markets)

needed. The supply is what the plants can produce at maximum capacity. The demand is what the markets want to buy and consume. The minimum cost allocation can be determined by the transportation model, which can be solved by using linear programming or various network methods. The method shown here is trial and error, but there are other systematic ways (rules called algorithms) for solving the transportation problem. Table 11-1 presents the data.

The matrix entries are the costs of transporting finished goods from factory plant i to market j. Factories are distinguished by rows, $i = 1, 2$. Markets are represented by columns, $j = A, B$. In this case, $i = 1$ stands for the Columbus, Ohio, plant location and $i = 2$ represents St. Louis, Missouri.

As for supply and demand, each market requires 40 units per day to be shipped from either P_1 or P_2, or a combination. Each plant can be designed to have a maximum productive capacity of 90 units per day—which in total is larger than the sum of the demands of both markets. This means that one plant could supply all demands. What is best—Columbus, St. Louis, or both?

Total daily supply potential of 180 units per day exceeds total daily demand of 80 units per day by 100 units. To correct the imbalance between supply and demand, a slack, or dummy, market (M_D) is created to absorb 100 units per day. The dummy market does not exist. A plant that is assigned the job of supplying only the dummy market would be eliminated. A possible pattern of shipments is shown in Table 11-2.

If this was the minimum cost solution, then P_2 would be the best plant location. It supplies the real markets M_A and M_B. It still has slack of 10, which is assigned to the dummy market (M_D) so P_2 will work at 8/9 of capacity, supplying only real demand. Further, the plant P_1 will be eliminated because it has been assigned the task of supplying only the dummy market.

Plant i	Supplier to Plant i Transport Costs	Plant i to Market j Transport Costs		Max Supply Quantities	**Table 11-1**
		$j = A$	$j = B$		Data for Transportation Analysis
$i = P_1$	$6/unit	$1/unit	$2/unit	90 units/day	
$i = P_2$	$3/unit	$3/unit	$4/unit	90 units/day	
Market demand (units/day)		40	40		

Table 11-2	Plants P_i	Markets M_j			Supply
		M_A	M_B	M_D	
Trial and Error Pattern of Shipments for Data in Table 11-1	P_1			90	90
	P_2	40	40	10	90
M_D is a dummy market	Demand	40	40	100	180

Table 11-3	Plants P_i	Markets M_j		
		M_A	M_B	M_D
Total per Unit Transportation Costs for Data in Table 11-1	P_1	6 + 1 = $7	6 + 2 = $8	0
	P_2	3 + 3 = $6	3 + 4 = $7	0

Is this shipping pattern the best solution—resulting in minimum total transportation costs? It is now necessary to test this pattern to find out if there is any better arrangement.

The matrix of total per unit transportation costs is shown in Table 11-3. See Table 11-1 for the basic data.

Supplier per unit transportation costs have been added to the finished goods per unit transportation costs. Shipments to the dummy market cost $0 because it does not exist.

11-5c Obtaining Total Transport Costs

Combine the data in Tables 11-2 and 11-3 by multiplying costs by quantities to derive Table 11-4. This shows a total cost of $520 for the specific shipping pattern of Table 11-2 that uses only plant 2.

Next, it is appropriate to develop the method for finding the optimal (minimum cost) solution.

11-5d Obtaining Minimum Total Transport Costs

To obtain minimum total transport costs, there is a 3-step procedure:

1   Start with a feasible solution. It should balance supply and demand. It also should leave some cells unassigned, as was done in Table 11-2. A method will be given shortly for getting started in a systematic way. It is called the **Northwest Corner (NWC) method**.

2   Select the lowest-cost, nonassigned cell. It is $7 at $P_1 M_A$. Determine the change in cost if one unit is moved to that cell. Make sure that the supply and demand totals are unchanged. This requires subtracting one unit and adding one unit at appropriate places in the matrix. If no saving is obtained (costs increase or stay

Northwest Corner (NWC) method

Put the largest possible shipment in the upper-left corner and move downward and toward the right as further assignments are made.

Table 11-4	Plants P_i	Markets M_j			Row Total Costs
		M_A	M_B	M_D	
Total Cost Transport Pattern Using Only Plant 2	P_1			90 × 0 = 0	0
	P_2	40 × 6 = 240	40 × 7 = 280	10 × 0 = 0	$520
	Column total	240	280	0	$520

Plants P_i	Markets M_j			Total Costs
	M_A	M_B	M_D	
P_1	$1 \times 7 = 7$		$89 \times 0 = 0$	$ 7
P_2	$39 \times 6 = 234$	$40 \times 7 = 280$	$11 \times 0 = 0$	$514
Totals	$241	$280	$0	$521

Table 11-5

Total Transportation Cost—One Unit at P_1–M_A

the same) go to the next lower cost cell and repeat step 2. Ultimately, every nonassigned cell will be tested.

3 If a decrease in total cost is obtained, then ship as many units as possible to the location where one unit produced a decrease.

11-5e Testing Unit Changes

What happens to the total cost of $520 if one unit is shipped from P_1 to M_A? Rearrange the total shipping schedule, as shown in Table 11-5. The total cost of this shipping arrangement is $521 per day. Because one unit shipped from P_1 to M_A produces a greater total cost, more than one unit shipped in this way will be even worse. Can the total cost be lowered by shipping one unit from P_1 to M_B? Refer to Table 11-6.

The total cost result is again $521 per day. No way to decrease total cost has been found. There are no other possibilities to study for alternate shipping routes. It can be concluded that the first solution shown in Table 11-2 is optimal. It provides a minimum total cost solution.

The location chosen is St. Louis, Missouri. The exact location of the plant has not been decided. Also, it has not been determined whether the plant will be rented or built. These issues are not addressed by this model. The plant selection was made on the basis of minimum transport costs. The strategic objectives can be criticized as being too restricted.

Another factory is now added to demonstrate some other points. The supply and demand quantities, and the per unit costs are given in Table 11-7.

11-6 Northwest Corner (NWC) Method

As before, the assumption is that transportation costs dominate the plant location decision. The initial assignment pattern shown in Table 11-8 is derived by the Northwest

Plants P_i	Markets M_j			Total Costs
	M_A	M_B	M_D	
P_1		$1 \times 8 = 8$	$89 \times 0 = 0$	$ 8
P_2	$40 \times 6 = 240$	$39 \times 7 = 273$	$11 \times 0 = 0$	$513
Totals	$240	$281	$0	$521

Table 11-6

Total Transportation Cost—One Unit at P_1–M_B

Plants P_i	Markets M_j			Supply
	M_A	M_B	M_D	
P_1	$7	$8	$0	50 units/day
P_2	$6	$7	$0	90 units/day
P_3	$8	$10	$0	90 units/day
Demand	40	40	150	230 units/day

Table 11-7

Supply, Demand, and per Unit Costs for Three Plants and Three Markets

Table 11-8	Plants P_i	Markets M_j			Supply
Northwest Corner (NWC)— Initial Feasible Assignment		M_A	M_B	M_D	
	P_1	40	10		50 units/day
	P_2		30	60	90 units/day
	P_3			90	90 units/day
	Demand	40	40	150	230 units/day

Corner method explained here. Supply and demand are balanced with a dummy market, called M_D.

To use the Northwest Corner (NWC) method, begin in the upper (northern) left-hand (western) corner of the matrix.

Allocate as many units as possible to P_1M_A—this is 40 units. More than 40 units exceeds demand. Assign as many units as possible without violating whichever constraint dominates—because it is smaller. The row constraint is 50 units; the column constraint dominates with 40 units.

P_1 still has 10 units of unassigned supply. Move east to allocate those 10 units at P_1M_B. All of P_1's supply is now allocated. M_B still requires 30 units to sum to the demand row value of 40. Moving south, these units are assigned from plant 2. Movement from the NWC is always either to the right or down.

P_2 still has 60 unallocated units remaining. These are assigned to the dummy market, M_D. They will not be made or shipped. To complete the matrix, P_3's supply of 90 units must be allocated. Place them in the P_3M_D cell. Supply and demand quantities tally now.

The NWC method always can be made to satisfy the requirement for an initial feasible solution. The procedure could start at any corner, but the NWC method is conventionally accepted as the way to start. Whatever method is used to obtain an initial feasible solution, it must produce $(M + N - 1)$ assignments for a matrix with N rows and M columns. The condition that there will be $(M + N - 1)$ assignments applies to the initial feasible solution, all intermediate solutions, and the final and optimal solution.

If upon testing the shipment of one unit into an empty cell, the result is an improvement, then all the units that can be moved are moved into the new cell. No change is made if there is no improvement. The NWC provides just enough shipments so that every shipment has at least one other shipment in its row or column. That is necessary for being able to move units to empty cells without changing the row and column totals.

11-6a Allocation Rule: $M + N - 1$

The total number of different paths assigned to shipments should never exceed $(M + N - 1)$. To remove any ambiguity, another way of saying this is that the number of shipment cells cannot exceed $(M + N - 1)$ where M = the number of destinations or markets and N = the number of origins or plants.

In Table 11-8, there are $3 + 3 - 1 = 5$ shipments. This is the number of shipments derived by means of the Northwest Corner (NWC) rules. A better solution can *never* be obtained *with more than five* shipments. In general, a solution with more than $(M + N - 1)$ active cells (assigned) would be worse.

There are $M \times N$ cells ($3 \times 3 = 9$) in total, with $M + N - 1 = 5$ assignments and $(M \times N) - M - N + 1 = 4$ boxes that are empty with no assignments.

The logic of the $M + N - 1$ assignments also is related to the mathematical nature of the system of equations that can be used to solve this problem. Thus, the problem is solvable using linear programming where each row and column is expressed as a separate inequation called a *constraint*. (An equation has an = sign. An inequation has either ≤ or ≥ sign.)

Plants P_i	Markets M_j			Supply
	M_A	M_B	M_D	
P_1 ($20)	$27	$28	$0	50 units/day
P_2 ($28)	$34	$35	$0	90 units/day
P_3 ($12)	$20	$22	$0	90 units/day
Demand	40	40	150	230 units/day

Table 11-9

Per Unit Transportation and Special Production Costs

There are supply and demand constraints. Because total supply and total demand sum to the same amount (using the dummy markets or, if needed, dummy plants), the number of independent constraints is one less than the sum of the number of rows and columns.

The exception to the rule that results in less than $(M + N - 1)$ assignments is known as *mathematical degeneracy*. The condition is purely mathematical and always can be resolved by adding a small extra amount to the appropriate row or column total. There should not be more than $(M + N - 1)$ assignments.

11-6b Plant Cost Differentials

The plants (being in different regions of the country or different countries in the world) might produce units at different costs. Some explanations for the differences might be:

1 Different type processes and cultural factors
2 Tax, tariff, and government regulation differentials
3 Different labor and material costs

Also, for the global setting, transportation costs between plants and markets might play a role in location decisions.

The per unit production cost differentials reflect any factors that relate to the source. They are simple to factor into the matrix of transport costs. To every element in a row, the cost is added that characterizes the source of that row.

Table 11-9 reflects the addition of the special production costs (shown in parentheses next to the plant) to the transportation costs of Table 11-7. Plant 2 has a per unit cost disadvantage of $16 as compared to plant 3, and $8 as compared to plant 1.

11-6c Maximizing Profit Including Market Differentials

Instead of using a cost matrix and minimizing total costs, the procedures can be reversed to permit maximization of a profit matrix. The power of including market-by-market revenues is shown here. For each cell, calculate the per unit revenue less the per unit shipping costs and other special per unit costs. This provides cell-by-cell data on per unit profit. Table 11-10 shows how this information is derived where per unit revenues are $50 for market A, $60 for market B, and the dummy market *MD* has zero profit.

Plants P_i	Markets M_j			Supply
	M_A	M_B	M_D	
P_1 ($20)	$50 − 27 = $23	$60 − 28 = $32	$0	50 units/day
P_2 ($28)	$50 − 34 = $16	$60 − 35 = $25	$0	90 units/day
P_3 ($12)	$50 − 20 = $30	$60 − 22 = $38	$0	90 units/day
Demand	40	40	150	230 units/day

Table 11-10

Supply, Demand, and per Unit Costs for Three Plants and Three Markets

Table 11-11	Original Matrix from Table 11-8				Unit Shift for Total Profit TPR_Δ		
Unit Shift for the Profit-Based Transportation Matrix	**Plants P_i**	M_A	M_B	M_D		M_A	M_B	M_D
	P_1	40	10	0	$\Rightarrow$	40	10	0
	P_2	0	30	60		0	29	61
	P_3	0	0	90		0	1	89

The 4-step procedure for profit maximization is

1 Start with a feasible solution that balances supply and demand and follows the ($M + N - 1$) rule. The NWC method yields the same result as Table 11-8. Using the per unit profit data from Table 11-10, calculate the total profit (TPR_1) for the first feasible (NWC) solution:

$$TPR1 = 40 \times 23 + 10 \times 32 + 30 \times 25 = 920 + 320 + 750 = \$1,990$$

2 Select the highest-profit, nonassigned cell. It is \$38 at P_3M_B. Determine the change in profit if one unit is moved to that cell. Make sure that the supply and demand total constraints are satisfied. This requires subtracting one unit and adding one unit at appropriate places in the matrix. If no profit increase is obtained, go to the next highest per unit profit cell and repeat step 2. Ultimately, every nonassigned cell will be tested.

Table 11-11 shows the unit shift to P_3M_B. The profit change based on shifting one unit (indicated by Δ) is calculated:

$$PR_\Delta = -(1 \times 25) + (1 \times 38) = +\$13$$

As a result, all 30 units are shifted to P_3M_B and the next calculation of total profit is called TPR_2.

The change in total profit (TRP_Δ) is calculated and shown to be positive.

Total profit change based on shifting one unit (indicated by Δ) is calculated:

$$TPR_\Delta = (40 \times 23) + (10 \times 32) + (29 \times 25) + (1 \times 38)$$
$$= 920 + 320 + 725 + 38 = \$2,003$$

Profit has increased by \$13 for the single unit change, so move as many units as possible to P_3M_B, as explained in step 3, which follows.

3 When an increase in total profit is obtained, ship as many units as possible to the location where a single unit produced a profit increase. The maximum amount that can be shifted for this example is 30 units, as shown in Table 11-12.

$$TPR_2 = (40 \times 23) + (10 \times 32) + (30 \times 38) = 920 + 320 + 1,140 = \$2,380$$

The increase in profit over TPR_1 is \$13 $\times$ 30 units = \$390.

4 Continue in this way, evaluating changes until profit cannot be increased any further. No further changes should be made because all evaluations of unit changes are negative and would decrease profits if used. The evaluation of unit changes that produces no further profit increase is shown in Table 11-13.

Table 11-12		Unit Shift				Basis for Total Profit TPR_2		
Unit Change Matrix to Total Change Matrix	**Plants$_i$**	M_A	M_B	M_D		M_A	M_B	M_D
	P_1	40	10	0	$\Rightarrow$	40	10	0
	P_2	0	29	61		0	0	90
	P_3	0	1	89		0	30	60

	Final Basis for Total Profit TPR₄				Evaluation of Unit Changes for the Fourth Matrix			**Table 11-13**
Plants$_i$	M_A	M_B	M_D		M_A	M_B	M_D	Per Unit Profit Changes for All Nonassigned Cells of the Fourth Matrix
P_1	0	0	50	⇒	–7	–6	*	
P_2	0	0	90		–14	–13	*	
P_3	40	40	10		*	*	*	

Note: Asterisks (*) are assigned shipments.

The final solution is called TPR_4 because it is the fourth iteration result. The basis for this result is shown in Table 11-13.

$$TPR_4 = 40 \times 30 + 40 \times 38 = 1,200 + 1,520 = \$2,720$$

The increase in profit of TPR_4 over TPR_1 is \$730, which is a 37 percent improvement in profit.

11-6d Flexibility of the Transportation Model (TM)

The TM can include much more than just transportation costs. It can reflect price differences in markets (regional, domestic, and international). Production efficiency differentials can be shown, as well as special location-based costs such as taxes, tariffs, and wage scales. The costs of governmental rules concerning pollution control, employee health and safety, and waste disposal vary widely around the world.

Imbalance in supply (S) and demand (D) can be handled by creating dummies to absorb whichever is greater. If S is greater than D ($S > D$, as was the case for all of the previous examples), create market dummies that can absorb part of the oversupply. In symbolic terms, create MD.

If $S < D$ (which is the case when peak demands are not being met), then create dummy plants to pretend to produce all of the demand. Markets that are shown to be supplied by dummy plants (PD) are not being supplied because the dummy plants do not exist. This raises a question of increasing capacity in optimal locations in order to satisfy demand most effectively. Trial and error may pay off in these investigations.

The TM is a systems organizer for more than just the distribution cost data. Market and process differentials can be represented, so their spokespeople also should be represented when the model is used. The TM as a profit maximizer is a good systems tool, whereas, as a cost minimizer it reflects the more tactical interests of P/OM.

11-6e Limitations of the Transportation Model

The limitations of the transportation method also should be understood by management. The cost equations and constraints on supply and demand are all linear. This means that the model does not allow discounts. It does not permit cost savings that learning curves and the experience horizon promise when larger volumes are handled. Basic discounts such as a car lot savings permit might be factored into the TM analysis by programmers familiar with methods for dealing with discontinuities in the cost functions.

The TM model does not shed light on other factors that influence location decisions such as the kind of community, weather, crime, and quality of schools, among others. Intangible factors are bypassed by this quantitative method. When intangibles are critical, then transportation cost differentials of the various alternatives can be combined with other relevant costs and combined with the intangible factors in a dimensional scoring model analysis.

11-7 Structure and Site Selection

It would be highly unusual to choose a structure without having carefully considered location preferences. It is quite usual to choose a location and then search for a specific structure and site. Often, the list consists of combinations. Various locations, each with attractive sites and/or structures, are cataloged. Location and structure-site decisions eventually are considered simultaneously.

Thus, North Carolina and Tennessee could be chosen as tax-advantage states in the United States. If market differentials exist, they also could play a part in the selection among regions of the country. After choosing location, the search for sites and structures becomes more specific. In comparing alternatives, all relevant elements of location, site, and structure should be included. If relocation is involved, the decision may be to select a new site or stay with the current one, and redesign and rebuild the facility.

11-7a Work Configuration Decisions Determine Structure Selection

Flow shop structures permit serialized, sequential assembly with materials being received and introduced to the line as close as possible to the point of use. Access by suppliers at many points along the walls of the building is needed. Gravity-feed conveyors can be used instead of mechanized conveyors when the structure is multistoried. There are many similar issues that arise that relate the building type with the work configuration. Part of the design of a good flow shop is the design of the structure.

Job shops do not entail large investments in the design of the process. In general, good flow shops do require large capital investment. The same large investment applies to extensive FPS systems. It follows that the kind of structure that will be adequate to house job shop processes is less restricted than for flow shops. More real-estate choices are suitable for job shops than for flow shops. Rentals are more likely to be feasible for job shops than for flow shops or for FMS systems.

Service industries are often associated with particular kinds and shapes of structures. Airports, hospitals, theaters, and educational institutions typify the site-structure demands for service specifics. Technological information and knowledge of real-process details are required to reach good decisions.

11-7b Facility Factors

Companies that build their own facilities to match work configuration requirements make fewer concessions. Continuous-process industries—like petrochemicals—have to build to process specifications. Even for the job shop, special requirements for space and strong floor supports—say for a large mixing vat—can influence the choice of structure. When renting, building, or buying, expert help from real-estate specialists, architects, and building engineers should be obtained to ensure proper evaluation of an existing facility or to plan a new structure. Among the facility elements to be considered are

- Is there enough floor space?
- Are the aisles wide enough?
- How many stories are desirable?
- Is the ceiling high enough?
- Are skylights in the roof useful?
- Roof shapes permit a degree of control over illumination, temperature, and ventilation. What are the maintenance requirements for roofs?

For new construction, in addition to costs, speed counts. Building codes may not be acceptable. Industrial parks may be appealing. Special-purpose facilities usually have

© 2007 Jupiterimages Corporation

Technical information and knowledge of real process details are needed to design service structures like airport terminals. What arrival and departure demands characterize the system? Airports must be designed for airline and flyer's utilities as plants are designed for manufacturing necessities.

lower resale value than general-purpose facilities. Good resale value can be critical, allowing a company flexibility to relocate when conditions change.

Company services should be listed. Capacities of parking lots, cafeterias, medical emergency facilities, male and female restrooms—in the right proportions—must be supplied. Adequate fire and police protection must be defined. Rail sidings, road access, and ship-docking facilities should be specified in the detailed facility-factor analysis.

External appearance and internal appearance are factors. An increasing number of companies are using the factory as a showroom. Some service industries use elegant offices to impress their clients. Others use simplicity to emphasize frugality and utilitarian policies. Some consider appearance to be a frill. Others take appearance seriously and illuminate their building at night. Japanese management stresses cleanliness as a requirement for maintaining employees' pride in their company. When Sanyo acquired dilapidated facilities, they painted the walls and polished the floors.

11-7c Rent, Buy, or Build—Cost Determinants

The costs of land, construction, rental rates, and existing structures are all numbers that can be obtained and compared with a suitable model. That model must be able to reflect the net present value of different payment schedules over time. An appropriate discount rate must be determined in conjunction with the financial officers of the firm.

Cost-benefit analysis is a model analogous to a ledger with dollar costs listed on one side and dollar equivalents for the benefits on the other side. The lists are summed. Net benefit is the difference. With intangibles such as community support, workers' loyalty and skill, union-management relations, and flexibility to relocate, it is difficult to get dollar figures. Thus, estimates of qualities need to be made and used in a scoring model.

Location, structure, and site come as a package of tangible and intangible conditions that have costs—some of which are difficult to determine but which are worth listing:

1   The opportunity cost of not relocating.
2   The cost of location and relocation studies. The collection of relevant data is facilitated through the cooperation of regional chambers of commerce.
3   The cost of moving may have to include temporary production stoppage costs. Inventory buildups may be able to help manufacturers offset the effects of stopping production. Inventory cannot help service stoppage.
4   The cost of land—often an investment. Renting, buying, or building has different tax consequences, which can play a part in reaching decisions.
5   The costs of changing lead times for incoming materials and outgoing products as a result of different locations.
6   Power and water costs differ markedly according to location.
7   Value-added taxes are used in many European countries. VAT is proportional to the value of manufactured goods.
8   Insurance rules and costs are location sensitive.
9   Labor scarcities can develop that carry intangible costs.
10 Union-management cooperation is an intangible cost factor.
11 The intangible cost of community discord can be significant.
12 Legal fees and other costs of specialists and consultants are location sensitive, especially for small- and medium-sized organizations.
13 Workmen's compensation payments and unemployment insurance costs differ by location.
14 The costs of waste disposal, pollution and smoke control, noise abatement, and other nuisance-prevention regulations differ by locations.
15 Compliance with environmental protection rules differs by location.
16 The costs of damage caused by natural phenomena are affected by location, which determines the probabilities of hurricanes and earthquakes, as well as

© 2008 Jupiterimages Corporation

This Norwegian oil rig in the North Sea is like a company town. Employee team members must work together on a variety of functions. There are always new problems such as those stemming from maintenance under the corrosive conditions of being at sea. Team members are part of production and operations as well as engineering and almost every service system that a small city requires.

floods and lightning. Insurance damage rates have risen markedly and do not cover production stoppages.

17 Costs of reducing disaster probabilities—such as using raised construction to reduce flood damage risk.

18 Normal weather conditions produce costs associated with location: heating, air conditioning, snow removal, frozen pipes, and more absentee days because of the common cold.

19 Extreme weather conditions, such as cold and heat, cause facilities to deteriorate faster than normal weather conditions. Extreme wind conditions, such as tornadoes and hurricanes, require special building protections.

How can the many tangible and intangible costs be brought together in a unified way? Scoring models provide a satisfying means for organizing and combining estimates and hard numbers. This topic is covered in the next section.

11-8 Facility Selection Using Scoring Models

If all of the facility costs were readily measurable, then an equation could be written for total costs—of the general form:

$$\text{Total Cost} = \sum_i x_i (i = A \text{ through } Z)$$

where *A* through *Z* includes costs associated with the location, structure, and site. Unfortunately, many factors cannot be reduced to dollars and cents. Part of the equation can be in dollars and the rest has to be cast as an estimation of costs. The total cost equation only can be symbolic:

$$\text{Total costs} = f(\text{Tangible costs } + \text{Intangible costs})$$

The objective is to choose the location/structure/site option or alternative that minimizes total costs.

The **scoring model** permits the simultaneous evaluation of tangible and intangible costs. The method allows intangibles to be dealt with in a quantitative fashion with as many factors considered as seems necessary. However, the most practical idea is to concentrate on the important factors.

The comparison among strategic location alternatives is equivalent to measuring the ratios of the cost estimates for the different intangible and tangible cost factors. This is a way of measuring relative advantage. Each ratio portrays opportunities to improve. The numerators and denominators are equivalent to the utilities of different options.

11-8a Intangible Factor Costs

The ratios measure the degree to which one option is better than, or preferred to, another. The dimension of *community attitude (CA)* is a good instance of an intangible factor. CA cannot be measured in a precise and nonambiguous way—as for example, dollars of rent. Therefore, an estimate is made by someone who knows the community attitude aspect of the location decision. In effect, the estimate states a preference for one community's attitude as compared to the other.

Assume that Orlando, Florida, has been given the top rating for CA. Because this problem is being stated in terms of costs, the best rating is "one," which is the smallest positive integer. Scoring models can be created with the goal of cost minimization or (alternatively) profit maximization. Terms must be consistent with whichever goal is used. For profits, the preference is large numbers. This will not apply to weighting factors that are used in the scoring model. Large weights are always more important than small weights. To sum up, the model presented now is a cost minimization formulation. The

Scoring model

Compares quantitatively alternative options for a broad variety of situations; there are reasons to prefer ratios that produce *pure numbers*. See http://www.myfico.com.

most important factors have large weights, and the most preferred situations have the smallest numbers.

It is possible to set the scoring model for any number of comparisons. However, to keep things simple for the current explanation, just two cities will be used. This model can be extended to three, four, five, or more without any changes in method. The value of the community attitude ratio for two cities will be called V_{CA}.

Orlando, Florida, is being compared with Edison, New Jersey, by a high-tech manufacturer currently located in Buffalo, New York. The old Buffalo facility is to be closed. There is general agreement to move south, but healthy debate about how far south to move. Edison, New Jersey, has been rated a 2 for supportive community attitude.

There are a number of ways to interpret the ratio:

$$V_{CA} = (Orlando) \div (Edison) = 1/2 \qquad (11\text{-}1)$$

First, the rater's preference for Orlando, with respect to community attitude, is two times greater than for Edison. The other side of the coin is that the rater's preference for Edison is half that of Orlando. Getting something that is less preferred is construed as a cost. The ratio of the cost estimate for the best alternative with respect to community attitude is obtained by dividing 1 by 2. Because costs are best when they are small, 1 is better than 2.

Second, the cost of choosing Edison instead of Orlando with respect to CA is $2/1 = 2$. This could be interpreted as any amount of money. The weighting factors will introduce a means of scaling the relative utilities. Ultimately, tangibles (such as dollars) and intangibles (such as community attitude) can be related in this way. See the next point.

Third, the scoring model deals with the importance (V_{CA}) of CA relative to all the other factors by weighting (W_{CA}) the value of the ratio, thus:

$$(V_{CA})^{W_{CA}} \qquad (11\text{-}2)$$

This enables the model to consider simultaneously the costs of both tangible and intangible factors. The preference measures and actual cost dimensions are weighted to express their importance to the total evaluation of the location alternative. To mix tangible costs with intangible costs, weights are used to express the relative importance of each. Then, all of the costs are combined. This treats measured values as though they also are preferences.

In fact, because apples and oranges are being compared, the scoring model can only work by combining the dimensionless ratios into a dimensionless value, V. This is a multiobjective model. Some of the objectives are in conflict. There is the objective to move to a location that has the best CA. This location might not be the one with the lowest taxes. A list of six objectives follows. They apply—three tangible and three intangible factors—to the two sample locations, sites, and structure problems.

Tangible Costs—Measured in Dollars:

1 Building costs—based on annual (straight line) depreciation—fully equipped with general-purpose equipment
2 Taxes per year
3 Energy costs per year

Another tangible factor is labor. Companies choose locations based on cheaper labor markets (including low-cost labor countries). Material costs also can differ according to location. To keep this scoring model manageable, labor and material costs have been treated as equivalent at both locations.

Intangible Costs—Measured in Preferences:

1 Ease of relocating if and when such becomes necessary
2 Product quality as a function of skills and morale
3 Community attitude

If one location is best for all six objectives, and the location planners agree that the list of objectives is correct and complete, then there is no need for the scoring model. The choice is obvious. If, however, as is more usual, one location is best for some of the six objectives, and the other location is best for the remaining objectives, then the use of the scoring model is not only warranted but needed. Six different dimensions, representing conflicting objectives, must be combined to provide a reasonable basis for evaluation.

11-8b Developing the Scoring Model

The tangible objectives are directly measurable. The other three objectives are intangible and require an estimate of preference. To systematize the scoring model, each objective can be assigned a scale position between 1 (best) and 10 (worst). Assume that the proposals for the Orlando and Edison locations have been evaluated as shown in Table 11-14.

The first three tangible factors are dollars that can be added together because all costs are based on a 1-year period. This yields $570,000 and $350,000 for the Orlando and Edison locations, respectively. Two additional dollar costs are not included because they are equivalent and cancel each other out. They are given zero weight.

Discounting methods can be used to compare net present values for time streams of money. Total tangible costs can be used as a single factor to represent all of the cost factors. It has the same weight of 4 as the other dollar factors. Companies will have different measures for the relative importance or utility of dollars. Organizations with large asset bases will consider small amounts of money to have low weights. Conversely, small- and even medium-sized companies usually treat cash-flow expenses as having large weights. In this case, management has evaluated dollars with an importance weight of 4, which is high.

Table 11-14	Objectives (a)	Orlando	Edison	Weight (d)
	Tangible costs (S)			
Factors for Comparison of Alternative Locations	Building costs (b)	$500,000	$300,000	4
	Taxes	$ 50,000	$ 20,000	4
	Energy Costs	$ 20,000	$ 30,000	4
	Labor costs	equivalent	equivalent	0
	Material costs	equivalent	equivalent	0
	Total tangible costs	$570,000	$350,000	4
	Intangible costs (c)			
	Relocation flexibility	1	6	3
	Workforce quality	2	3	5
	Community attitude	1	2	1
	Pollution regulations	equivalent	equivalent	0
	Room for expansion	equivalent	equivalent	0

Notes:

(a) Cost minimization objectives for all factors; 1 is best.

(b) Buildings and facilities use annual (straight line) depreciation. General-purpose equipment costs are also depreciated.

(c) Intangibles are measured by preferences with the scale of 1 to 10, where the most preferred has the lowest cost. Had the table been constructed for profits, value 10 would be optimal.

(d) The larger the weight, the more important the factor is considered to be relative to the other factors. This applies for both cost minimization and profit maximization. These weights have been chosen to go from 1 to 5. Other ranges could be selected. The weight of zero removes the factor from consideration because any factor to the zero power is equal to one.

This makes sense because to this company the purchase of a new building is a substantial investment. Edison has a cash outlay advantage over Orlando that is noteworthy at the outset.

Dollar expenditures are more important than any other factor—except workforce quality, which carries a weight of 5. The factor called *workforce quality* is considered to be a surrogate for product quality that results from a skilled workforce with high morale and pride of workmanship.

Consider the intangibles. Orlando leads in all cases. For workforce quality and community attitude, both Orlando and Edison have fine ratings although Orlando has the edge. When it comes to relocation flexibility, Edison does not seem to satisfy the company's expectations. As for pollution regulations and room for expansion, the two locations are equivalent and need not be considered (given zero weight) because they cancel out in ratio.

11-8c Weighting Scores

The fourth column of Table 11-14, captioned "Weight," presents weighting factors, or index numbers that have been scaled from 1 to 5. Choosing the weights is a subjective task that may not be easy to accomplish. The weights need to be chosen to capture the relative importance of each objective.

According to the weights assigned in Table 11-14, workforce quality (at 5) is the highest value that can be selected. Community attitude (at 1) is least important. Relocation flexibility (at 3) is somewhat less important than costs (all of which are at 4). It is expected that all costs are going to have an equal weight. However, very large costs that could bankrupt a firm may be given more weight with good reason. Also, it is implicit that costs to be paid tomorrow have higher weight than costs to be paid five years from now. The net present value model does the weighting for us in a sensible fashion.

The arrangement of weighting values could change if the company's capitalization were altered or if the location objectives were modified. It is useful to keep in mind that the numbers used for the scoring model were derived by a team of company managers after discussion and analysis of the situation.

The weighting is arbitrary, but not random. The same can be said about the preferences for the intangible factors. Say that the management team—composed of five executives including the CEO—agreed to accept the numbers in Table 11-14. Hopefully, such agreement means that there is consensus about both preferences and importance of those preferences. It could be that four out of five want to please the CEO.

If factors such as community attitude, product quality, and flexibility could be associated with dollar values, there would not be a dimensional problem to resolve. Everything would be measured in dollars, and there would be no need for weights.

11-8d Multiple Decision Makers

Each manager on the site-selection team will provide individual ratings (numbers) for all of the factors. If averages are used to combine the preference scores and the weights, the effect would be to decrease the differentials between locations. Averaging the scores of **multiple decision makers** reduces variability. This is because individual extremes tend to cancel each other. If the P/OM rated relocation flexibility for Edison as nil and gave it a 10 while the CFO considering it to be fair, rated it 4, then the average would be 7. If averaging is used, the results can be compared with the results for the individuals. The managers can identify problems and areas to be further studied by comparing their preference scores and weights.

This is similar to the Delphi method, which identifies differences in opinions and encourages convergence of informed opinion. Managers with dissimilar preferences and

Multiple decision makers
Quantitative scoring models can work with more than one person's evaluations of locations, suppliers, products, processes, etc.

weights can discuss why they selected the ratings they did. It is assumed that such transfers of information result in a leveling of opinion, i.e., more agreement.

Scoring models organize a lot of information that is relevant for location decisions. Managers can study what is known and what is not; what is agreed upon, and what is not; what is important and what is not; whether consensus exists about what is important; what appears to require additional research, etc. Ultimately, the decision has to be made about accepting or rejecting the solution indicated by the scoring model.

Pooling and polling opinions of many people in the company about location decisions increases involvement and builds pride in the company. It promotes interfunctional communication about facility decisions. If the company intends to relocate people who want that, the approach tends to motivate more people to participate in the move.

Information about the choices should be made available throughout the company. If feasible, cost factors should be shared. When the factor lists are made up, broad participation leads to better idea generation. Notions appear that otherwise might be overlooked and the process moves faster. The decision to relocate is better shared than sprung as a surprise.

11-8e Solving the Scoring Model

The scoring model takes ratios like the one previously developed for community attitude:

$$V_{CA} = (Orlando) \div (Edison) = 1/2 \tag{11-3}$$

and raises them to a power W_{CA}, which is the importance weight of the CA factor. These are called the *powers* of the factors. Thus, for the CA ratio of Orlando to Edison:

$$(V_{CA})^{W_{CA}} = (1/2)^1 \tag{11-4}$$

The powers of the factors are multiplied to derive the system's ratio, V, which is the combined score that is being sought.

$$V = (V_\$)^{W_\$} (V_{RF})^{W_{RF}} (V_{WQ})^{W_{WQ}} (V_{CA})^{W_{CA}} \tag{11-5}$$

where $\$$ = building costs and other dollar expenditures; RF = relocation flexibility; WQ = workforce quality; CA = community attitude.

Each ratio $V_j^{W_j}$ has Orlando in the numerator and Edison in the denominator. Therefore, if $V = 1$, then both locations have the same cost score. If $V < 1$, choose Orlando because it has a lower cost score than Edison. If $V > 1$, choose Edison because Orlando has a higher cost score than Edison.

This is the symbolic representation of the scoring model. It is a multiplicative model that derives the products of the preference (and cost) ratios raised to powers that represent the importance of each factor. In essence,

$$V = (preference\ for\ location\ a) \div (preference\ for\ location\ b) \tag{11-6}$$

V is a **pure number**, meaning that it has no dimensions. For example, if low cost, light weight, and small size are the desirable components of a product design, then a and b can be compared, as follows:

$$V = \frac{\text{preference for product design a}}{\text{preference for product design b}} = \frac{\text{dollars a}}{\text{dollars b}} \times \frac{\text{pounds a}}{\text{pounds b}} \times \frac{\text{centimeters a}}{\text{centimeters b}} \tag{11-7}$$

V = a pure number (dimensionless), which means that dollars, pounds, and centimeters cross out in each ratio. For conceptual understanding, note how price-earnings ratios are dimensionless ratios widely used to evaluate how pricey a stock is in the market. Another widely employed ratio measures actual capacity used as a percentage of the maximum capacity available.

Pure number

See **Scoring model**. Quantitative comparison of two options poses problems of combining multiple dimensions; ratios of the products of the powers yield a pure number because all dimensions are canceled.

Turning to the numbers given in Table 11-14:

$$V = \frac{\text{preference for location a}}{\text{preference for location b}} = \left(\frac{\$570,000}{\$350,000}\right)^4 \left(\frac{1}{6}\right)^3 \left(\frac{2}{3}\right)^5 \left(\frac{1}{2}\right)^1 = 0.002 = \frac{1}{500}$$

(11-8)

With this result, Orlando will be chosen because the ratio is less than 1. The combined weighted costs of Edison (in the denominator) are greater than the combined weighted costs of Orlando (in the numerator).

The scoring model is useful for a wide range of applications in addition to the location problem. It is appropriate for product-, process- and service-design decisions, equipment selection, warehouse-location plans, etc. The scoring model's multiplication method of evaluating alternatives by means of weighting factors is reasonable to handle multidimensional problems. It has a strong scientific foundation and is frequently used by those who are familiar with dimensional analysis.[1]

11-9 Equipment Selection

The building blocks for resolving the equipment selection problem have already been put into place. The first issue that has to be decided is: What work configuration is going to be used? This starts as a capacity-planning problem. The capacity required must be resolved before any equipment decisions can be made.

General-purpose equipment for the job shop and batch production come in many varieties and can be purchased new or used. There are more equipment selection constraints with continuous production processes and with flow shop systems. Equipment selection in the latter two cases requires careful and detailed engineering analysis. As a suggestion, the analysis along the lines of points 1 through 4 follows:

1   For choosing between specific machines, conveyors, forklift trucks, and other pieces of equipment, the net present value of the investments and operating costs should be determined. The reason that traditional financially discounted cash-flow analyses should be used is that it permits purchase price to be combined with the time stream of operating costs.

2   The classical breakeven model can provide critical data about equipment selection. This provides a benchmark regarding the volume of work that must be done on the alternatives before they start making a contribution to profit.

3   The scoring model, described for site selection, also is useful for evaluating some of the intangible factors that new equipment decisions involve. These include difficulty learning to use new equipment, assessing the competitive benefits of new equipment, improvements in quality and productivity that could be expected, and the variety of jobs that can be done on the new equipment.

4   Setup times of equipment alternatives must be compared. Using activity-based costing, it is possible to estimate downtime expenses as well as to determine the effect of setup costs and time on optimal lot sizes.

New equipment decisions are a P/OM responsibility. Still, the financial involvements require teamwork with financial control and accounting managers. Cooperation with engineers and R&D is warranted to make certain that all technical issues are properly addressed.

11-9a Design for Manufacturing—Variance and Volume

Without proper tools and equipment, even a skilled and motivated worker is hard pressed to do more than a mediocre job. Poor tools compromise quality. TQM requires that all the homework should be done concerning equipment performance, costs, and quality before reaching equipment selection decisions. The estimates of performance should not be naive. They must be used to explain expected variation in the qualities of the product.

Part of the work entailed in **design for manufacturing (DFM)** is equipment performance evaluation. First, the productivity of equipment must be related to the volume of work that has to be done. This means comparing the production rates of each alternative. Second, different degrees of variability are associated with the equipment alternatives. This relates quality of product to equipment selection.

Design for manufacturing (DFM)

Equipment performance evaluation is part of the DFM procedure. The inherent variability of the technology must be compatible with designers' tolerances.

Like fingerprints, each piece of equipment produces unique variations. Original equipment manufacturers (OEM) can categorize the tolerance capabilities of the machines that they sell. This helps to select equipment but tests must be conducted to determine the output variability of specific products made on the machines. The observed level of variability must be compatible with the designer's tolerances. It also must meet the DFM expectations of the process managers. There often is a great deal of difference between various manufacturers' equipment that otherwise appears to be of the same class. Equipment choice that ignores this information is selling process management short.

11-9b Equipment Selection and Layout Interactions

Equipment selection precedes facility layout. The two interact so strongly that it is logical to have an idea about layout requirements before facility choice. Size, weight, height, and number of pieces of equipment are critical layout parameters. Planning requires knowledge of equipments' footprints (space needed) and signatures (vibration, noise among others).

Movement of materials is another equipment factor. Elevated conveyors can carry materials near the ceiling whereas sufficient aisle clearance must be available for AGV and trucks. Equipment dictates facility layout design. It may influence facility location—when the ideal building exists somewhere.

P/OMs have a good idea of the equipment that will be required at the chosen facility and, therefore, of the general adequacy of a particular structure. The process of deciding what to do is interactive, going back and forth between facility selection, equipment selection, and facility layout. It is not unusual to find that equipment selection must accommodate an existing facility.

11-9c Life Cycle Stages

Life cycle stages

Facility decisions are a function of the life cycle stages of the items in the product line.

The effect of **life cycle stages** (start-up, growth, maturity, and withdrawal) on equipment selection is significant. Equipment selection is dominated by volume considerations. Volume increases are what life cycle stages are all about. Therefore, it is to be expected that equipment changes will be made over time in keeping with the life cycle stages.

The dynamics are hard to manage unless they have been consciously planned. It might seem reasonable to start off with machines that are economic to use at low volumes. Then, as growth in demand occurs, growth in supply would follow. However, if the risk is low that such growth will occur, then there is reason to start with equipment that has greater capacity than will be needed at first. The period of underutilization can be a short time in the life of a machine. As the equipment approaches full utilization, the costs per unit tend to decrease. With machines that are economic at low volumes, success brings volume increases. This leads to overtime, which inflates per unit costs.

Planning equipment selection should include timing of transitions in supply capability. Planning also must address the work configuration that will be attained eventually. The flow shop remains a worthy goal. When and if that state of affairs is achieved, low-volume general-purpose equipment will not be called upon unless the planning process includes the launching of new products at the proper points in time.

Replacement for wear is part of the planning. There is gradual deterioration in the performance of equipment that should be factored into the life cycle considerations. Maintenance can change the rate of deterioration and must be factored into the plan. Although some equipment is nearly maintenance-free, other equipment requires costly programs with skilled labor and downtime expenses. Appropriate equipment for start-up may not be able to be fully depreciated at replacement time. There is a market for used general-purpose equipment, which may be a consideration that can add flexibility in the early stages of product life. Planning is required to have used-up, and phased-out, low-volume equipment, or to have found new uses for it.

11-10 Layout of the Workplace and Job Design

It is hard to believe that until the 1980s, workers in American and European auto-assembly plants had to bend down to install the new tires on the wheels, and then tighten the tire bolts. The auto-assembly conveyors ran flat out near the ground. The layout made the job not much different from changing a flat tire on the road. Visitors to Japanese auto plants saw that the conveyor lifted the car up at the point of tire attachment. This carried the car above the worker and allowed putting the tire on at shoulder level. Workers could stand tall and attach the tires to the wheels without bending. Thereafter, conveyors that lifted the car were installed in world-class auto-assembly plants.

This simple anecdote illustrates how good layout interacts with good job design. It also shows that layout of the workplace is a 3-dimensional situation lending itself to creative solutions. It is evident how job design in the flow shop is partnered with layout.

Productivity increases and quality improves when the layout and job are properly designed in the job shop. Travel time and distance traveled are reduced. Paths are kept clear. Queues at workstations are reduced. Production scheduling, shop-floor layout, and job design are connected in a systems sense. The benefits of improved quality derived from better layout must be continuously monitored because process changes are constantly occurring.

11-10a Opportunity Costs for Layout Improvement

Proper workplace layout design can provide product and process quality improvements *(QI)*, throughput and **cost benefit** productivity improvements *(PI)*, and health benefits *(HB)* for employees. All of these result in higher profits. Evaluation of all jobs and workplaces along the supply chain will lead to layout improvements.

The paradigm used for such evaluations is like a balance scale or a seesaw. All of the costs of doing the job with the new layout *X* are put on one side of the ledger. All of the costs of not using layout *X* are put on the other side of the ledger. The lowest cost–highest benefit side (based on *QI, PI,* and *HB*) wins the contest. This describes the opportunity cost trade-off model succinctly.

Improving layout and job design involves **opportunity costs** trade-off analysis. Opportunity costs are the costs of doing less than best. By doing something that is not the best, the cost to be paid is the difference in net benefits. This follows the same kind of reasoning that underlies the improvement method of the transportation model.

In this case, there are opportunity costs for not having the best possible layout design. The equation for this trade-off model states that layout design improvement should be made if:

$CPI < OC(QI + PI + HB)$, where $CPI =$ Cost of layout plan improvement
$OC =$ Opportunity costs incurred for not having used the best possible layout with respect to *QI, PI,* and *HB*

Cost benefit
Comparison of costs and benefits that applies to alternative facility configuration decisions.

Opportunity costs
Costs of choosing options that are less than the best.

$OC(QI)$ = Opportunity costs for quality improvements that could have been obtained if layout design improvement had been made. If not made, they are the opportunity costs incurred by not rectifying quality deficiencies.

For example, improved conveyor layout would yield a better product, which is then translated into:

- Larger market share
- Greater revenues
- Fewer warranty claims
- Less service calls at company expense
- Higher prices that could be charged
- Smaller company discounts on ticket prices
- Better worker attitudes and morale
- Less dealer discontent
- More effective advertising campaigns

$OC(PI)$ = Opportunity costs for improved productivity.

These $OC(PI)$ could have been obtained if layout design improvement had been made. They also are the opportunity costs incurred by not rectifying factors that deteriorate productivity. Not having to bend down and work in a crouched position would enable workers to work faster as well as better. The cost of installing four tires to each car could be reduced. It is possible that one or more workers could be freed up to do other jobs in the time now allotted for the repetitive job at the production rate. Job observations and time studies can be used to get good estimates for the opportunity costs for productivity. Unlike $OC(QI)$, the costs $OC(PI)$ and $OC(HB)$, discussed next, are often measurable.

$OC(HB)$ = Opportunity costs for health benefit savings

$OC(HB)$ might have been obtained if layout design improvement had been made. For example, auto conveyors raise the cars so that tire assembly can be done without bending down. Costs associated with bending and crouching include back problems for workers that result in medical claims, higher health insurance, absenteeism, and lost time on the job. Computer operators have been experiencing a problem with their hands and wrists that is called *carpal tunnel syndrome*. Redesign of the computer keyboard, pads for the wrists to rest on, and other redesigns of the wrist support system have improved the situation. However, the strain of such repetitive work has led to the conclusion that keying jobs on the computer are best redesigned to include a regular rest period every hour. Job design, work schedules, and job layout must be treated together as an integrated system to deal with this issue.

11-10b Sensitivity Analysis of Opportunity Costs

Many opportunity costs are not easy to measure. Nevertheless, the costs are real and can be important. They do not disappear because they are difficult to measure with accuracy.

Estimates can be made more easily for a range running from a high to a low figure. By using high and low estimates, it is possible to test the sensitivity of the opportunity cost equation to the range of estimation. Also, it is possible to find out what values of $OC(QI)$, $OC(PI)$, and $OC(HB)$ can lead to equality:

$$CPI = OC(QI + PI + HB)$$

This is a systems breakeven value for layout improvement that takes into account quality, productivity, and employees' health.

There is a useful procedure, called **sensitivity analysis**, which tests the balance between the right- and left-hand sides of the opportunity cost equation. If the following inequation holds:

$$CPI < OC(QI + PI + HB)$$

then, the current design can be improved and should be altered. This is because the cost of layout improvement *(CPI)* is less than the total opportunity cost gain for improvements of the three kinds. If the cost of layout improvement *(CPI)* is more than the total opportunity cost for improvement of three kinds, as in the equation,

$$CPI > OC(QI + PI + HB)$$

then, cost justification is lacking to improve the current design.

There can be circumstances where the inequation indicates that no change should be made, but a change could be made anyway. The reason could be that the opportunity costs for health benefits, cannot be properly estimated. Safety comes under health benefits, and when threats to safety exist, the opportunity costs of *HB* can be regarded as infinite. This means that *CPI* is always less than the sum of the opportunity costs. Then, continuous layout design and workplace improvement are warranted.

Also, if managerial intuition rejects the model's solution, then deeper analysis of the quality and productivity opportunity costs is likely to show that one or both of these costs have been underestimated. The job and workplace design may be creating a situation that has not yet surfaced in traceable costs. Deterioration of worker morale is often detectable before it impacts quality/productivity on a measurable level. P/OM's hunches about negative interactions between layout and process design are worthy of respect.

11-11 Layout Types

There are at least five basic types of layouts that will be found in plants and offices. These are

1 *Job shop process layouts.* Similar types of equipment or jobs are grouped together. The lathes are in one place and the presses in another. For services, filing is in one room and copy machines are in another. Inspectors are in one place; designers are in another. Job shop process layouts should facilitate processing many different types of work in relatively small lots. Mobility of equipment enables P/OM to set up intermittent flow shops when that configuration is attainable. Space must be allocated for work completed at one station and waiting for access to another station. Equipment mobility and layout flexibility allow this configuration to be rearranged to suit the various order mixtures that can occur.

2 *Product-oriented layout.* This layout is typical of the flow shop. Equipment and transport systems are arranged to make the product as efficiently as possible. The layout is designed to prohibit disruptions to the flow. The product-oriented layout is most often associated with assembly lines.

3 *Cellular layout.* This layout is used with a team of people and machines working together to produce a dedicated family of parts, as in group technology. The layout is engineered to facilitate efficient transfer of work between stations in the cell. Setup and transfer are programmed by the system for fast changeovers that enable small runs of a limited number of parts or items.

4 *Group technology layout.* GT layout is used to efficiently produce families of parts without emphasis on computer programming controls as in cellular layouts. Layout is based on the advantage of having similarity of design features.

5 *Combinations of product and process orientation are very common.* Some of the products in the job shop achieve demand volumes that allow them to be run for

Sensitivity analysis
By using high and low estimates, it is possible to test the sensitivity of a business model (e.g., linear programming, scoring, and transportation models) to a range of conditions.

long periods of time as intermittent flow shops. Modular product-designed parts often have the high volumes that allow cellular manufacture or group technology layouts with, in some cases, serialized flow shop advantages. At the same time, other jobs in the shop remain at low volumes that are only suited to the process layout of job shops. The combination produces a mixed-layout orientation, which also is called a *hybrid layout.*

The complaint department of a large organization with a number of different products has the job shop process layout. Within that group, there are certain subgroups that handle high frequency requests with flow shop dedication. Sixty percent of the complaints can be treated in the highly repetitive fashion. The remaining 40 percent require special treatment for customer satisfaction. The analogy can be extended to families of complaint types and the use of group technology process layout.

Volvos are manufactured in Sweden on fixed platforms. The work does not move. Workers move to it and around it. Shipbuilders and homebuilders move around the work. Modular housing exemplifies hybrid layout where the parts are made in a factory and then brought to the site where they are assembled, similar to Volvos.

With fixed platforms, workers carry or drive their tools to where they are needed. Commercial airplanes are moved along a production line, albeit slowly. Commercial airline layout is a different form of hybrid, one that combines fixed and moving positions. The fixed-position layout is necessary for power plants, refineries, and locomotives. It is much more controversial (i.e., Volvo), so that deserves an extra word.

Volvo uses the fixed platform because Swedish workers find it more interesting to participate in building the whole car than doing a repetitive step along an assembly line. Worker motivation is improved. In Sweden, worker motivation is important because unemployment benefits are a large percentage of earned wages and readily available. Bored workers are likely to prefer the government benefits to the company wages.

The United Auto Workers (UAW) arranged an interesting experiment in which a group of GM workers were given the opportunity to work with Volvo for six months. Most of these workers said they preferred to work on the GM flow shop assembly layout in spite of, and because of, its repetitive nature. The Volvo layout required knowing and doing too many things. Some preferred the Volvo system and remained with Volvo.

Group technology (GT) for families of parts is a layout that many companies, such as Caterpillar, John Deere, and Cummins Engine, have found rewarding. GT cells are usually part of hybrid layouts. The group technology concept uses a product layout with the capability of producing an entire family of parts.

Special equipment is required that has rapid changeover capabilities to make parts that are identical except for size and/or other dimensional characteristics. Crankshafts, motors, and pumps are typical parts for GT. The production cells use flexible machine-tool organization. Group technology layout is usually a self-contained part of a process layout job shop.

11-12 Layout Models

The plant layout problem can be tackled with different kinds of models. There is good engineering knowledge for laying out flow shop processes. Usually, it is expensive to do the job well, and worth it. There is less solid knowledge about achieving excellence for job process layouts and less monetary justification. Four points to bear in mind:

1 Job shops and the batch production environment are subject to major changes in the product mix. What is optimal for one set of orders may be downright poor for the jobs in the shop one month later. Therefore, layouts that are likely to be good for the expected range of order types are better than those that are excellent for one type and not good for others.

2 The degree to which a few order types dominate the job shop will modify the statement in point 1 and allow some product layout to be mixed in with the process layout. It will be found that the per unit costs of operating product layouts will be significantly less than the costs associated with process layouts. The comparison is even more extreme if GT cells can be set up.

3 Flexibility is desirable, but on the other hand, it is expensive and disruptive to keep moving equipment around the plant. A balance has to be found between these two objectives. If the character of the batch work changes a great deal over time, it is best to go for the most general form of process layout. If layout is to be changed from time to time, it is essential to set up the layout system with this purpose in mind. Modular office layouts that are well planned have remarkable flexibility for making quick changes without paralyzing the workforce.

4 Use quantitative models with caution. Creative thinking and common sense pay off in achieving good layouts. Precise measurements count when trying to squeeze a machine into a tight spot. More questionable is the use of elaborate mathematical models to minimize total distance traveled or handling costs.

11-12a Layout Criteria

What criteria determine a satisfactory layout? Seven measures of layout effectiveness are

1 *Capacity*—throughput rate. Goal: Maximize total output volumes and rates.
2 *Balance*—The degree to which the throughput rates of consecutive operations are balanced. Applicable for flow shops and projects; more difficult to evaluate for job shops—although balancing work rates for job shops is always desirable. Goal: Perfect balance.
3 Amount of *investment and operating costs*. Goal: Minimum.
4 *Flexibility* to change layouts. Goal: Maximize ease of change.
5 Amount of *work in process* (*WIP*). Goal: Minimize units of inventory.
6 *Distance* that parts travel; saving an inch traveled thousands of times per day sums to sizeable savings. Goal: Minimize total travel time and distance.
7 *Storage for WIP and handling equipment* to move parts from one place in the facility to another. Goal: Minimize space used for storage and moving equipment.

11-12b Floor Plan Models

All seven of these criteria can be evaluated crudely yet with reasonably correct perceptions by using **floor plan models**. The floor plan drawings are graphic methods of trial and error that are used by interior decorators. They use little paper cutouts that represent the furniture. A dollhouse is the 3-dimensional deluxe version.

Plant layout models can be 2- or 3-dimensional. Often 2-dimensional floor plans, with cutouts made from templates, are used to represent the various pieces of equipment. When conveyors are employed, overhead space requirements may be important, and 3-dimensional "dollhouse" models are preferred.

These techniques are useful for an incremental approach to a satisfactory layout. They do not bring any quantitative power to bear. Although an optimal layout based on the numbers may be far from satisfactory, the quantitative information might assist creativity.

11-12c Layout Load Models

A relatively simple quantitative approach examines alternative layout plans in terms of the frequency with which certain paths are used. Usually, the highest frequency paths are

Floor plan model
Drawings of the plant floor are used to achieve capacity goals, obtain balanced workloads and minimum operating costs, low levels of work in process and least storage space, and minimum travel distance for people and parts.

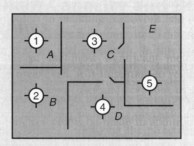

assigned the shortest plant floor path distances to travel. The objective is to minimize the total unit distances traveled.

The physical space is divided into areas that conform to floor layouts including stairs, elevators, rest rooms, etc. The locations are designated as *A*, *B*, *C*, *D*, and *E* in Figure 11-3.

The average distance that must be traveled between areas *A*, *B*, *C*, *D*, and *E* are shown in Table 11-15. These distances (in feet) are designated as d_{IJ}. They are physical measurements related to the floor plan shown in Figure 11-3. The matrix is read from row *I* to column *J* (both are capitalized letters).

This matrix is symmetric so the distance from *A* to *D* is 32. That is the same as the distance from *D* to *A*. However, symmetry does not always hold because of one-way passages, escalators, conveyor belts, and gravity feed delivery systems.

Work centers

Assignment of work centers to specific space locations on the plant or office floor should minimize costs (or times) of transport of materials, work in process, and finished goods.

Layout planning involves locating equipment and people to do certain kinds of jobs that are designated as **work centers** at specific locations on the plant floor. Work centers are equipped to do specific kinds of jobs—like the press shop, copy room, hamburger grill, and darkroom. Processing orders on-hand causes materials to move between the work centers and, therefore, between the physical locations. The materials are at different stages of work in process. Further, they represent various orders and job types. Also, order-batch sizes vary.

What is needed next is a measure of the amount of materials or the number of trips between the various work centers that different jobs entail. If order-process batches are of about the same size, then a random sample of jobs could be taken to estimate how many trips occur between each center.

If batches are not similar, then the idea is to capture those jobs that are most important either because they are the most frequent, involve the largest number of units, are the most difficult and costly to transport, or are the most profitable. Matrices appropriate to these special jobs should be created and studied. Perhaps no more that 20 percent of the jobs that are done in this batch production environment consume 80 percent of the transport resources. For the jobs that are most important, the objective is to minimize the total distance traveled.

Table 11-15

Distances (d_{IJ}) Measured
Between Locations *A*, *B*, *C*, *D*,
and *E*

Columns are Locations $J = A$, etc.	Rows are Locations $I = A$, etc.	A	B	C	D	E
	A	0	10	20	32	40
	B	10	0	16	18	20
	C	20	16	0	12	15
	D	32	18	12	0	10
	E	40	20	15	10	0

Note: Read from row *I* to column *J*.

Columns j and Row i	1	2	3	4	5
1	X	100	60	80	20
2	40	X	50	10	90
3	80	90	X	60	30
4	120	10	40	X	70
5	110	5	5	30	X

Note: Read from row i to column j.

Table 11-16

Number of Units Flowing Between Work Centers 1, 2, 3, 4, and 5 (wc_{ij})

Row i to Column j	A	B	C	D	E
1	X				
2		X			
3			X		
4				X	
5					X

The assignments are A1, B2, C3, D4, E5, with work centers 1, 2, 3, 4, and 5 to letter floor areas. There are $5 \times 4 \times 3 \times 2 \times 1 = 120$ different assignments of work centers to floor areas that are possible.

Table 11-17

Layout Assignments

Table 11-16 presents the information relating the number of units that move between work centers on an average day in a stable work-flow environment. These data are called wc_{ij}. The matrix is read from row i to column j (both are lowercase letters).

Table 11-17 shows the assignment of work centers (labeled 1 through 5) to the floor plan areas (with letter designations) given in Figure 11-3. This pairs up the floor plan locations A through E with the work centers 1 through 5. The assignments are: A1, B2, C3, D4, E5. Work centers are movable to different floor plan locations.

Multiplying the two matrices in Tables 11-15 and 11-16 is equivalent to multiplying $(d_{IJ})(wc_{ij})$, which yields unit-distances traveled. The equation for this volume of unit-distances of flow is written:

$$f_{IJ,ij} = (d_{IJ})(wc_{ij})$$

Table 11-18 shows the results for daily work flows on the shop floor.

The column totals in Table 11-18 are summed to give the grand total of the total daily work flows. The summing equation is

$$F_{IJ}^{ij} = \sum\nolimits_{IJ}^{ij} f_{IJ,ij} = \sum\nolimits_{IJ} \sum\nolimits_{ij} (d_{IJ})(wc_{ij}) \qquad (11\text{-}9)$$

	A1	B2	C3	D4	E5
A1	0	1,000	1,200	2,560	800
B2	400	0	800	180	1,800
C3	1,600	1,440	0	720	450
D4	3,840	180	480	0	700
E5	4,400	100	75	300	0
Totals	10,240	2,720	2,555	3,760	3,750

Number of Units Moving Between Work Centers Multiplied by the Distance Traveled From Rows Designated by Ii to Columns Designated by Jj

Table 11-18

Total Daily Work Flows

Table 11-19		A1	B4	C5	D3	E2
Total Daily Work Flows: A Reassignment Matrix	A1	0	800	400	1,920	4,000
	B4	1,200	0	1,120	720	200
	C5	2,200	480	0	60	75
	D3	2,560	1,080	360	0	900
	E2	1,600	200	1,350	500	0
	Totals	7,560	2,560	3,230	3,200	5,175

Number of Units Moving Between Work Centers Multiplied by the Distance Traveled Between Work Centers

The grand total of unit-feet traveled is the double sum of the multiplicative products as shown in the previous equation.

The total number of unit-feet traveled *in this layout* is 23,025. *There are better layouts*; a reassignment is suggested. Calculations show that an improvement results when the new assignments of A1, B4, C5, D3, and E2 are used. These numbers are the basis of Table 11-19, where the new assignments of work centers to plant floor locations is reflected by the column headings and row names.

Improvement results when A1, B4, C5, D3, and E2 are the new assignments.

The total number of unit-feet traveled per day in this layout is 21,725. Unit-feet traveled has been decreased by 1,300. That is an improvement of almost 6 percent. It is likely that additional decreases can be achieved by studying the matrices and trying to eliminate incorrect assignments of heavy-unit volumes to large distance movements.

This analysis has tested only two configurations out of 120 possibilities. How good was the original assignment? There is no way of telling. It could have been selected randomly. A starting point strategy and evaluation of that strategy are needed to achieve improvements. The starting point concept bears similarities to the NWC method for the TM.

In fact, the original was chosen because it could be improved with a sensible heuristic (rule of thumb). This explains the reassignment. There remain 118 other possible assignments of work centers to locations.

This is because there are 5! (factorial) ways ($5 \times 4 \times 3 \times 2 \times 1 = 120$) to assign five work centers to five locations.

The improved version is based on a reasonable heuristic. This means that it should be better than an alternative picked at random. Still other layouts exist that conform with the general idea of the heuristic. Because better is not best, more calculations are warranted.

How was Table 11-19 constructed? First, Table 11-20 is derived by literally rearranging the rows and the columns from the order 1, 2, 3, 4, and 5 in Table 11-16 to the new order of 1, 4, 5, 3, and 2, as shown in Table 11-20. A practical approach is to read off each entry in Table 11-16 and enter it in the appropriate cell in Table 11-20. For example,

Table 11-20	Columns are *j* and Rows are *i*	1	4	5	3	2
Number of Units Flowing Between Work Centers 1, 2, 3, 4, and 5 (wc_{ij})	1	X	80	20	60	100
	4	120	X	70	40	10
	5	110	30	X	5	5
	3	80	60	30	X	90
	2	40	10	90	50	X

Note: Read from row *i* to column *j*.

80 should appear at the intersection of $i = 1, j = 4$ in both tables. It may be useful to do a few of these transformations before continuing.

Second, multiply Table 11-20 by the numbers in Table 11-15 to derive Table 11-19. Again, it may be useful to do a few of these multiplications to get the understanding derived from doing operations rather than just reading about them.

11-12d Flow Costs

Say that the cost of a unit moving one foot is the same between all locations and work centers. Then, the costs of transporting units will not lead to a new matrix for total daily work-flow costs. However, if the costs of transport are different between either work centers, or floor locations, or both, then the following equation is needed to describe how these different transport costs arise for each cell in the matrix.

$$cf_{IJ,ij} = (d_{IJ})(wc_{ij})(c_{IJ,ij})$$

Total costs are obtained by summing across all of the cells.

$$CF^{i,j}_{I,J} = \sum^{i,j}_{I,J} cf_{IJ,ij} = \sum_{I,J} \sum_{i,j} (d_{IJ})(wc_{ij})(c_{IJ,ij}) \qquad (11\text{-}10)$$

Another way of stating this is to refer to matrix multiplication. Thus, if the costs of transporting units are different, then it is necessary to multiply the matrix of total daily work flows so that the appropriate costs per unit and per foot are expressed. Note that these transport costs need not be symmetric. The cost of down-moving gravity-flows is usually much less than the cost of carrying units up to higher floors.

If the cost is $1 per unit per foot traveled, then the matrices in Tables 11-18 and 11-19 also represent the total daily work-flow costs. These costs would be $23,025 for the first assignment tested and $21,725 for the second and improved assignment.

11-12e Heuristics to Improve Layout

Two **heuristics (rules of thumb** for improving the system's performance) come to mind when searching for policies that might help to improve plant or office layout.

1 Assign work centers with large unit flow rates between them to locations as close as possible.
2 Assign work centers with small unit flow rates between them to locations as distant as possible.

In Table 11-16, look at those pairs of work centers that have the largest work-flow rates between them. These are in descending order:

Work center 4 to work center 1 has a wc_{ij} of 120 units.
Work center 5 to work center 1 has a wc_{ij} of 110 units.
Work center 1 to work center 2 has a wc_{ij} of 100 units.

Assign these work centers to locations that are as close as possible. Note (in Table 11-15) that the distance between A and B is 10 feet and between C and D is 12 feet.

Using the D_{IJ} data in Table 11-15, the biggest distances are between locations A and D (32), and between A and E (40).

This means that the original layout of A1, B2, C3, D4, and E5 assigned 120 units to the second biggest distance (viz., 32 between A and D) in the matrix of Table 11-16. Further, the original layout assigned work center 1 to location A and work center 5 to location E. That means that 110 units were assigned to move the largest distance between locations—viz., 40 between A and E.

Heuristics (rules of thumb)
Methods for discovery, guides for problem-solving, and procedures for experimental learning. One of the most popular is the trial and error technique with feedback to reward steps in the right direction.

To follow the heuristic "assign the largest number of units to the shortest distance" would mean assigning work center 1 to *A* and work center 4 to *B*. That was done in the second matrix, which reassigned work center 4 to location *B*. Because work center 1 was already assigned to *A*, the next best distance from *A* is 20 at *C*. Therefore, work center 5 was assigned to *C* in the second matrix.

The second part of the heuristic calls for assigning the centers with the smallest work-flow rates between them to the locations that are as distant as possible.

The two smallest flow rates between centers (in the matrix of Table 11-16) are both 5, as follows:

Work center 5 to work center 2 has a wc_{ij} of 5 units.
Work center 5 to work center 3 has a wc_{ij} of 5 units.

Work center 1 has been assigned to location *A*. Work center 4 has been assigned to location *B* and work center 5 has been assigned to location *C*. The shortest distances from *C* are to *D* and *E*. These are 12 and 15, respectively. Assign work center 3 to location *D* and work center 2 to location *E*. This is the second matrix iteration (called the *reassignment matrix*) shown by Table 11-19.

The heuristic did its job, but it is not clear whether further improvement is still possible. Trial and error with the improved matrix can be used to test further shifts.

Spotlight 11-1 Bruce Richardson: Are Our Ports Safe?

A Conversation with Bruce Richardson, Chief Research Officer, AMR Research

In a post-911 world, the topic is safety and security of the port system, which links the global supply chain. The current port system is equivalent to thousands of unlocked doorways all over the world from which anything can be sent or received. Concern over the lack of security or visibility over what came in, what went out, and what moved about the shipping lanes is related to a 2002 initiative called *Operation Safe Commerce*.

Bruce Richardson is an AMR Research expert on supply chain management, including safe commerce. AMR is an independent research firm with its main office in Boston, with European headquarters in London, United Kingdom. The company's primary focus is on the enterprise software market.

Are our ports safe?

Eleven million containers are shipped into the United States every year. Traditionally, about 2 percent of these containers are inspected. That is equivalent to only 220,000 containers inspected per year or 604 inspected per day. There are not enough inspectors to sample a larger number and, even if there were, 100 percent inspection is not the right answer. A different approach is essential.

What new steps are being taken to improve security at U.S. ports?

In October 2006, President Bush signed the SAFE Port Act. This is designed to strengthen physical security at U.S. ports through the use of new inspection equipment. For example, the new technology would allow cargo inspection from the outside of the container. It also requires radiation detection equipment at the 22 most active ports by the end of 2007. In addition, U.S. inspectors have been deployed to foreign ports to screen cargo before it reaches the U.S.

What role does RFID play in port security?

The current buzz is around ISO 18185, the new standard for electronic cargo seals or "e-Seals." E-seals allow importers, shippers, port employees, and customs inspectors to determine whether anyone has tampered with the seal without having to conduct a complete physical inspection. While it seems like a logical idea, the process was delayed for years over debates about the standard and issues over who would bear the cost of the seal.

Will there be benefits to businesses resulting from firms complying with the regulations of Operation Safe Commerce and the SAFE Port Act?

Everyone benefits from compliance. Nobody wants a nuclear weapon to be smuggled into the United States under sacks of coffee beans. Emulating Operation Safe Commerce will permit other countries to secure their ports as well. Just as with ISO 9000 and ISO 14000, companies doing global business need to comply with regulatory requirements in other countries. For example, in Europe, environmental regulations require documentation that Tier 5 suppliers used hazardous chemicals to manufacture imported parts. This type of information will be required for Operation Safe Commerce, and it is already available through coordination and sharing of information sources.

Are there any other benefits?

Improvement of the supply chain as a result of increased visibility means that bottlenecks can be identified. Rapid correction of delays and interruptions will be facilitated by the online information system. The new initiatives will even enable producers to pinpoint the source of defective products as well as where damage occurs en route. Online awareness about the condition of the supply chain has long been the holy grail of supply chain managers. The new methods provide a significant improvement in the efficiency of the entire supply chain starting with production outputs through shipping logistics to warehouse arrival, receipt, and storage.

What are the keys to starting the Operation Safe Commerce program?

The first thing to realize is that security for transported cargo is not just a good idea waiting to happen. It is here. As a good analogy of how easy it is to miss the message, a lot of people saw the Sarbanes–Oxley Act coming but did not start the ball rolling until late in the game. That makes compliance very costly. Rushing project completions is messy and expensive. It is the antithesis of good project management.

How are companies implementing Operation Safe Commerce?

Successful implementation of Operation Safe Commerce requires an executive-level champion. Distribution center and warehouse managers are not accustomed to such roles.

There is a need for a chief of supply chain security (CSS) who understands how to work with both the U.S. and foreign customs organizations. That CSS must also be comfortable with port managers, transportation contractors, and the network of parties that are participants in supply chain logistics. Considering the situation, it also makes sense to partner with individuals and companies that have (or can develop) solid experience in the emerging technologies and business processes required to move materials securely and safely around the world. This is not something that you want to try learning from your mistakes.

What is happening in other countries?

China's exports reached $762 billion in 2005. This was up 28 percent from 2004, which had exports of $593.4 billion. The growth rate for 2006 is estimated at 27.8 percent based on total estimated exports of $974 billion in 2006. China's exports in 2004 were up 35 percent from 2003, which had exports of $439.6 billion. The growth rate continued from total exports of $326 billion in 2002, which is 22 percent greater than in 2001. Germany, along with China in the top 10 world exporters, grew 13.7 percent in the 2005–2006 time frame. These statistics exemplify the growth in shipping that is taking place worldwide. Companies must expand their IT global reach and achieve just-in-time delivery to be successful. Intensified problems of security make it imperative to know what is in the pipeline and where it is located. Developments in technology and business processes are making it possible to do just that.

Review Questions

1 How do you rate the safety and security of the port system that links the global supply chain post-9/11 as compared to pre-9/11? Google Maritime Domain Awareness (MDA). What was learned from some of these links?

2 If 100 percent inspection of containers shipped into the United States each year is mandated, how many containers will be inspected? Is 100 percent inspection the right way to guarantee security?

3 What is Operation Safe Commerce (OSC), and what role does technology play in its achievement? Google Operation Safe Commerce (OSC). What was learned from some of these links?

4 What are the immediate and long-term benefits of OSC?

5 How are companies implementing OSC, and who will coordinate the trade between countries?

Sources: 2007 correspondence with Bruce Richardson, Chief Research Officer, AMR Research, Inc. See also http://www.amr research.com. Interesting information about world trade can be found at the World Trade Organization: http://www.wto.org.

Spotlight 11-2 Don't Separate Strategy and Tactics

To gain a better understanding of the difference between enterprise systems and professional opportunities within them, consider what kind of company environment you would enjoy. A corporation is a cultural entity originally formed by decisions of its founder. The vision (or mission statement) of a company is shaped by the current CEO and board of executives. The degree of good decision-making, strategy and its implementation, business intelligence, and trust are important factors in choosing a workplace.

Any workplace can be exciting if company strategy includes development of its members' talents. Among employees, there may be a few who think, "Someday I'm going to be the one who barks out orders here." That employee might want to revise that vision after reading the rest of this Spotlight.

First of all, *strategy* and *tactics* are well-known words in military classrooms. *Strategy* is a plan for making, doing, or accomplishing an objective.

Tactics refers to the execution of a strategy. It means a procedure or set of maneuvers engaged in to carry out a plan, objective, or goal. In military terms, the word describes the science that deals with securing objectives set by strategy.

Lawrence Hrebiniak, a professor at the Wharton School of Management for more than 30 years, points out that MBA and undergraduate business programs teach how to plan but not to execute.

Hrebiniak is quoted as saying, "When companies separate the planning and doing—that's wrong. Strategic success really demands a simultaneous view of planning and doing. It is vital for managers to be thinking about execution as they are formulating the plans."

Some have used the analogy of a tree to explain the importance of strategy and tactics working together. The tree trunk can be viewed as a company, gaining strength from its roots and environmental resources. Branches are strategies, decisions that shape trees and companies. Twigs are tactical teams, the numerous small details, which, in trees, are the stems, leaves, flowers, fruit, and seeds that execute branch strategies. If a tree's strategy is to realize its biological potential, then twigs get top ranking. Tactical twigs absorb energy from light to make carbohydrates from CO_2 and water. Twigs also produce O_2 as a waste product. It could be said that all mammalian life depends on tactical photosynthesis.

In small, flat organizations where there is little hierarchy, strategy and tactics are usually integrated. They combine to make a force that multiplies the power of a company to reach sustainable and successful outcomes. In large, hierarchical companies, the executive strategy is implemented through a distant chain of command. When that happens, the burden falls on the immediate supervisors of the workforce. John Koenig, former president of O-Force, a business and education partnership focused on workforce development issues in the Orlando area, states, "Top management is certainly important for creating a consistent tone across an organization. In the end, though, employee attitudes and behaviors are shaped primarily by day-to-day interactions with immediate supervisors, and not by messages relayed from a corner office far away." John does not believe that immediate supervisors have the time, stamina, or commitment to build an effective team effort among workers who do not feel like valued partners in a shared enterprise.

As each of us enters the workforce, it is easy to look up the career ladder and envy those on the top rung of decision-making. It would be more useful to find out if the organization integrates strategy and tactics. If the top of the career ladder is considered the realm of strategic thinking—and if, at the bottom rungs, workers do the tactics without any idea of the strategies behind them—it might be wise to find another company to interview.

Vision, strategy, and tactics are as essential for one-person companies as for multinational corporations. The vision must be clear and concise so that everyone in the organization can understand and buy into it. The vision is the anchor that holds the entire system together. If you are thinking about going into business, develop the vision first and hold to it. Then, develop strategy. If there are internal or external changes that require a new strategy, make a new one before eliminating the old one. Develop flexible tactics that can move you toward fulfilling your strategy.

Review Questions

1 How does Spotlight 11-2 apply to educational institutions?
2 Have you ever worked for a company where you fully understood the strategies behind your work assignments? Was that part of your orientation?
3 Does your school experience support Professor Hrebiniak's belief that MBA and undergraduate business programs teach how to plan but not to execute?
4 How could management communicate its strategies to overcome the problem that John Koenig describes?
5 Has reading this Spotlight changed your opinion about choosing a job? Explain.

Sources: Lawrence Hrebiniak. "Making Strategy Work: Leading Effective Execution and Change." Wharton School Publishing, January 2005. Correspondence with John W. Koenig, former President of O-Force, http://www.o-force.org. Http://management.about.com/cs/adminaccounting/a/vst_2.htm. F. John Reh. "Vision, Strategy, and Tactics," August 2007.

Summary

The subject of facility management comprises choosing the location, determining the structure and the site, selecting equipment, and preparing the plant or office layout. There are numerous qualitative factors to take into account. Then, the quantitative modeling can begin. At the heart of facility decisions is recognition that each facility is part of a supply chain network. The big picture must be kept in mind to optimize the supply chain and not the facility alone.

The transportation model is used to minimize shipping costs or maximize profits where production location and market differentials exist. Scoring models are discussed, which can be applied for site or equipment selection. The layout of the workplace and job design interact strongly. Floor models that minimize distance traveled are explained.

After quantitative modeling, it is necessary to return to the qualitative factors to evaluate the relevance and quality of the solutions offered by the models. Throughout this facilities planning chapter, the systems approach is explained because teamwork among all participants in the supply chain is desired in making location, site, and equipment decisions.

The two Spotlight feature boxes that conclude this chapter illustrate real applications of facilities planning. Spotlight 11-1: Are Our Ports Safe? details that there can be no proper decision about where to locate that does not fully consider port location and the ramifications of achieving port safety. Spotlight 11-2: Don't Separate Strategy and Tactics is a warning that applies to every facilities plan conceived. Strategy precedes tactics but then is subject to review and change based on the success of the tactical systems used.

Key Terms

Best location (p. 423)
Build (p. 423)
Buy (p. 423)
Centroid location method (p. 425)
Cost benefit (p. 443)
Design for manufacturing (DFM) (p. 442)
Facilities planning (p. 421)
Floor plan models (p. 447)
Heuristics (rules of thumb) (p. 451)
Layout (p. 422)
Life cycle stages (p. 442)

Models (p. 423)
Multiple decision makers (p. 439)
Northwest Corner (NWC) method (p. 428)
Opportunity costs (p. 443)
Pure number (p. 440)
Rent (p. 423)
Scoring model (p. 436)
Sensitivity analysis (p. 445)
Transportation models (p. 423)
Work centers (p. 448)

Review Questions

1. What is meant by "The basis for location decisions differs according to which parts of the supply chain are involved"?

2. How many assignments of four work centers to floor locations can be made with a 4-story building? (No splitting of work centers is allowed.)

3. With four work centers, there are how many possible layouts?

4. Finding the best locations for police and fire stations is a pressing urban problem. Discuss the nature of this problem and what variables are likely to be important. How does this compare to the facility layout problem?

5. Is it true that plant selection should, at least in part, be based on estimates of labor costs for different areas of the country? Explain.

6. With the scoring model, what happens when a weight of zero is chosen for one of the factors?

7. What enables the horizontal and vertical "stepping-stone" pattern to work for shifting assignments when using the transportation model?

8 Some of the following industries tend to form high-density clusters in specific geographic areas. Identify those industries that have strong clusters and try to find the rational explanation for these specific clusters. In the same sense, identify those industries that do not have strong clusters and try to find the rational explanation for the lack of clustering.

a. Financial services

b. U.S. automobiles

c. Stockyards

d. Steel

e. Textiles-bathing suits

f. Semiconductors

g. Aerospace

h. Garlic processing

i. Motion pictures

j. Publishing

k. Tobacco products

l. Petroleum

m. Credit card processing

n. Non-U.S. automobiles

o. Theme parks and resorts

p. Advertising agencies

q. Soy products

r. Pharmaceuticals

9 Gasoline station location often is based on traffic density studies. What would be the criteria for a good location in terms of traffic density and patterns?

10 Recent emphasis on variety has led to flexible product layouts that can be quickly converted to produce mixed models. How can this be done using a product layout rather than the more typical process layout?

Problems Section

Note: This section has various problems that can be formulated and solved using QuantMethods Production/Operations Management software (QMpom). The appropriate model categories are indicated for each problem.

1 Use the trial and error heuristic to determine the best layout for the following data:

Locations

	A	B	C
A	0	4,000	2,000
B	4,000	0	3,000
C	2,000	3,000	0

Daily flow costs per unit distances from and to work centers:

	1	2	3
1	X	$50	$70
2	$20	X	$40
3	$30	$80	X

Using the QMpom module called Facilities Planning Models (Facilities Layout) will facilitate solving Problem 1.

2 Use the scoring model to resolve the following equipment selection problem. A choice is to be made between two alternative information technology (IT) systems. The following data apply:

	System 1	System 2	Weights
Investment cost	$5,050,000	$5,060,000	3
Operating costs (annual)	$ 400,000	$ 500,000	3
Downtime	3	2	7
Ease of repair	2	3	5
Ease of learning	4	5	2
Flexibility	4	2	4

Characteristics are scaled so that large numbers are less desirable than small numbers. Large weights are more important than small ones, and the scale runs from 1 to 7.

3   A matrix of supply and demand is shown here:

						Supply
						20
						30
						50
Demand	10	10	10	20	50	100

Use the Northwest Corner method to assign shipments for the first feasible solution. You will note that a twofold problem is encountered.

a. What are these conditions called?

b. What can be done about them?

To use QMpom Aggregate Scheduling Models (Transportation), enter supply and demand as indicated and enter all cost data as 1. Click on Northwest Corner Rule. The QMpom system will provide the NWC allocation and information about the special condition of this problem.

4   The American Company has two factories, A and B, located in Wilmington, Delaware, and San Francisco, California. Each has a production capacity of 550 units per week. American's markets are centered in Los Angeles, Chicago, and New York City. The demands of these markets are for 150, 350, and 400 units, respectively, in the coming week. A matrix of shipping distances is prepared. Determine the shipping schedule that minimizes total shipping distance. Estimates of shipping distances (in miles) are shown in the following matrix, along with supply and demand.

	Los Angeles	Chicago	New York City	Supply
Wilmington	3,000	1,000	300	550
San Francisco	400	2,000	3,000	550
Demand	150	350	400	

Using the QMpom module called Facilities Planning Models (Transportation) and the module called Aggregate Scheduling Models (Transportation) will facilitate solving the six (6) problems that are numbered 4 through 9.

5   The Northwest Corner (NWC) solution is shown here for a new plan that has been proposed for the 3-plant, 2-market problem.

Northwest Corner—Initial Feasible Assignment

Plants P_i	Markets M_j			Supply
	M_A	M_B	M_D	
P_1	40	20		60 units / day
P_2		40	30	70 units / day
P_3			60	60 units / day
Demand	40	60	90	

The profits per unit shipped are

Plants P_i	Markets M_j		
	M_A	M_B	M_D
P_1	$23	$32	$0
P_2	$16	$25	$0
P_3	$30	$38	$0

What is the total profit associated with the NWC assignment?

6   Using the information in Problem 5, ship as many units as possible into P_3M_B. How many units will that be? Draw the revised TM. Compare the profit of this shipping plan with that of the NWC assignment.

7   Using the information in Problem 5, ship as many units as possible into P_1M_D. How many units will that be? Draw the revised TM. What is the profit of that shipping plan? Compare the profit of this shipping plan with that of the NWC assignment.

8   Using the information in Problem 5, ship as many units as possible into P_2M_A. How many units will that be? Draw the revised TM. What is the profit of that shipping plan? Compare the profit of this shipping plan with that of the NWC assignment.

9   Using the information in Problem 5, ship as many units as possible into P_3M_A. The stepping pattern is more difficult but still uses horizontal and vertical moves from one shipping assignment to another. How many units will be shipped to $P_3 M_A$? Draw the revised TM. What is the profit of that shipping plan? Compare the profit of this shipping plan with that of the NWC assignment.

10   The cost of improving plant layout is $100,000 to be depreciated over a 5-year period. The estimated annual improvements in profit are $6,000 from better quality, $4,000 from higher productivity, and $11,000 from health benefits. Is the layout improvement recommended?

Using the QMpom module called Capacity Management Models (Breakeven) will facilitate solving Problem 10.

11   The cost of improving office layout is $27,000 to be treated as a one-time expense. The office manager does not have any way of estimating improved profits resulting from quality changes but says that the new layout will save time and miles of walking for the 40 office employees. She estimates that the new layout will cut the amount of walking for the average employee by 100 miles per year. How much will the layout improvement be worth?

12   Using the layout load model, determine a good arrangement for work centers at locations for the numbers given in the following matrices.

Distances measured between locations A, B, C, D, and E (d_{IJ}) from row I to column J:

I\J	A	B	C	D	E
A	0	10	20	32	40
B	10	0	16	18	20
C	20	16	0	12	15
D	32	18	12	0	10
E	40	20	15	10	0

Number of units flowing between work centers 1, 2, 3, 4, and 5 (w_{ij}) from row i to column j:

i\j	1	2	3	4	5
1	X	50	60	80	20
2	40	X	50	10	90
3	80	90	X	60	30
4	50	10	40	X	70
5	60	5	5	30	X

If the cost of a unit moving one foot is one dollar ($1 per unit per foot traveled), what is the total daily work-flow cost of the solution obtained?

13   Locate the central warehouse (centroid location) on an (x,y) grid so that the total distance from its location to the auto-discount stores that it serves will be the minimized. The four stores are located at (20,6), (3, 20), (10,10), and (5,0). The stores are considered to be of equal importance for delivery services.

Using the QMpom module called Facilities Planning Models (Site Location) will facilitate solving the three (3) problems that are numbered 13 through 15.

14   Locate the health clinic on an (x,y) grid with population centers: A at (100, 50) and B at (40,90) where B has twice the population of A.

15   Locate the fire station where the major fire hazards are located at (4,5), (3,4), (5,4), (4,3), and (1,1). All weights are equal for this problem because the fire department wants to avoid the appearance of partiality to any one site.

Practice Quiz

1 Facilities planning applies to plants, offices, customer service call centers, hospitals, and classrooms. Applications are as diverse as work systems. For all such planning, there are four fundamental components. Five are listed below. Which one of these is not applicable?

    a. Geographic location selection of the facility could be as broad as Europe, Asia, Africa, South America or North America. It could be by country within Europe or state within the United States. Part of the facility (say, fabrication) could be located in one place and another part (say, final assembly) could be located in another.

    b. Type of structure desired raises issues of build, buy, or rent. Interactions of existing structures with specific sites make it necessary to consider structure and site together. Build helps to disconnect structure and site.

    c. When structure and site decisions precede geographic location, the facilities planning effort is more effective. Time and money can be saved because lengthy analyses of geographic factors are essentially by-passed.

    d. Equipment choice is driven by process technology decisions. This consideration can become crucial in determining structure and site. Process technology may be a function of facility location. For example, if the market in Brazil is large enough to justify a flow shop being located there, then special-purpose equipment may require a new building close to a railroad siding.

    e. Planning moves up and down the hierarchy, and this includes feasible layouts of equipment and people. Layouts frequently involve decisions about materials moving via conveyors, forklift trucks, gravity chutes, AGVs (automatic guidance vehicles), etc., and people moving up and down stairs, or by elevators.

2 Six factors are well-known as critical determinants of location decisions. Several of these are discussed in choices a. to e. Which one statement is not logical for the location decision?

    a. Process inputs dominate location decisions when the cost of transporting raw materials and components to the production transformation process from distant locations is prohibitively high. Indonesian hardwood is an example, where trees are brought to lumber mills that are close to where they are harvested.

    b. Steps can be taken to reduce the large costs of transporting materials that will be discarded during production. For example, mine mouth processing plants grind ore to very fine particles. These "iron-rich fines" are separated from the rock using flotation methods or magnetically. They are then palletized for shipping to iron and steel plants, some at great distances. The production process for making steel and iron has been divided into two parts to reduce the shipment of unused materials.

    c. Process outputs become important to location decisions when companies want to inspect products before they are shipped to them. For example, it is difficult for buyers in New Orleans to determine the quality of products made in Nagoya.

    d. Many non-U.S. auto assembly plants have been located in states such as Alabama and Tennessee. This is partly because, by relocating their plants, they gain shipping cost advantages over manufacturing the cars abroad and sending them to the United States by sea. Although other factors are operating as well, this is an example of location decisions that are influenced by process outputs.

    e. The transplants are auto companies from abroad that moved their auto assembly to the southeastern United States. One of the reasons that have been given for so many firms making this move is that there are tax, tariff, trade, and legal advantages. There are also marketing factors when a company can say "made by American workers."

3 Discussion continues about the six well-known factors that are critical determinants of location decisions. Found in choices a. to e., which one statement is not logical for the location decision?

    a. In the automobile business, service is crucial. Acura and Lexus set up separate service facilities so as to differentiate themselves from Honda and Toyota. These companies view their process outputs as services (include parts and maintenance) that require locating very close to their customers.

    b. Special process requirements lead to location selection near energy supplies, water for hydro-power, cooling and runoffs, skilled labor force, ample labor supplies, lots of space, and for warehouse distribution centers, a location that is as close as possible to all major markets. That location can differ because markets vary by product types.

    c. Locations selected by grouping of like-industries have always turned out to have economic advantages. Tires stay in Akron; the diamond district in New York City is all within a few square miles; silicon valley is the place to be for semiconductors and their users; Detroit–Dearborn and environs have workers who know how to make cars, and their loyalty to the Big 3 is so great that the auto-assembly transplants had to go to Kentucky, Tennessee, and Alabama.

d. Top executives may have personal preferences for locations that override the logic of business location analysis. Studies have shown that managers (like other people) can put down deep roots that are difficult to dislocate. Location decision makers do not recognize that they are rationalizing reasons for location selection that overlook other places that should be considered. This applies as much to offices and plants as to hospitals, schools, restaurants, and gas stations.

e. The full-scale systems problem is addressed by including costs due to location with respect to both suppliers and customers. Such a business analysis method exists and it is called the transportation model.

4   The transportation model resolves location problems, quantitatively, on a large scale (i.e., with many alternatives, using computer programs such as the QMpom programs that are referenced in the Problems Section. QMpom has a transportation analysis model). Smaller problems can be solved with paper and pencil, or a spreadsheet. A small problem is presented here with all necessary data based on per unit output of the product. Two plants, called P_1 and P_2, have equal supply capabilities of 90 units per day. Two markets, called M_A and M_B, have equal demand requirements of 40 units per day. Plant to market (distributor) shipping costs are given as well as the supplier to plant transport costs for raw materials and components for one unit. Which one statement a. to e. is incorrect?

Plant	Supplier to Plant Transport Costs	Shipping Costs from Plant to M_A	Shipping Costs from Plant to M_B	Supply (units per day)
P_1	$6 per unit	$1 per unit	$2 per unit	90 units per day
P_2	$3 per unit	$3 per unit	$4 per unit	90 units per day
Market demand (units per day)		40 units per day	40 units per day	

a. A total of 80 units per day is demanded by the two markets. That demand level can be satisfied because each plant has a supply capability of 90 units per day. The total supply capability is 180 units per day.

b. The shipping costs to both markets are better for P_1 than for P_2. However, the supplier transport costs favor P_2. These costs have to be added together to make a comparison. That yields the following costs where M_D is a dummy market added to make total units demanded per day equal to total daily supply capability.

	M_A	M_B	M_D	Supply
P_1	6 + 1 = $7 per unit	6 + 2 = $8 per unit	$0 per unit	90 units
P_2	3 + 3 = $6 per unit	3 + 4 = $7 per unit	$0 per unit	90 units
Demand	40 units	40 units	100 units	180 units

c. If the decision is made to have P_1 ship 40 units to M_A and P_2 ship 40 units to M_B, then the total shipping cost will be $600 per day, which has the advantage of keeping both plants busy.

d. The dummy market M_D will not receive any units, which is how a dummy functions. It allows supply to equal demand, which the transportation model requires. A dummy production facility is required when demand is greater than supply. A dummy plant will make zero units. The market to which the dummy plant ships has a demand shortfall.

e. There is no direct information about the location of the two plants or where the markets are situated. There is no information about the location of the supplier. However, because shipping costs are given, it should be possible to make an informed guess about the respective locations. Note that specific locations are interesting for the storytelling, but they are not relevant to the analysis.

5   The shipping plan has not yet been decided for P_1 and P_2. The supply chain decision could be momentous because one of the plants might be shut down. The analysis continues with data unchanged. Results are stated in points a. through e. One report is wrong. Identify that report.

	M_A	M_B	M_D	Supply
P_1	6 + 1 = $7 per unit	6 + 2 = $8 per unit	$0 per unit	90 units
P_2	3 + 3 = $6 per unit	3 + 4 = $7 per unit	$0 per unit	90 units
Demand	40 units	40 units	100 units	180 units

a. There is an allocation rule that states with M markets and N plants there cannot be more than $M + N - 1$ shipments. The dummy satisfies the requirement that total supply equals total demand. Shipments $\leq (3 + 2 - 1 = 4)$.

b. Report 1 recommended the shipping pattern $(P_1 - M_A, P_1 - M_D, P_2 - M_B, P_2 - M_D)$. It has a total cost of \$560. Management rejected this report as too costly.

	M_A	M_B	M_D	Supply
P_1	40 units	0 units	50 units	90 units
P_2	0 units	40 units	50 units	90 units
Demand	40 units	40 units	100 units	180 units

c. Report 2 recommended the shipping pattern $(P_1 - M_B, P_1 - M_D, P_2 - M_A, P_2 - M_D)$. It has a total cost of \$560. Management rejected this report as too costly.

	M_A	M_B	M_D	Supply
P_1	0 units	40 units	50 units	90 units
P_2	40 units	0 units	50 units	90 units
Demand	40 units	40 units	100 units	180 units

d. Report 3 recommended the shipping pattern $(P_2 - M_A, P_1 - M_D, P_2 - M_B, P_2 - M_D)$. It has a total cost of \$520. Management rejected this report as too costly.

	M_A	M_B	M_D	Supply
P_1	0 units	0 units	90 units	90 units
P_2	40 units	40 units	10 units	90 units
Demand	40 units	40 units	100 units	180 units

e. The shipping costs to both markets are better for P_1 than for P_2. However, the supplier transport costs favor P_2. These costs have to be added together to make a comparison. That yields the following costs where M_D is a dummy market added to make total units demanded equal to total supply capability.

6 Structure and site selection generally follow the location decision. Some basic statements about structure and site are presented in points a. through e. Which one of these statements is unreasonable?

a. The fast-food industry searches for sites in all major cities, and all structures follow a prescribed architectural and interior plan. Thus, McDonald's, Wendy's, Chick-fil-A®, Koo Koo Roo, IHOP, and Fazoli's can be identified instantly from their characteristic features and the fact that for each brand one is almost exactly like another.

b. Structure and site decisions should be analyzed by a cost-benefit analysis that includes the costs of building and operating at a specific location, and the revenues that can be generated from the traffic pattern. In addition, the effects of competitors at present and likely to move into the neighborhood in the future should be included.

c. Location, structure, and site come as a package of tangible and intangible conditions that have costs. Some of these costs are difficult to determine but must be discussed. For example, neighborhood stores have been known to oppose attracting fast-food customers with 24/7 hours, loud music from cars at all hours, and complaints along similar lines.

d. Insurance rules and costs are structure and site sensitive.

e. Weather conditions have to be considered in determining operating costs in a geographic location. Site has its own issues related to specific conditions such as snow removal and drainage. In addition, fire and police protection can vary in accord with the site chosen.

7 Which location (structure and site) should be chosen? A scoring model has been created to capture the tangible and intangible factors that characterize these two locations, called Q and R. The choice will become the new call center for this large book and record retailer. Annual numeric costs are used. Intangible factors are scaled 1 to 10 with 1 being best. Decision objective is minimization so the best ratio will be as small as possible. Largest weights are most important. Findings are reported in points a. through e. Which one of the findings is incorrect?

	Location Q	Location R	Weight
Tangible Costs			
Buildings and land	$10 million	$ 15 million	3
Salaries	$500,000	$300,000	3
Other operations	$100,000	$100,000	3
Intangible Costs			
Telecommunication system	2	1	4
Workforce availability	3	2	2
Workforce skills	2	4	3
Community attitude	2	1	1

a. Total tangible costs for Q are $10.6 and for R are $15.4. Numbers have been rounded because the ratio of Q to R is 0.688 no matter how many millions of dollars is involved. Location Q is preferred to R. The ratio of 0.688 when raised to the power of 3 (importance weight) is 0.326. This gives Q about three times more advantage than R based on costs alone.

b. Telecommunication system's capability is important to this choice because it has the highest weight of 4. R has a two-to-one advantage with respect to this factor. When raised to the power of 4, that gives R 16 times more advantage than location Q. Combining the cost factor with that of telecommunication gives R more than five times the advantage of Q.

c. A discrepancy has arisen. One analyst states that the final ratio is 2.935, which means that location R is the winner, being almost 3 times more favored than Q.

d. A second analyst disagrees and states that the final ratio is 0.935, which means that location Q is the winner, but only by a hair's breadth.

e. It has been pointed out that workforce skills are not favorable for R. Location Q is preferred two to one and that is before using the weighting factor. After raising the ratio of 1?2 to the third power, R is at an eight-to-one advantage.

8 There are some basic rules for equipment selection. The first step is to agree on the work configuration to be used. Once the issues of special-purpose equipment versus general-purpose equipment are resolved, the points cited in a. to e. are guidelines. However, one of these is not correct. Which answer is wrong?

a. For choosing between specific machines, conveyors, forklift trucks, and computers as well, the net present value of the investments and operating costs should be determined. Discounted cash-flow analysis permits purchase price to be combined with a time stream of operating costs including maintenance costs.

b. Life cycle stages do not influence equipment selection because the tolerances required for products have nothing to do with stages in the marketplace.

c. The breakeven model provides a benchmark regarding the volume of work that must be done before profit can be made with the new equipment. Relationships between supply and demand should be examined when selecting equipment.

d. Scoring models are useful for equipment selection. They can help to organize the relevant data in much the same way that they were used for site choice. For example, scoring models can help with intangible factors such as how long will it take to train employees to use the equipment productively? How safe are the systems?

e. Setup times on alternative equipments should be compared. What variety of jobs is likely to be done on the new equipment?

9 There are at least five basic types of layouts that can be found in plants and offices around the world. Their identification and discussions about them are covered in points a. through e. One of these treatments is incorrect. Identify which of the different layout discussions is flawed.

a. Job shop process layouts are characterized by clusters of similar types of equipment such as lathes and drill presses. In offices, desks with phones are grouped in standard fashion. Computers, file cabinets, and copy machines are usually situated nearby. Kitchens of restaurants are filled with the general-purpose equipment that allows restaurants to produce to the menu.

b.   The product-oriented layout is typical of the flow shop where special-purpose equipment and transport systems move the product efficiently from workstation to workstation. This is the sequenced assembly that started with Henry Ford and which characterizes auto-assembly operations today.

c.   Cellular layouts are increasingly used as factories within a factory. They produce a quota of parts in an intermittent flow shop arrangement. Teamwork of cell members is particularly important. Because of cross-training, members can spell each other and shift between positions.

d.   Project layout charts are used to monitor and control the degree of completion of project steps and stages. Gantt and PERT layout charts reflect status and allow projections of future accomplishments. These layout charts send signals about likely troubles that are developing. They have been around for years and are considered to help report what is going on in complex project management situations.

e.   Group technology layouts can efficiently produce a family of parts. The computer may play a role in achieving changeovers but there is no emphasis on the tightly knit team-play found in cellular layouts. GT layout is focused on process abilities to produce similar parts using changes in fixtures, jigs, and equipment settings.

10   Every company must get down to the details of layout load models. It is the stage where interior decorating of the home, plant, office, or restaurant kitchen takes place. The difference in layout between McDonald's and Burger King is not coincidental. Layout criteria include capacity, balance, flexibility, volume flows, distance traveled, costs, and time. Gamma Company's matrix of distances measured between locations (A, B, C, D, and E) on the plant floor is shown next to the matrix of units flowing between work centers (1, 2, 3, 4, and 5). Number of units is on an average day with a stable work-flow environment. Where on the plant floor (A–E) should the work centers (1–5) be located so as to minimize the total unit-distances traveled?

	A	B	C	D	E		1	2	3	4	5
A	00	10	20	32	40	1	X	100	60	80	20
B	10	00	16	18	20	2	40	X	50	10	90
C	20	16	00	12	15	3	80	90	X	60	30
D	32	18	12	00	10	4	120	10	40	X	70
E	40	20	15	10	00	5	110	5	5	30	X

The discussion in points a. through e. makes pertinent observations that help to clarify what the layout load floor plan procedure is all about. However, one observation is wrong. Which is that?

a.   Equipment 1 is located on the floor plan at A. Equipment 2 is located at B. The matrix for A_1 and B_2 indicates that 1,400 unit-feet moved in a day.

	A_1	B_2
A_1	00	1,000
B_2	400	00

b.   For the assignment A_1, B_2, C_3, D_4, and E_5, the total number of unit-feet traveled in one day is 23, 025.

c.   Controversy exists between the reports of two analysts who disagree on the best solution found yet. One states that the assignment A_1, B_4, C_5, D_3, and E_5 is the best yet with unit-feet traveled per day equal to 21,725.

d.   The second analyst states that the assignment A_1, B_5, C_4, D_2, and E_3 is best yet with unit-feet traveled per day equal to 21,530.

e.   A heuristic approach pays heed to the fact that 120 units are shipped from work center 4 to work center 1 and assigns them to locations B and A because they are close to each other. The heuristic proceeds in the same way.

Additional Readings

Allen, Robinson, and Stewart (eds). *A Plant Floor Guide*, Dearborn, MI: Society of Manufacturing Engineers, 2001.

Bridgman, P. W. *Dimensional Analysis*. New Haven, CT: Yale University Press, 1922; paperback edition, 1963.

Burnham, John M. *Integrative Facilities Management*. Burr Ridge, IL: Irwin, 1994.

Cedarleaf, Jay. *Plant Layout and Plant Improvement*. Colville, WA: Bluecreek Publishing Co., 1997.

Chan, Yupo. *Location Theory and Decision Analysis*. Cincinnati, OH: Thomson/South-Western Publishing Co., 2001.

Davies, R. L., and D. Rogers. *Store Location and Assessment Research.* New York: Wiley, 1984.

Eislet, H. A. and C. L. Sandblom. *Decision Analysis, Location Models, and Scheduling Problems.* New York: Springer Publishing, 2004.

Gopal, Christopher, and Harold Cypress. *Integrated Distribution Management.* Burr Ridge, IL: Irwin, 1993.

Hauser, John R. *Applying Marketing Management: Four PC Simulations.* Danvers, MA: The Scientific Press, boyd & fraser publishing co (text with diskette for various kinds of scoring models), 1986.

Howard, Kevin. "Postponement of Packaging and Product Differentiation for Lower Logistics Costs." *Journal of Electronics Manufacturing*, vol. 4 (1994): 65–69.

Johansson, Henry J., Patrick McHugh, A. John Pendlebury, and William A. Wheeler III. *Business Process Reengineering.* New York: John Wiley, 1993, 180–186.

Karaska, G. J., and D. F. Bramhall. *Location Analysis for Manufacturing: A Selection of Readings.* Cambridge, MA: M.I.T. Press, 1969.

Koelsch, James R. "Work Smart." *Manufacturing Engineering* (November 1994): 65–67.

Lilien, Gary L. *Marketing Management: Analytic Exercises for Spreadsheets.* Danvers, MA: The Scientific Press, boyd & fraser publishing co (text with diskette for various kinds of scoring models), 1993.

Moore, James M. *Plant Layout and Design.* New York: McGraw-Hill, 1962.

Munton, A. G., N. Forster, Y. Altman, and L. Greenbury. *Job Relocation.* New York: Wiley, 1993.

Oliver, Mark. *Using AutoCAD Map 2000.* Albany, NY: Thomson Delmar Learning, 1999.

Owen, Jean V. "Making Virtual Manufacturing Real." *Manufacturing Engineering* (November 1994): 33–37.

Reed, Ruddell, Jr. *Plant Layout.* Homewood, IL: Irwin, 1961.

Schniederjans, Marc. J. *International Facility Acquisition and Location Analysis.* Westport, CT: Quorum Books, 1999.

Vincke, P. *Multicriteria Decision-Aid.* New York: Wiley, 1992.

Note

1. These references are presented for historical information. The "Additional Readings" section provides relatively current sources. L. Ivan Epstein. "A Proposed Measure for Determining the Value of a Design." *Operations Research,* vol. 5, no. 2 (April 1957) 297–299. The scoring method is used to evaluate alternative aircraft designs by a major aircraft manufacturer. Other applications are described by C. Radhakrishna Rao in the text *Advanced Statistical Methods in Biometric Research.* New York: Wiley, 1952, 103. Also, relevant to multidimensional modeling, see Walter R. Stahl. "Similarity and Dimensional Methods in Biology." *Science*, vol. 137, no. 20 (July 1962): 205–212. The basic explanation was stated by Paul W. Bridgman. *Dimensional Analysis.* New Haven, CT: Yale University Press, 1922; paperback edition, 1963. To update scoring, also see http://www.epic.org/privacy/creditscoring.

Enrichment Activity 11: Real and Spurious Correlations: A Deeper Look at Correlation Coefficients and Coefficients of Determination for a Location Scoring Model

Location Advisors, Inc., provides consulting advice to organizations seeking to relocate. The LAI scoring model (see Section 11-8) is reputed to provide buyers and builders with the appropriate amount to offer for the properties under consideration. Table EA11-1 shows the relationship for six LAI cases (*i*) for which location scores have been matched against actual selling prices.

The marketing division has collected the information in Table EA11-1 to help promote the performance benefits of LAI's product to new customers. The idea is to show how well the location scores match the selling price for various properties. In this case, the last six consulting jobs are represented in the table. A regression line is developed followed by a correlation coefficient (goodness of fit), and a coefficient of determination is calculated and explained.

Table EA11-2, which is used for this procedure, is similar to Table 3-4 in Chapter 3 of this text.

The equations EA11-1 and EA11-2 are similar to Equations 3-6 and 3-7 in Chapter 3. The numbers used in the equations were derived from the Table EA11-2. Thus:

$$b = \frac{\sum XY - n\bar{X}\bar{Y}}{\sum X^2 - n\bar{X}^2} = \frac{670.09 - 6(1.723333)(55.91667)}{20.5636 - 6(2.969878)} = 33.49144 \qquad (EA11\text{-}1)$$

Cases *i*	Location Score (*x*)	Actual Selling Price* ($ *y*)
1	690	21,000,000
2	1,650	44,000,000
3	1,650	49,000,000
4	2,900	95,000,000
5	2,100	74,500,000
6	1,350	52,000,000

Table EA11-1

History of Buying Prices
by Location Scores

* Location Scores have ranged between 150 and 5,000 but they have no theoretical upper limit. In Table EA11-2, they have been reduced by (10^3); selling prices have been reduced by (10^6) to keep computations simple.

	(000)	(000,000)			
i	x_i	y_i	$x_i y_i$	x_i^2	y_i^2
1	0.69	21	14.49	0.4761	441
2	1.65	44	72.60	2.7225	1,936
3	1.65	49	80.85	2.7225	2,401
4	2.90	95	275.50	8.4100	9,025
5	2.10	74.5	156.45	4.4100	5,550.25
6	1.35	52	70.20	1.8225	2,704
Sums	10.34	335.5	670.09	20.5636	22,057.25

Table EA11-2

Calculations Needed
to Parameterize the Normal
Equations

Note: Data for Normal Equations and Coefficients of Correlation and Determination: $\bar{X} = 1.723333$; $\bar{X}^2 = 2.969878$; $\bar{Y} = 55.91667$; $\bar{Y}^2 = 3126.674$; $\sum XY = 670.09$; $\sum X^2 = 20.5636$; $\sum Y^2 = 22,057.25$

$$a = \bar{Y} - b\bar{X} = 55.91667 - 33.49144(1.723333) = -1.80024 \qquad (EA11\text{-}2)$$

That provides the coefficients for the regression line estimating equation which is:

$$\hat{Y} = a + bX = -1.80024 + 33.49144X \qquad (EA11\text{-}3)$$

The question that the clients want answered is how good a fit does this straight line provide for the data point pairs that match location scores with actual selling prices? Does the line offer a sound method for predicting selling prices from location scores?

Two coefficients provide measures of the quality of predictions based on the regression line.

The two are the Coefficient of Determination and the Correlation Coefficient. Both measure the ratio of explained variation to total variation. Both answer the question, what percentage of the total variation is accounted for by the line that minimizes the squares of the deviations from that line (the least squares method)?

First, calculate the Coefficient of Determination (R^2) shown in Equation EA11-4.

$$R^2 = \frac{a \sum Y + b \sum XY - n\bar{Y}^2}{\sum Y^2 - n\bar{Y}^2} = \frac{-1.80024(335.5) + 33.49144(670.09) - 6(3126.674)}{22057.25 - 6(3126.674)} = 0.933594 \qquad (EA11\text{-}4)$$

This least-squares line has provided a very good fit. R^2 can only take values from 0 to 1.

When correlation is perfect, $R^2 = 1$. If there is no evidence of correlation between the two series of numbers, then $R^2 = 0$.

In this specific example, R^2 is quite near one so the location scoring method appears to be a good business opportunity for LAI.

The Coefficient of Determination (R^2) provides less information than the Coefficient of Correlation which is the square root of R^2. In this example, $R = 0.966227$, which is (again) very near one—and that implies strong predictive ability for the LAI method. Of course, this example was designed to substantiate the location scoring method. In the real-world, complex situations seldom obtain an $R = 1$ coefficient of correlation.

Note that $\sqrt{R^2} = \pm R$. The plus or minus sign is important. It is the arithmetic sign of the b-factor. When the correlation coefficient is positive, as x grows larger so does y. In the negative case, as x grows larger y gets smaller. Perfect positive correlation exists between ounces and pounds because they are measuring the same thing that is related by a scale transformation. As mountain climbers go up, the air pressure goes down which is an example of negative correlation.

An interesting case exists with respect to price elasticity. Usually, demand falls as prices rise. For some products that relationship does not hold. In fact, for silver tableware (often given as a wedding gift), a kink exists in the price elasticity curve. Demand rises as price goes up because gift-givers want it to be known that their gifts are expensive.

One more point: Causality is—at best—suggested, not guaranteed when R and R^2 are high. Spurious correlations are legion. For example, increased sun spot activity has been identified with rising stock market prices. In Holland, the number of stork nests has been found to correlate (but not cause) the number of human births. Hidden variables can account for x and y seeming to be highly correlated. Wikipedia explains that hot weather causes a high numbers of pool drownings and large volumes of ice cream sales. Finding intermediating causal factors is a Sherlock Holmes capability. Rapidly changing habits, styles, and tastes can mislead intrepid causality seekers. Last season's TV ratings may be high because reality shows are popular, but six months later that fad may have reached its zenith and been replaced by the popularity of unreality shows. The Journal of Spurious Correlations can be viewed at its website: http://www.jspurc.org (updated on March 20, 2007).

Enrichment Challenges 11

1 Is this model suspect because the R^2 and R coefficients are so close to 1.00?

2 What would be the estimated value of property with a location score of 5,000?

3 What would R^2 be if the data set produced the following results:

$$\bar{X} = 2.08; \bar{X}^2 = 4.34; \bar{Y} = 29.17; \bar{Y}^2 = 850.69;$$
$$\Sigma XY = 397.5; \Sigma X^2 = 31.25; \Sigma Y^2 = 5,375$$

4 What might explain the high correlation between sunspots and rising stock market prices?

5 What might explain the high correlation between stork nests and human births?

Operating the System

Do not separate strategy and tactics (Enrichment Activity 11-2) because they are connected by a continuous planning loop. As a well-known example, military tactics are concerned with *specific details* as contrasted with the *big strategic picture* that was the basis for planning and deciding *who* to battle, *when* to fight, and *how and where* to engage the enemy (competitor). Military tactics are related to the movement of troops and material. Maneuvering and logistics are often included as the descriptive part of the *details* concerning the use of resources. Tactics for P/OM are much the same as in the military situation.

P/OM recognizes as strategic the issues of *who* are the competitors, *what* markets are engaged, and *how, when,* and *where* are the products brought to the marketplace? Specific details about making products and delivering services must be decided after planning strategies are set. Doing the right thing must come before doing the thing right. Doing *the right thing* is the strategic part of the equation and doing it *the right way* is the tactical part of the story.

In Part 3, tactical responsibility takes over. Part 2 was a bridge connecting product line strategy and operating tactics. Part 3 is composed of six chapters which are dedicated to tactical planning issues. Specific details about making products and delivering services must be decided after planning strategies are set. Strategies precede tactics. When tactics fail to deliver strategic objectives, strategies must be revised. Figure PT3-1 accentuates the strong linkage of levels 2 and 4 as well as their close connection with levels 1 and 6. However, tactics are distanced from levels 3, 5 and 7.

Figure PT3-1   Operating Processes: Management Must Have *People and Technology* Skills

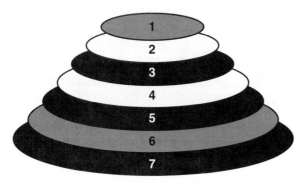

1. Product Design

2. Process Design

3. Project Management

4. Organizational Support

5. Technological Change

6. Competitive Marketplace

7. Sustainability: Ethics, Environment, and Security

Chapter 12 (Materials Management Impacts All Supply Chain Participants) uses the systems perspective to explore relevant elements of materials management (MM). Figure 12-1 shows the big (MM) picture. Information systems are crucial to MM. They control purchasing, receiving, inspection, storage, and the cash flow to pay for materials. The need for materials varies with process type. The systems perspective is essential to manage materials properly.

Chapter 13 (Aggregate Planning to Balance Supply and Demand) moves the focus to workforce planning of operations in the plant or service facility. Workforce planning is required for supply to satisfy demand. To balance supply and demand requires reasonable forecasts of demand. Constant workforce policies provide *level* production. This is contrasted with *chasing* policies that try to match supply to demand using hiring, layoffs, overtime, and subcontracting.

Chapter 14 (Inventory Management for Smooth and Continuous Demand Patterns) discusses how to manage inventories of materials with continuous demand such as toothpaste or gasoline. Economic order quantity (EOQ) models (continuous demand patterns) indicate when—and how much material—to buy. Economic lot size (ELS) models yield optimal production schedules for "make" rather than "buy" decisions. Operational aspects of running perpetual and periodic inventory systems are presented.

Chapter 15 (Material Requirements Planning (MRP) for Sporadic Demand Patterns) shows how to manage inventories of materials with irregular demands. MRP-type items often depend on which components go into what end-items, e.g., service kits or computer components. Successful MRP-inventory systems require good organization of well-managed information systems.

Chapter 16 (Production Scheduling for Manufacturing and Service Operations) shows how production scheduling permits loading and sequencing for the job shop. Loading and sequencing are critical tactical decisions for both services and manufacturing.

Loading is assignment of tasks to departments or nurses to wards. Sequencing follows loading. It specifies the order in which jobs are to be done or nursing shifts assigned.

Chapter 17 (Cycle-Time Management Increases Productivity) explains how cycle-time determines productivity and line-balancing makes the most efficient use of resources on the line. This applies to both manufacturing and service organizations. Differences are drawn between line balancing deterministic and stochastic processes. Stochastic cases can be line-balanced using queuing models and Monte Carlo simulations.

Materials Management Impacts All Supply Chain Participants

chapter 12

Chapter 12 starts the exploration of materials management in the supply chain. Whether making things with materials or using them to provide services, materials are the major circulation system of supply chains. Materials are used in making goods and providing services. They are also used to support the administrative infrastructure. Materials flow through the supply chains, which must always begin with raw materials. P/OM transforms the raw materials into materials that are work in process and finally into finished goods. Also, many supplies are needed for administrative purposes, e.g., to keep the offices and the bathrooms going. Materials can be made at home in the plant or outsourced. There is a lot of procurement outsourcing going on. The terminology has been fragmented to describe off-shore, near-shore, best-shore, and even all-shore sourcing. Canada has been called a secure near-shore location for U.S. companies. The taxonomy of names for various types of external supplier relationships will continue to reflect economic and political issues such as the relative costs of labor and the difficulty of getting a green card to enter the United States.

After reading this chapter, you should be able to:

- Explain what materials management (MM) is and how it connects many functions.
- Discuss the systems perspective applied to materials management.
- Explain the "big picture" of materials as part of the cost of goods sold (COGS).
- Discuss differences in materials management that apply to each kind of work configuration.
- Explain why the systems perspective is essential for successful materials management in both the job shop and the flow shop.
- Explain the materials management information system.
- Lower the risks that buyers take.
- Describe "turnover" and "days of inventory" and explain why they are critical measures of systems performance.
- Explain what is needed for successful centralization of the purchasing function.
- Discuss the receiving, inspection, and storage functions.
- Discuss why bids are often required before purchasing is allowed.
- Explain the management of spare parts.
- Describe the use of value analysis for materials management.
- Explain the management of critical parts.
- Describe why parts with high-dollar volume deserve special attention.
- Explain how to treat parts that have lower-dollar volume.
- Describe why certification of suppliers is important to materials management.

The Systems Viewpoint

Materials management is a system of broad-based planning and control over one of the most important components of the cost of goods sold (COGS). Two trends have been pervasive. The first is the marked decline of the direct labor component of the COGS. The second is the marked rise in the direct and indirect (overhead) cost of materials. Because materials costs are now critical to profitability, most organizations have created positions of high responsibility to oversee the many parts of the system that have to be integrated for materials management. The *integrator* that orchestrates the materials management system is the information system. It coordinates functions and enables purchasing to lower the buyer's risks.

Strategic Thinking

Materials management is a tactical system of planning and control. The strategic component came into play during start-up, when deciding what goods were to be made and what services were to be offered. However, strategies must always be reevaluated. If the system is not performing as it was intended, then changes in strategies may need to be made. In this regard, two systems measures—"turnover" and "days of inventory"—are very helpful for monitoring how well purchasing and inventory managers do their job. They are also helpful in assessing how well the strategic plans are faring. Strategies can be tweaked or changed significantly if they are not delivering according to plans.

These two measures can be useful in evaluating a system's performance under stressful conditions. In hard times, keeping inventories low is critical to cash-flow control. Insufficient cash flow can jeopardize the survival of the firm. Airline strategies with respect to materials management (e.g., cost of meals served, fuel consumed per passenger mile, etc.) were reevaluated after the bankruptcies of several major carriers.

12-1 What is Materials Management (MM)?

Materials management (MM) involves organizing and coordinating all management functions that are responsible for every aspect of materials movements and transformations—called the **materials management system (MMS)**. This system is triggered by demands (including those forecasted) that deplete stocks, causing inventory management to request replenishment through purchasing agents or direct contact with suppliers or vendors.

The distinction between vendors and suppliers is a matter of local usage. One or the other, or often both, are used by various companies and/or industries in different regions of the United States and the world. Before the Digital Equipment Corporation (DEC) was absorbed by Compaq Corporation, which later merged with Hewlett-Packard Corporation,[1] it used "vendors" to sell its products. The publication *VarBusiness* honors "Top Vendors" in an annual award event. Ford Motor Company employs "certification" of suppliers to assure quality and reliability. For selling, reselling, and servicing, many companies have channel partners (see http://telephonyworld.tradepub.com/free/var/).

12-1a The Systems Perspective for Materials Management

Materials management is an interlinked system, as shown in Figure 12-1. Note that the demand for stock is based on production needs and forecasts. MM connects the external sourcing of supplies to the internal scheduling of product to be delivered to the customer. Mismanage any part of the interlinked system and the adage that "a chain is as strong as its weakest link" applies.

The **internal MM system** requires control of production materials, which are process flows. Further, there is control of **work in process (WIP)** on the plant floor and finished goods in the warehouse. Some companies have external control over shipments of finished goods to distributors and customers as part of MM. Other companies limit MM to the regulation and use of incoming stock.

The materials management system must be synchronized and coordinated to be effective. The key to synchronization is in knowing "when" materials are needed and "where." Coordination results in meeting the deadlines. It is worth noting in Figure 12-1 how many functions must be coordinated. Each deals with different aspects of materials

© 2007 Jupiterimages Corporation

The tractor is digging in a gravel pit. This firm, which supplies gravel and stone to the construction industry, in turn must buy parts for its tractor as well as other supplies. The key is that firms that supply raw materials are themselves dependent on purchasing materials.

Materials management (MM)
Organizing and coordinating all management functions that are responsible for every aspect of materials movements, storage, acquisition, and transformation.

Materials management system (MMS)
Triggered by marketplace demands (via forecasts), which deplete stocks that cause inventory managers to place replenishment orders through purchasing agents with suppliers and vendors.

Internal MM system
Controls production materials flowing to and through the process.

Work in process (WIP)
Exists in the form of incomplete jobs that cannot be shipped or put into finished goods storage.

Figure 12-1

Systems Perspective of Materials Management for Incoming Stock Requirements

Demand for Stock by Offices, Maintenance, Cafeterias, Etc.	and	Demand for Stock by the Production Departments in Various Locations

Engineering, Design, Research & Development	Inventory Management
Purchasing Agents specialized by types of items, etc.	Purchasing Records computer tied in with Accounting
Suppliers from all over the world	Accounting takes care of Accounts Payable
The office of The Vice President of Materials Management Incoming stock management	Receiving keeps records of deliveries
	Inspection of all incoming materials before production's use or warehousing

Logistics

Tactics of materials management for buying, storing, and transporting materials of all kinds as required by the company's supply chain.

Value added

Raw materials have value added by the transformation process of P/OM, which makes them into parts.

© 2007 Jupiterimages Corporation

The farmer is working a field in Le Bic, Quebec, Canada. The farmer sends food along the supply chain but requires many materials, including seeds, fertilizer, fuel, and spare parts, to do the job.

management as part of the internal supply chain of the company. The incoming logistics system of the company is the outgoing logistics system of the supplier. **Logistics**, which are the tactics of materials management and product distribution, should always be in harmony with the company's strategies.

12-1b Taxonomy of Materials

Every business needs to acquire materials to function. The process of acquisition is known as *buying* or *purchasing*. There are three main classes of materials that have to be purchased and managed.

First, there are raw materials (RM). These are generally extracted from the ground and then refined, but they are still the basic ingredients. Examples include mined metals such as copper, gold, and platinum; chemicals such as sodium and potassium salts, manganese and phosphates; grains such as wheat and rye; beans such as coffee; natural gas, and petroleum.

Raw materials have **value added** by operations. Value adding occurs when purchased components are further transformed by the company's production process. Thus, refining, processing, packaging, and shipping when done by the organization are value-adding and profit-making processes.

All buyers of raw materials specify their required quality standards. Grains can be too dirty. All soy is not alike. Coffee prices vary with the perceived quality of the taste of the beans. Raw materials can be bulky and require special spacious storage bins. Companies prefer to locate their refining operations near the source of raw materials so they do not have to transport tons of materials from which pounds or even ounces are eventually derived for use.

Organizations that are in the business of supplying raw materials at the very start of the upstream acquisition process are themselves dependent on purchasing. A quick summary includes the equipment to dig in the mines or harvest the crop. The deposits in which the mines are located must be acquired. The land to be planted and farmed must be procured. Mining requires tools and lubricants, and farming demands seeds and fertilizer. This leads to the somewhat trite statement that "every organization has a supplier."

Both miners and farmers have offices to run to keep the records for themselves, their owners, and the tax office. Everyone needs to buy paper and clips. Few are without computers. Miners, refiners, farm workers, and office personnel all need the basic necessities for proper hygiene in the office or plant.

Second, components (C) and subassemblies (SA) are purchased materials that have greater value added than the raw materials. They are, in fact, composed of raw materials that already have experienced value adding. C and SA are characterized by some degree of fabrication, assembly, and manufacture. They are assembled into higher-order products by combining them with each other and with other parts made by the producer.

This produces the third class of materials that need to be managed. Work in process (WIP) can be stored and eventually shipped as finished goods (FG). WIP has more value added than the purchased subassemblies. There is a progression of value adding that starts at raw materials and moves up the supply chain to finished goods—sold and shipped.

Clearly defined quality standards for the components and subassemblies must be set by the materials managers for the producer. As some materials are transformed from raw materials to finished goods, they become less bulky. This characterizes the analytic processes, which start with tons of raw materials and reduce them to smaller amounts of work in process based on the thought that less bulky goods still require storage space.

The opposite effect occurs for many manufactured products, which employ synthetic processes. These assemble components into bigger and heavier subassemblies and eventually finished products like farm tractors, diesel locomotives, automobiles, and commercial airliners. There is clearly an advantage in having such large and heavy finished goods near to their marketplace so they do not have to be transported great distances to the customers.

Materials managers choose suppliers based on their locations. There has to be a balance between where to buy bulky raw materials and where to assemble big products. Decisions about where to buy materials and where to locate assembly for shipment to the marketplace are based on analyzing the costs of transport, handling, and storage. Being well-informed always represents an advantage because the alternatives being considered are better ones.

To illustrate, some organizations purchase all, or part, of the finished goods that they sell without acknowledging their use of outsourcing. The customer believes that the corporate brand name identifies the maker. This ploy may be because the organization does not have the capacity to meet demand and, therefore, contracts for the services of coproducers to augment their own output. The finished goods are either shipped directly to customers or put into finished goods inventory. There have to be tight quality controls on the standards and the meeting of those standards.

Coproduced (and copacked) products have much of their value added by the supplier. The purchaser's profits are related to marketing, selling, and shipping the product. There are instances of where firms buy finished goods for sale in certain countries while making them in others. Analysis is based on running the numbers for alternative taxes and tariffs in the countries where finished goods are purchased and sold.

12-1c Cost Leverage of Savings in Materials

Purchases from suppliers represent a large percentage of costs that must be recovered before the organization can start to make a profit. Looking at this issue in another way, if either direct labor or materials costs could be reduced by the same percentage, the average organization would save two or three times as much by choosing the materials costs reduction. The numbers differ by industry, ranging as shown in Table 12-1.

Say that the expenditure of $5,000 on an operations improvement study could reduce labor costs by 10 percent from $150,000 to $135,000. There is a *net saving* of $10,000. Making use of the percentages in Table 12-1, which apply to an "average" organization, materials costs would be seven times larger than the direct labor costs. "Average" is

Table 12-1	Components of COGS	Percent Range	Average%	Future%
Comparison of Labor and Materials Costs as an Average Percent of the Cost of Goods Sold (COGS) for a "Normal" Manufacturing Organization	Direct labor costs	05–15%	10	5
	Direct materials costs	60–80%	70	75
	Indirect costs	35–05%	20	20
	Totals	100%–100%	100%	100%

"now" but trends are evident that are moving the multiple closer to 15. That is basically for outsourced manufacturing. For service industries, a reasonable multiple of materials costs might be three times larger than labor costs. This would be $450,000.

If the $5,000 study could reduce materials costs by 10 percent, that would produce a saving of $45,000, or a *net saving* of $40,000. Spending to reduce materials costs provides savings four times greater than the study expense to reduce labor costs. Thus, investments in improving materials costs instead of labor costs are preferred because they have better leverage.

When only manufacturing industries are considered, direct materials costs in Table 12-1 range between 60 and 80 percent. The average percent for direct materials would be 70 percent of the cost of goods sold. An expense of $5,000 on an improvement study to reduce material costs by 10 percent would produce savings 7 times greater than the $15,000 savings associated with reduction of direct labor costs by 10 percent. The net saving would be $105,000 − $5,000 = $100,000. Spending to reduce materials costs provides savings that are 10 times greater than spending to reduce labor costs. For the most part, manufacturers should prefer investments that reduce materials costs rather than labor costs.

The examples lead to conjecture about the persisting pressures for downsizing labor. Are these efforts continuing in the year 2008? Do continued adversarial relationships between unions and management make sense? How can unions help to reduce materials costs? Back in 2002, the Los Angeles longshoremen's port strike epitomized the problem of management not knowing how to convince unions that the use of technology for very labor-intensive work could be in everyone's best interest. Seven years later management still seems to be unable to make the case in a convincing way.

Even before 1960, manufacturing was becoming less labor intensive as a result of technology. This same situation occurred in agriculture over the decades before 1960. The cost of labor for farming is far less than the cost of energy in the agricultural equation. It is estimated that less than 3 percent of the workforce is currently engaged in farming.

Still, manufacturers pursue inexpensive labor. Outsourcing the labor component, plants have moved to Mexico, Thailand, Indonesia, Pakistan, and the Republic of China. There has been rotation from one location to another as problems have surfaced in locations that are far from corporate headquarters. At the current time, China has become one of the largest sources for labor-intensive production.

Many services are labor intensive and although technology has had an impact, it has not alleviated the need for human contact. In some service industries, Table 12-1 is essentially reversed, with materials being the smaller percentage of the cost of services rendered. Efforts are being made to control service labor costs. Robots are being used increasingly. There are numerous examples of efforts to unionize service industries.

One key has been to make services so valuable to people that they are willing to spend an extra amount for clearly better investment advice, education, health care, hotel treatment (Four Seasons and Ritz-Carlton), and car service (Lexus and BMW). Marketing special service products may become increasingly essential to success. P/OM is called upon to fashion appropriate production systems to deliver high-value service products.

Information is one of the "materials" used by services. When properly managed, information can reduce the labor costs of services. A well-run travel agency uses the computer to provide quality service at low labor costs. Mail-order companies can trade off manual labor costs for computer input–output costs. The latter wins handily.

It should be noted that when purchasing pursues a high-quality, low-cost buying program, the pressure to control prices is passed to suppliers' firms, which are upstream from the producer in the supply chain. The expected pass-along reaction of suppliers will be to put their own suppliers, who are further upstream, under pressure to reduce prices. Thus, at each level suppliers first try to reduce costs by downsizing to control labor costs. Ultimately, they turn to their own suppliers, searching for additional cost advantages.

It is to be expected that analysis will continue to indicate that for all suppliers, their materials costs have greater leverage than their labor costs. This may not always hold true, but increasingly, replacement of labor with technology continues throughout most of industry.

These relationships will be found throughout most supply chains. At the raw materials level, technology and energy pay a much larger part of the bill than labor. It also is likely that when averaging across the whole supply chain, the major leverage factor is materials.

12-1d Penalties of Errors in Ordering Materials

Order errors include wrong specifications, incorrect quantities, and overpriced materials. Orders placed for materials should be as correct in every aspect as possible. Mistakes are more costly in some situations than in others, but in all cases, errors are to be avoided.

Worst cases are likely to be for start-ups and for the mature flow shop. In both of these cases, the process may have to be stopped until the materials problems are corrected. The least worst case is likely to be for the job shop where other jobs can be done while the materials errors are corrected.

Flexible and programmable systems also have some built-in advantages of being able to shift from one product to another, with minimum penalty, when materials problems are encountered. Projects, such as bringing out a new product (start-ups) or building an office tower, can be flexible or vulnerable depending upon the stage of the system.

Specifications of materials must be defined exactly. They must be priced right, delivered on time, and inspected for faults. Information about materials must be managed with skill. Stock outages can delay or halt production of goods and services. The need for on-time quality materials is as crucial for services as for manufacturing. There is no excuse for a factory that runs out of boxes to package products. A printer without paper is useless. The fast-food restaurant that runs out of french fries is heading toward extinction.

The costs of mistakes can be exorbitant. In an actual case, an Exxon refinery needed a replacement gasket costing $85. Several gaskets were listed as being in stock, but when examined, they turned out to be the wrong size. The cost to the refinery was substantial because it had to cut production and send a chartered plane 700 miles to get a proper gasket. The actual cost of this inspection error was not announced but it was costly. The penalty for mistakes depends on the kind of product, the life cycle stage of the product, and the process configuration that is being used.

12-2 Differences in Materials Management Are a Function of Work Configurations

Materials management requires unique rules and decision models for different markets, life cycle stages, and work configurations. That is, certain kinds of problems are posed by the materials requirements of flow shops that are not the same as for job shop and batch work systems. Differences also apply to projects and flexible processing systems.

12-2a Flow Shops

Flow shops require a continuous supply of a specific set of unchanging materials. The line must be shut down when stock outages occur. Alternatively, carrying large amounts of inventory can be unnecessarily costly, requiring more storage space than is justified. Obsolescence, deterioration, and pilferage (usually in that order) are the curse of carrying large amounts of inventories.

Trade-off models are needed to evaluate and balance the disadvantages of having large amounts of stock on-hand (SOH) against the benefits of large order quantities placed long in advance of delivery so that substantial quantity discounts can be obtained. The trade-off model also must consider the possibility that too little inventory on-hand followed by supplier strikes, delivery slowdowns, and acts of nature can lead to production shutdowns caused by a lack of supplies.

The management imperative of the supply chain is knowing when to order and how much to order. Therefore, an order policy that specifies "when" and "how much" to order for each item, independent of what is happening to other items, is a sensible approach to use for items that have smooth and continuous demands. The flow shop is the work configuration that satisfies this demand pattern.

The flow shop consumes supplies constantly. Its demand for supplies can be considered to be smooth and regular. This kind of a pattern applies also to the intermittent flow shop and to stable, big-batch order environments. Suppliers actively compete to supply the materials requirements of high-volume demand systems.

Trade-off models
Generic models in which raising the size of (*x*) brings increasing advantages of one kind (benefit) while creating larger penalties of another kind (costs).

12-2b Job Shops

Job shops have a varied and changing set of materials requirements. These may include certain materials, the uses of which are repeated with some degree of regularity, and others that are unique or infrequent orders. Frequency of usage is reflected in the dollar demand, which is a good measure of item importance.

Generally, job shops involve smaller order quantities of far more kinds of materials than flow shops. When discounts can be obtained, they are lower. Being able to track stock levels for many items is important. It requires an information management capability. One widely used information planning system—for job shops—is called *material requirements planning (MRP)*. The job shop work configuration can be viewed as having a continuing stream of minor projects with short start-ups, which lack the serious consideration given to major projects with complex start-ups.

The job shop needs to have planning done for materials requirements. Such planning involves having a good information system to track the components used for each job in the shop. The time when those components are required must be specified and acted upon with sufficient lead time, which is the replenishment time for an order. Lead-time data is part of the information system that materials management must track. Lead-time management is required to make certain that expected lead times are met and when possible to find ways to decrease the replenishment period.

Many suppliers are involved in job shop management. Changes from one to another are not unusual. A single decision that deviates from optimal materials planning cannot do too much harm. The cumulative effects of repeated instances of bad quality and/or late deliveries can impose significant penalties such as the loss of good customers.

12-2c Flexible Manufacturing Systems

Small penalties accrue to flexible manufacturing systems (FMS), especially if a large variety of products on the menu permit flexible shifting to other work orders while errors in materials are corrected. Minor penalties also characterize service-oriented job shops, where flexible processing routines enable switching to alternative tasks while corrective procedures are undertaken with suppliers.

Although there are special material requirements for flexible manufacturing systems, they reflect a blend of the flow shop and the job shop. If there are many different products produced on the same FMS, then the materials requirements are more like the job shop than the flow shop. On the other hand, if there are only a few items produced in large volumes, the flow shop character will prevail.

12-2d Projects

Project undertakings, such as building ships or theme parks, have stages when certain materials are used that will not be used again. Because project activity stages are nonrepetitive, the majority of orders are preplanned and placed once. Material requirements can be planned and information systems can be used to track the timing of materials needed for specific project activities.

Order policies concerning when to order and how much apply only to those project materials that are used consistently and uniformly throughout the project. Such ordering policies are appropriate when demands are independent of the specific project activities. This is the case for lubricants for machines, food for workers, paper for the office, and lightbulbs. In contrast, if material requirements are properly tracked, the right amount of cement can be ordered to be delivered on time for a specific construction job of known dimensions.

Often, much work on project materials is subcontracted to suppliers who as specialists are familiar with particular stages of materials requirements for the particular project. Cost of materials is often less crucial than on-time delivery. Sometimes, as with start-ups for new products, the materials required are unique. There is little experience in producing them. Discounts for quantity purchases are rare, whereas special set-up charges are not unusual. Careful follow-up with suppliers is essential when experience with their practices is limited.

When suppliers have minimum familiarity with the products they are supplying, this can lead to production difficulties. To illustrate, the supplier of the stage sets for a Broadway play may have never before dealt with some of the special effects that are to be used. Without follow-up, the director and cast may be in for some surprises when the dress rehearsals begin. Similarly, unseasoned entrepreneurs discover a succession of bugs that prevent smooth start-up and constancy of output. Professional training in P/OM leads to checklists and other procedures aimed at avoiding problems.

There are many tales or "war stories" that can be told about mistakes in materials management. The requirements are all the more difficult because of the fact that although purchasing and process management are part of the P/OM team, they are concentrating on different aspects of the system. Purchasing as a centralized or decentralized buying function is serving different product masters, various departments, diverse divisions, and even plants, not all in the same country.

When there is antagonism between the buyers and those for whom they buy, many problems can surface. To prevent this from happening, close communication should be established. Working with purchasing, a good relationship should be established with suppliers. There is increasing belief in a materials system with fewer suppliers and a greater trust relationship between all parties.

Expectations of buyers for the performance of their suppliers change when there is continuity of their supply-and-demand relationship. Buyers expect that improvements will occur in quality, price, and speed of delivery. Some buyers may expect that shipping patterns will move closer to *just-in-time* (meaning delivered as needed and often abbreviated *JIT*). The suppliers look for continuity and loyalty from their buyers. A good relationship is derived from mutual benefits perceived by both parties.

12-3 The Materials Management Information System

Materials management information system (MMIS)

Provides online information about stock levels for all materials and parts.

The **materials management information system (MMIS)** provides online information about stock levels for all materials and parts (RM, C, SA, WIP, and FG). Stock on order,

Intelligent information system
Captures the management issues of *what to buy, when to buy, from whom to buy, how much to buy, how much to pay,* etc.

lead times, supplier information, costs of materials, and discount schedules also are part of the MMIS. (RM = raw materials, FG = finished goods, C = components, WIP = work in process, SA = subassemblies)

An **intelligent information system** is desired rather than a system that acts like a ledger providing only the information that is specifically requested. An intelligent MMIS can provide unsolicited data that is timely for decision making. It can request action (i.e., noting that a withdrawal from stock should trigger a buy decision). That order may be automatically created and sent to the supplier's computer. The idea of a smart information system is not just user friendly. It is a system that can prompt decisions, detect errors, and provide a rapid-access, multifunctional systems database.

An intelligent information system is designed with parameters that capture the management issues of *what to buy, when to buy, from whom to buy, how much to buy,* and *how much to pay.* This MMIS is constantly working overtime. The same material management system may have to be able to consider when to make the parts instead of buying them and when to employ coproducers and copackers.

12-3a Global Information Systems—Centralized or Decentralized

Companies that can compete globally have achieved an organizational integration of the information required for materials control on a global basis. The past is gone where a variety of materials management activities existed as individual operations, each attended by managers who seldom communicated with each other. Inevitably, in the search for competitive effectiveness, a single, central materials control department has emerged for successful multinational and transnational organizations.

Centralization in purchasing may not be best for every organization, but it is more likely to be the best approach when the information systems infrastructure supports a global network. If the worldwide database is not properly organized, then decentralization is the only format that can cope with the numerous tasks that procurement entails.

Most organizations have a vice president in charge of materials control. This senior position is essential to permit the centralization of the global materials management tasks. The responsibilities vested in a materials control department include at least four subfunctions, each of which has major international implications.

Expediting
Actively following up on orders to make sure that deliveries will be on time. Expediters initiate remedial actions.

1 Purchasing from suppliers all over the world and having close relations with them. Regulating shipments as to carriers and delivery dates.

2 Maintaining stocks of inventory at various places worldwide, while knowing how much inventory is in place at each location (i.e., inventory stock control, on a global basis). Status in the warehouse includes control over the withdrawal procedures such as "first-in, first-out" or "last-in, first-out." **Expediting** means following up on orders and doing whatever can be done to move materials faster.

3 Inspecting incoming materials using various statistical methods of quality control for acceptance sampling. These inspections are taking place worldwide and must be coordinated by an information system that tracks location and status.

4 Running an international accounts payable department that can take advantage of terms for paying, such as 30 days before interest begins to be charged. Especially, in inflationary economies, such as those of Brazil (2000–2002) and Argentina (1960s–1990s), the interest rate terms can turn out to be as important as the buying price. The Brazilian annual inflation rate had been officially put at 6,000 percent—unofficially at 12,000 percent. Ford Motor Company's decision to build an auto plant in Sao Paulo may have been based on an accurate forecast that inflation would be under control and the economy thriving by the early 2000s. The Argentine oil company YPF overpurchased during the high-inflation period items such as rubber tires. Rubber does not store well for too many years.

Each materials management activity interfaces with the others. They are the mutual responsibility of many departments within the organization. Coordination of activities is needed, and that is why good information management is stressed.

12-3b Systems Communication Flows

Many forms of communication unite the various materials management groups within the larger organization. Some companies use paperless systems—at least in parts of the organization. Tandem non-Stop computer systems (part of Compaq and then Hewlett-Packard) developed a paperless factory in Texas as a role model. IBM in Santa Palomba, Italy, used electronic data interchange (EDI) to link up with other IBM European installations. The result was an online, real-time information system aimed at providing assembly instructions for order fulfillment. Hewlett-Packard in California pioneered the use of bar-code control of assemblies. RFID is increasingly used by factories and their warehouses. Communication networks are more robust with each passing day.

By 1990, the Internet was being employed by every major company to facilitate purchasing. There were exchanges and auction sites set up during the dot.com boom of the late 1990s. Many of these failed because of inadequate business plans. However, the function of the Internet has grown in leaps and bounds. B2B (business to business) via the Internet is widely used by internal purchasing departments all over the globe.

Even so, most companies have paper-rich trails that are coordinated with computer records. The objectives for paperless organizations remain worthy goals that are gradually being approached. Satellites enable e-mail transmissions to abound, raising communication levels by exponential amounts. EDI using computer-aided design permits The Limited to transmit clothing manufacturing patterns and materials requirements to suppliers in Hong Kong and Indonesia moments after finalizing patterns in Columbus, Ohio, and Waltham, Massachusetts.

Electronic information mixes with paper for invoicing accounts payable and for tracking stock withdrawals and stock on-hand. Verbal communications and TV pictures augment the multimedia system. The communications are especially helpful when problems arise due to contingencies, which in the course of otherwise normal materials management can be counted on to occur. Many times, contingencies lead the materials control department to seek help with problems from its own research and development department as well as the supplier's R&D department. Such interchanges can take place regularly on a global basis.

12-4 The Purchasing Function

Purchasing agents (PAs) and their buying organizations have the traditional role of bringing into the organization the needed supplies. Although this is very important, the role is changing, becoming more integrated within the organization and bringing in more important information, as well. Sourcing (which is the generic name for purchasing every kind of supply needed by the organization) has become a global system.

Purchasing agents (PAs)
PAs buy supplies the company requires.

12-4a The Twenty-First Century Learning Organization

The purchasing department in the twenty-first century is an information-gathering agency. Totally on the up-and-up, by being everywhere and able to listen, it is able to learn about new technologies being used by suppliers and the organizations they supply worldwide. It is on top of new materials, new suppliers, new distribution channels, new prices, and new processes that produce quality levels previously not attainable. It has a global reach via satellites and telecommunications capabilities that constantly expand horizons.

This purchasing department is responsive to the marketing strategies of the various suppliers from whom it obtains the required materials. The old and waning role of purchasing is to push suppliers on price. Shopping around for the best prices is no longer done. It is far from "best practice." The price-tag approach has been thrown out in favor of a long-term relationship with special trusted suppliers. In some cases there are many and in other cases just a few.

The importance of the buying function depends upon the extent to which the company requires outside suppliers. The determination of what to make and what to buy is a P/OM decision; however, purchasing department information can be crucial. It is evident that the decision often depends on the terms to buy, including price, quality, delivery, and innovations, among others, which purchasing learns about and communicates to the P/OM team.

When the production department cannot make the product, or deliver the service, then the importance of the buying function increases. Few mail-order companies and/or department stores produce any of the materials they offer for sale. Supermarkets use the capacity of copackers to offer products with their name. Purchasing provides the leverage for such products.

12-4b Buyers' Risks

Mail-order and department store purchasing agents (PAs) generate such large volumes that they are of equally great importance to the superstores (e.g., Wal-Mart) or the mail-order companies for which they work—and to the producers from whom they buy. Purchasing agents for flow shops also deal in such large volumes that making them happy is considered part of the supplier's business strategy. In many circumstances, purchasing managers are responsible for the success of their companies. Salaries of high-stake buyers are in line with the risks they accept. Even small mistakes are costly.

Purchasing for mail-order and retail business drives the logistics of the supply chain. This P/OM sales-service area is involved in a situation where the ability to shift rapidly to new product designs and suppliers is usually essential for success.

Fashion is fickle. Women's clothing styles change in complex ways. Manufacturers have been caught with large unsold inventories as a result of committing to a style that did not gain acceptance. When turnover is poor for retail or mail order, the goods are marked down and sold quickly at large discounts that provide no profit, and often at a loss. Books and toys that do not sell are marked down and remaindered.

12-4c Turnover and Days of Inventory—Crucial Measures of Performance

The performance of the purchasing agent in the supply chain is related to the speed (or velocity) with which goods sell and the amount of inventory that is on hand to be drawn down. There is also the replenishment rate. A small stock that is frequently replenished can satisfy large demand rates without entailing carrying charges for a stuffed warehouse.

Various ways exist for measuring these rates. Demand velocity (units per period like miles per hour) is measured as units sold—moved to the customer—per period of time. Average daily demand velocity is often called *average demand per day*.

Days of Inventory (DOI)

This measure is regularly reported internally by many firms. DOI is equivalent to dividing total stock on-hand by the average demand per day. It is the expected length of time before running out of stock—if no further stock is added. DOI changes when new stock is added (DOI goes up) and when daily demand speeds up (DOI goes down). When daily demand slows down (DOI goes up).

Automobile companies, furniture manufacturers, and makers of baby strollers reflect the broad spectrum of companies that customarily report DOI. There is a comfortable

© 2007 Jupiterimages Corporation

Best practice retailers strive to achieve large, double-digit inventory turns. For example, if the items in this warehouse are replaced 20 times a year, management might reasonably ask for turnover of 25 or even 30 times. Lower prices might do the trick.

level in each case, such that one month's supply of autos would usually be considered too little—six or more months of supply would be considered excessive. Ten months would be interpreted as a signal of dangerous inventory accumulation.

The computation of **days of inventory** is shown here, with a numerical example, where *Avg. inv.* stands for average dollar inventory (*Avg. $ inv.*). In the example that follows, *Avg. inv.* is $5 million. Also, the daily cost of goods sold (i.e., *Daily COGS*) is the annual cost of goods sold divided by (say) 365. *Annual COGS* is $50 million. If there are 250 selling days, then change 365 to 250.

$$Daily \ COGS = 50(10)^6 \div 365 = \$136,986.30$$

$$Days \ of \ inventory \ (DOI) = (Avg. \ inv.)$$

$$\div (Daily \ COGS) = \$5,000,000 \div \$136,986.30 = 36.5 \ days$$

An alternative way to compute this number would be

$$DOI = 365 \times (Avg. \ inv.) \div (Annual \ COGS)$$

$$= 365 \times 5(10)^6 \div 50(10)^6 = 36.5 \ days \ of \ inventory$$

Inventory Turns

Another measure that is used that captures the essence of supply chain objectives regarding throughput and value added is turnover. **Turnover** or **inventory turns** is measured as the number of times that the warehouse is emptied and refilled per year. Inventory turnovers can be measured with different time periods than a year, such as turns per month. If the summer months have low demand, then the inventory turns may decrease during that period speeding up in the fall.

The concept of turnover can be applied to retail stores, department stores, mail-order firms, and the family medicine chest. It is a very helpful performance measure to manufacturers and distributors moving goods off the factory floor to the customer.

The computation of inventory turnover is shown here, with a numerical example. The numbers used for this example are related to sales dollars rather than cost dollars. The latter were used to calculate days of inventory (DOI). Numbers for turnover are based on a sales price of $1.20 per dollar of the cost of goods sold. Also, average inventory is estimated in terms of sales dollars rather than cost dollars.

$$Annual \ net \ sales = \$50,000,000(1.2) = \$60,000,000$$

$$Avg. \ inv. (in \ sales \ dollars) = \$5,000,000(1.2) = \$6,000,000$$

$$Inventory \ turns = (Annual \ net \ sales) \div (Avg. \ inv.) = 60 \ million \div 6 \ million$$

$$Inventory \ turns = (Annual \ net \ sales) \div (Avg. \ inv.) = 10 \ turns \ per \ year$$

Note the relationship between 10 inventory turns and 36.5 days of inventory. Thirty-six and one-half days is the interval between turns. Both measures tell different but related stories about the same system. Inventory turns give a sense of the velocity with which inventory moves out of the warehouse. Days of inventory states the inventory backlog to be worked off in terms of how long that will take.

Using these measures, companies can determine how well they are doing in moving materials throughout the supply chain. If a soft drink company fails to make as many units of beverage as had been forecast, then days of inventory of sugar may grow too large and new orders will not be placed. For toys, books, VCR tapes, and autos, excessive days of inventory are costly.

12-4d Additional Turnover Examples

A manager of Limited Brands, Inc., said that LTD would like to achieve better than 100 turns per year in its warehouses. So would all of LTD's competitors. Wal-Mart targets as

Days of inventory (DOI)
Total stock on-hand divided by the average demand per day gives a measure of how long it will be before the stockroom and warehouse are empty.

Turnover
Turns are measured by annual net sales divided by total average stock on-hand.

Inventory turns
See **Turnover**.

SKU

Stock-keeping units where the SKU catalog numbers represent every different part carried, sold, or purchased by the company.

many turns as it can get, and it actually does better than eight, which means it sells every item on its shelves eight times a year. Thomasville, a furniture company, has taken the traditional two to four inventory turns for suites of furniture into ten or better per year.

Price can be a crucial factor. When an item does not move at Victoria's Secret, LTD drops its price. The item is put onto a bargain table. LTD does not sell on a **SKU** basis so turnover is hard to measure for a specific item. Rather, the DOI of an item is the measure of performance.

Good turnover brings large rewards and a reputation for purchasing success. On the other hand, there are great risks of failure. Poor measures mark the marginal competitor. Buyers and purchasing agents have to accept the risk of making errors such as overestimating demand or paying too high a price. Penalties of being wrong are high.

12-4e Purchasing Agents (PAs)

Purchasing records provide a history of what has been done in the past. Documenting history is useful, including what the costs were, who the major suppliers were, what discounts were obtained, what quality levels achieved, and delivery periods for specific items. Without documentation, the supplier history of a company can be lost.

The skills and experience of purchasing agents are not readily transferable between different industries. They may vary between companies even in the same industry. Differentiation exists by types of materials, buying and shipping terms, and supplier purchasing traditions.

It is not possible to discuss all of the intricate relationships that have been developed by buyers and suppliers in order to achieve maximum satisfaction for both parties. A number of important procedures are covered, but new ones are being developed all of the time that take advantage of changes in the information, storage, and transportation technologies.

The purchasing function is responsible for bringing the exact materials that production needs before they are needed, or just in time. Purchasing interfaces P/OM and its suppliers. P/OM may have some decisive requirements and some exceptional information for suppliers. It is not surprising, then, that this part of the supply chain is tightly coordinated with P/OM. Whatever the organization's structure, purchasing must be strongly linked to the P/OM team.

When the purchasing process is technical, the purchasing agent may be an engineer or a person who has worked with the production department. Purchasing is usually responsible for the following functions, which might be called the *purchasing mission*:

1 Ordering what is needed in the right quantities and then meeting all quality standards at the best possible prices—always achieving delivery reliability. This mission must be coordinated with P/OM and marketing with respect to what is going to be needed when. Purchasing must be assisted by P/OM in predicting the amount of scrap. By increasing order sizes to compensate, costly reorders can be avoided for a small number of units needed to complete orders.

2 Receiving inventories is part of the materials management function. Often, but not always, "receiving" is the responsibility of purchasing. Some organization must determine that deliveries are on time and that P/OM will have what it needs as it schedules production runs. Will it be just in time, or will extra stock be carried just in case? These decisions require communication and coordination between POM and the PAs.

3 Inspecting the incoming goods to make sure that their qualities meet specifications and that the right quantities have been delivered.

4 Purchasing is a specialist in knowing which suppliers to use. Sometimes, the PAs are in charge of certification of suppliers. See Enrichment Activity 12. Keep in touch with change. That is essential.

5 Purchasing is the materials management function to consult when engineering design changes (EDCs) occur that demand changes in the specifications of purchased materials. What happens to the stock on-hand that is outmoded? How fast can the new specifications be made and shipped? If the company is constantly changing designs (which many are doing) then knowing which suppliers can cope with shifting demands is crucial.

6 Stability of supply relationships can have inestimable value.

7 Purchasing must be adept at coordinating the materials that are needed for start-ups. The management dynamics that are associated with start-ups are entirely different from those that operate successfully for mature products.

Coordinating the goals of materials management with those of process management is one of P/OM's greatest responsibilities. Scenarios applicable to Functions 1 and 4 are common where a variety of suppliers are dealt with, and about one out of ten has serious failures. Consequently, there is regular shifting of suppliers over time, requiring P/OM adjustments.

A scenario applicable to Function 2 has the receiving dock forgetting to log in a shipment, which results in a "false" crisis when that item seems to have run out of stock. In some instances, the mistake is not traced and even though there is the necessary stock on-hand, it is lost in the warehouse.

The following story for Function 3 occurs repeatedly. Inspectors fail to check all of the quality standards and put defective received goods into inventory. The production line may be forced to shut down.

The situation that is involved with Function 5 is extremely serious in companies where technological change is moving at a rapid rate. Product malfunctions in the field lead to parts being redesigned and EDCs being issued, sometimes in bunches, in the hope that the problems will be corrected. Even with mature aircraft such as the Boeing 737, design changes in the reverse thruster were called for after it had been flying for many years.

© 2007 Jupiterimages Corporation

There is a *cultural difference* in the importance of legal contracts in the United States as compared to many other countries. For example, on a per capita basis, Japan has about 6 percent of the lawyers that practice in the United States. The Chinese do not value legal contracts in the same way that the United States does. These differences have significant impact on the way P/OM proceeds in other countries.

12-4f The Ethics of Purchasing

Purchasing agents make buying decisions that involve enormous amounts of money. As labor costs contract and material costs increase, the value of the job to buy materials becomes higher paid. The fact that suppliers influence purchasing decisions through gifts is not considered illegal or unethical in some places in the world. This disparity is an ethical conundrum. In the United States, it is neither ethical nor legal to bribe purchasing agents. The fact that it is okay elsewhere poses irreconcilable problems until all parties sit down at the same table to discuss the quandaries and their solutions (e.g., bidding).

The following section on bidding mentions the way in which companies use bids to provide the appearance of purchasing decisions that are not influenced by gifts of any kind. The only sure way to avoid problems is to make certain that purchasing agents are trustworthy and moral. It is understandable that purchasing agents achieve special arrangements with suppliers that they trust. After years of dealing with a supplier, a friendly relationship can develop that is an entirely ethical alliance. Both buyer and supplier value the long-term stability and goodwill of their relationship.

In the business environment of the United States, personal relationships are not considered to be a reasonable basis for enterprise decisions. They exist nevertheless in less blatant form than in other cultures. For example, in Latin America and the Middle East, personal friendships are held to be business assets that reduce risk and have monetary value. Part of this cultural difference can be traced to the importance placed upon legal contracts in the United States that does not exist elsewhere. With the growth of global business, cultural and legal factors can play major roles in determining P/OM's success in handling the affairs of subsidiaries outside the United States.[2]

12-5 Receiving, Inspection, and Storage

An important part of the materials management job is receiving shipments from suppliers. There is a need for a (receiving) unloading facility designed to take the supplies out of the shippers' conveyance. After unloading the supplies, there is usually a storage area to put them. The design of this facility differs depending upon what is to be unloaded (type of supplies), what the supplies are unloaded from (trucks, freight cars, hopper cars, ships, planes, etc.), and where they are to be unloaded.

The receiving facility is often called the *receiving dock*, and there is another location for shipping called a *shipping dock*. In many instances, these are the same place. In some instances, in the morning they are receiving docks and in the afternoon they are shipping docks.

Cross-docking

Transfer goods from incoming trucks at receiving docks to outgoing trucks at shipping docks. The docks are adjacent.

More often, they are completely separate facilities. Wal-Mart uses **cross-docking** to transfer goods from incoming trucks at the receiving dock to outgoing trucks at the shipping docks. This means that a large percentage of goods never enters the warehouse but crosses from one dock to the other. Such cross-docking has been credited with saving substantial amounts of money and time. It is often cited as an example of how P/OM's creativity improved the logistics of distribution operations.

It is not unusual for the freight cars or hopper cars to be used as storage facilities with materials being unloaded as needed. Instead of moving chemicals and plastics from the hopper car to the warehouse, the factory draws directly on the reserves in the hopper cars. The DuPont Corporation has successfully cut down on the number of hopper cars with inventory that are sitting around on sidings by coordinating customers' needs with shipping schedules.

Supplies must be inspected to control the quality and quantity of what was ordered. Is the shipment exactly correct and has it been received undamaged? Specific quality checks are made using acceptance sampling methods (see Chapter 7). Accepted materials are moved to storage facilities—often the company warehouse. Many materials deteriorate and must be monitored for age. Accordingly, order size must be adjusted for usage rates and time elapsed since receipt and storage.

12-6 Requiring Bids Before Purchase

Bidding

Buyer requests competitors to specify price and terms for their product.

Bidding is a process by which the buyer requests competing companies to specify how much they will charge for their product. Competitive bids can involve more than price. Sometimes, purchasing requests suppliers to submit competitive bids for both cost and delivery time.

In some industries and government systems, purchasing is required to use the bidding process. There are always two points of view with respect to bidding—the buyer's and the seller's. Materials management has the buyer's point of view of bidding, which is lowest costs, consistent quality, fastest delivery, vendor reliability, etc.

With discretionary bidding, purchasing agents might decide to use it to prevent charges of favoritism. It controls expenditures when there can be significant variation in supplier charges. Bid requests state specifically all of the conditions that must be met and ask for details of what the supplier intends, including prices, delivery dates, quality specifications, checks, and assurances.

Bidding can be a costly process for the materials management buyer. This is especially the case when there are many criteria upon which competing suppliers will be rated. Cost also rises when there are many firms that are bidders. On the other hand, for bidding to work, there must be at least two suppliers willing to bid for the job.

Bidding by government agencies is usually standardized. The IRS reviewed bids for updating its computer systems. The armed services utilize bids for military acquisitions. Bids are familiar in situations where industrial firms have no prior supplier arrangements and in which costly purchases (including engineering and construction jobs) are to be made. The federal government usually awards contracts to the lowest bidder subject to a set of external standards. Qualitative concerns that are taken into account by private industry are seldom permitted with government awards.

Bids can be requested where the price is fixed and the creativity and quality of the solution is at stake. Advertising agencies bid for accounts that have a set budget. Alternative bids are based on campaign creativity. The same applies to a P/OM request for proposals from a consulting organization where the budget allocation is fixed. Competing bids for a computerized materials management system are common.

With so much bidding action, it is not surprising that bidding (decision) models have been developed. Experienced e-Bay bidders use decision model software to guide them. Models can assist both the buyer who makes the requests for proposals (RFPs) and the sellers who offer the bids. Bidding models show that as the number of bidders competing increases, the size of the winning bid decreases. With more bidders, variability increases and so does competition.

Perhaps this is a good reason for the buyer to include many bidders. On the other hand, each extra bid adds to the ordering costs. There also is the fear that a low bid will be made by an organization that is less likely to produce quality work. Steps must be taken to ensure that quality is not compromised by price. Also, too many bidders may drive the expected profit so low that qualified suppliers refuse to join the bidding, leaving the field open to the less qualified.

A company may not choose to buy from the organization presenting the lowest bid. Price is almost never the only factor that needs to be taken into consideration when awarding a contract. Among other things, it is essential to consider quality and guarantees of quality, the experience of the supplier, the uncertainties of delivery, and the kind of long-term, supplier–producer relationship that is likely to develop. Certification may be required before a supplier is allowed to participate in a bidding contest.

Bidding is applicable for project procurement policies and for start-up purchase arrangements for the flow shop. It is less relevant for the job shop, although it may make sense when costly components and/or big batches are involved. Bidding is a useful protection when there is suspicion that special purchasing deals are being made between suppliers and company personnel.

12-7 Materials Management of Critical Parts

For projects and the flow shop, certain parts can fail that will shut down the line or seriously delay project completion. These are called *critical parts*. An entire refinery can be shut down. The cost of lost production may well run into millions of dollars.

How many spares of the various parts that are judged to be critical parts should be kept in stock? How likely is it that a spare part kept in stock for an emergency will ever be used? Often, severe technical problems are involved in purchasing critical parts for the maintenance function of complex technological systems.

This is a problem for the materials management–P/OM team that is familiar with the specific production equipment. It is able to evaluate the failure characteristics of the technology. Policies for stocking spare critical parts also are a function of the type of maintenance that is used. If preventive maintenance calls for replacing critical parts once every year, then that decision establishes the base requirements for stocking the part. When reliability is important, a technical basis must be used for purchasing spare parts.

For an important class of maintenance inventories, spare critical parts can be obtained inexpensively only at the installation of the start-up. If it turns out, later on, that an insufficient supply of these critical parts was acquired, the cost of obtaining additional spares can be much higher.

Failure models can be constructed to indicate how many spare parts should be obtained at start up. It is best to illustrate with a small specific case. Start with an accurate estimate from engineering data. Assume that failure data indicate that a particular critical part has a probability of i failures (p_i) over the lifetime of a flexible device called the *complex machine*.

There is a cost c for each spare part purchased at the time that the complex machine is acquired. When a spare part must be purchased at a later time, due to an insufficient supply purchased at the start-up, the cost is estimated to be c'.

c' can be much larger than c because it includes the cost of doing whatever has to be done to fill the production void caused by failure of the part. Thus, c' might reflect the cost of subcontracting work while the complex machine is out-of-order. There also is a large cost per replacement part charged by the OEM (original equipment manufacturer). As previously noted, it is common for OEMs to charge high prices for replacement spare parts not acquired at start up. Often, this is because a special setup is required.

Replacement part manufacturing may use different work configurations than the OEM used originally. Seldom can complex replacement parts be made economically.

12-7a How Many Spare Parts to Order

For the complex machine, the probability of i failures is (p_i).

Let $p_i \geq 0$ for $i = 0, 1, 2, 3$. If $p_0 = 0$, then there must be at least 1 failure and no more than 3 failures over the lifetime of the machine. If p_0 is large, then there may be no need to order spare parts at start up. The model must indicate how many spares to order.

The total probability of failure must sum to one; for the example, probabilities are distributed as follows:

$$i = 0 \text{ failure}; \quad p_0 = 0.00$$
$$i = 1 \text{ failure}; \quad p_1 = 0.50$$
$$i = 2 \text{ failures}; \quad p_2 = 0.33$$
$$i = 3 \text{ failures}; \quad p_3 = 0.17$$
$$\text{SUM} \qquad\quad 1.00$$

Let $c = \$5$ and $c' = \$400$. The question is: How many spare parts (k) should be ordered at the time of the original purchase? The spare part is only $5 if purchased initially. However, later replacement of the failed part costs 80 times the original price because of large setup costs and lost production time. The decision matrix for spare-part strategies is given in Table 12-2.

The steps required to obtain the expected values in Table 12-2 are as follows. The outcome entries in the matrix are computed by two different relationships. First, when the number of failures is equal to or is less than the number of parts originally ordered with the machine, then the cost is simply kc.

Table 12-2	Number of Failures i Occurring During Machine's Lifetime (column)	0	1	2	3	
Failure Cost Matrix for the Complex Machine	p_i	0	1/2	1/3	1/6	Expected Cost
	k					
	$k = 0$	0	400	800	1,200	$666.67
	$k = 1$	5	5	5 + 400	5 + 800	$271.67
	$k = 2$	10	10	10	10 + 400	$76.67
	$k = 3$	15	15	15	15	$15.00 MIN

Note: The initial number of spares = k; c is the cost/unit as originally purchased; c' is cost of replacement.

Second, when the number of failures is greater than the number of parts originally ordered, the cost is

$$kc + (i - k)c'$$

If 3 failures occur ($i = 3$) and only two parts were originally ordered ($k = 2$), then the cost is \$410, calculated as follows: $(2 \times 5) + (3 - 2)\,400 = 410$.

The minimum expected cost is obtained by ordering 3 spares—a result that could have been anticipated by the size of the numbers for c and c'. At least one failure will occur in line with the probability distribution given in the table. As is shown in the Problems Section (4, 5, 6 and 7), the result would differ if a substantial probability for zero failures exists.

After the matrix of total costs is completed, the expected values are obtained in the usual fashion:

Expected cost for $k = 0$: $400(1/2) + 800(1/3) + 1,200(1/6) = 666.67$
Expected cost for $k = 1$: $5(1/2) + 405(1/3) + 805(1/6) = 271.67$
Expected cost for $k = 2$: $10(1/2) + 10(1/3) + 410(1/6) = 76.67$
Expected cost for $k = 3$: $15(1/2) + 15(1/3) + 15(1/6) = 15.00$

For realism, assume that all numbers are in thousands. Having the lowest expected cost of \$15,000, three spares should be ordered with the complex machine. This is \$61,670 cheaper than ordering two, and more than a quarter of a million dollars cheaper than ordering only one spare part with the complex machine.

When the three parts arrive with the machine, they should be inspected carefully to make certain that they are properly made according to specifications. They must be able to do the job, if and when they are called upon.

The problem could be complicated and made more realistic by adding a charge for carrying a part in stock, changing the probabilities of failure after a failure occurs, allowing more than one spare to be reordered after failure, etc. All such issues, and others as well, can be treated in a more realistic albeit more complicated model.

The key, however, is to note the high cost of having three failures and not being prepared for that eventuality. This mistake pits a \$10,000 expenditure for two extra spares as insurance against having to pay more than a quarter of a million dollars to correct the problem. Different numbers would have other conclusions.

12-7b The Static Inventory Problem

This decision-matrix model effectively represents the **static inventory problem**. In materials management terms, the static case is deciding how much to buy *when only a one-time purchase* is allowed. The model is not representative of flow shop problems but it is fully applicable to the job shop and project manager. Variability of demand (in this case, the spare parts failure distribution) is only one way in which uncertainty about the order size can arise. Other causes are defectives (requiring additional parts to be made to fill the order), spoilage, and pilferage. All such factors can be accounted for with probability estimates and the decision-matrix methodology.

Static inventory problem
Classical inventory problem with some special characteristics, namely, how much to buy when there is only one purchase occasion allowed.

12-8 Value Analysis (Alternative Materials Analysis)

Value analysis has been a part of materials management for 55 years.[3] The idea behind **value analysis (VA)** is that

> **1** Materials are always being *improved* because of constant technological developments.

Value analysis (VA)
Search for alternative materials as replacements for the current ones with quality gains and cost advantages.

2   Unless a watch is kept on the relevance of materials, *opportunities to shift to new materials* that will improve the company's products will be missed.

3   Efforts should be made continuously to improve the material qualities of the product and to decrease product costs through *materials innovations.*

Value analysis is applied to all materials used by the process and for the product. VA works for materials in supply chains of all domains and industries including hospitals, hotels, restaurants, offices, manufacturers, and airlines. Airlines save every day by using electronic vouchers in place of paper tickets. This idea took many years to be accepted.

12-8a Methods Analysis (and Value Engineering)

Methods analysis

Systematic examination of all operations in every process. The objective is to search for better ways to do the jobs that the company requires.

Value analysis and **methods analysis** (MA) are often seen as close relatives. In fact, value engineering (VE) is part of the VA development which coincides with (MA) Methods analysis is the systematic examination of all operations in any process in search of a better way of doing things. It encourages alternative processing by combining operations, eliminating unnecessary steps, and making work easier. Method analysts are widely employed to help P/OM work smarter and not harder.

To distinguish value analysis from methods analysis, the latter is primarily concerned with process improvement and secondarily with materials. Specifically, value analysis is the "analysis of the value of alternative materials." Inevitably, value and methods analyses must share common ground. Starting with different perspectives, they converge on the same kind of situations, providing similar kinds of problem resolution.

Growth of interest in value analysis increases whenever new knowledge about materials technology arises (e.g., nanotechnology). Dramatic waves of change occur from time to time in metals, plastics (extended-chain aromatic polyamides—Spotlight 12-1), ceramics, solar panels, and glass.

On a related front, materials shortages raise interest in value analysis aspects of materials management. The petroleum shortage of the 1970s and the steeply rising prices in 2007 have led to major P/OM responses including alternate fuels (e.g., ethanol), and changes in products (hybrid cars). Companies were faced with the need to make swift alterations in the composition of their products. Goods and services were affected. Other commodity shortages that occurred during the last 30 years include yellow fats, paper products, lumber, copper, citrus, chocolate, and water.

Material shortages hit particularly hard at the flow shop, which is least flexible in adapting to changes in materials. Increasing numbers of organizations try to prepare for shortage situations by doing contingency planning. Often, this includes R&D efforts to prepare alternative formulations.

In addition to shortages, government agencies prohibit the use of well-established materials. The food industry has experienced bans on saccharine, cyclamates, food dyes, preservatives, and many other items. The detergent industry has reformulated its products at various times because of ecological effects of phosphorous and enzyme additives. Government regulation of plant and auto emissions are other examples. Such government restrictions will continue to grow in number and severity.

If proper value analysis of alternative materials has been done, then materials alternatives do not have to be hastily sought when shortages occur or when government edicts forbid the use of specific materials and/or change the way that they can be used. The procedures for value analysis should be applied to established products during their mature life cycle stages, and to new products during their early growth life cycle stages.

Successful value analysis requires a well-structured approach. This is reflected by the consistent application of a set of relevant questions. For example:

How do materials affect what this product or service is intended to do?

How do materials affect the cost of this product or service?

3 Have there been prior changes in the materials used?

4 What other materials could be used?

5 How do alternative materials affect Questions 1 and 2?

The value analysis approach has been designed to increase insights by providing a structural framework to encourage the development of alternative materials management strategies. The starting point is the methods analysis of existing outputs and processes.

Often, the most important materials in the product and process are labeled *primary classes*; others are called *secondary classes*. Major efforts are placed on primary classes, which are then related by analogy to other products, processes, and materials that have similar properties.

Both methods analysis and value analysis are used to discover new tactical, efficient alternatives. However, P/OM must be on guard against investments in efficiency studies before effectiveness issues have been thoroughly considered. Spotlight 11-2 warns "Don't Separate Strategy and Tactics."

12-9 ABC Classification—The Systems Context

Materials management—from the inception of the purchasing process all the way through production and the shipping of finished goods—can be improved by utilizing a powerful systems concept called the **ABC classification**. This concept alerts everyone: Some materials are more important than others—it is prudent to do what is important before doing what is less important. This concept applies to P/OM in a number of different ways. Two are discussed here.

12-9a Material Criticality

It is necessary for materials management to categorize the critical nature of parts, components, and other materials. There are various definitions of "critical" that fit different situations. When a part failure causes product or process failure, it is a critical part. Many parts of an airline engine may be critical, in this sense.

The following scenario is relevant. This airline considers parts to be most critical that have greater than a 10 percent probability of failing within one year. Membership in this top-ranking group is called *A-critical*. Perhaps the top 25 percent of all critical parts can be classified as being A-critical.

A second set, called *B-critical*, is identified by the airline as any part that has greater than a 10 percent probability of failing within five years. A-critical items are excluded. Perhaps the next 25 percent of all critical parts can be considered to be B-critical.

The third set, called *C-critical*, might be associated with greater than 10 percent probabilities of failing after five years. Because 50 percent of the parts are in the A and B groups, the remaining 50 percent of the parts are in the C group. The numbers can be adjusted so that A, B, and C are 25, 25, and 50 percent of the total number of parts.

As an alternative definition, part failure can have a probability (not a certainty) of stopping the process or product. Thus, a possible description of critical parts relates to the probability of total process or product failure when the part fails.

The parts are rank ordered by the probability of causing process or product failure. Say that if the first part fails there is a 30 percent probability of product failure. The next part might have a 20 percent probability.

Perhaps the top 25 percent of critical parts has an 80 percent probability of causing (each independently) product failure. This kind of situation is pictured in Figure 12-2.

Some processes do not fail as a result of part failure but instead the production output is reduced by a significant amount. Curves similar to Figure 12-2 can be created for such situations.

ABC classification
Inventory items in rank order by dollar volume. Generally, 25 percent of *all* items (SKU) contribute 75 percent of *total* dollar volume.

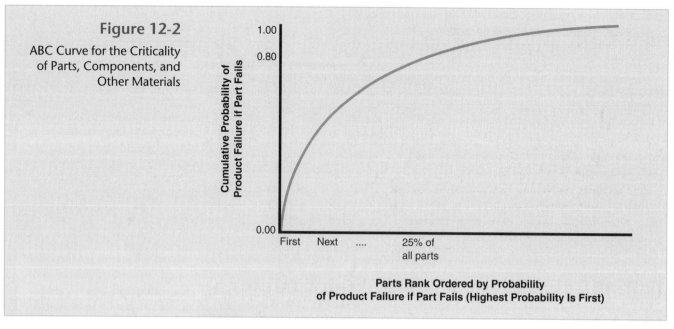

Figure 12-2

ABC Curve for the Criticality of Parts, Components, and Other Materials

Criticality

When part behavior causes process or product failure or a marked degradation in performance.

Criticality is a coined term that can mean *crucial to performance* or *dangerous to use*. Thus, an alternative definition of criticality could apply to the danger involved in using materials. Flammability, explosiveness, and toxicity of fumes are crucial safety factors for materials management.

Whichever definition of criticality is used, the procedure is to list first the most critical parts. Next, systematically rank-order parts according to their relative criticality. The concept of criticality should reflect the costs of failures, including safety dangers, loss of life, and losses in production output.

Spare parts and other backup materials should be provided to conform to remedial failure strategies. Also to be considered are replacement parts for preventive failure strategies. Further, spare parts must be inspected to ensure their continued integrity over time.

A large South American refinery decided to double its rubber spare parts inventory. Within two years, many of the parts had begun to deteriorate and could not be called upon to replace critical failed parts. The high penalty resulted in a return to the original policy. Organizations have found that poor spare parts policies can be an "Achilles' heel."

12-9b Annual Dollar Volume of Materials

More widely used is a second set of ABC categories based on sorting materials by their annual dollar volume. Dollar volume is the surrogate for potential savings that can be made by improving the inventory management of specific materials. Accordingly, all parts, components, and other materials used by a company should be listed and then rank ordered by their annual dollar volume. Thus:

$$DV_i(t = 1 \text{ year}) = c_i \sum_{t=0}^{t=1} q_i(t) \qquad (12\text{-}1)$$

where:

$DV_i =$ the annual dollar volume of the ith item for $t =$ year 1,

$c_i =$ the dollar cost per unit of i and $q_i(t)$ is the annual quantity of i ordered and used.

$$\sum_{t=0}^{t=1} q_i(t) = \text{ the number of units of the } i\text{th item ordered per year}$$

Start with those items that have the highest levels of dollar volume DV_i and rank order them from the highest to the lowest levels. The top 25 percent of these materials are called *A-type items*. The next 25 percent are called *B-type items*. The bottom 50 percent are called *C-type items*.

The ABC method requires individual study of each A-item in depth to improve its performance. Details include how much to order at one time, which determines how often to order; who to order from; what quality standards to set; delivery lead times; the consistency of lead times; as well as all special agreements with suppliers.

B-type items are studied in groups and with less attention to detail. Policies for C-type items are set to be as simple as possible to administer.

C-type items have low-dollar volume, which means that they have low price per unit or they may have low volume, or both. Most are C-type because of the low price. Small penalties are paid for overstocking such items so they do not have to be ordered as often. Still, it may turn out that a C-type item can lead to a critical situation. e.g., the CEO's bathroom runs out of toilet paper. TP is a typical C-type item.

If materials managers do not use this ABC systems approach, which sorts all materials into those that have more potential savings than others, then a major strategic capability for systematic and continuous improvement is being overlooked.

Companies differ with respect to what percent of all items stocked account for 75 percent of their total annual dollar volume. Usually, a small percentage of all items (such as 25 percent) accounts for a very large percentage of total annual dollar volume (such as 75 percent) as shown in Figure 12-3. The A-type items are labeled on Figure 12-3.

Figure 12-3 portrays a typical case where 20 to 30 percent of all items carried account for as much as 70 to 80 percent of the company's total dollar volume. Consider the hotel chain that stocks 1,000 different items for which the hotel spends $1 million annually. Twenty-five percent of these items cost $750,000 and constitute the A-class of inventory items.

That is, 250 items control 75 percent of the annual dollar volume and, conversely, 750 items control only 25 percent of the annual dollar volume. It is extremely unusual for the ABC curve to look like the one drawn in Figure 12-4. There, the percent of items always equals the percent of dollar volume. Rank order means nothing because all items are the same. Why is such a situation unlikely? It is because preference is not equally distributed among choices. Many people choose to live in cities so the population is not randomly distributed across all square miles. A small percentage of dogs (big ones) eat most of the dog food.

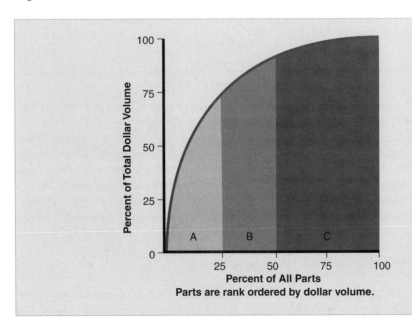

Figure 12-3

ABC Curve for Annual Dollar Volume of All Items Stocked

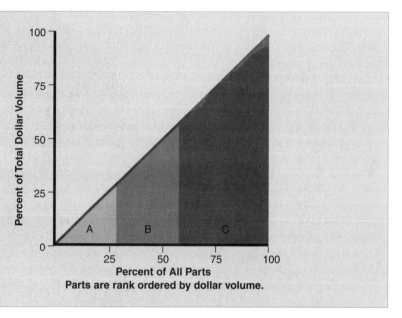

Figure 12-4

Straight Line ABC Curve with Equal Increments

Parts are rank ordered by dollar volume.

Consider the likely inventory of name tags at an airport kiosk. Some names are very popular and others are rare. Those favored one year are not found the next year. The following information is from the Social Security study of first names. In 2006, Emily was the most popular girl's name. Jessica was ranked 32nd. In 1990, Jessica was the most popular girl's name, and Michael was the first choice for a boy's name. In 2006, Jacob was the first choice for a boy, and Michael was second choice. Emily was not even on the list of the first 10 girls' names for 1990. In the United Kingdom, for 2006 Olivia knocked Jessica out of the number one spot, and Emily declined to fifth place. Jack, Thomas, and Joshua are in the top three. For the first time, Harry moved into fifth place.

The ABC curves of popular names for both boys and girls are highly skewed like Figure 12-3 and not like Figure 12-4. The items forming the A, B, and C classes are constantly changing. For further information, see the Social Security Administration webpage at http://www.ssa.gov/OACT/babynames.

Because the costs of inventory studies tend to be proportional to the number of items under consideration, MM always chooses to study and update A-class items. What is to be included in A-type classes will depend on β in the following equation:

$$y = x^{\beta}(1 \geq x \geq 0), (1 \geq \beta \geq 0)$$

y = percent of dollar volume

x = rank-ordered percent of all parts

Beta is 1 in Figure 12-4. Beta is less than one-half in Figure 12-3. The Problems Section (12-9 and 12-10) suggests that a curve be drawn for $\beta = 0.5$.

There is no fixed convention that A-, B-, and C-class breaks must occur at 25 and 50 percent. Some companies use only A and B classes. It is historically interesting that Del Harder of the Ford Motor Company is said to have developed the ABC concept in the 1940s. Still, almost 70 years later, it is not well-known among those who have not studied P/OM that inventories of materials conform to a curve that reflects disproportionately large effects (of criticality and dollar demand) derived from a small percent of all items in the supply chain.

Certification of suppliers
Process of grading (pass–fail) suppliers to assure conformance to standards set as necessary by P/OM. Grading can also be by ranked order.

12-10 Certification of Suppliers

Certification of Suppliers is a process for grading suppliers to ensure that suppliers' organizations conform to standards that are essential for meeting the buyer's needs. It is expensive and time-consuming to keep up-to-date. The certification process should be reserved for suppliers of A-type items with respect to both criticality and dollar volume.

In addition to establishing minimum standards that every supplier must meet, certification is like a bidding process for long-term relationships. Companies use the certification process to choose the best in the class—just like they use various criteria to hire students based on grades, dean's list, and personal evaluations. Most often, the requirements for suppliers are equivalent to the company's internal standards for itself with respect to excellence in quality and reliability.

The number of suppliers chosen can vary from one to several. Often, supplier organizations that do not make the grade are encouraged to improve. Many companies help potential suppliers upgrade those capabilities on which they are rated as deficient. Accepted suppliers are regularly reviewed to make certain that they maintain their "winning" status. Thus, although certification aims at long-term relationships, it is subject to reassessment. Often, smart buyers raise acceptance standards while assisting certified suppliers to meet the new and more stringent standards.

The rating procedures include formal evaluations of price, quality, delivery time, and the ability to improve all three, and more. Suppliers' productivity improvement programs are expected to result in lower prices. Suppliers' total quality management (TQM) programs are monitored for expected improvements. ISO 9000 standards and the Baldrige Award criteria provide the foundation. Lead-time management programs track delivery time reduction. Time-based management concepts form added bases for evaluation.

The buyer's materials management information system (MMIS) has to be able to handle many suppliers and potential suppliers for hundreds and even thousands of A-type items. Who does this successfully? The list is impressive. Chrysler, Dell, Ford, General Motors, Hewlett-Packard, Honda, IBM, Motorola, Texas Instruments, Toshiba, Toyota, and UPS are only a few of the companies that have made public their use of certification programs. Certification procedures blossom with the use of the systems approach (see Enrichment Activity 12).

Spotlight 12-1 Stephanie Louise Kwolek—Inventing Kevlar
Breakthrough Discovery—Inventing Kevlar

Photo courtesy of DuPont.

When Stephanie Louise Kwolek was a little girl, she wanted to be a fashion designer. She did not know at the time that she would ultimately create body armor that would save the lives of more than 3,000 police officers. Her father was an amateur naturalist and encouraged her scientific curiosity. Later, after her father died when she was 10, she decided to become a doctor. Pursuing that plan, she studied chemistry at Pittsburgh's Carnegie Institute of Technology, now known as Carnegie-Mellon University.

When Stephanie received her Bachelor of Science degree, she accepted a research job with DuPont until she could pursue her dream of medical school. She soon discovered that she liked the work so much, with its continuing challenges and academic environment, that she decided not to leave. In 1946, she was one of a few women working in chemical research. DuPont had already commercialized nylon successfully. Dacron polyester and Lycra Spandex were in the pipeline. DuPont was eager to develop next-generation high-performance fibers.

In 1964, Ms. Kwolek made an astounding breakthrough, discovering that molecules of extended-chain aromatic polyamides would form liquid-crystalline solutions. These solutions could be spun into highly orientated, very strong, and very stiff fibers. Dupont called this new material Kevlar, well-known for its use in bulletproof vests. It is also employed in more than 200 other end-use applications, including fiber

Spotlight 12-1 (Continued)

optic cable, radial tires, brake pads (a replacement for asbestos), skis, safety helmets, mooring and bridge cables and air-water-spacecraft outer shells. Many kitchens are equipped with hot surface handlers called "Ove" Gloves™.

Kwolek has earned 28 patents in her 40-year tenure as a research scientist and received highest honors in her field. She was inducted into the National Inventors Hall of Fame in 1995 and received the National Medal of Technology in 1996. In 1997 she was presented with the Perkin Medal from the American Section of the Society of Chemical Industry. The later two awards are rarely awarded to women. She has publicly supported and encouraged young people to believe in themselves and not to fear thinking differently. She believes that the creative process can be taught to a certain extent by exposing young people to books about creative people and by meeting and talking with creative people.

Today Stephanie Kwolek sees many people entering into research with the objective of quickly getting into management after acquiring some experience. This leaves little opportunity to make discoveries, particularly ones that open a new field. Such discoveries generally take more fundamental thinking and work than just making a modification to an existing product. New foundations have to be constructed from fresh observations.

Kwolek would like to see corporations place greater emphasis on long-term research. She does not see how people can be creative if they are constantly distracted. There must be time to read, think, and keep up with the literature. In her complex field of fiber research, she was given the freedom to amass a tremendous amount of knowledge that she used in making her discoveries. Without such a knowledge base, Kwolek thinks that it would be difficult for people to make breakthrough discoveries.

Even with a deep knowledge of fiber technology, Stephanie Kwolek had to use all her intuition, perseverance, and hard work to achieve her breakthrough. The moment of discovery was exciting because it was so unexpected. She had been assigned to look for the next-generation high-performance fiber. Kwolek started working with the more intractable para-orientated aromatic polyamides, which are made up of rod-like molecules, unlike the very flexible molecules in nylon. Not only did she have to make the polymers but she also had to find a solvent for them. She finally succeeded in finding a solvent, but the solutions turned out to be unlike anything she had previously seen in the laboratory. They were cloudy, opalescent upon being stirred, and of low viscosity, making them seem like poor candidates for successful new fibers. Normally, these questionable solutions would be discarded.

To get a fiber, a polymer solution must be forced through the very tiny holes of a spinneret. The person in charge of the spinning unit refused to spin Kwolek's cloudy, low-viscosity liquid-crystalline solution. He said it would plug up the holes of his spinneret and, furthermore, it had the viscosity of water, unlike regular polymer solutions. He believed the solution was cloudy because of particulate matter. After much discussion, he did spin it, and it spun with no problems. The first sign that Kwolek really had something unusual occurred as she stood by the spinning equipment and tried to break some of the newly spun fibers. Unlike nylon, this fiber was very difficult to break by hand. At that moment, Stephanie Kwolek knew she had found an extraordinary fiber. Her discovery created an entirely different field of polymer chemistry. Dupont immediately went to work on aspects of a product that is more than five times stronger than the same weight of steel.

This story of successful breakthrough discovery highlights why serious research scientists contend that it is a management responsibility to find ways to provide incentives for people to stay in research long enough to build a body of knowledge and experience for long-term research results.

Stephanie Kwolek retired in 1986, showing the world that science is not practiced by gender. It is a human enterprise, open to all. In 2007, Stephanie Kwolek is an 84-year-old hero who is honored now and then by visiting police officers who tell her she saved their lives. She spends her time actively promoting science and science education.

Review Questions

1 What did Stephanie Louise Kwolek do that is so remarkable?

2 Who uses Kevlar, and what is unique about it?

3 Ms. Kwolek believes that research results are slowed down and impaired because many who enter research have the objective of getting into management as soon as possible. Is this likely to become a widespread problem? If so, what can be done about fixing the problem?

4 How are breakthrough discoveries different from incremental steps of invention? Who was it that said "Eureka!" to signal an unexpected breakthrough?

5 Knowledge management is crucial to breakthrough discovery. Why is this so, and what can be done to enhance support for knowledge management?

Sources: "Hall of Fame Interview: Stephanie Kwolek," by Jim Quinn, *American Heritage of Invention & Technology*, Winter 2003, Volume 18, Number 3; http://www.chemheritage.org/EducationalServices/FACES/poly/readings/slk2.htm; http://www.usatoday.com/news/nation/2007-07-04-kevlar-inventor_N.htm; http://www.chemheritage.org/classroom/chemach/plastics/kwolek.html.

Spotlight 12-2 The Demand for Business Intelligence

An algorithm is a procedure for solving problems in a finite number of steps. Computer programs use algorithmic procedures with fast, accurate, and effortless efficiency. Because of advances in mathematics, we are enabling computers to imitate human behavior and in some cases replace it.

This is a story about the possibility of crossing the subtlety of human intellect with a processor's power. It is about how humans (smart, slow, and prone to error) are giving up some of their control in order to let machines (obedient, fast, and accurate) replace traditional business systems with on-demand data and retrieval systems that provide security while integrating, connecting, and analyzing all stages of a company's business plan. A system of autonomic business intelligence (BI) is analogous to a complex nervous system responding to internal stimuli. Utilizing such a system in a business environment can directly and positively affect a company's bottom line. The vocabulary of BI systems can be confusing. Web services, grid computing, service-oriented architecture (SOA), and virtualization are some of the terms developers use to describe their technologies. Different methods connect off-line data from local PCs to online connections, where proprietary operating systems and applications cease to be a problem. By connecting to an online integrated network, data can be accessed, analyzed, stored, and moved quickly and easily from server to computer to end-user and back.

By automating an entire company's disparate operations into one well-managed BI system, it is possible, for example, to analyze contracts with suppliers and negotiate better ones, see which regional offices are underperforming, and explain what factors caused sales to be *X* one day and *Y* on the same date the previous year. Instead of considering price alone, computers can weigh the relative merits of hundreds of variables. With software that can accurately negotiate deals digitally, BI systems can make use of an array of factors that people would not have considered, enabling satisfactory and fairly-achieved agreements between a company and its supply and demand chains. Today computers are in communication with each other all over the world.

Finding a reliable system that integrates all variables quickly and easily, and uses the enormous capabilities of the web to connect all parts of the business including the supply chain interactively on a global scale, is the ultimate goal. A good business intelligence system has to record, analyze, and extract insights from raw data so accurately that a CEO can be confident that decisions based on those insights would affect the bottom line profitably.

Companies like IBM, SAP, Oracle, and many others are businesses that sell these systems. They are continuously expanding and improving their BI software. Momentum is building within communities of digital knowledge professionals to partner with each other to create integration systems that will be the platform of choice. There is still much competition between these communities. A company that wants to outsource its old legacy systems will find a worldwide array of competing platforms and applications that are designed to replace or repair its own internal data systems, bearing in mind that overall standardization of methods is still a work in process.

Pushing demand for web-based data integration systems in public companies is the fear of noncompliance of government regulations. Errors in financial reporting can impose large penalties. Despite "integrate or disintegrate" slogans, some managers are wary. Decisions to delay are caused by high costs and reports of BI failures, although augmenting human logic with machine intelligence seems inevitable in a global environment.

One shining example of success comes from the restaurant industry. It is reported at http://www.cio.com/archive/031505/index.html in a March 15, 2005, news article by Meridith Levinson titled, "The Brain Behind the Big, Bad Burger and Other Tales of Business Intelligence." Levinson reports on CKE Restaurants, the chain that owns Hardee's. Hardee's customers were recently offered the "Monster Thickburger," consisting of two charbroiled 100 percent Angus beef patties (each weighing a third of a pound), three slices of American cheese, and four crispy strips of bacon on a toasted buttery sesame seed bun. The burger has 1,420 calories and 107 grams of fat, and customers were eating them as if there were no tomorrow. CKE introduced the Monster Thickburger on November 15, 2004, with confidence born from insights it had obtained from its business intelligence system, known inside the company as CPR (CKE Performance Reporting).

It would seem counterproductive to encourage obesity, but CKE was determined to monitor its sales in a test market using CPR. It also wanted its business intelligence software to clarify whether the monster hamburger was actually contributing to increases in sales or was it just cannibalizing sales of other, lesser burgers. CPR reported on this and a variety of other questions: Was the increase in Monster sales worth the cost? How do other burgers compare? What are advantages of various menu mixes? What are the gross profits and total sales for each of the test stores? What contribution does each menu item (including the Monster burger) make to total sales?

As a result of CPR test market insights, the company decided to roll out the Monster Thickburger nationwide on November 15, 2004. In one month, sales at Hardee's were

Spotlight 12-2 (Continued)

up 5.8 percent. Hardee's executive vice president announced that the Monster Thickburger was directly responsible for the increase in sales. The real winner was a good business intelligence system.

Review Questions

1 What are legacy systems and what do they have to do with business intelligence? If the term is murky, see http://en.wikipedia.org/wiki/Legacy_system.

2 Is there such a thing as a legacy manager and what does this question have to do with business intelligence?

3 Discuss the statement in the text, "Instead of considering price alone, computers can weigh the relative merits of hundreds of variables, including quantity, delivery time, and technical specifications."

4 What can an intelligent business network accomplish?

5 How does a company change an old business intelligence system to a new and better one?

Sources: http://en.wikipedia.org/wiki/Business_intelligence; http://www.cio.com/archive/011507/fea_scm.html; http://sloanreview.mit.edu/smr/issue/2005/spring/13; http://www.cio.com/archive/031505/index.html.

Summary

Chapter 12 starts with the query "What is materials management (MM)?" The answer is long and detailed. First, materials are used for the input–output transformation that produces goods and services. Second, materials managers design and operate linked systems functions, which are parts of the organization's internal and external supply chains. These many interlinked components must be coordinated to minimize all materials costs (including out-of-stock costs). A classification system for materials (RM, SA, WIP, etc.) is presented to cover the different kinds of materials that need to be managed. Then, the cost leverage of savings in materials and the penalties of errors in ordering materials are explored.

Materials management is unique for each of the various kinds of work configurations (flow shop, job shop, and project environment), as well as for flexible processing systems. All configurations require intelligent information systems, which is based on designing systems parameters that provide timely decision making for the right variables—often in a global information systems context.

Purchasing is a crucial player on the MM team. It can take advantage of the global reach provided by expanding telecommunications technologies. The learning organization uses purchasing to gain opportunities for improving competitiveness. "Turnover" and "days of inventory" are important measures of the competitive performance of material managers. From another point of view, quality assurances and trusted suppliers can be essential. Turnover and DOI capture part of the firm's success with customer satisfaction with quality. To be organized, supplier certification procedures are valuable.

Also covered are the MM functions of receiving, inspection, and storage. MM's use of bidding is discussed as well as the categorization of parts in terms of their criticality. A failure model for critical spare parts is presented. It is also shown how MM's capabilities are enhanced by the application of value analysis. To conclude, materials are categorized into ABC classes that rank order their criticality and then their importance in terms of the potential savings that can be made by improving the way they are managed.

Spotlight 12-1 describes a research breakthrough by a brilliant DuPont scientist who invents a new material—Kevlar. Stephanie Louise Kwolek demonstrated that good science knows no gender. Spotlight 12-2: The Demand for Business Intelligence is crucial in MM, the supply chain, P/OM, and general management planning. All of these functions require intelligent organized information to avoid being drowned in data chaos.

Key Terms

ABC classification (p. 491)
Bidding (p. 486)
Certification of suppliers (p. 494)
Criticality (p. 492)
Cross-docking (p. 486)
Days of inventory (p. 483)
Expediting (p. 480)
Intelligent information system (p. 480)
Internal MM system (p. 473)
Inventory turns (p. 483)
Logistics (p. 474)
Materials management (MM) (p. 473)
Materials management information system (MMIS) (p. 479)

Materials management system (MMS) (p. 473)
Methods analysis (p. 490)
Purchasing agents (PAs) (p. 481)
SKU (p. 484)
Static inventory problem (p. 489)
Trade-off models (p. 478)
Turnover (p. 483)
Value added (p. 474)
Value analysis (VA) (p. 489)
Work in process (WIP) (p. 473)

Review Questions

1 What is materials management (MM) and who does it?
2 Why is the systems approach important for MM in the supply chain?

3   Present the taxonomy of materials.

4   Why do materials have the greatest leverage for making cost savings?

5   What kinds of errors can be made in ordering materials and what are the penalties?

6   Explain differences in MM according to work configurations.

7   Describe the materials management information system (MMIS) and explain why it plays such an important role for P/OM.

8   Explain the difference between centralized and decentralized materials management.

9   Discuss how the information system participates in determining the degree of centralization of MM.

10 From the MM point of view, what is a global information system? Is it centralized or decentralized?

11 Discuss the effect of the systems communication flows.

12 Describe the purchasing function and the role of purchasing agents (PAs).

13 Why are PAs part of the twenty-first century learning organization?

14 Define turnover.

15 Define days of inventory (DOI).

16 What ethical problems must be resolved by purchasing?

17 Describe international issues that create ethical quandaries for purchasing agents.

18 Detail functions for receiving, inspecting, and storing. How are they a part of MM?

19 Explain why bids may be sought by P/OM.

20 Explain why materials costs often are a large percentage of both factory costs and operating costs of services.

21 Why does the low bid tend to decrease with more bidders?

22 Discuss the materials management of critical parts.

23 What is a static inventory problem? How often does it arise in the real world?

24 Explain the role played by value analysis for materials management. Why is value analysis part of the P/OM-team effort?

25 Explain the role played by methods analysis. Why is methods analysis part of the P/OM team effort?

26 Describe ABC classification as applied to material criticality.

27 Describe ABC classification as applied to material dollar volume.

28 Explain why supplier certification requires the systems approach to include all aspects of materials management. (Note: Do not overlook the use of bidding models, ABC concepts, and benchmarking, which permit comparison with the best in the class.)

Problems Section

Note: This section has various problems that can be formulated and solved using QuantMethods Production/Operations Management software (QMpom). The appropriate model categories are indicated for each problem.

1   Assume that downsizing could save the Market Research Store $5,000 in annual labor costs. The downsizing study costs $1,000. If, instead, the study focused on materials savings, what would be the net payoff for the first year—assuming average firm ratios for labor and materials costs?

2   If the ratio of labor costs to materials costs is 1/2 and labor costs are decreasing by 10 percent per year while material costs are increasing by 10 percent per year, what is the ratio at the end of the second year? (Note: This means that at the present time labor costs are 50 percent of materials costs.) Does the result seem reasonable?

3   If labor is 20 percent and materials 80 percent of COGS—say $20 and $80, then a 10 percent reduction in labor costs yields $18 added to $80 totals $98. This produces a 2 percent reduction in total costs [i.e., $(100 - 98)/100 = 0.02$]. Make the same comparison for a 10 percent reduction in materials costs.

4   Assume that the probability distribution has been changed for the decision matrix previously constructed for the complex machine spare parts failure problem. Thus, Table 12-2 should be altered to conform to the following data:

For the complex machine, let $p_i \geq 0$ for $i = 0, 1, 2, 3$. Note that now $p_0 = 1/6$, and that there can be no more than 3 failures over the lifetime of the machine. The probability of failure is distributed as follows:

$$i = 0 \text{ failure}; \quad p_0 = 1/6$$
$$i = 1 \text{ failure}; \quad p_1 = 1/3$$
$$i = 2 \text{ failures}; \quad p_2 = 1/3$$
$$i = 3 \text{ failures}; \quad p_3 = 1/6$$

How many spare parts should be ordered initially?

Using the QMpom module called Decision Theory Models (Decision Analysis) will facilitate solving the four (4) problems that are numbered 4 through 7.

5   Assume that the probability distribution has been changed again for the decision matrix previously constructed for the complex machine spare parts failure problem. Table 12-2 should be altered to conform to the following data:

For the complex machine, let $p_i \geq 0$ for $i = 0, 1, 2$. Note that $p_0 = 3/4$, and that now there can be no more than 2 failures over the lifetime of the machine.

The probability of failure is distributed as follows:

$$i = 0 \text{ failure;} \quad p_0 = 3/4$$
$$i = 1 \text{ failure;} \quad p_1 = 1/8$$
$$i = 2 \text{ failures;} \quad p_2 = 1/8$$
$$i = 3 \text{ failures;} \quad p_3 = 0.0$$

How many spare parts should be ordered initially?

QMpom module called Decision Theory Models (Decision Analysis) applies.

6   Referring again to Table 12-2, what would the decision be if zero failures are expected with 0.97 probability and the other failure rates for $i = 1, 2,$ and 3 are all 0.01?

QMpom module called Decision Theory Models (Decision Analysis) applies.

7   Again turning to the problem shown in Table 12-2, if $c = 5$, $c' = 20$, and

$$i = 0 \text{ failure;} \quad p_0 = 0.0$$
$$i = 1 \text{ failure;} \quad p_1 = 1/2$$
$$i = 2 \text{ failures;} \quad p_2 = 1/3$$
$$i = 3 \text{ failures;} \quad p_3 = 1/6$$

how many spares should be ordered? Note that the initial acquisition cost remains the same but is now only 1/4 the failure replacement cost.

QMpom module called Decision Theory Models (Decision Analysis) applies.

8   It has been stated that 16 percent of the beer drinkers drink 40 percent of all the beer that is consumed. Is this likely to be the case?

Would the curve that passes through these points be described by ß equal to 0.5?

Draw the curve for the equation

$$\text{where } y = x^{\beta}(1 \geq x \geq 0), (1 \geq \beta \geq 0)$$

$y =$ percent of dollar demand, $x =$ rank-ordered percent of all items, and $\beta = 0.5$
This is equivalent to $y = \sqrt{x}$

9   For the β in Problem 8, determine the percent of total dollar demand that occurs when the A category is set at 25 percent of all items.

10   Calculate the inventory turnover rate when monthly net sales are $120 million and average inventory evaluated at the selling price is $240 million. What might this product be and comment on this level of turnover for such a product.

11   Continuing with Problem 10, calculate the days of inventory (DOI) if average inventory is $120 million (calculated in terms of costs) and the monthly cost of goods sold (COGS) is $60 million. Use 30 days per month. What product might be described by these data? Comment on what might be an adequate level of DOI (days of inventory) for such a product.

12   Compare the answers obtained in Problems 10 and 11. Explain how these answers might relate to each other.

Practice Quiz

1   Materials management is an important supply chain function in companies that have a large percent of their costs allocated to buying raw materials. These are value-adding production companies that transform materials into finished products. At the other extreme, there are companies that just buy and assemble components, and subassemblies made by another company. The discussion that follows in points a. through e. is transcribed observations of company executives in a meeting with the vice president in charge of materials management. The vice president of materials management agreed with all but one statement. Which one is that?

a. When the cost of materials is a large percent of the cost of goods sold, then purchasing needs strong management support. A materials management function reporting at the top level of the company is vital because materials policies are strategic.

b. Inventory management is not the purchasing agent's job. The materials manager should have an inventory department in addition to a purchasing department. The activities of these two departments should be coordinated because purchasing should be given guidelines about how many units to buy at a time.

c. Accounts payable are important when materials constitute a major part of the cost of goods sold. Invoices need to be paid before suppliers will ship. Because production is dependent on bills being paid in a timely fashion, it is necessary for P/OM to establish an office for accounts payable.

d. Coproduced and/or copacked products have much of their value added by a contract supplier. Because profit goes to those who do the value-adding, contract packing and producing should only be used when the company's production capacity is unable to satisfy market demand.

e. On average, direct material costs for job shop manufacturers has risen to 70 percent of the cost of goods sold. That is a high percentage and a big change, given that in 1950 labor costs were about 70 percent of the cost of goods sold. This information is important to both the company and union managers.

2 Turnover and days of inventory have been called crucial measures of performance. The following table presents a number of factors that are useful for calculating these important benchmarks. There is also commentary about the interpretation of the measures under different circumstances. With which statements in parts a. to e. do you disagree?

1	Average total dollar inventory	$ 60,000,000
2	Annual total cost of goods sold (COGS)	$400,000,000
3	Sales price per dollar of cost of goods sold	$1.80
4	Annual net sales	$720,000,000
5	Average inventory in sales dollars	$108,000,000
6	Annual net profit	$220,000,000
7	Annual general administration and overhead costs	$100,000,000

a. Days of inventory are calculated in two steps. First, divide line 2 by 365. That equals $1.0959, which is the daily total cost of goods sold (in millions). Second, divide line 1 by 1.0959. That equals 54.75 days of inventory. Using a 30-day month, 54.75 days is equivalent to 1.825 months. A good way to calculate inventory turns is to divide 365 days by 54.75 days, and that equals 6 and 2/3 turnovers per year.

b. Inventory turns are calculated by dividing line 4 by line 6, and that equals 3 and 3/11. The difference occurs because the cost dollars have been converted into sales dollars.

c. Days of inventory are calculated by dividing line 4 by line 3, which equals line 2. Then, divide line 5 by line 3, and that equals line 1. Next divide line 1 by line 2, and that equals 0.15. Multiply that result by 365 to obtain 54.75 days.

d. Inventory turns are calculated dividing line 2 by line 1, equaling 6 and 2/3 turns per year.

e. Six and 2/3 inventory turns per year is not a lot for a retail business like Wal-Mart or Kmart. It might be considered a threshold of acceptability for a furniture retail outlet like Thomasville. *The Wall Street Journal* in the local vending machine is always sold out by 10 A.M., which indicates that on 260 weekdays, a 100 percent turnover occurs. The WSJ, at this box, gets 260 turns per year. That is what the stocking policy for the vending machine aims to get. If more papers were filled each day, there might be days when turnover is not complete.

3 Materials management of critical parts is a significant responsibility of P/OM. There is likely to be no greater cost to a production system than the need to slow down or (worse yet) shut down the process. To drive home this point, the production manager has listed a number of issues for management to discuss at a roundtable retreat that is being held in a few weeks. The list has circulated with a surprising result. Three managers have objected to one of the points listed in a. through e. What would likely be the point in contention?

a. Criticality needs to be defined. The definition of "critical" should be: When a part (component, subassembly) failure causes the product or process to fail, that part is critical. In addition, if a part malfunctions in such a way as to partially impair or disable the associated product or process, then that part is critical.

b. Critical parts need to be identified by all the players. In addition to the obvious list of maintenance personnel, process engineers, and production managers, there is a need to interview customers, suppliers, workers (related to product or process), and product designers.

c. Failure records that allow review of all product and process incidents should be examined in detail. There may be cover-ups that are reported as aberrations rather than failures. Also, procedures need to be tightened for recording complaints of every kind with respect to the product and the process. Incidents for service products are particularly vulnerable to subjective errors.

d. Spare parts policies need to be reformulated in terms of the probabilities of failure and the distribution of times to failure. Regular inspections of critical spare parts inventories should be scheduled. Two problems occur often. First, the wrong part is received as if it were the critical spare part. It is given the SKU number of the critical spare. That unfortunate fact is not discovered until that critical spare is required. Second, the correct part is logged in but deteriorates in storage, or it is pilfered.

e. Spare part policies need to be reexamined when only one purchase order occasion exists. As a variant, spare parts can only be ordered at a reasonable price at the time the unit requiring spares is placed.

4 The custom-made steering engine for a large tanker ship has a high cost. Bidding specifications for building and installing the engine are not yet completed. (A ship's steering engine is akin to the power steering system for a car. The hydraulic system that moves the ship's giant rudder is similar in principle but not in scale.) At the same time that the steering engine is being built, spares can be made for parts that wear out and have to be replaced. The cost of spares at the time of initial ordering is relatively low, viz., $500. Spares cost a great deal more after installation of the steering engine, viz., $40,000. Data have been compiled by the maritime engineers before the bidding begins so that the shipping company can include a specific number of spare parts in the request for proposal (RFP). Spare part strategies are order none, one, two, or three. The probabilities of part failure are good estimates based on engineering pragmatics. There is zero probability of no failures; 1/2 for one failure; 1/3 for two failures; 1/6 for three failures. As they must, these sum to one.

Using the QMpom module called Decision Theory Models (Decision Analysis) will facilitate solving Problem 4.

Failure Cost Matrix

	0 Failures	1 Failure	2 Failures	3 Failures
0 spares	0	$40,000	$80,000	$120,000
1 spare	$500	$500	$40,500	$80,500
2 spares	$1,000	$1,000	$1,000	$41,000
3 spares	$1,500	$1,500	$1,500	$1,500

At the meeting to decide on how many spare parts to request with the RFP, a number of good points were made. These are listed as a. through e. There is agreement that one of the five points is heading in the wrong direction. Before proceeding further, identify the statement that needs to be dismissed.

a. The strategy to order three spares is the safest course of action. For the lifetime of the steering engine there has never been a case reported of more than three failures. However, three failures have been reported more than 16 percent of the time. This is causing concern for some of the managers who have suggested that the data are not showing a fourth failure, but the probabilities suggest that four failures could occur.

b. Management fears that it will be called to account for wasting money if three (or four) spare parts are ordered. The purchasing agent has found out that two is the average number of spare parts ordered with this steering engine. This information disturbs some of the project managers who are leaning toward three spares.

c. Using the decision-matrix approach, the optimal number of spare parts to request in the RFP is three. That strategy has the lowest expected cost of $1,500.

d. It is not reasonable to order zero spare parts. Data indicate that there has always been at least one failure. The average number ordered is two. If the company orders two spare parts, no one can get upset. They will say that management has been cautious and not wasteful.

e. If more than one spare is ordered, that would permit one to be kept on board the ship. Only one spare part is needed at a time. The extra spare(s) will be stored at the home dock. It seems logical that the probability of two failures within a short time is low. The reason for failures occurring needs to be studied. The purchasing agent has stated that use is the primary cause of failure. Age plays a part as well.

5 Another company has proposed bidding on the steering engine using new technology. The costs are the same but the probabilities of failure have shifted significantly. With the new design, there is an 80 percent probability of no failure; 10 percent of one failure; 10 percent of two failures; and zero percent of more than two failures. These probabilities sum to one. Another meeting was called to decide on how many spare parts to request with the RFP. A number of good points were made at the meeting. These are listed as a. through e. There remains one incorrect statement. Identify the point of contention and the statement that needs to be dismissed.

Using the QMpom module called Decision Theory Models (Decision Analysis) will facilitate solving Problem 5.

a. Using the decision-matrix approach, the optimal number of spare parts to request in the RFP is two. That strategy has the lowest expected cost of $1,000.

b. The strategy to order three spares remains the safest course of action. This is in spite of the fact that new company has estimated that for the lifetime of the steering engine, there is zero probability of more than two failures.

c. Management may be called to account for wasting money if three spare parts are ordered. The purchasing agent points out no data exists for the average number of spare parts ordered with the new steering engine. This fact underscores the uneasiness of some of the project managers about going with relatively untried new technology. At the meeting, a manager asked, "What if the company is wrong about these probabilities?"

d. It is not reasonable to order less than two spare parts. The expected cost of one spare after failure is $4,500. The expected cost of three spares is only $500 more than the minimum expected cost of two spares. Because the probabilities are uncertain, and the cost of an extra spare part is only $500, the best course of action is to go with three spares and temper the decision-matrix result with caution.

e. Because the design is based on new technology and the probabilities of part failure are not certain, the old steering engine should be purchased and the new one should wait for others to try out.

6 An ABC database of annual dollar volume per SKU (stock-keeping unit) in the company's inventory can be drawn as curves to reflect graphically the cumulative ranked order contribution of each item's dollar volume to the total dollar volume of the firm. Knowledge of this information can be helpful in many ways to production and operations managers. The kinds of insights that are available from this information are given in statements a. through e. Which one of these is not proper for ABC?

a. C-class items are called the *trivial many*. They constitute about 50 percent of all item SKUs carried in stock, but they account for less than 10 percent of total dollar volume. Ordering policy for C-types can be as needed or on a regular periodic basis, e.g., on the third Monday of every week. Stock on-hand level is noted. Orders are placed to cover demand for the next interval of time.

b. Most of the time, if there is a stock-out, replenishments can be obtained for C-type items with minimal lead time. Customers will wait a short time without complaining. However, in some cases, it can be inconvenient to run out of stock (e.g., rest room supplies). The reason that items are classed as C-type is that optimal order policies will not save enough money to pay the bill for creating them.

c. B-type items are in the middle 25 percent of all items carried, and they account for about 15 percent of total dollar volume. That makes B-type items a little more worthy of analysis. It pays to watch them because some B-type items are increasing in dollar volume and could become A-types in the future. Also, at the top of B-type items in their rank order are almost A-types. It may pay to regroup the A- and B-types from time to time. There is no hard and fast rule as to where A's end and B's begin.

d. Neither growth in demand volume for a company's products nor price alterations can change the rank order of an item's dollar volume. This removes pressure on the part of the inventory managers to constantly update their records, which could become an ongoing clerical and analytic requirement.

e. A-type SKU are the cash users and cash generators for the company. They are called the *significant few*. The top 25 percent of all the company's SKUs account for about 75 percent of the total dollar volume. For these items with large cash flow, bad order policies penalize the company. Good ordering policies reward the company.

7 As a training exercise for its materials managers, AutoParts Retailers, Inc., has designed a table of eight items with their daily sales volume and price per unit. The manager-students are asked to arrange this table so as to create a standard (25%A–25%B–50%C) ABC curve. The answers in parts a. through e. are given to the manager-students for them to mark true or false. There is only one false answer. Which one is it?

AutoPart Item (SKU)	Daily Volume (SKU)	Price per Unit
X303	200 units	$2.49
X664	3 units	$39.50
Y829	5 units	$9.89
X155	16 units	$149.99

AutoPart Item (SKU)	Daily Volume (SKU)	Price per Unit
Y447	7 units	$30.50
X721	20 units	$4.12
X267	1,003 units	$0.99
Y595	61 units	$3.25

a.   The average *daily volume* of the A-type SKUs is 509.50 units, and the average price per unit of the A-type SKUs is $75.49.

b.   The average *daily volume* of the B-type SKUs is 103.50 units, and the average price per unit of the B-type SKUs is $16.50.

c.   The average *daily volume* of the C-type SKUs is 22.25 units, and the average price per unit of the C-type SKUs is $14.19.

d.   The average *daily dollar volume* of the A-type SKUs is $1,696.41, as compared to the average *daily dollar volume* of the B-type SKUs, which is $355.75.

e.   The average *daily dollar volume* of the A-type SKUs is $1,696.41, as compared to the average *daily dollar volume* of the C-type SKUs, which is $49.45.

8   The ABC data from AutoParts Retailers, Inc., given in Problem 7, have yet to be classified in the traditional way. Manager-students have been asked to do this. They have been instructed to draw the ABC curve before answering the company's true or false quiz (statements a. through e). There is only one false answer. Which one is it?

a.   The top 25 percent of items (A-type, ranked by largest daily dollar volume) contributes 74.52 percent of total dollar volume in AutoParts Retailers, Inc., database.

b.   B-type items are the next 25 percent of items (ranked by daily dollar volume). These B-types must be listed after the A-types because they occupy the range from 25 percent to 50 percent of all items in the rank-order hierarchy. This B-type group contributes 15.63 percent of total dollar volume. The cumulative percent of total daily dollar volume has reached 74.52 + 15.63 = 90.15 percent.

c.·   These numbers confirm the fact that C-type items (which are the next 50 percent of items ranked by daily dollar volume) account for 9.85 percent of total dollar volume. Note that the cumulative percent of total daily dollar volume has reached 100 percent, i.e., 74.52 + 15.63 + 9.85 = 100.00 percent.

d.   The A-type items are X155 and X267. X155, which is a starter motor, is first in rank order with daily dollar volume of $2,399.84. That is 52.71 percent of total dollar volume. Because 16 starter motors are sold per day at a price of $150 each, it is crucial for AutoParts Retailers to find out if there are always enough parts on hand. Does the customer ever walk away because there are none on hand? The order policy for X155 and X267 must result from detailed study of how much to order at one time, which determines how often to order, who to order from (are there backup suppliers), what quality standards are set by the buyer, how long and how variable are the lead times, etc. There is no room for error in this A-type category.

e.   X267 is second in rank order and contributes 21.81 percent to the total dollar volume. It too is important and deserves detailed study. X303, which is third in rank and at the top of the rank-ordered B-type items, accounts for only 10.94 percent of total daily dollar volume. It does not require detailed study.

9   ABC is a powerful concept that applies to many different kinds of inventories. Regarding the inventory of land and people, a small percent of the total land area of the United States (less than 25 percent of the total resource) supports a large percent of Americans. As an estimate, that number is 75 percent. From an alternative viewpoint, a small percent of all dogs (rank ordered by weight) eat most of the dog food consumed in the world. Beer drinkers and dessert gourmands closely fit the canine ABC curve. At a symposium on the inventory aspects of materials management, a number of points were stated (a. through e.) about disproportionality of resource utilization and its impact on materials management. Which one of these statements is flawed?

a.   A mathematical model for the ABC effect is $y = x^\beta$, where y is percent of dollar demand ($0 \leq y \leq 1$), x is percent of all rank-ordered items ($0 \leq x \leq 1$), and β is the coefficient of disproportionality ($0 \leq \beta \leq 1$). When $\beta = 1$, the disproportionality effect is minimized. The result is a straight line where $y = x$.

b.   Designers of mail-order catalogs strive to have β as close to 1 as possible.

c.   Using Excel, the curve in point a. can be derived by clicking on the "insert function" icon f_x; go to *Math and Trig* in the left-hand window that opens. In the right-hand window, scroll down to *POWER* and click OK. A new window opens asking for *Number* (*x*) and *Power* (β). Let *x* change as it goes from zero to 100 percent. For the sake of illustration, let $x = 0.70$ and $\beta = 0.3$. Click on OK, and the result shown in the window gets placed in the cell. The value is 89.85 percent.

   d. Data drive the curve and not vice versa. In other words, actual dollar demand data are collected. Then, the appropriate ABC curve can be drawn to match the data by the method described in c.

   e. A company with 100,000 SKUs would use a random sampling of SKU data to get a picture of its ABC curve.

10 Certification is a process for grading suppliers. It is aimed at discovering which vendors excel in quality, consistency, delivery, etc., and which ones are most likely to match the company's culture and fit into its family of partners. Certification often is a necessary but not sufficient condition to assure a long-term supplier relationship. It is a growing requirement of a number of larger firms. A major chemical products company has invited a group of potential buyers to a symposium dedicated to explaining how this company will help the buyer certify its qualifications. The following list highlights some of the points that were covered. There is a consensus that one of the points is not acceptable. Which statement is not acceptable?

   a. Because it is a costly process, certification should be used only for suppliers of A-type items. The A-types should cover both criticality and dollar volume.

   b. Certification should set minimum standards for factors such as percent defectives and lead time.

   c. Certification should permit comparisons between suppliers so that the "best in class" can be identified and selected. Scoring models can assist in the comparison and can provide tracking over time. That which passes today may slip, falter, and fail by the same criteria over time. Further, what is best today can be bested tomorrow.

   d. Most companies have internal standards for the individual departments. The level of the internal standards can be used for external assessment.

   e. Scoring for certification should not include the supplier's ISO 9000 certification. The fact that the supplier has achieved ISO certification can cause bad judgment and bias the company's own certification process.

Additional Readings

Arnold, J. R. Tony, and Stephen N. Chapman. *Introduction to Materials Management*, 4e. Upper Saddle River, NJ: Prentice-Hall, May 2000.

Burt, D. N. *Proactive Purchasing*. Englewood Cliffs, NJ: Prentice-Hall, 1984.

Dobler, D. W., L. Lee, Jr., and D. N. Burt. *Purchasing and Materials Management*. New York: McGraw-Hill, 1984.

Ellram, Lisa M., and Laura M. Birou. *Purchasing for Bottom Line Impact*, vol. 4. National Association of Purchasing Management (NAPM), Homewood, IL: Irwin, 1995.

Hazardous Materials Management Magazine (as of November 2003): http://www.hazmatmag.com.

Heinritz, S. F., P. V. Farrell, L. Giunipero, and M. Kolchin. *Purchasing: Principles and Applications*, 8e. Englewood Cliffs, NJ: Prentice-Hall, 1991.

Hickman, Thomas K., and William M. Hickman. *Global Purchasing: How to Buy Goods and Services in Foreign Markets*. Homewood, IL: Business One Irwin/APICS Series in Production Management, 1992.

International Federation of Purchasing and Materials Management (as of November 2003): http://www.ifpmm.org.

Killen, Kenneth H., and John W. Kamauff. *Managing Purchasing*, vol. 2. National Association of Purchasing Management (NAPM), Homewood: IL, Irwin, 1994.

Leenders, Michiel R., and H. Fearon. *Purchasing and Materials Management*, 10e. Homewood, IL: Irwin, 1993.

Leenders, Michiel R., and Anna E. Flynn. *Value-Driven Purchasing*, vol. 1. National Association of Purchasing Management (NAPM), Homewood, IL: Irwin, 1994. *Materials Management in Health Care Magazine* (as of November 2003): http://www.matmanmag.com.

Miles, L. D. *Techniques of Value Analysis*. New York: McGraw-Hill, 1961.

———. *Techniques of Value Analysis and Engineering*. New York: McGraw-Hill, 1972.

Raedels, Alan R. *Value-Focused Supply Management*, vol. 3. National Association of Purchasing Management (NAPM), Homewood, IL: Irwin, 1994.

Schonberger, R., and J. Gilbert. "Just-In-Time Purchasing: A Challenge for U.S. Industry." *California Management Review*, vol. 26, no. 1 (Fall 1983): 54–68.

Tersine, R. J. *Materials Management and Inventory Systems*, 3e. New York: Elsevier North-Holland Publishing, 1987.

Notes

1. The New York Stock Exchange (NYSE) symbol for the merged HP and Compaq Company is HPQ. The merger took place in 2002.
2. Important insight is available from Edward T. Hall. "The Silent Language in Overseas Business." *Harvard Business Review,* vol. 38, no. 3 (May–June 1960): 87–96. Things change, but this is a classic article about the cultural settings of business. The French say, "plus ça change, plus c'est la meme chose" and this means "The more things change, the more things stay the same."
3. Value analysis is attributed to the work of Lawrence D. Miles whose 1961 book, *Techniques of Value Analysis and Engineering*, was the seminal work in the field. For the third edition (online) see: http://wendt.library.wisc.edu/miles/milesbook.html. In a quote from Chapter 5, "*Value Engineering* is a system, but instead of parts, it consists of approaches, understandings, and techniques—for one sole purpose, *the efficient identification of unnecessary cost.*"

Enrichment Activity 12: Scoring Model for Certification of Suppliers

The generic vendor scoring system shown here is based on ten factors. These should be arrived at on a consensus basis by materials managers. After there is agreement about the dimensions for certification, this form can be circulated. It may be best for managers to fill out the form shown in Table EA12-1 before consultation with each other. Then, they should get together and discuss their differences of opinion with respect to weights and the actual scores that they have given to each vendor. That results in Table EA12-2.

This entire process is a remarkable exercise in teamwork. Managers must find out what their colleagues consider important factors in choosing vendors. The factors may differ according to the types of materials (e.g., raw materials, WIP, finished

Table EA12-1

Generic Vendor Scoring
Certification Model

Weights add to 100; best cell score is 10; each score is identified by the vendor letter and the factor number, e.g., C4 is vendor C's rating on delivery reliability.

Factors	Weights	Vendor A	Vendor B	Vendor C	Vendor D
Price/Unit (1)					
Average Quality Level (2)					
Quality Consistency (3)					
Delivery LT (4)					
JIT Ability (5)					
Design Flexibility (6)					
Design Change Speed (7)					
Product Line Diversity (8)					
Services Promised (9)					
Attitude Perceived (10)					

Scored by_____

Date _____

Location _____

Weight Scale Used: 1 to 10 for each category with 10 being best.

Factor Scale Used: 1 to 10 for each cell entry with 10 being best.

Create a company handbook for definitions of Factors.

The best that any vendor can do with this system is to receive scores of 10 in each of the ten benchmarking categories. No matter how the weights are distributed, that vendor will receive a total score of 1000 if the scoring system is sum of weighted values.

Weights add to 100; best score is 10; each score is identified by the vendor letter and the factor number, e.g., C4 is vendor C's rating on delivery reliability.

Factors	Weights	Vendor A	Vendor B	Vendor C	Vendor D
Price/Unit (1)	30	9	5	5	7
Average Quality Level (2)	20	7	3	6	7
Quality Consistency (3)	10	5	3	7	7
Delivery LT (4)	7	8	5	5	7
JIT Ability (5)	2	4	3	6	7
Design Flexibility (6)	1	4	4	7	7
Design Change Speed (7)	5	3	6	4	7
Product Line Diversity (8)	8	6	7	6	7
Services Promised (9)	6	5	8	7	7
Attitude Perceived (10)	11	6	10	4	7

Scored by_____

Date _____

Location _____

Weight Scale Used: 1 to 10 for each category with 10 being best.
Factor Scale Used: 1 to 10 for each cell entry with 10 being best.

Table EA12-2

Specific Vendor Scoring
Certification Model

goods, mining commodities, food grown on the farm, petroleum products, etc.). The weights given to each factor by different managers may reveal important personality characteristics that team players need to understand in dealing with each other.

Enrichment Challenges 12

1 Which vendor should be chosen because it has the best score?
   For sample calculations, note for vendor A:

   Weighted sum measure is calculated by: $(30 \times 9) + (20 \times 7) + (10 \times 5) + (7 \times 8) + \cdots + = 687$.

   Product of the powers measure is calculated by: $9^{30}7^{20}5^{10}8^{7}4^{2}4^{1}3^{5}6^{8}5^{6}6^{11} = 1.026 \, (10)^{82}$

2 What kind of a vendor is D? How might vendor D be used for benchmarking?
3 Create a perfect vendor. Explain how to do that and how to use the "perfect vendor" for benchmarking.

Aggregate Planning to Balance Supply and Demand

Chapter Outline

Level production

A well-trained workforce of constant size operating with throughput standards produces a fixed level of units, or delivers a fixed level of services per day. This is the basis of level production over long periods of time.

Chapter 13 moves the focus onto the floor where work is done. This can be inside the plant or the service facility. Operations managers must deal with workforce planning. The number of employees is strongly related to the outputs required from the input–output transformation process. Workforce planning is directly related to the control of inventories based on forecasts of demand. Although this discussion epitomizes tactical planning, nevertheless, there is an apparent interaction with strategic planning.

When should plant managers pursue the idea of having a hiring policy consistent with a constant workforce size—with the goal of **level production**? Similarly, when should the goal be to adopt a chasing policy with workforce size adjustments? Flexible workforce size is better fitted to the configuration of job shops and batch production than it is to flow shop production. The constant workforce is better suited to continuous, high-volume throughputs that characterize flow shop output. In contrast, a chasing policy using hiring, layoffs, overtime, and subcontracting is an effort to be flexible in order to match variable and even volatile demand forecasts. Combination policies (hybrids of constant and chasing workforce size) are alternatives worth exploring.

The methodology to find optimal resource allocations is known as *aggregate scheduling*. Aggregate scheduling with a flexible workforce size applies to batch production and mixed-model flow shop environments. Line-balancing methodology for planning to run an optimal continuous production system with a constant workforce is discussed in Chapter 17 on Cycle-Time Management.

After reading this chapter, you should be able to:

- Explain the function of aggregate planning (AP).
- Discuss the systems nature of AP in terms of classes of resources and product-mix families.
- Explain standard units of work.
- Relate the importance of forecasting to AP.
- Compare constant (or level) production with a chasing policy—where supply chases demand.
- Detail the cost structure for aggregate planning.
- Describe how to use linear programming for AP.
- Describe how to use the transportation matrix for AP.
- Explain why a nonlinear cost model can be used as a benchmark for other AP models.

The Systems Viewpoint

Aggregate planning (AP) is resource planning for the job shop. AP matches types of jobs with the supportive resources needed to produce each of them. The concepts of "what does it take to make this class of items" or "what skills, know-how, and technologies are used to provide this class of services" are successful if based on broad systems thinking. Aggregate planning takes the expected demand for the job shop product mix and assigns available resources in an optimal *tactical* way (say, minimum total costs or times). Using the systems point of view, it is also necessary to extend the study to include alternative product mixes and other available resources. AP provides a critical link between tactics and strategic thinking for the job shop.

Strategic Thinking

Strategic thinking is engaged when the tactical performance of the system is not considered to be worthy of the investment of resources. Perhaps the company should rethink its product lines because the costs of doing business do not provide a satisfactory cash flow and/or return on the investments. Alternatively, the current product line might be acceptable if the system's capacity is altered with additional investments or by outsourcing some part of the production function. Good tactics are only as good as their performance measures indicate. When that is not good enough, P/OM must return to the beginning and reevaluate the strategic plans that are being utilized.

13-1 What Is Aggregate Planning (AP)?

Aggregate planning (AP) is a method used to design a generalized production schedule across a variety of job types. If the same workforce can make Xs and Ys, provide services for Ws and Zs, and handle different materials using different machines, then AP is needed to find a commonality between them all so that hours of work can be estimated to prepare the full menu. A generalized schedule is determined to comprehend the great variety of types. Variety is reduced by expressing work to be accomplished in standard units. Rather than planning for $X, Y, W,$ and Z, standard units are used. That is what the term *aggregation* means. By collecting an assemblage of specific identities, all individuals are merged into a *common pool of standard units* or standard hours.

Supply is stated in these aggregated units, and demand also is estimated in the same aggregated units. Demand is generated by a variety of customers for the different kinds of products made by the job shop or the different kinds of services offered by job shops such as a market research company, a restaurant serving many kinds of meals, or a hospital with tests and treatments for all kinds of cases. *Congeries* is another term for aggregation. Both mean collections within which many details of identities are lost.

It is important to note that aggregate planning is an internal production management function that leads to detailed internal production scheduling in later stages. The specific purpose of AP is to decide when to schedule work and under what conditions to schedule it. The conditions can vary such as second shift, overtime work, and subcontracting.

In Figure 13-1, aggregate planning (the middle box) is shown as following strategic business planning (the top box—called the *Company Plan*). Aggregate planning is the producer's general plan for getting work done. It is not detailed scheduling (the bottom box—called the *Production Schedule*), which follows aggregate planning.

Aggregate planning starts a chain reaction in the supply chain of suppliers-producers-customers. Once the internal assignments that relate to the factory and the office are scheduled, then the external flows begin to function. These are flows of materials from the factory to the warehouses by trucks and other transport systems, which must be coordinated. Transport from the warehouses to the customers must be organized. External flows from suppliers to the production transformation system must be activated. Equipment may have to be rented or bought and people hired and trained, or workforce reductions may be initiated.

The driver of AP is forecasted customer demand. This can take the form of customer orders and/or inventory plans. The forecasts are translated into production plans. The goal is to be prepared to make the product and deliver it when the actual demands are on hand. The same applies to delivering services to the customer at the optimum time.

Material flows inside the company can be scheduled in detail for specific items, or in categories of specific items that have been aggregated. Before trying to do detailed, tactical scheduling, aggregate planning (which is generic) should be used to avoid costly mistakes arising from not being prepared with the proper resources at the right time.

Aggregate planning (AP)
The specific purpose of AP is to schedule production for the job shop with a set of common denominators (e.g., standard hours).

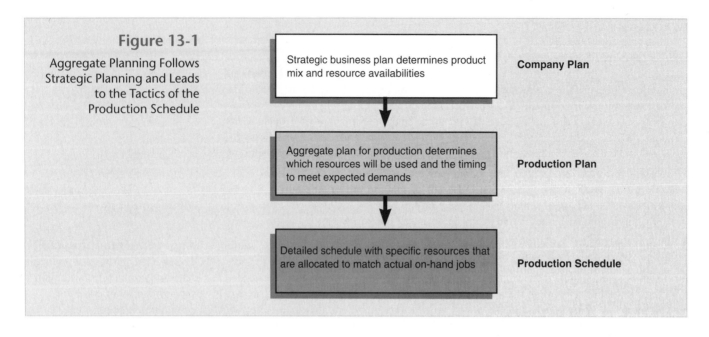

Figure 13-1

Aggregate Planning Follows Strategic Planning and Leads to the Tactics of the Production Schedule

Strategic business plan determines product mix and resource availabilities — **Company Plan**

Aggregate plan for production determines which resources will be used and the timing to meet expected demands — **Production Plan**

Detailed schedule with specific resources that are allocated to match actual on-hand jobs — **Production Schedule**

13-1a Aggregation of Units

When the specific classes of production items to be made are called apples, oranges, and pears, there is too much detail required for planning *n*-periods ahead for each category. It is much simpler to schedule the production of one aggregated item, called "fruit." Later on, the decision can be made about what kind of fruit to plant. This method is not without weaknesses. Some fruits will not grow on the same land with other fruits. Different fertilizers may be required. Irrigation requirements may differ. Harvesting can be a conflict between crops competing for attention or a lucky sequence of resource availabilities.

Service (1) products and manufactured (2) products are similar enough to farm (3) products to draw this analogy. These three categories share some characteristics and they differ in others. Aggregation methods take advantage of the similarities. Differences can be accounted for at a later time.

Standard units
Jobs are converted from pieces of work (order size) into standard hours on a designated machine called the standard machine.

Standard units are used as the common denominator for aggregated units in the production-scheduling problem. Forecasts of specific items such as sweaters of different colors, cotton, wool, and mixtures are converted into the standard machine hours required to make each type of sweater. This is referred to as aggregation of the mixed-model product line of the job shop. It is the aggregation of finished goods used as the basis for planning what will be made in the period starting *n*-months ahead.

If the planning period is for *one quarter*, then it starts at the beginning of t_1 and it finishes at the end of t_3. Assume that planning starts one month ahead (lead time $n = 1$), and it is now January 1; then the planning period starts February 1 and ends April 30.

Aggregate planning is achieved by collecting and lumping all items to be produced together. The idea is to strip away the specifics while retaining the aggregate properties of the product. The purpose is to match aggregate capacity against aggregate demand. This results in generalized determination of workforce requirements, including the possible use of multiple shifts, overtime, and part-time work to satisfy demand across a great variety of stock-keeping units.

Planning horizon
Determine the appropriate planning horizon for forecasting demand.

Consider the paint manufacturer with a product line that includes water-based, oil-based, and acrylic paints. They come in many colors and can sizes. For aggregate planning, the standard product unit might be gallons of paint; the time period could be monthly; the **planning horizon** could be one year ahead. Alternatively, it might have been decided to separate aggregate planning for each type of paint—water-based, oil-based, and acrylic—on a week-by-week basis, for half a year.

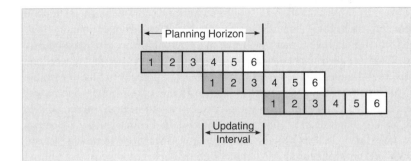

Figure 13-2

Aggregate Planning with Planning Horizon of Six Months and Updating Interval of Three Months

The idea is to aggregate demands that use essentially the same resources. This allows effective utilization of resources across competing demands. By the same resources, it is meant that essentially the same equipment, materials, people, space, and experience are transferable between the different items to satisfy demand as capacity allows in an optimal manner.

Aggregate planning methods can derive better solutions when P/OM can find:

1 Ways to expand the number of products that can be made by a specific class of resources (group technology)
2 Ways to expand the number of resources that can make a class of products (flexibility)

Points 1 and 2 provide increased resources and flexibility to satisfy demand. Also, planning results can be improved by investing in more capacity of the right kind. This makes scarce resources less scarce. Changing the product line and the order mix can result in other benefits. These are systems-oriented concepts for improvements using aggregate planning.

Also, to be effective, the forecast interval has to provide sufficient lead time to allow the resource mix to be changed in accordance with the plan. The paint company might decide to do aggregate planning using monthly time buckets with a planning horizon of six months and updating the conclusions once every three months. Figure 13-2 illustrates these time-planning concepts with the numbers just given.

13-1b Standard Units of Work

It was said that "aggregate planning is achieved by collecting and lumping all items to be produced together." This should be amended to "... lumping all items together that share the use of common resources." This point, which was previously made, is emphasized by the process of creating standard units.

This process requires that different parts, activities, products, and services all be described and accounted for in terms of an arbitrarily chosen, but agreed-upon standard unit of work. For example, assume that a paint department has resource availability of 100 standard units per hour. To make a pint of deluxe external white paint, it requires two standard units of work; to make a gallon of green latex paint, it requires five standard units. Start playing with the options. The company can make 20 gallons of green per hour, or 50 pints of white, or 10 gallons of green and 25 pints of white, etc. Other departments and other products are combined in line with resource interchangeability and demand requirements.

The aggregated total will be used for workforce planning. Seven standard units of workforce time are required to make one pint of white and one gallon of green paint. Workforce planning is of great importance to all service industries. It applies to crew scheduling for airlines, hospitals, and banks. Because many job shops provide services and not goods, it pays to emphasize the fact that AP is useful to all kinds of job shops. It also can apply to intermittent flow shops, which have lumpy demands over time.

The Blackfeet Indian Pencil Company in Browning, Montana, was a small company selling a variety of writing instruments such as markers and pencils. Demands were too sporadic to permit sound aggregate planning. Book publishers having to plan for erratic demand patterns have learned to do aggregate planning. Theme parks, hotels, and resorts have shifting demands as a function of seasons and events, and they have learned how to do successful aggregate planning. They cannot inventory low-season, unused capacities to accommodate peak demands. Nevertheless, they can use AP for workforce scheduling.

In addition to workforce planning, AP treats inventory and equipment availability. The AP model cannot always satisfy demand. Sometimes capacity is insufficient. At other times, some part of the system's resources will be idle because supply is greater than demand. As the AP models are developed, note in particular how certain kinds of supply (like overtime) provide protection against not being able to deliver the goods and services. However, P/OM is usually happy to see that overtime supply is seldom utilized.

The direct approach for understanding standard hour computations is to work through an example of how planners aggregate demands for different products or services. This means changing actual hours of work into standard units of required production capacity. For the example that follows, the standard unit is selected as a standard machine hour (SMH). A machine can be chosen to be the standard arbitrarily or because it is the newest or the fastest. Thereafter, the standard machine (SM) is the standard for comparison with all other machines.

For this example, total production capacity is based on four machines (departments, people, etc., can be used when appropriate). The four machines, called M1, M2, M3 and M4, work at different rates. It must be noted that the rate differentials apply across all of the jobs that these machines are assigned.

That is: M2 is fastest—for all of the jobs, and by the same amount in comparison with the other machines. It is logical to choose M2 as the standard machine (SM). It will be assigned an SM index of 1.0. All of the other machines in comparison will have fractional SM indexes. Thus:

Machine Number	SM Index	Description
1	0.5	50% as fast as M2
2	1.0	Standard Machine
3	0.8	80% as fast as M2
4	0.6	60% as fast as M2

Each machine, department, or person is ranked by an index number that when multiplied by the actual machine hours available per week yields the standard machine hours (SMH) available per week. Thus, Table 13-1 provides the actual machine hours that are

Table 13-1	Machine	SMH Index	SMH per Week	Actual Hours
Supply of Actual and SMH Hours Available per Week	M1	0.5	18 SM hours	36
	M2*	1.0	54 SM hours	54
	M3	0.8	64 SM hours	80
	M4	0.6	20 SM hours	33.3
	Total SMH		**156 SM hours**	

M2* with the asterisk is the standard machine (SM). If M1 had been chosen as SM, the indexes would have been (1.0, 2.0, 1.6, 1.2), which is the result of multiplying the SMH index by 2. This kind of relationship is not unusual between machines. It often applies to skills. Some variations from perfect index relations can be tolerated as long as they provide a reasonable approximation.

Job	A	B	C	D	E
Units demanded	300	210	240	1,800	400

Table 13-2

A Forecast of Demand *D* in Actual Units for Next Week

Job	A	B	C	D	E
Production rate of the standard machine in units per standard machine hour (SMH)	6	7	6	30	25

Table 13-3

Productivity Rates of Standard Machine

available per week converted by means of the SMH index into standard machine hours available per week.

The total of 156 standard machine hours (SMH) is available per week. How many standard hours are in demand? The fact that there are 203.3 actual machine hours available per week has no significance for the resolution of the problem. Actual hours must first be converted to standard hours for application to the jobs that need to be done. This will be understood by examining the job requirements in Table 13-2, which represents a forecast of demand for next week.

Table 13-3 provides the *productivity rate* (i.e., the production output rate) of the standard machine for each of the jobs listed in Table 13-2. These data are obtained from the production department and have not been previously furnished.

The computations for converting demand in actual units into demand in standard units are guided by the following equation where unit dimensions are shown in parentheses. The dimension of *units* is in the numerator and denominator and cancels out. The remaining dimension is *SMH* (standard machine hours). Thus, demand in units has been transformed to demand in standard machine hours.

$$D(actual\ units) \div PR\left(\frac{units}{SMH}\right) = D(SMH)$$

$$D(actual\ units) \div PROD(units/SMH) = D(SMH\ units)$$

(13-1)

$D(actual\ units)$ = demand in actual units for each kind of job (e.g., 4 lamps, 6 chairs)
$PROD(units/SMH)$ = the production rate of units per SMH
$D(SMH\ units)$ = demand in units of standard hours

Table 13-4 converts actual units of demand for jobs A through E into standard machine hours (SMH) of demand, as follows:

	SMH of Demand—by Jobs		
A	300/6	=	50 SM hours
B	210/7	=	30 SM hours
C	240/6	=	40 SM hours
D	1800/30	=	60 SM hours
E	400/25	=	16 SM hours
	Sum	=	**196 SM hours**

Table 13-4

Demand in Units Converted into Standard Hours

To satisfy demand, 196 standard machine hours (SMH) are needed. The transformation of the dimension *actual units* to *SMH units* should be noted. It makes the generalized nature of standard machine hours understandable. Both supply and demand have been converted to the common terms of SMH. As shown in Table 13-1, there are 156 standard machine hours available. So, $196 - 156 = 40$ SMH of demand that will *not* be met.

The same reasoning applies to standard workforce hours (people hours) and to combinations of people and machines working together. Various weighting schemes can be used to bring different kinds of estimates of supply and demand into a *common framework*.

13-2 The Importance of Forecasts

Production planning

First level is aggregate planning; it is the only level that requires a forecast. The second level is loading; level three is sequencing.

Figure 13-3 shows the connection between the three activity levels of **production planning**. Note that the top box—called Level 1—aggregate planning—is the *only one* that requires a forecast. This will be used in addition to orders that are on hand. Activity Level 2 is **loading**, and activity Level 3 is **sequencing**, all to be explained shortly.

If all three levels of production scheduling are well managed, job shop profitability is significantly enhanced. Doing this complex job well requires total attention to detail and understanding the system.

13-2a Planning Horizon for Aggregate Scheduling

Loading

Assign jobs to departments before sequencing jobs within departments.

First level. Set the planning horizon for forecasting demand, as required by AP, equal to or greater than the longest lead time. If it takes eight months to have an order filled for materials needed to make the product, or to hire five computer programmers, no plan can be carried out until eight months have elapsed. Lead times include the interval required to train the workforce, obtain needed facilities, and be able to do the jobs that are forecast.

Sequencing

Primary basis for establishing optimal sequence is to minimize the time jobs spend waiting. There are other bases, too.

13-2b Loading Is Assigning Jobs to Departments

Second level. Assigning jobs to departments is called *loading*. These departments have been equipped and staffed according to the aggregate plan. The jobs are bound to deviate in number and kind from the AP forecast. The estimate of required total standard hours

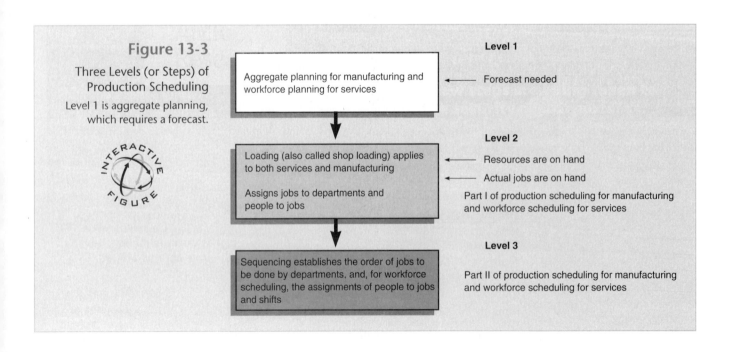

Figure 13-3

Three Levels (or Steps) of Production Scheduling

Level 1 is aggregate planning, which requires a forecast.

INTERACTIVE FIGURE

Level 1

Aggregate planning for manufacturing and workforce planning for services   ←— Forecast needed

Level 2

Loading (also called shop loading) applies to both services and manufacturing

Assigns jobs to departments and people to jobs

←— Resources are on hand
←— Actual jobs are on hand

Part I of production scheduling for manufacturing and workforce scheduling for services

Level 3

Sequencing establishes the order of jobs to be done by departments, and, for workforce scheduling, the assignments of people to jobs and shifts

Part II of production scheduling for manufacturing and workforce scheduling for services

may be fairly good, but how jobs get allocated to specific departments will have greater uncertainty. As is usual, errors tend to cancel out. The second level of production scheduling permits a comparison to be made of forecast versus actual demand. Feedback concerning accuracy may be helpful in improving future forecasts. Further, at the second level, the real resources that were collected and prepared, based on the aggregate plan, must now be used to deal with the actual demand on hand.

13-2c Sequencing Sets the Order for Doing Jobs at the Department

Third level. Sequence work according to a good shop-floor (or service-floor) policy. This rule determines the order in which jobs will be done by each department. Intervals between loading and sequencing are short (days or hours), whereas the intervals between AP and loading are long (months). Sequencing decisions have an important effect on customer satisfaction. They are determinants of delivery schedules and affect costs as well. The quality of sequencing decisions is always a consequence of AP and loading decisions; however, sequencing skills and knowledge are based on experience with customers wants and process requirements.

13-2d Integration of the Three Levels

If the three levels of the job shop are not recognized, a number of problems and possible crises can result. Job shop "veterans" call it "organized chaos." Lack of careful attention to the three levels leads to random management of the system. Job shop management involves so many details (different jobs, machines, workers) that strong information management capabilities are essential.

At the aggregate planning level, forecasting plays a crucial role. It is not possible to do aggregate planning without a forecast. Therefore, if the company lacks the means to get a method-based forecast, all that remains is to guess. Common sense works.

If management is not in control of the situation, losses occur because of neglect at all three levels. The costs are cumulative. They impair an organization's competitiveness. Errors made at the first level create unnecessary costs at the second and third levels. Errors made at the second level create unnecessary costs at the third level. That is what is meant by cumulative costs.

Information is essential for forecasting and planning at level one and for decision making at levels two and three where the aggregate units have become specific jobs. Most companies maintain the necessary information about processing in the form of blueprints, bills of materials, operations sheets, and routing sheets. Most of these are available as printouts from computerized databases.

Methods for ordering materials required for the job shop follow aggregate planning. These include developing master production schedules, which are precise commitments of what is to be made in the shop or done by the service organization.

Aggregate planning gains utility from a statistical advantage of forecasting for aggregate phenomena as compared to forecasting values for specific components of the aggregation. For example, sales forecasts of the category "cameras" are more accurate than for any specific camera within the category.

Aggregate forecasts are always better than the set of component forecasts because the standard deviation of the total (T) of (n) components is equal to the square root of n multiplied by the standard deviation of the individual components. The equations are shown here. Consider as another example the sales estimates for the spring quarter. First, the variance of the estimate for the quarter is equal to the sum of the variances of the three months of April, May, and June.

$$\sigma^2_{Spring} = \sigma^2_{April} + \sigma^2_{May} + \sigma^2_{June} \text{ or more generally, } \sigma^2_{Total} = \sigma^2_1 + \sigma^2_2 + ... + \sigma^2_n$$

For simplicity, assume the variances of the components ($i = 1, 2, 3, \ldots, n$) are all about equal. Then, $\sigma_T^2 = n\sigma_i^2$ and $\sigma_T = \sigma_i\sqrt{n}$.

The square root effect makes the standard deviation of the total significantly smaller than the linear sum of n standard deviations. The standard deviation of three months is $\sigma_T = \sigma_i\sqrt{3} = 1.732\sigma_i$, which is 0.58 of the sum of three months taken separately, i.e., $(1.73)/(3.00) = 0.58$. Forecast enhancement is one of the AP model's advantages.

13-3 Basic Aggregate Planning Model

Job shops require a strong methodological approach for planning ahead. There is much detail needed to capture the variety. Aggregate planning provides just the approach that the job shop requires. Demand and production output are treated in aggregation across a variety of different work facilities and output jobs. The aggregate is treated as one job made by one facility operating under several different modes, e.g., regular and overtime production, with and without subcontractors.

The organization's facilities are used to satisfy varying demand levels over time and in whatever way promises to minimize total costs. These total costs vary according to the work schedule used. Demands for different outputs are aggregated by considering them all to be a unified demand for the output capacity of the facility.

Figure 13-4 shows the demand side of the system. Varying demands for different items (1, 2, and 3) have been aggregated into a single demand called S_t. Previously, the forecast components were months of the quarter. This time the components are different items. The sum of item demands in period t results in total sales called S_t.

Figure 13-5 shows the production factors of aggregate planning:

1 Demand aggregated over time (e.g., sales = S_t).
2 Supply aggregated over time (e.g., production = P_t).
3 Overtime production occurs when the normal time production capacity level (*ntc*) is exceeded, ($P_t \geq ntc$).
4 Workforce level = W_t, measures human resources required to meet demand.

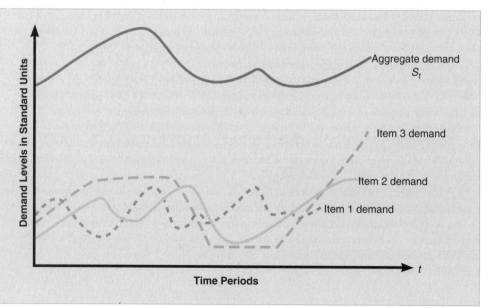

Figure 13-4

Aggregate Demand as the Sum of the Demand of Three Items in Standard Units over Time Period *t*

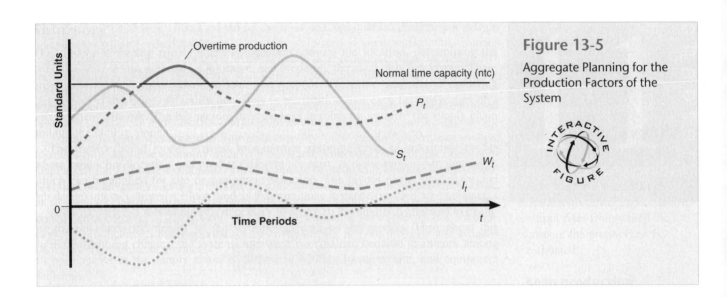

Figure 13-5

Aggregate Planning for the Production Factors of the System

5   Inventory level = positive I_t is the result of supply being greater than demand—stock accumulates; negative I_t results when demand exceeds supply and out-of-stock or backorder conditions occur.

6   All factors are measured against *ntc* stated in standard units.

The aggregate supply resulting from production during period t is P_t. Both the facilities used and the organization's workforce are likely to vary over time. The workforce level during time t is called W_t. For the prior period, called $t - 1$, the workforce level is called $W_t - 1$. The same time considerations apply to supply, demand, and inventory levels. Production managers need to control inventory levels over time. Thus: $I_t, I_{t-1}, I_{t-2}, \ldots I_{t-n} \ldots$, which is also shown in Figure 13-5.

Using the forecast for aggregate demand S_t over time, the aggregate planning problem is: What values of P_t, W_t, and I_t will optimize this supply chain system's performance?

More specifically, the aggregate planning problem requires period-by-period solutions that will optimize the total system's performance. There are interperiod dependencies, which mean that one period might not be as good as it could be in order that the total result for the entire planning horizon is best. This is classic systems thinking in which component performance may have to be suboptimized to obtain the system's optimal. (Note Tables 13-5, 13-6, and 13-7 as good examples of aggregate systems planning. Also see Figures 13-6a, 13-6b, 13-6c, and 13-6. These tables and figures provide much information.)

Month t	S_t	P_t	I_t	$\sum_{t=1}^{t} I_t$	W_t	$W_t - W_{t-1}$
1	420	380	−40	−40	38	0
2	360	380	+20	−20	38	0
3	390	380	−10	−30	38	0
4	350	380	+30	0	38	0
5	420	380	−40	−40	38	0
6	340	380	+40	0	38	0
Totals	**2,280**	**2,280**			**228**	**0**

Table 13-5

Pattern A—Constant

Table 13-6	**Month** t	S_t	P_t	I_t	$\sum_{t=1}^{t} I_t$	W_t	$W_t - W_{t-1}$
Pattern B—Chasing	1	420	420	0	0	42	0
	2	360	360	0	0	36	−6
	3	390	390	0	0	39	+3
	4	350	350	0	0	35	−4
	5	420	420	0	0	42	+7
	6	340	340	0	0	34	−8
	Totals	2,280	2,280	0	0	228	−8

Table 13-7	**Month** t	S_t	P_t	I_t	$\sum_{t=1}^{t} I_t$	W_t	$W_t - W_{t-1}$
Pattern C_1—Slightly Chasing—One of Many Combinations	1	420	390	−30	−30	39	+1
	2	360	370	+10	−20	37	−2
	3	390	390	0	−20	39	+2
	4	350	370	+20	0	37	−2
	5	420	390	−30	−30	39	+2
	6	340	370	+30	0	37	−2
	Totals	2,280	2,280			228	−1

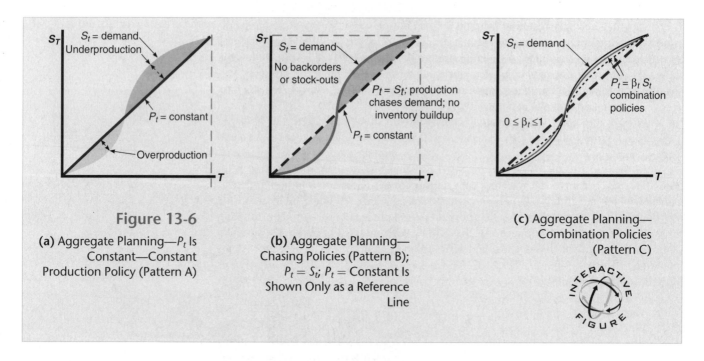

Figure 13-6

(a) Aggregate Planning—P_t Is Constant—Constant Production Policy (Pattern A)

(b) Aggregate Planning—Chasing Policies (Pattern B); $P_t = S_t$; $P_t =$ Constant Is Shown Only as a Reference Line

(c) Aggregate Planning—Combination Policies (Pattern C)

13-4 Three Aggregate Planning Policies

Constant production strategy

The sum of costs associated with a constant workforce must be less than the sum of costs associated with a variable workforce.

Three policies are considered here:

1 *Do not vary the workforce.* This means keeping P_t constant over time. By formula: $P_t = k$ for the entire period, $t = T$. Keeping a constant workforce is called a *level policy*. In Figure 13-6a, P_t is constant. This is the condition for a **constant production strategy**.

Both overproduction and underproduction occur when production is constant and demand varies. For most circumstances, keeping the workforce constant makes it easier to keep output constant. Then, the variability of demand determines whether overproduction (being overstocked) or underproduction (being understocked) is the problem to be faced at any point in time. Figure 13-6a calls this *Pattern A*.

The policy that creates Pattern A is a constant, fixed, and level volume of production. Routine production sequences can be followed every day. This saves money because process alterations are avoided. Setups, takedowns, and changeovers, which can be costly, are minimized. However, there are likely to be costs associated with the fact that the "level policy" does not match demand.

2 *Vary the workforce, W_t, so that production output, P_t matches demand, S_t as closely as possible*. Figure 13-6b calls this option *Pattern B*. It is labeled a **chasing policy** because P_t strives to match S_t at all times. Because the demand occurs before the supply can satisfy it, there is a lag in fulfilling the goal. That is the reason why production chases demand.

Pattern B (the *chasing policy*) is the solid line in Figure 13-6b. Because P_t cannot exactly match S_t, the actual production line would approach but not fall on the solid line in Figure 13-6b. This kind of situation will be shown later as a combination policy. Meanwhile, the pure chasing policy has as its paramount objective the avoidance of over- and understock inventory costs.

Pattern B strives to chase and match supply with demand—as exactly as possible—for every time period. This goal is represented by $P_t = S_t$. In this situation, workers are hired, fired, or furloughed in each time period according to the expected demand of the particular time period. Workforce changes are made according to the flexibility of the industry. In some situations, changes are daily. In others, they are weekly, monthly, or longer.

With perfect forecasts for an actionable lead time, there can be a perfect match. Perfect forecasts are hard to come by except where there are contracts that specify demand. Even in the case of contracts, it may be difficult to control the workforce size because of shortages caused by illness, weather, and lack of availability of certain skill sets. Also, overstaffing places burdens on the human resources managers who have to deal with personnel needs and the long-term repercussions of asking people to leave without notice.

Fixed-volume, level production shops—as in Pattern A—create a more stable job shop environment than the variable-volume, chasing production policy shops of Pattern B. Greater investments in training can be justified for Pattern A. As a result, the level shop has less start-up and learning waste. It is associated with higher quality products and services. A drawback to Pattern A is that it creates unneeded inventory when supply is greater than demand. It causes out-of-stocks and backorders when supply is less than demand. However, if properly managed, the inventory build-up is used to prevent out-of-stocks and backorders. When inventory build-up beyond a certain point is economically unfeasible, part of the constant workforce is idled.

Such idle time is minimized by the variable-volume job shop of Pattern B. When there is a large amount of demand fluctuation, a variable workforce capability is appealing but there are offsetting costs, which include information systems to keep track of workforce changes. That is the bookkeeping part of the problem. Being able to hire and lay off involves human resources management with a lot of detail. There are unpleasant aspects to layoffs. The use of temporary employees for peak loads and subcontracting can reduce the need for layoffs.

3 *Find superior combinations of policies (Patterns A and B)*. There are many different variable-volume lines that could connect zero and S_t. Some of these lines are shown in Figure 13-6c. Each is a partial chasing policy and a partial level policy. They are labeled *combination policies* in Figure 13-6c.

Chasing policy
The sum of costs of a variable workforce and underutilized equipment should be less than the sum of costs of overstocks and backorders.

© 2007 Jupiterimages Corporation

Workforce size is a variable that is often a function of the volume of business, revenues, and profits. This variability is characteristic of labor intensive planning meetings, creative brainstorming, and other kinds of knowledge work. It also occurs in the billing department, purchasing offices, with R & D, and the sales force. It used to be characteristic of production on the plant floor, but increasingly, machines are replacing workers, and they are idle when not needed.

The models for AP can provide guidance about minimum cost policies using tangible cost factors. Less tangible factors may have to be included qualitatively. In trying to find the best policy, there may be a cost of spreading management too thin. The systems approach can enable P/OM to do aggregate planning with costs that reflect human resources management limitations. Companies may prefer to use mixtures of policies (A + B = C) that come closer to being realistic than pure policies. Combination (C) policies have different patterns for production (partially) chasing demand. What is represented is greater reluctance to react rapidly to match demand. There is more systems inertia.

Each line in Figure 13-6c has different costs. Certain costs disappear when Pattern B is followed instead of Pattern A. At the same time, another set of costs appears. The cost-mixtures are greater for the lines in Figure 13-6c that deviate further from either of the pure policies. Each curve-solution represents some combination of changing production rates, changing workforce size, varying degrees of overtime utilization, fluctuating inventory levels, and overstocks as well as out-of-stocks.

Combination policies fall between two pure policies. Assume that P/OM would be happiest with level work conditions because it is never easy to hire and/or let workers go. On the other hand, marketing would be happiest with perfect chasing because it would not produce stock outages. Human resources management is the department that facilitates hiring and downsizing. Therefore, it might be on the same side as P/OM. Warehouse managers might prefer the marketing point of view because they can achieve better performance measures by avoiding overstocking given limited space. In view of this, combination policies produce the need for negotiations between different parts of the organization.

13-4a Pattern A—Policy: Supply Is Constant

Consider a numerical example of Pattern A. Assume that the workforce is maintained at a constant level ($W_t = 38$ workers) and that each worker can produce $k = 10$ units per time period. Then, production will be constant at $P_t = 380$. This in turn means that inventory will fluctuate as demand sometimes exceeds and sometimes falls below the constant supply of output units.

In Table 13-5, total supply equals total demand (2,280 units) for the 6-month planning horizon.

At the end of the first period, production has fallen short of demand by 40 units. The lack of inventory that requires **backordering** is indicated by $I_t = -40$. Backordered work is shown as negative inventory.

The cumulative inventory for month 1 is $\Sigma I_t = -40$ units. It is assumed that prior to period 1 there was zero inventory accumulation and no backorders. When cumulative inventory changes signs from minus to plus, it means that backorders have been filled and accumulation of stock has occurred. The details for this example are shown in Table 13-5.

In reality, it is impossible to tell which purchases will be backordered since inventory is stated in terms of aggregates. Also, some buyers refuse to accept backorders. These orders are known as *fill or kill*. In Table 13-5, all backordered jobs are filled eventually (by the sixth month). The cumulative inventory column shows backorders occurring in four out of six periods, but the value is zero in month 6. That means that all cases of demand greater than supply that have been backordered have been filled. There are no more backorders.

In certain product classes, "fill or kill" is more likely than in others. An airline is not likely to cancel an order for a Boeing 787. Even though Boeing 787s are always back-ordered, a bankrupt airline has no choice but to cancel. However, an order for a recent Harry Potter DVD has to be filled. Children are said to have little patience with a local

Backordering
Because there is no stock on-hand to fill an order, customers are asked to wait a specific period of time. When stock is made, or received from a supplier at time t, the order from time $t - 1$ is filled. Some customers do not accept backorder status.

Blockbuster store that cannot fill an order. Yet, the Netflix business model is based on people's willingness to wait "a few" days.

It is customary to "fill or kill" orders for CDs, DVDs, and video games not available in the first store of choice. Customers are seldom willing to accept backorders for nail polish, lipsticks, other cosmetics, and gourmet foods. Brazilian hearts of palm and real caviar are often fill or kill items. Because they are needed "now," the buyer will travel far and wide to find what is wanted.

Note that in period 2, production, P_t is larger than demand S_t by 20 units. This adds 20 units to inventory, I_t. These units will be shipped to reduce backorders from 40 to 20. The remaining 20 backordered units are shown in row 2 under the cumulative inventory column as -20 units. The equation for *cum. inv.* is shown in the column heading of Tables 13-5, 13-6, and 13-7.

Summing up, Pattern A has understocks occurring in three of the six months, and it has overproduction in three of the six months. There is good news for this company. At the end of six months, the ups and the downs balance out. Cumulative inventory is measured as zero. It looks good to have a constant workforce of 38.

13-4b Pattern B—Policy: Supply Chases Demand

Consider Pattern B, where supply chases demand perfectly. What happens to costs when the workforce level is changed in order to allow production to match demand?

Because $(W_t - W_{t-1})$ will not always equal zero, as in Table 13-5, the production Pattern B $(P_t = S_t)$ can be followed by altering the workforce levels. Monthly variation of the workforce is used to match supply and demand. There will be no inventory accumulation if demand can be perfectly predicted so that workforce size can be perfectly adjusted. If perfection is elusive, then production always will be chasing demand, trying to reduce overstocks and decrease backorders.

If perfection is obtainable, then backordering and overstocking costs will not occur. In general, forecasts of demand will deviate from being perfect. Unexpected orders and cancellations are usual. Also, estimates of supply will not match the requirements. Workforce adjustments are difficult to achieve. New workers with specific skills cannot be found. The untrained take time to be brought up to speed.

Running the numbers, again, assume that each worker produces 10 units per time period. Demand in the first period is 420 units and 42 workers have been employed. Perfect forecasts of demand can be made. The results are shown in Table 13-6.

Production in the first period is 420 units, i.e., $P_1 = 420$. Production exactly matches demand, so there is no inventory, i.e., $I_1 = 0$. Cumulative inventory is shown in the fifth column heading of Tables 13-5, 13-6, and 13-7.

No change in workforce size $(\Delta W_t = W_t - W_{t-1})$ is assumed for the first period. Had there been fewer than 42 workers, then backorders would have arisen, and the workforce size in the next period would have been increased to catch up with demand. Whenever a forecast error causes overstocking or backordering, the workforce will be adjusted to catch up and produce zeros in the inventory columns.

In the second period, because the demand is 360, the workforce contracts to 36, which is a reduction of 6. Thus, $\Delta W_t = -6$. Then, the workforce expands to 39 in the third period. The remainder of the record is read from the table in the same way. W_t goes from 35 to 42 to 34. $P_t = S_t$, so there are neither inventories nor stock-outs and all orders are filled with minimum delay. The table portrays production perfectly chasing demand.

The supply chain is value adding continuously and in synchronization with demand. There are no unfilled orders, and there is no inventory sitting around waiting for demand to increase. On the other hand, the costs for changing workforce size can be substantial.

In addition to costs for changing W_t (i.e., related to ΔW_t), there are other costs that include alterations of space requirements and services (such as cafeteria and restrooms) for the workforce. More people need more room and more services. Further, $-\Delta W_t$

© 2008 Jupiterimages Corporation

Supply chasing demand is unlike a bike race. If the leader is demand and the laggard is supply, when demand slows up so does supply. The aggregate planning goal is for supply and demand to be as equal as possible—or neck-and-neck for bikes and horse races.

causes group morale problems and teamwork failures. These expenses are difficult to estimate, but they must be considered nevertheless.

Contrasting the two cases of A and B, the constant workforce has produced three instances of supply being less than demand. The total shortfall is 90 units. However, backorders never exceed 40, as seen from the cumulative inventory column. It should be remembered that cumulative inventory is the measure of actual stock on-hand, which is net stock on-hand.

In the constant workforce case, there is no positive accumulation of inventory. That is by chance because there is nothing to have prevented it from occurring. If the first period had been deleted, there would have been positive inventory to report. Note that for the constant workforce of 38, total demand for 6 periods equals total supply, which is 2,280 units.

The same totals apply to the figures for the chasing policy. In trade for no inventory or backorders, the organization is required to hire 10 workers and lay off 18. The costs of workforce changes need to be contrasted with the savings that result from having no backorders and no inventory accumulation.

Which approach has the lowest expected cost, Pattern A, B, or C? Recall that C-type patterns allow many different combinations of A and B. Thus, it is important to consider configurations that are logical mixtures of Patterns A and B.

13-4c Pattern C₁—Policy: Increase Workforce Size by One

Begin with a simple rule for change. Test the workforce level using the stable workforce size of 38 as a basis:

1 Increase the number of workers from 38 to 39 whenever demand > 380.
2 Decrease the number of workers from 38 to 37 whenever demand < 380.

Making unit changes is a sensible way to begin. Results are shown in Table 13-7. This plan *slightly* chases demand when $S_t > P_t$, and reduces backorders a little. This plan *slightly* reduces overstocks when $S_t < P_t$.

The resulting sum of the cumulative inventory for six periods of this *slightly* chasing policy (C_1) is shown in Equation 13-2 as −100 for total backorders and +0 for total stock on-hand.

$$\sum_{t=1}^{t=6} \sum_{t=1}^{t=6} I_t = -100 \tag{13-2}$$

Next, the sum of workforce changes is −1, as shown in Equation 13-3.

$$\sum_{t=1}^{t=6} \Delta W_t = -1 \tag{13-3}$$

That result is derived from +5 for hires and −6 for workforce reductions. There are charges for both types of changes. There are no additional labor charges because the average number of workers for the 6 periods in C_1 is 38.

Comparable figures for Pattern A (with a stable workforce policy where $W_t = 38$) are −130, as shown in Equation 13-4. That is the sum of −130 for total backorders and +0 for total stock on-hand.

$$\sum_{t=1}^{t=6} \sum_{t=1}^{t=6} I_t = -130 \tag{13-4}$$

By definition, for Pattern A, Equation 13-5 shows workforce change equals zero. That is zero for hires and zero for workforce reductions.

$$\sum_{t=1}^{t=6} \Delta W_t = 0 \tag{13-5}$$

Comparable figures for Pattern B (the chasing policy where no inventory costs occur) are shown in Equation 13-6 as zero:

$$\sum_{t=1}^{t=6}\sum_{t=1}^{t=6} I_t = 0 \tag{13-6}$$

The double sum equals zero, and this number is composed of two parts. There is -0 for total backorders and $+0$ for total stock on-hand. This result is predictable by the definition of perfect chasing.

The next calculation is the sum of workforce changes for Pattern B, which are -8, as shown in Equation 13-7.

$$\sum_{t=1}^{t=6} \Delta W_t = -8 \tag{13-7}$$

That sum is also composed of two parts. There is $+10$ for workforce hires and -18 for workforce reductions, which then net out to -8.

13-4d The Cost Structure

The costs that apply must be used to decide which is best. Comparing the stable policy A with the slightly chasing policy C_1, there is a reduction of backorders by 30, an increase of 5 for hires, and a decrease of 6 people for workforce reductions.

Say that backorders cost \$100 per occurrence, costs for carrying inventory are \$25 per unit, hires cost \$200 per instance, and reductions cost \$300 per event—all occurring within the time period. Then, for the C_1 policy, the total variable cost, $TVC(C_1)$, is

$$TVC(C_1) = (100 \times 100) + (0 \times 25) + (5 \times 200) + (6 \times 300) = \$12,800$$

Compare this to the total variable costs of the stable workforce of 38 workers. For policy A, the total variable cost, $TVC(A)$, is

$$TVC(A) = (130 \times 100) + (0 \times 25) + (0 \times 200) + (0 \times 300) = \$13,000$$

Preference is for C_1, the *slightly* chasing policy, which has reduced costly backorders at the expense of increased hires and layoffs. The difference is only \$200, but the policy was only slightly chasing. Because backorders are driving the preference, it is logical to examine policy B, which completely eliminated inventory costs by chasing demand perfectly (perhaps unrealistically). Total variable cost $TVC(B)$ for the B policy is the winner.

$$TVC(B) = (0 \times 100) + (0 \times 25) + (10 \times 200) + (18 \times 300) = \$7,400$$

Chasing as much as possible seems to be the preferred way to go for the particular costs that have been assumed. Other costs would lead to entirely different conclusions.

The comparisons are examples of **cost trade-off analysis** using only the variable portions of total cost. The variable portions are those costs that differ between alternative choices. The total variable costs do not include the costs of the workforce size, W_t, so long as there are no additional wages to be paid. If a policy required hiring a 39th worker, the cost of the individual's wages would have to be included as a variable component.

Another factor to consider is the difference in the costs of increasing the workforce size and of decreasing the workforce size. There is no reason for them to be equivalent. Hiring involves orientation and training. There are many forms of workforce reduction. Some ways are temporary; others are permanent.

Also, note that when supply (P_t) varies with demand (S_t), workforce adjustment costs could represent overtime costs with a constant size workforce, or a fluctuating workforce

Cost trade-off analysis
Different mixtures of the two pure strategies are feasible. Each blended strategy has a unique total cost, which may be less than the total costs of either pure strategy.

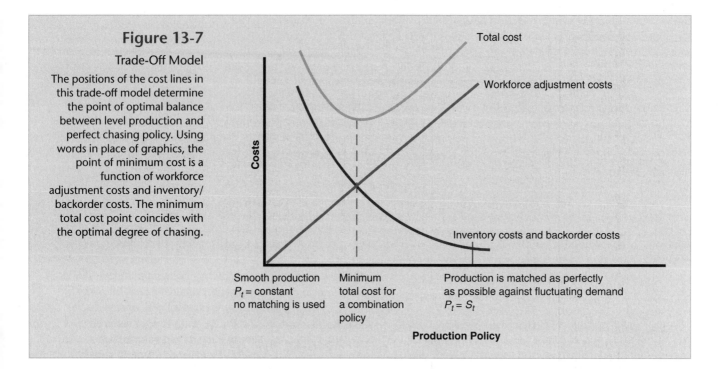

Figure 13-7

Trade-Off Model

The positions of the cost lines in this trade-off model determine the point of optimal balance between level production and perfect chasing policy. Using words in place of graphics, the point of minimum cost is a function of workforce adjustment costs and inventory/backorder costs. The minimum total cost point coincides with the optimal degree of chasing.

size, without the use of overtime. The cost structures must apply to the policies that are followed.

There is a trade-off between workforce adjustment costs and inventory/backorder costs. The **trade-off model** is shown in Figure 13-7, where the x-axis runs from level production at the left to perfect chasing (production matches demand) at the right.

Workforce adjustment costs and inventory/backorder costs are added together to create the total cost curve, which has a minimum point. That minimum total cost is associated with the concept of a combination policy, which is not specific. The idea of a 50 percent chasing policy is ambiguous.

Looking at Figure 13-7, imagine that the line describing workforce adjustment costs rises more steeply. Because there are two kinds of workforce adjustment costs, perhaps two lines should have been used. Because only one line is used in this case, an assumption has been made that the two kinds of costs are equivalent. Possible reasons that the slope of the workforce adjustment cost line has increased could include new government regulations requiring more training and larger severance packages.

When the slope of this line rises more steeply, the effect is to move the minimum cost point of the total cost line (the optimal combination) closer to constant (level) production. If the inventory and backorder cost curve rises, that curve moves upward and to the right. The effect is to move the optimal combination closer to perfect matching of production and demand.

Trade-off model
See **Cost trade-off analysis**.

13-5 Linear Programming (LP) for Aggregate Planning

Figure 13-7 illustrated the way in which total cost reaches a minimum value for some particular production schedule. The goal is to find that **minimum cost assignment schedule**. This is equivalent to identifying the production policy for the minimum cost point on the x-axis of Figure 13-7.

Minimum cost assignment schedule
Search for the production schedule that has the minimum total cost along the scale that starts with smooth production and ends with perfect matching of supply and demand.

A linear equation can be written for the minimum total cost objective. Also, a set of constraints will be needed to characterize patterns such as those previously described as A, B, and C_1. The advantage of LP for aggregate planning is that computer programs can quickly solve problems with a large number of variables and many constraints. Check out the power of Solver in Microsoft's Excel to provide LP solutions. This is explained in expanded form in Section 10-10. Also, QMpom has a module called Mathematical Programming Models, which includes Linear Programming, Integer Linear Programming, Product Mix, Diet Problem and Transportation Models.

The nature of **linear programming (LP)** variables and LP constraints now will be explained in terms of symbols, many of which have already been introduced in this chapter. Repetition has its benefits.

Linear programming (LP)
See **Fundamental theorem of linear programming (LP)**.

S_t = sales in period t (sales demand is forecast on definite orders). If supply < demand, some part of S_t will not be satisfied. LP selects the best demands to fill. Best is defined as achieving the minimum cost solution (and/or the maximum profit solution).

t = the planning horizon that is chosen in terms of *need to plan ahead* and *believability of the forecast*. Time periods can be in days, weeks, months, quarters, or years, depending upon the way that the data are collected and other circumstances of measurement.

Five variables that can be controlled for optimal aggregate planning are:

1 W_t = the number of workers at the beginning of each period t. $P_t = kW_t$ = normal production output in period t (k is the output per worker in period t). Ordinarily k is not considered to be a decision variable. However, by selecting different equipment, and by using different skill levels, it is possible to affect productivity. In this case, P_t is derived from W_t and k is considered to be a constant. W_t is the variable that will be used in the LP equation.

2 A_t = workforce additions (number of people) at the beginning of period t.

3 R_t = workforce reductions (number of people) at the beginning of period t.

4 I_t = inventory (number of units in stock, or out-of-stock) at the beginning of period t.

5 O_t = overtime production (units of output) in period t.

Seven reasonable constraints for each period are

1 $W_t \leq W$, which places limits on the workforce because of space, payroll, and other resource availability.

2 $A_t \leq A$, which places limits on additions to the workforce because of constraints imposed by training facilities and the ability to absorb additional workers.

3 $R_t \leq R$, which places limits on reductions to the workforce because of constraints on ability to process layoffs and company policy regarding the number of layoffs and furloughs that will be permitted in a time period.

4 $W_t = W_{t-1} + A_t - R_t$. This equation describes the size of the workforce at the beginning of each time period t. It is subject to constraints 1, 2, and 3.

5 $I_{min} \leq I_t \leq I_{max}$ places limits on how large or small the inventory held in each period can become. If backorders are allowed, I_{min} can be a negative number. Storage limitations can be the basis for the maximum inventory level at time t.

6 $O_t \leq O$ places a limit on how much overtime is acceptable.

7 $I_t = I_{t-1} + P_t + O_t - S_t = I_{t-1} + kW_t + O_t - S_t$

This describes the amount of inventory (net stock on-hand, or out-of-stock) at the beginning of each time period t imposed by constraints 5 and 6.

There are five variables and seven constraints for each time period. Say that the time period is months. Then, with a planning horizon of six months there would be 30 variables and 42 constraints. In practice, some of the constraints that have been listed as possibilities would not be exercised. Say that half of them are real constraints. This would result in 30 variables and 21 constraints.

For reasons that are described here, only 21 variables will have values greater than zero. This means that $(30 - 21) = 9$ variables will have zero values. They will not be active variables.

13-5a The Fundamental Theorem of LP

Fundamental theorem of linear programming (LP)

For aggregate planning, supplies and demands will determine the number of different active production assignments that can be made to minimize total costs.

Crucial to understanding LP is the fact that it is a mathematical method consisting of equations that are interdependent. The dependencies are expressed by the **fundamental theorem of linear programming (LP)**. It states that there cannot be more *active variables* than *real constraints*. From the previous paragraph, the assumption has been made that there are 21 real constraints. From the fundamental theorem, there can be only 21 active variables. Twelve of these can be accounted for at the outset.

There are six time periods for the five variables (W_t, A_t, R_t, I_t, and O_t). This results in 30 variables that could be active. Workforce will be positive for all six t. That is six active variables. Inventory levels are likely to be positive for all six t. The result is that 12 active variables have been noted. This means that at least nine uses of overtime, or additions to the workforce, or reductions to the workforce, will be inactive (e.g., set at zero). Inactive variables will not be used.

To obtain a minimum cost LP solution, individual costs must be assigned to the variables, as follows:

c_W = earnings of each worker per time period t
c_A = cost of adding a worker
c_R = cost of reducing the workforce—removing a worker
C_c = cost of carrying a unit for the time period t
c_o = cost of production for an overtime unit

The total cost objective function to be minimized is an all-linear set of equations, as shown in Equation 13-8. Note that there is an equation for each time period t, as t goes from one to T.

$$TC = \sum_{t=1}^{t=T} (c_W W_t + c_A A_t + c_R R_t + C_c I_t + c_o O_t) \qquad (13\text{-}8)$$

This cost minimization is subject to satisfying the demands, S_t. If supply < demand, the most costly demands will not be met.

A common objection to use of the LP model is that it has a linear structure for the costs of the objective function and for the constraints. A pioneering aggregate planning model called **HMMS**, after its creators, allows nonlinear costs. This requires much more work. The advantage is that results obtained from a better model of reality are more likely to provide rewards instead of penalties. The problem is that the nonlinear costs require great amounts of tracking and even then are elusive and change in the blink of an eye. Also, the computational burden is so large that most analysts demur at using the model.

HMMS

Pioneering aggregate planning model that uses nonlinear costs for its resource constraints.

Another important issue is that production output is sensitive to the k in $P_t = kW_t$. P/OM carefully considers how k can be increased by introducing new technology and by improving training methods. This is not part of the LP solution. However, by increasing k, different solutions will be obtained. Overtime costs can be scaled back, workforce additions can be decreased, and workforce decreases may be possible. The minimum total cost can be reduced considerably by using improved process methods. From the systems perspective, coordination with human resources management for training improvements, and marketing for better product-mix alternatives, can significantly decrease costs. In fact, this kind of application may make sense for airline crew scheduling and airline flight schedules, but even so, it is not used.

13-6 Transportation Model (TM) for Aggregate Planning

The transportation matrix provides a convenient representation of the aggregate planning problem. It can provide an optimal aggregate solution based on relatively simple assumptions. Computer software can solve these transportation problems using network algorithms[1] or linear programming (LP) software. As previously mentioned, QMpom covers this application within its module called Mathematical Programming Models.

Two versions of transportation matrices are presented. The first one allows no backorders and is relatively easy to solve by hand, if it is not too large. The second one, which permits backorders and their special costs, is presented as Enrichment Activity 13. When backorders are allowed, the solution is too laborious to solve by hand if there are more than a few variables and constraints. Computer software is recommended in Enrichment Activity 13.

Costs that apply to one, or the other, or both versions of the transportation matrix are listed here:

r = normal production labor costs per unit made during the regular work shift
v = overtime or second-shift production costs per unit made
c = inventory carrying costs, per dollar of expenditure over a given time period
b = backorder costs per unit and per time period backordered
I_0 = initial inventory (for the beginning of period $t = 1$)
I_f = final inventory (for the end of period $t = f$)

Table 13-8 presents the first version of the aggregate-planning transportation matrix, which does not allow backorders. Table EA13-1 in Enrichment Activity 13 presents the second version of the TM, which permits backorders.

With respect to Table 13-8, demand is shown as the column totals for the first three columns. D_1, D_2, and D_3 are demand levels in the first, second, and third periods.

Final inventory (called I_f) is specified at the bottom of the fourth column. Slack (SL)—which balances supply and demand—is listed at the bottom of the fifth column.

Supply is shown as row totals. The first row is initial inventory (called I_0). Thereafter, rows alternate in presenting production supply for regular time and for overtime, called R_1 and O_1, R_2 and O_2, R_3 and O_3.

The objective is to minimize total cost. Constraints reflect the limited availability of regular and overtime production capacity in hours. As another version of the problem, alternative configurations can be studied where capacity is added or removed by additional hires and/or new equipment technology.

Standard units are required to aggregate different kinds of product where the same resources are used to make diverse models such as small and large cans (aggregated as "cans"), or white, red, and green paint (aggregated as "paint"), or 40, 60, 75, and 100 watt bulbs (aggregated as "bulbs" even though "bulbs" include tungsten, CFLs, LCDs, etc.).

The transportation model (TM) is flexible. *It does not require a square matrix.* Each matrix applies to a specific period of time. Table 13-8 has eight rows and six columns—one of which is a slack column. In this case, a slack column is added instead of a slack row because supply is greater than demand. Thus, $S > D$, so $S - D > 0$ and $S - D = SL$. Then: $S = D + SL$. Slack costs are all zero.

Table 13-8

Transportation Model for Aggregate Planning—No Backorders Allowed

		Sales Periods					
		1	2	3	Final Inv.	Slack	Supply
Initial Inv.		0	c	$2c$	$3c$	0	I_0
Regular 1		r	$r+c$	$r+2c$	$r+3c$	0	R_1
Overtime 1		v	$v+c$	$v+2c$	$v+3c$	0	O_1
Regular 2	x		r	$r+c$	$r+2c$	0	R_2
Overtime 2	x		v	$v+c$	$v+2c$	0	O_2
Regular 3	x	x		r	$r+c$	0	R_3
Overtime 3	x	x		v	$v+c$	0	O_3
Demand	D_1	D_2	D_3	I_f	SL	Grand Total	

The model is linear. This means that unit costs or profits are not able to be changed as a function of volume. Profit saturation and nonlinear cost increases cannot be represented.

Normal transportation methods are used to obtain the minimum cost solution. In this case, however, backorders are prohibited (by the x's in six cells). Each x represents a situation where production units made in the nth period are intended for delivery in the $(n - 1)$ period. This is equivalent to making units in February that are intended to satisfy January demands that were backordered. To have the computer program block assignments, backorders are assigned large unit transport costs in the x-marked cells.

Several simple numerical examples are assigned in the Problems Section at the end of this chapter. Calling the time period months, the transportation matrices in Tables 13-8 and EA13-1 cover a planning horizon of one quarter. Note how the carrying costs are zero for the first month. For the second month c is charged per unit carried in that month. For the third month, $2c$ is charged because inventory has been carried two months. Back-order costs are like carrying costs. They grow with each additional month that a unit is being backordered.

13-6a Network and LP Solutions

The AP problem in Table 13-8 has unique characteristics because no backorders are allowed. It can be solved by assigning as many units as possible to the lowest cost cells in each column. Start the process with column 1. When the supply in a row is used up, go to the next lowest cost in the column and assign as many units as possible in that row. The constraints that must be met are the row and column totals. More units cannot be assigned to the lowest cost cells than row and column totals allow.

When column allocations equal the column 1 total, move to column 2. Proceed in the same way, making sure not to assign more units to lowest cost cells than the row and column totals can support. The lowest cost assignments in column 2 may be blocked by assignments already made in column 1. These blocked assignments cannot be violated. Continue until all columns have been assigned. Solutions obtained in this way are optimal.

It is useful to understand the LP equations for solving transportation problems because LP organizes the input data correctly for software applications. The constraining equations or supply inequalities (which are also called *in-equations*) are

$$\sum_{j=1}^{M} x_{ij} \leq S_i \tag{13-9}$$

where i = rows (supply); $i = 1, 2, \ldots, N$; and where j = columns (demand); $j = 1, 2, \ldots, M$. This applies to one row at a time.

The demand constraint is

$$\sum_{i=1}^{N} x_{ij} \leq D_j \tag{13-10}$$

where i = rows (supply); $i = 1, 2, \ldots, N$; and where j = columns (demand); $j = 1, 2, \ldots, M$. This applies to one column at a time.

The grand total is the sum of all active cell assignments and is the total number of units of supply or demand, whichever is larger. The larger value includes active slack values.

$$\sum_{i}^{N} \sum_{j}^{M} x_{ij} = \text{Grand Total} \tag{13-11}$$

The objective function to be minimized is

$$TC = \sum_{i}^{N} \sum_{j}^{M} c_{ij} x_{ij} \tag{13-12}$$

where TC = total cost of all active x_{ij} assignments.

Data requirements include row totals for all S_i, column totals for all D_j, the number of rows, N, the number of columns, M, and the costs c_{ij} for all i and j. LP software has built-in methods for finding the first feasible solution, which is the starting point for the iterative improvement methodology. In addition, most software permits **sensitivity analysis**, which allows investigation of the effect of altering supply capacities, demand levels, and costs on a "what if" basis. (QMpom permits the full range of sensitivity analysis.)

Sensitivity analysis
Allows investigation of the effect of altering supply capacities, demand requirements, costs of carrying, backordering, etc.

13-7 Nonlinear Cost Model for Aggregate Planning (AP)

The linear limitations of LP and the transportation model (TP) are so often cited that it is important to explain what a nonlinear structure might look like. A well-known nonlinear method, called HMMS after its four developers, Holt, Modigliani, Muth, and Simon, was developed at PPG's paint factory.[2] The HMMS model addresses four separate issues.

1 What are nonlinear costs and what nonlinear costs apply to AP?
2 How complex is the HMMS model?
3 How much difference will it make?
4 In practice, how much is it used?

A linear cost equation is $y = cx$. A quadratic (second order), cost equation is $y = cx^2$. The quadratic cost equation is just one form of nonlinear cost equation. With linear costs, when x doubles, the cost y doubles. For example, y goes from c to $2c$ or from $2c$ to $4c$. With nonlinear costs, when x doubles, cost y might be squared. For example, y goes from c to $4c$ or from $4c$ to $16c$.

HMMS uses both linear and quadratic cost equations to approximate the actual cost system of the PPG job shop. The approximations are shown as grey dashed lines in Figure 13-8. The only linear cost line among these approximations is *payroll costs*. The solid black lines are generic assumptions that are frequently made about the "true" character of these specific cost functions.

Overtime costs increase in a nonlinear fashion as the production rate increases. The question is how rapid is that increase? The quadratic approximating cost function for overtime increases faster than the curve that was initially assumed. The specific rate of increase for overtime costs must be studied for the specific application as the production rate increases.

Hiring and firing costs were previously discussed. In Figure 13-8, the comparison is being made between the quadratic approximating cost and the linear assumption that is frequently used. Slopes of the linear estimates are different with the discontinuity occurring at the zero point. The quadratic approximation gets better as the number of people being hired and/or fired increases. Distortions around the zero point may not matter too much because the costs are small in that neighborhood.

The *inventory costs* curve takes into account not only stock on-hand and backorders, but also the setup costs that are associated with changing production from one product to another. The approximations are acceptable until the inventory on-hand, or backordered, is large. Good management can keep the actual costs experienced within the range of approximation (and before the costs escalate significantly).

The dashed grey lines in Figure 13-8 are based on the HMMS equations with specific values set for the cost coefficients. These coefficients were supplied by PPG managers to provide the best fit for each product line in the PPG job shop. Thus, payroll is linear and described by $(C_1 W_t)$.

The bifurcated costs of hiring and laying off are captured by one quadratic cost function $C_2 (W_t - W_{t-1})^2$ instead of two lines with different slopes. Only one cost coefficient, namely, C_2, is used to describe the required shape of the curve.

Similar descriptions apply to the other costs. The HMMS model requires four cost coefficients for the overtime payroll. These are C_3, C_4, C_5, C_6. Further discussion about costs and demand follow.

To evaluate the complexity of the HMMS model, a good starting point is the total cost equation.

$$\text{Minimize TC} = \sum_{t=1}^{t=T} C_t \tag{13-13}$$

T is the end period of the planning horizon, and C_t in the two equations is now spelled out.

$$C_t = C_1 W_t + C_2(\Delta W_t)^2 + C_3(P_t - C_4 W_t)^2 + C_5 P_t - C_6 W_t + C_7\left(\sum I_t - C_8 - C_9 S_t\right)^2 \tag{13-14}$$

Next is the critical constraint requirement for the rational balancing of inventory over consecutive periods:

$$\sum_{t=1}^{t=t^*} I_{t-1} + P_t - S_t = \sum_{t=1}^{t=t^*} I_t. \tag{13-15}$$

Cumulative inventory from period to period equals inventory at the end of the previous period $(t - 1)$ plus production added to inventory minus shipments from inventory, during the period t. This equality applies for all values of t, called t^*.

Figure 13-8

Cost Functions—Used for the
HMMS Aggregate Planning
Model

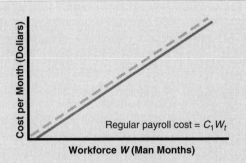

Regular payroll cost = $C_1 W_t$

Workforce *W* (Man Months)

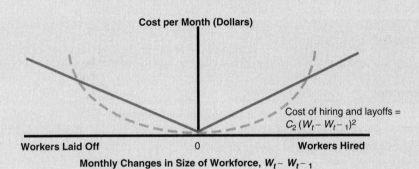

Cost per Month (Dollars)

Cost of hiring and layoffs =
$C_2 (W_t - W_{t-1})^2$

Workers Laid Off   0   **Workers Hired**

Monthly Changes in Size of Workforce, $W_t - W_{t-1}$

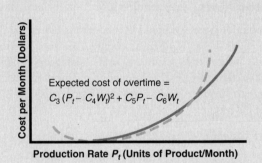

Expected cost of overtime =
$C_3 (P_t - C_4 W_t)^2 + C_5 P_t - C_6 W_t$

Production Rate P_t (Units of Product/Month)

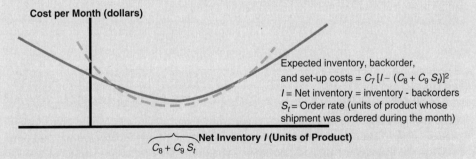

Cost per Month (dollars)

Expected inventory, backorder,
and set-up costs = $C_7 [I - (C_8 + C_9 S_t)]^2$
I = Net inventory = inventory - backorders
S_t = Order rate (units of product whose
    shipment was ordered during the month)

Net Inventory I (Units of Product)
$C_8 + C_9 S_t$

Source: From Charles C. Holt, Franco Modigliani, and Herbert A. Simon. "A Linear Decision Rule for Production and Employment Scheduling." *Management Science,* vol. 2, no. 1 (October 1955). Permission required
and granted.

The costs, forecast, and variables, as shown in the equation, are identified as follows:

Costs

C_1 = costs related to payroll (i.e., size of the workforce); as C_1 increases, the slope of the payroll line rises.

C_2 = hiring and layoff costs; workforce changes cause exponential increases in cost; C_2 is not exponential.

C_3, C_4, C_5, C_6 = four components of overtime costs; increases in C_4 and C_6 slow the rise in overtime costs.

C_7, C_8, C_9 = three different kinds of inventory costs; increases in C_8 and C_9 slow the inventory cost rise.

ΣC_t = total costs over t periods ($t = 1, 2, \ldots T$)

Given by Forecast

S_t = demand in units for period t; increases in S_t will reduce the net inventory costs.

Variables

ΣI_t = on-hand inventory minus backorders—end of period t

P_t = aggregate unit production rate—period t

W_t = workforce size—beginning of period t

13-7a Methodology for HMMS

The method for obtaining the optimal solution is detailed in the HMMS text. See Notes at the end of this chapter. The HMMS procedure uses the calculus of partial derivatives, which can be done quite readily with computers. Optimum values of W_t, P_t, and I_t must be obtained for each time period. The computational work to set up the computer for this approach, let alone to obtain correct estimates of nonlinear costs is significantly greater than anything that LP requires.

How much difference will the use of HMMS make? Using LP properly, good linear approximations of nonlinear functions can be made. To illustrate, note how the LP model treats workforce additions (hiring) and reductions (layoffs) separately. The HMMS approximation, in this case, may be less accurate. Also, there are additional techniques that can be used with LP to further the cause of approximating nonlinear cost functions.

No organizations are known to be users of the HMMS model. This is probably because data collection for HMMS and inputting data for solution are prone to errors. The only reason for explaining the HMMS model is to provide important insight into the use of alternative models for nonlinear costs.

13-7b Benchmarking the TM, LP, and HMMS Models for AP

The HMMS model stresses the need to get correct cost functions. It provides a basis for management to put costs under a microscope. The accounting department will not have a way to shed light on the real cost structure. Therefore, the discussion will entail a plan to obtain the actual costs experienced by the production department. Lean and activity-based accounting methods may make it easier to discard irrelevant costs and to get better fixes on those that are relevant.

HMMS also offers a benchmark for comparison of models. Because it is not linear, and the other models are linear, management must evaluate the consequences of making the linearity assumption. It is believed that the linear hypothesis is often quite acceptable. If distortions from linearity assumption are acceptable, then for ease of use the TM gets first place. It costs much less to use TM than HMMS. For overall ratings, LP gets a strong second place while HMMS is a far-distant third.

The old-fashioned balance scale was a better benchmarking symbol than a modern scale that tells the weight. The comparison between LP, TM, and HMMS requires sets of comparisons, and the scales reflect how much better one method is than another according to the dimension being judged.

In conclusion, it is useful for operations managers to suggest to aggregate planners that they examine all cost functions for linearity. When significant curvature characterizes a cost curve, the LP model should be designed—as much as possible—to take that into account.

Spotlight 13-1 Changing the Way We Pay
ATMs and Smart Cards

A major revolution in banking operations began in the 1970s with the advent of the automated teller machine (ATM). The traditional customer-to-teller relationship was replaced by customer-to-machine interface. Although customers primarily use ATMs for basic banking transactions, such as cash withdrawals and verification of account balances, this was still a trust transaction. It took time for many people to feel secure with the loss of person-to-person contact. A growing number of bank customers have demonstrated willingness to pay for the convenience of automated banking because an automated relationship permits access on a 24/7 basis.

In the back rooms of banks, P/OM has learned how to utilize automated operations to obtain significant savings in time and labor costs while extending banking hours. As an example of the progress made, in 1977, it was reported that the cost of processing ATM transactions was eight times the cost for paper checks.[3] Thirty years later, banks consider ATMs to be profit centers. Banks obtain income directly from ATM usage fees (including surcharges) and from increased banking activities. Unlike tellers, ATMs are at work 24/7. Bankrate.com estimated (in 2005) that American consumers pay more than $4.3 billion in withdrawal fees for using ATMs not owned by their own bank.

For a brief history, the ATM was invented 40 years ago by John Shepherd-Barron. It was installed in Barclay's in North London in 1967. Plastic cards had not been invented so special cheques (British spelling) were impregnated with carbon 14. The mildly radioactive substance was detected by the ATM, which matched the check number against a PIN number. The rest of the story is an outstanding example of P/OM working hand-in-glove with technology development experts.

Not resting on laurels, the banking industry continues to search for ways to expand the use of ATMs so as to generate new sources of revenues. For example, on-screen advertising is being tested, as is ATM use by customers for in-store payments for purchases. Additional revenue opportunities include airline passengers who are choosing to buy their tickets at (ATM) kiosks in the airports. Experiments with kiosks located in downtown areas can generate traffic for multiple purposes including deposits, payments, tickets for airlines, shows, and cash withdrawals. ATMs are on cruise ships and sell lottery tickets in convenience stores.

Gas station customers have become comfortable making credit and debit card payments at credit card ATMs that can ask the customer "Do you want a carwash?" Wal-Mart, Home Depot, Target, King Soopers, etc., have developed customer self-service systems for adding up the bill, bagging, paying, and checking out. Other sources of ATM income such as coupon use, recognition of supermarket loyalty cards, phone cards, Mobile Top-Up (using mobile phones with ATMs to make payments—such as adding to balances on prepaid cards), toll booth payments including automated charging via RFID (radio frequency identification), etc., are being used somewhere. Wikipedia places ATMs as far south as McMurdo Station in Antarctica, and as far north as Longyearbyen in Svalbard, Norway.

Most traditional ATMs are freestanding but other designs include through-the-wall models that can be fitted for either drive-up or walk-up kiosks. The U.K. colloquial for ATMs is "hole-in-the-wall." Outdoor units withstand extreme weather conditions. Maintenance and repair costs, as well as transaction costs, are often outsourced as well.

In Malaysia, topping-up a smart travel card (such as ez-link) involves a service charge of about 3 percent. In Singapore, ez-link is a contactless, stored-value smart card (CSC) that has replaced the magnetic farecard with impressive operational results. "Twenty people can now board the bus in one minute using the ez-link card, as compared to 12 if they were to pay cash and 15 if they were to use the magnetic farecard." This "improves boarding time for buses by as much as 50 percent." The increased speed in fareloading for rail is as much as 60 percent. The ez-link card uses an antenna and an IC chip for wireless radio communication.

Smart card (RFID) technology interacting with ATMs is changing one of the most accepted features of hundreds of years of history. Money may not disappear but it is undergoing a huge metamorphosis based on electronic payment systems. Wireless transactions allow secure identification because the smart cards transmit a significant amount of information using seamless communications between buyers and sellers.

Spotlight 13-1 (Continued)

In Britain, smart cards support dual currencies, i.e., the euro and the pound sterling. Also, new systems provide standards that allow the smart chip to have the same interoperability as the magnetic strip. Europay, MasterCard, and Visa jointly defined an international standard for smart card payment systems—called *EMV* for the sponsors' names. EMVCo, LLC, has managed and enhanced the integrated circuit card specifications since February 1999, which fosters secure transactions and ensures international interoperability.

The new card service can be used to shop on the web by means of an electronic purse, which is an instrument that facilitates payments between merchants and their customers. There is support for the notion that the electronic purse may one day replace currency in routine transactions.

Level Four Software, Ltd. (a U.K. company with its registered office in Dunfermline, Scotland) has been globalizing ATM use. With offices in Charlotte, North Carolina, Dubai Internet City, and Maidenhead, United Kingdom, the goal of geographic expansion is evident. Level Four's Bridge product is "a holistic solution for ATM software."

From the Level Four website http://www.levelfour.com/bridge_home.htm, we read:

"A rethink of the ATM and self-service 'network landscape' is required to bring new services to market faster and more efficiently." There is no doubt that new technology is emerging that will foster large changes in our monetary transaction systems.

Sources: Brian Milligan. "The Man Who Invented the Cash Machine." BBC News. June 25, 2007.
See http://news.bbc.co.uk/2/hi/business/6230194.stm
For Speedpass: http://www.speedpass.com/home.jsp.
For a global view of the ATM business, visit the industry association of ATM users: http://www.atmia.com.
For ez-link in Singapore, see http://www.ezlink.com.sg.
For EMV card, see http://international.visa.com/fb/downloads.
For electronic purse information, click on "Joint Specifications for Common Electronic Purse Cards."
For electronic purse, also see the top of page 5 in the report written by John Wenninger and David Laster (April 1995): http://www.newyorkfed.org/research/publication_annuals/por95.pdf.

Spotlight 13-2 Chick-fil-A®, Inc: A Great Business Model
Independent Operators and the Loyalty Effect

Courtesy of CFA Properties, Inc.

S. Truett Cathy, founder and chairman of Chick-fil-A®, Inc., looks back to 1967 when the first Chick-fil-A restaurant opened and says of himself at that time, "I did not expect . . . to be running a chain of 1,000 restaurants. I grew into it one day at a time with help from talented people around me. When you get this big, you grow through the talent of others." Truett Cathy learned to divide tasks and trust other people to do the job well. In 2006, Chick-fil-A's system-wide sales reached $2.275 billion. This figure reflects a 15.16 percent increase over the chain's

performance over the previous year and a same-store sales increase of 8.52 percent. Since 1967, the company has posted 39 consecutive annual sales increases, with double digit increases for the past 13 straight years. There are currently more than 1,300 restaurants in 37 states.

In 2006, Chick-fil-A was voted as having the best drive-through operation in America by *QSR Magazine* (Quality and Speed for Restaurant Success). Among other top honors, *Fast Company Magazine* gave Chick-fil-A its "Customers First" award, and noted Chick-fil-A as the "Customer-Centered Leader" among all types of businesses in recognition of its success in areas of service, satisfaction, and loyalty. *Restaurants and Institutions* magazine gave Chick-fil-A their "Choice in Chains" Customers Satisfaction Award (2006).

If there is a secret in such success, it is hiding in plain sight. The company keeps a well-managed and informative website, http://www.chick-fil-a.com, including the story of the original Chick-fil-A Sandwich and how it was created. (The blend of spices remains a secret). S. Truett Cathy's influence can be condensed into three simple rules: listen to the customer, get better before getting bigger, and focus on quality. Beyond these rules, however, lies a deeper philosophy that makes Chick-fil-A truly unique and is briefly described in this Spotlight. The books that Cathy has authored can provide a better understanding. (See under "Sources.") If there is any secret, it can be found in the personality and spirit of the man who has inspired so many lives.

Creating a "loyalty effect" through a lifetime commitment to the success and well-being of its franchised operators, the company buys real estate, builds a restaurant, and turns over the responsibility of a multimillion-dollar business ownership to a franchisee; many Chick-fil-A franchisees are under 30 years of age. Truett explains to each applicant that a commitment to Chick-fil-A is like a marriage with no consideration given to divorce. Each new operator runs a single restaurant and holds no outside employment or other business interest. Unlike some franchisees who might think of themselves as investors with no direct contact with the store itself, Chick-fil-A expects operators to make a full-time commitment to the restaurant the company has built for them. The operator is CEO, operations manager, president, and treasurer of his or her own business.

The Cathy family's loyalty to their operators is evident. Operators are supported with training, technology, and anything else they need. Chick-fil-A is on the leading edge of information technology. Because each restaurant is a separate legal and tax entity, the company offers hundreds of separate tax filings as a service to operators. Its payroll system is web-based, allowing operators to write checks in their restaurant. Trust develops as it becomes clear that everyone is working together, depending on each other, and not just bound by a franchise agreement. In 1973, Cathy established the Leadership Scholarship Program. Since then more than $23 million has been awarded—$1,000 scholarships to qualifying restaurant employees to the school of their choice. In 2007, Chick-fil-A awarded $1.3 million to its restaurant team.

The Chick-fil-A franchise agreement has not changed since 1967. The only money required from an operator is a $5,000 refundable initial capital commitment. The company supplies the initial capital for the restaurant. The agreement calls for the operator to sublease the restaurant, paying Chick-fil-A 15 percent of gross sales plus 50 percent of net profits from the restaurant as a franchise fee. Operators own their own business even though they work closely with Chick-fil-A, Inc. More than half earn more than $100,000 annually; many earn more than $200,000; and some top $300,000.

Cathy looks for several specific traits in seeking operators. Character is paramount. According to Cathy, everything else can be learned. Applicants must demonstrate that they really want the opportunity with an entrepreneurial attitude. They must set high standards of excellence for themselves. Their appearance must be neat and clean. They must demonstrate their ability to make long-term commitments and handle financial responsibility. Cathy encourages his operators to think and experiment under reasonable circumstances. Otherwise, he writes, "We will end up with a bunch of timid operators." Approximately 65 percent of current operator selections come from former Chick-fil-A team members who are eager to succeed and ready to pour their hearts and souls into their own restaurant.

One operator from Mesquite, Texas, says of his business, "The most important people are our employees. Some people will say customers are most important, but if we create the right atmosphere where our employees enjoy their jobs and have opportunities for growth, they will get a kick out of their work. They're part of a winning team. That feeling will spill right over to the customer." This Texas operator used his initiative to get involved with the entire school system in town. He sometimes surprises teachers with a party tray of Chick-fil-A® Nuggets or a brownie tray to thank them for the work they do. Giving creates a level of loyalty that leads to long-term success.

The most important part of an operator's role is selecting his or her people. It is similar to organizing a baseball team. There are 50,000 team members. One operator in Dayton, Ohio, writes, "Sometimes during an interview I will 'accidentally' knock a stack of papers off my desk and see if the interviewee will pick them up. If the person is service-oriented, they'll immediately reach down for them." She continues, "We also learn whether potential employees can think for themselves and react appropriately to an irate customer through role-playing situations."

Thousands of teenagers work as part-time employees of Chick-fil-A restaurants at one time or another. Truett expects his operators to teach them good permanent work habits and attitudes. To make a positive impact on the people around us, he urges us to avoid complacency as we measure ourselves against the national average. "Look what it means to be average," he writes. "You're the worst of the best and the best of the worst."

A caveat from Cathy to seekers of success: "Never overextend yourself." Cathy would rather have 70 restaurants operating efficiently and professionally than 500 restaurants where only one-half are run well. He warns against the formula of borrowing as much money as you can, renting a fancy office, and starting out with the image of success. He believes that the most common reason companies fail is their desire to grow faster than they can manage, especially companies that make a public offering and find themselves staring at a pile of money. Truett writes, "All they want to do is to grow. But you have to digest growth as you go. Slight economic downturns can force layoffs of employees to salvage the company. You don't build a good reputation by discharging people, but rather by developing

Spotlight 13-2 (Continued)

people." He continues, "I want everyone who works at Chick-fil-A to feel secure that we will not resort to layoffs because we are overextended."

The company's record speaks for itself. Chick-fil-A, advertised by a few spelling-challenged cows climbing on billboards, is the second-largest quick-service chicken restaurant chain in the nation based on sales. It has consistently maintained its 39-year consecutive sales growth. Dan Cathy, one of Truett's sons, said that posting sales gains every year since the first outlet opened in 1967 is a testament to the chain's restaurant operators and "our prudent expansion policy."

Deciding to give employees and their families a chance to be together at least one day a week illustrates the company's profound commitment to family. No Chick-fil-A store is open on Sunday. The Cathy sons [Dan is president and COO and Don (Bubba) is senior vice president] and daughter, Trudy Cathy White, have signed a covenant with their parents, pledging to stay closed on Sundays and keep the company private. Dan says his father has laid out a solid business blueprint he intends to follow closely, adding, "He's been an incredible role model as a business person."

Review Questions

1 What products does Chick-fil-A®, Inc., sell?
2 How does Chick-fil-A's business model relate to *QSR Magazine* rating the company as "The Best in Drive-Thru in '07"?
3 This Atlanta-based quick service restaurant (QSR) is closed on Sundays, which is a busy revenue-generating day since many families go out to eat together. What explains this policy from a P/OM point of view?
4 What can you learn about Chick-fil-A, Inc., by going to the *QSR Magazine* website (http://www.qsrmagazine.com)?
5 What can you learn about Chick-fil-A, Inc., by going to the company's website: http://www.chick-fil-a.com?

Sources: S. Truett Cathy. *Eat Mor Chikin: Inspire More People. Doing Business the Chick-fil-A Way.* Decatur, GA: Looking Glass Books, 2002.http://www.Chick-fil-Apressroom.com; Don Perry, Vice President of Public Relations, Chick-fil-A®, Inc., September 2007.

Summary

Everyone leads a job shop life. There are many things to accomplish. Flow shop type routines are partial, at best, and changing all of the time. Everyone must do aggregate planning to cope with such great variety for the use of their time and money. Aggregate planning (AP) for the commercial job shop is an internal production management function. It constantly matches classes of jobs with the resources needed to produce each of them. Its relationship to business planning and production scheduling is essential. Chapter 13 explores the methods for aggregate planning. Three aggregate planning policies are developed and compared. These are (1) level production with problems of making too much or having too little, (2) supply chasing sales, and (3) combinations of (1) and (2). Linear programming (LP) is a great method for solving AP problems. The LP model is an effective means of achieving optimal aggregate plans. Occasionally there is trepidation that the assumption of a linear cost structure may lead to poor planning. Most of the time, there are ways around the linear constraint.

Akin to LP, the TM is ideal for many AP applications. It has the same linear cost constraints as LP, but is even easier to use. The transportation model for aggregate planning (backorders not allowed) can be solved with the simplest network rules. When backorders are allowed, the TM can be solved either as an LP or network model and simple Excel spreadsheets or QMpom-type software can be used. Chapter 13 also explains how the nonlinear HMMS model introduces second-order equations to describe costs more accurately. The three AP models are benchmarked against each other.

Two Spotlights illustrate applications of aggregate planning. Spotlight 13-1: Changing the Way We Pay explains how payment technology is changing. Opportunities are being created for a new aggregation of banking activities. Firms now experience a constant stream of payments. These are 24/7/365 and globally dispersed. Counting money (payable and receivable) used to be confined to "bankers hours." Spotlight 13-2: Chick-fil-A®, Inc.: A Great Business Model explains how independent operators have generated great business success for this aggregation of Chick-fil-A® quick service restaurants. The operators of these stores have staffing problems related to level versus chasing strategies. Their loyalty has produced stable systems with great learning about how to keep employees and, thereby, customers happy.

Key Terms

Aggregate planning (AP) (p. 511)   Linear programming (LP) (p. 527)
Backordering (p. 522)   Loading (p. 516)
Chasing policy (p. 521)   Minimum cost assignment schedule (p. 526)
Constant production strategy (p. 520)   Planning horizon (p. 512)
Cost trade-off analysis (p. 525)   Production planning (p. 516)
Fundamental theorem of linear   Sensitivity analysis (p. 531)
   programming (LP) (p. 528)   Sequencing (p. 516)
HMMS (p. 528)   Standard units (p. 512)
Level production (p. 510)   Trade-off model (p. 526)

Review Questions

1   Why is aggregate planning (AP) used? What does it do?
2   What is meant by aggregation of units?
3   Explain standard units of work.
4   Explain the use of backordering for goods.
5   Give one or more examples of how backordering can be used for services.
6   Explain the significance of "fill or kill" and give some examples.

7   Describe the system's nature of aggregate planning from the point of view of classes of resources and product-mix families.

8   Explain why aggregate planning follows strategic planning.

9   Explain the statement that aggregate planning starts a chain reaction in the supply chain of suppliers-producer-customers.

10 Discuss the importance of forecasting for AP.

11 Explain the planning horizon and the updating interval.

12 A job shop manager said, "For the average job shop product, the best planning interval would range from 3 to 6 months." Might this statement provide a reasonable rule of thumb?

13 Why do forecasts for aggregated jobs have an advantage over forecasts for individual (disaggregated) jobs?

14 How can the effects of seasonal demands be taken into account for aggregate planning? Explain.

15 In some job shop industries, a smooth production rate is the preferred choice. Explain what this means and when it can be true.

16 In some job shop industries, the workforce size is altered to chase the expected demands. Explain what this means.

17 Compare smooth or level aggregate production policies with chasing policies. Explain when each is likely to be preferred.

18 At one time, the canning industry was totally dependent on harvest dates. As a result, major workforce alterations occurred sporadically. After careful study, steps were taken to smooth the demand patterns. What measures might have helped?

19 Explain the meaning of this question: How should P_t, W_t, and I_t, be varied so as to optimize the systems performance?

20 What is a combination aggregate policy and why is it called partially chasing?

21 Explain how the trade-off model for workforce adjustment costs and inventory costs yields an optimal aggregate planning policy.

22 What is meant by a slightly chasing policy?

23 Describe the use of linear programming for AP.

24 What does the fundamental theorem of linear programming state? How does this theorem provide important guidance?

Problems Section

Note: This section has various problems that can be formulated and solved using QuantMethods Production/Operations Management software (QMpom). The appropriate model categories are indicated for each problem.

1   Seven jobs will be in the shop next week. The demand in units for each job (called d_j) and the production rates of the standard operator in pieces per standard operator hour for each type of job (called PR_j) are given as follows:

Job	A	B	C	D	E	F	G
d_j	600	1,000	500	50	2,000	20	800
PR_j	60	20	25	10	40	2	40

What production capacity is required to complete all of these jobs? (Use standard operator hours.)

Using the QMpom module called Production Scheduling (Shortest Processing Time [SPT]) will provide some useful insights concerning the best sequence for completing the work in Problem 1.

2   Six service calls are on hand for next week. The number of steps required for each has been determined and is listed as d_j. The supervisor is designated as the standard operator. Her output rates are labeled as PR_j. They are measured in steps per standard operator hour for each type of job.

Job	A	B	C	D	E	F
d_j	500	400	200	150	2,000	48
PR_j	100	20	25	75	400	12

What workforce capacity in standard operator hours is needed to complete all service calls?

3   It has been estimated that annual demand for five types of soup made by The Big Soup Company are as follows:

Soup	A	B	C	D	E
d_j	900	630	240	1800	1,200

There are three plants located in the United States. The most productive plant has been chosen as the standard plant. Its output is listed in standard plant output per day.

PR_j	6	7	2	10	25

The other two plants have indexes of 0.9 and 0.7. There are 250 working days in the year, and all numbers are given in thousands of cases. Is it likely that the three plants can handle the annual demand?

4 Using the information in Problem 3, assume that the two other plants have indexes of 0.8 and 0.7. Is it likely that the three plants can handle the annual demand?

5 Complete Table 13-9 for the 6-month period shown. What kind of aggregate planning policy is this?

T	S_t	P_t	I_t	ΣI_t	W_t	$W_t - W_{t-1}$
1	340	380			38	0
2	420	380			38	0
3	350	380			38	0
4	390	380			38	0
5	360	380			38	0
6	420	380			38	0

Table 13-9

An Alternative Workforce Pattern

6 Compare the results obtained by completing Table 13-9 in Problem 5 with the results obtained from Table 13-5 in the text. Describe similarities and differences between these problems and the results.

7 Using the information in Problem 5, what would be the effect of adding another person to the workforce? Specifically, this means increasing the number of workers from 38 to 39. Is this a sensible move?

8 Using Table 13-5 in the text, what would be the effect of adding another person to the workforce? Specifically, this means increasing the number of workers from 38 to 39. Is this a sensible move?

9 Using the information in Table 13-9 in Problem 5, calculate the total variable costs for the 6-month period. Backorders cost $100, and carrying inventory costs $25 per unit per time period. Hires cost $200 per person added, and layoffs cost $300 per person. The cost of an additional person working is $2,000 per month. Fractional payroll amounts can be calculated and used as well. In addition to stating the total variable costs, show the components that make up this value.

10 Using the conditions stated in Problem 7, determine the total variable cost. Compare this total variable cost with that derived in Problem 9. Present your recommendations concerning adding one person to the workforce.

11 Using the conditions stated in Problem 8, determine the total variable cost. Compare this total variable cost with that derived in the text for Table 13-5. Present your recommendations concerning the addition of one more person to the workforce.

12 Complete Table 13-10. What kind of aggregate planning policy is this? Be as specific as possible in the description of this AP.

T	S_t	P_t	I_t	ΣI_t	W_t	$W_t - W_{t-1}$
1	340	380			38	
2	420	390			39	
3	350	360			36	
4	390	370			37	
5	360	360			36	
6	420	400			40	

Table 13-10

An Alternative Workforce Pattern

13 Write the linear programming (LP) equations for aggregate planning using $k = 500$ and the demand forecast of {17,000, 21,000, 17,500, 19,500, 18,000, 21,000} for the first six months of the year. What additional data is needed to solve the LP aggregate planning problem?

14 There is sufficient data in Table 13-11 to solve this aggregate-planning transportation model. Assume that carrying costs per unit, c, are stated as dollars per month. Note: Because no backorders are allowed, this particular TM can be solved directly. Starting inventory, $I_0 = 50$, and final inventory, $I_f = 200$.

Table 13-11

Transportation Model for Aggregate Planning—No Backorders Allowed

| | Sales Periods | | | | | |
	1	2	3	Final Inv.	Slack	Supply
Initial Inv.	0	c	$2c$	$3c$	0	I_0
Regular 1	r	$r+c$	$r+2c$	$r+3c$	0	$R_1 = 100$
Overtime 1	v	$v+c$	$v+2c$	$v+3c$	0	$O_1 = 200$
Regular 2	x	r	$r+c$	$r+2c$	0	$R_2 = 300$
Overtime 2	x	v	$v+c$	$v+2c$	0	$O_2 = 200$
Regular 3	x	x	r	$r+c$	0	$R_3 = 100$
Overtime 3	x	x	v	$v+c$	0	$O_3 = 50$
Demand	$D_1 = 200$	$D_2 = 300$	$D_3 = 200$	$I_f = 200$	SL	Grand Total

c = \$1/unit per month; r = regular production cost/unit = \$2; v = overtime cost/unit = \$3

Using the QMpom module called Aggregate Scheduling Models (Transportation) will facilitate solving the two (2) problems that are numbered 14 through 15.

15 For the aggregate planning TM presented in Problem 14, assume that carrying costs per month rise from \$1.00 to \$1.50 and overtime costs decrease from \$3.00 to \$2.50 per unit. Specify the solution and comment on the following question: How sensitive is the solution to these changes in costs?

16 Refer to Figure 13-8, which presents three kinds of nonlinear (second order) costs and one kind of linear cost function used by the HMMS–AP model. Make a table of (or plot on graph paper) the regular payroll cost per month for $C_1 =$ \$100 per day. Let the workforce range between 35 and 45 workers.

17 Refer to Figure 13-8, which presents three kinds of nonlinear (second order) costs and one kind of linear cost function used by the HMMS–AP model. Make a table of (or draw on graph paper) the costs of hiring and laying off per month where $C_2 =$ \$200 per change. The workforce starts at 35 workers and grows to 45 workers.

18 Refer to Figure 13-8, which presents three kinds of nonlinear (second order) costs used by the HMMS–AP model. Make a table or plot on graph paper the expected cost of overtime where the production rate follows Pattern A but overtime is used to match demand. The costs are $C_3 =$ \$50/unit and $C_5 =$ \$20/unit, C_4 and $C_6 =$ \$10/unit. Remember the relationship between P_t and W_t.

19 Refer to Figure 13-8, which presents three kinds of nonlinear (second order) costs used by the HMMS–AP model. Make a table or plot on graph paper the expected sum of inventory carrying costs, backorder costs, and setup costs where $[(C_8) + (C_9 S)] = 40$/unit when $I = 50$. For this case, treat the sum costs $(C_8 + C_9 S)$ as a constant. Also, $C_7 =$ \$30/unit. Let I range from -50 to 150 units.

Practice Quiz

1 A production and operations management class has turned to Section 13-1 of Chapter 13. The students discover that the title of that section is "What Is Aggregate Planning (AP)?" Initially, most students do not have a clue as to how to answer that question. However, after reading, discussing, and thinking about the material in this section, these students should be able to answer the question and explain when AP is used and what function it serves. The following points a. to e. cover the subject, but one item is incorrect to permit the student to differentiate between right and wrong. Which letter marks the wrong statement?

a. Aggregate planning follows strategic planning. Strategic planning determines the product-mix and resource availabilities. AP determines the production plan.

b. The driver of AP is forecasted customer demand. When some orders are on hand at the beginning of the planning horizon, there is less probability of forecasting error.

c. Because the application is the job shop and forecasts are being made for items that take different amounts of work and time, a separate forecast is made for each item.

d. To be effective, the forecast interval has to provide sufficient lead time to allow the resource mix to be changed. In other words, the planning horizon has to be long enough to permit satisfaction of forecasted demand.

e. The planning horizon might be six months, which is the shortest period of time that will allow actions to be taken in response to the forecast. Corrections of the forecasts could be done every three months. However, the corrections would apply to the 6-month planning horizon. For example, at the end of the third month a projection would be made for the end of the ninth month.

2   An aggregate planning problem is no surprise to the Omicron Corporation. OC's job shop is based on converting orders (on-hand and expected for the next week) into standard hours. The shop has enough production capacity to allow a 1-week planning horizon, and materials can be obtained within a few days. There are four departments that can do the same kind of general-purpose work; however, the newest department D(1) is twice as fast as the oldest department D(4). All of the departments are shown in the table where $D(x)$ is the department number. The production manager has been running an aggregate planning workshop for new employees. The list of statements in a. through e. are correct except for one of the points. Identify the flawed statement.

D(x)	SDH Index	SDH/Week	AH/week
1	1.00	54.0	54.0
2	0.80	64.0	80.0
3	0.60	20.0	33.3
4	0.50	18.0	36.0
Totals		156.0	203.3

a. A standard department hour (SDH) index has been derived for each department relative to D(1), which is designated as the standard department (index of 1.00).

b. Department D(1) is the standard department against which the other indexes are created. If any of the other departments work faster on some jobs than D(1), and slower on other jobs than D(1), then the concept of the standard department is even more applicable to such otherwise difficult situations.

c. Actual hours (AH) per week are the real amounts of time that each department has available in the next week. For example, department D(2) is prepared to work two 40-hour shifts yielding 80 hours.

d. Department D(2) works at only 80 percent of the rate that the standard department D(1) regularly achieves. Therefore, multiplying the index of 0.80 by the actual hours available yields $0.80 \times 80 = 64$ standard department hours.

e. There is a total of 203.3 actual hours available from the four departments, but the method of aggregate planning requires use of the total of 156 standard department hours.

3   The Omicron Corporation has five jobs scheduled for next week. They are named A, B, C, D, and E (in row 1). The table shows how many units of each job are ordered (in row 2). The table then shows the production rate of the standard department on each job (row 3). Row 4 shows demand in units converted into demand in standard departmental hours. The production manager is very pleased with the results of the training program to date. Extending the pop quiz makes sense. What item listed in a. through e. is off-base?

Job	A	B	C	D	E	Totals
Units ordered	300	210	240	1800	400	2,950
D(1) production rate	6/hr.	7/hr.	6/hr.	30/hr.	25/hr.	
Demand in SDH	50 hrs	30 hrs	40 hrs	60 hrs	16 hrs	196 SDH

a. Dividing the units ordered (for the week ahead) by the production rate of the standard department D(1) converts demand for jobs A through E from units into standard department hours (SDH).

b. The aggregation of entirely different order sizes and unit work requirements has homogenized A, B, C, D, and E into a common dimension of SDH.

c.   From the table in problem 2, there are 156 standard department hours available for the coming week. Orders on-hand require 196 SDH. There is a shortfall of 40 SDH.

d.   Because there is a shortfall of SDH, the problem is changed from aggregate scheduling to adding capacity to meet requirements.

e.   Because there is a shortfall of SDH, the significance is that some order will not be completed. For example, if job C is not done, then standard hours of supply equals standard hours of demand.

4 Based on the data in Problems 2 and 3, and the conclusions drawn, it is not clear which job or jobs should be backordered in order to match supply and demand. The production manager has given the company trainees a matrix of production rates. These data, which are not in standard hours, were derived directly from the tables in Problems 2 and 3. The manager also prepared a list of suggestions concerning how to proceed.

   The trainees have been asked to study the list of suggestions, a. through e., concerning how to resolve the problem of too much demand. They are asked to consider using the good ideas, rejecting the one bad one that exists in the list. Identify the bad suggestion.

a.   Derive the costs, revenues, or profits that count. If possible, go for the profits per unit because maximizing them is our goal and minimizing costs is a secondary goal. Once the profits per unit are obtained, convert them to profits per standard hour.

b.   The suggestion in a. seems right, but if it cannot be accomplished quickly enough to deal with the situation for next week; find a heuristic that might help.

Matrix of Production Rates (Units per Hour)						
	D(1)	D(2)	D(3)	D(4)	Demand (units)	Demand (SDH)
A	6	4.8	3.6	3	300	50
B	7	5.6	4.2	3.5	210	30
C	6	4.8	3.6	3	240	40
D	30	24	18	15	1,800	60
E	25	20	15	12.5	400	16
AH	54	80	33.3	36	Totals	196
SDH	54	64	20	18	156	
Index	1.0	0.8	0.6	0.5	Difference	40

c.   One heuristic that has been suggested is to look for the smallest number in the matrix of production rates and backorder that job. Here, there is a tie for lowest productivity for job A (value 3) and for job C (value 3).

d.   Only part of job A must be backordered because it requires 50 SDH and only 40 SDH are needed to balance supply and demand. That fact may please marketing because the A customer will receive part of the order. All of C must be backordered. Probably, both B and E are poor candidates. If either is backordered, another job must still be chosen. B has only 30 SDH and E has only 16 SDH.

e.   A solution to the problem is announced by the management science department. It has used linear programming to optimize profits. According to this solution, 40 SDH have been assigned to the dummy and that means backordered. The customer will receive a partial shipment of 60 units instead of the 300 units in the original order. Note that it was not coincidental that Job A with low productivity in D(4) was chosen for backordering. However, that fact only played a part in the bigger picture.

Final LP Solution in Standard Department Hours						
	D(1)	D(2)	D(3)	D(4)	Dummy	Demand
A				10	40	50
B	22			8		30
C	32	8				40
D		40	20			60
E		16				16
Total	54	64	20	18	40	196
Index	1.0	0.8	0.6	0.5		

5   In aggregate planning, information is essential for planning and forecasting at level one. The same can be said about information for decision making at levels two and three, where aggregate units have the tangible form of being real jobs in the shop. An aspect of aggregate planning (level one) that is often overlooked is the advantage of forecasting for aggregations as compared to forecasting for individual components of the aggregation. Four of the following five statements concerning this subject are correct and one is not. Which is the incorrect statement?

   a.   Aggregate forecasts have less variability (uncertainty) than the combined variability of the forecasts for the individual components in the aggregation.

   b.   The variability of a forecast is related to the spread around the expected value (mean value) of the distribution. When a statistical distribution is postulated as a forecast, the mean value and the standard deviation (σ) are stated. Plus or minus one standard deviation ($\pm \sigma$) is related to the range that encompasses about 68 percent of the area of a normal distribution. If the range is $\pm 2\sigma$ standard deviations, then the area covers about 95 percent of the distribution. Two σ means that the forecast will lie within that range 95 percent of the time. This discussion is intended to explain what is meant by the variability of a forecast.

   c.   If n sales forecasts are made, one for each floor in a Sears store, then the variability of the n sales forecasts relates to the uncertainty regarding the exact amount of sales on each floor. Taken floor by floor, uncertainties add up so that a forecast of the total store sales would have a large range that would be roughly proportional to $n\sigma$.

   d.   On the other hand, aggregate the floors so that a single forecast is made for the store. This will have a significantly smaller range that will be approximated by $\sigma\sqrt{n}$.

   e.   This effect of reducing variability of forecasts through aggregation would not apply to forecasting sales for the year, as compared to adding together forecasts for individual months of the year.

6   The table shows the changes in inventory levels that occur over six time periods when a constant workforce is used. The policy of constant workforce was suggested to Alpha Corporation by their consultants because workforce alterations are costly to this technology-oriented company. The production team has come up with a list of considerations a. through e. The vice president in charge of materials management has faulted one of the points as being wrong. Which one is the incorrect statement?

Constant Size Workforce

T	S(t)	P(t)	I(t)	ΣI_t	W(t)	$\Delta W(t)$
1	420	380	−40	−40	38	0
2	360	380	+20	−20	38	0
3	390	380	−10	−30	38	0
4	350	380	+30	0	38	0
5	420	380	−40	−40	38	0
6	340	380	+40	0	38	0
Total	2,280	2,280				

Note: $\Delta W(t) = W(t) - W(t-1)$; $P(t) = 10\ W(t)$

   a.   Per unit time period, the cost of overstock is $10 per unit and the cost of being out of stock is $20 per unit, all per unit time period; the cost of the constant workforce policy is $2,600 over six time periods.

   b.   The cost of the workforce change should be examined. To do this, measure the effects of making an *incremental change*. Reduce the workforce in the second period by one person. Then, to satisfy demand, increase the workforce to 39 in period three and return the workforce size to 38 in the fourth period. The result is

Incremental Change to the Constant Size Workforce

T	S(t)	P(t)	I(t)	ΣI_t	W(t)	$\Delta W(t)$
1	420	380	−40	−40	38	0
2	360	370	+10	−30	37	− 1
3	390	390	0	−30	39	+ 1
4	350	380	+30	0	38	− 1
5	420	380	−40	−40	38	0
6	340	380	+40	0	38	0
Total	2,280	2,280				

Note: $\Delta W(t) = W(t) - W(t-1)$; $P(t) = 10\ W(t)$

Because the cost of overstock is $10 per unit and the cost of being out of stock is $20 per unit, the cost of inventory adjustments is now $2,800 for the six time periods. In addition, the cost of workforce adjustment is 2 times the cost of reducing size (say $150), plus the cost of one increase (say $250). The total of $3,200 is larger than the cost ($2,600) of the constant workforce policy.

c. The cost of matching production and demand can be calculated readily given that this policy is shown in Table 13-6 in the text. There are no inventory adjustment costs, and the workforce adjustment costs are ($150)(18) + ($250)(10) = $5,200. The chasing strategy costs twice as much as the constant workforce policy.

d. The preference of Alpha Corporation for the constant workforce size is not a surprise given the fact that workers can produce only 10 units per day.

e. It is unlikely, with these particular costs, that the optimal aggregate-scheduling solution will shift from the constant workforce to a solution that blends inventory adjustments with workforce alterations.

7 Linear programming can be used for aggregate scheduling. Some facts about this method are listed in points a. through e. Purposefully, one is incorrect and it is requested that the wrong one be identified.

a. The objective function is to find the minimum cost aggregate schedule. This is equivalent to determining which production policy has the lowest total cost.

b. Variables that can be controlled are familiar to aggregate planners. They are $W(t)$, $P(t) = kW(t)$. Changes in workforce size are $A(t)$ for additions and $R(t)$ for reductions. There are also inventory adjustments where $I(t)$ is the inventory at the beginning of period t.

c. If overtime is used during period t, there is a variable, $O(t)$.

d. Data inputs are $S(t)$, which are sales in period t. These must be known with relative certainty beforehand. Otherwise the LP will solve for fictitious conditions.

e. Reasonable constraints must be written for $W(t)$, $A(t)$, $R(t)$, $O(t)$, and $I(t)$. LP must have constraints. In fact, the fundamental theorem of linear programming states that the number of active work assignments in the workforce schedule cannot exceed the number of real constraints.

8 The transportation model is a popular choice for aggregate planning for a number of reasons. Some of these reasons are listed in points a. through e. However, one explanation is off the mark. Which one is that?

a. Transportation models are less mathematical and easier to understand and use than LP equations, which form an alternate solution method. In other words, these are two roads to the same place.

b. Transportation models are useful in many applications of which aggregate scheduling is only one. The obvious use is to minimize the cost of transporting goods between origins and destinations. It is beneficial for management to be comfortable with the transportation model because of its broad application base.

c. A disadvantage of the transportation model is that it requires a "square" matrix, which means that there must be the same number of rows as columns. If the rows are supplies and the columns are demands, then this constraint means that there must be the same number of supply rows as demand columns.

d. The transportation model is a linear model, which means that the cost per unit is multiplied by the number of units scheduled to be made in a cell. This is not different from linear programming.

e. The HMMS aggregate-scheduling model permits cost per unit to increase or decrease as more units are scheduled to be made in a cell. The great benefit of nonlinearity is that many "real" costs are not linear. However, the drawback is that the system of equations is large and the work effort is demanding. For most cases that are not academic, managers prefer to get a good enough solution without a major investment in problem-solving.

9 A transportation model for aggregate planning (TAP) has been created by Aviation Parts Suppliers, Inc. (APS). It covers two sales periods of one month each. The demand for period 1 is called D(1) and similar treatment for D(2). The model is named TAP-NOBO—because no backorders are allowed. The X costs in the matrix are assumed to be so large that no assigned units of production will occur there. TAP-NOBO is being used as a training exercise for its job shop production schedule team. Their first task is to become familiar with the elements of the model and to understand how it works. A list of facts about TAP-NOBO has been circulated to the team members. They have been asked to separate true from false statements. In the list of a. to e. there is one false observation about TAP-NOBO. Which one is it?

Transportation Model for AP with Costs in Cells

	1	2	INV(F)	Slack	Supply
INV(0)	0	c	$2c$	0	INV(0)
PR(1)	r	$r+c$	$r+2c$	0	REG(1)
PO(1)	v	$v+c$	$v+2c$	0	OVT(1)
PR(2)	X	r	$r+c$	0	REG(2)
PO(2)	X	v	$v+c$	0	OVT(2)
Demand	$D(1)$	$D(2)$	$D(\text{FINV})$	$D(\text{SL})$	Total

a. The final inventory of period 1 is the initial inventory of period 2. Symbolically, the final inventory, called INV(F)—from the prior period, is the initial inventory, called INV(0), of the next period. The reason for setting a stock level at final inventory is that the job shop is expected to be able to fill certain kinds of orders on demand. Not all items are like that, so final inventory for some types of items is zero. APS should not be out of stock on items regularly (though sporadically) demanded by loyal customers. Without final inventory, there would be backorders. Customers would have to wait for the next production run in either regular time during the first period—called PR(1), or in overtime during the first period—which is called PO(1). The amount of stock that could be produced in regular time during the first period is called REG(1) in the matrix. The amount of stock that can be produced using overtime is called OVT(1) in the matrix. The same statements apply to REG(2) and OVT(2).

b. If all or part of the initial inventory INV(0) is shipped to the customer during the first period to satisfy at least part of the demand D(1), no carrying charge is levied. However, if all or part of INV(0) is kept in stock to be shipped during the second demand period—called D(2), then a carrying cost of c dollars per unit is charged to APS for items shipped. *Customers are not charged.* The model charges APS, thereby increasing its total costs, which the company is trying to minimize. Similar considerations apply to the other costs that are in the matrix.

c. For items made using regular production in the *first period*, there is a variable cost per unit of r dollars. Items made using regular production in the first period that are *not shipped until the second period* carry a charge to TAP of $r + c$ dollars.

d. For items made using overtime production in the *first period*, there is a variable cost per unit of v dollars. For items made using overtime production in the *first period* that are *not shipped until the second period*, there is a charge to TAP of $v + c$ dollars. Final inventory is charged for an additional carrying cost, e.g., $r + 2c$ and $v + 2c$.

e. There is a charge of X dollars per unit backordered. If an item produced in the second production period PR(2) is shipped to satisfy a first period order, then the backorder charge of X must be included as part of the total cost solution for the model. It is logical that for some industries X is not prohibitively large. If there is enough production capacity, fill the unsatisfied demand.

10 AviationParts Suppliers, Inc. (APS) has supplied data for use of the TAP-NOBO model. Conclusions about optimum schedules, which minimize total costs, are made in this phase of the training program. Team members have been asked to analyze the matrix of costs, production capacities, and market demands. A list of conclusions (a. to e.) has been published. There is one false conclusion in that list. Which one is it? As a reminder, the model called TAP-NOBO does not allow backorders.

Transportation Model for AP with Costs in Cells

	1	2	INV(F)	Slack	Supply
INV(0)	0	$2	$4	0	10 units
PR(1)	$5	$7	$9	0	20 units
PO(1)	$8	$10	$11	0	15 units
PR(2)	X	$5	$7	0	25 units
PO(2)	X	$8	$10	0	15 units
Demand	35 units	30 units	15 units	5 units	85 units

a. As a starting point, the team set up an initial feasible solution by simply making row and column entries starting at the top left and moving down toward the right (which is called the Northwest Corner method). This is shown in the matrix label *units assigned*. Next to that matrix is another matrix, which shows costs of assignments.

Units Assigned				
10				10
20				20
5	10			15
	20	5		25
		10	5	15
35	30	15	5	85

Costs of Assignments				
$0				
100				
40	100			
	100	35		
		100	0	
$140	$200	$135	0	$475

b. This solution satisfies demands and uses all production capacities except five units of overtime production in the second period. Those five units are assigned to the dummy market because supply is greater than demand. The total cost of this schedule is $475.

c. The question arises—is there a better solution (lower total cost)? There are methods, including linear programming and transportation network analysis, for determining, unequivocally, the optimal solution. These methods are not available at this time, but this is a small problem. There is a logical way of using cut and try to solve the problem.

d. Using the trial and error method, with some heuristics to help, four iterations were required to reach the solution shown in the matrix. The saving is $15, which is a little more than 3 percent.

Units Assigned				
10				10
20				20
5		5	5	15
	25			25
	5	10		15
35	30	15	5	85

Costs of Assignments				
$0				
100				
40		55	0	
	125			
	40	100		
$140	$165	$155	0	$460

e. The fact that only 3 percent was saved after so much analysis may indicate that the method is not robust and will cost APS more money than it is worth.

Additional Readings

[Aggregate planning models were fully developed by 1970. Therefore, a few citations are early, going back to the basics. What is new is the software that can be used to solve large AP problems. Some of these are cited here. In addition, more recent references with present-day perspectives about mathematical programming are given.]

Attaran, M. *OMIS: Operations Management Information Systems.* NY: Wiley, 1992.

Bowman, E. H. "Production Scheduling by the Transportation Method of Linear Programming." *Operations Research*, vol. 4, no. 1 (February 1956).

Excel Solver for LP solutions.

Holt, C. C., F. Modigliani, J. F. Muth, and H. A. Simon. *Planning Production Inventories and Work Force*. Englewood Cliffs, NJ: Prentice-Hall, Inc., 1960.

Holt, C. C., F. Modigliani, and H. A. Simon. "A Linear Decision Rule for Production and Employment Scheduling." *Management Science*, vol. 2, no. 1 (October 1955).

Interfaces. "Special Issue: The Practice of Mathematical Programming." (15 articles covering various aspects of linear and mathematical programming), vol. 20, no. 4 (July–August 1990).

Lasdon, L., and A. Waren. "Gino: General Interactive Optimizer." (software) and J. Liebman, L. Lasdon, A. Waren, and L. Schrage. *Modeling and Optimization with GINO*. Danvers, MA: boyd & fraser publishing co., 1986.

Nemhauser G. L., and L. A. Wolsey. *Integer and Combinatorial Optimization*. New York: Wiley, 1988.

Plane, Donald R. *Management Science: A Spreadsheet Approach*. Danvers, MA: The Scientific Press Series, boyd & fraser publishing co., 1994 (Solvers apply to LP spreadsheets).

———. *Management Science: A Spreadsheet Approach for Windows*. Danvers, MA: The Scientific Press Series, boyd & fraser publishing co., 1995 (Solvers apply to LP spreadsheets).

Pinney, W., Mark Atchison, Edward Nowotny, and Randy McElroy. QMpom QuantMethods Production/Operations Management software, Version 1.1.0, 2006 (http://www.quantmethods.com).

Schrage, L. Lindo: *An Optimization Modeling System*, 4e. (text and software) Danvers, MA: boyd & fraser publishing co., 1991.

Vollmann, T. E., W. L. Berry, and D. Clay Whybark. *Manufacturing Planning and Control Systems*, 3e. Homewood, IL: Irwin, 1992.

Wallace, Thomas F., and Michael H. Kremzar. *ERP: Making It Happen*, 3e. New York: John Wiley & Sons, 2001.

Notes

1. For archival purposes, one of the first citations to solution by LP was E. H. Bowman. "Production Scheduling by the Transportation Method of Linear Programming." *Operations Research*, vol. 4, no. 1 (February 1956): 100–103. Computer programming solutions were massive undertakings at this time.

2. C. C. Holt, F. Modigliani, J. F. Muth, and H. A. Simon. *Planning Production Inventories and Work Force*. Englewood Cliffs, NJ: Prentice-Hall, Inc., 1960. This is also cited for archival purposes.

3. David Lawrence Mason. *From Buildings and Loans to Bail-outs: A History of the American Savings and Loan Industry*, 1831–1995. Cambridge, UK: Cambridge University Press, 2004.

Enrichment Activity 13: Using the Transportation Model (TM) for Aggregate Planning with Backorders Allowed

The transportation model was introduced in Section 13-6 to allow solution of the aggregate planning problem. At the time, a specific constraint was introduced to prevent backorders such as using production capacity in April to fill orders that were due in February or March. This is equivalent to a row of the TM matrix with supply generated at time $(t + n)$ shipping units into a column with demand requested at an earlier time $(t + n - 1)$, $(t + n - 2)$, etc.

Using the QMpom module called Mathematical Programming Models (Transportation) will facilitate solving these problems. Dedicated software will save time, but it does not preclude the possibility of using the stepping stone method described in Sections 13-5 and 13-6. It is also feasible to transform the TM problem into its linear programming equivalent described in Section 13-6a. For learning about how the TM works, the stepping stone method is recommended with a small problem such as Problem 1 in the Enrichment Challenges 13 section that follows. Doing this will instill confidence in the method and in TM-software-generated solutions. As a reminder, Table 13-8 in the text presents the version of the aggregate-planning transportation matrix which does not allow backorders. To accomplish this goal, the backorder costs b are made so large that shipments into backorder cells are prohibitive.

Table EA13-1 presents the backorders-allowed version of the aggregate planning transportation matrix. This matrix has costs, b, which are backorder costs per unit backordered. Backorder costs are integrated without disruption. The model can be solved by conventional transportation techniques including stepping stone network algorithms, linear programming, or computer analysis using QMpom.

To understand Enrichment Activity 13, it may help to reread Section 13-6 and to study Table 13-8. A brief review of the structure is presented here. Demand in three periods is shown by column totals D_1, D_2, and D_3. Final inventory (called I_f) is at

Table EA13-1

Transportation Model for
Aggregate Planning—
Backorders Allowed

		Sales Periods					
		1	2	3	Final Inv.	Slack	Supply
Initial Inv.		0	c	$2c$	$3c$	0	I_0
Regular 1		r	$r + c$	$r + 2c$	$r + 3c$	0	R_1
Overtime 1		v	$v + c$	$v + 2c$	$v + 3c$	0	O_1
Regular 2		$r + b$	r	$r + c$	$r + 2c$	0	R_2
Overtime 2		$v + b$	v	$v + c$	$v + 2c$	0	O_2
Regular 3		$r + 2b$	$r + b$	r	$r + c$	0	R_3
Overtime 3		$v + 2b$	$v + b$	v	$v + c$	0	O_3
Demand		D_1	D_2	D_3	$I_f = 200$	SL	Grand Total

the bottom of the fourth column. Slack (*SL*), which balances supply and demand, is at the bottom of the fifth column. Supply is shown as row totals. The top row is initial inventory (called I_0). Thereafter, rows alternate in presenting production supply for regular time and for overtime, called R_1 and O_1, R_2 and O_2, R_3 and O_3. The objective is to minimize total cost. Constraints reflect the limited availability of regular and overtime production capacity in standard hours. Slack costs are all zero.

Table EA13-1 presents the version of the aggregate planning model that allows backorders. The new costs, *b*, are backorder costs per unit backordered. Backorder costs are like carrying costs. They grow with each additional month that a unit is backordered.

Enrichment Challenges 13

The data in Table EA13-1 show only supply and demand. The costs supplied in the problems here are identical to those given in Problem 14 of the Problems Section. The difference is that the backorder costs in Problem 1 are set very high so as to prohibit selection of any of the backorder options. In Problem 2 they are set to a reasonable level.

1 What is the optimal assignment of regular and overtime production for the costs and conditions given here?

r = normal production labor costs per unit (regular work shift) = $2.00
v = overtime or second-shift production costs per unit made = $3.00
c = carrying costs in dollars per unit per month = $1.00
b = backorder costs in dollars per unit per months backordered = $100.00
I_0 = initial inventory (for the beginning of period $t = 1$) = 50
I_f = final inventory (for the end of period $t = f$) = 200

2 How does the solution change if the backorder costs are reduced to $1.00 per unit per month?

3 The conditions of Problem 1 hold with the exception that a special deal has been arranged with the union and the buyers. It will enable overtime production in the second period O_2 to cost $1.30 per unit per month when backordered to Sales Period 1.

   Does the solution change with this special backordering arrangement?

Inventory Management for Smooth and Continuous Demand Patterns

Chapter Outline

Chapter 14 explains how to manage inventories of materials that have continuous demand that typifies flow shop production. This class of inventory models is known by the acronym OPP (order point policies). These materials are independent, which means they are not components of (high-variety) job shop *end* items. The economic order quantity model (EOQ) is designed for buying items to satisfy flow shop replenishment requirements. The economic lot size model (ELS) is designed for intermittent flow shop production. The make or buy problem is analyzed with EOQ and ELS. These concepts are fundamental to understanding how perpetual and periodic inventory systems work and when each is preferred. Quantity discount models are a by-product of the EOQ model, providing further insights for inventory managers.

After reading this chapter, you should be able to:

- Explain what inventory management entails.
- Describe the difference between static and dynamic inventory models.
- Discuss demand distribution effects on inventory situations.
- Discuss lead-time effects on inventory situations.
- Describe all costs relevant to inventory models.
- Differentiate inventory costs by process types.
- Explain order point policies (OPP) and when they are used.
- Discuss the use of economic order quantity (EOQ) models for determining the optimal order size for batch delivery.
- Discuss the use of economic lot size (ELS) models for determining the optimal production run for continuous delivery.
- Explain the operation of the perpetual inventory model and explain why it is the most widely used inventory control system.
- Explain the operation of the periodic inventory model and describe the special circumstances that make its use desirable.
- Describe the discount model and explain how it indicates when a discount should be taken.

The Systems Viewpoint

Inventory management encompasses the widest spectrum of activities related to materials. The activities include when and how much to make or purchase. Timing replenishments and decisions about storage are systems issues as well. Materials are used by everyone in the organization. That encourages the systems viewpoint. The purpose of having these materials is to create and distribute the finished products or services to customers. Suppliers are an integral part of the system. The materials can play a direct role as part of the product or an indirect role such as documentation in the office or food for the spirit in the cafeteria. This chapter focuses on an important aspect of the total inventory required by companies. That aspect is to focus on items that are used continuously and consistently for flow shop operations over long periods of time. Continuous need indicates such inventory is crucial to the strategic plans of the company. The penalty for ignoring the systems point of view ranges from substantial inefficiencies to costly chaos.

Strategic Thinking

Without the systems perspective, everyone, everywhere will be ordering what they need as they need it. Lack of coordination diminishes buying power and loses the knowledge-based benefits of the centralized system. Strategic thinking is required to optimize the production plans of suppliers and producers to best meet the needs of their customers throughout the supply chain. In that way the lowest costs and best deliveries can be achieved for mutual benefit. The information system of a multinational company with a centralized inventory management system has to keep track globally of where everything is, where and when it will be needed, when to order it, and where to store it. It is an enormous system to manage. The strategic thinking that went into designing any such system must be robust and not casual. The need for change is always there when things do not work out as planned. This is revisiting the initial strategies.

© 2007 Jupiterimages Corporation

When business is slow, management cuts back on inventory. Note the empty areas in this warehouse. That may mean that some customers are going to be told that they will have to wait for delivery of the products they have ordered. Alternatively, inventory carrying costs are charged for inventory that is not turning over and moving out of the warehouse. Determining optimal inventory policies is a major P/OM job.

Inventory
Stock on-hand for every practical reason that materials are needed to run an organization.

14-1 Types of Inventory Situations

Inventory is those stocks or items used to support production (raw materials and work in process items), supporting activities (maintenance, repair, and operating supplies), and customer service (finished goods and spare parts).[1] [This definition, taken from the *APICS Dictionary*, is just part of the definition that is written there. The rest is more technical and requires understanding issues that will be discussed later in this chapter. The American Production and Inventory Control Society (APICS) is a professional society that has played an influential role in the inventory management area.]

Who manages inventory? APICS has established the fact that the management of inventory is a major P/OM responsibility. How to manage inventory is dependent on the type of inventory that is involved. Most types of inventory situations are best handled by well-designed computer systems that utilize as much centralization of record keeping and order placement as is feasible. The manifold advantages of the systems perspective with centralized buying includes the fact that larger quantities provide stronger supplier relationships, bigger discounts, a more informed choice of suppliers, and less chance for mistakes.

Each of the seven classes of inventory situations described here requires its own type of management even though they can all be centralized or decentralized according to the dispersion of use for producers, suppliers, and customers.

1 Order repetition—static versus dynamic situations.
2 Make or buy decisions—outside or self-supplier.
3 Demand distribution—certainty, risk, and uncertainty.
4 Stability of demand distribution—fixed or varying.
5 Demand continuity—smoothly continuous or sporadic and occurring as lumpy demand; independent.
6 Lead-time distributions—fixed or varying. **Lead time (LT)** is the interval between order placement and order receipt (including recognized need and write up).
7 Dependent or independent demand—when components are dependent on one or more end items, the information system must be able to calculate linked demands.

Lead time (LT)
Interval between order placement and order receipt (including time to recognize need and write up).

Static inventory models
In the static situation, how much to order is a one-shot decision.

Dynamic inventory models
Places orders repetitively over a long period of time.

14-1a Static Versus Dynamic Inventory Models

To explain order repetition, **static inventory models** have no repetition. They portray "one-shot" ordering situations, whereas **dynamic inventory models** place orders repetitively over long periods of time. A few examples underscore the practical nature of this distinction between one order only, or a repetitive stream of orders for the same item placed over time. The introduction to this chapter noted that dynamic models apply to flow shop production. It was also pointed out that this was the primary focus of this chapter.

The pure static case also is called a one-period model even though under some circumstances a corrective "second shot" may be allowed. The "Christmas tree problem" is a good illustration of the static situation. The owner of a tree nursery that sells Christmas trees locally said that she placed her orders with a Canadian tree farm north of Montreal back in July. Reasoning that it would be a good year—because people were feeling more prosperous than the prior year—she had bought the maximum number of trees that her organization could truck and accommodate.

Unfortunately, the two weeks before Christmas were unusually rainy. This discouraged people from buying trees for the holiday. In the last week before Christmas, the owner had posted sale signs slashing prices. She felt that helped but nevertheless, 25 percent of the trees remained unsold on Christmas eve. Five percent of them were live trees that could be saved, but 20 percent would have to be scrapped.

The seller's problem: how many trees to order in July for next December? Most of the sales take place a few days before Christmas. There is no time to take corrective action. What is to be done if too few trees are stocked? Driving up to Canada to replenish supplies is impractical. Also, there may not be any trees left there to sell. If sales are unexpectedly strong, buying locally will cost too much.

If too many trees are stocked, the best alternative is to advertise discounts, hoping to get anyone who was going to buy a tree to buy it from the overstocked dealer. The dealer never really knows whether the order size was over or under, or just right, until Christmas day.

Other static examples include the storekeeper who has to decide how many *Wall Street Journal* newspapers to buy for each day. Only one decision can be made to buy *n* newspapers. In its purest form, there is no opportunity to correct that decision based on later information. Another example is the problem of the hot dog vendor at the ballpark.

Consider the department store buyer who places an order in July for toys to be sold at Christmas time. If the toy is a dud, there is severe overstock. If the toy is hot, there will not be enough stock to meet demand. Both types of situations occur regularly. Another example is the spare-parts order for the complex machine. When placed with the original order, the parts are relatively inexpensive. When required later, because of unanticipated failure, the costs are exorbitant. This spare-parts model is a static decision problem.

In the case of overestimated demand, salvage value is sometimes available. For example, a department store that overbuys on toys, shipped from abroad in time for the holiday season, may be able to sell those toys at a discount after the selling season is finished.

Dynamic situations require different considerations because the demand for such items is constant. Orders are placed repetitively over time. The problem becomes one of adjusting inventory levels to balance the various costs so that total variable costs are minimized. Variable, in this case, means these costs change with order size.

Dynamic models apply to inventories that are used for flow shops, intermittent flow shops, batch work that occurs fairly regularly, and supplies that are used for ongoing support systems—no matter what work configurations are typical of the process. The models developed in this chapter address dynamic situations. Service systems use many kinds of supplies with dynamic demand patterns (as in hospitals, hotels, restaurants, theme parks, airlines, and educational institutions).

14-1b Make or Buy Decisions—Outside or Self-Supplier

Make or buy decision
Purchase from outside (outsource) or make it internally (self-supplier).

Inventory is either purchased externally or made internally. The decision about which way to go is dictated by many factors. Cost and quality are among the most important considerations. The choice is called the **make or buy decision**. Make is self-supply; buy is outsourced. One reason for self-supply is that profit paid to the supplier can be saved by being your own supplier. This requires being as efficient as the best of the suppliers (or nearly so). If the volume that the self-supplier produces is significantly lower than the volumes produced by the leading suppliers, it is doubtful that self-supply will be as efficient and, therefore, able to be justified.

Costs can be compared using breakeven analysis. Making the product has significant fixed costs—much larger than the buy option. The variable costs have to be low enough to offset the fixed costs of the investment. With a new process, it is reasonable to assume that variable costs will start high and gradually decrease. They may never decrease enough to warrant choosing the make option on a strictly cost basis.

A car company that has never made windshield glass faces an awesome task if it decides to learn how to do it. An enormous amount of experience is required. During the education period, which can last a long time, costs will be excessive and quality will be erratic. Vertical integration could be used, which entails buying a windshield producer. Vertical integration means buying companies able to provide components that are otherwise purchased from suppliers. The other option is to buy from an expert supplier.

Learning about new process technology—to be up to par or better—is another reason for reaching the decision to make the product rather than to buy it. Eventually, cost and quality advantages are expected to make the buy decision worthwhile. By learning, the company may be better able to deal with suppliers.

14-1c Type of Demand Distribution—Certainty, Risk, and Uncertainty

Decision problems that have certain outcomes do not have a probability distribution. Signing a contract to supply a given number of units converts demand from a risk to a certainty. Locating a supplier down the block reduces delivery time uncertainty. Generally, there is a cost for certainty. Because contracts reduce the producer's risk, the buyer expects the price will reflect this fact. The supplier that locates across the street from the buyer expects compensation for being at that location.

Sometimes certainty is a reasonable assumption. This only works when the degree of variability will not affect the solution. Then, certainty is assumed for convenience and it does not violate the spirit of the model. Linear programming methods and transportation models make this assumption. Lead time for delivery is often treated in this way. Say that two weeks is the average for a specific case. The variability around the average will determine if two weeks can be used as if it were certain. It is important that users of inventory models know when the certainty assumptions are allowable. When lead time variability could cause a stock-out, it cannot be treated as constant.

Buffer stock is stock carried to prevent outages when demand exceeds expectations. Basic inventory methods dealing with order point policy (OPP) make assumptions about the demand distribution that get translated into buffer-stock levels. The OPP models on which Chapter 14 focuses are based on order point policies. Order points are stock levels at which new orders are triggered and placed. Explanations will be detailed. Differences with other inventory models will be highlighted in Section 14-4.

Uncertainty means that there is no good forecast for the probabilities of demand and/or lead-time distributions. When uncertainty exists, the probabilities for various levels of demand occurring are speculative. However, when there is a known risk, some planning can be done. Delivery of critical materials from the port city of Kobe in Japan always was totally reliable until the January 18, 1995, earthquake caused serious delays. Some companies factor such possibilities into their planning and can react quickly.[2] Another example is the 2003 strike in Venezuela, which led to an increase in the price of oil from $23 to $33 per barrel.[3] As an important benchmark, the price of oil surpassed $100 per barrel for the first time during January 2008. August 29, 2005, hurricane Katrina devastated New Orleans and closed its busy port for months.[4] Serious damage had been predicted years in advance. A number of companies including BMW, Hyundai, P&G, Home Depot, and Wal-Mart had plans in place to deal with the situation. Finite probabilities always exist for various catastrophes. Having a team on hand, ready to assess the situation and find solutions can provide significant advantage.

Buffer stock
Additional stock carried to prevent outages arising from demand exceeding expectations.

Order cancellations may be a less severe disaster, but they are usually costly enough to make planning for the event worthwhile. Many production departments have exposure to the risk that an order in process will be cancelled. Contingency planning for cancellations is better production management than reacting to cancellations after the fact.

When forecasting is difficult because there is no history, systems are developed to search for advance warning. They are tuned in to whomever might have information about orders. Every effort is made to find the key players who originate the orders and to keep them in the communication loop at all times. Other factors that might trigger orders also are tracked. Efforts are made to gain some control over the uncertain occurrences.

14-1d Stability of Demand Distribution—Fixed or Varying

Uncertainty about setting the right capacity for supply includes the possibility that the demand distribution is changing over time. This could be caused by a stable shift factor such as seasonality. On the other hand, the drivers of change could also be unknown. In the latter case, the instability of causal factors is generally acknowledged to reflect high risk.

If it is known how demand is changing, then the risk levels may be controllable because forecasts of some merit are possible. OPP methods are applicable to predictable demand distributions. The best of these is stable demand, but forecasts can be modified if it is known how the distributions are changing. Otherwise, the system is searching in the dark. Other methods than OPP should be used to manage these situations. Material requirements planning (MRP) is the most favored alternative when the demand distribution is unknown or unstable.

14-1e Demand Continuity—Smoothly Continuous or Lumpy

Much of the prior discussion applies to demand continuity. OPP needs demand continuity that can be described as persistence of the stable demand pattern over a relatively long time period. MRP as an alternative inventory methodology can deal with the lack of smoothly continuous demand. It should be noted that assuming smooth and continuous demand is akin to converting a known risk situation into one of certainty. The assumption is usually valid and can be tested by simulating different patterns that are more or less smooth and continuous and measuring the extra costs incurred for assuming perfect smoothness when, in fact, it is good but not perfect. Such testing is most readily done with computer simulation programs. It is called **sensitivity analysis** whether it is done by hand or computer.

14-1f Lead-Time (LT) Distributions—Fixed or Varying

Lead time is the interval between order placement and receipt (order need recognition and write up times are included). Variability of the lead time will be a factor in setting the size of the buffer (safety) stock. As lead times get longer, inventory systems become more sensitive to problems that can arise in the supply chain. One of the main reasons is that with long lead times, correction of errors takes longer. The more critical the materials are for production, the worse this situation becomes. For materials that are not critical, the assumption of fixed lead times does not do too much damage. When materials are critical, inventory planning had best take into account forecasts for the lead-time distribution. In that event, lead-time distributions will assign additional units to buffer stocks. Another name for buffer stock is safety stock because these units are held to provide protection against variability in demand and (where applicable) lead times. Simulation testing for sensitivity is advised for this situation as well as the one covered in Secton 14-1e.

14-1g Independent or Dependent Demand

Chapter 14 focuses on independent-demand systems. This means that orders can be placed for nondependent items without considering what demand is forecast for the end

Sensitivity analysis
Allows diagnostic analysis of the effects of changing inventory costs.

products of which they are part. For example, labels for a specific kind of jam are dependent on the demand for that particular kind of jam. Beach plum jam is highly seasonal because of the nature of that crop. This part does not meet the criteria for stable, continuous demand that characterizes OPP models. Alternatives to OPP should be used when dependent demand systems are involved. This is applicable for components and subassemblies that are used as parts of one or more finished products that have sporadic demand. The dependency is greatest when both the timing and the quantity for end-product demands is not predictable.

14-2 Costs of Inventory

The core of inventory analysis lies in finding and measuring relevant costs. Six main types of costs are discussed and then, in a seventh category, a few others are mentioned.

The six costs that will be discussed are:

1 Costs of ordering
2 Costs of setups and changeovers
3 Costs of carrying inventory
4 Costs of discounts
5 Out-of-stock costs
6 Costs of running the inventory system

14-2a Costs of Ordering

The best way to determine the cost of an order is to do a systems study of the elements that go into making up and placing an order. The elements are then given costs related to materials and labor used, space required, and equipment charges. It is easy to say how to do the cost analysis, but difficult to get the correct cost allocations. Assume that the purchasing department can process 100 orders per day, but things are slow and so it processes only 50 orders per day. Does that mean that the cost of an order is twice as great when things are slow? It does mean that if things stay slow, redesigning the purchasing department makes sense. Those dictates would arise with activity-based and lean accounting procedures.

What is needed is the determination of the variable costs of ordering. Those costs will be twice as large for two orders as for one. How long does it take; what skill levels are involved? The fixed costs of ordering have to be separated from the variable costs. Fixed costs are not changed by the order size or frequency of ordering, so they are not included in the inventory policy model. They are inherent costs of operating the purchasing department.

It is possible to evaluate the fixed costs to determine if purchasing is carrying too much capacity. Activity-based costing can help to ascertain an optimal size for the order department. If union regulations allow, purchasing people can do other things when they are not occupied with purchasing. This converts fixed costs to variable costs.

With variable costs defined, the systems study of the ordering process continues. It consists of writing up the purchase requisition form, making phone calls in connection with specifications, and ordering, faxing, or mailing purchase orders to the supplier. All costs that increase as a function of the number of purchase requisitions and the size of the orders qualify for inclusion.

Finally, a specific example helps to illustrate how the ordering cost relates to under-capacity of service orders. Assume that the order department now processes 100 orders per week. A new inventory policy requires that 150 purchase requisitions be processed in a week. It is agreed that the ordering department must be enlarged. The increase in labor costs, equipment, and overhead is considered to be an addition to variable costs. Thus, the ordering cost is determined on top of a base-ordering system.

14-2b Costs of Setups and Changeovers

When self-supply is being used, the ordering cost is replaced by the cost of setting up the equipment to do the run. This requires cleaning up from the prior job, which also is called *taking down*. The process is known as *changeover*, and the costs can be significant.

A number of parts may have to be made before the setup is complete. The cost of learning is involved and defectives play a role. When acquiring equipment, changeover times and costs can be as important to consider as output rates. Flexible manufacturing systems (FMS) are notable for their ability to provide fast changeovers, but the expense of the equipment makes the costs of the changeovers high.

14-2c Costs of Carrying Inventory

Good inventory policy maintains the minimum necessary stock on-hand. When demand slackens, companies cut back further on their inventory. They do this because of the belief that the minimum necessary level is going down.

Also, inventory is a form of investment. Capital is tied up in materials and goods. If the capital were free, alternative uses might be found for it. The alternatives include spending for R&D, new product and/or process development, advertising, promotion, and going global. Some firms even put the money into financial instruments, the stock market, or the savings bank.

Expanded capacity and diversification are typical opportunities that, when ignored, incur the cost of not doing that much better with the investment funds. By holding inventory, the company foregoes investing its capital in these alternative ways. Such opportunity costs account for a large part of the costs of carrying inventory.

Inventory carrying costs are variable costs that depend upon the average number of units stocked ($Q/2$), the cost per unit (c), and the carrying cost interest rate that is applicable (C_c). These costs vary with the number of units per order, Q.

Inventory carrying costs also include the expense of storing inventory. As was the case for the ordering department, costs should be measured from a fixed base. The key is to find the variable cost component that is associated with storage.

These are the costs over which P/OM can exercise control using inventory policies. Thus, if a company has shelf space for 1,000 units, but can get a discount if it purchases at least 2,000 units, then to get this discount it must expand storage capacity. It can buy or rent additional space.

There are options for ordering large quantities to obtain discounts without requiring expanded storage capacity. One of these is *vendor releasing*, whereby the supplier agrees to deliver small increments of the larger order over time. It will be mentioned again in connection with inventory deliveries for the flow shop.

Another method for reducing storage space requirements is the use of *cooperative storage*. Commonly used supplies are ordered at discount in large quantities, stored in co-operative warehouses, and dispensed to participating hospitals, in the same metropolitan area, on an as-needed basis. Airlines share the storage costs and investment-based carrying costs of commonly used parts such as jet engines. Cooperative sharing reduces storage costs and increases the availability of expensive components that require large dollar expenditures.

Items carried in stock are subject to costs of pilferage, obsolescence, deterioration, and damage. These costs represent real losses in the value of inventory. Pilferage, which is petty theft, is characteristic of small items such as tools. Department stores suffer extensively from stolen merchandise. Hotels lose ashtrays and towels. Pencils and stamps disappear in offices.

Obsolescence may be the most important component of carrying cost because it happens so often and so fast. Obsolescence occurs quite suddenly because a competitor introduces technological change. Also, it can be the kind of loss that is associated with style goods, toys, and Christmas trees. Out-of-season and out-of-style items can lose value and must be sold at a special reduced rate. The determination of how much inventory to carry will be affected by the nature of the inventories and the way in which units lose value over time.

Deterioration affects the carrying cost of a broad range of products. Industrial products that deteriorate with advancing age include adhesives, chemicals, textiles, and rubber. Weather deteriorates iron and wood. Rubber gaskets in pumps can fail. Food is date stamped, but even without that documentation the owners of restaurants are keenly aware of the effects of sour milk and stale bread.

Companies put spoilage retardants in foods, but increasingly customers avoid additives. Adding ingredients to prevent spoilage increases material and production costs while decreasing the carrying cost for product deterioration. The net market effect must be factored in as well. Spoiled milk and stale bread are quickly perceived, but customers can avoid buying products before they spoil by noting freshness dating information as required for milk and bread. Whatever cannot be sold because of real or dated deterioration is added to the carrying cost. Some drugs like aspirin are dated. Although drugs are vulnerable to spoilage, many people use them anyway because though ineffective they do not taste bad.

Some products that are not required to use freshness dating are testing its effect on their market share. Consumer advocacy groups are suggesting regulations that automobile tires be dated because there is age deterioration in tire materials. Freshness dating not only increases the carrying cost component, but it also increases demands on operations to make and deliver product as much before the freshness date as possible. Delays in getting dated products to market will decrease productivity and increase carrying costs. It is evident that consumers want many product categories to show elapsed time. Freshness dating increases production and inventory costs.

An added component of carrying cost is both taxes and insurance. If insurance rates and taxes are determined on a per unit basis, then the amount of inventory that is stocked will determine directly the insurance and tax components of the carrying costs.

Determination of Carrying Cost

Table 14-1 is furnished as a guide. Numbers have been provided that are similar to the carrying cost computations of most companies in the United States. Each situation is different, so the accountants and operating managers must assess those costs that apply to their particular situation. The estimates are particularly susceptible to interest rates.

14-2d Costs of Discounts

Accepting discounts by buying at least a certain amount of material involves extra costs that may make taking the discount unprofitable. An appropriate inventory cost analysis must be used (and is furnished in a later section of this chapter) to determine whether a

Category	High	Medium	Low
Lost opportunity costs*	15.00	9.00	6.00
Obsolescence	3.00	1.00	0.00
Deterioration	3.00	1.00	0.25
Shipping and handling	2.00	1.00	0.25
Taxes	0.25	0.10	0.05
Storage cost	0.25	0.10	0.05
Insurance	0.25	0.10	0.05
Miscellaneous	0.25	0.10	0.05
Theft	6.00	0.10	0.05
C_c Totals	30.00 %	12.50 %	6.75%

* Loss due to inability to invest funds in profit-making ventures, including loss of interest.

Table 14-1

Past History of High, Medium, and Low Estimates of Total Carrying Costs Rates (C_c).

The Components of Total C_c are Shown (All are percents per dollar per year.)

discount that is offered should be taken. The extra costs for taking the discount are compared to the savings obtained from the discount. Extra expenses include additional carrying costs. Part of these carrying costs is incurred for additional storage space. Table 14-1 can be consulted for other variable cost components associated with holding extra inventory.

14-2e Out-of-Stock Costs

When the firm does not have stock to fill an order, there is a penalty to be paid. Perhaps the customer goes elsewhere, but will return for the next purchase. Then the penalty is only the value of the order that is lost. If the customer is irritated by the out-of-stock situation and finds a new supplier, the customer may be lost forever. The loss of goodwill must be translated into a cost that is equivalent to the termination of the revenue generation of that customer. The specific cost is how much lower the **lifetime value** of that customer becomes, or the revenue from that customer may terminate entirely.

If the buyer is willing to wait to have the order filled, the company creates a backorder. This calls for filling the order as soon as capacity is available or materials arrive. Backorder costs include the penalties of alienated customers. To avoid this penalty, some mail-order companies prefer to fill customers' orders with a more expensive substitute instead of creating a backorder. The outage cost is related to the decrease in profit margin. However, the goodwill generated by the gesture is an intangible addition to long-term profit. Depending on the system that is used (i.e., backordering, substitutions, fill or kill, and so on), various costs of being out of stock will occur. The lost-goodwill cost is most difficult to evaluate.

Organizations that are not close to their customers frequently ignore lost goodwill. This may occur because the firm does not know how to measure or recognize goodwill. Many bureaucracies are identified as neglecting customer satisfaction inadvertently by overlooking the job satisfaction of their employees who in turn deal with the customers. Disgruntled employees do not make happy customers.

14-2f Costs of Running the Inventory System

Processing costs that are associated with running the inventory system are referred to here as *systemic costs*. This category of costs is usually a function of the size of the inventory that is carried and the importance of knowing exact stock levels on-line immediately.

A big part of systemic expense is keeping up with incessant supplier cost changes, customer demand alterations, carrying cost modifications, labor costs for keeping records, and technology alteration costs. Costs are related to the number of people operating the inventory system. Operating costs also include systems assistance and programming that are needed. There are training costs. The amount of time that the system operates (round-the-clock) and the number of locations that are networked into the centralized data system (round-the-world) will have to be factored into this cost.

Systems involving many stock-keeping units (SKUs) are dependent upon having an organized information system. There are different SKU part numbers for each model type, as well as for each size and color. Part numbers for SKUs identify specific suppliers and where the inventory is stored. When there are frequent online transactions with many SKUs, the amount of detail is great. Such systems are labor-intensive and expensive.

It makes sense to focus on the SKUs for materials and items that are critical for production. Also, it makes sense to pay special attention to items that have high dollar volume. A-type items waste the most money if handled badly. If the A-category of the ABC inventory system is large and if there are many critical items to manage, then keeping all the information up-to-date is important, costly and rewarding.

The status of work in process (WIP) can be monitored by means of *bar codes, RFID*, and *optical readers*. Often, these technologies are combined. There still is no sign of an entirely paperless factory. Oticon Holding S/A tried it and failed (see Section 19-6c). Systemic costs continue to be formidable.

Lifetime value

Estimate of how much revenue and profit will be generated by a loyal customer who keeps on rebuying the product (e.g., returns to the same hotel) over the lifetime of sales to that customer. Called LTV, abuse them and lose them—and their entire LTV.

14-2g Additional Inventory Policy Costs

The six costs previously discussed are generally the most relevant in determining inventory policy. However, other costs can play a part in specific cases. The costs of delay in processing orders can take on great significance when a heart transplant is involved. Not quite as dramatic, every manufacturer recognizes the costs of delay when lengthy setups are required. Service organizations are sensitive to the costs of delay. Organizations set goals for the maximum time that can be allowed to elapse before answering a ringing phone.

The costs of production interruptions have previously been related to the critical nature of inventory items. Salvage costs can play important roles, as can the costs required for expediting orders. The costs of spoilage for food might be better handled as separate costs instead of as a part of the carrying cost related to obsolescence. The costs of central warehousing as compared to dispersed warehousing can be crucial. In various circumstances, one or more of these costs can dominate the inventory policy evaluation. A strong systems study will look outside the typical boundaries of inventory costs to spot those factors that are influencing the cost/benefit system.

14-3 Differentiation of Inventory Costs by Process Type

Significantly different inventory costs characterize each type of work configuration. These cost differentials play an important part in P/OM planning. They are fundamental to selecting best process types to achieve strategic objectives.

14-3a Flow Shop

Serialized production of the flow shop has low costs of ordering. This is because orders for the same items are placed with regularity. Uncertainty and variability are costly, and they are minimized for flow shop inventory.

The carrying cost of inventory reflects industry profitability. The reason for this relationship is that the carrying cost rate Cc is larger where reinvestments in the process or in marketing and distribution can bring excellent returns on investment. Out-of-stock costs tend to be severe. The line may have to shut down or run at some fraction of total capacity. For this reason, large buffer stocks are usually held in the inventory, in spite of the fact that carrying costs are high. Because of the large quantities of similar materials, purchases can qualify for discounts.

On the other hand, many companies—striving to be lean producers (low waste)—have made efforts to move toward just-in-time (JIT) deliveries of required materials (see Enrichment Activity 14). The goal is to count on trusted relations with few suppliers. The reliability of the supplier is viewed *as if* the supplier were part of the company being supplied. Serialized processes lend themselves to being well balanced and having synchronized flows of materials. Maintaining the balance is dependent upon the actual reliability of the supplier.

There is a loophole for JIT enthusiasts who want discounts. A large amount of material can be purchased at one time to be delivered in small JIT quantities. This agreement, called **vendor releasing**, is not available from all suppliers. Buyers must negotiate with suppliers to achieve it.

14-3b Job Shop

Ordering cost tends to be high for the job shop. There are many jobs and a great variety of materials used in small quantities. The right vendors have to be located for new work. Quantities are too small to build trust relations with a few suppliers. Vendors may not

Vendor releasing
Supplier agrees to deliver small portions of the larger order on a specified schedule.

value the business and take liberties, including not delivering when bigger and better opportunities come their way.

It is difficult to get engineering and R&D's attention to develop new materials and components because the order sizes are too small. Carrying costs will tend to be lower than those of the flow shop to the degree that the job shop is less profitable. Overordering to provide protection against defectives leaves an increasing accumulation of small amounts of materials that are difficult to sell as salvage. This increases the costs of obsolescence.

14-3c Projects

Ordering costs for projects are usually high. Bidding, which is expensive, is often used. Project managers may have to buy from a variety of vendors with whom they have had little experience. Projects are unique and project purchasing is often not repeated.

For small items that are essentially one-shot, minimum effort is made to bring efficiency and control to the purchasing function. Carrying costs are relatively unimportant, because the inventory is quickly used up. Time minimization drives project management.

The importance of being on time with the project has led to the development of critical path methods. The computer-based critical path calculation facilitates project planning and reporting of project status. These reports to P/OM permit a great deal of control over out-of-stock items. Though such project-control methods are costly, they are warranted by the high out-of-stock costs. Critical-path methods (Sections 18-8 and 18-9) help to minimize (or entirely eliminate) the number of outages to which high out-of-stock costs can be applied.

Inventory management of projects is a unique reflection of costs related to work configurations. Missing the special inventory requirements of projects can be costly.

14-3d Flexible Process Systems (FPS) Including FMS

Flexible manufacturing systems (FMSs) have low ordering costs. This is because there is considerable homogeneity of materials used for products by processes. The variety of materials used more nearly matches the flow shop than the job shop. Flexible process systems (FPSs) have high carrying cost rates because of the large capital investment and the profitability of the technology when it is properly managed.

Out-of-stock costs are less significant than for the flow shop because FMSs run small batches. Other products can be made while waiting for delivery of out-of-stock materials. FMS lot sizes are small, allowing air delivery. Obsolescence of small amounts of inventory are less likely than for the job shop because materials controls are monitored by computers that run the show.

FPS situations are a cross between flow shop and job shop characteristics. However, these processes have additional unique advantages that are directly attributable to the flexibility of FPS technology. FPS permits better cost control than is available for more traditional work configurations.

14-4 Order Point Policies (OPP)

Order point policies (OPP) define the stock level at which an order will be placed. In other words, as withdrawals decrease the number of units on hand, a particular stock level is reached. That number of units, called the **reorder point (RP)**, triggers an order for more stock to be placed with the appropriate supplier. OPP models specify the number of units to order. The time between orders varies depending on the order quantity and the rate at which demand depletes the stock on-hand. So, order size is fixed and the interval between orders varies. This discussion is about one type of order point system called the **perpetual inventory system**. It continuously records inventory withdrawals. Most often it is used online and in real time.

Order point policies (OPP)

Define the stock level at which a new order will be placed.

Reorder point (RP)

Triggers an order for more stock.

Perpetual inventory system

The interval between orders is variable and the order quantity is fixed.

Next, another type of order point policy will be described. It is called a **periodic inventory system**. On consecutive specific dates separated by the same amount of time, the item's record is called up and an order is placed for a variable number of units. The order size is determined by the amount of stock on-hand when the record is read. It is the date that triggers the review and the order being placed. Therefore, in the periodic case, the interval between orders is fixed while the ordered amount varies. The order amount is a function of the rate at which demand occurred in the period between reviews of the item's records.

Periodic OPP has become outmoded in some companies because computer systems enable the perpetual inventory system to be used inexpensively. The perpetual system has advantages that will be explained. Nevertheless, the periodic system will be described for two reasons. *First*, it is used to order certain items together from the same supplier. This may be done by small- and medium-sized organizations to obtain carload freight rates because they do not have sufficient volume to fill a freight car with one item. They may also want to deliver a number of different items to retailers on (for example) a once-a-week basis. Having a truck run to fulfill requirements of the perpetual inventory system could be far too costly. *Second*, some advanced inventory models mix the use of the perpetual and the periodic systems with the result that costs are further reduced. Therefore, it is useful to understand the mechanism of the periodic model.

Models such as the two mentioned here are based on the concepts and mathematical structure of an **economic order quantity (EOQ)**—the fixed amount to order, or an **economic lot size (ELS)**—the fixed amount to produce. An engineer named Ford Whitman Harris first developed the EOQ concept in 1913.[5] The ideas behind OPP inventory management have been expanded in many ways to give P/OM a powerful set of order point inventory models, but Harris' basic structure remains the same.

There is another set of problems that are not resolved by OPP inventory models. Those "other" situations are dealt with by *material requirements planning (MRP)* in Chapter 15. At this moment, the point to make is that MRP is used when the assumptions about order continuity and consistency of demand that are required by EOQ and ELS are not met. Table 14-2 indicates conditions for OPP models and for MRP models.

The most important requirements for EOQ and ELS (which are OPP models) are consistency of independent demand over time with relatively smooth and regular withdrawal patterns of units from stock. MRP works for sporadic dependent demand by using information systems control of messy demand patterns. MRP requires detailed information processing capabilities, which have grown enormously since MRP was first developed in the 1960s. When OPP is an online system, dealing with the perpetual inventory management of large numbers of SKUs, significant information capabilities are also required.

14-5 Economic Order Quantity (EOQ) Models—Batch Delivery

EOQ models, also called *square root models*, form the basis of most order point policies. They can be related to Japanese inventory methods, which stress small lot production and

Periodic inventory system
The interval between orders is fixed and the order quantity is variable.

Economic order quantity (EOQ)
How many units to order when purchasing items for batch delivery; needed to support flow shop production.

Economic lot size (ELS)
How many units to make in a production run; designed for the intermittent flow shop.

Continuity Requirement	Model Type
Static order	One-shot, single period (see Table 12-2)
Dynamic orders	OPP
Continuous smooth demand	OPP
Sporadic demand in clusters	MRP (see Chapter 15)
Demand Dependency Requirement	**Model Type**
Independent	OPP
Components dependent on end item	MRP (see Chapter 15)

Table 14-2

Conditions for OPP and MRP

just-in-time (JIT) deliveries. EOQ calls for JIT order quantities (as shown in Enrichment Activity 14) when there is:

1 Extreme reduction of the cost of ordering
2 Extreme reduction of the cost of setting up jobs
3 Very high costs of carrying inventory

The Japanese inventory methods also emphasize supplier relationships to accomplish goals that are not directly represented by the inventory models—namely, high product quality, communication of impending problems, short lead times, and delivery reliability. How do the costs defined in Sections 14-2 and 14-3 operate in an inventory system where deliveries of purchased supplies are made at regular intervals? The quantities will be delivered in batches of Q units (the order quantity). Also, it is assumed that the production system uses up the inventory at a *constant rate* and that there is *no variability* in this rate or in the delivery intervals. Because of these assumptions, all units that are ordered will be consumed in a fixed period. There will be no salvage costs for excess units, and no stock-outages. Later on, variability in the rate of inventory usage and in the lead-time replenishment interval will be included.

The proposed conditions apply to many inventory systems. They are applicable to FPS and the flow shop, which receive materials in batches that can be small and delivered just-in-time. They also are relevant for the job shop, or the project or the intermittent flow shop, where the question arises: Should the entire inventory needed to meet demand be purchased at one time, or in several lots, over time?

Although it is assumed that consumption occurs at a uniform, continuous rate, it is seldom a serious problem if the conditions are not exactly met. The objective is to balance opposing costs so that an optimal inventory procedure can be designed. Figure 14-1 shows the relationship of the order quantity, Q, with carrying costs having the linear form aQ, labeled Line A. Figure 14-1 also shows the order cost curve having the nonlinear form b/Q, labeled Line B. Note that a and b are generic constants that will be defined for both EOQ and ELS.

As the number of units (Q) purchased per order increases, carrying costs rise. This is Line A. As the number of units per order increases, the number of orders placed per year will decrease, lowering the ordering costs as shown in Line B.

If the demand (D) for a particular item amounts to 1,000 units per year, all of the units could be ordered at one time. $Q = 1,000$ and only one order would be placed per year. The 1,000 units gradually decrease to zero from the beginning to the end of the year so

Figure 14-1

Variable Carrying Cost Line (A) Increases as Variable Ordering Cost Curve (B) Decreases

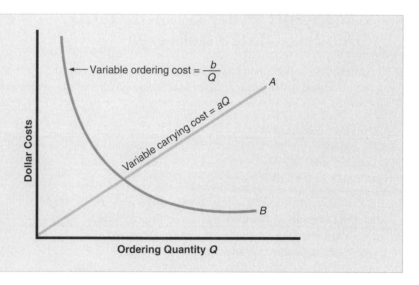

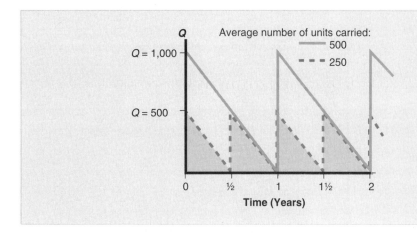

Figure 14-2

Constant Withdrawl Order Policies for $Q = 1,000$ and $Q = 500$ units; Demand $(D) = 1,000$ units/year

that the average annual stock would be 500 units. Two orders per year cuts the average annual number of units in half to 250.

$$\overline{Q} = \text{Average inventory with smooth withdrawl} = \frac{Q}{2} \qquad (14\text{-}1)$$

Figure 14-2 illustrates the continuous withdrawal pattern that is an important OPP assumption.

Figure 14-2 shows withdrawal patterns for two different order size policies, both of which satisfy demand of $D = 1,000$ units per year. The first policy places a single order of $Q = 1,000$ units once a year. Then, the average inventory is $\overline{Q} = 500$ units.

The second policy places two orders a year so $Q = 500$ and $\overline{Q} = 250$ units. Note that demand per year (D) divided by the number of units per order (Q) equals the number of orders per year (n).

$$\frac{D}{Q} = n \quad \text{or} \quad D = nQ \qquad (14\text{-}2)$$

The progression is evident: as Q is halved, n is doubled. Thus: when $Q = 250$, $\overline{Q} = 125$ units, $n = 4$ orders/year. And when $Q = 125$, $\overline{Q} = 62.5$ units, $n = 8$ orders/year.

Although the ordering cost (related to n) is doubling, the carrying cost is being cut in half because the average inventory $\overline{Q}$ is cut in half.

14-5a Total Variable Cost

Total variable cost is the sum of the ordering cost and the carrying cost. Thus:

$$TVC = CC + OC \quad \text{where:}$$

$TVC = $ total variable cost; $CC = $ carrying cost; and $OC = $ ordering cost. The reason that TVC is used instead of TC is that only costs that change (are variable) with different order sizes are included. The goal is to write the total variable cost equation and then minimize it with respect to the order size Q.

Figure 14-3 shows TVC as the sum of the two cost factors (CC and OC) previously shown in Figure 14-1. The TVC curve results from the sum of the carrying cost (Line A) and the ordering cost (Line B).

Minimum total variable cost (min TVC) is associated with an order quantity $Q = Q_o$, where Q_o is referred to as Q (*optimal*). Some parts of the equation are already familiar.

1. Average number of units carried in stock is $Q/2$, where Q is the number of units purchased/ordered.
2. Average dollar inventory carried is $cQ/2$, where c is the item's per unit cost.

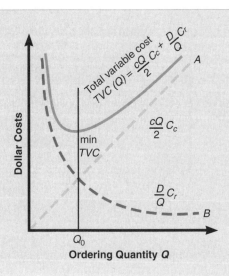

Figure 14-3

Total Variable Cost: $TVC = \sum (Carrying\ Costs + Ordering\ Costs)$ in Dollars/Year as a Function of Q

3 The total variable carrying cost per year is ($cC_cQ/2$), where C_c is the carrying cost rate, per dollar per time periods. This is the first term of the total variable cost equation written earlier.

4 Number of orders placed per year is D/Q, where D is the total demand per year.

5 The total variable ordering cost per year is ($D/Q)C_r$, where C_r is the cost per order. This is the second term of the total variable cost equation, *TVC*.

6 The time interval most often used is a year. This is consistent with the stability of the flow shop and the conceptualization of carrying cost rates and interest rates per year. Adjustments can always be made if needed. For example, if interest rates are volatile a 6-month period may be more accurate. It is essential that all time periods in the equation be the same.

Using math symbols, the total variable cost *TVC* is described as follows:

$$TVC = C_c(cQ/2) + C_r(D/Q)$$

This equation appears within Figure 14-3 where costs are shown individually and summed.

The minimum value of *TVC* can be obtained by trial and error methods. Finding the minimum can be done visually using Figure 14-3. There is no need to use trial and error because the *minimum total variable cost always occurs at the* crosspoint *of Lines A and B*. This statement applies to all linear equations of the form $y = aQ + b/Q$. This is the structure of the *TVC* equation shown here and in Figure 14-3.

The minimum total variable cost also can be derived by taking the derivative of y, setting that derivative equal to zero, and solving for the optimal value of Q (i.e., Q_o) as follows:

$$\frac{dy}{dQ} = a - \frac{b}{Q^2} = 0 \quad \text{or} \quad Q_o^2 = \frac{b}{a} \quad \text{and} \quad Q_o = \sqrt{\frac{b}{a}} \qquad (14\text{-}3)$$

By showing it in this way with just a, b, and Q, there are far fewer letters and the structure can be readily seen. This representation assumes that calculus has been studied. If that is not so, there is the graphical approach to derive the position of the minimum value of *TVC* (see Figure 14-3). There is also the method of setting the two terms of the equation equal to each other.

The general equation can now be applied to the derivation of optimal order quantity, Q_o, substituting *TVC* for y.

$$\frac{d(TVC)}{dQ} = \left(\frac{c}{2}\right)C_c - \left(\frac{D}{Q^2}\right)C_r = 0 \qquad (14\text{-}4)$$

Solving:

$$Q_o^2 = 2DC_r/cC_c \quad \text{and} \quad Q_o = \sqrt{\frac{2DC_r}{cC_c}} \qquad (14\text{-}5)$$

The same result is obtained by setting the two terms of the equation equal to each other. They are equal at the crosspoint. Thus, set $(cQ/2)C_c + (D/Q)C_r$ and solve for Q to obtain the economic order quantity (Q_o). The result is the same as Q_o, as shown earlier.

This **square root inventory model** is basic. It is the foundation equation for all inventory modeling of the OPP type and applies to flow shops, job shops, flexible processing, and projects. Human intuition tends to extrapolate linearly and does not empathize with square root relationships. That is why people do not get best results when managing inventories by guessing.

If one of the variables under the square root is doubled, what happens to Q_o? As a specific illustration, if demand (D) in the numerator is increased to $2D$, it is not instinctive that Q_o should increase by $\sqrt{2} = 1.41421356$.

When risk exists in the system because of demand or lead-time variability, a version of the EOQ model can be built in which buffer stock is added to Q_o. Other alterations of the basic model permit discount policies to be examined to ascertain whether the company should take or refuse a discount. When inventory is self-supplied instead of purchased from an external vendor, the model can be converted to indicate optimal run size. This variant is called the *economic lot size (ELS) model*. In all of these cases, which will be addressed shortly, the foundation is the square root model.

14-5b An Application of EOQ

Assume that the carrying cost rate is 6 percent per year. This is in the low category. According to Table 14-1, 6.75 percent would be an average figure for carrying cost rates in a low interest period, such as during 2006–7. Probably, 6 percent is a conservative estimate in a low interest era.

$C_c = 0.06$ per year or 6 percent per year
$c = \$0.005$ per unit (this is price paid for a unit of a bulk item—1,000 units cost
     5.00; i.e., items such as nails, napkins, and noodles)
$D = 3,000$ units per month $= 36,000$ units per year
$C_r = \$2$ cost per order

The total annual variable cost equation is

$$TVC = (0.005)(Q/2)(0.06) + (36,000/Q)(2) = 0.00015Q + 72,000/Q$$

$$Q_o = \sqrt{\frac{(2)(36,000)(2)}{(0.005)(0.06)}} = \sqrt{(480)(10)^6} = 21,909$$

This indicates that 21,909 units should be ordered at one time. This number could be rounded off to 22,000 without disturbing anything. To find the number of orders per year, divide demand by order size.

$n_o = D/Q_o = 36,000/21,909 = 1.643$ orders per year, or per 12 months
$t_o = Q_o/D = 21,909/3,000 = 7.3$ months between orders
$t = 1/n$ is introduced for the first time. It is the period of time in months that elapses
     between placing successive orders.
t could be calculated in years, or in other time periods. It is shown in months between
     orders. Note: in the denominator, $D = 3,000$ units per month.

Square root inventory model
Optimal order quantity for make or buy with continuous demand is a function of the square root of the ratio of ordering cost to carrying cost when that ratio is multiplied by annual demand.

Accordingly, n in months is calculated: n_o (*annual*) $/12 = n_o$ (*monthly*) or $1.643/12 = 0.13692$ orders per month

QMpom module called Inventory and Production Models (Economic Order Quantity) can be applied. (Set LT $= 1$ day, working days per year $= 365$, price $= \$0.005$)

Assume that the current ordering policy is to order 3,000 units every month to exactly match demand and approximate a just-in-time ordering policy. Call this a *demand matching policy*. How does the demand matching policy $TVC_{3,000}$ compare with the optimal policy, $TVC_{21,909}$?

$$TVC_{3,000} = 0.00015(3000) + 72,000/(3000) = \$0.450 + \$24.00 = \$24.45$$
$$TVC_{21,909} = 0.00015(21,909) + 72,000/(21,909) = \$3.286 + \$3.286 = \$3.286(2) = \$6.57$$

The optimal policy always has equal carrying and ordering costs. In this case, they are both $3.286. The optimal TVC saves a considerable amount, namely, $24.45 - 6.57 = \$17.88$. If the same kind of savings can be made on many other purchased items, total savings can be substantial.

Optimal TVC is 270 percent lower than the *demand matching policy*. This is because Q for demand matching is small, which associates it with the steeply rising (left of optimal Q) portion of the total variable cost curve in Figure 14-3. It should be noted that the total cost curve is steep only when the optimal ordering quantity, Q_o is small. Otherwise, there is room for the total cost curve to spread out on both sides of the minimal value.

The TVC curve flattens out as the order quantity gets larger. From the sentence before, the TVC curve is flatter when the minimum point occurs at a large order quantity. For the flatter curves, there is less cost difference between the minimum cost at Q_o and the costs associated with small changes ($\in$) in the order quantity. On the other hand, when measured from small values of Q_o, such minimal changes as $Q_o \pm \in$ produce large cost changes, especially $Q_o - \in$. Examples of both low and high cost sensitivity are illustrated in the Problems Section for Chapter 14.

Application of the systems point of view leads to questions: Where should the $t_o = 7.3$ months' supply of these bulk items be stored? Will these bulk items age and deteriorate, or become obsolescent? Why is it that *matching demand* does not provide the just-in-time cost benefits that have been popularized?

Small sums are involved. It may well be that the use of EOQ is not worth the bother. For this particular item, the annual expense is $36,000(0.005) = \$180.00$ a year. This is a C-type item in the ABC categories. The savings for going optimal are tremendous on a per unit basis but trivial from the systems point of view.

Now, the questions can be addressed. Where should the 7.3 months' supply of the bulk items be stored? The answer depends on the size, weight, and volume of the items to be stored. Thousands of paper clips can be placed in a very small space, and they require minimum care. If bulky items are likely to age, deteriorate, or become obsolescent, the cost of storage may be so great as to warrant ordering less. Logically, answers depend on the kind of items with respect to size and care. Some items are more vulnerable than others, and the carrying cost calculation should reflect this fact. Paper clips and pencils will be taken home. That adds to the cost of the remaining pencils. Cherries will deteriorate. Computer chips will become obsolete. Inventory management must be logical.

Why is it that matching demand with monthly orders does not provide the just-in-time benefits that are indicated in the popular press? The answer is twofold. The carrying cost, as reflected by the combination of cost per unit and carrying cost rate, cC_c is too low to rule out stock on-hand. The cost of half a cent per unit, and a 0.06 rate for carrying stock, together are so small that JIT is not a needed strategy. The *combination* of low unit cost and low carrying cost rate make matching demand with supply unnecessarily costly. On the other hand, low ordering and setup costs, large unit costs, and high carrying costs are conditions that foster JIT.

Instead of EOQ batch delivery at fixed intervals, a serialized process that can deliver product (or services) on a continuous basis now will be explored. It will be seen that batch production is one extreme of this more general model of production. At the other extreme is continuous non-stop production. In between are run lengths determined by the same factors that drive the EOQ model.

14-6 Economic Lot Size (ELS) Models

Explaining the ELS model is best accomplished by comparing it with the EOQ model. ELS models provide continuous delivery of product (say, hourly or daily) instead of delivery in batches (say, every three days or once a week). The two options are pictured in Figure 14-4, where a batch delivery of 6 units is made every third day. This is called BATCH delivery. The second option is regular and constant delivery of 2 units every day. This is called CONTINUOUS delivery.

Generally, batch delivery is the result of batch manufacture where work is done in stages within the job shop. Six units are delivered every 3 days. Batches of work are completed in 3 stages. No units can be delivered until the entire batch is completed on days 3, 6, and 9. Eighteen units are delivered in nine days.

The other possibility is that work is continuous using a flow shop process, and deliveries are made on a relatively continuous basis. The important distinction to be made is that the batch of 6 units is only available at the end of day 3, whereas 2 flow shop units are available at the end of each and every day.

The constant output in Figure 14-4, labeled CONTINUOUS, could only be delivered in daily batches of two. Some flow shops can deliver a finished product as frequently as every minute, while in others it might be every hour. The producer might decide to deliver the continuously produced product in batches of six as shown in Figure 14-4, labeled BATCH. Various reasons account for the producer storing continuous output for

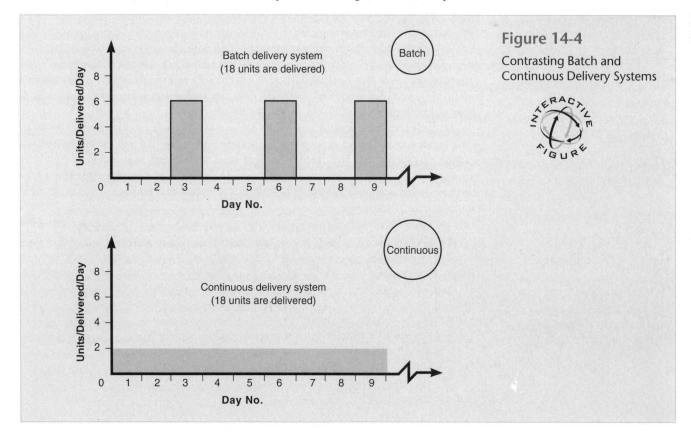

Figure 14-4

Contrasting Batch and Continuous Delivery Systems

batch delivery. Among these reasons might be a JIT agreement between buyer and supplier. This JIT agreement could be based on lack of storage space at the buyer's site, and delivery economics where less than fully-filled shipping containers, trucks, or railroad cars are too costly a way to ship product.

Some of these points hold true whether units are delivered by an outside supplier or produced internally. Production delivery systems are often designed to permit delivery of units only when they are called for by the user. This is called a "pull" system in contrast to a "push" system. The pull system of production does not allow deliveries to be made to a workstation until that workstation calls for a unit or units of supplies. Some pull systems permit a batch size of no more than one unit to be delivered. (See Section 17-7.)

14-6a The Intermittent Flow Shop (IFS) Model

When a flow shop does not have sufficient demand to warrant running it continuously, it can be converted with new setups and changeovers to run other products. It is an intermittent flow shop where run time is called *online* and non-run time is called *off-line*.

Figure 14-5 pictures the way that an IFS functions for one product. It shows the length of time of the production run [(t_1) goes from 0 to the 400th day]. The time that the system is free to run other kinds of units is shown by the negative sloping line [(t_2) goes from the 400th to the 500th day]. At the 500th day, production of the original product is resumed. The horizontal dashed line at 200 units is labeled *average number of units carried in stock*. This average value is determined by the production rate, the run time, and the demand rate. In the figure, there is another horizontal dashed line at 400 units. It is labeled *maximum storage required*. The size of the storage facility that is required to accommodate units at their stock-level peak is of practical importance. Peak storage quantity occurs just as the production system goes off-line for the original product and switches to another product.

Note that Figure 14-5 shows the production rate. The production rate line has a greater slope than the unit accumulation rate line (positive slope between 0 and 400). This is because the net rate of addition to stock on-hand must account for the daily withdrawals from inventories that are being made.

The ELS model portrays intermittent production with continuous deliveries. The stock level continuously increases until the apex is reached, which sets the maximum storage requirement. Then, stock on-hand begins to decrease because production for the item is off-line. Eventually, stock on-hand (SOH) reaches zero (or some protected level of stock—if buffer units are held for service safety reasons).

The math formulation of the economic lot size (ELS) model is the same as the EOQ model with an extra term. This model gets its name from the fact that the production run quantity is called a *lot*. The model is used to determine the optimal production lot size, which translates into run time as a function of the production output rate (p). The model also can be used to study the effect of varying the production output rate (p), e.g., more units per hour.

Figure 14-5

The Operation of the Economic Lot Size (ELS) Model for Intermittent Flow Shop Planning

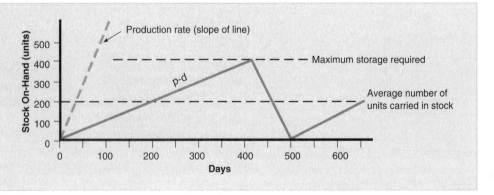

First, read the caption of Figure 14-6. Then, it may be evident that if the production output rate (p) is increased, then the positive slope of the line rising to the apex increases. In other words, the left side of the SOH triangle rises faster. Also, the production rate dashed line (in Figure 14-5) rises faster.

This means that run time could be shortened leaving longer free times on the production line for other products. Furthermore, note that as the slope of the left side of the SOH triangle increases—rising faster—this triangle looks more and more like the right triangles that characterize EOQ batch models (see Figure 14-2).

Figure 14-6 shows the ELS triangle divided into two right triangles called A and B. The upward slope of the left side of the A triangle represents the net rate of accumulation of the stock on-hand. It is the production rate per day (p) minus the demand rate per day (d), which is labeled ($p - d$). That rate of net accumulation lasts for a time interval labeled t_1.

The downward slope of the right side of the B triangle represents the demand per day (d). There is no production going on during the interval called t_2. Although other production activities are going on, their graphs are not displayed. Each of them would have an A-type triangle to represent net accumulation of the particular item that is sharing the production line with the item in Figure 14-6.

The ELS model's ability to determine optimal production run size seems of primary interest to suppliers and producers. The EOQ model's calculation of the optimal order quantity would seem to be of primary interest to buyers and customers. The systems perspective refutes this concept of limited self-interest. The ability of suppliers and producers to obtain minimum cost solutions via adequate production runs operates to the advantage of buyers and customers. The benefits of lower costs and satisfactory delivery times create new markets and get passed on to the customers. The buyer's EOQ solution and the supplier's ELS solution should be complementary and congruent.

The ELS model provides continuous JIT-type delivery with intermittent production. The discontinuity in production is behind the scenes. This characterizes flexible production systems and intermittent flow shops designed to run one item, and then change over to run another item, using the same or similar equipment, the same workstations, and the same workers. The ELS solution is encountered with flexible NC, CNC, and other computer-controlled equipment. Because of the ability to change over more rapidly and at lower cost than manually, the economic lot size can be reduced.

The ELS model can run the gamut from the continuous production of the flow shop to short production runs. When the supplier delivers the economic order quantity to the buyer, the production of the required batch can be thought of as being instantaneous. The ELS math model developed below shows the broad range of these properties.

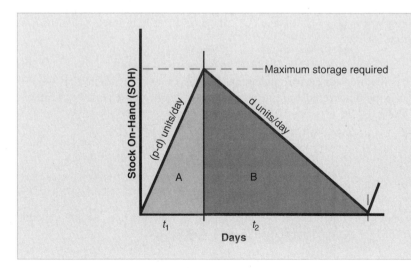

Figure 14-6

The ELS triangle is divided into two right triangles called A and B: A shows stock accumulation at the rate of ($p - d$), and B reflects continuous deliveries at the rate of (d) units per time period.

The cost of preparing to produce a product or to provide a service (run the lot) includes setup costs, C_S. Setup costs are producers' costs for preparing the process to do the job. Setup costs are generally significantly larger than order costs that are experienced when buying from suppliers. However, when dealing with FPS (flexible process systems) the setups are pre-engineered. The costs are not repetitive. Ability to achieve rapid setups at low costs, C_S, is the result of large original investments in design and engineering prior to building the equipment.

Setup costs are composed of two main parts:

1 Cost of labor that is required to prepare the facility for the new production run
2 Cost of lost production created by the facility's downtime while being prepared for the new job

Optimal run size is derived in a manner similar to the derivation of the economic order quantity. Many of the variables are the same. The two new variables are p and d: p = production rate in units per day; d = demand rate in units per day.

The total variable cost equation is

$$TVC = \left(\frac{cQ}{2}\right)\left(\frac{p-d}{p}\right)C_c + \left(\frac{D}{Q}\right)C_s \qquad (14\text{-}6)$$

Where

$$\left(\frac{p-d}{p}\right)\left(\frac{Q}{2}\right) = \text{the average number of units in inventory} \qquad (14\text{-}7)$$

As with the EOQ model, the minimum total cost can be derived by taking the derivative of TVC for ELS, setting it equal to zero, and solving for the optimal value, Q_o:

$$\frac{d(TVC)}{dQ} = \left(\frac{c}{2}\right)\left(\frac{p-d}{p}\right)C_c - \left(\frac{D}{Q^2}\right)C_s = 0$$

$$(14\text{-}8)$$

$$Q_o^2 = \left(\frac{2DC_s}{cC_c}\right)\left(\frac{p}{p-d}\right) \quad \text{and} \quad Q_o = \sqrt{\left(\frac{2DC_s}{cC_c}\right)\frac{p}{p-d}}$$

Alternatively, setting the two terms of the ELS equation for TVC equal to each other produces the same result because minimum TVC occurs at the Q_o value where the two lines in Figure 14-3 cross.

$$\frac{cC_cQ}{2}\left[\frac{p-d}{p}\right] = \frac{D}{Q}C_s \text{ and so } Q_o = \sqrt{\frac{2DC_s}{cC_c}\left[\frac{p}{p-d}\right]} \qquad (14\text{-}9)$$

Production run size is $Q_o = pt_1$ (where t_1 = run time or on-line time). Solve for t_1 as shown in Equation 14-10:

$$t_1 = Q_o \div p \qquad (14\text{-}10)$$

Total time t is required for each complete cycle; thus, $t = t_1 + t_2$ where t_2 is the off-line time. Because the run size (Q_o) must satisfy demand for the entire period t, it follows that: $Q_o = dt$. Then:

$$t = Q_o \div d \qquad (14\text{-}11)$$

Subtracting Equation 14-10 from Equation 14-11 yields the off-line time (t_2):

$$t_2 = t - t_1 = \frac{Q_o}{d} - \frac{Q_o}{p} = Q_o\left(\frac{p-d}{pd}\right) \qquad (14\text{-}12)$$

Figure 14-6 provides graphic meaning to the online (t_1) and off-line (t_2) intervals that have been described for the fundamental relationships of ELS.

14-6b An Application of ELS: Mixed-Model Systems Running on the Same Line

Units of different colors are to be made on the same equipment using an intermittent flow shop that runs 250 days per year. Different colors are run successively on the same line. Production capacity for all units run on this line is 1,800 units per day. Setups are needed to change colors. Blue has the largest market share.

Data for blue have been assembled as follows:

Yearly demand for blue $= D = 200{,}000$ units per year; and $D = 250d$
Daily demand for blue $= d = 800$ units per day $= D/250$
Daily production of blue $= p = 1800$ units per day
Setup cost for blue $= C_s = \$20$ per setup
Carrying cost rate $= C_c = 0.15 = 15\%$ of the unit cost per year
Cost of blue $= c = \$0.06$ per unit

Calculating the optimal lot size:

$$Q_o = \sqrt{\frac{(2)(200{,}000)(20)(1800)}{(0.06)(0.15)(1000)}} = \sqrt{\frac{(144)(10)^8}{(9)}} = \frac{(12)(10)^4}{3}$$

$$= 40{,}000 \text{ units}$$

Production run time (t_1) for blue is

$$t_1 = \frac{Q_o}{p} = \frac{40{,}000}{1{,}800} = 22.22 \text{ days}$$

Cycle period (t) is determined:

$$t = t_1 + t_2 = \frac{Q_o}{d} = \frac{40{,}000}{800} = 50 \text{ days}$$

Off-line period between runs is

$$t_2 = Q_o\left(\frac{p-d}{pd}\right) = 40{,}000\left(\frac{1000}{800 \times 1800}\right) = 27.78 \text{ days}$$

This means that 22 days (rounding) are required for the blue run and $50 - 22 = 28$ days (rounding) are available for other colors. The problem of *fitting* **mixed-model systems** on the same production line is seldom easy. An approach that is used is to start with the individual product optimal assignments. Then modify them with the "cut and try" method. More sophisticated mathematical models also can be used.

QMpom module called Inventory and Production Models (Economic Production Lot Size) can be applied. (Set LT = 1 day)

When can all items of a mixed-model set achieve optimal runs that minimize each of their *TVC*s? The answer is only when there is sufficient capacity so that none of the items (say, colors) are constrained. When demand levels overtax existing capacity of a mixed-model flow line, it is rare that each item of a mixed-model set can have an optimal run.

For this example, blue is optimal when it has control of 44 percent of the flow shop time. Note: $22.22/50 = 0.44$. If red and green split the remaining time equally, each would have about 28 percent of the available time.

Imagine what would happen if blue, red, and yellow had very similar characteristics. How could all three items be run on the same system? The only way that they can all be run is by cutting down on the run sizes. This means that each of the items will have *TVC*s that are suboptimal. Thus, overall costs for the system will be minimized but each item would have lower costs if there were no resource constraints. The best that can be done is

Mixed-model systems
Ford's black-colored Model T epitomizes a single-model production system. As soon as multicolored cars begin being made on the same line, mixed-model problems arose.

to achieve the systems' optimal, which is less good than the sum of individual item optimals.

14-6c From EOQ Through ELS to Continuous Production

The ELS model for optimal run size is shown in Equation 14-13

$$Q_o = \sqrt{\left(\frac{2DC_s}{cC_c}\right)\left(\frac{p}{p-d}\right)} \qquad (14\text{-}13)$$

The optimal run size (and length of production time) lends itself to analysis of extremes. First, if d were almost equal to p, then $(p - d)$ would approach zero. This means that Q_o would become very large. In notation, if $(p - d) \rightarrow 0$, then $Q_o \rightarrow \infty$.

Numbers grow infinitely large (∞) as the denominator of a fraction approaches zero. The conclusion is that if the demand rate is as great as the production rate, then the process should be run continuously without inventory buildup. The slope of the solid line in Figure 14-5 would decrease so that the SOH line would be flat against the x-axis line, which represents time. Maximum stock on-hand is thereby zero.

On the other hand, if p is much greater than d, i.e., $(p >>> d)$, then Equation 14-13 becomes Equation 14-14 which is almost like Equation 14-5. The EOQ model conditions prevail with one exception.

$$Q_o = \sqrt{\left(\frac{2DC_s}{cC_c}\right)\left(\frac{p}{p-0}\right)} = \sqrt{\frac{2DC_s}{cC_c}} \qquad (14\text{-}14)$$

The model in Equation 14-14 has setup cost, C_s, in place of order cost, C_r. This producer can supply the entire order quantity, Q_o, as a batch, on demand, but with a lead time based on other jobs that are competing for the same equipment. There really is no difference from the point of view of Figure 14-2 as shown in Figure 14-7.

Between the two extremes for p and d, many online–offline arrangements of mixed-model production throughputs are feasible.

14-6d Lead-Time Determination

Lead time (LT) is the interval that elapses between the recognition that an order should be placed and the delivery of that order. For both EOQ and ELS models, required lead times can be identified by studying their respective graphs as shown in Figure 14-7.

Note how the diminishing stock level reaches a threshold (or limen) called Q_{RP} on both diagrams. Q_{RP} stands for the stock level of the reorder point. That threshold triggers the order for replenishment. The level of stock that is at the reorder point, RP, is based on having enough stock on-hand to meet orders until the replenishment supply arrives and is ready to be used. The interval between reordering and receiving that order, and readying the units for use, is called the lead time (LT). Figure 14-7 shows how the horizontal Q_{RP}

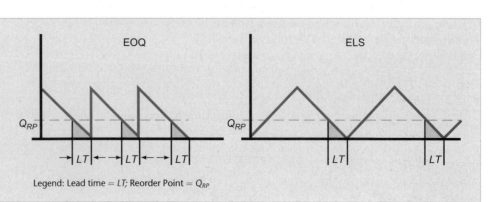

Figure 14-7

Lead Time Determines the Reorder Point for Both EOQ and ELS Models

Legend: Lead time = *LT*; Reorder Point = Q_{RP}

line intersects the *place order and initiate lead time* line on the down-sloping side of both the EOQ and the ELS models.

Eight lead-time (LT) considerations that apply to EOQ or ELS or both:

1 *The amount of time required to recognize the need to reorder.* If the reorder point is monitored continuously, then this period is as close to zero time as the system permits. If the stock level is read at intervals, then the average interval for noting that the reorder point has been reached is part of the LT interval.

2 *The interval for doing whatever clerical work is needed to prepare the order.* This includes determining how much to order and from whom to order. It might even include preparing for bidding. If multiple suppliers are to be used, this also includes determining how to divide the order. Self-supply with ELS pertains.

3 *Mail, e-mail, EDI, or telephone intervals to communicate with the supplier (or suppliers) and to place the order(s).*

4 *How long does the supplier's organization take to react to the placement of an order?* Is a system in place for communicating with everyone who participates in filling the order? How long does it take to find out if the requested items are in stock? If the items are not in stock, how long will it take for the supplier to set up the process to make them? How long will it take to produce, pack, and ship?

5 *Delivery time includes loading, transit, and unloading transporters.* If **transshipment** is needed, the lead-time period must be extended to take that into account. This period begins when the product leaves the supplier's control and ends when the buyer takes control of the items.

6 *Processing of delivered items by the receiving department includes quantity and quality checks as well determining storage locations and moving items.*

7 *Inspection to be sure items match specifications either by sampling or 100 percent inspection is generally required.* Time may be required to deal with problems uncovered by the inspection.

8 Computers used for updating records are sometimes unavailable until after normal office hours. The *effect of such delays* on the production schedule must be considered.

These eight lead-time components, when added together, form the total lead time. Determination of good lead-time estimates requires awareness of all relevant systems factors. Proper lead-time determination requires a systems study that traces out all contributing factors including the averages and variances of these factors. Each situation requires familiarity with what is actually being done and what needs to be done.

14-6e Expediting to Control Lead Time

Expediting is part of the P/OM function. It is used to control and improve lead times in the plant, in the office, and with outside suppliers and shippers. Expediting is the process of keeping track of the state of an order. It includes reminding and following up with anyone who could be delaying order processing.

Expediters are accountable for making certain that due dates are met. Often, there are many dates and places to be tracked. For example, the Association of American Railroads (AAR) uses sensing systems that include data tags and their readers (called automatic equipment identification—AEI) to provide car location messages (CLM). Transport Canada (TC) uses integrated AEI/OCR (optical character recognition). All tracking systems provide "carAt" location data that states where the car is located. Also they specify "loadIs." These are details about the cargo. Additionally, there is shipper information and data that distinguishes type of rail cars (e.g., boxcars, hoppers, flat cars, stock cars, and gondolas). The vision for future tracking of rolling stock and cargo is impressive. See the World Bank Transport Forum 2006 presentation titled, "Network Centric Railroading Utilizing Intelligent Railroad Systems."[6]

Transshipment

FedEx picks up packages from senders' locations in the United States and routes them to the transshipment hub in Memphis, as well as some smaller hubs, too. From the hub they are redirected to the receivers' addresses. Many companies use similar transshipment logistics.

© 2007 Jupiterimages Corporation

Imagine that the inventory stored in cardboard boxes behind the forklift truck is freshness dated. That procedure has marketing advantages, but the inventory costs are higher. A computerized tracking system can help to control the costs of obsolete and out-of-date stock.

Expediters also are trained to prevent and remedy problems. Delays are addressed as to causes and corrections. Using information systems to track and evaluate situations, the expediters know how to take action and when to use special capabilities (such as using FedEx) to speed things up. This also applies to tracking orders in a supplier's factory where knowledge about the degree of completion of an order can be vitally useful.

There is contingency training required in the use of equipment such as radio frequency identification (RFID) systems and techniques to take effective action. Such expediting techniques are increasingly used in project management where slippage along time lines is considered to carry high monetary penalties.

14-6f Lead-Time Variability

Lead times are usually variable. There are delays of varying length in each of the eight lead-time components listed earlier. When variance is significant, estimates must be made of the degree of variability.

Appropriate steps should be taken to include the effects of variability in the analyses. Expediting can be considered management's attention to decrease delays (Latin, 15th Century; *expeditus*). It is also the effort to decrease variability. Expediting deals with the causes of variability and attempts to keep those causes under control so that due dates can be met. Expediters strive to keep management and suppliers informed about slippage (due dates that will not be met). Expediting is delay control for lead times, but it also applies to project activities. In addition, expediting is also information dissemination so that all participants are aware of what is happening.

Although lead times are usually variable, they are often treated as if they were fixed, single values. There are two reasons for this:

1 The amount of variability is considered to be small and relatively negligible.
2 It is complex to assume variable demand and variable LT simultaneously.

Then, to take variable lead time into account in a quick and easy way, the idea of increasing protection against stock-outs is used. This is accomplished by assuming a larger (worse case) average than the actual average for the LT. To illustrate, if lead time is known to average 10 days, and it is also known to range ± 2 days almost all of the time, then an estimate of 12 days for LT might be a self-protective move. Extra inventory would be carried to buffer the two days that LT might slip. Airlines add extra minutes to their flight schedules to reduce the regularly reported frequency of being late.

The uses of safety (buffer) stock is a just-in-case, rather than a just-in-time, tactic. The much-used *perpetual inventory system* always employs some amount of extra stock as protection against surges in demand and delays in delivery. The question is "how much extra stock?"

14-7 Perpetual Inventory Systems

Perpetual inventory systems continuously record inventory received from suppliers and withdrawn by employees. Most perpetual inventory systems are used online, in real time with some demand variability. The EOQ and ELS models discussed so far do not include demand variability. In many practical situations, this assumption is unrealistic. With modifications, the EOQ and ELS models can deal with demand variability.

Variability of demand arises from variations in order sizes. Variability is passed along the supply chain, affecting everyone. Customers are the primary cause of demand variability. There are other causes of demand variability as well. These include stock on-hand replacement to make up for items lost as a result of warehouse fires, employee pilferage, and the discovery that items in stock cannot be shipped because they are defective.

Consider what occurs when a machine setting changes, creating a large number of rejects that cannot be reworked. Production must run larger numbers of items to compensate for the scrap. More materials must be withdrawn from inventory to be used by the process. The supplier furnished the usual number of units per order that was based on the estimate of the expected demand (D). Because demand is larger than expected, the reorder point Q_{RP} will be reached sooner.

The perspective that will be used to explain how the EOQ model can be modified to protect the buyer will assume batch delivery of the quantity:

$$Q_o = \sqrt{\frac{2DC_r}{cC_c}} \qquad (14\text{-}15)$$

The same conditions apply. The processes must be ongoing with item demand being relatively constant over time. It is evident that such modeling does not apply to job shops with small orders because they lack continuity of demand.

The focus now is on items that are stocked regularly, where the demand can vary. The buyer orders the economic order quantity, but has on hand some buffer stock (which is sometimes called *reserve stock* or *safety stock*). The buffer stock is extra stock so that when demand is heavier than expected, orders can still be filled.

An option is to design a perpetual inventory system. It is perpetual because it is an online system, tracking the stock on-hand (SOH) at each transaction of withdrawal or stock entry. To design the system, it will be useful to answer the following questions:

1 How many buffer stock units should be carried?
   The answer involves balancing the added carrying costs for extra stock against the costs of running out of stock. As one cost goes up, the other comes down.
2 When should an order be placed for the buffer stock?
   The buffer stock should be created as soon as it is determined that it is beneficial to have it. It does not have to be replenished when it has been drawn on to avoid stock-outs because the use of buffer stock is expected to average out at zero. The only times that this will not apply will be if the demand system is changing over time or is unstable.
3 How often should an order be placed for buffer stock?
   Once, and then whenever the buffer-stock level needs to be updated.
4 How many units should be ordered to meet expected demand?
   Use the same economic order quantity, Q_o.
5 How often and when should the orders be placed for units to meet the demand?
   An order is placed whenever the reorder point, Q_{RP}, is reached.
6 How does this perpetual system work?
   Withdrawal quantities are entered in the computer each time one or more units are taken out of stock. These quantities are subtracted from the previous stock-level balance to determine the new balance quantity of stock on-hand.

© 2008 Jupiterimages Corporation

Global package delivery systems have logistic problems to overcome. It is inevitable that they will become low cost, fast, and efficient. Global information delivery systems are already in widespread use.

14-7a Reorder Point and Buffer-Stock Calculations

The reorder point quantity is designated for each item and is entered in the computer program. When the reorder point has been reached, the program recognizes this fact and an order is placed for the economic order quantity, Q_o.

The stock level of the reorder point (Q_{RP}) is equal to the expected demand in the lead-time period called $\bar{D}_{LT}$, plus the buffer (or safety) stock (BS) quantity. Thus:

$$Q_{RP} = \bar{D}_{LT} + BS \qquad (14\text{-}16)$$

Figure 14-8 shows the *distribution of demand in the lead-time period*. It also provides a physical interpretation of the components of Equation 14-16.

Figure 14-8

Determination of the
Reorder Point Q_{RP}

It is measured from the
expected demand in the lead
time period $\bar{D}_{LT}$.

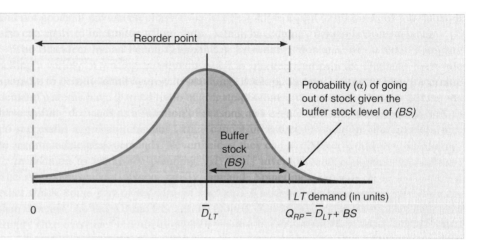

There are two parts to the construction of the reorder point. The first part is the left-hand side of the bell-shaped curve shown in Figure 14-8. The second part of the construction is the right-hand side of Figure 14-8 that is labeled "Buffer Stock."

The left-hand section of the reorder point goes from zero (at the left side of the diagram) to the mean of the lead-time distribution, which is $\bar{D}_{LT}$

The right-hand side of bell-shaped curve is divided into two parts. There is the section called *buffer stock (BS)*. It starts at $\bar{D}_{LT}$ and, moving to the right, spans a distance $+ k_\alpha \sigma_{LT}$, which is, in words, "*k standard deviations of the lead-time distribution.*" This, adds $+ k_\alpha \sigma_{LT}$, units of stock (called buffer stock–*BS*), to the mean of the lead-time distribution, $\bar{D}_{LT}$.

Equation 14-17 defines the reorder point, Q_{RP}. The value of $+ k_\alpha$ in $+ k_\alpha \sigma_{LT}$ represents a probability design decision regarding stock-out frequencies. The right-hand side tail of the lead-time distribution is labeled the probability (α) of going out of stock when the reorder point is set at $Q_{RP.}$

$$Q_{RP} = \bar{D}_{LT} + (BS = + k_\alpha \sigma_{LT}) \qquad (14\text{-}17)$$

The α-size of the tail of the distribution in Equation 14-17 is carefully chosen. When it is a large tail area, there will be many stock-outs. If a stock-out represents a life and death situation (e.g., no Type-A blood for critical surgery) or a difficult economic problem (e.g., no spare jet engine available) then the allowed probability of going out of stock may have been set too high. There is an economic balancing situation here in which the cost of going out of stock versus the cost of carrying more inventory.

Outages happen whenever actual demand in the lead-time period exceeds Q_{RP}. The value of α sets the k-value which when multiplied by the standard deviation of the distribution creates the tail size.

The likelihood of an outage occurring will be decreased by increasing the value of k. When $k = 1$, there is about a 16 percent probability of an outage happening during a lead-time period. When $k = 1.645$, there is a 5 percent probability of an outage happening during a lead-time period. When $k = 2$, the number decreases to 2.3 percent. When $k = 3$, the tail area is small at 0.13 percent.

When the tail area is small, then the buffer stock is large, and the likelihood of going out of stock is small. The large buffer stock means that the *carrying cost of stock is high to make sure that the actual cost of stock-outages is small*. When the tail area is large, then the amount of buffer stock that is being carried is small and the carrying cost is small, but the outage penalties are going to have to be paid more often.

How is lead time determined? The best way to determine the lead-time distribution is by observation. First, take as large a number of past lead times as the computer records make available and calculate the average lead time (say it is 10 days). Then, as a second step, record demand over successive 10-day intervals. Plot the distribution and determine the standard deviation.

If the successive 10-day periods are independently distributed, as they usually are, the lead-time distribution obtained by observation will be a reasonable approximation. This requires using the same supplier and delivery system over the sample period. If a change occurs, then new lead-time parameters will have to be estimated again.

Enough intervals should be collected in the sample to provide a smooth, nearly normal shape for the lead-time distribution when it is plotted. If the distribution appears bimodal or skewed, further statistical investigation is needed. Bimodal may mean that two different delivery systems are operating without being apparent. Skewed distributions may indicate that delays tend to reinforce further delays.

14-7b Imputing Stock-Outage Costs

Buffer stock is designed to prevent out-of-stock situations some percent of the time. The size of the alpha tail of the distribution in Figure 14-8 indicates the level of protection being sought. The buffer-stock level that is chosen is based on balancing the costs of stock-outs with those of carrying costs. Thus:

$$\text{Carrying cost of buffer stock } (BS) = cC_c(k_\alpha \sigma_{LT}) \qquad (14\text{-}18)$$

$c = $ cost of the unit in dollars/unit

$C_c = $ the carrying cost *rate* as a percent per dollar per year

$cC_c = $ carrying cost in dollars per unit per year

$k_\alpha \sigma_{LT} = $ number of units carried in the buffer stock; k_α has been chosen to limit the probability (α) that demand in the lead time will exceed $k_\alpha \sigma_{LT}$

$cC_c(k_\alpha \sigma_{LT}) = $ carrying cost in dollars per year for buffer stock designed to offer an (α) level of protection

The cost of stock-outages relates to their frequency. As k_α gets larger, the frequency of stock-outages decreases. Say that the tail of the distribution with $k_\alpha = 1.645$ provides protection against demand levels exceeding buffer stock 95 percent of the time. That means that five out of 100 lead-time intervals (or one out of 20 LTs) will experience a stock-outage, thus: $\alpha = 0.05$.

The number of lead-time intervals is the same as the number of orders placed. Say that $n = 5$ orders are placed per year. Then, an outage is expected once every four years. Stated in an alternative way, it is expected that four years will elapse between stock-outs. Finally, assume that the carrying cost per year for buffer stock is $2,500 obtained by using Equation 14-18. In four years, this sums to a value of $10,000 without discounting.

The value of k_α chosen $(k_\alpha = 1.645)$ has an *imputed stock-out cost* of $10,000. Imputed means attributed in the sense that an action attributes value. It is now up to management to decide whether that implied cost seems sensible and is acceptable. In many instances, it is very difficult to determine stock-out costs directly. The direct measure requires finding all of the consequences of the stock-out and then measuring the impact of those consequences. Therefore, the use of imputation of costs provides an appealing alternative. If the imputed cost is accepted, then:

$$\text{Outage cost (imputed by the choice of } \alpha \text{ level)} = \$10,000$$

14-7c Operating the Perpetual Inventory System

The first step to understanding how the perpetual inventory system works is by studying the graphic representation of it. Figure 14-9 illustrates the two parts that have been put together. The EOQ model sits on top of the buffer stock (which is the shaded rectangle).

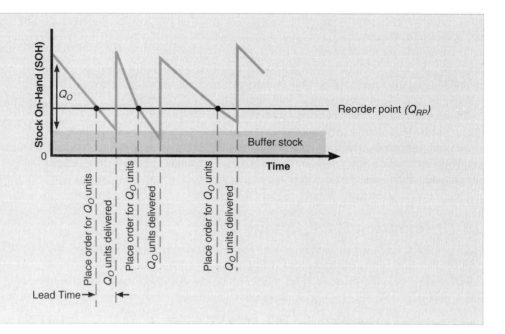

Figure 14-9

A Perpetual Inventory System—SOH Is Reduced with Each Withdrawal

When the reorder point is reached, a new order is placed. Stock level continues to decrease during the lead-time interval. The stock level rises when the replenishment order is received.

Follow the stock on-hand line as it forms an irregular sawtooth pattern. When demand becomes greater, the line moves down faster, and when the demand rate decreases, the line moves down more slowly. In other words, when the slope of the line becomes steeper, the reorder point (Q_{RP}) is reached more quickly.

Note that the interval between orders is variable depending on whether the demand has been faster or slower than the average rate. When the demand is consistently at the average rate the spacing between orders will be constant and unchanging at: $t_o = Q_o \div D$.

Note in Figure 14-9, the first of the replenishment cycles stops right at the buffer-stock line. At that point, SOH is zero and no buffer stock is withdrawn. Demand dips into the buffer-stock region only for the second replenishment cycle. In other words, buffer stock is called upon once in three replenishment cycles. The buffer stock withdrawn will be replaced when the next order is received and the units are put in stock.

The third of the three replenishment cycles shows an order arriving when the stock level is above the buffer-stock level. If the demand distribution is stable over time, then the buffer-stock level will average out to the planned number of units for buffer stock.

14-7d Two-Bin Perpetual Inventory Control System

The two-bin system is a smart way of continuously monitoring the order point. It is a simple self-operating perpetual inventory system. Figure 14-10 shows the two bins with familiar labels.

Two bins are marked 1 and 2. The optimal order size of Q_o units has been delivered. First, Bin 1 is filled to the reorder-point level (see Equation 14-17). Bin 1 now contains units to cover expected demand in the lead-time period plus safety stock. The remaining units from the delivery of EOQ = Q_o units are put into Bin 2. The bottom of Bin 2 is labeled the reorder point. When Bin 2 is emptied the number of units remaining are all in Bin 1 and they are the reorder point in number. Spending a few minutes with Figure 14-10 will make clear the delineation of the reorder points in Bins 1 and 2.

Withdrawals are made from Bin 2 first. When Bin 2 is depleted, an order is placed for the EOQ, and further units are taken from Bin 1. Each time Bin 2 is emptied, a new order is placed—it is equivalent to reaching the reorder point.

The two-bin system is not feasible for many kinds of items. When applicable, much clerical work is eliminated. This two-bin system is well suited to small items like nuts,

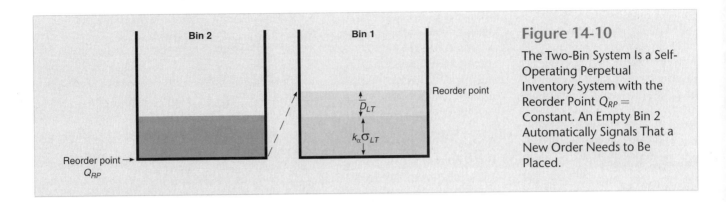

Figure 14-10

The Two-Bin System Is a Self-Operating Perpetual Inventory System with the Reorder Point $Q_{RP} =$ Constant. An Empty Bin 2 Automatically Signals That a New Order Needs to Be Placed.

bolts, and fasteners. These are items too small and too numerous to make withdrawal entries for each transaction. The same reasoning applies to recording withdrawals of liquids, for which the two-bin system approach is also ideal. Spotlight 10-2 discusses how the two-bin system is applicable for hospital inventories.

14-8 Periodic Inventory Systems

Periodic inventory systems were more popular than perpetual inventory systems before inventory information was digitized and put online. Periodic inventory systems are based on regular fixed review periods that were ideally suited for manual entries. They are also needed when actions should be taken periodically rather than randomly.

Computers outmoded periodic manual systems primarily designed to save money on the clerical aspects of tracking inventory. However, periodic inventory systems continue to be used for other reasons. These include requirements of suppliers concerning the timing for accepting new orders, requirements of shippers about timing deliveries, meeting the schedules of customers, fulfilling the need to combine orders to obtain volumes sufficient for shipment discounts.

Some organizations have central warehouses that will only accept orders from their regional distributors once a week. Each region expects deliveries on a different day of the week. Further, some industries prefer the regularity of the periodic method, which can be linked to changeover intervals for production processes as well as the phases of projects. For example, the stages of buildings must be synchronized with what suppliers deliver.

Periodic inventory systems also play a part in an advanced class of inventory models (called *Ss policies*) that combine the ordering rules of perpetual and periodic order systems to obtain lower total costs. These blended methods can be encountered in big inventory systems installations such as the Armed Forces use.

The optimal interval, t_o, for periodic review is based on the square root relationship shown in Equation 14-19, where the lower case oh's stand for optimal.

$$t_o = \frac{Q_o}{D} = D\sqrt{\frac{2DC_r}{cC_c}} = \sqrt{\frac{2C_r}{DcC_c}} \qquad (14\text{-}19)$$

High-cost items and large carrying costs increase the desirability of short review periods. High ordering costs and/or large setup costs call for long review periods.

To use the periodic model, first find and set the review interval. Then, at each review, determine SOH by adding total receipts and subtracting total withdrawals. An order is placed for a variable quantity contrasting with the perpetual inventory model where the order was a fixed quantity at variable intervals.

Figure 14-11 illustrates the way that the periodic order system functions. Note the upper line marked M. Summing the order quantity Q and the stock on-hand, including the buffer stock, sets the value of M. Thus:

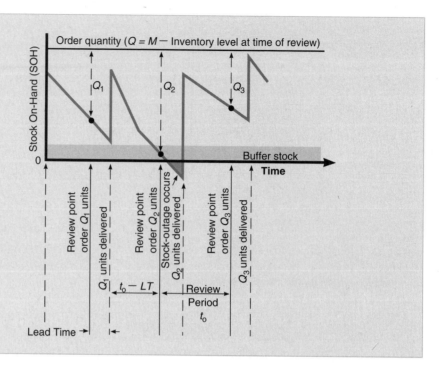

Figure 14-11

The Periodic Inventory
System Where SOH Is
Computed at Fixed Intervals
and Q Is Variable

$$M = Q + SOH \tag{14-20}$$

As seen in Figure 14-11, SOH includes the expected demand in the lead-time period plus the buffer stock. In this case, the buffer stock must protect against larger than average demand in the lead-time period plus the review period. This is:

$$SOH = \bar{D}_{LT} + BS_{t_o+LT} \tag{14-21}$$

Observe that the order quantity Q is the expected demand, $\bar{D}_{t_o}$ in the review period. The review period is also called t_o, and it is so-labeled in Figure 14-11. Functionally, the review period is the fixed interval between successive reviews by the inventory managers. Using this information, Equation 14-20 is rewritten based on Equation 14-21. It becomes Equation 14-22, as follows:

$$M = \bar{D}_{t_o} + \bar{D}_{LT} + BS_{t_o+LT} \tag{14-22}$$

The size of the buffer stock for the periodic review system must include protection against unexpectedly great demand—in a review period plus one lead-time interval. This is shown in Equation 14-23.

$$BS_{LT+t_o} = k_\alpha \sigma_{LT+t_o} \tag{14-23}$$

M is calculated as shown in Equation 14-24.

$$M = \bar{D}_{t_o} + \bar{D}_{LT} + BS_{t_o+LT} = \bar{D}_{LT+t_o} + k_\alpha \sigma_{LT+t_o} \tag{14-24}$$

Periodic buffer stock is calculated using the distribution of $(LT + t_o)$ because after an order is placed, variations in demand can be experienced during the period t_o. Then a review occurs and an order is placed. Demand variations can continue during the LT. Therefore, exposure to variable demand before correction can be made occurs over a review period and a lead time. This requires extra stock for protection, which is a major drawback of the periodic model.

The operation of the periodic model is to first determine the review dates using Equation 14-19. Then, at the review date, calculate *SOH* (Equation 14-21) and subtract it from *M* as in Equation 14-25. The result is the order quantity, *Q*.

$$M - SOH = Q \qquad (14\text{-}25)$$

The periodic model appeals to managers who like bookkeeping and regularity of actions. On the review date, the books are opened. The ledger is added up and the order is placed. The market drives actions in the perpetual; the calendar drives actions in the periodic. The difference is both economic and psychological.

14-9 Quantity Discount Model

Accept a quantity discount only when it lowers the total costs. Therefore, to determine when the discounted order quantity should replace the optimal undiscounted order quantity Q_o, it is necessary to derive the total cost curves. Note that it is necessary to compare *total costs* instead of *total variable costs* because for discount analysis the cost of goods purchased must play a significant role in the decision to accept or reject a discount. Lowering the price paid for goods is the purpose of taking the discount, but the true criterion must be total costs.

The discounting situation is directly reflected by the schedule shown in Table 14-3.

Total cost is TC using TVC, as previously defined, plus dollar demand (cD, and $c'D$) for undiscounted and then discounted costs. In this example, there is only one price break, viz., Q_1.

$$TC(c) = TVC(c) + cD = (cQ/2)C_c + (D/Q)C_r + cD(0 \le Q < Q_1)$$
$$TC(c') = TVC(c') + c'D = (c'Q/2)C_c + (D/Q)C_r + c'D(Q \ge Q_1)$$

These two total cost curves are drawn in Figure 14-12—curve without discounts includes point a; curve with discounts includes point b.

The quantity discount model involves more than one total cost equation but only one line segment is applicable in each cost break's range, i.e., c and c'. The discontinuities of the curves $TC(c)$ and $TC(c')$ are shown in Figure 14-12. There are two sets of curves in the left figure.

There is the upper curve and there is the lower one. In the upper curve, $TC(c)$ applies to the left of the vertical line Q_1. It is the higher of the two curves that occupy that space. It has the point a on it.

As shown in the bottom curve, $TC(c')$ applies on the vertical line Q_1 and to the right of the vertical line Q_1. It has point b on it as well as other letter-designated points. Because the discount price break occurs at Q_1(and for greater quantities), $TC(c')$ starts at the Q_1 vertical line and moves to the right.

The right-hand figure shows the resultant curves when the nonapplicable parts of each curve are removed. We say that this figure shows a curve with a discontinuity. Each curve includes its own respective dollar volume, that is, cD for the first curve and $c'D$ for the second curve. The entire top curve, $TC(c)$ is based on an undiscounted cost c. Therefore, that curve is imaginary in the right-hand space, which is on or above the discounted quantity Q_1. The bottom curve, $TC(c')$ is applicable when a discount is available, but it is only applicable at and above the quantity needed to obtain the discount. It is imaginary in the left-hand space, which is less than Q_1.

$Q \ge Q_1$ is the specified quantity required to obtain the discount. Q_1 is the discount quantity break point. The figure on the right shows that the discount must be taken

Quantity (Q units)	Cost per Unit	Total Cost	
Q = zero up to Q_1	c	$TC(c)$	**Table 14-3**
$Q = Q_1$ and greater	c'	$TC(c')$	Discount Schedule with One Quantity Price Break
Note: There can be any number of price breaks.			

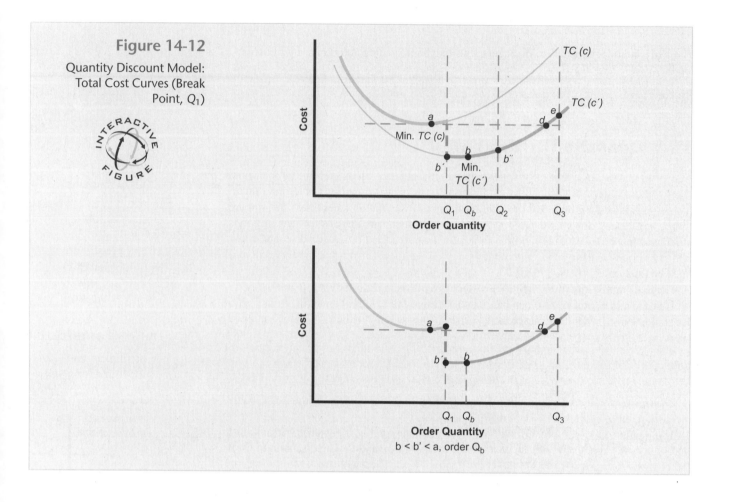

Figure 14-12

Quantity Discount Model:
Total Cost Curves (Break
Point, Q_1)

because the *TC* at b' is lower than the *TC* at *a*. Point *a* is the minimum total cost without the discount. It is the optimal point for that total cost curve based on the square root inventory model. It is not the optimal point under the discounting conditions.

In fact, the order quantity should be increased from Q_1 to Q_b, which is the order quantity at point *b*. Point *b* is lower than b''. Point b is the minimum total cost with the discount. It is the optimal point for that total cost curve based on the square root inventory model.

Reference to the upper and lower sets of curves in Figure 14-12 is essential to note the positions of points a, b', and b. Summarizing, for this discount schedule, point *b* is the lowest total cost that can be obtained. The discount should be taken and the optimal order quantity Q_b should be purchased at the discounted price of c'.

However, a materials manager may say "no" to the idea of the quantity *b* instead of the quantity b'. Several reasons could explain this position. The savings in *TC* appear to be negligible, but more cash will be tied up and more storage space required. On the other hand, if there is a possibility of a shortage of materials from a delivery disruption, then the larger order will be preferred. If a tie exists (and, in this case, that appears to be almost the case), then qualitative factors become more important. No matter what the curves indicate about taking or passing up a discount, qualitative factors must be used to scrutinize the decision.

With a tie, the issue of choosing the larger order size may reflect fear of a competitor cornering the market. Choosing a smaller order size may indicate an intuition that in the future prices will fall. Similar thinking should always come into play when qualitative factors impinge on making a good decision.

Some *factors that make a larger purchase attractive* could include

- Is there a possibility of a strike?
- Can the purchase of a large quantity make it difficult for competitors to buy it?
- Can the purchase of a large quantity promote further price reductions?

Some *factors that make a smaller purchase attractive* could include

- Should there be a change in the material being used?
- Does this item spoil easily?
- Does it have to be protected against pilferage?
- Does it experience obsolescence?

According to which points seem to apply, the manager is more likely to favor purchasing larger or smaller quantities associated with points a, b', and b.

The reasoning process that has been applied, and the curves that have been drawn, can be extended to any number of price breaks for quantity discounts. It is recommended to draw the total cost curves, mark the price break ranges, and examine where the minimum cost points fall. On the other hand, a purely mathematical approach can be computerized for rapid decision making when faced with many discount offerings.

QMpom provides a discounting module. See Inventory and Production Models (Economic Order Quantity with Discounts).

Spotlight 14-1 Evolution of the Single Global Electronic Market

Improving business processes has a long and remarkable history. In Babylonia, 2285–2242 B.C., compliance with the Code of Hammurabi required clay records for all commercial transactions. Use of papyrus instead of clay tablets improved recordkeeping in ancient Egypt. A system for evaluating government programs and administrators was developed in China by 256 B.C. In ancient Rome, household expenses had to be documented in a codebook called a *codex accepti et expensi* and used as a basis of taxation and civil rights. Using an annual budget was a business innovation to control fiscal operations as well as financing Roman wars of conquest.

In England, an ingenious system of marking wood sticks was devised to update records. William the Conqueror (1027–1087) had taken possession of all property in 1066 and needed an inventory system. Twice a year, wood tally sticks were placed on a counting table covered by a checkered tablecloth, each check representing a county. We inherit the word "exchequer" from King William. (*Webster's Encyclopedic Unabridged Dictionary* defines "exchequer" as "a treasury, as of a state or nation" or more informally, as "one's financial resources.")

In 1494, two years after Columbus discovered America, Luca Bartolomes Pacioli (born in 1445 in Tuscany) invented and disseminated his method of double entry bookkeeping, ushering in a new era of accounting. The Italians were the first to use Arabic numerals regularly in business—an important improvement over Roman numerals. Luca Pacioli, knowledgeable in literature, art, business, and sciences, and believing in the interrelatedness of all subjects, was a Renaissance man. Pacioli's friend, Leonardo da Vinci, helped him with illustrations in one of his writings and, in turn, Pacioli helped da Vinci by calculating the amount of bronze needed for one of da Vinci's huge statues.

Dissemination of printed information was expensive. Gutenberg had invented the metal type printing press only 25 years before Pacioli wrote his famous *Summa de Arithmetica, Geometria, Proportioni et Proportionalita*. In one chapter of this book, Pacioli provides complete instructions for the conduct of business, giving traders his improved and timely method of accessing information about their assets and liabilities. Translation of the "Summa" into five languages over the next century spread the "Italian method" throughout Europe.

Charles Babbage (1791–1871) is the "Father of Computing." Born in Teignmouth, Devonshire, United Kingdom, he designed calculating engines. In 1991, 200 years after his birth, the Science Museum in Kensington, England, constructed a calculating machine called the Difference Engine from drawings left behind by Babbage. Babbage's

Spotlight 14-1 (Continued)

plan to build an improved device he called the Analytical Engine, capable of any mathematical operation, could not be funded by a government short of cash in the 1840s. Babbage believed in standardization. He standardized railroad gauge, postal rates, and screw threads, among other achievements.

Pacioli and Babbage would probably puzzle over web services on the list of 10 top technologies of 2004 published by the American Institute of Certified Public Accountants (AICPA). Further samplings on the list would be total mysteries: spam technology, digital optimization, data mining, virtual office, ID authentication, radio frequency identification (RFID), 3G wireless, and simple object access protocol (SOAP), a message-based protocol using XML for accessing services on the Internet.

From 2004 to 2007, web services expanded to encompass tools and strategies to manage and maintain all systems across the enterprise. These technologies connected companies, vendors, and customers instantly and interactively from anywhere in the world. It was no longer necessary to go to the web to get useful information. For example, to obtain a car's location from the GPS satellite network, an in-car computer obtains information from an Internet services mapping site. The site knows the auto's location and sends a message back to the vehicle's dashboard display. Web connections enable computers to talk to computers as well as different applications or devices such as mobile phones.

By 2007, the designation "web services" had become an omnibus term that include all of the web-issues. The term has split into specialized sectors. Information Security Management was ranked number 1 on the AICPA's top 10 technology list for 2007, followed by Identity and Access Management. Developers are constantly challenged to create common standards in the use of web services. Charles Babbage would surely applaud this standardization effort. A fast, intelligent, interactive, and safe central repository of business information is the goal of every company. Standardization promotes a single global electronic market.

Examples of web services and network connection capabilities can be found everywhere. Bekins, a moving company founded in 1891, now has a state-of-the-art information system. Incorporating web services is saving the company about $75 million annually. Web-based tools provide real-time tracking of shipments from the time of order to delivery.

Bekins uses the latest standards in the industry for a complete business solution within their own intranet as well as the Internet. Their web services–based company includes everything from satellite tracking to a complete wall-to-wall asset and data management system. Trucking agents no longer compete for jobs. Jobs are posted via Internet services simultaneously to all agents who sign up for the system. Any agent can accept the job, and once accepted, it becomes unavailable to others. Because the system is so efficient, Bekins can accept lower-margin moving jobs that it would have refused in the past.

The last word goes to Charles Babbage. Although he lived 217 years ago, he left a message for future builders [and users] of calculating machines: "[You] alone will be fully able to appreciate the nature of my efforts and the value of their results."

Review Questions

1. What is meant by "web services?"
2. Why must developers of web services agree to a set of common standards to obtain the benefits of a single global electronic market?
3. There is a long and noble history of data management that shows how persistent the effort has been to learn about a system's status. Recently, a threshold has been crossed that alters the structure of information recovery and analysis. What characterizes the new plateau of information control and decision mastery?
4. Given the present advanced state of computers and the Internet, has programming web services run its course? Can we expect that companies will start to take these capabilities for granted?
5. The moving company, Bekins, is an example of a web service–oriented company. Why does Bekins say that as a result of web services, it is able to accept lower margin moving jobs?
6. Has the status of Disaster Discovery Management been changing over time? (Refer to the last URL in the Source list.)

Source: http://acaus.org/acc_his.html#2; http://ei.cs.vt.edu/history/babbage.2.html; http://www.bekins.com; http://infotech.aicpa.org/NR/rdonlyres/8AD36EA9-18E8-4BBC-B776-2905085AE5D1/0/Information_Security_Management_02_07.pdf

Spotlight 14-2 Starbucks
Blending Quality Coffee and Best Practice Ideas

Blending coffee, people, and brilliant business ideas, Starbucks has endeared itself to customers all over the world. The company is the leading global retailer, roaster, and brand of specialty coffee. Washington Rodriguez, an Ipanema Farm general director in Brazil, has nothing but praise for his 15-year relationship with Starbucks. With Starbucks help, he says, "We have increased the quality of our coffee while ensuring our land will grow the same high-quality coffee 100 years from now."

In early 2007, there were more than 13,000 retail Starbucks store locations in North America, Latin America, Europe, the Middle East, and the Pacific Rim. Recently, the company revised its ultimate projected growth from 30,000 to 40,000 stores worldwide, with at least one-half that number in locations outside the United States. At present, there are over 9,400 stores in the United States and over 3,700 in its international operations.

At the end of fiscal year 2006, Starbucks consolidated net revenue was $7.8 billion, an increase of 22 percent over 2005. Net earnings in 2006 were increased by 14 percent to $564 million. Since the company's initial public offering in 1992, Starbucks has had five 2-for-1 stock splits.

The World Environment Center (WEC), an independent, not-for-profit, non-advocacy organization, chose Starbucks as the 2005 recipient of its 21st Annual Gold Medal for International Corporate Achievement in Sustainable Development. WEC ideals are exemplified by the company's innovative Coffee and Farmer Equity Practices Buying Guidelines (C.A.F.E. Practices). This program provides a set of environmentally, socially, and economically responsible guidelines and offers incentives to growers who are willing to meet them. The WEC's Gold Medal Jury believes that Starbucks achievements stand as a model to

be emulated by agribusinesses throughout the world. On May 13, 2005, Howard Schultz, chairman of the board of Starbucks Corporation, received the Gold Medal Award at the National Building Museum in Washington, D.C., on behalf of Starbucks' approximately 100,000 partners (employees) around the world. Two years later, the number of partners had grown to 110,000. By the end of 2007, Starbucks will have a presence in more than 37 countries. The company has recently opened stores in Brazil and Egypt and plans to expand into Russia and India.

More than thirty years ago in 1971, Starbucks opened its first location in Seattle's Pike Place Market. Howard Schultz joined the company in 1982 as director of retail operations and marketing. Through Howard's efforts, Starbucks began to provide coffee to fine restaurants. After a trip to Italy where he was impressed with the espresso bars in Milan, Howard Schultz convinced the founders of Starbucks to test the coffee bar concept in a new location in Seattle. The experiment succeeded, spreading to other states, to Canada, and then to many countries around the world.

Howard Schultz and Orin C. Smith (former president and CEO) worked together for years to shape and develop Starbucks into a respected brand, recognized around the world for its commitment to people, coffee, and the quality of relationships with farmers and suppliers in coffee-origin countries. Orin Smith retired in March 2005, after a tribute from Howard Schultz, who thanked Orin for his guidance along "the road less traveled."

In 2007, Starbucks has 39 senior officers. Howard Shultz is chairman of the board. Jim Donald replaced Orin Smith as CEO. Peter Bocian, a new team member with a strong global operations orientation, has been invited aboard as executive VP and CFO, replacing outgoing CFO Michael Casey. The company values its stakeholders with whom it maintains open communications. See Starbucks Investor Relations online at http://www.starbucks.com.

Innovations are always being added at Starbucks. The Starbucks brand is expanding to include music, books, and movies all carefully selected to represent best-quality cultural products at the cutting edge. The company intends to focus on introducing new products as part of the *Starbucks Experience*. Starbucks stores continue to serve as reliable T-Mobile HotSpots®, providing high-speed wireless Internet service in coffeehouse comfort. Supermarkets carry Starbucks® coffees, cans of Starbucks DoubleShot® Espresso Drink, and bottled Frappuccino® Coffee Drinks.

It is fascinating to learn how Starbucks executive leadership connects with its own partners. Every partner is given

Spotlight 14-2 (Continued)

the task of improving day-to-day processes, leading to better quality control. The resulting two-way communication and feedback represent partnership in the full sense of the word. Mishaps are valued as learning experiences that constantly change and improve company operations. In 2007, Starbucks was rated by *Fortune Magazine* as sixteenth in their list of "100 Best Places to Work."

"Black Apron Exclusives™" is a line of rare coffees that represent the best of the best. A black apron is worn by Coffee Masters who have attained a deep understanding of the intricacies and nuances of coffee through the Coffee Master certification program. The goal is to increase the number of Coffee Masters until at least one black-apron Coffee Master is present in every company-operated Starbucks around the globe. Why? The answer is simple. Whenever employees add to their wealth of knowledge, customers benefit as well.

Starbucks success is based on quality products and care—of people and relationships. In 2006, the company donated $36.1 million in contributions to charities and non-profit organizations worldwide. In Nicaragua, Starbucks helped to improve sanitary conditions and water quality at the Modesto Armijo School, which is attended by 1,200 elementary school children from San Juan de Rio Coco. Teaming with five Guatemalan coffee farms, Starbucks helped to fund and continues to maintain health clinics, day-care centers, and schools that serve thousands of people in local farming communities. In Ethiopia, Starbucks helped fund a bridge connecting two communities, benefiting the people that live there.

Relationships with people in Starbucks' coffee-farming communities are long-term and aimed at encouraging social development and sustainability. Clean water initiatives in many countries and the China Education Project to train teachers are ongoing.

A world away from coffee's origins, in the small town of Winter Park, Florida, the dean of a prestigious business school had a problem. In his busy schedule, there was no time during the day to have uninterrupted conversations with faculty members or to mentor students who needed his undivided attention. The dean requested his assistant to start making appointments for him at the local Starbucks, where problems could be quickly solved and relationships improved over a favorite Starbucks beverage.

Review Questions

1 What accounts for Howard Schultz returning as CEO of SBUX in January, 2008? (See the URL below.)

2 Despite the premium price for coffee, customers say that they get good value from shopping at Starbucks. What does providing "value" mean? What is the company's core competency?

3 How does Starbucks maintain high standards of excellence for coffee, tea, and cocoa beans from suppliers who live and work in farming communities that are located throughout the world?

4 Should Starbucks expand store offerings to include additional products, such as hot breakfasts and luncheon sandwiches? Should the company continue to expand its sales of music, books, and movies at the "media bar"?

5 How do you rate Starbucks quality (1 to 10, where 10 is excellent)?

Printed with permission of Starbucks Corporation.
Source: http://www.starbucks.com Check on latest news re Schultz' Transformation Agenda Communication.

Summary

This chapter addresses "independent demand" inventory management. It explains order point policy (OPP) models in terms of demand continuity. The costs of inventory are treated. These include costs of ordering, setups, and changeovers, carrying inventory, discounts, stock-outages, and running the inventory system. Process types differentiate inventory costs.

Then, economic order quantity models (EOQ) are developed for batch delivery. The total variable cost equations are set up and solved. Economic lot size models (ELS) for continuous delivery of product are contrasted to EOQ models. The ELS are applied to intermittent flow shops (IFS). There is discussion of lead-time structure, uncertainty, and variability.

Next, the perpetual inventory system with its reorder point and buffer-stock calculations is detailed. This includes operation of the two-bin perpetual inventory control system. The periodic inventory system is explained, including why this system is being outmoded by computer capabilities—yet it still is needed in certain situations. The chapter ends with an explanation of how quantity discount models work.

Spotlight 14-1: Evolution of the Single Global Electronic Market spells out the future for dealing with the potential of many suppliers from all over the globe. Product qualities and prices will change. Discount schedules will be revised. Delivery terms will be altered. The new information needs to be utilized immediately to correct future inventory policies. Spotlight 14-2 on Starbucks pictures a gigantic OPP-type situation. The supply chain for coffee must keep thousands of Starbucks stores stocked with customers' favorites as the green bean (unroasted coffee) market changes with each passing weather system.

Key Terms

Buffer stock (p. 555)
Dynamic inventory models (p. 553)
Economic lot size (ELS) (p. 563)
Economic order quantity (EOQ) (p. 563)
Inventory (p. 553)
Lead time (LT) (p. 553)
Lifetime value (p. 560)
Make or buy decision (p. 554)
Mixed-model systems (p. 573)

Order point policies (OPP) (p. 562)
Periodic inventory system (p. 563)
Perpetual inventory system (p. 562)
Reorder point (RP) (p. 562)
Sensitivity analysis (p. 556)
Square root inventory model (p. 567)
Static inventory models (p. 553)
Transshipment (p. 575)
Vendor releasing (p. 561)

Review Questions

1 It has been stated that, as a rule of thumb, "the best inventory is no inventory." Discuss this heuristic.

2 How does this rule of thumb apply to gasoline? Is gasoline an OPP commodity?

3 For a toothpaste manufacturer, how is the decision made concerning how many caps should be ordered? Could it be a different number than the number of tubes that are ordered at one time?

4 How often should an order size be updated?

5 What method should be used to determine the order quantity for a raw material that is used continuously within a flow shop?

6 What method should be used to determine the order quantity for a raw material that is used continuously within an intermittent flow shop?

7 Who are the people that are responsible for placing orders?

8 Electronic data interchange (EDI) makes communication between connected supply chain participants immediate. How does the use of EDI reduce the order quantity?

9   Using the information in Problem 7, how does the use of EDI reduce the buffer stock?

10 A manufacturer of costume jewelry has a sales force that uses handheld computers with modems. Salespeople take stock at each retail establishment and then call the factory with stock-level data. How does this procedure affect the manufacturing schedule of the company? Explain your answer in terms of ELS models.

11 Benetton is a well-known manufacturer and retailer of clothing all over the world. The Benetton factories are tied in with retailers so that demand information is relatively immediate and complete concerning what is selling and what is not. How does this information affect lot-size planning?

12 Salespeople use handheld telecommunications devices to communicate inventory status to the warehouse in a major toy company. Why is this system needed and what does it affect?

13 What is carrying cost composed of and what is the range of values that will be found for it?

14 What is the logic for a buyer accepting a discount?

15 What is the logic for a seller offering a discount?

16 Why is there an ordering cost and of what is it composed?

17 What is the difference between an ordering cost and a setup cost?

18 When is it likely that an ordering cost will be larger than a setup cost?

19 When is it likely that a setup cost will be larger than an ordering cost?

20 Relate the number of orders placed and the order quantity.

21 Why are order point policies (OPP) called by that name?

22 Why are total variable cost equations written for OPP models instead of total cost equations?

23 When discounts are being considered, total cost equations must be used instead of total variable cost equations. Why is this so?

24 Differentiate between EOQ and ELS models.

25 When is lead-time variability a problem and what can be done about it?

26 How can lead-time variability be modeled?

27 What is a two-bin system? When is it applicable?

28 Describe a perpetual inventory system.

29 When is a perpetual inventory system preferred?

30 Describe a periodic inventory system.

31 When is a periodic inventory system preferred?

32 How can a quantity discount model be used by a buyer and supplier to negotiate a price break point schedule that benefits both of them?

33 Why is it that multiple price break points for many discount levels can be examined in the same fashion as one price break point for a single discount?

34 Is the two-bin inventory system perpetual or periodic?

35 Assume that a new IFS has been set up to make a baby stroller. The ELS analysis is completed and the run size and run time are determined. Discuss what to do with the time, t_2, when the process is not running the product.

36 Distinguish between inventory problems under certainty, risk, and uncertainty.

Problems Section

Note: This section has various problems that can be formulated and solved using QuantMethods Production/Operations Management software (QMpom). The appropriate model categories are indicated for each problem.

1   Water testing at the Croton reservoir requires a chemical reagent that costs $500 per gallon. Use is constant at 1/3 gallon per week. Carrying cost rate is considered to be 12 percent per year, and the cost of an order is $125.

   What is the optimal order quantity for the reagent? (EOQ model)

   Using the QMpom module called Inventory and Production Models (Economic Order Quantity) will facilitate solving Problem 1.

2   Continuing with the information about the Croton reservoir given in Problem 1, the city could make this reagent at the rate of 1/8 gallon per day, at a cost of $300 per gallon. The setup cost is $150. Use a 7-day week.

   Compare using the EOQ and the ELS systems. What course of action do you recommend? (EOQ and ELS models)

   Using the QMpom module called Inventory and Production Models (Economic Production Lot Size) will facilitate solving Problem 2.

3   Water testing at the Delaware reservoir requires a chemical reagent that costs $400 per gallon. Use is constant at 1/3 gallon per week. Carrying cost rate is considered to be 10 percent per year, and the cost of an order is $100.

What is the optimal order quantity for the reagent? (EOQ model)

Using the QMpom module called Inventory and Production Models will facilitate solving the ten (10) problems that are numbered 3 through 12.

4   Continuing with the information about the Delaware reservoir given in Problem 3, the town could make this reagent at the rate of 1/4 gallon per day, at a cost of $500 per gallon. The setup cost is $125. Use a 7-day week.

Compare using the EOQ and the ELS systems. What course of action do you recommend? (EOQ and ELS models)

5   The Drug Store carries Deodorant R, which has an expected demand of 15,000 jars per year (or 60 jars per day with 250 days per year). Lead time from the distributor is three days. It has been determined that demand in any 3-day period exceeds 200 jars only once out of every 100 3-day periods. This outage level (of 1 in 100 LT periods) is considered acceptable by P/OM and their marketing colleagues. The economic order quantity has been derived as 2,820 jars. Set up the perpetual inventory system. (EOQ with stock-outs)

6   Use the information given in Problem 5, plus the fact that it has been determined that demand in any 50-day period exceeds 4,000 jars only once out of every 100 50-day periods. This outage level (of 1 in 100 LT periods) is considered acceptable by P/OM and their marketing colleagues. Set up the periodic inventory system. (EOQ with stock-outs)

7   Compare the results derived in Problems 5 and 6. What do you recommend doing? Explain how you have taken into account all of the important differentiating characteristics of perpetual and periodic inventory systems. (EOQ with stock-outs)

8   Consider the recommendation made in Problem 5, taking into account the fact that The Drug Store must combine orders for Deodorant R with other items in order to have sufficient volume to qualify for the distributor's shipping without charge. With this constraint, what are your recommendations?

9   The information required to solve an EOQ inventory problem is as follows: $c = \$10$ per unit, $C_c = 16$ percent per year, $D = 5,000$ units per year, and $C_r = \$10$ per order. What is the optimal order quantity? (EOQ model)

10   Using the information in Problem 9, instead of buying from a supplier the decision is to make the item in the company's factory. The new equipment is able to produce $p = 30$ units per day. Costs are changed to $c = \$6$ per unit and $C_s = \$150$ per setup. What is the optimal run size? (EOQ and ELS models)

11   Using the information in Problems 9 and 10, which is better: make or buy? (EOQ and ELS models)

12   Using the information in Problems 9, 10, and 11, what factors that are not in the equations might shift the decision?

13   The following quantity discount schedule has been offered for the situation described in Problem 9.

$c = 10$	$Q =$ up to 300
$c' = 9$	$Q = 300$ to 499
$c'' = 8$	$Q = 500$ and up

Should either of these discounts be accepted? (EOQ with discounts)

Using the QMpom module called Inventory and Production Models (Economic Order Quantity with Discounts) will facilitate solving the three (3) problems that are numbered 13 through 15.

14   The quantity discount schedule offered in Problem 13 prompted a competitor to offer the following discount schedule:

$c = 10$	$Q =$ up to 250
$c' = 9$	$Q = 251$ to 599
$c'' = 7$	$Q = 600$ and up

Should any of these discounts be accepted? (EOQ with discounts)

15   Compare the answers to Problems 13 and 14 and discuss these results, making appropriate recommendations.

16   Murphy's is famous for their coffee blend. The company buys and roasts the beans and then packs the coffee in foil bags. It buys the beans periodically in quantities of 120,000 pounds and assumes this to be the optimal order quantity. This year it has been paying $2.40 per pound on a fairly constant basis.

The company ships 1,200,000 1-pound bags of its blended coffee per year to its distributors. This is equivalent to shipping 24,000 1-pound foil bags in each of 50 weeks of the year. This can be considered to be constant and continuous demand over time.

What carrying cost in percent per year is implied (or imputed) by this policy if an order costs $100 on the average? Discuss the results. (EOC model)

$$Q_o = \sqrt{(2DC_r) \div (cC_c)}$$

Using the QMpom module called Inventory and Production Models (Economic Order Quantity) will facilitate solving the two (2) problems that are numbered 16 through 17.

17 Using the information in Problem 16, suggest a better ordering policy. (EOQ model)

18 What production run lengths are individually optimal for each item in the following table? (ELS model)

Item i	Annual D_i	Setup C_{S_i}	Unit Cost c_i	p_i (per day)
1	200	100	6	10
2	400	50	10	12
3	600	20	15	14
4	800	80	9	20

Note: D_i is demand per year; p_i = production run size, $C_c = 0.24$ per year, and $D_i = 250d_i$ for changing daily demand into yearly demand.

Using the QMpom module called Inventory and Production Models (Economic Production Lot Size) will facilitate solving the three (3) problems that are numbered 18 through 20.

19 Using the information in Problem 18, can all of these items be scheduled to run on the same equipment? Discuss.

20 Using the data in Problem 18, employ cut and try methods to determine a reasonable set of production run lengths so that all items can be scheduled to run consecutively on the same equipment. Compare these results with the individual optimal values obtained in Problem 18.

21 The manager of the greeting card production department has been buying two rolls of acetate at a time. They cost $200 each. Card production requires 10 rolls per year. Ordering cost is estimated to be $4 per order. What carrying cost rate is imputed? Is it reasonable?

Using the QMpom module called Inventory and Production Models (Economic Order Quantity) will facilitate solving the four (4) problems that are numbered 21 through 24.

22 Using the information in Problem 21, if the cost of rolls of acetate increases to $250 each, what happens to the imputed carrying cost rate? Is this reasonable?

23 Refer to Figure 14-3 in the text and the example upon which it was based. Illustrating the flatness of the total cost curve when Q_o is large, determine the TVC for $Q = 20,000$. Recall that the optimal value presented in the text and related to Figure 14-3 was $6.57 associated with $Q_o = 21,909$ units. The calculations were as follows: $TVC_{21,909} = 0.00015(21,909) + 72,000/(21,909) = \$3.286 + \$3.286 = \$6.57$

Determine the percent increase in TVC and decrease in Q. Discuss your findings.

24 Using the information in Problem 23, calculate TVC for $Q = 25,000$. What percent increase has occurred in TVC? Calculate the percent increase in Q from the optimal value of $Q_o = 21,909$ units. Does this back up the statement: "The total variable cost curve flattens out as Q_o gets larger. There is less difference between the minimum cost at Q_o and the costs associated with small changes ($\in$) in Q_o such as $Q_o \pm \in$." Note: This requires analysis of the cost effects of making small changes around the point $Q = 25,000$ as compared to the cost effects of small changes around $Q_o = 21,909$.

25 Masters of Travel, Inc. (MTI) gives customers who have purchased travel arrangements a soft canvas shoulder-strap bag. Bags Limited, the company that furnishes these bags to MTI, has suggested that if the order quantity is doubled, it would discount the cost per bag by 20 percent. At present, MTI buys 600 bags imprinted with MTI at a time for $1.50 per bag. This represents a 2-month supply.

Should the discount be taken?

Using the QMpom module called Inventory and Production Models (Economic Order Quantity with Discounts) will facilitate solving the two (2) problems that are numbered 25 through 26.

26 Using the information in Problem 25, a competitor to Bags Limited has made the following offer:

Number of Shoulder Bags	Price
600	at $1.45 each
800	at $1.35 each
1,000	at $1.25 each

What should MTI do?

Practice Quiz

1 There are many different types of inventory models. When starting an application, the first thing to do is recognize the category of inventory problem so that the appropriate model can be examined and fitted to the specific situation. One of the great benefits of inventory models is that students can practice using them. Savings obtained practicing model building are theoretical. However, the effort is worthwhile and begins to build confidence that a real application could make significant savings for actual companies. Read the list of salient points (a. through e.) about various types of inventory situations. Identify the one point not suitable for the inventory taxonomy (classification system).

a. Inventory systems are classified by whether their demand distributions are linked to their lead-time distributions. For example, if the lead time required for delivery is long, then the demand will be great. This is one of the reasons that companies often tell their customers that repair will take a longer time than is really needed.

b. Dynamic inventory models deal with a repetitive stream of orders as compared to static inventory models, which have little or no repetition. As an example of repetitive demand, Tropicana must have cartons (month after month) to fill with orange juice. In contrast, the hot dog vendor puts in one order for the number of hot dogs that he or she thinks can be sold at the final game of the World Series.

c. At one time, Ford Motor Company made all of its own windshield glass. In the make or buy decision at that time, upstream vertical integration seemed to be justified by many factors, including cost and control. Ford no longer makes its own windshield glass because the analysis years later showed different results. Make or buy stock decisions must be reviewed over time because internal and external factors change.

d. Inventory problems can be categorized by different kinds of risk distributions. Linear programming assumes that demand and lead times are known with certainty. Other types of inventory models such as the perpetual and periodic kind assume demands (and lead times) are distributed according to well-known, well-behaved distributions such as the normal or Poisson distributions. Inventory models that must cope with uncertainty of demand (and lead time) are rare but not unknown. New products may have uncertain demands, which lead to strategic decisions to begin with a "safe" or conservative inventory policy. Then, as more information becomes available, the investments in capacity and stock are increased. Simulation is often used to analyze worst-case scenarios and "what if" situations when uncertainty prevails. Uncertainty can take the form of unstable demand and lead-time distributions that change in erratic ways.

e. Demand continuity will affect the kind of inventory model that applies. OPP models are applicable when there is continuity of demand. MRP models are used when the demand is sporadic, but not one-time. Table 14-2 shows the conditions for OPP and for MRP in terms of continuity and dependence.

2 Costs are the crucial measurable elements of every inventory model. There are other factors, but if the costs have not been included, and measured correctly, then the inventory situation cannot be resolved. Which statement of a. through e. is not part of proper inventory methodology?

a. The best way to get the cost of an order is to do a systems study of the steps and procedures that are used by the organization to place an order. It is essential to determine if the same procedures are always followed and if not, when do the variants apply? Divide the fixed costs per year by the number of orders placed per year. Variable costs are added to the applicable fixed costs to obtain the total costs. However, before announcing the cost of an order, in a proper systems study, work simplification is applied. The "best" methods for placing orders should be the basis of the cost of an order. The ordering cost, C_r, is in the numerator of the economic order quantity (EOQ) equation. Therefore, the order quantity, Q, changes with the square root of C_r. When ordering cost doubles (100 percent increase), the order size increases 41.4 percent.

b. Costs of designing, setting up, and running inventory systems must be balanced against the lost benefit of not using them. Also, high systemic costs of computerized perpetual inventory systems frequently lead managers to prefer periodic inventory systems using workbooks.

c. The setup cost, C_S, is used with the economic lot size model (ELS). It is measured by dividing the fixed costs per year by the number of setups used per year. Variable costs are added to the applicable fixed costs to obtain the total costs. The "best" methods for setups should be determined. Often, there is a lot of opportunity for improvement because traditional ideas about setups have changed as a result of different attitudes and new technology. The setup cost, C_S, is in the numerator of the ELS equation. The run lot size, Q, changes with the square root of C_S. When the setup cost doubles (100 percent increase), the run size increases 41.4 percent.

d. The total cost of carrying inventory, cC_C, is composed of the carrying cost rate, C_C, and the per unit cost, c. The carrying cost rate is composed of lost opportunities to use funds in other ways plus charges for storage, taxes, obsolescence, deterioration, pilferage, and insurance. If carrying cost rates are set high, the effect is to decrease the value of Q by the square root of the increase in C_C (which is in the denominator of the EOQ and ELS equations). Carrying cost rates are low when interest rates are low and opportunities for the use of money are limited.

e. Out-of-stock costs are dependent on the expectations of the market. For "fill or kill" systems with high volume items (like lipstick), the cost can be significant if lead time to restock is long. The problem is not the single lipstick sale that is lost. The loss of customer loyalty as a result of sustained out-of-stocks is really damaging. Another aspect often found with catalogue sales is the use of upgraded substitutions. The cost of the upgrade is often smaller to the mail order firm than the cost of disgruntled customers. Markets that accept backorders tend to include much larger ticket items like expensive refrigerators, large airplanes and subway cars. Out-of-stock costs are built into setting levels of safety stock where a balance is struck between carrying additional buffer stock and outage penalties.

3   Delta Corporation has an inventory managers' training program. One exercise is to show how the total cost curve for the economic order quantity (EOQ) is derived for one item in one department. A simple numerical example has been created to avoid computational complexity while driving home important concepts. The data are furnished in the table marked *Data for EOQ Computation*. Delta has set the demand for the item at $D = 12$ units per month; the cost is $c = \$2,000$ per unit. Identify the incorrect statement in points a. through e.

Data for EOQ Computation

Q	aQ	b/Q	TVC
1	10	24	34
2	20	12	
3	30	8	
4	40	6	

Note: Legend: Q = units per order; $a = cC_c \div 2$; $b = DC_r$ and $Q_o = \sqrt{(2DC_r) \div (cC_c)}$; $b = DC_r$; TVC = total variable cost per month; D = demand per month; c = cost per unit; C_c = carrying cost rate per month; C_r = cost of an order.

a.   The table indicates that the order size can vary from 1 to 4, as shown in the left-hand column of the table.

b.   Coefficient $b = 24$. This information is directly available from row 1, where $Q = 1$ and $b/Q = 24$. Because $b = DC_r$ or $24 = 12C_r$, the cost of an order is $2.00.

c.   Coefficient $a = 10$. This information is directly available from row 1, where $Q = 1$ and $aQ = 10$. Because $a = cC_c \div 2$, and $20 = 2,000C_c = 0.01$, the carrying cost rate per month is 0.01.

d.   Filling out the total cost column (4) requires summing columns 2 and 3. The minimum total cost occurs when Q is equal to 3 units per order.

e.   The part of total cost (TC) that reflects variable carrying cost increases linearly as order quantity, Q, increases. The other part of the total cost is called the *variable ordering cost*. It declines geometrically as Q increases. There will be a minimum total cost point in the table but it may not be the same as the actual minimum total cost.

4   Delta Corporation is pleased with the training results. The decision is made to continue the training program for inventory managers by extending the analyses of Problem 3. All of the data are the same. Use any parameter values previously derived. Statements made in points a. through e. include one incorrect observation. Please identify which one is incorrect.

a.   The table called *Data for EOQ Computation* presents enough information to plot a total cost curve. When the curve is drawn, there is evidence of a minimum total cost point in the neighborhood of $Q = 2$. Neighborhood means that the minimum could occur somewhere between Q greater than 1 and less than 3. Drawing the curve is useful. Graphs provide different kinds of information such as the rate of change of TC with Q.

b.   To find out the exact value of Q_o (called Q-optimal) is impossible, but the approximate value of the optimal order quantity can be derived.

c.   The EOQ equation indicates the optimal value is the square root of 2.4, which is 1.549. That may be a difficult number to order unless there is a scale transformation (such as all numbers should be multiplied by one thousand).

d.   Because the table has Q values of only integer numbers, the square root derivation is essential to understand the situation. Delta has never explained what kinds of units are involved in this inventory problem. If the units are gallons, it is possible to order one and a half gallons to come close the minimum total cost associated with the optimal order quantity, Q_o. It is more likely that it would be thousands of gallons because of the high price.

e.   The total cost associated with the optimal order quantity, Q_o, is

$$TC_o = b/Q_o + aQ_o = 15.49(2) = 30.99 = 31$$

5 Some general concepts have been learned by the Delta Corporation teams. Management has created a list of points to consider. There is one item that should be corrected before the list is sent to the participants. Which item in a. to e. must be corrected?

a. The EOQ equation is a good example of a trade-off model in which, as the controlling (independent) variable increases, the dependent variable increases for one function and decreases for another function. In this case, the carrying cost, $CC = aQ$ increases linearly with the order quantity. The ordering cost, $OC = b/Q$ decreases geometrically with increasing order quantity.

a. The square root solution $Q_o = \sqrt{b \div a}$ indicates where the minimum point occurs on the total cost curve.

b. It would appear from the graph that the minimum point on the total cost curve occurs at the same location as the crosspoint of the two curves. This is a graphical illusion if they cross close to the minimum point, which occurs as a coincidence.

c. Lacking good estimates of the four factors that produce the total cost curve, managers will give their best guess. A guess that is likely to produce an underestimate of Q is less desirable than a guess that is likely to produce an overestimate of Q. The reason is that the total cost curve is much steeper as it gets near to the y-axis. This is called the "under- and overestimation effect."

d. The (optimal) number of orders placed (n_o) when the optimal order quantity is Q_o is determined by $n_o = D/Q_o$. Using the data from problem 3, $n_o = 6/(1.549) = 3.87$, or rounding at 4 orders per month. Alternatively, multiplying 3.87 by 12 months, there are 46.5 orders per year. This is equivalent to $52/46.5 = 1.12$ orders per week.

e. The EOQ model is a major component of both the perpetual and periodic inventory models. However, there is no indicator in the EOQ model as to when to order. That is the function of the perpetual and periodic inventory models where lead time (LT) plays an important role.

6 Delta Corporation's managers' inventory training program has been successful. The decision was made to expand it to include economic lot size modeling (ELS). The same type of exercise that was used to show how the total cost curve is derived for the economic order quantity (EOQ) model is going to be used for ELS modeling. As before, the total cost will be derived for one item in one department. Another numerical example has been created for the ELS situation. It is intended to avoid computational complexity while driving home important concepts. The data are furnished in the table marked *Data for ELS Computation*. Delta has set the demand for this item at $D = 20{,}000$ units per year and the cost per unit is $c = \$6.00$. Note in the legend under the table that demand per day, $d = 80$ units. Production capacity is $p = 150$ units per day. One of the statements in the list prepared for the trainees (which goes from a. to e.) is incorrect. Identify the incorrect statement.

Data for ELS Computation

Q	aQ	b/Q	TC
500	84	800	884
1,000	168	400	
1,500	252	266.67	
2,000	336	200	

Note: Legend: Q = units made per production run (called the *lot size*); $a = (cC_c)(p - d) \div 2p$; $b = DC_s$; $Q_o = \sqrt{(2DC_r)(p - d) \div (pcC_c)}$; TC = total cost per year; TC is the sum of columns 2 and 3; D = demand in units per 250 day work year; d = demand in units per day based on $D = 250d$ so $d = 20{,}000/250 = 80$ units per day; p = production per day = 150 units; $c = \$6.00$, which is the cost to make a unit (includes all relevant factors); C_c = carrying cost rate per year; C_s = setup cost (changeover); the ELS equation for run size is shown above as Q_o. n = number of orders per year; $t(1)$ = length of run time in days; $t(2)$ length of wait between runs; $t = t(1) + t(2)$ = production cycle of run and off-line.

a. The table indicates that the number of units that can be made per run (per lot) can vary from 500 to 2,000, as shown in the left-hand column of the table. Although the table is set up for 500 unit increments, additional rows could be added (say, by 100 unit increments).

b. Coefficient $b = 400{,}000$, obtained from row 2, where $Q = 1{,}000$ and $b/Q = 400$. Because $b = DC_s$, it follows that setup cost, $C_s = b/D = 20.0$.

c. Coefficient $a = 0.168$, obtained directly from row 2 where $Q = 1{,}000$ and $aQ = 168$. Solving:
$C_c = 2ap \div (p - d)(c) = 2(0.168)(150) \div (150 - 80)(6) = 0.12$. The carrying cost rate per year is 0.12.

d. Filling out the total cost column (4) requires summing columns 2 and 3. The minimum total cost ($TC = \$518.67$ or 519) occurs when Q is equal to 1,500 units per order.

e. Total cost (TC) increases by a larger increment (49.33) as Q moves from 1,500 to 2,000 units than when Q decreases by 500 units. Moving from 1,500 to 1,000 units increases TC by 17.33.

7 The table in Problem 6 was built with Q increments of 500 units—ranging from 500 to 2,000. A better minimum exists than associated with $Q = 1,500$ units (as found in Problem 6) but it must be found by analysis. Also, an expanded table has been presented to the Delta team. They have been asked to provide the run time, off-line time, cycle time, and the number of runs per year. Delta team is presented with options a. through e. Which one of these is incorrect?

a. Minimum total cost occurs when Q equals a lot size of 1,543.03. The total cost at that point is 518.46. The two components of this minimum total variable cost (TVC) change in opposite directions as Q changes. The costs of these two are 159.23 for the carry cost factor and 359.23 for the setup cost factor.

b. In the *Solutions for ELS Computation* table, it is apparent that $Q = 1,500$ is near the minimum total cost because the two components (aQ and b/Q) are almost equal. They are equal when at $Q_o = 1543.03$. Another row has been added to the table to show the $Q_o = 1543.03$ solution.

Solutions for ELS Computation							
Q	aQ	b/Q	TC	$t(1)$ days	$t(2)$ days	t days	n
500	84	800	884	3.33	2.92	6.25	40
1,000	168	400	568	6.67	5.83	12.50	20
1,500	252	266.67	518.67	10.00	8.75	18.75	13.3
1,543.03	259.23	259.23	518.46	10.29	9.00	19.29	12.96
2,000	336	200	536	13.33	11.67	25.00	10

c. Running the selected lot size (Q) takes a given number of days that are linearly related to the quantity. The optimal run time is 10.29 days with 9 days between runs. The full cycle is 19.29 days. For the 250 working days per year, that means there will be 12.96, or 13 runs per year. See the number of orders, n.

d. If there is a reason to run smaller lot sizes (such as a lack of storage space), that may mean that a cost was not included, or incorrectly estimated. The best candidates for these complaints are the carrying cost and the setup cost. In the case of the carrying cost, perhaps it should have been larger to include extra costs of finding storage space. In the case of the setup cost, perhaps a method has been invented to reduce it, and thereby justify smaller Q-values.

e. The solutions table shows how run time, off-line time, and cycle time are related to the run size and to the number of production runs. With relatively small lot sizes of 500, the number of runs is 40, which is almost weekly. There are limits to reduction of the run size, and 500 units is likely to be very close to that limit.

8 Perpetual inventory models are a powerful means of controlling cost-benefit trade-offs of inventory policies. Instead of doing complex numerical analyses, Delta trainers decided that the first step would be to acquaint all trainees with the fundamental concepts of perpetual methods. In that regard, a list of propositions (a. through e.) was submitted to the team members with the understanding that everyone would read each point carefully to absorb its message. As a team member, please determine which statement is not correct.

a. Most perpetual inventory systems are online. As items are withdrawn from stock, the stock level is reduced immediately. The new stock level is compared to the reorder point, which is equal to the expected demand in the lead-time period. This procedure is applied to all items of the ABC curve.

b. The EOQ model is a fundamental part of the perpetual inventory model. The other fundamental part is the buffer (or safety) stock. Determination of the buffer stock is based on balancing carrying cost against outage costs.

c. Buffer stock is carried like an insurance policy. When needed, because demand (a random variable around a stable mean) is excessive, buffer stock is called upon to fill orders and take care of needs. After the rush on the buffer stock is over, these units are replaced. In effect, it is an extra load of stock, not intended to meet regular demand, which is a prevailing extra carrying cost expense.

d. How much buffer stock to carry is determined by the tail of the distribution of demand in the lead-time period. Perpetual inventory models are favored because the buffer stock need only protect against excessive demand after the reorder point is reached. That is when the replenishment lead time begins.

e. The larger the buffer stock, the further out on the tail of the lead-time distribution is the protection level. When the tail is very small because the buffer stock is large, the probability of ever going out of stock is statistically quite small. A big buffer stock raises the level of the reorder point, which is the sum of the buffer stock and the demand in the lead-time period.

9   Periodic inventory models are an absolute necessity under certain distribution constraints. Periodic systems appeal to many people because of their time-line consistency. Delta trainers concluded that the next step would be to acquaint all trainees with the fundamental concepts of periodic methods. To do that, a list of propositions (a, to g.) was submitted to team members with the understanding that everyone would read each point carefully to absorb its message. As a team member, please determine which statement is not correct.

a.   Perpetual and periodic models have pros and cons. One might wish to be able to put perpetual and periodic inventory models together to take advantage of the best of both. That has been done in certain high-investment inventory environments (such as stocks of the U.S. Navy) where the combination models have been studied. *(This statement has been certified to be correct by Delta.)*

b.   Most periodic inventory systems are online. If the manager decides to "open the books" early on an item scheduled to be reviewed later, the system will provide all of the information needed to place an order.

c.   The reorder point of the perpetual inventory model is a stock level, whereas, for the periodic model it is a point in time, i.e., the reorder point time. The optimal time period equation is Equation 14-19 in the text.

d.   Buffer stock required by the periodic model is larger than for the perpetual model to yield the same statistical level of protection against stock-outs. The reason is that the periodic model has to carry buffer stock for the expected demand in the lead time period (LT) plus one complete replenishment period (t_o).

e.   The amount to reorder is the difference between stock on-hand at the reorder time and the M-level, which is the expected demand in the reorder period plus the lead time plus the buffer stock. The equation is Equation 14-25 in the text.

f.   Buffer stock to protect the inventory system from going out of stock is determined by the selected tail of the distribution of demand in the lead-time period plus demand in the reorder period. The equation shows how the measure of demand variability (sigma:σ) includes both lead time and reorder period. $BS = k_\alpha \sigma_{LT+to}$. When alpha ($\alpha$) is small, k is large, so the probability of going out of stock is low.

g.   A primary use of the periodic inventory model is to match the periodicity of the demand or delivery systems. For an example of delivery system requirements, the Frito-Lay truck delivers potato chips to retailers on Route 66 twice a week, on Mondays and Thursdays. For an example of demand system requirements, the manager of the theater has announced that delivery of theater supplies must be made on Saturday evening only.

10   Delta often takes advantage of discounts offered by suppliers. Training inventory managers to recognize when discounts are viable is an important part of the program. On the other side of the coin, Delta produces products that it offers with discounts to its customers. Therefore, the company is interested in taking the inventory discount recognition skills and teaching them to its marketing department pricing managers. The idea is that if you know when to take a discount, you should know when to offer a discount. One SKU is chosen for which discounts have been offered but never taken. Delta buys the economic order quantity for that SKU at the current time.

Data about demand per year, order cost, unit cost, and carrying rate are in the first column of the table. The next two columns show some useful computations.

The managers have asked the trainee team whether they should accept the vendor's offer to drop the price by 12.5 percent if the company will increase the purchased amount by 36 percent. The discussion about this matter is found in points a. through e., one of which is incorrect. Identify the wrong point.

Demand/yr. (D)	200	Q (opt.)	220.48	cD	$800
Order cost	175	aQ	158.75	TC	$1,117.49
Unit cost (c)	$4.00	b/Q	158.75		
Carrying rate	36%/yr.	TVC	317.49		

a.   The 36 percent increase in quantity, Q changes the order quantity from optimal to non-optimal for both the current price and the proposed price.

b.   The 12.5 percent decrease in price takes it from $4.00 per unit to $3.50. At the lower price, the optimal order quantity is 236 units. This will work out nicely with the new order quantity that the vendor proposes Delta should buy in the future.

c.   The total cost of the current buying strategy is shown in the table as $1,117.49. This includes the two kinds of variable costs and the undiscounted cost per unit times the yearly demand.

d. The vendor's recommended buying strategy with the discount has a total cost of $1,005.67. This is a real saving of $111.82, $100 of which is directly attributable to the 50 cent reduction per unit.

e. What is bothersome is the size of the order quantities, with and without the discount. At present, Delta is buying in each order 10 percent more units than the annual item demand. If it is assumed that storage, obsolescence, deterioration, pilferage, etc., are not costly, there still is the capital tied up as inventory. With the discounted policy, Delta is buying in each order 50 percent more units than the annual item demand. The savings reported of $111.82 might not be enough to compensate Delta for pursuing the discounted policy.

Additional Readings

Arnold, Tony, Stephen N. Chapman, and Lloyd Clive. *Introduction to Materials Management*, 6e. Englewood Cliffs, NJ: Prentice-Hall, 2007.

Ellram, Lisa M., and Laura M. Birou. *Purchasing for Bottom Line Impact*, vol. 4. National Association of Purchasing Management (NAPM). Homewood, IL: Irwin, 1995.

Fogarty, D. W., and T. R. Hoffmann. *Production and Inventory Management*. Cincinnati, OH: South-Western Publishing Co., 1983.

Hickman, Thomas K., and William M. Hickman. *Global Purchasing: How to Buy Goods and Services in Foreign Markets*. Business One Irwin/APICS Series in Production Management, Homewood, IL, 1992.

Hyer, Nancy, and Urban Wemmerlov. *Competing Through Cellular Manufacturing*. (Winner of the 2003 Shingo Prize). Productivity Press, 2002.

Killen Kenneth H., and John W. Kamauff. *Managing Purchasing*, vol. 2. National Association of Purchasing Management (NAPM). Homewood, IL: Irwin, 1994.

Leenders, Michiel R., and Anna E. Flynn. *Value-Driven Purchasing*, vol. 1. National Association of Purchasing Management (NAPM). Homewood, IL: Irwin, 1994.

Peterson, R., and E. A. Silver. *Decision Systems for Inventory Management and Production Planning*, 2e. New York: Wiley, 1984.

Plane, Donald R. *Management Science: A Spreadsheet Approach*. Danvers, MA: boyd & fraser publishing co., 1994.

Raedels, Alan R. *Value-Focused Supply Management*, vol. 3. National Association of Purchasing Management (NAPM). Homewood, IL: Irwin, 1994.

Ragsdale, Cliff T. *Spreadsheet Modeling & Decision Analysis: A Practical Introduction to Management Science*, 4e. Cincinnati: Thomson, South-Western Learning, 2004.

Tersine, R. J. *Principles of Inventory and Materials Management*, 3e. New York: Elsevier-North Holland Publishing, 1987.

Vollmann, T. E., W. L. Berry, and D. C. Whybark. *Manufacturing Planning and Control Systems*, 3e. Homewood, IL: Irwin, 1992.

Notes

1. John H. Blackstone Jr., and James F. Cox, III (eds). *APICS Dictionary*, 11e. APICS Educational and Research Foundation Publishers, 2004.
2. "Sea-Land Beats the Odds in Kobe, Company Is Ready to Resume Shipping." *The New York Times* (February 4, 1995).
3. "Venezuela's Chávez Asked Brazil's President Lula da Silva to Send Oil Technicians to Break a Month-Old General Strike." *The Wall Street Journal* (January 3, 2003).
4. Hurricane Katrina was a category 5 storm that shut the Port of New Orleans down on August 29, 2005. During February 2006, the Port, operating with only 70 percent of its facilities operational, achieved 100 percent of its pre-Katrina ship calls. The name Katrina was officially retired by the World Meteorological Organization on April 6, 2006.
5. Donald Erlenkotter. "Ford Whitman Harris and the Economic Order Quantity Model." *Operations Research*, vol. 38, no. 6 (November–December 1990): 937–946. Erlenkotter reports that Harris published the EOQ model in *Factory, The Magazine of Management*, 1913.
6. This is the link to the paper that is referenced. If it does not open, paste it into your browser window: http://www.worldbank.org/transport/learning/tf2006/railways%20day/presentations/ditmeyer2.ppt#261,1,Network Centric Railroading Utilizing Intelligent Railroad Systems

Enrichment Activity 14: When Should Just-in-Time (JIT) Be Part of the Buyer's Deal?

Just-in-time has different meanings for job shops and flow shops. For the job shop where repetitions of orders are irregular and volumes of batches are on average about 50 units, getting the materials needed to make or service those 50 units requires an information control system. Knowing when buyers will need specific materials and how long it will take to get those materials from appropriate suppliers is what the MRP system is designed to do. Lead times of suppliers to produce and deliver materials to buyers is part of every MRP system's data base. Material requirements planning (MRP) is the subject of Chapter 15. Suffice it to say that MRP is a just-in-time system for sporadic and irregular demand systems, so there is no need to address that problem before Chapter 15.

Just-in-time delivery of materials is used for the flow shop when it promises to lower inventory levels, and thereby, inventory carrying costs. That advantage must be balanced against the increased risk of going out-of-stock because safety stock has been eliminated. The trade-off brings up the question of how many units are delivered with a JIT system. Does JIT mean one-at-a-time and just as needed? Alternatively, how about two-at-a-time with the additional one unit for safety just in case something happens to the delivery van. Extreme JIT means just-as-needed (one-at-a-time) but sensible JIT means a few-at-a-time. The flow shop will grind to a halt if materials needed at any one workstation are not available from delivery or as a backup from inventory.

There are many levels of just-in-timeliness. P/OM must find a sensible JIT balance. If 80 units are being processes per hour, and the supplier of components is across the street from the producer, eight deliveries of ten units (one hour of inventory) might be fine. However, too many deliveries tie up the shipping dock, create start-and-stop inspection, and almost continuous bookkeeping. Instead of benefiting, a steady flow is interrupted. The decision might better be five deliveries per week of 80 units per day.

The fundamental JIT model must compare the costs of being out-of-stock with having too much stock, including all of the costs discussed above. A simulation model can be built in which the risks of interrupted delivery for a period of time have a cost that is balanced against costs of carrying spare parts in case of interrupted delivery. Systemic costs should be added to this model.

Another approach is to adapt the static inventory decision model explained in Section 12-8-1. For revising this model, the number of failures requiring spares would be the frequency of failures to deliver just-in-time. The spares ordered in advance would be analogous to safety stock carried in the event of JIT-failures. Costs in the matrix would be carrying costs for safety stock and out-of-stock costs that occur when safety stock does not compensate for JIT failures.

If buyers are using the EOQ model described in Section 14-6, then it will be seen from the equation below that JIT is called for increasingly as annual demand and the order cost rise. The same effect occurs as the cost per unit and the carrying cost rate decrease. n_o = the optimal number of orders of optimal size Q_o.

$$n_o = D/Q_o = D \div \sqrt{\frac{2DC_r}{cC_c}} = \sqrt{\frac{DcC_c}{2C_r}}$$

Enrichment Challenges 14

1   The purchase details for a component in lipstick cases are as follows: Order cost is $8 per order placed; demand is 1600 units per year; cost per unit is $4; carrying cost rate is 0.09 per dollar per year. How many orders should be placed per year?

2   When the P/OM director learns the answer to Question 1, she points out that using the modular production concept (explained in Section 10-11) it is sensible to combine orders for that component because it is used in 400 other lipstick cases that the company sells. This raises the annual demand to 640,000 units. How many orders should be placed per year? How many days between orders? Does this look more like a JIT ordering system?

3   It is pointed out that because of the new ordering policy, the cost of an order has decreased from $8 to $2. What does this change do to the number of orders? How many days elapse between orders? Is this a JIT ordering system?

4   What other factors could drive this system toward daily ordering?
    Note: QMpom models for EOQ can provide helpful insights quickly.

Material Requirements Planning (MRP) for Sporadic Demand Patterns

Chapter Outline

Chapter 15 explains MRP, which is needed to manage inventories of materials that have sporadic demands. This is in contrast to OPP (Chapter 14), which has continuous and consistent demands. Sporadic demands are often associated with dependencies on one or more job shop end-items. For example, an HDTV is comprised of many parts that are used in other HDTV models too. The basis of MRP is good organization of information. Appropriate information systems facilitate the timing of orders to make sure that everything needed to make (say) 1,000 Model X–HDTV is on hand at the right moment in time. The methods, strengths, and weaknesses of MRP are evaluated. The chapter also examines capacity requirements planning, known as CRP, and distribution requirements planning, known as DRP.

After reading this chapter, you should be able to:

- Explain the difference between dependent and independent demand systems.
- Distinguish between the foundations and fundamentals of OPP and MRP.
- Describe when MRP is preferred to the OPP approach for materials planning.
- Explain the importance of the master production schedule (MPS).
- Discuss the role of the bill of material and describe different forms that are used for the BOM.
- Detail the data inputs and information outputs of material requirements planning (MRP).
- Talk about lot sizing methods used for ordering with MRP.
- Describe capacity requirements planning (CRP).
- Explain distribution requirements planning (DRP = DRP1) and relate it to replenishing inventory at the branch warehouses.
- Explain distribution resource planning (DRP = DRP2) and relate it to planning for the key resources of the supply chain.
- Discuss how information systems use coding to connect parts from more than one product into a cohesive planning whole.
- Distinguish between two extensions of basic MRP, namely, closed-loop MRP and MRP II.

The Systems Viewpoint

Material requirements planning (MRP)

An information system that organizes all factors that determine production-scheduling decisions and all support functions including vendors.

Material requirements planning (MRP) is inherently a systems approach to the management of the entire supply chain. The method addresses a broad range of P/OM situations for inventory planning using information systems to connect parts from many products in an overall plan of action. MRP employs detail about customers, suppliers, and producer's capabilities to provide guidance for actions of when to order and how much to order, among other things. Time-dependent factors are an integral part of the analysis and solution development.

Systems that require MRP include interdependencies between final assembly products (parents) and parts (components that include subassemblies). In other words, the same part occurs in various products and so when planning production runs, over time the different demand patterns for the parts (or components) in each product must be linked to determine the overall demand for the part. Good systems analysis is essential for achieving the goals of having *what* is needed, *when* needed, and *where* needed.

An interesting aspect of the MRP acronym is that it is used in a multitude of closely related ways. For example, manufacturing resource planning is associated with MRP II, which is addressed in Section 15-13.

Strategic Thinking

The ultimate systems plan is manufacturing resource planning (MRP II), which links P/OM production planning with marketing goals, financial policies, accounting procedures, R&D plans, human resources management constraints, and so on. Put in an alternative context, MRP II is responsive to the strategic business plan of the company. Thus, new product introductions are most likely to be successful if the total organization is communicating and coordinated. The organization as a whole can mobilize to handle serious problems as they arise, such as large numbers of defectives and major equipment failures.

In line with the need for strategic thinking, reactions to predicaments may include adding physical space and production capacity as well as coproducing, which means subcontracting work to firms having the requisite capabilities. The production budget will have to be changed. From both the strategic and the systems point of view, MRP, in its various forms, helps to achieve functionally coordinated organizations. By noting the degree of information completeness regarding all functions, it is possible to ascertain at what level of coordination the firm is functioning. MRP II operates at the highest level of coordination. That is very demanding and difficult to achieve. It is a goal worth striving for because it provides one of the most powerful platforms for finding best solutions to the dynamics of change.

15-1 The Background for MRP

There always has been a need for a method to deal with the great complexity of inventory control for job shops that have many interdependent parts. The method had to be able to organize all of the data on stock-keeping units (SKUs). It had to keep track of stock levels, and order timing, while coordinating process scheduling with delivery dates for customers. The challenge of organizing all of this information continued to grow with the increasing size of markets, product line variety, and production capabilities.

The first book on MRP, written by Joseph Orlicky, was published in 1975. In the preface to this book, Orlicky states that the development and installation of computer-based MRP systems began in 1960—over 48 years ago.[1] Also, he points out that "the number of MRP systems used in American industry gradually grew to about 150 in 1971, when the growth curve began a steep rise as a result of the 'MRP Crusade,' a national program of publicity and education sponsored by the American Production and Inventory Control Society (APICS)." Today, there are tens of thousands of companies using various kinds of MRPs, and they are located all over the world.

MRP could not work in a practical way without the powerful computer capabilities that were emerging by the 1970s. The need to be able to manage the massive amount of information required for ordering and scheduling in large job shops became pressing. The ability to meet that need grew even faster.

MRP has drawn broad national attention and support as computer power has become increasingly available at significantly lower prices. It continues to be true that the pros and cons of specific MRP software must be discussed separately from the principles that drive the methodology. In-house programming as well as many software packages are alternatives that need to be evaluated according to circumstances.

15-2 Dependent Demand Systems Characterize MRP

MRP applies to a dissimilar class of problems than order point policy (OPP) models, which are used under distinctly different circumstances. OPP models (which are represented by EOQ and ELS) are powerful as long as the assumptions for their applicability hold true. MRP is used when the following OPP assumptions do not hold.

OPP Assumptions

DVR

Digital video recorder supplied by cable companies. See also TIVO at http://www.tivo.com.

End products

Also see **Parent products**. End-product demand can be sporadic. MRP is the information system that details what must be done to produce the required number of end products. The BOM lists parts and comparisons.

Parent products

Final products (like cars or fans) have many parts assembled to create them. These final parent products are also called "end products."

1   Demand is independent. This is true of end products like cars and digital video recorders (**DVR**), whose demand is driven by the marketplace. In contrast, the demand for the raw materials, subassemblies, and components used in the automobiles and DVRs are dependent on the number and types of cars and DVRs that are made. **End products**, which also are called **parent products**, are considered to have independent demand systems.

2   Demand for the item has to be regular and relatively continuous over time for order point models and policies to be applicable. If demand for an end-item is sporadic, so that stock on-hand for components that the end-item uses might sit around waiting for unknown periods of time, then that item does not fit the mode for an OPP application. When this is not the case, so that the inventory gets used up and needs to be reordered on a repetitive basis, the OPP conditions exist.

MRP Assumptions

MRP should be used for inventory management of any items that do not satisfy both of the two OPP assumptions. Alternatively, MRP is used when the following two points apply.

1   Demand is dependent because it will organize and control bringing together the kit of interdependent parts and subassemblies to make up the end product. The more complex the dependencies, the more critical is the use of MRP.

2   Demand for the item is sporadic and lumpy. This can occur for end products that have demand patterns that are not smooth and regular. However, quite often sporadic and lumpy conditions occur for parts that are dependent on end products that have regular and smooth demands. The various reasons why this is true include the fact that the part appears in several end products.

Sometimes the part is used by different end products that are produced simultaneously on parallel lines. In other circumstances, the common part is used in different end products that are scheduled to be made at widely separated times. Part demands can change according to which special options of the parent product are being produced.

To illustrate this last point, say that DVRs with different options (one model has 200 GB—called H2, and the other model has 400 GB—called H4) are run on the same line. The line switches from one model to the other on alternating weeks. The demand is fairly constant for DVRs so that 200 are made every day. Note how the demand for the 200 GB and the 400 GB hard drive changes on a weekly basis. Every other week there is no need to have stock on-hand for both the H2 and the H4.

Table 15-1 illustrates the sporadic character of the dependent demands for H2 and H4. Although DVR production is smooth and continuous, the demands for HD components H2 and H4 are discontinuous—fluctuating between needing 1,000 units one week and none the next week.

Week	1					2					3...	
Day	1	2	3	4	5	1	2	3	4	5	1	
DVRs	200	200	200	200	200	200	200	200	200	200	200...	
H2	200	200	200	200	200						200...	
H4						200	200	200	200	200		

Week 1	Need 1,000 H2s	Need 0 H2s
Week 2	Need 0 H4s	Need 1,000 H4s
Week 3	Need 1,000 H2s	Need 0 H2s

Table 15-1

Demand for End-Product DVRs Is Smooth While Demand for HD, Components H2 and H4 Pulses

Dependencies are seldom as regular as in Table 15-1 because the components are used in different end products, each of which has its own demand pattern. Most are only relatively continuous and not as stable as the DVR pattern shown here.

The comparison with regard to stock on-hand for independent and dependent demand systems is shown in Figure 15-1. When reorder point models are used to control stock on-hand for linked parts, parent demand systems often produce inventory swings that lead to overstocks and out-of-stocks. This occurs because the information about the products and the parts are not properly merged. The result is that the inventory levels are mismanaged. Lump withdrawals of parts to supply their parent products create demand surges, which overpower the steady demand pattern required for reorder point models.

MRP reflects the systems viewpoint by connecting the parent products and the dependent parts. This linkage is made by managing the combined information concerning dependent demands, SOH, deliveries, and lead times.

15-2a Forecasting Considerations

Reorder point models require that demand distributions exist for their forecasting requirements. When such reliable, long-term forecasts are not feasible, MRP is indicated. This accounts for a broad range of P/OM situations that require MRP because they have irregular demands—and do not have stable distributions.

Even though MRP demands are sporadic and lumpy, they can be predicted as discrete order events when there is advance knowledge about probable order placements. Predictions about the demand for parts are often based on forecasts for the end product. This is the result of dependent demand. The distinction that is being made is between predictions that are generated by customer notification of intentions to buy (use MRP), as compared to forecasts based on demand distributions that exist in a steady state over time (use OPP).

Actual customer orders (CO) on-hand provide relatively solid information about future demands. However, cancellations of orders are not uncommon, so risk factors still

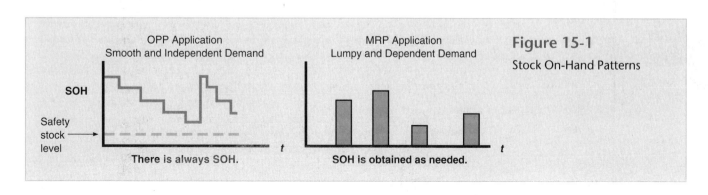

Figure 15-1

Stock On-Hand Patterns

play a part in the determination of future events. Often, there are many customers with a variety of types of products (associated with the job shop). This creates numerous interdependencies and sources of change long after order entry for the customer's order. Change also can take place after orders are placed with suppliers for the parts needed to make the end products.

Ollie Wight wrote in 1970, "... the number of pages written on independent demand-type inventory systems outnumbers the pages written on material requirements planning by well over 100 to 1. The number of items in inventory that can best be controlled by material requirements planning outnumbers those that can be controlled effectively by order point in about the same ratio."[2] The ratio of papers written for OPP as compared to MRP is now closer to 50/50, but the number of items in inventory that fit MRP instead of OPP is not much changed.

15-3 The Master Production Schedule (MPS)

Master production schedule (MPS)

Converts aggregate plans into a time-phased plan that indicates exactly when each SKU should be made and how much should be run; responsive to customer orders on hand and forecasts.

The **master production schedule (MPS)** is one of three inputs to the MRP information system. The other two are the bill of material (BOM), which describes what constitutes the end product, and inventory stock-level reports.

Aggregate production planning determines the resource capability and capacity to produce generic product in standard hours or in some other generalized dimension. For example, the aggregate plan might specify the number of gallons of paint to be made in January. The master production schedule converts this number into a time-phased plan, which indicates exactly when each type and color of paint and size of can should be made, and how much of it should be made.

Table 15-2 shows the planning only for January. Similar plans will be made by the MPS for February, March, and all succeeding months.

The basis for the assignments of MPS—quantity to be made of specific models at chosen times—are customer orders and forecasts of orders to come that are considered highly probable. The MPS makes the assignments in response to sales department commitments, which are called **order promising**.

Order promising

Sales department commitments for delivery; answers the question "When can you ship?"

Order promising is defined as "The process of making a delivery commitment, i.e., answering the question, 'When can you ship?' For make-to-order products, this usually involves a check of uncommitted material and availability of capacity. *Syn.* customer order promising, order dating."[3]

Figure 15-2 relates order promising to the time line that characterizes all production scheduling. It shows that the drivers (or inputs) of the MRP system are the customers' orders for parent products, which have been scheduled by the master production schedule (MPS). These are drawn above the parent product process time line.

Table 15-2

Converting the Aggregate Planning Schedule into the Master Production Schedule for January—130,000 Gallons Are Required

January Master Production Schedule Paint Code (Color, Size, Type) (Table Entries Are in 000)							
Week	WGF	WHGF	WGO	RGGL	RHGF	WPGL	YGF	SUM
1	10	10	10					30
2	10		10	15	5			40
3			20			10		30
4			10			10	10	30
SUM	20	10	50	15	5	20	10	130

Note: Legend for paint codes: First letter in sequence is color: W = white, R = red, Y = yellow. Second code place is size: G = gallon, HG = half gallon, P = pint. Third code place is type: F = flat, O = outdoor, GL = glossy. Five letters are possible, as in WHGGL.

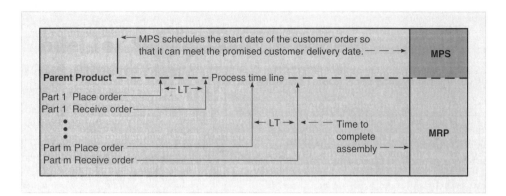

Figure 15-2

The Time-Phased MPS Function

Note relationship to later use of the terms: Place order = planned-order release; receive order = planned-order receipt. Examples of parent products include mobile phones, DVD players, DVRs, digital cameras, laptops, bicycles, autos, farm equipment, and industrial machines.

Figure 15-2 also shows that the MRP system determines what parts are used by the parent product (Parts 1 through *m*). It indicates when they are required by the process. It physically represents the lead times (LT) between placing orders and receiving them. MRP assignments are shown below the parent product process time line.

Total or cumulative lead time (LT) is defined by APICS as follows: "In a logistics context, the time between recognition of the need for an order and the receipt of goods. Individual components of lead time can include order preparation time, queue time, move or transportation time, and receiving and inspection time. *Syn.* total lead time."[4]

The cumulative lead time for a parent product is found by looking at the longest lead-time path to obtain all of the parts that go into it as the end-item. To assemble A in Figure 15-3 requires ordering B one week before the assembly operation is to begin. Part C must be ordered two weeks before assembly is to begin on part A. Parts D and E are necessary components for part C. Part D has $LT = 2$ and part E has $LT = 4$. The longest path results from A + C + E and that has $LT = 6$, and it dominates cumulative lead time.

However, if part E is a *standard* item, which means it is stocked, then E should not be considered when calculating total lead time. If D is a *special* item, which means there is no stock on-hand for D, then the lead time $LT = A + C + D = 4$ dominates the cumulative lead time. If both D and E are standard items, then $LT = A + C = 2$ has a longer path than $LT = A + B = 1$. As a final consideration, if C is a standard item, the longest lead-time path is $LT = A + B = 1$.

15-3a Total Manufacturing Planning and Control System (MPCS)

The manufacturing planning procedure started with resource evaluation and forecasting at the aggregate scheduling stages of manufacturing planning. Based on an authorized

Total or cumulative lead time (LT)

Time between recognition of the need for an order and the acknowledged, genuine receipt of goods.

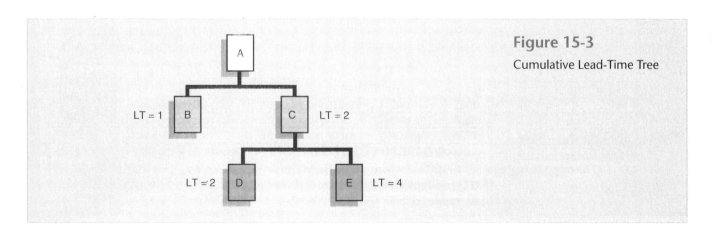

Figure 15-3

Cumulative Lead-Time Tree

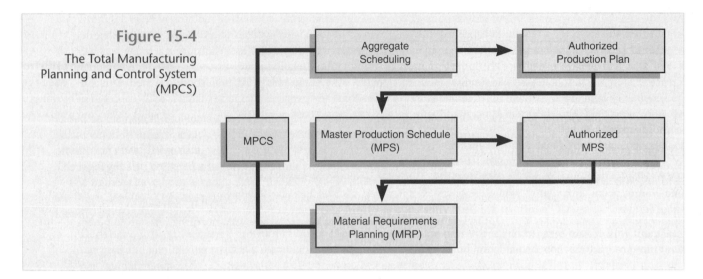

Figure 15-4

The Total Manufacturing Planning and Control System (MPCS)

© 2008 Jupiterimages Corporation

Details are the essence of MRP in which every number drives actions concerning the timing of orders—placed with whom; for how many; when delivered at what price and with what discounts.

production plan, it moved to master production scheduling (MPS), which reacts to specific customer order expectations and orders on hand. Once the MPS is accepted and authorized, the planning process proceeds to details of scheduling that are the province of the material requirements planning (MRP) system.

These steps are flowcharted in Figure 15-4. The system called the *total manufacturing planning and control system (MPCS)* captures what takes place in job shops all over the world.

The MPS stage needs to be documented. In Figure 15-5, an MPS chart is shown that is created for every parent product. It represents the middle step—MPS—in the total MPCS shown in Figure 15-4. This MPS chart goes nine weeks into the future with parent-product requirements scheduled for weeks 2, 5, and 9. The MPS must project gross requirements far enough ahead to permit actions to be taken that are needed for the success of parent-product production.

Weeks are the intervals, or time buckets, most often used. However, other periods can be required. Some organizations use short- and long-term master production schedules where the short-term schedules are in days or weeks and the long-term schedules are in months or quarters. The time buckets used reflect the rapidity of changes to schedule, lead-time lengths, and how far ahead it is possible to forecast.

The MPS chart in Table 15-3 has 20 units of parent product to be made in the second week ahead from *now*. If it takes 4 weeks (total lead time, $LT = 4$) to order parts that are

Figure 15-5

Inputs and Outputs of MPS

Weeks Ahead	1	2	3	4	5	6	7	8	9	**Table 15-3**
Gross (amount) requirements		20			45				60	MPS Chart for *Specific* Parent Product

needed for the parent product, then the order should have been placed already. Note that this chart is updated each week.

The gross amount required moves from the *nth week ahead* to the *n* – 1 week ahead of *now*. Thus, the second week from now at one time appeared as week 5. When it was in the week 5 position, the parts were ordered during week 1. Therefore, it is expected that the necessary order for parts already has been placed for the present *week 2 ahead* gross requirements of 20.

In Table 15-3, there are 45 units required for the *present week 5 ahead*. The planned order should be released now, in week 1. There are 60 units required for the *present week 9 ahead*. Perhaps there should be a planned-order release *in week 5 ahead* for these 60 units. However, the ordering policy, which will be discussed shortly, may determine that the order for week 5 ahead (which is released in week 1) should cover some (or all) of the week 9 ahead requirements. There is a point to be made; namely, the master production schedule is required to have a planning horizon as long as the longest cumulative lead-time function.

15-3b MPS: Inputs and Outputs

Master production schedulers set down the make-build schedule for specific parent products. Their scheduling function moves beyond the generic units of time and money that were the limitations of aggregate scheduling. They deal with real-time and specific SKUs. The master production schedules are partially driven by the sales forecast, which is one of the usual inputs to the production plan. It also is driven by actual orders on hand. It takes into account priorities for orders based on urgency and customer importance. Master production schedulers always seek to make the best use of actual capacity and resources. These considerations are brought together in Figure 15-5.

15-3c Changes in Order Promising

Order promising by sales and marketing and order fulfillment goals of production are matched and coordinated by the MPS. If marketing promises dates that production cannot deliver, changes are required either in the due dates promised to customers or in the production schedules for the plant.

In a **make-to-stock (MTS) environment**, there is some latitude in what is scheduled. Also, there may be sufficient inventory in stock to help fulfill order promising. The emphasis is on having sufficient stock on-hand to provide excellent service with minimum delivery times. The MRP emphasis is on finished product, which is usually smaller in number than the number of components that make up the finished product. This is typical of automobiles, homeowners' tools, and DVRs.

In a **make-to-order (MTO) inventory environment**, there is no finished goods inventory to call upon. End-items are produced to customers' orders. Consequently, greater dependency exists between sales, which promises delivery, and P/OM, which has to produce what is to be delivered. Customers expect finished goods to be delivered on time. This characterizes small- and medium-sized job shops—often called *machine shops*—that work from blueprints and do not have product lines. Carpenters and plumbers live in an MTO environment. On a larger scale, auto replacement part manufacturers including windshield glass have a significant percent of their business as MTO.

Make-to-stock (MTS) environment

There is latitude in what to make and the quantities to produce because various items have finished goods inventories; marketing can (to some extent) meet customers' demands by selling what is in stock.

Make-to-order (MTO) inventory environment

There is no finished goods inventory to meet demand.

Assemble-to-order (ATO) environment

End-items are built from parts and subassemblies. The MPS insures availability of all components to fulfill promised due dates.

The **assemble-to-order (ATO) environment** is one where end-items are built from subassemblies. Master production schedules ensure that these subassemblies are available to meet demand within promised due dates. Often the number of components is smaller than the number of finished products, and master production schedules operate at the components or subassembly level. This means that parts and subassemblies are scheduled instead of parent products. In this case, the MPS is only secondarily concerned with parent end products and primarily with making the parts to complete the subassemblies. The master production schedule is focused on the subassemblies much like the modular BOM concentrates on options (see Section 15-4). The heavy equipment industry uses assemble-to-order.

15-3d The Bill of Material (BOM)

The bill of material (BOM) for a dinner party is the cook's shopping list. Job shop production managers used the BOM long before MRP was developed. Now, as 2010 approaches, MRP is widely used. MRP cannot be used without the BOM. The social dinner party was fun, but McDonald's and Burger King have a more serious view about the materials required for the manufactured food service business. The bill of material for an automobile is so extensive that it has to be subdivided into subassemblies of components.

Bill of material (BOM)

Lists all of the subassemblies, parts, and raw materials that go into a parent assembly showing the quantities required.

The APICS definition is quite complete. A **bill of material (BOM)** is "a listing of all of the subassemblies, intermediates, parts, and raw materials that go into a parent assembly showing the quantity of each required to make an assembly. It is used in conjunction with the master production schedule to determine the items for which purchase requisitions and production orders must be released. There is a variety of display formats for bills of materials, including the single-level bill of material, indented bill of material, modular (planning) bill of material, transient bill of material, matrix bill of material, and costed bill of material. It may also be called the 'formula,' 'recipe,' 'ingredients list,' in certain industries."[5]

BOMs include every material that goes into or onto a product. It can also be applied to every material that is needed to deliver a service. This is epitomized by "meals on wheels." In manufacturing, the materials may be screws, nails, rivets, glue, paint, and packaging. Figures 15-6, 15-7, and 15-8, and Table 15-4 display a number of the commonly used BOMs. Each of the different kinds of bills of materials mentioned in the APICS definition captures some important aspects of the MRP process. BOMs are the starting point for actual use of MRP, and the varieties are consequently instructive.

The multi-level BOM (as a tree or in the indented form) is essential for MRP purposes because it captures everything that must be ordered to complete the parent product. The APICS definition is precise, namely "a display of all the components directly or indirectly used in a parent, together with the quantity required of each part. If a component is a subassembly, blend, intermediate, etc., all of its parts will also be exhibited and all of their components, down to purchased parts and materials."[6]

Modular BOMs are organized so that product options can serve in place of single-product parents. This BOM is associated with products that can be assembled in

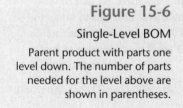

Figure 15-6

Single-Level BOM

Parent product with parts one level down. The number of parts needed for the level above are shown in parentheses.

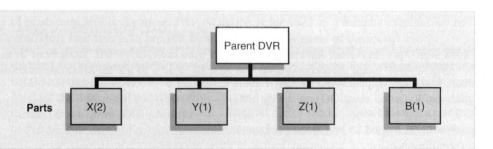

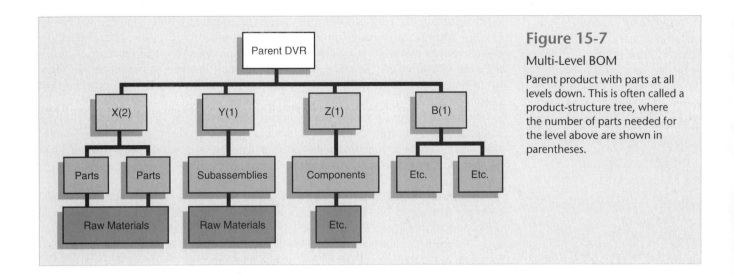

Figure 15-7

Multi-Level BOM

Parent product with parts at all levels down. This is often called a product-structure tree, where the number of parts needed for the level above are shown in parentheses.

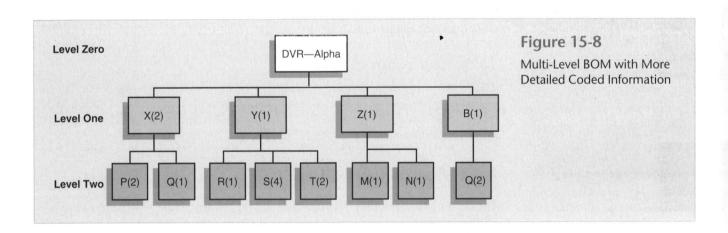

Figure 15-8

Multi-Level BOM with More Detailed Coded Information

Table 15-4

Multi-Level Indented BOM

Parent product and parts are carried at levels (0, 1, 2, and 3) for two DVR models (the alpha and the beta) as shown here. The number of parts needed for the level above are indicated in parentheses. (See Figure 15-12 for the DVR-beta product structure and note that because B(1) is low-level coded at level 2, E(2) is at the third level. Low-level coding will be explained shortly.)

DVR Alpha		Level (0)	DVR Beta		Level (0)
X(2)		1	G(2)		1
	P(2)	2		P(2)	2
	Q(1)	2		B(1)	2
Y(1)		1	Y(1)		1
	R(1)	2		R(1)	2
	S(4)	2		S(4)	2
	T(2)	2		T(2)	2
Z(1)		1	V(1)		1
	M(1)	2		C(1)	2
	N(1)	2		D(1)	2
B(1)		1	B(1)		1 (Code 2)
	Q(2)	2		E(2)	2 (Code 3)

many different ways. Thus, assemble-to-order is common with computers that can be configured in many ways using different boards and drives. It also is characteristic of automobile assembly with different packages of features. The options are fewer than the end products, which can combine options in many different ways. Thus, by using options, fewer bills of materials are required to control the ordering and inventories.

The matrix BOM is a special chart constructed by analyzing the BOMs of a family of similar products. It arranges parts in columns and parent products in rows. This is useful where the objective is to make the greatest number of products with the minimum number of parts. This matrix characterizes what is called the *modular product design objective*.

Cost BOMs show complete parent-part hierarchical product structures with the latest costs per part appended. The costs must be regularly updated to prevent incorrect and misleading information. Cost BOMs are useful for purchasing decisions when alternative suppliers are being considered. They are also important to determine the costs of parts including raw materials, subassemblies, and components.

Transient or phantom BOMs are used for subassemblies that are not kept in stock. Note that phantoms are assigned zero lead time and lot-for-lot order quantities (concepts that will be discussed). This permits the MRP system to bypass the subassemblies and go directly to their components.

15-3e Explosion of Parts

The multi-level product structure was called an *explosion* by Orlicky who wrote, "In executing the explosion, the task is to identify the components of a given parent item and to ascertain the location (address) of their inventory records in computer storage so that they may be retrieved and processed."[7]

Inventory record files (IRF)

Stock on-hand levels; suppliers' prices and delivery lead times must be current.

15-4 Operation of the MRP

The **inventory record files (IRF)** are the third major input to the MRP computer system. The inputs are shown in Figure 15-9 along with the outputs from the MRP system that are about to be discussed.

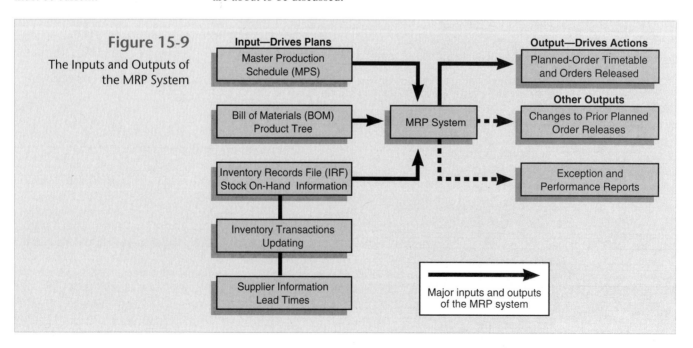

Figure 15-9

The Inputs and Outputs of the MRP System

Stock on-hand levels need to be up-to-date. So should all ordering information, including the suppliers' lead times. The roles of the MPS and the BOM have been discussed already. It is noted that preparation of the MPS involves knowledge of the BOMs as well as the inventory and supplier information.

15-4a Coding and Low-Level Coding

When various parent items have had their parts explosion accomplished, **coding** provides a means of identifying the fact that some parts belong to more than one parent. In Table 15-4, note that the indented BOMs of the alpha and beta DVR models share Y(1) subassemblies at level one. All components of Y(1) are similarly shared at the next level down. These are R(1), S(4), and T(2). Further, P(2) is used by both models at the second level. The SKU numbers can include coding such as Y(1) for code 1 and P(2) for code 2.

When the master production schedule calls for various amounts of alpha and beta DVRs, the MRP must combine the demands of commonly shared parts. For the specific example that is being discussed here (Table 15-4), the MRP program must be able to recognize that one alpha DVR and one beta DVR call for 2Y(1)s, 2R(1)s, 8 S(4)s, 4 T(2)s, and 4 P(2)s. Increased demand for parts shared in common will affect the order quantities in different ways, depending upon the method used to determine order lot sizes.

Coding techniques capture other relevant information about parts, such as data about suppliers, storage locations, and what substitutes exist. Coding of part names is the foundation for an effective information system to link the components and the parents together. It also is the best means of identifying families of parts that can be made with minimal setup changes. Such part-family-oriented processes are the subject that is identified by the name "group technology."

Part numbers should not be chosen randomly. There is so much useful information that can be instantly gleaned from carefully coded part numbers. It is best to code part numbers so that they reflect the level of the part and the product parents of the part. Additionally, as suggested earlier, codes show who are current suppliers of the part, who might be future suppliers of the part, alternative locations for storage, and the type of materials of which the part is made.

The method called **low-level coding** is commonly used to organize order quantity calculations for parts with combined demands. Top-level parents, such as the DVR sets, are called the level zero. Parts and components that are one level down are coded level one. Those two levels down are coded level two, etc. This coding scheme shows how distant parts are (in their linkage) from their parent products.

"Once low-level codes are established, MRP record processing proceeds from one level code to the next, starting at level code 0. This ensures all gross requirements have been passed down to a part before its MRP record is processed. The result is planning of component parts coordinated with the needs of all higher-level part numbers. Within a level, the MRP record processing is typically done in part number sequence."[8]

Low-level coding uses the principle that the lowest position of a part should determine where that part is located for computer scanning. Part B of DVR beta appears as B(1) at both the first and second levels of the multi-level indented BOM in Table 15-4. The MRP software counts down from the level zero to determine order quantities and when to release the orders for parts. Thus, for the beta DVR, it will carry B(1) at level one down to level two, where it will combine it with the level two B(1). (This is shown in Figure 15-12.)

Figure 15-10 shows the product structure for a hall coat rack tree where a G part appears at both levels one and two. Figure 15-11 redraws to accommodate the low-level coding requirement. The graphics aside, low-level coding is simply an organizing rule for computing materials requirements.

Exception codes are used to identify important items. This is equivalent to adding on to the part number an exception code indicator to reflect the fact that checks should be

Coding
Provides a means of identifying the fact that some parts are required by more than one parent.

Low-level coding
Organizes order quantity calculations for parts with combined (multi-level) demands; the lowest position of a part determines where the calculation of gross cumulative requirements is made.

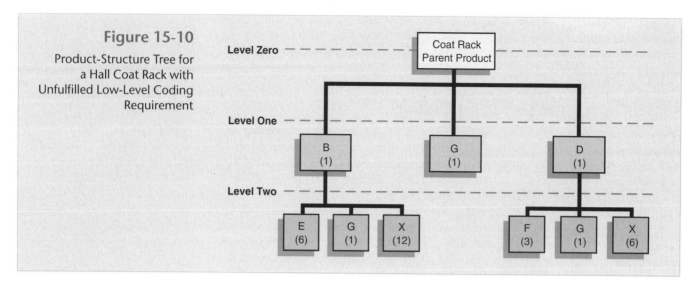

Figure 15-10

Product-Structure Tree for a Hall Coat Rack with Unfulfilled Low-Level Coding Requirement

Figure 15-11

Product-Structure Tree for a Hall Coat Rack with Low-Level Coding Requirement Fulfilled

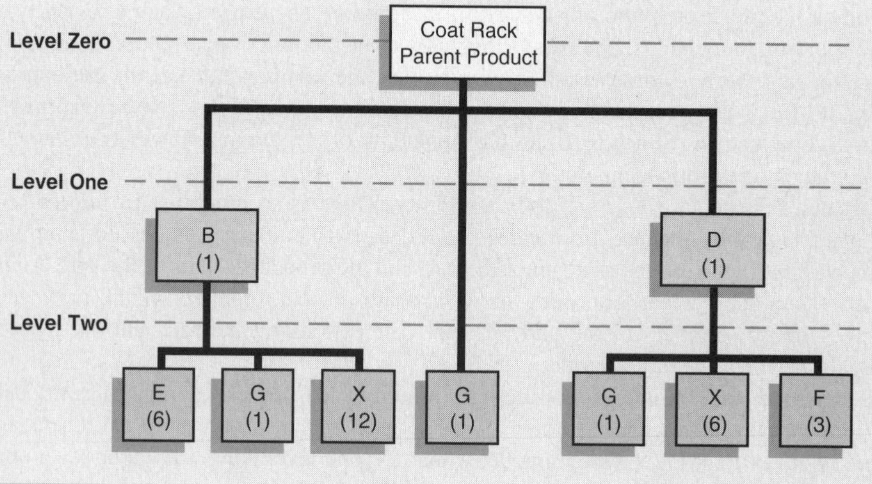

made for the accuracy of the data and the status of the part. Ten percent of all items might receive such special coding; this depends on the importance of the customer, the difficulty of the job, or the fact that MRP cannot schedule completion of a level zero product because something has gone awry.

15-5 MRP Basic Calculations and Concepts

Gross requirements GR_t for end-items for week t are required by MRP and stated by the MPS. Inventory information is on file for the prior week's stock on-hand (SOH_{t-1}). There may be some open orders that will be received at the beginning of week t, and these are called scheduled receipts, SR_t.

$$\text{Projected stock on-hand at time } t = SOH_{t-1} + SR_t \qquad (15\text{-}1)$$

The gross requirements less the projected stock on-hand, at time t, are called the *net requirements*, NR_t, thus:

$$NR_t = GR_t - (SOH_{t-1} + SR_t) \qquad (15\text{-}2)$$

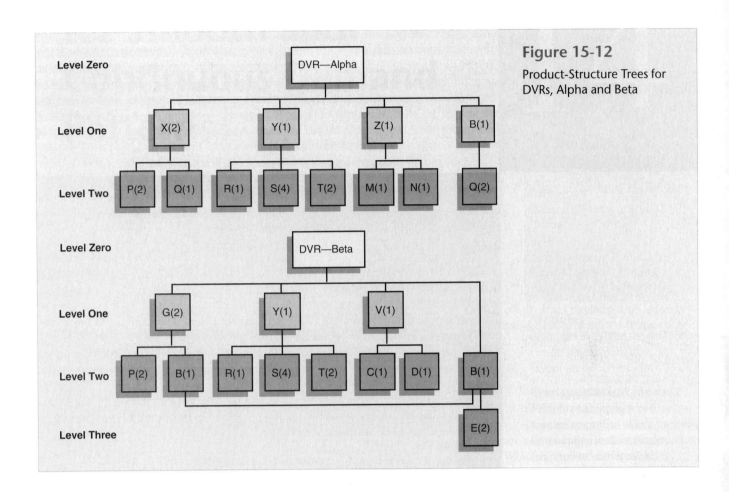

Figure 15-12

Product-Structure Trees for DVRs, Alpha and Beta

The process of determining net requirements is called *netting*. Based on net requirements and order policies, *planned-order receipt times* and *planned-order release times* can be determined, using the following equations.

If projected stock on-hand at time t is larger than the gross requirements:

$$(SOH_{t-1} + SR_t) > GR_t \qquad (15\text{-}3)$$

then, there would be stock on-hand at the end of period t. Thus:

$$SOH_t = SOH_{t-1} + SR_t - GR_t > 0 \qquad (15\text{-}4)$$

Net requirements (Equation 15-2) would be zero in Equation 15-4 because there was more stock on-hand than gross requirements. However, if

$$GR_t > (SOH_{t-1} + SR_t) \qquad (15\text{-}5)$$

then, $NR_t > 0$, and an order must be placed early enough so that with the lead time, delivery can be made at the beginning of period t. This order is called a *planned-order receipt*, PR_t.

In Equation 15-6, set $PR_t = 0$ when projected stock on-hand (Equation 15-1) is greater than gross requirements.

$$SOH_t = SOH_{t-1} + SR_t + PR_t - GR_t \qquad (15\text{-}6)$$

However, when there is a shortfall, the size of the *planned-order receipt*, PR_t must be decided. Often, **lot-for-lot ordering** is used. This means that the planned-order receipt is equal to the net requirements, as in Equation 15-7.

$$PR_t = NR_t \text{ with lot-for-lot ordering} \qquad (15\text{-}7)$$

Lot-for-lot ordering

Planned-order receipt will equal the required amounts at each point in time.

Table 15-5	Week										
Master DVR Schedule—Alpha and Beta Models	Net requirements	1	2	3	4	5	6	7	8	9	10
	Alpha model	-	60	-	-	-	80	-	-	40	-
	Beta model	-	-	50	-	-	20	-	-	-	60

If other methods are used for ordering, then the order size can exceed net requirements, and the planned-order receipt, PR_t will be greater than the net requirements.

To keep the charts simple in the examples that follow, scheduled receipts are set to zero. Therefore, projected stock on-hand is the same as SOH_{t-1}.

15-6 MRP in Action

The easiest way to understand MRP is to simulate the action. Here are some sample scenarios that provide an operational explanation of the workings of MRP.

First, create the MPS for the alpha and beta models. Use rough-cut capacity planning (RCCP) to make certain there is enough capacity to produce Table 15-5 specifications. Rough-cut means approximate rather than precise.

Second, develop the product structure for both alpha and beta models, as in Figure 15-12.

Note that because of low-level coding, B(1) is at level two, placing E(2) at level three. See also the indented BOM in Table 15-4.

Scenario 1: Lot-for-Lot Ordering with No Parts Sharing Parents—Level One

MRP methods will be used to determine order timing for part Z in the alpha model of the DVR. Note that Z(1) occurs only in the alpha model, and at level one. There is one unit per DVR. Lead time (LT) = 2 weeks, which means that LTs for both M(1) and N(1) are less than two weeks. There must be time for the Z component to be assembled after receiving the parts M and N.

Initial SOH = 80. Lot sizing follows a lot-for-lot policy. This means that both the planned-order receipt and the planned-order release exactly match net requirements (number of units). See Table 15-6.

The conclusion is to have an order release (place the order) for 60 units of Z in week 4 for receipt in week 6. Also, order 40 units of Z in week 7 for receipt in week 9. There are two orders, and once the initial stock on-hand is used up, there are no carrying costs. This is due to the fact that lot sizing is done on a lot-by-lot basis. The short lead time makes this feasible.

Table 15-6		End Week									
		1	2	3	4	5	6	7	8	9	10
MRP Plan for DVR Alpha—Z(1)	**Gross requirements**	-	60	-	-	-	80	-	-	40	-
	Stock on-hand (SOH)	80	20	20	20	20	-	-	-	-	-
	Net requirements	-	-	-	-	-	60	-	-	40	-
	Planned-order receipt	-	-	-	-	-	60	-	-	40	-
	Planned-order release	-	-	-	60	-	-	40	-	-	-

		End Week									
	1	**2**	**3**	**4**	**5**	**6**	**7**	**8**	**9**	**10**	
Gross requirements	-	-	-	60	-	-	40	-	-	-	
Stock on-hand (SOH)	40	40	40	-	-	-	-	-	-	-	
Net requirements	-	-	-	20	-	-	40	-	-	-	
Planned-order receipt	-	-	-	20	-	-	40	-	-	-	
Planned-order release	-	-	20	-	-	40	-	-	-	-	

Table 15-7

MRP Plan for DVR Alpha—N(1)

Scenario 2: Lot-for-Lot Ordering with No Parts Sharing Parents—Level Two

Part N(1) is dependent on part Z(1). One N and one M are needed to make one Z. The use of MRP methods will determine order timing for part N in level two of the alpha model of the DVR. Lead time is one week, and SOH is 40 units. See Table 15-7.

Forty units of stock are carried for three weeks. Two orders are placed. One order is in week 3 and the other order is in week 6. Planned receipt is in weeks 4 and 7.

Scenario 3: Lot-for-Lot Ordering with No Parts Sharing Parents—Level Two and no SOH

Part M(1) is dependent on part Z(1). The difference between the scenarios for N (shown earlier) and M (now) is that part M has no SOH (SOH = 0 units). Again, MRP methods will be used to determine order timing for part M in level two of the alpha model of the DVR. LT is one week as it was for part N. See Table 15-8.

There is no stock carried. Two orders are placed in weeks 3 and 6 with planned receipt in week 4 and week 7. Table 15-9 summarizes the first three scenarios, which are related in the DVR hierarchy.

Having stock on-hand for Z(1) deferred the need for an order until week 4. Thereafter, the lot-for-lot ordering policy took over. On the other hand, the fact that N(1) had some stock on-hand did not defer an order. It just made it a smaller one. The pattern of dependency is evident in that M and N need to be ordered in weeks 3 and 6 to satisfy Z's need for stock in weeks 4 and 7.

		End Week									
	1	**2**	**3**	**4**	**5**	**6**	**7**	**8**	**9**	**10**	
Gross requirements	-	-	-	60	-	-	40	-	-	-	
Stock on-hand (SOH)	-	-	-	-	-	-	-	-	-	-	
Net requirements	-	-	-	60	-	-	40	-	-	-	
Planned-order receipt	-	-	-	60	-	-	40	-	-	-	
Planned-order release	-	-	60	-	-	40	-	-	-	-	

Table 15-8

MRP Plan for DVR Alpha—M(1)

			End Week								
SOH	**Name**	**1**	**2**	**3**	**4**	**5**	**6**	**7**	**8**	**9**	**10**
0	DVR	-	60	-	-	-	80	-	-	40	-
80	Z(1)	-	-	-	60	-	-	40	-	-	-
40	N(1)	-	-	20	-	-	40	-	-	-	-
0	M(1)	-	-	60	-	-	40	-	-	-	-

Table 15-9

Summary of MRP Orders Placed

Table 15-10

MRP Plan for DVR Alpha and Beta—Y(1)

		End Week									
		1	2	3	4	5	6	7	8	9	10
Gross requirements		-	60	50	-	-	100	-	-	40	60
Stock on-hand (SOH)		80	20	-	60	60	-	50	50	10	-
Net requirements		-	-	30	-	-	40	-	-	-	50
Planned-order receipt		-	-	90	-	-	90	-	-	-	90
Planned-order release		-	90	-	-	90	-	-	-	90	-

The next, and final, scenario assumes that an economic order quantity Q_o has been determined to set the order size. Note it is used because it minimizes the sum of ordering and carrying costs. Also, it is not the basis for a continuous (dynamic) ordering system with a reorder point.

Scenario 4: Economic Order Quantity for a Part That Shares Parents

Y(1) subassemblies occur in both the alpha and the beta model. Therefore, the demands in the MPS are combined. There is one unit used whichever model is made. $LT = 1$ week, which means that R(1), S(4), and T(2) all have lead times that are one week or less.

The initial SOH = 80. Lot sizing is done using the economic order quantity (EOQ) model. The optimal lot size has been determined to be $Q_o = 90$ units. See Table 15-10.

Y(1) total demand (combines demand for both the alpha and beta models) drives the planned-order releases and receipts. There are three orders, and 230 units are carried over the 7-week period. This 7-week period (which stretches from the end of week 3 to the end of week 10) starts once the initial (SOH) inventory of 80 units is used up.

The average number of units that are carried is equal to 230/7 = 32.86, or 33. For the 10-week period, it is the same (330/10 = 33). Also, there will be 90 − 50 = 40 units carried during week 11.

Note: Enrichment Activity 15 supplements the MRP calculations to allow comparison of the total costs of all scenarios. That comparison helps operations managers make a choice between alternatives.

15-7 Lot Sizing

Lot-for-lot sizing is among the simplest ordering methods, but it places more orders than other methods that order less frequently in larger quantities. Lot-for-lot is as close an approximation to just-in-time as it makes sense to get with an MRP model. However, if there are setups required, then the costs associated with lot-for-lot are likely to be too high, and alternative methods that order less frequently will prevail.

The cost of this policy can be obtained by multiplying the number of orders that are made using lot-for-lot by the cost of an order or setup. As revealed by the simulations (scenarios), with lot-for-lot sizing and no order cancellations, the amount of inventory carried would be zero. MRP systems are not immune to last-minute changes that result in stranding inventory that was earmarked for make-to-order. When orders are canceled, there is stock left, and this might have to be carried for quite awhile.

Grouping periods require summing the demands to cover various fixed periods of time, the length of which is selected based on the concept of an optimal period t_o as shown here. The period also can reflect accounting conveniences and policies of the supplier concerning how often it is able to deliver.

The idea is to decrease the number of orders. If a 4-week fixed period is chosen, 13 orders will be placed per year. It is not difficult to keep track of average inventory carried and to put a cost on carrying stock. If this cost is close to the cost of an order, or setup, multiplied by 13, then a good balance has been established. This approach, called the *part-period model* using an economic part-period criterion, is examined in the supplement to this chapter.

Economic order quantity is calculated for items using the traditional OPP method:

$$Q_o = \sqrt{2DC_r \div cC_c}$$

The annual demand, D, can be estimated. The cost per unit, c, is known. The carrying cost, C_c, and the ordering cost, C_r, both must be estimated. The economic order quantity sets the order size. The equivalent to the reorder point is that positive net requirements signal the need to place an order. It is expected that the number of such orders placed will average out to be $n_o = D/Q_o$, and the average interval between orders will be $t_o = 1/n_o$, as calculated here:

$$t_o = \sqrt{2C_r \div cDC_c}$$

The sensible approach for important items is to compare the costs obtained by using the various methods. The methods that have been discussed for economic part period balancing (ppb) are only able to approximate the optimal. Over a long planning horizon the dynamic programming approach based on the Wagner-Whitin algorithm comes closest to minimizing the total costs which are the sum of the carrying and ordering costs. Computing intricacies, which have been a stumbling block to implementation of this model for very large inventory systems, have been reduced to a practical level.[9] This is for various reasons including better computing algorithms, faster computers, and experience with what counts.

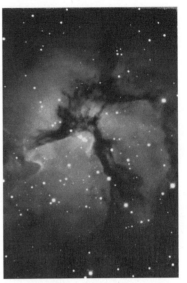

© 2008 Jupiterimages Corporation

How many stars are in the sky? There are so many that the inventory ledgers are huge. Nevertheless, they are all catalogued and have labels similar to stock-keeping units (SKUs) that are fundamental for identification of all parts in company inventories.

15-8 Updating

There are two approaches for updating the MRP files and records. The first of these is called *regeneration MRP* and the second is called *net change MRP*. APICS definitions should be used as a standard for the field. They are precise and concise.

"**Regeneration MRP**—An MRP processing approach where the master production schedule is totally reexploded down through all bills of material, to maintain valid priorities. New requirements and planned orders are completely recalculated or 'regenerated' at that time. *Ant.* net change MRP, requirements alteration."[10]

"**Net change MRP**—An approach in which the material requirements plan is continually retained in the computer. Whenever a change is needed in requirements, open order inventory status, or bill of material, a partial explosion and netting is made for only those parts affected by the change."[11]

The MRP records are usually regenerated once a week. However, the variation that exists in practice can be traced to the degree to which change affects the system and how frequently it occurs. Because net change systems respond to transactions and only calculate the effects of that transaction, it is a simpler system requiring less time. Net change systems can be programmed to be activated by exception reports. This allows the system to react quickly to problems that arise.

It is not common practice to rely upon the net change system for all transactions over time. There are too many runs required for small and local effects. The many runs can lead to accumulation of errors instead of corrections. The systems for correction may not have received the same amount of thought and attention as the regeneration program. Consequently, it is often the case that net change is reserved for exceptions and regeneration is used on a regular basis.

Regeneration MRP

Thorough, time-demanding method of updating the MRP information system; master production schedule is totally reexploded down through all bills of material.

Net change MRP

Fast and economical method of updating the MRP information system; a partial explosion and netting is made for only those parts affected by the change.

15-9 Capacity Requirements Planning (CRP)

Capacity requirements planning (CRP)
Readjust capacity when the MRP system delivers a plan that is not feasible because of capacity limitations.

Capacity requirements planning (CRP) is an extension of MRP. Sometimes it is necessary to readjust capacity when the MRP system delivers a plan that is not feasible because of capacity limitations.

Capacity requirements planning (CRP) is "the function of establishing, measuring, and adjusting limits or levels of capacity . . . (it) is the process of determining how much labor and machine resources are required to accomplish the tasks of production. Open shop orders and planned orders in the MRP system are input to CRP, which 'translates' these orders into hours of work by work center by time period. *Syn.* capacity planning."[12]

There is the short-range picture of shifting capacities and the long-range view of commitments to strategic alterations. CRP addresses the former, which can be called "the more immediate problems." The latter, which is treated in Section 15-13, is called *manufacturing resource planning*, or *MRP II*.

CRP is generally applied to short-term modifications for capacity problems that are encountered as a result of infeasible MRP plans. Specifically, capacity changes can be affected by using overtime, longer and extra shifts, renting more space, and hiring part-time workers. Subcontracting often is used when backlogs arise.

Bottlenecks can be removed by methods studies. Changes can be made in the way that purchasing functions. Priorities can be altered, and sales can be asked to emphasize certain products and not take orders for others. For the most part, these are considered to be stopgap measures that can be employed until the problems are solved in a more permanent fashion.

Figure 15-13 illustrates the way in which capacity requirements planning (CRP) is used to modify the MPS and the MRP system when supply called *resource availabilities* (RA)—and demand called *material requirements* (MR)—do not match.

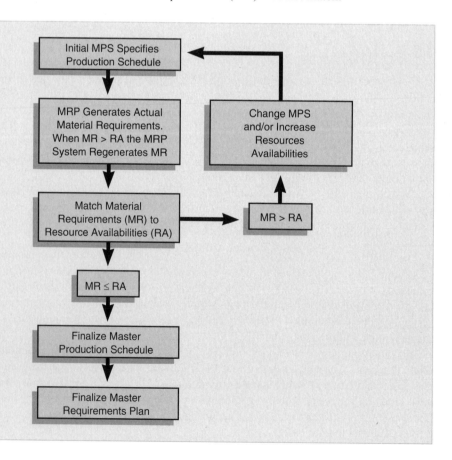

Figure 15-13

The Capacity Requirements Planning (CRP) System

The fact that CRP operates at a higher level than MRP is an important first step in realizing potentials for the organization. Thus, capacity planning permits consideration of alternative sources of product. What is being made can be shifted to what will be bought, and vice versa. Nevertheless, as will be noted when MRP II is discussed, CRP looks outside the boundaries of MRP on a relatively short-term basis.

15-9a Rough-Cut Capacity Planning (RCCP)

Rough-cut capacity planning (RCCP) uses approximation to determine whether there is sufficient capacity to accomplish objectives. It serves as a precursor of the CRP process. RCCP occurs when the aggregate plan is being transformed into the master production schedule. In order to authorize the MPS (as shown in Figure 15-4), it is essential to check that there is enough capacity to do the job that the MPS describes.

RCCP is used to be certain that realistic objectives are being transmitted to the MRP process. If there is insufficient capacity to produce the MPS, then steps are taken to bring in additional key resources and/or to use subcontracting and/or co-processing.

Bills of resources (BOR) are used to accomplish these objectives. The **bill of resources (BOR)** is a listing of the key resources needed to make one unit of the selected items (or family of items as in group technology). Resource requirements are identified with a lead-time offset to show the impact of the requirements on resource availability with respect to the time line. RCCP makes use of BOR to determine the expected capacity requirements of the MPS. The BOR also is called the *product load profile* or the *bill of capacity*.

Capacity requirements planning is post-MRP planning. However, capacity planning is going on before this stage in the form of rough-cut capacity planning. It is used to disaggregate the aggregate schedule in order to develop the master production schedule. It also should be noted that the MPS is the basis for the manufacturing budget. If there is not enough production capacity to fulfill orders promised, capacity has to be changed. This will alter the manufacturing budget.

15-10 Distribution Resource Planning (DRP)

When the acronym DRP is used, it refers to *distribution resource planning*, which is akin to MRP II (described later). DRP is the essence of supply chain management. A total systems point of view prevails. The basic distribution system is extended to consider not only how to keep the warehouse supplied but, also, how to configure the key resources of the distribution supply chain including the manufacturing supply. **Distribution resource planning** is referred to as **DRP2** in the following discussion.

Distribution resources can be modified once the underlying *distribution requirements planning* system (defined in the following paragraph) is charted and understood. Note that the distribution requirements planning system is akin to MRP. The acronym DRP is sometimes used to label this extension to MRP. For clarity, distribution requirements planning can be called DRP1 and defined as follows:

"(1) The function of determining the needs to replenish inventory at branch warehouses. A time-phased order point approach is used where the planned orders at the branch warehouse level are 'exploded' via MRP logic to become gross requirements on the supplying source. In the case of multi-level distribution networks, this explosion process can continue down through the various levels of regional warehouses, master warehouse, factory warehouse, etc., and become input to the master production schedule. Demand on the supplying source(s) is recognized as dependent, and standard MRP logic applies.

"(2) More generally, replenishment inventory calculations may be based on other planning approaches such as 'period order quantities' or 'replace exactly what was used' rather than being limited to solely the time-phased order point approach."[13]

Rough-cut capacity planning (RCCP)

Used to check that there is sufficient capacity to produce what is needed.

Bill of resources (BOR)

Lists the key resources needed to make a unit of various selected SKUs.

© 2008 Jupiterimages Corporation

The bill of resources may be found captured in both books and on the computer screens of the MRP department. Because of hackers, MRP managers require strong backup systems since there is great dependency on viable data systems. Ultimately, books are too cumbersome.

Distribution resource planning (DRP2)

Operates as an extension of distribution requirements planning (DRP1) by addressing what additional resources are needed in the distribution system.

The analogy of DRP1 to MRP is evident. Material requirements connect the supply chain participants. Lead-time dependencies exist as factories feed central warehouses and these, in turn, supply regional warehouses. It will be noted that shipping quantities are much like lot sizing. Lot-for-lot replacement is a potential strategy.

DRP2 is a higher order planning system than the distribution requirements planning system because it also plans for resource availability such as storage space in warehouses, trucking capacity, railroad boxcar availabilities, distribution workforce commitments and training, and cash flow needed to keep the distribution system moving. Thus, DRP2 operates as an extension of **distribution requirements planning (DRP1)** by addressing what resources are needed in the distribution system.

15-11 Weaknesses of MRP

MRP is vulnerable to variability in lead times. The parent product cannot be made if any one of the items on the lower levels is not delivered on time for the scheduled production runs. This raises the point that a sensible policy might require some safety stock.

MRP is supposed to do away with the need for safety stock. However, P/OM must evaluate the risk of delayed supplier deliveries and take adequate protective measures. This is done by increasing the lead time by an amount that should cover delivery contingencies. Such "safety time" translates into added stock being carried.

The fact that a production or delivery problem at any level in the hierarchy can shut down the system cannot be treated as an MRP weakness. Whether MRP is used or not, the lack of materials will result in stopping the process. MRP helps to keep problems from arising by documenting the time-phasing for all parts that are needed. Follow-up calls can be made to ascertain the status of orders. Other forms of *expediting* can be used when slippage seems to be occurring. The weakness of MRP, in this regard, is that it does not automatically check status of orders and expedite them. That remains an organizational matter related to how information is used. Expediting should be treated as an integral part of the MRP organization.

There are problems evaluating MRP software. Many kinds of MRP software are available off-the-shelf. Some companies buy these and then modify them to suit their own particular systems' needs. Large firms often build their own systems. Failures with MRP can often be traced to having chosen software that was not well-suited to the applications.

MRPs are information systems that are vulnerable to data errors. Data entry must be checked carefully for original records, and then for updates. Errors can creep into net-change systems that are difficult to detect. Many organizations have so many parts that it is difficult to be sure that all changes are recorded. Engineering design changes occur so frequently in some companies that it is hard to keep up with them. With MRP, the system for keeping up with changes had better be as good as the MRP system.

One of the worst problems that MRP faces is last-minute changes in orders. It is inevitable that the size of orders will be altered, and that cancellations will occur. To illustrate, assume that the order for 90 Y(1) subassemblies has been placed in week 2 for scenario 4. A week later, sales cancels the beta model DVR run of 50 units. It is possible that no more betas will be made. There is a frantic effort to cancel the 90 Y(1) subassemblies to no avail. Fortunately, the Y(1) subassemblies also are used in the alpha model. The dependent nature of shared parts adds to the complexity of resolving errors and to the severity of potential problems. It also increases the safety net when cancellations occur.

15-12 Closed-Loop MRP

Closed-loop MRP is "A system built around material requirements planning that includes the additional planning functions of sales and operations (production planning,

---

Distribution requirements planning (DRP1)

Time-phased order point approach is used to "explode" planned orders at the branch warehouse level via MRP logic.

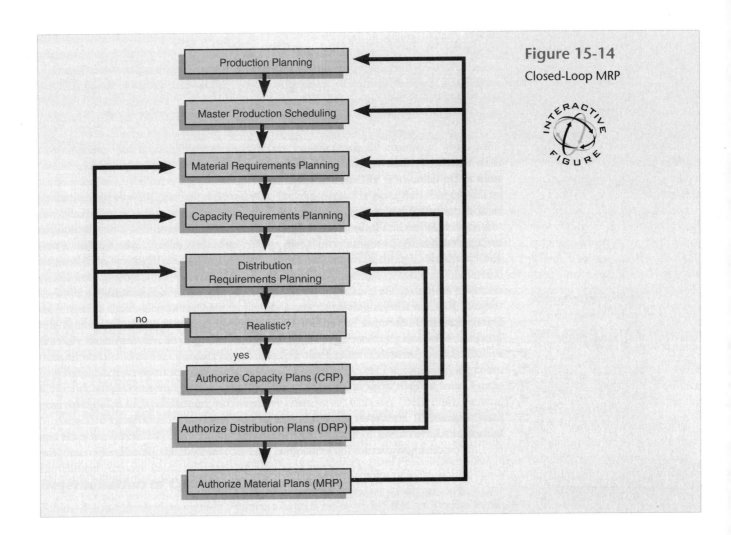

Figure 15-14

Closed-Loop MRP

master production scheduling, and capacity requirements planning). Once this planning phase is complete and the plans have been accepted as realistic and attainable, the execution functions come into play. These include the manufacturing control functions of input–output (capacity) measurement, detailed scheduling and dispatching, as well as anticipated delay reports from both the plant and suppliers, supplier scheduling, etc. The term **closed-loop MRP** implies that not only is each of these elements included in the overall system, but also that feedback is provided by the execution functions so that the planning can be kept valid at all times."[14]

The closed-loop MRP has material requirements planning as one of its steps. It is replete with feedback loops that permit planning and replanning. It extends the MRP concept to include capacity requirements planning, shop scheduling, and supplier scheduling. The first step in the planning hierarchy is production planning, which indicates that master production scheduling is based on more than open orders and sales forecasts.

The essence of the closed-loop MRP systems approach is represented by Figure 15-14. Some diagrams of closed-loop MRPs do not include distribution requirements planning, but good systems thinking endorses its inclusion. MRP becomes more powerful with the additions of closed-loop MRP.

Closed-loop MRP changes into the more powerful MRP II with the addition of business resource planning as discussed in Section 15-13 and shown in Figure 15-15.

Closed-loop MRP

Feedback prevails at many levels, and over time, for planning and replanning scheduling, capacity requirements, and sales strategies.

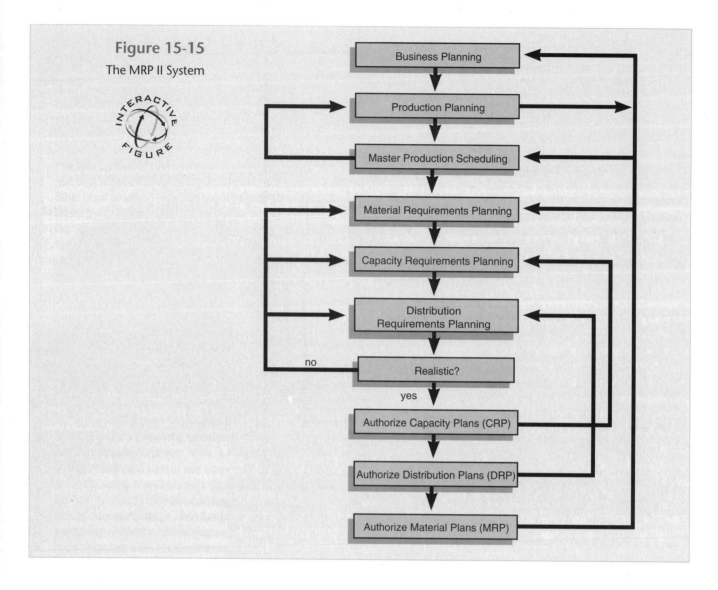

Figure 15-15

The MRP II System

INTERACTIVE FIGURE

15-13 Strengths of MRP II (Manufacturing Resource Planning)

MRP II

Systems plan for operating effectively at the plant level; links P/OM and production planning with marketing goals, financial policies, R&D plans, accounting procedures, and human resource management goals.

MRP II entails total manufacturing resource planning as part of the strategic business plan. Thus, minor capacity adjustments can be made on a short-term basis (CRP); however, longer-term and broader systems perspectives should prevail. For example, marketing considerations raise the possibility of changing the master production schedule to allow for the introduction of new products and the alteration of the company's product mix.

Financial planning can access and control what is being done and determine what will be done in the future. Accounting is linked directly to the MRP II cost systems so that accounts payable, accounts receivable, and cash flow are online with production. R&D's agenda is linked to long-term plans for the company and the architecture of its MRP II.

Technology is constantly changing. MRP II encourages and supports reevaluation of the way that work is being done. It permits assessment of the product mix and the input–output processes that are being used.

Competitive shifts in strategy produce forces to alter what is being done. This can be brought up for consideration by any of the systems players—finance, marketing, R&D,

HRM, P/OM, and purchasing. Concretely, MRP II puts business planning into a box hierarchically above that of production planning.

Compare Figures 15-14 and 15-15. The business planning box is not present in Figure 15-14, which depicts closed-loop MRP. The diagram for "closed-loop planning" starts with production planning. In contrast, in Figure 15-15 there is a *feedback loop* connecting the business planning function with the production planning function. The hierarchical stature of "business planning" for all functions elevates MRP II into the highest levels of strategic thinking.

Because strategic business plans drive the MRP II system, this allows consideration of the effect of buying new machines, changing computer equipment, building new plants, altering the product mix, and modifying advertising and promotion campaigns, among others. Based on systems thinking, changes to any part of the planning process shown in Figure 15-14 should be in line with strategic business plans as developed in Figure 15-15.

Toward this end, note that there is another feedback loop for MRP II from master production scheduling to production planning. This permits coordination of plans and actions to assure achievement of the best plan for manufacturing resources and, thereby, materials requirements. The long-range viewpoint in search of optimal configurations is the essence of MRP II.

Ollie Wight said, "… the theme of MRP II (is) managing all of the resources of a manufacturing company more productively." In his book,[15] he then proceeds to develop Chapters 8–15 as follows:

Chapter 8—"The CEO's Role in MRP II"
Chapters 9, 10, 11, 12, 13—"MRP II in Marketing, Manufacturing, Purchasing, Finance, and Engineering (respectively)"
Chapter 14—"DRP: Distribution Resource Planning"
Chapter 15—"MRP II in Data Processing Systems"

The scope of MRP II is fully revealed by Ollie Wight throughout his book. He developed MRP II with the broadest systems scope in mind.

15-14 Emerging Power of ERP

MRPII is the foundation for **Enterprise Resource Planning (ERP)**. Transformation of MRPII to ERP in its most far-reaching form is accomplished by converting the Business Planning box at the top of Figure 15-15 into an Enterprise-Wide Planning box. Following the path in Figure 15-15 produces an integrated marketing-production strategy, which is intended to combine resources of the company in an optimal fashion.

Reported experiences of ERP providers such as SAP, Oracle (which absorbed People-Soft in January 2005), IBM, Manugistics, Sun Microsystems, MicroSoft, Arriba, i2 Technologies, and many consulting firms indicate how difficult it is to achieve a seamless information system that properly amalgamates P/OM, finance, marketing, human resources, etc., into a unified, coordinated management entity. Many firms find that small steps toward the long-run goal of integrating all departments and functions, as well as suppliers, is the wisest course of action. Departments that are advanced may adopt integrating systems in the hope that eventually other departments will join in the consortium.

Whether it is tackled on a small scale or a total systems scale, the ERP goal is to integrate customer-order information with financial data, human resource information, and marketing knowledge. This combines predictions about sales and cash flow with production capacities and capabilities. Among the many logical objectives of using such systems is to lower inventory costs, cut inventory levels, reduce cycle times, increase productivity, improve customer relations, and expand tie-ins with the Internet. The achievements of some ERP systems show that although the price is high, the

© 2008 Jupiterimages Corporation

MRP II is considered to be the highest level of all MRP systems, but ERP includes all aspects of MRP II and extends even further into every aspect of enterprise strategic planning.

Enterprise Resource Planning (ERP)

Company-wide integration of the information system for seamless planning across all functions.

rewards can be many times greater if the project is successful. Failures have extreme penalties.

Visits to http://www.sap.com, http://www.oracle.com, http://www.aajtech.com, etc., can prove valuable in promoting an understanding of ERP.[16]

Spotlight 15-1 Trading Stability for Mobility

According to extensive and ongoing research by RainmakerThinking, Inc., a consulting firm in New Haven, Connecticut, that studies young workers, there has been a profound "generational shift" in the American workplace, a revolution that has had worldwide effects. Bruce Tulgan, founder of RainmakerThinking, Inc., has focused his company's attention on changing relationships between employers and employees. In a 10-year study between 1993 and 2003, he and his firm studied trends that were first noticed in the 1990s. Globalization of business and technology, with its high-risk business environment, erratic markets, and unpredictable need for resources, has shaped new necessities for employers. Bruce Tulgan's study concluded, "To remain viable, employers have been forced to adopt extremely flexible and efficient hiring practices. In turn, employees have adjusted by adopting more aggressive attitudes, expectations, and behaviors."

A sense of free agency has given young workers expectations of creating lifetime careers not with one or two companies, but as independent contractors, selling their services on a project basis to many employers. Each job change means a new negotiation, not only for pay but also for control of the working environment, balance between work and private life, and training for the next job. Free agents quickly realize that survival depends on keeping their skills current. Heather Neely, a former consultant at RainmakerThinking, said, "They want to learn constantly because once they stop learning, they stop being viable." By 2004, Tulgan found that free agency had swept across the entire workforce. Skilled workers of all ages were trading stability for mobility.

The new work preferences are most highly developed in the 30-something workers who have never known a stable workplace and grew up mainly as self-reliant, latchkey children. Bruce Tulgan says that Generation Xers (born 1965–1977) are accustomed to facing problems on their own and have confidence in their ability to fend for themselves. If these young workers seem to be self-centered in their approach, it is prompted by a workplace without job security. "These workers choose employers based on benefits, rewards, and career opportunities. They are all *me* related, rather than where the company will be in 10 to 15 years," said a recruiter.

Peter Cappelli, author of *The New Deal at Work: Managing the Market-Driven Workforce* and professor of management at the Wharton School, has studied Generation X and their younger counterparts, Generation Y (born 1978–1986). In his opinion, both groups believe there is no reward for loyalty and are not eager to make long-term commitments. If they are seen as disloyal and unwilling to contribute, the reality is that they are adapting to a workplace in which "corporations broke the old arrangement unilaterally. They've seen what's gone on with their parents' generation, and a lack of trust in the corporation is a perfectly rational response to that."

Complicating life for employers is Generation Xers' attitude that everything is open for negotiation. Instead of accepting company policy, they will say, "Let's talk about making an exception" or "Let's change the policies." One healthcare recruiter said, "These people think outside of the box."

A frequent point of negotiation is the work–life balance. As Ann Fishman, president of Generational Targeted Marketing, a research company in New Orleans, describes it, "No matter how bad the economy gets, these workers won't work in an environment they don't like. They are willing to give up salaries to have quality of life in the workplace."

These trends are neither sudden nor exclusive to generational factors. As far back as 1994, the September 19 cover of *Fortune* magazine proclaimed, "The End of the Job" and announced that the traditional job is becoming a social artifact. Today traditional jobs continue to disappear because of technology changes, integrated information systems, a teamwork mind-set, and global diversity. Such issues interact with generational factors. Bruce Tulgan's description of the difference between the X and Y generations is interesting. He says that the Y's are super X's in every way. Y's are super-high performers and demand very high maintenance.

Managing younger workers can be challenging. Short attention spans, cell phone conversations, instant messaging, iPods, and downloading music while engaged in job-related tasks can drive a boss crazy. The belief that one should be given special projects rather than dues-paying jobs can be annoying to an employer as well. All this falls heavily on immediate supervisors of independent young workers. Are supervisors up to the task? Bruce Tulgan and his company decided to find an answer.

Over an 18-month period from December 2002 to June 2004, RainmakerThinking, Inc., conducted surveys, questionnaires, and personal interviews within hundreds of companies. The Tulgan team focused on management and the performance of immediate supervisors at every level. The results are disturbing as well as dramatic. The findings present a clear picture of what RainmakerThinking calls "The Under-Management Epidemic."

Tulgan considers under-management a disease similar to a pathological condition with clear signs, painful symptoms, and harmful effects. He defines under-management "as a condition in which a leader with supervisory authority *fails to provide regularly and consistently* to employees who are directly subject to that authority any of the following five management basics:

1 Clear statements of performance requirements and standard operating procedures related to recurring tasks and responsibilities.

2 Clear statements of defined parameters, measurable goals, and concrete deadlines for all work assignments for which the employee will be held accountable.

3 Accurate monitoring, evaluation, and documentation of work performance.

4 Clear statements of specific feedback on work performance with guidance for improvement.

5 Rewards distributed fairly."

His research showed that only 1 percent of managers provided all of the above at least once a day. Even in an entire year, 35 percent of managers did not provide all of the above. Under-management was found to be the common denominator in most cases of sub-optimal workplace performance of all types and at all levels.

Low performers are the great beneficiaries of under-management. Low performers look for a boss who doesn't tell them what to do and how to do it. Low performers do not want bosses to spell out expectations every step of the way. If managers are hands-off and treat everybody the same, the result will be under-managing most employees into a slow downward spiral.

On the other hand, when managers are strong and highly engaged, most employees will be managed into a steady upward spiral of performance. High performers want a boss who knows exactly who they are and exactly what they are doing every step of the way. High performers want to know that they are important and look for managers who will clear the low performers out of the way. They want a boss who will set them up for success, who spells out expectations clearly, who teaches them best practices, who warns them of pitfalls, who helps them solve small problems before they grow, and rewards them when they go the extra mile. To combat the under-management epidemic, Tulgan and his team originated seminars and training programs where managers could learn better habits.

In 2007, Bruce Tulgan authored his 16th book, *It's OK to Be the Boss: The Step-by-Step Guide to Becoming the Manager Your Employees Need*. His book contains eight techniques for winning the fight against the under-management epidemic. See Spotlight 15-2 to continue this discussion.

Review Questions

1 What profound "generational shift" has occurred in the American workplace?

2 What are some of the causes of this significant generational shift?

3 How did Bruce Tulgan of RainmakerThinking describe the problem of under-management? Does his diagnosis make sense to you? Give examples from your own experience.

4 What does the generational shift have to do with P/OM?

Source: "Managing the Generation Mix: From Urgency to Opportunity," authored by Carolyn H. Martin and Bruce Tulgan, HRD Press, Inc. ©2006. *"It's Okay to Be the Boss: The Step-by-Step Guide to Becoming the Manager Your Employees Need,"* authored by Bruce Tulgan, HarperCollins Publishers, 2007.

Spotlight 15-2 It's Okay to Be the Boss

Bruce Tulgan

"Get in the habit of managing every day" is first of eight techniques that Bruce Tulgan describes in his 2007 book, *It's Okay to be the Boss: The Step-by-Step Guide to Becoming the Manager Your Employees Need*. It is a technique that practice can improve. Many managers describe themselves as "hands off." They don't want to be viewed as a "jerk," so they empower their employees to handle responsibilities with little guidance. Tulgan's term for this situation is "false empowerment." Generation Y does not want to be left alone. Real empowerment is high engagement. It is not an easy course of action to follow but it works. Tulgan reminds managers that doing their job every day will put out fires that otherwise would grow huge with neglect.

Tulgan writes that most managers operate in a crisis mode. If managers develop the habit of spending an hour a day with their employees or even 15 minutes per day setting up an employee for success, it makes an amazing difference. Instead of giving orders, Tulgan suggests asking employees what they will focus on and what they plan to do. He says to managers, "Be brief, straight, and simple in a non-crisis dialog. New habits take time. Try practicing this one for at least 3 weeks." That gives enough time to review and improve on the first results.

Managers can get employees in the habit of giving an account of their work by explaining to them that measuring their work is meaningless unless it is under the employee's control. Spelling out a manager's expectations has to be done up close. Many times a manager has no knowledge of the work an employee does. In such cases, Bruce Tulgan suggests taking the role of a patient. Ask questions as if the employee were your doctor. Be a rigorous consumer of the employee's work. Try to learn what each employee wants. Help employees do better work from that knowledge. Being a great manager can happen only when performance is

tracked every step of the way through a daily working relationship as well as helping employees move toward what they want. The Tulgan techniques, if practiced regularly, may well be a cure for the under-management epidemic.

John Koenig, ex-president of O-Force, a business and education partnership focused on workforce development issues in the Orlando area, summed up his reaction to Tulgan's findings as follows: "Top management is certainly important for creating a consistent tone across an organization. In the end, though, employee attitudes and behaviors are shaped primarily by day-to-day interactions with immediate supervisors, and not by messages relayed from a corner office far away."

An interesting view of the future of the workplace comes from Monster.com. John Sumser, a Monster contributing writer, calls attention to the fact that the U.S. skilled workforce is shrinking. Driven by declines in family size, the American workforce is growing by a mere 1 percent, down from 2.6 percent in the 1980s. Currently, there is a shortage of healthcare professionals and security experts, to name just a few critically under-staffed areas. Newcomers and immigrants enter the workforce at the lower end of the skills spectrum, keeping up positive growth, small as it is. However, a decreasing birthrate is causing most of the overall shrinkage of talented workers.

Sumser believes that the true Talent War has just begun and will be with us for a very long time. Brought about by new technology and global competition, the shift in organizations now favors employees who possess attributes associated with "knowledge work," i.e., high-level cognitive skills, abstract reasoning, problem-solving, communication, and collaboration. These valued employees need an environment that can enhance and develop their talents. Unlike publishing houses that provide authors with developmental editors to meet production deadlines, many companies are not yet willing to give their young talent the tools and support they need to succeed. Instead, management is investing in digital technology to monitor employees, work areas, cash registers, and use of the Internet in the attempt to reduce liability.

Influence of lawyers rather than belief that the company will run more efficiently has promoted this corporate monitoring. Robert Siciliano, an author and personal security expert for IDTheftSecurity.com in Boston, describes it this way, "Just assume there's a video camera looking over your shoulder all day long."

Working under the rule of a video camera may produce discipline and efficiency for awhile but, at the same time, corporations are reducing their returns by de-motivating most employees. Deborah Stephens, co-founder and managing partner of the Center for Innovative Leadership in

Silicon Valley, states, "There is a hidden cost that most leaders are overlooking when they decide to watch their employees." By breaking the bond of trust, she writes, companies destroy what is essential for success. She finds it hard to imagine how an environment where employees are spied upon can strengthen a work culture or produce results that are needed in a workplace.

A picture emerges from the efforts of many sources, pinpointing where companies need improvement. Monitoring with "spy" technology, with all its security benefits, is not a solution for overcoming the disease of under-management as defined by Bruce Tulgan. What is needed is an environment that allows personal interaction, cohesion, and mutual trust between young workers and their immediate supervisors. Organizations filled with talented, capable, enthusiastic people can succeed where lawsuits, intimidation, lack of caring, and distrust cannot. It has been argued for many years that strong, nontraditional middle managers are the essential ingredient.

Howard Schultz gives us a tip from his successful company, Starbucks Corporation (See Spotlight 14-2). He states, "We do not run a business that serves coffee. We run a coffee business that serves people." Starbucks employees value themselves as partners. The company has created a workplace where cohesion and even loyalty can grow.

A word from Greek antiquity is "myrmidon." It means "a faithful follower who carries out orders without question." Today no one in the workforce is a myrmidon. Only computers qualify. The concept of workforce free agency is being put to the test. John Koenig, who is currently Director of Market Positioning with Holland & Knight, LLP, raised an interesting question regarding this issue. As Gen Xers and a few Y's are already moving into middle management ranks, he asks, "Are they bringing with them the attitudes that the corporate world found so challenging? Or is the corporate world merely promoting to middle management those who surrender or suppress their 'free agent' tendencies? The question is whether Gen Xers are managing any differently?" The answers will be evident as young talent chooses between mobility and stability.

Review Questions

1   In your current job (or the last one you had), how are you being managed?

2   How do you want to be managed?

3   Describe the best supervision you ever had.

4   Describe the worst supervisor you ever had.

5   Discuss Bruce Tulgan's remedies for the problem of under-management. Do they make sense to you? Give examples, if possible.

6   As the current Baby Boomer managers get ready for retirement, do you think that Gen Xers and Gen Y's will manage any differently as they move into middle management ranks?

Sources: http://www.RainmakerThinking.com.

William Bridges. "The End of the Job." *Fortune* (September 19, 1994): 62–74.

Douglas Coupland. *Generation X: Tales for an Accelerated Culture.* New York: St. Martin's Press, October 1992.

http://www.monster.com

http://www.annfishman.com; Look for the intergenerational chart 1900 to present.

http://knowledge.wharton.upenn.edu; Search Dr. Peter Cappelli/ Books.

http://www.cfil.com; Deborah C. Stephens at The Center for Innovative Leadership.

Correspondence with John W. Koenig, 2004 through 2007.

Summary

Chapter 15 presents the means for appreciating the utility of material requirements planning—widely referred to as MRP. Demands for parts, components, and subassemblies that are dependent on the demands for end-items to which they belong characterize MRP. The first major tool of MRP is the master production schedule (MPS), which fits within the framework of the total manufacturing planning and control system (MPCS). Differences between make-to-stock (MTS), make-to-order (MTO), and assemble-to-order (ATO) are described. Converting gross requirements into net requirements is explained.

A major component of the information system is the bill of material (BOM), which leads to a product-structure tree reflecting the explosion of parts. Coding and low-level coding are detailed for operating the MRP system. Lot-sizing scenarios are described. Updating the system is discussed. Then higher orders of MRP systems are presented. These are CRP (capacity requirements planning), DRP [distribution resource planning (DRP2), which is a higher order planning system than the distribution requirements planning system (DRP1) because it also plans for resource availability], closed-loop MRP, and finally, MRP II, which is manufacturing resource planning.

ERP is the logical extension of MRP II. It calls for an expanded view of the firm. It requires seeing the firm as a total system. That point of view is advocated by this text, which has repeatedly shown that marketing and financial planning are absolute essentials to adequate P/OM planning, and vice versa. A firm faces an enormous burden when it attempts to integrate all of its activities into a coherent whole. The strategies and tactics that coordinate and synchronize financial decisions, marketing initiatives, HR capabilities, and P/OM planning are so various and complex that a structure is needed. MRP provides the initial concepts from which an enterprise solution can be approached. ERP undertakes to create the expanded view of the firm. That is why an in-depth study to achieve real ERP requires great amounts of resources and organizational commitment from top to bottom. See Spotlight 18-2 on the Balanced Scorecard.

Spotlight 15-1: Trading Stability for Mobility provides a profile of different generations of workers who are currently engaged with companies all over the world. The MRP work environment is entirely demanding because there are so many things that can go wrong and only dedicated employees are likely to be able to handle the stress. Spotlight 15-2: It's Okay to Be the Boss continues with prescription for the managers. "Get in the habit of managing every day," says Bruce Tolgan. Successful MRP really needs the kind of boss who is on top of it all, and who will tell it like it is—consistently and regularly.

Key Terms

Assemble-to-order (ATO) environment (p. 610)

Bill of material (BOM) (p. 610)

Bill of resources (BOR) (p. 621)

Capacity requirements planning (CRP) (p. 620)

Closed-loop MRP (p. 623)

Coding (p. 613)

Distribution requirements planning (DRP1) (p. 622)

Distribution resource planning (DRP2) (p. 621)

DVR (p. 604)

End products (p. 604)

Enterprise Resource Planning (ERP) (p. 625)

Inventory record files (IRF) (p. 612)

Lot-for-lot ordering (p. 615)

Low-level coding (p. 613)

Make-to-order (MTO) inventory environment (p. 609)

Make-to-stock (MTS) environment (p. 609)

Master production schedule (MPS) (p. 606)

Material requirements planning (MRP) (p. 602)

MRP II (p. 624)

Net change MRP (p. 619)

Order promising (p. 606)

Parent products (p. 604)

Regeneration MRP (p. 619)

Rough-cut capacity planning (RCCP) (p. 621)

Total or cumulative lead time (LT) (p. 607)

Review Questions

1 How does inventory planning differ for the flow shop and the job shop?
2 Explain how MRP relates to the job shop and the flow shop.
3 What is meant by time-phased requirements planning for MRP?
4 What is the difference between updating by "regeneration" and updating by the "net change" method for MRP? Discuss the pros and cons of each method.
5 Explain net requirement, planned-order receipt, and planned-order release. When are they equal and when are they not equal?
6 What is CRP?
7 What is DRP? How does it relate it to distribution requirements planning?
8 Distinguish between MRP, closed-loop MRP, and MRP II.
9 What characterizes dependent demand systems?
10 How do forecasting considerations apply to MRP?
11 Explain the master production schedule (MPS).
12 What is meant by the total manufacturing planning and control system (MPCS)?
13 Explain the bill of material (BOM). How does it relate to the product-structure tree?
14 What purpose is served by the explosion of parts?
15 How does coding and low-level coding impact order policies?
16 What is lot sizing?
17 What are some of the different methods that are used for lot sizing? Describe those that you know.
18 What is the difference between gross and net requirements?
19 Describe the make-to-stock (MTS) environment.
20 Explain the make-to-order (MTO) inventory environment.
21 Explain the assemble-to-order (ATO) inventory environment.
22 How is rough-cut capacity planning (RCCP) used?
23 Explain bills of resources (BOR).
24 What is ERP?
25 Why does ERP require "great amounts of resources and organizational commitment from top to bottom"?

Problems Section

Note: This section has various problems that can be formulated and solved using QuantMethods Production/Operations Management software (QMpom). The QMpom module called Material Requirements Planning can be used in a variety of ways to facilitate solving the twenty two (22) problems that are presented below.

1 The master schedule for end product P is as follows:

Week	Gross Requirements
1	400
2	200
3	200
4	300
5	500
6	100
7	600
8	400

Stock on-hand for p_1, a component of P, is 700. Develop the planned-order release schedule for p_1, assuming a lot-for-lot sizing policy and lead time $LT =$ two weeks.

2 Use the information in Problem 1 to address the following issue: SOH of 700 units is always maintained because there is unreliability of delivery. How does the lot-for-lot sizing policy deal with this issue?

3 With further reference to Problem 1, the cost of a unit of p_1 is $12. The carrying cost rate is 0.25 percent per week (0.0025). The setup cost to produce p_1 is $48. Demand per year can be estimated from the table in Problem 1. Use the economic order quantity (EOQ) to set the order size whenever an order is triggered by positive net requirements. Describe the performance of this system.

4   Using the information in Problem 3, what is the expected interval between orders?

5   The master schedule for parent product M is as follows:

Week	Gross Requirements
1	3,400
2	4,200
3	5,200
4	6,300
5	7,500
6	3,100
7	4,600
8	5,400
9	6,600
10	7,800

The policy is to carry no stock on-hand for m_1, which is a subassembly of M. Develop the planned-order release schedule for m_1, assuming a lot-for-lot sizing policy and lead time $LT =$ one week.

6   Use the information in Problem 5 to address the decision of the MRP manager who wants to try 2-period ordering. She requests that you compare your lot-for-lot plan with the 2-period plan. Also, she asks, "Would it help to have some SOH?" Make the comparison and answer the question.

7   With further reference to Problem 5, the cost of a unit of m_1 is $1. The carrying cost rate is 24 percent per year. The ordering cost for m_1 is $25. Demand per year can be estimated from the table in Problem 5. Use the economic order quantity (EOQ) to set the order size whenever an order is triggered by positive net requirements. Describe the performance of this system.

8   Using the information in Problem 7, what is the expected interval between orders?

9   Develop the lot-for-lot ordering scenario for DVR-alpha part Q, using Table 15-5 in the text and the product-structure tree in Figure 15-12. Note: Q appears more than once in the product-structure tree. Also, observe the number of units of Q that are required for each unit of X and for each unit of B. The lead times for both X and B are zero because they can be assembled immediately. The lead time for Q is one week. Part Q has no other parents or end-items than DVR-alpha.

In addition to providing the quantitative ordering instructions, evaluate the performance of the ordering system. Hint: Include in the planned-order release chart levels 0, 1, and 2.

10   Develop the lot-for-lot ordering scenario for DVR-alpha part Q, using Table 15-5 in the text and the product-structure tree given by Figure 15-12. As in Problem 9, note that Q appears more than once in the product-structure tree. Also, observe the number of units of Q that are required for each unit of X and for each unit of B. The lead times for both X and B are one week to assemble. The lead time for Q is one week. Part Q has no other parents or end-items than DVR-alpha.

In addition to providing the quantitative ordering instructions, evaluate the performance of the ordering system. Hint: Include in the chart for planned-order release, levels 0, 1, and 2.

11   Develop the lot-for-lot ordering scenario for DVR-beta part B using Table 15-5 in the text and the product-structure tree given in Figure 15-12. Note that B appears more than once and on different levels of the product-structure tree. Also, observe that only one unit of B is required in both cases. The lead time for G is zero and the lead time for B is two weeks. Assume that part B has no other parents or end-items.

Provide quantitative ordering instructions and an evaluation of the behavior of the ordering system. Hint: Include in the chart for planned-order release levels 0, 1, and 2.

12   Develop the lot-for-lot ordering scenario for DVR-beta part B using Table 15-5 in the text and the product-structure tree given in Figure 15-12. Note that B appears more than once and on different levels of the product-structure tree. Also, observe that only one unit of B is required in both cases. The lead time for both G and B is one week. Assume that part B has no other parents or end-items.

Provide quantitative ordering instructions and an evaluation of the behavior of the ordering system. Hint: Include in the chart for planned-order release levels 0, 1, and 2.

13   Determine what happens to Y(1) subassemblies if 50 DVR-beta units ordered for week 3 are canceled. Use Table 15-5 and Table 15-10. Note that Y(1) subassemblies are used in both alpha and beta end-items.

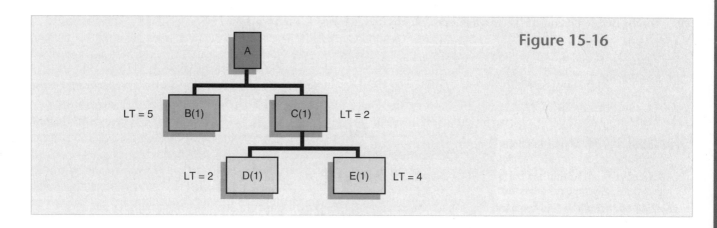

Figure 15-16

14 What is the maximum cumulative lead time for parent assembly A where subassemblies B, C, D, and E are all special items with lead times as marked? The usage quantities shown in parentheses are all one-for-one, meaning one B and one C subassembly are required for A. One D and one E are required for C. (Use Figure 15-16.)

15 Using Figure 15-16 and information in Problem 14, what is the maximum cumulative lead time for parent assembly A if subassembly E is a standard item and there is SOH?

   Note: Subassemblies B, C, and D are all special items.

16 Using Figure 15-16 and information in Problem 14, what is the maximum cumulative lead time for parent assembly A where subassembly B is a standard item with SOH? All other components are special.

17 The product structure BOM in Figure 15-17 does not account for low-level coding. Redraw Figure 15-17 so that it is consistent with low-level coding.

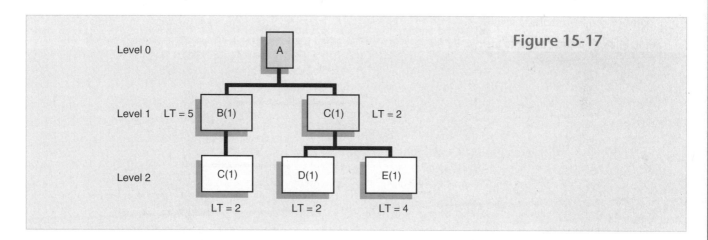

Figure 15-17

18 Using Figure 15-17 in Problem 17, what is the maximum cumulative lead time for parent assembly A where subassemblies B, C, D, and E are all special items with lead times as marked? The usage quantities are shown in parentheses.

19 Using Figure 15-17 in Problem 17, what is the maximum cumulative lead time for parent assembly A where subassembly C is a standard item for which there is ample SOH? Subassemblies B, D, and E are all special items. The usage quantities are shown in parentheses.

20 For the BOM in Figure 15-18, to which subassembly does the planned-order release chart apply?

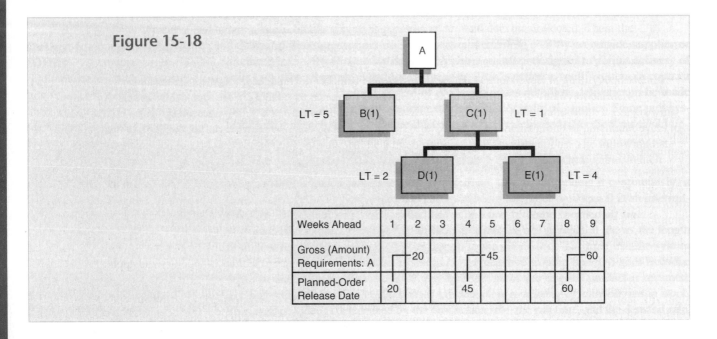

Figure 15-18

Weeks Ahead	1	2	3	4	5	6	7	8	9
Gross (Amount) Requirements: A		20			45				60
Planned-Order Release Date	20			45				60	

21 Complete the planned-order release chart in Figure 15-19 (marked *work sheet*) so that it applies to subassembly C, which requires two-for-one as shown in the following BOM.

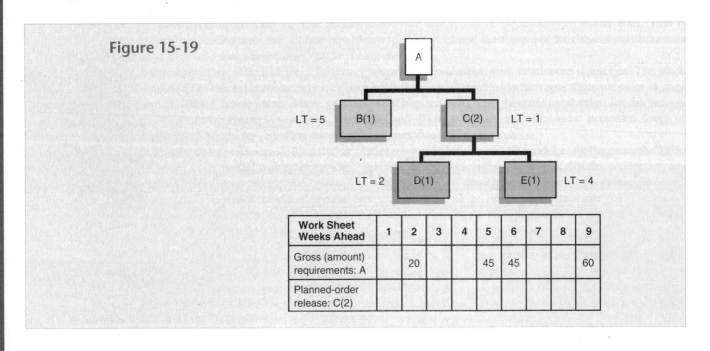

Figure 15-19

Work Sheet Weeks Ahead	1	2	3	4	5	6	7	8	9
Gross (amount) requirements: A		20			45	45			60
Planned-order release: C(2)									

22 Using Figure 15-19 in Problem 21, complete the following planned-order release chart below (marked *work sheet*) so that it applies to component D.

Work Sheet Weeks ahead	1	2	3	4	5	6	7	8	9
Gross (amount) requirements: A			25	35	40		20		60
Planned-order release: C(2)									
Planned-order release: D(1)									

Practice Quiz

1 MRP *evolutionized* the field of inventory management. There were major quantitative developments in the inventory-modeling field for order point policies during the late 1940s and early 1950s. Much research led to important extensions of methodology along the same line from 1950–1970. However, starting in the 1960s, and accelerating throughout the 1970s, MRP began to capture the imagination of inventory managers throughout the world. P/OM needs to be able to explain the differences between MRP and OPP to business students and executives alike. Toward that end, points a. to e. have been developed to provide a lexicon of ideas about these two branches of inventory theory and application. Identify the one point that is not suitable for the comparison of inventory systems.

   a. As much as 80 percent of manufactured goods is made in batches. Close to 100 percent of office operations conform to job shop methods. With the exception of quick-service restaurants, service functions vary between custom work and small batch production. Inventory systems for dealing with job shops and batched outputs are MRP-oriented.

   b. To explain why OPP inventory systems were the major focus of early research in inventory modeling requires understanding that analytic work in the 1940s and 1950s was influenced and paid for by military organizations. Military needs for *material* are both substantial and continuous over time. The logistics of supplying the Army, Navy, and Air Force are like the requirements of a flow shop production system. OPP is able to provide answers to such continuous demand systems.

   c. One of the main assumptions of OPP is that demand is driven by the marketplace, whereas a main assumption of MRP is that demand is driven by the number of end units to be made. OPP systems require a continuous and regular supply of units each and every day. MRP systems are designed to handle sporadic and irregular demand patterns.

   d. MRP part demands are dependent on the number of parent products scheduled to be made. However, if an MRP part is used by more than one parent-SKU, it is given a different part number and treated independently. Thus, production of the parent is not held up.

   e. The reason that demand for a parent product can be smooth while demand for components of that parent product are lumpy or pulsed is that different models of the parent product use different parts. For just this reason, Henry Ford always wanted to make only black Model T automobiles. That is because it is less expensive to deal with smooth demand than with irregular demand.

2 Material requirements planning operates as an intelligent information system. Understanding MRP inputs and MRP outputs is the first step to understanding what has to be done to make the system work. Choose the one statement (a. through e.) not appropriate to MRP as a proper inventory model.

   a. Input: Inventory information about stock on-hand levels, certified suppliers, prices, supplier lead times, problems, and complaints are part of the inventory record file (IRF). When a change occurs in these files, the information should be updated.

   b. Input: Bills of material with specifications of what goes into the makeup of the product. Also information on product-structure trees which includes part numbers, required number of each part, and level coding, including low-level capture. A part specification might be six screws, designated by B[6] at level 3.

   c. Input: Planned-order timetable with all indicated order release information. Definition of order release is that full specification of the vendor and the item is documented. Items are listed by SKU and each SKU shows the number of units ordered. This has been released to the vendor with confirmation requested.

   d. Input: The master production schedule (MPS) takes into account customer orders on-hand as well as forecasts for the parent products. The master production schedule takes into account the demand for capacity and allocates the capacity delivered by the aggregate planning model for the planning horizon that applied. The MPS makes the best use of the available resources for the actual market demands.

e. Output: Changes to earlier planned-order releases that may be needed because orders are canceled or due dates are changed. Also, performance reports are prepared and delivered including any exceptions that may have occurred.

3 A strong interaction exists between marketing and P/OM in a variety of business functions. One of the most apparent cases occurs when MRP receives its basic plan of action from the master production schedule (MPS). Choose the one statement (a. through e.) that does not appropriately describe the relationship between marketing and P/OM.

a. Order promising dates for delivery of items to customers is done by sales. Order fulfillment is done by P/OM using master production scheduling. If promised dates and fulfillment dates do not match, production has to accept what marketing says.

b. Establishing a make-to-stock environment may require adding capacity so that P/P/OM can build up inventories to provide a buffer against periods of heightened demand.

c. Having the best possible forecasts helps both marketing and P/P/OM to plan to deliver product as promised to important customers. It also helps marketing avoid making promises that cannot be fulfilled. Finally, it establishes a basis for assigning priorities to customers. The prioritizing methods could include keeping promises to customers who generate the most revenue. Many alternatives exist. One of the favorites is to increase priority customers who have been most delayed.

d. Especially in a make-to-order (MTO) environment, there is no inventory for sales to call upon for a customer. There is a lead time for production to make the promised items, which includes finishing the jobs that are being worked on. Priorities may be needed to establish who goes first in a queue of orders. Make-to-order is a tougher situation than make-to-stock and sell-from-stock.

e. Assemble-to-order environments pose different managerial problems than make-to-order ones. If the components and subassemblies are sourced from outside, led by reasonable forecasts, the right materials can be on hand in time for assembly. MRP systems provide lead-time guidance. Because there is less value-adding going on, the ability of production to react to new orders is enhanced as compared to fabrication from scratch. Nevertheless, there are problems that require that marketing and P/OM coordinate promises made and delivery schedules.

4 Interpreting a multilevel indented bill of material chart is necessary for inventory trainees working for MRP certification. The chart is accompanied by a list of points about BOM graphics, charts, and tables. Which one of these points is in error?

Multi-Level Indented BOM for CNB Corporation								
1	2	3	4	5	6	7	8	9
		Level	Code				Level	Code
CNBR		0			CNBD		0	
X(2)		1			G(2)		1	
	P(2)	2				P(2)	2	
	Q(1)	2				B(1)	2	
Y(1)		1			Y(1)		1	
	R(1)	2				R(1)	2	
	S(4)	2				S(4)	2	
	T(2)	2				T(2)	2	
Z(1)		1			V(1)		1	
	M(1)	2				C(1)	2	
	N(1)	2				D(1)	2	
B(1)		1			B(1)		1	2
	Q(2)	2				Q(2)	2	3

Note: Figures within parentheses are the number of units required.

a. The chart called *Multi-Level Indented BOM for CNB Corporation* presents subassemblies in columns 1 and 6, and parts in columns 2 and 7, for the newest computer notebooks of the CNB company. Two models are in production: the regular (CNBR) and the deluxe (CNBD). Alternative representation is available using structured trees instead of this tabular arrangement. In either case, the parent products CNBD and CNBR are at the top with level 0 designation. Level is shown in columns 3 and 8. The indented chart has four columns for each model. The two columns (4 and 9) marked *code* represent low-level coding for parts that require that designation.

b. There are four major subassemblies in each model. Two of them are shared by each notebook, viz., Y(1) and B(1). The demand levels for the shared subassemblies in each model will be added together by the MRP system. The same applies to the total demand for the shared parts that go into each of the subassemblies. MRP is able to cull out and integrate hundreds of shared parts, e.g., common nuts, bolts, and rivets.

c. Both notebook models draw on a set of shared parts. These are P, Q, R, S, and T. The number of units required for each model is the same except in the case of Q. One part Q is required for each subassembly X, and this only applies the CNBR. Two Xs are required for each CNBR, so two part Qs will be needed at level 2.

d. Levels for both models begin at zero. Subassemblies at level 1 proceed to parts at level. Two exceptions occur for model CNBD. In the first, low-level coding of 2 is required for the B subassembly. This is because B units are part of G subassemblies. MRP captures demand for B units at the lowest level and combines all demand for B, above that point. B also is a subassembly of the regular model. MRP will capture the demand for B in this usage as it searches for common part numbers across all models.

e. The second low-level code exception applies to the two units of Q in model CNBD. These Q are parts joining with subassembly B. Because B is low-level coded at two, Q must be low-level coded at 3. In this case, low-level coding requirements have moved B and Q each one level lower for the deluxe model. The effect on lead time is to delay the order by an additional time period. For example, order these parts one week earlier to allow the MRP system the extra time to move down the hierarchy to capture total demand for B and Q.

5 MRP has a basic structure that can be represented by mathematical equations. Not everyone enjoys the algebra, but it is essential to be able to recognize that these equations are the means by which MRP logic is translated from records into actions. There is one item that should be corrected before this list is shared with trainees from the company's inventory training program. Which item in a. to e. must be corrected?

a. For each parent or end-item, subassembly, part, etc., gross requirements (GR_t) are the total number of units demanded for week t. Inventory information is on file for the prior week's stock on-hand (SOH_{t-1}). Open orders that will be received at the beginning of week t are called: (SR_t). Then, projected stock on-hand at time t is $\hat{SOH}_t = SOH_{t-1} + SR_t$.

b. Gross requirements less projected stock on-hand at time t is called *net requirements*. Thus, $NR_t = GR_t - \hat{SOH}_t = GR_t - SOH_{t-1} - SR_t$. The process of determining net requirements is called *netting*.

c. Based on net requirements and ordering policies, the planned-order receipt times and planned-order release times are determined. If $\hat{SOH}_t > GR_t$, there would be stock on-hand at the end of period t. Thus, $\hat{SOH}_t = SOH_{t-1} + SR_t - GR_t > 0$. Net requirement would be zero because there is more stock on-hand than gross requirements. This means that gross requirements can be met out of inventory.

d. If gross requirements are greater than projected stock on-hand, then an order must be placed for the net requirements. In equations: $GR_t > \hat{SOH}_t$, then, $NR_t = 0$.

e. When an order is needed, it must be placed early enough so that delivery can be made in time. Lead time specifies what "early enough" means. Working backwards from planned-order receipt date, subtract lead time to determine planned-order release date. Planned-order receipt (PR_t) is zero when projected stock on-hand is greater than gross requirements. When projected stock on-hand is less than gross requirements, the size of PR_t must be determined: $\hat{SOH}_t = SOH_{t-1} + SR_t + PR_t - GR_t$. If lot-for-lot ordering is used, then planned-order receipt exactly equals the net requirements. Thus, $PR_t = NR_t$.

6 MRP has a basic structure that can be represented in tabular form. Although mathematical equations are responsible for triggering actions that are indicated by the table, it is feasible to operate the table manually. The MRP inventory trainees are taught to read the tables and to interpret what is taking place. They are being tested with a list of statements about the MRP tables. There is one item that should be corrected before this list is published and distributed. Which item in a. to e. must be corrected?

a. The table shows stock on-hand for Q at the beginning and end of period 1 is 100 units. Because Q(2) is the indicated usage, the number of end-items that can be made is 50 units of either CNBR or CNBD (or combinations).

b. Period 2 has gross requirements of 80 units. Satisfying this demand reduces the stock on-hand to 20 units and that SOH will continue through period 4.

Part Q										
End week	1	2	3	4	5	6	7	8	9	10
Gross requirements		80			100	100			70	
Stock on-hand	100	20	20	20	100					
Net requirements					80	100			70	
Planned-order receipt					180				70	
Planned-order release			180				70			

Stock on-hand at the start of $t = 1$ is 100 units; lead time is two weeks; 2 units of Q are need for each end item, i.e., Q(2); Q demand is accumulated from CNBR and CNBD; the lot sizing policy is lot-for-lot except where net requirements are greater than zero for two consecutive weeks, in which case, combine the two weeks net requirements.

c. The gross requirements of 100 units in period 5 draw down the SOH $= 20$ units to zero units. GR_5 triggered NR_5 of 80 units, and these in turn required a planned-order receipt of 80 units. That led to a planned-order release of 80 units in period 3 because the $LT = 2$ weeks. The table is not correct and needs to be redrawn to show that planned order release in period 3 is 80 units.

d. The fact that planned-order release is 180 units in period 3 stems from the rule in the legend that lot-for-lot sizing would be bypassed if net requirements are greater than zero for two consecutive weeks. That occurred for NR_5 and NR_6. As a result, the planned-order release is 180 units in week 3 for planned-order receipt of 180 units in week 5.

e. In week 5, $GR_5 = 100$; SOH contributes 20; 180 units received; 80 used for gross requirements; leaving 100 units as new SOH.

7 Another type of MRP table puts together a summary of the ordering status of end products, subassemblies, and parts. Because of interactions between parts and dependencies between parents, this table requires understanding and patience on the part of the user. An example of the format has been created for use by the inventory manager training program. The summary table is a reporting form rather than a calculation sheet for updating information. The table reports on the number of units expected to be delivered (planned-order receipts) over an 8-week period. It is important to confirm that the units required will be on hand to meet the gross requirements, which are shown in the parent row of the table. Students understand that to fulfill planned-order receipts, planned-order releases have been activated with the appropriate lead times. Inventory trainees are taught to read the tables and to interpret situations. Trainees are being tested with a list of statements about the MRP summary table. There is one item that should be corrected before this list is published and distributed. Which item in a. to e. must be corrected?

MRP Summary—Schedule of Planned-Order Receipts									
SOH	End Week	1	2	3	4	5	6	7	8
	SKU Name								
10	Parent–CNBD		80			100			70
80	Subassembly—G(2)		60			200			140
00	Part P(2)	120			400			280	
30	Part B(1)	30			200			140	
00	Subassembly—B (1)		70			100			70
25	Part Q(2)	115			200			140	

Parent gross requirements are 80 in week 2, 100 in week 5, and 70 in week 8; lead time is one week to obtain parts P, B, and Q, and assemble them into subassemblies. Figures in parentheses indicate the number of units required for assembly.

a. Left-hand column of the table shows SOH for parent, subassemblies G(2) and B(1), and parts that go into subassemblies. Two G(2) and one B(1) are needed to assemble each parent unit by the due dates. The parent-CNBD has 10 units of SOH. Therefore, only 70 units will be needed in week 2.

b.   Part B is both a subassembly of the parent-CNBD, and a part of the G(2) subassembly. SOH for part B is shown as 30 units. The error being looked for in the table is that SOH for the subassembly is shown as zero. This should be corrected by showing 30 units of SOH for both the subassembly and for the part.

c.   SOH for subassembly G(2) is 80. Because two units of G are required for each parent unit, and 70 parent units are required in week 2, then, 140 units of G are needed. 80 units can be drawn from stock. Then, 60 units have planned-order receipt in week 2.

d.   To make 60 units of G, 120 units of part P(2) are needed (two Ps for one G). No SOH exists for P. Therefore, a planned-order receipt is required for P in week 1.

e.   If there was no SOH for Part B(1), 60 units would be required. However, part B has 30 units of SOH. The net requirement for Part B(1) is 30 units.

8   The analysis of the MRP summary table in Problem 7 has not been completed. Inventory trainees are assigned a new list of statements concerning the information in that table. One item should be corrected before this list is finalized and placed in the trainee's binders. Which item in a. to e. must be corrected?

a.   SOH for subassembly B(1) is zero. The SOH for part B(1) has been assigned to the subassembly G(2). Then, 70 units of B(1) are required in week 2 because one unit of B (the subassembly) is required for each parent unit, and 70 parent units are required in week 2.

b.   To make 70 units of B(1), a planned-order receipt of 115 units will be required in week 1 for part Q(2). Because two Q parts are required for each subassembly, B(1), there are 140 units to be supplied. SOH for part Q is 25 units. Therefore, $140 - 25 = 115$ units.

c.   The remainder of the schedule functions on a lot-for-lot basis. Thus, week 5 gross requirement for the parent-CNBD is 100 units. There is no stock on-hand for any of the parts or subassemblies. This leads to speculation about ordering policy. Might it have been better to order larger quantities of parts (and subassemblies) in the period of weeks 1 and 2?

d.   If larger quantities had been ordered of parts and subassemblies in weeks 1 and 2, there would have been additional carrying costs. The week before the start of this MRP summary table showed significant amounts of SOH. This means that larger than lot-for-lot orders had been policy before weeks 1 through 8.

e.   There is a lot of volatility in the gross requirements stated for CNBD. If the other model had been included in the MRP summary table, it might have smoothed demand for commonly shared parts and subassemblies. In fact, Bs, Ps, and Qs are known to be common with model CNBR. These should have been included in the MRP analysis. Unless, some unknown other factor has intervened, there is a possible error in the MRP system because shared parts have not been represented.

9   A series of statements has been prepared to describe various aspects of MRP. These cover a number of issues that the well-rounded inventory manager should be able to discuss with comfort. Statements a. through f. are circulating within the company, and one of them is not correct. Which is the flawed statement?

a.   If there are significant setup costs, lot-for-lot sizing is not going to deliver a minimum cost method of order sizing. Multiply the number of lot-for-lot orders in a given time period by the setup cost (or the order cost). That gives the inventory cost because there are no carrying costs with lot-for-lot. Carrying some inventory during that same period can reduce the number of setups, which might offset some of the setup costs. Cut and try to get an equitable balance between the number of orders and the carrying costs.

b.   MRP is not immune to last-minute changes that strand inventory developed on a make-to-order basis. Stranded inventory units can be carried for long periods of time, or sold as salvage, or destroyed. Real-life scenarios may favor ordering policies that are closer to lot-for-lot because they reduce exposure to the costs of stranded units.

c.   The part-period model uses an economic part-period criterion based on annual demand (D) and economic reorder interval (t_o) which is the inverse of the economic number of orders, $t_o = 1/n_o = \sqrt{2C_r \div cC_cD}$.

c.   The other symbols are familiar from the EOQ model. Part-period balancing divides the year by t_o (say $t_o = $ 4 weeks), which means there will be 13 orders. The average inventory carried during the 4 weeks is calculated and compared to the cost of an order. If the inventory carrying cost is greater than the ordering cost, increase the number of orders. Continuing in this way, a nonoptimal heuristic-type solution is obtained.

d.   The economic part-period is an attempt to achieve a minimum total cost policy for planned-order release size. Lot-for-lot is one extreme where no carrying charges are incurred. More than lot-for-lot order size results in carrying costs. The minimum total cost policy occurs when setup or ordering costs are equal to carrying costs. The estimate of economic part-period is an effort to achieve this state.

$$\text{Economic Part-Period} = \frac{\text{Total Setup Costs}}{\text{Unit Carrying Cost per Period}}$$

e. Calculations of all kinds must be checked frequently because conditions change. The two most-used methods of updating MRP data sets are regeneration MRP and net change MRP. Regeneration is more time-consuming but it is to be avoided because it can introduce new errors as the total data system undergoes revision.

f. There is a short-range picture of shifting capacities and the long-range view of commitments to strategic alterations. Capacity requirements planning (CRP) addresses the former, which are "the more immediate problems." MRP II is the approach used for the longer-range, strategic solutions to capacity imbalance.

10 The series of statements about MRP that began with Problem 9 has been continued by the training staff because they have been well-received as discussion points. The idea has prevailed that an inventory manager should not be viewed as a specialist but as a generalist with a systems perspective that encompasses business strategy. Discussion statements a. through e. are designed to raise issues about the evolution of MRP to higher and higher decision and control levels within the enterprise. There is a flawed statement. Which one is it?

a. Although rough-cut capacity planning (RCCP) uses approximation to determine if there is sufficient capacity to accomplish objectives, it is viewed by management as a strategic heuristic.

b. Distribution resource planning (DRP) provides a strategic view of supply chain management. It is very much akin to MRP II, but the emphasis is on logistics rather than on manufacturing. The distinction is useful because distribution requirements planning is more like MRP. Thus, distribution resource planning is an extension of distribution requirements planning. It addresses what additional resources are needed in the distribution system.

c. One of the major weaknesses of MRP systems is the vulnerability to variability in lead time. The MRP report states that parent-CNBD can be made but the delivery trucks with part Q have not arrived. The MRP schedule can be searched to find alternative options for the facilities. However, operating under uncertainty is not one of MRP's strong points.

d. Closed-loop MRP operates at a cut below strategic planning. It is able to include all elements that bear on scheduling decisions as they are currently structured in the system. Strategy contemplates restructuring opportunities, whereas closed-loop MRP includes executive functions for the overall system with feedback fully operative. It is a strong managerial MRP system.

e. MRP II was the precursor of ERP. In many ways, MRP II provided a better structure than ERP because it centered on the production operations of the firm. ERP has a loftier vantage point, but it also may be too far removed for dealing effectively with issues "where the rubber meets the road."

Additional Readings

AGRA Software. *FastMan* (MRP software). (613-596-3344). Ottawa, Ontario, Canada, 1993.

Baker, K. R. "Requirements Planning," in S. C. Graves, A. H. G. Rinnooy Khan, and P. Zipkin (eds.). *Logistics of Production and Inventory*. Amsterdam: North-Holland Publishing Company, 1993.

Berry, William, Thomas E. Vollman, and D. Clay Whybark. *Master Production Scheduling: Principles and Practice*. Washington, DC: American Production and Inventory Control Society, 1979.

Buzacott, J. A., and J. G. Shanthikumar. "Safety Stock Versus Safety Time in MRP Controlled Production Systems." *Management Science*, vol. 40, no. 12 (December 1994): 1678–1689.

Cox, James F., John H. Blackstone, Michael S. Spencer. *APICS Dictionary*, 7e. APICS Educational and Research Foundation, 1992.

Donath, Bob. The IOMA Handbook of Logistics and Inventory Management. Institute of Management and Administration. Hoboken, NJ: John Wiley & Sons, Inc., 2002. Pages 396–400 emphasize constraint-based MRP where M is taken as "manufacturing" instead of "material."

Hamilton, Scott. *Maximizing Your ERP System: A Practical Guide for Managers*. New York: McGraw-Hill, 2003.

Heady, R. B., and Z. Zhu. "An Improved Implementation of the Wagner-Whitin Algorithm." *Production and Operations Management Journal*, vol. 3, no. 1 (Winter 1994).

Martin, Andre. *Distribution Resource Planning*. Williston, VT: Owl Publications, Inc., 1982.

MRP and ERP White Papers—2007. http://www.knowledgestorm.com. At the search window enter the keyword MRP to find various appropriate white papers.

Orlicky, Joseph. *Material Requirements Planning*. New York: McGraw-Hill, 1975.

Stern, Joel M., and John S. Shiely (with Irwin Ross). *The EVA Challenge: Implementing Value Added Change in an Organization*. New York: John Wiley & Sons, February 2001. (Chapter 6 extends EVA to the Shop Floor.)

Vollman, Thomas E., William L. Berry, and D. Clay Whybark. *Manufacturing Planning and Control Systems*, 3e. Homewood, IL: Irwin, 1992.

Wight, Oliver W. *The Executive's Guide to Successful MRP II*. Williston, VT: Owl Publications, Inc., 1981.

———. *MRP II, Unlocking America's Productivity Potential*. Boston: CBI Publishing Co., 1982.

Young, S. David, and Stephen F. O'Byrne. *EVA and Value-Based Management: A Practical Guide to Implementation*. New York: McGraw-Hill Trade, November 2000. (MRP in this text is market risk premium; however, economic value-adding is highly related to the goals of MRP II.)

Notes

1. Joseph Orlicky. *Material Requirements Planning*. New York: McGraw-Hill, 1975, p. ix.

2. Oliver W. Wight. "Designing and Implementing a Material Requirements Planning System." *Proceedings of the 13th International Conference of APICS, 1970*. The quote appears in Joseph Orlicky, *Material Requirements Planning*. New York: McGraw-Hill, 1975, p. 1.

3. James F. Cox and John H. Blackstone (eds). *APICS Dictionary,* 11e. APICS Educational and Research Foundation, 2004.

4. Ibid.

5. Ibid.

6. Ibid.

7. Orlicky, op. cit., p. 56.

8. Thomas E. Vollman, William L. Berry and D. Clay Whybark. *Manufacturing Planning and Control Systems,* 3e. Homewood, IL: 1992, p. 34.

9. R. B. Heady and Z. Zhu. "An Improved Implementation of the Wagner-Whitin Algorithm." *Production and Operations Management Journal,* vol. 3, no. 1 (Winter 1994), pp. 55–63.

10. APICS Dictionary, 11e, 2004.

11. Ibid.

12. Ibid.

13. Ibid.

14. Ibid.

15. Oliver W. Wight. *MRP II: Unlocking America's Productivity Potential.* Boston: CBI Publishing Co., 1982.

16. Scott Hamilton. *Maximizing Your ERP System: A Practical Guide for Managers.* New York: McGraw-Hill, 2003.

Enrichment Activity 15: Part-Period, Lot-Sizing Policy for MRP

The lot-for-lot policy—without errors, cancellations, or changes in order size—exactly matches orders to requirements. Therefore, there would be no carrying cost and many orders. If placing orders is expensive because a new setup is required in each case, then there would be a preference for fewer orders and some carrying costs. Consequently, a lot-sizing policy that is worthy of consideration is one that balances setup costs with carrying costs.

Ordering more than lot-for-lot results in parts being carried over periods of time. This statement is the basis for the part-period lot-sizing policy. It is an attempt to achieve the minimum total cost policy, which occurs when setup, or ordering, costs are equal to carrying costs. An estimate can be made of the economic part-period. Thus:

$$\text{Economic Part-Period} = \frac{\text{Total Setup Costs}}{\text{Unit Carrying Cost per Period}} \qquad (EA15\text{-}1)$$

The dimensions of this measure are unit months, or whatever time period the carrying costs embody.

Assume that the following costs have been estimated: The unit cost of the part is $10, the carrying cost rate is 1.00 percent per month, and the unit carrying cost for one month is then $10(0.01) = $0.10. The setup cost to produce this component is $15.

$$\text{Economic Part Period} = \frac{\text{Total Setup Costs}}{\text{Unit Carrying Costs per Period}} = \frac{\$15.00}{\$0.10} = 150 \text{ Unit Months} \qquad (EA15\text{-}2)$$

	Month	Net Requirements	Cumulative Lot Size	Months Carried	Carrying Cost/ Unit	Policy Is: Order for Months Numbered
Table EA15-1 Data Required for Part-Period Lot Sizing	1	20	20	0	$0	1
	2	40	60	1	$4	1+2
	3	60	120	2	$16	1+2+3
	4	30	150	3	$25	1+2+3+4

Next, calculate the number of unit months (part-periods) of each possible ordering policy.

Table EA15-1 lists monthly net requirements. These are summed in the column titled "Cumulative Lot Size." Thus, if the order is to produce enough for the first month only, then the lot size will be 20 units. If the order is to produce enough for the first 4 months, then the lot size will be 150 units, etc. The carrying cost per unit calculations is shown here.

The carrying cost is determined for each policy. If the policy is to produce or order enough for only the first month, then there are no carrying costs:

$$20 \text{ units carried for 0 months} = 0 \text{ part-periods or unit months}$$

Producing or ordering for 2 months entails no carrying charges for the first 20 units. They will be used for production in month 1. There are carrying costs of $4 per unit for the second month. Thus:

$$20 \text{ units} \times \$10/\text{unit} \times (0.01) \times 0 \text{ months carried} = \$0$$
$$40 \text{ units} \times \$10/\text{unit} \times (0.01) \times 1 \text{ month carried} = \$4$$
Total units ordered for 2 months = 60 units
Part-periods = $(40 \times 1) = 40$ unit months
Total cost = $4

Producing or ordering 120 units for the first 3 months requires:

$$0 \text{ units} \times \$10/\text{unit} \times (0.01) \times 0 \text{ months carried} = \$0$$
$$40 \text{ units} \times \$10/\text{unit} \times (0.01) \times 1 \text{ month carried} = \$4$$
$$60 \text{ units} \times \$10/\text{unit} \times (0.01) \times 2 \text{ months carried} = \$12$$
Total units ordered for 3 months = 120 units
Part-periods = $(40 \times 1) + (60 \times 2) = 160$ unit months
Total cost = $16

This ordering policy for the first 3 months comes close to matching the prior determination of the economic part-period, which was 150 unit months. It is necessary to see whether the next ordering policy for the first 4 months can come as close.

To determine the carrying cost of producing 150 units for 4 months' requirements, simply add the 3-month total to the carrying cost of the fourth month's net requirements.

$$30 \text{ units} \times \$10/\text{unit} \times (0.01) \times 3 \text{ months carried} = \$9$$
Carried forward from 3-month lot-size policy = $16
Total units ordered for 4 months = 150 units
Part-periods = $(40 \times 1) + (60 \times 2) + (30 \times 3) = 250$ part-periods
Total cost = $25

The 3-month ordering policy is indicated in two related ways. First, its economic part-period policy is closest (150 versus 160). Second, the setup cost of $15 is closest to the carrying-cost charges of $16 for a lot size of 3 months' requirements. That meets the criterion of balancing these two opposing costs. Consequently, produce or order 120 units.

The deviation between the economic part-period measure and the chosen order size will vary as a function of the actual net requirements, as shown in Table EA15-1.

Enrichment Challenges 15

1 Determine the production or order quantity for Table EA15-1 when the setup, or ordering, cost is $24.

2 Assume that the following costs have been estimated: The per unit cost of the part is $50, the carrying-cost rate is 2 percent per month, and the setup cost to produce this part is $75. What is the economic part-period?

3 Using the information in Problem 2, calculate the number of unit months (part-periods) of each possible ordering policy for the following table.

Month	Net Requirements	Cumulative Lot Size	Months Carried	Carrying Cost/Unit	Policy Is: Order for Months Numbered
1	30		0		1
2	50		1		1+2
3	20		2		1+2+3
4	40		3		1+2+3+4
5	30		4		1+2+3+4+5
6	25		5		1+2+3+4+5+6

Then, determine the production or order quantity to be used.

4 When the order is placed in Problem 3, start the calculations again from that point. Derive the next order quantity and continue in this way until the data are used up.

5 Use the part-period lot-sizing method for the data in Problem 1 of the Problems Section in Chapter 15.

Production Scheduling for Manufacturing and Service Operations

16

Chapter 16 presents the important topic of production scheduling for both manufacturers and service organizations. In essence, production scheduling is planning when jobs are to be started and finished, who is going to do them, where, and in what order. These production-scheduling plans are accomplished by the shop loading function and by the sequencing function for the job shop. *Loading* consists of assigning jobs that are on hand to departments or work centers. Loading is done by P/OM for both services and manufacturing. Load charting is detailed and three loading methods are explained. These are based on the assignment method, the transportation method, and a particular heuristic method. *Sequencing* for both services and manufacturing is the next logical procedure. It completes assignments by specifying the *order* in which jobs are to be done. Various sequencing policies are described.

After reading this chapter, you should be able to:

- Explain why production scheduling must be done by every organization whether it manufactures or provides services.
- Discuss the application of loading to the job shop (often called *job shop loading* or *shop loading*).
- Draw a Gantt load chart and explain its information display.
- Describe how to resolve the loading problem where teams compete for permanent assignment to the best facilities.
- Explain why "best assignments" require the systems approach.
- Relate best-loading assignments to opportunity costs in terms of lowest cost, greatest profit, or fastest completion time.
- Detail the strengths and weaknesses of the assignment model.
- Describe how the transportation model resolves the "no splitting" problem of the assignment model.
- Detail strengths and weaknesses of the transportation model.
- Describe the role of sequencing and how to apply sequencing rules for one facility and for more than one facility.
- Explain the purpose of priority sequencing rules and the means for using them.
- Describe the critical ratio and other priority rules for sequencing.
- Explain how finite scheduling and the TOC/OPT concept take bottlenecks into account.
- Discuss changing the capacity of bottlenecks.
- Explain queue control and synchronized manufacturing.

The Systems Viewpoint

Department scheduling decisions rarely achieve optimal assignments for every job at every facility. Best assignments can seldom be made on a one-by-one basis. Instead, the problem must be looked at as a whole. As an analogy, NASA found that if every component of a space vehicle is optimized with respect to its function and only its function, the "bird will not fly." Instead, the vehicle must be designed together as a coordinated system of components. The same applies to scheduling for the job shop. The assignment of work and its timing need to be orchestrated. Bottlenecks need to be taken into account, and the goal of synchronized manufacturing requires coordination of the entire job shop with respect to the mix of jobs that is being orchestrated.

The systems approach is called for so that the total set of assignments is optimized. The system's total costs are minimized or the total profits are maximized. Total quality (the sum of individual item qualities) and total productivity (the sum of individual item productivities) are maximized. This means that each and every item is not at maximum quality and productivity. The nature of the goal is to select assignments that—although less than best individually—result in the overall system's best.

Strategic Thinking

Production scheduling is always a system's problem because jobs, people, and teams compete with each other for best facilities. Jobs (as surrogates for customers) also compete with each other concerning which gets done first. Facilities contend with each other for jobs. Departments that do similar work compete with each other for preferred work. Orders placed with suppliers are tied to priorities with respect to jobs and customers—so suppliers' orders also rival each other in terms of importance and how they are treated.

Strategic planning is required to design the facilities, staff the departments, select suppliers, and design the product mix—for the expected blend of job shop orders. In contrast, the flow shop has a specific set of items to be made in volume on dedicated facilities. The flow shop system is predesigned to optimize through synchronization the production schedule.

With the job shop, the company must achieve systems optimization to rationalize the various preferences in a way that is not self-defeating. When the systems point of view prevails, the solutions are company-wide optimizations even though people and facilities experience suboptimal assignments. Over time, the facilities need to be altered in such a way as to minimize the degree of suboptimization. That requires strategic thinking.

16-1 Production Scheduling: Overview

The final step of **production scheduling** assigns actual jobs to designated facilities with unambiguous stipulations that they be completed at specific times. The steps in scheduling will be reviewed here, moving from generic resource planning to actual assignments at workstations.

1 *Aggregate scheduling* developed resource plans based on forecasts of orders in generic units such as standard hours.
2 Later, with actual orders on hand or with reasonable predictions about orders, the *master production schedule (MPS)* assigned jobs to time slots to permit orders to be placed for required materials using *material requirements planning (MRP)*. These time period assignments are so well defined that they are referred to as *time buckets.*
3 The next step in production scheduling is to load facilities, which means taking the actual orders and assigning them to designated facilities. **Loading** answers the question: Which department is going to do what work? **Sequencing** answers the question: What is the order in which the work will be done?

To summarize, the third step in production scheduling does both loading and sequencing. Loading assumes that the material requirement analysis has been done and that orders have been properly placed for required materials and for needed parts and subassemblies. It further assumes that the parts will be on hand, as planned. A problem in supplier shipments will delay scheduling production of the affected order.

Specifically, loading assigns the work to divisions, departments, work centers, load centers, stations, and people. Whatever names are used in a given organization, orders

Production scheduling
Consists of loading and sequencing; used to deal with the difficulty of optimizing detailed complex arrays of data for all possible schedules.

Loading
Which jobs are to be assigned to which teams or facilities.

Sequencing
Job order can make a big difference in the flow time, which is the length of time it takes to process a sequence of *n* jobs.

are assigned to those who will be responsible for performing the work. Loading releases jobs to facilities.

At this point, sequencing will be explained so that the entire process of production scheduling will be clear to the reader. Sequencing models and methods follow the discussion of loading models and methods. Sequencing involves **shop floor control**, which consists of communicating the status of orders and the productivity of workstations. Sequencing assigns priorities that determine the order with which work will be done. Say that Jobs *x, y,* and *z* have been assigned to workstation 1 (loading). Jobs *x, y,* and *z* are in a queue (waiting line). Sequencing rules determine which job should be first in line, which second, etc. The objective function can be to minimize system's costs, or to minimize total system's time, or (if margin data are available) to maximize total system's profit.

Shop floor control

Tracking and communicating the status of orders; monitoring and reporting on the productivity of workstations.

16-2 Loading

Loading, also called *shop loading*, is required to assign specific jobs or teams to specific facilities. Loading is needed for machine shops, hospitals, and offices. Although loading assigns work to facilities, it does not specify the order in which jobs should be done at the facility. Sequencing methods (described later) determine the order of work at the facility.

16-2a Plan to Load Real Jobs—Not Forecasts

Aggregate scheduling used standard hours based on forecasts to determine what resources should be assembled over the planning horizon. Loading takes place in the job shop when the real orders are on hand. If the aggregate scheduling job was done well, then the appropriate kinds and amounts of resources are available for loading. The master production schedule also made resource assignments that could be modified if capacity was not adequate. Planning actual shop assignments is a regular, repetitive managerial responsibility. Releasing the jobs, as per assignment, is another.

Each facility carries a backlog of work, which is its "load"—hardly a case of perfect just-in-time in which no waiting occurs. The backlog is generally much larger than the work in process, which can be seen on the shop floor. This is because work not assigned yet is waiting, but not visible. A major objective of loading is to spread the load so that waiting is minimized, flow is smooth and rapid, and congestion is avoided.

These objectives are constrained by the fact that not all workstations can do all kinds of jobs. Even though the job shop uses general-purpose equipment, some workstations and people are better suited for specific jobs than are others. Some stations cannot do jobs that others can do. Some are faster than others and tend to be overloaded. The scheduling objective is to smooth the load with balanced work assignments at stations.

Gantt load charts

Load charts provide a graphic system to visualize how much work has been assigned to each facility.

© 2008 Jupiterimages Corporation

Gantt load charts lead to discussions about many factors that go into their creation, such as suppliers that have not delivered, machines that are not working, and absent employees who have certain skills.

16-3 Gantt Load Charts

The use of Gantt charts for loading dates to the early 1900s when Henry L. Gantt (1861–1919) developed them as a formal means for assigning jobs to facilities and charting job progress. **Gantt load charts** provide a graphic system that is easy to follow by visualizing the progress of jobs and the load on departments. Often these two purposes are combined on one chart. Too much job waiting (overloading), facilities not working at full utilization (underloading), or load imbalances between stations (some busy, others idle) could be seen immediately by someone familiar with these charts.

Gantt charts deal with the system's realities of loading for production scheduling. These are issues such as which jobs have not started that should have started, how much progress toward completion has been made, which departments are overloaded, and which ones are underloaded.

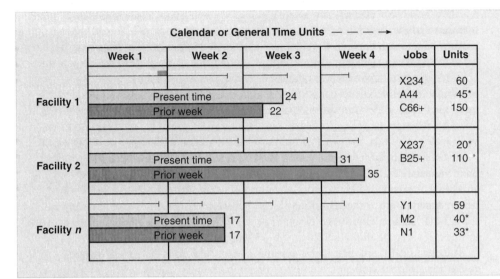

Figure 16-1

Gantt Load Chart

This traditional Gantt load chart has been used for over 100 years in essentially the same form. The legend explaining lines, bars, and other chart marks is given in Section 16-3a.

The ideal situation is creative customization (of load scheduling charts) that meets the needs of the process managers and the sales department. Proper charts reflect the interests of customers and the impact of suppliers. Figure 16-1 illustrates the Gantt load chart and the discussion that follows explains it.

The Gantt load chart in Figure 16-1 has a time scale running along the top. The rows represent resources: people, machines, stations, departments, or whatever facilities will be required to do the job. The time scale is labeled in either dated calendar time or with general intervals ahead, such as weeks.

The left-hand side of the chart is the start time. Depending on the time scale, a specific date can be used, or it can be called *time zero*. Bars and lines, running from left to right, convey various kinds of information designed to help the department schedule its production needs.

16-3a Gantt Chart Legend

- For each facility, and week, there is a box that contains a horizontal line and two bars under that line. The lines and bars for each week are divided into 10 units of time. For all four weeks, there are 40 units of time.
- The single horizontal line is the workload percent by the week. All lines start at the left. Moving to the right represents higher percentages of utilization. If the line runs from one side of the box to the other side, then that facility is 100 percent loaded for the week.
- Sequencing decisions have been reached with respect to weekly assignments as per the master production schedule. Orders have been placed with suppliers. Lead times have been calculated so that materials will be received in time to permit production to begin the job in that week. The order in which jobs will be done within each week has not yet been determined. Note: If the time buckets are monthly, then all times are monthly to be consistent.
- The jobs column describes all of the jobs that are waiting at that facility. To the right of the job name is the number of units to be made for that order. The load consists of on-time jobs and backlogged jobs. Work is on time when it is scheduled for production so that delivery can be made on or before the promised **due date**. Work is backlogged when it is going to be late. This is shown by an asterisk in the units column. An additional column can be added to the Gantt load chart to explain the causes and extent of delays.
- The top bar (light gray) is the cumulative workload at the present time.
- The bottom bar (dark gray) is the cumulative workload at the beginning of the prior week.

Due date

Order promising shows up as a due date on the production schedule.

The cumulative load at each facility is presented in two ways. First, there is the load that exists at the beginning of the current week. Second, there is the load that existed at the beginning of the prior week. Comparing these can be useful to determine where and when the load is increasing, decreasing, or staying the same. This helps the scheduler to assign load where it can be best processed.

Which departments are underutilized *can be seen at a glance.* That is one of the primary purposes of the Gantt chart, which makes no pretense at being a method for optimizing assignments. In management science terms, *Gantt graphics facilitate heuristic methods*—which rely on "rules of thumb" and sound generalizations developed from experience. OM decisions must often be made with fast data scans ("eyeballing") that rely on the assistance of charts such as the Gantt load chart.

The charts can deliver additional information as well. They can show that certain departments have reserved time for preventive maintenance. This would be indicated by blocking off time along the horizontal line. Facility 1 has blocked 10 percent of its time in week 1 with a small box to indicate preventive maintenance.

The charts can show that particular jobs cannot be split up. This is shown by a + sign in the jobs column. Running one job in two departments would mean two setups, which can take too much time, cost a lot, and adversely impact quality control. Two different setups cannot have the same statistical fingerprints. For some jobs, this lack of homogeneity can be a serious problem. Good Gantt charting prevents split assignments that impair productivity and quality.

When jobs cannot be split, for the economic and quality reasons mentioned earlier, they must wait until there is sufficient time available in appropriate departments. Note that facility 2 has 10 percent idle time in the second week. If it does not require scheduled maintenance, this time could be used for process improvement, training, and cross-training exercises.

When meeting due dates is a problem, it is useful to add cumulative backlog of jobs to the Gantt chart. As with total load, the cumulative backlog data should be shown for the current week and the prior week. This information will indicate whether the backlog is increasing, decreasing, or staying about the same. Note: At facility 1, load has increased from 22/40 to 24/40. At facility 2, load has decreased from 35/40 to 31/40. However, it could be that backlog has decreased at the first facility and increased at the second one. Thus, when due date problems are a concern, the Gantt chart should reflect that fact.

As an illustration, the load scenario for facility 1 with due date considerations might be as follows:

Week Number	Load Level Percent of Capacity	Cumulative Load: Current	Cumulative Load: Prior	Cumulative Backlog: Current	Cumulative Backlog: Prior
1	90	9/10	10/10	3/10	2/10
2	70	16/20	15/20	5/20	4/20
3	50	24/30	19/30	6/30	6/30
4	30	24/40	22/40	6/40	7/40

The load at facility 1 in week 3 has increased from 22/30 to 24/30. Cumulative work load in week 4 shows signs of decreasing. Due date problems (backlog) have diminished, in week 4 going from 7/40 to 6/40. Accompanying notes can indicate which backlog situations are considered to be the most serious.

Studying load charts can reveal whether there is a long-term capacity problem. It highlights bottlenecks and problem areas. When work that is scheduled is not completed on time, either the scheduler underestimated the time required for completion, or there is a process problem to be determined.

Constant matching of estimated and actual times improves the database for estimation, monitors process productivity, and reflects on the knowledge and skill of the schedulers.

It is important to strive for the load being equally distributed among facilities. Overloaded departments suffer morale problems, especially when they see other departments that have idle capacity. Long-term solutions may be needed to provide capacity balance.

This kind of information must be fed back to the MRP departments and the master production schedulers. Often, the original scheduling concepts were applicable but the character of the jobs changed. Shifting job requirements can lead to an imbalance in load among departments. The changes can favor different materials, machines, and skills. The variability of the order mix is a factor in planning capacity and taking corrective actions during aggregate scheduling. Variability in the loading mix is a difficult problem because the time for resource planning is long past.

Without knowing what the jobs are and the capabilities of the departments, it is not possible to evaluate how good a scheduling job has been done—both in the current week and in the weeks ahead. In a company where management knows its processes and its people, everyone in the organization should be aware of the schedule. Teamwork is the key to successfully adjusting to variability.

Employing the systems perspective, anyone who has some special knowledge that affects quality and/or productivity should feel empowered to communicate with those doing the scheduling. Inputs from various suppliers regarding schedules can be useful. Open lines to learn about customer needs may be essential and lead to schedule revisions.

16-4 The Assignment Method for Loading

The **assignment method** provides production scheduling with a decision model for matching jobs with facilities in an optimal way. Such loading of facilities determined by this model is subject to a variety of conditions.

The first scheduling question is always which facility, person, or department is best-suited to do the job. That raises another question: If the best-suited facility is occupied, or for any other reason unavailable, what facility is next best?

Using systems thinking, it becomes clear that these questions beg the issue, which is: What set of assignments will produce the overall best schedule? "Best" can be defined in many ways, including highest output quality, greatest productivity, lowest cost, fastest completion, or greatest profit. Best assignments (on a pair-by-pair basis) are unlikely to add up to optimal systems-wide solutions. The assignment problem must be visualized as a collection of paired assignments that interact as a whole.

The assignment model provides solutions when jobs compete for facilities where it is uneconomic to split the job. No splitting means that whichever facility, person, or team gets the job does the whole job. Usually this is because split job setup costs are prohibitive and/or quality control at two facilities is not manageable.

There may be tooling or equipment for only one location. Many factory jobs cannot be worked on at two locations simultaneously. Project assignments are generally of this singular-assignment type.

It is uncommon for department-loading decisions to achieve optimal assignments for every job at every facility. Therefore, it is the set of assignments that is to be optimized. The concessions—which make some assignments that are less than the best—should result in an overall systems best.

The assignment model is based on **opportunity costs**, which are the costs of not making the best possible assignments of jobs to facilities and vice versa. The reason that the best possible assignments cannot be made for every job is that jobs compete with each other for available time on those facilities for which they are best-suited. Thus, consider Table 16-1, which shows the cost per part for jobs 1, 2, and 3 at facilities A, B, and C.

Jobs 1 and 2 have their lowest cost per part when made at facility B. They are in direct competition with each other for the use of this facility. Job 3 has the lowest cost per part

Assignment method
A decision model for matching *n* resources with *n* resource users.

Opportunity costs
Costs of not making the best possible assignments of a set of resources to a set of resource users.

Table 16-1			Facilities		
Cost per Part for Jobs at Facilities			A	B	C
		1	0.10	0.09	0.12
	Jobs	2	0.08	0.07	0.09
		3	0.15	0.18	0.20

Table 16-2			Facilities		
Job Opportunity Costs— Using Row Subtraction			A	B	C
		1	0.01	0	0.03
	Jobs	2	0.01	0	0.02
		3	0	0.03	0.05

when assigned to facility A. It is not competing with any other job for that facility. However, this assignment cannot be made until the conflict between jobs 1 and 2 has been resolved. The reason is that whichever job is not assigned to facility B might be better assigned to facility A than job 3.

All the numbers in the matrix are interrelated. This is a systems problem. Assignments should not be made on an individual basis. The assignment model develops comparisons of penalties (opportunity costs) for making an assignment other than the best possible one. To make the necessary comparisons, subtract the smallest number in each row from all other numbers in that row. This yields Table 16-2, which is a matrix of the opportunity costs for not assigning each job to the best possible facility for that job. There is a zero in each job row.

All of the zeros in Table 16-2 are best possible job assignments. Because of the conflict between jobs 1 and 2 at facility B, the solution is stymied. Also, there is an assumption that the orders are of the same size. Otherwise, the matrix should represent total costs, not costs per unit as in Table 16-1. This means that the assignment problem would start with a matrix of total costs.

16-4a Column Subtraction—Best Job at a Specific Facility

Column subtraction yields the opportunity costs at a given facility for assigning jobs that are not the best jobs. These are facility opportunity costs. Using Table 16-1, subtract the smallest number in each column from all other numbers in that column. The opportunity costs of each facility with respect to jobs are shown in Table 16-3. There is a zero in each column.

Job 2 has all zero opportunity costs in its row. It is the preferred job at each facility. The facilities are in competition with each other for job 2. Therefore, thus far, there is no feasible assignment.

16-4b Row Subtraction—Best Facility for a Specific Job

The next step is to subtract the smallest number in each row of Table 16-3 from all other numbers in that row. The instruction is applicable only for rows 1 and 3 because row 2 has all zeros in it. Row subtraction provides the combined opportunity cost matrix in Table 16-4. It represents the penalty for each job being assigned to less than the best facility—and for each facility being assigned to less than the best job. Table 16-4 presents the total opportunity cost matrix.

Table 16-4 states that all jobs can be assigned to facility A with zero opportunity cost. If this were acceptable (assuming that there was other work to be done at facilities

		Facilities			Table 16-3
		A	B	C	Facility Opportunity
	1	0.02	0.02	0.03	Costs—Using Column
Jobs	2	0	0	0	Subtraction
	3	0.07	0.11	0.11	

		Facilities			Table 16-4
		A	B	C	Column Subtraction First,
	1	0	0*	0.01	Row Subtraction Second—
Jobs	2	0	0	0*	Yield Total Opportunity Cost
	3	0*	0.04	0.04	Matrix

(0^* = zeros chosen for assignment of jobs to facilities)

B and C), then a sequencing problem exists at facility A. That is, which job goes first, which goes second, and which goes third?

All jobs being assigned to facility A is not an acceptable option for this problem. Given that a job must be assigned to each facility without splitting, there is a feasible set of zero opportunity cost assignments. They are shown in the cells of Table 16-4 as asterisks on zeros, with the footnoted statement (* = zeros chosen for assignment of jobs to facilities).

The logic of this assignment starts with the fact that there is only one zero in column C and that is row 2. So, job 2 must be assigned to facility C. There is only one zero in row 3. Job 3 must be assigned to facility A. That forces the assignment of job 1 to facility B.

Note that Table 16-2 was derived by using row subtraction first. This yielded the opportunity costs of each job being assigned to less than the best facility. Using Table 16-2, apply column subtraction to derive the results of Table 16-5.

The same set of assignments as in Table 16-4 results. Although the final matrices are not identical, it is equally correct to use either row or column subtraction first. However, sometimes it turns out to be easier to use one first instead of the other to reduce the matrix to an assignable set of zeroes. There is no way of prejudging, which will be easier beforehand. Also, other complications can be encountered. To deal with them requires understanding all opportunity cost relationships of the cells of the assignment model or being able to use appropriate "assignment method" software.

It should be noted that if profit maximization is the goal, and the matrix in Table 16-1 had been profit data, then all profit numbers should be subtracted from a number larger than any one of them. To illustrate, if the profit per part, given by the matrix in Table 16-1, is subtracted from $1.00, the result is shown in Table 16-6.

Use the assignment method to minimize profit opportunity costs. The solution can be obtained by using row subtraction first—followed by column. The assignment remains

		Facilities			Table 16-5
		A	B	C	Row Subtraction First and
	1	0.01	0*	0.01	Then Column Subtraction
Jobs	2	0.01	0	0*	Second—Yield Another Valid
	3	0*	0.03	0.03	Total Opportunity Cost

(0^* = zeros chosen for assignment of jobs to facilities)

Matrix

Table 16-6		Facilities		
Matrix of Profit per Part (Related to Table 16-1)		**A**	**B**	**C**
	1	0.90	0.91	0.88
Jobs	2	0.92	0.93	0.91
	3	0.85	0.82	0.80

A3, B1, C2. It will be noted that if column subtraction is used first—followed by row subtraction—then an impasse occurs because all of column 1 and all of row 3 have zeros. There is a method for creating a new zero at the lowest value entry that remains. That change is compensated for by adding an opportunity cost to all existing zeros (twice at the intersection of the row and column of zeros). Then, row and column subtraction procedures previously described will continue until a final assignment solution is found.

The definition of profit opportunity cost is the cost of assigning a job to a facility that does not result in having the best possible profit. In Table 16-6, the assignment of job 2 to facility B results in the largest amount of missed profit, viz., 93 cents. When the matrix of costs in Table 16-6 is minimized, the total amount of missed profit is minimized.

Using the assignment method demonstrates the importance of opportunity costs for loading. The weakness (or strength, when it applies) of the assignment model is that only one job or team can be assigned to each department, facility, or machine at a time. No splitting of assignments is permitted. This condition accurately describes the permanent post of managers to stores, pilots to planes, and chefs to restaurants (i.e., splitting a row assignment between two columns). Also, two pilots cannot be assigned to one plane (i.e., splitting a column assignment between two rows).

16-5 The Transportation Method For Shop Loading

Under certain circumstances, a weakness of the assignment method was that no splits are allowed. When split assignments are allowed, the transportation method can be used. The transportation model embodies the transportation method, which permits assigning more than one job to a machine or team. In Table 16-7, machine 1 is assigned three jobs called A1, B1, and C1. Loading involves matching supply of available machine time, $S(i)$ with demand of jobs for machine time $D(j)$.

Another type of split prohibited by the assignment method is that no job can be divided with that method. In Table 16-7, job C has been split into three parts: C1, C2, and C3.

Although the transportation method overcomes assignment method difficulties, it has certain restrictive assumptions of its own. Split assignments are easy to make, but when demand in units, [called $D(j)$] is loaded against supply in machine hours [called $S(i)$], the amounts of supply and demand must be put into common terms. A convenient common terminology is to express supply and demand in standard hours.

Table 16-7	Jobs Are Columns (*j*)		Job A	Job B	Job C	Supply *S(i)* Actual Hours
Split Assignments of Two Kinds with the Transportation Model Used for Job Shop Loading		M1	A1	B1	C1	S(1) = 36
	Machines Are	M2			C2	S(2) = 54
	Rows (*i*)	M3			C3	S(3) = 80
	Demand D(*j*)		D(A)	D(B)	D(C)	

Machine (*i*)	SMH Index	Relative Productivity	Table 16-8
M1	0.5	Half as fast as the SM	Relative Productivity and the Equivalent SMH Index (for each machine *i*) SMH = standard machine hours
M2 (SM)	1.0	Standard machine	
M3	0.8	80% as fast as the SM	

To create standard hours *it is necessary to assume that strict proportionality exists between the productivity rates of the machines*. To review this concept (developed when explaining aggregate scheduling), note that in Table 16-8, machine 1 is half as fast as machine 2—which has arbitrarily been chosen to be the standard machine (SM). Similarly, M3 is 0.8 as fast as the SM.

The restrictive assumption is that the SMH index for each machine *applies to all jobs*. It is called the *presumption of productive proportionality*. Thus, M2 is fastest—*for all of the jobs*—by the same amount, in comparison with the other machines. M1 is half as fast as M2 *for all jobs*. The equation for the SMH index is derived in more general terms, as follows:

$$\text{SMH Index of } M(i,j) = \frac{\text{production output of } M(i,j)}{\text{production output of } M(SM,j)} \text{ (for all } j \text{ jobs)}$$

For each machine, when the SMH index is multiplied by the actual machine hours available per week, the standard machine hours (SMH) available per week are obtained. Table 16-9 provides the actual machine hours that are available per week converted by means of the SMH index into standard machine hours available per week. Table 16-9 concludes that total SMH = 136 per week. Note that a week was chosen as a convenient period. It could have been a day or a month.

The fact that there are 170 actual machine hours available per week has significance after the resolution of the standard hour problem. The transportation model is solved using the 136 standard hours that are available per week.

Table 16-10 provides production output rates (in pieces/hour) for each machine for every job. The entries in the matrix are labeled $PR(i,j)$ where i = machine and j = job, which is consistent with the notation throughout this section. The production rate of the standard machine for the jth job is $PR(SM,j)$. See the second row (machine M2) in Table 16-10.

Now, turning to Table 16-11, demands are initially stated as the *number of units ordered per job*. These can vary greatly because there are many different types of orders. For example, simple, small gears may be needed in large numbers whereas complex, large gears are expensive to make and have low demand. Orders such as these can put loads on the facilities for various lengths of time. An order for 300 C-type units would take 10 hours on the standard machine, M2. It would take 20 hours on M1.

Demand quantities for goods or services of type j, called $D(j)$, must be turned into standard hours to match the amount of supply available from machines of type I, called $S(i)$. Standard hours are also essential to balance out the production differences between making simple and complex products.

Machine	SMH Index	Actual Hours/Week	SMH per Week	Table 16-9
1	0.5	36	18	Department Time Converted into SMH
2 (SM)	1.0	54	54	
3	0.8	80	64	
Total:	Total actual hours/Week = 170 hours		Total SMH/Week = 136 SM hours	

Table 16-10	Jobs		A	B	C	SM Index
Production Rates *PR(i,j)* in Pieces per Hour for Machines *i* and Jobs *j*	**Machines**	M1	3	3.5	15	0.5
		M2	6	7	30	1.0 (SM)
		M3	4.8	5.6	24	0.8

Table 16-11	Calculation	Actual Units	Standard Hours of Demand
Convert Job Demands from Units to Standard Hours	$D(j) \div PR(SM, j) = D'(j)$		
	$D(A) \div PR(SM,A) = D'(A)$	300 A units ÷ 6 =	50 standard hours
	$D(B) \div PR(SM,B) = D'(B)$	210 B units ÷ 7 =	30 standard hours
	$D(C) \div PR(SM,C) = D'(C)$	1800 C units ÷ 30 =	60 standard hours
	Total standard hours of demand = 140		

To accomplish the transformation of all dimensions to standard hours, start by dividing the number of units demanded for job x by the production rate of the standard machine for job x. This yields demand in standard hours $D'(j)$ instead of demand in units $D(j)$. The equations for units of demand into standard hours of demand are shown on the left side of Table 16-11.

On the right side of Table 16-11 is the numerical calculation of units demanded divided by the production rates of the standard machine (SM) for each job. This produces numerical values of demand in standard hours. For example, 300 units of A when divided by 6 units per standard hour yields 50 standard hours.

Now, both supply and demand have been converted to the common terms of standard machine hours (SMH). There are only 136 standard machine hours available per week and 140 hours demanded to complete the orders. Therefore, $140 - 136 = 4$ standard machine hours of demand will not be satisfied this week. Specifically, supply is less than demand. A backorder will be created if allowed.

A dummy machine is created to pick up the slack. It is called MD (for machine dummy). By definition, MD has zero output for all jobs. Some part of whichever job is assigned to the dummy will not be done. The balanced supply and demand system with all numbers in standard hours including the output rates per standard hour in the upper right-hand corners of each assignment cell is given in Table 16-12.

As with the assignment method, profit can be used instead of cost with the transportation model. Profit per piece, π_j, is calculated for each job j. When π_j is multiplied by the product output rates $PR(i,j)$, the result is $\Pi_{ij} = \pi_j PR(i,j)$, which is profit per standard hour for each machine i. This formulation assumes that costs per piece are the same on all machines. If not, it would be necessary to use $\pi_{i,j}$ for each cell.

Specifically, when that assumption is incorrect, the revenue r_{ij} less the cost c_{ij} is multiplied by the product output rates $PR(i,j)$ for each cell in the matrix. Thus, where $\pi_{ij} =$ profit per piece for each cell i,j, and $\Pi_{ij} =$ profit per standard hour for each cell i,j:

$$\prod_{ij} = \pi_{ij}PR(i, j) = (r_{ij} - c_{ij})PR(i, j) \tag{16-1}$$

Often, the revenue is simply r_j because it is a function of the job and not the machine. However, if quality differences occur as a result of the machine used, which affects price charged, then Equation 16-1 should be used. Often, costs are unique, i.e., c_{ij}, and Equation 16-1 applies.

When the profit per piece is independent of the machine used, as shown in Table 16-13, then the optimal load assignments are as indicated by the numbers in the matrix

The bold numbers for supply and demand are in standard hours. The internal matrix values in the small boxes in the upper right-hand corner of each assignment cell are output/standard hour; internal numbers in the second row for M2 are the outputs of the standard machine with index = 1. The internal matrix values apply to each job on a specific machine.

Table 16-12

Transportation Model

	Job A	Job B	Job C	Supply $S(i)$
M1	3	3.5	15	**18**
M2	6	7	30	**54**
M3	4.8	5.6	24	**64**
MD	0	0	0	**4**
Demand $D(j)$	**50**	**30**	**60**	**140**

that sum to match the supply capabilities and the demand requirements. Note that the product output rates per standard hour have been multiplied by profit per piece to reflect the profit per standard hour. These are shown in the small boxes in the upper right-hand corner of each assignment cell.

The goal is to find the loading arrangement that uses the resources available to maximize total profit. The optimal loading schedule is shown in Table 16-13 in standard machine hours with the

$$\text{Maximum total profit } \left(\Sigma_i \, \Sigma_j \, \Pi_{ij} \right) = (18 \times 6) + (54 \times 15) + (32 \times 9.6)$$
$$+ (26 \times 5.6) + (6 \times 12) + (4 \times 0) = \$1,442.80$$

There are four rows and three columns, which means that $M + N - 1 = 6$ assignments should be made for the transportation model. The requisite six are in place. The optimal has been found for this example using the standard techniques employed to solve the

Table 16-13

Transportation Model: Matrix Adjusted for Profits, $\pi_{i,j}$

Profit per Piece	$2.00	$1.00	$0.50	
	Job A	Job B	Job C	Supply $S(i)$
M1	18 6	3.5	7.5	18
M2	12	7	54 15	54
M3	32 9.6	26 5.6	6 12	64
MD	0	4 0	0	4
Demand $D(j)$	50	30	60	140

Table 16-14

Transportation Model: Actual Assignments

	Job A	Job B	Job C	Supply $S(i)$
M1	36 ⟨3⟩	⟨3.5⟩	⟨15⟩	36
M2	⟨6⟩	⟨7⟩	54 ⟨30⟩	54
M3	40 ⟨4.8⟩	32.5 ⟨5.6⟩	7.5 ⟨24⟩	80
MD	⟨0⟩	4 ⟨0⟩	⟨0⟩	4
Demand Filled	300	182	1800	
Shortages	0	28	0	
Demand $D(j)$	300	210	1800	

transportation model. Software is readily available to solve transportation problems involving many variables. It also can be solved as a linear programming problem.

The solution in terms of standard hours must now be converted back into actual machine hours and actual job units. Divide the standard hour assignments by the SMH index for each machine. This is shown in Table 16-14.

- *For Job A: The load is established by consulting Tables 16-13 and 16-14:*

    18 SMH ÷ SMH index of 1/2 equals 36 actual hours assigned on machine 1 for job A. This yields $36 \times 3 = 108$ units of A.

    32 SMH ÷ SMH index of 0.8 equals 40 actual hours assigned on machine 3 for job A. This yields $40 \times 4.8 = 192$ units of A.

    Total $108 + 192 = 300$ units as required for job A.

- *For Job B: The load is established by consulting Tables 16-13 and 16-14:*

    26 SMH ÷ SMH index of 0.8 equals 32.5 actual hours assigned on machine 3 for job B. This yields $32.5 \times 5.6 = 182$ units of B.

    4 SMH are assigned to the dummy machine MD so job B will be partially completed.

    There is a shortage of $(210 - 182) = 28$ units for job B.

- *For Job C: The load is established by consulting Tables 16-13 and 16-14:*

    54 SMH ÷ SMH index of 1.0 equals 54 actual hours assigned on machine 2 for job C. This yields $54 \times 30 = 1,620$ units of C.

    6 SMH ÷ SMH index of 0.8 equals 7.5 actual hours assigned on machine 3 for job C. This yields $7.5 \times 24 = 180$ units of C.

    Total $= 1620 + 180 = 1800$ units as required for job C.

The transportation model has been solved for total profit maximization. It is as simple to use costs and solve for total cost minimization. Total time minimization, productivity maximization, and other goals can be chosen as well.

A criterion that must be satisfied for using the transportation approach to shop loading is that reasonable proportionality exists between machine output rates. When the SMH index does not apply, a heuristic modification of the transportation method can be tried. If one machine is especially efficient for job A and another machine is best for job B, the heuristic could make those assignments more profitable, or less costly. In other words, some assignments would be made a priori based on clear advantages. As another alternative, the loading problem can be dealt with by linear programming. It does not have the constraint of proportionality.

16-6 Sequencing Operations

Loading assigns work to facilities without regard to the *order* in which the jobs will be done. Sequencing establishes the order for doing the jobs at each facility. Sequencing reflects job priorities according to the way that jobs are arranged in the queues. There are different costs associated with the various orderings of jobs. Proper loading should precede the sequencing of operations.

Loading and sequencing in a typical job shop are done over and over again. Each time, doing it the right way provides a small savings. This has been demonstrated for loading where doing it the right way can provide better profit or lower costs. The accumulation of small benefits over highly repetitive environments can add up to a substantial cost savings or profit accumulation.

Good sequencing provides less waiting time, decreased delivery delays, and better due date performance. There are costs associated with waiting and delays. Total savings from regularly doing it the right way the first time can accumulate to substantial sums. Rescheduling can be significantly more costly. When there are many jobs and facilities, sequencing rules have considerable economic importance.

© 2008 Jupiterimages Corporation

With a roller-coaster, which car goes first is not an option. As people board the ride, they have some leeway in how they choose their cars. Going first or going last or being in the middle is a matter of preference. The sequence in which work is done is also a matter of choice, which can make a big economic difference.

FIFO
The first jobs into the shop get worked on first.

LIFO
The "last-in, first out" rule for providing service.

16-6a First-In, First-Out (FIFO) Sequence Rule

The most natural ordering for doing work is in the order that the jobs are received. That means that the first jobs into the shop get worked on first. This is called **FIFO** for "first-in, first-out." Supermarkets like to use FIFO for their late-dated products (for example, do not use after 04/04/04). There is a cost advantage in getting older products to be purchased first.

LIFO, which is "last-in, first-out," frequently causes spoiled milk problems. That is because the first-in with the earliest date is waiting until all of the later-date items are shipped. If there is no age-spoilage problem then, as its advocates point out, LIFO can save warehouse handling costs. LIFO items are more readily accessible. So, where the product date does not matter; and where you have to move a lot of things away to gain access to the first one in, LIFO may save money.

FIFO is an appealing sequencing policy because it seems to be the fairest rule to follow. Sometimes—to emphasize the fair treatment sense—it is called "first-come, first-served" (FCFS). Customers can get angry when someone seems to jump to the head of the line. The cost of angry customers is not to be trivialized.

However, by at least one measure that will be discussed in this section, FIFO is unfair because it penalizes the average customer. The penalty is extra waiting time for the setup and processing time of the average order. This means that on-average regular customers will wait longer—even though FIFO satisfies first-come, first-serve.

Customers who regularly submit orders with short setup and processing times will benefit if the job shop does not employ the FIFO rule, but uses instead a shortest processing time (SPT) priority rule. Customers who regularly submit long orders may be discriminated against by the shortest processing rule. If so, compensatory steps can be taken at the discretion of those doing the sequencing. Note Section 16-10 on modified SPT rules.

16-7 Gantt Layout Charts

It is useful to visualize the conversion of loading information to sequencing decisions. Loading, in this case, means that each department has a list of assigned jobs. The Gantt layout chart arranges the list in order of processing, i.e., an optimal sequence.

Figure 16-2

The Gantt Layout Chart (A Reserved Time-Planning System)

Status: (1) job P-284 at facility 4 (F4) is ahead 2 days; (2) job J20 (F5) is ahead 3.0 days; (3) job O22 is ahead 6.0 days; (4) job M21 is ahead 1.1 days; (5) job R-65 (F1) is 2 days short of completion and 2.5 days late waiting for M (materials); (6) job P-285 at F3 is 1.5 days late with 5,000 units; (7) job T10-X at F5 is 1.5 days short and about 3.5 days late (M) and (E); (8) facility 2 is unscheduled for 7 more days.

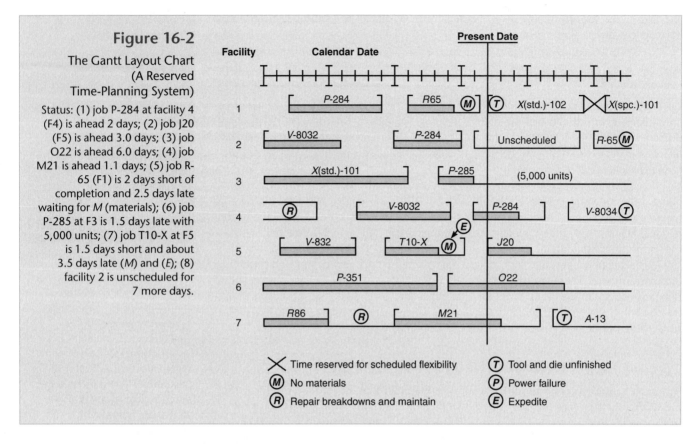

Sequencing chart
See **Gantt layout chart.**

Gantt layout charts
Layout charts establish the exact order in which jobs are to be done at each facility.

Gantt, the master chart maker, developed the Gantt layout chart to show sequence assignments. Also called a **sequencing chart**, it reserves specific times on the various facilities for the actual jobs that have been assigned. It appears in a number of different forms depending upon the sequencing applications. In any of its forms, it accomplishes specific job assignments.

Figure 16-2 shows how the Gantt layout chart assigns the specific jobs to the particular facilities, over some given period of time.

Past sequences of work can be monitored, concurrently, to discover the state of completion of those jobs that were scheduled to be run in prior time periods. Although **Gantt layout charts** provide work-schedule control, they offer little help in determining the best-work sequences.

The chart shows the job schedule at each facility and the state of completion of all jobs. The current date is shown by the arrow and its associated vertical line on the chart. Thereby, the chart is divided into time past, present, and future.

It is easy to see which jobs have been finished and which should have been finished but are not. It is simple to look ahead to observe which jobs are coming up and in what order. Thus, the difference between loading and sequencing is that sequencing specifies the precise timing of assignments. Thereby, it allows customers to be notified of delivery dates.

Once an assignment is made it blocks other assignments from being made. Because sequencing charts are revised regularly, assigned time can be unblocked if it appears to permit a better schedule. A correct amount of time is allowed between jobs to account for machine maintenance, to absorb divergences from estimates, and to allow for setups and takedowns.

Frequently, additional symbols are attached to Gantt charts to indicate why a job has not been completed and which jobs are being expedited. Some of these symbols are shown in Figure 16-2. A lot of useful information can be conveyed by means of succinct shorthand notations. Each organization develops its own conventions. Consultants learn a great deal about a company by studying its Gantt charts.

The Gantt layout chart is continually updated. Jobs must be rescheduled because things happen. Machines break down and customers start screaming when priorities change. A good chart must be easy to alter for contingencies such as tool breakage, materials that do not arrive as scheduled, and customers suddenly canceling deliveries because of special circumstances. Sequencing flexibility is easier to accept when the updating of charts (redrawing them) is supported by software. However, there are commercial products that permit some flexibility using on-the-wall Gantt charting.

Jobs are indicated by i, and the symbol n is used to refer to the number of jobs ($i = 1$, $2, \ldots\ldots, n$) that are waiting to be sequenced through a facility. In the typical job shop, n varies a great deal over time. Also, it is necessary to specify the number of facilities, m, through which the jobs must pass. The character of the sequencing problem is often specified as the n by m problem and represented by $n \times m$.

It is necessary to know how much time every job (i) will spend at each facility. For a given facility, this time is called t_i for the ith job. It is usual for t_i to include job setup time and the work processing or operations times. (From here on, the combination of setup and operations times will be referred to as processing time, t_i.) This does not include waiting time, W_i. The waiting time is nonproductive, as everyone knows who sits in the dentist's waiting room, or waits for the help line to answer.

The degree to which varying patterns of demand requiring different kinds of machines occur in the job shop cannot be underestimated. When a set of jobs follows a fixed ordering, the conditions exist for an intermittent flow shop. Knowledge of technological orderings is required for job shop sequencing. The sizes of orders, the number of alternative facilities for doing each job, the length of production runs, and the setup costs and times, among other things, are the determinants of what type of job shop systems exist.

16-7a Evaluation Criteria

Many criteria exist for evaluating production schedule sequencing. To determine how good a production sequence is, evaluation measures called *total flow time* and *mean flow time* are used. These are defined in the following way.

Total flow time is the cumulative time required to complete a group of jobs. It is composed of the sum of the complete-to-ship times (including waiting time) for each job in the group.

Mean flow time is the average amount of time required to complete each job in the group. It is the average of the wait-to-start and processing times for every job in the group.

The equation for total flow time is the sum of the completion times, C_i for all i jobs that are in the queue:

$$\sum_{i=1}^{i=n} C_i \tag{16-2}$$

The equation for mean flow time is total flow time divided by n:

$$\sum_{i=1}^{i=n} C_i/n \tag{16-3}$$

To sequence a group of jobs at a specific facility, define for each job i a waiting time W_i, and a processing time, t_i. These sum to C_i.

$$C_i = W_i + t_i \tag{16-4}$$

If job $i = 1$ begins at time zero, then its waiting time is zero and its C_i is its processing time, t_i. Thus:

Total flow time
Cumulative time required to complete a group of jobs.

Mean flow time
Average amount of time required to complete each job in a group of n jobs that have been sequenced at a facility.

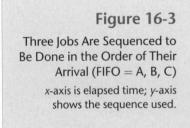

Table 16-15	FIFO	Job_i	W_i	t_i	C_i
Three Jobs Sequenced According to First Come-First Served	1 (first)	A	00	05	05
	2	B	05	03	08
	3 (last)	C	08	04	12
	Sum		13	12	25

$$C_1 = W_1 + t_1 = 0 + t_1 = t_1 \tag{16-5}$$

Beginning at time zero is the same as saying that the *release time*, called r_i, equals zero. This might be the start of a day or a week, etc.

Table 16-15 is constructed for three jobs A, B, and C, which were received in that order. They are to be processed in that order under the FIFO criterion. This means that job A has a release time, $r_A = 0$.

$\Sigma_i C_i$ = the total flow time. It is 25. Mean flow time with $n = 3$ is 8.333 as follows:

$$\sum_i (C_i / n) = 25/3 = 8.333$$

Part of flow time and mean flow time is job waiting time, W_i. The goal is to make the total waiting time as small as possible on the assumption that all customers want to have their orders filled as quickly as possible. Therefore, if mean flow time is minimized, this is equivalent to minimizing the mean waiting time because the processing times t_i are fixed by the nature of the jobs to be done.

If the average completion time, $\sum_i (C_i / n)$, is as small as possible, the average customer's order is delayed the minimum necessary time. This can be a primary objective in determining rational sequence priorities.

Figure 16-3 shows the three jobs (A, B, and C) that have been sequenced to be processed in the order of arrival which is the FIFO (first in-first out) criterion.

The *x*-axis is elapsed time. The *y*-axis shows the sequence used, which is A first, B second, C last. It is the same information given in Table 16-12. Because A goes first, it starts at the top-left. B is the next step down and to the right. C is the final step down and to the right. The steps are all of unit value down, because all jobs are considered to be of equal importance. In Section 16-9, dealing with priority-modified job sequences, the step-down size will be greater for important jobs.

Along the *x*-axis, job A is completed after 5 minutes. Jobs B and C have to wait that 5-minute period. Then job B is done in 3 minutes while job C waits 3 minutes more for a total of 8 minutes. Next job C is completed at 12 minutes. The completion times of 5, 8, and 12 are added together to obtain total flow time for the group of three jobs.

Other measures used in evaluating the performance of order processing sequences include promised delivery dates. Define d_i as the due date of a job. Then, $L_i = C_i - d_i$ is a

Figure 16-3

Three Jobs Are Sequenced to Be Done in the Order of Their Arrival (FIFO = A, B, C)

x-axis is elapsed time; *y*-axis shows the sequence used.

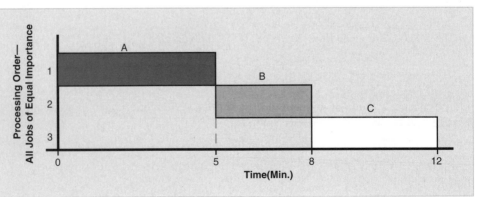

measure of lateness of job i when $d_i < C_i$. To minimize average lateness, minimize mean flow time, assuming that promised dates are reasonably determined.

Facility idleness also may play a critical role in sequence determination. However, sequencing models become increasingly difficult to handle with optimizing models, as the number of facilities through which jobs must pass becomes large. Because jobs take different times at each facility, the best sequence at one location may not be best at another.

In sequencing, the degree of data complexity is large. Consequently, heuristics have been developed to cope with the high levels of detail involved in making repetitive sequencing decisions required by many job shops.

16-8 The SPT Rule for n Jobs and $m = 1$ Facility ($n \times m = n \times 1$)

The common objective of job-facility sequencing—to minimize mean flow time—is usually equivalent to minimizing average job waiting times, as follows:

$$\min \frac{\sum_i^n C_i}{n} = \min \frac{\sum_i^n (W_i + t_i)}{n} = \min \frac{\sum_i^n W_i}{n} \qquad (16\text{-}6)$$

A simple rule achieves this objective. Namely, if a set of n jobs in one facility's queue ($m = 1$) are arranged so that the operations having the shortest processing times (SPT) are done first, then mean flow time and mean waiting time will both be minimized. Sequencing jobs according to their shortest processing times is called the **SPT rule**.

Using the shortest processing time rule (SPT) to sequence Table 16-15 for jobs A, B, and C results in the following decrease in total flow time.

SPT rule

Jobs are rank-ordered in their processing times, t. The job with the smallest t goes first. The job with the next-smallest t goes second, and so forth.

SPT	Job$_i$	W$_i$	t$_i$	C$_i$
1 (first)	B	00	03	03
2	C	03	04	07
3 (last)	A	07	05	12
Sum		10	12	22

$\Sigma_i C_i$ = the total flow time = 22. Mean flow time with $n = 3$ is 7.333 as follows:

$$\sum_i \frac{C_i}{n} = \frac{22}{3} = 7\frac{1}{3}$$

There is 12 percent reduction in total and mean flow times.

For further contrast, note the effect of sequencing by longest processing time, called *LPT*.

LPT	Job$_i$	W$_i$	t$_i$	C$_i$
1 (first)	A	00	05	05
2	C	05	04	09
3 (last)	B	09	03	12
Sum		14	12	26

$\Sigma_i C_i$ = the total flow time = 26. Mean flow time with $n = 3$ is 8.667 as follows:

$$\sum_i \frac{C_i}{n} = \frac{26}{3} = 8\frac{2}{3}$$

With respect to the SPT result, there is an increase of 18 percent in the total flow time.

Figure 16-4

Six Jobs Are Processed in the Order of Their Shortest Processing Times (SPT)

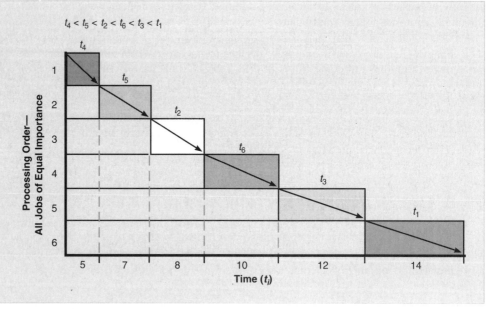

Figure 16-4 provides a larger example of SPT, where six jobs have been rank-ordered by their shortest processing times. Thus:

$$t_4 < t_5 < t_2 < t_6 < t_3 < t_1$$

There are $n = 6$ jobs and $m = 1$ facility, as shown in Table 16-16.

$\Sigma_i C_i$ = the total flow time = 165. Mean flow time with $n = 6$ is 27.5 as follows:

$$\Sigma_i \frac{C_i}{n} = \frac{165}{6} = 27\frac{3}{6}$$

Note that the curve in Figure 16-4 has its convex (curving outward) surface down. This minimizes the area of waiting time, which lies under the curve. This observation is important because it relates the physical character of the graphic approach to the conceptual ideas of minimizing the waiting time of jobs.

In Figure 16-5 the same jobs shown in Figure 16-4 and Table 16-16 are processed according to the rule of customer perceived fairness, which is first-in, first-out (FIFO).

In terms of processing times, FIFO is often a random sequence—without regard to SPT. This is true when any length job is as likely to enter the shop first as any other. Take a ticket and wait your turn, so these orders are processed according to the FIFO rule. Neither the area under the curve nor the mean flow time is minimized. Table 16-17 presents the FIFO waiting times, processing times, and flow time calculations.

$\Sigma_i C_i$ = the total flow time = 211. Mean flow time with $n = 6$ is 35.1667, as follows:

$$\Sigma_i \frac{C_i}{n} = \frac{211}{6} = 35\frac{1}{6}$$

Table 16-16

Total Waiting Time and Flow Time with SPT

SPT	Job_i	W_i	t_i	C_i
1 (first)	4	00	05	05
2	5	05	07	12
3	2	12	08	20
4	6	20	10	30
5	3	30	12	42
6 (last)	1	42	14	56
Sum		109	56	165

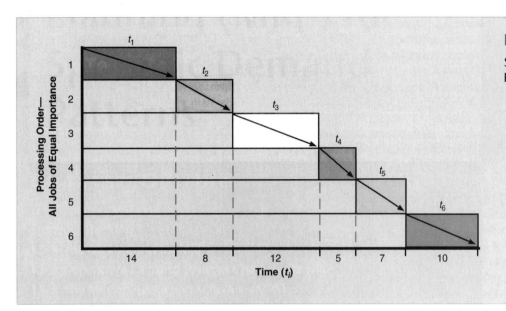

Figure 16-5

Six Jobs Are Processed in the FIFO Sequence

This is an increase in mean and total flow times of 27.88 percent, which is a significant deterioration of customer service.

The waiting time areas under the curves in Figures 16-4 and 16-5 can be determined by multiplying each job's processing time t_i by the number of jobs waiting for that job to finish, and summing them all.

In each figure, there are columns of blocks that represent the number of jobs waiting plus being processed. Each job carries its stack of waiting jobs, except the last one. When the stack size is multiplied by the processing times, the result is total job time spent in the system. It is equal to flow time.

Table 16-18 shows the computations for Figure 16-4, which is based on the SPT rule.

This is the identical value obtained for waiting time in Table 16-16. Note how the larger values of t_i are multiplied by the smaller values of the number of jobs waiting. That is the SPT effect. If jobs working and waiting had been used, then the stacks would start with 6 jobs waiting and working. Continuing in this way, the number 165 would have been derived for total waiting and working time in the system.

Comparing the results of this stack analysis with that applicable to Figure 16-5, where FIFO sequencing was used, Table 16-19 is obtained.

This is the same value that was obtained earlier in Table 16-17 for total waiting time. Continuing in this way, the number 211 would have been derived for total waiting and working time in the system. In this case, the largest value of t_i happens to be multiplied by the largest value of the number of jobs waiting. FIFO is not a logical sequence if the goal is to minimize waiting time or total time spent in the system.

Sequencing jobs by the SPT rule can help to minimize average delivery lateness, L_i, and maximize fulfillment of delivery promises. It cannot overcome delivery promising

FIFO	*Job$_i$*	*W$_i$*	*t$_i$*	*C$_i$*
1 (first)	1	00	14	14
2	2	14	08	22
3	3	22	12	34
4	4	34	05	39
5	5	39	07	46
6 (last)	6	46	10	56
Sum		155	56	211

Table 16-17

Six Jobs Are Processed in the FIFO Sequence

Table 16-18

Total Job Waiting Time Spent in the System with the SPT Sequencing Rule

Job ID	t_i	Multiplied by	Number of Jobs Waiting	=	Job Waiting Time in the System
4	05	X	5	=	25
5	07	X	4	=	28
2	08	X	3	=	24
6	10	X	2	=	20
3	12	X	1	=	12
1	14	X	0	=	00
Total	56	Total waiting time in the system		=	109

Table 16-19

Total Job Waiting Time Spent in the System with the FIFO Sequencing Rule

Job ID	t_i	Multiplied by	Number of Jobs Waiting	=	Job Waiting Time in the System
1	14	X	5	=	70
2	08	X	4	=	32
3	12	X	3	=	36
4	05	X	2	=	10
5	07	X	1	=	07
6	10	X	0	=	00
Total	56	Total waiting time in the system		=	155

that is physically unrealizable. The beneficial effects of SPT follow from the fact that wasted time, W_i, is minimized under that rule.

Note: Because total processing time, $\sum_{i=1}^{n} t_i$, is fixed, when flow time, $\sum_{i=1}^{n} C_i$, is minimized so is waiting time, and average lateness, L_i.

16-9 Priority-Modified SPT Rules: Job Importance

The SPT rule may need to be modified to take into account the fact that some jobs are more *important* than others. Factors such as a customer's long-term importance, or not wanting to be faulted for failing to keep the promised due date, or needing to avoid lateness (and other issues related to setting special priorities) can be taken care of by dividing each job's time t_i by the relative importance of that job, w_i.

Thus, *priority ratios* $= t_i/w_i$ are rank ordered. The job having the smallest value of t_i/w_i is placed first. The job having the next smallest value of is placed second, and so on.

An important job will have a large value of w_i resulting in a small number t_i/w_i. This will place the job earlier in the priority-modified SPT sequence than would otherwise have been the case. Importance may be assigned a number from 1 to 10 depending on the potential lifetime value of the customer, the profitability or margin contribution of each job, the probability of making an occasional customer into a long-term loyal one, or responding to who yells the loudest.

Alternative interpretations of w_i include lateness such that t_i/w_i is the ratio used for SPT. A job that is not late carries an $L_i = 1$. Another system is to let w_i equal the number of days that the job has been waiting to be processed.

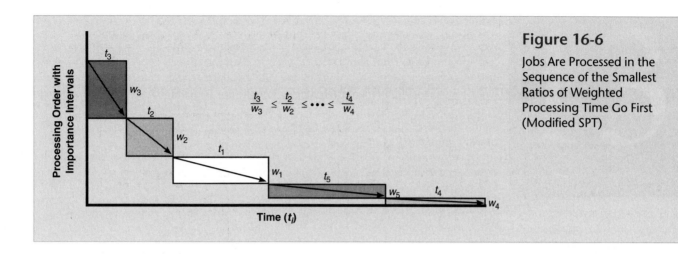

Figure 16-6

Jobs Are Processed in the Sequence of the Smallest Ratios of Weighted Processing Time Go First (Modified SPT)

16-9a Critical Ratio for Due Dates

As another variant, due date, d_i, is the number of days remaining before promised delivery. A sequencing rule—called *critical ratio*—rank orders the ratios d_i/t_i. Jobs are sequenced according to the SPT rule applied to these ratios. The smallest ratio is first in line, etc. The first in line will have some combination of least time available until due date divided by longest processing times that obstruct on-time delivery.

Figure 16-6 illustrates the modified SPT rule for priority ratios of t_i/w_i but it applies as well to d_i/t_i.

The importance weight, w_i, alters the height of the blocks, which is the step size, and thereby the slope of the arrows. Previously, in Figures 16-4 and 16-5, the w_i were all equal to one. Now, the most vertical arrow (which has the largest slope) will belong to the job with the smallest ratio t_i/w_i. The same reasoning applies to the critical ratios.

As shown in Figure 16-6, the ratio of t_3/w_3 is smallest. Therefore, job 3 with processing time t_3 is placed first in the sequence. This ratio rule assures a smooth (convex) function that will minimize the area under the curve.

By using a ratio, the production scheduler who is doing the sequencing gains greater control over the factors. Processing time is an important sequencing factor, but other factors can drive priorities as well.

16-10 Sequencing with More Than One Facility ($m > 1$)

The SPT characteristic of the sequencing problem is easy to understand with n jobs and 1 facility. The optimal sequence through a single facility can be calculated without an ambiguity. There are $n! = (n)(n-1)(n-2)\ldots(1)$ ways to sequence n jobs through *one* facility.

The complexity of finding the minimum flow-time sequence becomes increasingly difficult as a larger number of facilities process each job in successive order. However, when there are n jobs with $m = 2$ facilities, the method for finding the minimum waiting-time sequence is still fast and concise.

With the $n \times 3$ problem, the optimal sequence cannot always be derived. There are certain conditions that must be met. When m is 4 or greater, heuristic methods must be used to find a satisfactory sequence. Optimization methods cannot be used to minimize flow time. The number of sequencing combinations $(n!)^m$ grows large quickly. Thus, when $n = 5$ and $m = 4, \ldots (n!)^m$ is larger than 200 million.

The SPT concept can still be applied when jobs must pass through two facilities in a given technological ordering. For example, (say) the first facility (F1) drills a hole in the

Table 16-20

HMO Sequencing Problem—
What Is the Best Order for
Processing Persons (or Jobs)?
(Time Is in Minutes)

Job (Person)	F1 (Diagnosis)	F2 (Treatment)
a	6	3
b	8	2
c	7	5
d	3	9
e	5	4

Figure 16-7

Gantt Sequencing Chart for
$n \times 2$ Problem Where $n = 5$
Persons Being Processed by
$m = 2$ Facilities

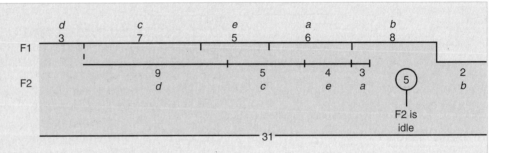

part. This is followed by the second facility (F2), which de-burrs the part after drilling. Technological ordering is set by the process. It is not possible to reverse that order.

Technological ordering also applies to services. In the health care situation, an HMO clinic schedules 5 people for diagnosis to be followed by treatment. Table 16-20 presents the data (in minutes).

S. M. Johnson's algorithm derives the minimum completion times for all "no passing" cases.[1] "No passing" means that the order of processing jobs through the first facility must be preserved for all subsequent facilities.

To use the modified SPT sequencing rule for Table 16-20, where F1 must be done first, select the job (in this case, person) with the shortest processing time in either the F1 or the F2 columns. If this minimum value is in the F2 column, place that person last in sequence (here in fifth place). If the minimum is in the F1 column, put that person in first place. Specifics for this example are that person b requires 2 minutes in the F2 column and will, therefore, be treated last. The next step is to remove person b from the data set and then continue in the same way. In other words, cross out row 2. This removes "b" from the matrix.

Select the smallest number remaining in the matrix. If it is in the F2 column, assign that person to the last place—if it is available—or the next to last place if not. If the smallest number remaining is in column F1, that person is given first place—or next to first place if first place is taken.

Resolve ties by randomly selecting either position for assignment unless some other factors exist for preferring one arrangement or the other. For the previous example, person b goes last, person d goes first, person a goes next to last, person e is treated next to next to last, and person c fills the remaining slot. Note that the smallest number after 2 was 3. Person a has 3 in F2 and person d has 3 in F1. This creates a non-conflicting tie because d goes first and a goes next to last.

The minimum total completion time is 31, as shown by the Gantt chart in Figure 16-7. There is idle time at F2 of 5 minutes. There is no idle time for F1.

16-11 Finite Scheduling of Bottlenecks— TOC Concept

Bottlenecks

Slowest machine in the line sets
the pace of the process.

Bottlenecks are well described by their name. The narrowing of the bottle's neck constricts the flow of output. In terms that are more germane to production, the slowest machine sets the pace of the process flow. When the pace of a person or machine is exceeded by the demand for his, her, or its time, waiting lines begin to grow.

Everyone has experienced the feeling of keeping people waiting because other assignments must be completed first. People who are bottlenecks in their organizations (often because of the design of the system and through no fault of their own) are placed under stress. Workstations that are bottlenecks create tension. Job shops always have one or more bottlenecks. These change according to the product mix in the shop.

16-11a Flow Shops and Continuous Processes Are Designed Without Bottlenecks

Properly designed flow shops and continuous processes, such as a refinery, have no bottlenecks. Fluid mechanics describes how various liquids increase their flow velocities and decrease their pressures when encountering pipe constrictions. Severe constrictions can cause choked flows, which limit the amount of liquid passing through. These are akin to bottlenecks.[2]

Flow shops eliminate all bottlenecks by pre-engineering. Their process flows are fully balanced. In the flow shop, machines are timed to supply each other at just the right rate. When people and machines interact at workstations, a paced conveyor belt carries the work between stations. The timing of the conveyor (how fast it moves between stations and how long it stays at the station) is the *drumbeat* of the processing system.

Bottlenecks are caused by mismatching of process rates. The flow shop eliminates unbalances by design. Often, the mismatch is not the result of bad management. It occurs because of the mixture of orders that are received and already in process for a particular shop configuration. As job mixtures change, shop configurations can be altered but that takes time.

However, because bottlenecks are a fact of life for the job shop, it is worth learning to control where and when they occur—and particularly their severity. Thus, bottleneck control is an expected and routine part of job shop management. When time allows, it is best to turn attention to the causes of scheduling problems instead of dealing with the symptoms, which are the problems of filling orders on time.

© 2008 Jupiterimages Corporation

Traffic funnels into a tunnel, which means that methods for merging lanes of traffic must be developed. The tunnel is a bottleneck, and funnels help channel many items into an opening that admits few. The same applies to bridge entrances and runways at the airport.

16-11b Queue Control (TOC, OPT, and Other Approaches)

Multiple bottlenecks usually exist within any process. When processes are being altered from hour to hour, as is the case with batch work, the potential for clogging the pipeline is large. The damaging effects of queues multiply as the number and length of the waiting lines grow. Orders get misplaced and materials are lost. The chaos level crescendos. The need for queue control becomes apparent. Studying the queuing situation at the bottlenecks can result in improved production scheduling.

As discussed in Chapter 17, queuing systems and their waiting lines are most often associated with arrival time and service time variabilities. However, waiting lines form even when there is a constant period between requests for service and constant service times. For example, assume that a merry-go-round has 45 seats, each ride lasts five minutes, and exactly 15 people arrive every minute and enter the queue for the ride. Starting from scratch, after 3 minutes a waiting line begins to form. At 4 minutes that line consists of 15 people. When the ride stops, a total of 75 people are in line waiting and only 45 can be seated for the next ride. This will not continue if, after one minute, management closes the line because there were already 30 people waiting. Even if the managers did not do this, new arrivals spot the waiting situation and refuse to join the line. The merry-go-round bottleneck arose without any variability being present.

To reduce the wastefulness of queues, the OPT (optimum production technique, also known as optimized production technology)[3] system recommends feeding the bottleneck. This is equivalent to saying that all prior operations should be able to supply the bottleneck with what it needs, when it needs it. Having identified the bottlenecks removes part of the problem. Seeing that they are kept working removes another part of the problem.

OPT

Developed to deal rationally with bottleneck-based finite production scheduling. OPT controls queues by supplying the bottleneck with sufficient batches of work.

Theory of Constraints

A mind-set for determining the core problems in production scheduling, project management, and other P/OM activities. Optimizing production scheduling in isolation from other business variables usually does not lead to higher productivity. See **Finite scheduling**.

TOC

Theory of Constraints provides best finite scheduling and concepts for managing bottlenecks. See **Theory of Constraints**.

Synchronization

Flow shops are predesigned to have perfect synchronization of workstations. Job shops require major efforts to synchronize manufacturing.

Finite scheduling

Controlling the flow of work so that lot sizes and frequency of setups result in minimum total costs.

Finally, when the bottleneck-capacity constraints are unacceptable, they can usually be removed. Then, other bottlenecks emerge.

The creator of TOC (originally **OPT**) was Dr. Eliyahu M. Goldratt (see Spotlight 16-2). After a time, OPT was discarded as a name. Practitioners preferred the analogical **Theory of Constraints** (**TOC**). The bottleneck's processing rate is called (in both OPT and TOC terms) the drum because it sets the production rate for all of the upstream and downstream activities. For synthetic processes (which assemble items), work begins upstream at the tributaries and flows downstream to the trunk encountering various bottlenecks along the way. This is called the *V process* because work moves in the direction of the V-point flowing from upstream to downstream.

Upstream activities (which occur prior to the bottleneck) should be slowed down or stopped to synchronize with the drum. In the stream analogy, if dams cannot slow the flow, then flooding occurs. Floods are waiting lines composed of excess water that cannot be serviced by the existing runoff and containment systems. Levees are built to contain the backed up waters. This is one form of flood control. Similarly, work in process backs up and needs a place to stay. Containment of excess work to which value is not being added is simply less desirable than slowing the flow to the bottleneck. Flow control can result in smaller lot sizes being made more often.

For production of goods, the specification of *when to perform specific operations* is called *finite scheduling*. The topic of *finite scheduling* follows two important TOC rules. First, the transfer batch (which can be part of the production run sent to the next workstation) may be smaller than the total process batch. This production rule increases flexibility and lowers cost. Second, the process batch should be variable and not fixed. Relatively small transfer batches can be used effectively to provide inventory buffers for the bottleneck (drum). The span of protection (called the *time buffer*) is varied to protect the plant against disruptions. For example, the time buffer can be increased from four to five days when there is greater risk of not being able to supply the bottleneck.

Downstream activities cannot expect to receive more work than the fully utilized bottleneck can deliver. The bottleneck sets the course for the rest of the process—that is, until the next bottleneck is encountered—as the work flow moves downstream. In process terms, excess capacity located downstream from the bottleneck may be wasted investment in capacity. If the bottleneck throughput rate is increased, it may not be wasted investment.

16-11c Synchronized Manufacturing

Synchronization requires control of the timing of flows. This includes how much is made at one time and transferred to the next station. Transfer amounts and storage amounts are determined by control mechanisms that can be viewed as valves or gates that can be opened and closed by sending electronic signals to control the flow of materials to the bottlenecks and to the operations that follow the bottleneck. Ropes (ala TOC) are communication links that synchronize the flow rates throughout the system. The controlled flow rates establish the time buffers.

Figure 16-8 illustrates the *drum-buffer-rope* concept, which is the queue-control mechanism designed by Goldratt. It applies to both deterministic and stochastic TOC systems. For the expected case, queue (flow) control over time and space between stations is essential. It is why these methods are described as being synchronized production-scheduling methodology. The flows are units of work. The methods remain standard P/OM practice. The key to success is **finite scheduling**, which is defined as production scheduled in optimal batches (finite size runs for a variety of jobs in the shop). These might coincide with lot-for-lot scheduling.

Variability can disrupt the smooth flow of product. Consequently, it is necessary to provide bottlenecks with assurance that their suppliers will increase production when there are signs that one or more of the bottlenecks could be idled. When any one of the bottlenecks is idled, the existing system is not producing to its maximum.

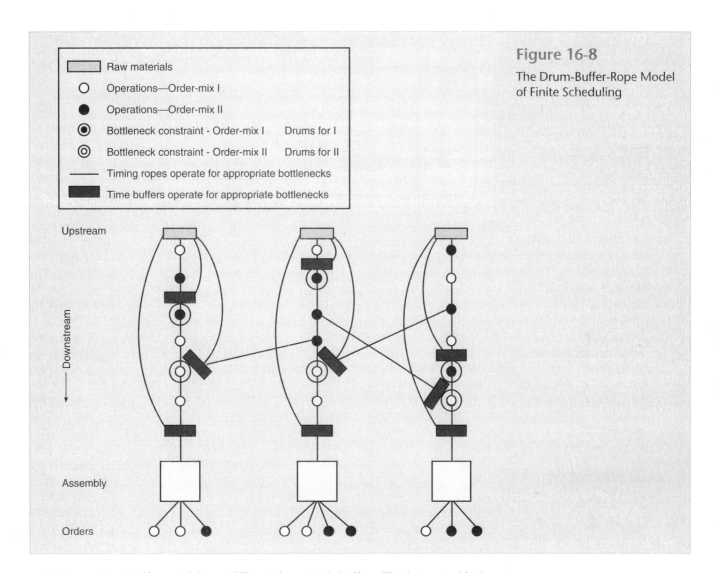

Figure 16-8

The Drum-Buffer-Rope Model of Finite Scheduling

TOC uses time buffers, which are different from stock buffers. The latter specify the number of units of stock that should be kept in reserve, whereas the former specify the amount of time that the bottleneck can keep working if any of its suppliers are shut off. Time reserves are maintained by means of the communication links that the managers of finite scheduling call *ropes* (see the timing ropes in Figure 16-8).

The bottleneck-feeder stations are aware of the need to monitor and allow for statistical variation in the process. TOC time buffers are maintained by regulating the outputs of all feeder stations in line with the status of each time buffer. Being constantly in communication with each other assures that the bottleneck and its feeder systems are integrated. The rope is similar to a ship's telegraph, which can signal the desired speeds of the engine. In this case, the signals indicate the production output rate that is required to prevent idling the bottleneck facilities.

This is symbolically represented in Figure 16-8, which shows shifting bottlenecks for two different order mixes. Order-mix I consists of five jobs and order-mix II consists of five different jobs. There are time buffers before three bottleneck operations in each case. Also, there are time buffers before the three batch assembly operations. Notice how this job shop is in communication with its bottleneck-constraint system. As the order mix changes, the system shifts bottlenecks (new drums alter timing) and it calculates new time buffers. Finite scheduling requires that with changing conditions, production mastery exercises control of upstream production and establishes new ropes as needed.

Spotlight 16-1 The Challenge of Scheduling Production and Operations

Discussion Based on the Ancient Puzzle Game, The Tower of Brahma (also known as the Tower of Hanoi)

"In the great temple at Benares beneath the dome which marks the center of the world, rests a brass plate in which are fixed three diamond needles, each a cubit high and as thick as the body of a bee. On one of these needles, at the creation, God placed sixty-four discs of pure gold, the largest disc resting on the brass plate and the others getting smaller and smaller up to the top one. This is the Tower of Brahma. Day and night unceasingly, the priests transfer the discs from one diamond needle to another, according to the fixed and immutable laws of Brahma, which require that the priest on duty must not move more than one disc at a time and that he must place this disc on a needle so that there is no smaller disc below it. When the sixty-four discs shall have been thus transferred from the needle on which, at the creation, God placed them, to one of the other needles, tower, temple, and Brahmans alike will crumble into dust, and with a thunderclap, the world will vanish."*

Operational Conclusions

The process is clearly explained in detail. Move the disks subject to the placement rules. The objective is to take all of the disks from one needle and move them to another needle following the rules. The complexity of this seemingly simple set of tasks is underscored by the following conclusions:

The number of transfers required to fulfill the prophecy is $2^{64} - 1$, that is 18,446,744,073,709,551,615. If the priests were to effect one transfer every second, and work 24 hours a day for each of the 365 days in a year, it would take them 58,454,204,609 centuries plus slightly more than 6 years to perform the feat, assuming they never made a mistake—for one small slip would undo all their work.**

Production scheduling is reflected in various aspects of this ancient puzzle game. There are repetitive rules that apply, although the identical production steps do not reoccur as the stack of disks is reduced on one needle and increased on another. In that regard, there are also rules that apply with respect to which empty needle is to become the fully loaded needle. The first move made will determine where the final stack resides and that depends upon whether the number of disks is odd or even.

A typical factory system involves so many options that it is not possible to determine an optimal production schedule. Instead of optimization, heuristic methods are used to "satisfice." Heuristics are rules of thumb that are intended to produce the most satisfactory solution (called *satisficing*) that can be found in a reasonable time. There is no heuristic for the tower of Brahma because there is only one solution algorithm. However, the number of steps to achieve the objective corresponds to the levels of complexity that arise when trying to make a number of different items using general-purpose equipment.

There is another analogy. Computer programmers recognize that the disk-moving rules of the Tower of Brahma are based on recursive functions (i.e., repeating the same kinds of steps on a succession of results) to move a stack of disks from one needle to another. Recursion is a commonly used programming practice. There are many instances in production and operations scheduling where recurrence relations are the basis of the methodology. For example, the assignment method in Section 16-5, "The Assignment Method for Loading," uses a recursive algorithm that differs from the algorithm used to solve the transportation model of Section 16-6, "The Transportation Method for Shop Loading."

How likely is it to make a mistake in managing the activities required by this project? The disk-moving algorithm is a simple routine for a computer—even when the number of disks is large. However, humans tend to get preoccupied, and if you have a momentary lapse, one mistake sets the entire program back to the beginning.

Try a simple example using three poles (in place of diamond needles) and three disks of cardboard (large, medium, and small) in place of golden disks. Also, there are various Towers on the web that can be accessed. Go to Google and search for Tower of Hanoi. It is easier to find a simulator for Hanoi than for the Tower of Brahma. Click on Maze-Works or go directly to http://www.mazeworks.com/hanoi.

There is a counter for the number of moves and a clock to time how fast you can schedule these operations. Start with three disks and learn the algorithms before attempting more than three disks. The range from MazeWorks is 3 to 12. Note the assignment is to move all the disks from the left peg to the right peg. What would be different in the algorithm if the assignment had called for moving all of the disks from the left peg to the middle peg? Do the number of disks have any effect on the rules for final position? Note that the MazeWorks Tower of Hanoi tells you how many moves are required and how many moves you have made. If you do it right it says "Congratulations." The timer allows you to compete against yourself or a friend in how rapidly you can move the disks correctly.

Author's Note Concerning Names and Systems for Large Numbers

The number of transfers in the U.S. and French numbering system is 18.4 quintillion (18.4×10^{18}). In the English and German numbering system, it is 18.4 trillion. The following table shows the different number of zeros in each counting system. They are the same at the million mark.

Name	U.S. and French Systems	English and German Systems
quintillion	10^{18}	10^{30}
quadrillion	10^{15}	10^{24}
trillion	10^{12}	10^{18}
billion	10^{9}	10^{12}
million	10^{6}	10^{6}

For further reference, a gigabyte is 1,000 megabytes (mb = 10^{6}), which is 1 billion bytes in the U.S. and French systems. A terabyte is 1,000 gigabytes or 1 billion bytes in the U.S. and French systems. When the Germans refer to a billion euros, that is a trillion euros to Americans. The British government converted to the U.S. system in 1974. The British press is altering too.

Review Questions

1   What is the Tower of Brahma, and how does it differ from the Tower of Hanoi?

2   Why is Spotlight 16-1 titled, "The Challenge of Scheduling Production and Operations"?

3   How good are you at manipulating the disks without making a mistake? According to the legend, a mistake with the Tower of Brahma means starting over. Such a disk-scheduling mistake can be costly. How fast are you at moving disks to complete the transfers?

4   Observe that scheduling time increases exponentially with each additional disk in the Tower of Brahma. How many moves are required to move 5 disks? What does this say about the complexity of a shop with many jobs and many workstations?

5   With increased complexity, it gets harder for people to avoid making mistakes. This is especially true when speed is required. What can be done to maintain control of a complex system where rapid response is essential? See Spotlight 17-1, where the case of fighter pilots (and their O.O.D.A. loops) is explained.

*Tower of Hanoi (also known as the Tower of Brahma) from Volume 4 of the *World of Mathematics*. "Pastimes of Past and Present Times," by Edward Kasner and James R. Newman, published by Simon & Schuster, 1956, page 2425. The quoted material is sourced by Kasner and Newman from W.W.R. Ball, *Mathematical Recreations and Essays*, 11e. New York: Macmillan, 1939.
**World of Mathematics, op. cit.

Spotlight 16-2   Dr. Eli Goldratt: The Fallacy of Pursuing Local Optimums

An Interview with Dr. Eliyahu M. Goldratt, Author of
The Goal, It's Not Luck, *and* The Race

Dr. Eliyahu M. Goldratt

Dr. Eliyahu M. Goldratt, renowned worldwide for developing new production control and management philosophies and systems, challenges companies to "break outside of the box" of conventional practices in their ongoing efforts to achieve business goals. In his early work, Goldratt developed the concept and technology for bottleneck-based finite scheduling. From this he concluded that optimizing production scheduling in isolation from other business variables usually does not lead to higher productivity or achievement of company goals. As his work evolved, he called his ideas the Theory of Constraints (TOC).

Based on systematic thinking processes, TOC studies the cause and effect relationships between dependent aspects of a given problem or project. It provides an overall framework for determining (1) what not to change (not everything is broken); (2) how to change (what are the simple, practical solutions); and (3) how to implement change (overcoming the inherent resistance to change). TOC enables

Spotlight 16-2 (Continued)

the determination of core problems, construction of detailed solutions, and devising of implementation plans. TOC has major applications in production, project management, distribution, finance, marketing and sales, and management strategy but can be used as well to solve any problems that arise in life.

Dr. Goldratt brings his finite scheduling theory and TOC framework to life in his books *The Goal: Excellence in Manufacturing* and its sequel, *It's Not Luck.* He wrote these two business textbooks as novels "to give the content in a way people can absorb it," he said. The books give students and practitioners of business a "real-life" context for applying Goldratt's ideas for achieving business excellence. (He does not accept credit for inventing this creative genre, however, attributing inspiration to novelist/philosopher Ayn Rand.) Goldratt has written several traditional texts as well, including *The Haystack Syndrome, The Race,* and *The Theory of Constraints.* In *The Haystack Syndrome,* Goldratt presents evidence that "cost accounting is public enemy number one of productivity." In *It's Not Luck,* he asserts that balance sheets are "nothing more than the liquidation

value of the company . . . and should not be used to judge an ongoing operation."

Application of Goldratt's theories have proven that "the core problem right now in most of the industry is a lack of a systems approach." This core problem is referred to throughout his work as "striving to run the whole system based on local optimums." Goldratt teaches that one area of a business may need to sacrifice its own local optimums for the greater good of the entire system. Goldratt sees an eagerness among the business community to embrace systems thinking, but finds major resistance to this approach in academia. He believes that academics who do not present a systems perspective are "sending graduates into the market totally unprepared." Goldratt's theories have met with widespread acceptance, as evidenced through sales of over two million copies of *The Goal*—with no advertising expense incurred! When he's not consulting with managers of the world's largest corporations, Goldratt lives in Israel.

Sources: A conversation with Dr. Eliyahu M. Goldratt and correspondence, August 1, 2003, and September 2007.

chapter 16

Summary

Production scheduling is the culminating series of steps that determines *when* orders are to be worked on, *where*, and *by whom*. The function goes back to the earliest days of systematic production and assignment of service jobs to work crews. The Gantt load chart was developed at that time, and it is still used. Loading decisions concern which jobs are to be assigned to which teams or facilities. Jobs on-hand are relatively risk free to schedule. Jobs that are on the books as forecasts are problematic. Depending upon the real situation, they may not be scheduled because there is too high a risk of cancellation.

Chapter 16 explains that the assignment method for loading jobs at facilities is powerful but limited to a real class of situations where job splitting is not permitted. Assignment models can maximize profits or minimize costs. More flexible, the TM (transportation model) is developed for shop loading. It permits job splitting and multiple job assignments at one facility. The drawback of the transportation model is the requirement to use standard units and the presumption of *productive proportionality*.

Loading is nonspecific to job order, so it is always followed by sequencing. There is strong methodology to determine the best order for job processing. Which job goes first, second, and so on? Service system managers often require first-come, first-serve so that their customers do not get upset. The same applies to production deliveries. Customer systems are criticized when the "fairness criterion" [first-in, first-out; (FIFO)] is violated. Nevertheless, the alternative of processing orders so that shortest processing times (SPT) go first provides benefits to everyone *except* those who regularly have orders that take a long time to process.

Gantt layout charts are used to organize sequencing assignments. The sequencing situation depends on the number of jobs (n) and the number of machines (m) that are available to work on the jobs. Solution methods differ according to the number of facilities (machines, m). In general, the problem size is given by $n \times m$. In Chapter 16, SPT rules are developed for $n \times 1$ and $n \times 2$. The SPT rule can be modified to reflect various forms of priorities including job and customer importance, due date, and lateness. Modified SPT incorporates priorities within the goal of reducing job-waiting times.

Chapter 16 concludes with a discussion about identifying bottlenecks and using the Theory of Constraints—TOC—to deal with bottlenecks. TOC manages bottlenecks using finite scheduling based on the drum-buffer-rope method for synchronized manufacturing. Bottlenecks set the pace of production. Bottlenecks are protected from idleness caused by variability using time-based stock buffers. The rest of the system is synchronized to match the input–output performance of the bottleneck.

Spotlight 16-1: The Challenge of Scheduling Production and Operations presents a discussion of a complex production-scheduling problem based on an ancient puzzle game known as The Tower of Brahma. In fact, the production-scheduling rules are simple, but carrying them out with an awareness of the size of the problem is complex. This game epitomizes the simple but complex nature of production scheduling. Spotlight 16-2: The Fallacy of Pursuing Local Optimums is an interview with Dr. Eliyahu M. Goldratt, author of *The Goal*, *It's Not Luck*, and *The Race*. Dr. Goldratt, the creator of TOC, has revolutionized the treatment of finite scheduling problems. His insights are invaluable.

Key Terms

Assignment method (p. 651)

Bottlenecks (p. 668)

Due date (p. 649)

FIFO (p. 659)

Finite scheduling (p. 670)

Gantt layout charts (p. 660)

Gantt load charts (p. 648)

LIFO (p. 659)

Loading (p. 647)

Mean flow time (p. 661)

Opportunity costs (p. 651)

OPT (p. 670)

Production scheduling (p. 647)

Sequencing (p. 647)

Sequencing chart (p. 660)

Shop floor control (p. 648)

SPT rule (p. 663)

Synchronization (p. 670)

Theory of Constraints (p. 670)

TOC (p. 670)

Total flow time (p. 661)

Review Questions

1   The Gantt load chart can be used to determine whether the "load" is equally distributed among facilities. To which jobs and responsibilities is balanced loading important?

2   Explain the statement: "Load real jobs, not forecasts."

3   Opportunity costs are instrumental for loading models and decisions. Are these real costs? Explain.

4   What is the assignment method of loading? What special conditions apply?

5   Distinguish between the maximization model for the assignment problem and the minimization model. Explain the differences.

6   What is the transportation model (TM) for loading? What special conditions apply?

7   Distinguish between the conditions necessary for using the assignment model and the transportation model.

8   How do Gantt load charts differ from Gantt layout charts?

9   When does FIFO make sense as a sequencing rule?

10   When does LIFO make sense as a sequencing rule?

11   When should SPT be used?

12   What are priority-modified SPT rules? Give examples; explain when they should be used.

13   Explain the use of critical ratios for due dates.

14   What is the significance that sequencing charts are convex (curving downward) when the sequencing rule is SPT?

15   What is the significance that sequencing charts are not purposefully convex (curving downward) when the sequencing rule is FIFO?

16   What is the $n \times 1$ sequencing problem?

17   What is the $n \times m$ sequencing problem?

18   What is the $n \times 2$ sequencing problem? How can it be resolved?

19   What are time buffers?

20   Explain the meaning of drum-buffer-rope for scheduling.

21   What is meant by synchronized manufacturing?

22   What is the scheduling theory of constraints (TOC)?

23   Why is finite scheduling concerned with bottlenecks?

24   Discuss the reasons that job shops and not flow shops are associated with the problem of bottlenecks.

25   When does it pay to remove a bottleneck? What is entailed?

26   Explain why the removal of a bottleneck creates a new one.

27   Describe what is meant by "feed the bottleneck."

Problems Section

Note: This section has various problems that can be formulated and solved using QuantMethods Production/Operations Management software (QMpom). The appropriate model categories are indicated for each problem.

 The matrix of *total costs per day* for jobs 1, 2, and 3—if assigned at facilities A, B, and C of the Rivet and Nail Factory—is

		Facilities		
		A	**B**	**C**
Jobs	1	$1,000	$ 900	$1,200
	2	800	700	900
	3	1,500	1,800	2,000

What relatively permanent assignments will minimize total costs per day?

Using the QMpom module called Aggregate Scheduling Models (Assignment) will facilitate solving the six (6) problems that are numbered 1 through 6.

2 The matrix of *costs per part* for jobs 4, 5, and 6—if assigned at facilities A, B, and C of the Rivet and Nail Factory—is

		Facilities		
		A	B	C
Jobs	4	$0.10	$0.19	$0.12
	5	0.16	0.14	0.18
	6	0.30	0.36	0.40

The jobs are all of the same size (5,000) and duration. What relatively permanent assignments will minimize total costs?

3 The matrix of costs per part for jobs 7, 8, and 9 if assigned at facilities A, B, and C of the Rivet and Nail Factory is described by the matrix:

		Facilities		
		A	B	C
Jobs	7	$0.10	0.09	$0.12
	8	0.08	0.07	0.09
	9	0.30	0.36	0.40

The jobs are all of the same size (5,000 units) and duration. What relatively permanent assignments will minimize total costs?

4 The executive offices for five vice presidents of an airline are on the tenth floor of the airline's building. The decision is made to assign the offices in such a way as to maximize total satisfaction. Each VP is asked to rank his or her preferences for the available offices. One is the most preferred location and five is the least preferred. The data are as follows:

Office	VP1	VP2	VP3	VP4	VP5
O1	1	1	2	3	2
O2	5	3	1	2	3
O3	4	2	5	1	1
O4	3	5	4	3	4
O5	2	4	3	5	5

a. What is the best assignment plan from the company's viewpoint?
b. How does this problem relate to production schedules?
c. How does this problem relate to service scheduling?

5 Use the assignment model to achieve an optimal shop-loading arrangement for an intermittent flow shop. Jobs are 1–5 and the facilities are A–E. The per unit profits are given in the following matrix. Relatively continuous production can be expected for each assignment over the next quarter.

Jobs	A	B	C	D	E
1	19	17	15	15	13
2	12	30	18	18	15
3	13	21	29	19	21
4	49	56	53	55	43
5	33	41	39	39	40

6 For the data in Problem 5, a new facility F has become available that can only work on jobs 1, 2, or 3, with unit profits of 14, 11, and 12, respectively.

a. Should one of the current facilities be replaced with F?
b. What information is lacking that could help make the recommendations more definitive?

7 The following matrix has productivity per standard machine hour [PR(i,j)] filled into each box within a machine-job cell. The revenue per piece is given by column and the cost per piece is given by row.

Revenue per Piece		$2.00	$1.00	$0.50	
Cost per Piece		Job A	Job B	Job C	Supply S(i)
$0.20	M1	3	3.5	15	
$0.10	M2	6	7	30	
$0.30	M3	4.8	5.6	24	
$0.00	MD	0	0	0	
Demand D(j)					

Determine the profit per standard hour values that should be used. Draw up some blank matrices (without the corner entries) so that these results can be entered, and used for later calculations. These numbers can be filled into the empty boxes within each machine-job cell in the matrix and used for Problem 8.

Using the QMpom module called Mathematical Programming Models (Transportation) will facilitate solving the five (5) problems that are numbered 7 through 11.

8 The following matrix has the supply of available standard machine hours in the right-hand column. It has demand in standard hours in the bottom row. Fill in the Northwest Corner (NWC) assignments. This means starting at the upper left-hand box and entering as many units as the row or column sums allow. Then, move to the east or to the south, depending upon whether it is the row or column sum that still needs to be satisfied. Continue in this way until the NWC assignment is complete.

Revenue per Piece		$2.00	$1.00	$0.50	
Cost per Piece		Job A	Job B	Job C	Supply S(i)
$0.20	M1				18
$0.10	M2				54
$0.30	M3				64
$0.00	MD				4
Demand D(j)		50	30	60	140

What is the total profit associated with the NWC assignment?

9 The following matrix has been derived after a number of shifts from the NWC assignment aimed at improving profit.

Revenue per Piece	$2.00	$1.00	$0.50	
Cost per Piece	Job A	Job B	Job C	Supply S(i)
$0.20 M1		12	6	18
$0.10 M2			54	54
$0.30 M3	50	14		64
$0.00 MD		4		4
Demand D(j)	50	30	60	140

What is the total profit associated with the "improved" assignment? By how much has it improved the solution obtained with the NWC assignment?

10 Convert the solution obtained for Problem 8—the NWC solution—into actual assignment hours and units.

11 Convert the solution obtained for Problem 9—the improved solution—into actual assignment hours and units. Can you tell if this is the optimal solution?

12 The Door Knob Company has four orders on hand, and each must be processed in the sequential order:

First: Department A—press shop
Second: Department B—plating and finishing

The following table lists the number of days required for each job in each department. For example, job IV requires one day in the press shop and one day in the finishing department.

	Job I	Job II	Job III	Job IV
Department A	8	6	5	1
Department B	8	3	4	1

Assume that no other work is being done by the departments and that "no passing" of jobs is allowed.

Use a Gantt sequencing chart (see Figure 16-7) to show the best-work schedule. (Best-work schedule means minimum time to finish all four jobs.)

Using the QMpom module called Production Scheduling Models (Shortest Processing Time [SPT]) will facilitate solving the fourteen (14) problems that are numbered 12 through 25.

13 Using the information in Problem 12, find the best sequence for each department separately.

14 How do the solutions obtained for Problems 12 and 13 compare?

15 The Market Research Store has four orders on hand, and each must be processed in the sequential order:

First: Department A—computer analysis
Second: Department B—report writing and printing

The following table lists the number of days required by each job in each department. For example, job IV requires two days during computer analysis and one day in report writing and printing.

	Job I	Job II	Job III	Job IV
Department A	3	6	5	2
Department B	8	3	4	1

Assume that no other work is being done by the departments and that "no passing" of jobs is allowed.

Use a Gantt sequencing chart to show the best-work schedule. (Best-work schedule means minimum time to finish all four jobs.)

16   Using the information in Problem 15, find the best sequence for each department separately.

17   How do the solutions obtained for Problems 15 and 16 compare?

18   Examine the sequences for the following $n \times 1$ system. There are six jobs with processing times t_i. As these jobs arrived they were named in alphabetical order (A, B, C, . . . , F).

Job i	t_i
A	5
B	4
C	6
D	9
E	12
F	8

What is the SPT sequence? Derive the SPT solution. What are the total and mean flow times for that sequence?

19   Using the information in Problem 18, derive the LPT (longest processing time) solution. What is the LPT sequence? What are the total and mean flow times for that sequence? Compare the SPT and the LPT solutions.

20   Using the information in Problem 18, derive the first-come, first-serve (or FIFO) effect. What is the FIFO sequence? What are the total and mean flow times for that sequence? Compare SPT and FIFO.

21   For Problem 18, what effect does the information that jobs A, B, and C are half as important as jobs D, E, and F have on the sequence solution?

22   For the following $n \times 1$ problem, use a priority-modified SPT rule where the priority is based upon reducing lateness L_i. Work times t_i and lateness are given in the following table for jobs A, B, . . . F.

I	t_i	L_i
A	5	1
B	4	2
C	6	1
D	9	3
E	12	1
F	8	1

What is the optimal sequence and what are its total and mean flow times? Compare the answer with the one obtained for Problem 18.

23   For the following $n \times 1$ problem, use a priority-modified SPT rule where the priority is based upon the critical ratio using due dates d_i and work times t_i as given in the following table.

i	t_i	d_i
A	5	10
B	4	16
C	6	18
D	9	18
E	12	36
F	8	25

What is the optimal sequence and what are its total and mean flow times? Compare the answer with the one obtained for Problem 18.

24   For the following $n \times 1$ problem, use a priority-modified SPT rule, where the priority is based on the additional information about customer importance called w_i (given in the following table).

i	t_i	w_i
A	5	6
B	4	5
C	6	4
D	9	3
E	12	2
F	8	1

The more important the customer, the larger the value of w_i.

What is the optimal sequence and what are its total and mean flow times?

25 The problem faced by Information Search, Inc. (ISI) has the processing times shown here:

	Jobs (A–E)				
	A	*B*	*C*	*D*	*E*
1. Look up references	4	8	9	4	6
2. Write report	3	2	5	7	4

What is the optimal sequence and what are its total and mean flow times?

Practice Quiz

1 Production scheduling must be done by any organization that does work in batches or lots. Familiar to manufacturing, it is equally necessary for service functions. In some instances, it might be called by other names. P/OM is responsible for knowing how, when, and what to schedule. City Hall has come to realize that many municipal functions would profit from understanding production scheduling. A consultant has been hired from the private sector, and she has prepared a test for the city managers. It consists of five statements (a. to e.), one of which is wrong. Assume the role of a city manager and take this test. Which statement about production scheduling is wrong?

   a. The police department writes an average of 500 tickets per day. The variability is very high. On certain days, it is twice that number and on other days it is half as much. The resources required to be scheduled include the ticket writers, the ticket processors, the court requirements, the collection functions, etc. Production scheduling is involved with all of these activities.

   b. Sanitation is a production function. Fortunately, the pickups are already scheduled, as are the drop-offs at the disposal dump. This area does not require additional attention.

   c. Every election seems to be treated as a new project when in fact elections are repeats of batch production operations separated by a year for local elections, two years for state and federal elections, and four years for presidential elections. It is recommended that elections be studied as candidates for production scheduling.

   d. Tax collection by the city is very inefficient, whereas the state is very fast and makes few errors. The state production schedulers need to sit down with the city folks. That is a beginning.

   e. The fire department faces uncertain demand. Sometimes there are no calls or simple ones that take a few minutes to correct. At other times, there are requests for help with big fires that can take a long time to subdue. Production scheduling can help a great deal once it has access to the real data.

2 Gantt load charts are 100 years old, but they are still used because they work well. Five statements have been prepared for the City Hall management team about load charting. Most of the managers say that they have been using load charts to obtain reasonable (not quite optimal) capacity utilization in the systems for which they are responsible. Comfort is expressed with these graphic methods. Choose the one statement (a. through f.) not appropriate to load charts.

   a. Proper charts reflect the interests of customers and the impact of suppliers. For example, with respect to security at City Hall, "which jobs have not started that should have begun"? Alternatively, "what progress toward completion has been made"? If the answer is "The security system at City Hall will be installed as soon as possible, but protocols have not yet been created, nor tested," these statements make it quite evident that layout charts have not been drawn. Gantt project charts are in order before the layout charts can be drawn. (*This statement has been accepted as being true by the mayor.*)

b.   Layout charts can show either calendar time or general time units along the *x*-axis. For each department, there is a line indicating workload percent by the week (or day, etc.). In each time bucket, lines start at the left and move to the right, representing a percent of the range. A solid line that spans the box indicates 100 percent load.

c.   Jobs are listed for each department in a separate box at the right of the chart. The number of units to be completed for each job may be shown. The order in which jobs will be done has not yet been determined.

d.   It is helpful to show the cumulative load for each department (facility). It is helpful to see the load for the current week and the prior week. Which departments are falling behind and which are catching up?

e.   Work that has been promised, where the due date is past, is labeled "backlogged." An asterisk can be used to highlight the situation. Backlogged jobs are given top priority. They will be the first ones to be assigned to the department as soon as the current jobs are completed.

f.   The load chart reveals at a glance which departments are underutilized. That is a primary purpose. Gantt load chart users make no pretense that the method will enable optimization of schedules. The load chart graphics facilitate heuristic methods for reaching better generalizations with fast data scans. "Eyeballing" is a key use of the load charts.

3   The assignment method for loading facilities is useful in actual application and also conceptually because of its reliance on opportunity costs with no splitting allowed. An example has been built around the assignment of office spaces (A, B, C) to managers (1, 2, 3) at City Hall. Each manager has stated his or her preference for each office based on a scale of one to ten with one (lowest cost) being best. Which statement a. through e. is wrong?

		Offices		
		A	B	C
	1	9	5	2
Managers	2	8	3	5
	3	8	7	3

a.   No splitting means that each manager must have only one office. Thus, manager 1 cannot be assigned to offices A and B, even part of the time. Also, office A cannot be shared by managers 1 and 2.

b.   Opportunity costs are the costs of managers not having their preferences satisfied. Then, there would be zero total opportunity cost and maximum total satisfaction if the assignments C1, B2, and C3 could be granted. That is impossible because the rule is no splitting and no sharing. As a benchmark, the total preference value if each manager got his or her first choice would be 11. This results from summing the smallest cell value for each manager.

c.   If row subtraction is used first, there are no zero opportunity costs (*zoc*) in column A. B2 is an uncontested *zoc*. There is a conflict in column C between C1 and C3, both of which have *zoc*.

d.   To resolve the assignment conflicts, column subtraction is used next. It results in an unambiguous set of assignments, namely, A3, B2, and C1. These have a total preference value of 13. There is no assignment that can be made that will have a lower total preference cost.

e.   If column subtraction is used first, the assignment solution appears without conflict. There are zeros at A3, B2, and C1. This is the same solution that occurred when row subtraction was used first and followed by column subtraction.

4   City Hall realizes that there is a great deal more learning available from the simple three-by-three assignment problem set forth in Problem 3. The example is now continued with some different assumptions about the preferences. In this case, each manager has stated his or her preference for each office based on a scale of one to ten with ten (highest revenue) being best. Which statement a. through e. is wrong?

		Offices		
		A	B	C
	1	9	5	2
Managers	2	8	3	5
	3	8	7	3

a. The objective function has been reversed so that the largest numbers represent the managers' greatest preferences. Then, row subtraction produces a total stalemate with all zeros in column 1.

b. If the matrix derived in a. (which is a matrix of opportunity costs) is followed by column subtraction, the result is an unambiguous solution. A1 is uncontested in the first row. B3 is uncontested in the second column. That eliminates the other zeros except for C2.

c. The assignment from operations in b. has total satisfaction value of $9 + 7 + 5 = 21$, which is the maximum that can be obtained with these data.

d. If every number in the matrix is multiplied by k, the solution will change. A new set of analyses is required.

e. If every number in the matrix has an added value of k, the solution will not change. A new set of analyses is not required.

5 The transportation model or method is a more powerful alternative than the assignment model or method for shop loading. City Hospital has always done its manpower planning (a generic name that has not been replaced by peoplepower planning) by cut and try on a large whiteboard. They have been persuaded to try using the transportation method in one of its load planning formats. The resulting example illustrates how the method works, although real problems are significantly larger in size and use more realistic numbers. The list of observations (a. to e.) about the method contains one erroneous statement. Identify the flawed statement.

	D(1)	D(2)	D(3)	Supply
P(1)	40			40 hrs.
P(2)	5	35		40 hrs.
P(3)		30	10	40 hrs.
P(D)			40	40 hrs.
Demand	45 hrs.	65 hrs.	50 hrs.	160 hrs.

a. D(1), D(2), and D(3) are departments of City Hospital. D(1) requires 45 hours per week of medical assistance. D(2) requires 65 hours and D(3) requires 50 hours. There are three medical assistants that can be assigned to these departments. They are called P(1), P(2), and P(3). Each has 40 hours of time available per week. The problem is to find the best manpower plan.

b. The transportation matrix shows an initial feasible solution obtained by using the Northwest Corner allocation method. The next matrix has the costs of assigning P(1) to D(1), P(1) to D(2), P(2) to D(1), etc. The costs are purposely single digit to make the illustration simple to follow.

	D(1)	D(2)	D(3)	Supply
P(1)	$5/hr.	$6/hr.	$7/hr.	40 hrs.
P(2)	$6/hr.	$7/hr.	$8/hr.	40 hrs.
P(3)	$7/hr.	$6/hr.	$5/hr.	40 hrs.
P(D)	$0/hr.	$0/hr.	$0/hr.	40 hrs.
Demand	45 hrs.	65 hrs.	50 hrs.	160 hrs.

c. There are more hours demanded than are available. Consequently, a dummy assistant P(D) is created. Whichever department the dummy is assigned to will have a labor shortage. The dummy is given costs of $0 per hour for all departments because it will not be paid. The dummy is indifferent as to which department it is assigned.

d. There is still not enough information to use the transportation model. What is missing is the preference of the assistants for the various departments.

e. The cost of the first feasible assignment solution is $[40(5) + 5(6) + 35(7) + 30(6) + 10(5) + 40(0)] = \$705$. It places the dummy entirely in D(3), which requires 50 hours of work. D(3) does get 10 hours of work from P(3). The assistant P(3) splits his or her time spending 30 hours in department D(2). Note how the transportation model employs splitting a worker's time between departments and how departments share more than one worker.

6 City Hospital is not about to settle for manpower assignments that just happened by dint of a method called Northwest Corner. Hospital schedulers now wish to show how they can manipulate the matrix to provide an optimum (minimum total cost) solution. What are the next steps? A list has been prepared with statements a. to e., and one of these statements is wrong. Which statement is in error?

a. Each cell in the Northwest Corner solution matrix that does *not contain* an assignment is analyzed to determine if costs would increase or decrease if one unit was assigned to that cell in lieu of the current assignment.

b. Put one unit into cell P(1), D(2). Take one unit out of P(1), D(1). Put one unit into P(2), D(1). Take one unit out of P(2), D(2). Shifting that one unit results in $12 of added costs and $12 of subtracted costs. It is a tie, which means that an alternative solution will exist with the same cost. Then, using the same technique, evaluate cell P(D), D(2). The result is that a savings of $1 per unit moved to that cell is available.

c. The maximum number of units that can be moved to cell P(D), D(2) is 40 units. That move should lower the total cost by 40($1) = $40. The discussion ensued as to whether $40 is worth the trouble because it is a savings of 4.3 percent at best.

d. The final assignment solution is shown in the matrix. It has a total cost of $675. One of the managers got very enthusiastic about the transportation method for manpower planning. He stated that it could be used for City Hospital's Call-A-Medic business unit, which is a call center run by the hospital. Call centers are very labor intensive, yet they have major technology interfaces. The discussion touched on call centers, widely used by public utilities (power providers), airline and train reservation systems, and technology purveyors such as Dell, Nextel, and D-link.

Final Assignment Solution				
	D(1)	D(2)	D(3)	Supply
P(1)	40			40 hrs.
P(2)	5	35		40 hrs.
P(3)			40	40 hrs.
P(D)		30	10	40 hrs.
Demand	45 hrs.	65 hrs.	50 hrs.	160 hrs.

e. The transportation model cannot be solved by hand with cut and try when it is of large size. Manpower planning for City Hospital involves hundreds of nurses being assigned to dozens of departments. Linear programming will solve problems of such size (once the data inputs are well organized) with remarkable speed. It will permit sensitivity analyses to be run regarding other factors that drive the manpower-loading problem for the hospital.

7 If the loading situation applies to manufacturing with jobs assigned to machines (or work areas such as the foundry, press shop, plating, and assembly), then the transportation model requires transforming job units into standard hours. Hospital schedulers are convinced that this applies to their Hematology Department, where jobs are measured in units that require different amounts of time. Hematology testing facilities take different amounts of time to complete each of the different types of jobs. Hospital schedulers have prepared a list of six statements that relate to the classical facility-loading problem. Which single statement in the list (a. to f.) is in error?

a. There are n different kinds of hematology jobs to be done. Each one can be done by the m lab teams, which have different levels of technology at their disposal and various amounts of training.

b. The head of the lab has stated that it is reasonable to assume that proportionality exists between the productivity rates of the m teams. The fastest team has been selected as the standard team. The way that the other teams relate to the standard team is shown in the table.

Simple Example of Shop Loading for Three Teams in the Hematology Department				
(*i*)	Team Standard Index	Relative Productivity	Actual Hours/Week	Standard Team Hours/Week
T(S)	1.0	Standard team	54 (Saturday with 9-hour shifts)	54
T(1)	0.8	80% as fast as T(S)	80 (double shift)	64
T(2)	0.5	Half as fast as T(S)	36 (department maintenance)	18
Totals			170 actual hours	136 standard hours

c. The actual hours that each team has available is converted to standard team hours by multiplying the index times the actual hours. This is shown in the table.

d. Three jobs (A = 300 units, B = 210 units, and C = 1800 units) are waiting to be done by the Hematology Department. They have not yet been assigned to teams for shop loading. Jobs A, B, and C have to be converted to standard team hours. This is done by dividing actual job units by the productivity of the standard team. This is shown as part of the transportation matrix in the following table.

Matrix of Productive Output for Each Team on Each Job				
	Job A	Job B	Job C	Supply in Std. Hrs.
T(S)	6 units/hr.	7 units/hr.	30 units/hr.	54 std. hrs.
T(1)	0.8(6) = 4.8	0.8(7) = 5.6	0.8(30) = 24	64 std. hrs.
T(2)	0.5(6) = 3.0	0.5(7) = 3.5	0.5(30) = 15	18 std. hrs.
T(D)	0.0(6) = 0	0.0(7) = 0	0.0(30) = 0	4 std. hrs.
Dummy team				
Demand in std. hrs.	300/6 = 50	210/7 = 30	1800/30 = 60	Total = 140 std. hrs

e. The transportation method can now be used to find the maximum total productive output solution. This best shop loading is not restricted to no-splitting of jobs. Jobs assigned to the dummy team will not be done. Four standard hours will not be done at one of the jobs.

f. This problem cannot be done by linear programming because it is a maximization problem with constraints. LP can only deal with minimization problems with constraints. The nature of the constraints is related to the field of hematology.

8 Once the loading problem has been resolved, City Hospital schedulers know that the detailed aspects of assignment ordering must be made. Which nurses will be assigned morning shifts in each department? Who will follow in the afternoons and evenings? Sequences of who follows whom must be established in each department to satisfy the manpower scheduling requirements. Loading decisions did not determine shift assignments. Loading assigned people to departments without their shift designations. City Hospital schedulers decided to use the X-ray Department and sequence the work assigned to it. The list was prepared with relevant points a. through e. Unfortunately, one point on that list is incorrect. Which point is that?

a. Three jobs are in the X-ray Department queue. All that is known about them is the order in which they arrived for processing (A, B, C) and how long they each will take to accomplish. That is the operation times, t_i.

Sequencing Table (LPT)				
Arrival Order	Job (i)	W_i Minutes	t_i Minutes	C_i Minutes
First	A	0	17	17
Second	B	17	12	29
Third	C	29	9	38
Total		46 minutes	38 minutes	84 minutes

b. The table shows that by chance the first job to arrive is the longest one. The second is the next longest, and the third is the shortest. Sequencing experts know that this arrangement, which is called longest processing time (LPT), will lead to the longest total wait time (and the highest average wait time) for the set of $n = 3$ jobs. Managers prefer to use FIFO (first-in, first-out) when possible because it seems fair to their customers.

c. The table shows that when the processing order is LPT, the total waiting time is 46 minutes. Processing time is 38 minutes, and that will not change no matter in what order the jobs will be done. The total completion time is 84 minutes, which is the sum:

$$\sum_{i=1}^{i=n} C_i = \sum_{i=1}^{i=n} (W_i + t_i)$$

d.   A familiar objective in sequencing is to minimize mean flow time, which is

$$\overset{i=n}{\Sigma}\, C_i/n = \overset{i=n}{\Sigma}\, (W_i + t_i)/n$$

e.   The specific value of mean flow time in this case is 21 minutes.

9   Shortest processing time (SPT) will minimize the average waiting time for all jobs. This raises questions about the fairness of FIFO if it penalizes the average job on the waiting line. That was the case in Problem 8 because the FIFO order happened to be the longest processing time (LPT). In general, if random arrivals are serviced with the FIFO rule, then the result will seldom be optimal and will generally fall between the SPT optimal and the LPT worse case. The City Hospital schedulers wanted to demonstrate the truth of this point to all department heads in the hospital. They have drawn up a table based on SPT for the X-ray Department. The new table retained the LPT totals so that a comparison could be made between LPT and SPT. Based on the new table, a list was prepared with relevant points a. through e. One point on that list is incorrect. Which point is that?

a.   The same three jobs are in the X-ray Department queue. The schedulers decided to ignore the FIFO rule because A arrived before B, which arrived before C. The first column is now processing order and not arrival order. In this case, the last to arrive, C, is the first to receive processing.

Processing Order	Job (i)	Sequencing Table (LPT)		
		W_i Minutes	t_i Minutes	C_i Minutes
First	C	0	9	9
Second	B	9	12	21
Third	A	21	17	38
Total Flow-Time-LPT		46 minutes	38 minutes	84 minutes
Total Flow-Time-SPT		30 minutes	38 minutes	68 minutes
Percent Improved		34.8%	No change	19%

b.   Sequencing experts know that shortest processing time (SPT) will lead to minimum total waiting time (and the lowest average wait time) for the set of $n = 3$ jobs.

c.   The table shows that when the processing order is SPT, the total waiting time is 30 minutes. Processing time is 38 minutes. The total completion time is 68 minutes, which is the sum:

$$\sum_{i=1}^{i=n} C_i = \sum_{i=1}^{i=n} (W_i + t_i)$$

d.   The mean flow time is $68/3 = 22.67$ minutes, as shown in the equation.

$$\sum_{i=1}^{i=n} C_i/n = \sum_{i=1}^{i=n} (W_i + t_i)/n = (30 + 38)/3 = 22.67$$

e.   The improvement must be viewed in terms of the frequency with which a small but significant saving is obtained. There is a reduction in waiting time of almost 20 percent as a result of using SPT as compared to the worst case LPT situation. The benchmark is extreme because FIFO will seldom produce an LPT ordering.

10   The SPT rule is a benefit to the average customer. However, it penalizes customers with long jobs. In the X-ray Department, there are jobs that take extensive periods of time to prepare. These jobs may constantly be passed over in favor of the short jobs. To avoid problems of this sort, City Hospital's schedulers have decided to use critical ratio procedures (for due dates) and priorities based on cumulative delays to modify SPT rules. The intention is to cover a number of issues that a well-trained production schedule manager should be comfortable discussing. The list of points a. through e. have been sent around the company for observations and comments. One of them is not correct. Which is the flawed statement?

a.   Optimal sequencing can be found when there is one facility ($m = 1$) and any number of jobs (n) to be processed through that facility. When more than one facility exists for processing jobs, i.e., $m > 1$, the problem is too complex. There are no optimal solutions. Simulation must be used with heuristics.

b. Priority-modified SPT rules can take into account the fact that some jobs are more important to the company than others. This is done by dividing each job's processing time, t_i, by the relative importance of the job, w_i. Thus, t_i/w_i, are rank ordered. The job with the smallest ratio, t_i/w_i, is placed first. Continue in the same way with the next smallest ratios. Important jobs have the smallest modified SPT value.

c. Alternative interpretations of w_i include lateness, L_i. If a job is not late, $L_i = 1$. Otherwise, the ratios, t_i/L_i, put late jobs at the top of the processing order.

d. Another system lets w_i equal the number of days that the job has been waiting to be processed. As delay mounts up, the ratio, t_i/w_i, rises quickly to the top of the list.

e. A sequencing rule that is called the critical ratio rank orders d_i/t_i, where d_i is the number of days remaining before the promised delivery.

Additional Readings

Conway, Richard W., William L. Maxwell, and Louis W. Miller. *Theory of Scheduling.* Mineola, NY: Dover Publications (a classic, reissued in paperback), June 2003.

Conway, Richard W. "Priority Dispatching and Job Lateness in a Job Shop." *Journal of Industrial Engineering*, vol. 16, no. 4 (July 1965).

Digital Equipment Corporation. *Factory Scheduler.* Oregon Licensed to the Mitron Corp. of Beaverton (503-690-8350), 1994.

Goldratt, Eliyahu M. *The Haystack Syndrome.* Great Barrington, MA: North River Press, Inc., 1990.

———. *The Theory of Constraints Journals.* volumes 1–6. Great Barrington, MA: North River Press, Inc., 1990.

———. *It's Not Luck.* Great Barrington, MA: North River Press, Inc., 1994.

Goldratt, Eliyahu M., and Jeff Cox. *The Goal: A Process of Ongoing Improvement*, 2e. Great Barrington, MA: North River Press, 1992.

Goldratt, Eliyahu M., and Robert E. Fox. *The Race.* Great Barrington, MA: North River Press, 1986.

Herrmann, Jeffrey W. (ed.). *Handbook of Production Scheduling.* New York: Springer, 2006.

Plenert, Gerhard, and Bill Kirchmier. *Finite Capacity Scheduling: Management, Selection, and Implementation.* New York: John Wiley & Sons, January 2000.

Red Pepper Software. *ResponseAgents (Optimizing Production Scheduler).* San Mateo, CA John Wiley & Sons (415-960-4095), 1994.

Umble, M. Michael, and M. L. Srikanth. *Synchronous Manufacturing: Principles for World Class Excellence.* Cincinnati, OH: South-Western Publishing Co., 1990.

Notes

1. S. M. Johnson. "Optimal Two- and Three-Stage Production Schedules with Set-up Times Included." *Naval Research Logistics Quarterly*, vol. 1, no. 1 (March 1954): 61–68. This article laid the foundation for later work in sequencing theory. It is historically of interest.

2. See http://en.wikipedia.org/wiki/Venturi_effect for a diagram of a Venturi meter and a picture of a Venturi tube.

3. Eliyahu Goldratt and R. Fox. *The Race.* North River Press, 1986. The OPT system was developed by Eliyahu Goldratt as a commercial product for best scheduling practice. Also visit http://www.goldratt.com for 2003 up-to-date information about AGI and TOC, including its project management (critical chain) developments. The AGI is the Goldratt Institute.

4. Costliest and deadliest hurricane in the history of the United States. This storm of August 29, 2005, shut the port of New Orleans for over six months.

Enrichment Activity 16: Increasing Bottleneck Capacity

It is an everyday problem. Bottlenecks constrain throughput in offices, plants, stores, and kitchens throughout the world. People learn to live with them, but true competitors do not accept them without analyzing the alternatives. Assume it is known where a particular bottleneck exists. Are people the cause? For example, they do not work fast enough or they are making mistakes that create defects and rework. Is technology the cause? Perhaps bad weather has slowed traffic. Maybe the economy is the cause. People have stopped buying high-priced items and shifted to lower-priced items that cannot be produced in sufficient volume. Natural disasters are bottleneck creators that deserve prior contingency planning (as in the case of the port of New Orleans shut by hurricane Katrina[4]).

Unacceptable bottlenecks prevent daily demand levels from being filled, which has costs that can be very large threatening survival. For example, a new drug is being tested and has been found to have promising results. However, the U.S. Food and

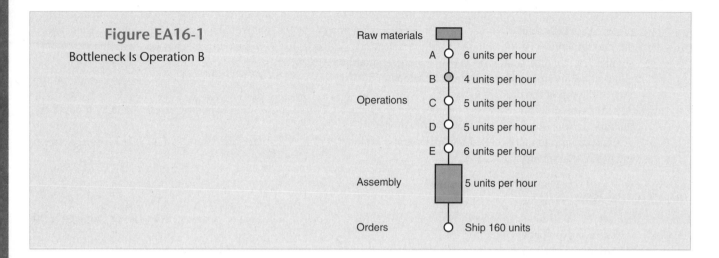

Figure EA16-1

Bottleneck Is Operation B

Raw materials

A	6 units per hour
B	4 units per hour
Operations C	5 units per hour
D	5 units per hour
E	6 units per hour
Assembly	5 units per hour
Orders	Ship 160 units

Drug Administration (FDA) requires procedures that delay the availability of this drug to numerous individuals dying of the disease that this drug may cure. The delay (bottleneck) will be justified if it turns out (after extensive testing) that the drug kills more people than it cures. Raising the bottleneck capacity in this case would mean finding a way to cut testing time.

Flow rates should be studied using flow process charts, as in Figure EA16-1, to permit bottleneck analysis of specific situations. In this figure, flow is from upstream (A) to downstream (E, assembly and shipping). Bottleneck B is the drum because it has the smallest constant processing or throughput rate of four units per hour.

In general, it is sensible to consider the impact of increasing the capacity of every bottleneck facility. Sometimes by using new technology or more people, a greater volume of work can be done inexpensively. This may result in shifting the bottleneck to another part of the process where it is not economically feasible to further increase throughputs.

Operation A has unused capacity of two units per hour. It is instructed to feed the bottleneck, and the time buffer is set to provide an hour of protection in the event that operation A breaks down. B needs four units every hour, which means that between A and B there should be a reserve of four units. This is equivalent to A working 2/3 of an hour. However, the first two hours A will work at full speed to create the necessary time buffer. Thereafter, if B works faster and draws down on the hour of buffer stock, A can work longer than the usual 40 minutes to make up the difference. It should be noted that C, D, and "Assembly" all can work at five units per hour. E can produce six units per hour. None of them will be able to work faster than B. The bottleneck B sets the pace, and B cannot be allowed to run out of stock because that would result in lower profits.

The basic assumptions of this bottleneck problem are the simplest ones that exist. B works at a steady pace and A feeds B at a constant rate of 4 per hour. Unexpected events such as a breakdown of A are covered with buffer stock and a breakdown of B is not even mentioned. Variable work rates on the part of both A and B are not allowed. These simple assumptions describe a deterministic process. When variabilities exist, this more complex process is described as a stochastic process.

Deterministic flow patterns through bottlenecks are discussed in this Enrichment Activity 16. Stochastic flow patterns through bottlenecks are discussed in Enrichment Activity 17. Deterministic bottlenecks should be analyzed as follow:

1 *Locate the bottleneck.* This is called prospecting for bottlenecks. It involves developing detailed flow-process charts for all important orders in the shop and measuring or estimating the processing rates. Every operation must be included and associated with its processing rate. Workstation B will be found in this way.

2 *Determine appropriate time buffers for the bottlenecks.* Then control the transfer lot sizes and the frequency of delivery from all upstream operations (in this case only operation A needs to be controlled).

3 *Is it feasible to increase the throughput rate of the bottleneck?* Analyze the costs and benefits of increasing the throughput rate (capacity) of the bottleneck. The bottleneck will shift to another place of constraint. Will the new bottleneck be preferred to the prior one? Is the shift acceptable?

Example I

With regard to point 3, if the use of new technology, costing $150,000, could increase operation B's output to five units per hour, B, C, D, and "Assembly" all become bottlenecks. A time buffer must now be built up between the many bottlenecks so that B can feed C, then, C can feed D, and so on. It is considerably easier to have only one bottleneck to tend. Consequently, using overtime with the existing bottleneck might be a better solution.

The system can now produce 160 units per week. The additional 40 units (8×5) per week times 50 weeks per year yields 2,000 extra units per year. Assume that each of these 2,000 units delivers a $50 profit. The investment in bottleneck reconfiguration will pay for itself in one and a half years. Thus: V = investment to increase production by Δp, where Δp = extra production per year; and π = profit per unit. Then, alter the bottleneck when:

$$\left(\frac{V}{\pi(\Delta p)}\right) \leq n \qquad\qquad (EA16\text{-}1)$$

where n is the chosen payback period.

For these numbers, $150,000/($50)(2,000) = 1.5$ year payback period, which is likely to be an acceptable investment in bottleneck repair.

Example II

Removing bottlenecks (or diminishing their effects) may cost more than the resulting improvement is worth. Assume this firm buys an automatic feeder (AF) to speed throughput at workstation B (the bottleneck in Figure EA16-1) from four to six units per hour. However, downstream stations can only process five units per hour, which limits workstation B to produce five also. The benefit of the AF can be quickly calculated from the fact that profit for this part is $50. Therefore, the AF raises profit by $100,000 per year (1 unit per hour $\times$ 40 hours per week $\times$ 50 weeks per year $\times$ $50 profit per unit). This AF costs $2,000,000. It will take 20 years to payback this AF. If net present value is used with 3% interest, it will take 31 years. This is an unreasonable investment. If downstream bottlenecks can be adjusted to increase their capacity to six units, without additional cost, then, the AF can achieve payback in half the time. However, net present value estimation with a discount rate of 3%—see Enrichment Activity 8—shows more than 12 years to recoup the investment.

Example III

Still referring to Figure EA16-1, if demand calls for shipping 200 units, that falls 40 short of the 160 units that will be made in the present 40-hour week. Without any new technology, 10 more hours of production are required. As before, each unit generates $50 of profit, or a total of $2,000 per week. The cost of overtime for ten hours at workstation B must be less than $2,000 or $200 per hour. The other workstations must be factored into this calculation. It they require overtime, that will diminish the $2,000 per week of extra profit. It is quite likely that for the entire system of workstations, overtime cost will turn profit to loss.

Example IV

By training people to do jobs of standard quality at a faster pace, bottleneck capacity can be increased. Supporting technology can help. Another approach is to view bottlenecks as delays in deliveries to customers. Referring to SPT rules in Section 16-8, assume that three jobs are to be completed every eight hour day. They are called R, G, and B requiring 1 hour, 3 hours, and 4 hours, respectively. If these jobs are done in LPT fashion because management believes that you should get the toughest jobs done first, then, the matrix below applies. If management believes in SPT, then the delivery bottleneck effect is reduced by 55% which is substantial. Using SPT, it will be found that total W_i is five hours.

Job	W_i	t_i	C_i
R	0	4	4
G	4	3	7
B	7	1	8
Total	11	8	19

Enrichment Challenges 16

1 New technology can be purchased that will cut the four hour time (t) required by R in Example 4 (above) to three hours. As shown in the matrix below, this reduces the waiting time to nine hours from eleven hours for LPT. That is an 18% reduction in the delivery delay of the bottleneck when the LPT schedule is followed. If the new technology costs $10,000, is it worth it?

2 What is the effect on the SPT result? Is the $10,000 investment worthwhile? Discuss this issue from a systems perspective.

Job	W_i	t_i	C_i
R	0	3	3
G	3	3	6
B	6	1	7
Total	9	7	16

3 Workstation B is the bottleneck (see Figure EA16-1). B has a throughput rate of four units per hour, which constrains the system's output rate to 160 units per week. An order has been received for 240 units, which led to the decision to buy an automatic feeder machine. This machine can raise B's output rate to six units per hour.

  What output rate will be achieved? How long will it take to fill the order?

4 Using the information in Problem 3 and in Figure EA16-1, what time buffers should be set for workstation A? Are there any other time buffers to be set?

5 Combine the information in Problem 3 with the fact that the feeder machine will cost $25,000. The profit per unit for extra units will be $2.00. Do you agree with the decision to buy the new machine? Explain your response.

6 Combine the information in Problem 3 with the fact that for $50,000 all of the units can be connected with a paced-conveyor belt and run at six units per hour. Will this investment pay off? Discuss the problem of feeding multiple bottlenecks.

Chapter 17 explains what cycle-time management is and why it has become so important to both manufacturing and service organizations. Cycles are intervals of time during which events repeat themselves. Cycle time determines productivity. When operations produce a stream of outputs *repetitively over time, as in the flow shop*, it is necessary to determine how long the process takes from start to finish. That is a benchmark against which further improvement is measured. It is of paramount importance to analyze the process to find out if any time periods (no matter how short) can be shaved from that cycle time. As cycle time decreases, output rises (see Table 17-4).

Line balancing for cycle-time control is one kind of effort to smooth the availability of resources along the path of production so that no slowdown occurs. Waiting is waste in the cycle time. These ideas apply to intermittent and continuous flow shops. Differences are drawn between deterministic, stochastic, and heuristic line-balancing situations. The management of cycle time is shown to be an important aspect of time-based management (TBM). Waiting line or queuing models are introduced in this context of balanced work flows when arrivals and servicing times are random variables. The Enrichment Activity 17 provides simulation of queuing models reflecting line-balancing objectives and the waiting line phenomenon.

After reading this chapter, you should be able to:

- Explain the nature of cycle-time management.
- Illustrate the relationship between the line balancing of serialized production systems and cycle-time management.
- Explain when line balancing is essential.
- Detail different kinds of line-balancing situations that exist with respect to labor-intensive and technology-oriented workstations.
- Describe the difference between deterministic, stochastic, and heuristic line-balancing situations.
- Explain what must be done to balance a production line.
- Relate cycle-time management to time-based management (TBM) and distinguish between tactical and strategic TBM.
- Draw a precedence diagram and calculate output rates for different numbers of stations.
- Describe perfect balance, measure-balance delay and line efficiency, and explain why they are useful measures.
- Demonstrate a heuristic line-balancing algorithm and explain why the use of computer software is desirable.
- Relate stochastic line-balancing and queuing models.
- Explain why all service systems can be viewed as queuing systems that must be balanced to satisfy customer expectations.
- Demonstrate how single-channel queuing models can be used to estimate average length of waiting lines and waiting times.
- Describe the role of suppliers in cycle-time management.
- Discuss the advantages and conversion of push-production systems to pull-production systems.

The Systems Viewpoint

Cycle time provides a measure of the output rates of different parts of the system. For the system as a whole, CT is a common denominator that interrelates the timing of activities and flows of materials. Timing is as important to the performance of repetitive production systems (flow shops) as it is to the performance of a symphony orchestra. Cycle time is directly related to the interval that work stays at each workstation, and to the rate at which items are finished and ship to customers. The big systems perspective connects customers' demand rates and suppliers' delivery rates with management's control over production output cycle time. Supply chain management (SCM) and CTM are partners in the system. Cycle-time management will reflect decisions about how much to make to ship and how much to make to stock under normal and peak demand conditions. The systems view requires inclusion of the cycle times of internal functions that support the production process, such as production scheduling for components and subassemblies, materials inspection, maintenance, and billing for accounts receivable. The systems viewpoint requires inclusion of cycle times related to delivery of materials and distribution along the supply chain. Time-based management is dependent on cycle time design and control.

Strategic Thinking

When plans are being formulated concerning how to convert money into productive resources, product and service strategies are the focus of attention. The concept of using flow shops to achieve volumes of output that have substantial cost savings is part of that strategy. The signature of a flow shop is its cycle time. There is a theoretical cycle time and a realistic cycle time. Competitive advantage is gained by firms that can decrease the cycle time of an established process. The higher level of margin that results can be used to support marketing, design even better process cycle times, decrease the price of the product line, and to create new products. When cycle-time management is applied to various work configurations, it is feasible to determine which comes closest to satisfying the strategic plans, which can include flow shops that are relatively permanent or the shorter durations of intermittent flow shops (IFS) producing large batches of work. Strategic thinking should include time-based and cycle-time management (TBM and CTM). Just-in-time (JIT) considerations are supply chain support for CTM. Synchronization and orchestration are strategic issues of cycle-time management. Spotlight 17-1 on the O.O.D.A. loop brings home the strategic importance of short cycle (or loop) time in being successful under stressful competitive conditions.

17-1 Cycle-Time Management (CTM)

Cycle time is defined as the interval of time that elapses between successive units of finished product coming off the production line. **Cycle-Time Management (CTM)** is the design and control of that interval for making goods and providing servicing operations. Cycle time is always managed but it is not always managed well.

17-1a Automobiles: Cycle Times

If a completed Subaru comes off the production line in Lafayette, Indiana, every 1.5 minutes, then one and one-half minutes would be the cycle time (*C*) for that assembly line. Using this figure, every hour 40 cars (60/1.5 = 40) would be driven off the end of the line. Output per day would be 720-cars using two 9-hour shifts per day. With two 9-hour shifts per day for 26 days per month, 18,720 cars would be produced per month and 224,640 cars per year. (In this example, each regular shift is 8 hours with 1-hour overtime—and one overtime weekend might be worked per month.)

Cycle time

The interval, *C*, that elapses between successive units of finished work coming off the production line.

Cycle-Time Management (CTM)

Setting and maintaining the interval of time that service is rendered, or that it takes to make a complete production unit. See **Cycle time**.

In addition, *if* there are 300 workstations, then to make a car would take 450 minutes, or 7.5 hours, from start to finish. Perhaps 900 employees are on the line and supporting the 300 workstations. Numerical estimates, such as those shown here, help to model the cost of making an automobile. They assist, as well, in establishing rough benchmarks and refining those benchmarks. Additionally, standards need to be set with production methods put in place to achieve the standards and then improve upon them.

From the definition given here, cycle time must be the length of time that a unit spends at each stop point along the (conveyor belted) production line. This means that if the process can be altered so that work in process spends less time at each workstation, then the interval between successive units of finished goods coming off the line can be shortened, resulting in an increased production output rate.

As another example, if a completed Subaru comes off the production line in Lafayette, Indiana, every 1.0 minutes, then one minute would be the cycle time for that assembly line. Using this figure, every hour 60 cars ($60/1.0 = 60$) would be driven off the end of the line. Output per day would be 1,080 cars using two 9-hour shifts per day. With two 9-hour shifts per day for 26 days per month, 28,080 cars would be produced per month and 336,960 per year. In addition, if there are 300 workstations, then to make a car would take 300 minutes, or 5.0 hours, from start to finish. These numbers are not meant to describe actual Subaru production. However, they are meant to provoke discussion about how cycle time relates to the production output.

When cycle time went from 1.5 minutes to 1.0 minute, this was a reduction of cycle time by 33 percent. That led to a 50 percent increase in the number of cars produced. Productivity increased. The time required to build a car decreased by 33 percent (going from 7.5 hours to 5.0 hours). Cycle-time reductions go right to the bottom line, which is why management is focused on process improvements. It makes good sense to spend money on training and new technology if those expenditures can significantly decrease the cycle time. There is ample evidence that such expenditures can deliver significant improvements in cycle time.

When production rate cycle time is altered up or down, this will change the cycle times for many activities that support the production system. More or less materials may be needed from the automotive suppliers to feed the production line. Fewer or more workers doing their own inspection may be needed to deal with quality and quantity checks. More or fewer auto carriers may be wanted to carry finished autos to retailers and distributors' warehouses. Cycle times of inbound and outbound supplies are interconnected with the fundamentals of the production line. Balanced production systems require understanding cycle timing.

It is not surprising that in recent years, cycle time has become one of the most important P/OM topics for executives from a broadly diverse set of industries. With pressure on profits, cycle-time improvements can provide financial leverage at the relatively low cost of thinking creatively. Big improvements in output and revenue can be gained at low cost and (often) fairly quickly. Decreasing cycle time by working smarter and not harder has the effect of increasing productivity, decreasing the breakeven point, and increasing the system's effective capacity.

Rolls-Royce provides another example of how improving process design decreases cycle time and raises output. Often, but not always, the extra input costs are minor in comparison to the output gains. The Rolls-Royce manufacturing plant was antiquated and inefficient. Using consultants familiar with Japanese lean methods, they were able to cut the cycle time for making a Rolls-Royce from 50 to 30 days. Although this 40 percent improvement reduced the breakeven point from 2,600 cars in 1992 to 1,300 cars in 1994, the firm did not achieve profitability. Thirty days is still far too long a time to build a car, even a Rolls-Royce. It became evident that a new plant would be needed to alter the situation. They call it a *greenfield* plant, meaning it is start-up from scratch with all new systems. Greenfield plants in the United States include the Saturn plant located in Spring Hill, Tennessee; the Honda plant in Marysville, Ohio; and Toyota plants in Princeton, Indiana, and Georgetown, Kentucky. Greenfield plants generally produce a car a minute.

The improvement just described was not enough to keep the U.K. Rolls-Royce in business. Volkswagen took control of the company, but they used the same plant that had been producing the car for 60 years, viz., the manufacturing facility at Crewe in Cheshire. That did not work out. As pointed out earlier, it can be difficult to cut cycle time significantly without radically changing the factory environment.

BMW then took over Rolls-Royce production from its German rival Volkswagen, which produced its last Rolls in August 2002. BMW built a new Rolls-Royce manufacturing plant for £65 million at Goodwood in West Sussex. By 2003, BMW announced that the company achieved a breakeven point well below 1,000 cars per year. The plan called for production of 4 cars per day to sell for about £240,000. A 2-hour cycle time ($C = 120$ minutes) is still long when compared to U.S. greenfield plant standards of 1 or 2 minutes. However, the Rolls-Royce sells at 10 times the price of an expensive American SUV. $C = 120$ minutes is significantly better than $C = 30$ days for the cycle time that Rolls-Royce achieved after major improvement of their manufacturing facility at Crewe in Cheshire.

17-1b Airlines: Cycle Times

To apply cycle time to airline flights, treat each time the *next* plane takes off on the same runway as the *next* finished unit coming off the production line. The interval between takeoffs is the cycle time of the airport for the specific runway. U.S. Airways realized that its cost structure was not competitive (and this was before 9/11). Using good P/OM practice, they cut the ground time between flights from 45 minutes to 20 minutes. This is equivalent to saying that cycle time was reduced by $25/45 = 55.56 = 56$ percent. That would appear to be outstanding but not enough to compensate for the fact that U.S. Airways had too much debt.

From a P/OM point of view, there is much interest in the fact that cycle time was reduced by 56 percent. This was done by decreasing the number of crew changes, speeding up the check-in procedures, and loading planes with enough food and drinks for several trips. The resulting productivity improvement increased the available seating capacity for the fleet of planes by 3,500 seats per day. There are a number of ways of looking at this improvement. The most direct might be to estimate increased revenues at between $100 and $200 per extra seat yielding a range for additional revenue from $350,000 to $700,000 per day. The conservative yearly estimate is impressive being 365 × $300,000, which is in excess of 10 million dollars.

In fact, much of this estimated revenue would not be realized for a variety of reasons, including the fact that the airlines adhere to their published flight schedules. Less time on the ground and a shorter cycle time might save operating costs and help achieve on-time performance with higher customer satisfaction.

This airline example is particularly useful because it changes perspective. It broadens the applicability of the concept of cycles from the traditional, and entirely correct, notion that cycle time applies to repetitive operations such as an assembly line. In this case, cycle time is appropriate for a set of operations that are linked together as a chain of repetitive activities such as supporting airplane takeoffs.

© 2007 Jupiterimages Corporation

Intervals between takeoffs are cycle times fixed by safety concerns for separation of aircraft. This interval differs for 747 jets and Cessna prop planes. The starting position on runways is equivalent to an initial workstation on the line. Lift-off is equivalent to preparation of the product for delivery.

17-1c Other Applications of Cycle Times

In setting time standards, there are short and long cycles that comprise the job. Having to go to the storeroom to get materials, such as rolls of tape to seal boxes, may have to be done once every 1,000 boxes sealed. Nevertheless, it is a legitimate cycle that deserves to be studied and that can be improved. Perhaps getting two rolls of tape at a time, or one double roll, would decrease the frequency of work interruption. That change might lower the cost of the job and increase the productivity of the worker.

Industrial engineers are trained to question the methods being employed to perform a task. How far does Joe have to walk to obtain a role of tape? Can storage be moved

© 2008 Jupiterimages Corporation

In Quebec, this roller-coaster makes its loops during a fixed cycle time, and any variability would be dangerous. Amusements parks run like clockwork, which epitomizes flow shop cycle times.

Time-based management (TBM)

Managers are concerned about timelines, schedules, deliveries, and project completions; their goals are to be fast-moving rapid-responders; they want to achieve high velocity without quality losses.

© 2008 Jupiterimages Corporation

Keeping the records for the start and finish times of track events is a crucial task. The same applies to running an efficient production process. How long it takes to make a part or provide a service is critical information for managers.

closer, decreasing the distance? Value analysis raises the question "Is there some better material to use than tape?" Can a glue gun improve the seal and reduce the cost of this operation? Cycle-time improvements often result from worker suggestions.

Cycles exist in the repetitive intervals between placing an order and receiving supplies. Inspection cycles exist between receiving and accepting materials for use on the production line. Just-in-time (JIT) systems can make deliveries faster by providing automatic (computerized) procedures for recognizing that stock levels need replenishment. Bigger trucks require fewer trips but lengthen cycle times. Conversely, smaller trucks have shorter cycle times with less materials being stocked more often. The frequency of deliveries and the stock that is carried as a result are most often viewed as inventory management problems. The decision to use just-in-time deliveries alters the production cycle of suppliers as well as their shipping schedules.

Cycle time is of critical importance to the designers of theme park rides. Disney and Universal design rides to maximize throughput rates. Disney's Tower of Terror has two elevators working side-by-side doing the double (now triple) drop in the dark that is the core experience. "Guests," however, are only aware of the elevator that they occupy.

Because guests do not enjoy waiting time, FastPass was created by Disney. FastPass allows guests to make reservations on particular rides to avoid waiting on long lines. It is not a far cry to consider the New York City subway as much a ride as the Hulk coaster at Universal's Islands of Adventure or Kraken at Sea World in Orlando. In New York City, the Metropolitan Transit Authority (MTA) is totally aware of cycle time to load and unload the crowded subways at Times Square. In office buildings, the elevator is designed to pick up and drop off crowds of people with different patterns in accord with the time of day. Cycle times are at center stage, influencing productivity, cost, and quality.

17-2 Time-Based Management (TBM) and Synchronization of Flows

Cycle-time management is one facet of **time-based management (TBM)**. It is the aspect of TBM that applies to running a better production process for a flow shop. Better means balanced (as will become evident from materials ahead). Better also can mean a shorter cycle time. This was explained for autos, airlines, and other applications.

Cycle time-based management is generally regarded to be tactical in scope, given that the system has been designed, built, and it is up-and-running. It needs controlling. The reason that it is tactical is that it entails management of the existing production process. To further clarify, tactics are applied to military situations with respect to "small scale" actions serving a larger purpose. Tactical vision is usually applied to situations with limited and/or immediate ends in view.

In contrast to tactical steps and procedures, there are strategic plans and decisions that precede tactical activities. For example, when alternative process designs are under consideration, the decisions about which way to go are strategic ones. The best strategic decisions are made with an understanding of the tactics that will be used under that strategic umbrella. Using retail business as an illustration, strategies relate to where to locate, how big a store, and what to sell. Tactics might be where to advertise, how to price products, when to have sales, how to display merchandise, and what the sale force should say.

Cycle times include how long it takes to make a sale, intervals required for checking out and paying, time to restock the shelves, replenishment intervals, coupon expiration dating, and other details that make that business function. TBM is at work determining the optimal timing through synchronization of the factors. Don't advertise until there is sufficient stock on-hand. Have enough cash register operators so customers are not upset waiting. That is what is meant by tactical aspects of TBM.

The concept of continuous process improvement, instead of reengineering (or radical change), often, but not always, applies to cycle-time reduction. For instance, BMW's success in cutting cycle time for Rolls-Royce required literal interpretation of the green-field concept. It was necessary to start the new building on a vacant lot. When talking about reengineering, it means starting from scratch. On the other hand, continuous improvement is associated with the idea that "practice makes perfect." The old tried and true recipe prevails but it must be tweaked because the critic wrote a review in *The New York Times*, and he said that rosemary should be added to the broth. In that vein, reengineering restaurants is very difficult in the same location.

Location experts need to think about this. Certain locations are said to be "cursed." For example, every restaurant that opens at a certain location fails. Could it be that the first restaurant at that location failed and thereby put a *blight* on every subsequent restaurant at that location? Customers do not associate a trip to that location for a "good meal" as supportable. A bookstore at the same location might be a big success. Greenfield gives a boost to reengineering the entire system to conform to a clearer strategy.

Another facet of TBM that is increasingly important to operations management is project management. Project management has a different interpretation of cycle time than the flow shop. Often, projects deal with developing a new product or process as quickly as possible. Such developments are considered strategic because they represent a major change in resource usage and company policy. Managing a project would apply to the way in which BMW handled the project of building, installing, and starting up its new production process for Rolls-Royce.

Tactical timing goals must synchronize cycles of all participants. The flows of materials used on the line must get to where they are needed on time. Shipping schedules of finished goods must be synchronized so that inventory pileups do not occur on the shipping docks. When the cycle times of parts of processes are reduced in one place, other places in the process must be adjusted so that balance is maintained and the flows are synchronized. This aspect of cycle-time management is inherent in proper control of the supply chain.

The management of the broad range of activities that can be defined as cycles puts the spotlight on the timing. Substantial reduction of intervals between successive outputs from the production line can usually be obtained by rethinking the way that things are done. Cycle-time management and quality management have a lot of similarities. The reduction of cycle time and the reduction of defectives can result from being clever about process design. Conversely, poor processes result from a lack of teamwork and a shortage of team members' suggestions. Thus, as it is said that some part of quality improvement is free, some part of cycle-time improvement also is free.

In building confidence that one can improve cycle times, the place to start is with line-balancing serialized work configurations. This includes intermittent flow shops. There is often reluctance to spend as freely on line balancing temporary flow shops as compared to permanent ones. Line balancing is the main cycle-management technique in both cases—whether the system of supporting machines, conveyors, and training are for dedicated or temporary production purposes.

17-3 Line-Balancing (LB) Methods

Line balancing (LB) is the effort to *nearly equalize* the output rate capabilities of successive workstations on the production line. LB also is the effort to reduce and match excess idle time at the workstations. Line balancing has to take into consideration constraints that include the order in which work can be done and the impossibility of splitting some operations between different stations. The overriding objective of LB is to achieve a balance of production resources that can deliver the right amount of production to satisfy demand requirements with minimum waste of resources.

This goal can be directly translated into supply chain terms. LB synchronizes material flows by properly assigning required resources. These include people, production equipment, storage space, and transportation facilities. When production equipment is part of a

Line balancing (LB)
Effort to divide total work content into equal (or nearly equal) balanced parts for assignment at each of *n* workstations. Bad design loads stations unevenly.

dedicated flow shop (as in automobile assembly), engineers provide perfect line balance for such mechanized manufacturing systems.

Unlike the engineering of dedicated flow shops, the use of LB for intermittent flow shops (IFS) is common when batch sizes are large enough to warrant a temporary serial form of production. A manufacturer of baby strollers runs different models on the same production line for varying times according to demand. Each model has unique characteristics that change the line-balance requirements. A manufacturer of electric switch boxes makes most models on a job shop basis in batches. When an order is received for batch sizes that tie up machines for more than two days, an intermittent flow shop setup is used. Market research operators use IFS processing when a report has many regions and a variety of products being compared. The intermittent flow shop is the process of choice for growth firms and product situations where short life cycles characterize the market. They are so prevalent that line balancing for cycle management is a necessity for competitive capability.

With IFS, people often are an important part of the production system. The participation of people at the workstations in manufacturing, service systems, and along the supply chain increases the variability of output rates. The effect of worker variability is particularly important for cycle management using line balancing of service systems. Variability of service systems is noticeable in both the arrival rate of people and work for servicing, and in the rates at which services are administered.

People and work wait in line, which is inefficient. Then, at other times, the service system is idle, which is inefficient. These aspects of line balancing will be covered in Section 17-5 on stochastic line balancing, which is another way of saying line-balancing systems that have random arrivals and/or service times.

Serialized processes are composed of operations that are repetitive and sequential. They are linked together—usually by a conveyor that moves the pieces and then stops—so that work can be done at each station. Line balancing requires assigning operations ($i = 1, 2, \ldots, k$) to workstations ($j = 1, 2, \ldots, n$) so that all of the workstations are about equally busy (previously described as *nearly equalized*). This terminology of line balancing can be applied to supply chain and service systems.

Some workstation activities are labor intensive. Others are highly mechanized. The spectrum is constantly moving closer to automation. Glasstech's Advanced In-Line Windshield Forming System is entirely mechanized. People pollution is the bane of *clean rooms* for semiconductor manufacturing. Yet, people are needed in clean rooms, and windshield manufacturing provides labor servicing and supporting robot equipment. The nursing profession delivers hands-on assistance, which patients require. The social ethic would have it no other way. Although the trend is technologically driven toward increasing automation in volume manufacturing systems, for most service systems it remains labor intensive.

Volume production of semiconductors reflects a unique combination of labor and technology in manufacturing. The production process takes place in a clean room. Workers in full containment garb are part of the process. The slightest bit of dirt on computer chips ruins circuitry. Clean-room technology constantly filters away the smallest particles. Workers interact with machines at workstations within this special environment.

Automotive-assembly line balancing reflects a broad range of technology and workers. Installing window glass and upholstery is relatively labor intensive, whereas painting and welding are primarily computer and machine driven. Timing is set for the assembly-line conveyors that travel at rates carefully set by engineering and management design. When there are unions, they participate in agreeing to the rate of the **paced conveyor** system.

The history of line balancing deserves attention. In the 1940s at the Louisville, Kentucky, plant of General Electric, which manufactures appliances, a group called *Operations Research and Synthesis (OR & S)* led by Mel Salveson decided to investigate the line-balancing problem. Their studies began a stream of activities that led many

Paced conveyor

A transporter, usually a belt, moving materials between workstations at a fixed rate of speed. Station stop-time equals cycle time.

researchers to contribute results to the line-balancing literature. By the 1960s, a fine body of work existed in all three classes of line balancing. The three classes, which are deterministic, heuristic, and stochastic line balancing, are described here.

Deterministic line balancing is based on the assumption that each total process takes an exact amount of time, which is known and not variable. The total process is made up of operations. The operations' times when added together constitute the total process or total job time. The operations' times are all fixed. If they were not, then the total process time would not be deterministic.

Heuristic line-balancing methods employ "rules of thumb," common sense, logical thinking, and experience to find near-optimal solutions for large problems. These are problems that involve too many operations to allow enumerating and testing all of the possibilities. The number of possible configurations in line balancing grows rapidly with operations and stations. Only heuristic methods are economically feasible for many real problems.

Heuristics are used when complexity of size is an issue and the flow shop is temporary. When the flow shop is relatively permanent, as in computer-chip manufacturing and automobile assembly, engineering efforts can be justified to design perfectly balanced flow shops. That level of expense is not often acceptable for intermittent flow shops, which have sufficient complexity to require heuristic methods and sufficient volume to pay for the application of the heuristic. Under these circumstances, the line-balancing problem offers one of the best examples of a real need for heuristic methods. Heuristic LB can be used in both deterministic and stochastic line-balancing situations.

Stochastic line balancing exists when the assumption of fixed and deterministic times for operations and total process time is not correct. As previously noted, this might be especially relevant for workstations where labor-intensive operations dominate. It also can be critically important where the variability makes it impossible to complete the work at a station. When the conveyor carries defective work to the next station, it often shuts off production for the rest of the downstream line. Thus, bottlenecks emerge that limit the benefits to be gained from serialized flow shop configurations.

Some assembly lines permit workers to stop the conveyors from moving work further when a serious problem arises at their station. This will be discussed later. Also, it is worth noting that the stochastic line-balancing problem is related to queuing models. These models describe the length of queues and the average waiting times that can occur when lines are not balanced. In effect, the demand for service becomes greater than the supply. Queue length is greater when requests for service occur randomly than when requests are evenly spaced.

If demand volume justifies it, the *high-volume, properly balanced flow shop* is the best work configuration to obtain lowest costs and best quality. A smooth running, conveyor-driven flow shop, with its well-timed stream of product, has low WIP (work in process) levels and enjoys economies of scale. It is a production system that moves just the right amount of material between stations.

Serialized production systems, without conveyors to set the pace, can push uncontrolled amounts of materials from one station to another. Line imbalances get translated into uneven workloads. Stations are not designed to handle inventory overloads. The result of worker overloads is the production of poor quality work as the operators speed up to compensate for the extra materials they must process. Push-type production systems create bottlenecks that cause disruptive backups of costly WIP to form. When stations push materials, there is no consistency in what is being delivered for processing by adjacent stations. On the other hand, pulling product along the line with a goal of being just-in-time is part of proper line balancing.

17-3a Basic Concepts for Line Balancing

Step 1 is to detail the process to be balanced. This means listing all of the operations that need to be done to make the product or deliver the service. Detailing requires specifying

Deterministic line balancing

Total process time for making the product is exactly the same for every unit of product that is completed. To achieve that goal, all operation times are fixed and never vary.

Heuristic line-balancing methods

So many combinations for assigning work to stations that ordinary mathematical optimization solutions do not apply; various rules of thumb constitute a common sense approach to line balancing.

Stochastic line balancing

Occurs when variability exists in the form of statistical distributions of operation and/or transport times.

Precedence diagram
Chart all relevant operations indicating which operations must follow others.

the order in which all operations are to be done. This includes stating which operations must be done before others can be started. A **precedence diagram**, used to chart the sequence, will be described shortly. Knowledge of the process technology is essential to successfully carry out step 1.

It is useful to have a number of people review the list of operations and their sequence. Even great chefs have different recipes for baking the same kind of cake. One recipe might be better than another for different volumes of production. Team responsibility for accepting the list of operations and the order for doing the operations is desirable. That team may be called upon to revise the set of operations and the precedence diagram in order to better balance the line.

This first step is often taken for granted. How the job will be accomplished must be precisely stated. The "devil" is in the details. For making toothpaste, it is not enough to state "mix the slurry for 20 minutes." The details include the mixing rate, the quantity mixed, the way the materials to be mixed are loaded and unloaded, and how and when other materials are added.

Other examples of deciding in detail how each of the operations is to be done include which adhesive will be used and how much at what temperature. How will the adhesive be applied? What software will be used and which version on which computer? Such a set of decisions constitutes the first feasible enumeration of the process. Accepting exactly how the job is to be done is the inception of intelligent line balancing. There is ample proof that it pays to question every facet of the stated procedure before beginning the next step.

Step 2 requires estimating how long the operations will take. Getting these operation times right is important and will be discussed shortly. Step 3 follows acceptance of the process and estimation of the operation times.

Step 3 is to assign the specific operations to workstations. As a goal, **perfect balance (pb)** is sought. PB can seldom be achieved. It is difficult to design processes in which every station along the production line has the same amount of work to do. With pb there is no idle time at any station—no waste exists. Another way of saying this is that the *sum* of the operation times for each station *would be the same*, and all available time is completely utilized at each station. A constraint to the achievement of perfect balance arises because workstation assignments cannot violate precedence conditions. Before the bread is baked, the dough must be kneaded.

Having equal sums of operation times at each station is not easily achieved because:

Perfect balance (pb)
See **Balance delay**.

© 2007 Jupiterimages Corporation

To P/OM, balance is an important operational objective sought in various ways. When production lines are in *perfect* balance, there is optimal use of resources. Each workstation requires the same amount of time to complete its tasks. With perfect balance (pb), the flow shop has no idle time. Even when perfect balance (pb) is not attainable, the effort to improve line balance is worthwhile. Better line balance prevents some workers from being too overloaded while others are inactive.

1 *Precedence constraints limit flexibility.* Some operations must be done in specific sequences. Others must be done together at the same station (see Section 17-3f), which discusses zoning constraints). Exact arrangements are detailed, drawn, and analyzed using precedence diagrams. Precedence diagrams are discussed later.

2 *Operation times can be increased and decreased in various ways.* The degree of flexibility is limited by the physical process, management policies and practices, technology, and training. When some operations are speeded up, there is a loss in quality. Other operations cannot be done faster unless an entirely new technology is available to be used.

3 *Human performance is variable.* Individuals and teams shift rates over time. These problems, which are pronounced for the intermittent flow shop, can often be circumvented by the use of technology and proper design of the dedicated flow shop. When the flow shop is dedicated, equipment can be designed to be balanced because the expense will be amortized over high production volumes for a long period of time.

The step 3 goal is to assign operations so that the sums of operation times at all stations are about equal. Thus, starting up the process: Raw materials enter station 1 at 9:00 A.M. Stations 2, 3, and 4 are idle. The start-up routine is always involved in the domino effect of prior adjacent workstations passing along their work in process to the next downstream workstation. Between 9:00 and 9:03 A.M., the raw materials are worked on at station 1. Precise operational details must be specified for station 1 activities.

The materials (now, work in process) move from station 1 to station 2 at 9:03 A.M. Station 2 adds value to the work in process it has received from station 1 by using its set of operations. Precise operational details must be specified for station 2 activities. At the same time, new raw materials enter station 1, and the description in the previous paragraph applies. Station 1 repeats the same operations every 3 minutes.

At 9:06 A.M., station 3 begins to operate on WIP passed from station 2. Continue in this way until all stations are actively engaged. Every 3 minutes, raw materials enter at station 1, and finished goods leave the final station every 3 minutes. Cycle time is $C = 3$. Table 17-1 provides the start-up log. Figure 17-1 pictures the situation.

After start-up has been accomplished, each of the $n = 4$ stations has operations that take approximately 3 minutes to perform. This is shown in Figure 17-1. However, this system had to go through start-up where, at first, only station 1 is busy; then stations 1 and 2, and so on. Finally all 4 stations are operating, as shown in Figure 17-1. Because constant (deterministic—not statistical) operation times are assumed at each station, the idle times are also constant at each station.

There has been no allowance made for workers to *rest and delay*. There is little slack (elbow room) at any of the stations and none at station 4. If there are people working at the stations, they have needs. Perhaps some person is available to relieve employees who want to use the rest rooms.

		Table 17-1
9:00 A.M.	Station 1 begins working. Station 1 is scheduled to take 2.9 minutes to complete its operations. Idle time at station 1 is 0.1 minute.	Log of 4-Station Start-Up
9:03 A.M.	Station 1 repeats its operations. Station 2 begins working. Station 2 is scheduled to take 2.7 minutes to complete its operations. Idle time at station 1 is 0.1 minute and at station 2 is 0.3 minute.	
9:06 A.M.	Stations 1 and 2 repeat their operations. Station 3 begins working. Station 3 is scheduled to take 2.8 minutes to complete its operations. Idle time at station 1 is 0.1 minute, at station 2 it is 0.3 minute, at station 3 it is 0.2 minute.	
9:09 A.M.	Stations 1, 2, and 3 repeat their operations. Station 4 begins working. Station 4 is scheduled to take 3.0 minutes to complete its operations. Idle time at station 1 is 0.1 minute, at station 2 it is 0.3 minute, at station 3 it is 0.2 minute, and it is 0.0 minute at station 4.	
9:12 A.M.	All stations repeat their operations until shutdown.	

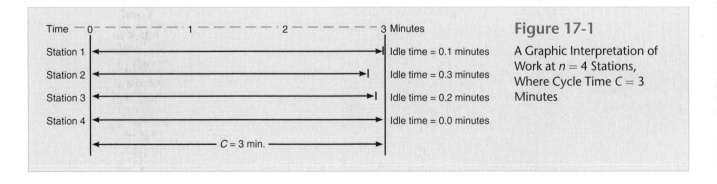

Figure 17-1

A Graphic Interpretation of Work at $n = 4$ Stations, Where Cycle Time $C = 3$ Minutes

Having developed a way to visualize the operation times at stations and their comparative idle time, the best way to understand the concept of line balancing is to study a small problem. It is useful to bear in mind that real line-balancing problems are seldom so small.

For an example, The Photo Lab is a mail-order film processor. It has developed a computer-controlled color film process that improves the quality of work while speeding up film developing and printing time. The process designers have created a flow shop that starts with mail receipt of film and money. Each cycle ends with an envelope of photo prints and negatives ready for mailing and control of payments for deposit to The Photo Lab's account. At the end of each cycle, the order is completed and shipped.

17-3b The Precedence Diagram of the Serialized, Flow Shop Process

The first version submitted by the process designers to the operations team was changed after detailed discussion of contingencies that might arise. The next version was rejected by the plant manager as being difficult to service. The final process version is shown by the precedence diagram in Figure 17-2. It shows the order of operations. *Precedence diagrams are important graphic displays*, which show what operations *must* be done before others.

This sequence specifies operations that are antecedents and successors. The precedence diagram specifies the progression such that A follows or precedes B. However, the numbers on the nodes do not specify the order in which work must be done. Thus, (1) must precede (3) and (4), but (4) might be done before (3). Similarly, (2) could be done before (1) or vice versa. The lines of the diagram establish the precedence constraints. The diagram shows when precedence must be taken into account and when it does not constrain the system.

The operations that constitute the process are labeled i where $i = 1, 2, \ldots, k$. For each operation, an operation time, t_i, has been estimated. These times are shown in the precedence diagram of Figure 17-2 and in Table 17-2.

Operation times are estimates because the line has not been set up yet. The actual times can be estimated in various ways. For example, the estimates can be based on simulations that come close to emulating the situation that will hold after the line is running. Having correct estimates is crucial for line balancing. Therefore, the design will first be balanced; when the system is up and running, the actual line will be rebalanced.

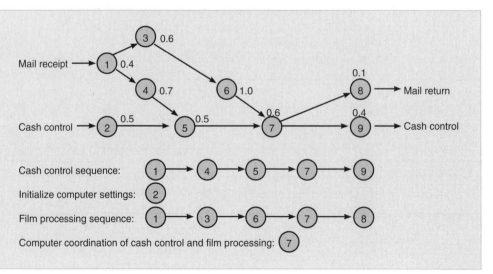

Figure 17-2

Precedence Diagram for The Photo Lab

Operation (*i*)	Operation Time (*t_i*) in Minutes
1	0.4
2	0.5
3	0.6
4	0.7
5	0.5
6	$1.0 = t_{max}$
7	0.6
8	0.1
9	0.4

Table 17-2

Operation Times for The Photo Lab

Note: $t_{max} = 1.0$ minute is the longest operation time.

The design of the process, and thereby of the precedence diagram, must be approximately right. Then, the estimates of the operation times will be relatively good ones.

Next, the operations team must estimate how many orders will have to be processed per hour. Say that The Photo Lab currently processes 40 orders (envelopes) per hour, which is 320 orders per 8-hour day or 1,600 orders per week. If more orders than that are received, there will be a waiting line, which will begin to disappear when less than 320 orders are received per day.

With a processing capacity of 320 orders per 8-hour day, if 400 orders are received on a particular day, a waiting line of 80 orders will result. If, on the following day, 260 orders are received, the backlog of 80 will be reduced to 20 orders waiting. These estimates assume that overtime is not used. However, as an alternative to having a waiting line, the process can be run for more than 8 hours per day.

Mail-order film customers do not like to wait, but overtime is costly. Consequently, if the probability that more than 320 orders will be received per day is significant, then the process should be restudied and adjusted. This could arise if the business grows as customers tell their friends about the good service and prices of The Photo Shop. If 320 orders per day is reasonable, then it is sensible to proceed with line balancing. Perhaps the rate of 40 orders per hour will be attainable under line-balanced conditions.

17-3c Cycle Time (C) and the Number of Stations (*n*)

Product (completion) output rate O is equal to the time period T divided by the cycle time C. The cycle time has been defined earlier as the time interval that the conveyor stays at each station. It is represented by Equation 17-1.

Cycle Time (C)

T is the time period (e.g., minutes per hour) used to *match* the time dimension of the cycle time (minutes at a workstation) with the time dimension of the output rate (orders per hour).

t_i is the number of minutes required to do the ith operation at the jth station. It will always be true that $t_i \leq C$. To do the entire job (complete the order) requires $\sum_i t_i$. The output to cycle time relationship is:

$$O = T/C \quad \text{and} \quad C = T/O \qquad (17-1)$$

If $O = 40$ orders per hour, and $T = 60$ minutes per hour, then, cycle time is $C = 60/40 = 1.5$ minutes per order. See Figure 17-3.

C is the desired cycle time if the demand rate of 40 orders per hour is to be achieved. The process will be designed to have this cycle time as a lower bound. The actual cycle time chosen may be longer to allow for some idle time and to provide workers with an opportunity to rest.

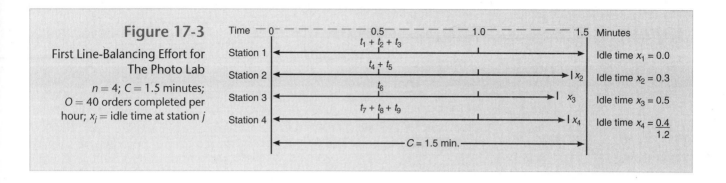

Figure 17-3

First Line-Balancing Effort for The Photo Lab

$n = 4$; $C = 1.5$ minutes; $O = 40$ orders completed per hour; $x_j =$ idle time at station j

Cycle time, C, in this instance, has been calculated to satisfy demand—with the assumption of perfect balance.

As another example, if daily output (8-hour day) of 300 units was required, then the cycle time would be $480/300 = 1.6$ minutes. In Figure 17-4 with $n = 3$ perfect balance exists, which means that there is no idle time. In contrast, Figure 17-1 has idle time and the line balance is not perfect.

The problem that must next be resolved is the number of workstations (n) to be chosen to deliver the finished units in the required cycle time. The technology of the process will determine how feasible it is to divide operations evenly among the workstations.

Reference to Figure 17-2 and Table 17-2 indicates that the selected output rate of 40 orders per hour may be possible. Every operation time (t_i) is shorter than the cycle time of 1.5 minutes per unit. This includes the longest time of $t_{max} = 1.0$, as shown in Table 17-2. One or more operations can be completed at any of the j stations. For example, $\sum_i t_i$ for the specific operations $i = 1$, 2, and 3 sums to $C = 1.5$ minutes. They could all be done at station 1 without violating precedence constraints.

Number of Stations (n) and Total Work Content (TWC)

It is a physical reality that the number of stations n must always be an integer. For each integer number of stations, there is an associated cycle time. Consider the product $nC =$ *constant*. As n rises, C decreases.

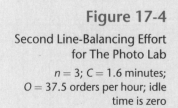

Total work content (TWC)

The sum of all operation times required to make a finished product or deliver completed service.

In this case, the right-hand side constant is the **total work content (TWC)** required to make a completed order (ship a finished unit or, in a service example, complete cleaning the house). *TWC* is defined in Table 17-3 as 4.8 minutes. Creative ideas about how else to do the job may change that number.

Table 17-3 shows that nine operations (i) must be completed to fill an order for The Photo Lab. The operation times to complete an order range from the shortest activity, which is operation $i = 8$ with a time of $t_i = 0.1$, to the longest operation (identified as t_{max}) for operation $i = 6$.

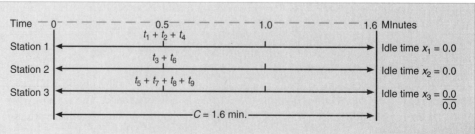

Figure 17-4

Second Line-Balancing Effort for The Photo Lab

$n = 3$; $C = 1.6$ minutes; $O = 37.5$ orders per hour; idle time is zero

Operation (*i*)	Operation Time (t_i) in Minutes	**Table 17-3**
1	0.4	The Photo Lab's Processing Times
2	0.5	
3	0.6	
4	0.7	
5	0.5	
6	$1.0 = t_{max}$	
7	0.6	
8	0.1	
9	0.4	
TWC	$4.8 = \sum_i t_i$	

Note: *TWC* = total work content = $\sum_i t_i$ = 4.8 minutes.

This sum of operation times, which is equal to 4.8 minutes, is called *total work content* (*TWC*). The equation relating cycle time (*C*), the number of workstations (*n*), and the total work content (*TWC*) is equal to *nc*, as follows:

$$n^*C = \sum_i t_i = \text{minutes, and this is perfect balance.} (n^* \text{ is explained next.})$$

Start with the desired output (*O*) of 40 completed orders per hour. Next, determine the cycle time to deliver that output. That is, $C = 60/40 = 1.5$ minutes per unit. The total work content is 4.8 minutes. All of the relevant data are shown in Table 17-4.

When total work content is divided by the desired cycle time, it is possible to derive a noninteger value for *n* (called *n**). This case is illustrated by using the data in Table 17-4.

$$n^* = TWC/C = \sum_i t_i/C = 4.8/1.5 = 3.2 \text{ stations}$$

This result of 3.2 stations can be viewed as a minimum (ideal, but infeasible) number of workstations. The actual number of stations *n* will have to be a larger integer to accommodate all operations in a physically feasible system. Going backwards, *TWC* cannot be changed unless the job is redesigned. So, the new cycle time for perfect balance is $C = 1.2$ minutes. This is feasible but not necessarily doable because of the assumption of perfect balance. The value of *C* is obtained by dividing the same total work content by the larger integer number of stations, as shown below Equation 17-2, which is the equation for perfect balance.

$$nC = TWC = \sum_i t_i \text{ for all } i \text{ operations}$$
$$C = (TWC)/4 = (4.8)/4 = 1.2 \tag{17-2}$$

Dividing the total work content time (4.8 minutes) by the new integer number (4) of stations determines the number of minutes, *C*, spent by an order at each station. The cycle time $C = 1.2$ is also the number of minutes occurring between completion of orders.

Line balancing divides up the total work content, making assignments of various operations *i* to each workstation. This has the effect of assigning differing amounts of t_i to the workstations.

Summing up, the desired output rate *O* drives the system. *O* is used to determine a satisfactory cycle time, *C*. This first value of cycle time may not be feasible because it leads to a noninteger number of stations. It may not be doable because the assumption of perfect balance is not tenable for the set of operation times. *C* and $TWC = \sum_i t_i$ are used together in Equation 17-2 to determine the number of stations *n*, working on different operations to fill the orders.

	$C = \sum_i t_i/n$	$O = T/C = 60/C$	Total Idle Time
Table 17-4			
	n	in Minutes	Orders/Hour	in Minutes
The Photo Lab's Chart	1	4.8	12.5	0
of Possible Cycle Times, C,	2	2.4	25.0	0
Also Hourly Output Rates,	3	1.6	37.5	0
$O = T/C$, for Number of	4	1.2	50.0	0
Stations, n	*5	0.96	62.5	0
	*6	0.80	75.0	0
	*7	0.69	87.5	0
	*8	0.60	100.0	0
	*9	0.53	112.5	0

Note: (* = infeasible)

Each order is at a different stage of work in process and completion. The greater the number of stations, the shorter the cycle time. In general, the smaller the cycle time, the larger the output rate. But this will depend on the ability to assign work to stations so as to minimize idle time and approach perfect balance. The various options will be examined, and the most preferred line-balancing architecture will be chosen.

17-3d Cycle-Time Limits

Limits on cycle time can be established. Cycle time can be no less than the longest operation time. It can be no more than total work content time. The alternative statement is also correct and follows the symbols in Equation 17-3, namely, the longest operation time must be equal to or less than the cycle time, and the cycle time must be equal to or less than the total work content.

$$t_{\max} \leq C \leq TWC \tag{17-3}$$

In Tables 17-2 and 17-3, the sixth operation has been marked $t_{\max}$ because it is the longest operation time. Cycle time must be equal to or longer than $t_{\max}$. If $C < 1.0$, then the $t_{6 \text{ is max}}$ operation must be completed at more than one station. In this case, $t_6 = 1.0$ would have to be broken into two segments.

It is reasonable to ask if any t_i can be further divided, but especially the long ones. If $t_{\max}$ can be divided after the system is set up and running, that should have been done when the process was in the design phase. It *always* is beneficial to have shorter operations that can be assigned to workstations more readily than longer ones. Large t_i are difficult to assign, and they reduce line-balancing flexibility.

Cycle time must be equal to or less than total work content. This follows from using the smallest integer value of $n = 1$ in Equation 17-2, where $C = 4.8/n$. The Volvo method of production in Sweden assembles an entire car at one station. The cycle time that Volvo uses to assemble the car is that of the total work content. By using parallel "lines," more than one car can be assembled at the same time.

Table 17-4 presents The Photo Lab's chart of all possible cycle times C and hourly output rates O for an integer number of stations $n = 1$ through 9. Note that this chart is based on perfect balance (pb) so for each n, the total idle time is zero. Figure 17-1 does not have pb and pb may not be able to be achieved!

Several points need to be discussed about Table 17-4, Equation 17-3, and Figure 17-2. Then, references will be made to Figures 17-3, 17-4, and 17-5 because they illustrate related aspects of line-balancing situations.

1 When the number of stations is $n = 5$, or greater, the cycle time C is less than one. This is denoted by asterisks (*) in Table 17-4. Because $t_{(\max)} = 1.0$, $n \geq 5$ is not feasible. See Equation 17-3, which states that C must be equal to or greater than t_{max}, which is 1.0.

2 The desired output $O = 40$ orders completed per hour cannot be achieved directly with less than four stations. $O = 37.5$ with $n = 3$, which is a shortfall. Whereas, $O = 50$ when $n = 4$. If three stations are to be used, some overtime (OT) would be required, but not much, and (OT) might be approved.

3 From Table 17-4, with four stations, the cycle time is 1.2 minutes if perfect balance can be achieved. However, this line cannot be balanced with $C = 1.2$, $n = 4$, and $O = 50$. There is no way to assign the operations to four stations for perfect balance.

4 Note that in Figure 17-3 the cycle time has been enlarged to be 1.5 minutes. Then, the operations can be assigned to the four stations. There is total idle time of 1.2 minutes. Total work content plus idle time $(4.8 + 1.2 = 6.0)$ is equal to the maximum capacity to do work, which is $nC = 4 \times 1.5 = 6.0$.

5 As will be seen shortly, the measure of line-balance goodness that has been achieved in Figure 17-3 is 20 percent. This is not too bad given the fact that rest and delay is usually allocated about 10 percent. However, station 1 has no idle time whereas stations 2, 3, and 4 average 0.4 minute per 1.5-minute stop. That is an average of 27 percent of the total stop time. This unbalanced allocation of idle times in Figure 17-3 is not acceptable.

6 The nonworking time at each station has been denoted by $x_j = idle\ time$. The sum of idle times is $\sum_{j=1}^{j=4} x_j = 1.2$ minutes. This number is derived in Figure 17-3 at the right-hand side of the chart.

7 If the arrangement in Figure 17-3 can be adjusted so that idle times are more evenly distributed, the situation might be acceptable because a cycle time of $C = 1.5$ produces an output of $O = 40$ completed orders per hour, viz., $O = T/C = 60/1.5 = 40$. That satisfies the stated demand requirement.

8 The question now arises: Is there a better arrangement of the operations at the stations that conforms to the requirements of the precedence diagram in Figure 17-2?

9 To begin, note that the arrangement shown in Figure 17-4 is feasible with respect to precedence constraints. In that scenario, cycle time has been increased to 1.6 minutes. There are $n = 3$ stations instead of $n = 4$. Output has decreased to 37.5 orders per hour, which falls short of the required 40, but there is perfect balance, which means there is no idle time. If cycle time is increased by 12.5 percent, that would yield $C = 1.8$ minutes per stop. Output decreases further to $60/1.8 = 33.33$ orders per hour. The one weakness of the scenario is the fact that 9.6 hours instead of 8 hours of production are required per day. Overtime cost has to be applied to 1.6 hours per day. This amounts to an extra 8-hour day per week at overtime.

10 Another possibility is to set up parallel production lines. For example, with perfect balance, two parallel production lines with two stations each would be able to process 50 orders per hour. This is shown in Figure 17-5. It is only practical to have perfect balance if machines and no people work at each station.

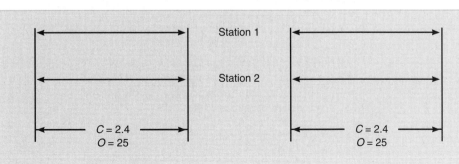

Station 1

Station 2

$C = 2.4$
$O = 25$

$C = 2.4$
$O = 25$

Figure 17-5

Perfect Balance with Two Parallel Production Lines

$n = 2$ for each production line; $C = 2.4$ minutes; $O = 25$ orders for a total of 50 orders per hour

Assume that people are employed and increase the cycle time by 12.5 percent for rest and delay. This raises the cycle time to $C = 2.7$ minutes. Output decreases from 25 orders per hour at each of the two parallel production lines to 22.22 for a total of 44.44 completed orders per hour. The new arrangement meets the demand of 40 orders per hour and leaves 4.44 orders per hour of excess capacity.

11 Note, for the two stations in parallel production, when $C = 3.0$, $O = 20$ with a total of 40 orders per hour. That is an increase of 25 percent in C, which is excessive for rest and delay. It matches the demand but $n = 1.6$ is infeasible.

12 There is a systems interaction to consider! If it turns out that two parallel lines, each with two stations, lowers production costs while raising the capacity of the process, then P/OM and marketing could set a reduced price strategy for film processing. This might increase the volume of business and total profit.

13 For cost analysis, the variable costs of production include the number of stations being managed (c_1n), the use of t amount of overtime (c_2t), and the cost of total idle time, $\sum_{j=1}^{j=n} x_j$. The total cost is $TC = c_1n + c_2t + c_3 \sum_{j=1}^{j=n} x_j$.

14 It is usually assumed that operation times cannot be shortened, having been chosen as the smallest reasonable components into which the total process or job can be subdivided. This assumption can be relaxed when technological factors permit alternative arrangements. It is important to check out this assumption.

17-3e Developing Station Layouts

Henceforth, stations will be labeled with Roman numerals to distinguish them from operation numbers. The procedure for developing station layouts is based on the use of precedence diagrams. Place in station I (the first column) all operations that need not follow others. Reference to Figure 17-2 shows that operations (1) and (2) can be placed in station I. See also Figure 17-6.

Then, place in station II operations that must follow those in station I. These are operations (3) and (4). Note that (5) must follow (4) and, therefore, cannot be in the second station (II). Continue to the other station columns in the same way. Thus, in Figure 17-6, The Photo Lab's operations have been placed into the maximum number of stations required by operational sequence, not by operation times.

Sequence is fully specified but column position is not fixed. For example, operation (2) could be done in either station I or II. This first feasible set of five stations is determined by the longest chain of sequenced operations, not in time, but by the number of operations in the chain.

Various orderings exist that can satisfy the precedence requirements. Intracolumn movement is totally free between operations that are mutually independent (not connected by arrows). Thus, at station II, operation (3) could be done before operation (4) or

Figure 17-6

The Photo Lab's Precedence Diagram with Five Stations (A First Feasible Solution)

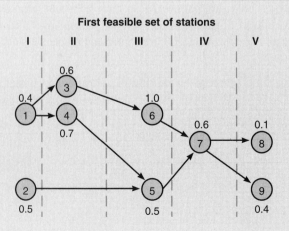

Station	I	II	III	IV	V
Operations	(1), (2)	(3), (4)	(5), (6)	(7)	(8), (9)
Total operation times	0.9	1.3	1.5	0.6	0.5
Idle times	0.6	0.2	0.0	0.9	1.0

Table 17-5

The Photo Lab's 5-Station Line-Balanced Layout with $C = 1.5$ and Total Idle Time = 2.7 Minutes

Station	i	t_i	Station Sum	Cumulative Sum	Idle Time
I	1	0.4			
	2	0.5	0.9	0.9	0.6
II	3	0.6			
	4	0.7	1.3	2.2	0.2
III	5	0.5			
	6	1.0	1.5	3.7	0.0
IV	7	0.6	0.6	4.3	0.9
V	8	0.1			
	9	0.4	0.5	4.8	1.0
Totals		4.8	4.8		2.7

Table 17-6

The Photo Lab's 5-Station Line-Balanced Layout

vice versa. This kind of flexibility with respect to the order with which operations are completed at a station is called **permutability of columns**.

Also, operations can be moved sideways from their columns to positions to their right without disturbing the precedence restrictions. Operations (3) and (6) could be done at the third workstation, but (3) must always precede (6). Flexibility to move sideways is called **lateral transferability**.

With this 5-station layout, the cycle time would be set at 1.5 minutes (or more) by the assigned operation times at station III. The total station operation times and idle times are shown in Table 17-5.

There is a great deal of idle time at stations I, IV, and V. Another way of representing this assignment pattern is illustrated in Table 17-6.

Using trial and error methods, efforts should be made to improve upon this line-balancing arrangement. The most promising approach is to turn to heuristic methods for line balancing, which will be explained in Section 17-4. First, however, this section dealing with concepts of line balancing is concluded with consideration of perfect and imperfect balance, and a new term, which is **balance delay (*d*)**.

17-3f Perfect Balance with Zero Balance Delay (*d*)

With cycle time *C* fixed by design (1.5 minutes for The Photo Lab), the number of stations under perfect balance would be $\Sigma_i t_i \div C = n$, or $4.8/1.5 = 3.2$ stations, which is not feasible. The integer number of stations $n = 3$ or $n = 4$ might qualify. Three stations yield a lower production rate. Four stations provide a challenge to make use of excess capacity.

Perfect balance is not a realistic objective for a number of reasons. First, it is difficult to group operations into stations such that the total operation times at all stations are equal. Also, technological factors exist that do not permit operations to be split. Such physical restrictions are referred to as **zoning constraints**.

The system's inefficiency (or imperfect balance) is measured by a quantity *d*, called the *balance delay*. This term refers to the *percent of unproductive time* at the stations. Unproductive time is another name for idle time in a line-balanced system.

$$d = 100\left(nC - \sum_i t_i\right) \div nC \qquad (17\text{-}4)$$

Permutability of columns

Flexibility within a workstation concerning the order in which operations will be done.

Lateral transferability

When precedence diagrams permit operations to be assigned to earlier or later workstations.

Balance delay (*d*)

A percentage measure of idle time across all of the workstations that participate in the complete process cycle.

Zoning constraints

Technological factors exist that do not permit operations to be split between workstations.

Figure 17-7

The Photo Lab's Flow Shop with Balance Delay of 20 Percent

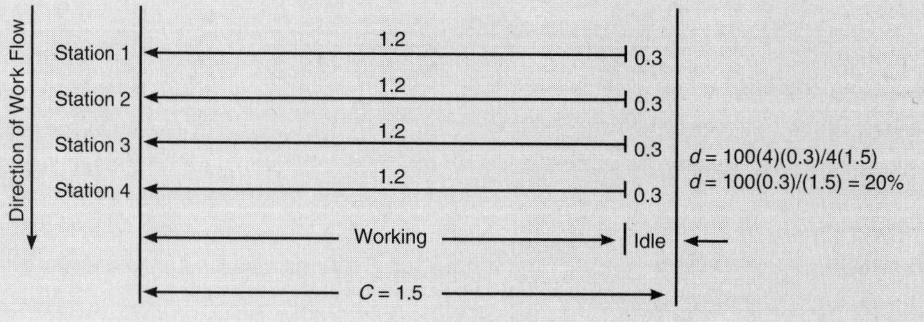

Balance delay d equals zero for all cycle times listed in Table 17-4. That is because total capacity (nC) is equal to total work content. Equation 17-5 describes the condition of perfect balance.

$$nC = \sum_i t_i \qquad (17\text{-}5)$$

For The Photo Lab's cycle time of 1.5 minutes, $n = 3.2$ was derived for perfect balance. Even though a noninteger value for the number of stations, $n = 3.2$, is not physically feasible, the calculations with that theoretical n demonstrate that $d = 0$.

$$d = 100[(3.2)(1.5) - (4.8)] \div (3.2)(1.5) = 0 \text{ percent}$$

If the integer value of $n = 4$ is used with the cycle time of 1.5 minutes, balance delay would be

$$d = 100[(4)(1.5) - (4.8)] \div (4)(1.5) = 20 \text{ percent}$$

The illustration in Figure 17-7 aims to show that balance delay is the total idle time of all stations as a percentage of total available working time of all stations. Thus,

$$d = \sum_{j=1}^{j=n} x_j / nC = (Total\ Idle\ Time)/Total\ Available\ Time$$

Tables 17-5 and 17-6 show the 5-station line-balanced layout for The Photo Lab. Total idle time is 2.7 minutes out of a total work time of $5 \times 1.5 = 7.5$ minutes, which is balance delay, $d = 36$ percent. This degree of balance delay is excessive.

Balance delay is characterized as a systems measure of idle time because it relates total idle time to the total work content of the entire process. For cycle-time management, the cost of balance delay $c_4 d$ may be a better measure than the cost of total idle time $c_3 \sum_{j=1}^{j=n} x_j$ because $c_4 d$ describes the percent of processing time that is idle.

17-3g Line Efficiency (Λ)

Line efficiency (Λ)
Total work content divided by the total capacity to do work.

Line efficiency (Λ) is a related measure used to assess how well the line is balanced. It is

$$\Lambda = TWC/nC = \sum_i t_i \quad where \quad 0 \le \Lambda \le 1 \quad and \quad i = all\ operations \qquad (17\text{-}6)$$

Balance delay and line efficiency expressed as a percent (i.e., 100Λ) have a linear relationship with a negative slope as follows:

$d = 100(1 - \Lambda)$. When line efficiency is one, balance delay is zero and both describe the condition of perfect balance. In the example of Tables 17-5 and 17-6, $\Lambda = 0.64$ and $100\Lambda = 64$ percent, whereas $d = 36$ percent.

17-3h Rest and Delay (r & d)

Perfect balance without idle time for rest is expected for a serialized system of interconnected machines, but people require time for rest and delay. Between 10 and 20 percent of station work time normally is added to a perfectly balanced line. If the work at the station is strenuous or fatiguing (e.g., eye strain), then more *r & d* is added. It is common to call this allowance *r & d*, but it is in no way related to the R&D of "research and development."

From a systems perspective, cycle-time management has trade-offs to consider between longer cycle times using people and shorter cycle times using technology. Also, with technology it is easier to achieve perfect balance and to maintain greater control over variability. Machines require maintenance and often that can be provided during an off-shift. Also, flexible computer-controlled machines allow using modular product designs, which provides greater market variety while enjoying the benefits of dedicated flow shop technology.

17-4 Heuristic Line Balancing

The term *heuristic* has been used by Simon and Newell[1] to describe a common-sense approach to problem solving and decision making. Heuristic models utilize logic derived by observation and introspection. Heuristic approaches replace mathematical optimization efforts when optimization is not sensible or feasible. Heuristic line balancing uses rules of thumb to set near-equal workloads at successive stations.

Complex formulations of linear programming have been devised to obtain solutions to the line-balancing problem, but in practice they are not acceptable. Heuristic approaches are faster and offer more opportunities for testing alternative solutions. For practicality, they require computer software.

The essence of the heuristic approach is in the application of selective routines that reduce the complexity of a problem. Thus, the assembly line-balancing problem can be treated by simulating the decision-making pattern of managers when faced with this problem. The advantages of this approach are consistency of the decision rules, speed of application, and, by using the computer, the ability to cope with large systems.

The key is to trace out and then embody the thinking process that an intelligent decision maker uses to resolve the line-balancing problem. A few popular heuristics will be described. References will be given to other heuristics with brief descriptions of what they do.

If the product or service output of the flow shop is expected to have a long and stable life cycle, then engineering design will be the preferred method for line balancing. On the other hand, when the output life cycle is not stable over a long time, shorter-term flow shops (including intermittent flow shops) are needed. These are ideally suited for heuristic resolution.

17-4a Kilbridge and Wester's (K & W) Heuristic

Kilbridge and Wester[2] proposed a heuristic procedure that *assigns a number* to each operation describing how many predecessors it has. This is done using the appropriate precedence diagram. The operations are *rank ordered* according to the number of predecessors each has. Operations with zero predecessors are ranked first in line. They are followed by operations with 1 predecessor, then 2 predecessors, etc.

Then, the *assignments to stations* are made. First operations assigned to workstations are those with lowest predecessor numbers. Zero is first, then 1, then 2, etc. The procedure is illustrated in Tables 17-7 and 17-8, where The Photo Lab is trying the K & W heuristic for an $n = 3$ station design with cycle time $C = 4.8/3 = 1.6$ minutes. The number of predecessors for each operation is obtained using Figure 17-2. The results are listed in Table 17-7.

Operations are assigned to stations in the order of the least number of predecessors. For station I, select operations (2) and (1) in that order because of the following rule for ties. They have a total operation time of 0.9, which leaves 0.7 free time in station I. This follows from $C = 1.6$.

Next, based on tied predecessor numbers, either introduce operation (3) with $t_i = 0.6$ or operation (4) with $t_i = 0.7$ into station I. Following the rule for ties, choose operation (4).

Table 17-7	Operation	Number of Predecessors	t_i
The Photo Lab Operations Ranked by the Number of Predecessors	1	0	0.4
	2	0	0.5
	3	1	0.6
	4	1	0.7
	6	2	1.0
	5	3	0.5
	7	6	0.6
	8	7	0.1
	9	7	0.4

Table 17-8	Station	I	t_i	Station Sum	Cumulative Sum	Idle Time
K & W Heuristic with Cycle Time 1.6 Minutes	I	2	0.5			
		1	0.4			
		4	0.7	1.6	1.6	0
	II	3	0.6			
		6	1.0	1.6	3.2	0
	III	5	0.5			
		7	0.6			
		9	0.4			
		8	0.1	1.6	4.8	0
	Totals		4.8	4.8		0

The Rule for Ties

When ties exist, the following rule applies. Choose first the *longest* operation times *that can be used*. Short operations are saved because they are easier to fit into stations later. In this way, upstream stations (with earlier work) are given the least idle time possible. As a result of this rule, in Table 17-8 operation (2) is assigned before (1). Also operation (4) is assigned before operation (3).

Continuing with K & W Assignments

Because operation (4) is assigned to station I, this results in total work time of 1.6 for station I, which is now fully assigned and has no idle time.

Attending to station II, of the remaining nonassigned operations, number (3) has the least number of predecessors (1). It is assigned to station II. Next comes operation (6) with two predecessors. Station II with operations (3) and (6) has a total working time of 1.6. Station II is fully assigned with no idle time.

If operation (6) had required more time than was available at station II, then operation (5) would have been chosen. Operations (7), (8), and (9) could not be used until both operations (5) and (6) are used. That is the information shown in Figure 17-2 about precedent constraints. Operations (7), (8), and (9) will be placed in a station further downstream (later work).

When an operation with the smallest number of predecessors has too long an operation time to be included in the station, the heuristic is programmed to look for the operation with the next smallest number of predecessors that fits the available time at the station and observes precedent constraints. Thus, operations (5), (7), (9), and (8) are assigned at station III, which is fully assigned and has no idle time. Note that operation (9) is assigned before (8) because of the rule concerning ties.

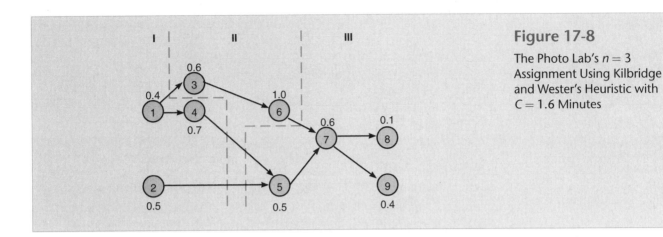

Figure 17-8

The Photo Lab's $n = 3$ Assignment Using Kilbridge and Wester's Heuristic with $C = 1.6$ Minutes

Perfect balance has been achieved using the K & W heuristic. This is shown in Table 17-8. The precedence diagram in Figure 17-8 is subdivided in accordance with Table 17-8 assignments. Three perfectly balanced stations can be used if the technology permits. Assume that people work at the stations. Then, add (say) 0.2 for rest and delay. This adds 12.5 percent to the cycle time. Perfect balance output would be $60/1.6 = 37.5$ orders per hour (see Table 17-4). With rest and delay, the output would be further reduced to $60/1.8 = 33\ 1/3$ orders per hour.

At the end of the day, instead of 320 orders being processed, there would be 266 2/3 orders completed. That is 53 1/3 orders shy of expected demand. Dividing 53 1/3 by 33 1/3 yields 1.6 hours of overtime per day (or 8 hours per week) to correct the situation. There are lots of other alternatives including use of the $n = 4$ station line-balance solution.

17-4b Other Heuristics

H & B Assignments

Helgeson and Birnie's (H & B) heuristic suggested first assigning to stations those operations whose followers have the largest total time. This is the sum of all successors' operations times.[3]

$$\sum_i t_i \quad i = \text{all followers of } i \qquad (17\text{-}7)$$

H & B called their approach the "ranked positional weight" method.

In Table 17-9 each operation of The Photo Lab example is associated with a weight equal to the sum of all operation times that follow it. Operations are then ranked by descending order of the weight measure.

Station	Operation in Ranked Order	Station Weight W_t	Station Time t_i	Station Sum	Station Idle Time
I	1	3.9	0.4		
	3	2.1	0.6		
	2	1.6	0.5	1.5	0.1
II	4	1.6	0.7		
	5	1.1	0.5	1.2	0.4
III	6	1.1	1.0		
	7	0.5	0.6	1.6	0.0
IV	8	0	0.1		
	9	0	0.4	0.5	1.1
Totals				4.8	1.6

Table 17-9

H & B Heuristic with Cycle Time = 1.6 Minutes

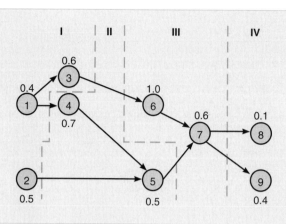

Figure 17-9

The Photo Lab Assignment
Using Helgeson and
Birnie's Heuristic $n = 4$;
$C = 1.6$ Minutes

Check Figure 17-2 to develop the set of weights that appear in Table 17-9. As one example, operations (3), (4), (5), (6), (7), (8), and (9), (not 2), follow operation (1). The sum of these operations' times is 3.9. This is the weight given to operation (1) in Table 17-9. Similarly, operations (8) and (9) follow operation (7). The sum of their operations' times is 0.5, which is the weight for operation (7) in Table 17-9. One more example uses operation (5), followed by (8) and (9) as well as (7). Adding (7)'s time of 0.6 to those of (8) and (9) yields 1.1, which is the weight assigned to operation (5) in Table 17-9.

The operations have been assigned to the stations in accordance with the weights. The largest weight is 3.9 for operation (1) and it goes first. Next is operation (3) with a weight of 2.1, and so on. Note that the cycle time of 1.6 minutes was selected to allow comparison with the results of the Kilbridge and Wester heuristic. Four stations are required to use $C = 1.6$ minutes.

Figure 17-9 shows the precedence diagram divided into four station sectors.

Operations are assigned without violating precedence or zoning constraints. When the total time for a station is exceeded, the attempt is made to find an operation further down the list that is feasible. In the case of station I, there are no other downstream operations that are feasible.

The heuristic requires that operations (1) and (3) be included as part of station I. Operations (2), (4), and (6) are the only ones that might then be assigned without violating precedence. The total time for operations (1), (3), and (4) is 1.7 minutes. For (1), (3), and (6), it is two minutes. For (1), (3), and (2), it is 1.5 minutes, and so that was used.

With $n = 3$, the cycle time of 1.6 minutes is fully used up at station III. At station I, the idle time is 0.1, which is close to zero. If stations III and I are not staffed by people but entirely run by machines, then this arrangement might have possibilities. However, station IV is badly underutilized. Perhaps a later inspection or packaging activity could be added to station IV.

The H & B approach does not yield three stations but results in four stations operating under the cycle time of 1.6. Overall, the four stations are unbalanced, and idle time (balance delay) is uneven and high:

$$d = 100(4 \times 1.6 - 4.8)/(4 \times 1.6) = 25 \text{ percent}$$

This same result is obtained by adding up the total idle time in Table 17-9, dividing it by total station time, and making it a percent, i.e., $100[1.6/(4 \times 1.6)] = 25$ percent.

Tonge's Heuristic for Line Balancing

Tonge's heuristic develops a learning procedure[4] that rewards success and penalizes failure by increasing and decreasing the probability of selecting a heuristic randomly from a catalog of heuristics. Each heuristic assigns operations to stations on its own basis. Those heuristics that require the least number of stations are rewarded. Those that require a greater number of stations are penalized.

Among the set of heuristics employed to establish preference for choosing the next operation to be assigned to a station are

A. Longest operation time, t_i
B. Largest number of immediate followers
C. Random choice of the next operation, i

All assignments are made subject to non-violations of precedence and zoning constraints. The choice of heuristic is determined by $p(A)$, $p(B)$, and $p(C)$. These probabilities sum to one. Initially they are all equal, i.e., 1/3. Then, according to the success of the heuristic chosen, the associated probabilities are increased or decreased.

Tonge concludes that this probabilistic approach results in fewer workstations than any single heuristic taken alone—or by random choice of operations.

Arcus' Heuristic for Line Balancing

Arcus' heuristic[5] sets the pattern for random generation of feasible sequences. All assignments are made subject to not violating any constraints based on precedence, zoning, and feasibility relations. The computer program generates 1,000 line-balance arrangements. The line-balance arrangement chosen is that one out of a 1,000 that requires the minimum number of stations.

On computers in the decade 2010, large problems take a very few minutes to generate thousands of sequences. It is historically interesting to note Arcus' experience in 1966 with a relatively small problem. Arcus reported that the generation of 1,000 sequences for a system of 70 operations on an IBM 7090 required 30 minutes.

It should be noted that for very large problems, the objective of minimizing the number of workstations—with cycle time given—makes good sense. The cycle time is chosen with the output rate in mind.

Also, in spite of its antiquity, E.J. Ignall's article[6] is one of the best summaries of line-balancing approaches.

17-5 Stochastic Line Balancing

Another facet of the line-balancing problem occurs when operation times at the workstations are variable. Most machines have relatively constant operation times; workers do not. Without planning for variability, bottlenecks can arise. Then, a WIP buildup occurs. If a paced conveyor is being used, it may have to be stopped, or other steps must be taken to keep the line moving.

When operation times are randomly distributed, rather than fixed, they are said to be stochastic. To illustrate, The Photo Lab's operation (6) might vary 95 percent of the time between 0.6 minute and 1.4 minutes with the average time being 1.0 minute. In a system such as shown in Figure 17-7, where the line balance (including idle time) is perfect, consider the effect if operation (6) shifts from 1.0 to 1.4. The built-in leeway is only 0.3, so this production line must stop.

When task time at a station can exceed the allotted time, a plan is needed. The alternatives are:

1 Let the unfinished or defective item move on to the next station. Depending on the nature of the problem, successive stations may or may not continue to work on the item.
2 Develop a group of special workers who can shift from station to station to provide extra help as needed.

© 2008 Jupiterimages Corporation

Games of chance epitomize stochastic processes. In business, risk is reduced as much as possible. P/OM does not practice gambling, however, when risk cannot be removed, it must be understood.

3 Label this item so it can be removed at the end of the line and reworked then. Stations will not continue to work on items so labeled.

4 Stop the line and correct the problem. This applies not only to the product but also to the part of the process that created the problem.

5 Remove the defective item as soon as it is discovered and let the line move on without it. Downstream stations will have to wait until good items start to reach them again. Take the item to a rework area.

Each plan has a cost that can be determined with analysis. Other plans can be developed that might be more appropriate.

As far as line balancing is concerned, operation times should be increased to reflect longest times that might be experienced with each operation. The number of standard deviations used will depend on the severity of the penalty that will be paid for having exceeded the cycle time of the paced conveyor. Severe penalties might require more than 3-sigma protection.

The longer operation times used for planning will lead to more stations being required in order to deliver the specified output. The cost for protection against extra long operation times is more stations to manage and increased idle time at those stations. The trade-off analysis must be done with reasonable estimates of the costs to determine what policies to follow.

Generally, methods of statistical process control can be used effectively to control, and sometimes reduce, the variability of the operation times. Programs of total quality management can be started with emphasis on seeking suggestions for improvement from those working on the process.

17-5a Queuing Aspects of Line Balancing

Queues can form when stochastic behavior characterizes any operation time t_i. The word *stochastic* is commonly used to describe the process that causes a waiting line for service to form. Say that t_2 and t_4 in Figure 17-6 can vary. This means that operation (5) in station III is sometimes idle, while at other times there is a queue made up of different numbers of completed twos (2) and fours (4).

In the same way, assume that t_5 of operation (5) is variable. This affects station IV, and consequently V, with fluctuations of arrivals leading to queues sometimes and idleness at other times. Queuing theory has the ability to describe what happens in such systems.

Queuing theory begins by characterizing arrival rates according to their type of variability. The classic case is random arrivals (Poisson distributed) and random service intervals (exponentially distributed). Although that is frequently a good descriptor, sometimes arrivals are constant (or fall between random and constant). Special cycle-time management is required when variability characterizes operation times.

The paced conveyor is not practical when variability exists for either arrival times or service times. Then, line balancing is achieved by putting the right amount of service power in place to handle the arrivals. Such balance changes over time as demand cycles from peak loads to normal and below normal loads.

The behavior of **single-channel system** (e.g., a single workstation; $N = 1$) can be described as an input–output system with variable arrivals and variable service times. It is illustrated in Figure 17-10 with an arrival rate λ and a service rate μ. The figure shows that a queue of four has formed in front of the station.

Single-channel system

With variable service times and variable arrival rates, a line starts to form when the number of arrivals is greater than one during an average service period because $N = 1$.

Figure 17-10

A Single-Channel Workstation; $N = 1$

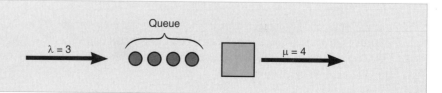

Queue

$\lambda = 3$ $\mu = 4$

Assume that the workstation has an average output capability of four units per hour ($\mu = 4.0$). μ is the average of a Poisson distribution. The arrival rate of orders averages three per hour ($\lambda = 3.0$). λ is the average of a Poisson distribution.

Assumptions for N = 1 Queuing Models in 17-5b

The use of this queuing model makes certain specific assumptions. First, the source of arrivals is large enough to be considered infinite. Second, there are unlimited accommodations for a waiting line. Third, service is granted on a first-come, first-served or FIFO basis. Fourth, it already has been stated that this analysis and the equations that follow apply to single-service channels. Fifth, the arrival and service distributions are Poisson. If intervals between arrivals and between services are used (instead of the numbers of events), then both distributions are exponential.

Standard nomenclature describes assumptions about the model in the form M/M/1 where the first M stands for Markovian (Poisson) arrivals; the second M is Markovian (Poisson) service times and the third place 1 means that N (called s here) is one server. The M/G/s system has a general service time distribution that includes specification of the standard deviation of the distribution. In this text M/M/s are treated and QMpom programs will solve that class of problems.

17-5b Single-Channel Equations[7]

$$\rho = \lambda/\mu = the\ systems\ utilization\ factor \qquad (17\text{-}8)$$

The meaning of the **systems utilization factor**, for the single channel, is the average number of orders being serviced over time. With a single-channel system, ρ (rho) is the average percent of time that the station is providing service. ρ must be less than one because if it is one or greater, then the system is always occupied and the waiting line will grow indefinitely. Thus: $\rho < 1.0$ is required.

L, the average number of orders in a single-channel service system, is defined by Equation 17-9.

$$L = L_q + \rho \qquad (17\text{-}9)$$

Note that L is the sum of (L_q) the average number of orders waiting in the queue line, and (ρ) the average number of orders being served.

The average time that an order waits on line is W_q as shown in Equation 17-10.

$$W_q = L_q/\lambda \qquad (17\text{-}10)$$

The average time that an order spends in the system—waiting and receiving service—is called W. It is shown in Equation 17-11.

$$W = W_q + 1/\mu \qquad (17\text{-}11)$$

W consists of W_q, which is the average time spent waiting in queue plus the average service time, $1/\mu$.

L_q is defined in terms of ρ as shown in Equation 17-12.

$$L_q = \rho^2/(1 - \rho) \qquad (17\text{-}12)$$

Figure 17-10 depicts a single-channel situation where $\lambda = 3$ and $\mu. = 4$. Although the station's output capacity (of four units per hour) is greater than the demand rate (of three units per hour), a waiting line will develop from time to time. This occurs when either the variable demand becomes greater than the average lambda (λ) and/or the variable service rate falls below the average μ (mu). If both occur simultaneously, the resultant queue can be of formidable size.

Equations 17-8 through 17-12 provide the system's characteristics as follows:

Systems utilization factor
Average percent of time that the M-server system is providing service.

$\rho = \lambda/\mu = 3/4 = 0.75$ (from Equation 17-8)
$L_q = (3/4)^2/(1 - 3/4) = 9(16)(1/4) = 9/4 = 2.25$ orders (from Equation 17-12)
$L = 2.25 + 0.75 = 3.00$ orders (from Equation 17-9)
$W_q = L_q/\lambda = 2.25/3 = 0.75$ hours (from Equation 17-10)
$W = 0.75 + (1/4) = 1.00$ hours (from Equation 17-11)

A lot has been learned about waiting times and the numbers of orders that are in queue. If not acceptable because there are too many delays (there are ways to put costs on waiting times, number of servers, and idle time of servers), changes can be made in the process configurations.

Note that as long as there is a waiting line, the *average* cycle time between successive completed orders is 0.25 hour or 15 minutes. This means that when there is a waiting line, the station's output rate averages four orders per hour. However, output drops to zero when there are no orders in the system. To find out what percent of the time the station is not working, it is useful to determine the probability distribution of system occupancy. Using that distribution some additional insights can be gained.

The probability distribution is denoted by (P_n), where (P_n) equals the probability that the total number of orders in the system is (n). When $n = 0$, there are no orders and the station is idle. When $n = 1$, the station is working but no orders are waiting. When $n = 2$, the station is working (setup times included) and one order is waiting. The pattern continues for $n > 2$.

The values of P_n are derived from Equation 17-13.

$$P_n = (1 - \rho)\rho^n \qquad (17\text{-}13)$$

Table 17-10 shows the calculations for $\rho = 0.75$.

Figure 17-11 shows the probability distribution for n orders being in the system. The area of the tail of this distribution is the probability (α) that the queue length will exceed (n) for $\rho = 0.75$.

The right-hand tail of the graph states the probability that the queue will be longer than nine (i.e., 10 and greater) is 0.0563. This is determined by

$$P_{n>9} = 1 - \sum_{n=0}^{n=9} P_n = 1 - 0.9437 = 0.0563$$

Work waiting for processing can be expected to be greater than eight more than 5 percent of the time. If only eight units can be stored in front of the station, then at least

Table 17-10	n	P_n		Probability Density	Cumulative Probability (Sum)
Distributions of P_n for Single-Channel Queuing Model with Assumptions Stated Above and $\rho = 0.75$ (Probability Density and Cumulative Probability Distributions)	0	$P_0 = (1 - \rho)$	=	0.2500	0.2500
	1	$P_1 = (1 - \rho)\rho$		0.1875	0.4375
	2	$P_2 = (1 - \rho)\rho^2$	=	0.1406	0.5781
	3	$P_3 = (1 - \rho)\rho^3$	=	0.1055	0.6836
	4	*	=	0.0791	0.7627
	5	*	=	0.0593	0.8220
	6	*	=	0.0445	0.8665
	7	*	=	0.0334	0.8999
	8	*	=	0.0250	0.9249
	9	*	=	0.0188	0.9437
	10	*	=	0.0141	0.9578
	*	*	=	*	*
	*	*	=	*	*
	*	*	=	*	*
	n	$P_n = (1 - \rho)\rho^n$	etc.	etc.	etc.

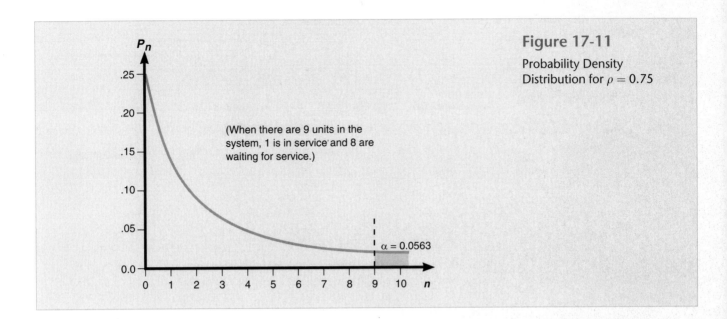

Figure 17-11

Probability Density
Distribution for $\rho = 0.75$

5 percent of the time the system will turn away arriving orders and/or shut down. Because this is clearly undesirable, steps should be taken to decrease the probability of exceeding eight units in queue, or to provide more storage space. Storage and waiting problems that can stop production typify cycle-time management for stochastic systems.

Other performance characteristics of this system are apparent from Table 17-10. The station will be idle 25 percent of the time as reflected by $P_0 = 0.25$.

Workstation output is given by Equation 17-14.

$$\text{Expected output} = (1 - P_0)\mu = (0.75)(4) = 3 \text{ units per hour} \qquad (17\text{-}14)$$

Expected daily output is $3(8) = 24$ units per day. Cycle-time management can take on the task of increasing μ. This might be done by adding an additional station.

17-5c Multiple-Channel ($N > 1$) Equations[8]

Figure 17-12 shows a queue of four orders with arrival rate μ waiting for service by N **multiple-channel system**, which have service rates of $\mu_1, \mu_2, \ldots, \mu_N$. This kind of waiting system, used by many banks, airline ticket windows, and the post office, is called a **Red Carpet system**. The number of channels or servers is sometimes represented by $s, S, m,$ or M.

The system utilization factor when there are N servers is

$$\rho = \lambda/N\mu = \text{the systems utilization factor} \qquad (17\text{-}15)$$

To avoid infinite waiting lines $\lambda < N\mu$, which insures that $\rho < 1$ will hold. If the decision is made to use two parallel stations, then $N = 2$ and

$$\rho = \lambda/2\mu = 3/8 \qquad (17\text{-}16)$$

when $\lambda = 3$ and $\mu = 4$, as before.

The multiple-channel equations for L, W, L_q, etc., are much more complex than for single-channel systems. QMpom programs make it simpler. The results now shown of adding another station are based on QMpom calculations. Table 17-11 compares the total number of orders (L) that are in the system—waiting and being serviced. It also compares P_0, which for $N = 1$ means one station is idle and for $N = 2$ means both stations are idle. Using the QMpom software, we easily make additional comparisons as shown for $\rho, L_q,$ $W, W_q, P_1, P_{n>1},$ and $P_{n>9}$. System utilization decreases by 50 percent with two servers. Orders in the system decrease by 72 percent and orders on line by 61.2 percent. Waiting time in queue decreases by 94.6 percent and total waiting time in the system decreases

Multiple-channel system
Effect of multiple channels (stations, servers, systems) is to provide greater systems capacity and to lower the system's utilization.

Red Carpet system
A single waiting line feeds multiple servers. Whoever is at the head of the line goes to the first free server. This system is quite frequently used for airport queues.

Figure 17-12

Multiple-Channel Workstations (N) with Single Queue (called a Red Carpet)

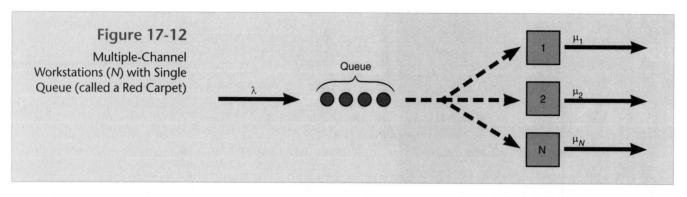

Table 17-11

Comparison of One and Two Stations with $\lambda = 3$ and $\mu = 4$

	N = 1	N = 2	Percent Change
ρ	0.75	0.375	−50.0%
L	3.00 orders	0.85 orders	−72.0%
L_q	2.25 orders	0.8727 orders	−61.2%
W	1.00 hour = 60 min.	17.4545 minutes	−70.9%
W_q	0.75 hours = 45 min.	2.4545 minutes	−94.6%
P_0	0.2500	0.4545	+81.8%
P_1	0.1875	0.3409	+81.8%
$P_{n>1}$	0.5625	0.2045	−63.6%
$P_{n>9}$	0.0563	0.00008	−99.86

by 70.9 percent. The probability that all servers are idle increases by 81.8 percent as does the probability that one server is occupied. The probability that all servers are busy diminishes by 63.6 percent with two servers as compared to one. Knowing the cost of servers and estimating the cost of orders waiting permits good decisions to be made about how many servers to employ.

An additional strategy is available for cycle-time management. If the single-channel workstation can be mechanized so that the service intervals are constant, then L will be reduced by about 35 to 45 percent. Less variability of service times produces significant reductions in waiting lines and in cycle time.

Finally, the kind of system that is being managed can vary greatly. The service units can be part of a job shop. Each station stands alone as an individual, stochastic input–output system providing batch service. When the flow shop configuration is used, then the various service units are interrelated, and the outputs of one system become the inputs to another. This requires careful coordination and matching of the stochastic behaviors of systems that are depending upon each other.

Queues can be comprised of customers' orders waiting for service, WIP waiting for the next machine, airplanes waiting to be cleared to land, or cars waiting at the tollbooth. The waiting line is invisible but present when a busy signal is encountered on the telephone line. Express checkout lanes in supermarkets alter the FIFO priority and would require other models. Parking garages put up the sign "Sorry Full," which turns away arrivals.

Queuing models do not provide optimum solutions for output rates and cycle times. They provide descriptive measures. P/OM evaluates various designs using these descriptive measurements of queuing criteria and incorporating them with costs. Design changes are made based on test results, and the system is retested and re-costed. This goes on until a satisfactory production line is obtained.

Many different models exist, and most of them have been fully explored in the literature. When the situation does not lend itself to mathematical analysis, then simulation can be used to determine the behavior of the service system (see Enrichment Activity 17).

17-6 Just-In-Time (JIT) Delivery

In line-balance terminology, each station is a customer for the "supplier" station that precedes it. Just-in-time is a cycle-time management principle that states that delivery to the next station of a specified amount of material is to be made when and *only when that next station is ready* to receive that delivery. Just-in-time (JIT) delivery requires agreement between suppliers and buyers of what, when, where, and how much. It should be noted that JIT puts production at risk in the event that something happens to the supplier or to the supplier's shipper. Thus, risk reduction is achieved by carrying extra stock. This policy is referred to as *just-in-case*.

A **kanban** is any method that calls attention to the fact that the next station wishes to receive a JIT delivery. Kanban is a card used in Japanese manufacturing plants to signal that a delivery will be needed. The word has been adopted worldwide to describe an array of signaling devices that include colorful squares that indicate a need for supplies when uncovered. Other signals are ping-pong balls dropping through tubes, and lights flashing.

The same concept applies to outside suppliers making deliveries as required by what is needed by the producer. The details require specification of when, where, and how much. Various plants and distributors' warehouses are built with walls that open anywhere along the production line. In this way, supplies can be delivered where they are needed on the production line. Automobile-assembly plants reduce JIT delivery risks by having suppliers located on adjacent land right outside the plant.

Production systems that signal for delivery from upstream stations (including from outside suppliers) are known as **pull-production systems**. They pull materials as they need them to work on. In contrast, production systems that push materials on the downstream stations are regarded as impeding productivity. The smooth flows and balanced cycle times of pull-production systems are gradually replacing the **push-production systems** of earlier production eras.

What accounts for workstations pushing as much WIP as possible onto the next workstation? The motivating factor for such performance is often the accounting system, which records the utilization of workers and equipment and rewards people for using equipment and producing product. The focus is on keeping busy. The result is process bottlenecks and storage space filled with unfinished product, which has carrying costs. Smooth running JIT-type pull systems have multiplicative advantages over the management accounting model, which encourages full utilization of all resources and facilities.

Serialized production systems, which are not connected by paced-conveyor belts, must often compensate for variable arrival and service rates. These systems are free wheeling but coordinated by a kanban serving as the communication link to synchronize the interdependent activities. Such systems are line balanced so that there is the same average amount of work at each station. They also are balanced as much as possible with respect to the amount of variability that characterizes each station.

The previous description also applies to balancing the flows in the supply chain. When strong relationships have been developed with suppliers, the effect of the externality of the supplier to the producer can be minimized. There is rapid communication, trust, and a sense of mutual responsibility. Also, there is less difference between adjacent stations that are entirely within the plant, and adjacent stations that are in two different plants.

There is shared confidence that the quality control system of the supplier will ensure that standards are met or bettered. Deliveries are regular and reliable. Problems at either end are immediately shared. Improvements are suggested by both parties for the other's plants. Suppliers operating in this environment are regarded as part of the buyer's team. The supplier's cycle-time management is the buyer's concern and vice versa.

Another form of cycle-time management that connects suppliers and buyers is *vendor releasing*. This is an agreement that the buyer makes to purchase a quantity that entitles the buyer to a discount. However, the supplier makes regular deliveries of parts of the

Kanban
Calls attention to a workstation's need to receive a just-in-time (JIT) delivery.

Pull-production systems
Systems that call for delivery of materials from upstream stations (including outside suppliers) are pulling materials as needed.

Push-production systems
Workstations pushing materials on the downstream stations are impeding productivity. Poor line balance aggravates the situation, causing uneven output.

total quantity purchased. To illustrate, six months of supply can be purchased at one time with weekly deliveries of specific amounts that can be changed as per agreement.

Suppliers that offer vendor releasing often can do so because they have other customers, which allows them to produce in larger volumes. By producing either continuously or in substantial economic lot quantities, shipments are permitted directly from the line and only occasionally from stock. Steel and aluminum companies use this delivery cycle-control technique to sell big quantities of product to customers who could not otherwise buy large amounts to earn discounts because they lack storage space.

Volkswagen AG has a plant in the rural town of Resende, Brazil, that is a modular-based consortium.[9] A dozen suppliers coexist within the plant, each contributing their specialized parts to the 1,000 trucks per day that are output. Modularity of design allows a number of different models to be constructed without having to redesign the way that parts from different suppliers (seats, dashboards, chassis) fit together. The production line is well balanced, and the system functions well because of good communications and trust between the parties. VW Resende announced doubling its investment in the plant as of April 1, 2002. A new multibillion-dollar Mexican plant (Puebla) was announced in 2006 based on VW's assembly operation in Resende.[10]

17-7 Push- Versus Pull-Process Discipline

As an example of the conversion from a push-production system to a pull-production system, consider the following situation. Say that Joe toasts hamburger buns and Josephine puts the burger between the buns and adds tomatoes, pickles, relish, and sauce. Further, assume that Joe's toaster produces 10 finished crowns and heels per minute while Josephine's production is 6 burgers per minute.

If both work at their top capacities, Joe is pushing 4 extra buns per minute on Josephine; her queue will grow to 240 buns in an hour and to almost 2,000 by the end of the 8-hour shift. Push-production processes are relentless in their overfeeding of the bottleneck process, which in this case is Josephine's operation. To prevent absurd queues from growing, Joe shifts to the french fries department whenever there is no more space left on which to push the finished buns.

Josephine is a student of P/OM. She has learned about a manufacturing process that uses kanban to signal the need for supplies. From Josephine's point of view, the simplest kanban would be a yellow square on which Joe placed toasted buns whenever the square had no buns on it. The ideal quantity to be called for would be one bun at a time.

To produce this result, Joe's conventional toaster, which delivers all finished goods in a batch, should be replaced with a circular toaster, as shown in Figure 17-13.

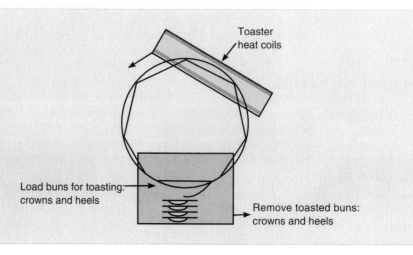

Figure 17-13

Serialized Toasting Permits Pull Process

Toaster heat coils

Load buns for toasting: crowns and heels

Remove toasted buns: crowns and heels

Like a Ferris wheel that stops every so often to let passengers depart and new ones embark, the circular toaster deposits a finished bun (crown and heel) and is reloaded to start toasting every 10 seconds. This permits Joe to feed buns to Josephine as they are needed. When the demand drops off, because the peak period is past, Josephine slows down and makes fewer burgers per minute. Joe must then adjust the bun-loading pattern to feed the bottleneck activity at the rate that it needs to be fed. Josephine has succeeded in pulling buns as needed.

If demand exceeds the capacity of Josephine to make burgers, then a swing person (such as the manager) starts to work alongside Josephine. The setting is turned up on the toaster and its speed of rotation is increased. This effectively increases its throughput rate without jeopardizing quality. The flexibility of the pull system is dependent upon the speed control of the feeding systems.

The pop-up toaster that was formerly used produced a batch of 10 finished buns every minute, and these were delivered en masse to Josephine. Joe thought that he was doing a great job when he really loaded up Josephine's workstation because that is the criterion of high productivity when using a push system. Customers are much happier with the pull one-at-a-time system initiated by Josephine. The buns are fresher. Josephine is happier too because she sets the pace and is not always working to reduce the bun inventory that swamps her workplace.

There is more than ample evidence that pushing output on the next workstation is counterproductive. The pull number does not have to be one. Josephine might have preferred to have two buns delivered to her every time her kanban square was empty.

Pushing production is based on two concepts:

1 The independence of adjacent workstations in the process
2 The objective of having everyone, and every facility, work at maximum capacity

Both points represent non-systems thinking. Adjacent workstations in any process should be viewed as interdependent. They are connected by material transfer systems, and successive stages of work entail product design dependencies. Workstations always are connected by common systems objectives, which include waste reduction of all kinds including space, WIP, and time.

Hewlett-Packard (HP) has made an exceptional videotape (titled *Stockless Production*) at their Greeley Division in Colorado. It has been used internally to demonstrate to HP employees the effectiveness of moving from push- to pull-type production systems.

An intermittent flow shop was set up to make a mock product. The production line consisted of five stations, each with one person doing simple operations to a styrofoam insert that was then put into a cardboard box. The line did not appear to be balanced, but each of the five stations had about the same amount of work to do.

Three different production arrangements were tested. The first pushed six completed units from each station to the next one. The second pulled three units and the third pulled one unit.

The five evaluation measures used were space required, work in process, cycle time, rework quantity, and problem visibility. HP measured cycle time as the interval between start work on a part and its completion. It is shown to be correlated with both work in process and the rework quantity. To determine rework quantity, defective material inserted into the line was detected at the fifth and final station. All work in process queued up between stations was counted to determine how much rework would be required once the problem was spotted.

Table 17-12 shows the results of these push versus pull comparisons.

There is a decrease of 90 percent in cycle time between push 6 and pull 1. The decrease in WIP and rework quantity also is 87 and 89 percent respectively. Space needs are cut in half because WIP is down to four units. Problems can be spotted immediately because the WIP clutter is removed. Everyone who views this tape agrees that the

Table 17-12		Push 6	Pull 3	Pull 1	Percent (6:1)
Results of the Push Versus Pull Comparison	Space used	2 tables	2 tables	1 table	−50.0%
	Work in progress (WIP)	30 units	12 units	4 units	−86.7%
	Cycle times	3' 17"	1' 40"	0' 19"	−90.4%
	Rework quantity	26 units	10 units	3 units	−88.5%
	Problem visibility	Hidden	Hidden	Visible	0 to 1

push versus pull pilot experiment is impressive. Process visibility had improved so much that the production manager commented, "it might be possible to automate the line."

JIT processing was a by-product of the switch from push to pull-one production. Cycle-time management is enhanced by this transformation of the process. Line balancing is a natural outgrowth of the change. No investment was required other than the will to change. There were no costs and the savings are evident and significant. The applicability of this method to real production systems and supply chain functions is immense.

Spotlight 17-1 The O.O.D.A. Loop
How Fast Can You React? (Asking Fighter Pilots and Business Managers)

The late Colonel John R. Boyd of the U.S. Air Force is credited with developing time-based theories about achieving successful military operations. His strategies have engaged many military strategists in discussions about implementing his ideas. At the same time, many business school academics and industry executives have been impressed with the applicability of Colonel Boyd's ideas when transferred to a competitive business context.

Part of Boyd's core thinking relates to the O.O.D.A. loop. This is a repetitive cycle of activities that starts with *observation* of the situation. The second O in the loop stands for *orientation*. This consists of assessing our (fighter plane's) position relative to the orientation of the adversary. The D stands for using the information obtained in OO to make a *decision* about which maneuvers will provide an advantage in a dogfight. The A in the OODA loop is the *action* of carrying out the decision.

Before Boyd identified and named the O.O.D.A. loop in 1986, dogfights were a matter of honed instinct and fast reactions for fighter pilots. John Boyd advocated a conscious effort to accelerate the time to complete the loop using new training and technology.

Quoting from Boyd's military briefing (titled "Patterns of Conflict" and posted at http://www.d-n-i.net/boyd/pdf/poc.pdf), "to win, we should operate at a faster tempo or rhythm than our adversaries, or better yet, get inside our adversary's Observation-Orientation-Decision-Action time cycle or loop." His explanation is that being faster unnerves the adversary. Whoever has the fastest O.O.D.A. loop

appears to the adversary to be unpredictable, which generates confusion and disorder. Military aircraft in the United States are now designed to provide pilots with superior O.O.D.A. loop performance. Pilot training amplifies that advantage.

Brigadier General Mark T. Matthews, 48th Fighter Wing Commander of the Royal Air Force, wrote a note for the *Commander's Forum of the Royal Air Force Lakenheath, England Newsletter* (03/26/04), which stated he had attended a lecture of Colonel Boyd and that it had taken him years to "come to appreciate—if not fully agree with—his observations." General Matthews says, "Colonel Boyd referred to the second letter of the acronym as the 'Big O' because he believed that proper orientation was critical in making rapid, accurate decisions." Dictionaries define orientation in terms of both psychological as well as physical positioning.

The O.O.D.A. loop is not restricted to military applications. O.O.D.A. loop awareness will be found in sports and business. For example, quarterbacks of winning football teams go through O.O.D.A. loops in completing passes that lead to touchdowns.

In business, competitive decisions must be made rapidly and correctly. Once made, they are hard to reverse. Recognition of the importance to business of Colonel Boyd's O.O.D.A. loop thesis appeared quickly after its publication in December 1986. In a 1987 *New York Times* article, Thomas Hout and Mark Blaxill stated, "Build an organization with fast response time in serving customers and preempting competitors, and you will grow profitably."

The O.O.D.A. loop is preemptive when new products are developed faster and better than those of competitors who cannot get a fix on the intentions of fast-movers. The initiative is seized when your orders can be delivered to customers ahead of those of your competitors. Firms that deal with fast-delivery system vendors have a competitive advantage. The speed of just-in-time is just-right. It reduces waste and increases margins. Timing can be the suppliers' contribution to the firm's O.O.D.A. loop. There is a clear advantage when production and operations managers work closely with product and process designers. Logically, these two activities should be congruent so that quality can be maximized; redesign and retooling can be minimized. Rapid and accurate were Boyd's objectives.

Hout and Blaxill recommend a tight-knit operations architecture "rooted in systems thinking. If each working part of the company is closely linked with others and work is done right the first time, the company will do everything faster than its competitors."

Dogfight winners have the faster O.O.D.A. loop. (See: Norman Franks, *Dog-Fight: Aerial Tactics of the Aces of World War I*, Greenhill Books, London, July 2003.) The same competitive advantage holds for companies that break out of traditional bureaucratic modes. Operational decisions made on the plant floor without requiring upward review provide significant competitive advantage. Also, employees so empowered are happier with their jobs. What organizational structures help companies move faster through the O.O.D.A. loop?

Value-adding is going on at higher rates in firms that reach decisions without stalling. Jobs waiting for sign-offs are reduced in number. Projects move to completion at a faster rate. Implications of marketing decisions (such as pricing) can be discussed by everyone concerned without having to justify crossing boundaries.

With the O.O.D.A. philosophy, three questions need answers. How slow is our company's loop? How fast are our competitors' loops? What can we do to speed up our loop?

Review Questions

1   What is the O.O.D.A. loop principle?
2   What role did Colonel John R. Boyd of the U.S. Air Force play in developing time-based strategies for military operations?
3   What variables determine the rapid-response of a fast O.O.D.A. loop?
4   Is the O.O.D.A. loop a strategic or tactical principle?
5   What do O.O.D.A. loops have to do with business and P/OM?

Sources: Thomas Hout and Mark Blaxill. "Managing for Increased Competitiveness: Make Decisions Like a Fighter Pilot." *The New York Times* (November 15, 1987); John Boyd's articles can be found at http://www.belisarius.com/boyd.htm. Click on "Defense and the National Interest" and then on "Boyd's complete Discourse"; also, note the over subscription to the Boyd Conference at Quantico (4/10/2007) on the Belisarius webpage.

Brigadier General Mark T. Matthews article, "Of OODA Loops, Gorillas and Hand Grenades," originally (but no longer) posted at http://www.lakenheath.af.mil/Jet48/2004Folders/032604/ccintent_ooda.htm>; Also read, Richards, Chet. *Certain to Win.* Xlibris Corp., Outskirts Press, Inc., Parker, CO. 2004.

Spotlight 17-2 Innovation
Everyone Has Something to Say About It

Innovations deliver improvements. Opinions differ about what constitutes improvement. Mapping a path to innovation starts with a fork in the road. The question is whether to innovate or defend the status quo. Both require strong commitments and dedicated work. Military concepts of defense or offense are surrogates for the business analogy. Static defenses (like the Maginot line) can be outflanked by innovators.

If the choice selected is to change things, then the scope of innovation is the next decision point. The Japanese kaizen concept is one of continuous incremental improvement. Kaizen has had a significant effect on American manufacturers and service providers. Continuous improvements are likely to be minor changes accomplished slowly. This is in contrast to radical redesign of a process that is called reengineering (REE). The term, REE, is not commonly applied for radical product redesign although it might be a good application of the same process-changing rules.

Good results can occur when radical innovations are adopted to reengineer processes that seem flawed beyond redemption. However, "extreme" innovation has had its share of failures as well as successes. To go for the gold, one starts with a clean slate. Old baggage is discarded. Such start-ups for manufacturing are called *greenfield plants*. Saturn's plant in Spring Hill, Tennessee, is one example; Toyota's Georgetown, Kentucky, plant is another.

The pros and cons of reengineering have been argued. The reward for using radical surgery with an existing system can be high, but the failure penalty is severe. Reengineering is essential if the existing system is unacceptable and cannot be fixed by kaizen.

Spotlight 17-2 (Continued)

Alternatively, continuous improvement is rejected when it further institutionalizes a failed product or process. That is like continuous improvement of the slide rule or the buggy whip. On the other hand, continuous improvement is desirable when "good is getting better." Auto safety may require both approaches. In the near term, improve on crash results. In the long term, build cars that drive themselves on smart highways with total safety. An overriding rule is "Don't do better what shouldn't be done at all."

Continuous improvement works best with what is familiar. Attempts to change the ground rules to *make the familiar strange* and *the strange familiar* are called synectics. The latter term is usually defined as a theory or system of problem stating and problem solving based on creative thinking that involves metaphor and analogy in informal interchange within a group of individuals of diverse personality and areas of specialization. The http://www. synecticsworld.com site is worth visiting.

Course corrections make sense when you know where you are going. They are not helpful when you are deciding where you want to go. The firm's probabilities of success are significantly lower for radical innovations than for course corrections.

Disruptive technology creates radical, discontinuous changes in market structure. For example, refrigerators replaced iceboxes swiftly. A more current example would be nonconventional fuel systems to power cars. Many companies support separate research efforts to work on disruptive technologies such as low-fat foods and e-books. The reason for separation is that disruptive technologies threaten existing technologies and can create hostile internal competition. When there is a split message in the organization, it is best to separate the radical innovators from the status quo group.

There remains the question about whether innovation is always a good thing. Bill Moran as vice president of market research for Lever Brothers found that among large companies, the 70:30 rule applied. This means that 7 out of 10 new products do not achieve breakeven. Don't count on the 30 percent to make a fortune either. ABC curves describe the disproportionately large contributions of the critical few. On average, 10 percent of new product launches account for 90 percent of additional revenues.

Is innovation worth the effort? A good business model can help to answer the question. Two major factors are (1) how much does it cost on average to develop new ideas and launch an innovation; (2) how much return does the average successful innovation generate?

In consumer package goods, the payoff for one successful new product launch out of 10 tries may provide suffi-cient reward to compensate for the costs of developing and launching 9 failures. When the odds slip to 1 in 20, the innovation program is unlikely to pay off. Meanwhile, efforts can be made to cut costs, raise margins, and improve probabilities of winning.

The costs and risks of managing innovations in different ways are discussed by Andrew and Sirkin. They identify three different organizational approaches to innovation.

1 Self-manage all aspects of the total system.
2 Create one or more alliances with logical partners.
3 License the innovation with companies better suited to market successfully.

The first approach has high costs, significant risks, and large payoffs when successful. Second, alliances provide equitable benefits to all parties when there is too much risk and/or not enough knowledge to go it alone (global corporate alliances). Third, minimal investor requirements of licensing make this approach a safe haven (with low payoffs) when marketing and manufacturing competencies are not sufficient.

One new innovation catches the imagination. Rensselaer Polytechnic Institute, in Troy, New York, is our nation's oldest technological university. In 2007, the faculty and students of three departments collaborated in producing a piece of paper that could make our present battery systems obsolete. Using nanotechnology (the science of the small), they have created a flexible device, 90 percent cellulose, like newsprint, into which is infused a nanotechnology material called carbon nanotubes. These act as the plus and minus terminals of a battery. With no toxic chemicals, this paper battery also acts as a super capacitor, allowing bursts of high energy. It is lightweight, ultra thin, completely flexible and able to function in temperatures from 300 degrees Fahrenheit to 100 degrees below zero because it contains no water. The paper can be twisted, folded, cut, or stacked. It can meet the most difficult design and energy requirements of tomorrow's vehicles, gadgets, iPhones, and implantable medical equipment. The inventors look forward to manufacturing their patented nanocomposite paper (see Sources) with methods used by newspaper publishing.

The last words on innovation belong to two famous men. It was Buckminster Fuller who said: "There is nothing in a caterpillar that tells you it's going to be a butterfly." Equally relevant is another point of view from the great American General, George S. Patton, who said, "Never tell people how to do things. Tell them what to do and they will surprise you with their ingenuity."

Review Questions

1 What is innovation, and why do managers make such a fuss about it?

2 Is continuous improvement a method for achieving real innovation?

3 Is radical reengineering (REE) of a product or a process the same?

4 Under what circumstance is application of the innovation process a mistake?

5 Are inventions innovations? What are the greatest innovations of all time?

6 Information technology (IT) is accused of slowing down innovation while others see it as spurring innovation. Explain and explore these diverse points of view.

Sources: James P. Andrew and Harold L. Sirkin. "Innovating for Cash." *Harvard Business Review* (September 2003): 76–83; Michael Hammer and James A. Champy. *Reengineering the Corporation: A Manifesto for Business.* New York: Harper Business, May 1994; Jeff Mauzy and Richard Harriman. *Creativity, Inc.: Building an Inventive Organization.* Cambridge, MA: Harvard Business School Press, April 2003; Martin K. Starr. *Global Corporate Alliances and the Competitive Edge.* Westport, CT: Quorum Books, 1991, pp.135–160; Clayton M. Christensen, Scott D. Anthony, and Erik A. Roth. *Seeing What's Next.* Cambridge, MA: Harvard Business School Press, 2004. http://www.maginot-line.com/index.htm; http://www.synecticsworld.com; http://www.synecticsworld.com/system/popups/articles/5waystokillanidea.htm; http://www.synecticsworld.com/system/exploringcreativity.htm; http://www.newswise.com/articles/view/532367/ (Nanocomposite paper)

Summary

Cycle-time management is the management of the interval between finished goods coming off the production line or the interval between completion of servicing operations. Cycle-time management also is the management of how long work remains at workstations and how much idle time there is at the stations. Line balancing is used to provide near-equal assignments to all workstations. This prevents some stations from being overloaded while others are idle. Cycle-time management is a form of TBM (time-based management) related to synchronization of material flows including those from suppliers.

The different approaches to line balancing consist of the deterministic, heuristic, and stochastic models. All require designing the best possible processes using precedence diagrams of serialized flow systems. The general objective is to obtain the desired production output with the minimum number of stations and the least amount of idle time.

Perfect balance, which has zero balance delay, still needs rest time added if people are working on the line. Heuristic models include Kilbridge and Wester's (K & W) line-balancing techniques. This heuristic approach—as well as others—is discussed. The heuristic models are needed for complex intermittent flow shop systems because the problems are too large for optimization models, and they are too important to ignore the benefits of line balancing.

Stochastic line balancing deals with the effects of variability in cycle management. This includes consideration of a variety of queuing models. It should be pointed out that a primary function of queuing models is to facilitate the design of balanced-service systems (requests for service and servicing capabilities) throughout the supply chain. The discussion includes suppliers' participation in effective cycle-time management.

Chapter 17 contains two examples of the conversion of push-production systems to pull-one-unit production systems. The advantages of pull-one unit are detailed. The Chapter 17 supplement deals with simulation of stochastic line-balanced queuing models.

Spotlight 17-1: The O.O.D.A. Loop is a fast-paced balancing act where competitors are viewed as being on the same line. The first to complete the cycle is the favored winner. Spotlight 17-2: Innovation is an O.O.D.A. loop of its own special kind. **Disruptive technology** is both a competitive opportunity and a competitive threat.

Disruptive technology
Abruptly replaces established and dominant technology with unexpected speed. Also called disruptive innovation.

Key Terms

Balance delay (d) (p. 709)

Cycle time (p. 693)

Cycle-Time Management (CTM) (p. 693)

Deterministic line balancing (p. 699)

Disruptive technology (p. 728)

Heuristic line-balancing methods (p. 699)

Kanban (p. 721)

Lateral transferability (p. 709)

Line balancing (LB) (p. 697)

Line efficiency (Λ) (p. 710)

Multiple-channel system (p. 719)

Paced conveyor (p. 698)

Perfect balance (pb) (p. 700)

Permutability of columns (p. 709)

Precedence diagram (p. 700)

Pull-production systems (p. 721)

Push-production systems (p. 721)

Red Carpet system (p. 719)

Single-channel system (p. 716)

Stochastic line balancing (p. 699)

Systems utilization factor (p. 717)

Time-based management (TBM) (p. 696)

Total work content (*TWC*) (p. 704)

Zoning constraints (p. 709)

Review Questions

1   What is cycle-time management?

2   What is line balancing?

3   How does line balancing relate to cycle-time management?

4   Do line balancing and cycle-time management apply to services as well as material products?

5 What is the difference between deterministic and stochastic line balancing? Can a paced conveyor be used for either one? Explain your answer.

6 Why is it said that heuristic line balancing is a practical approach to achieving a reasonably good intermittent flow shop? Can a paced conveyor be used for the resulting production line? Explain your answer.

7 Explain why heuristic line balancing is associated with computer software to run the algorithms.

8 Why is perfect balance often regarded as an unrealistic goal? When is that not the case?

9 Explain permutability of columns.

10 What does lateral transferability mean for line balancing?

11 What are zoning constraints for line balancing?

12 Why is it essential to design the best possible process before starting line balancing?

13 Why is it important to get good estimates for operation times before starting line balancing?

14 An automated teller machine (ATM) corresponds to a stochastic input–output flow shop system. As such, queuing theory can be used to study the behavior of the system and to provide cycle-time management. Explain.

15 The flow shop is designed to remove stochastic behaviors. Explain this statement and comment on how this objective can be accomplished. When is this objective unrealistic?

16 How do queuing models relate to cycle-time management?

17 For single-channel systems, why is $\lambda > \mu$ a violation?

18 For single-channel systems, why is it necessary to assume that the source population is very large?

19 For single-channel systems, why is it necessary to assume that the storage space can accommodate any number of units?

20 What distinguishes single-channel configurations from multiple-channel configurations?

21 Would the FIFO order of entry make sense for an automated teller machine?

22 For multiple-channel systems, why is $\lambda > N\mu$ a violation?

23 What are the characteristics of Poisson arrivals?

24 What is meant by exponential service times?

25 How can the exponential distribution be stated in terms of the Poisson distribution?

26 Does FIFO hold for supermarket checkout counters?

27 What kind of stochastic situation occurs in a supermarket with *n* different checkout lanes?

28 What constitutes cycle time in the supermarket checkout situation?

29 What is the supplier's role in cycle-time management?

30 Explain vendor releasing from the point of view of both the buyer and the supplier.

31 When is a push-production system desirable?

32 Explain how to use kanban to convert a push-production system to a pull-one-unit production system.

Problems Section

Note: This section has various problems that can be formulated and solved using QuantMethods Production/Operations Management software (QMpom). The appropriate model categories are indicated for each problem e.g., see problems 3 and 20.

1 Assume that you are going into business selling replacement tires. Draw a precedence diagram for changing tires. Discuss the way in which this job could be done with a flow shop configuration. Why would a flow shop be preferred? Suggest a possible division of labor that could produce a reasonable line balance.

2 Draw a precedence diagram for the way in which tellers handle withdrawals at the bank. Can this job be accomplished by tellers in flow shop configurations?

3 Line efficiency (Λ) is a measure used to assess line balance. It is given by Equation 17-6. Determine line efficiency for The Photo Lab where $n = 4$, $C = 1.5$ minutes, and total work content is 4.8.

   Using the QMpom module called Production Scheduling (Line-balancing and Cycle-time Controls) will facilitate solving the seventeen (17) problems that are numbered 3 through 19.

4 Determine line efficiency (described in Problem 3) and relate it to the balance delay measure (given in Equation 17-4) for the following conditions: Total work content is 3 hours; there are 180 stations operating with a cycle time of one minute. Compare the results and meanings of *d* and Λ.

5 For The Photo Lab, what happens if t_{max} can be reduced from 1.0 to 0.7 by improving the technology of the film development step $i = 6$? Refer to Figure 17-2 and Tables 17-2 and 17-3.

6 Using the information in Problem 5, what occurs if t_{max} is reduced from 1.0 to 0.6 by installing two photo developing units in parallel for operation (6)? Develop a table similar to Table 17-4.

7   Use The Photo Lab's precedence diagram in Figure 17-2, but change the operation times in Table 17-2 as follows:

Operation (i)	Operation Time (t_i), Minutes
1	1.4
2	1.5
3	1.6
4	1.7
5	1.5
6	2.0
7	1.6
8	1.1
9	1.4

   What productivity rates are possible with perfect balance?

8   Using the information in Problem 7, develop a feasible station layout for $n = 5$. What are the characteristics of this arrangement, i.e., cycle time, productivity, and balance delay?

9   With the information in Problem 7, use Kilbridge & Wester's heuristic line-balancing algorithm. Assume that $n = 4$. What are the characteristics of this arrangement, i.e., cycle time, productivity, and balance delay?

10   Drop operation (9) from The Photo Lab's precedence diagram in Figure 17-2, and alter Table 17-2 as follows:

Operation (i)	Operation Time (t_i), Minutes
1	0.4
2	0.5
3	0.6
4	0.7
5	0.5
6	1.0
7	0.6
8	0.1

   What productivity rates are possible with perfect balance?

11   With the information in Problem 10, develop a feasible station layout for $n = 3$. What are the characteristics of this arrangement, i.e., cycle time, productivity, and balance delay?

12   With the information in Problem 10, use Kilbridge & Wester's heuristic line-balancing algorithm. Assume that $n = 4$. What are the characteristics of this arrangement, i.e., cycle time, productivity, and balance delay?

13   Solve The Photo Lab's problem after multiplying all operation times in Table 17-2 by 10. Use the Kilbridge & Wester's heuristic to achieve a productivity level of 20 finished units per 8-hour day.

14   Obtain the solution for Problem 13 using Kilbridge & Wester's heuristic with $n = 4$.

   a. What is the cycle time?
   b. What is the productivity rate?
   c. How much idle time results?

15   Using the information from Problems 13 and 14, do you recommend three or four stations?

16   Using the information from Problems 13, 14, and 15, evaluate working 9 hours per day with $n = 3$.

17   Use the information from Problems 13 and 14, plus the fact—just known—that the system can be totally mechanized. Would it be worthwhile to try to speed up certain operations so that an output rate of 40 units per hour is achieved?

18   Use the information from Problem 17. Is it possible to design a balanced flow shop that can deliver hourly output rates of 37.5, 40.0, and 42.5 at the flick of a switch?

19   Figure 17-14 depicts the current line balance used by the Baby's Stroller Company for an intermittent flow shop that makes convertible strollers. These strollers, which can be made into baby car seats, have become increasingly popular. The IFS is now run twice a month for four to five days, and all of the work is done with five stations.

   a. What is the productive output per hour?
   b. What is the balance delay?

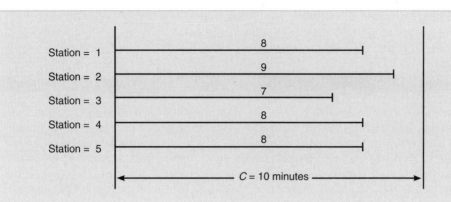

Figure 17-14

Baby's Stroller Line Balance

20 Viewing the automated teller machine (ATM) as a stochastic, single-channel, input–output system with Poisson arrivals and exponential service times, determine the values of W_q and L_q when $\lambda = 8$ and $\mu = 10$. Note: FIFO holds as well as the other assumptions required for single-channel queuing models.

  Using the QMpom module called Queueing System Models (Queues) will facilitate solving the five (5) problems that are numbered 20 through 24.

21 Viewing a vending machine as a stochastic, single-channel, input–output system with Poisson arrivals and exponential service times, determine the values of and W and L for $\lambda = 8$ and $\mu = 10$. Note: FIFO holds as well as the other assumptions required for the single-channel queuing model.

22 View the painting booth in an automobile-assembly plant as a stochastic, single-channel, input–output system with Poisson arrivals and exponential service times. Determine the values of P_0 and P_1, and $P_{n>1}$ for $\lambda = 8$ and $\mu = 10$. Note: FIFO holds as well as the other assumptions required for the single-channel queuing model.

23 For the painting booth described in Problem 22, what kind of in-process (WIP) storage will be needed? Where should it be located?

24 If an assembly line is mechanized with two workstations such that the first station's output rate is three units per minute and the second station's output rate is four units per minute, what is the output rate of the system—assuming deterministic performance?

25 At The Burger Place, Jane's toaster produces 20 finished crowns and heels per minute while Jim dresses 10 burgers per minute. They have been trained to use push-production methods. When Jane sees that Jim has no more space, she helps out at the drive-through window. What is the waiting line if they both work at rated speed for 15 minutes? How big a storage space does Jim need? How is quality affected?

26 Using the information in Problem 25, convert Jane's operation to a pull-five system. What delivery rate will apply?

27 Using the information in Problems 25 and 26, what kind of a kanban do you recommend for times when demand for burgers drops off to less than 10 per minute? Would it make sense for both Jane and Jim to combine the toast and dress operations and work in parallel? What maximum demand rate could they satisfy?

Practice Quiz

1 Cycle-time management is crucial in both manufacturing and services. Understanding the opportunities for competitive advantage can provide major tactical advantages. It is easy to overlook the fact that cycle-time management can lower costs for municipalities (police, fire, sanitation, and hospital services, the post office, tax collectors, etc.). To bring this into focus, the local business school has developed a seminar on cycle-time management and has invited the mayor's office, chief of the post office (http://www.USPS.com), bankers, regional industrialists, and hospitality managers to attend at the same time. Before the seminar, a list of points to be covered is circulated among the participants. Calls have been coming in to the seminar leader questioning one of the statements a. to f. Which statement is causing trouble?

   a. Cycle-time management is one facet of time-based management (TBM). This aspect of TBM is tactical in nature. Other aspects of TBM, such as FedEx developed with its Memphis hub for next-day delivery, are strategic. FedEx is the largest single employer in Memphis. As of 2006, FedEx worldwide has 280,000 employees and contractors. It owns 669 aircraft serving 375 airports. Its tactics follow the best P/OM and its strategic impact is enormous.

   b. The concept of continuous process improvement, instead of reengineering (or radical change), often, but not always, applies to cycle-time reduction. There are many examples of long cycle-times being reduced. For example, call center technology and training have led to shorter wait times for customers; Amazon decreased warehouse cycle times (from order receipt to ship) and thereby obtained significant savings; U.S. Airways improved its cycle times by cutting waiting time on the ground from 45 minutes to 20 minutes. This is a 56 percent reduction in cycle time.

c. Reengineering (REE) is a strategic initiative. By definition, REE is *once again* starting from scratch. Do it right the first time has to be modified to "do it right the second time around." However, even though short cycle times can often be obtained by redesign, the cost may be too high because the old infrastructure is hard to shed.

d. First-time start-ups *can* do it right the first time. That has obvious as well as hidden benefits. The obvious advantages are learning from competitors' mistakes and new technology. The hidden start-up advantage over existing competition is no prior infrastructure and few preconceived notions. At the outset, Southwest Airlines (SWA) chose time-based strategic goals that ran counter to industry practice. SWA set goals for achieving fast turnaround from ground to air. Southwest's costs have always been lower than industry benchmarks. Volume of business is well above breakeven.

e. Nummi in Fremont, California, is a reengineered plant. Originally, it was a General Motors plant that closed for a variety of serious reasons that made it a quality nightmare. After being reengineered by Toyota, Nummi became a model plant, receiving very high ratings in productivity and quality. Over time, as labor costs began to increase, Toyota has indicated it may leave General Motors alone to fend for itself in this one-of-a- kind joint venture.

f. Every parcel distribution system has a cycle time that starts with customers sending packages and ends with other customers receiving packages. Delivery of parcels has these dual customers at the input and the output of the transport transformation. It is, however, a production process with no analogies to workstations. Consequently, the concept of line balancing is not applicable.

2 Continuing along the same line, the faculty seminar leader prepared another set of discussion points regarding cycle-time management and line balancing. Again, a single statement was introduced that was not correct. Identify the incorrect statement.

a. The intermittent flow shop (IFS) is the work configuration of choice for newly founded firms that are starting up a new product line. After sufficient demand is developed, a permanent flow shop can be put into place. If the new product does not grow demand as expected, investment losses in expensive, serial production technology is avoided.

b. Deterministic line balancing will not work with the intermittent flow shop. It is intended to be used with dedicated flow shops that employ a lot of technology. The IFS, on the other hand, requires almost all labor. The variability of workers is hard to control, and with several workstations, the amount of idle time will be set by the fastest workers.

c. Deterministic line balancing calls upon everyone to consider how to make the jobs at the workstations as consistent as possible. For example, a worker holding a part with the left hand while polishing the surface with the right hand will experience fatigue faster than if the part is held by a fixture on the work table. Fatigue increases the variability of the times required to accomplish a task. Fatigue sets in quickly when an employee has to bend down to work. Auto assembly engineers found that raising the entire car by conveyor increased the productivity of workers putting tires on the car.

d. Heuristic line balancing of an IFS may not be productive unless that IFS has many activities at a large number of stations. The heuristic is used when the complexity of the line is an issue. Most likely, this applies to a dedicated flow shop that employs more labor than technology to maintain a productive output rate.

e. Stochastic line balancing of an IFS is unlikely to be productive because there is a great deal of analysis and analytic reasoning involved. The IFS is not permanent enough to warrant that kind of approach. On the other hand, if the IFS is used fairly regularly, although not continuously, these comments should be subjected to scrutiny.

3 A task force of the seminar group prepared a statement about the differences between large companies and small- and medium-sized companies. It began by noting that large firms launch new products with big television budgets, as well as magazine and newspaper ad budgets. The TV ads may be coordinated with extensive product sampling to potential consumers' mailboxes. Seminar attendees represented a mixture of large-, medium-, and small-sized companies as well as nonprofit hospital, educational, and municipal managers. Everyone was interested in the task force conclusions published as a. to f. Which point in particular was cited as being incorrect?

a. Large company rollouts, often on a national scope, are not likely to have production based on an intermittent flow shop. Instead, commitment will be to a dedicated flow shop with proper line balance for a range of volumes.

b. Large firms can commit to a technology-based flow shop, whereas a small start-up firm cannot readily do so. One reason for the difference is that large, established firms have experience with the product line. That coupled with extensive market research gives large-firm product managers the confidence to use a "full-scale" (dedicated) flow shop (FS) strategy.

c.   For large firms, there are high costs of moving from a "hedge-your-bets" (IFS) strategy to a "full-scale" (FS) strategy. One of these is that large firms have much visibility and keep track of each other's projects. If competitors see a marketing opportunity in a situation that has minimum barriers to entry, they will enter that market. The first company into the market with a dedicated flow shop has erected a significant barrier to entry. A dedicated flow shop provides the "first into the market" with tangible cost and quality advantages.

d.   Large firms have sufficient cash to deal with changes in strategies and tactics as they are needed to fine-tune product success. Smaller firms seldom have a cushion to fall back on when changes are required. Therefore, small- and medium-sized enterprises (SMEs) prefer to use a hedging strategy.

e.   Large firms are not likely to face bankruptcy resulting from a product failure. A smaller-sized business has to husband its resources because permanent flow shops require big investments, whereas intermittent flow shops are a hedge investment. SMEs can make mistakes at the IFS level of investment but not at the FS level.

f.   Process engineers in large firms can help find alternative uses for flow shop investments that have not been successful. If green speckled detergent does not make it in the market, perhaps red speckled detergent will. The process is the same.

4   Specific elements of line balancing for cycle-time management are being examined by the seminar group's tax collection and sanitation engineering groups. Which statement in the list from a. to f. is not correct?

a.   In line balancing, step 1 is to detail the process to be balanced. For example, spell out what must be done by the tax collection department. It is essential to list all activities that must be done—start to finish. Documentation is needed. Detail all operations and specify the precise order for doing these activities. Based on these data, the precedence diagram can be drawn to show which activities have to be completed before the next activity can be started.

b.   Before going to step 2, it is recommended that a team of colleagues review the list, the sequences, and the precedence constraints. It is better to have tax collectors review tax collection, and sanitation workers review waste management. The reason is that specific process knowledge is essential. Encourage colleagues to add details that may have been missed in the first statement of the process.

c.   Step 2 is to estimate how long the various activities will take, bearing in mind that different amounts of resources can be brought to the table. Questions arise such as is it worthwhile buying or leasing a machine? For example, Pitney Bowes' small business digital mailstation™ postage machine can process 18 letters per minute. Can the tax collector's office justify acquiring that technology for the premailing workstation? Would the time to do a job change enough to warrant training? These issues will be addressed again, when changing activity times could help balance workloads at stations.

d.   Step 3 is to assign each of the listed activities to appropriate workstations. The effort is made initially to achieve perfect balance (i.e., $d = 0$, which means there is no idle time at any station). If this is a large-scale problem with many operations, a method for assigning jobs to stations should be chosen. Possible candidates are the heuristic approaches. Software systems are available for accomplishing line balancing.

e.   Step 3 assumes that the number of workstations to use has been properly determined. The tax office manager has derived four workstations from studying the precedence diagram as follows: B follows A; C follows B; and D follows C. The tax office manager states that four stations will accommodate the precedence constraints. Because the activities are people-oriented, at least four tax office employees will be required to run the workstations.

f.   The sanitation engineer has made an effort to determine workstations for the waste management situation. He observes that the collection function normally requires one driver and two truck loaders who move as a team from one workstation to another. The truck is like the conveyor belt. This is an interesting variation of the normal view of the flow shop.

5   The bank manager in the class has taken great interest in cycle-time management. She states that the bank already uses line-balanced flow shop work configurations to process checks. In her opinion, the bank has many other opportunities to create a flow shop for operations that are now being done in batches. Seminar classmates agree that this possibility exists in their firms too and that it deserves attention. The issue of determining the number of workstations for cycle-time management has been raised by many in the class. Seminar faculty agree—this area needs attention. They release new statements that deal with this issue. Which one of the statements (a. through e.) is incorrect? Equation 17-2 for perfect balance with no idle time will help in addressing Problem 5.

a. The determination of how many workstations n to use is based on how much product is needed per time interval. The more workstations used, the shorter the cycle time, C. As the cycle time gets shorter, the output rate goes up. $O = T/C$.

b. The work content for check processing is small. It is reasonable to set the cycle time equal to the work content time and have one person do the entire job. Then, each person functions as a workstation. Many individuals doing check processing would be acting as parallel workstations. This model might work effectively for parking ticket processing.

c. A manufacturing manager in the class describes how his firm (Expensive Shoe Company—ESC) uses the IFS work configuration to fill orders for 90 pairs of very stylish, high-heeled women's shoes. They are expensive and made in limited quantities. They are of top quality with customized handwork. The market is strong. There is a shortage of these shoes and a waiting line for them. The shortage is intentional, being based on limitations of production runs.

d. Assume that each shoe requires an hour of labor, and 80 shoes are to be made in an 8-hour day. Ten shoes per hour is the desired output rate from which the cycle time is derived as 6 minutes per shoe, i.e., $C = T/O = 60/10 = 6$. From the equation $nC = TWC$, or $n6 = 60$ minutes, $n = 10$ workstations.

e. The shoemaker points out that breaking up the job into 10 separate sections will not yield perfect balance, i.e., there will be idle time at some workstations. This fact is not evident from the data, but it is known to the shoe process specialists of this firm. Also, six minutes is too short for an ideal cycle time. A preferable configuration is two parallel production lines of five workstations, each with a cycle time of 12 minutes. It would produce an output rate of five shoes per hour, or 50 pairs of shoes per day.

6   Class representatives of the hotel and hospitality industry are convinced that cycle-time management is applicable to their business. There is no doubt about the fact that theme park designers and managers are totally aware of ride cycle times and throughput rates, which impact on both theoretical and actual hourly ride capacities. The group believes that there are many opportunities to create flow shop type operations that are currently being done in batches. The seminar classmates agree to work together to capitalize on this opportunity, and they have made a list of items for discussion. Which one of the statements (a. through f.) is incorrect?

a. The first item on the agenda is the reduction of work content when 10 workstations are used as compared to one person doing the entire job. Assume that one craftsperson required an hour of labor to make a fancy shoe. For the theme park, substitute Cinderella's glass slipper. Assume that with 10 stations, work content is reduced by 25 percent so that each shoe requires only 45 minutes of labor.

b. Cycle time decreases to 4.5 minutes because $10C = 45$ (with perfect balance—pb). Output is equal to $60/4.5 = 13\ 1/3$ shoes per hour. If 80 shoes are the goal, that will take 6 hours. A 25 percent reduction in work content has translated into a comparable work time reduction. Another style of fancy shoe or glass slipper can be made in the remaining two hours per day.

c. Flow shop configurations produce efficiencies, derived from specialization at workstations, with significant payoffs. British economist Adam Smith (1723—1790), in his book, *The Wealth of Nations* (1776), first proposed using the division of labor to produce substantial savings for industrializing countries. Called the *father of modern economics and capitalism*, Smith predicted factories that would benefit from the increasing productivity of specialized labor.

d. Even without productivity gains, flow shops permit delivery of finished product at the end of every cycle. Originally, this meant that a finished shoe could be delivered every 6 minutes. With five workstations, delivery could be made every 12 minutes. With two parallel 5-station flow shops, a complete pair of shoes is ready for delivery every 12 minutes. In part a., with 10 workstations, a finished shoe is available every 4.5 minutes.

e. Assume that 20 percent reduction of total work content is available with four stations. Then, $4C = 48$ (assuming pb) and cycle time, $C = 12$ minutes. That is the same cycle time associated with five stations before benefits from division of labor occurred.

f. As additional workstations are added to the flow configuration, the efficiencies of specialization get better and better. This is because the job is further divided, allowing specialization of ever-smaller fractions of operations.

7   Representatives from the manufacturer of the Expensive Shoe Company (ESC) point out that breaking up the production line into 10 separate work sections will not make sense. They have divided the process into 9 operational steps, many of which can be done together at a single workstation. They are also keenly aware of the desirability of getting close to perfect balance. Bill and Nancy have shown that the actual process being used for one of the most elaborate shoe designs made by the company has total work content of 4 hours and 48 minutes—with their flow shop specialization. Nancy estimates that work content would be 6 1/2 hours without flow shop specialization. Bill tabulated the operations A

through J (he skipped I because it looked too much like "one" or "el." He also put into the table the operation times (t_i) and precedence information. The faculty leader of the seminar considered this to be an excellent exercise in line balancing. He circulated the table with a list of observations, a. to f., one of which is wrong. Which is incorrect?

Operation (i)	Preceded by	t_i (minutes)	No. of Predecessors	Notes
A	Nothing	24	0	
B	Nothing	30	0	
C	A	36	1	
D	A	42	1	
E	B, D	30	3	
F	C	60	2	t_{max}
G	E, F	36	6	
H	G	06	7	
J	G	24	7	
Total $\sum_i t_i$		288		

Legend: The entry t_{max} is the longest operation and it is not divisible at this time. $\sum_i t_i$ is the total work content.

a. Operation F and the total work content are the upper and lower boundaries on cycle time, C. The situation is described by Equation 17-3 and by the numbers, $60 \leq C \leq 288$.
b. A line balance can be found with $n = 5$, and $C = 90$ minutes:

Operation (i)	Station Name	t_i (minutes)	Station Sum	Idle Time
A	I	24		
B	I	30	I–54 out of 90 minutes	36 minutes
C	II	36		
D	II	42	II–78 out of 90 minutes	12 minutes
E	III	30		
F	III	60	III–90 out of 90 minutes	Zero
G	IV	36	IV–36 out of 90 minutes	54 minutes
H	V	06		
J	V	24	V–30 out of 90 minutes	60 minutes
Total	Five stations	288 minutes	288 out of 450 minutes	162 minutes

This solution is not looked upon favorably. It was obtained by taking the longest chain of operations in the precedence diagram. That is four links connecting five operations, such as $A \rightarrow D \rightarrow E \rightarrow G \rightarrow J$. It has a balance delay measure of $d = 36\%$. That is excessive idle time. The output rate is 2/3 unit per hour or one finished item every 90 minutes.

c. For perfect balance (with the situation in b), it can be shown that $n = 4$.
d. A better line balance was obtained by using the Kilbridge and Wester heuristic. The K & W method is based on a number of rules, the first of which is to label each operation with the number of predecessors it has. Operations are assigned to stations in the order of the least number of predecessors. For workstation I, select operations B and A, in that order because of the rule for ties (both have zero number). When a tie exists, select the operation with the longest processing time first, saving short operation times for ease of later fitting.
e. The K & W method yields perfect balance when $C = 96$ minutes with three stations. The output rate is 0.625 finished items per hour, so 1.6 hours is required for a finished unit to be delivered.

Operation (*i*)	Station Name	t_i (minutes)	Station Sum	Idle Time
B	I	30		
A	I	24		
D	I	42	I: 96 out of 96 minutes	Zero
C	II	36		
F	II	60	II: 96 out of 96 minutes	Zero
E	III	30		
G	III	36		
J	III	24		
H	III	6	III: 96 out of 96 minutes	Zero
Total	Three stations	288 minutes	288 out of 288 minutes	Zero

f.   There is a problem, however. No time has been provided for worker R & R (rest and relaxation). If 10 percent is added (say 10 minutes instead of 9.6 minutes), then cycle time becomes 106 minutes. The output rate is 0.566 finished items per hour, so 1.8 hours is required for a finished unit to be delivered. Productivity is negatively affected, but the morale will be sustained.

8   The seminar was demanding. There was a good deal of homework and yet many questions remained unanswered. As a result, it was decided to prepare a list of issues that still needed attention. Which two of the points a. to f. are incorrect?

a.   In Problem 7, there were five stations with a cycle time of 90 minutes, which means that total station time available for work was 5 x 90 = 450 minutes. Idle time added up to 162 minutes. Balance delay was derived from the ratio of idle time to total available work time, viz., 162/450 = .36 or 36 percent.

b.   There are a variety of line-balancing heuristics, including Helgeson and Birnie (H & B). They chose to assign first those operations whose following operations have the least total time.

c.   Queuing aspects of line balancing are related to stochastic factors such as workers that sometimes are faster and sometimes slower.

d.   Arrival rates at each workstation are not stochastic if a paced conveyor belt is being used to transport work in process, unless the pace is under the control of workers at each of the stations. In the Toyota plant, a worker can stop the line from moving if that becomes necessary. It is interesting to note that although this capability exists, the Toyota lines are seldom down for more than a half minute and even that is very rare.

e.   Service rates at the workstations upstream are viewed as arrival rates at stations that are downstream from them. If these arrival rates are Poisson distributed around a mean value, it is likely that the variabilities will cancel each other out and the workstations downstream will experience almost constant arrivals.

9   Josephine and Joe are designing a new quick service restaurant. Their purpose is to take the push out of fast-food production and convert it to a pull system. Joe toasts chicken–tofu burger buns. Josephine puts the chicken–tofu burger between the buns and adds sun-dried tomatoes, gherkins, and barbecue sauce. An MBA-friend has written out things to watch for and Josephine is sure that one of them is wrong. If she is right, which one is wrong?

a.   Joe's toaster produces 10 finished crowns and heels (of buns) per minute. Josephine's production rate is 6 completed units per minute. Joe is pushing four extra buns per minute on Josephine. Her queue will grow to 240 buns in an hour even though there are no statistical distributions involved.

b.   Assume that Joe's workstation has a variable Poisson output rate with a mean of five buns. Assume that Josephine has a variable service rate of 6 completed chicken–tofu burgers (also Poisson, with 10 seconds on average between completions). Then, the systems utilization factor, (*rho*), $\rho = 0.833$ and the waiting line for Josephine is 6.167.

c.   Serialized production systems that are not connected by paced-conveyor belts must compensate for variable and arrival rates. These systems work well when the arrival rate is controlled by a call for items that is often done using a kanban signal such as a withdrawal card, a light flashing, or a ping-pong ball rolling down a track.

d.   Just-in-time deliveries by a supplier are frequently prearranged where only a change of plans calls for intervention to alter the schedule. Where contract agreements prevail, the method is called *vendor releasing*.

    e.   Pull numbers do not have to be one-at-a-time, which epitomizes just-in-time. Several units can be delivered together, which does not require great amounts of storage space and keeps carrying costs on the low side. At the same time, a few-at-a-time is not the same as all-at-once, which is associated with fear of delivery problems termed *just-in-case*.

10   Arrivals, departures, and queues are a fundamental phenomenon in everyday life as well as P/OM. The regularities apply to batch production as well as flow shops. The final seminar of the series dealt with variability of the input–output production system. Some truths about this area of study were set down and circulated for discussion with all members of the seminar. Which one statement on the list is incorrect?

    a.   In line-balancing terminology, each workstation is a "customer" for a "supplier." The first station (most upstream in the line) is exposed to the most risk because materials for it come from outside sources. Except in highly engineered flow shops (working like clockwork), variability is always a problem. In batch work environments, materials are moved in lots to the next workstation. Bottlenecks become evident because the work flow stops and takes a place on the waiting line.

    b.   When parking garages cannot accept more cars, the sign "Sorry Full" appears. It causes cars to turn away and seek alternative parking spaces. The problem is one of storage. In push-production systems, the inability to store upstream materials moving downstream tends to occur when the work in process is big and bulky. It also occurs when the receiving station experiences slowdowns caused by quality problems, bad materials, equipment breakdowns, and employee difficulties. Storage problems also occur when the supplier speeds up output as a result of new methods and improved materials. Periodic studies are required to rebalance systems subject to change.

    c.   Pushing production is based on two concepts: (1) the independence of adjacent workstations and (2) the objective of having all resources fully utilized and never idle. The first point is never questionable in any system. Also, the second point is always valid.

    d.   Line efficiency (Λ) is related to balance delay (d). This ratio falls between zero and one. The ratio subtracted from one could be called *line-balancing inefficiency*. This measure is not related to stochastic line balancing or queuing, except that if workstation times are variable, then ($1 - \Lambda$) should be large enough to buffer imbalances.

    e.   Another way of looking at the trade-offs between skills and technology is the need to have rest and relaxation (also called *rest and delay*) for people to endure repetitive work. With technology, the cost of queues can be avoided; the costs of extra cycle time can be eliminated; variability of quality can be reduced; and sometimes, in addition to improved consistency, other quality standards can be raised.

Additional Readings

Ahmadi, Reza H., and Hernan Wurgaft. "Design for Synchronized Flow Manufacturing." *Management Science*, vol. 40, no. 11 (November 1994): 1469–1483.

Chow, W. M. *Assembly Line Design*. Amsterdam: Marcel Dekker, 1990.

Christensen, Clayton, Scott D. Anthony, and Erik A Roth. *Seeing What's Next: Using the Theories of Innovation to Predict Industry Change*. Cambridge, MA: Harvard Business School Press, 2004.

Cooper, R. B. *Introduction to Queueing Theory*, 2e. New York: Elsevier North-Holland Publishing, 1981.

Ghosh, S., and R. Gagnon. "A Comprehensive Literature Review and Analysis of the Design, Balancing and Scheduling of Assembly Systems." *International Journal of Production Research*, vol. 27, no. 4 (1989).

Graves, S. C. "A Review of Production Scheduling." *Operations Research*, vol. 29, no. 4 (July–August 1981).

Gross, D., and C. H. Harris. *Fundamentals of Queuing Theory*, 2e. New York: Wiley, 1985.

Hopp, Wallace J., and Mark L. Spearman. *Factory Physics*, 2e. New York: McGraw-Hill/Irwin, 2004.

Hirano, Hiroyuki. *JIT Implementation Manual: The Complete Guide to Just-In-Time Manufacturing*. Cambridge, MA: Productivity Press, 1990.

Ignall, Edward J. "A Review of Assembly Line Balancing." *Journal of Industrial Engineering*, vol. 16, no. 4 (July–August, 1965).

Japan Management Association (ed.). *Kanban and Just-in-Time at Toyota: Management Begins at the Workplace*. Trans. by D. J. Lu, Cambridge MA: Productivity Press, 1989.

Law, A. M., and W. D. Kelton. *Simulation Modeling and Analysis*. New York: McGraw-Hill, 1982.

Plane, D. R. *Management Science, A Spreadsheet Approach*. Danvers, MA: boyd & fraser publishing co., 1994.

Pritsker, A. A. B., C. E. Sigal, and R. D. J. Hammesfahr. *SLAM II, Network Models for Decision Support*. Pacific Grove, CA: Duxbury Press, 1994.

Ragsdale, C. T. *Spreadsheet Modeling & Decision Analysis*, 5e. Cincinnati, OH: Thomson South-Western, 2008, pp. 668–702.

Vollmann, T. E., W. L. Berry, and D. C. Whybark. *Manufacturing Planning and Control Systems*, 3e. Homewood, IL: Irwin, 1992.

Notes

1. H. A. Simon and A. Newell. "Heuristic Problem Solving: The Next Advance in Operations Research." *Operations Research,* vol. 6, no. 1 (January–February 1958): 1–10.
2. M. D. Kilbridge and L. Wester. "A Heuristic Model of Assembly Line Balancing." *Journal of Industrial Engineering,* vol. 12, no. 4 (July–August 1961): 292–99.
3. W. B. Helgeson and D. P. Birnie. "Assembly Line Balancing Using the Ranked Positional Weight Technique." *Journal of Industrial Engineering*, vol. XII, no. 6 (November–December 1961): 394–398.
4. Fred M. Tonge. "Assembly Line Balancing Using Probabilistic Combinations of Heuristics." *Management Science*, vol. 11, no. 7 (May 1965): 727–735.
5. A. L. Arcus. "Comsoal: A Computer Method of Sequencing Operations for Assembly Lines." See Elwood S. Buffa (ed.). *Readings in Production and Operations Management*. New York: Wiley, 1966, 336–360.
6. E. J. Ignall. "A Review of Assembly Line Balancing." *Journal of Industrial Engineering*, vol. 16, no. 4 (July–August 1965): 244–254.
7. For complete coverage of queuing equations, see D. Gross and C. H. Harris. *Fundamentals of Queuing Theory*, 2e. New York: Wiley, 1985. Also, see Kleinrock, Leonard, and Richard Gail. *Queuing Systems: Problems and Solutions*. New York: Wiley-Interscience, 1996.
8. David G. Dannenbring and Martin K. Starr. *Management Science: An Introduction*. New York: McGraw-Hill, 1981, 603–607. See also, D. Gross and C. H. Harris, note 7.
9. Corrêa, Henrique L. "The VW Resende (Brazil) Plant Modular Consortium SCM Model After 5 Years of Operation." *Proceedings of the POMS Conference*. Orlando, FL, 2001.
10. *Ward's Auto World*, April 1, 2002. Also, John McCormick. *Automotive Industries*. February 2005.

Enrichment Activity 17: Simulation of Queuing Models

The Post Office has proposed that a 2-station system such as the one shown in Figure EA17-1 be used by the postal system to sort bulk mail.

The output rates of the first and second stations are expected to vary, as shown in Table EA17-1.

The average Poisson output rate for station I is 3.4 units per minute and for station II it is 3.6 units per minute. Although II processes at a faster rate than I, a queue will develop, and the storage facility between I and II is needed. The intervals between arrivals and service completions are exponentially distributed.

Station I must stop working when the storage queue gets larger than *ST*. This is a variable that could be changed at a cost if analysis indicates net benefit.

Output rates are converted to intervals between inputs from station I and to service durations at station II by taking the reciprocals. This is column 2 of Table EA17-1. Column 3 provides data for the probability density distribution values. Column 4 shows these data converted into cumulative probability distributions values.

Monte Carlo numbers (MCN) are assigned in Table EA17-2. They translate the cumulative probability distribution estimates of column 4 in Table EA17-1 into number clusters that are like labels for the different output rates and their associated intervals. MCN can be used to generate random sequences of arrivals with different input intervals from station I and service intervals at station II. These generated patterns conform to the respective probability distributions of outputs and inputs at the stations.

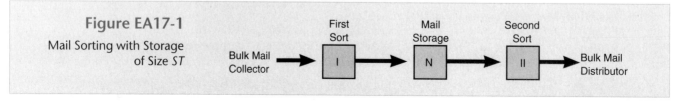

Figure EA17-1

Mail Sorting with Storage of Size *ST*

	Output Rate (units/min)	Interval Between Inputs to Station II (minutes)	Probability Distribution Density	Probability Distribution Cumulative
	Column 1	Column 2	Column 3	Column 4
Station I	2	0.500	0.10	0.10
	3	0.333	0.50	0.60
	4	0.250	0.30	0.90
	5	0.200	0.10	1.00
		Service Duration at Station II (minutes)		
Station II	2	0.500	0.10	0.10
	3	0.333	0.30	0.40
	4	0.250	0.50	0.90
	5	0.200	0.10	1.00

Table EA17-1

STATION II—Arrival and Service Rate Distributions

Station I			Station II		
Input Interval (min.)	Monte Carlo Numbers	Quantity	Service Interval (min.)	Monte Carlo Numbers	Quantity
0.500	00–09	10	0.500	00–09	10
0.333	10–59	50	0.333	10-39	30
0.250	60–89	30	0.250	40-89	50
0.200	90–99	10	0.200	90-99	10

Table EA17-2

Monte Carlo Number (MCN) Assignments

By using a random process for selecting numbers, there are 10 chances to pick a Monte Carlo number 00–09, which is associated with an input interval from station I of 0.500 minutes. Similarly, there are 50 chances of picking a MCN 10–59. This is the right proportion of station I input intervals of 0.333 minutes.

Note that instead of Monte Carlo Numbers, colored chips could be used in the right quantities. There might be 10 red chips, 50 blue chips, 30 green chips, and 10 yellow chips. Working with the computer and tables, the MC numbers are preferable.

An *abbreviated* table of random numbers is used to generate a series of random events. Table EA17-3 shows a small set of random numbers produced by computer. The character of the numbers in that table is such that any digit 0 through 9 is as likely to appear as any other. Because each 2-digit MCN is associated with a particular event, the occurrence of all events is similarly random.

Random number tables are useful for instructive purposes, but computer programs can generate the numbers as needed for the various algorithms and applications.

A systematic pattern of reading the numbers in the table (i.e., vertically, diagonally, horizontally) must be used so that no bias is introduced in the way that the numbers are selected. Then, reading successive pairs of digits from Table EA17-3: The first pair is equivalent to an input interval from station I, and the second pair is equivalent to a service interval at station II.

Note: Successive triplets of digits 000–999 would be used if the probabilities were stated in three places, such that 1.000 would be the sum of those figures. Probabilities expressed to four, five, or more places would be dealing with phenomena that are rare. Then, an important distinction exists between events that can occur (say) one in 10,000 or one in 100,000 times.

05621	64483	38549	62908	71579	19203	83546	05917	51905
82773	76475	60896	93681	03327	49250	78355	78582	20869
66592	69112	64499	63939	75944	59053	14086	60716	70017
44474	90319	74480	73857	62484	38228	87185	73667	24870
50983	46638	81624	40012	35426	04146	22613	76275	00250
10052	03550	59144	59468	37984	77892	89766	86489	46619
50263	91130	22188	81205	99699	84260	19693	36701	43233

Table EA17-3

Abbreviated Table of Random Numbers

Pencil and paper simulations are good for instructional purposes. However, in a real case, the simulation of the 2-station flow shop for sorting bulk mail would be computerized. The details given here reflect the pedagogical approach for students of the method.

The simulation consists of choosing successive pairs of random numbers and matching these against the input interval and the service interval Monte Carlo number assignments specified in Table EA17-2.

The first pair of random numbers indicates the period of time between the start of the simulation and the first arrival at station II. That interval is 0.5 minutes. The second pair of random numbers specifies how long servicing will take. That service duration is 0.25. Four more random numbers are drawn. The first pair of these random numbers is used to specify the interval until the next arrival at station II. The second pair of these random numbers details the second service time.

When a sufficient sample is drawn, the behavior of this system can be evaluated. The maximum and average length of the waiting line can be estimated. The bottleneck effect of limited storage ST between stations can be assessed. The idle time of station II can be estimated, and the overall quality of this stochastic flow shop configuration can be observed to determine whether an acceptable line balance has been achieved.

Cycle-time management will depend on what strategies are available to alter λ and μ. Can station II be faster? Can another station II sorter be added at peak load times? Are there new technologies that might be brought to bear? Perhaps some of the load from station I can be directed to another sorter location.

A left-to-right scan of the top line of the random number table, Table EA17-3, shows the following:

05621　64483　38549　62908　71579　19203　83546　05917　51905

The first two pairs of digits are 05 and 62, representing an input arrival interval of 0.500 and a service duration of 0.250. The simulation continues in Table EA17-4. This table builds a scenario with the focus on arrival time, completion time, idle time, and queue size.

Table EA17-4 Eight Steps of the Simulation	Sample Number	Random Numbers		Input Interval	Arrival Time at Station II	Service Duration at Station II	Completion Time at Station II	Idle Time	Queue Size
	1	05	62	0.500	0.500	0.250	0.750a	0	0
	2	16	44	0.333	0.833a	0.250	1.083	0.083a	0
	3	83	38	0.250	1.083	0.333	1.416	0	0
	4	54	96	0.333	1.416	0.200	1.616b	0	0
	5	29	08	0.333	1.749b	0.500	2.249c,d	0.133b	0
	6	71	57e	0.250	1.999c,d	—	—	0	1c
	7	91	92f	0.200	2.199d,f	—	—	0	2d
	6				2.249d,e	0.250e	2.499d	0	1e
	7				2.499f	0.200f	2.699	0	0g
	8	03	83	0.500	2.699	0.250	2.949	0	0

Legend:

a —Station II is idle from 0.750 until 0.833 (0.083 minute).

b —Station II is idle from 1.616 until 1.749 (0.133 minute).

c —Station II is busy so arrival number six must wait from 1.999 until 2.249 (0.250 minute).

d —A second unit, arrival number seven, joins the line at 2.199. Assume that there is storage space for it. Otherwise, station I would have to stop at 2.199 and wait until 2.499 before it could begin again. One unit waits from 1.999 until 2.249 (0.250 minute). The other unit waits from 2.199 until 2.249 (0.050 minute).

e —The random number 57 in the sixth sample indicates a service duration of 0.250. So, the sixth arrival begins to be serviced at 2.249.

f —The seventh arrival waits from 2.199 until 2.499 to be serviced. The random number 92 indicates a service duration of 0.200.

g —The line is cleared of waiting units. To this time, station II has been idle a total of 0.216 minute. The waiting line has been occupied by a single unit for 0.200 minute, by two units for 0.050 minute (together 0.100), then by a single unit for 0.250 minute, for a total waiting time of 0.550. There has been no shutdown of station I.

All of the different performance characteristics of the system can be simulated. Complex assumptions can be made that defy mathematical analyses. To illustrate, it has been assumed that the input and service intervals are independently distributed. If this is not so, and they are conditional upon each other, or on prior states, these conditional dependencies can be modeled in a simulation. Math analysis of complex dependencies can be more difficult when discontinuous dependencies account for the systems behavior. With a computer simulation program, is not as difficult to simulate stochastic line-balancing problems involving hundreds of activities.

Enrichment Challenges 17

1 Use the following random numbers to simulate the behavior of the 2-station mail-sorting system.

> 10052   03550   59144   59468   37984   77892   89766   86489   46619

2 Use the following random numbers to simulate the behavior of the 2-station mail-sorting system.

> 50263   91130   22188   81205   99699   84260   19693   36701   43233

3 What happens if storage space *ST* is limited to one unit in the queue? See Table EA17-4.

Changing the System

part

4

Figure PT4-1 Management at Level 4 is the Gatekeeper Observing Forces For Change From Below and Using Projects (3) as the Means to Organize Changes Above

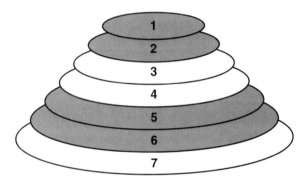

1. Product Design

2. Process Design

3. Project Management

4. Organizational Support

5. Technological Change

6. Competitive Marketplace

7. Sustainability: Ethics, Environment, and Security

Part 4 is composed of three chapters which are fundamental to making changes in the product line and/or the processes used to make goods and deliver services. Figure PT4-1 emphasizes the strong linkage between levels 3, 4 and 7. There are important connections between them and levels 1, 2, 5 and 6. When changing the system there are no distant levels and the whole system is in play.

Management at level 4 operates as the doorway between forces for change (from below) and the things that are being changed (above). Project management at level 3 is the means used to bring about change.

These three chapters build a structure for understanding transitions that organizations are always undergoing. Starting from scratch—called "greenfield"—is a transition; recovery from "bankruptcy" is another. Total changeover of product line and process is another major transition as compared to gradual alteration of product line and processes.

Post-9/11, security systems at airports changed substantially. Traditional inspection methods were replaced by a nonstop wave of new ones. Security technology blossomed. Inventions to improve security accelerated. Security is a good example of transitions being jump-started by an external event. Hectic change will not diminish for the TSA (Transportation Security Administration) until technology reins in a myriad of dangers.

The relevance of Figure PT4-1 to Part 4 resides in the fact that management (level 4) acts as a gatekeeper. Gatekeepers need to look in two directions. Not only is there a Janus (doorway) effect, there is also complexity that must be traversed to integrate strategies and tactics across all seven levels (see Spotlight 11-2). Management must reach up three levels and down three levels to make tactics congruent with strategies. Congruence is achieved when the goals and objectives of tactics conform with those of the strategies.

Chapter 18 (Project Management for New Products and Processes) encompasses products (goods and/or services) and congruent processes. Processes must reflect the drivers of product strategy. Project management is the enabler of the product/process development cycle. Stages and phases of the development process play critical roles. Understanding how to manage projects is essential. Toward that end, critical path methods (CPMs) are explored. Attention is paid to completion times, and the use of resource leveling.

Chapter 19 (Change Management with Faster Project Completions) explores the need to achieve rapid change. An organization development model (Gleicher's Formula) looks at factors that facilitate change as opposed to conditions that tend to maintain the status quo. Projects can be designed to support continuous gradual improvement. An alternative is to design reengineering projects which develop radical changes that eradicate what was done in the past. Neither "*step-by-step*" change nor "*revolutionary*" change methods guarantee success. Project methods are detailed to achieve project continuity yielding uninterrupted streams of new product and processes.

Chapter 20 (Sustainability Issues: Environment, Ethics, and Security) has a 21st Century title. It will not be found in other texts on P/OM, until it is emulated in one form or another. The point is that there are increasingly powerful global forces for change. Processes have major impacts on the environment. Design for reuse and recycling are examples of P/OM contributions to ethical practice. There must be integrity with respect to safety and health of all customers, employees, and suppliers. Ethical benchmarks are changing. There is worldwide convergence on acceptable environmental standards (ISO 14,000). Safety and security have assumed paramount importance to every person in the world since the ethic of fairness has been temporarily compromised by a battle for dominance.

Project Management for New Products and Processes

A need to change may be driven by forces from *outside* the firm such as competitive actions or customer dissatisfaction. The force may originate *inside* the firm as a result of R&D, creative product development, innovative process management, and other sources of compelling new ideas that will provide competitive advantage. In the decade from 1995 until 2005, forces for substantial and rapid change were emerging. In the decade of 2005–2015, these conditions are accelerating. As a result, projects can no longer be treated as special situations, limited to Stage IV adventurous firms. Projects have become a necessity—an ongoing way of life for all organizations. Projects, as time-based structures for planning activities to bring about change, should be supported by permanent systems in the organization. To be effective, projects should be planned proactively—not managed reactively. Without adequate project planning, major transitions will be arbitrary, casual, and less successful.

After reading this chapter, you should be able to:

- Design an effective way of planning new product initiatives.
- Understand the important role of knowledge management (KM).
- Describe the difference between tacit and explicit knowledge in KM.
- Evaluate product development programs.
- Explain the unique work configurations known as *projects*.
- Classify projects by their various types.
- Describe the life cycle stages of projects. At what stage do engineering change orders (ECOs) play a part?
- Explain how project managers differ from process managers.
- Discuss project-management leadership and teamwork.
- Explain the basic rules for project management.
- Describe pros and cons of parallel-path project management.
- Describe Gantt project-planning charts.
- Explain the advantages and disadvantages of Gantt project-planning charts.
- Describe how critical-path methods differ from Gantt chart procedures.
- Explain how to use forward-pass calculations to determine the shortest feasible time for project completion.
- Explain how to use backward-pass calculations to determine which project activities are on the critical path.
- Describe what *slack* means; explain how to derive it.
- Explain when deterministic and probabilistic estimates for activity times apply.
- Show how to use optimistic and pessimistic activity time estimates to obtain a variance measure for activity times.
- Describe the penalty–reward system that is used for motivating on-time (or better) project completion.
- Determine when to use resource leveling to reduce project-completion time.
- Discuss the challenges and opportunities for managing multiple projects.
- Explain why computers are essential for adequate project management.

The Systems Viewpoint

Projects have life cycle stages, which means that the project environment is dynamic and changing. It is like a race through an obstacle course where there is planning to "get ready," steps to be taken to "get set," and at the command "go," the race begins. It may take months or years to complete the project, but time to completion is a crucial factor. Many projects are involved with thinking up a new product, building a prototype, testing a new concept, evaluating prototypes, and determining what process will be used to make or deliver products. At each early stage of a new product, a decision is required to stop, or continue with the same, or changed, design specifications. Projects encompass products and processes together.

What are the early stages of the product? **New product development** is entirely different from altering an existing product or process, or both. Project management has different demands placed on it according to the product's life cycle stages. The project to bring out a new product is a race against the competition. As competitors become faster, the time factor becomes more than an economic issue of how long will it be until return on investment begins. It becomes an issue of whoever is first into the marketplace with a new quality product gains significant competitive advantage. It is known that systems-wide cooperation speeds up project completion while improving the quality of the new product. Companies that do not have the systems viewpoint lack the ability to achieve the level of cooperation necessary to win this race.

New product development
Stages include concept selection, process specification, pilot plant, market research, and business modeling.

Strategic Thinking

Strategy begins with the planning of new products and processes. Think about the steps that went into the planning for Apple's iPhone; a first-time MBA course on security operations; chef Mario Batali's new menu at Babbo Ristorante e Enoteca; and DayJet's Air Taxis Fleet of very light jets (VLJs). The strategy is followed by the tactics of making it happen. Project management, in such cases, requires simultaneous attention to strategic and tactical issues. The product development project system is visionary, but it must also include checking the crucial details. As is often said, "The devil is in the details." Can it be made, will they buy it, how much will they pay, what margin can it deliver, when can it be ready to roll out? Information gathered from every part of the organization as well as suppliers must be analyzed. The tactical details must be congruent with the strategic plans. Until tactics are thought through thoroughly, it is not feasible to evaluate strategic platforms to select the best one to follow. Strategic thinking helps to determine how many projects can be ongoing at the same time. See Spotlight 18-2 on Balanced Scorecards and refer back to Spotlight 11-2: Don't Separate Strategy and Tactics.

18-1 Designing New Product-Planning Initiatives

Products are goods and services that are made and delivered by operations management. New products are required to replace old products that are becoming unprofitable. In addition, new products can help increase the cash flow that sustains a company. New products also provide an opportunity to extend a successful product line, which supports marketing efforts. In short, there are many reasons for a company to be working on line extensions as well as new products that represent different forms of endeavor.

Several rules apply to the new product area. One of these is to choose products that have attributes that are familiar to management because of existing experiences. In other words, try to incorporate what the company is already good at doing, i.e., play to the company's strengths. The following sections on **knowledge management (KM)** relate to methods for systematizing the company's strengths.

Knowledge management (KM)
Managing the inventory of knowledge that exists in the company; the ability to find, select, and absorb new knowledge to add to the prior encyclopedic storehouse.

18-1a Market Research Inputs to Knowledge

Market research

Many techniques exist including interviews with customers and focus groups. Care must be taken not to bias surveys or generalize based on inadequate sample sizes.

Another rule that applies to the new product area is to offer only what customers will want to buy at a price that provides an attractive margin to the seller. Information about what customers will buy that fits the company's capability profile and margin requirements is complex. **Market research** supplies valuable information. Also essential for success is competent analysis of the complete and appropriate business model.

This requires knowledge of company **capabilities** (with business processes) and company **core competencies** (with technology) to be matched with marketing awareness. Correct information gathering is the function of marketing intelligence. Often, this information is available through the market research department. Working closely with operations, market research can help process management improve existing products (changes in taste and appearance, for example). Knowledge about process capabilities interacts with knowledge of the marketplace in helping to fashion new market entries. The systems approach has marketing and operations functioning together. Their combined expertise is a form of knowledge that differs from their individual expertise.

Capabilities

Management expertise in areas such as purchasing and inventory as compared with technological core competencies.

Core competencies

Technical, technological, and production skills possessed by a company interacting with that company's product line.

18-1b Knowledge Management Systems

Knowledge management requires having access to an inventory of expertise and skills that can be examined for possible application to a new endeavor. Some call this knowledge directory the *yellow pages of in-company expertise*. In effect, the company has to document its intellectual capital and special skills. The company has to know *what it knows, who has this knowledge*, and *how this knowledge has helped it succeed*. For example, if existing products are successful (at least, in part) because these products embody particular knowledge and understanding of distribution channels, then new market entries might have an advantage if they embody this special expertise.

The same idea works for special capabilities in sales, marketing, operations, engineering (say, in physics, chemistry, or other technical specialties), service, repair, and maintenance. In each case, there may be unique management skills, and/or technical information, in the company's experiential databases. This is the intellectual property of the company gained through its investment in people and their research and experiences. It can exist in people's minds, or on their computers, or stored as paper in files.

Explicit Knowledge

Explicit knowledge

Form of knowledge that describes what must be done to make things work; can be transferred from teachers to students in words or diagrams.

One of the problems of downsizing has been that HR departments may be unaware of the firm's skill and knowledge inventories. There are ample anecdotes about how firms lose critical knowledge when knowledgeable people accept company severance packages. Too late, the company finds out that only Joe knew how to run a machine that is crucial to complete an important customer's order. Taking an inventory of the firm's skills, experiences, and other explicit forms of special abilities is an essential starting point for a knowledge management system.

Explicit knowledge is the description of what must be done to make things work. Two examples are how to fix a leaky washer on the sink or how to determine the amount of inventory to order from a supplier. The character of **explicit knowledge** is that it allows a successful transfer of "how to" information between the expert and anyone who wants to learn how. Transfer agents can be written words, equations, graphics, icons, spoken words, pictures, and movies.

From a distance learning point of view, explicit information can be studied and used at any time. It is termed *asynchronous information* because the sender and the user do not have to be online together for it to be effective. The asynchronous characteristic of explicit knowledge allows it to be studied as needed. It is in the files and (at least, in theory) recoverable. Intel, IBM, Oracle, SAP, and other firms have systems for dealing with information recovery when there are hundreds of thousands of pages of data.

The problem of recovering this explicit knowledge is that the database is so large that careful coding is required to use data mining effectively. An Intel paper (2002) titled "Information Overload: Inaccessible Data and a Knowledge Management Solution" lays out a systematic approach for discovery and access of the desired explicit information. The web address is: http://cache-www.intel.com/cd/00/00/10/28/102849_pp023204_sum.pdf.

Tacit Knowledge

Knowledge management of complex systems is seldom satisfied by explicit information alone. There is a great deal of information conveyed by facial expressions such as a raised eyebrow. Body language is often mentioned as a clue to purpose and intentions. There are other clues about what is happening in a system. These can include sights, odors, noises, tastes, tactile memories, temperatures, pressures, and other tacit forms of knowledge.

Distance learning systems have long enjoyed the ease of transferring explicit knowledge via the Internet, by CD, DVD, written texts, audiotapes, and combinations. However, distance-learning systems have long contended with the difficulty (often verging on the impossibility) of transferring **tacit knowledge** using such media. It is reassuring to know that in-person, classroom teaching remains one of the best ways to successfully transfer information of the tacit type of knowledge. Consulting visits and apprenticeships are also strong means of transferring tacit knowledge.

Unlike explicit knowledge, tacit knowledge often requires synchronous transmission. This means that the people have to be in the same room, talking face-to-face, to absorb the knowledge. That is the classroom in schools, the meeting room in companies, or the focus group seated around a table helping to plan designs for new products and services.

Tacit knowledge
Unstated, implicit, inferred, and unspoken; to access tacit knowledge, consult with people who are seen as being intuitive, instinctive, and perspective.

Core Competencies

Hamel and Prahalad described the benefits of core competencies in their 1990 *Harvard Business Review* article.[1] In the knowledge management arena, these would be described as technical, technological, and production skills possessed by a company. For example, the special expertise that Polaroid had developed for producing instant photography materials focused their competitive efforts on film-makers (Kodak, Fuji), whose product took longer times to develop. At the same time, although Polaroid was the leader in digital cameras, the company misread the future of that product line. Meanwhile, many factors were making the Polaroid process obsolete. See Spotlight 18-1 about Polaroid.

For many years, Eastman Kodak was the technical and manufacturing leader in photographic films. Eventually, Fuji built its expertise to the point where the rivalry with Kodak was unceasing and intense. However, the film market was disintegrating in favor of digital camera technology. Gilette and Schick spend a great deal of money on research and advertising to gain share in the "razor wars." Favorite restaurants exist because chefs have "technical" core competencies with their recipes and cooking methods. However, another class of capabilities that is not dependent on the technical and production process expertise, but is instead the result of knowing how to manage a system, is described in the following sections.

Capabilities Advantages

Two years after the article by Hamal and Prahalad, George Stalk, Philip Evans, and Lawrence E. Shulman distinguished between capabilities and core competencies in their 1992 *Harvard Business Review* article.[2] They identified management expertise as providing competitive advantages. Such expertise can take a variety of forms, including smarter procurement, better inventory management, faster new product development, and cross-docking distribution (a la Wal-Mart). Taken together, the core competencies and special capabilities need to be considered when analyzing new product opportunities. W. L. Gore and Company has developed a management style designed to bring a constant stream of successful new products into the product line. That is a capability that few organizations (except perhaps W. L. Gore and 3M) can boast about. Because recipes make a great chef, they are the core of favorite restaurant competencies. The other side of the coin would be that ambiance and service are examples of managerial capabilities.

Synergistic Advantages

Synergism is the interaction of elements that, when combined, produce a total effect that is greater than the sum of the individual elements. Knowledge management strives for combinations of expertise where one plus one is equal to a lot more than two. For example, Wal-Mart's cross-docking combines expertise in the retail business with expertise in purchasing, distribution, and logistics. McDonald's original key to success was the development of its to-go (single-use, all-in-one) packaging. The combination of fast food and the package to carry that food required smart marketing working hand-in-glove with adroit package designers, purchasing, and operations managers. See also Spotlight 19-1 on smart packaging at HP.

18-1c Designing New Products

Some steps for designing new products occur before the product introduction. Two new product introductions are shown in Figure 18-1. The second new product, called P_2, is introduced at a time of restaging the first new product, called P_1. On the other hand, P_1 may be withdrawn when P_2 is ready to take over and generate sales in the market segment formerly occupied by P_1. Similarities exist between designing new products and redesigning old ones. Timing is critical for maintenance and restaging of P_1, and for launching the introduction of new product P_2. Figure 18-1 is meant to reflect the issues of coordinating introductions and replacements to preserve market share.

The first stage is *concept selection*, *development*, and *testing*. An example has been chosen that can be worked through to illustrate the steps. It is in the form of a small case about the Sticky Edge Company (SEC).

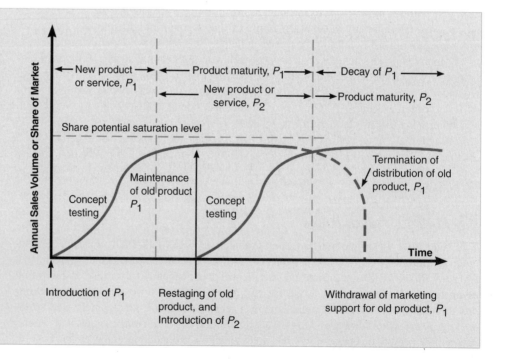

Figure 18-1

Coordinating Life Cycle Stages of New Product Introductions

The Sticky Edge case reflects on the present-day state of the art of stick-on note pads. In general, these pads have a sticky edge of about 0.5 inches in width. SEC is considering developing a new product. It is a new pad with a 1.0-inch sticky edge. A team has been selected and, through talking with the operations manager, it has discovered that production will (probably) be able to reset (quickly and easily) the machinery being used for the standard sticky note. Talks with marketing indicate that a need exists for stronger bonding of notes to paper and cardboard—as well as walls and doors. Marketing is eager to develop a campaign for "industrial strength" stick-on notes, which have been labeled "power notes."

The following list of stages will be discussed:

1st—Concept selection, development, and testing
2nd—Estimation and business modeling (using spreadsheets)
3rd—Prototype construction and testing
4th—Process specification and pilot plant

Concept Selection, Development, and Testing

The elements that are discussed in the sections on knowledge management play a significant role in *concept selection*. To identify winning concepts (which is the first step in the process of new product development), core competences and special capabilities of the firm need to be examined in terms of market readiness.

Where do good concepts come from? They often originate with the sales force, which is likely to be the first to know that something has changed or needs changing. Perhaps the old product version is no longer the best product available. The sales force is likely to be the first to learn that customers want something different. Competitors often lead the way to change.

Sometimes, change originates with operations. Material prices may have decreased. New technology that is superior to existing technology becomes available. Perhaps competitors are using new materials.

Competitive analysis is always a source of good ideas. Apple Computer provides wonderful examples of product redesign that affects market segments outside of its market sphere. Dell, IBM, Hewlett-Packard, Lenova, etc., have copied some of Apple's superior appearance features. To date, Apple's market segments are separated by fundamental differences from competitors. For the time being, there are good opportunities to imitate Apple in non-Apple market segments.

Estimation and Business Modeling (Using Spreadsheets)

The note pad with a 1-inch sticky edge is discussed by all project participants in the company—as well as with suppliers. The project team develops estimates for two different quality concepts. All investments and operating costs are based on given specifications of quality. It is not difficult to build the spreadsheet model in Table 18-1. However, the estimates in that table are known to be rough. The spreadsheets are meant to be changed. Better numbers will be used as the new product development team learns more about the project.

Concept 1 has lower quality and price than concept 2. Stickiness for concept 1 will last up to three years. After that, the adhesive will begin to dry up. Concept 2 has a 5-year quality horizon. Table 18-1 presents a draft spreadsheet of the estimates for (a) price per package of five pads; (b) package demand per year in thousands (Note: Demand falls off as price increases, reflecting estimates of price elasticity that could be geographically sensitive. Production quantities are based on demand expectations.); (c) annual revenue in thousands (the result of multiplication of the two row cells above); (d) cost per package (depreciation is included for the fixed cost component); (e) annual profit in thousands (calculated on the spreadsheet by subtracting cost per pack from price per pack and then multiplying that quantity by the annual demand).

Concept 1						
Price/pack	$10.00	$11.00	$12.00	$13.00	$14.00	$15.00
Demand (000)	200	190	180	165	150	130
Revenue (000)	$2,000.00	$2,090.00	$2,160.00	$2,145.00	$2,100.00	$1,950.00
Cost/pack	$8.00	$8.20	$8.40	$8.65	$8.80	$9.10
Profit (000)	400	532	648	717.75	780	767
Concept 2						
Price/pack	$10.50	$12.00	$12.50	$13.50	$14.50	$15.50
Demand (000)	195	183	170	153	135	114
Revenue (000)	$2,047.50	$2,196.00	$2,125.00	$2,065.50	$1,957.50	$1,767.00
Cost/pack	$8.10	$8.11	$8.12	$8.15	$8.80	$9.00
Profit (000)	468	711.87	744.6	818.55	769.5	741

Table 18-1

Spreadsheet Summary of the First-Year Business Model for Two Different Concepts

From Table 18-1, note that concept 1 has highest revenue of $2,160,000 at the $12/package price with demand of 180,000 packs. Concept 2's highest revenue occurs at the $12 price with demand of 183,000 packs. It is $2,196,000, which is $36,000 higher than concept 1's revenue. That is only 1.67 percent higher.

Concept 2 profits are higher for the price range of $10.50 through $13.50. It would have been easier to make comparisons if the two tables for concepts 1 and 2 had used the same price points. For various reasons, real situations are often like this. A similar set of prices could have been developed using interpolation. The highest profit for concept 2 is $818,550 at a price of $13.50 and production of 153,000 packages.

The best profit for concept 1 is $780,000 at a price of $14, with 150,000 packages required from production. No decision will be made at this stage, but prototypes will be manufactured and samples distributed to improve on both sets of tabled estimates.

Prototype Construction and Testing

The decision has been made to create the two kinds of stick-on note pads in the laboratory. If the team had confidence in the estimates of Table 18-1, it might have opted to go straight to the pilot plant that would manufacture the sample quantities on the production floor. Lacking confidence that the market of users will find the 1-inch sticky edge an advantage, the decision is taken to proceed with caution.

Once the prototypes are built, they will be distributed to in-company executives as well as to some other company executives in the neighborhood. Simple market research results will be collected to determine customer satisfaction and to get an idea about how much to charge. The famous Post-it® Notes were actually tested in this way.

To keep on track, assume that the results thus far are positive. There is interest in the product, and the estimates in Table 18-1 remain unchanged. The next step is important because assumptions about the production system (easy to shift from a 0.5-inch to a 1.0-inch sticky edge) will be tested by the pilot plant manager. Also, the costs per unit become clearer.

Process Specification and Pilot Plant

The operations manager for the 0.5-inch sticky edge process runs into difficulty when trying to convert the edge width to 1.0 inch. An alteration of the machinery would make the conversion easier and less costly. However, the fixed cost for the alteration will add 50 cents to each package of five pads. This is based on a 3-year horizon. The production run (even though under pilot plant conditions) indicates that output rate must be slowed down, which adds 85 cents to each package of five pads. Thus, there is a total increase in the cost per package of $1.35.

Concept 1							
Price/pack	$10.00	$11.00	$12.00	$13.00	$14.00	$15.00	$16.00
Demand (000)	180	171	162	148.5	135	117	100
Revenue (000)	$1,800.00	$1,881.00	$1,944.00	$1,930.50	$1,890.00	$1,755.00	$1,600.00
Cost/pack	$9.35	$9.55	$9.75	$10.00	$10.15	$10.45	$11.50
Profit (000)	117	247.95	364.5	445.5	519.75	532.35	450

Table 18-2

Spreadsheet Summary of the First-Year Business Model for Concept 1

Further, the quality envisioned for concept 2 is not feasible for the equipment being used. The product development team agrees to drop the concept 2 version of the product. Concept 1 will be produced on a pilot basis in a lot size of 50,000 units, or 10,000 packages. Results will be collected by market research, and together the management team will make a final decision about this new product.

18-2 Evaluating the Product Development Program

Various techniques have been used to test consumer response to the product in the marketplace. Early on it was learned that the price might be too low, and a $16 price for a package of 5 pads was added. It was noted that demand elasticity took a jump around that price. People liked the increase in sticky area for certain applications. In particular, where there was a fear of losing the note, an extra-wide edge gave an added sense of security. The fact that notes might not adhere for more than 3 years did not disturb many customers, nor did the idea of paying a premium for extra security.

Nevertheless, the team's analysis of Table 18-2 with its revised estimates led to a sense of prudence. Although revenue peaked at the same $12 price, it was down by 10 percent, caused by the 10 percent drop in demand that had surprised market research.

Profit was now maximized at $15, whereas previously, it was at $14. Maximum profit in Table 18-1 was $780,000 as compared to $532,350 in Table 18-2. This quarter of a million dollar decrease is significant. The decline in profitability is 32 percent.

What really bothered the team was the severe drop in profit at $16. Any miscalculation in estimates that would suggest a price increase to fix the problem would not be feasible. Also, there was work going on by the R&D department that would lead to greater stickiness without requiring a larger sticky edge. This led to the suggestion that two varieties be marketed when the new technology was feasible—hold and super-hold—the latter with a premium price. The cost of this alternative would be the same as the current costs. Furthermore, failure of any new entry in this product line could affect the way that customers view other products in the stick-on note product line. The team concluded that caution was the better part of valor.

18-3 Defining Projects

Projects are special work configurations designed to accomplish singular or nearly singular goals such as putting on one play, writing new software, creating a mail-order catalog, and constructing a building. Bringing out a new product, building a factory, and developing a new service belong to the same category of unique activities and qualify as projects. Each of these projects consists of a set of goal-oriented activities that end when the goal is achieved. Such undertakings have a finite planning horizon. This is in contrast to the character of batch and flow shop production. Projects have many attributes that are similar to custom work. However, the scale of projects is much greater, involving many participants and resources.

© 2007 Jupiterimages Corporation

Building the Golden Gate Bridge in San Francisco was a major project. Imagine what it was like to be project manager in charge of creating this magnificent bridge. The construction time (from January 5, 1933, to May 28, 1937) and bridge statistics can be found at http://www.goldengatebridge. org. Click on the "Did You Know" question. Use the Research Library to find "seismic retrofit," which is a continuing aspect of the project. The photos are worth the visit to this webpage.

Projects

Time-based endeavors that bring together skills and technology to accomplish major goals.

Engineering change orders (ECOs)

May appear to be minor alterations in the product design or in the process used, but there are interactions that can lead to severe systems complexities.

Projects can include some repetitive activities. Building several houses on one land subdivision is a project. Software programming is a project even though use is made of modular components (object-oriented programming). Projects may entail some batch work and even some intermittent flow shop work. However, the project itself integrates activities as it moves toward completion, much as each additional chapter is written for a book or floors are added to buildings.

Projects can be classified by degree of simplicity. Many engineering design changes, which result in **engineering change orders (ECOs)**, appear to be minor alterations in the product design. However, even simple changes require alterations of the process that can lead to systems complexities. A small design change can destroy the ability of fixtures to hold the parts for all downstream activities. Also ECOs can multiply in number and lead to severe quality problems. These problems are especially noticeable if there is insufficient time to test the interactions of the proposed changes. Having too many ECOs can disrupt the normal business of an organization.

Projects can be classified by frequency of repetition. Although NASA has launched many shuttle flights, they are not all the same. *Challenger* blew up on launching (January 28, 1986) because of special conditions. Seventeen years later (February 1, 2003), Columbia burned up during reentry. Again, unique conditions applied. Between these dates, hundreds of successful missions were flown. In space programs, what part can be deemed repetitive; what part is unique and unknown?

Housing developments consist of the same house design being built many times. There are benefits from having repetitive activities within a project. Parts can be purchased with quantity discounts. Training for repetitive activities is justified. The same activity plan (charts) can be used. As the project frequency increases, the project mind-set must remain in place. Plan for contingencies. We are also reminded that object-oriented programming calls upon similar repetitive modules for computer software development.

That mind-set is goal oriented with completion planned for a specific time. If the activities begin to be treated as a repetitive system, then the project orientation has been replaced by one of repetitive scheduling as used by job shops and intermittent flow shops. Note that even though many houses of the same design are being built, there are unique site considerations that must be taken into account. Nevertheless, some builders have produced houses in volume to reduce the costly project factors and replace them with lower manufacturing costs. Modularity of components is a supply chain factor that brings significant economies of scale to projects that are properly planned in this way.

Projects can be classified by degree of complexity. Often, the number of issues to consider is very large. Building a new factory is complex. It requires doing a great variety of things that have not been done before. Building another McDonald's may seem at first glance to be highly repetitive. However, locations are different. Community officials and their rules are different. Time is different and things change over time (see "Select Country/Market" at http://www.mcdonalds.com).

New product developments are not all the same. Bringing out a new automobile model may seem to be highly repetitive, but there are new elements to deal with every time. The same applies to bringing a new movie to its marketplace. There are lessons learned from prior experiences and then there are the new and different factors to consider. The distinction that is being drawn is between making the last car of a run of 2,000 made that day and the third animated movie brought to a world market by Pixar. It may be the same old thing to a few people who are skilled at planning a dinner party. For most people, that remains a daunting project. Although everyone would agree that a dinner party is simpler than launching a shuttle, for many, if not most, it still qualifies as a challenging project.

Projects can be classified by how many really new activities are involved. Some projects have activities never done before. Examples of such projects might include NASA building an international space station together with Russia. The construction of a monorail train from Tampa to Orlando might not be that different from the Shanghai monorail since the same technology will be used.

On a scale of one to ten, where would the construction of the Eurotunnel fall? Called the *Chunnel*, this transportation system under the English Channel connects England to France: Folkestone to Calais in 35 minutes; 4 times an hour; 24 hours a day. Simulation was used a lot to try to understand things that had never been encountered before. Maybe a rating of seven or eight would be appropriate. Still, there was a lot of basic engineering information transferred from other tunnels (see http://www.eurotunnel.com).

18-4 Managing Projects

Good project management methods keep track of what has been done and what still needs to be done. Also, good project methods point to activities that are critical for completion. They expedite those activities that seem to be slipping. These points are part of the five project life cycle stages described here:

1 *Describing the goals* requires developing and specifying the desired project outcomes. (Architects lay out plans for building and thereby set the goals of the project.)

2 *Planning the project* requires specifying the activities that are essential to accomplish the goals. It involves planning the management of the project including the timing of the activities. (The project manager lays out the charts of sequenced activities and estimates how long it will take to do them. The time frame sets in motion the execution of the plan. The builder is usually the project planner.)

3 *Carrying out the project* requires doing the activities as scheduled. (Getting building permits, ordering materials, assembling different kinds of work crews required at the right times, and constructing the building. The builder is usually the project manager.)

4 *Completing the project* can mean disbanding work groups and closing down the project-management team. However, firms that are in the business of project management, such as companies that build refineries, move their crews from project to project. Each project is goal specific and finite. That is the mission of project management companies as compared to organizations that need to use project management from time to time. The latter cannot avoid the fact that an ECO is a project and needs to be managed as such.

5 *Continuous project teams* is an increasingly attractive option. Companies that are not in the project business might bring out a new product and then disband the project teams when the job is done. As will be discussed later, organizations increasingly opt to maintain continuous project capability.

18-4a Project Managers Are Leaders

Organizations encounter the need for project management whenever they consider introducing a new product or service. Often, they turn to their process managers and appoint them to deal with the project over its lifetime. The kinds of problems encountered in projects are different from those encountered in the job shop and flow shop. Time is money in several ways.

First, until the project is completed there is seldom any return on investment (ROI). Second, when projects are new products, the first into the marketplace with a quality product gets a substantial market advantage. In the same way, when the project is a major process improvement, there may be a cost or quality advantage that also translates into a market differential.

The project manager is constantly trying to reduce the cycle time from inception to completion of the project. This is quite different from the job shop manager who is trying to reduce the cycle time of batches of work waiting to be delivered to customers. It also is different from the intermittent flow shop manager who sets the process-cycle time to deliver the required output to satisfy demand. Although one person can be good at both, a different hat should be worn for each mode.

The project manager is guided by strategic planning, which is tuned to windows of opportunity in the marketplace. This often means putting more resources to work to speed up project completion. Problems arise that slow the project. The costs of such delays can be in the many millions of dollars, whereas the batch shop manager can accept delays that cost much less and are correctable the next time around. Usually, there is no next time around for the project manager.

The ability to manage under pressure and crises is a leadership issue that should be recognized when selecting project managers. Tracy Kidder's description[3] of the enormous stress that was experienced by Tom West's project group when they developed a new computer for Data General (no longer in business) makes memorable reading.

Project managers are accustomed to living with great risk and the threat of large penalties. Their goals are strategic and usually vitally important to top management and the success of the company. Often, their goals are the change management plans for the company. Thus, the profile of a successful project manager is different from that of job shop and flow shop process managers. Further, project managers often require rapid systems-wide cooperation to resolve their problems quickly. This is a different kind of leadership than that required by process managers who are control-oriented.

18-5 Contrasting Projects and Processes

A major dichotomy of P/OM activities is between change management projects and control management processes. Change management projects—called (α)—require planning, designing, building, testing, redesigning, and implementing the system. This term refers to the management of change. Control management processes—called (β)—entail running the system and shielding it from external disturbances. Running the system means controlling inputs, the transformation process, and outputs. Protecting the system involves security and safety.

These are the two main types of P/OM activities. α-type activities are the domain of project managers. β-type activities are the domain of process managers. Organizations such as Bechtel, Computer Science Corporation, URS, Foster Wheeler and BE&K devote a lot of their resources to managing projects. They develop managers with high-level expertise in α-type activities. These organizations and their project management knowledge are often hired by β-type companies that require projects to remain competitive.

18-6 Basic Rules for Managing Projects

The following basic rules apply to project management:

1   State project objectives clearly. They should be reduced to the simplest terms and communicated to all team members. There often are many participants in a project, and knowledge about objectives must be shared.

2   It should be made clear to everyone that **change management projects** (α) are a unique work configuration that demands specific capabilities, including leadership and teamwork. The contrast should be drawn between (α) and **control management processes** (β).

3   Expertise is required to outline the activities of the project and sequence them correctly. These activities are what must be done to achieve the goals. As a simple example of what happens if the right steps and sequences are not known, when the walls are plastered and painted before the electrical wiring and plumbing are done,

Change management projects (α)
Refers to the management of change, which requires planning, designing, building, testing, redesigning, and implementing the system.

Control management processes (β)
Refers to the management of existing systems, which requires operating that system, controlling the inputs, the transformation process, and the outputs.

the house will have to be unbuilt (going backwards) and then rebuilt to achieve goal completion.

4　Accurate time and cost estimates for all project activities are essential. Slippage from schedule often means real trouble, whereas at other times it can be tolerated because there is sufficient slack. Slack is a time buffer and will be precisely defined in a later section. Project management requires knowing which activities to monitor and expedite.

5　Duplication of activities, in general, should be eliminated. Under some circumstances, however, parallel-path project activities are warranted, namely:

　a.　If a major conflict of ideas exists and there is urgency to achieve the objectives, then it is sometimes reasonable to allow two or more groups to work independently on the different approaches. Preplanned evaluation procedures should exist so that as soon as it is possible the program can be trimmed back to a single path.

　b.　At the inception of a program (during what might be called the exploratory stage), parallel-path research is frequently warranted and can be encouraged. All possible approaches should be considered and evaluated before large commitments of funds have been made.

　c.　Parallel-path research is warranted when the risk of failure is high, for example, survival is at stake. When the payoff incentive is sufficiently great with respect to the costs of achieving it, then parallel-path activities can be justified for as long a period of time as is deemed necessary to achieve the objectives.

6　One systems-oriented person should be responsible for all major decisions. The project manager must be able to lead a team that understands technological, marketing, and production constraints. Multiple project leaders are not advisable.

7　Project management methods are based on information systems that utilize databases that are updated on a regular basis.

　a.　Project methods categorize and summarize a body of information that relates to precedence of activities, and their time and cost.

　b.　Project methods can assess the effects of possible errors in estimates.

18-7 Gantt Project-Planning Charts

The great chartist, Henry L. Gantt, developed a planning graphic in the early 1900s that is still used in much the same form. Gantt's chart permits a basic project plan to be set down. Then, using trial and error, improvements in project scheduling can be attempted. The Gantt chart does not computerize complex project situations, nor does it permit the mathematical analysis of project paths. PERT and CPM methods, which have these capabilities, will be described after Gantt charts are covered.

A Gantt chart is good for small projects and for visualizing the basic structure of any project. Large projects require other techniques where the power of computer-driven project-planning programs can be used.

Figure 18-2 shows successive steps of a Gantt project-planning chart for a manufacturing system. This chart starts with planning, moves through assemblies, and ends with certification. Figure 18-3 shows a chart that describes in general terms the activities required to launch a redesigned automobile. Time lines for both the generic project and the 30-month auto redesign are critical to the Gantt charting method.

Project planners use Gantt charts in two steps. First, set down the necessary activities (*project stages*) to accomplish the project objectives; second, track the status of the project's activities over time. Referring to Figure 18-2, the conventional symbols are bars that show planned start and finish times. The bars are all shaded initially. As work proceeds, a

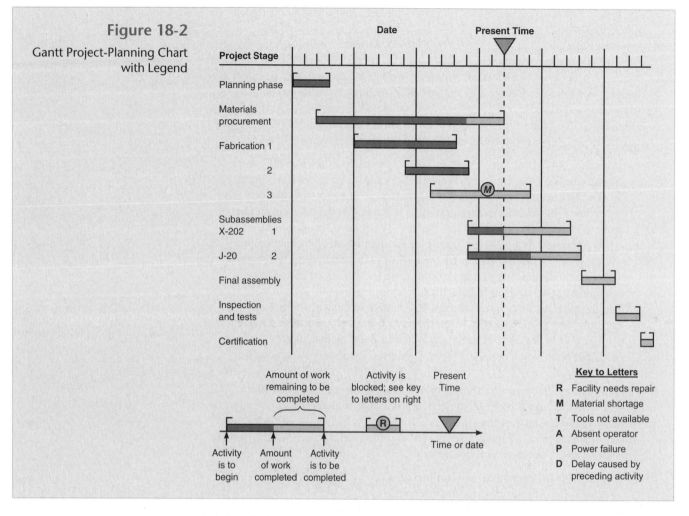

Figure 18-2

Gantt Project-Planning Chart with Legend

darker shade moves over the lighter one to show the activity's percent completion. The dashed vertical line is current time, which moves one unit to the right as each day ends.

Project stages are listed along the left side of the chart. The planning phase has been completed as scheduled. Materials procurement is behind time. It was supposed to have been completed today. Presumably, the project manager knows what is missing, when it is expected, and what is being affected. Apparently, the materials for fabrication activity 1 arrived because it has been completed on time. The same is true of fabrication activity 2.

Fabrication activity 3 has not been started, and the letter M indicates the problem is material shortage. The delay started six days ago and might seriously compromise the completion time of this project. However, the two subassemblies do not seem to be affected. One is on time and the other is ahead of schedule. Final assembly is scheduled in six days from now. Fabrication activity 3 requires eight days. Unless some way is found to speed it up, the project will be delayed two days. Inspection and certification will be delayed.

The Gantt chart in Figure 18-2 is helpful in tracking a project's progress. The Gantt chart in Figure 18-3 is useful in a different way. It plans a car that requires 30 months from general product specifications and market positioning to public introduction. This is a major reduction in the time traditionally (1950–1980) required from start to finish of an auto. This cycle took four to five years in the 1960s. Detailed attention to how a project is developed will pay off, as a general rule, with significant cycle-time reduction.

Figure 18-3 shows the broad categories of activities that need to be completed to achieve product assembly and launch. Each bar on the chart in Figure 18-3 could be detailed with specific notes and information, as in Figure 18-2. Sometimes, however, too

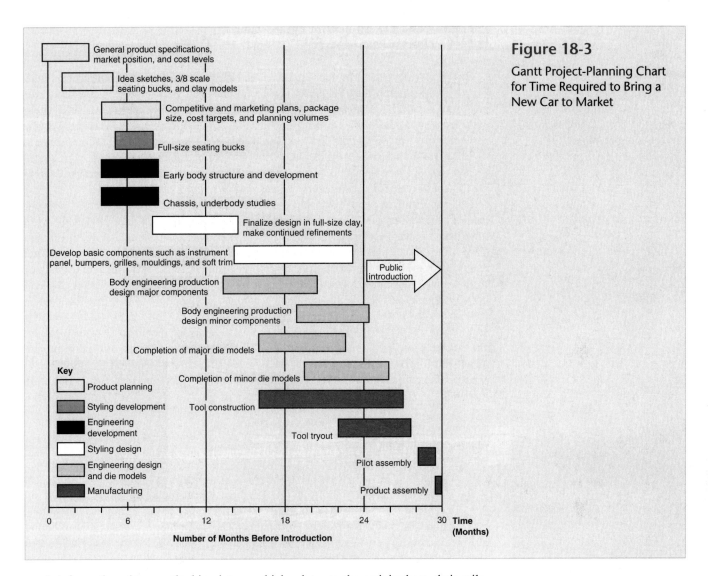

Figure 18-3

Gantt Project-Planning Chart for Time Required to Bring a New Car to Market

much information obscures the big picture, which relates to the activity bars, their milestones, and project completion.

The variables that account for bar length are related to the amount of resources used. Certain activities can be accomplished faster or slower, depending upon the number of people employed, the kinds of facilities that are utilized, and so on. Resource allocations determine time and cost. There are various options. Therefore, for any project there is at least one best sequence to be followed and one best use of resources with respect to cost and time objectives.

Gantt project-planning methods, based on graphical analysis, cannot (1) *lead to optimal resource utilization* or (2) *provide sufficient project-tracking capability* for the complex projects that now are undertaken by large organizations. Because **critical-path methods (CPM)** and PERT (both are described here) are methods programmed for computers, they can achieve (1) and (2). The programming methodology is powerful, which justifies careful study of PERT and CPM methods.

18-8 Critical-Path Methods

Starting about 1957, two similar approaches to large-scale project network planning and tracking were begun at separate locations and for different reasons. These were

Critical-path methods (CPM)

The longest time-path from start to finish of the project; determines completion date of the project.

PERT—program evaluation review technique
CPM—critical path method

PERT

Identifies the longest time-path in the project. Emphasis is on estimation as the determinant of project completion time.

PERT was developed by the U.S. Navy Special Projects Office in conjunction with Booz Allen Hamilton for the Polaris submarine launched missile project. This cold war project was considered urgent by the government and time was a critical variable. There were about 100,000 activities divided amongst thousands of suppliers. PERT set up activity networks, ideal for large projects, which could be systematically analyzed by computers.

CPM was a similar method developed by DuPont and Remington Rand, which later became Unisys. It was used to design and coordinate chemical plant operations. Even at the time of development, computers were essential.

Both applications were very successful in reducing project time. Before network methods existed, project slippage was a fact of life. Projects often took 20 percent more time than expected and cost 20 percent more than budget estimates. With PERT and CPM, 20 percent reductions in expected values were experienced. The adoption of the new project methods was immediate within the United States. Many different kinds of software were developed that could be used for very large projects, including year-end budget preparation. (See the "Additional Readings" section at the end of this chapter.)

PERT and CPM differ only in details. Because *both methods share the notion of a critical path*, Section 18-8 is called *critical-path methods* for the property of the network and not the name of the program. Further, PERT is the most familiar method to project managers. It was adapted by NASA as NASA-PERT and is required by government agencies for participation in U.S. government projects. Therefore, this discussion refers to PERT.

18-8a Constructing PERT Networks

Three steps are required to utilize these network models.

1 *Detail all of the activities* that are required to complete the project.
2 *Draw a precedence diagram* for the precise sequencing to be used based on technological feasibility, managerial objectives, administrative capabilities, equipment, and workforce constraints. The rationale for sequential ordering should be documented so that all teammates can share it and the historical record is permanent and explicit.
3 *Estimate the time to perform each task or activity*. The method of estimation for activity times needs to be detailed and related to project quality. For example, more time is required to use double-error checking—to be sure that no project defects occur. Double-error checking means that two different people (and/or methods) are used to verify that no errors occur. Two options are treated with respect to step 3.

Option 1: *deterministic estimates* for activity times are used.
Option 2: *probabilistic estimates* for activity times are used.

Critical path is defined in terms of time. PERT is a time-based method. Time and cost estimates will be related at a later point. For now, time is the crucial parameter. The goal is reduction of planned project completion time—and then, control of project-cycle time to meet the goals of the plan.

18-8b Deterministic Estimates

After the project has been planned, the activities and their sequence are known so the project-precedence diagram can be drawn. Figure 18-4 shows a precedence diagram for a construction project. This diagram spells out the sequence of what should be done next in the construction of successive floors of a multistory building.

© 2008 Jupiterimages Corporation

Project management is essential for the construction of buildings because fundamental conditions such as location and weather differ even when building plans seem to be the same. Architects and construction engineers must incorporate every detail in the building blueprints and precedence diagrams (see Figure 18-4, which is an abstract version of an actual precedence diagram).

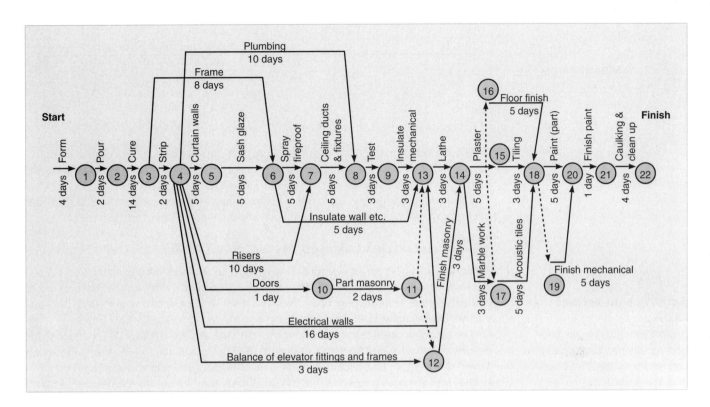

Figure 18-4

A Precedence Diagram for Construction of Floors of an Office Building (Abstract Version from an Actual Diagram)

Each activity has a time estimate written on its arrow. That number is sometimes derived by requesting an engineering estimate. It may be an average based on historical records of the time required for that activity. Because it is one number, there is no way of inferring variability. Later, two parameters (the average and the variance) for probabilistic estimates will be discussed.

PERT charts are introduced with deterministic estimates to keep the discussion focused on their construction and on the determination of the critical path. Two kinds of charts can be drawn. The first is where activities are represented by circles called nodes.

Activities-on-nodes (AON)
Numbered nodes are the project activities; arrows between nodes show the precedence on activities.

18-8c Activities Labeled on Nodes (AON)

Networks consist of arrows and nodes. One form of network chart assigns activities to nodes. This is shown in Figure 18-5. There, the arrows describe the order or precedence of the activities. For example, activity C follows completion of activity A. This is called an **activities-on-nodes (AON)** network.

Figure 18-5

Activities Are Drawn as Nodes Called "Activities-on-Nodes (AON)"

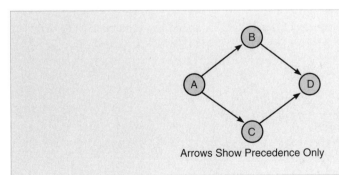

Arrows Show Precedence Only

Table 18-3	Activity	Activities That Must *Immediately* Precede
AON for Figure 18-5	A	None
	B	A
	C	A
	D	Both B and C

Put another way, the AON chart in Figure 18-5 shows that activity A precedes activities B and C. It also states that activity D cannot be done until both B and C are completed. The relationships are summarized in Table 18-3.

There is no ambiguity about these instructions. However, when the activities are drawn on the arrows, there can be confusion about the precedence instructions.

18-8d   Activities Labeled on Arrows (AOA)

When the activities are represented as arrows, then the node circles are called events. Each node marks either the starting event of one or more activities, or the finishing event of one or more activities, or both. This is shown in the event-oriented, **activities-on-arrows (AOA)** network of Figure 18-6.

This chart is ambiguous because there are two arrows labeled D. One arrow for activity D has to follow the arrow of activity B. The second activity D arrow follows the arrow of activity C. Consideration of the non-ambiguous precedence rules in Figure 18-5 reveals one of several problems that can arise when transferring from activities-on-nodes (AON) to activities-on-arrows (AOA).

This situation cannot be permitted for computational reasons. The computer (using the PERT-network algorithm) cannot distinguish between these two D arrows. The ambiguity is removed by redrawing this network, as shown in Figure 18-7, where a dummy arrow has been added.

The dummy activity in Figure 18-7 is represented by the dashed line inserted between nodes 2 and 3. Dummy activities take zero time to accomplish. This dummy allows activities B and C to join at a single node (4), which precedes activity D. It will not affect time

Activities-on-arrows (AOA)

Project activities are the connecting arrows. They start with one numbered node and end with the other node.

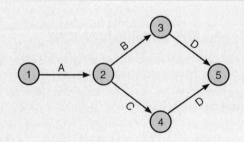

Figure 18-6

Activities Are Drawn as Arrows, Called "Activities-on-Arrows (AOA)"

In this case, ambiguity is created about activity D.

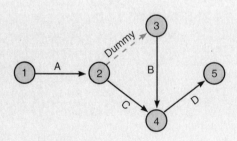

Figure 18-7

Ambiguity of the AOA Network in Figure 18-6 Is Removed by Using a Dummy Activity

Node	Event That Is Tracked	Time	Activity Time
1	Start activity A	t_1	
2	Finish activity A	t_2	$t_A = t_2 - t_1$
	Start activity C	t_2	
	Start dummy activity	t_2	
3	Finish dummy activity	t_3	$t_{dummy} = 0$
	Start activity B	t_3	
4	Finish activity B	t_4	$t_B = t_4 - t_3$
	Finish activity C	t_4	$t_C = t_4 - t_2$
	Start activity D	t_4	
5	Finish activity D	t_5	$t_D = t_5 - t_4$

Table 18-4

Computer Record of Project Data for Start and Finish Times

computations along the network paths. However, it allows the computer to keep track of the nodes, as shown in Figure 18-7 and Table 18-4.

In Figure 18-6, note that nodes 3 and 4 are both starting nodes for activity D. Without the dummy activity, computations would stop. The program cannot resolve this ambiguity. Observe that $t_3 = t_2$ in Figure 18-7 because the dummy activity requires zero time.

Note that in Figure 18-7 the dummy activity could as well have preceded activity C instead of activity B. Examining this alternative will provide a better understanding of how dummy activities are created. Also, it becomes apparent why there is no need for dummy activities when AON is employed. However, computers cannot use the information in the AON diagram because those data lack start and finish times. AOA supplies the start and finish times and is therefore required for the PERT method. The need to create dummy activities arises only when there is ambiguity about start or finish nodes for an activity—as in Figure 18-6. Dummy activities can be developed by trial and error to address situations of ambiguity with AOA.

The PERT algorithm (rules for calculation) uses the nodes and the activity times to compute four different measures of project timing, (e.g., early start, late finish). Thus, the data in Table 18-4 are the starting point for further computations. This will be explained right after some other network conditions are stated.

18-8e Activity Cycles

In planning a project, some activities go through a cycle of steps. For example, a test on a new product design can result in pass or fail. If the product fails the test, then rework is required, and a retest is scheduled after rework completion. Looping back and forth between test, rework, and retest, as shown in Figure 18-8, is not permitted in PERT networks.

The test/redesign cycle shown in Figure 18-8 could occur more than once before the project is completed. Project planners can seldom pre-specify the amount of redesign, rework, and testing that will be needed before project completion. Therefore, estimates are made of the likely rework requirements, and the PERT network is drawn in extensive form as shown in Figure 18-9. This *extensive network* illustrates that activities are always moving forward

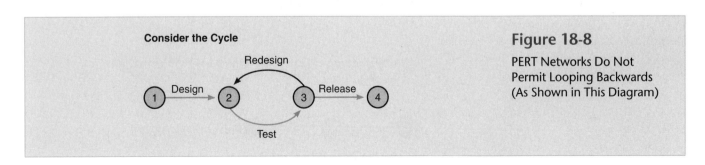

Consider the Cycle

Figure 18-8

PERT Networks Do Not Permit Looping Backwards (As Shown in This Diagram)

Figure 18-9

PERT Networks Must Be
Drawn in Extensive Form

This figure indicates that
redesign is expected to occur
twice. The network must be
redrawn if changes occur.

with no arrows allowed to loop backwards. If the estimate is not correct, then the PERT network is redrawn and recalculated. Such updating of PERT networks is normal.

Figure 18-9 presents the project network in extensive form with two test–redesign occurrences followed by product acceptance and release after a third test. Assume that the project planner's best guess was that it was equally likely that one, two, or three redesigns would be needed. The average of two redesigns was used for Figure 18-9. Probabilities can be recalculated as the project proceeds and more information becomes available.

Projects of realistic size have thousands of different activities. Whenever an activity starts or finishes, an event node must be created. The project designer may use few or many activities to represent the same project elements. For effective project design, more activities are better than few because that allows greater activity control. However, activities should not be divided when they are interdependent and indivisible.

18-9 Critical-Path Computations

Figure 18-10 depicts a project network with three main branches called A, B, and C. The PERT network is drawn for computer use with activities on the arrows.

The project network cannot be used as drawn here. There are two arrows labeled A_2. They were both drawn to show that neither A_3 nor B_2 could begin until A_2 was finished. Figure 18-11 corrects the situation by constructing a dummy activity.

In this reality-based project example, the activities A_1, A_2, and A_3 might be marketing activities needed to launch the new product. Branch B might be production process activities B_1 and B_2. Branch C might be activities C_1, C_2, and C_3, used to develop distribution channels. The branches move ahead together, which is considered good practice. It will help to decrease time to market. The PERT information system has no way of showing that team members are in communication with each other. It can show that teams are monitoring progress.

All activities are labeled with an activity time t (in days). In addition to the dummy constraint, which insures that A_2 will be completed before either A_3 or B_2 can start, it should be noted that A_3, B_2, and C_3 must be completed before product launch can occur at the last node. There are four unique paths leading to the launch node.

(Marketing)	Top path: A_1, A_2, A_3
(Marketing and production)	Mixed path: A_1, A_2, dummy, B_2
(Production)	Middle path: B_1, B_2
(Distribution)	Bottom path: C_1, C_2, C_3

Figure 18-10

Basic PERT Chart with an
Infeasible Network

There are two arrows labeled A_2;
the dummy activity in
Figure 18-11 is needed.

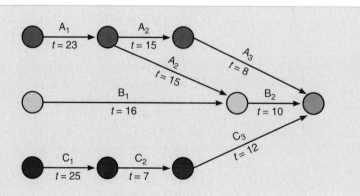

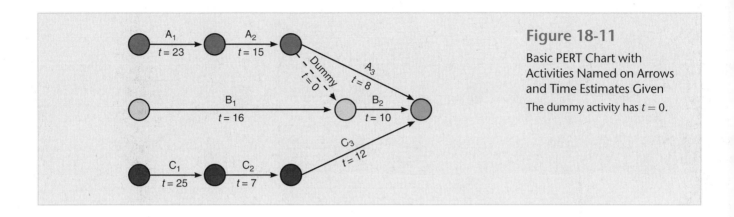

Figure 18-11

Basic PERT Chart with Activities Named on Arrows and Time Estimates Given

The dummy activity has $t = 0$.

18-9a Forward Pass for Completion Time

Every event node in the PERT network will be identified with the following 4-part scorecard. That scorecard shows earliest and latest starts and finishes. Activity time t accompanies the scorecard.

ES = earliest start; dependent on preceding activities
EF = earliest finish; dependent on ES and activity time
EF = ES + t (t = activity time)

ES	EF
LS	LF

LS = latest start, without delaying project
LF = latest finish, without delaying project
LS = LF − t (t = activity time)

The node scorecards are now explained in terms of Figure 18-12, which starts scoring ES, the earliest start, and EF, the earliest finish, for the first nodes along each path. For every arrow, the left-hand node is its start time and the right-hand node is its finish time.

The earliest start for each beginning node is zero, which is therefore entered in the upper left-hand box of the scorecard. Next, note that the earliest finish EF is equal to ES plus the activity time (t) along the arrow that connects two nodes. Adding $t = 23$, the activity time for A_1 to zero yields 23, which is entered into the upper right-hand box of the scorecard. Doing the same for branches B and C produces pairs of numbers (ES, EF) of (0, 16) and (0, 25), respectively.

Figure 18-13 completes the calculations for the top two boxes (ES, EF) of every node.

The value of EF for each preceding node becomes the value of ES in the next node. In other words, the earliest finish for C_1 becomes earliest start for C_2.

For activity A_2, ES is 23, $t = 15$, and so EF is 38, which is entered in the upper right-hand scorecard for A_2. The same operation is performed for A_3. Carry the previous EF to the new ES. Add the activity time and the entry pair is (38, 46). This is consistent for the dummy activity, which carries forward the same EF of 38 for earliest finish time of A_2 and puts that number into ES for the dummy. Then, 38 plus the dummy's activity time of zero makes EF for the dummy equal to 38 (unchanged).

Skip the B-path momentarily because a second scoring rule applies there. Instead, calculate the values for the C-path. For C_2, (32 = 25 + 7). For C_3, (44 = 32 + 12). The top two boxes of all scorecards have been completed except for the B-path.

When two arrows converge at a single node, which occurs at the start node for B_2 (which is also the finish node for the dummy and for the B_1 arrow), always carry forward

Figure 18-12

PERT Chart with First Scorecard Calculations for Earliest Finish (EF)

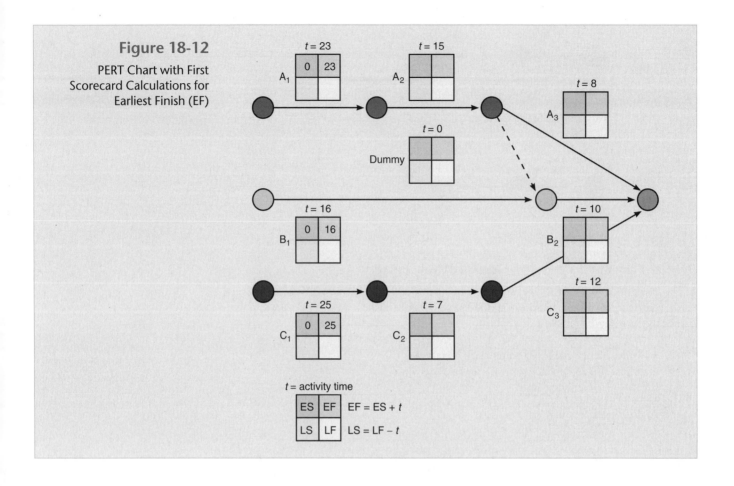

to the next earliest start (ES) the largest prior value of earliest finish (EF). Figure 18-14 focuses on just this one part of the network.

Figure 18-14 shows EF circled for both the dummy and B_1. The circled EF is 38 for the dummy. The circled EF is 16 for B_1. The largest value of the two is 38 and so that is entered as ES for B_2.

Forward pass rule

Enables the project managers to determine how long it will take to complete the project; a necessary precursor to use of the backward pass rule.

The **forward pass rule** for arrows converging at a node: *When two or more arrows converge at a single node, choose the largest value of EF among the converging arrows for the ES value of the next activity.* All further accumulation proceeds with this larger number, because it is the earliest possible starting time for the next event in the network. It is the earliest possible starting time for all successive events thereafter. That is why ES = *earliest start, dependent upon preceding activities.*

Note that in Figure 18-15, three arrows converge on the last node of the network. The forward pass rule for arrows converging on a node applies here in a different way.

The arrows converging on the last node are A_3, B_2, and C_3. Their EF values are 46, 48, and 44, respectively. There is no next node to carry them to, and therefore the largest one specifies the earliest finish time for the project. That number is 48 for the example in Figure 18-15, and it is entered on the final node. It has now been determined that this project requires 48 days for completion.

The procedure just followed is called the *forward pass* through the project network to determine the earliest start and earliest finish times at all nodes. The largest value of the earliest finish (EF) at the last node also is the latest finish time possible for the last node. Thus, EF = 48 days = LF, and 48 is entered for the latest finish (LF) in the bottom right-hand box of the scorecard *for all three arrows* converging at the last node in Figure 18-15. If LF is chosen to be later than 48 days, it would delay the project.

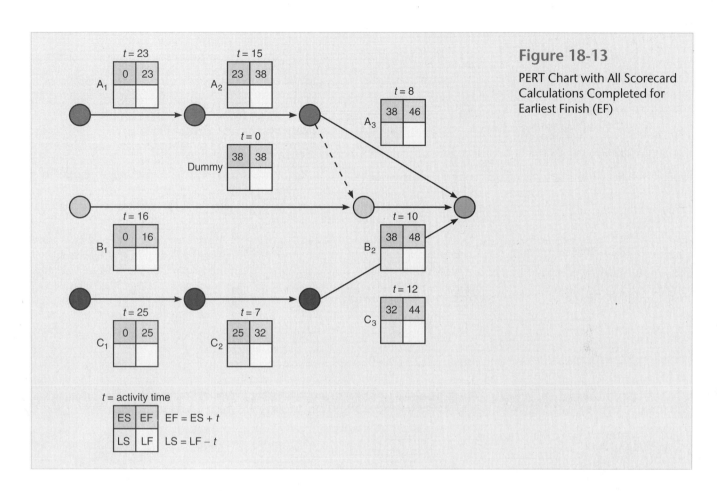

Figure 18-13

PERT Chart with All Scorecard Calculations Completed for Earliest Finish (EF)

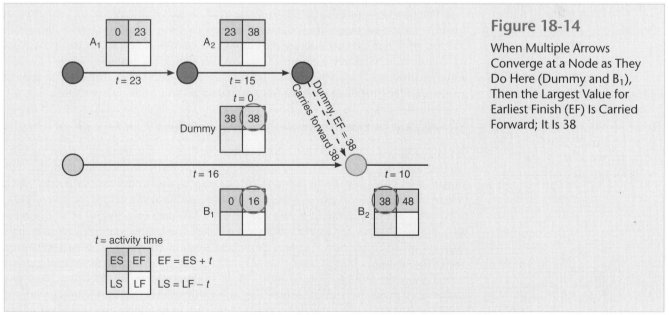

Figure 18-14

When Multiple Arrows Converge at a Node as They Do Here (Dummy and B_1), Then the Largest Value for Earliest Finish (EF) Is Carried Forward; It Is 38

This largest value of EF and LF at the last node in the network is the project-completion time, assuming that nothing unexpected occurs. It also is a measure of the maximum cumulative time of any path through the network, i.e., the longest time sequence of consecutive linked activities through the network.

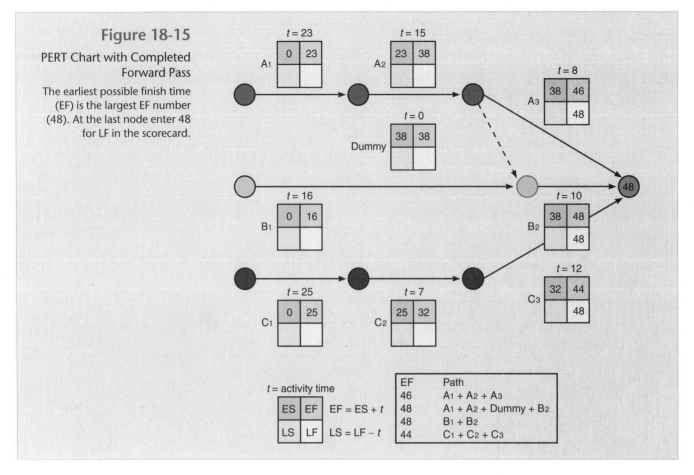

Figure 18-15

PERT Chart with Completed Forward Pass

The earliest possible finish time (EF) is the largest EF number (48). At the last node enter 48 for LF in the scorecard.

Although shorter paths exist (for example, all C-branch activities can be completed in $25 + 7 + 12 = 44$ days), the longest path dominates all plans concerned with project completion. If this example was the PERT chart for building a new home, don't try to get the certificate of occupancy before 48 days. As an alternative example, failure results if advertising occurs before the new product is on the supermarket shelves. The project team advised marketing to assume 48 *working* days if there are no late penalties.

18-9b Backward Pass to Get the Critical Path

The next step is to determine the activities that constitute the critical path. Start with the final node of the last activity and move backwards. For example, which of the four unique paths previously listed accounts for the longest time sequence of 48 days? That path is called the *critical path*. There is at *least one* path that constitutes the critical path. For a small project network, it is easy to find out which path (or paths) of activities is responsible for the final EF and LF. With real project complexity, the PERT computations (forward and then backward) cannot be done without a computer. The backward-pass part of the algorithm is as follows.

Start with the largest value of latest finish. In the example, this is LF = 48. Move backwards through the network, subtracting activity times in accordance with LS = LF − t. The latest start time (LS) of the $(n + 1)$ node becomes the latest finish time (LF) of the prior nth node. LF is the bottom right-hand box of the scorecard. LS is the bottom left-hand box of the scorecard. Thus, for activity B_2, $(38 = 48 - 10)$.

Note the B_2 scorecard in Figure 18-16. It shows that LF was entered as 48 and $t = 10$ was subtracted yielding LS = 38. This becomes LF for the DUMMY. In Figure 18-16, two arrows emanate from the finish node of activity A_2. These arrows come out of the

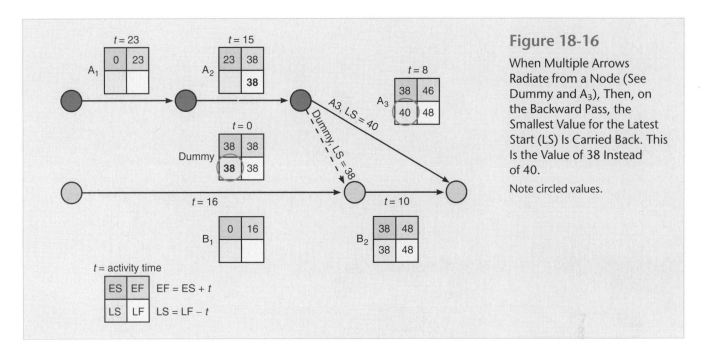

Figure 18-16

When Multiple Arrows Radiate from a Node (See Dummy and A_3), Then, on the Backward Pass, the Smallest Value for the Latest Start (LS) Is Carried Back. This Is the Value of 38 Instead of 40.

Note circled values.

node, moving from start to finish. This means that in going backwards, these two arrows converge on that same node.

There is a backwards convergence rule that is similar and opposite to the forward convergence rule. It is opposite because it carries back the smallest value of LS. The **backward pass rule** for multiple arrows emanating from a single node: *When two or more arrows meet at a single node, choose the smallest value of LS among the converging arrows for the LF value of the preceding activity's arrow.* All further accumulation proceeds with this smaller number, which is the latest possible finishing time for the preceding activity without delaying the project.

In Figure 18-16, the calculation for the dummy's latest start (LS = LF − t) is (38 = 38 − 0). LS for A_3 is 48 − 8 = 40. Because 38 is smaller than 40, 38 becomes LF for A_2. See the circles in Figure 18-16 and the boldfaced 38 for LF of A_2.

Figure 18-17 shows all node scorecards filled in with latest starts. The backward pass has been completed. Table 18-5 shows all these results as well as those for EF.

Table 18-6 tabulates the results for latest start (LS) and latest finish (LF) for all three branches of the project network. This includes results previously calculated on the backward pass. In addition, to put all relevant information together in one place, Table 18-6 includes the data for earliest finish (EF) and earliest start (ES) for all three branches of the network.

The results in Table 18-6 are used in three ways. First, they are used to calculate *slack*, which is allowable slippage. **Slack**, by definition, can be wasted without changing project-completion time. Note how the previously discussed C-branch takes 44 days to complete, whereas the critical path takes 48 days. There is slack of four days along branch C. Second, Table 18-6 can be used to identify the critical path c, which is the path of zero slack. Third, Table 18-6 allows identification of where slack resides.

18-9c Slack Is Allowable Slippage

Table 18-6 calculates slack in two ways. Slack = (LS − ES) = (LF − EF). Note that both subtractions produce the same result for each activity. Also, the column marked CP has an x in it if that activity is on the critical path.

The slack of an activity describes the amount of time (here in days) that can be viewed as a safety buffer for slippage. The project manager views small amounts of slack and

Backward pass rule

Enables the critical path to be identified; also permits the determination of slack.

Slack

Translates to allowable slippage in an activity's schedule along a slack path; the amount of time that it is safe to be late in delivering a completed activity. Safe means no addition to project completion time.

Figure 18-17

PERT Chart with All Latest Starts (LS) Completed

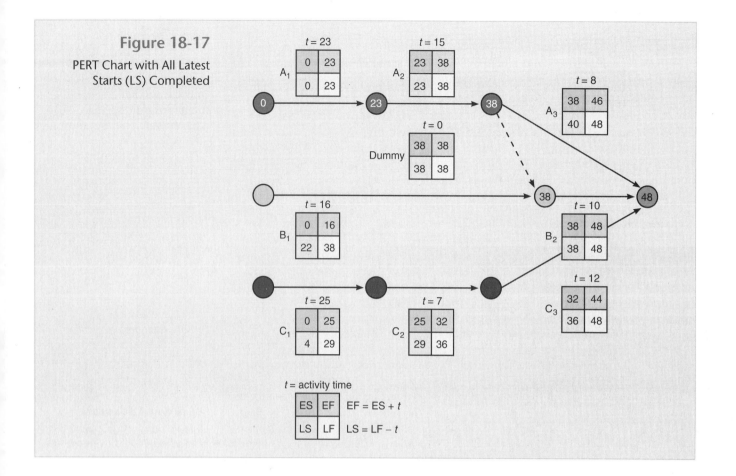

t = activity time

ES	EF	EF = ES + t
LS	LF	LS = LF − t

Table 18-5

Latest Start (LS) from Latest Finish (LF) for All Activities and from Figure 18-15 Earliest Finish (EF) and Earliest Start (ES)

Activity	LS = LF − t	EF = ES + t
A_3	40 = 48 − 08	46 = 38 + 08
A_2	23 = 38 − 15	38 = 23 + 15
A_1	00 = 23 − 23	23 = 00 + 23
B_2	38 = 48 − 10	48 = 38 + 10
B_1	22 = 38 − 16	16 = 00 + 16
C_3	36 = 48 − 12	44 = 32 + 12
C_2	29 = 36 − 07	32 = 25 + 07
C_1	04 = 29 − 25	25 = 00 + 25
DUMMY	38 = 38 − 00	38 = 38 + 00

Table 18-6

Calculating Slack in Days, Two Methods Are Used: LS − ES and LF − EF

Activity	LS	ES	Slack	LF	EF	CP
A_1	0	0	0	23	23	x
A_2	23	23	0	38	38	x
A_3	40	38	2	48	46	
B_1	22	0	22	38	16	
B_2	38	38	0	48	48	x
C_1	4	0	4	29	25	
C_2	29	25	4	36	32	
C_3	36	32	4	48	44	
DUMMY	38	38	0	38	38	x

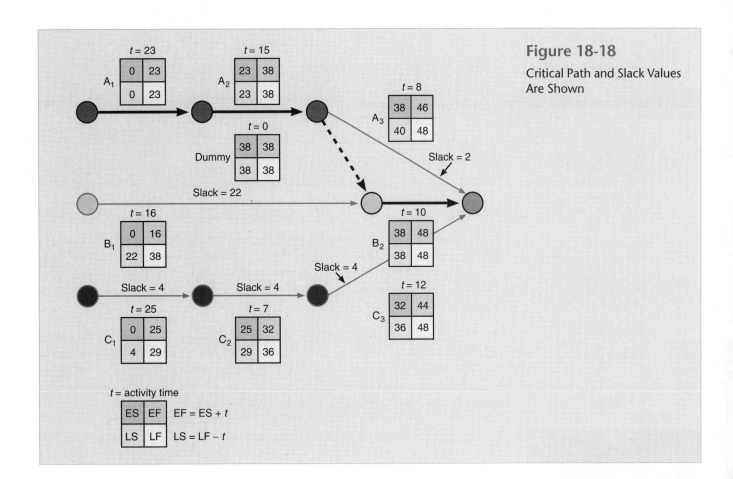

Figure 18-18

Critical Path and Slack Values Are Shown

zero slack as activities that demand constant attention because slippage there results in project delay. Also, reallocation of resources can affect slack, which puts discretionary powers for what is critical, and what is not, in the hands of project planners.

Note the activities with zero slack follow the path $A_1 + A_2 + DUMMY + B_2$. *This is the critical path.* It is the set of activities that define the shortest time in which the project can be completed without slippage. Figure 18-18 shows the critical path with darker lines than the rest of the network.

In Figure 18-18, where slack exists, the amount is indicated. The C-path has slack equal to 4 for all three C activities. If C_1 starts four days late, all the slack is used up for C_2 and C_3. Contiguous slack along a path is shared slack.

If activity A_3 is delayed two days, it becomes part of the critical path. Activity B_1 has 22 days of slack. That is a great deal of slack for a project with a critical path of 48. B_1 can be delayed in starting or take much longer to be done than expected. The project manager might think about transferring some people from B_1 to one of the critical activities to relieve the stress. That tactic is called *resource leveling* and it will be discussed later.

Using the 3-branch example of marketing, production, and distribution brings up the question of Best Practice. Because production has 22 days of slack at B_1, it might seem acceptable for P/OM not to get involved in the project immediately. However, that is no longer acceptable practice. Instead, production should get involved with marketing issues to help expedite work along the critical path and to share insights and systems perspectives. From a systems point of view, note how the dummy activity shows an important systems linkage between A_2 and B_2. Production has the opportunity to work on marketing issues, and then marketing has a little leeway to work on production issues. This is termed *concurrent project management*.

Figure 18-19

When B_1 and C_1 Are Delayed 22 and 4 Days, Respectively, Before Starting, Then All Activities Except A_3 Become Critical

All activities except A_3 now have the same shading because they are all on the critical path.

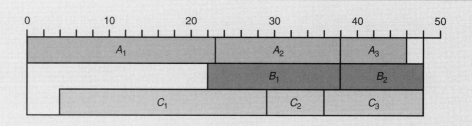

The slack situation is represented by Figure 18-19 in a concise way where both B's and C's slack are allowed to be used up. Then, both paths of the project become critical. Only activity A_3 can be allowed to slip without increasing project-completion time. This illustrates how more than one project path can be critical. Management is hard pressed to handle projects that have a large percent of critical activities.

Knowing which activities have slack is important. It is probably wasteful to expedite activities A_3, B_1, C_1, C_2, and C_3. It is likely to be useful to expedite along the critical path. Note that such information about slack and the critical path are not available using the Gantt chart.

18-10 Estimates of Time and Cost

Project management requires good estimates of time to manage the critical path and use slack resources in a proper fashion. Delivery of the finished project must be on time. As will be explained shortly, there can be penalties for being late.

As for cost estimates, when project bidding is used, underestimating the cost of a job results in lower bids with higher probabilities of the bid being accepted. The actual higher cost of the job reduces profit. A good estimator increases the organization's revenues by not overestimating costs, which produces bids that are too high, resulting in lower probabilities of winning the bid.

Management relies upon its ability to estimate before hard data are available. Organizations that deal in projects track the estimating capabilities of their employees by maintaining historical records of their estimation errors. The following equation can be maintained for all project managers who make estimates.

$$\text{Estimate} - \text{Actual result} = \text{Error}$$

Using this equation to collect data, it is possible to evaluate estimators in terms of

1 How close their *average error* is to zero
2 How dispersed (*variability*) are their errors
3 Whether their errors tend to be overestimates or underestimates (error bias)

Basically, there are three different methods for obtaining estimates: First is a person's opinion derived from his/her experiences. Second is the pooling of several individuals' opinions derived from their experiences. Many different pooling techniques are available, the most obvious being to use the average value. Third, several parameters of estimation are requested from an individual, and these are combined by a computing formula (called *multiparameter estimation*). As in the second method, the pooling of several persons' opinions can be achieved.

For PERT, the prevalent estimation procedure is either the first or the third method. The U.S. Navy helped to develop multiparameter estimation, which uses the beta (three

© 2008 Jupiterimages Corporation

The level of detail for a NASA space flight is enormous. The estimates for project launch are a mixture of engineering knowledge and estimates concerning weather. Each launch has a window of possibilities. If the window is missed, the launch must be postponed until the next window appears.

parameter) distribution. The PERT system requires three different estimates of time for each activity. These are

1 An optimistic estimate, called a
2 A pessimistic estimate, called b
3 A most likely estimate, called m

The three estimates are combined to give an expected (mean) elapsed time, called t_e.

$$t_e = \frac{1}{6}(a + b) + \frac{2}{3}(m) \qquad (18\text{-}1)$$

If a single number is given as an estimate, it is the mode value, m. The computing formula adds variance information by providing a range between shortest likely and longest likely times. A possible distribution for these three elapsed time estimates is shown in Figure 18-20.

The three values a, b, and m are used to estimate the mean of a unimodal beta distribution. For the unimodal beta distribution, if a and b are equally spaced above and below m, then $m = t_e$. That is

$$t_e = \frac{1}{6}[(a = m - x) + (b = m + x)] + \frac{4}{6}(m) = m \qquad (18\text{-}2)$$

When a and b are not symmetric around m, the mean, t_e, is moved in the direction of the greatest interval.

A beta estimate of the variance (σ^2) associated with the mean value t_e is given by:

$$\sigma^2 = \left[\frac{1}{6}(b - a)\right]^2 \qquad (18\text{-}3)$$

This method of estimating the variance is appealing because a single estimate of variance without historical data is difficult to make and hard to believe. Beta provides a logical and consistent basis for estimating variability.

The sum of the means of successive activities is the mean of the path. Thus, for the top (marketing) path:

$$t_{(A1+A2+A3)} = t_{A1} + t_{A2} + t_{A3}$$

Figure 18-20

A Possible Distribution for Activity Time Estimates Using the Beta Distribution

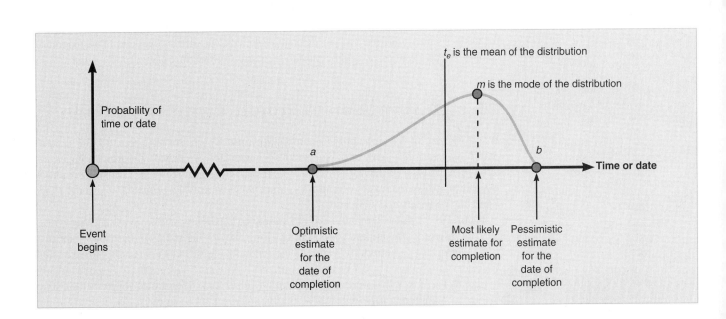

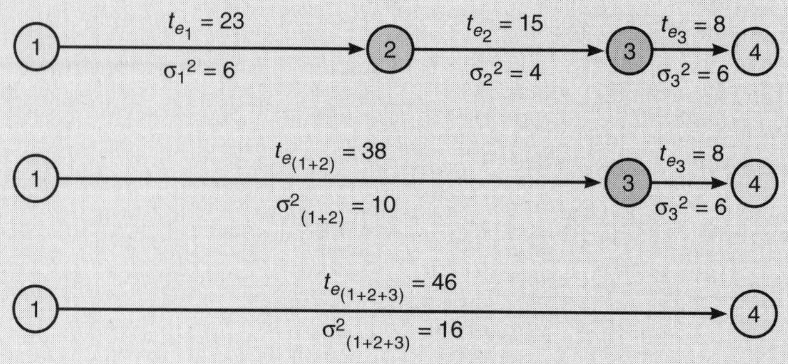

Figure 18-21

The Variance of the Path Is
Equal to the Sum of the
Variances of the Individual
Activities. The Mean of the
Path Is Equal to the Sum of
the Means of the Individual
Activities. (Note: Variances
Are the Same as Those Used
in Figure 18-22.)

The same kind of equation can be written for all the other paths. The sum of the variances of successive activities is the variance of the total path.

Figure 18-21 illustrates how the mean and the *variance* are combined by summation.

The rule concerning the sum of activity *variances* requires that the activities should be independent. This means that if one activity is late, it will not affect any other activity's completion time. The next equation describes the variance of the (top) marketing path:

$$\sigma^2_{(A1+A2+A3)} = \sigma^2_{A1} + \sigma^2_{A2} + \sigma^2_{A3}$$

The variance of the *critical path* (mixed-marketing and production) is

$$\sigma^2_{(A1+A2+Dummy+B2)} = \sigma^2_{A1} + \sigma^2_{A2} + \sigma^2_{Dummy} + \sigma^2_{B2}$$

The variance of the (middle) production path is

$$\sigma^2_{(B1+B2)} = \sigma^2_{B1} + \sigma^2_{B2}$$

The variance of the (bottom) distribution path is

$$\sigma^2_{(C1+C2+C3)} = \sigma^2_{C1} + \sigma^2_{C2} + \sigma^2_{C3}$$

Note that the paths share activities, so that the *variances of the paths* are not independent. This is not a problem as long as the *variances of the activities* do not affect other activities.

When the variance of a noncritical path (based on t_e) is larger than the variance along the critical path, it is possible that the noncritical path will become critical. This means that the original critical path switches to the new one. Simulations can be run using the mean and variance information to determine the percent of time that each path becomes critical. Much attention should be paid to the paths that become critical most often.

18-11 Distribution of Project-Completion Times

When activity times vary, project-completion time varies. Assume that off the critical path there is enough slack to make variances along the critical path the main point of interest. An analysis of the variation of critical-path time provides risk estimates of major interest to project managers who promise to deliver the finished project at a specific time. There are penalties for being late.

Figure 18-22 shows the mean and the variance (in parentheses) for each activity.

The variances are summed proceeding along the critical path. At the final node that signals project completion, the mean of the critical path (48) is shown with the estimated variance (16).

Figure 18-22 is based on a normal distribution. It illustrates a probability of 0.95 that the actual completion time will fall within the range of 40 to 56 days. The left tail of the

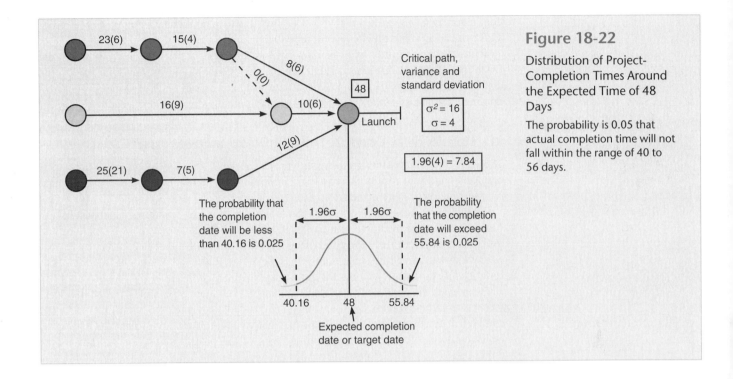

Figure 18-22

Distribution of Project-Completion Times Around the Expected Time of 48 Days

The probability is 0.05 that actual completion time will not fall within the range of 40 to 56 days.

distribution reflects the 0.25 probability of an early completion of the project. The right tail of the distribution reflects the 0.25 probability of being late in completing the project. The figure shows that 48 days $\pm 1.96s$ ranges from 40.16 days to 55.84 days. Also, it is interesting to note that the probability is 50 percent that the actual project-completion time will exceed 48 days or, conversely, be less than 48 days.

To summarize, there is a 95 percent probability that the actual completion date will fall within the range of 48 days $\pm 1.96\sigma$. Because $\sigma = 4$, $1.96s = 7.84$, and $48 + 7.84 = 55.84$, and $48 - 7.84 = 40.16$, providing the means to discuss penalties for being late and rewards for being early. This range can be used to specify an earliest and latest project-completion date for contract negotiations.[4] For readers' convenience, a table is provided in Note 4 at the end of Chapter 18 that shows useful ranges for different values of k in $k\sigma$.

18-11a The Effect of Estimated Variance

The analysis of project-completion times can be extended to reflect the effect of variance on all of the paths in any project network.

Path		Expected Completion Time	Total Variance	95% Range (1.96σ)
1	A1, A2, A3	46 days	16	38.16—53.84
2*	A1, A2, Dummy, B2	48 days	16	40.16—55.84*
3	B1, B2	26 days	15	18.40—33.59
4	C1, C2, C3	44 days	35	32.40—55.60

*Path 2 is the critical path.

The variance of path 4 is so large that the upper limit of 55.60 is almost the same as the upper limit of the critical path (55.84). If the activities along the critical path remain as expected, but the path 4 activities require excessive times, then completion will be dominated by a new critical path, C_1, C_2, and C_3, which could take as much as 55.6 days. This can occur within the 95 percent probability range.

Path 4 is near-critical with 44 days (versus 48 days), and its variance is more than twice that of path 2. This means that careful managerial attention should be paid to the distribution activities of path 4. These path 4 activities can shift to critical. They can dominate the situation and cause the targeted completion date of the project to be missed.

18-11b Why Is Completion Time So Important?

There are three dimensions for assessing project success. These are completion time, total cost, and quality of results. All three are important, but, often, meeting the targeted date for finishing the project is the first factor considered.

This is not surprising. Certain products have marketing "windows of opportunity." Textbooks must be available in time for adoption, toys must be ready for Christmas, and roses need to bloom for Valentine's Day. Projects to launch planetary probes have specific windows defined by such factors as closeness to Earth and position of the Sun. Seasonal factors produce a window for the Alaska pipeline and for new TV shows.

Even when the window concept does not apply, "as soon as possible" frequently does. Projects usually involve large investments that do not start paying off until the project is completed. When viewing project costs against when return on investment (ROI) begins, managers have come to prefer spending more of the project investment in the present rather than in the future. Spending now to decrease completion time makes sense if a positive cash flow (or other benefits, such as hospital beds) can be obtained as soon as possible. In bidding situations, project-completion time is a major determinant for winning the award. Frequently, contract terms include stiff penalties for failing to bring the project in on time.

18-11c Progress Reports and Schedule Control

At all stages of the project, the manager will ask for progress reports. Each activity, especially those with suppliers, should report status on a regular, predetermined basis. Usually, daily computer printouts indicate activities that are ahead, those that are behind, and by how much. Shifts in the critical path are reported. New slack values appear and are constantly monitored. Continually updated, the network reflects project progress and problems.

Teamwork requires that progress reports be shared by all. When problems arise, there is mutual concern. Shared efforts can be made to move resources from one part of the network to another to keep on schedule. The topic of allocating resources is relevant at the beginning design stage of the project. It also applies continuously during the project's lifetime when redesign is referred to as *reallocation of resources*.

One aspect of reallocation is *resource leveling*. Before resource leveling could be addressed, it was necessary that the PERT method be thoroughly understood. It is also reasonable to address trade-offs between time and cost, which will be done in Enrichment Activity 18, after resource leveling is discussed.

18-12 Redesigning Projects

There are methods for designing projects so that resources can be used in the best way. Redesign can result in improving the performance of projects such as shortening the critical path, getting closer to target-completion time, and meeting the budget. Stringent project quality goals have to be set, monitored, and met. Steps to make project-completion dates earlier should not be permitted to damage project quality and/or project quality control.

18-12a Resource Leveling

Resource leveling is an important concept for project design. The fundamental idea of **resource leveling** is to switch extra resources from places where they are not essential to places where they could be used immediately. Alternatively, resource leveling aims to balance resource assignments across activities over time. It also provides some control for time-based management (TBM) of project life cycles and facilitates shortening the critical path. It is a method for improving the speed of project achievements and for being able to implement rapid-attainment project management.

The *beginning game* is thoughtful and deliberate. The design of many projects is such that they start slowly while many ideas are being considered. There is much slack in activities that are off the critical path as reports are written and approvals are sought. There seems no need for urgency. The critical path is itself stretched out by bureaucratic organization of the project. This point of view has been undergoing change because of competitive pressures. See Section 19-7.

The *end game* has everything coming to a head very quickly. The end game has a time deadline that begins to appear to be looming. Then, it is decided that time must be made up. There is a surge in spending to speed up the project. Often, in the rush, mistakes are made and damage control uses up time that was meant for thoughtful and deliberate means to bring the project to a successful conclusion. It is well-known to project managers that this type of pattern is not desirable. Unless caught by circumstances, present-day project management avoids this damaging scenario.

In search of shorter project cycles, the newer approach to projects uses a multifunctional team with rapid communication to secure approvals. The cash-flow pattern is far more balanced from start to finish. Resources are assigned along all paths so that the critical path can be shortened and slack imbalances can be corrected before the beginning, or early on in the project's time line.

Resource leveling seeks to move people from overstaffed activities to those that are understaffed. It attempts to reallocate money from where there is overspending to where there is under spending. These efforts at leveling must make sense in technological and process terms. Similarly, the project manager would prefer smooth demand for cash instead of sporadic cash outflows. If, among a set of simultaneous activities, a few are receiving the greatest percentage of project expenditures, it often is desirable to level these allocations.

The existence of slack is an important basis for resource leveling. To illustrate, three people have been shifted from activity B_1, which has 22 days of slack, to activity A_1 on the critical path of Figure 18-18. The assumption is made that each added person decreases activity time by one day. Similarly, it is assumed that each removed person increases activity time by one day. The assumptions are applied to the two activities, A_1 and B_1. The result is resource leveling, as shown in Figure 18-23.

Several effects are to be noted. The critical path remains unchanged with respect to nodes and activities. However, the length of the critical path has decreased from 48 to 45. Project manager and clients will be pleased. Slack for B_1 has decreased from 22 to 16. Because 22 seemed excessive, no one is likely to object, except the C-branch manager. Shared slack along the C-path has been reduced from 4 to 1. This could lead to some objections because the distribution branch of the project has three activities that are urgent (with near-zero slack).

It is worth pointing out that simple assumptions about the effects of trading off resources (such as the one-for-one assumption made earlier about workers and days) need to be replaced with knowledgeable estimates of the effects of resource changes. This requires balancing cost and time trade-offs.

The term "resource leveling" implies that the amount of resources is held constant. It is only the allocation of resources that is altered. The term "resource management" denotes more flexibility. It provides the option to *withdraw resources* or to *add new*

Resource leveling
Where slack exists, there is potential for resource trade-offs that can reduce nonvalue-adding time while decreasing the time required for completion of the project.

Figure 18-23

Resource Leveling

Three employees shifted from B_1 to A_1. Critical path is reduced from 48 to 45. Slack for B_1 is reduced from 22 to 16. (Compare with Figure 18-18.)

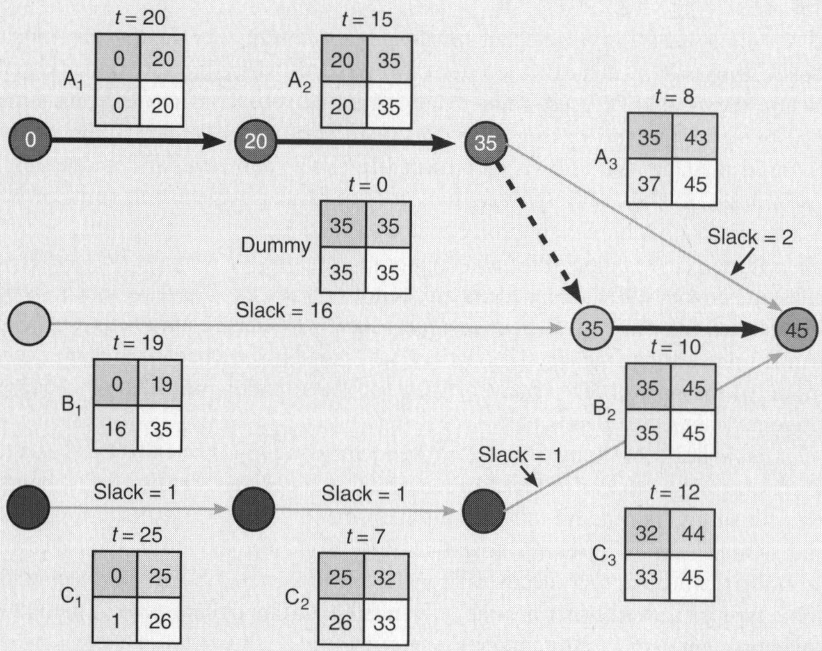

resources. This approach changes budgetary constraints. Changing the budget is a strategic decision.

The tactical aspect of resource leveling is that it can affect the entire system without changing the budget. All project team members are impacted when resources are shifted, and they should be kept informed of project alterations. Good resource allocation decisions are a P/OM project management responsibility. This is another example of where tactical changes have far-reaching impact on strategic issues.

18-13 Cost and Time Trade-Offs

Project approaches that deal only with time are called PERT/Time or CPM/Time. Another way to consider changing critical paths and slack time is by means of **trade-offs** of cost and time. It is often possible to reduce the critical path duration by spending more money. Resource leveling shifts costs among activities but does not add new funds or reduce existing funds. The project manager transfers funds from activities with slack to activities on the critical path.

What must be known is how adding or decreasing the resources employed (and their costs) affects the times required to complete activities. Then, comparisons can be made between **crash time** programs (using peak resource allotments) and **normal time** programs with minimum resource utilization.

Assume that the project plan is to run all activities on a crash basis. This means that each activity will be done in the least possible or minimum time. Crash planning can entail substantial cost additions to the project budget. If the alternative objective to minimize cost is used, this will stretch out project time and reduce spending. The objectives of minimum cost and minimum time are negatively correlated. Usually, crashing to achieve minimum time has maximum costs. Minimum cost activities have maximum times associated with them and are called normal times. One can dream up exceptions to the rule; but, in general, more resources cost more money. When properly used, more resources decrease the time required to finish a project so that return on the project investment can begin sooner.

Trade-offs

Spend more money on project resources, and finish sooner, or vice versa.

Crash time

Crashing an activity means spending as much as it takes to achieve *minimum* activity time. Crashing is generally used to decrease the length of the critical path.

Normal time

Normal activity time is associated with the minimum necessary spending on project activities because there is no great stress on completing the project as soon as possible.

Maximum quality (qualities) attainment is a third objective that project managers take very seriously. As the *Challenger* and *Columbia* space shuttle tragedies showed, project-quality goals are not guaranteed. They do not take care of themselves. Project quality is a design, engineering, and P/OM responsibility. Flawed technology, bad weather, faulty design standards, poor building techniques, and improper materials can be ignored as a result of pressure to do more, faster. Project crashing must be done with great care. It is essential that crash-time spending should be sufficient to avoid mistakes (e.g., cutting corners to meet a deadline).

Cost-cutting with normal-time project procedures can also inflict penalties. Failures in bringing a new product or service to the marketplace often can be traced to the project instead of the product. This is a systems problem requiring extensive coordination between engineering, marketing, distribution, and P/OM. The project team is accountable.

18-14 Multiple Project Management

In an environment that is totally supportive of managed change, project management takes on organizational dimensions that are significantly expanded. This is because many Stage IV companies expect their people to have more than one project assignment. Chapter 19, on change management, discusses various methods for dealing with many new products and/or process changes. Firms, in search of improvements, have subscribed to doing a great number of process improvement initiatives. These tend to be going on simultaneously and require competent **multiple project management**. Mostly, this is a twenty-first century topic since the concept did not gain real support until after Y2K. However, companies like W. L. Gore & Associates have been successful with myriads of projects for almost 50 years (see Section 19-8a).

Multiple projects create challenges and opportunities. One of the challenges is to compartmentalize the assignments so that time lines are not sacrificed on one project at the expense of another project. Multitasking, which generation Y is said to excel at, is a requirement of manifold project management. Organization is essential because the old saying that "too many cooks spoil the broth" remains substantially correct.

Resource leveling has been described within a single project. In that case, the resources are traded off between branches of the one project. It is not difficult to extend resource leveling so that skills are borrowed and loaned between different projects as needed. As in single project management, the idea is to look for "free" resources that can be shifted to a borrowing project without damaging the time line and quality of the lending project.

Employees have to be supported in making such shifts. Confusion is an enemy of efficiency that often appears when the juggler is not trained in that skill. For handling multiple projects, software is available that can help organize efficient collaboration. See http://crn.channelsupersearch.com/news/crn/39739.asp. Also, see http://www/teamworkzone.com.

In Redmond, Washington, April 8, 2005—"Microsoft today completed its acquisition of Groove Networks, the Beverly, Mass.-based provider of collaboration software for ad-hoc workgroups, and will add Groove's products to the lineup of Microsoft Office System products, servers and services. The acquisition makes the Groove product and team part of Microsoft's Information Worker Business." See http://www.microsoft.com/midsizebusiness/businessvalue/projectcollaboration.mspx. As Microsoft states, "Collaboration products typically come in two flavors: as Web-based tools or as packaged software (although subscription-based collaboration software is likely not far behind)." There are many options and care must be exercised in choosing.

In addition to resource leveling, cost/time trade-offs can be analyzed with respect to budget allocations across multiple projects. Using cost/time trade-offs permits the firm to set reasonable limits on how many projects can be handled at one time. It allows setting

Multiple project management
Management of multiple projects calls on all of the skills required to manage a very complex project that has many suppliers and workers. Resource leveling can be used effectively between projects.

time lines for project completions that are consonant with the company's resources. Balancing new product needs and process change improvements against resources available is an essential planning discipline.

Big projects contain subprojects that are often concerned with quite disparate physical and aesthetic characteristics. At a point, the design of the wing and the design of the airplane seats must be related to each other, if in no other way than in terms of a shared weight limit. Communications between the team members working on wings and those working on seats can be optimized by sharing developments in each subproject.

Multiple project management faces challenges and *opportunities*. Among the challenges is the need to juggle ideas and schedules. Sharing information in an efficient way is an opportunity for coordination, synergy, and serendipity. The coordination of big projects can be enhanced by use of a control room where the walls are display panels showing the progress of various project teams. Projects that are tracked by good information systems require less management time to produce controlled innovative success stories.

Spotlight 18-1 The Polaroid Story

"Over the years, I have learned that every significant invention has several characteristics. It must be startling, unexpected, and must come to a world that is not prepared for it."

—Edwin H. Land

In the fast-paced technological world of digital imaging and smart machines, no one would have believed that Polaroid Corporation, the world leader in instant imaging, would not be able to overcome its rivals (HP, Kodak, Olympus, Canon, and Sony, among others) in the production of digital cameras and related products. Unfortunately, Polaroid ran out of cash and on April 30, 2002, filed a reorganization plan in bankruptcy court. Why did this happen?

Polaroid's founder, Edwin H. Land (1909–1991), was a prolific inventor from the day he left Harvard at the end of his freshman year in 1926. He conducted research on light polarization and filed for his first patent in 1929 after inventing the first synthetic sheet polarizer. With his scientific and entrepreneurial genius, Land conceived and produced his own products and marketed them for use in sunglasses, glare-free auto headlights, and 3-D stereoscopic photography.

One day, the story goes, he was inspired by his 3-year-old daughter, who asked him why she couldn't see a photo he had taken of her right away. It was through his Polaroid Corporation, founded in 1937 in Massachusetts, that Land was immortalized for his invention and marketing of instant photography. The first Polaroid camera was sold to the public in November 1948. Today the word "Polaroid" has two definitions in *Webster's New World Dictionary*: a trademark for transparent material capable of polarizing light; and the Polaroid (Land) camera that produces a print within seconds.

Land spent his entire adult life experimenting and innovating in the field of optics. As a science advisor to Eisen-

hower during the Cold War, he spearheaded the development of the U-2 spy plane and helped design NASA. His 535 U.S. patents stand second only to Thomas Edison. Land was awarded the Medal of Freedom, the highest honor granted to civilians in the United States. In 1980, Edwin Land retired as CEO of Polaroid, having given the world a camera that had revolutionized photography. He also left a company culture based on science, patents, and a proud and honorable tradition.

Another revolution was underway in the early 1980s. Polaroid Corporation was aware of the challenge of digital camera technology and had commenced work in this field of innovation before many of its competitors. The company had a great brand, brilliant scientists and engineers, and a large global marketing and distribution system. Polaroid knew what intense competition it would face. Somehow it failed to realize that a radical change in company culture and methods of manufacturing and marketing would be needed. Long product development cycles and decades-long patent protection became liabilities.

A different style of management was necessary in a new manufacturing environment where the cost and capabilities of computer chips constantly change. (See "Moore's Law" under *Sources* at the end of this Spotlight.) Also, Polaroid's core capabilities and skills were in optics and films. They were not in software, storage technologies, and electronic digital signal processing.

In order to enter the digital market, Polaroid had to make large investments. Its first digital offerings did not catch on. Helios, a digital laser-imaging system designed to replace printing of X-rays, was launched in 1993. Several hundred million dollars in investment did not bring the expected return. In 1996, Polaroid launched its first digital camera, the PDC-2000, aiming at professional photographers as customers. It retailed for between $2,995 and $4,995. Other digital cameras from competitors were available for less than $1,000. The company's real effort to enter the consumer market came in late 1997. It was too late. With declining instant-film sales, inability to generate sufficient profits from the digital business, and demands for investment in technology, the company had trapped itself by incurring dramatic losses of revenue.

Switching its strategy, Polaroid focused on becoming a "new products" company in 1998. By year's end, it showed a net loss of $51 million despite its $1.8 billion in net sales.

In 1999, the company switched again, deciding to refocus on its core business and exiting its new-products approach. That year showed a record sale of 9.7 billion instant cameras along with 400,000 digital cameras. Although its revenues were great (Polaroid's net sales were $1.9 billion, its highest on record), its earnings were miniscule. Statements made to investors in October 2000 by Polaroid's chairman and CEO, Gary T. DiCamillo, did not seem to reflect the company's cash drains and increasing competition. In reality, Polaroid's business plan was perfectly suited for a world that no longer existed. On October 12, 2001, the company ceased conducting commercial business, had no employees, and was more than 900 million in debt.

On April 30, 2002, Polaroid was in bankruptcy court. A tidal surge of competition in digital media had broken Polaroid apart, washing away a wonderful company that tried, up to the last moment, to survive. The last press releases give the impression of a great Titanic, unable to either stay or correct its course. Criticism has been raised over the way this process was undertaken, because it left the executives of the company with healthy bonuses, leaving stockholders, as well as current and retired employees, with nothing.

On July 31, 2002, all of Polaroid's assets including its name were under control of One Equity Partners, a division of Bank One (now JP Morgan Chase). Under the bank's authority, the OEP Imaging Operating Corporation renamed itself the Polaroid Holding Corporation (PHC), taking over sales, assets, and rights to the Polaroid name. The old Polaroid Corporation became Primary PDC, operating under the protection of Chapter 11 bankruptcy code to settle claims.

For the next three years at PHC, Jacques Nasser, the former CEO of Ford Motor Company, held the position of Chairman and non-exec CEO along with CEO J. Michael Pocock. Nasser's job was to develop and commercialize new products. PHC was well-equipped to design, develop, manufacture, and market photographic hardware accessories for the instant photography market. Other products and services consisted of eyewear, principally sunglasses, DVD players, and secure identification systems for commercial applications. PHC performed contract manufacturing for and licensed its brand and technology to third parties.

In September 2002, PHC granted exclusive rights to the Polaroid name to World Wide Licenses (WWL) to sell digital cameras under the Polaroid brand for distribution internationally. Giovanni Thomaselli, WWL's managing director, said, "This agreement allows us to combine strong and innovative design with one of the strongest camera brands in the world ... and to improve Polaroid's market share in digital cameras for the future." Polaroid 2-go sold a related but broad line of items via the Internet. At the end of three years, Chairman Jacques Nasser, and CEO, J. Michael Pocock left PHC with reimbursements considered by some to be excessive. Under the directorship of Nasser and Pocock, 4,000 retirees from the original Polaroid Corporation received one-time checks for 47 dollars and lost their medical and life insurance benefits.

On January 7, 2005, a privately held company, Petters Group Worldwide, agreed to pay $426 million to acquire Polaroid Holding Company by merger. Polaroid's board of directors unanimously approved the merger agreement. Renamed Polaroid Corporation following the merger, the company became a wholly owned subsidiary of Petters and was no longer a publicly traded company.

Petters Group Worldwide invests in a variety of companies, and its core portfolio includes retail and wholesale firms. Since 2002, Petters has been a licensee in North America for consumer electronics including DVD players and plasma, LCD, and traditional TVs. Petters' website is a marvel of media "sell." It highlights Polaroid as one of its many brands. At the time of the merger, Chairman Tom Petters said, "Polaroid will become a strategic cornerstone along with our unique business model and attention to our customers needs. This will position us as a global leader in ... innovative imaging and consumer electronics products at an outstanding value." Polaroid's I-Zone instant camera continued to be the nation's top seller, with a price of approximately $15 in 2005. During 2005, Flextronics bought Polaroid's manufacturing operations, deciding to send most of the manufacturing to China.

In bits and pieces, Polaroid's brand name has found its way into a new century of global manufacturing and marketing.

Review Questions

1 At one time, the (original) Polaroid Corporation was considered an ideal model of what a company should be like. What characteristics made it so enviable? Note: After bankruptcy, one of Polaroid's assets was its name, and that was sold to another company (i.e., the new Polaroid Corporation).

2 What major management mistakes destroyed Polaroid's growing dominance over a significant segment of the photographic field?

Spotlight 18-1 (Continued)

3 What happened to the Polaroid patents?

4 What happened to Polaroid's leadership of the digital camera technology?

5 Why is there a new Polaroid company, and what has been learned?

Sources: http://inventors.about.com/library/inventors/blpolaroid.htm; http://web.mit.edu/invent/iow/land.html; http://www.pettersgroup.com/EN/manufacturing.html; http://www.polaroid.com; http://www.primarypdc.com; http://www.intel.com/research/silicon/

mooreslaw.htm. Moore's Law: According to Moore's Law, the number of transistors (semiconductors) on a chip roughly doubles every two years, resulting in more features, increased performance, and decreased cost. Gordon E. Moore received a Ph.D. from Cal Tech and was one of the founders of Fairchild Semiconductor Division of Fairchild Cameras and Instrument Corporation, becoming the director of the Fairchild Research and Development Laboratories. In 1965, he wrote his famous paper predicting an evolution of larger and larger circuit functions on a single semiconductor substrate.

Spotlight 18-2 Balanced Scorecards
Benchmarking the Strategy-Focused Organization

The landmark book *In Search of Excellence: Lessons from America's Best-Run Companies*, started by selecting firms using the 7-S McKinsey Framework, which translates into "comfort slogans" about being close to the customer and keeping things simple, e.g., lean staff and walk-around management. The selection procedure was not based on hard measures except in the finance area, where six numerical scores served as an ultimate screening. Firms that flunked the financial tests were dropped.

Two years later, *Business Week* ran its famous November 5, 1984, "OOPS" cover, which noted that more than one-third of the "excellent 43" firms had fallen on hard times. Critics of the original study were quick to point out that the method of selection was flawed. Many of them advocated expanding the scope and range of the metrics that were employed.

In spite of "OOPS," a follow-up volume, *A Passion for Excellence: The Leadership Difference*, was a resounding success. Another winner of that genre is *Good to Great: Why Some Companies Make the Leap . . . and Others Don't*. These books are replete with anecdotal material and conclusions that managers take seriously. *Good to Great* is assigned reading in a number of companies. However, these books do not represent scholarly work of academics using scientific methods even though the authors often refer to their studies as research.

If hallmarks of excellence could be identified and made part of a theory of management, then emulation of those characteristics would ensure large profits, long-term survivability, and sustainability. Such a theory is not likely to be achieved in the complex, counterintuitive, economic, and psychological domains. An appealing alternative to management fads was initially conceived as an organizational performance measure tool to overcome the limitations of historical accounting-based measures and metrics.

In the early 1990s, Drs. Robert Kaplan (Harvard Business School) and David Norton (president, Balanced Scorecard Collaborative, Inc.) developed a broad-based system of measurement that they called the "Balanced Scorecard." It was tailored to a company's mission statement, strategies and execution, aligning the entire executive management into a collaborative effort from the top down to bring about performance objectives. Without clear communication at every level of the chain of command, management by objective has often proven to be little more than wishes.

Introduced in 1992, the Balanced Scorecard (BSC) has become widely used by western corporations. Intended to create a strategic management model that would counterbalance financial measures, this model included marketing and production excellence. It emphasized the systems connections that tie together all relevant elements of business performance. Kaplan and Norton have pointed out that the balanced scorecard recognizes that financial measures tell the story of the past. Dr. Edwards Deming use to call this style of management "rearview mirror steering."

Steve Kerr, former Chief Learning Officer of Goldman Sachs, has said, "The future is moving so quickly that you can't anticipate it. We have put a tremendous emphasis on quick response instead of planning." Kerr indicated that aware firms will continue to be surprised, but they will be anticipating surprises and prepared for them. Helping to plan for surprises, the Balanced Scorecard can be defined as an integrated framework describing company strategy using four balanced perspectives that have evolved over the years. This framework is a strategic measurement system and communication tool to link all performance measures. In 2007, the following four related activities, measured by the Balanced Scorecard, are critical to nearly all organizations and levels within them.

1 Investing in learning, growth, and innovation capabilities
2 Improving efficiency and productivity of internal business processes
3 Providing and improving customer value
4 Increasing financial value, success, and sustainability

Point 1 covers management of change and transitions. How many successful new products (goods and services) have been created? Is management promoting people out of innovation teams before their efforts pay off? How many day-by-day interactions occur between employees and supervisors?

Point 2 focuses on those business processes that are core competencies. Is P/OM personnel part of the family? Pursuing this vision, do strategies empower employees to strive for continuous improvement?

Point 3 requires specifying how we want customers to see and communicate with us. What are the marketing essentials? Market research is a good basis for measuring customer perception.

Point 4 uses past financial track records to benchmark future achievements, using windshields as well as rearview mirrors. Does evaluation of plans made in points 1, 2, and 3 promise better financial outcomes in the future?

Quality improvement relies on feedback loops that interconnect points 1, 2, 3, and 4 in all possible paths. Process improvement is measurable in terms of better quality, more throughput, and increased product variety (with lower setup costs). Because the BSC is a self-improving metric-based information system with continuous feedback, a company can continuously reappraise its strengths, weaknesses, opportunities, and threats.

P/OM enjoys using the BSC method, and related software, because it brings all parties (marketing, finance, human resources, and accounting) to the same table. Production and operations issues are not well discussed in traditional executive meetings. BSC gives P/OM an ongoing voice in company objectives. After all, BSC defines "excellence" in terms of many P/OM measurements.

Robert Kaplan and David Norton authored their latest book titled *Alignment*, published by Harvard Business School Publishing, 2006. The book addresses the question: "Is every part of your organization marching in the strategic direction you've defined?"

Whether the BSC method and model will give corporations what they need in the long-term future or be replaced by something else remains open. More than 60 large companies are said to be currently using it with success.

Review Questions

1 What is a BSC and who thinks that it has any value?
2 What are the components of the BSC?
3 What has the BSC to do with transition management?
4 What has the BSC to do with business processes?
5 How do BSC components interact to provide P/OM benchmarks?
6 What are the sources of expertise for applications of BSC?

Sources: http://www.bscol.com; Jim Collins. *Good to Great: Why Some Companies Make the Leap ... and Others Don't.* New York: Harper Business, 2001; Robert S. Kaplan and David P. Norton. "Using the Balanced Scorecard as a Strategic Management System." *Harvard Business Review* (January–February 1996); Thomas J. Peters and Robert H. Waterman, Jr. *In Search of Excellence: Lessons from America's Best-Run Companies.* New York: Warner Books, 1982; Thomas J. Peters and Nancy Austin. *A Passion for Excellence: The Leadership Difference.* New York: Warner Books, 1985; Robert S. Kaplan and David P. Norton. Information about *Hall of Fame Reports*, from Balanced Scorecard Collaborative, April 2005.

chapter 8

Summary

Chapter 18 begins with an explanation of new product development, which is a classic example of a crucial project. The chapter emphasizes the relationship between product development and project management. New products (comprised of goods and services) are best chosen to benefit from the special skills and experiences that have been significant in the success of other products for the company. The inventory of knowledge is connected to the knowledge management system, which has core competencies and capabilities as its foundation. Management of both explicit and tacit knowledge is discussed with respect to the stages of new product development, which are concept selection, development, and testing. To promote evaluation of the product-development program, estimation and business modeling are used. A spreadsheet model is created to exemplify the power of a proper business model. If the spreadsheet passes muster, the next stages are prototype construction, testing, process specification, and pilot plant operation.

All of this does not happen by chance. Good project management is essential. Chapter 18 explains that projects are sets of activities designed to accomplish goals. These goals, when achieved, terminate the project. Projects constitute a unique P/OM work configuration. Gantt project-planning charts are introduced and then critical-path methods and PERT are examined. Networks of activities are constructed leading to the determination of critical paths, which are the set of activities that determine project duration being the longest time path from the beginning to the end of the project. Slack is calculated and used for resource leveling aimed at reducing project time.

Some other details of project management that are covered include differences between deterministic and probabilistic time estimates for activity times, different network-construction methods, activities labeled on nodes (AON), activities labeled on arrows (AOA), forward and backward passes to determine the critical path, and the distribution of project-completion times. The topic of multiple projects is introduced, and this is prior to materials in Chapters 19 and 20 that deal with management under forces of change.

Spotlight 18-1 tells a story of projects gone awry. In spite of wonderful new products, the old Polaroid Company went bankrupt. Perhaps the new Polaroid Company will have more luck. Spotlight 18-2 describes balanced scorecards as a means to benchmark the strategy-focused organization. One of the most critical aspects of the BSC is the ability to use project management to develop and launch new products that will keep the firm vital. Enrichment Activity 18 provides an extension of the concepts and methods behind Cost/Time trade-off analysis. Even if these methods are seldom applied with software, because that is difficult to do, the trade-off concepts are valid and support or do not support decisions to pursue more rapid completion of the projects.

Key Terms

Activities-on-arrows (AOA) (p. 762)

Activities-on-nodes (AON) (p. 761)

Backward pass rule (p. 769)

Capabilities (p. 748)

Change management projects (α) (p. 756)

Control management processes (β) (p. 756)

Core competencies (p. 748)

Crash time (p. 778)

Critical-path methods (CPM) (p. 759)

Engineering change orders (ECOs) (p. 754)

Explicit knowledge (p. 748)

Forward pass rule (p. 766)

Knowledge management (KM) (p. 747)

Market research (p. 748)

Multiple project management (p. 779)

New product development (p. 747)

Normal time (p. 778)

PERT (p. 760)

PERT/Cost/Time (p. 795)

Project/Cost/Time (p. 795)

Projects (p. 753)

Resource leveling (p. 777)

Slack (p. 769)

Tacit knowledge (p. 749)

Trade-offs (p. 778)

Review Questions

1 How does new product development relate to project management?
2 Why is knowledge management a foundation for new product development?
3 What is the difference between explicit and tacit knowledge? Why does it matter?
4 What is the difference between core competencies and management capabilities?
5 How do the differences in Question 4 relate to the differences in Question 3?
6 How are spreadsheet-based business models used to evaluate new product quality?
7 What is a pilot plant? How does a pilot plant link new product development and project management?
8 What are the unique attributes of project management? Frame the answer in terms of other P/OM work configurations.
9 Explain the construction and use of Gantt project-planning charts.
10 What are the strengths and weaknesses of Gantt project-planning charts?
11 Classify projects by type and describe project life cycles.
12 Why is the project manager considered a leader?
13 Why is teamwork repeatedly mentioned when discussing good project management?
14 The current air-traffic control system is one of two systems that were funded using the concept of parallel-path project development. Can this dual expenditure be justified?
15 What is PERT's relationship to critical-path methods?
16 What does the forward pass accomplish in critical-path methods?
17 What does the backward pass accomplish in critical-path methods?
18 What is the critical path and how does knowing it help project managers?
19 What is slack and how does knowing it help project managers?
20 What are the differences between deterministic and probabilistic activity time estimates?
21 Evaluate the strengths and weaknesses of the beta method for obtaining activity time estimates.
22 What are the strengths and weaknesses of PERT?
23 Explain how resource leveling is done and for what purposes.
24 Describe how Cost/Time trade-off methods can be used given the decision to spend an additional 10 percent on the project.
25 Describe project crashing and contrast it to normal time.
26 What advantages can be gained by, and what are the dangers of, using crashing?
27 What are the challenges and opportunities of managing multiple projects?

Problems Section

Note: This section has various problems that can be formulated and solved using QuantMethods Production/Operations Management software (QMpom). Using the QMpom module called Project Management Models (CPM/PERT) will facilitate solving all of the problems that are in this section.

1 Set up teams to work together on the construction of a Gantt chart for the project of implementing the introduction of a new product on a national rollout basis. This new product is a shampoo that claims that it stimulates the growth of thick hair. Market research reports that the new product will obtain more than 50 percent of the market by year's end if the store price of $1.50 is used. The problem that marketing foresees is not having enough product to meet supermarket demands. The suggestion has been made to hold back the demand by charging $10.50 per bottle initially. The price would be reduced gradually as production grows to meet the potential demand.

   First, sketch out an approach. Note how working with a team improves the creativity of solutions and the quality of problem solving.

2 Set up teams to work together on the construction of a Gantt chart for the project of implementing the engineering change order (ECO) to replace the faulty motherboard in 500 computers. The steps, setup times (SUT), and times per unit (t) are given in minutes. One person is doing the work in batches of 500, i.e., step a is completed on 500 computers before step b is begun.

   a. Remove 4 screws and lift off case: $SUT = 60$, $t = 2$.
   b. Detach cables: $SUT = 70$, $t = 1$.
   c. Remove faulty motherboard: $SUT = 15$, $t = 0.5$.
   d. Replace with new motherboard: $SUT = 15$, $t = 0.5$.

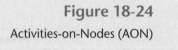

Figure 18-24

Activities-on-Nodes (AON)

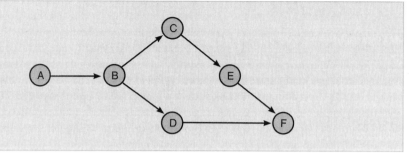

e. Attach cables: SUT $= 45$, $t = 3$.
f. Put cover on with four screws: SUT $= 60$, $t = 4$.
g. Inspection check: plug in and turn on: SUT $= 20$, $t = 3$.
h. Mark computers that do not pass test: SUT $= 30$, $t = 1$.

First, sketch out an approach. Note how working with a team improves the creativity of solutions and the quality of problem solving.

3 Use the team approach to draw a Gantt project chart (for Problem 2 data) but in this case two people are working at adjacent stations. The second person starts to work on step b as soon as the first person completes step a on 10 computers. Thereafter, let the two people operate in a logical way. Note that the second person has 80 minutes to set up for step b. Setup time for step a is 60 minutes, and 10 units take two minutes each for an additional 20 minutes.

4 Convert the Gantt project-planning chart of steps required to bring a new car to market (Figure 18-3) into an appropriate critical-path, PERT-type diagram. Make whatever assumptions you require. Discuss the advantages and disadvantages of each form of representation.

5 Convert Figure 18-24, where activities are labeled on nodes (AON), into an equivalent figure where activities are labeled on arrows (AOA).

6 The Gantt project chart in Figure 18-25 has vertical lines drawn upward from the upper left-hand corner of each activity bar. Where these lines intersect the prior (upper) activity is the "milestone" that when reached allows that next activity to begin. To illustrate, the activity "order materials" is 13/20 finished when the activity "receive materials" becomes active presumably because materials ordered earlier begin to be received. Note that the position of "Build A" is triggered by a milestone in the "Design" activity. There is no overlap with "Receive Materials." How can this be explained?

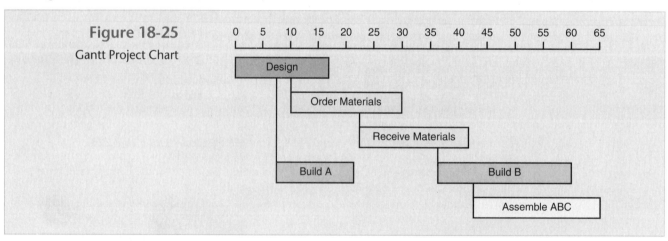

Figure 18-25

Gantt Project Chart

7 Using the information in Problem 6, draw a PERT diagram with activities-on-nodes (AON).

8 Using the information in Problems 6 and 7, draw a PERT diagram with activities-on-arrows (AOA).

9 The Delta Company manufactures a full line of cosmetics. A competitor recently developed a new skin rejuvenating cream that appears to be successful and potentially damaging to Delta's skin care position in the marketplace. The sales manager has asked the operations manager (P/OM) what the shortest possible time would be for Delta to reach the marketplace with a new product packaged in a competitively redesigned container. The P/OM has drawn up the following table:

Activity	Initial Event	Terminal Event	Duration (Days)
Design product	1	2	30
Design package	1	3	15
Test market package	3	5	20
Distribute to dealers	5	6	20
Order package materials	3	4	15
Fabricate package	4	5	30
Order materials for product	2	4	3
Test-market product	2	7	25
Fabricate product	4	7	20
Package product	7	5	4

  a. Construct the appropriate PERT diagram.

  b. Apply the estimates of activity duration to the arrows.

10   Using information in Problem 9, make the forward pass to fill out the ES and EF part of the 4-box scorecard. As a reminder: ES = earliest start, EF = earliest finish, LS = latest start, LF = latest finish, and EF = ES + t, LS = LF − t, t = activity time.

ES	EF
LS	LF

What is the shortest feasible completion time for this project?

11   Using the information in Problems 9 and 10, make the backward pass to fill out the LS and LF part of the 4-box scorecard. As a reminder: LS = latest start, LF = latest finish. Identify the activities on the critical path.

12   Use the information in Problems 9, 10, and 11 to determine the slack for each activity. Neither the sales manager nor the P/OM is satisfied with the way the project is designed. However, the P/OM insists that because of the pressure of time, the company will be forced to follow this plan. In what ways does this plan violate good practice?

13   Use the information in Problems 9, 10, 11, and 12. The decision is made to form an engineering task force with people from sales, production, distribution, engineering, and R&D. The first recommendation of this team is to use resource leveling in the initial design-product and design-package phases. It is noted that one-for-one applies, which means that if a person is moved from package to product design, the package-design activity time will increase by one day and the product-design activity time will decrease by one day. Up to 10 people can be shifted in this way. Do you recommend doing so?

    Hint: the only way to tell is to try some applications of smart resource leveling.

14   The engineering task force has redesigned the project for the Delta Company as follows:

    The product and package will be test-marketed together, which has necessitated adding a dummy activity for test-market package.

Activity	Initial Event	Terminal Event	Duration (Days)
Design product	1	2	30
Design package	1	3	15
Test-market package	3	2	0
Distribute to dealers	5	6	20
Order package materials	3	4	15
Fabricate package	4	5	30
Order materials for product	2	4	3
Test-market product and package	2	7	25
Fabricate product	4	7	20
Package product	7	5	4

a. Construct the appropriate PERT diagram.

b. Apply the estimates of activity duration to the arrows.

15 Make the forward pass using the information in Problem 14. Complete the ES and EF boxes (part of the 4-box scorecard). What is the shortest feasible completion time for this project?

16 Make the backward pass using the information in Problems 14 and 15, to fill out the LS and LF part of the 4-box scorecard. Identify the activities on the critical path.

17 Use the information in Problems 14, 15, and 16.

a. Determine the slack for each activity.

b. Evaluate the project design.

c. Compare the results of Problems 9–13 with the results for Problems 14–17.

18 Although dummy arrows are a finer point of PERT construction, they play an important role when needed as in Problem 14 where the engineering task force recommended that test-marketing the product and the package could be done together. When dummies were discussed in Figure 18-7, it was stated that the dummy activity could as well have preceded activity C, instead of activity B. Redraw Figure 18-7 to create this alternative. Does it make a difference?

19 Three people were shifted from activity B_1, which has 22 days of slack, to activity A_1 on the critical path of Figure 18-18. The assumption was made that each added person decreases activity time t by one day. Similarly, it was assumed that each removed person increases activity time t by one day. The results of this resource leveling were shown in Figure 18-23. Using the same assumptions with respect to the same two activities, A_1 and B_1, shift four people (instead of three) from B_1 to A_1. Discuss the results.

20 Using the information in Problem 19, shift two people from B_1 to A_1. Discuss the results.

21 You are requested to make a model of a PERT network out of string. Use the PERT chart for filmmaking in Figure 18-26. String models of a project network require that the length of the pieces of string be cut to scale. The length of string should be proportional to the time of the activity. The pieces are tied together in conformance with the PERT precedence diagram. When the strings are pulled taut (between the starting node and the final node), the critical path is revealed as the tight part of the string model. The other strings show their degree of slack by drooping. Comment on the applicability of this analog model (a) for solving real problems; (b) for teaching the concepts.

Figure 18-26

PERT Chart for Filmmaking

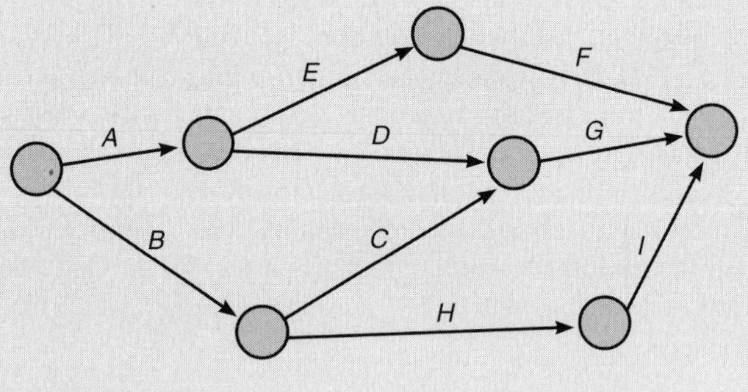

Practice Quiz

1 Every book that The Famous Publisher (TFP) brings to market is a project of many activities. There are various people who manage the stages of publication. Selection of the authors and the subject of the book is the beginning of a chain of events that results in bound, printed paper, or a CD/DVD, or an Internet text, or all three. TFP's managers recognize that they are dealing with projects all of the time, but they do not employ project management methods. The general manager and the chief editor have assembled their top managers for analysis of this situation. A list of topics has been circulated for the meeting containing points a. through f. Which one of these points is incorrect?

a. The publishing business does not have time lines like other projects. This is because authors are like artists. They work when they are inspired and the clock does not keep time as it does for a construction job.

b. Knowledge management is applicable to the publishing business in several ways. TFP needs to catalog who are the experts in the various activities that make book publishers successful. A directory of these people needs to be created so that issues can be resolved as quickly as possible.

    c.   TFP's KM experts can be categorized by the amount of explicit knowledge versus tacit knowledge that their specialization represents. For example, the editors and the production people can set standards for the condition of the manuscript when it is submitted. That way, less editorial and styling work is required. Production schedule methods are entirely explicit.

    d.   On the other hand, issues of permissions and royalties for copyright-protected materials may involve negotiations. Similarly, requesting authors to make changes that reviewers suggest might be better handled by people experienced in the tacit knowledge domain of personalities and negotiating techniques.

    e.   There are core competencies with respect to manuscript preparation in special page preparation software. There are also managing capabilities for keeping production teams on time and running quality control on the transformed manuscript, which epitomizes the input–output transformation model of P/OM.

    f.   Core competencies are particularly important to manuscripts that are transformed into Internet-available texts. The Internet permits links to be explored by readers, and interactive dialogs can be embedded in the manuscripts.

2   Continuing with The Famous Publisher's quest for structured project management, the chief editor suggests that the assembled group start with the idea that new books should be treated as if they were new products. This means developing new books according to marketing principles rather than waiting for book ideas to be brought to the publisher by agents and authors. A list of applicable concepts (a. through f.) was drawn up and circulated. Identify the single incorrect statement.

    a.   Concept selection would read like a publisher's wish list of titles. Perhaps 10 such titles would be developed with a page description of what that title would entail.

    b.   Idea development would determine which authors are most suitable and what it would take to enlist their support for the project, i.e., assign writers to books (title by title).

    c.   Market research would now be used to test the concepts and the titles. A book failure would be defined by market research results indicating that sales volume would be below the breakeven point.

    d.   An interesting issue arises as to whether the publisher would be better off paying the writer by time instead of paying royalties on sales. The business model would make estimates of cost, time, and the risk of failure (defined as an expected sales volume below the breakeven volume). If the expected volume of sales is low, then the royalty payment method is probably preferred. If the expected volume of sales is high, then a single payment to the writer is likely to be chosen.

    e.   Authors selected to write specific books may not agree to the chosen method of reimbursement. This is an area for negotiation. The process of selecting authors should take into account the type of payment that is likely and the type of author that has been selected. An issue for discussion is why should TFP accept books that have low expected sales volume? If TFP adopts the *new product development* (NPD) model used by *consumer package goods* companies (CPG), then books that have low sales-volume estimates (and poor profitability) will be rejected.

    f.   NPD for CPG companies (see e. for acronyms) includes testing prototypes (such as a new shampoo and its container). The final step in the NPD is the process specification and the pilot plant. Both of these steps still need to be taken by TFP.

3   A large consumer package goods company (CPG) is getting ready to launch its newest bar soap. The marketing–production task force has met with the CEO, and he has raised a series of issues about preparations for the launch. This is the list a. to e. Which one statement is incorrect?

    a.   There are four project (not product) life cycle stages. The first stage is to fully specify the goals of the project. For example, specify how many cases are to be sold in the first three months of the national rollout. That kind of detail is required.

    b.   Stage 2 is planning all the activities that are required to fulfill the goals. Activities and their time lines need to be comprehensive. For example, explain where and how this much product will be made. Give the pros and cons of using an intermittent flow shop as compared to a dedicated flow shop. Discuss project characteristics including completion time, costs, critical path, slack amounts and with which activity branches slacks exist, opportunities to speed things up, and threats to the plan.

    c.   Carrying out project activities comes next. Full reporting is needed of how resources are being utilized. For example, track how many people are working on the various component parts of this project over time. Show the payroll and material expenses on a daily and cumulative basis. Project managers must report on exceptions, missed deadlines, and new threats to successful completion. If expediting is required, explain what is being done.

    d.   Project-completion reporting can sum up goals exceeded, matched, and not realized. This is for time, money, quality, and competitive responses. Plans for disbanding or for continuing teams with other goals and objectives should be outlined. For example, if there are going to be further NPD for bar soaps, this project team would be ideal for the next assignment.

e. Performance reports on all team members are needed to finalize the project. Grades should be given so that future teams can be drawn from the very best. Top project managers should be given increased process-management responsibilities. The best project managers could now be given the production lines for the new bar soap.

4 According to the CPG project manager, there are a number of important guidelines for the effective management of projects. The marketing–production task force responded to the CEO and has now prepared a list of additional facts to consider. They have circulated this list amongst themselves and sent copies to the project manager and to the CEO. Both are complimentary, but the project manager takes issue with one of the team's points a. through e. Which statement is bothering the project manager?

a. Often there are many participants working on some aspect of the same project. For example, there is a team working on packaging the soap so that it stays attractive. Packages on display get shabby from customer handling. Other teams are working on marketing, advertising, and speeding up the production process while maintaining high quality. The key to success is communication so that everyone is reminded about the project goals and is informed about the current status.

b. Duplication of project activities should be eliminated except if major differences of opinion exist about how to do something. Also, parallel-path activities are warranted if there is no opinion about how to achieve some goal or if there is serious risk of failure if the wrong fork in the road is taken.

c. Multiple project managers are better than one alone. Having several people running the show broadens perspective. It shares stress and lets several sets of shoulders carry the burden. Projects are so rich in detail that one person cannot be blamed for everything.

d. Project management is based on well-designed information systems. The system reports regularly on status for each ongoing activity, which includes many supplier activities. Errors in estimates such as how long a given activity would take need to be corrected as soon as the new information is obtained.

e. Gantt project-planning charts are helpful. They provide graphic evidence of project activities, sequences, time status, and problem areas. As soon as the project is defined, a Gantt chart should be created, and it needs to be kept up-to-date. There needs to be one dedicated Gantt charter on the project team.

5 The pizza chain manager in the seminar class has taken great interest in Gantt charts for project planning as well as critical-path methods (CPM) and PERT. Every time a new product is offered, all employees go through a series of training steps related to making the product and serving it to the customers. The ideal way to handle the new product introduction is in the form of a project. The manager realizes that Gantt charts do not optimize resource utilization, whereas PERT charts can be used for that purpose. Yet, he feels that there is a special utility derived from Gantt charting that makes it the best way to start a project, even when it is planned to follow Gantt with PERT. The pizza chain manager has written down some points (a. through j.) that seem relevant and has asked his teammates to provide feedback. Team members do this and report two errors. What two points are in error?

a. PERT and CPM are both methods for determining the critical path, which is the *longest time path through the network of precedence-sequenced activities* required for the project. PERT and CPM are so similar that only one or the other needs to be mentioned. The pizza manager prefers PERT because of its use by NASA.

b. The features that differentiate PERT from CPM include their histories and their methods of estimation. First, their histories: PERT was developed by the Special Projects Office of the U.S. Navy with the assist of Booz Allen Hamilton and Lockheed Missile Systems, for the Polaris missile program. CPM was developed by DuPont and Remington Rand (now Unisys) for construction of a chemical plant. Dates of development for both PERT and CPM were about the same—1957–1958.

c. One explanation for the nearly simultaneous creation of two critical-path methods was the need to deal effectively with increasingly complex projects. Prior to the mid-1950s, the state of the art in computing was not up to the task.

d. The second distinguishing feature is that PERT has provisions for using the beta distribution for estimation purposes. Beta has three parameters, which take the form of pessimistic, optimistic, and most likely (modal) estimates. The beta distribution is remarkably well-suited to conflate these three disparate points of view.

e. The equations for conflation can be exemplified with a simple numerical illustration. Assume that the pessimist estimates two hours to hang a picture on the wall; the optimist estimates 18 minutes. Records show that (for this class of picture-hanging parameters) most often this activity takes 45 minutes. The estimate of the mean of the distribution (called t_e) is $1/6(18 + 120) + 2/3(45) = 55$ minutes.

f. The variance of the beta distribution is $[1/6(120 - 18)]^2 = 289$, which means that the standard deviation is 17. There is a 68 percent probability that the true value of the time to hang the picture will range between 38 and 75 minutes.

g. The Gantt chart, as well as PERT charts, indicates when project completion will occur. The problem with Gantt charts is that they do not indicate which activities are on the critical path. Guesses could be made, but not if the project has many activities.

h. The reason that project managers (who advocate use of computers for projects) like to start with Gantt charting is that Gantt brings project managers closer to the core of the problem. Gantt provides a hands-on feeling for project planners.

i. Gantt encourages visualization of project activities. This allows better insight about the need for doing activities in a different way than they are currently being done.

j. Milestones trigger the start of next-in-line activities in the sequence of activities that are part of the Gantt project-planning system. PERT charts need to create activities that end before and start after a milestone. There are pros and cons for both types of situations.

6 The managers of Oil Changers, Inc. (OCI) have told the class that their company has been using PERT for customer-based projects. They classify a project as a set of activities bundled together to meet customer demand. For example, a project might be to change and rotate tires or replace a muffler assembly. The managers presented a typical situation to the class members that permits calculations of forward pass, backward pass, critical path, and slack. The precedence diagram can be stated in terms of AON and then converted to AOA by the students. Thus, for AON, A precedes B, which precedes D; also, A precedes C, which precedes D.

The OCI managers point out that every aspect of the problem is simplified by creating the AON graph for these relationships. That way, a visual understanding of the problem develops. Then, an AOA graph can be drawn from the AON graph. After all class members had drawn their graphs, the OCI managers handed out a list of points (a. to e.) concerning important calculations that can be made and problems that project planners can expect to encounter. The faculty leader has noted that there are two erroneous statements. Class members are asked to identify the incorrect statements.

a. When the AON chart is converted to AOA, a problem will be encountered. Namely, two arrows will have been labeled activity D. This situation cannot be permitted. The computer will not be able to distinguish between the two D arrows.

b. Ambiguity can be removed by redrawing the AOA network with a dummy activity that requires zero time. The dummy is inserted between the end of arrow A and the beginning of arrow B. This alters the prior precedence chart to: A precedes dummy, which precedes B, which precedes D; also, A precedes C, which precedes D.

c. With the dummy in place, the forward pass algorithm produces the "earliest" results in the table. The earliest start (ES) and earliest finish (EF) boxes can be completed, but the latest start (LS) and latest finish (LF) cannot be completed until the backward pass is done.

Activities	Earliest Start (ES)	Latest Start (LS)	Slack	Earliest Finish (EF)	Latest Finish (EF)
A	0			5	
Dummy	5			5	
B	5			9	
C	5			12	
D	12			15	

d. It is evident that the project as currently designed will take 12 days. Also, the time required for each activity is evident from the subtraction of EF minus ES. Thus, A = 5 days, dummy = 0 days, B = 4 days, C = 7 days, and D = 3 days.

e. Slack cannot be determined until the sideways pass is complete. Once that is done, it will be possible to specify the critical path. The length of the critical path is already known.

7 Managers from the Expensive Shoe Company (ESC) ask that the exercise started by their classmates from Oil Changers, Inc. (OCI) be continued so that the PERT table can be completed. Everyone agrees that they have enough information to use the precedence diagram for the backward pass. They have continued the practice of creating a list of conclusions (a. to e.) and, as in Problem 6, point out there are two mistakes to be noted. Which points contain the errors?

Activities	Earliest Start (ES)	Latest Start (LS)	Slack	Earliest Finish (EF)	Latest Finish (LF)
A	0	0	0	5	5
Dummy	5	8		5	8
B	5	8	3	9	12
C	5	5	0	12	12
D	12	12	0	15	15

a.   The forward pass rule encountered the special situation of two or more arrows converging at a single node. Convergence occurred when the ends of arrows B and C (indicating conclusions of activities B and C) entered the node from which activity D's arrow begins. The rule is to choose the largest value of EF; the choice is between B's EF = 9 and C's EF = 12. The latter becomes D's ES = 12.

b.   The backward pass rule encountered the special situation of two or more arrows emanating from a single node. That occurred where the dummy arrow and activity C's arrow begin at the conclusion of activity A. The rule is to choose the smallest value of LS; the choice is between the dummy's LS = 8 and C's LS = 5. The latter becomes A's LF = 5.

c.   Slack can only be calculated by subtracting (for each activity) the earliest start time from the latest start time, i.e., LS – ES. Slack is associated with an activity, but if a sequence of activities has slack, that is called a slack path.

d.   The critical path, by definition, has zero slack. It is the longest time path of activities for the project that defines project completion. Any slippage along the critical path will delay the project. Therefore, in this example, the critical path is A⇒C⇒D.

e.   Activities that are not on the critical path are the dummy and activity B. The dummy always requires zero activity time, so slack is meaningless for that arrow. Slack is simply a computational convenience. However, slack of 5 days that is associated with activity B is meaningful and useful. This is demonstrated in Problem 8.

8   Everyone in the class is happy to learn how project managers determine critical paths. Organizational awareness about project management is low. When that fact is recognized, then the large body of knowledge about projects can be brought to the table. Understanding how to determine the longest time path of a project becomes a management necessity. But, that raises the issue of how to modify the critical path. Students in this class already know how to calculate the amount of project slack that is available. Now, they need to understand how slack can be used to modify the time length of the critical path. All class members agree to create a list of discussion points about this topic. The faculty leader edits these statements, noting that there is one point that should be changed because it is not true. Which point should be changed?

a.   Slack is often an underutilized resource. This is especially true when conscious project management is not practiced. Those aware of critical paths do not overlook or ignore slack. However, if project managers are happy with the critical path (time of completion), and with the proposed budget, consideration of slack is unnecessary. In this case, "ignorance is bliss."

b.   The data used in Problem 7 apply to Problem 8. An additional fact is that C's activity time of $t = 7$ days can be changed to $t - 1 = 6$ days by transferring one worker from activity B to activity C. In turn, the activity time for B goes from $t = 4$ days to $t + 1 = 5$ days because B has one less worker. This process is known as resource leveling.

c.   Resource leveling can only take place when there is slack. The resource is moved from the activity with slack to the critical path. The best trade-off rule is to move slack resources to that activity on the critical path that will result in the largest decrease in activity time.

d.   Specifically, transfer workers from slack activities so as to achieve the largest reduction in critical-path time. If all activities on the critical path are shortened by the same amount of time, then there is no special place along the critical path to favor in awarding the extra resources.

e.   If the project is large and has nearly-zero slack activities throughout, then the project is a challenge for management. Managers can only handle (monitor for slippage) a limited number of critical activities at one time. When there is slippage at a critical activity, the manager has immediate responsibilities to expedite (e.g., get suppliers to deliver on time, replace faulty o-rings, etc.). Under these circumstances, it is good project management to bring in new resources so that the entire project is not critical.

9   Students have requested that Problem 9 address issues raised but not treated in Problem 8. For example, the effects on the critical path of moving slack to critical activities. The question has arisen about using resource leveling for multiple projects because it works so successfully on the multiple paths within a single project. Another issue is the question of using mean and variance to account for variability of critical-path measures. A new list of statements is created by the class members. It has five points, a. to e., and two of these points are wrong. Where are these errors?

a.   The one-for-one assumption is: Take a worker away—add a day; add a worker and subtract a day. Using the one-for-one assumption, when a worker from B is moved to C, the effect is to decrease the length of the critical path from 15 to 14 days without changing the critical path (i.e., A⇒C⇒D) and without increasing project costs.

b.   Using the one-for-one assumption, when two workers are moved from activity B to activity C, the effect is to switch the critical path to A⇒dummy⇒B⇒D, which yields a completion time of 13 days.

c.   Multiple projects are equivalent to independent paths within one project. One launching by NASA typifies this multiplicity of ongoing activities that join at (or near) the end of the project. Independence is the same as saying that nodes are not shared. There is good reason to use resource leveling between multiple projects. Efficient employment of resources benefits the overall organization.

d.   An issue must be faced that is not unlike one that occurs within any single project. Namely, how truly transferable are resources between activities? The one-for-one assumption is more likely to exist for intertwined paths of a single project than for the independent paths of multiple projects. Nevertheless, cross-training for somewhat similar activities can be viewed as an option for project management.

e.   Multiple projects are usually totally independent of each other. Nevertheless, to a limited extent, resource leveling can be used in spite of the independence between projects. Trading resources between activities is possible when the activities are functionally equivalent. For example, a welder on the Brooklyn Bridge can weld as well on the George Washington Bridge. A stone and marble mason could work on the cathedral at Notre Dame de Chartres as well as Notre-Dame Cathedral in Paris.

10   Before this seminar class graduates and gets a certificate indicating efforts to become accomplished project managers, the faculty insisted that one more set of exercises be assigned. These are the issues that often get missed during project-management instructions. A series of points (a. to g.) were developed and provided to all members of the seminar class. The question is, "If any of these points are incorrect, which are they?"

a.   Testing activity results is a familiar part of project management. Sometimes, it turns out that the system fails the test. For example, the pipe leaks, or the meat is still tough. Because of the extensive nature of PERT diagrams, it is not possible to cycle back to an earlier node. Therefore, it is necessary to build test failures, repair, and retesting into the PERT charts initially. A risk-averse strategy is to assume failure and extend the time of the risky activity accordingly.

b.   The *failure-repair-retest* sequence may not have affected the critical path. If it seems to be prudent, because failures are common to this activity, two or more of these redo loops can be included in the extensive network form. When the redo loop impacts the critical path, then the critical path should be calculated with and without the *failure-repair-retest* sequence. As soon as the activity passes the test, the safety provision should be dropped out.

c.   When an earthquake severely damaged a California freeway, Caltran made a contract with a construction company that penalized that company if completion of the repair took longer than an agreed-upon date. This is not an unusual provision. What was different was a reward for early completion. The reward increased as the completion became earlier. The actual completion date was sooner than anyone had expected.

d.   To exemplify the penalty–reward situation, assume that activities A, B, C, and D are associated with a mean time for completion and the variance of the distribution. This is in contrast to the beta distribution, which has optimistic, pessimistic, and most likely estimates that conflate to provide an estimate of the mean.

Activity	Mean Time	Variance
A	5	1
B	4	6
C	7	1
D	3	2
Dummy	0	0

For the path A⇒C⇒D, the total mean time is 15 and the total variance is 4. For the path A⇒dummy⇒B⇒D, the total mean time is 12 and the total variance is 9.

Variances are the square of the standard deviation, and these can be summed for well-behaved distributions (e.g., the normal distribution is assumed in this case).

e. The standard deviation of path A⇒C⇒D is 2. The range for plus and minus one standard deviation for this path could produce a value as high or higher than 15 + 2. It could produce a value as low or lower than 15 − 2. There is a 32 percent probability that one or the other of these extremes will occur.

f. The standard deviation of path A⇒dummy⇒B⇒D is 3. The range for plus and minus one standard deviation for this path could produce a value as high or higher than 12 + 3. It could produce a value as low or lower than 12 − 3. There is a 32 percent probability that one or the other of these extremes will occur.

g. From points e. and f., there is a reasonable possibility that the current critical path, A⇒C⇒D, could take on the value 13, and the other path could become the critical path with a value of 15. When there is variability, it is essential to monitor all paths that could become critical if the dice roll that way.

Additional Readings

Burke, R. *Project Management: Planning and Control*, 2e. New York: Wiley, 1994.

Hartley, J. R. *Concurrent Engineering: Shortening Lead Times, Raising Quality, and Lowering Costs.* Cambridge, MA: Productivity Press, 1992.

Heldman, K. PMP: *Project Management Professional Study Guide.* Alameda, CA: Sybex Publishing, April 2002.

Kerzner, H. *Project Management: A Systems Approach to Planning, Scheduling and Control*, 8e. New York: Wiley, 2003.

Meridith, J. R., and S. J. Mantel. *Project Management: A Managerial Approach.* New York: Wiley, 1995.

Project Management Institute. *Essentials of Project Management.* Philadelphia, PA: PMI, 2003.

———. *A Guide to the Project Management Body of Knowledge.* Philadelphia, PA: PMI, 2000.

Pyron, T., et al. *Using Microsoft Project 2002.* Indianapolis, IN: Que Publishing, September 2000.

Scholtes, P. R., et al. *The Team Handbook.* Joiner Associates (608-238-8134). Madison, WI: Que Publishing, 1989.

Shaughnessy, H. *Collaboration Management: New Project and Partnering Techniques.* New York: Wiley, 1994.

Tabaka, Jean. *Collaboration Explained: Facilitation Skills for Software Project Leaders.* Boston, MA: Addison-Wesley Professional. 2006. (While this book focuses on software projects of which there are myriads, the ideas and anecdotes are valuable for all applications of project collaboration.)

Uyttewaal, E. *Dynamic Scheduling with Microsoft Project 2000: The Book By and For Professionals.* New York: International Institute for Learning, Inc., June 2001.

Project Software:

Thousands of options exist. See http://www.project-management-software.org

Click on Project Management. Many options work with Microsoft Office Project Standard (or Professional) 2007. Numerous options are web-based.

Notes

1. Gary Hamel and C. K. Prahalad. "The Core Competence of the Corporation." *Harvard Business Review* (May–June 1990).
2. George Stalk, Philip Evans, and Lawrence E. Shulman. "Competing on Capabilities: The New Rules of Corporate Strategy." *Harvard Business Review* (March–April 1992).
3. Tracy Kidder. *The Soul of a New Machine.* Boston, MA: Little, Brown & Co., 1981.
4. This table assumes a normal distribution, which would result if a number of beta distributions were added together to form a single distribution for the project as a whole. See the Appendix for the entire Normal Distribution Table.

Number of Standard Deviations ± ($k\sigma$) from the Mean	Probability That the Actual Time Falls Within the Specified Range
1.00	0.680
1.64	0.900
1.96	0.950
3.00	0.997

Enrichment Activity 18: Project/Cost/Time (and Quality)

Project/Cost/Time relationships are often referred to as **PERT/Cost/Time**. They begin in the same way that standard Pert/Time starts, i.e., with the precedence-based network of activities. However, in this case, two separate estimates for each activity are derived. These are:

Crash time: A minimum time estimate for each activity and the associated cost.
Normal time: A minimum cost estimate for each activity and its associated time.

Figure EA18-1 shows the relationships between some sample pairs of estimates.

The data for these Cost/Time relationships are presented in Table EA18-1 for numerical clarity.

The best way to understand how to use these numbers is to apply them. This is done in Figure EA18-2, where activities A, B, C, and D are illustrated in normal-time and crash-time networks. The network on the left is based on the normal (minimum cost, max-time) estimates for each activity. The network on the right is based on crash-time estimates.

The critical path (shown by darker lines) for normal times is CD. The Earliest Finish (EF) for the upper branch of the network is 17. EF is 22 for the bottom branch which, being longer, is the critical path. Shortest completion time for this network is 22.

The network on the right is based on the crash-time (maximum cost, minimum-time) estimates for each activity. The critical path remains CD. Earliest finish in the two-box scorecards is 9 for the upper branch and 17 for the lower branch. Thus, 17 is the length of the critical path under crash-time conditions.

If 22 days until project completion is unacceptable—then, crashing C and D will increase costs from 14 to 20. This is a 43 percent increase. The decrease in time from 22 to 17 is a 23 percent decrease. It should be noted that there may be no advantage in crashing A and B, which in normal time is 17. However, the entire network becomes the critical path if A and B remain at normal time while C and D are crashed. Slack of 5 shared by A and B in the all-normal configuration is removed when only C and D are crashed.

Project/Cost/Time

Measuring and modeling the trade-offs between short activity times and costly methods to achieve them. Similarly, long activity times save money.

PERT/Cost/Time

Spend more—finish faster; spend less—finish in normal time.

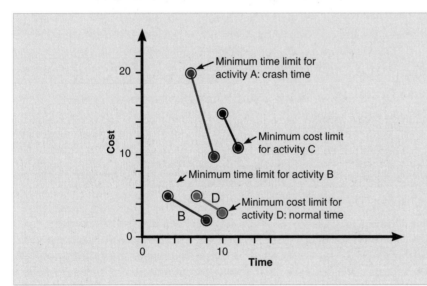

Figure EA18-1

Cost/Time Relationships

Linearity is assumed over the specified ranges of costs and times. End points of each line are assumed to be limits for activities A, B, C, and D.

Activity	Normal max *t*	Normal min *c*	Crash min *t*	Crash max *c*
A	9	10	6	20
B	8	2	3	5
C	12	11	10	15
D	10	3	7	5

Table EA18-1

Data Table for Normal and Crash Times (*t*) and Normal and Crash Costs (c)

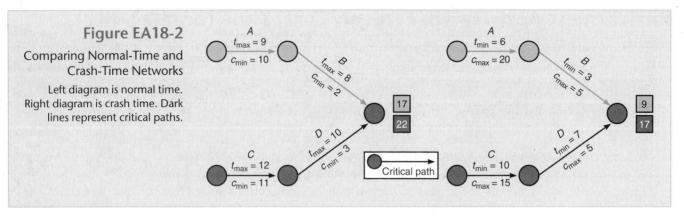

Figure EA18-2

Comparing Normal-Time and Crash-Time Networks

Left diagram is normal time. Right diagram is crash time. Dark lines represent critical paths.

Another alternative is to crash specific activities along the normal-time critical path but not all activities on that path. In this case, crash either C or D. In this way, the critical path can be shortened selectively until such time that

1 Another path becomes critical, and then it is selectively reduced, or
2 The modified critical path is acceptable

As a rule of thumb, select first those activities along the critical path where the ratio of cost increases (Δ) to time reductions (Δ) is smallest. Thus, select those activities on the critical path where

$$|\Delta Cost| \div |\Delta Time|$$

is smallest. Then the next-to-smallest ratio is used, and so on, until a satisfactory compromise between time and cost is achieved. If the critical path switches, the next alterations are made along the new path. Absolute signs $|\Delta C| \div |\Delta T|$ are used so that plus changes in the numerator and minus changes in the denominator do not confuse the selection of the smallest ratio number.

Trade-off models in project planning represent an advanced aspect of P/OM capabilities. Project management abilities enable changes to be made to the product line, to the organization, and to the environment.

Enrichment Challenges 18

Using the QMpom module called Project Management Models (CPM/PERT) will facilitate solving the five (5) problems that are numbered 1 through 5.

1 Entertainment is a service area that has demonstrated growing awareness of the importance of P/OM for improving productivity and quality. Filmmaking uses P/OM for various scheduling activities as well as layout on location. Movies and films are costly and complex projects that benefit from the application of critical-path methods.

   The PERT network in Figure 18-26 (which appears in the end-of-chapter Problems Section) has been developed by the film's producer. It goes hand-in-glove with the following table, which provides crash times and normal times. It also gives cost information for the activities required to make the next major box-office winner.

Activity	t_{min}	t_{max}	c_{min}	c_{max}
A	5	9	5	12
B	10	12	4	10
C	3	8	9	15
D	6	7	3	8
E	4	14	12	20
F	5	7	9	12
G	2	3	6	11
H	7	10	2	9
I	3	5	7	9

Find the critical path if all activities follow normal time.

2 Using the information in Problem 1, find the critical path if all activities are crashed.

3 Using the information in Problems 1 and 2, compare the slack that exists in normal time versus crash time.

4 Consistent with Problem 3, what are the total costs of normal time versus crash time?

5 Use the information in Problem 1. Assume that the director wants a target date halfway between the required total project times of crash-time and normal-time planning.

    a. Use resource leveling with cost and time trade-offs to achieve the objective.

    b. How can resource leveling over time and between activities be applied to the project of filming a movie? Treat both the overtime and between activities aspects of shifting resources. Note the degrees of freedom that exist for the time order of scenes.

Change Management with Faster Project Completions

Change is always occurring in the way that business is conducted. It is noticeable if you pick up a book on P/OM written 20 years ago how little reference is made to certain topics that are in the spotlight these days (e.g., supply chain management, new product development, and sustainability). Another aspect of change is the recognition that certain topics that had much attention paid to them 20 years ago are no longer of major concern and importance (e.g., time and motion study with clipboards and stopwatches, standard symbols for process flow analysis, and work simplification).

More subtle is the change in the way that some topics are treated. For example, project management has been an important part of P/OM since 1950; however, projects were assumed to be constrained by engineering and subject to immutable laws concerning how long it takes to construct a building or bring out a new car. Project scheduling was an onerous manual task that has now been extended and amplified for communicating and tracking with many vendors linked to the core computer systems.

Change occurred when management recognized that it could affect completion times, project costs, and quality by reorganizing the way that jobs are done. Concurrent management of project activities can be used now in place of sequential management to speed project completion. Continuous multiple project systems are able to produce a stream of new product developments. Communication among project participants has been amplified by email. Procurement using the Internet has altered project inventories and selection of suppliers. Geographically dispersed teams work round-the-clock using technology that did not exist 20 years ago to communicate about project management, production, and research. Methods for continuous improvement are mixed with reengineering to bring about fundamental changes in the business model.

After reading this chapter, you should be able to:

- Explain why organizations must be able to adapt to change.
- Explain why projects at one time were constrained by engineering assumptions and/or geographic boundaries.
- Explain why projects are no longer constrained by engineering assumptions and/or geographic boundaries.
- Describe how e-mail changes the way in which project participants communicate.
- Discuss the effect e-mail has on project teamwork.
- Describe what special contributions P/OM can make to change management for adopting new technologies, and the timing of change. Discuss concurrent engineering in this regard.
- Describe three factors that must exist for change to take place, and explain how they combine into a powerful force for change.
- Describe the operations manager as a change agent and—at the same time—as a team player.
- Explain why a vision of what the future can become must be understood by the team players and supported by top management.
- Describe various forms of benchmarking including by process type and self-benchmarking.
- Provide a list of "smart" benchmarks that capture essential P/OM characteristics of processes.
- Relate benchmarking to both continuous improvement (CI) and reengineering (REE) aspects of change management.
- Describe continuous improvement methods.
- Explain reengineering and business process redesign.
- Discuss the principles of reengineering.
- Categorize procurement over the Internet as continuous improvement or REE.
- Give some examples of companies that live by the principles of continuous improvement.
- Describe the kind of change that the Internet brought to project and process management.

The Systems Viewpoint

To be successful, change managers must adopt the broadest systems perspective. New forces arise continuously, and in response to them, strategic adaptation must occur. External change must be met by internal adaptation. Change is met by counterchange, and stimulus by response. Teamwork is essential because even small changes ripple through the system, creating new conditions that have to be managed.

The change management team communicates with employees at every level from top to bottom. Strong teams attempt to determine how a change strategy might affect every activity of the organization. Tracing cause and effect is a systems task particularly well-suited to P/OM talents and abilities. Permissions must be granted explicitly and implicitly that allow cutting across all functional boundaries (e.g., marketing).

Five of the most important factors that force change in this area are environmental, ethical, technological, global, and security. The proper response of the organization to challenges and opportunities in each of these areas is to bring change management capabilities into focus. Change management is able to use combinations of continuous, incremental improvement (CI) and reengineering. REE reexamines all assumptions and starts from scratch to bring about change. Grading performance does not stop when the manager gets the diploma. All activities of a Stage IV company (see Chapter 1) are constantly being graded and being compared with who is best in class. That comparison, known as *benchmarking*, has become increasingly more complex as the global framework—for whom to benchmark—has expanded.

Benchmarking is the trigger for dissatisfaction when the system being graded falls short of what has been determined to be best-practice achievements. Such dissatisfaction leads to both continuous improvement and REE. Managing change requires implementing modifications that will have the most desirable performance improvement. To benchmark successfully, it is necessary to know what goals are being sought and how they are being measured. The runner's goal of coming in first is frequently supplanted by a higher goal of breaking the record. A profit goal can be confusing in the same way. How much profit is enough profit? Stock market evaluations penalize not breaking records. Success stories, however, are often based on sustainability of resources and stable growth.

Strategic Thinking

Bureaucracies tend to develop strategies dedicated to protecting the status quo. Dissatisfaction with this strategy occurs when the status quo becomes unacceptable, which can occur for many reasons. Social disapproval (concerning environmental impact and ethical factors related to customers, employees, and stockholders) can call for a different strategy. Similarly, failure to compete successfully can be indicated by falling profits, failure to maintain technological leadership, and global miscalculations in markets and/or plant locations. P/OM must be part of the change (or transition) management team. It can provide a "vision" of what operations and technology might be like in the future. Such vision is derived from benchmarking other companies used as models of excellence.

Strategies are often created by emulation of companies that have been rated excellent. Business periodicals regularly publish information that describes the "best managed" companies. Lists today are gone tomorrow, indicating that what led to past excellence may not continue in the future. Prior reference has been made to *Business Week's* cover on November 5, 1984, stating, "OOPS!" The article went on to say, "*In Search of Excellence* quickly became a best-seller.... The authors name America's best-run companies—and claimed to have found the reasons for their success. But some of those companies aren't looking so excellent any more."[1]

19-1 Adaptation to External Changes

When **change management** is discussed, what is meant is that managers will reach strategic decisions leading to actions that will help their organizations adapt to significant

Change management
Managing modification of the transformation process, including the inputs and the outputs, is a major challenge and opportunity.

External Changes	Company Adaptation
New technology becomes available rapidly	Company strives to adopt the new technology
New environmental regulations are created	Company meets or beats the new regulations
Ethical problems receive public attention	Company changes procedures to match new ethical expectations
Competitor adopts higher ethical and/or environmental standards	Company changes procedures to meet or raise ethical and/or environmental standards
There are new global competitors and new competitive methods	Company changes to become more effective as a global competitor
Competitor invents new global initiatives	Company responds with new counterinitiatives that increase the intensity of global competitiveness

Table 19-1

Change Management

External changes force management to adapt by selecting strategies to manage transition.

changes in the competitive realm. Success demands systems thinking and cooperation. Table 19-1 illustrates company adaptation to several types of external changes.

New competitors appear with no old investment burdens. They start without the old designs and obsolete equipment their competitors have. Newcomers can put all of their investments into new technology, deriving improved products from better processes. P/OM is able to evaluate the competitive advantage.

The old barriers to entry that kept competitors out of a market included

1 Lack of experience with the technology
2 A learning curve to become as good as the existing suppliers
3 Difficulty in taking customers away from existing suppliers
4 Large investments to become as good as existing suppliers

These four principles no longer apply. Technology changes continuously and rapidly. It transfers almost immediately. The owner of the latest technology has cost and quality advantages, which the old supplier's customers find irresistible. There are global sources of capital that are constantly searching for best return on investment. Start-up companies have distinct advantages over established companies because experience with the old technology drags down innovative use of the new technology. P/OM is fully apprised of the technological advantages of start-ups and the importance of timing when upgrading old technology.

New technology forces established companies to find ways to adapt. The transition from old to new technology must be managed. Timing is crucial. Old facilities are modified or closed down. On a global scale, many of the old auto assembly plants have been closed by DaimlerChrysler, Ford, and GM to keep pace with what new plants can achieve in quality and cost. Theme parks must upgrade their technologies to keep pace with competitive attractions. Hospitals are involved in continuous change of technology. P/OM's participation is critical on the technology management team.

New rules and regulations regarding environmental impacts of both processes (smokestack emissions) and products (auto-engine emissions) force change and adaptation. P/OM is the change manager in charge of meeting pollution controls and recycling requirements.

Customers change in what they expect. Health and safety considerations have forced entire industries (such as food and automobiles) to adapt to new customer levels of needs and wants. Customer-driven changes have occurred in what is considered to be acceptable quality. Raising standards of quality is part of a continuing dynamic that new competitors turn to their advantage. If P/OM cannot help the company adapt quickly enough, the market falters and the financial system withdraws its support.

Employees change in what they expect. In the first half of the twentieth century, they were told what to do and they did what they were told. After 1950, a desire to participate in planning and decision making became more immediate. Increasingly, P/OM could justify replacing people with technology. Some managers did tasks that computers could do faster and more accurately. Many causes have led to company downsizing and a sense of alienation. Trust in the company, formerly repaid with loyalty, has been damaged.

Suppliers change what they make, how they manufacture, what services they offer, their quality standards, and what they charge. The buyer now goes to the global market. New organizations appear continuously. Start-ups have the new technology advantage, which was discussed earlier in terms of "cost and quality advantages that . . . customers find irresistible." The advantages of dealing with established suppliers certified by P/OM for their current *capabilities* and likely future improvements must be weighed against the strategy of switching suppliers. P/OM is needed on that strategy planning team. (For more discussion of capabilities advantages, see Chapter 18, "Project Management for New Products and Processes.")

Community expectations change. Environmental expectations are real. The ethical conduct of the company is important. To derive *The 100 Best Companies to Work for in America*, and later on the *Fortune Magazine* (2007) list of 100 best companies, high among the rating characteristics is pride in work and company.[2] There can be no pride in working for a company considered lacking in ethics by employees.

Global activity is changing. It is increasing for every one of the preceding factors. Companies are becoming global in activities and mind-set. This forces continuous and substantial change. The communities mentioned earlier can be anywhere in the world. Customers, employees, and suppliers speak many different languages and use a variety of currencies. Rules and regulations change by crossing borders. Because teamwork is essential to manage such change, P/OM has a major role to play on that team.

© 2008 Jupiterimages Corporation

Smokestacks are beginning to vanish, and, where they exist, plumes of smoke emanating from the stacks are disappearing. Emission controls are old technology that is being replaced by new fuel systems that do not require the smokestacks that are the hallmark of traditional pictures of industrial pollution.

19-2 P/OM's Part in Change Management

P/OM brings special knowledge to the change management team; this knowledge consists of three parts.

1 *Familiarity with technology* and the timing of technological change, which includes technological forecasting and knowing when it is best to adopt a new technology and leave behind an old one. If a new start-up company has a technological advantage, there may be a benefit to not imitating that technology. Instead, by waiting for further technological development the company can "leapfrog the competition." To retain customers during the transition may require price cuts and full disclosure of the intended strategy. There are other scenarios that P/OM is uniquely suited to suggest and evaluate. Knowledge of timing is complex and critical. The P/OM advantage stems from experience with the technology of processes.

2 *Understanding the interaction between technology and environmental protection* takes the form of pollution controls for land, air, and water. It applies to processes and products. P/OM contains the body of knowledge that is essential for greening the globe. Whether the reference is to replenishment in forestry, preventing oil spills, or nuclear contamination, the issues arise from operations and technology, which are both in the comfort zone of P/OM.

3 *Understanding the responsibility for ethical production practices*: A major area of ethics is related to the honest effort to deliver a safe and healthy product to customers. The quality of products is the responsibility of P/OM. Shipments of cans that might explode or foods that might be tainted often can only be stopped

by operations managers. Other managers do not know the specifics of each day's production output.

If adequate standards are not maintained during production, and these problems are ignored, it is likely that deliveries will be made of unsafe food, toys that are dangerous, and cars that should not be driven. The design of the product also plays a part. Design is acknowledged to be a responsibility shared by P/OM and others. Design for manufacturability (DFM) and design for assembly (DFA) are subject to the conditions of design for safe use by customers and design for nonspoilage during manufacture.

The product must be safe to make. Ethics of the workplace reflect integrity to protect employees from noxious fumes, toxic substances, unsafe machines, unsanitary facilities, jumbled storage, and combustible materials. The factories and offices must be nice places to work. Care of the environment is free but takes caring from P/OM. The costs of not caring can be significant. Employees leave and/or morale is low. Regulatory penalties can include shutdown. Chiron Corp.'s plant manufacturing flu vaccine near the Mersey River in England was shut down by the Medicines and Healthcare Products Regulatory Agency (MHRA), which is the British equivalent of the U.S. Food and Drug Administration. The closure occurred during the most sensitive flu epidemic months during 2004–2005. Costs of special vaccination programs were not announced and many people went without flu shots, which has unknown costs. The supply of flu vaccine for 2006–2007 was far greater than demand. The supply chain being off-kilter either way gets its full share of critics.

P/OM also encounters ethical issues when dealing with suppliers. In many places in the world, incentives to purchase from a particular supplier are not called bribes. There are ample examples of companies using inferior materials to save money. P/OM can oversee and enforce honest dealings with suppliers, maintain the integrity of government contracts, and end the need for whistle-blowers. It may be impossible to put an exact cost on the damage done to workforce morale when management practice is unethical, but it is too high a cost to pay at any time.

19-3 Factors That Enable Organizational Change

Having established some of the reasons that P/OM has a special role in dealing with transitions and change management, it is important to point out that changing strategies for products and processes often require organizational changes. These organizational changes are not readily achieved by a bureaucracy that champions the status quo. There are specific conditions that must be fulfilled for change to occur. Various models describing the conditions for change have been proposed. The Gleicher model described here is an accepted change model, which means it describes circumstances that allow for transformation. The **Gleicher Model (conditions for change)** is explained directly.

Gleicher Model (Conditions for change)

The product of three factors, D, V, and P, must be greater than the cost of change, C.

Dr. David B. Gleicher's model was used to structure a meeting of the American Assembly aimed at change management. The 3-day conference was convened to discuss reversing the declining competitiveness of the United States.[3] The meeting addressed the issue of increasing the values of each of the three factors that promote change.

The model proposes that the product of three factors (D, V, P) must be greater than C to allow organizational change to take place. C is the total cost of bringing about the planned changes.

$$\text{Thus: } D \times V \times P > C$$

The factors are

1 *Dissatisfaction* with the current situation (D)
2 *Vision* of what the future can become (V)
3 *Practical first steps* to achieve the vision (P)

Note that because the three factors are multiplicative, if one of them is zero, then there can be no change. Further, when all three factors are greater than zero, their product might be greater than the cost (C) of changing the situation. If $D \times V \times P > C$, then change is likely, assuming that no other factors negatively impact the change.

Increasing **dissatisfaction** with the current situation is often the result of comparing a company with its competitors. If it is learned from the comparison that "they" can build a car in 20 hours while it takes "us" 40 hours, the seeds for dissatisfaction (D) have been sown. Methodical comparisons called *benchmarks* are developed by the P/OM benchmarking function, to be discussed shortly.

The cause of dissatisfaction with the current situation (20 versus 40) also provides a vision (here, a productivity target) of what the future can become. Benchmarking usually has the ability to indicate the causes of dissatisfaction (cycle-time needs reduction) and targets to shoot for (20 hours per car). **Vision** has various meanings but the one intended here is "something seen otherwise than by ordinary sight." Two words that often accompany this nonordinary sight are "wisdom" and "imagination."

Practical first steps include design studies aimed at using fewer parts and allowing quicker assembly; process improvement studies to replace workers with faster machines for tedious and repetitive work; and work simplification studies to redesign workstations so that teamwork can make the job more productive and less arduous. P/OM can be expected to be involved in this change management situation from beginning to end.

The American auto industry has changed a great deal. It benchmarked itself against the Japanese auto industry, resulting in high *Dissatisfaction* and clear vision as to where it must go. Various efforts were made to find practical first steps and, over time, good answers were found. For a variety of reasons, problems still remain. More change management is needed. Industries that have used downsizing extensively have noted that it has the effect of eliminating dissatisfaction. Those remaining in the workforce are happy to still be employed. But downsizing increases dissatisfaction because the threat of further downsizing obscures vision unless it is clearly identified as a means to the vision of stable employment in a successful company.

The kind of vision that is obscured is the need for new product innovations and new state-of-the-art plants. It also is significant that both unions and management in the U.S. auto industry have had different visions, which in systems terms is equivalent to turning competition inward instead of keeping it external. The first practical steps would be to get everyone playing on the same team with a shared set of clearly stated objectives.

The activities in Table 19-2 are basic P/OM contributions to change management. For example, vision is not useful unless it has real support from above. P/OM can serve as a

Dissatisfaction
Benchmarking is the trigger for dissatisfaction with the status quo.

Vision
Clear and unambiguous view of what the future can become.

Practical first steps
"The devil is in the details" captures the essence of practical first steps; requires articulated goals and believable tactics for realizing initial goals.

Factor P/OM	Activity
Dissatisfaction (D)	Benchmarking (comparing your own, or your department's, performance with Best Practices in other firms and/or other departments of the same firm)
Vision (V)	Best conceivable practice (creative visioning is realistic imagination of what the process and the products can be like; estimates derived from benchmarking about possible future conditions; found by proposing product and process innovations)
Practical first steps (P)	Project management with short-term goals that can lead to long-term visions; often realized by implementing new technology and/or replacing old technology; or a procedural change that promises to lead to other more sweeping changes.

Table 19-2

P/OM Activities for Change Management Factors

© 2008 Jupiterimages Corporation

Wind turbines produce emission-free electricity but not free power. Investments and upkeep are substantial but as costs improve, greater use is made of nature's resources. Electrical power storage is required to deal with windless times as well as peak demand intervals. Location selection is a critical variable. P/OM knowledge about such alternative sources of energy is growing at an accelerating rate. As the efficiency of various energy-alternative systems improves, global pollution issues draw more attention.

strong change agent when it is part of a team. Many companies stress teamwork for change management. Concurrent engineering, which is widely used for project management, requires the team-oriented approach. Project management allows P/OM to provide a practical means for moving toward the realization of a goal. P/OM is often the only solution provider for practical first steps (*P*).

19-3a Mastering Change

With instantaneous global communication, transitions speed up. Change is now the core of competitiveness. Learning how to change has become a critical ability for personal and corporate life. John W. Gardner wrote in his book *Self Renewal: The Individual and the Innovative Society*, "Most men and women out there in the world of work are more stale than they know, more bored than they care to admit."[4] John A. Byrnes, editor of *Fast Company*, describes these people, many of whom may be one's own colleagues. He writes, "Somewhere along the line, they were disappointed by dumb decisions, passed over for key promotions or raises, or just beaten down by banging their heads against a bureaucratic wall day after day."[5]

Convincing disillusioned people to change their behavior and commit to any meaningful transformation almost always fails. Only one of nine people with heart disease succeeds in making a permanent shift to a healthy lifestyle. Despite the knowledge of disaster if they do not change, the other eight cannot make the transition. Severe health problems provide powerful examples of major personal threats that are ignored, but there are others as well. Shifting from the status quo in business is difficult for most and impossible for many.

Myths about Change

Altering the culture or direction of an enterprise populated by thousands of different people with diverse agendas is an enormous project. Leaders who have beaten the odds are usually willing to explain how they did it. However, the forces for status quo are significant. Alan Deutschman's important article titled "Change" in the May 2005 issue of *Fast Company*, states that crises and fear do not usually bring about change.[6]

Enron (see Spotlight 20-1) denied a crisis existed even after the firm declared bankruptcy. Lawyers have changed the equation so that crises are opportunities that are not to be feared by some executives in the company. Facts become fiction in the hands of knowledge manipulators. Truth is in the eye of the beholder, which means the truth is at times determined by the best lawyer. Doctors do not always agree, which is why second opinions are sought by patients and insurance companies.

The dot.com bubble is a good example of missed cues and denial of crisis conditions. That situation time line is epitomized by Webvan, which intended to take over and replace the supermarket business with home delivery. But years before, and after, the Internet-related phenomenon, Sears Roebuck, Monroe Calculators, Keuffel and Esser, American Motors, MCI, Digital Equipment Corporation, Westinghouse Corporation, and many others had gone from top to bottom, from good to bad, and in some cases from existence to nonexistence. Crises may have energized these companies to refocus, but in the long run, denial blocked corrective actions.

Facts did not help the Sony Corporation recognize that its strategy for keeping the BetaMax format alive lost the company its advantage gained from being first into the VCR market. Facts did not help General Motors Corporation executives who believed that Japanese auto manufacturers could not attract and hold market share. They also did not expect hybrid vehicles to amount to anything. Krispy Kreme could not believe that health and diet issues would eventually emerge with such force that its revenues would suddenly plummet in spite of all the new stores that it had opened.

There is a substantial body of literature that deals with problems of misperception. See http://www.psu.edu/dus/md/mdmisper.htm; googling "misperceptions" results in

1,430,000 hits. When facts seem to contradict each other, people find a way to make them consonant, according to Leon Festinger. He developed the theory of cognitive dissonance to deal with this issue.[7] Not everyone has agreed. Opponents of cognitive dissonance cite the ability of many people to reconcile contradictory beliefs with no apparent stress. John Kotter (Harvard Business School professor) has studied dozens of organizations in the midst of upheaval. He writes, "The central issue is never strategy, structure, culture, or systems. The core of the matter is always about changing the behavior of people."[8] The need to change is not sufficient to bring about change, because people resist change. Kotter advocates developing a coalition of managers that is imbued with the vision of what can be achieved.

The need for behavioral change arises because of marketplace dynamics. There are global competitors with new strategies, shifts occur in technology, government regulations are revised, etc. Firms must be constantly in flux to stay competitive. Yet, CEOs may be more resistant to change than middle managers. The power that they exercise insulates them from feeling and sharing. In that regard, Kotter and Cohen[9] provide valuable insights. Behavioral change occurs when people's feelings are altered. That kind of persuasion is not part of the curriculum of business schools. It is not in the job description of engineers, lawyers, doctors, accountants, scientists, or managers, let alone CEOs who pride themselves on dispassionate and analytic thinking.

Range of Responses to Demands for Change

There is a continuum of responses expressed by typical statements of people when confronted with the need to change: Never–Someday–Soon–Maybe tomorrow–Perhaps later today–Shortly–Now. Between 70 and 80 percent of people who have to change their behavior for health reasons never get to "Soon," or beyond "Soon." It may be valuable for P/OM to note how Dr. Dean Ornish reversed these probabilities.

Dr. Ornish, professor of medicine at the University of California–San Francisco, and founder, president, and director of the Preventative Medicine Research Institute in Sausalito, California, put his patients through a 1-year program of vegetarian food, support group sessions, relaxation, yoga, and aerobic exercise. After 3 years, the study found 77 percent of 333 patients who had started with severely clogged arteries had avoided surgery.[10]

What Dr. Ornish achieved was the substitution of fear (of dying) with enthusiasm for living. He says, "Joy is a more powerful motivator than fear." There are ample examples of successful companies whose employees are optimistic about the future. Pessimistic employees do not create an environment that encourages employer loyalty. There may be no examples of successful companies whose employees are pessimistic about the future.

Researchers believe that Ornish's success results from how he changes the way his patients view the world. In a business context, employees at W. L. Gore & Associates have a different perspective about what work entails than employees in most other companies (see Section 19-8a). W. L. Gore & Associates has transformed traditional models of the workplace, relying on self-directed employees making their own choices about joining one another in small teams. The 3M Company provides another example (see Section 19-8b).

How IBM Changed

Getting people to change one frame for another is especially hard for companies that have enjoyed great success—until their business model began to fail. IBM made a remarkable turnaround in the 1990s under Louis V. Gerstner, Jr. He exemplified the art of emotional persuasion. At first he used all the usual techniques that had succeeded in the past but quickly discovered that the old methods (selling assets and cutting costs) were not enough. IBM had become hidebound and bureaucratic. Behaviors of hundreds of thousands of employees had to be changed. In his memoir, Gerstner wrote that he had to "shake them out of their depressed stupor, remind them of who they were—you're IBM, damn it!"[11]

He made thousands of personal appearances, which engaged his audiences. IBM began to change into a company that sold services, not hardware. If customers needed other companies' products, IBM recommended them. As IBM employees learned to provide their customers with integrated data and information systems, IBM's business model changed to allow for flexibility and knowledge acquisition.

Although IBM has shifted strategies successfully once, that does not mean that it can sustain its customer base in the future. Technology follows Moore's Law and customers' needs change over time. "Change or die" is a mantra that cannot be ignored by any company. Digital Equipment Corporation (DEC) ignored it. DEC was a great company. Many DEC executives and consultants tried to save it, but they failed to do so. It is clear that top decision makers refused to believe that their firm was becoming obsolete. The CEO rejected the concept of DEC as a doomed dinosaur. One consultant who was invited to give a presentation to top management came away amazed at the arrogance and denial in the room. He learned that success in the past breeds a certain deaf ear to current realities. It is wise to listen most carefully to what you don't want to hear.

Small incremental changes to improve often do not produce satisfactory results. People who make small to moderate changes in their diets get the worst of both worlds. They feel deprived and hungry with nothing much to show for it. Patients on the Ornish radical program noted rapid, dramatic results. Almost all patients reported a decrease in chest pain in one month. Ornish said, "Rapid improvements are a powerful motivator."

Supporting Change

Companies need to support their employees as they learn how to change, just as Ornish's patients were bolstered with regular support groups and attention from dieticians, psychologists, nurses, and yoga instructors. Similar support systems are essential success factors in companies that are rewiring themselves for new competencies.

When Xerox was in deep crisis a decade ago, its executives came up with a new vision that required salespeople to change the way they had worked for years. The sales force of 5,400 had been accustomed to knocking on doors, looking to see how old the copy machines were, and suggesting replacements. They knew how to do that. Suddenly top management told them to change their methods. They were instructed to engage in conversations with customers in order to learn and understand the complexities of their clients' operation and find opportunities to sell other products, such as scanners and printers.

Learning about clients' needs meant taking a longer time and required real communication with the customer. As normal routines and habits were discarded, sales representatives experienced confusion and lack of confidence in the new approach. This was further heightened by the failure of Xerox to provide transitional support. Training was not available for months, and it took two years to implement an incentive pay system that reflected extra time and effort expended on closing deals. Eventually, however, the change effort opened up the sales focus to a larger range of products. Xerox adapted the product line to customers' needs and experienced a turnaround that avoided bankruptcy.

Internal organizational support (sometimes called *internal alignment*) is the key to facilitating new learning. Even if change starts at the top level, it will often die in the middle if there is no confidence in the company's internal support system. Xerox now holds "alignment workshops" that ask middle managers—the people who make processes work—to study and identify areas that could hinder the company's plan for change so that improvements can be made. P/OM has played a major role in these efforts.

Habits and Change

What made it so difficult for the Xerox sales representatives to change their routine? Dr. Michael Merzenich, a professor at the University of California at San Francisco, has studied how animals form habits through training. A rat can be trained to solve a puzzle using food rewards, but after 200 times, it can remember how to solve the puzzle for a lifetime. It is a habit. Habits can actually change physical brain patterns. Flutists develop large representations in their brains in the areas that control the fingers, tongue, and lips. Businesspeople are also highly trained specialists and, according to Professor Merzenich, have distorted their brains, too. Specialists are valuable to organizations but specialization instills rigidity. The cumulative weight of experience makes it hard to change.

Competitive Advantage of Learning

Dr. Merzenich wants us to restart our brain's machinery for learning. Doing so will overcome the disadvantages of specialization. We become stultified when we stop learning. We stop using the brain's machinery, so it starts to die. "People mistake being active for continuous learning," Merzenich says. "The brain's machinery is only activated by learning. People think they are leading an interesting life when they haven't learned anything in 20 or 30 years."[12] He suggests that leaders of a company need a business strategy for continuous mental rejuvenation and new learning.

A company called "Posit Science Corp" is working on ways to prevent, stop, or reverse cognitive decline. They have developed a "fifth day" strategy where everyone spends one day a week working in a different discipline. For example, a software engineer could get involved with marketing, designers could try their hand at P/OM, and vice versa. Everyone gets a new project without sacrificing the core business. W. L. Gore & Associates use a variant of this multi-team strategy (see Section 19-8a). A rejuvenated staff is important at every level. Ideally, new challenges will produce complex new learning. Merzenich states, "Innovation comes about when people are enabled to use their full brains and intelligence instead of being put in boxes and controlled."

BP, as a widely diversified international company, espoused corporate learning in a number of ways including **peer-assist**, which meant that small groups from various parts of the company could share ideas and knowledge.

Peer-assist
An initiative to bring colleagues with new ideas into a specific project-oriented meeting to seek their fresh ideas about how to proceed. The duration of the assist depends on the situation.

Competitive Advantage of Cooperation

As an example, British Petroleum wished to measure the effectiveness of its horizontal well-drilling processes, but there was no available device to do so. BP pooled intellectual and financial resources with Schlumberger, the oil field services company, to build such a tool. BP shared its ideas on how to do this. The result was of benefit to everyone. Much was learned about "Unlocking tight gas . . . by drilling on a deviated path to bypass obstacles; or they can be horizontal or multilateral, where several horizontal wells are drilled in different directions originating from a single vertical well."[13]

John W. Gardner, 1912–2002, in his famous *Self-Renewal* book, reflected on individual and societal renewal. "Failure to face the realities of change brings heavy penalties," he said. "Individuals become imprisoned in their own rigidities. Great institutions deteriorate . . . yet decay is not inevitable. There is also renewal."

19-4 P/OM's Benchmarking Role in Change Management

Systematic comparative measurements made between similar processes (functions, departments, products, services, and so on) are benchmarks. The procedure for making comparative measurements is called *benchmarking*. Comparisons can be made between different industries. IBM, when developing mail and telephone-order services, benchmarked that process with Lands' End, which is known to be a leader in mail-order service. Disney is frequently benchmarked for comparisons in customer relations.

Xerox played an important role in bringing serious attention to benchmarking. It remains committed to benchmarking. See http://www.benchnet.com. This is the Benchmarking Exchange's homepage, where it is easy to explore a variety of benchmarking issues. For current member organizations, click on X and up comes 28 countries in which Xerox operates. Xerox has had some difficult times in spite of its commitment to benchmarking. Perhaps it would have been one of the companies that disappeared by 2008 had it not been for those early benchmarking initiatives. In fact, there is reason to believe that because of their benchmarking initiative, creative concepts have been developed resulting in improved conditions for Xerox.

The history of benchmarking starts before 1990, when a Xerox executive sent a group of managers to Japan to determine quality goals. The group concluded that "Competitive benchmarking resulted in specific performance targets rather than someone's guess or intuitive feel of what needs to be done—which is the real power of the process."[14] The benchmarks were effective. Xerox stated that its production line defects were decreased by 84 percent using new targets that were commonly held in Japan.

It is noteworthy how benchmarks permit global comparisons. Benchmarking is most useful when there is a clear correspondence of processes and their purposes and goals. The accounts payable function of Mazda and Ford led to improvements for the latter. Other processes that could benefit include the productivity of specific production processes. Anheuser-Busch regularly benchmarks all of its plants. Credit approval, repair and maintenance, accounts receivable, performance appraisal, salary reviews, and so on, are other examples of processes that lend themselves to benchmarking.

Comparisons require at least two parties. Access must be available for the comparison to be made. Companies that would like to benchmark themselves against the competition can only use measures that are available through information in the public domain, such as annual reports and newspaper and magazine articles. Data from newspapers and magazines must be used with care. Sometimes information is obtained from suppliers that are shared with competitors. There is an ethical question that arises. If competitors share information, there are legal issues about collusion. Benchmarks are sometimes available when there are joint ventures, as was the case with Ford/Mazda and Chrysler/ Mitsubishi.

Benchmarking similar departments in the same organization is a teamwork concept as long as it is used to encourage cooperative improvement and not as a basis for penalizing the lower-grade departments. In the Anheuser-Busch case, it is expected that the newer plants will have higher benchmark grades.

Self-benchmarking over time provides useful insights concerning self-improvement. Individual athletes in every kind of sport track themselves. Coaches use detailed team statistics to guide them in their efforts to design winning teams. Government departments track trade, productivity, unemployment benefits, the velocity of money, and so on.

Benchmarking can only be as good as the relevance of the measures that are used. There are three determinants. First, the measure must be appropriate. Second, measurement must be done properly. Third, the entities being compared must be comparable. Even if all three conditions are met, some benchmarks provide more insight than others. If they capture the competitive factor, they are "smart."

Smart benchmarks
Based on those dimensions that are most valuable for steering tactics and for redirecting strategies.

A list of **smart benchmarks** might include the following 10 target variables:

1 *Cycle time*. The inverse is output rate. Choose short cycle times to increase output rates.
2 *Net margins* (after-tax income as a percent of revenue). Detroit became obsessed with the use of net margins to reflect its quest to improve the way it designs and builds cars and trucks. "It's a good management tool to keep everyone focused on where we need to go," according to Jack Smith, General Motors CEO, in 1995.[15] However, there are benchmark fads. What is smart one year may not be as popular the next year.
3 *Return on equity*. Increasingly popular among CFOs.

4 *Inventory turns* per year, measured by net annual sales divided by average inventory level. It is increasingly used in preference to direct measures of profit by retailers.

5 *Days of inventory.* 365 divided by inventory turns. Also popular with retailers.

6 *Delivery speed.* How many days, hours, or minutes does it take to deliver? Fast-track deliveries are typically next-day instead of parts of a week.

7 *Project life cycle intervals.* Rapid completion is often half the customary response time. Old standards are constantly being slashed.

8 *Breakeven volume.* Comparisons are made with industry norms. Also, comparing the organization's BEP over time is considered beneficial.

9 *Breakeven time.* Hewlett-Packard developed this measure to indicate how long a period is required for a new product to reach breakeven volume.

10 Other insight-building benchmarks include multidimensional quality mapping, which shows the position of competing products on more than one dimension, team accomplishments, and levels of core competencies. (For more discussion of this term, see Chapter 18, "Project Management for New Products and Processes.")

Some Best-Practice measures should reflect long-term survival of the enterprise. These measures can relate to environmental concerns, ethics, mastery of global business practices, and grasp of future technological developments.

Benchmarks have been criticized for various reasons. Government measures (such as unemployment, productivity, and the consumer price index) have been changed from time to time, which makes them difficult to track over time. Company measures of resource utilization (machine and people) can be counterproductive. Measures of overhead can be misleading. Quarterly financial report statements are cited as a cause of short-term decisions. End-of-month shipments are used to meet quotas, distorting production schedules and adversely impacting quality.

The systems complexity of benchmarking is exemplified by the U.S. government's monthly publication of flights that are delayed more than 15 minutes. The airlines that come out on top use this data in their marketing campaigns. Delays due to mechanical problems originally were excluded but later were made part of the on-time measure of performance. Various airlines have complained that this causes pressure to defer repairs to keep good grades.

An airline analyst says that a better measure of reliability is the percentage of flight miles canceled, because a canceled trip irks travelers far more than minor delays.[16] Cancellations are measured by the percentage of scheduled miles that are actually flown. Criticism of a cancellation benchmark could be made if airlines failed to cancel flights (because of weather and mechanical problems) in order to maintain good grades. What starts out as a good idea to benchmark airline performance becomes complicated by issues of how these benchmarks are used and possibly abused. The power of benchmarking to influence behavior in unexpected ways must be taken into account.

19-5 Continuous Improvement (CI) for Change Management

Two approaches are used to accomplish planned change. P/OM is comfortable and involved with both kinds of change. First is **continuous improvement (CI)**, which is a constant effort to find better ways to produce the products and deliver the services.[17] This is often local with conversions being done to the existing process. Because it is incremental, gradual, and tactical, P/OM plays a large role in originating, implementing, and evaluating the results. (For more discussion of this term, see Chapter 6, "Process Analysis and Redesign.") In this category, both **products, continuous development**, and **projects, continuous development**, are relevant terms. The second approach is REE.

Continuous improvement (CI)
Uses constant effort to find better ways to produce a product and deliver a service. Scope is local, limited to incremental change, and persistent.

Products, Continuous development
See **Continuity** and **Ferris Wheel model**.

Projects, Continuous development
See **Continuity** and **Ferris Wheel model**.

Reengineering (REE)
Starts from scratch with practical first steps. Radical changes occur when the design process begins with a blank piece of paper.

Within the scope and surveillance of P/OM, a continuous improvement program should be reviewed by the change management team. Decisions to make simple changes can obscure opportunities for fundamental and sweeping changes associated with **reengineering (REE)**. Adherents to the continuous improvement track have made commitments that place them in opposition to REE. One of the first decisions that change management faces is which track to take—the gradual or the extensive road to change.

The administration of specific improvements can be as simple as a new method for deciding when machine adjustments are to be made. It should not be as complex as the implementation of a new technology. A change of real magnitude deserves a total systems study, which is characteristic of reengineering (examined in the next section).

Because continuous improvement changes are improvements to existing processes, a systems study to question goals and purposes is not undertaken. Benchmarking plays the guiding role in continuous improvement activities. It provides the basis for making course corrections on the journey to excellence. Work simplification, inventory reductions, and information system changes are typical of continuous improvement programs.

19-5a Planning Transitions

The prescription for successful continuous improvement changes includes total management involvement for implementation. When Chemical Bank (JP Morgan Chase, Inc.) introduced new technology for its stock transfer system, senior management sat down with members of the workforce to provide hands-on training in the new procedures.

A lot of careful thought went into planning the transition. There was recognition of the fact that it is normal to resist change. Therefore, senior managers listened to the employees' problems related to changing. Adjustments could be made when warranted because those who had planned the changeover were on the production line with those who do the work. That also signaled the importance of the changes being made.

When the (change) managers of the Royal Bank of Canada developed an expert system for monitoring risk with sophisticated technology, they stressed the importance of dialogue with members of the workforce. One of their purposes was to prevent employees from feeling threatened by the new technology. They did this by emphasizing employee ownership of the new technology and methods. They accented the need for teamwork to successfully facilitate making the changeover. The implementation team was aware of the need to listen, hear, and make adjustments during the transition period.

19-6 Reengineering (REE) for Change Management

Reengineering (REE)—also called *business process redesign*—seeks radical improvements over a reasonable period of time. REE is at the opposite pole from continuous improvement. Reengineering (REE) requires total replacement of existing systems with new systems that have been designed from scratch. What is meant by "reasonable period of time"? The answer is: Reengineering is not associated with long-term, theoretical research. Reengineering is associated with short-term, application-oriented research.

Reengineering has disturbed even its adherents because of extreme claims. Hammer and Champy wrote the original book in 1993, which started an REE crusade.[18] In 1995, Champy writes, "on the whole ... reengineering payoffs appear to have fallen well short of their potential. *Reengineering the Corporation* set big goals: 70 percent decreases in cycle time and 40 percent decreases in costs; 40 percent increases in customer satisfaction, quality and revenue; and 25 percent growth in market share."[19] Studies done by Champy showed that "participants failed to attain these benchmarks by as much as 30 percent."

Such failures would be successes for many companies. In addition, the causes of failures can be traced to doing REE incorrectly. Champy's book strives to right that wrong by elaborating on the requirements for success. These have to do with identifying the core processes of the business (such as new product development for the pharmaceutical business and customer service for a bank). "Identify those key operational processes, reassemble the work that goes into them in line with the core mission of the business."[20] This is operations management territory, and P/OM knowledge is a crucial ingredient for success.

One important variant of REE highlights a different purpose using the same methodology. **Breakpoint business process redesign** "focuses on creating strategic-level competitive advantages through breakthroughs in the *core business processes that most affect customers and shareholders*."[21] The idea is to select functions to reengineer that can create market response that is much greater than the resources required to achieve it. Emphasis is placed on competency-based competition, which almost always involves P/OM and logistics-type capabilities.

Time-based management (including rapid-response project life cycle management and fast-delivery cycle times) is one form of special **capabilities**. Four principles of capabilities-based management are stated by George Stalk, Philip Evans, and Lawrence E. Shulman in their seminal article, "Competing on Capabilities,"[22] as follows:

1 The building blocks of corporate strategy are not products and markets but business processes.

2 Competitive success depends on transforming a company's key processes into strategic capabilities that consistently provide superior value to the customer.

3 Companies create these capabilities by making strategic investments in a support infrastructure that links together and transcends traditional SBUs and functions. (SBUs are strategic business units.)

4 Because capabilities necessarily cross functions, the champion of a capabilities-based strategy is the CEO.

P/OM is central to a capabilities-based strategy. What is happening is that fundamental axioms of business, which have been followed with great success for 100 years, are no longer valid. Those axioms can be replaced by reengineering business processes. This change management methodology entails great responsibility for P/OM. As Booz Allen Hamilton states, "Where once the challenge was to find ways to be more competitive with the products or services you produced, it now lies in figuring out how to produce better products or services with which to compete."[23] The shift is from marketing and sales reliance to the systems approach with project teams composed of P/OM, marketing and sales, R&D, engineering, and everyone else involved.

General principles of reengineering and redesigning business processes are listed as a sequential set of steps:

General Principles of REE

1 *Identify special core qualities, competencies, and capabilities* of the company. Some companies have developed unique ability to turn over inventory; others have developed a manufacturing skill in working with special materials. Rare process skills are required for making fine chocolate, and the same applies to automotive windshield glass. A company that will be mentioned shortly has people with special knowledge and a mind-set about hearing-aid technology.

2 *Identify core processes* that deliver the special capabilities described in step 1. Core processes are broad-based. For example, merchandising methods and pricing might be credited with the achievement of fast inventory turnover. Alternatively, electronic data interchange (EDI) linking retail stores, distribution, and delivery systems might be the core process responsible for delivering fast turnovers.

3 *Trace cross-functional transactions* (between P/OM, marketing, distribution, suppliers, and so on) in detailed systems terms—for the core processes. To

Breakpoint business process redesign
Strategic-level competitive advantages in the areas of the company's core business processes.

Capabilities
Capabilities-based strategies are reflected in smart management of business processes.

illustrate, assume that Fidelity Investments wants to examine how their computer systems are used by customers to make unassisted, discounted stock trades by telephone. P/OM's backroom operations handle the calls, which would then be related to cash management, marketing activities, accounts receivable, accounts payable, customer services, and so on.

4 *Develop detailed process analyses*, including activities that are part of cross-functional transactions. Process components consist of people, machines, and workstations.

5 *Benchmark* cost, time, and quality for each process component. Include such measures as customer satisfaction, cycle times, productivity, and complaints and errors. Some benchmarks will be broad-based and others detailed. Fidelity Investments will probably want to benchmark against Charles Schwab & Co., and vice versa. They might be able to do this on broad measures, such as customer satisfaction derived from market research. Data for operations are not likely to be shared by these competitors. Each can propose target-improvement levels for process components. This is done in the next two steps.

6 *Select processes to be redesigned.* Figure 19-1 (adapted from a Booz Allen Hamilton figure)[24] provides a sensible way to prioritize processes with respect to their impact on the desired capabilities and the degree to which each process can be improved.

7 *Set target levels* for improved performance, such as—cut customer waiting time in half, reduce cycle time by 70 percent, decrease perceived difficulty for customers to order online so that it takes half as long, increase inventory turnovers from 6 to 10, set the maximum number of times that the phone should ring before being answered at 3 rings, and so on. Many of the targets listed in this paragraph are typical CRM (customer relationship management) goals. See http://www.crm2day.com.

8 *Reengineer the process.*

9 *Test, evaluate, and replan* (stop REE when satisfied).

19-6a Process Role in Delivering Special Capabilities

Step 2 of the general principles of reengineering is to identify the core processes that deliver the special capabilities. As seen in Figure 19-1, processes do not deliver special

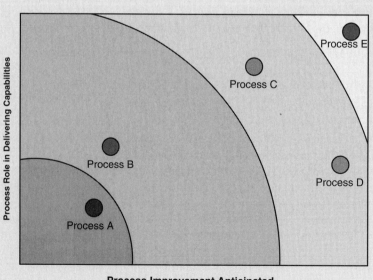

Figure 19-1

Priorities Using Efficiency Frontiers for Reengineering Different Processes (Based on Process Role in Delivering Capabilities and Process Improvement Anticipated)

Process Role in Delivering Capabilities (vertical axis)

Process E

Process C

Process B

Process A

Process D

Process Improvement Anticipated

capabilities equally. Process A has the least ability to deliver the special capabilities chosen in step 1. Process E has the best ability. Process C is next best. Process B is better than D. These five processes have been chosen because they deliver the special capabilities in varying degrees. In other words, the value of the origin of the *y*-axis is not known.

19-6b Process Improvement

The *x*-axis reflects the degree to which each process can be improved. This evaluation is based on the information that was developed using steps 4 and 5. Process E promises the greatest improvement, followed by processes D, C, B, and A, in that order.

The arcs shown in Figure 19-1 are called **efficiency frontiers** because they separate the regions with respect to their combined power to deliver improved capabilities. In effect, these frontiers represent combinations of delivery capabilities (DC) and improvements anticipated (IA) that are considered to be equally desirable. In equation form, they might be approximated by arcs of circles:

$$(DC)^2 + (IA)^2 = R^2 \quad (R \text{ is the circle's radius})$$

Financial analysis uses risk–return efficiency frontiers in much the same way that reengineering employs the DC-IA frontiers. Four regions have been demarcated. Process A is in the worst region. Process E is in the best region and should be chosen for reengineering. Note that efficiency frontiers drawn through processes C and D provide minimal differentiation.

Figure 19-2 provides another way of prioritizing the projects, which clears up the ambiguity for choosing processes C or D.

Using quadrant differentiation, processes in quadrant I are the most important processes for delivering the capability and have the greatest potential for improvement. That makes them ideal subjects for REE. Quadrant II is high on special capabilities but low on improvement potential. As noted here, this may be because these processes have already been reengineered. Quadrant III is low in delivering the selected capabilities but high in improvement potential. Processes A and B in quadrant IV are not attractive candidates for reengineering. They promise little improvement of low-level capabilities.

After reengineering, process E will move from its position in quadrant I to quadrant II, as shown in the right-hand matrix of Figure 19-2. E is located high up in the left-hand corner, indicating that little opportunity remains for this process to be further improved. Process E continues to play a major role in delivering special capabilities. Successful reengineering will result in a cluster of processes in the upper left-hand corner of the right-hand matrix in Figure 19-2. The potential for process improvement will have been used up, and the company's special capability is as good as it is going to get under the current set of systems conditions, i.e., core assets (capabilities, such as intellectual capital) are being used to the best of the company's ability.

Figure 19-3 is a concise rendering of the reengineering process. Feedback loops go from step 9 to steps 6, 7, and 8. This is consistent with *test, evaluate, and replan* (step 9).

It is necessary to be able to reconsider what processes to redesign (6). It is usual practice to reset the target levels (7) and to continue reengineering the process originally selected (8). To accomplish step 8 (reengineer the process), some additional heuristics (rules of thumb—from A to Z) should be considered. These are not intended to be applied sequentially, and a number of the heuristics overlap.

REE Heuristics—a Through z

a. Question the current task structure. For each task ask: Why is this done? Why is this done this way?

b. Before deciding to use reengineering, check the benefits of using continuous improvement methods instead. Continuous improvement and REE should not be used simultaneously.

Efficiency frontiers

These are boundary lines reflecting combinations of variables such as risk and reward or potential improvements and ability to realize them. If a process can be improved a great deal and that will help company performance significantly, it will fall on a high-priority (large radius) efficiency frontier.

The pastry chef is highly trained but not everyone can have the combination of special capabilities that include dexterity, imagination, and ability to deal with stress and pressure.

Figure 19-2

Priorities Using Quadrant Differentiation for Reengineering Different Processes (Based on Process Role in Delivering Capabilities and Process Improvement Anticipated)

After REE: Process E moves from quadrant I to II.

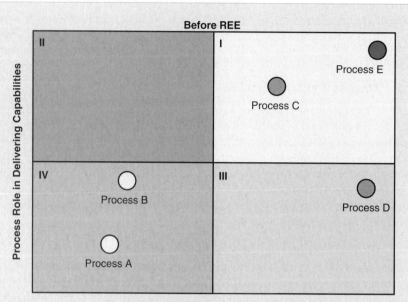

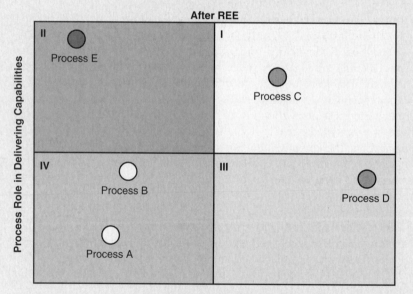

c. When the core processes, goals, and subgoals are understood (steps 1 through 6) and the targets are set (step 7), REE starts with a clean sheet of paper in an effort to achieve the targets. Because benchmarking is an ongoing activity, the processes selected and/or the targets may change.

d. For reengineering, focus on *task design*, not on task execution.

e. Search for radically different approaches. Thinking outside the box is encouraged because almost everything in the box is worn out. Innovative thinking is easier for some people than others. Methods exist for making the strange familiar (familiarization) and the familiar strange (defamiliarization) that are applicable to students in kindergarten.

f. Empower people to consider leading creative projects. (Note the discussions of Oticon Holding S/A, W. L. Gore & Associates, Inc., and MMM, which follow

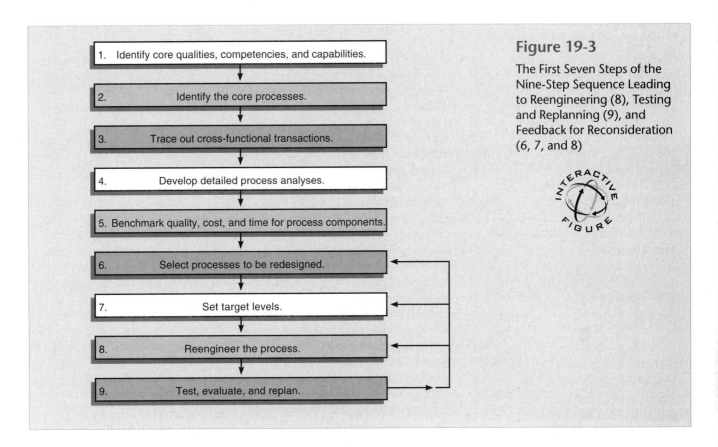

Figure 19-3

The First Seven Steps of the Nine-Step Sequence Leading to Reengineering (8), Testing and Replanning (9), and Feedback for Reconsideration (6, 7, and 8)

1. Identify core qualities, competencies, and capabilities.
2. Identify the core processes.
3. Trace out cross-functional transactions.
4. Develop detailed process analyses.
5. Benchmark quality, cost, and time for process components.
6. Select processes to be redesigned.
7. Set target levels.
8. Reengineer the process.
9. Test, evaluate, and replan.

(see Section 19-6c). These cases provide a small window on what is known about the creative process and organizational catalysts of creativity, such as leadership.)

g. Organize processes around outcomes, not tasks. (If the process to be reengineered is "grant credit," then organize to grant credit and not to do a sequence of tasks such as check on credit history, request credit references, check on credit references, analyze references, analyze income, etc.)

h. Using team collaboration, simultaneously work on as many activities as possible. Strive to avoid sequential activities where one must be finished before another can begin. Experience with **concurrent engineering (CE)** has shown how CE speeds up project completion. When team members work in parallel, individuals can coordinate tasks that are various parts of the job. Another way of stating this is: Delinearize the process for rapid completion with the highest project quality.

i. When possible, make those who use the output of a process part of the group creating that output.

j. Combine information processing with output-producing work. In other words, quantity and quality data should be recorded and analyzed by the same people that produce the product or service. Thus, someone who does credit accounting should be part of the process for setting credit ratings and granting credit.

k. Employ geographically dispersed resources as though they were centralized (using computer technology).

l. Make decisions where the work is done.

m. Place quality controls with the people who do the work.

n. Capture information only once and as close to its source as possible.

o. Develop detailed process flowcharts for the existing processes and for the proposed new processes. "An indispensable tool in Business Process Re-engineering is process mapping. Competitive realignment . . . requires an extensive understanding of the activities that constitute core business processes and the

Concurrent engineering (CE)

Parallel and simultaneous work along many project paths; more resources early in the project's evolution. CE uses a team-oriented framework.

processes that support them, in terms of their purpose, trigger points, inputs and outputs and constraining influences."[25]

p. Successful reengineering emphasizes balancing process flows—not maximizing production flow rates. Increasing output rates can be accomplished in many ways—after the balanced flow has been achieved.

q. Stress every employee's right to choose to do what needs to be done—instead of fulfilling a job description.

r. Experiment with alternatives before finalizing new process configurations to avoid suboptimization.

s. Use **pilot studies** of proposed changes. These can be run in parallel to existing processes. Pilot plants are scaled-down models of the factory or service system.

t. Implement REE changes for only part of the system before expanding the application to the entire system. This requires choosing a sample set of items to manufacture in the new way, a sample of accounts payable to be handled in the reengineered fashion, and a sample set of credit applications to be approved or rejected by the new methods. Then, if the experiment is successful, extend implementation to a larger subset and eventually to the entire system. Call this *partial applications*.

u. Have patience! Efforts that do not work out can be learned from and should encourage further creative experimentation.

v. Institute a continuous reengineering program. This means that steps 6 through 9 in Figure 19-3 should be ongoing.

w. Continuous benchmarking is a learning process (step 5 and heuristic rule C). Search for new benchmarks and continue to measure existing benchmarks over time. Translate benchmarks into targets.

x. Select new processes to be redesigned (step 6). Successes and failures are indicators for new REE opportunities.

y. Constantly reset the target levels (step 7).

z. Successful reengineering often requires reorganization.

19-6c Oticon Holding S/A

In 1991, Lars Kolind, then president of Oticon Holding S/A,[26] reorganized this 89-year-old Danish hearing-aid company. His reengineering of Oticon satisfies the 26 heuristics listed here. Kolind has left Oticon, now, but his out-of-the-box legacy remains. See Chapter 2, Spotlight 2-2: Transformation of Ideas into Sustainable Businesses.

Oticon Holding S/A, home-based in Hellerup, Denmark, had its entire set of business processes reengineered. Oticon embraced radical redesign using continuous project management without labeling it reengineering.

To compete with Siemens, Philips, and Sony, Kolind (as CEO) freed everyone in the organization to generate and develop new ideas. He called his plan the "disorganization" of Oticon with the goal of achieving the "ultimate flexible organization." Departments and titles disappeared. All activities became projects initiated and pursued by informal groups of motivated individuals. Jobs were reconfigured to be fluid, matching individual abilities and company needs. Project leaders were empowered to find and hire the right people.

All offices were eradicated and replaced with open spaces filled with uniform workstations, each consisting of a desk without drawers and a desktop computer. (In Section 20-5, "Readying Operations Management for Future Conditions," the growing use of the "hotel office" concept is described along with that of the "virtual office.") Everyone has access to all information with few exceptions. Incoming mail is optically scanned and then shredded. As a constant reminder of the no-paper policy, the remains of the shredded paper plunge into a glass cylinder, which is a centerpiece of the company's cafeteria.

Kolind changed how people communicate in the organization. Informal dialogue became the accepted mode of communication, replacing all memos and other formal

Pilot studies
Small-scale systems used to test feasibility of the process. The assumption is that if the pilot scale works, then the full-scale system will work.

documentation, including electronic messages. All Oticon employees were described as thinking twice before sending e-mail to Kolind. They opted to avoid his deeming them "superfluous" by electronic return. Kolind believes that oral communication is "ten times more powerful, more creative, quicker, and nicer" than memo writing.

Because it had almost entirely done away with paper, Oticon required employee computer fluency. A computer identical to those in Oticon workstations was offered to every employee for home use in exchange for a commitment to learn to use it. The staff leaped at the opportunity, forming a "PC Club" to train each other outside of working hours. With computers installed at home, the concept of working hours disappeared. Kolind observed that "everyone works more and they're much more flexible."

Two aspects of this company's continuous reengineering process tell the tale. Traditionally, hearing-aid companies focus on the technology required to make small hearing aids smaller. Oticon generated the vision to be the best in any hearing-aid user-satisfaction survey in the world. A successful Oticon design was a bigger unit for hearing better. Aimed at looking like a modern communications system, it was not pink, but silver-gray like a mobile phone.

Second, Oticon is now the third largest hearing-aid manufacturer in the world. It grew 23 percent in a declining market and increased its gross profits by 25 percent. Price per unit was reduced 20 percent in two years. Startling new designs account for the excellent earnings growth. There are about 100 ongoing projects of various magnitude, which have been rated with high probabilities of success. (See Enrichment Activity 19 regarding probability of project success.)

This innovative company, which has earned ISO 9001 certification, epitomizes change management. *Industry Week* reports that Oticon is "now observed as a prototype for the company of the future," providing "vital strategies for survival" in a "knowledge-based era." Lars Kolind believes this applies in 2008, and ahead as well.

19-7 Rapid Completion of Projects: Time-Based Management (TBM)

An area of capability called **time-based management (TBM)** has captured increasing attention because of the success that companies have had using it. TBM elevates time to a position that is equal in importance to cost, quality, and productivity. Time is considered a surrogate for profitability, market share, customers' satisfaction, and so on. Being able to deliver product to customers quickly is one form of TBM. Cutting project duration by a significant amount is another valued form of TBM. Whoever is able to be first into the marketplace with a quality product gains a significant advantage.

The need for speed in project completion has increased as global competitors are empowered by technology. Some are new companies having the advantage of not being encumbered with old plants and old ideas. The time between technological feasibility and new products that embody the new technology has been cut between a third and a half by practitioners of TBM. Technological diffusion concerning the state of the art, and what is feasible, is nearly instantaneous among high-technology players. Many of these companies are home-based in Asia and Europe, and they set up new facilities in North America.

The methods for shortening project life cycle time include PERT analysis with particular emphasis on cutting the critical-path time without jeopardizing quality. Resource management includes resource leveling and COST/TIME trade-offs, which previously have been discussed. Utilization of project funds is often directed toward the goal of minimizing project duration.

The way that the resources are managed has changed considerably as rapid-completion project management has gained adherents because of its clear-cut competitive advantages. The use of more resources at the beginning of the project is encouraged. Project managers used to defer resource utilization until quite late in the project's life cycle.

Time-based management (TBM)

Responsible for fast delivery of goods and services to customers and rapid development of new products.

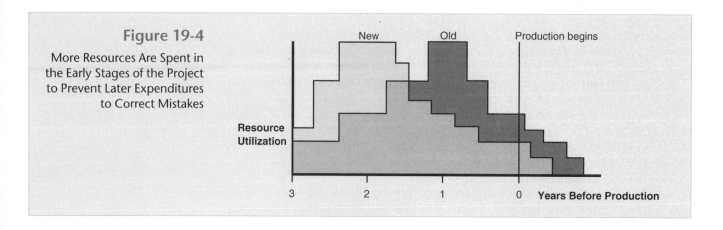

Figure 19-4

More Resources Are Spent in the Early Stages of the Project to Prevent Later Expenditures to Correct Mistakes

Projects, rapid completion

From scratch, design, build, and produce a car in one year, instead of three years.

A main reason for this delay in the early allocation of resources was the compartmentalization of authority, which meant that each group would be left alone to conclude its assignment. Not until approval had been granted for that part of the project would the next stage be authorized to proceed.

Figure 19-4 shows the difference in timing of resource utilization under the time-based project management scenario (new) as compared to the traditional (old) project system. Design for manufacture (DFM) and design for assembly (DFA) are examples of outcomes of using this early resource-allocation orientation of rapid-completion project management. It is useful to note that the appropriate index listing for this subject is **projects, rapid completion**.

It is directed toward preventing the need for later changes by thinking everything through as early as possible. The concept requires many points of view being used in the initial stages of the project. The idea is to dream up (conjecture about) contingencies leading to engineering design changes that could arise and delay the project. The management of resources to achieve early-spending benefits of early project completion is called *concurrent engineering*.

19-7a Concurrent Engineering (CE)

Concurrent engineering (CE) is a time-based management approach that employs more resources earlier in a team-oriented framework than the sequential, compartmentalized project engineering method. The CE approach spends money faster at the start, but it usually reduces project time and improves project quality.

Concurrent engineering is also defined as multifunctional, parallel-path project management. The comparison is made between a football team or a rugby team and a relay race. In rugby, all team players work together to carry the ball down the field. The conventional project management analogy is the relay race, where compartmentalized project groups complete their activities in isolation before handing the baton over to the next group. Every segment runs its own race, i.e., obtains separate approvals that are required before the next one in line is allowed to run.

Figure 19-5 aims to portray the managing team concept for concurrent engineering used to develop a new product (a new production system, etc.). The essential difference with the traditional way is that all channels now communicate with each other from start to finish. The noncompartmentalized structure has to be carefully orchestrated and monitored because there is a tendency to stray back to the old way.

The early use of noncompartmentalized resources has been adopted by many high technology and aerospace companies. In these industries, there is a long history for simultaneous engineering, which put various engineering skills on the same team. Automotive and heavy industry companies also relate to the "simultaneous engineering"

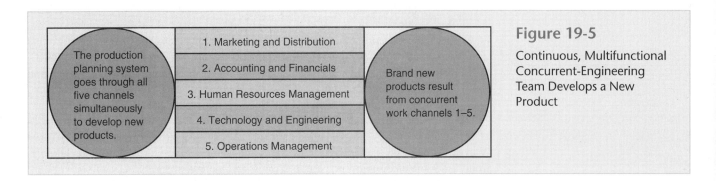

Figure 19-5

Continuous, Multifunctional Concurrent-Engineering Team Develops a New Product

approach. The idea is for technical teams to share their knowledge with the focus on joint problem solving.

The terms *parallel planning* and *parallel engineering* are used because they highlight the fact that a multifunctional team is a permanent part of the project-resource plan. This team (or task force) is in many instances multidisciplinary when various branches of science and engineering are called upon to play a part. The team is expected to define the project goals in great detail and depth. The team is responsible for uncovering potential problems and for taking whatever steps are necessary to avoid them. Quality issues are therefore at the top of the task force's agenda. CE requires a culture in which everyone is responsible for quality.[27]

CE is a way of assuring project quality. It strives to achieve team-based, seamless transfers of information. Successful teams have strong leaders who are experimental innovators. Teams often include customers' and suppliers' organizations. Principles of disassembly are used to accelerate learning. Benchmarking is widespread to provide best-practice standards.

CE methods are known to be used by companies such as Airbus (EADS), Boeing, DaimlerChrysler, Deere & Company, Eastman Kodak, Ford, General Dynamics, GE, GM, Hewlett-Packard, Honda of America, IBM, Ingersoll-Rand, Komatsu, Lockheed-Martin, Nissan, Northrop, Siemens, Toyota, and the U.S. Air Force. This list of 20 organizations represents far less than 1 percent of the companies that are known to use CE for project management.

19-8 Continuous Project Development Model

Global competitors have used CE to develop *continuous* project management systems. **Continuity** refers to project teams that complete one project and then move to another. In this way, project skills are not dissipated when a project is completed. Because product and process improvement is an ongoing effort, the task force often supports the use of continuous improvement.

Continuity in project management also refers to the use of project teams in different parts of the world so that the work can progress as it follows the sun. Teams using distance-learning technologies can transfer information about the status of projects. The media are the Internet, interactive video, etc. Data travels from east to west as team specialists communicate what has been learned and what needs to be done.

Engineers at General Electric–Fanuc (a long-term U.S.–Japan joint venture) design devices used to control factory operations that function around the clock, using a telelink with Japan.[28] Each day's accomplishments are downloaded from GE in the United States to Fanuc in Japan in the afternoon, and uploaded from Japan the next morning. See http://www.gefanuc.com. Global companies are using round-the-clock shifts with CAD/CAM to design and manufacture textiles. Bells and whistles are not really needed. Two-shift project management is a major step ahead of one-shift in cutting project time.

Continuity

Refers to project teams that upon completing a project, or even during the activities of a project, begin another project; benefit of not dissipating project skills and knowledge.

19-8a W. L. Gore & Associates, Inc.

W. L. Gore & Associates[29] has been practicing continuous reengineering long before that term was invented. The company is best known for consumer products including GORE-TEX® brand fabric and ELIXER® guitar strings. GORE-TEX fabric is a synthetic material that is popular for outdoor (and camping) use because of its waterproof and breathable qualities. It is made of an expanded form of polytetrafluoroethylene (PTFE) or Teflon.

The company was founded in 1958 by Wilbert L. (Bill) Gore, a former research chemist with DuPont in Newark, Delaware, and by his wife and business manager Genevieve (Vieve). Today, W. L. Gore & Associates makes thousands of advanced technology products for the electronics, industrial, fabrics, and medical markets.

Products have been developed by the 8,000 associates in facilities throughout the world. There are 4500 in the U.S. No one is an employee—everyone is an associate. Gore uses a "lattice organization," which connotes freedom to move in any direction: to lead, to grow, or to commit to new projects. Many of the associates have developed ideas that have garnered supporters. Leaders arise when their ideas inspire others to follow them. Everyone is encouraged to develop projects leading to new products.

This continuous project development method has achieved great results. The company has experienced steady growth with 2006 worldwide sales reaching $2 billion. The company has generated more than 700 U.S. patents in its 50 years of operation, which is more than 14 domestic patents per year. Based on its **core competencies** with PTFE and Gore-Tex expanded PTFE, the company has more than 50 plants and sales locations worldwide and, on average, 160 associates per location.

This indicates another lattice organization principle, which is to stay under 200 people per plant. Small plants with no authoritarian hierarchy encourage people to communicate with each other in creative ways. Because there are no bosses, sponsors act as advocates for associates in compensation matters. Advice flows freely in all directions because there are no titles and there is no formal organization. Gore's facilities in the U.K., Italy, and Germany have been named as one of the Best Companies to Work For as well as in the United States, where it has earned 10th place in *Fortune*'s January 8, 2007, list where W. L. Gore & Associates has appeared for the 10th consecutive year. See http://www.greatplacetowork.com/best/list-bestusa.htm.

The key values of this global company can be summed up as fairness, freedom to grow and innovate, self-commitment, and communication. Gore President and CEO Terri Kelly, in 2007, described the unique corporate structure as follows: "All of our practices stress maximizing individual potential, maintaining an emphasis on product integrity, and cultivating an environment that fosters creativity. Despite our growth and expansion worldwide, we continue to believe that our people and their abilities are the key to our success."

19-8b Ceaseless Reengineering—Project Management Cycles

Oticon and W. L. Gore are two companies that provide useful models of ceaseless reengineering driven by means of continuous project development. Both companies have an internal focus that is insistent on pleasing customers. Oticon and Gore avoid hierarchies and grant employees freedom to be creative and to search for better ways to satisfy customers. Both firms are continuously reinventing themselves without needing special names such as "reengineering."

Another innovative organization is 3M (MMM—also known as the Minnesota Mining and Manufacturing Co.). 3M has an astounding record of new product development, and the organization supports the same kind of personal creativity that characterizes Oticon and Gore. A useful self-assignment for students who are interested in being champions of innovation within their firms is to research 3M using search engines on the web.

Figure 19-6 is an explanation of how continuous project management systems function.

Core competencies

Focus on competitive technological advantages with processes, materials, and product designs. Contrast with (management) **Capabilities**.

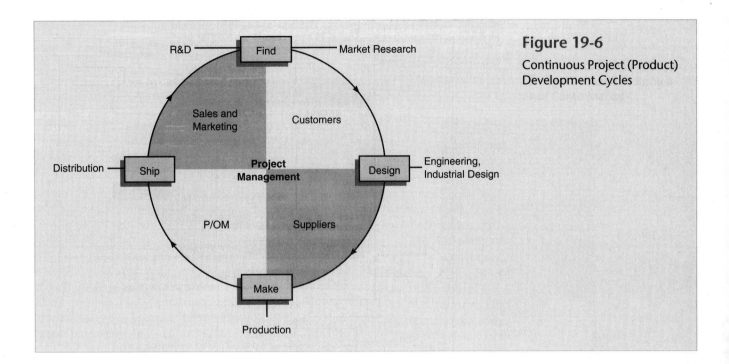

Figure 19-6

Continuous Project (Product) Development Cycles

The project management team is multifunctional, which facilitates the coordination of finding, designing, making, and shipping the product. The *find-design-make-ship* cycle must be supported by appropriate functions. All functions participate in each stage, but some of the main effects are as follows: Find and design are best done while everyone "listens to the voice of the customer." Design and make should be coordinated with suppliers. P/OM connects make and ship. Sales and marketing drive shipping. Market research and R&D back up the creative impulses of the project-oriented management. Only a systems attitude (state of mind) can adequately relate all of these cross-functional considerations.

When one project leader finishes the cycle, another can take over the released resources. Alternatively, the same project leader can go through another product development cycle with the purpose of making new contributions or further improvements. The same model applies to the dynamics of projects starting and finishing. A well-managed project wheel is constantly turning. The number of turns of this wheel measures the revenue-generating energy of the system. Still some failures are bound to occur. When properly viewed, these provide learning experiences that improve the probabilities of future successes.

The Ferris Wheel is always spelled with a capital F because it is named after its creator. George W. Ferris built the Ferris Wheel for the 1893 World's Fair in Chicago. The ride cost 50 cents and made $727,000, which was a lot of money for that time. Ferris Wheels serve as analog models for continuous project management. The idea of spacing project completions so that resources can be shifted from a completed project to one that is just starting is portrayed by the Ferris Wheel. Enrichment Activity 19 shows how this works. It also uses probability of project success to determine net profits of project development programs.

© 2008 Jupiterimages Corporation

A Ferris Wheel is an analog model of a perfectly continuous project development system. Of course, nothing about project management is totally controllable and so perfection must be tempered with humility.

Spotlight 19-1 Kevin Howard: Saving Time and Money by Postponement

An Interview with Kevin Howard, Consultant, Packnomics, LLC

Kevin Howard

What do Burger King and the Hewlett-Packard Company have in common that earns both companies P/OM accolades? The answer is postponement of customized product and packaging differentiation. Kevin Howard worked at HP from 1988–2005, where he initiated the concept of packaging postponement for inkjet (DeskJet) printers.

Burger King prepares its Whopper or burger sandwich and then places it under the cover of a steam table for up to 10 minutes so that it can be finalized to satisfy the customer's request. Other items are stored in a Henny Penny warmer for up to 30 minutes. These work-in-process (WIP), inventoried items enable Burger King to make good on their marketing statement, "Have it your way."

The Hewlett-Packard postponement strategy was begun in 1989 when HP decided to ship generic models of ink-jet printers from their factories in Vancouver, Washington, and Singapore. These boxed printers were shipped to three distribution centers (DCs) around the world where they were "localized" for their final destination. Localization means adding country-specific power modules and language-specific software and manuals to the boxes at the DC sites. Before 1989, printers were made and packaged in line with forecasts for country and language-specific SKUs.

To better respond to fluctuating demands for specific localized configurations of printers without increasing inventory levels, analyses were done by HP engineers and P/OM consultants from academia. Some of the people who worked on this project were Brent Carter, Manager for Special Projects, Kevin Howard, HP packaging logistics engineer, and Hau Lee, a professor at the Stanford Business School. To avoid forecasting, which had sizeable errors of both types

(overstocks and out-of-stocks), they studied various systems of postponing fulfillment until actual orders were on-hand.

Kevin Howard's assignment was to determine a way to localize printer shipments This was first accomplished by using a new box design to ship the printers from the manufacturing plants to the distribution centers (DCs). These boxes had a flap that could be opened and the localizing materials inserted at the DC without removing the printers from the pallets. This allowed DCs to localize the units at a point in the distribution process when demand was known which resulted in major savings. However, as Howard said, "It was clear to me we were paying a lot for shipping this empty space in the boxes. . . . and were spending (for Europe, at that time) almost $400,000 a year on repackaging boxes that had been damaged during distribution overseas."

Considerable product damage resulted from repetitive handling of boxes. Some damage was caused by forklift trucks as the boxed printers were moved on wood pallets. Who would have guessed that forklift truck operators would take greater care with printers they could see than with boxes that made the product invisible? Packaging experts might confirm that large anonymous cardboard boxes are a natural target for lift forks and a convenient place for warehouse workers to stand on for stacking boxes. With a visible product, damage rates decreased to near-zero, representing significant savings.

Howard's second improvement was accomplished in 1991. Instead of palletizing half-empty printer boxes, unboxed printers were packed on cavitated foam trays so that more could fit on a wood pallet. Elimination of boxes and protective foam cushioning allowed pallet density to increase from 32 to 60 units per pallet. This process permitted shipping more printers. It also decreased product damage. Prior to bulk packing the printers, individually boxed printers were commonly stripped off of pallets by air freight forwarders and stacked one at a time onto air cargo cookie sheets. This individual handling resulted in drops and crushing when workers stepped on boxes. The new design interlocked all the printers into one unitized load that could not easily be broken apart. The thousand pound load could only be moved with mechanical assistance, thus eliminating free fall drops of individual units.

A third improvement replaced heavy wood pallets with plastic (polyethylene) slip sheets that provided flexible platforms for shipping. Special fork lift truck adapters to handle slip sheets and elimination of the wooden pallets allowed HP to get 25 percent more printers in the stack and to reduce transportation, storage, and materials handling costs by 25 percent.

Kevin Howard believed that the use of wood pallets was "a tragic misuse of our natural resources." He said that a significant amount of lumber cutting goes into the production of wood pallets, measuring in the hundreds of millions annually, many of which are thrown away after one use. The reuse rate in Europe is better because of standardized pallet designs and agreements to re-employ these pallets.

In the 1990s, the high-density polyethylene (HDPE) sheets, which are the thickness of a cardboard cereal box, were made of 100 percent recycled milk jugs. Also during that period, HP returned many of the used slip sheets to the manufacturer for recycling in the United States, while other locations could recycle this material locally. These plastic slip sheets continue to be recycled.

When this study was first undertaken, HP was shipping about 150,000 printers per month. More than a decade later, that number has grown to more than 3 million per month. Densifying the loads from 32 boxed printers on a pallet to 75 unboxed printers on a slip sheet saved tens of millions of dollars in logistics costs. Adding language-specific accessories and electrical connections at the DC rather than at the factory reduced inventory carrying costs about 20 percent, saving many millions of dollars annually. Additionally, inventory levels decreased for the supply chain pipeline and for the safety stock required to keep out-of-stocks at a specified service level.

Currently, HP has many plants in many places in the world, but it continues to use postponement of final packaging and country-specific product differentiation. The systems approach, as described here, continues to increase flexibility and reduce unnecessary waste. Contrary to the old maxim, he who hesitates may be consciously avoiding irreversible mistakes by using the postponement method.

Review Questions

1 What do Home Depot, Dell, Wendy's, Xilinx, and Burger King have in common with Hewlett-Packard that earns them all high P/OM grades?

2 In October 2003, Oracle Corporation and Cap Gemini Ernst & Young U.S. LLC jointly sponsored an in-depth study of emerging trends in postponement. More than 350 supply chain professionals took part in the survey conducted with APICS. What did this survey discover? See http://www.us.capgemini.com/news/current_news.asp?ID=335&PRyear=2003.

3 What does postponement have to do with push versus pull process methods?

4 How did Kevin Howard improve packaging of generic printers at the factory to permit localizing the product at the distribution center?

5 What kinds of products would be good candidates for localization? What kinds of savings could be made from postponement strategies? To answer the second part of this question, note the savings made by Howard at HP. Also, the article at the URL given in Question 2 can be of some help in answering this question.

Sources: Kevin Howard. "Postponement of Packaging and Product Differentiation for Lower Logistics Costs." Invited paper presented to the Council of Logistics Management Conference, Michigan State University, May 1991. Conversations and correspondence with Kevin Howard, December 2003, March 2005, April 2007. In the April 2007 communication, Kevin Howard pointed out that, "the postponement concept eventually spread throughout HP to virtually every high volume product made in the 1990s. Also, during that time, Canon, Apple and Lexmark employed the concept, and perhaps others." At the same time, Kevin Howard made the following crucial statement, "It should be realized there are practical limits to the use of packaging and product differentiation postponement. The characteristics that made packaging postponement practical for HP printers were the combination of two factors. First, the ratio of product size to package size was small. With small ratios, pallet load density can be increased substantially by postponing packaging. Second, when shipping costs are large because distances are great and air cargo is used, postponement provides great savings. When HP began to utilize maritime cargo transport instead of air cargo transport, the scales tipped away from postponement for lower valued items that did not require customization. Ocean shipping costs 80 to 90 percent less than air shipping per unit. Smaller printers were designed with greater printing, scanning, and copying capabilities with less damage vulnerabilities. Good systems analysis that takes all factors into account is essential to determine when to use postponement."

Spotlight 19-2 The Pursuit of Clean Air

In 1952, the Great Smog of London killed 4000 people in four days. Air pollution control found a champion in Dr. Arie Haagen-Smit, a biologist and researcher at the California Institute of Technology. By 1954, he had demonstrated in his laboratory that nitrogen oxides and hydrocarbons (greenhouse gases) in the presence of ultraviolet radiation from the sun interact to form smog, a key component of which is ozone. Ozone is good in our stratosphere (protects

Spotlight 19-2 (Continued)

us from the sun's ultraviolet waves) but at ground level, ozone from smog damages people, animals, and crops. By 1955, England had passed its first Clean Air Act.

In the same year, the U.S. federal government under President Dwight D. Eisenhower decided to deal with air pollution on a national level. The Air Pollution Control Act of 1955 was the first federal legislation of its kind, following pollution-reduction efforts from state and local governments. The federal act identified air pollution as an environmental hazard and assigned Congress the right to control this growing problem. However, the act did little to prevent air pollution, despite Dr. Haagen-Smit's findings that exhaust from motor vehicles and industrial facilities become part of the greenhouse gases (GHG) that create smog.

Eight years later, the Clean Air Act of 1963 under President John F. Kennedy set emissions standards for stationary sources. Power plants and steel mills were regulated, but the act did not take into account mobile sources of pollution. Under President Lyndon Johnson (1963–1968), the 1965, 1966, 1967, and 1969 (Nixon) amendments authorized governmental departments to set standards for auto emissions and to set air quality standards.

Nixon, in his State of the Union Address in January 1970, said that the American people had entered a "historic period when, by conscious choice, [we] transform our land into what we want it to become." He signed the National Environmental Policy Act, creating a new Council on Environmental Quality. The environmental movement was underway. April 22, 1970, marked the first Earth Day. On July 9, Nixon called for the creation of the Environmental Protection Agency.

In the same month, Nixon signed the Clean Air Act of 1970, which some compared to President John F. Kennedy's 1961 challenge to put a man on the moon before the end of the decade. The 1970 act presented an extreme challenge, ensuring that all Americans would have air that is safe to breathe within a time frame that initially seemed impossible. It also mandated removal of toxic lead in gasoline. The goal was a 90 percent reduction in automobile emissions measured against pre-1968 standards. The deadline was the end of 1974, when new model cars for 1975 would be on the market.

An extraordinary crash program of research and development followed. Engineers knew that factories would have to be ready to produce emission controls before the deadline for a mass market. To most engineers, it looked hopeless. However, one man had been working on gasoline emission problems since the end of World War II.

That man was Eugene Houdry. He would have welcomed the Clean Air Act, but his death had occurred eight years earlier. As an engineer, he developed catalytic cracking in the 1920s and 1930s. Houdry's process provided a large part of the aviation fuel needed for the Allied victory in World War II. He was convinced that unburned hydrocarbons from automobile exhaust gases caused lung cancer, and he thought he had a solution.

In 1948, Houdry founded Oxy-Catalyst in Wayne, Pennsylvania, to develop catalyst systems that would oxidize and convert unburned hydrocarbons into water and harmless carbon dioxide (CO_2). No one knew that CO_2 would be debated as a global warming issue in the future. By 1959, his catalytic mufflers were fitted into the exhaust system of automobiles. He is quoted as saying, "Put them on all cars and watch the lung cancer curve dip." His catalytic muffler was awarded a patent in 1962, the same year he died at the age of 70.

At that time, drivers were accustomed to using leaded gas in their cars to achieve higher octane and to prevent engine knocking. However, leaded gasoline limits the effectiveness of catalytic converters. Converters use a combination of catalysts (platinum, aluminum oxide, and palladium) spread out over a honeycomb structure through which exhaust gases must flow to turn harmful gases into water and CO_2. Emissions from leaded gasoline coated the catalysts with lead, making it necessary to replace converters about every 12,000 miles at a cost of approximately $150. That was not considered acceptable to the American public.

By 1969, smog over California freeways was so bad that the state created its own standards. The Engelhard Company in New Jersey was working on a project to reduce carbon monoxide emissions from forklifts in mines and warehouses. Carl Keith of Engelhard (who knew Eugene Houdry's work) began experimenting with unleaded gasoline. Spurred on by the Clean Air Act of 1970, which specified converter effectiveness for at least 50,000 miles, scientists from Corning Glass Works also joined the search for a device that would clean a car's exhaust gases.

Each impossible challenge was met. The government raised standards again and again, and this remarkable handful of company scientists and engineers kept meeting them. The resulting catalytic converter has been called one of the greatest environmental achievements of the twentieth century.

The Clean Air Act of 1990 strengthened and improved existing regulations in many areas: air quality standards, motor vehicle emissions and alternative fuels, toxic air pollutants, acid rain, and stratospheric ozone depletion. The Eurozone had even more stringent regulations than the United States. China imposed the most rigorous standards of any country based on a brilliant strategy. China's tough rules were intended to pressure their auto companies and dealers to introduce hybrids and other cleaner alternative technologies to minimize dependence on foreign oil. In hybrids, an electric motor's battery is charged by the gas engine while braking or idling, saving fuel and energy. China's population, with a potential market of millions of hybrid cars, could support high production at low cost. In the United States, hybrid cars account for only slightly more than one percent of all vehicles. In 2007, U.S. government tax benefits for purchasing a hybrid were cancelled.

Smog abatement strategies include non-polluting biofuel. Ethanol, made from sugarcane in Brazil, is used in 18 percent of Brazilian cars (2008). In this country, corn is the usual feedstock. Gasoline in the United States already contains up to 10 percent ethanol by law. A 2007 study by Mark Jacobson, a Stanford University civil and environmental engineering professor, says switching from gasoline to ethanol may create dirtier air, causing slightly more smog-related deaths. Other experts disagree. Forty percent of the current U.S. production of biofuel is made up of small businesses. One company in Georgia uses watermelons in its fermentation plant. The future of ethanol is not clear but there is a lot of entrepreneurial kinetic energy being expended.

Hydrogen, the most common element in the universe, can be obtained from a wide variety of renewable sources. No one knows if hydrogen-powered cars are practical, but experiments are going on. Four hydrogen-powered Ford buses are now in service in Orlando, Florida, with four more to come. A Shell and GM partnership is in process of building two large-scale demonstration models including service station infrastructure due to be on display in the United States in 2009.

Currently, the temperature of our earth's surface has become the subject of worldwide controversy. Fear of continued global warming is at the core of the debate. Measurement of greenhouse gases shows that the amount of carbon dioxide in our atmosphere is 35 percent higher than 200 years ago. One should keep in mind that correlation is not necessarily causation. Otherwise it would be easy to conclude that man-made CO_2 is surely the cause of global warming. That issue can be debated in light of geologic history. A 1500-year cycle of heating and cooling goes back a million years. Research from the Ocean University School of Marine Science in China shows evidence of a rapid buildup of natural GHG in the early Jurassic period (180,000 years ago). Temperatures rose by 9 degrees Fahrenheit. Being cautious makes good sense. Why produce more CO_2 if it can be just as cost efficient—or even more cost efficient—to produce less CO_2?

Many countries have agreed to limit the amount of man-made GHG that reaches the atmosphere. Plans to collect and store CO_2 at large industrial sites are underway. "Clean coal" plants are being built. Nuclear energy sources are reappearing. Solar, wind and tidal energy recovery systems are being discussed. With good research, all of these methods are likely to hold promise.

The Kyoto Protocol has put a cap on allowable emissions. Committing to this agreement, 160 member countries have joined in a United Nations effort, using a complex credit-trading plan (creating potential for both hostility and cooperation). The United States, Australia, and a few other countries have not joined the Kyoto agreement but have a plan of their own. Since the global average air temperature near Earth's surface has increased 1.33 degrees Fahrenheit in the last 100 years, many fear that an increase over 3.6 degrees Fahrenheit will make global warming much more difficult to curb. More solid research needs to be done.

California is the world leader in its efforts to manage air quality and fight global warming. In 2006, Governor Schwarzenegger signed landmark legislation to reduce greenhouse gas emissions. The press release from the governor's office quoted him as saying, "I wanted to make California No. 1 in the fight against global warming. This is something we owe our children and grandchildren.... I say unquestionably it is good for businesses. Not only large, well-established businesses, but small businesses that will harness their entrepreneurial spirit to help us achieve our climate goal.... By 2050 we will reduce emissions to 80 percent below 1990 levels. We simply must do everything in our power to slow down global warming before it is too late." Business thrives in this creative environment if it is sincere and not political.

Business organizations should prepare for change in both climate and smog control. Unlike the global warming debate, the effects of smog are not controversial. In pursuit of clean air, there is good reason to be optimistic in light of our historic ingenuity and the fact that well-founded solutions will benefit all.

Review Questions

1 What is the federal government's history of air pollution control in the United States from 1955 through 1970?

2 What is the history of automotive emissions, including origination of efforts to control substances discharged into the air by internal combustion engines?

3 Which people and companies were responsible for the development of the catalytic systems for auto emission control?

4 What country has imposed the most rigorous and demanding standards on automotive emissions?

5 What is the systems approach to providing clean air?

Sources: Tim Palucka. "Doing the Impossible." *Invention & Technology* (Winter 2004): 22–31; "Legislation: A Look at U.S. Air Pollution Laws and Their Amendments." http://www.ametsoc .org/sloan/cleanair/index.html; http://www.cleanairtrust.org/cleanairact .html; http://www.ametsoc.org/sloan/cleanair/cleanairlegisl.html; http:// www.answers.com/topic/what-are-greenhouse-gases; http://www.cbc .ca/news/background/environment/smog.html; http://www.hydrogen .energy.gov/pdfs/review06/tv_7_sell.pdf; http://en.wikipedia.org/wiki/ Global_warming http://gov.ca.gov/index.php?/press-release/4111 http://www.calepa.ca.gov/About/History01/arb.htm (last updated 2006).

Summary

The need for change (transition, modification, and alteration) is often apparent, but managers of organizations are not able to shift directions. Bureaucracy deflects efforts to change but that does not make bureaucracy bad or evil. Most often, it is a guardian of the status quo. The key point is that when fundamental change is required to survive, sticking to the status quo may destroy a company that could have met the challenge if it had recognized the need to change.

Chapter 19 explains a change model composed of four factors. Using these factors, P/OM can develop systems that encourage change when change is needed. The approach for determining what to—and how much to—change is related to the method of learning from comparison—using benchmarking. Technology is advancing at an incredible rate, creating new global competitors. The Internet has created a cohort of young millionaires. It has permanently altered the way that supply chain procurement operates.

Further, it produced an advantage for the swift. Rapid completion of new products can spell the difference between profit or loss. Continuous new product project development provides major competitive advantage. Descriptions of three companies that engage in one form or another of continuous product development are presented. Also, P/OM has mastery over continuous improvement methods for incremental alteration as well as the radical reengineering approach. P/OM can fix a broken system either way. The trick is to figure out when to discard the old and do reengineering (starting with a clean slate requires top-down support to remake the system).

Spotlight 19-1: Saving Time and Money by Postponement presents an interview with Kevin Howard, who explains how his packaging projects completely changed the way that printers were packed and shipped by Hewlett-Packard. This remarkable story epitomizes the power of persistent project management to "evolutionize" an otherwise static and traditional method of shipping product. Spotlight 19-2: Pursuit of Clean Air is an ongoing story of point and counterpoint. Indications of change are occurring with possible causes and probable consequences that may demand major projects on a worldwide stage. Results to date indicate actions being taken in bits and pieces at every hierarchical level including on the local companies plant floor and offices.

Key Terms

Breakpoint business process redesign (p. 813)

Capabilities (p. 813)

Change management (p. 801)

Concurrent engineering (CE) (p. 817)

Continuity (p. 821)

Continuous improvement (CI) (p. 811)

Core competencies (p. 822)

Dissatisfaction (p. 805)

Efficiency frontiers (p. 815)

Ferris Wheel model (p. 838)

Gleicher Model (Conditions for change) (p. 804)

Peer-assist (p. 809)

Pilot studies (p. 818)

Practical first steps (p. 805)

Products, Continuous development (p. 811)

Projects, Continuous development (p. 811)

Projects, Probability of success (p. 838)

Projects, rapid completion (p. 820)

Reengineering (REE) (p. 812)

Smart benchmarks (p. 810)

Time-based management (TBM) (p. 819)

Vision (p. 805)

Review Questions

1 What is P/OM's role in change management?
2 What eight factors are forcing the organization to change?
3 How do the four elements of the Gleicher change model work?
4 Use the Gleicher change model to explain why a new CEO might say that another vision statement is not needed.

5 What is the effect of downsizing on change management?

6 Why do schools teach that downsizing is not reengineering?

7 The elevators are kept locked at Oticon in Denmark to encourage meetings on the stairwells. What purposes are served?

8 What are the various kinds of benchmarking that are used?

9 What is continuous benchmarking?

10 How do smart benchmarks differ from other ones? Exemplify.

11 Why should continuous improvement programs be regularly reviewed by a change management team?

12 It has been said that transition planning and training should include senior management. Explain this and give examples.

13 Provide nine reengineering principles and explain them.

14 What purpose is served by the reengineering heuristics, A through Z. Pick the half you like the most, and explain why.

15 What is the purpose of time-based management (TBM)?

16 How does concurrent engineering relate to project management?

17 Explain the resource-management principle that CE uses.

18 What is the special role of teamwork for CE?

19 Why is it said that computers are essential for project management?

20 What are the usual goals of rapid-completion project management?

21 Why is it pointed out that Oticon Holding S/A and W. L. Gore & Associates, Inc., do not use the term *reengineering* even though both companies are excellent examples of continuous reengineering?

22 What are the benefits of continuous project development?

23 Peer-assist arises when a project team seeks to enlist colleagues from other sites to bring special knowledge to bear. How does peer-assist differ from peer review? (A web search is suggested to answer this question.)

Problems Section

1 Using the Gleicher model, if: $D = 9$, $V = 7$, $P = 1$, and $C = 40$. Will the organization be likely to accept change? Assume D and V are scaled 0 to 10 and that P is either 1 or 0. Also, assume that C is measured from 0 to 100.

2 In Problem 1, there is a lot of dissatisfaction and a reasonable vision of what the future could be like. There is much resistance to change. C is more than four times larger than D. Practical first steps are unknown ($P = 1$ rather than 0). Then, a consulting firm is hired that recommends a 15 percent workforce reduction. What changes might be expected in the original set of numbers?

3 *Business Week* and *Forbes Magazine* benchmark business schools regularly. *U.S. News & World Report* ranks undergraduate and graduate schools. *The Financial Times* ranks executive education programs. There has been criticism of the benchmarks used.

   a. Develop the lines of the criticism that are deserved.

   b. Develop a set of criteria that you believe would permit an accurate comparison of business schools.

   c. Do the same as in b. for executive education programs.

4 Make a chart for the benchmarks developed in Problem 3b. Then rate your own school on each of the criteria from 1 to 7, where 7 is best. If you have friends attending other business schools, ask them to rate their schools using your benchmark criteria. Compare the ratings and discuss what they mean.

5 Referring to Problem 4, if you want to combine the numbers in some way to get a single number (as *Business Week* and *Forbes Magazine* do), a scoring model will have to be developed. One possibility is to multiply the $j = 1 \ldots n$ ratings for each school. For school A this would be: R_{jA}. Then the index value for school A is

   a. $Index_A = R_{1A} \times R_{2A} \times R_{3A} \times \cdots \times R_{nA}$. Use this scoring model and explain your results.
   More complex scoring systems weight the ratings before multiplying them. For example:

   b. $Index_A = R_{1A}{}^{w1} \times R_{2A}{}^{w2} \times R_{3A}{}^{w3} \times \cdots \times R_{nA}{}^{wn}$. Use this scoring model and explain your results.

   c. Compare the results in a. and b.

6 To improve the school, which factors should be changed first? (Use the information developed for Problems 3, 4, and 5.)

7 Ferris Wheel, Inc., has generated over 1,200 patents worldwide in its 37 years of operation—better than 32 per year.

   a. What is the average interval in days between patents granted?

   b. What kind of system could generate this number of projects for products that are unique enough to be awarded patents?

8 Various methods are used by companies to determine their best candidates for significant improvement using process reengineering. Efficiency frontiers (Figure 19-1 in the text) are approximated by the equation $(DC)^2 + (IA)^2 = R^2$ where

DC = delivery capabilities; IA = improvements anticipated, and the radius, R, reflects the combined power of the efficiency frontier.

a. Calculate the efficiency frontier values for the following table:

Project	A	B	C	D	E
R^2	4	4	9	9	16
DC	1.414		2.122	3	3
IA		2			

b. Rank order preference for these projects and explain.

9   Draw the chart indicating the appropriate efficiency frontiers and the points for each project as obtained in the table for Problem 8. Rank order preference for projects.

10 Construct a quadrant differentiation chart using the data in Problem 8 and the quadrant center point of 2.2. Compare the results with those from the chart in Problem 9.

11 Set up the best possible schedule for project continuity using concurrent-engineering methods. The company and its suppliers have research offices in New York City (0), San Francisco (–3), Tokyo (+14), and London (+5). The number of hours that separates each city is within parentheses. Is there any way of maintaining perfect project continuity?

12 Major revisions of U.S. patent law are under consideration. The expectation in 2008 was that it will become increasingly more difficult to sue for infringement. Explains what this means. Does the assumption hold true? Bring to bear research on the number of patents granted in the United States over the past five years.

Practice Quiz

1   Change in external business conditions is always occurring. There is a question about whether change is happening more often and if the changes are more extreme. The Famous Publisher (TFP) has taken the classes for project management and has now set up an Adaptability Management Council (AMC) to deal with rapid changes in the textbook publishing field. AMC has issued a list of topics for debate at a meeting next week. The list is being sent to all textbook editors and managers before the meeting. Which points a. to e. are incorrect?

a. Transitions in the publishing business are taking place but at a speed that allows everyone in the field to evaluate the situation and devise plans for eventualities. For example, e-books were first heralded as replacing paper books, distance learning was proclaimed as the classroom replacement, and the Internet was going to deliver most classroom materials, including textbooks. None of this has happened, yet.

b. New technology is streaming into place in publishing. Few authors write books with quill in hand. Harry Potter's author, J. K. Rowling, is an exception. The students at Hogwarts School for Witchcraft and Wizardry, not surprisingly, use quills and not computers. On the contrary, the technology of editors, compositors, graphic designers, and printers is changing at a remarkable rate. Yet, the publishing industry has tamed the technology. It has used it to do what it always has done, in somewhat faster and better ways, rather than being changed by it in any fundamental way.

c. Start-up publishing companies have an opportunity to use technological innovations (such as the Internet) in unique ways that are likely to set new standards for textbook publications. There can be significantly lower text prices, which will provide market entry to companies that have not been able to compete with the Big Guys before.

d. Price alone will not make the difference. At least part of the education market has a kinked elasticity curve, which means that demand goes up when price is increased. Kinked elasticity is associated with customers that want high quality and use price as proof that they are getting it. Wedding gifts and the best schools need to be priced high to convey this message.

e. Technology change supports new processes that deliver higher quality products. For example, graphics will be dynamic, quizzes will be interactive, and Internet links will be active connections to the real world. Perhaps most important of all, there can be constant updating of materials. This replaces the traditional 3-year revision cycle for textbooks.

2   Some large, quick-service restaurants (QSR) have been studying the possibilities of using robotic servers as part of the preparation and counter-delivery operations. Advances in robotic technology have made this option reasonable to consider. This purpose is to obtain cost efficiencies, increased service speed, and other quality improvements. A SWOT analysis has been done by one of the major chains. Their task force report has been circulated to top planners, and it has gotten a great deal of response, including identification of faulty conclusions. Which points a. to e. are not correct?

a. Strengths include being among the first to test the new restaurant concept. Marketing sees the new technology appealing to children. Being first to market is generally a significant advantage. Robots could act as a barrier to entry if their costs are significant. Copycat QSRs might find duplicating the robotic technology of established chains too costly, lacking the advantage of being first with unique appeal. P/OM input to the design of the new server technologies is essential for productivity, maintenance, costs, and quality controls.

b. Weaknesses caused by ignoring robotics include the likelihood that new firms will enter the business and be first to market with a new customer appeal. A reverse weakness occurs if an ethical problem arises as a result of using the robots for customer service in lieu of the current workforce. Layoffs will be criticized, generating ill will. Any dangers that exist in contact between robots and customers must be fully explored because an accident of any kind will be exploited.

c. Opportunities exist with respect to health claims. Robots will not carry infectious Hepatitis A, which is a fairly common food handler safety issue. Robots will not get surly if someone criticizes their performance and does not leave a tip. Programmed machines can be used to clean up rest rooms and to maintain strict rules of sanitary food handling.

d. Threats (*challenges* is a preferred way of viewing this) arise because machines are often associated with environmental pollution. It takes energy to operate a robot, but the amount of energy would probably be far less than a person needs to drive to work. It will be a challenge to establish the benefits to the environment of employing robots, but that case is worth exploring.

e. The SWOT summary is positive for robots. The task force will likely conclude that several experimental sites should be developed to examine the effects of robots on all of the factors in a. through d. Market research with both parents and their children could provide benchmarks for establishing levels of robotics that would be suitable at the start. This level might be increased over time, and that is another subject for study.

3 The American Assembly (in conjunction with Columbia University) held a seminar of several days, in 1988, at Arden House in the Ramapo Mountains of New York to discuss how to get the United States back on track with respect to global competitiveness and world-class productivity. Dr. David Gleicher's model was used to analyze the situation because it explains conditions for achieving organizational transformation. Seminar attendees agreed that the model captured fundamental elements necessary to bring about change. An evaluation of the success of the model was made after the seminar. This evaluation was published and circulated among the attendees, who agreed with four of the following five points. Which point was considered to be incorrect?

a. Dissatisfaction of business and society with the competitive situation that existed during the 1980s was rampant because customers in the United States were buying products (such as automobiles) made abroad. There was more purchasing by U.S. consumers from foreign companies than vice versa, so there was a trade deficit. That situation has now been rectified because of efforts like the Arden House seminar.

b. Michigan University's Surveys of Consumer Confidence can be a surrogate measure of dissatisfaction (D) in the Gleicher model. The same applies to the Conference Board's Index of Consumer Confidence. Some estimates are given here that reflect the 2007 situation but are not data received from either source for publication.

Date	Index of Consumer Confidence
January 2007	110.0
June 2007	105.0
August 2007	105.5
September 2007	99.9
Base Year: 1985	100.0

When D decreases markedly, only one of four factors is in place to trigger change.

c. A clear vision (V) of a better state of affairs is another one of four factors that must be in place to permit change to occur. An articulated vision for a company might be measured in terms of an achieved return on investment (or return on equity), an employment level, market shares, margin contributions, and inventory turns.

d. What constitutes practical first steps (P) toward achieving the vision is unique to each situation. It is assumed that practical first steps are congruent with long-term strategies of the organization. They must also be consistent with the short-term, tactical activities that are taking place. Practical first steps are tactics that may not be scrutinized for their short-term benefits because they are stepping-stones toward a goal. However, because they are practical, they can be achieved without risk of long-term damage to the company.

e.   The influence of substantial dissatisfaction, multiplied by the strength of an attractive vision of the future, is a compelling force for change. However, until the two change agents are empowered by practical first steps, the combination will not be a viable force for change. Even then, the energy for change must overcome the inertia that is embodied in the cost of change. There is a great cumulative cost incurred when all of the players agree to change their way of life. The force for change, $D \times V \times P$, must overpower the cost of changing, C, i.e., $(D \times V \times P) > C$.

4   A group of managers meets regularly to consider various ways to improve individual member's performance. These managers come from all of the familiar functional areas within a firm. There are about equal numbers from operations, finance, marketing, HRM, accounting, engineering, and R&D. They agree to build a list of *smart* benchmarks. Meeting together, they pare the list to the top five benchmarks to determine whether each function has its own best benchmarks or whether all areas of the business benefit by using the same smart benchmarks. Which benchmark listed in a. through e. is not so smart?

a.   *Breakeven volume* is interesting to managers of all functional areas because it is a common goal in any organization to achieve the demand volume at which level loss stops. For example, every employee of a museum profits from knowing how many visitors per month are required to pay for their salaries and all other costs.

b.   *Return on investment* is important to financial managers, who use this measure to determine if the capital investments of the company are sufficiently rewarding. *Return on equity* is also used by financial managers to benchmark themselves against other companies with equity financing. *Return on assets* is also used for benchmarking by financial executives. These are all ratios and permit determination of the balance between output and input of investments.

c.   *Delivery quality* is a measure of how many units arrive in unsatisfactory condition. This is an important measure of performance for marketing and logistics managers. Poor delivery quality is related to items that are damaged in transit. These must be returned for replacement. The process of replacing damaged items is costly. Some companies do not replace items and instead refund the customer's payment after the item is returned. This complexity makes c. a smart benchmark.

d.   *Days of inventory* or *inventory turns* are measuring many complex interactive factors. These measures are of primary interest to the P/OM, marketing, and financial managers. In other words, most managers want to know if there is a slowdown in inventory turns. Change management is called for when the inventory begins to accumulate. The first question to answer is why has inventory begun to accumulate? The second question concerns what to do about that.

e.   *Cycle time* is a smart benchmark that reflects a complex of factors. Because those factors are primarily production- and operations-oriented, cycle time is considered to be a smart P/OM benchmark. However, a look underneath the cloak reveals that marketing's ability to deliver on time is a function of the cycle time. More study shows that return on assets will be conditioned by cycle time. There are other aspects to cycle time as well, including the ability to finish a project and get to market first.

5   "Dent Free (DF) takes the dings out." The radio jingle is widely known. DF's regional manager has participated in the process management seminar class. He has expressed great interest in applying continuous improvement methods to the operations of the hundreds of stores that the company operates all over the United States, beginning with the Southeast region. The DF manager says continuous improvement is a natural evolution of the long-term commitment of the company to offer better services at lower prices. Another manager in the seminar is in charge of maintenance for the Always-on Power Company (APC). It has recently experienced serious outages. In fact APC was considered to be at the core of a series of events that led to widespread blackouts in the Midwest and the East Coast in August 2003. In class, the APC manager discussed the fact that power companies have used continuous improvement for many years. That has led to patching networks, which she stated has contributed to serious power failures for companies all over the world. Recently, this was reinforced by an extensive power failure in the London (UK) power grid, which had been the recipient of conscientious continuous improvement. The APC manager went on record as a staunch advocate for total reengineering (REE) based on employing new technology to produce coherent innovative systems rather than patched and "band-aided" systems. The seminar faculty leader saw this difference in approach as an opportunity to examine the pros and cons of continuous improvement versus REE. Accordingly, each manager was asked to create three top reasons for using the system that he or she advocated. There is one error in the continuous improvement list (a., b., and c.) and one error in the REE list (d., e., and f.). Identify the two flaws.

a.   Continuous improvement requires a constant effort to find better ways to produce products and deliver services. This is often a local effort where team members will ask for suggestions from a variety of individuals. There is no requirement that all parts of a production line be included in the system under study. It is expected, though, that upstream and downstream neighbors of the process path being improved will be consulted when changes are being considered. That is another way of describing a "local effort."

b. Dent Free is an organization ideally suited to using continuous improvement. This stems from the fact that no DF store is big enough to undertake a major project. However, ideas are readily transferred from one location to another. DF's manager has recommended that a Suggestion Team be created to review ideas and check out the consequences of implementing a continuous improvement proposal on a company-wide basis.

c. The DF manager has recognized that resistance to continuous improvement-type changes is likely to be greater than resistance to the more sweeping changes of a total reengineering (REE). This, he states, is because the backing of management is not as evident in small changes as in large ones. To counter this effect, he has developed a newsletter issued by the general manager that proclaims and supports the continuous improvement list of the month.

d. APC prefers the broad systems approach of REE because patching the energy grid is a stopgap measure. It does not address the fundamental issue of matching energy supply when surges of demand for power occur that are above peak capacity. The production supply of energy can become insufficient if a transformer breaks down or a power line is broken.

e. The energy network must be made smart by employing algorithms that match existing capacity to demand without shutting down power-generating systems. Smart algorithms are required to determine how to measure and ration all existing capacity. The operation of such algorithms requires a variety of technological capabilities to monitor and control the system. The smart power system that results cannot be put into place by methods of continuous improvement. Neither power plants nor power management systems are constructed by continuous improvement. "Reengineer the power system," says the APC manager. "It is not the same as improving Dent Free."

f. The Dent Free manager disagrees. He states his beliefs as follows: "It is very rare that several of our stores experience peak demand at the same time. That is why power outages have occurred so infrequently. Major blackouts in the Northeastern United States happened in 1959, 1961, 1965, 1977, and in 2003. The record speaks for itself. The intervals between the episodes were 2, 4, 12, and 26 years. Continuous improvement is working. Conservatively, the next expected blackout is 52 years, or 2055."

6 The discussion about when to use continuous improvement or REE that was developed in Problem 5 has captured a great deal of attention. The district manager of Oil Changers, Inc. (OCI) told the class that his firm has been using continuous improvement for years. Recently, a new CEO was hired who decided to employ breakpoint business process redesign. The procedure has just begun, so the result is unknown. The OCI manager asked if anyone else in the class had utilized this system. No one had a similar experience, but there were many issues raised in the ensuing discussion. Points a. through j. have been written down, and at least one of these 10 items is not held to be correct. Identify the incorrect point or points of conjecture.

a. Breakpoint business process redesign (BPR) is a variant of REE, which ignores ordinary returns on improvement investments. Instead, it seeks out exceptional returns stemming from breakthroughs such as developing a new market based on much lower price but higher quality resulting from converting a batch process into a flow shop.

b. Special capabilities in time-based management (for exceptionally fast delivery or rapid development of new products) are additional examples of business process breakthroughs. In this regard, it has been pointed out that the foundation of corporate strategy is neither products nor markets but business processes. Special capabilities support BPR.

c. P/OM can be the portal to process breakthroughs. Working with R&D, engineering and materials management, suppliers, and customers, production and operations managers are on the firing line. They can be stodgy bureaucrats who view change with distaste (no BPR), or risk-taking innovators who embrace the concept of breakthrough design. When human resource managers hire production and operations managers, they are determining the probable direction for future innovation in that organization.

d. Innovations will not be accepted by an organization that fears change. An innovator working for the company has to strive hard to create the factors that support change, i.e., dissatisfaction with the current situation, a vision of what the future can become, practical first steps to move toward goals of the vision, and an ability to demonstrate that the costs of change are less than the benefits of transition.

e. Efficiency frontiers exist with respect to REE and BPR that are similar to those used by finance for risk–reward combinations. Everybody prefers low risk and high return. Most people will accept higher risk levels if, and only if, there is sufficient increase in the potential return on the investment. The same trade-off considerations apply to the changes that might be accomplished by reengineering. When breakthrough results are sought, the risk levels of the project failing to accomplish its objectives can be expected to increase.

f. In a risk–reward hierarchy, continuous improvement projects are least risky and least rewarding. Next in line are the higher risks and larger rewards that are associated with starting from scratch with REE. Maximum risk and commensurate largest rewards are coupled with extraordinary breakthroughs using BPR.

g. It is the OCI manager's opinion that BPR is far too risky for the oil-change business. Customers come to locations expecting fast and traditional procedures to be used to change their oil. Innovations in process are likely to create a feeling of insecurity that the job is being done in the right fashion.

h. The manager of the Always-on Power Company states that for her industry, the time has come to move toward a set of higher-risk, revolutionary (rather than evolutionary) changes to the power grid. Among other considerations, the use of solar panels has been significant in Japan but not the rest of the world. The use of windmills is not new, but they have been faulted because they are so often disabled by lightning. In fact, lightning is another source of power that has been overlooked. She advocates new smart algorithms for monitoring and controlling the flows of powers between sections of the power grid.

i. The Dent Free manager is in favor of choosing projects that have a high probability of success. He believes that his firm benefits most from the clever use by management "improvement patches" and the use of band-aid solutions to keep things going when troubles arise. His experience with "disruptive REE-type projects" is that they cause more trouble than they are worth. He calls everyone's attention to the fact that the U.S. power grid did a great job for 28 years.

j. The Dent Free manager also states that he is in favor of a change-management team to determine if a seemingly small change could possibly lead to an unsuspected big problem somewhere else in the system. He recommends the change-management team to act as a check on continuous improvement systems that are not well-thought-out.

7 The Big-Width Shoe Company (BWSC) manager requests the faculty leader to help the seminar class develop a set of principles for reengineering and for developing breakthrough business process redesigns. The exercise was completed with five principles having been stated. These were handed to the faculty leader, who complimented the class on four out of five, saying that only one of the five was incorrect. Which one of a. through e. is not right?

a. Identify and define the special core qualities, abilities, and competencies of the men and women who work for the company. Also, review the information and experience stored by the company in the form of documents, blueprints, bills of material, special supplier relationships, etc. Similarly, list advantages of the company such as facilities, locations, customers, and suppliers. REE and BPR should focus on these knowledge management strengths.

b. Identify and define the special process capabilities of the firm. Examine every function that the company requires and rate the processes that it uses to fulfill the functions. With respect to each process, it is useful to know if the company is less good than others, as good as others, better than any others, and uniquely superior to others. REE and BPR should focus on any processes that could be converted from less good and as good to uniquely superior to others.

c. Do not get involved with cross-functional transactions because departmental opposition to REE and BPR is the kiss of doom for achieving successful change. A successful strategy is to use P/OM as the core function that needs to be reengineered. When the problem crosses into another functional area, then it is time to sit down with a managerial counterpart to negotiate a reasonable accommodation between parties.

d. Develop detailed process analyses of all activities including cross-functional events. Benchmark cost, time, and quality for each process component. Propose and set target improvement levels for each process component.

e. Select the processes to be redesigned after prioritizing projects with respect to their impact on desired capability goals and the degree to which each process can be improved. Focus on task design and not task execution.

8 Rapid completion of projects is a new frontier that has begun to accelerate. The mind-set of project management in the twentieth century was inspired by engineering estimates of how long it should take to do a job that was based on pre-computer time lines. After 1950, the rapid growth of computer capabilities changed that time line, but project managers stayed with the conventions that they had grown up with because that made them comfortable. This discussion began with an in-house seminar group being held for Bridge-Builders, Ltd. This firm builds refineries, theme park rides, large warehouses, bridges, etc. Management wants to know if their planning horizons are based on old concepts, as described by the faculty leader in terms of pre-computer time lines. The CEO asks, "Are we operating by early twentieth century standards?" A project management team has drawn up a list of seven relevant facts (a. through g.). How much of this list is correct?

a. A project-oriented organization should have concurrent engineering capabilities. That enables it to bring all functional knowledge to bear on the project at the outset. As a result, development speed will be increased significantly. For example, Boeing's 777 was designed completely by computer. This bypassed the wind tunnel experiments that used to take great amounts of time to collect and analyze.

b.   A project-oriented organization should have continuity capabilities, which means that it has a variety of projects going on at the same time. This means that efficiencies of redundant information and experience are built into the project system.

c.   With continuity, some projects are later stages of earlier ones. Project overlaps are preplanned design features. For example, models 245 and 255 of a Hewlett-Packard calculator were designed at the same time. The 245 was to be released six months before the 255. Both used all the same components except for a different chip. The 255 had a more powerful chip that would replace the less powerful 245 chip when the new model was introduced to the market as an entirely new unit.

d.   The continuous project (product) development cycle always starts with sales making a suggestion for a new product based on a competitive product that has come to the attention of marketing. If this new product is still in development, then the information is like an intelligence report, which gives the company additional time to react. It is crucial to get a competitive offering on the shelves as soon as possible so that the "first to market" advantage of the competitor is diluted.

e.   The continuous project (product) development cycle can start in many different ways. For example, "finding" can happen in any functional part of the organization. P/OM can develop new process abilities. These can cut production costs, increase quality of the product or service, and decrease time to delivery.

f.   R&D is often the source of such changes, as is market research, which discovers things that customers want. There are examples of customers not knowing what they want until they are shown what they can have. Customers may need instructions before they know what is good for themselves.

g.   The find–design–make–ship cycle involves almost everyone in the organization. It is vital to understand that a company following this plan moves toward becoming a flow shop for the *production of projects*. Lower costs and shorter times to completion with higher quality achievements are some advantages of flow shops—as compared to batch shops. On the other hand, if projects prosper by being treated as relatively unique situations, then the customized approach of the "artisan" project manager has advantages over attempts to shoehorn projects into a mold that does not properly fit their distinctiveness. Managers of Bridge-Builders, Ltd., are intrigued by statement g. and encourage further discussion in pursuit of agreement, accord, and consensus.

Note to Students: Skip the next two Practice Quiz questions unless Enrichment Activity 19 has been assigned or independently studied.

9   The Ferris Wheel provides a useful model for those wishing to move their project management methods from the twentieth century to the twenty-first century. The wheel developed by bridge builder George W. Ferris for the 1893 Chicago World's Fair was an answer to the Eiffel Tower built for the Paris Exposition of 1889. There is more historical information to be gleaned with a little research, but for the moment, it is worth noting that the wheel was a money-maker. Charging 50 cents for a ride grossed $726,805.50, and that helped with breakeven. That amounts to 1,453,611 riders in 36 wooden cars, each one holding up to 60 people. That means there could have been more than 2,000 people on the wheel at any one time. See http://inventors.about.com/library/inventors/blrollercoaster .htm.

   Package Goods Masters (PGM) had a line of shampoos, dentifrices, soaps, and mouthwash products that were regularly renewed with new containers, perfumes, tastes, cleaners, ingredients, and claims. The new product launch process involved teams that carried R&D concepts into market testing. Then pilot plant product was market tested with its packaging. New products with successful tests were released to production and launched with advertising and coupons. PGM ran simulations of continuous project management based on a development time per new product of 18 months. The objective was to launch a new product every three months. To determine management's understanding of the continuous new product method, a fact sheet from a. through f. was prepared. Which of these facts might be in error?

a.   Cycle time (C) for the Ferris Wheel is the time between cars stopping for passengers to get on and off. Cycle time (C) for the project "wheel" is the time between new product start-ups. Similarly, it is also the time between successive new product launchings. PGM requested that $C = 3$ months.

b.   For the Ferris Wheel, the time between complete rotations is T. Cycle time, $C = T/n$. There will be n cars to fill. For PGM, $C = 3$ months and $T = 18$ months. Then, $n = T/C = 18/3 = 6$ projects underway at all times.

c.   Management wants to know how many new projects will be started per year. This is equivalent to how many new products will be launched per year. The output will be O and $O = 12$ months per year. Divide O by C (which is months between launchings). That is $12/3 = 4$ new product launches per year.

d. For the Ferris Wheel, O is equivalent to how many cars will be emptied and refilled (say) in an hour. To get Ferris Wheel figures, assume that a complete rotation of the Ferris wheel takes $T = 1.5$ hours (90 minutes). With $n = 6$ cars, $C = 90/6 = 15$ minutes between each car stop.

e. Also, $O = 60$ minutes per hour divided by C (minutes between stops) $= 60/15 = 4$ car stops per hour.

f. The strength of the Ferris Wheel model is that the amusement park wheel will perform as calculated. The project wheel will also be precisely correct as if it were a well-made timepiece.

10 Package Goods Masters (PGM) has a new product failure ratio of five out of ten. Failure is acknowledged when management cancels introduction or withdraws the item from inventory. There are many factors that define a new product failure. One of these is that gross margin does not reach at least $1 million per year. (Gross margin is sales revenue per year less all manufacturing costs per year.) This PGM requirement is said to be necessary but not sufficient for the definition of success. In other words, if gross margin meets the requirement but market share is not large enough, or if nonmanufacturing costs are too great, that project can be canceled. Average project development costs are $150,000 per year. If these costs grow too large, the project is withdrawn and counts as a failure. Project teams are asked to evaluate the analysis that is presented in points a. through j. The question is asked: Which of these points is incorrect?

a. On average, $T = 18$ months. The plan calls for $n = 6$ new product projects. As a result, $900,000 is tied up in project development investments per year.

b. Project output per year is four. Of these, two projects are deemed successful.

c. Successful projects will generate $2 million of total gross margin per year.

d. Gross profit (total gross margin less total project costs per year) is calculated to be $1.1 million.

e. Management is not thrilled with these performance numbers and has asked for an assessment of the effect of changing n from six to ten projects. They have also asked for new project selection and development methods that can raise the probability of success to 75 percent. The revised results are shown in f. through j.

f. If $T = 18$ months and $n = 10$ new product projects, then $1,500,000 is tied up in project development investments per year.

g. Project output per year is now 6.67. Of these, five projects are deemed successful.

h. Successful projects will generate $5 million of total gross margin per year.

i. Gross profit (total gross margin less total project costs per year) is calculated to be $3.5 million per year. This is more than three times the profit previously obtained.

j. Management is very pleased with this result and intends to announce that continuous project management will be adopted by PGM.

Additional Readings

Beckhard, R., and R. Harris. *Organizational Transitions*. Reading, MA: Addison-Wesley, 1987. (An old but venerable treatise)

Biztech Network provides interesting readings pro and con business process reengineering at http://www.brint.com/BPR.htm. There are articles and references to books that deal with BPR and benchmarking.

Carr, D. K., K. S. Dougherty, H. J. Johansson, R. A. King, and D. E. Moran. *Breakpoint: Business Process Redesign*. Arlington, VA: Coopers & Lybrand Series, 1992.

Champy, James. *Re-Engineering Management: The Mandate for New Leadership*. New York: Harper Business, 1995.

Debevoise, Tom. *Business Process Management with a Business Rules Approach: Implementing the Service Oriented Architecture*. New York: Business Knowledge Architects. Brint Institute, 2005.

———. *Beyond Re-Engineering*. New York: Harper Collins, 1995.

Hammer, Michael. "Forward to Basics." *Fast Company* (November 2002) (insights with a radical flavor). See http://www.hammerandco.com. Click on the article in the lower right-hand margin.

Hammer, Michael, and James Champy. *Re-Engineering the Corporation*. New York: Harper Business, 1993.

Imai, Masaaki. *Kaizen: The Key to Japan's Competitive Success*. New York: Random House Business Division, 1986.

Johansson, Henry J., Patrick McHugh, A. John Pendlebury, and William A. Wheeler III. *Business Process Re-Engineering: Breakpoint Strategies for Market Dominance*. New York: Wiley, 1993.

McGrath, Michael E. *Product Strategy for High-Technology Companies: How to Achieve Growth, Competitive Advantage, and Increased Profits*. Burr Ridge, IL: Irwin Professional Publishing, 1995.

Miller, Jeffrey G., Arnoud De Meyer, and Jinichiro Nakane. *Benchmarking Global Manufacturing: Understanding International Suppliers, Customers, and Competitors*. The Irwin/APICS Series in Production Management, Burr Ridge, IL: Irwin, 1992.

Puchek, Vladimir, Noel Tichy, and Carole K. Barnett (eds.). *Globalizing Management: Creating and Leading the Competitive Organization*. New York: Wiley, 1993.

Stalk, G., P. Evans, and L. E. Shulman. "Competing on Capabilities: The New Rules of Corporate Strategy." *Harvard Business Review* (March–April 1992).

Tabor, Richard. *Global Quality: A Synthesis of the World's Best Management Methods.* Burr Ridge, IL: Irwin, 1993.

Notes

1. Tom Peters and Robert Waterman, Jr. *In Search of Excellence: Lessons from America's Best Run Companies.* Warner Books, November 1982.
2. R. Levering and M. Moskowitz. *The 100 Best Companies to Work for in America*, rev. ed. A Plume Book. New York: Penguin Group, 1994. When this book was no longer reissued, *Fortune Magazine* began its own survey. It publishes results yearly. Google was number 1 in 2007. W. L. Gore & Associates (see Section 19-8a) was tenth. Starbucks (see Spotlight 14-2) was sixteenth.
3. "Running Out of Time: Reversing America's Declining Competitiveness." Conference held at Arden House, Harriman, New York, November 19–22, 1987. For details, see M. K. Starr (ed). *Global Competitiveness: Getting the U.S. Back on Track.* 74th American Assembly, New York: W.W. Norton, 1988.
4. John W. Gardner. *Self-Renewal: The Individual and the Innovative Society.* New York: W.W. Norton, 1995.
5. John Byrne. "Letter from the Editor: The Case for Change." *Fast Company* (May 2005): 12.
6. Alan Deutschman. "Change: New Insights from Psychology and Neuroscience Offer Some Surprising Answers—And Ways to Improve the Odds." *Fast Company* (May, 2005): 53.
7. L. Festinger. *A Theory of Cognitive Dissonance.* Stanford, CA: Stanford University Press, 1957.
8. John Kotter. *Leading Change.* Harvard Business School Press, 1996.
9. John Kotter and Dan S. Cohen, *The Heart of Change: Real-Life Stories of How People Change Their Organization.* Harvard Business School Press, 2002.
10. Dean Ornish, MD. *Dr. Dean Ornish's Program for Reversing Heart Disease.* Ballentine Books, 1996. Also see http://webmd.com and Search for "Ornish." Ornish served as a consultant to alter the menu that McDonald's serves: "Is a Trip to McDonald's Just What the Doctor Ordered?" *The New York Times,* Business Day (May 2, 2005): C1, C6.
11. Louis V. Gerstner. *Who Says Elephants Can't Dance: Leading a Great Enterprise Through Dramatic Change.* Harper-Collins Publishers, 2002.
12. "Making the Connection Between Science and Learning: A Conversation with Michael Merzenich," November 2000; http://www.brainconnection.com/gen/?main=conf/nov00/merzenich-int.
13. See http://www.bp.com. In the search box (upper right), key "Horizontal Wells" and click "go." Under "Search Results," click on and read "Unlocking tight gas."
14. C. J. McNair and K.H.J. Leibfried. *Benchmarking: A Tool for Continuous Improvement.* New York: Harper Business, 1992, p. 20.
15. *USA Today* (March 1, 1995): 4B.
16. The quote from Julius Maldutis at Salomon Brothers is reported in *The New York Times*, March 7, 1995, in an article by Adam Bryant, p. C5.
17. Continuous improvement also is called *kaizen.* See Masaaki Imai. *Kaizen: The Key to Japan's Competitive Success.* New York: Random House, 1986. The Kaizen Institute, in Zug, Switzerland, held its annual Kaizen Tour (October 2007). See http://www.kaizen.com.
18. Michael Hammer and James Champy. *Re-Engineering the Corporation.* New York: Harper Business, 1993.
19. James Champy. *Re-Engineering Management: The Mandate for New Leadership.* New York: Harper Business, 1995, p. 3.
20. Ibid., p. 112.
21. D. K. Carr, K. S. Dougherty, H. J. Johansson, R. A. King, and D. E. Moran. *Breakpoint: Business Process Redesign.* Arlington, VA: Coopers & Lybrand, 1992, p. v.
22. G. Stalk, P. Evans, and L. E. Shulman. "Competing on Capabilities: The New Rules of Corporate Strategy." *Harvard Business Review* (March–April 1992): 57–69.
23. Booz Allen Hamilton. "Understanding the New Environment." *Business Process Redesign: An Owner's Guide.* OPER 401, 13M, 1993, p. 4.
24. Ibid., p. 14.
25. Henry J. Johansson, Patrick McHugh, A. John Pendlebury, and William A. Wheeler III. *Business Process Re-Engineering: Breakpoint Strategies for Market Dominance.* New York: Wiley, 1993, p. 209.
26. Information about Oticon was originally derived directly from conversations with employees of the firm in Copenhagen, Denmark and Somerset, New Jersey. The article by Polly LaBarre, "The Dis-Organization of Oticon," *Industry Week*

(July 18, 1994): 23–28 was very helpful. Oticon, Inc., the U.S. branch of the Danish parent, shares many of the innovations developed in Denmark. In 2007, conversations with Lars Kolind continued earlier dialog capturing many changes in company activities.

27. J. R. Hartley. *Concurrent Engineering: Shortening Lead Times, Raising Quality, and Lowering Costs.* Cambridge, MA: Productivity Press, 1992, p. 19.

28. C. R. Morris. "The Coming Global Boom." *The Atlantic* (October 1989): 56.

29. The information on W. L. Gore & Associates was derived by speaking directly with individuals who work for the firm and from write-ups of this company appearing in *Fortune Magazine*'s *The 100 Best Companies to Work for in America.* Originally, this was a book by Robert Levering and Milton Moskowitz, rev. ed. A. Plume Book. New York: Penguin Group, 1994. In 2006, W. L. Gore & Associates was listed as the number 5 company among the best 100. Also see http://www.gore.com.

30. London Eye is run by The Tussaud's Group with partners British Airways and Marks Barfield Architects as of 2004.

Enrichment Activity 19: Ferris Wheel Model for Continuous New Product Development

The Ferris Wheel is an ideal model of continuous, multiple-project systems for new product development. Project starts and completions are modeled by occupants getting on and off the Ferris Wheel in Figure EA19-1. Timing the wheel is management's strategy.

The **Ferris Wheel model** for project management is based on the amusement park ride, which has n separate seating compartments. The wheel makes a complete rotation in T minutes and stops every C minutes to let the riders get off and others get on.

If one is in London, a visit to the London Eye[30] will provide an up-to-date view of what a Ferris wheel can be like. See http://www.londoneye.com/default.asp.

To apply the model to projects, let T equal an average project's total development time (in days) and let n equal the number of projects that are actively being pursued. Then, the average interval between project completions (in days) C is given by:

$$C = T/n$$

Say that $T = 730$ days (2 years) and $n = 100$ projects; then, on average, a project is completed every 7.3 days. That is kind of amazing for even a dedicated new product system. Recapping, it takes 2 years on average to complete a new product timeline (start-up to release). This company has 100 real projects in process. For most companies, that is an exceptionally heavy load.

$$C = 730/100 = 7.3 \text{ days}$$

Also, O, the output per year (the number of projects completed per year), is given by

$$O = 365/C = 365/7.3 = 50 \text{ projects completed per year}$$

When the numerator (365 days per year) is divided by C, the result is projects completed per year. If the numerator was set at 30 days per month, then $30/7.3 = 4.1$ projects completed per month. Similarly, with 7 days per week, there would be $7.0/7.3 = 0.96$ projects completed per week. That is quite a feat—worthy of being called prodigious project production.

Probability of Project Success

Not all projects succeed. This is especially the case for new product development projects. The bottom line can be stated in equation form, but it is easier to understand when numbers are used. Say that on average 70 percent of this class of new product projects fail. Although it is a high number, it is likely to be in the right arena. Alternatively, the probability of success is denoted by p_s and

$$p_s = 0.30$$

Then, the number of project successes would be

$$O p_s = 50(0.30) = 15$$

The output in projects completed per year, $O = 50$, was derived in the prior section. Given the probability of success and the expected output, there would be 15 project successes per year. It should now be apparent why the appropriate index term for this subject is **projects, probability of success.**

Ferris Wheel model

Provides a model of continuous, new product development, and ceaseless project management.

Projects, Probability of Success

p_s is the probability of product success. Given O project completions per year, $p_s O$ is the number of successes.

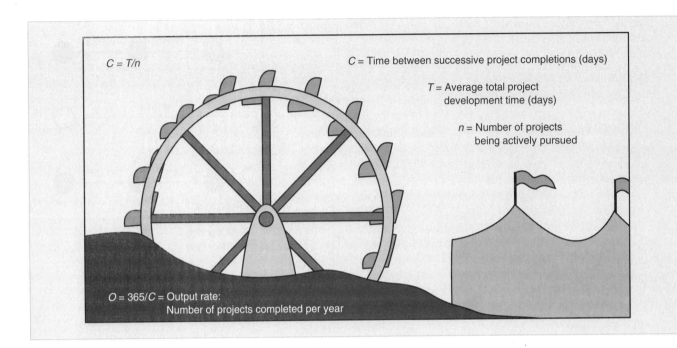

Figure EA19-1

The Ferris Wheel Model of Continuous Project (Product) Development

Net Profit of Continuous Project Development Program

If each project has an average cost of $100,000 per year, then the average load of $n = 100$ projects has a total cost of $10,000,000 per year.

Assume that average gross margin for each *successful* project is $1,000,000 per year. (Gross margin is sales revenue less manufacturing costs but not including selling, administrative, and development costs.)

The 15 successful projects will generate total gross margin of $15,000,000. Subtracting from this amount the total development costs of $10,000,000 yields a profit of $5,000,000. Even after administrative and sales costs are subtracted, there is substantial profit from engaging in continuous project development.

Note: It more than compensates for the cost of failed projects. Further, the development costs for successful products rapidly diminish, while the revenue stream grows. Also, the pool of successful products increases so that total gross margin continues to climb in successful companies.

Small increases in $p_s = 0.30$ will improve the net profit figures substantially. The organizational models used by Oticon, W. L. Gore & Associates, and 3M are geared to have high values of p_s. Success means that revenue will be generated that outstrips costs so that net profit results. Otherwise the business model for continuous product development will indicate firm failure.

High values occur when people are motivated to use teamwork to create new revenue-generating ideas, a pattern that is successful only in a nonauthoritarian change-management setting. (It is suggested that a great deal can be learned from a sensitivity analysis using simulation that varies values of p_s.)

Enrichment Challenges 19

1 For the economic analysis of continuous project development, the probability that a project is successful is $p_s = 0.30$; $T = 730$ days (average total project development time in days); $n = 100$ projects (number of active projects). The average cost of projects is $100,000 per year. Average gross margins of successful projects is $800,000 per year.

   a. What is the estimated total gross margin?
   b. What percent increase of p_s is required to increase the estimated total gross margin by 50 percent?
   c. What percent increase of p_s is required to increase estimated total gross margin by 100 percent?

2 For the economic analysis of continuous project development, $p_s = 0.50$. Also, $T = 500$ days (average total project development time in days); $n = 100$ projects (number of projects actively being pursued); projects have an average cost of $50,000 per year. Successful projects have average gross margins of $100,000 per year.

    a. How many successful projects will occur per year?

    b. Do you recommend this arrangement?

Sustainability Issues: Environment, Ethics, and Security

Chapter Outline

Chapter 20 deals with environment, ethics, and security. These topics are involved with technological developments and contingency planning. Chapter 20 starts out by reviewing environmental issues that increasingly impact organizations on worldwide scale. To provide environmental protection, constraints on processes, plant locations, and products are imposed by court and governmental agencies. Since these constraints are advocated by the Greenpeace organization (http://www.greenpeace.org/international; and click on one of more than 40 countries) and by political parties that often take the designation of *green* (especially in Europe), they are lumped together and termed *green* initiatives. The *green* agenda as carried out by courts' judgments and by governmental regulations often impact P/OM processes far more than other organizational functions. In fact, existing process designs can be vetoed because making goods as planned, or delivering services as planned, negatively impacts the environment—or society's sense of ethics. This puts another layer of acceptability on process design. It should be cleared environmentally, ethically, and not be a security risk—before approval.

Chapter 20 puts ethics and environmental issues together—they are strongly related. From the *American Heritage Dictionary*: "Ethics is (a) A set of principles of right conduct. (b) A theory or a system of moral values." That definition unites ethical and environmental goals. Since it is morally correct to protect customers and employees, security is also part of the obligation.

Production and operations managers recognize that the definition of ethics has critical and persistent importance to their responsibilities. Damage to the environment as a result of process contamination is unethical. There are no counterbalancing circumstances. Similarly, producing dangerous product is ethically bad. A company may not be aware of the harmful potential but as soon as it learns about dangerous properties, warnings must be given and corrective actions taken on the spot. The word "ethics" has been interpreted to have a moral equivalence way above the importance of profit. In fact, there is much evidence that profit is not sustainable in a moral vacuum. That translates into ethical issues having value and contributing to profit in a manner that traditional business models may overlook because it is not customary to think in that fashion.

The subject of ethics may have once seemed far removed from making goods and delivering services. No longer the case, it is part of the P/OM system of responsibility now. The field of P/OM has obligations above and beyond other functional areas, in this regard. Chapter 20 treats ethical issues concerning environmental and technology effects from both legal and psychological perspectives.

Security and ethics are bound together. There is a personal right to be safe and secure. Chapter 20 considers the impact of 9/11/01 on safety and security for citizens of the world, customers, employees, suppliers, and bystanders. This category of security brings to mind questions about crisis management and contingency planning. It is a P/OM obligation to oversee safety and security and to manage systems in crisis by various means, including the premeditated activities of contingency planning. These subjects are treated together under the security umbrella. In the P/OM profession, Chapter 20's topics are at the forefront of research and attention. These topics pose difficult but exciting places to be working.

After reading this chapter, you should be able to:

- Describe the special capabilities and core competencies that P/OM offers that can support greening the environment, i.e., how P/OM contributes to greening the environment.
- Discuss limitations on P/OM contributions to greening the environment.
- Explain how maintenance affects the environment.

- Describe how OSHA, CDC, FDA, and other governmental organizations relate to environment.
- Describe how OSHA, CDC, FDA, and other governmental organizations relate to ethics.
- Describe the four parts of design for disassembly (DFD) and relate DFD to reverse supply chains.
- Explain applications of design for disassembly (DFD) and its role in environmental protection.
- Explain water-jetting and why this technology is important for environmental protection.
- Explain recycling concrete and asphalt, and how this technology protects the environment.
- Explain how P/OM can maintain or change ethical standards (nationally and internationally).
- Relate ethics and quality integrity.
- Relate quality integrity and the Hazard Analysis and Critical Control Point (HACCP) system.
- Describe the workings of the Hazard Analysis and Critical Control Point (HACCP) system and what this has to do with P/OM.
- Describe the application of food and drug testing by the Food and Drug Administration and explain what this has to do with P/OM.
- Explain what it means to ready the organization for future technology (e.g., vision-able robots).
- Describe P/OM's role in doing business on a global scale. Draw on ISO 14000 and the SME Enterprise Wheel.
- Explain the consequences of using ISO 14000/14001 and their limitations.
- Explain how P/OM relates to safety and security for customers and employees.
- Discuss P/OM's role in crisis management.
- Explain how contingency planning relates to crisis management.

The Systems Viewpoint

An important kind of change is forced from the outside. It is not the result of "our" strategic planning, but it could be the result of "someone else" creating a new competitive situation. The Twin Tower catastrophe (9/11/01) led to a chain of consequences for the airlines that had to be dealt with in a systems fashion. Newer airlines like Jet Blue and AirTran had an easier time than giant bureaucracies like United, Delta, and American. The big picture has to be grasped right away. Waiting for a series of pieces to fit together as with a jigsaw puzzle is too little too late. *Once the systems picture is understood*, then creative strategic thinking is the only way to survive. Survival always precedes winning. Crisis management with contingency planning is a preview method that attempts preparations for hurricanes, earthquakes, senseless acts of terrorism, war, incompetence, and crime. There are sound reasons to invest in an operations management point of view.

Strategic Thinking

The business organization works with two kinds of change forces. There are those that arise inside the firm in response to the desire to advance company success. Continuous product development is an example of the company striving to become better, bigger, and richer. This occurs when a Stage III company seeks to become a Stage IV company (see Section 1-8, "The Stages of P/OM Development," and Figure 1-8). *Good to Great: Why Some Companies Make the Leap ... and Others Don't* (Jim Collins, Harper Business, 2001) is a book that epitomizes the urge to excel. The title of Chapter 1 of Collins' book provides insight by itself. It is "Good Is the Enemy of Great." To transform an organization so that it achieves constancy of superior achievement requires, at the outset,

© 2008 Jupiterimages Corporation

Polyurethane foam from automotive seating as well as reusable plastics from other auto interior components can be reprocessed, and then molded again into new seat cushions, dashboards, and other auto parts. P/OM strives to find ways to reuse materials because in most well-thought-out cases, reusing is good for the environment and is cost-saving for the company.

Reuse

A reusable part can quickly be returned to inventory. Reusable plastics, glass, paper, and metal may require more value-adding than a nut, bolt, or gear that can be reused with just cleanup.

Ethics

Ethical standards must be established in multicultural environments that satisfy the various participants.

sound strategic planning to bring about change. If times are considered to be good, it is difficult to risk going from "good to worse."

The second kind of force for change is from outside the firm. It is what happens when an act of nature (e.g., a hurricane or earthquake makes it impossible to conduct business). It is when an act of governments and their courts set restrictions on process effluents and emissions, on wages paid, taxes levied, and patents honored. The range of issues that a firm can face changes with politics and economics. These include nationalization of property, accusations of anti-competitive behavior and monopolistic policies, as well as unsafe products. Security issues arise as another external force for change. Safety of facilities and transportation (of cargo and people) has become a major concern because of forces that have intent to harm, damage, and destroy.

20-1 Adapting to External Forces

Unanticipated external forces imposed from outside allow only a reactive mode. The key word in that sentence is "unanticipated." It is now considered appropriate to imagine what can possibly happen in order to prepare a response. This is called contingency planning. For example, without explicit warning a law is passed that reduces smokestack emissions. Using contingency planning, the company would have pre-thought that possibility and documented a strategy to deal with the situation. Contingency plans permit managers to anticipate a range of happenings and even to prepare proactive responses in the event that one of them occurs. It should be noted that companies like BMW, Home Depot, Hyundai, Wal-Mart, and Toyota have successfully developed strong contingency plans for handling low probability but severely damaging events (e.g., hurricane Katrina).

Historical records indicate that environmental standards will continue to increase in scope and rigor. The environmental effects of operations (e.g., pollution control and take-back laws for material reuse) will be impacted by society with increasing frequency and severity. Pre-thinking creative **reuse** of recycled parts can lower costs, improve products, and meet new stringent laws about the percent reuse of a car's components that are current in parts of Europe—and coming to North America. Technology is making some major shifts occur as research for reuse of materials is funded.

Laws passed to achieve environmental goals can take many forms such as prohibition on cutting trees, drilling for oil, and limits on effluents. **Ethics** of operational constraints have become another factor of growing concern to P/OM. Ethical issues, like environmental issues, take the form of external forces of limitation and constraint. However, there are examples of such constraints surprising the constrained by producing great profits rather than excessive costs. In other words, the consequences of unexpected ethical issues can be positive as well as negative. Ethics do not have to be external forces. Chick-Fil-A® (Spotlight 13-2) is a successful quick-service restaurant (QSR) that closes on Sundays. Take a look at http://www.chick-fil-A.com. Click on "History" at the bottom and then on "Why we are closed on Sundays" in the left-hand navigation pane. Research at http://www.QSRmagazine.com reveals how successful Chick-Fil-A® is in the QSR business. Chick-fil-A's "Eat Mor Chikin" cows won a place on New York's Madison Avenue Advertising Walk of Fame on September 26, 2007, when more than one million online voters selected the cows. Bloggers said they like the message and the company.

There is also a lot of uncertainty about what is ethical in a diverse and disparate multination cultural milieu. This necessitates understanding how disparate cultures view work, gifts and bribes, pay, holidays, unions, syndicates, the Internet, and contracts (to choose a few of many issues). It also highlights the communication problems when customers, suppliers, and fabricators speak different languages. There has been deep interest in the ethics of the food industry's commitment to provide healthful food and drugs. Chapter 20 looks into some operational aspects of this commitment.

Readying the organization for technology developments is an operations management responsibility. For example, if health care is going to employ hospital robots for various orderly and even nursing functions, the training requirements are part of the P/OM job. Technology issues get tentacles into every aspect of this chapter. Examples are presented of the reuse of materials (recycling) and a cleaning method (water-jetting) that reduces pollutants. Technology interacts with safety and security in many ways that can be cited and many more ways that are unfolding.

Chapter 20 examines the consequences of external events that have occurred recently. For example, the destruction of the World Trade Center in New York City on September 11, 2001, has altered more than the budget for safety and security. It has changed the methods, processes, and procedures that are associated with the management of security operations. Airlines' operations are an obvious illustration. Among the many operational issues that need to be considered: What items get on board as cargo? Which people get on board as passengers (or, when do the shoes come off before boarding the plane)? Issues continue once on board the plane. What are the rules for passengers waiting to use bathrooms? Are cockpit doors locked and unbreachable? Are there marshals on board? What technology is monitoring which events about every flight?

Four factors that underlie adapting to external forces will continue to be the environment, ethics, technological developments, and doing business in the global community. These factors cross over and interact with security and contingency planning. For example, new environmental laws in Germany change the cost structure of cars in Japan. U.S. decisions to prohibit oil drilling in Alaska alter the research agenda for car designers and engineers in Detroit, Tokyo, and Seoul.

Ethic laws that prohibit giving bribes (called *gifts*, in some countries) can lead to a change in the method of doing business. For example, aircraft firms have share-based arrangements with parts manufacturers in the countries where there will be product purchase support, and that is not considered unethical at this time. Technological development of computers brought the end of the world for Keuffel and Esser. Global methods (like Japanese car manufacturing) changed the way that cars were designed and made by GM, DaimlerChrysler, and Ford. Advanced methods are more productive, less costly, less polluting, and more recyclable. New materials and technology produce a change in conditions, e.g., nanotechnology has altered what are fashionable trends in fabrics with microfibers and processes that make clothes spill-resistant. MSNBC reported on "smart textiles" during December 2004.

20-2 Greening the Environment: Maintenance

Environmental upgrading is called **greening the environment**. P/OM has capabilities for both protecting and upgrading the environment. Without P/OM's awareness and technical knowledge, the environment can be degraded irreversibly. With increasing ecological damage, proactive steps to repair the situation fall on P/OM shoulders. Using technology and good management, and driven by a sense of what is ethically correct, P/OM can help limit, if not prevent, ecological harm. Often, it can do more than that by cleaning up messes (say, in lakes and rivers) that were brought about by forces long gone and even natural (not man-made) disasters.

Following are some examples of initiatives that can be taken to prevent environmental damage. Most of these methods are cost-effective as well.

Greening the environment
Greening is meant to connote that efforts are successful to achieve sustainable land and water resources.

20-2a Water-Jetting Maintenance

Water-jetting exemplifies a technology that has now been developed to a point where it can replace toxic maintenance methods that are used to remove paints and other coatings. It is also used for cutting shapes with water and abrasives. The ThomasNet (2007) lists more than 600 companies that provide waterjet cutting and cleaning applications. The **water-jetting** method has been used to strip paint from planes and marine hulls before repainting them.

Water-jetting
High water pressure technology that replaces toxic maintenance methods used to remove paints and coatings. Also, cuts shapes with water and abrasives.

A journal article dated August 2007[1] makes the relevance of the process evident: "Water jetting is becoming an acceptable and many times preferable method of surface preparation. (It) provides many benefits over abrasive blasting including lower overall project cost, less environmental impact, and the ability for other trades to work side by side with the water jetting operation."

The traditional method is to blast the coatings with abrasive grit. There are six major problems with that process. These are (1) large volumes of potentially toxic airborne particulate (lead and chromate laden dust); (2) machinery failures caused by the dust and grit; (3) reduced visibility in dry docks; (4) inability of other trades to work in the vicinity of blasting; (5) massive labor-intensive cleanup effort after blasting and prior to painting; (6) waste collection and disposal. Old methods need to be reconsidered. New technology methods do not suffer problems 1 through 6.

The Lydia Frenzel Conference Center provides newsletters and white papers on various cleaning applications at http://www.lydiafrenzel.com. These companies design ultra-high pressure (UHP) systems (20,000–55,000 psi) that can remove paint and asbestos as well as heavy metals.

Water-jetting is a cost-effective and environmentally sound alternative approach to many conventional coating removal methods such as chemical stripping, incineration, machining, and abrasive blasting. The conventional technique for removing paint from aircraft skin is by applying methylene chloride, a toxic solvent that requires that workers use protective latex clothing and special breathing apparatus. Aircraft engine parts are dipped in toxic chemical baths, whereas high-pressure water-jet technology uses only water to achieve effective cleaning and de-coating.

The water-jet system has many potential applications. It has been researched as a method for cleaning airport runways. It can be a replacement technology for machine cutting tools, concrete cutters, and shoe leather and carpet cutting. It has been suggested for radioactive waste removal and as a coal mining method. An experimental application that has been discussed is surgical removal of basal cell carcinomas.

20-2b Water Supply Maintenance

It is a P/OM responsibility to choose the best maintenance functions. Maintenance decisions are often flawed because of a preference for what is familiar. There is a strong tendency to believe that what was done in the past was carefully chosen as best. In fact, once procedures are installed, it takes a point of view (such as value analysis) to recheck for new materials and methods. Although it is sensible to test the old way against the new, it is not always done. Maintenance seems an old-fashioned function in a society that uses things up and then throws them away. However, maintenance should be viewed as being on the cutting edge along with new materials and methods.

Water maintenance is a good example. Treatment of pools with chlorine is standard in the United States. There are some adventurous users of alternatives such as bromine and the combination of ozone with chlorine or bromine. Distillation and various forms of filtration are used for drinking water. NASA developed a silver iodide system for drinking water that has been adopted by some European municipalities for pool and spa maintenance. Individual users of this new technology also can be found in the United States.

When comparing systems, what should matter is not that maintenance prefers the "tried and true" but the comparative qualities of the results and the costs incurred. There is some evidence that silver iodide is a strong contender for "Best Practice." Still, it is not surprising that most pool maintenance follows traditional chlorine treatment plans. Research on cost/benefits of alternative water treatments is ongoing.

Reference to the AWWA webpage indicates the breadth of issues that relate to water maintenance (see http://www.awwa.org, Click on e-Journal, Vol. 99, No. 8, AWWA, August 2007). The Benchmarking Clearinghouse covers outstanding practices for water and wastewater utilities of all sizes. It provides 22 key performance indicators and support for sections, which are the states and regional groupings of states. The association has created the Self-Assessment and Peer Review Forum (SA/PRF) in addition to the quality program for utilities called *QualServe*.™ The increasingly important topic of security for water systems is included under education and training as the new vulnerability assessment.

The National Association of Clean Water Agencies (NACWA) represents the interests of the country's wastewater treatment agencies. They acknowledge their responsibility as "true environmental practitioners that serve the majority of the sewered population in the United States, and collectively treat and reclaim more than 18 billion gallons of wastewater each day." See http://www.nacwa.org. NACWA is organized for purposes of information dissemination as well as lobbying. The sewerage function is an operations management arena that is often overlooked. NACWA provides conferences and workshops. During 2007 there were a number of events on Clean Water Law and a Workshop on Pretreatment and Pollution Prevention.

In its political activities, NACWA is an enabling organization for the legislation unanimously approved by the U.S. House of Representatives on October 7, 2002. This is The Wastewater Treatment Works Security Act, H.R. 5169, which authorized $200 million in grants to EPA (Environmental Protection Agency) for vulnerability assessments and security enhancements at POTWs (publicly-owned treatment works). Maintenance managers may be the most reluctant operations managers to adapt new technologies. Why is this so? Maintenance is what keeps old systems running. For example, the condition of elevators needs to be checked and often breakdowns occur so that both preventive and remedial maintenance seem to be required. Some countries buy used airplanes and buses that are not kept up to par.

The upkeep of old plants is difficult without replacement parts and budget for them. Often, old facilities are installed with maintenance instructions that are ambiguous. Such older facilities abound in third world countries, but there are many of them in the United States as well. Innovative maintenance is tough to support under such circumstances. OSHA (Occupational Safety and Health Administration of the U.S. Department of Labor) has been said to dictate (occasionally) procedures that management would like changed, but alteration of methods is not easy to accomplish. Otherwise, a visit to http://www.osha.gov reveals important contributions made by government agencies to health and safety, e.g., September 27, 2007, OSHA issues Draft Ergonomics Guidelines on Preventing Musculoskeletal Injuries in Shipyards. See Enrichment Activity 9 on Ergonomics (also known as) Human Factors.

20-3 Greening the Environment: Design for Disassembly (DFD)

Many associations are devoted to various aspects of recycling. Some representative ones will be included in this discussion. In the United States, the Vehicle Recycling Partnership (VRP) was formed in 1991 "to promote and conduct research to aid in the development of technology for the recovery, reuse and disposal of materials from retired vehicles. The partnership falls under the United States Council for Automotive Research or USCAR, an organization set up to facilitate, monitor and promote pre-competitive research and development activities among DaimlerChrysler, Ford and General Motors."

A press release dated June 25, 2007, states, "The USCAR Vehicle Recycling Partnership (VRP) composed of researchers from (the above-named three companies) is taking a leadership role in optimizing the recycling of ALL materials in shredder residue, regardless of their source." At the webpage http://www.uscar.org, click on "Consortia" to view the many initiatives that are underway.

Press release, Southfield, Michigan, April 20, 2007: "According to statistics published by the U.S. Environmental Protection Agency on its http://www.epa.gov website, 50 percent of all paper, 34 percent of all plastic soft drink bottles, 45 percent of all aluminum beer and soft drink cans, 63 percent of all steel packaging and 67 percent of all major appliances are now recycled." The announcement goes on to say that cars and trucks outstrip these figures. In fact, "more than 95 percent of all vehicles in the United States go through a market-driven recycling infrastructure, with no added cost or tax to consumers. More than 84 percent, by weight, of each **end-of-life-of-vehicle (ELV)** is recycled." Plans are for USCAR's VRP to increase the recycled percentage of each ELV to almost 100 percent.

End-of-life-of-vehicle (ELV)

Eventually close to 100 percent of vehicles, computers, etc., will be returned for recycling and/or disposal by the manufactures.

Substances of concern (SOC)

Agreement has been reached to entirely remove Cr(VI) by January 2007.

This is a huge job since every year there are about 12 million vehicles that are scrapped in the United States. European countries used to lead the way for ELV disposability. The U.S. has caught up and is also very good with elimination of **substances of concern (SOC)**. These include lead, mercury, cadmium, and hexavalent chromium, Cr(VI). Hexavalent chromium has been entirely eliminated by all major auto companies as of July 1, 2007.

The VRP goals of USCAR are:

- Reduce the total environmental impact of vehicle disposal.
- Increase the efficiency of the disassembly of components and materials to enhance vehicle recyclability.
- Develop material selection and design guidelines.
- Promote socially responsible and economically achievable solutions to vehicle disposal.

In the United Kingdom, BMRA (British Metals Recycling Association) tackles a wide range of green issues. See http://www.eco-web.com/register/01886.html. Its Green Pages list 7,000 suppliers located in 149 countries that participate in recycling programs.

In Canada, the Ontario Automotive Recycling Association (OARA) links hundreds of associations and committees with its waste management program and its recycling trade associations. OARA has committees working on salvage problems and a collision industry action group (CIAG). To see the linkage and diversity, visit http//www.oara.com.

In Australia, there are estimated to be 500,000 ELVs per year with 70 percent being shredded and recycled. The Auto Parts Recyclers Association of Australia Inc. (APRAA) sets standards for car recyclers.

© 2008 Jupiterimages Corporation

United States Code, Title 23–Highways; Ch 1; Sub-ch1; Section 138; January 1, 1968, provides for control of junkyards and refers specifically to "automobile graveyards." The code provides hefty penalties for states that do not abide by the code with respect to location and appearance of such scrap metal facilities.

20-3a Take-Back Laws

One purpose of many of these organizations is to learn how to design robust take-back functions. The system under study is a reverse supply chain. Materials flow from consumers with end of life (used up, or damaged) products back to the manufacturer who made that product in the first place. The manufacturer is held accountable to do the best possible thing with the returned materials. The government may hold the manufacturer responsible, but the trade associations are often the basis of industry agreements that are intended to head off more legislation about take-backs. The five elements of accomplishment for products in general are

- *Products that can be dismantled quickly and easily.* It is not enough that these materials are easily recycled. If it is difficult to get at those materials, they will go to the "dump." Economical dismantling is essential.
- *Components that can be reused* (sometimes for a second time without any additional operations). At other times, process refurbishing is needed, and it must be economically justifiable.
- *Parts that can be disposed of safely.* When reuse is not possible, then destruction and reduction must lead to safe disposal. The process can include pulverization, making the material liquid, putting it into containers, and burying it in caves thousands of feet below the surface (like depleted uranium). The ultimate question is where can

dangerous used-up materials be safely stored? Safely means out of harm's way. The caves under Yucca Mountain, Nevada, are a suggested solution for depleted uranium.

- *Materials that can be recycled.* This brings up a distinction between materials that are reused and materials that are recycled. The recycling process for paper is a good example. All qualifying paper products (the commodity) are mixed together and treated chemically to form a substance that can be transformed into paper. The benefit is that fewer trees are needed to make a given amount of paper. Tire and glass recycling follow the same pattern.
- *Materials that can be reused* (where reuse, in comparison to recycle, is related to the amount of reprocessing required). In recycling paper, there is a good deal of reprocessing. In contrast, a disposable camera is returned by the customer with the film in it for film processing. That camera has parts that can be used again with a minimum amount of reprocessing. Parts such as spool take-ups for the film, and lens components that are undamaged, can be collected from the spent camera and put into the new camera. Perhaps a component like this needs a part replaced or resized for a new model. Initial design can significantly increase the percent of reusable parts.

In 1995, *Fortune* magazine stated that the people working in the five bullet-point areas discussed here "are riding the hottest new production trend in the world: **design for disassembly (DFD)**."[2] It has gotten hotter with each passing day. The pressure has been building for many reasons. One factor that accounts for the growing importance of DFD is the *increasing cost of the disposal of waste.* A second factor is the tough (and getting tougher) European **take-back laws.** They compel manufacturers to take back used product. As a direct result, manufacturers are forced to design cars, telephones, copy machines, and refrigerators that are quick to disassemble and, as much as possible, reusable. BMW has led in disassembly with recycling goals of better than 95 percent (by weight) of its cars.

Equally important are the cost savings that can be realized. Economic and ecological benefits are so well correlated that in the United States, without take-back laws, Detroit's carmakers work with auto-part recyclers to reuse more than 84 percent of the weight of American cars. The effort to increase this percent will result in continuous innovations using new materials and principles of assembly–disassembly. The United States is on board with the European Union and with Japan.

DFD innovations are exemplified by the Saturn Corporation (wholly-owned subsidiary of GM). Saturn developed a new disassembly line that was more energy efficient than the previous method of shredding cars. The new method of recycling had the capability to recycle 83 percent (by weight) of Saturn cars with a goal of 95 percent by 2010.[3]

The design of the car promotes recycling. Thermoplastic side panels for Saturn doors is an industry first. The panels do not dent, which has been an effective advertising selling point. The plastic can be recycled, which pleases environmentalists. Saturn returns damaged accident parts from retailers nationwide using the roundtrip of its repair-parts trucks to Spring Hill, Tennessee, for recycling.

The methods and tools of life cycle management are well thought out at Saturn. The company is a model of corporate commitment to environmental protection. The Saturn initiative spans design and construction of the manufacturing/assembly facility through the entire product life cycle. Saturn describes the cycle as:

$$\text{Design} \rightarrow \text{Manufacture} \rightarrow \text{Consumer Use} \rightarrow \text{Post-Consumer Disposal}$$

The Saturn Vue Green Line Hybrid has been chosen by Enterprise Rent-A-Car for its California market in 2007.

P/OM coordination of design for manufacturing, assembly, and disassembly is paramount in many industry applications: Xerox and Panasonic (copy machines), Kodak and Fuji (cameras), John Deere and Caterpillar (tractors), and IBM and HP (computers). HP recycles 3.5 million pounds of electronic equipment per month. Sony has developed a cooperative take-back program with the state of Minnesota.

Design for disassembly (DFD)
DFD innovations can be rewarding in terms of rapid disassembly, reduction in the number of parts required, reuse (rework and remanufacture), and recycle (with safe disposal).

Take-back laws
Governmental rules are being invoked in Europe and in the United States (at a slightly slower rate) to ensure material reuse and/or proper disposal.

Table 20-1	1 Rapid disassembly.
Four R Categories as P/OM Objectives of the DFD Initiative	2 Reducing the number of parts needed.
	3 Reusing, reworking, and **remanufacturing** parts. If step 3 can only be done n times, then after the nth time . . .
	4 Recycle the material or dispose of it safely.

Remanufacturing

Disassemble the returned product. Reuse good parts, repair damaged parts, replace unusable parts to make a new product.

In the United States, Springfield Remanufacturing Corporation has achieved remarkable remanufacturing statistics (see http://www.srcreman.com). The company's slide show makes a major point about "not rebuilding" but remanufacturing. The latter, it is stated, means total disassembly, cleaning and inspecting all parts—whereas the former is disassembling only to the point of failure. The URL starts with the acronym that the company has come to be known by and followed by "reman" for remanufacturing. Customers include Case, Mitsubishi, New Holland, General Motors, Cummins, Isuzu, and International.

Hewlett-Packard (HP) continues to be a leader in the DFD area. It rebuilds and recycles every workstation that is returned to the company. HP's manager of product stewardship stated: "In the hierarchy of the three R's of design for the environment, the first two—reduce [the number of product parts] and reuse [the parts]—rank above recycling." Table 20-1 expands the usual three R categories of DFD into four P/OM objectives.

The Silicon Valley Toxics Coalition (SVTC) is devoted to informing its members about current events for these topics. In a strongly worded announcement at http://www.svtc.org, the SVTC pointed out that the European Parliament passed two laws on February 18, 2003, that will affect U.S. companies doing business in any country of the European Union. The laws deal with extended producer responsibility. The first, known as WEEE (waste from electronic and electrical equipment), requires free take-back of e-waste by final owners and demands that equipment producers be completely responsible for financing the collection, treatment, recovery, and disposal of all waste. The second law, known as RoHS (restriction of the use of certain hazardous substances), requires ending the use of lead, mercury, cadmium, and other toxic materials on a timetable that extends over nearly six years.

It is beneficial to review the effects of some reuse strategies. Eastman Kodak converted its throwaway camera concept to recyclable cameras because environmentalists were disturbed and planning to take action. Internal parts are now reused up to 10 times, and 87 percent of the camera (by weight) is reused or recycled. These products have been reported to be among Kodak's most profitable products.

For Xerox, remanufacturing and recycling of parts was saving approximately $500 million per year. Xerox had a team called *Asset Recycle Management Organization* that worked exclusively on DFD. Xerox, today, may have turned its attention to other matters. Once its financial stability is ensured, it may return to the DFD initiative it helped to create.

Design for assembly (DFA) has lowered production costs and is related to DFD. That which is easier to put together, generally is easier to take apart. With thoughtful design, DFA and DFD become symmetrical functions. Bearing this in mind, lowering assembly costs is often a prelude to allowing robotic assembly.

Design for automation (DFAU) raises another level of accomplishment if the same robot can disassemble returned units. Computer PCs and laptops are a natural candidate, which is to be kept in mind when reviewing the EU challenges listed earlier with respect to the Silicon Valley Toxics Coalition.

Design for assembly (DFA)

Product is designed to be put together efficiently, meaning at minimum cost and with higher quality standards.

Design for automation (DFAU)

Robots can decrease assembly costs and bear the brunt of difficult work such as welding and painting with toxic materials. Quality and speed of assembly work increases while the cost goes down.

20-3b Reverse Supply Chains

The attention that has been paid to improving supply chain performance has been outstanding. As a result, whether the supply chain is efficient or not, it could be made so if there is organizational buy-in. The supply chain of consumer products (e.g., to supermarkets) is quite efficient. On the other hand, the supply chain of the healthcare industry is highly inefficient. In 1998, the EHCR (Efficient Healthcare Consumer Response) tried to model its supply chain on that of the grocery industry's ECR and failed in the United States.

The Canadian EHCR remains as an organization dedicated to the idea of manufacturers, hospitals, and group buying organizations promoting efficient health care through the use of electronic commerce-enabling technologies including bar codes and EDI. There is some evidence that the Canadian EHCR is successful. At least, it is not following the debacle of EHCR in the United States.

The take-back movement has grown stronger for several reasons, including the unexpected monetary gains that companies have experienced once they agree to participate in end-of-life product recovery. The imposition of intelligent end-of-life (EOL) objectives for products has made a difference.

Reverse supply chains manifest themselves in a number of ways. For example, "smart" remanufacturing can lower costs and improve quality. Resource recovery has the potential to reduce the cost of materials. There is also a reduction in the cost of failures, which require repair or replacement. Add the realization that governments will be increasingly holding fabricators responsible for end-of-product life disposal and additional forces emerge for planned reverse logistics.

The average return rate of products is substantial (about 20 percent). The variability is also significant. Working with a mail-order firm provided an estimate for catalog item returns of about 30 percent. Department stores may have less than 8 percent returns. Most of the returns are not brought or sent back because they are defective. A charge of 10 percent or 15 percent for so-called "restocking" has not been well-received by customers. Therefore, a good number of stores consider returns as a cost of doing business. However, it is not evident that many managers know how much returns cost.

Companies do not use process analysis to determine the costs of various strategies for dealing with returned goods. Companies like Home Depot and Costco have return policies that do not require receipts as long as the product is carried by the company. Analyses of what happens to the stream of returned products is not available. However, with some observation and logic, it is easy to conjecture that a significant percent of returns that are not faulty are put back on the shelves. Faulty products are returned to vendors for credit. The vendor's process with returned items is more complex.

Information about take-back to vendor remanufacturing is available through strong sources such as the National Center for Remanufacturing & Resource Recovery (cleverly called NC3R in 2005). It is located at the Rochester Institute of Technology (see the wonderful timeline of the remanufacturing industry at http://www.reman.rit.edu). A reasonable estimate for 2007 is that (all categories of) remanufacturing is more than a $100 billion industry in the United States. When looked at on a worldwide basis, remanufacturing is estimated to be three times the amount just stated for the United States.

In Table 20-2, the location of remanufacturing in the reverse supply chain is shown in two parts. There is the traditional outbound system that moves to the customer. But first, the customer must return product to the company. The latter is the nontraditional inbound system. The supply loop is formed when the two parts are taken together. *Supply loop management* is a newer term used to describe managing the forward and reverse loops in a strategic way.

An informative website with respect to end-of-life (EOL) generic product directives and supply loop management is available from Cardone Industries at http://www.cardone.com. In 2007, Cardone remanufactured 38 different product lines. They are specialists in **reverse engineering**. As an estimate, (just automotive) remanufacturing is a $37 billion dollar category.

Delving deeper into an often-asked question "What is meant by reverse logistics?" Specifically, the term means the take-back, send-back, and receive-back portion of the supply chain. Reasons for the reverse flow include normal customer returns, government rules to take back and dispose of pollutants, and cost benefits to the company if it can save money by retrieving and reusing materials.

Reverse supply chains
There is a reverse delivery logistic at end-of-life for both used up and damaged products.

Reverse engineering
Method for discovering the technological principles of a device that are hidden by its assembly. It is taken apart. Interactions of components are analyzed. Often much is learned in reassembly.

	Outbound: Suppliers→Manufacture→Ship to Consumers Inbound: Consumer Returns Product or Company Retrieval Occurs→Inspect Returned Product→Repair, Refurbish, and Relabel→Post-Consumer Disposal	
Table 20-2 Supply Loop Management— Forward Supply Chain Called *Outbound*; Reverse Supply Chain Called *Inbound*; Taken Together, Forward and Reverse Are Called the *Supply Loop*	**Some Ideas for Efficient Reverse Supply Chains**	
	Step Number	**Step Description**
	1	Company takes back old parts in the same truck that delivers new product.
	1A	Persuade customers to return used-up products for disposal.
	1B	Analyze trade-in potentials as a reverse supply chain marketing strategy.
	1C	Develop a remarketing strategy for replacement?
	2	Take-backs must be sorted by part types, model, age, condition, etc.
	2A	Evaluation process requires testing and smart decisions to refurbish or dispose.
	3	New, reused, and refurbished parts are put together in an assembly kit.
	3A	Assemble, relabel, and repackage.
	4	Steps 2., 2A., 3., and 3A. are remanufacturing. That process can be optimized.
	5	Remarketing of the refurbished product if not replacement.
	6	Redistribution of the remarketed product starts the outbound supply chain.

Customers return products for a variety of reasons. There are expected rates of return by industry type. *Abnormal return rates might be symptoms of serious defects* in manufacturing and delivery. Knowing what the expected return rate should be is important. When this is exceeded, understanding the cause of abnormal returns is critical for quality control. Returns must be inspected to find out what is wrong with the take-backs.

The economics of repair and refurbishment change over time. A refurbished computer from an old era might be an interesting antique, but it might not be suitable as a business machine for data processing and keeping spreadsheet accounts. Once upon a time, repairing old phones (Merlin) by AT&T at Little Rock was cost-beneficial. When phone prices dropped significantly, and wireless phones took a solid share of the telephone set market, the economic benefits of remanufacturing this product shifted. AT&T gave up on this business and sold its Little Rock repair operations.

Good original design helps to ensure that remanufacturing is feasible. There are many pressures to use design as the first step toward remanufacturing, not the least of which is the fact that the city dump will not be permitted to serve as the ultimate destination of all defunct products. Thereby, the life expectancy of old products will be extended. In the medical and dental fields, this also applies to patients with artificial body parts. Transportation is a critical component of both forward and reverse supply chain management. As in the case of Saturn Corporation, where the auto-delivery carrier becomes the vehicle for returning used parts, integration can occur between forward and reverse planning. Consider the logistics planning required by all appliance manufacturers as laws for reverse supply chains kick into action.

20-3c Construction and Demolition (C&D) Reverse Supply Chain

"Publicity-wise, C&D recycling is a poor stepchild to the more famous recovery and reuse of paper, plastics, aluminum cans, etc.... But by weight and volume, C&D

recycling is the biggest recycling industry in North America. According to CMRA ... 325 million tons per year (2007) of recoverable construction and demolition materials are generated in the U.S.A. annually. C&D is made up primarily of concrete, asphalt, wood, gypsum, demolition metals and asphalt shingles. It is generated from roadbuilding and highway maintenance, plus from building renovation, demolition and construction."[4]

Recycling of paper, cans, etc., has not been easy to fund because it does not readily turn a profit. On the other hand, C&D is generally a profitable enterprise. **Recycling concrete** and asphalt is important for its sheer volume and the difficulty of disposal without the reuse capability. There are economic advantages as well. The Construction Materials Recycling Association (CMRA) estimates that 105 millions tons of concrete are recycled every year. Read the accomplishment of CMRA at http://www.cdrecycling.org.

Recycling concrete

Recycling concrete from the old road to the new road is an excellent example of end-of-life (ELV) product recovery.

20-4 Ethics and Operations Management

Greening the plant environment should come naturally to P/OM because health and safety start with workers on the production line. Discussions about methods for establishing workstation safety can be found in the earliest industrial engineering literature. However, the Occupational Safety and Health Administration of the U.S. Department of Labor (see prior reference to OSHA; http://www.osha.gov) has met with a lot of problems in fulfilling its mission—basically, to save lives, prevent injuries, and protect the health of America's workers. For the complete mission statement, see the webpage.

20-4a Ethics: Health and Safety of Employees and Customers

There are many causes of safety lapses and health threats. Ignorance, incompetence, and indifference are some of the culprits. Although these three situations are all bad for responsible production system behavior, they are not directly greed-based. Where greed is a root cause, it is correct to state that ethical failure is immediately responsible. For example, if managers perceive an opportunity to save money by cutting corners, which may affect customers deleteriously, then they have clearly violated ethical standards. Ignorance of the law is no excuse from a legal point of view, but when it comes to ethics, if the managers were ignorant of the ill effects caused by their decisions, there is a basis for debate. It could be an ethical failing not to be educated or to be ill-informed about the consequences of decisions. Management can be blamed for an ethical failure when job responsibilities are given to incompetent people.

It is always a crucial question: What effect do innocent bad decisions and not-so-innocent decisions to cut corners have on the health and well-being of employees and customers? It was bad judgment to have big investments in a company 401(k). The fact is that bad investments in a retirement plan do affect health and welfare of employees. Management has an ethical obligation to show that all possible contingencies were examined in matters related to employee and customer health and safety.

Retirement plans may be the core of ethical study and research in the future because many companies have indicated interest in abrogating their "contracts" with employees after many years of employment. It may be that due diligence and proper performance of management will be required to fulfill employees' expectations regarding pensions. It is likely that if corners have been cut that jeopardize the pensions of employees (already and soon to be) retired, there will be legal recourse.

Starting with Enron and continuing with WorldCom, Tyco, etc., the meltdown of the stock market in the period from 2000 through 2003 was accompanied by a host of ethical horrors. These are not just accounting errors. See Spotlight 20-1: Ethics by Regulation.

The P/OM area is impacted by improper funding to produce the product and/or service. Deals are made that bypass customers, stockholders, and employees. One of the worst aspects of management failures are the rewards bestowed on the stewards of bankruptcy.

20-4b Ethics and the Supply Chain

There are no examples, on record, of where inside trading in stock is done by operations managers. The financial area is not the domain of operations. On the other hand, purchasing agents are not expected to accept substantial presents that are intended to influence the choice of suppliers. Many companies have strict rules that require gift-refusals by buyers. For example, the U.S. government is adamant about the ethical standard of "take no gifts." This strict standard is interesting when compared with the unwritten rules of many non-American companies that believe that gifts are a proper way to start a relationship.

How can policies be so out-of-kilter with each other? When business relations are viewed as a matter of personal trust rather than legal obligations, then gifts are not hard to understand. Friends and families interchange gifts throughout the year as a sign of caring. The family basis for a gift-giving business culture does not exist in the United States and many other parts of the world. Therefore, in gift-giving business culture countries, the United States is not considered to be polite, kind, or trustworthy. A dilemma exists in this situation because the legal mind-set is not considered to be ethical in these cultures. The result is a culture split between what is considered ethical and what is felt to be friendly and trustworthy.

Inventory managers have been cited for ethical crimes in a variety of circumstances. In an actual non-U.S. situation, order sizes were triple economic order quantities. Investigation indicated that payoffs were given to executives for large order sizes, but no price discounts were awarded to the company. The ethical violation is evident, and yet it was argued that in this culture, the salary of managers was expected to be augmented by payoffs. The excess materials were deteriorating as a result of aging. Overbuying created an ethical problem because individuals benefited while the company was damaged. The same would apply if the supply chain was used for personal gain at the expense of product obsolescence and product deterioration. In the example given earlier, the products were rubber and synthetic tires.

In the supply chain, the ethical problems are related to over-ordering, paying too much, and accepting poor qualities—for personal gain. Ethical issues can take on other forms such as pocketing discounts instead of passing them to the company; making deals with uncertified vendors; eliminating the best bids from consideration; and refusing to consider eligible competitors.

In the international supply chain, there are some additional ethical factors. The supply chain distance can be greater and transit times longer. This is especially true when sea transportation is used. Hewlett-Packard ships printers from the West Coast of the United States to Europe and Asia. Lead times are extensive and pipeline inventory substantial. See Spotlight 19-1: Saving Time and Money by Postponement. Lead times must also include delays that are sometimes a function of legal requirements and interpersonal activities including payoffs to customs and to other regulators of the flow of goods across national boundaries. Lead-time management often interacts with ethical issues.

There is another gray area related to selling expensive products (like airplanes) without using bribery. *The Wall Street Journal* reported ... that Airbus was in talks with China for the sale of between 30 and 50 A320 airliners, worth up to US$2.7 billion." The issue of ethics arises when reading on: "Airbus has spent some US$80 million in setting up a training and support center in Beijing, (and) also signed a deal with China on co-producing wing parts for A320 planes" (*China Daily*, August 28, 2001).[5] Bribes are illegal in many countries, but training investments and coproducing deals are widely used by many companies. Airbus is not alone; Boeing has the same kind of partner-sharing arrangements.

20-4c Ethics and Environment

Enlightened companies take great pains to be ethical in every respect. This begins by management setting examples of doing what is known to be right when confronted with opportunities to gain advantage by using non-ethical behaviors. This is why many auto companies in the United States work together to reduce pollution in the environment.

The same applies to the internal environment, i.e., in the plant. A good example of successful interactions between OSHA, management, unions, and workers is found in counteracting dangers caused by painting autos. Significant strides have been made by the automobile industry to protect employees from the harmful fumes and chemicals of paint. Painting exemplifies systems that pollute both internal and external environments.

Saturn was the first car manufacturer to use water-based rather than solvent-based paints. Water-based paints have about one-fourth of the emissions of solvent-based paints. Painting is done in a clean room using paint booths and robots to do the spraying. Extra paint flows into a water river under the paint room, and the paint is later separated from the water using electric charges with special chemicals that cause the paint to float. Workers are not put in harm's way, and the effluent that reaches the ground is not polluted. There are two points to discuss that derive from the Saturn example.

First, a greenfield plant (like Saturn) has the advantage of being able to do things right the first time. Second, an old plant must be redesigned and rebuilt at high costs, including the cost of lost production while changing over from one system to the other. The ethical issues in going from old to new are further complicated by legal differences that arise when new laws are enacted that only apply to new structures. This type of law, called a *grandfather clause*, exempts old businesses from new government regulations.

It is not unusual that established systems are regulated under different rules than new systems because greenfield facilities can embody new technologies and meet new standards within reasonable economic parameters, whereas old systems would go bankrupt. Grandfather clauses are the explanation for old nightclubs being responsible for many tragic fires where hundreds of people are killed or injured (e.g., in West Warwick, Rhode Island, in 2003 and Sheffield, England, in 2007). Old clubs have not been held to the same standards as the new ones with respect to building materials, smoke detectors, and sprinkler systems.

Hazard reduction for workers, customers, and communities is a matter of ethics. These ethics are a set of acceptable social standards for proper behavior. In the United States, standards have been moving toward higher ideals of winning on merit in a community sense, in the plant/office, and in the supermarket. Consumer examples include increasingly stringent labeling of food ingredients, cigarette package warnings, expiration dating, tamper-proof drug packaging, seat belts, and front/side airbags. OSHA has been strict in demanding safety in the workplace.

Ethics is not a separate part of business. When ethical precepts are treated as separate, it is not possible to build an ethical infrastructure. Ethics requires the systems point of view because the standards must be known and accepted by everyone who works for the company. It is not possible to conform to an ethical standard if some of the employees think it is all right to cut corners on quality, ship inferior product, overcharge some customers, solicit kickbacks, take bribes, and even steal office supplies. Pilferage ranging from minor items to large-scale theft significantly reduces a company's profitability. No matter how small, the business environment is damaged by a culture that permits theft.

20-4d Ethics and Quality Integrity

When accepted practice is bypassed, it is critical to document the reasons for changing procedures. An acceptable explanation for the change is that there is a better way to do that job. Striving for continuous improvement is to be rewarded. On the other hand, if ignorance, incompetence, and/or indifference are responsible for changing procedures, the ethical response is to require an explanation. Then, when it is clear that the original procedure was best, reset the system and eliminate the causes of the problems.

Were the wrong people hired to do the job? Were the people who were hired fine but their training on the job was not up to par? There are times when motivation is missing.

An unmotivated workforce is often the cause of business problems. This explains why downsizing for cost reduction becomes a possible cause of reduced customer loyalty, and that translates into lower market share and reduced revenues. The critics of downsizing refer to it as an ethical breach with employees. Supporters of downsizing point to the fact that with the existing workforce, the firm would be forced into bankruptcy. This indicates an ethical dilemma. Decisions to downsize have to be based on competent evaluations of the pros and cons.

If the problem stems from the fact that customers perceive that they are receiving less quality for the price of the product and, thereby, lower value, the question must be raised about the cause of the perception. The size and weight of the product may have been downsized. The taste or effectiveness of the product may have been changed. There is an ethical question about the consistency of quality (and quantity) that customers have come to expect. Changes of this sort are seldom seen as life threatening but they can be when a new ingredient is added to a product that produces allergic reactions in some percent of users. If the ingredient was added to save money, that raises further ethical questions.

Contaminated food is responsible for a great deal of illness and death. Sources of the contamination are traceable to operations associated with preparing and handling that food. The ethical standards are clear. Because they fail quite often, what are the possible explanations? Causes could be managerial ineptness, or incompetence, or managerial ignorance. As stated in a prior section, ignorance of what is required for safe and healthy operations is not an excuse. Therefore an ethical boundary is crossed when an operator does not know how to run a safe plant, or airline. Inebriated pilots (as reported from time to time in the United States and almost never in many other countries) are intolerable examples of unethical behavior.

When quality problems arise for customers because of employee self-interest, the worst form of ethical failure has occurred. When bad decisions for company quality turn out to be motivated by self-interested managers, the focus of the ethical transgressions becomes a legal matter. For example, there are documented stories about managers who have been stressed by their bosses to ship production units to meet quotas while looking the other way on quality requirements. There are cases in the courts filed by customers (honestly and falsely) claiming personal loss caused by poor quality for tires, auto gas tanks, hot coffee, and bugs in soda. Claims are not proof of quality malfeasance. Each situation must be judged on its own merits.

It is difficult to keep employees' morale high when the company they work for is under siege for asbestos litigation. By end of the first quarter of 2003, the asbestos litigation cost was over \$200 billion, and nine defendants had gone out of business.[6] See http://www.kazanlaw.com/search/home.cfm. Enter "asbestos" in the search window. Many settlements have been reached but the interaction of ethics and asbestos goes on and on. For example, in a class-action lawsuit, ABB (facing 220,000 claimants) agreed to pay the lawyer in the case in addition to the plaintiffs to obtain an agreement for an end to legal actions. The suits arose from the boiler work done by the Combustion Engineering division of ABB. *The New York Times* has the headline "A Caldron of Ethics and Asbestos."[7]

Similar reasoning applies to tobacco companies faced with the attorneys general for tobacco-caused illness. The settlement with the states' attorneys general was hundreds of billions of dollars in 1998, and lawsuits by individuals continue. Exxon employees were unhappy about the *Valdez* oil spill in Alaska. That was March 24, 1989. See the turn of events by visiting the Exxon Valdez Oil Spill Trustee Council at http://www.evostc.state.ak.us. The entire working plan is there, including the Draft Work Plan for year 2008.

Although it was not Pan Am's fault, there was a quality integrity problem after the bomb blast destroyed Flight 103 in December 1988 over Lockerbie, Scotland. Travelers on Pan American Airlines did not feel safe. Airline revenues went into a major decline. Pan Am ultimately filed for bankruptcy. All employees lost their jobs. Common stockholders lost every cent of their investments. It has been speculated that a change of name might have helped the airline survive. Would it have been unethical to change the airline's name?

In a variety of cases, there are potential whistle-blowers who do not speak up because the ethics of tattling on fellow managers frequently overrides the ethic of righting a wrong. How often that situation occurs is unknown because the whistle-blowers do not speak up. What is evident is that when whistle-blowers do speak up, management often ignores those warnings. Enron and Arthur Andersen might still be in business if top management had listened to their whistle-blowers. WorldCom might be healthier if evidence of wrongdoing had not been swept under the rug.

In the short term, unethical management may get away with bad practice. In the long run, it is reasonable to believe that unethical management will not prosper. Management, employees, stockholders, and customers lose as company stock values plunge, products are unavailable, and jobs are gone. Visit Management Malpractice for "the ten worst companies" at http://www.managementmalpractice.com/10_worst_companies.php.

Ethics, Quality Integrity, and CDC/FDA

For P/OM, one of the most important ethical issues is to deliver safe and healthy products and services. That standard is called **quality integrity**. The definitions of integrity are many, including honesty, veracity, and truthfulness. For business, this may mean producing the product according to standards that have been set by government regulators. It also means not shipping product to customers that deviates from standards. One of the most sensitive areas to monitor for ethical adherence to standards is in foods and drugs. This includes meat and poultry processing plants, food canning operations, egg production, food shops, and restaurants. At the same time, the CDC-related Agency for Toxic Substances and Disease Registry (ATSDR) was set up in 1980 by the Comprehensive Environmental Response, Compensation, and Liability Act, which is known as the Superfund. ATSDR prevents exposure to hazardous wastes and deals with environmental spills of hazardous materials. See http://www.atsdr.cdc.gov.

The U.S. Department of Health and Human Services includes the Food and Drug Administration (**FDA**) and the Centers for Disease Control and Prevention (CDC). As of April 2005, the **CDC** had 15,000 people and contractors employed in 12 centers, institutes, and offices. Dr. Julie Gerberding has been the CDC director since 2002. See http://www.cdc.gov for various topics such as avian flu pandemics.

The centers are used to identify trends and new concerns about diseases (such as botulism). Between 2004 and 2007, the CDC estimated that annually 76 million people got sick; 325,000 were hospitalized; and between 5,000 and 8,000 people died as a result of food-borne illness. The identification of causes is difficult and the estimates are rough. This is a difficult area for estimation because many cases are not reported. Also, a common cause has to be identified if there is an outbreak of illness in an area of the country. CDC estimated that seafood accounted for 4.8 percent of reported cases of food-borne illness (from 1987 to 1994, and that probably holds for the next decade as well).

Hazard Analysis and Critical Control Point (HACCP) System

The FDA has taken numerous steps to provide consumers with protection against tainted foods and food poisoning. The causes of such illness are associated with the quality integrity of food products from a number of points of view, including sources and handling. One of the strongest initiatives is the operation and the application of Hazard Analysis and Critical Control Point (HACCP) principles to establish procedures for safe processing and importing of fish and fishery products. See http://www.haccpweb.com. This is a private company webpage (not the U.S. government).

HACCP also monitors unpasteurized fruit juices and dairy products. In 1998, the U.S. Department of Agriculture established HACCP for meat and poultry processing plants. The FDA intends to extend HACCP "to eventually use it for much of the U.S. food

Quality integrity
Ensure delivery of products and services good for the safety and health of customers. P/OM must also provide a secure and accident-free working environment for employees. Such standards are the foundation of quality integrity.

FDA
The FDA monitors quality integrity for food producers, warehouses, distributors, retailers, and restaurants.

CDC
Centers for Disease Control and Prevention, located in Atlanta, Georgia; the lead federal agency for protecting the health and safety of people—at home and abroad. CDC has responsibilities that are new and not well-defined since the potential of bioterrorism has emerged as a global threat.

supply" (from the *FDA Backgrounder*, "HACCP: A State-of-the-Art Approach to Food Safety," October 2001). See http://vm.cfsan.fda.gov/lrd/haccp.html for 2006 approaches to HACCP. This is the U.S. Food and Drug Administration webpage.

HACCP is a combination of an early-warning system for troubles that could occur and contingency planning about what to do if one or another form of trouble does occur.

It is not necessary to restrict discussion of the **Hazard Analysis and Critical Control Point (HACCP) system** to the seafood industry, which is comprised of organizations engaged in fishing, aquaculture, fish farming, fish and shellfish processing, and packing. It applies to all foods and drugs and can be extended to hazard analysis for all products and services. How much effort should go into the control of hazards is an ethical issue. The government sets standards that companies can elect to surpass. The FDA's evaluation of the HACCP seafood program for fiscal years 2000/2001 (September 23, 2002) reveals positive improvements with an average compliance of 88 percent (see http://www.cfsan.fda.gov/comm/seaeval2.html). For later developments through 2007, see http://www.saferpak.com/haccp.htm. Browsers will encounter flow diagramming and six-sigma among many other P/OM terms.

Hazard analysis and critical control point's application as a preventive system for hazard control was pioneered by the Pillsbury Company in the 1960s to create safe food for the space program. The program was applied successfully and since that time has been consistently extended and developed. It is one of the largest scale quality-control programs that can be found in the field of operations management. HACCP is an excellent example of total quality management where inspection and testing are not sufficient by themselves to achieve satisfactory quality.

"HACCP is a science-based system of preventive controls for food safety that commercial food processors develop and operate to identify potential problems and keep them from occurring. The evaluation covers implementation of the HACCP program by about 4,100 U.S. seafood processors.... This report shows that the seafood HACCP program has increased the margin of safety for American consumers.... But this report also identifies segments of the industry that need continued focus and government oversight."[8]

Online interactive quality monitoring is needed to assure that food poisoning does not occur at all. The FDA intended to make HACCP mandatory for the seafood industry. Nevertheless, only a small percent of the industry is obliged to take remedial steps to correct problems.

Seven steps for using HACCP's principles are:

1 *Analyze hazards.* These are causes of food being unsafe for consumption. The key is to identify potential hazards associated with a food and identify measures to control those hazards. Hazards include biological, such as a microbe; chemical, such as a toxin; or physical, such as ground glass or metal fragments. The principal seafood-related hazards that cause food-borne illnesses are bacteria, viruses, and natural toxins.

2 *Identify critical control points in the process.* The CCP are points in a food's production where the potential hazard can be controlled or eliminated. The CCP start with the raw state and go through processing, shipping, and point-of-consumption by consumers. CCPs could be cooking, cooling, chilling, packaging, sanitation procedures, or employee and plant hygiene. The CCPs are identified with respect to the hazards analyzed in step 1.

3 *Establish preventive measures with critical limits for each control point.* Critical limits are boundaries of safety for each critical control point. They specify thresholds for preventive measures to be taken for temperatures, times, moisture levels, available chlorine, pH, etc. The critical limits can be derived from sources such as regulatory standards and guidelines, experimental studies, literature surveys, and experts. For example, this could include setting a minimum cooking temperature (to ensure the elimination of harmful microbes).

4 *Establish procedures to monitor critical control points.* This is a planned sequence of observations or measurements to assess whether a critical control point is under

Hazard Analysis and Critical Control Point (HACCP) system

Designed to prevent food hazards from arising without detection. It is a quality control system that discerns the presence of defective process management.

Courtesy: NASA.

Blast-off into the clouds brings to mind that HACCP was developed by NASA in its pioneering work in the 1960s to create safe food for the astronauts in the space program. Later it was applied by the FDA as a preventive system of food hazard control in the sale and preparation of fish and, later, orange juice, dairy, and other foods to consumers. It is now widely used by P/OM in appropriate contamination-control applications.

control and to produce an accurate record for future use in verification. As with quality control charts, this system monitors the process at critical prevention points to spot trends indicative of potential trouble, or of real trouble. It is expected that corrective action will be taken to bring the process back into control before a real problem deviation occurs, or to correct a real problem. Also important is the written documentation for use in verification of the HACCP plan. For example, identify how, and by whom, cooking times and temperatures are to be set and monitored.

5 *Establish corrective actions to be taken when monitoring shows that a critical limit has been exceeded.* For example, what should be done if the minimum cooking temperature is not fulfilled? Three things need to be done:

   a. Determine the disposition of food produced during a deviation. Should the food be disposed of, and how should that be done safely? Can the food be reprocessed?

   b. Correct the cause of noncompliance to ensure that the critical control point is under control.

   c. Maintain records of food disposal, reprocessing, and the corrective actions for noncompliance.

Because food poisoning is an unacceptable quality deviation, the disposition of spoiled food becomes an obvious subject to be determined and documented. Spoiled food can be salvaged by the unwary. This is an interesting aspect of the reverse supply chain. HACCP sets down good methods for industry to utilize. What happens to defective product should be decided as part of every quality control system. This is an ethical commitment, too.

6 *Establish procedures to verify that the HACCP system is working properly.* This step includes verification that the critical limits are appropriate and functioning as intended. The step also is used to make sure that all aspects of HACCP are being followed. Finally, it ensures periodic revalidation of the plan to make certain that it is still relevant to raw materials, technology, and all other process factors and conditions. For example, the recording devices for time and temperature must be tested to verify that the cooking unit is working properly.

7 *Establish effective record-keeping systems to document all significant aspects of the HACCP system.* Maintain records of hazards and their control methods. Document monitoring of safety requirements and actions taken to correct potential problems. Basic principles must be backed by sound scientific knowledge. For example, use correct, published microbiological studies on time and temperature factors to control food-borne pathogens. The records show critical control points, critical limits, and all relevant data generated by the process during its operation.[9]

The implications of the HACCP system for assuring the quality of outputs of processing technologies are significant. The essence of the ethics in this case is to employ the system to protect customers and employees. The design of process technology should have as an objective minimum costs for achieving the HACCP objectives. The attention to documentation and methods for updating changes in conditions make HACCP a superior operational system.

All organizations entering the seafood industry and related businesses (as the use of HACCP grows for foods in general) will learn the HACCP regulations in order to be in compliance. This adds another dimension when planning and choosing process technologies. It is *design for compliance*. The rules must be understandable and compliance must be possible using reasonable technology and training.

Appropriate information technology makes the record-keeping system a boon and not a burden. HACCP is a pragmatic system that has the potential to cure some basic problems. The shellfish industry is being destroyed by the fear of toxic poisoning. People who like to eat raw oysters and clams are giving them up because of misgivings. If HACCP can save the shellfish business, jobs would be saved and consumers' health protected. The rewards are far larger than the costs.

© 2008 Jupiterimages Corporation

The shellfish business has been severely damaged by health department warnings regarding toxins. At the same time, shellfish harvests have been depleted by runoffs that pollute the beds. Despite investing more than $7 million, the Mohegan Tribe in Connecticut gave up on the idea of cultivating clams, oysters, and scallops in local waters. As of September 2005, the tribe abandoned its aquaculture business. It had been restarted in 2000. The Mohegan Tribe had traditionally harvested shellfish and had much expertise. If HACCP rules were totally in place with restaurants and distributors, and if the runoffs from fields and waste were controlled, the industry might have been saved.

The HACCP model reflects good management of ethics. It might well be adopted by those who manage new food processes that use genetic materials and biotechnology. Hormones fed to cows to increase milk supplies and irradiation of food products to retard spoilage are two areas of concern. If they are definitely established to be safe, then HACCP can be used to monitor and control the process dosages of biological materials and radiation. For environmental processes, it may be useful to consider the application of the HACCP principles and seven steps to pollution control and hazardous waste disposal management.

For process technologies in general, HACCP has relevance as an application of TQM under governmental regulation. Quality, a primary P/OM responsibility, always has been regulated, to some degree, by the federal government. Examples are weight, purity, and honest labeling. New rules make change management essential.

Quality has been under constant discussion in the courts (product liability cases, etc). The difference is that HACCP regulates QC methodology whereas, previously, quality was only regulated as an end result. HACCP regulates quality at the process level.

The Occupational Safety and Health Act of 1970 (OSHA) provides precedence for governmental regulation of systems and processes. Inspectors are used to check workplace conformance to safety rules. There have been many complaints about bureaucracy, and strenuous efforts have been made to have OSHA function as a positive complement and not antagonistically with business. It is hoped that HACCP regulators can learn from the OSHA experiences. This is an excellent example of the dynamics of ethics. Improvements in ethics are aided and abetted by proper governmental regulation.

While OSHA is concerned with the safety of the process, HACCP deals with the quality of outputs from the process. Related to HACCP goals is product liability, which is increasingly associated with HACCP-type rules. Currently, courts require documentation of efforts to "design for safety" and the use of QC methodology to assure safety.

From these trends, it is evident that the systems perspective is necessary. It is required to deal with changes that are occurring in the regulatory and legal systems that promote ethical business in the United States and globally. P/OM has the lead role with HACCP. It must coordinate activities with R&D, process engineering, the legal departments, and the government regulators. The customer must not be lost in a regulatory jungle.

Food and Drug Testing

Food and Drug Administration regulations for testing new drugs are extensive. Running counter to the fast-track project management theme, pharmaceutical product cycles take many years. During that time, P/OM fabricates test materials (in batches) working with R&D and prepares suitable facilities and quality-control methods for each stage. Many quality tests and drug effectiveness tests are required. New drugs go through years of laboratory studies followed by three phases of clinical testing with people.[10]

"The Tufts Center for the Study of Drug Development (CSDD) has been tracking drug development costs for 25 years. The newest research on development costs reveals a price tag of $802 million per drug.... The average drug takes 12 years and must overcome a very selective process. Tufts research reports that of every 5,000 potential new drugs tested in animals, only five are promising enough to be tested in humans; only one of those five is eventually approved for marketing."[11] The CSDD also found that contract research organizations are being increasingly outsourced and this results in faster drug development.[12]

Some consider the FDA to have overly conservative testing standards and requirements. The main pros and cons associated with stringent test specifications, requirements, and standards are captured by the following two points:

- *Undertesting* includes inadequate testing methods and deficient testing technology. Both can lead to disasters. The ethics of approving drugs with insufficient evidence is contrasted with the ethical issue of having a drug that might cure an illness but withholding it from a patient who will die without it.

- *Overtesting* delays the acceptance of effective drugs. The dilemma is that if the drug works, then people are dying unnecessarily.

Two examples are presented for the undertesting situation.

1   A vaccine was rushed into production to counter a predicted swine flu epidemic. One of the vaccine manufacturers, operating under crash project conditions, made process-technology errors that were not picked up in testing because that would have delayed the vaccination program. The result was that a far larger number of people died from the vaccine than from the swine flu, which never became an epidemic. The coincidence of failures in this case can all be attributed to the axiom that "haste makes waste."

2   The drug thalidomide reflects the complicated trade-off between the risks and benefits of testing delays. European governments have organizations equivalent to the FDA in the United States. Some of them had approved the use of thalidomide as a tranquilizer after a shorter period of testing with a smaller sample than was permitted in the United States. The drug was never legally accepted by the FDA for the United States. It turned out that this drug adversely affected the fetus if taken by women in the early months of their pregnancy. European testing had overlooked the early months even though use of tranquilizers was common during that period. Thalidomide children were born with serious deformities, which reinforced the conservative nature of the FDA in the United States.

There are two kinds of potential errors that pose ethical quandaries for P/OM and the organization. Should undertesting errors be preferred to overtesting errors? Some pharmaceutical and biotechnology firms would like FDA standards to be less stringent. They feel testing costs too much and takes too long. They believe that more funds would be invested in R&D for new drugs if test standards were relaxed. Patients tend to be on the side of faster is better, saying that people are suffering and dying unnecessarily while the testing is proceeding. In fact, they propose delivering test products to those suffering serious illnesses. The counterargument to this last point is that test results get confused when controlled experimentation is waived in favor of humanitarian considerations. The opposition states that pharmaceutical firms will say and do anything to shorten test periods to make more money.

The FDA, in recognition of the humanitarian-ethical issue, has speeded up the testing of AIDS drugs and cancer treatments. It has permitted their use for seriously ill patients before approval is granted. Aside from that, many reject the claim that the high cost of testing discourages the development of new drug technologies. They cite the fact that the pharmaceutical industry in the United States has done an excellent job of creating new drugs while making a great deal of money.

P/OM in the pharmaceutical industry emphasizes quality control as much as, or more than, any other industry. The cost of quality in pharmaceutical production is very high and there is pressure to find ways to cut these costs while increasing quality standards. Test methods are ideal candidates for reengineering. Because the FDA is known to accept change slowly and with great care, the topic of how ethics relates to the policies of change and transition management is totally relevant.

20-5 Preparing Operations Management for Future Conditions

Factories and offices of the future will look very different from their present-day counterparts. P/OM will be practiced under different circumstances and in different ways. Today's management has to be prepared for substantial change. Predictions of changes to expect are useful but hardly likely to hit the bull's-eye. The only way to benchmark these expectations is by noting current state and then extrapolating patterns of development. Some directions for change seem to be evident. Benchmarking against fundamental trends produces the following insights.

The September 19, 1994, cover of *Fortune* proclaimed, "The End of the Job: No longer the best way to organize work, the traditional job is becoming a social artifact. Its decline creates unfamiliar risks—and rich opportunities."[13] More than a decade has gone by since this article was published. Traditional jobs continue to disappear as a result of new technology, integrated information systems, a different mind-set that strives for teamwork with much involvement in projects, and the global network of business. See Spotlights 15-1 and 15-2 for a broad view of jobs and generations.

Historic events changed the frozen landscape of superpowers vying with each other until 1990. The Berlin Wall was built August 13, 1961. East Germany opened the wall November 9, 1989, and by the end of 1990 it was torn down. For more historical detail see http://www.dailysoft.com/berlinwall. Since that time, the development of the Internet fostered the instant and inexpensive communication required for a global community. However, the events of September 11, 2001, triggered a new set of conditions that put in jeopardy common safety and security. Protection from hidden terrorists moved to the top of the list for priorities in social and economic development. The new threats changed the character of global development.

20-5a Mobile Robots: Increasing Use in the Future

Many repetitive, unpleasant, and dangerous jobs can now be assigned to machines. Fixed machines can do some jobs, but they are limited by the lack of mobility. Robots[14] that move along in-floor guidewires are less constrained, but still restricted compared to freely moving people. With better sight, robots play a greater role in factory and office designs. Contributions come from many sources worldwide.

The Purdue Robot Vision Laboratory (part of Purdue University's School of Electrical and Computer Engineering) "performs state-of-the-art research in sensory intelligence for the machines of the future. This laboratory has made pioneering contributions in 3D object recognition, vision-guided navigation for indoor **mobile robots**, task and assembly planning" (http://rvl.www.ecn.purdue.edu/RVL).

The Robot Vision Group at Technische Universität München is part of the Institute for Real-Time Computer Systems (RCS) at the Department of Electrical Engineering and Information Technology. On their website, they list many research projects including Human and Robot Hand-Eye Coordination, and they show Marvin (Mobile Autonomous Robot with Vision-based Navigation) at http://www.rcs.ei.tum.de/research/marvin/index_html. For the general webpage, see http://www.rcs.ei.tum.de/research/index_html.

The Robot Vision Group, which is part of the Intelligent Systems Lab at the School of Engineering, University of Guelph, Ontario, Canada, explores "real-time dynamic visual processes (e.g., tracking, optical flow, binocular vision) . . . for various applications such as elderly or disabled aids, search and rescue robotics, intelligent automobiles . . . tracking animals (e.g., pigs), traffic surveillance and wearable computing for the disabled" (http://www.eos.uoguelph.ca/webfiles/robotvision).

A significant text, written by Professor Berthold Horn, called *Robot Vision*,[15] was developed as part of an MIT course on robot design. The ability to move about freely is dependent upon sensory inputs, spatial localization, mapping functions, and landmark identification. *Computational Principles of Mobile Robotics* by Gregory Dudek and Michael Jenkin exemplifies efforts in this direction.[16]

iRobot was founded in 1990 by Helen Greiner, Colin Angle, and Rodney Brooks. The firm's Roomba vacuum-robot with vision based on bump sensors has sold more than 2 million units as of May 2006. The firm's PackBots are used by the military to search for ammunition stores in Iraq and Afghanistan. These sales have led to a successful IPO in November 2005. (See http://knowledge.wharton.upenn.edu. Use the

Mobile robots

Robots with mobility are especially useful for safety and security. Service robots are being built smaller, smarter, more mobile, and less expensively. Mobile nurse and orderly robots are increasingly used in healthcare services.

searchword iRobot in the upper left-hand search window for Greiner interview dated June 2, 2006).

Past predictions about robot advances have fallen short of reality. However, it would be a mistake to overlook the true state of affairs, which is that steady advances are being made in improving machine capabilities. Robots can perceive objects in color and in three dimensions with speed and accuracy. With high performance vision, robots can achieve significant mobility and dexterity. This is transforming the fields of manufacturing, logistics, mining, space prospecting, and service operations.

Some robots are able to see objects in their path in 3D. That allows them to react intelligently to avoid obstacles, find targets, recognize patterns, and provide intelligent human services for the elderly and handicapped. Additionally, they can provide remote virtual reality displays of actual environments that are deadly for people. For example a robot can go inside volcanic craters, nuclear reactors, the depths of the ocean, airless space, and can defuse a bomb.

20-5b Operational Issues for Safety and Security

Security has become one of the most important P/OM service concerns. The P/OM responsibility for quality extends to the safety of travelers on planes, buses, and subways. Quality covers the well-being of people at the opera, theater, concert, visiting a theme park, or in the supermarket. Quality covers the well-being of people when they pick up their mail. Other forms of transportation, water and air quality systems, office buildings, and theme parks are undergoing similar alterations of operations to provide customer and citizen safety under potential terrorist attack conditions.

Prior to the World Trade Center attack, industrial security was considered to be a special calling that was not the concern of all managers. Today, security is a general management concern. It is also a field in which operations management should be involved. Entirely new approaches now have to confront the problems of industrial insecurity. Much more must be known before there is satisfaction that all systems are as secure as they can be made.

The American Society for Industrial Security (ASIS) would be likely to take exception to the idea that security has only recently emerged as an operational concern. It is the P/OM field that has not been aware of developments in security and not ASIS, which was founded in 1955. ASIS International has 35,000 members in 204 chapters worldwide.

ASIS is very active in training and education. Courses include assets protection, securing the global workplace, emerging trends in security, and in providing certification programs. The CPP (Certified Protection Professional) program has two types of certification, viz., PCI (professional certified investigator) and PSP (physical security professional). See http://www.asisonline.org.

New P/OM Developments to Enhance Safety and Security

How secure is the mail room? The health threat of anthrax (sent through the mail after September 11) closed major buildings in Washington, DC, and post office facilities. Scientists have determined that the anthrax powder had been made recently (within two years). Investigators said that the theory it had been stolen from an old batch in a lab could be dismissed. The threat that the perpetrator could do it again was evident from the dating. The forensics are good but not sufficient to have identified the culprit. Could Sherlock Holmes have done better without radiocarbon dating but having great inferential capabilities?

In companies, someone has to take responsibility for detecting dangerous packages in mail rooms. The United States Postal Service (USPS) states, "The mail center is a major gateway into any business or government agency." USPS provides a Mail Center Security Handbook and a quick reference guide for *Best Practices for Mail Center Security*. Security of packages shipped via FedEx, UPS, and DHL—from the point of view of the recipient rather than from the point of view of the shipper—is not evident. The neighbors of recipients might also be concerned.

An option to be encouraged is the use of smart robots designed specifically to help deal with threats of these kinds. Technological innovation, after September 11, 2001, is accelerating developments related to increased security. There are a number of promising areas for forensic technological systems. These include DNA identification, fingerprint data-mining, retinal identification, and face and body-shape identification. Pre-911 privacy protection has changed to allowing identification as a requirement for entrance to systems that are vulnerable to those who would do them harm. There will continue to be many debates concerning individual rights to privacy and secrecy as well as societal rights to protect citizens. Technology may make the issue moot by being able to identify those who are about to break the law. An article dated July, 2007 in *Government Technology*, is titled: "The Unblinking Eye: Behavior recognition technology adds intelligence to surveillance cameras." The company that has developed Perceptrak (the smart mind behind the unblinking eye) is Cernium, master of perception-based analytics.

P/OM always benefits from transparency. Secrecy in operations is not about to become a contentious issue. There is no benefit in hiding sources of pollution or machines that are unsafe. There are no advocates for protecting the source of contamination of a food production process. Terrorism thrives on obfuscation; transparency diminishes surprise.

One security focus that has dominated the press and the mind-set of people is the freedom from danger of airline passengers. Anxiety from fears of attack and sabotage are alleviated by concerted efforts to provide protection. Transportation Security Administration (TSA: http://www.tsa.gov) screening of all passengers is increasingly effective. Air marshals are placed on many planes. Mobile robots might someday take their place because they can outperform their human counterparts. Cockpit doors are built to prohibit forced entry. In addition, vision systems are being installed by some airlines. For example, Jet Blue Airlines has installed them in its planes so the pilot can watch the passengers.

In Times Square, there are over 200 surveillance cameras. New York City has over 1,000 video cameras and 3,000 motion sensors in place. In Washington, DC, when the police chief was asked how many cameras he can hook into, he replied, "It's . . . practically unlimited."[17] That is because of networking between the DC police department and traffic cameras of Virginia's DOT and Maryland's DOT. The networks are extendable. Surveillance cameras are ubiquitous in stores, ATM machines, and national monuments. In England, more than 2 million cameras were installed to counter IRA terrorism. Estimates range between 300 and 500 for the number of times a day that the average Londoner is recorded on film.

The utility of cameras is questionable until they become part of a data-mining system that can compare items to sort out potential dangers. For example, Tampa police used face recognition surveillance at Super Bowl XXXV (January 28, 2001). Cameras scanned faces in the audience and compared them with the facial phenotypes of people known to pose problems. There were no reports of any "hits."

Although this technology is rudimentary, taxonomies are developing along various lines. Johns Hopkins School of Medicine–CCDD lists eight craniofacial dimensions to observe. These are presented on the webpage of the Center for Craniofacial Development and Disorders. There is a great deal to be learned about what makes a face unique at http://www.hopkinsmedicine.org/craniofacial/Physician/GrowthChartsFaceMeasure.cfm.

TSA security steps taken before emplaning are constantly changing as innovative technology is provided by a growing new industry. This safety assurance service operation (run by the U.S. government) combines human and technology-based inspections with guidelines for continuous improvement. Who will be responsible for benchmarking this quality control system? Methods of operations management combined with research on technology and methodology that could improve security are required. For example, computer simulations of scenarios of security breaches could help determine the effectiveness of various strategies in lowering probabilities of foiling culprits.

Following the Columbine High School massacre (April 20, 1999), there has been dedicated interest and deep concern about preparations for problem management in schools. The Crisis Prevention Institute (CPI) provides training for administrators, teachers, and instructional aides in the "management of disruptive, assaultive, and out-of-control behavior in a school setting." This P/OM service area is gaining attention. CPI's webpage heading is "School-Community Partnerships: Building a safer, healthier and brighter future for our children" (http://kcsos.kern.org/schcom/stories/storyReader$70).

Since 9/11, corporate security officers (CSOs) have been appointed in many major companies. These corporate security officers are on the constant lookout for booby traps, loaded guns, and opportunities for mischief, malfeasance, and mayhem. At the same time, security in many locations, such as theme parks and theaters, is capable of providing cardiopulmonary resuscitation (CPR) and first aid while awaiting EMS (emergency medical services). EMS is an operations management service application that requires strong P/OM capabilities. EMS as operations is another window on P/OM opportunities.

Dogs have been used for drug-sniffing and more recently for bomb material sniffing. There are machines that are also capable of sniffing bomb materials. It is hoped that, eventually, mobile robots will have even greater effectiveness. There is also the development of very small robots related to basic microbiological nanotechnology. See the website http://www.nano.org.uk.

The Columbia shuttle accident that occurred in January 2003 is an event likely to promote the use of robots for space exploration. There has always been pressure to move more manned space exploration toward robotic sojourns. The drones that filled the sky over Afghanistan and then over Iraq are another example of robots replacing old methods of warfare. It is worrisome that drones are available to all sides in a conflict. Increasingly, aerial robots are being perfected to have incredible mobility and vision.

Robot-controlled cars are likely to have far fewer accidents. Radar back-up beeping increases in frequency the closer the vehicle comes to an object. Back-up cameras are safety steps along the way. Enormous auto accident rates will be reduced by technology since training does not seem to appeal to drivers. As will be discussed shortly, robots in the healthcare field also reduce accidents by preventing mismatches of many kinds.

Evidently, major changes are on the horizon as business computers gain sensory capabilities for seeing, hearing, feeling (temperatures and pressures) and even smelling. Most significantly, computers with mobility will have profound effects on society. People and machines will move and communicate without wires over large distances using nonmobile databases that are securely protected. Computers lifting, pushing, and grasping can work as robots on the line 24/7 without outsourcing problems while achieving setup and changeover events in nanoseconds. Once appropriately engineered and programmed, robots will repeal the laws governing economies of scope (changeover costs and times).

20-5c Crisis Management of Operations: Contingency Planning

Ensuring safety and security have become a normal part of everyday life. However, when an event occurs that is an act of nature (like a powerful earthquake or hurricane), a crisis occurs. Contingency planning for such situations is essential. However, often there are surprises about the size or strength and the location of the epicenter, as well as the path of the storm. If all possible scenarios could have been anticipated, preparations for dealing with each of them might have been available. Crisis management is most effective when the assumption of worst cases is made. The biggest storms are a good beginning (Sebastian Junger. *The Perfect Storm*. St. Helens, Oregon: Perennial Press, 1999). Hurricane Katrina's severity surprised New Orleans (8/29/05).

Crisis events can result from a failure of technology. All phones are down because a cable has been cut. This happened in New York City in the 1900s. What happens if the IT system is down because a giant power failure has occurred? The company that has done contingency planning knows what to do in such a situation. The response to great stress is likely to be expensive, but the costs of losses due to crises are far greater.

Crises of the two types described here are manageable because they are imaginable. To some extent, the scenarios of what will happen when nature erupts and technology fails can be defined. The steps for dealing with them can be logical. What must be understood is that terrorist attacks are not illogical, but they are diabolical. Movie scriptwriters know how to dream up the diabolical. Original credits for the World Trade Center destruction do not go to the terrorists who copied the story from Hollywood movie scripts.

When one seeks protection from home burglars, the best advice can be obtained from a home burglar turned consultant. When the nation seeks protection from terror, it is probably best to go to the source of most of the deadly ideas. Hollywood scriptwriters and the community of science fiction authors qualify.

The issue of importance, according to *Contingency Planning & Management* magazine (January–February 2003), is business continuity planning (BCP). How much downtime can a business survive? How much backup, replication, and redundancy can the firm afford? Disaster recovery is another way of stating the problem (see http://www .disasterrecoveryworld.com and http://www.contingencyplanning.com).

The ultimate question is how do we create successful contingency plans and operational contingency planning teams? Toyota management figured that out 43 years ago.[18] They set up teams called *quality circles*. These teams were assigned the task of naming and describing in as much detail as possible everything that the team members could think of that could go wrong on the production line. Any one person can think of a few things—but teams can write novels about how many things can go wrong. Team members recall situations that went awry and they serve as talking points for conjuring up unthought-of situations.

Things that "could go wrong" are contingencies. *American Heritage* dictionary defines "contingency" as "(a) An event that may occur but that is not likely or intended; a possibility; and (b) A possibility that must be prepared for; a future emergency."

Having specified what can go wrong, the next step in contingency planning is to prepare for these situations. Preparing for these conditions requires remembering that the errors and faults leading to crises are possible, but unlikely to occur. Further, there is a domino effect where many things have to go wrong so as to cancel preventions and safeguards. Also, there will be many possible scenarios since imagination has no bounds concerning what can go wrong. Therefore, great diligence is required to anticipate all contingencies in order to be prepared for every eventuality.

Yet, contingencies are possibilities that must be prepared for—to some degree—because if and when they occur, the penalties are large. On balance, to be prepared, methodology must be used to deal with the crisis in combination with generic technology. For example, a fire extinguisher is a generic contingency tool because it can be used for many situations in which a fire that must be extinguished occurs. Generic counter-contingency technology needs to be enumerated, inventoried, and monitored for performance worthiness over time.

Teams are assigned to each and every contingency situation. Members are asked to refine plans continually aimed at preventing the disastrous consequences of each scenario—to circumvent its occurring, to diffuse the impact of the condition, to remove the problem, to remedy its costs, to alleviate its penalties, and to avoid the punishments.

Team solutions are compared and the best ones are reexamined by all members at every level in the company. The best ones are chosen, but never fixed in stone. Regular reviews are conducted to check that best procedures remain "the best." New ideas and new materials may surface to improve methodologies. Technological developments can appear that will be used to alter the practice drills. Unexpected problems may arise that suggest new scenarios for contingency planning. Contingency planning situations must be treated as fluid and dynamic.

As important as the fire extinguisher is the fire alarm. Critical to contingency planning is the communication that a problem exists. That communication must include information about the nature of the problem and what plan will be followed to deal with the problem.

For example, on an auto production line, Toyota has a board mounted in a location where everyone can see it. Colored lights on that board signal when something is wrong. Color connotes where the problem exists, its type and severity. That board is called the "Andon" (problem display board). Because of much practice with existing contingency plans, when the "Andon" lights up each member on line knows what interventions are called for by proximity and training. See http://www.isixsigma.com/dictionary/Andon-585.htm (dated January 2004).

ISO 17799 for Operational Security

The International Organization for Standardization is a thriving community of academics, politicians, and practitioners. See their front page on the web: http://www.iso.org/iso/home.htm.

Useful information about ISO 17799 is found on the web at http://www.computersecuritynow.com. This company provides software and an ISO 17799 Toolkit. There is an informative slideshow available under General ISO 17799 Information. Click on *presentation*. An explanation about ISO 17799 (summarized here) is explained in more detail on that webpage.

There are ten points:

1   Business continuity planning
2   System access control
3   System development and maintenance
4   Physical and environmental security
5   Compliance
6   Personnel security
7   Security organization
8   Computer and operations management
9   Asset classification and control
10 Security policy

The ethics of information systems are sorely tested by the absurd belief that computers are fair game for one who can outsmart them. In fact, destruction and damage of information systems brings the most costly harm to people who can ill afford disruptions of their paychecks. Reciprocity of trust should be taught in much the same way that the Hippocratic Oath is required for medical doctors.

There have been many discussions about protecting privacy on computers that are connected to the Internet. Intrusion detection of web perversions includes (1) stealing intellectual property, (2) e-shop lifting (by altering information), (3) hijacking information (taking over a website), and (4) defacing and disabling a website. Companies are turning to vulnerability assessments. As in quality of manufactured goods and providing services, fixing a mistake costs much more than preventing it from happening.

For all IT applications, ISO user guides have been prepared. They are also used as training materials. These guides can be found at the URL at http://www.iso.org/iso/standards_development/it_tools.htm. Most key IT applications have been developed and are maintained by project teams operating under ISO's Information Technology Strategies Implementation Group (ITSIG), which consists of individuals who have been appointed by ISO member bodies.

The conflict between secure and private Internet connections and open platforms will be a challenge for operations managers and their information systems support teams over the next decade. Probable solutions will derive from the ability of technology to keep private that which is entrusted while sharing that which is of mutual benefit. This is a major IT initiative that will be ongoing for the foreseeable future.

20-5d Service Robots: Growing Utilization

Industrial and manufacturing robots are a multibillion-dollar industry worldwide, whereas the service robot industry is at an earlier stage of development. There are few commercially viable service robots on the market today. Those that do exist provide real services and should not be confused with consumer "toys, pets, and gadgetry."

Entertainment robots sell more for their "wow" factor than for their ability to perform useful tasks. For example, the entertainment robot that Sony named AIBO was discontinued in March 2006.

The book *Service Robots*[19] by Gernot Schmierer and Rolf Dieter Schraft explores specific robots that provide service functions, including refueling, cleaning, surveillance, firefighting, sorting, cooking, marketing, nursing care, and space exploration. Note the previous section where robots were used for paint removal and cleaning by water-jetting. Also, no list is complete that does not include a robotic system that provides information about flight arrivals and departures for all the major airlines—as though the caller is speaking with a charming operator.

Other robotic issues are related to cyborgs and autonomous robots. Cyborgs are combinations of human beings and robots that result from implants such as pacemakers and hearing aids. A text that explores the autonomous (self-willed robots that improve their own design) is *Robo Sapiens: Evolution of New Species*.[20] This book has been praised for its excellent photographs. It has great reviewers' quotes from Sir Arthur C. Clarke, author of *2001: A Space Odyssey* ("mind-stretching, frightening"), and Ray Kurzweil, author of *The Age of Spiritual Machines: When Computers Exceed Human Intelligence* ("inevitable merger of human and machine").

The actual state of affairs is that despite a great deal of interest, both academic and practical, there are only a few significant service robots that are commercially available. Joseph Engelberger, the "father of robots" and a pioneer in both industrial and service robots in the United States, continues to believe that the tipping point is coming soon. See http://en.wikipedia.org/wiki/Joseph_F._Engelberger. The Joseph F. Engelberger Robotics Award Fact Sheet is available on the website of the Robotic Industries Association (RIA) (http://www.robotics.org). Awards are listed through 2006. Enter "awards" in the search window. Over 100 awards have been given through 2006. Engelberger was instrumental in developing HelpMate robots for elder care.[21]

The majority of the awards are given for factory automation. However, vision and mobility capabilities are being further developed and, eventually, they can translate into service provider capabilities. In 2005, North American manufacturing firms ordered 18,228 robot units valued at $1.16 billion in revenue from North American suppliers. This is a 23 percent increase over 2004. From Roboticsonline.com, "Robot Sales Jump 39% in North America in First Half of 2007." RIA estimates that more than 171,000 robots are working in the United States, second only to Japan. There are over one million industrial robots working worldwide.

Pyxis HelpMate® SP (previously mentioned in the Engelberger discussion) is a mobile service courier robot from Cardinal Health. It moves around healthcare facilities without tracks or guidewires, delivering medications, meals, lab specimens, and more, wherever needed. Pyxis HelpMate SP is shown in Figure 20-1.

People working in hospitals are more comfortable when they give names to their robots. That is why in Durham, North Carolina, Pyxis HelpMate SP is called TOBOR. The 400-pound robot has a safe in its midsection for medicines and bags of intravenous fluids labeled with the name and bar code of the intended patients.

Pyxis HelpMate SP works around the clock, costing the hospital less than $5 an hour to lease. "Whenever a new patient is admitted to the Veterans Affairs Medical Center, . . . a 4-foot 8-inch talking robot rolls up to the nurses' station nearest to the patient's room, bringing doses of whatever drugs the doctor ordered. TOBOR, the robot, is a delivery 'droid' that glides along the corridors day and night ferrying medicines from the hospital's central pharmacy to its wards."[22]

Pyxis HelpMate SP's computer brain plots its routes to over 30 possible destinations within the Veterans Affairs Medical Center. Pyxis HelpMate SP employs sonar and infrared sensors, and communicates via RF Ethernet. It avoids people and obstacles and proclaims to patients and visitors in the elevator or corridor, "I am about to move; please stand clear."

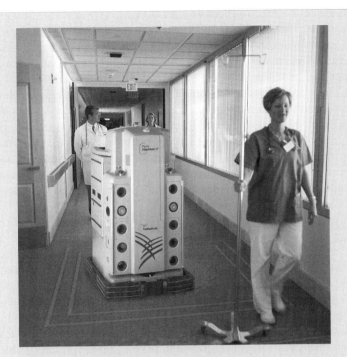

Figure 20-1

Pyxis HelpMate® SP Is Stepping Ahead of the Doctors in a Hospital Corridor

Photo is courtesy of Cardinal Health, Inc.

Cardinal Health has placed hundreds of its Pyxis HelpMate SP robots in more than 100 U.S. hospitals. Pyxis HelpMate SP provides hospitals with an economical way to better service the nursing units, allowing nurses more time for patient care. Pyxis HelpMate SP is reliable (with no history of absenteeism), and it is as content with night shifts as day shifts. Also, Pyxis HelpMate SP is bilingual in English and Spanish. Pyxis HelpMate SP is assisted by other computer (information monitoring) systems, such as Pyxis Homerus (nonmobile drug dispensing system) and Pyxis Veri5 (handheld bar scanner) to bring a level of quality controlled safety to the nurse-patient healthcare interaction that typifies advances from new technologies.[23]

Pyxis HelpMate SP can be compared to its cousins in the industrial robot sector, which are trackless industrial AGVSs (automated guided vehicle systems). Both require extensive navigational abilities. Using walls and ceilings as guides, they access internal maps that confine them to preprogrammed routes. Total attention to details is required for success in both applications.

Glimpsing the future, production people will be accustomed to working with mobile service robots (MSRs) that can navigate corridors and carry materials between stations. Mobile service robots will alter service industries, providing rapid setups, maintenance, deliveries, repair, and cleaning services. MSRs have a role to play in both developed economies and underdeveloped economies. There are economic and cultural issues about jobs in the service sector that portend shortages in service functions all over the world.

Mobile service robots with vision and speech can transform the service sector much as industrial robots with flexibility in changeovers and multiple setups have revolutionized manufacturing. Note that robots are particularly well-suited when second- and third-shift staffing is a problem. They are almost error-free, whereas human caretakers are prone to error. MSRs can change the cost structure and delivered quality of services industries.

Employee contact with customers and clients is the service interface. Young customers' expectations may not be similar to those of their elders. Seniors show signs of shifting their values. Most customers have adapted to using ATMs (automated teller machines), which are non-mobile robots. Preferences are changing. People are choosing to buy their airline tickets on the web. By 2008, most airlines have discontinued paper tickets. People prefer to use kiosks to check in at the airport to avoid waiting on line for a person. See Spotlight 13-1: Changing the Way We Pay.

Other examples of the swing to using computers and robots rather than clerks—given the choice—are self-service check-out, e.g., Albertsons, Home Depot, Sam's Club—online banking, grocery shopping and game-playing, distance learning, and blogging, The next generation of far more service-oriented robots will be viewed by the post-Y generation as being very "cool." New levels of creativity are due with artificial intelligence (AI),[24] robot mobility, voice recognition, and memory sorting that knows what everyone likes before they request it. The result is a plausible revolution for service delivery systems.

20-5e Virtual Offices: The Trend Is Ever-Greater Tactical Use

Offices become virtual when no space is dedicated to specific individuals. They are like mobile offices and have an equivalency to mobile robots. The trend to what have been called *nonterritorial offices* has been going on for a long time. Many companies have developed a great deal of experience with work at a distance, called telework. Perhaps a better term is *tele-computing-commuting*. The crucial ingredient is the substitution of communication and computer work from a virtual office instead of a centralized office. The virtual office can be at one's home, or in a car, hotel, restaurant, or a distant office from the home office.

Before new technology made it easy to do, many companies tried decentralized branch offices that would reduce the amount of commutation required by employees. Communication technology has connected the globe, while transportation technology struggles with traffic and delays. For the most part, someone else pays the rent for virtual offices. Even the telephone part of telework is no longer constraining as wireless access to the Internet becomes the prevalent system of communication.

This raises an important distinction. Tactical telework is an informal arrangement or a non-policy alternative work arrangement. Strategic telework is a formal component of a firm's business strategy. Most organizations use tactical telework when their people are traveling, or working from home. The strategic approach is a formal commitment to non-assigned office space, roaming desks, and the assumption that the office is where the manager's BlackBerry or laptop is found. Table 20-3, a communication–commuting table, depicts a number of relationships as centralized, traditional offices move up and to the right along the diagonal of the matrix.

The left-hand column of the matrix reflects the present-day "informal and tactical" use of wired and wireless communication systems. The main effort takes place in the office, which is the lowest left-hand box. Still, some work is done outside of the office— by phone (usually cell phone, handheld PDA, or laptop wireless computer). Occasionally teleworking is done from hotels or home. These occasional tactics are shown in the center and upper boxes of the left-hand column.

The middle-row box of the middle column in the matrix reflects a combination of work patterns. There is a mixture of both "informal" and "formal" telecommuting. There is a partial commitment to virtual office communications. The "informal" is occasional use as needed. This system lacks the efficiency of "formal" commitments.

The upper right-hand box in the right-hand column of the matrix reflects a "formal" commitment to the virtual office. This is where planned telecommuting occurs. The system is operative 24/7 and a knowledge-based corporate memory must support the system. In addition, this can link suppliers' data with home-based information systems.

Most activities occur along the reverse diagonal (bolded italicized words) of the matrix. In the upper-right box is the work configuration that approaches the status of an office-less company. The knowledge base of that company is embodied in its systems of

	Traditional Files and Folders in a Nonintegrated Tactical System	Evolving to a Unified Computerized Information System	Knowledge-Based Corporate Memory Accessible Anytime from Anywhere	Table 20-3 Tele-Computing–Commuting Table
Virtual office	Sales force may be on the road	Conscious effort to use some virtual office workers in a learning mode	*Virtual office strategy removes need to commute and provides 24/7 availability*	
Decentralized offices	An option for traffic-delayed commuting employees	*Combination of telecommuting and in-office systems*	Some need remains for decentralized offices	
Centralized office	*Tactical, traditional office system*	Determination to improve the information systems in support of transition	No need for the centralized office remains	

computers, which may be located in scattered locations for security purposes and to provide backup when needed. (See Oticon Holding S/A in Section 19-7c.) The middle of the diagonal represents mixed-mode offices, which are probably the most numerous type at this time. Mixed-mode offices have some traditional (informal) telework, while other parts of the organization are strategically virtual. Still, many organizations are in the lower-left box, which is the tactical, traditional office system. However, as Internet utility becomes more apparent, and increasingly powerful, there is progress moving up and to the right along the diagonal.

Varieties of virtual offices include

1 *Working at home.* This transfers the cost of space from company to worker. It is being used to decrease commuting by car. Sun Microsystems, IBM, and other organizations have experimented with this plan in California, where increasingly tough regulations are expected to be passed requiring companies to limit the number of employees permitted to travel to a particular work site (to reduce environmental pollution). Note the Valley Metro, Maricopa telecommuting report at http://www.valleymetro.org/Rideshare/Telework/Resources/index.htm. Click on Cases in the left hand navigation pane and then on IBM (for example). "Working at home moms" (WAHM) are independent operators and entrepreneurs as contrasted with large companies using telework methods as cost savers (see http://www.wahm.com).

2 *Working from cars, hotels, and customers' offices.* These are all mobile offices staffed by mobile workers. Pressure for office mobility is associated with jobs that require extensive travel. Salespeople, accountants, auditors, consultants, and service team members are logical candidates for mobile-office assignments. The effect is to increase the amount of time that these professionals spend with their customers, which both parties usually find rewarding.

3 *Working in nonassigned spaces at the company site.* Called *hoteling.* There are companies all over the world that provide rented space for this purpose. Some use "doubling up," which means that a number of people are assigned to the same space. That method was used by Oticon S/A (in Denmark), American Express,

3 COM, Catalyst 400, and others. Companies have reported increasing the employee-to-desk ratio in a range of from 2-to-1 to 5-to-1. There is also *hot desking*, which allows many employees to share the same desk, computer, or phone. Technology is aligned to recognize the PIN numbers of each employee and to furnish the right database. See http://servicedoffices.mwbex.com/about-our-offices/hot-desks.html.

4 *Renting virtual offices* from companies such as Regus, with 950 office locations in 400 cities in 70 countries (http://www.regus.com), makes hoteling a simple fact of life around the world. Officescape, with 500 office suites and 150 conference facilities, is another example; see http://www.officescape.com/services.asp. For an all U.K. virtual office, there is e-office at http://www.eoffice.net.

The advantages of virtual offices are increased operational efficiency, agility to adapt to change, flexibility to increase or decrease space on a seasonal basis, and to grow with the business. Upsizing and downsizing are readily accomplished.

At a point in time, the advertising agency TBWA/Chiat/Day reengineered its offices using combinations of the four points shown here, proclaiming satisfaction with the results. Later, the firm changed its mind. IBM's seven regional U.S. markets converted to virtual office configurations. Private offices were replaced by "small team rooms" for use by the mobile executives.[25] Companies that have used virtual offices note that management changes are required to make this major shift in working modes effective and productive. Some companies have slowed the pace of virtualizing, and telecommunication is not always lauded. When virtualizing is used properly, it is reported that "the amount of office space needed for certain types of employees—those who travel a good deal—has declined to 48 square feet a person from 200 square feet."[26]

Technology makes the virtual office possible. Economics makes it desirable in many cases. Knowing when to use it is part of the challenge for P/OM. Change management methods of P/OM are needed to adopt technologies that make the virtual office work. There is also a need to get people to accept the new modus operandi and to have them use the new systems with comfort—and that translates into "effectively."

20-6 Environmental Quality: ISO 14000/14001 (and More)

ISO 14000/14001 series

ISO 9000 series is acknowledged worldwide as the accepted set of standards for quality management. ISO 14000/14001 sets similar standards for environmental management. The ISO 17799 Toolkit addresses operational security.

Global environmental (and ethical) benchmarks will change the way that business is done worldwide. ISO launched Series 14000 for environmental management in 1996. These standards have grown to encompass **ISO 14000 / 14001 / 14004 / 14010 / 14011 / 14012 / 14030 / 14031** and more. In Chapter 4, the great success of the ISO 9000 series was discussed. With that certification in place, the International Organization for Standardization in Geneva aimed for environmental management guidelines."[27] These ISO 14000/14001 (and more) guidelines are now fully developed, highly accepted, and being used broadly. See the manuals and training software of AQA Press at http://www.aqapress.com (updated June 2005).

"Many organizations have undertaken environmental reviews or audits to assess their environmental performance. On their own, however, these reviews and audits will seldom be sufficient to provide an organization with the assurance that its performance not only meets, but will continue to meet, its policy requirements. To be effective, they need to be conducted within a structured management system, integrated with overall management activity and addressing significant environmental impacts."[28]

The ISO 14000 series is designed to set standards for conformity assessment leading to certification. It is designed to provide organizational structure and management discipline for achieving excellence in environmental performance. ISO 9000 does not deal with specific product qualities. ISO 14000 does not deal with specific environmental qualities, such as emission levels. Like ISO 9000 standards, ISO 14000 standards are coordinated by the American National Standards Institute (ANSI) in cooperation with the American Society for Quality Control (ASQC).

ISO 14001 is the accepted specification for the EMS (environmental management system). It starts with a generic environmental policy with flexible management systems to plan the environmental program. Management provides for operations and implementation (e.g., training, means of communication, documentation, and emergency preparedness). ISO 14004 elaborates with guidance for ISO 14001 requirements. ISO 14020 provides labels to be used. ISO 14030 details environmental assessment methods. ISO 14031 gives the basis for Evaluation of Environmental Performance. ISO 19011 replaces ISO 14011 with a single audit protocol, which can be used for both the 9000 and the 14000 series. ISO 14010, 14011, and 14012 are audit guidelines, audit procedures, and information.

ISO 14000 is a good way to wind down this chapter because it embodies care for the environment and highlights ethics in an organizational and management context. The idea of a uniform codification for environmental protection prevents the operational nightmare of trying to satisfy the environmental requirements of many different countries. Standardization is a blessing.

Reengineering and continuous improvement can have substantial environmental impacts. Every TQM and JIT program can affect the environment. Companies having earned ISO 14000/14001 certification will not be forced to select which country's standards it will follow in process improvement. ISO 14000 has done away with wasteful conflicts of standards between countries. ISO 14000 has been accepted as a unified global standard and certification procedure. Like ISO 9000, ISO 14000 has been adopted by all countries.

20-7 Vision of a Fully Integrated Global Company

Readying operations management for future conditions requires understanding new demands of society and new developments in technology. Implementing world-class performance in a dynamically evolving system requires the systems point of view, which brings all-important elements to the table.

Comprehensive vision must be supported by a totally interconnected informing system (communicating information system). A picture of what this infrastructure might look like is shown in Figure 20-2. It is named the SME Manufacturing Enterprise Wheel. A similar wheel of six concentric circles can be drawn for service industries. Differences between the integrating wheel for manufacturing and customer services should be thought out in detail. Creating the service enterprise wheel is a worthwhile project.

(1) Start with the customer, who could be located anywhere in the world. (2) Move out to the next ring, where people are organized for teamwork. (3) Next ring, the organization is designed to share knowledge by using the systems approach. (4) Next ring, employs the systems approach to tie together customer support, product/process factors, and manufacturing (or customer services). (5) The next ring connects resources (information, people, materials, etc.) and responsibilities to employees, investors, and community with criteria for ethical behavior and environmental protection. The wheel is surrounded by (6) which is labeled the manufacturing (or service) infrastructure.

In the summer of 1993, CASA/SME (the Computer and Automated Systems Association of the Society of Manufacturing Engineers) announced this new version of the enterprise wheel. The old wheel (1985) was called the CIM Enterprise Wheel. CIM stood for *computer-integrated manufacturing*. The center of that wheel focused on information systems architecture and databases. The SME wheel was linked to 2006 CASA/SME home and membership.

World-class manufacturers organize, integrate, and invest their resources to achieve new levels of customer satisfaction. The new manufacturing enterprise wheel is a

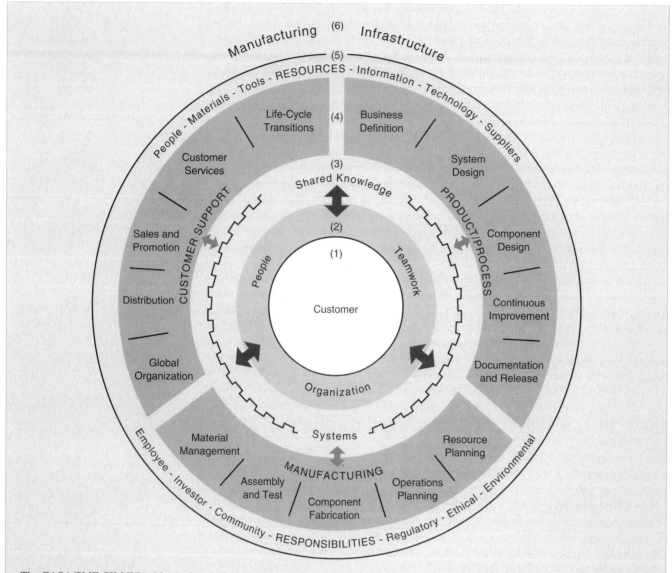

The CASA/SME CIM Wheel is reprinted with permission of the Computer and Automated Systems Association of the Society of Manufacturing Engineers, Copyright 1993.

Figure 20-2

SME Manufacturing
Enterprise Wheel

recognition of the significant progress to date, and the progress yet to be made, in manufacturing. It serves as an overview of today's Best Practice in total enterprise integration.

This new wheel centers on the customer. It considers "the virtual enterprise," which is the inclusive system of all of the people who are teamed together to achieve company objectives. The new wheel stresses "the need to integrate an understanding of the external environment, including customers, competitors, suppliers, and the global manufacturing infrastructure."[29] The **SME enterprise wheel** provides a vision of a fully integrated global company system. More than 12 years have elapsed since the new SME enterprise wheel was launched. It is more relevant than ever.

SME enterprise wheel
Graphic provides a "vision" of a fully integrated global company; links resources and responsibilities.

Spotlight 20-1 Ethics by Regulation

Enron and the Sarbanes–Oxley Act

Mark Twain once said, "Always do right. This will gratify some and astonish the rest." If he were here to comment on the technology and telecommunications boom of the 1990s, Twain would have been the first to point out the delusional expectations that governed behavior of top executives and investors in corporate America. It was irrational to believe that stock prices could rise indefinitely, along with profits, salaries, and ROI. Goldman Sachs, swept up by euphoria, took Internet grocer Webvan public, investing over $100 million of its own money in Webvan before it failed.

The delusional expectations of that era were based on the commonly held conviction that a sea change in economic fundamentals had occurred. Enron Corporation's attempt to hide mounting losses by placing its stock in secret partnerships would have been illogical if the company feared that its stock value would drop significantly.

Created through the merger of two midsize natural-gas pipeline companies in the late 1980s, Enron reinvented itself as an energy-trading giant in the 1990s. At one point in 2000, its value approached $100 billion, with its natural-gas pipeline business representing less than 10 percent of the company's imputed worth. Unfortunately for employees and shareholders, Enron's other businesses (power plants, risk management, trading commodities, etc.) ate up cash at an astounding rate with no prospect of turning a profit.

The difficulty of separating the delusional from the dishonest has given prosecutors a hard time in even the most obvious cases of fraud. It provides a challenge for ethicists and social historians to explain what actually happened when the bubble burst in March 2000.

Information is one of the most vital, strategic assets any organization possesses. When record-keeping practices of U.S. corporations, professional service firms, or other business entities come under suspicion, trust in the corporate system is damaged. Examples of corporate unethical behavior include shredding documents to obstruct justice by Enron, falsification of financial statements by WorldCom, and the criminal trial of Arthur Andersen for destruction of audit records. The Andersen trial led to the sudden and dramatic demise of one of America's best-known professional service firms. It shows the significance of record-keeping issues and the necessity for systematic compliance with record retention policies and procedures.

In November 2001, the SEC issued a subpoena to Arthur Andersen, requesting records related to public accounting work it performed for Enron. In January 2002, Andersen officials disclosed that the company had destroyed a number of records related to Enron audits. The officials said that the records were destroyed before receiving the subpoena.

If shown to be true, this was in conformity with company policy, which permitted the destruction of nonessential records relating to specific audits, without criminal intent.

Federal prosecutors alleged that Andersen destroyed the audit records after the SEC investigation had begun and that Andersen officials were fully aware that they would be asked to produce records. It is illegal to destroy records relevant to pending or ongoing litigation. Many leading clients of Arthur Andersen withdrew their business from that firm after criminal charges were disclosed. Arthur Andersen drastically reduced its workforce and sold several of its operations to competitors before going out of business. Even though the U.S. Supreme Court eventually overturned the conviction due to flaws in jury instructions, Arthur Andersen LLP, once a synonym for accounting honesty under the leadership of its founder, has little chance of making a comeback.

Strong reaction from public officials, legislators, regulatory authorities, shareholders, and law enforcement agencies (because of the Andersen case and other high-profile incidents) led to the Sarbanes–Oxley (SOX) Act of 2002. It is widely viewed as the most important corporate reform legislation since the Securities and Exchange Act of 1934. Signed into law on July 20, 2002, SOX specifies requirements and penalties that address corporate accountability issues raised by the Andersen case, WorldCom, Tyco, etc. The SOX Act applies to all U.S. public companies and public accounting firms, including those that perform audit work for foreign subsidiaries of U.S. companies. All public company CEOs and CFOs must personally certify that periodic financial disclosures accurately reflect the company's financial condition and fully comply with applicable securities laws.

The SOX Act criminalizes destroying or tampering with corporate accounting records. It created a new federal crime: the destruction, mutilation, or alteration of corporate records with the intent to impede or influence a government investigation or other official proceeding, including the simple contemplation of such an event. Violations by executives and employees are punishable by fines of up to $5 million and up to 20 years in prison.

Noncompliance with specified minimum retention periods for accountants' work papers, correspondence, and other records that contain analyses, opinions, conclusions, financial data, or other information about corporate audits can result in large fines and prison sentences of up to 10 years. The act creates a Public Company Accounting Oversight Board (PCAOB) with broad authority to subpoena records produced by public accounting firms and their clients. See http://www.pcaobus.org.

Spotlight 20-1 (Continued)

In the wake of the Sarbanes–Oxley Act, there was a tidal wave of complaints. In 2005, after two years of SOX compliance, 33 percent of respondents to a Financial Executive International (FEI) survey agreed that compliance has helped prevent or detect fraud, although 85 percent of all respondents believed the costs of SOX still outweigh the benefits. Large companies were paying an average compliance cost of 3.5 million and spending an average of 23,000 staff hours internally to comply. Following an all-day roundtable discussion organized by the SEC and the PCAOB in May 2006, federal regulators said they would consider modifying rules and auditing standards relating to the Sarbanes–Oxley Act. In November of 2006, Alan Greenspan, former chairman of the U.S. Federal Reserve, referred to Section 404 of the Sarbanes–Oxley Act as a "nightmare and extremely costly." As time goes on, there are no signs of modification.

As for Enron, complex litigation from class actions and appeals finally reached the U.S. Supreme Court in 2007, all stemming from the disastrous fall of a fraudulent giant. The company no longer exists except as a shell to process claims, but the name of Enron lives on. T-shirts are being sold on the Internet showing Enron's logo with the caption: "Endless Opportunities."

The Securities and Exchange Commission requires companies to disclose whether they have a code of ethics for their CEO, CFO, and senior accounting personnel. It may never be known whether ethics by regulation can produce better company policies, but it is clear that honest business practices are instrumental in building long-term trust in our corporate systems.

Review Questions

1 Why did Enron Corporation, formerly a Fortune 500 company, hide its mounting losses during the end of the technology and telecommunications boom of the 1990s?

2 What is the Sarbanes–Oxley Act (called the SOX Act) of 2002?

3 Do you think that the SOX Act will accomplish its intent to reform public company policies?

4 What are some company benefits that might result from the high cost of assiduously adhering to the SOX Act?

5 What happened to Enron after bankruptcy?

Sources: Jonathan A. Knee. *New York Times Book Review* (October 26, 2003); Bethany McLean and Peter Elkind. *The Smartest Guys in the Room: The Amazing Rise and Scandalous Fall of Enron.* New York: Portfolio, 2003; http://www.sec.gov/news/press/2003-89a.htm; http://www.arma.org; Ann Bednarz, *Sarbanes–Oxley: Too Much for Too Little?* Network World, May 15, 2006 or use link http://www.networkworld.com/news/2006/051506-sox.html; http://www.en.wikipedia.org/wiki/enron; http://www.arma.org.

Spotlight 20-2 Crisis Management: Securing the Right Decision
Humpty Dumpty Might Still Be in One Piece

Considering his fragile state, if Humpty Dumpty had thought through his decision to sit on the wall, he might still be in one piece. The same goes for top executives who fail to consider both the unintended as well as intended consequences of a decision. The first wrong move will topple the others, says crisis management advisor Robin Cohn. That's why she calls these actions "domino decisions."

No matter the industry or problem, a domino decision can impact security. The resulting anger of those negatively affected, including employees, protest groups, and victims, will cause them to act out in some way, Robin explains. Theft, damaging media leaks, and sabotage are all possible by-products.

Unfortunately, many executives don't understand that all decisions have ramifications, notes Robin, author of the *PR*

Crisis Bible and president of Robin Cohn and Company. She's seen the consequences. With more than 20 years of advising top executives, she has managed such crises as a plane crash, hijackings, government investigations, product boycotts, and corporate scandals.

A domino decision can bring down companies and top executives, Robin warns. Too often, executives look for short-term results without thinking of their impact down the road. For example, what if the auditing firm Arthur Andersen had resigned the Enron account when its internal auditors warned of Enron's illegal accounting practices? Yes, the company would have lost a top client, but it would still be in business.

What if Firestone had recalled its tires when it first saw growing claims of tire separation in 1992? A recall would have been expensive. However, in 2000, a National Highway Traffic Safety Administration investigation and a massive public uproar led to a recall of 6.5 million tires. Firestone's once sterling brand name was irrevocably damaged.

Another pitfall in decision making is not looking at the big picture, Robin explains. For example, a domino decision brought down Don Carty, American Airline's former chairman and CEO. To avoid bankruptcy, American Airlines asked three unions to make painful and costly concessions. At the same time, the company approved retention bonuses and pension payments for top executives. The unions were outraged when they learned of the executive perks and threatened to vote against concessions. The controversy forced the airline to drop its plans to compensate top executives, and Mr. Carty was fired. The unions later approved the concessions. "This crisis could have been avoided if decision makers had seriously considered the ramifications of granting bonus packages while asking their own employees to make sacrifices," Robin says.

Such is the problem of executive entitlement. Robin warns top executives about acting upon the belief that "some are more equal than others." In addition, many make the false assumption that actions can be kept quiet or won't be noticed. This ivory tower mind-set often skews decisions to benefit top management at the company's expense. Take Enron. The company began facing losses. The top executives realized that telling the truth would be bad for the stock and their own enrichment. Private partnerships were created to get the debt off the balance sheet. Six years later, the domino decision to hide losses wound up costing billions of dollars, with executive jail terms, and nonrecoverable failure for both Arthur Andersen and Enron.

"While top executives might have control in the executive suite, they don't in the outside world," Robin concludes.

Damaging domino decisions don't only occur in the corporate suite. Robin points to the case of the Augusta National Golf Club, when it refused women membership in 2002. This domino decision had ramifications that went beyond a golf club's membership rules to ultimately hurt Augusta's economy. The club hosts the prestigious Masters Tournament. Due to the decision, many corporate leaders stayed away, not wanting to be perceived as supporting the club's policy. Sponsors canceled, protesters were outside the gates, and overall attendance fell. Hotels, restaurants, and other services were left feeling the pinch during what should have been the biggest money-making event of the year.

Not all domino decisions are bad. In some cases, a good decision can contain a crisis and win praise, Robin points out. Facing the 1982 scare over Tylenol capsules laced with cyanide, Johnson & Johnson CEO James Burke made the decision to own up to the problem and fix it. That domino decision to act responsibly wound up enhancing both the company's and Mr. Burke's reputation. "Ultimately, the right ethical decision is also the right business decision," Robin emphasizes.

Whether it is product tampering, angry unions, protesters, a company going out of business, or accidents, a company needs to have security plans in place for internal and external consequences.

The pressures of a crisis situation can often affect judgment. Yet, that's the time when clear thinking is essential. To avoid a damaging domino decision, Robin recommends the following:

- Think things through. What are you trying to accomplish? Who will be affected? How will this decision be perceived? Do you have all the information? What are the alternatives? What could go wrong?
- Examine what could really happen versus what you would like to have happen.
- Consider which way the public-opinion wind is blowing.
- Get feedback: Encourage others to play devil's advocates.

Review Questions

1 Who was Humpty Dumpty, and what does he/she/it have to do with the subject of "securing the right decision"?

2 Robin Cohn (a leading crisis expert) says that top executives who fail to consider the unintended (as well as intended) consequences of a critical decision put themselves and their companies at great risk. What is the nature of this risk?

3 If something goes wrong (e.g., product tampering), the effort to avert a crisis can lead to the domino effect. What is this effect?

4 Why is it that "looking at the big picture" is essential if management is to avoid severe damage from an inadvertent crisis?

Sources: Robin Cohn, author of *The PR Crisis Bible*, is a nationally recognized crisis management advisor who works with executive decision makers to avoid or contain any problem that affects a company's reputation and bottom line. Conversation and correspondence, March 2005 and April 2007. Robin Cohn and Company, 20 W. 64th Street, #11-U, New York, NY 10023 212-874-6108, jnfo@crisiscontrol.com; http://www.crisiscontrol.com.

Spotlight 20-3 Scarce Resources Lead to the Controversy of the Commons

In a crowded world, every rational person by the age of 20 is aware of controversy regarding the management of our basic resources. Each country has differing laws regarding the environment. Air, water, and space pollution, congested highways, blighted neighborhoods, loud noises, obnoxious smells, biting dogs, potholes, and offensive advertisements come to mind.

All people including astronauts reside and work in Earth's environment. From the 1500s to the present, a population explosion has resulted in 6.5 billion people inhabiting the planet. Many are malnourished and most live in poverty. Many reputable sources, including some scientists from the U.S. National Academy of Sciences, claim that humanity is reaching a crisis point with respect to the interlocking issues of population, natural resources, and sustainability.

What would you think about curtailing population by limiting human reproduction under legal mandate agreed upon by a majority of voters? Would it also be prudent to stop immigration and halt donations of foreign aid completely? If our country donates aid, should acceptance of it require a commitment from the aided country to limit its own population?

These questions were taken seriously by a remarkable man. Dr. Garrett James Hardin (1915–2003) leaves a legacy that will continue to be debated. As a famous scientist, ecologist, and author of 27 books and 350 articles, he dedicated his life to the branch of biology that deals with the relations between living organisms and their environment. Excerpts from "The Tragedy of the Commons," which follow, illustrate Dr. Hardin's conclusion that most of the misery of the world is caused by overuse of our common earth resources. Like most prophets throughout history, his message has been ignored, ridiculed, or hated by his opponents. Nevertheless, he is one of the most quoted scholars in the field.

His pejorative view of the future is dismal unless world societies agree to set limits on population and the use of our planet's resources. In his writings, Dr. Hardin compares our world to a lifeboat filled to more than its carrying capacity. Solutions in the area of science and technology, he argues, will intensify the problem and create more misery. Despite his view of global crisis, a friend remembers him "as a generous and perpetually cheerful individual, with an infectious zest for life—for knowledge, for art, and for human companionship."

In his famous 1968 paper, published in *Science* by the American Association for the Advancement of Science, Dr. Hardin referred to a pamphlet written in 1833 by a political economist, William Forster Lloyd (1795–1852), who held the Drummond Chair at Oxford in the 1830s. Dr. Hardin paraphrased a portion of Lloyd's pamphlet as follows:

"The tragedy of the commons develops in this way. Picture a pasture open to all. It is to be expected that each herdsman will try to keep as many cattle as possible on the commons. Such an arrangement may work reasonably satisfactorily for centuries because tribal wars, poaching, and disease keep the numbers of both man and beast well below the carrying capacity of the land. Finally, however, comes the day of reckoning, that is, the day when the long-desired goal of social stability becomes a reality. At this point, the inherent logic of the commons remorselessly generates tragedy."

Dr. Hardin describes what causes this crisis. Times are good and each person decides to maximize his gains. "Therein is the tragedy. Each man is locked into a system that compels him to increase his herd without limit—in a world that is limited. Ruin is the destination toward which all men rush, each pursuing his own best interest in a society that believes in the freedom of the commons. Freedom in a commons brings ruin to all."

Even in our age of ecological sensibility where we recognize the value of controlling auto emissions, purifying water, and effective waste disposal, the preceding paragraph is extremely controversial. In Dr. Hardin's view, the effects of overpopulation, immigration, and pollution cannot be limited by any means short of governmental legislation. Volunteerism, Dr. Hardin emphasizes, will not work because "those who restrain their demands ... lose out in competition with short-term 'maximizers.'"

Is the tragedy of the commons so inescapably ruinous that our human condition can only be improved by laws limiting population growth? It is a fair but controversial question.

A systems point of view says that there are balancing forces, operating over long periods of time that limit the occurrence of extreme situations. One example is the elimination of inefficient users of resources by long-term marketing forces. International regulations with incentives for cooperation, such as ISO 14001 (a worldwide standard for environmental business conditions), can help to curb excessive oscillations of resource availability. These standards may help to control critical situations earlier than might otherwise be the case. (See the discussion of ISO 14001 in this chapter.) Even in unregulated situations, free market forces tend to penalize actions harmful to the goal of sustainability.

These are basically self-regulating trends, a correction mechanism observable before and after a market bubble bursts.

New information on the subject of population growth has recently appeared in an article titled "Environmental Heresies," by Stewart Brand, the founder of *The Whole Earth Catalog*. His article was published in the May 2005, issue of *Technology Review, MIT's Magazine of Innovation*. He announced that world population is leveling off rapidly, even precipitously, in developed countries with the rest of the world soon to follow. He said that the world population growth rate actually peaked at 2 percent in 1968, the same year that Paul Ehrlich published *The Population Bomb*. It has taken a long time to realize we are experiencing a decline in birthrate. According to Stewart Brand, women, worldwide, have chosen to move to the city, where children are a liability. He states, "A global tipping point in urbanization is what stopped the population explosion. As of 2008, more than 50 percent of the world's population lives in cities with at least 61 percent expected by 2030. In 1800 it was 3 percent; in 1900 it was 14 percent."

Can the world stop worrying about the population explosion? Does the declining birthrate mean that we will not endure the ruinous fate of the commons? It is true that investor enthusiasm for business expansion in a growing economy can encourage a company to expand too fast, overextending its resources without regard to eventual downturns or unforeseen competition? (See Spotlight 20-2: "Securing the Right Decisions," which discusses domino effects.) The story of the commons might be a lesson in not making assumptions too soon. If there are self-inflicted traps ahead, there are also cycles, tipping points, and surprises that will energize our capacity for sustainability and renewal in an increasingly interdependent world.

Review Questions

1 What information about world population, regional populations, and U.S population projections can you find online?

2 What is the population dilemma? Why is it important for P/OM to understand it?

3 What are the arguments of the Malthus advocates? Concerning Malthus, see http://www.ac.wwu.edu/stephan/malthus/malthus.0.html and http://www.blupete.com/Literature/Biographies/Philosophy/Malthus.htm.

4 What are the arguments of the anti-Malthus advocates?

5 What is the controversy of the commons?

Sources: "The Tragedy of the Commons," Garrett J. Hardin, *Science* 162 (1968): 243–248. Interview with Otis Graham on March 9, 1997. http://www.garretthardinsociety.org/tributes/tributes.html, March 2005 and April 2007. "Living on a Lifeboat," by Garrett Hardin, 1974, The Garrett Hardin Society. "Tribute to Garrett Hardin," by Leon Kolandiewicz, October 11, 2003, Minnesotans for Sustainability. "Garrett Hardin, 1915-2003—A Tribute," Ernest Partridge, The Online Gadfly http://www.igc.org/gadfly; http://www.garretthardinsociety.org/gh/about_gh.html

Summary

Chapter 20 highlights environmental issues that are both threats and opportunities for companies. The weakness of many companies is that environmental regulations and restrictions happen before the firm is prepared to match the rules. It is a strength to be ready for the expectations as they arise so that fines can be avoided and processes to achieve the goals can be developed at a reasonable price. Chapter 20 also focuses on ethical problems. In particular, there are ethical issues when quality is sacrificed to save money. It may not be a grave example, but when a package size is unchanged although the weight of the unseen contents is reduced, there is quality issue. Spoiled food and contaminated water and lead-painted toys are operational responsibilities. Problems stemming from lack of know-how or indifference are unacceptable.

Examples of environmentally sound P/OM processes are presented. With care and attention to ecological impacts, companies can save money and improve the environment at the same time. Similar results apply to benefits from being ethical. There is a cost, but the gains are greater. In this regard, quality integrity is an ethical issue. The HACCP program for seafood quality is a model of effective FDA regulation of total quality. Time to test and release new drugs is another issue for debate. Chapter 20 examines the impact of 9/11 on safety, security, crisis management, and contingency planning. All are P/OM responsibilities.

P/OM is on the team that can prepare the organization for future technology. Trends include smart robots that can move without wires. Technological developments are changing services and manufacturing. The virtual office is possible because of new technology. Learning to use it is a P/OM responsibility.

Spotlight 20-1: Ethics by Regulation is the story of how the Sarbanes–Oxley law came into being. How does P/OM evaluate the impact of the SOX laws? Spotlight 20-2: Securing the Right Decision discusses an increasingly critical issue: How to react when a crisis threatens the most basic issues of safety and credibility for crucially important products in the product line. This spotlight was written by a crisis expert and consultant whose advice has been borne out repeatedly over time. In spite of intelligent preparation for contingencies, crises continue to occur. Spotlight 20-2 sets down guidelines for securing the right decisions when crises happen. Spotlight 20-3 describes the controversy of the commons (usually a tract of land owned equally by all members of the community). A problem arises when the "commons" as a shared resource becomes overused. As examples, substitute for "overused" the terms "overgrazed" or "overfished." Such situations can go from "bad to worse" or systems can get triggered that provide self-correcting feedback. It is a P/OM responsibility to initiate adjustments for preventing tragedy.

Key Terms

CDC (p. 857)
Design for assembly (DFA) (p. 850)
Design for automation (DFAU) (p. 850)
Design for disassembly (DFD) (p. 849)
End-of-life-of-vehicle (ELV) (p. 848)
Ethics (p. 844)
FDA (p. 857)
Greening the environment (p. 845)
Hazard Analysis and Critical Control Point (HACCP) system (p. 858)
ISO 14000 / 14001 Series (p. 872)

Mobile robots (p. 862)
Quality integrity (p. 857)
Recycling concrete (p. 853)
Remanufacturing (p. 850)
Reuse (p. 844)
Reverse engineering (p. 851)
Reverse supply chains (p. 851)
SME enterprise wheel (p. 874)
Substances of concern (SOC) (p. 848)
Take-back laws (p. 849)
Water-jetting (p. 845)

Review Questions

1 Would simulated attacks on buildings, reservoirs, theaters, cruise ships, etc., help to evaluate existing security procedures? Explain. If this simulation includes glimpses of the attackers planning and preparing their attacks, would the defenders obtain early warning information that an attack might be imminent?

2 It is said that operations management is the one functional area closest to Best Practice of ethics. Why would this be so?

3 P/OM is the harshest critic of ethical failures. Why?

4 Describe the history of ethics as practiced by operations, financial, and marketing management.

5 Explain what take-back means. How is take-back changing the way that the supply chain operates?

6 What are the four aspects of DFD? Explain the role of DFD.

7 Why does water-jetting qualify as an OM greening technique?

8 Why is recycling concrete used as an example of OM greening the environment?

9 What five phases are used for environmental evaluations?

10 Explain the lack of quality integrity as an ethical issue.

11 Describe the Hazard Analysis and Critical Control Point (HACCP) system. What are the HACCP objectives? What are the seven recommended steps of HACCP?

12 How does HACCP relate to TQC and TQM?

13 Why is HACCP called a custodian of social ethics?

14 Explain the problems associated with overtesting and undertesting the safety and effectiveness of food and drug products.

15 What is the role of the CDC? How does the FDA relate to CDC?

16 What is the potential impact of healthcare robots?

17 What are the advantages of mobile robots that can move without wires?

18 Explain the impact of the virtual office on operations management decisions.

19 TBWA/Chiat/Day, an advertising agency, used hoteling. American Express uses hot desking. "Standard Life chooses VMware for hot-desking within its IT department, as it reduces the number of offices it operates." (by Cliff Aran, July 10, 2007, *Computer Weekly.com*). When are these office configurations beneficial?

20 Relate the virtual office to the "end of the job" concept.

21 How can P/OM help globalize operations?

22 Explain how ISO 14001 helps P/OM support firm success in global opportunities.

23 Explain the power of the SME wheel. If time allows, include an explanation of each concentric ring.

Problems Section

1 When office space is reengineered using hoteling, the square feet needed per employee may decrease from 200 to 48.

    a. What is the percent decline in space?

    b. At $12 per square foot per month, what is the saving per employee?

    c. If there are 1,000 employees, what is the total monthly saving?

    d. What business functions are best suited to hoteling?

2 Knowing that you have completed a P/OM course, the principal of your high school invites you to give a presentation to a high school class about global careers in P/OM. Show an outline of the presentation.

3 What is hot desking?

4 Benchmark the recycling system currently used by your community against the ideal one that you envision. Explain the factors that count and the criteria that you believe would permit an accurate comparison of systems.

5 Benchmark the ethics system that is currently used by your company (or community) against the ideal one that you envision. Explain the factors that count and the criteria that you believe would permit an accurate comparison of systems.

6 Over time, the 1-pound can of coffee appears to have remained the same size, but the contents have gone from 16 ounces to 13 ounces, and more recently to 10 or 11 ounces. Meanwhile, the printed weight of the contents has gotten noticeably smaller.

    a. Determine the percent decrease from 16 to 13 ounces. If the price of a pound of coffee is $8 and law requires that the same price per ounce be maintained, what would be the price for 13 ounces?

    b. Is there an ethical issue in this case? Can the argument for maintaining package size be justified?

7   Over the years, yogurt containers have remained about the same size but contents by weight have decreased. Can this fact be discerned by the customer? Is there an ethical issue in this case?

8   Set up a flowchart to indicate how the HACCP system could be applied to a large fish restaurant. (If you get a chance, get to know The Fish Market in Birmingham, Alabama.) Note the seven steps for HACCP and make certain that all seven are represented on the chart.

9   Develop a scoring model for comparing alternative reverse supply chain systems for:

   a. Paint cans where the paint has been used up and the cans have to be discarded
   b. Old computers that include the monitor, the hard drive, and the printer
   c. Worn tires for automobiles; for 18-wheel trucks
   d. Totaled automobiles (*totaled* means damaged so badly they are sent to the junk yard; however, parts can still be reused)

10 There are claims that teleworking is inefficient. Argue both the pros and cons of this statement.

11 What is the current rate of use of teleworking? Is it likely to increase or decrease in the future?

12 What does teleworking have to do with P/OM?

13 Create the Hazard Analysis and Critical Control Point (HACCP) system using the seven recommended steps for:

   a. A fishing boat
   b. Trucks carrying fish to the distributor
   c. The retailer of fish

14 What is the long-term effect of vision improvements on robots?

15 Detail an operations management plan for opening a quick-service restaurant in:

   a. Japan
   b. The United Kingdom
   c. The United States

16 Research the steps that need to be taken to obtain ISO 14000/14001 for a new branch in Australia.

17 7-Eleven food stores in Japan have used JIT deliveries to such an extent that the company has been accused of creating road pollution. How would application of ISO 14000–14001 help to sort this problem out?

Practice Quiz

1   The IQ (intelligence quotient) test is well-known, widely-used, and considered to be only one possible measure of intelligence. Other measures have emerged, one of which is called the EIQ (emotional intelligence quotient). Developed by Daniel Goleman and Richard Boyatis (see the EI Consortium at http://www.eiconsortium.org), it offers tests of EI competencies. The relationship of EI to ethics is apparent from examining the emotional competence framework. There are two parts to this framework in the Goleman system. The first component is personal competence. The second component is social competence. Points a. through e., related to personal competence, highlight the ways in which ethical decision making is dependent upon the level of an individual's personal emotional competency. Which one of these points is not consistent with the fundamentals of personal emotional competencies?

   a. Three building blocks of personal competence are self-awareness, self-regulation, and motivation. (This is certified to be a correct EI Consortium answer.)
   b. Self-awareness requires accurate self-assessment. It is unethical for someone to do a job that requires competence that they do not have. If someone flies a plane who is posing as a licensed pilot, that may be no more unethical than a CEO who does not take proper care of company business.
   c. Self-regulation includes self-control, trustworthiness, and taking responsibility for personal performance. It is unethical for a manager to hire a person known to be incompetent to do the job for which they are hired, e.g., nepotism or more.
   d. Motivation is the third component of personal competence. It includes the drive for achievement, which can include the desire for power, personal advancement, and increased earnings. Greed is neither condoned nor condemned as an attribute of emotional intelligence, because it is a basic human emotion.
   e. Motivation also includes commitment. This permits the individual to align with the goals of the group, and with the organizational objectives.

2   The EIQ (emotional intelligence quotient) test measures a different kind of intelligence than traditional IQ tests, which do not capture many of the elements of ethical behavior. From Problem 1, the first component of the EIQ is personal

competence—how we manage ourselves. The second component is social competence—how we handle relationships. In Problem 2, points a. through e. are related to social competence. The points highlight ways in which ethical decision making is dependent upon the social aspects of an individual's emotional competency. Which of these points is not consistent with the fundamentals of social emotional competencies?

a. Two building blocks of social competence are empathy and social skills. (This is certified to be a correct answer.)

b. Empathy is awareness of others' feelings, needs, and concerns. It leads to a service orientation, which anticipates, recognizes, and thereby permits meeting customers' needs. Ethical issues about customers' needs also include health and safety factors. The same service orientation applies to employees, suppliers, and the communities in which the company operates.

c. An additional factor that relates to the emotional intelligence of an individual in a social system is empathy to help another person bolster his or her abilities. However, issues of competitiveness arise. Situations occur where a person must fend for him- or herself at the expense of others in the organization. It is not intelligent to give assistance to another person who may be promoted and become the boss.

d. Social skills is the second building block of social competence. There are many components to include. Among these are team capabilities, negotiation skills, change management expertise, and good communication proficiency.

e. Returning to empathy as an ingredient of social competence, emotional intelligence is strongly related to cultivating diversity opportunities.

3 Protecting the environment is an ethical issue that managers of every company must consider. There is a tendency to jump to the conclusion that only large manufacturing companies can impact the environment. Yet, in Japan, 11,500 7-Eleven stores are owned by Seven & i-Holdings, which was responsive to complaints that too many trucks were making just-in-time deliveries, causing road congestion and pollution. 7-Eleven changed its delivery schedules to remove objections. 7-Eleven was started in 1927 by the Southland Ice Co. of Dallas, Texas. It was named for its hours of doing business. In 2007, about 6,000 stores operate in North America, making 7-Eleven number 11 in the "Top 75 North American Food Retailers" with $15 billion in sales (*Supermarket News*). Assume that a company in the convenience store category (like 7-Eleven) convenes a worldwide meeting of its managers to discuss environmental issues. The agenda has been listed in points a. through e. One of these points is unacceptable to the general manager. Which point is objectionable?

a. Maintenance is a major aspect of environmental protection, i.e., greening the environment.

b. Other major topics that relate to greening the environment include production take-back rules, which require disassembling products and recycling an increasing percent of products. For example, BMW has created an experimental plant with the goal of recycling 95 percent (by weight) of its automobiles.

c. The Green Party is a major advocate of political action to achieve more productive maintenance of facilities. For example, how are roads, bridges, and tunnels maintained? Although Green Parties can be found all over the globe, productive aspects of maintenance is their main concern.

d. A serious maintenance problem is related to stripping old paints and coatings from ships, buildings, and airplanes. An important new opportunity for coating and surface removal uses water-jetting technology to replace old surfaces with new protective surfaces.

e. The *Thomas Register* (2003) lists more than 20 companies that provide marine hull treatment. There are many other applications for water-jetting, including gas turbine coatings and airplane surfaces.

4 The ways in which business organizations affect the environment are useful to enumerate. As a result of the conference of convenience store managers, a task force was set up to list some of the impact zones. This list is presented here for approval. There is one point that was rejected by the steering committee of the conference. Which point a. through e. deserves to be reworked?

a. A short list regarding air quality includes smokestacks, delivery trucks, company cars, ships and boats, airplanes' exhausts, air-conditioners, air-blowers, windmills, wind vanes and wind turbines. See http://www.ndseed.org/htmls/past_vanes.htm. In addition to the North Dakota seed URL, see the URL concerning green power purchasing: http://www.eere.energy.gov/greenpower/home.shtml. Many items on this list not only affect air quality, but they also have significant noise levels.

b. Water is used and altered by industry in various ways. As a coolant and refrigerant, it is employed by trucks, cars, boats, and airplanes. It participates in many chemical processes. Water is treated for purification (pools and drinking water), distillation, and pressure hosing including water-jetting. As another example of multiple impacts, jet ski complaints include their effect on air, water, and noise levels.

c. Waste and sewage are major environmental factors that affect air and water as well as requiring special disposal methods. The Environmental Protection Agency has received hundreds of millions in grants as a result of the Wastewater Treatment Works Security Act, H.R. 5169. The European Union (EU) Land Directive banned disposal of whole tires in July 2003 and "shredded tyres from July, 2006." Bicycle tires are not subject to this ban. See http://www.tyredisposal.co.uk.

d. Asbestos has not been used as a building material for over 30 years. It is not treated as an environmental problem as a result. The same applies to pesticides like DDT (banned in the United States in 1972) and PCBs (banned in the United States in 1976). Radon is not considered a problem at present.

e. Pesticides can affect the water table and impair the safety of drinking water. Oil and gas drilling activities have contaminated water tables in Colorado and New Mexico. Oil and natural gas pipelines have ruptured with greater frequency than one expects. The effects of radiation exposure from high voltage lines, X-rays, high-altitude flying, and (naturally occurring) radon are being scrutinized. The effects of spills at sea (such as the Exxon *Valdez*) and by railroads and trucks have promoted litigation long after the events occurred. Dumping of medical products at sea creates hazards when they are washed ashore.

5 USCAR stands for United States Council for Automotive Research. This organization is sponsored by DaimlerChrysler, Ford, and General Motors. USCAR is the umbrella organization of the three companies, formed in 1992 to strengthen the technology base of the U.S. domestic auto industry. This is accomplished using precompetitive, cooperative research. Using the website http://www.uscar.com, determine which one of the following points, a. through e., is wrong.

a. USCAR and the U.S. Department of Energy have joined an industry/government research initiative that is aimed at freeing the nation's personal transportation system from petroleum dependence and from harmful vehicle emissions.

b. The FreedomCAR partnership was announced January 9, 2002. There is no single strategy to solve the dependence problem. The United States buys 26 percent of the world's oil to satisfy 55 percent of its market requirements. In other words, the United States produces only 45 percent of the petroleum it uses. Supply and demand are out of synchronization and will get worse unless various steps are taken. The current gap between supply and demand is projected to more than double by 2030 if no steps are taken to remedy the situation.

c. Detailed results of R&D are documented. Significant results will be reported at the website http://www.cartech.doe.gov. Clicking on "What's New," the categories are progress reports, materials research, batteries research, fuels research, and an archive.

d. The Vehicle Recycling Partnership (VRP) was formed November 1991. It has P/OM goals to reduce the environmental impact of vehicle disposal. It calls for the efficient disassembly of components and materials to enhance vehicle recyclability.

e. The Institute of Electrical and Electronic Engineers Standards Association has developed a universal standard for motor vehicle event data recorders (MVDER). This black box is similar to those that monitor airplane crashes. Data include date, time, location, velocity, heading, number of occupants, and seat belt usage. This works for personal autos, trucks, buses, ambulances, fire trucks, and other vehicles. The black box that is being installed by auto companies can establish personal blame in court cases.

6 Take-back laws and regulations are predicated on careful and clever preplanned DFD (design for disassembly). Five essential elements have been listed by the managers of Contronics, which provides electronics manufacturing services to OEMs for mobile phones, computers, workstations, and computer peripherals. The tide is changing. More attention is being placed on DFD than on DFA. In fact, the head designer has told a conference group that they are the same thing. He lists the five essentials and throws in a sixth for a ringer. "Keep awake," he tells the audience. "I have included one statement in a. to f. that is not good advice." Which is that statement?

a. Design products without using super-adhesives to hold parts together. The best adhesives are those that hold until instructed otherwise.

b. Create a manual of fastenings and fastening methods. Rank them in terms of how well they hold things together under vibration, heat, etc., and how readily they come apart when that state is required. It may help to examine children's blocks and construction sets.

c. Choose components that can be reused with minimum rework (or, if possible, with no rework). Set the target price for a component that can be used *n* times at a multiplier of *n* times the cost that would be paid for that component if it would be used once. For example, be willing to pay $3 for a spool that can be reused three times, if a single-use spool was acceptably priced at $1. (Target price is determined by the amount that the buyer will be willing to pay to the seller. It applies to auctions as well as bids for project awards.)

d. Components that require hazardous-care disposal should be priced at the cost of the component plus the disposal cost per unit. If that is not acceptable, search for an alternative material. If possible, get away from designs that require special care for disposal. Examine new processes as often as possible for recycling and disposal.

e. Use analysis to identify materials that can be moved through the reverse supply chain as inexpensively as possible. The total systems cost is the logistics cost of original transport (to the customer), plus the reverse supply chain take-back logistics cost to return the material to be recycled, plus the costs of recycling that material. (The costs of the entire supply loop are relevant.)

f. Consider the advantages of locating a recycling facility close to the customers' return-of-product access points rather than at the remanufacturing plant. For example, melt down car doors before returning them in the reverse supply loop to the door-making location.

7 Ethics and operations management are inextricably related to each other. Safety, security, and health (SS&H) have gone from being mundane expectations in a time of peace to being seriously threatened prospects in a time of war. Of the five statements a. through e., one is not correct. Which one is incorrect?

a. The assignment to protect safety, security and health (SS&H) falls squarely on the shoulders of P/OM. Innovative two-way cooperation is required with IT (information technology) to select and monitor variables that capture and preserve the well-being of employees and customers. Companies with products that provide explosive detection systems (EDS) are being rewarded by higher stock market valuations since airports, buildings, and theaters are considering installing this line of products. Visit http://www.mistralgroup.com/SEC_exdetect.asp.

b. Accidents need to be fully documented and studied for both employees and customers. OSHA (Occupational Safety and Health Administration) of the U.S. Department of Labor establishes protective standards guidelines. OSHA enforces these standards and provides outreach and technical assistance to employers and employees, and charters an advisory committee to identify research opportunities. Visit http://www.osha.gov.

c. OSHA has a four-pronged comprehensive approach to ergonomics, which is the art and science of designing and arranging physical interfaces with the human body (e.g., chairs) and senses (e.g., dials) for effective, efficient, safe and healthful use by people. For example, OSHA addresses musculoskeletal disorders (MSDs) in the workplace. The four segments of OSHA's strategy for reducing injuries and illnesses are listed in point b.

d. ISO 14000 provides OSHA guidelines for employees' safety and health. ISO 14001 embodies the security aspects of SS&H by requiring measures to prevent willful acts by employees that are harmful to other employees. OSHA does not include issues related to terrorism in its guidelines.

e. Innovative technologies are being developed that will bring about major changes in security. In point a., cooperation of P/OM and IT are stressed. An example of this would be the use of Perceptrak,™ which utilizes content analysis and behavior recognition software to identify "potentially suspicious people, vehicles, and objects." Visit http://www.cernium.com. Click on Minnesota Daily (9/18/2007).

8 Eras have tipping points. Calm and tranquil eras can tip to stormy and violent epochs. The cold war was filled with tension. When it ended, there was conjecture that a calm and peaceful time would begin. In retrospect, it was a mistake to believe that hard times were over when the Berlin War fell. Historian Francis Fukuyama (*The End of History*, Free Press, January 1992) believed that the liberal democratic, capitalistic system had triumphed once and for all. That meant that the U.S. form of government would be unchallenged, hence the end of history. However, new wicked problems that society and management faced after the end of the Soviet Union were threats from terrorism, ecological–technological disaster potentials, global warming, computer virus assaults, cyberterrorism, and SARS-like plagues. In response, government agencies and international organizations created some operations-oriented steps to deal with the shift in types of threats from the cold war era to the post-9/11 era. Discussion and examples are included in points a. through e. Which one of these statements is not correct?

a. ISO 17799:2000 is a set of guidelines for the security of information systems. Although this is broadly applicable, it was drawn up to apply to operations. ISO 17799 is intended to minimize the risk of systems failure and to protect the integrity of software and information. Application to e-business systems is evident. ISO 17799:2000 was developed by the same International Organization for Standardization in Geneva, Switzerland, that created ISO 9000.

b. There are 10 major sections in ISO 17799:2000. These are designed to facilitate trading in a trusted environment. Three of the major sections in ISO 17799:2000 are (1) business continuity planning to counteract interruptions caused by disasters, (2) physical security to prevent unauthorized access, damage, and interference, and (3) personnel security to reduce risks of human error, theft, fraud, or misuse of facilities. Visit http://www.computersecuritynow.com.

c. ISO 17666:2003 is an ISO guideline for reducing project risks. Although it is designed to apply to space programs, it is also intended to be used by any industry that wishes to minimize project risks. This ISO guideline provides templates to systematically assess, plan, measure, and report risks throughout the development of the projects.

d. The Department of Homeland Security issues threat-level warnings. Visit http://www.dhs.gov. Click on "National Threat Advisory" in the left-hand navigation pane for details on these threat conditions. These advisories apply to municipal services [police, fire, EMS, and TSA (Transportation Security Administration)], but have no bearing on industrial, commercial, or service operations. Visit http://www.emsmagazine.com for timely updates on EMS systems.

e. Hazardous waste operations and emergency response (HAZWOPER) training is required by OSHA. This is for employees who are designated by their companies to respond to hazardous material emergencies. Organizations that are in compliance with other OSHA safety requirements and trained for HAZWOPER have a great head start in coping with natural disasters (e.g., earthquakes or hurricanes) or willful violence (e.g., terrorism).

9 Some business benefits of ISO 14000 are listed here. They have been provided by the International Organization for Standardization in Geneva, Switzerland, at http://www.iso.org, using "Search" on ISO 14000. The posted concepts have been interpreted and expanded to fit the interests of P/OM. Four of the five listed points are correct. Which one is in error?

a. Some managers will do what is necessary to avoid legal penalties for polluting. They will do only what is required to comply with legislation. This is a reactive P/OM strategy based on spending as little as possible to conform. For example, contamination of air and water is kept just below the allowable threshold. There is usually a large opportunity cost for using this strategy.

b. The opportunity cost for not being proactive by keeping contamination levels far below allowable thresholds is related to low community esteem and lack of customer admiration for the company. Regulators may look longer and harder at a company that is known to barely comply with regulations.

c. Additional benefits accrue to companies that consider part of their mission to be reduction of waste products by encouraging reuse, remanufacture, rework, and recycling. There are usually material and energy savings from reuse strategies.

d. The drawback for companies using ISO 14000 is that different rules apply in various parts of the world. If two countries subscribe to ISO 14000, there is less likelihood that each country will demand that its own regulations be followed. Nevertheless, the ISO 14000 in one place may not be acceptable in another.

e. ISO 14000 can help to lower distribution costs. If too many trucks are delivering too few items, causing unacceptable pollution, the company EMS should detect that fact. The EMS will provide faster alert than would be available from environmental activists who break the news.

10 Technology is being developed to counteract high threat levels. Defense and protection require analysis of threats. Security-technology for EDS (explosive detection systems) is in process. Fingerprint and face identification systems are being improved. See http://www.l1id.com for automated biometric identification, mobile, remote, and continuous scan ID platforms. Robot technology provides access that is least life-threatening and invasive. Technology is also being developed to improve safety in healthcare systems. In addition to technology, there are many algorithms for improving the quality of life that are on the drawing boards or in test. A list of potential applications of new technology and improved systems has been developed by the P/OM students in a distance-learning class. They have assembled this list and circulated it amongst themselves for verification. Several of the 16 points a. through p. are incorrect. Identify which ones are wrong.

a. Hazard Analysis and Critical Control Point (HACCP) system is an airport security system that is able to detect explosives and gases. It is based on 3-sigma quality control charts. It can automatically send a signal when an out-of-control point is detected.

b. Mobile robots have been used successfully for various kinds of police work including bomb squad operations.

c. HACCP was pioneered by the Pillsbury Company (http://www.pillsbury.com) in the 1960s to create safe food for the space program.

d. Dogs have been successfully used for detecting drugs and explosives.

e. Service robots have been developed (see http://www.pyxis.com) for use in hospitals, which has significantly reduced healthcare errors.

f. Pillsbury, not the Food and Drug Administration (FDA), uses the Doughboy to promote their products.

g. HACCP requires that companies handling spoiled foods develop safe ways to dispose of them. This is called a *food deviation*. HACCP also required that records of food disposal be maintained.

h. Thalidomide unexpectedly caused severely adverse birth defects. This drug (used for morning sickness) never received approval by the U.S. Food and Drug Administration. Many problems arose because it had been approved for use in Europe. See http://www.fda.gov/cder/news/thalidomide.htm.

i. Pyxis Homerus® is an integrated centralized pharmacy with automated dispensing systems. It retrieves pharmaceuticals from its own storage system and packages appropriate doses with information bar codes for accuracy.

j. Pyxis Homerus® addresses the 5Rs as stated in *Nursing Responsibilities Regarding Drugs*. These are entirely operational issues, as follows: Use the right drug, right dose, and route, at the right time for the right person.

k. Security has unique problems to address when telecommuting and telework are used either from home base or with hot-desking or hoteling (aka virtual offices). Among the dangers is the transfer of confidential information under insecure conditions. Also, unknown occupants can examine files and computer records. For hot-desking, see http://www.eoffice.net, and for hoteling, see http://www.dea.com/Hot.asp.

l. The website http://manufacturing.stanford.edu provides virtual online plant tours that can be used to provide information about increasing security.

m. The SME Manufacturing Enterprise Wheel is a total systems approach that centers on the customer. Among the factors that need to be added when the next update of the wheel appears are safety, security, and health issues.

n. IDs can be accurate without being invasive. Fingerprints, facial structure, retina prints, etc., provide reliable information.

o. Robots of many kinds could help to repatriate jobs that are currently going abroad. However, new techno-robots will not bring people-jobs back to the United States. The hourly wage for robots may not please the union leaders.

p. Contingency planning is planning for the possible, not the inevitable, nor only the probable. The possible includes the improbable, and it may be wise to take another look at the impossible. Contingency planning deals with more than forecasts of events to come. It can alter the probabilities of future events.

Additional Readings

Barnes, Nick, and Zhi-Qiang Liu. *Knowledge-Based Vision-Guided Robots*. Heidelberg, Germany: Physica-Verlag, 2002.

Čapek, Karel. *Rossum's Universal Robots (R.U.R.)*. 1920. For a list of up-to-date references to R.U.R., see http://www.uwec.edu/Academic/Curric/jerzdg/RUR. Note: The Czech word "robota" means drudgery or servitude; "robotnik" is a serf. R.U.R. was first published in English in 1923. It has been performed on stage for many years.

Collins, Jim. *Good to Great*. New York: Harper Collins, October 2001.

Department of Health and Human Services, Food and Drug Administration (FDA). *Proposal to Establish Procedures for the Safe Processing and Importing of Fish and Fishery Products*, 21 CFR Parts 123 and 1240 [Docket Nos. 90N-0199 and 93N-0195]. Also, U.S. FDA Center for Food Safety and Applied Nutrition (CFSAN), Office of Seafood, "FDA's Evaluation of the Seafood HACCP Program for Fiscal Years 2000/2001," September 30, 2002.

Engelberger, Joseph F. *Robotics in Practice: Management and Application of Industrial Robots*. New York: AMACOM, 1980.

Greene, Richard Tabor. *Global Quality: A Synthesis of the World's Best Management Methods*. Burr Ridge, IL: Irwin, 1993.

Historical information for the HACCP program. *Federal Register*, vol. 59, no. 19 (January 28, 1994). Companion document: "Fish and Fishery Products Hazards and Controls Guide." FDA Draft Document, PB94-140-985.

Horn, Berthold K. P. *Robot Vision*. Cambridge, MA: MIT Press, March 1986. Also, see Chae, H. An, Christopher G. Atkeson, and John Hollerbach. *Model-Based Control of a Robot Manipulator*. Cambridge, MA: MIT Press, March 2003.

Imai, Masaaki. *Kaizen: The Key to Japan's Competitive Success*. New York: McGraw-Hill/Irwin, November 1986.

———. *Gemba Kaizen: A Commonsense, Low-Cost Approach to Management*. New York: McGraw-Hill Trade, March 1997.

Langenwalter, Gary. *The Squeeze: A Novel Approach to Business Sustainability*. Dearborn, MI. Society of Manufacturing Engineers. 2006.

McGrath, Michael E. *Product Strategy for High-Technology Companies: How to Achieve Growth, Competitive Advantage, and Increased Profits*. Burr Ridge, IL: Irwin Professional Publishing, 1995.

Menzel Peter, and Faith D'Aluisio. *Robo Sapiens: Evolution of New Species*. Cambridge, MA: MIT Press, September 2000.

Puchek, Vladimir, Noel Tichy, and Carole K. Barnett (eds). *Globalizing Management: Creating and Leading the Competitive Organization*. New York: Wiley, 1993.

Schmierer, Germot, and Rolf Schraft. *Service Robots* (German edition, 1996). A. K. Peters, Ltd., July 2000.

Stalk, G., P. Evans, and L. E. Shulman. "Competing on Capabilities: The New Rules of Corporate Strategy." *Harvard Business Review* (March–April 1992).

Summers, David A. *Waterjetting Technology*. London, England: E. F. Spon, Ltd., Division of Chapman & Hall, 1995.

Yeung, Andy C. L., and Charles Corbett (special issue editors), "Call for Papers." *International Journal of Production Economics, Special Issue: Meta-Standards in Operations Management.* Abstract: "The widespread use of meta-standards such as ISO 9000 and ISO 14000, HACCP, and others represents a new 'management technology' in operations management." Publication date: January 31, 2007.

Notes

1. Rick Schmid, Dr., Lydia Frenzel, and Rich Burgess, "Problem Solving Forum: On Water Quality for UHP Water-Jetting." *PaintSquare Portal to the Coatings Industry* (August 2007): 47–56.
2. Gene Bylinsky. "Manufacturing for Reuse." *Fortune* (February 6, 1995).
3. This information was obtained in conversation with John J. Resslar, Champion, Designs for the Environment, Saturn Corporation. Update, March 2000. Later, he was manager of the Design for the Environment at the World Wide Facilities of the General Motors Corporation. At present, John J. Resslar is President of Wolverene Applied Research (Updated, October 2007).
4. William Turley. *Headline News* at http://www.recyclingtoday.com, March 2, 2003. Also, "9/11 Clean-Up Memories Linger." *C&D News* (October 22, 2002).
5. "Airbus to Deepen Investment, Cooperation in China." *China* Info*Flash* (August 2001): 1.
6. "Economic Cancer." *Lawyer News* (September 23, 2002).
7. Alex Berenson. "A Caldron of Ethics and Asbestos." *The New York Times, Business Day* (March 12, 2003): C1, 22.
8. Department of Health and Human Services, Food and Drug Administration. *Proposal to Establish Procedures for the Safe Processing and Importing of Fish and Fishery Products*, 21 CFR Parts 123 and 1240 [Docket Nos. 90N-0199 and 93N-0195]. Also, U.S. FDA Center for Food Safety and Applied Nutrition (CFSAN), Office of Seafood, FDA's Evaluation of the Seafood HAACP Program for Fiscal Years 2000/2001, September 30, 2002.
9. For steps 1–7, many of the phrases are taken directly from government documents such as "HACCP: A State of the Art Approach to Food Safety." *FDA Backgrounder* (October 2001). At the same time, liberal paraphrasing has been used.
10. J. A. DiMasi. "Cost of Innovation in the Pharmaceutical Industry." *Journal of Health Economics*, Amsterdam, Elsevier Publishing Co., vol. 10, no. 2 (July 1991): 107–142. The breakdown is: Laboratory studies: 3.5 years; 1st Phase—Safety, 1.0 year; 2nd Phase—Testing Effectiveness, 2.0 years; 3rd Phase—Extensive Clinical Testing, 3.0 years; FDA Review, 2.5 years; Total Time: 12.0 years.
11. For 2002 data, see the article by J. A. DiMasi. "The Economics of Pharmaceutical Innovation: Trends in Costs, Risks and Returns." *CPSA 2002 Digest* (October 8, 2002). Proceedings at http://www.milestonedevelopment.com/CPSA/2002. Report on 2005 symposium: http://www.milestonedevelopment.com/CPSA/2005. For report on 2006, put appropriate date in the 2005 URL.
12. Medical News Today.com. 24 Jan. 2006.
13. William Bridges. "The End of the Job." *Fortune* (September 19, 1994): 62–74.
14. The word *robot* was derived from the Czech words *robota*, meaning "work" and *robotnick*, meaning "worker," by Karel Čapek for his play, "RUR (Rossum's Universal Robots)," written in 1920.
15. Berthold K. P. Horn. *Robot Vision.* MIT Press, March 1986. Also, see Chae H. An, Christopher G. Atkeson, and John Hollerbach. *Model-Based Control of a Robot Manipulator.* MIT Press, March 2003.
16. Gregory Dudek and Michael Jenkin. *Computational Principles of Mobile Robotics.* Cambridge, UK: Cambridge University Press, 2000.
17. *CBS News Sunday Morning.* "Close Watch." April 21, 2002, http://www.cbsnews.com/stories/2002/04/19/sunday/main506739.shtml.
18. The Deming Prize was awarded to the Toyota Motor Corporation in 1965. The A1 prototype vehicle was developed by the company's founder, Kiichiro Toyoda, in 1935.
19. Gernot Schmierer and Rolf Dieter Schraft. *Service Robots.* London, England: A. K. Peters, Ltd., July 2000. This book was first published in German in 1996.
20. Peter Menzel (photography) and Faith D'Aluisio. *Robo Sapiens: Evolution of New Species.* MIT Press, September 1, 2000.
21. Joseph F. Engelberger. *Robotics in Service.* Cambridge, MA: MIT Press, 1989.
22. Susan Okie. "Robots Make the Rounds to Ease Hospitals' Costs." *The Washington Post* (April 3, 2002).
23. "Robotics and Electronic Health Record (EHR)." *Virtual Medical Worlds*, October 2005.

24. Described in *Computer Models of the Fundamental Mechanisms of Thought*, by Douglas Hofstadter and the Fluid Analogies Research Group, New York: Basic Books, 1995.

25. Montieth M. Illingworth. "Virtual Managers." *Information Week* (June 13, 1994): 44. For the Virtual Assistant, see *Business Week* (Enterprise), (September 14, 1998).

26. Susan Diesenhouse. "Price Waterhouse Tries Check-In-and-Out Office." *The New York Times* (December 7, 1994). Also see Business Bulletin, *The Wall Street Journal* (March 9, 1995): 1.

27. Quote from International Standards Organization (ISO) working paper *ISO/TC 207/SC 1/N 47 for ISO/CD 14001 Environmental Management Systems—Specification with Guidance for Use*, Geneva, Switzerland, September 2000.

28. Ibid.

29. Computer and Automated Systems Association of the Society of Manufacturing Engineers (CASA/SME). *The New Manufacturing Enterprise Wheel*, 3e. Publication of CASA/SME, Dearborn, MI, 1993. CASA/SME Technology Trends Report for 1999 was presented in Detroit at the CASA/SME State of the Industry Reception, September 15, 1999.

Enrichment Activity 20: The Calculation of Lifetime Value (LTV) Losses

The LTV calculation is important to everyone who manages the company, but it is especially critical for P/OM because customer complaints are most frequently the result of a quality failure. The impact of different kinds of defects is special to each industry. For example, a room robbery is a far more serious complaint than a room not made up. The probability of losing a customer forever in the former is almost always 100 percent. The probability of losing a customer in the latter case will vary by the demographics of the customer (business or resort) and by the way in which it is remedied.

Assigning probabilities of losing a customer forever (or for some period of time) for each type of complaint situation is the first step in calculating LTV lost. For each customer lost, there is a revenue stream that is suddenly terminated. It is pretty straightforward to calculate unearned profits. The company can afford to spend foregone profit to correct the causes of lost customers. For example, a big, well-known hotel has calculated that it loses $14 million per year because of problems that can be corrected with expenditures of less than $2 million per year. Management also believes that some complaints will not be resolved no matter how much is spent because the complainants are habitual and the circumstances are not under management control. These complainants may never return again to any place they have ever been. A few scenarios will be presented to demonstrate the calculation of LTV losses.

Pizza Scenario:

The company delivers a full range of pizzas with a promised delivery within 30 minutes. The company believes that any delivery within 45 minutes incurs no customer annoyance. However, it is believed that the probability of losing a customer forever increases as delivery delays occur beyond 45 minutes. To make this example simple, one probability estimate will be used for deliveries between 45 and 60 minutes. Ten percent (10%) of all customers experiencing that delay will switch to another pizza company. Note that a table of probabilities could be determined for different times of day, locations, delay intervals, and various demographics. Such detail does not promote a good example but it is essential for making decisions about real problems. Now, a critical point is the estimate that 25 percent of all orders experience delays between 45 and 60 minutes.

Data and Analysis:

An average family loyal to this company purchases 50 pizzas per year at an average price of $20 per order. Company profit is $8 per order after all costs including delivery. Thus, the net profit per year to the company for this one customer is $400. An expected lifetime of purchasing by this family is 20 years. A calculation that does not take into account the lesser value of purchases made in the future is $20 \times \$400 = \$8,000$ dollars of foregone profit. If net present value (NPV) calculations were used, the profit stream that has been lost has a present value of $4,705.70 with 5.69% interest. (See Enrichment Activity 8 for the NPV model.) The big question now is "How many families are there that fit this category?" Say that there are 100,000 families and that 25 percent (or 25,000) experience the 45 to 60 minute late delivery. Further assume that ten percent of these (2,500) never order again. The loss using NPV is almost $11,764,250.

The pizza company has ample opportunity to improve without wasting money. If it spends $3 million to prevent 95 percent of the unnecessary loss, it still retains $8,176,037.50. It has been unable to eliminate $588,212.50 of lost business (at least right away, although with experience it may do better). The $3 million spent on improving might include the use of new GPS technology to avoid traffic stalemates, smarter locations for the pizza stores, better training of drivers, faster procedures for making and packing the pizzas, "call ahead" empowerment of drivers, and the use of gift certificates for customers experiencing late deliveries.

Enrichment Challenges 20

It is a straightforward exercise to make a table of the relevant numbers in an Excel spreadsheet. For example, enter 400 in A1 and pull down the box to A20. Get the sum in A21. Select A22 and click on the f_x symbol and write "NPV" in the window of "Insert Function." Say OK for NPV. Enter "5.69%" in the "Rate" window of the "Function Arguments" Window. In the "Value 1" window select boxes A1:A20, and say OK. $4,705.70 appears within box A22. Now, all of the "iffy" estimates can be tested using sensitivity analysis. Examples are suggested in the following Enrichment Challenges.

1   What happens to these decisions when the cost of pizza goes up by 10 percent and profits drop accordingly?
2   What occurs if the interest rate is 4.962 percent? If the difference of the national market is 1 million families per year?
3   What is the difference if the NPV interest rate is 4 percent?

AutoZone, Inc.
Case Study

Case Study Significance

This case study is significant because it illustrates the impact of teaming of logistics providers and academia with a goal of providing leading-edge world-class solutions to an involved customer. The project combined the capabilities of Global Concepts (a logistics process consulting and software firm), Transplace (a transportation third-party logistics provider, called 3PL, with expanded services of a 4PL—see References to 3PL/4PL at the end of this case), and the extended industrial engineering resources of the University of Oklahoma under the direction of Dean of Engineering, Tom Landers. The customer, AutoZone, Inc., is a very large client operating in a high volume supply chain management (SCM) situation. The ultimate SCM design concepts and systems development were implemented in a phased approach that was accomplished on time and on budget without negatively impacting AutoZone's store deliveries. The final results allowed AutoZone to improve customer service and increase throughput while decreasing costs. The team's efforts are credited by AutoZone's position as a Standard & Poor's leader in performance for several years. This project and its success has become a foundation on which AutoZone has expanded at a phenomenal rate, moving into the international arena.

Company Profile

AutoZone is the nation's leading auto parts retailer. As of early 2007, it operated 3,955 stores in the United States, Mexico, and Puerto Rico, employing over 56,000 people. A Fortune 500 company with 2006 sales exceeding $5,948,400,000, AutoZone is opening more stores per year than any other retail auto parts chain in the nation. The company sells auto parts and accessories, e.g., A/C compressors, alternators, batteries and accessories, brake drums, rotors, shoes and pads, carburetors, clutches, CV axles, engines, fuel pumps, mufflers, shock absorbers and struts, starters, and water pumps. AutoZone's stores generally offer approximately 21,000 stock-keeping units (SKU), covering a range of vehicle types and year models. Each store carries a basic product line tailored to parts inventories that mirror the makes and models of the vehicles in individual store's trade area. Hub stores carry a larger assortment of products available for delivery to commercial customers or local satellite stores. More than 750,000 additional SKU of slower selling products are available through a vendor direct program (VDP) offering overnight delivery, or through salvage and original equipment manufacturer (OEM) parts programs.

AutoZone's supply chain consists of eight distribution centers (DCs) with a combined footprint of over six million square feet. Large DC's process more than a million radio frequency identification (RFID) transactions per day. The transactions result in the shipment of a daily average of over 4,000,000 pieces from those locations. Additionally, one of the large distribution centers provides in-bound and low-demand cross-dock operations to support other DCs. This multi-echelon network provides an optimized blend of excellent customer service with a supply chain cost that also serves as a benchmark by which other retailers are measured.

Warehouse Management Re-engineering and System Results

At the time AutoZone selected Global Concepts as a partner, the distribution centers were capable of supporting approximately 200-250 stores. Following implementation of process re-engineering supported by Global Concepts' warehouse management system (WMS), using GCI's Logistics Engine (LE), the larger AutoZone DCs now support over 1000 stores. This higher level of capability is the result of a 400% increase in throughput achieved while reducing operating costs 20% and maintaining inventory accuracies near 99.9% (see Figures C-4, C-5, and C-6 in the Appendix of this case). The increased capability removed warehouse capacity as a growth constraint and allowed greater focus on improving transportation economy.

World-class cross-dock strategies, and dependable, high-quality transportation services developed by Transplace allowed Global to reduce inventories 20% throughout the supply chain without reducing customer service or increasing stock-out situations. Finally, the new found capital made available as a result of the foregoing successes combined with world-class transportation and supply chain management allowed unprecedented expansion of operations and store density in a short period of time.

SCM Needs

AutoZone planned aggressive expansion and recognized the need for new logistics processes to support that growth. Because of the size and complexity of their operations, AutoZone required that the SCM:

- *Be highly configurable* – Because SCM procedures vary based on the different types of products supported in each region, AutoZone demanded that a single SCM system handle all the various situations
- *Offer robust functionality* – Because of their aggressive growth plans, AutoZone required a SCM system with strong functionality that would be able to support operations for many years while reducing costs and improving efficiencies. They demanded a SCM with depth and breadth of functionality across many areas. A high level of coordination of the incremental details of processes was required to provide AutoZone the resource it needed to aggressively cut costs
- *Provide complete visibility of operations* – With the average DC exceeding 500,000 square feet, a system that simplified management and monitoring of activities to ensure timely completion. Also required was visibility of store inventory and inventory in transit
- *Be extremely user friendly* – AutoZone's employee turnover rate exceeded 50% per year at the worker level. A SCM system was needed that was easy to learn and use. They specified a SCM system that provided management tools that could simplify functions so management could concentrate on more value-added tasks rather than firefighting
- *Provide fast system response transaction times* – Because of the volume of the supply chain, AutoZone demanded the SCM system be capable of fast transaction times even with extreme volumes
- *Be easy to implement* – Because stores stocked a minimal amount of inventory, they demanded that the new SCM system be quick and easy to implement, and that the new SCM would not impact DC operation during implementation
- *Be capable of being modified* – Due to the growth planned and the recognition that enhancements would be required, they demanded a scalable SCM system capable of supporting future needs.

AutoZone investigated the in-house development of a new SCM system as well as the implementation of an off the shelf solution. An attempt to purchase services to implement a more standard SCM from one of the larger companies failed for a number of reasons. The off-the-shelf SCM system was not flexible enough to meet their arduous requirements. Further, there was a lack of qualified support, and the off-the-shelf solutions available did not provide the required visibility into operations and the competitive advantage desired.

After an in-depth and costly study it was determined that the expertise to re-engineer the entire supply chain was lacking. Based on the study, the decision was made to search out a partner or partners having the necessary experience to accomplish the defined goals and objectives. As a result, Global Concepts and Transplace were chosen to focus on areas that were constraining AutoZone's supply chain.

Project Management

Program Management Organization

Global Concepts' project management approach was to form integrated teams and work together with AutoZone representatives directly involved with specific activities to solve issues. True partnerships were formed at every stage of the process. Unlike many vendors, Global Concepts' personnel are well versed in best-in-breed logistics practices, including systems support software. Global Concepts as a company is based on the belief that "*processes drive systems.*" Software products are enablers to enhance/simplify the processes; hence, their goal is to tailor the SCM system to support advanced processes to provide world-class performance. This is considered to be preferred to changing processes to match the available system support. If AutoZone processes were not solid, it was necessary to change them, but the changes needed to reflect what was best for AutoZone and not simply what any given system might provide.

Global Concepts formed two types of teams within AutoZone operations. A functional level team that dealt with the day-to-day requirements met and discussed issues on a regular basis. It consisted of subject matter experts from Global Concepts and AutoZone that worked together to implement the new SCM process. A team of senior management from Global Concepts, Transplace, and AutoZone acted as a "Steering Committee" involved in making significant decisions and keeping the project focused, on time and on budget. This approach was used at AutoZone on a grand scale because of the size and complexity of their operations.

Because AutoZone has multiple distribution centers in North America, over 3,900 stores, and extended vendors supplying over 250,000 SKU, several super users were trained. This cross-training provided redundancy within AutoZone and allowed each member of the team a break without impacting the status of the project.

Program Control

The steering committee and project managers from both Global Concepts and AutoZone were responsible for monitoring the status, timeline, and costs of the project. The project managers worked together, taking significant decisions to the steering committee for approval and keeping the steering committee posted as to status. The managers were also responsible for the quality of the implementation to ensure that the installation of the new SCM would not negatively impact DC operations.

The Critical Path Method (CPM) of project management was used to plan and track the project. Microsoft Project was employed to manage the installation as well as other project activities. An extract of the project's Gantt chart is shown in Figure C-1.

Risk Management

AutoZone was very sensitive to risk management because of past failed implementation attempts. The Global Concepts and Transplace team was tasked with being able to implement without deteriorating operations. Global Concepts met this challenging assignment by planning in three areas viewed as critical to a smooth implementation:

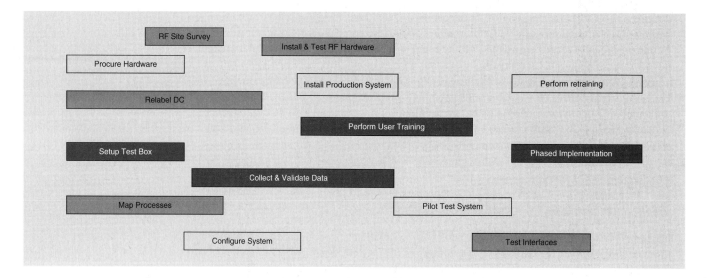

Figure C-1

Implementation Example
GANTT Chart

- Data Validation
- Enhanced Training
- Phased Implementation

The old adage "*garbage in/garbage out*" was the first hurdle to be overcome. This was addressed by creating data validation tools. Three levels of data validation are:

- Required reference data analysis
- Optional reference data analysis
- Prescriptive reference data analysis

The required reference data analysis checks over 250 different elements to ensure they are properly setup within the SCM system. If the analysis finds errors, then it reports the problems in the form of a report for the user to correct. For example, a new location is setup within the supply chain for inventory buffers. The analysis would ensure that:

- Each SKU was assigned to a location
- The location had a minimum and maximum quantity assigned
- The locations had minimum and maximum quantities that were not zero
- The locations' minimum quantity is less than the maximum
- The reserve locations had appropriate minimum or maximum quantities in the event procurement from the reserve location was needed
- Only valid SKU or acceptable substitutes are assigned to the location
- Locations are not unnecessarily duplicated in another part of the supply chain
- The location had an appropriate material storage media and internal process control
- The location was included in all SCM analysis

Such controls checked for proper SCM configurations and correct data throughout the setup phase, or whenever changes were made. The project managers continually worked to the available data using the progress of validation as a management device to quickly assess the status of the project and establish work priorities. The analysis of optional and prescriptive reference data was used to check SCM data and settings for configurable processes.

Global Concepts' experts know that no matter how well designed a system—if users are unable to make proper use of the tool its successful integration is doubtful. Therefore, rigorous training standards were put into place for every level of user:

- Production users
- Frontline supervisors
- Management
- Super users/technical support staff
- General support staff in related areas
- I.T. Training

The skills and knowledge of the production and supervisor users are key to mitigating risks during implementation. For frontline supervisors, a specialized training class called ADS (Advanced Decision Support) was developed. This class focused on the most common problems experienced when implementing a new SCM system. The goal of this class was to teach the supervisors how to use system tools to diagnose and correct problems. Production users attended training sessions specific to the functions they performed. The goal of these classes was to teach users the details of the new SCM system so that they could perform their roles following changeover. All users were required to attend training classes before they were allowed to work with any new system. Certification tests were developed for the user community in areas such as operation of the new WMS. The certification training was useful not only to verify the user's understanding but additionally to determine knowledge gaps for retraining.

The WMS test is given to each functional area. Within that area, test questions are clustered by type. To receive certification, a minimum score of 80% must be achieved. The certification test computes the final score as well as the score the user obtained for each of the functional areas within the test. For example, a supervisor taking the ADS exam may score a 90%; therefore, a passing score. However, detailed analysis of the test reveals that the person did not score as well in questions about the receiving function. This person would be retrained in that subject to improve his or her understanding in that area. Traditional certification tests would not have revealed the knowledge gap, which may have resulted in problems after implementation. Certification tests are required for all training areas, and functional knowledge retraining is conducted when warranted. While standard tests exist for many commercially available software applications, these tests should be tailored to be appropriate to specific operations.

Training alone cannot truly prepare an individual to work with unfamiliar processes and a new supporting system. Users forget things or may have gotten lucky and guessed correctly on enough questions on the certification tests. The only true test of proficiency is performance in the "line of fire." To reduce the risk associated with an ever-present learning curve inherent in process and system changes, Global Concepts used a phased approach. Phased implementation consists of turning on portions of the system while in parallel continuing to run the legacy system. This plan offers many advantages over the flash cut. A flash cut is accomplished by turning off the old system and simultaneously bringing up the new and is the process frequently used by integrators because of its simplicity. Phased implementation allows:

- "Live" testing of the interfaces at increasing volumes.
- "Live" training for the users and supervisors
- An immediate fallback in the event a serious problem does occur
- Simplification of the change management process

Phased implementation almost eliminates risk because of the safety net of having the old system available and running. Global Concepts has implemented many tools to make running both systems in parallel simple, with no impact on operations and minimal additional labor required. This approach allowed AutoZone to implement very high volume distribution centers with no impact on customer service and no drop in worker productivity while allowing critical process testing for interfaces in a low stress situation.

AutoZone used this process to implement their new DC process and system supports. The phased implementation would occur over the course of one to two months depending upon the size and complexity of the DC and its operations. The number of users also affects the length of implementation; AutoZone operated three shifts—around the clock on weekdays and weekends.

The phased approach made the implementations very smooth, greatly reduced pressure, and ensured high customer service during the transition. Anecdotal evidence of the success of this process was a call made by one DC manager to the implementation project managers. The manager called on Wednesday to ask when the DC was going completely "live" because he had not seen the implementation staff that day. In fact, the DC had gone completely live the previous Friday, but the transition was so smooth the manager was not aware it had taken place.

Change Management

Change management is a significant issue that is sometimes overlooked when installing software. The most important element of the system, people, must buy into the product to make it truly successful. AutoZone, Global Concepts, and Transplace proactively addressed this issue on a number of fronts. A side benefit of phased implementation is improved change management. Allowing the user to get hands-on experience with the new processes and system support in a real environment without the pressure associated with true production gave them the time they needed to get comfortable, and ask the necessary questions.

AutoZone senior management at a corporate level showed their commitment by touring the operations and actually learning to use many features within the software support. Global Concepts and AutoZone's management team taught many of the training classes to illustrate management's understanding and to highlight the advantages it provided AutoZone. During the training classes, Global Concepts' representatives developed relationships with users and supervisors. This led to the user community feeling as if they could ask questions and express concerns. This open-door policy allowed operations personnel, throughout the supply chain, to feel a part of the project.

Process Mapping – Obtaining AutoZone Specific Knowledge

It is a challenging task to completely document the requirements for any project. Because of AutoZone's size, complex supply chain configuration, and many requirements the process was doubly difficult. The problem was approached by addressing operations within each node of the supply chain.

Global Concepts' and Transplace's consulting experience with AutoZone positioned them to be aware of many of the day-to-day operations, and that experience allowed them to recommend proper systems support. Global Concepts also spent additional time performing detailed interviews and site visits to collect current customer information.

Appropriate subject matter experts within each area were selected from all involved companies. During the design phase of the project, teams began the process of identifying and understanding the details of AutoZone's processes and preparing the operations for implementation. Project teams consisted of logistics experts from industry and academia, and AutoZone subject matter experts. These teams analyzed each process step to determine if it was in line with the best-in-breed project objective, and if so, did the required system support the process? If the process was solid and the system could be configured to support the process, then the appropriate configuration decisions were made. If the system as proposed could not support the preferred process, then Global Concepts worked with AutoZone to determine the impact of the gaps and if enhancements were required or alternative processes were possible.

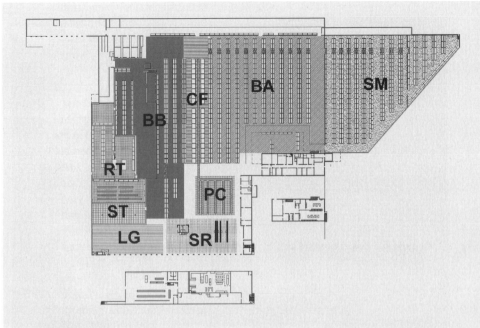

Figure C-2
DC Zone Map

RT: Returns
BB: Batch Area B
CF: Carton Flow
BA: Batch Area A
SM: Slow Moving
ST: Staging
PC: Package Consolidation
LG: Large Orders
SR: Shipping & Receiving

ZONE: The warehouse is generally a single entity, like a building. Typically, within the building there are a number of storage characteristics. For example, rows of shelves, high-bay racks, narrow aisles are some. Even more exist in those warehouses that support a manufacturing environment as well as a distribution operation.

Some areas within the facility may be either physically separated from the others, or restricted to storage of only certain products. All of these areas are called zones. Zones may be defined for a hazardous storage area, raw materials storage areas, shipping and receiving docks, production areas etc.

Each functional area was mapped, and individual configurations set for each key area. Figure C-2 illustrates a high-level zone map of a representative distribution center. This "zoning" is the first line of configuration options settings. Each different color or shading represents an area that must be distinctly configured to meet AutoZone's processes.

The close integration of both companies allowed Global Concepts to obtain the knowledge from AutoZone to gain an accurate understanding of their processes. This understanding, combined with Global Concepts' past experience and logistics expertise, positioned them to ensure that the SCM solution met AutoZone's needs.

Management Tools

System management tools as developed by Global Concepts had many features that simplified operations for AutoZone and allowed for the reduction of costs. Global Concepts uses an approach called, "Control Tower." Control Tower provides a graphical display of all of the critical work within the SCM allowing complete visibility of inventory, orders, people, and vehicles. The physical AutoZone Control Tower is illustrated in Figure C-3.

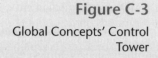

Figure C-3

Global Concepts' Control
Tower

Control tower is a bank of monitors powered by a single PC that displays the critical processes in real time. A single person operates this station. For AutoZone this single process overseer saved nearly $400,000 dollars in middle management salaries because of the visibility, decision support and control capability of the Control Tower.

Global Concepts' approach to provide such detailed visibility allowed AutoZone to reduce its management structure significantly. Prior to implementation, AutoZone had a distribution center manager at each of its sites. When installed, Control Tower's increased visibility into the operations reduced this level of management needed and subsequently AutoZone reduced staff to two managers for all distribution centers in the system. Their roles remain unchanged but with Global's and Transplace's advanced tools they can accomplish the same work with much less effort and without being onsite.

Metrics Advantages

At AutoZone, Global Concept's designed systems collect a tremendous amount of data. Data is a useful management tool only if its analysis is quick and provides a true view of operations. To assist managers, Global Concepts created an application called Metrics Advantages (MA). MA summarizes all of the raw data from the LE into useful formats that managers can use to improve operations. All of the data is statistically analyzed to make sure it is statistically significant, and is not swayed by outliers. MA contains all of the summarized information, while LE contains the actual real-time information.

MA tracks the progress of an AutoZone warehouse by illustrating trend analysis on the key metrics of the DC. At a high level, MA tracks the productivity, customer service, and inventory accuracy of the DC. Users can drill down to the next level of detail at the sub-zone level and operational levels, e.g., picking, receiving and still further into individual data elements.

AutoZone uses the data MA provides to address many issues. First, AutoZone management uses it to track the key metrics for their DC. They can tell how well the DC is performing over time and take steps to improve performance. AutoZone's engineering group uses MA to benchmark the operations of each of its eight warehouses. If it is noticed that one warehouse is better than another, a root cause analysis will attempt to bring the other warehouses to the same level by implementing the improvements. Before MA, this benchmarking was not possible because the level of detail was not available, and it was too expensive to perform the work by traveling to each site. The third area where AutoZone uses MA is for a labor management system.

MA summarizes all the work performed within the LE and reports it on an individual level. This allows managers to see which employees are performing well. AutoZone does not use MA as a true-engineered labor management system with defined standards. For dedicated workers that perform the same function every day it would be possible; however, many of AutoZone's workers have flexible assignments. Engineered labor standards tend to penalize these people for being flexible (they are AutoZone's best people), and attempting to create realistic goals is extremely difficult. AutoZone's employees also do much work outside the system that is difficult to track. They do use the system to make sure people are working. On a recent visit to AutoZone, management was able to identify two orders that had been shipped short. Drilling down into the detail, they realized that two new employees in the back of the warehouse had not been working because they picked only a few items for the entire night. They were able to take action with documented details, and correct the problem almost immediately.

Summary

Graphical representations in Figures C-4, C-5 and C-6 (all in the AutoZone Appendix) summarize financial results.

References

3PL describes third-party logistics providers. 3PL organizations provide services which are not part of the core competency of the business owner. Such services might include one or more of the following: distribution, transportation, and warehousing. 3PL/4PL refers to third-parties that offer expanded services such as customization, re-packaging, and minor-levels of assembly.

Review Questions

1 What are the major contributions of Global Concepts to managing the AutoZone supply chain?
2 What is phased implementation?
3 What is flash cut implementation?
4 What are the pros and cons of "phased" as compared to "flash cut" implementation?
5 What are the advantages of the Global Concepts' Control Tower?

Appendix

Figure C-4

➤ Increased throughput 200%

➤ Decreased labor costs 20%

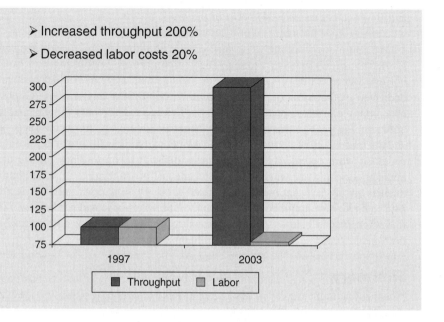

Figure C-5

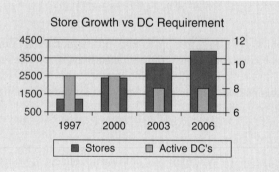

Figure C-6

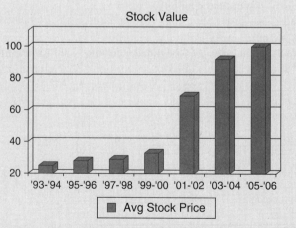

Source: Developed by the GCI team. April, 2006 through October, 2007. Correspondence with Don Stuart and his team over the same dates; *Arkansas Business* (*The States Business Weekly*), by Jeffrey Wood, "Global Going National with Software Rollout," April 21–27, 2003, Volume 20, Number 16.

One Tail Area and Critical Values of the Standard Normal Distribution (z)

Table A-1
Normal Distribution Table

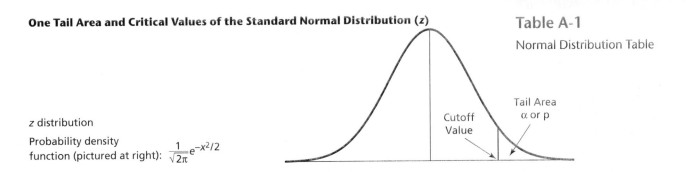

z distribution

Probability density
function (pictured at right): $\frac{1}{\sqrt{2\pi}}e^{-x^2/2}$

Cutoff Value

Tail Area
α or p

z	0.00	0.01	0.02	0.03	0.04	0.05	0.06	0.07	0.08	0.09
0.0	0.5	0.4960	0.4920	0.4880	0.4840	0.4801	0.4761	0.4721	0.4681	0.4641
0.1	0.4602	0.4562	0.4522	0.4483	0.4443	0.4404	0.4364	0.4325	0.4286	0.4247
0.2	0.4207	0.4168	0.4129	0.4090	0.4052	0.4013	0.3974	0.3936	0.3897	0.3859
0.3	0.3821	0.3783	0.3745	0.3707	0.3669	0.3632	0.3594	0.3557	0.3520	0.3483
0.4	0.3446	0.3409	0.3372	0.3336	0.3300	0.3264	0.3228	0.3192	0.3156	0.3121
0.5	0.3085	0.3050	0.3015	0.2981	0.2946	0.2912	0.2877	0.2843	0.2810	0.2776
0.6	0.2743	0.2709	0.2676	0.2643	0.2611	0.2578	0.2546	0.2514	0.2483	0.2451
0.7	0.2420	0.2389	0.2358	0.2327	0.2296	0.2266	0.2236	0.2206	0.2177	0.2148
0.8	0.2119	0.2090	0.2061	0.2033	0.2005	0.1977	0.1949	0.1922	0.1894	0.1867
0.9	0.1841	0.1814	0.1788	0.1762	0.1736	0.1711	0.1685	0.1660	0.1635	0.1611
1.0	0.1587	0.1562	0.1539	0.1515	0.1492	0.1469	0.1446	0.1423	0.1401	0.1379
1.1	0.1357	0.1335	0.1314	0.1292	0.1271	0.1251	0.1230	0.1210	0.1190	0.1170
1.2	0.1151	0.1131	0.1112	0.1093	0.1075	0.1056	0.1038	0.1020	0.1003	0.0985
1.3	0.0968	0.0951	0.0934	0.0918	0.0901	0.0885	0.0869	0.0853	0.0838	0.0823
1.4	0.0808	0.0793	0.0778	0.0764	0.0749	0.0735	0.0721	0.0708	0.0694	0.0681
1.5	0.0668	0.0655	0.0643	0.0630	0.0618	0.0606	0.0594	0.0582	0.0571	0.0559
1.6	0.0548	0.0537	0.0526	0.0516	0.0505	0.0495	0.0485	0.0475	0.0465	0.0455
1.7	0.0446	0.0436	0.0427	0.0418	0.0409	0.0401	0.0392	0.0384	0.0375	0.0367
1.8	0.0359	0.0351	0.0344	0.0336	0.0329	0.0322	0.0314	0.0307	0.0301	0.0294
1.9	0.0287	0.0281	0.0274	0.0268	0.0262	0.0256	0.0250	0.0244	0.0239	0.0233
2.0	0.0228	0.0222	0.0217	0.0212	0.0207	0.0202	0.0197	0.0192	0.0188	0.0183
2.1	0.0179	0.0174	0.0170	0.0166	0.0162	0.0158	0.0154	0.0150	0.0146	0.0143
2.2	0.0139	0.0136	0.0132	0.0129	0.0125	0.0122	0.0119	0.0116	0.0113	0.0110
2.3	0.0107	0.0104	0.0102	0.0099	0.0096	0.0094	0.0091	0.0089	0.0087	0.0084
2.4	0.0082	0.0080	0.0078	0.0075	0.0073	0.0071	0.0069	0.0068	0.0066	0.0064
2.5	0.0062	0.0060	0.0059	0.0057	0.0055	0.0054	0.0052	0.0051	0.0049	0.0048
2.6	0.0047	0.0045	0.0044	0.0043	0.0041	0.0040	0.0039	0.0038	0.0037	0.0036
2.7	0.0035	0.0034	0.0033	0.0032	0.0031	0.0030	0.0029	0.0028	0.0027	0.0026
2.8	0.0026	0.0025	0.0024	0.0023	0.0023	0.0022	0.0021	0.0021	0.0020	0.0019
2.9	0.0019	0.0018	0.0018	0.0017	0.0016	0.0016	0.0015	0.0015	0.0014	0.0014

z	0.0	0.1	0.2	0.3	0.4	0.5	0.6	0.7	0.8	0.9
3	1.35E-03	9.68E-04	6.87E-04	4.83E-04	3.37E-04	2.33E-04	1.59E-04	1.08E-04	7.23E-05	4.81E-05
4	3.17E-05	2.07E-05	1.33E-05	8.54E-06	5.41E-06	3.40E-06	2.11E-06	1.30E-06	7.93E-07	4.79E-07
5	2.87E-07	1.70E-07	9.96E-08	5.79E-08	3.33E-08	1.90E-08	1.07E-08	5.99E-09	3.32E-09	1.82E-09
6	9.87E-10	5.30E-10	2.82E-10	1.49E-10	7.77E-11	4.02E-11	2.06E-11	1.04E-11	5.23E-12	2.60E-12

Table A-2   **Two Tail Areas and Critical Values of the Standard Normal Distribution (z)**

Normal Distribution Table

z	0.00	0.01	0.02	0.03	0.04	0.05	0.06	0.07	0.08	0.09
0.0	1	0.9920	0.9840	0.9761	0.9681	0.9601	0.9522	0.9442	0.9362	0.9283
0.1	0.9203	0.9124	0.9045	0.8966	0.8887	0.8808	0.8729	0.8650	0.8572	0.8493
0.2	0.8415	0.8337	0.8259	0.8181	0.8103	0.8026	0.7949	0.7872	0.7795	0.7718
0.3	0.7642	0.7566	0.7490	0.7414	0.7339	0.7263	0.7188	0.7114	0.7039	0.6965
0.4	0.6892	0.6818	0.6745	0.6672	0.6599	0.6527	0.6455	0.6384	0.6312	0.6241
0.5	0.6171	0.6101	0.6031	0.5961	0.5892	0.5823	0.5755	0.5687	0.5619	0.5552
0.6	0.5485	0.5419	0.5353	0.5287	0.5222	0.5157	0.5093	0.5029	0.4965	0.4902
0.7	0.4839	0.4777	0.4715	0.4654	0.4593	0.4533	0.4473	0.4413	0.4354	0.4295
0.8	0.4237	0.4179	0.4122	0.4065	0.4009	0.3953	0.3898	0.3843	0.3789	0.3735
0.9	0.3681	0.3628	0.3576	0.3524	0.3472	0.3421	0.3371	0.3320	0.3271	0.3222
1.0	0.3173	0.3125	0.3077	0.3030	0.2983	0.2937	0.2891	0.2846	0.2801	0.2757
1.1	0.2713	0.2670	0.2627	0.2585	0.2543	0.2501	0.2460	0.2420	0.2380	0.2340
1.2	0.2301	0.2263	0.2225	0.2187	0.2150	0.2113	0.2077	0.2041	0.2005	0.1971
1.3	0.1936	0.1902	0.1868	0.1835	0.1802	0.1770	0.1738	0.1707	0.1676	0.1645
1.4	0.1615	0.1585	0.1556	0.1527	0.1499	0.1471	0.1443	0.1416	0.1389	0.1362
1.5	0.1336	0.1310	0.1285	0.1260	0.1236	0.1211	0.1188	0.1164	0.1141	0.1118
1.6	0.1096	0.1074	0.1052	0.1031	0.1010	0.0989	0.0969	0.0949	0.0930	0.0910
1.7	0.0891	0.0873	0.0854	0.0836	0.0819	0.0801	0.0784	0.0767	0.0751	0.0735
1.8	0.0719	0.0703	0.0688	0.0672	0.0658	0.0643	0.0629	0.0615	0.0601	0.0588
1.9	0.0574	0.0561	0.0549	0.0536	0.0524	0.0512	0.0500	0.0488	0.0477	0.0466
2.0	0.0455	0.0444	0.0434	0.0424	0.0414	0.0404	0.0394	0.0385	0.0375	0.0366
2.1	0.0357	0.0349	0.0340	0.0332	0.0324	0.0316	0.0308	0.0300	0.0293	0.0285
2.2	0.0278	0.0271	0.0264	0.0257	0.0251	0.0244	0.0238	0.0232	0.0226	0.0220
2.3	0.0214	0.0209	0.0203	0.0198	0.0193	0.0188	0.0183	0.0178	0.0173	0.0168
2.4	0.0164	0.0160	0.0155	0.0151	0.0147	0.0143	0.0139	0.0135	0.0131	0.0128
2.5	0.0124	0.0121	0.0117	0.0114	0.0111	0.0108	0.0105	0.0102	0.0099	0.0096
2.6	0.0093	0.0091	0.0088	0.0085	0.0083	0.0080	0.0078	0.0076	0.0074	0.0071
2.7	0.0069	0.0067	0.0065	0.0063	0.0061	0.0060	0.0058	0.0056	0.0054	0.0053
2.8	0.0051	0.0050	0.0048	0.0047	0.0045	0.0044	0.0042	0.0041	0.0040	0.0039
2.9	0.0037	0.0036	0.0035	0.0034	0.0033	0.0032	0.0031	0.0030	0.0029	0.0028

z	0.0	0.1	0.2	0.3	0.4	0.5	0.6	0.7	0.8	0.9
3	2.70E-03	1.94E-03	1.37E-03	9.67E-04	6.74E-04	4.65E-04	3.18E-04	2.16E-04	1.45E-04	9.62E-05
4	6.33E-05	4.13E-05	2.67E-05	1.71E-05	1.08E-05	6.80E-06	4.22E-06	2.60E-06	1.59E-06	9.58E-07
5	5.73E-07	3.40E-07	1.99E-07	1.16E-07	6.66E-08	3.80E-08	2.14E-08	1.20E-08	6.63E-09	3.64E-09
6	1.97E-09	1.06E-09	5.65E-10	2.98E-10	1.55E-10	8.03E-11	4.11E-11	2.08E-11	1.05E-11	5.20E-12

Capital Letter	Small Letter	Name	English Translitration
A	α	Alpha	a
B	β	Beta	b
Γ	γ	Gamma	g
Δ	δ	Delta	d
E	ε	Epsilon	e
Z	ζ	Zeta	z
H	η	Eta	e, $\bar{e}$
Θ	θ	Theta	th
I	ι	Iota	i
K	κ	Kappa	k
Λ	λ	Lambda	l
M	μ	Mu	m
N	ν	Nu	n
Ξ	ξ	Xi	x
O	o	Omicron	o
Π	π	Pi	p
P	ρ	Rho	r
Σ	σ	Sigma	s
T	τ	Tau	t
Y	υ	Upsilon	u, y
Φ	φ	Phi	ph
X	χ	Chi	ch
Ψ	ψ	Psi	ps
Ω	ω	Omega	o, $\bar{o}$

Table A-3

The Greek Alphabet

Source: Adapted from Fred M. Feinberg, Thomas C. Kinnear, and James R. Taylor. *Modern Marketing Research: Concepts, Methods and Cases.* Cengage Learning, 2008.

Glossary

20:80 rule: Twenty percent of the total number of problems (complaints) that have been checked off (on the data check sheet) are likely to occur 80 percent of the time. Pareto charts call attention to these high-frequency events. It is often necessary to separate the critical minority of complaints from the inconsequential majority. Call-A-Nurse is constantly faced with sorting out the requests for advice about health problems that are not life threatening (but frequent) from the few that are critical life or death matters requiring immediate hospital emergency room attention. The quality issues in this instance demand great diagnostic abilities being exercised over the phone.

ABC classification: Materials purchased for use by P/OM processes can be classified by their importance in several ways. For one of these ways, see **Criticality**. The most widely used ABC classification of inventory is by dollar volume, which drives cash flow "in" and "out." ABC classifies inventory items in rank order by dollar volume. Generally, 25 percent of *all* items (SKUs) contribute 75 percent of *total* dollar volume. These are called A-type SKU. That means 75 percent of *all* items (SKU) represent only 25 percent of the *total* dollar volume. These are called B- and C-types, which although labeled the *insignificant many*, for some purposes they are hardly trivial. ABC relationships do bring awareness to materials management of the critical importance of the few. The ABC contribution to production methods is attributed to Del Harder of the Ford Motor Company.

Acceptance sampling: Inspecting acceptability of suppliers' shipments by using sampling of required qualities instead of 100 percent inspection. The sampling plan is a statistical method for estimating the probability of accepting a production batch (many units) by sampling a small number of units from the batch. If a certain number of defectives are found in the sample, the batch will be rejected because of the statistical relationship of defectives in the sample to defectives in the batch. Statistical design of acceptance sampling plans requires knowledge of how these parameters relate to the average percent defectives in the batches.

Acceptance sampling methods: Set the inspection parameters for drawing a sample from a production lot. If the sample fails to pass the test because it has too many defectives, then the entire lot is inspected. Defectives are removed, which is called *detailing*. The result is a defect-free lot. If the sample passes the test, there may be some defectives according to the design of the test. Acceptance sampling assumes that the production process is stable.

Action learning: (1) A training technique that rotates employees through a variety of jobs in pursuit of broader understanding of the company's goals and methods. Action learning is a systems-oriented pedagogical method. For example, marketing managers are assigned to machines on the plant floor, and production managers are asked to collect market research data at local supermarkets. When purchasing is switched to accounting and human resource managers are assigned to purchasing, remarkable insights can develop. (2) Trading jobs for a period of time allows one to stand in the other's shoes and encourages systems-wide thinking. Action learning spurs team building and has the advantage of role-playing for more than a few minutes. Companies that use action learning are at the training forefront because it seems disruptive to managers who want to maintain the status quo.

Activities-on-arrows (AOA): Also known as activities-on-arcs, the project network is structured with numbered node circles connected by arrows. The project activities are the connecting arrows. They start with one numbered node and end with the other node. Sometimes more than one activity (arrow) converges at a node (use the forward pass rule) or more than one activity (arrow) leaves a node (use the backward pass rule). See **Activities-on-nodes, Backward pass rule,** and **Forward pass rule.**

Activities-on-nodes (AON): The project network is structured with numbered node circles connected by arrows. The numbered nodes are the project activities. Arrows between nodes show the precedence of activities. Project software can be read easily as AON, but forward and backward pass computations require AOA concepts. See **Activities-on-arrows, Backward pass rule**, and **Forward pass rule**.

Activity-based accounting: See **Activity-based costing (ABC) systems.**

Activity-based costing (ABC) systems: Replaces traditional, volume-driven cost accounting methods with expenses only for resources actually used by the production system. ABC systems make clear the labor costs that would not have been incurred if the job had not been done. These costs must be incurred when the job is done. Further, ABC makes evident the labor costs that would have occurred whether or not the job is done. These costs are divided into used and unused portions. ABC can be credited with raising awareness about making cost allocations that are representative of the actual labor and materials that an activity uses.

Actual capacity: The realistic maximum amount of storage space or output rate that can be achieved with the existing configuration of resources and the accepted product or service mix plans. Strategic planners know that decisions about capacity are among the most important P/OM activities. In the hierarchy of capacity measurement, volume and volume flow rates trump measures of area and length. Capacity breakeven area relates to the number of tables in a restaurant that are allowed and can be serviced. Linear capacity relates to the number of cars that can travel on a 4-lane highway. Capacity of an elevator or a swimming pool is a volumetric concept. Similarly, the actual capacity of a warehouse might be stated as the number of cubic feet the warehouse holds. The ultimate measure of the production system is its actual throughput capacity—the number of units that the P/OM system can produce and ship. Engineers design systems with theoretical flow specifications that assume everything works perfectly. P/OM deals with the fact that nothing works perfectly all of the time. Actual capacity is the realistic interpretation of the theoretical maximum capacity.

Aggregate planning (AP): The specific purpose of AP is to schedule production for the job shop. When there are a variety of machines and workers with (some) crossover capabilities, it is essential to develop a set of common denominators (e.g., standard hours). Then, resources can be grouped and schedules developed for jobs to be done. Resource utilization (e.g., second shift and/or overtime) affect job completion times. Specifically, different job–machine combinations are transformed into standard hours of supply and demand. Standard hours of supply are measured by the output of a designated standard machine. Aggregate planning converts strategic *company plans* into *production plans*, which then lead to the tactical determination of production schedules. See **Standard units.**

Agile manufacturing: Term applied to an organization that can change tactics (including process details) and strategies (including process types) rapidly when necessary because of competitive, technological and situational changes.

Analytic process: A production process that starts with one ingredient. Using appropriate transformation techniques, the process turns a single, basic ingredient into several or (even) many products. For example, cabbage can be transformed into coleslaw, sauerkraut, and the cabbage that goes with corn beef. Also, some single basic ingredients, SBI's, can be taken apart for various uses, e.g., cream and milk. Further, analytic processes can start with a few rather than only one basic ingredient.

Analytic reduction: The systems approach (called *introspection*) employs analytic reduction of a system into its parts to scrutinize the behavior of components and to determine their fundamental characteristics. This approach epitomizes *the sciences*.

Artificial intelligence (AI):   Based on copying the nervous system of human beings to develop mechanisms that have the capability of sensing and learning. More broadly, aimed at understanding the nature of intelligence, including the ability to compute, remember, and to make good decisions. The purpose is to engineer systems analogous to neural networks that exhibit such intelligence.

Assemble-to-order (ATO) environment: Setting where end-items are built from subassemblies. Master production schedules ensure that the subassemblies are available to meet demand within promised due dates. Fabrication of parts takes place off-line. Common to computers and cell phone assembly. Contrast with **make-to-stock (MTS)** and **make-to-order (MTO).** Heavy equipment industry prefers to use ATO; however, market realities and competitive actions have created need for inventories of finished goods for many (standard) types of equipment.

Assignable causes: Identifiable causes of process problems that create variability. They are traceable and can be removed. This is in contrast to chance causes. Also called *special causes*, methods of statistical quality control are aimed at identifying and removing them to reduce variability. The aim is for only chance cause variability to remain.

Assignment method: A decision model for matching n resources with n resource users. Examples of assignment problems are legion: how to assign n jobs requiring various skills to n workers possessing various skills. Assign managers to stores, boats to slips, horses to starting positions, etc. The method provides the *best* assignment where *best* can be lowest total cost, highest total revenue or profit, and greatest total satisfaction. The square matrix epitomizes the constraint of no splitting of a resource between users and no sharing of several resources by any one user. The method minimizes the sum of the opportunity costs. See **Opportunity cost.**

Autocorrelation: Term applied to a time series that is correlated with itself with a specific time-shift. For humans, conception and birth are well-correlated, but not perfectly, with a 9-month lead time.

Average performance: There are various uses for the phrase. One applies to performance evaluation where judgment of the evaluator is that performance is average. A more specific meaning is associated with time studies where many observations are taken by an observer using a stopwatch or by a computer timing operations. Sum N numbers and divide by N to obtain average performance (or average time), which is then adjusted to obtain productivity standards.

Backordering: Because stock to fill the order is lacking, delivery is deferred until a later time when inventory levels permit fulfillment.

Backward pass rule: Also known as the backward convergence rule, it is similar and opposite to the forward pass (or convergence) rule. The backward pass rule: When two or more arrows emanate from a single node, choose the arrow with the smallest value of the latest start time. The backward pass rule enables the critical path to be identified. It also permits the determination of slack. Taken together with the forward pass rule, the fundamental parameters of the project can be calculated. These calculations for the network can be manual, but for projects of realistic size, software is essential to manage the network algorithms and the information system that underlies them. For details of the methods, the text should be consulted. See **Critical path methods (CPM), Forward pass rule,** and **Slack.**

Balance delay (d):   A percentage measure of idle time across all of the workstations that participate in the complete process cycle. Perfect balance is when $d = 0$. Anything other than perfect balance delay is an assessment of the system's inefficiency. When $d > 0$, imperfect balance prevails. This equation calculates the percent of unproductive time at the total set of flow shop process stations that accounts for the process cycle time, C. Thus, $d = 100(nC - \Sigma_i t_i)/nC$ where n = number of work stations; C = cycle time; $\Sigma_i t_i$ = total work content, also called TWC; and nC = total flow shop workstation time available. Note that $nC - TWC$ = idle time across all workstations. See **Cycle time** and **Line efficiency.**

Baldrige Award: Public Law 100–107 is the Malcolm Baldrige National Quality Improvement Act signed into law on August 20, 1987, by the U.S. Congress. This award for quality management (in the sense of TQM) resulted from the fact that the United States had been sensitized to the high costs of inferior quality by Japanese successes in making automotive products within the United States.

Bar chart: Graphical method that uses bars of different lengths to present numerical and/or statistical data. For example, along the x-axis are different types of events such as various spectator sports. The height of the bars might indicate the number of people who attended each type of sport in the prior year. That number is measured along the y-axis. Bar charts are considered to be among the easiest graphical representations to understand.

Benchmark: A measure taken to provide a standard against which other measures can be made to show progress or deterioration in revenue, cost, quality, speed, value, etc. Origin: A bench mark was a surveyor's notch in a landmark of a previously determined position.

Benchmarking: (1) A method for comparing processes with one that is considered to be the best. The secret is to choose significant dimensions for comparison and then to measure those dimensions in an accurate way. Customer satisfaction is a popular benchmark with many service firms. This dimension is difficult to measure. (2) A systematic method for comparing one process with another. The idea is to use what is learned to improve. Comparing our systems with the "best" can assist the effort to emulate the leaders. It is not easy to identify leaders in similar processes. The secret is to choose significant dimensions for comparison and measure those dimensions in an accurate way. For some, the goal is to get "better than the best."

Best in class: The top choice for the benchmarking standard. It is the candidate to beat. Note the benchmarking reference to "better than the best." It fits the World Series in baseball or the Super Bowl in football.

Best location: Location, location, location ... what are they talking about? This answer is based on pragmatic (observed) information: A *necessary* but *not sufficient* condition for success in business is to get the right location. The right (or best) location is defined by the function of the facility and the characteristics of its products and services. For example, in the retail business, best locations generate high-contact frequencies with "potential customers." Location is best when it is specially tailored to the particulars of the situation, e.g., close to the market, near suppliers, able to draw on highly skilled work pools, facilitates joining about 12,000 other maquiladoras (U.S. and others-owned and operated assembly factories located along the 2,100 mile border that separates Mexico and the United States, employing over 1 million workers). See http://www.uwec.edu/geography/Ivogeler/w188/border/maquil.htm. A popular alternative: Be in Beijing.

Best practice: A process standard based on identifying those who perform the process in the best way yet known. Benchmarking should set best practice as the standard for comparison.

Bidding: Provides the appearance (and allows the reality) of purchasing decisions that are not influenced by donations or outright gifts. Suppliers meet specifications, including costs and delivery dates, and the buyer chooses the offer that is preferred. Selection includes many factors, including vendor reliability. Quality can suffer from buying on price alone. Government requirements often specify the manner in which bidding is to be conducted, including number of bidders.

Bill of material (BOM): Describes in detail what constitutes the end product. One of three inputs to the MRP information system, viz., MPS, IRF, and BOM. For a dinner party, it is the cook's shopping list. BOM lists all of the subassemblies, parts, and raw materials that go into a parent assembly showing the quantities required. A variety of display formats for BOM exist, including single-level, indented, modular, transient, matrix form, and "costed" bill. It is called the "formula, "recipe," or "list of ingredients" in some industries.

Bill of resources (BOR): Lists the key resources needed to make a unit of a specific SKU or various selected SKUs (or a family of items, as in group technology). Resource requirements are identified with a lead time to show the impact of requirements on resource availability. The BOR is also called the *bill of capacity* and the *product load profile*.

Bottlenecks: Well described by the narrowing of the bottle's neck, which constricts the flow of output. In production terms, the slowest machine in the line sets the pace of the process. When the throughput rate of the bottleneck is exceeded, a waiting line or queue starts to develop.

Breakeven: In casual discussion, breakeven connotes the fact that enough units of product were sold to offset the costs and begin to make a profit. Airlines talk about their load factor, which is the percent of total seats filled. For example, U.K. carrier easyJet reported that from 2001 to 2002 their load factor increased from 82.6 percent to 85.9 percent. The breakeven load factor is dependent upon the type of aircraft; its fuel efficiency; other operating costs, including food and crew salaries; length of flight; and ticket prices (including discounts for revenue management). Every system has the goal of operating at volume levels above breakeven. The more above the BEP, the better.

Breakeven point (BEP): The sales volume point at which total costs exactly equal revenues. Profit is zero. Then, as sales volume increases, profit > 0. Models of breakeven are at the crux of capacity decisions. With overcapacity, it takes patience to grow the business to breakeven and beyond. Undercapacity may mean that the breakeven point cannot be reached until the company expands its capacity. Attention must be paid to the forecast probabilities that supply volumes to meet demand will be above or below the BEP. Decision modeling combines the location of the BEP and the slope of the profit-loss line to permit selection of the optimal process.

Breakpoint business process redesign: Finding strategic-level competitive advantages in the areas of the company's core business processes. Breakthroughs at that level become core competencies of the organization. These innovations will have the greatest impact on the customers and shareholders of the firm. Competency-based competition is almost always related to P/OM. An important variant of reengineering.

Buffer stock: Additional stock carried to prevent outages arising from demand exceeding expectations. The forecast is for the expected stock requirements. Buffer stock (BS) is held in inventory just in case the demand is above the forecast. Also called safety stock, these extra units can also be called upon when lead time for deliveries is greater than had been anticipated. Overall protection against the effects of variability on supply.

Build: Alternatives to "build a new facility" would be either "rent" or "buy." There are many examples of "buy, tear down, and rebuild." This choice is needed when undeveloped land is not available in the right location.

Buy: Make a list of all potential sites and buildings. Then, do a rent or buy (and build) analysis. See **Build** and **Rent.**

c-chart: Control chart for multiple numbers of defectives in a single unit. For all control charts, there is an upper-control limit and a lower-control limit around a process average. With c-charts the process average is for the number of defects found per unit. For example, mail order catalogues have printing-run defects that can be counted. Before the presses are set up to do a final run, it is useful to take a pilot-run sample. Using the pilot-run sample, create the c-chart and provide good SQC analysis to see if the process is stable (under control).

Capabilities: Capabilities-based strategies are reflected in management of business processes, for example, production scheduling and inventory management. Core competency-based strategies are applied to management of process technologies, for example, large, laminated glass windshields.

Capacity: There are two basic types of capacity. One is storage space and the other is throughput flow rates. Mental capacity is not part of this treatise. Storage capacity is exemplified by "maximum loading" for the school auditorium. That is a measure of how many people are permitted to be seated at one time in a given square area by the fire department. In contrast, warehouse storage space is often volumetric because products can be piled to the roof. The two storage examples differ because of the way that each facility is filled and emptied. Dynamic capacity measures relate to the flow rate of liquid through pipes and product output from the production process. Flow shop throughput rates reflect cycle time, C. For any particular job, C is a function of the number of workstations.

Capacity requirements planning (CRP): (1) This is an extension of MRP. It is necessary to readjust capacity when the MRP system delivers a plan that is not feasible because of capacity limitations. CRP is the process of determining how much labor, equipment, and facilities resources are needed to fulfill the production schedule. Open shop orders and planned orders in the MRP system are input to CRP, which is the function that establishes, measures, and adjusts levels of capacity. (2) There are two aspects to CRP. First is strategic. Second is tactical. Section 10-2c differentiates between strategic and tactical issues of CRP. The strategic issues relate to long-term planning for capacity including breakeven points and optimal allocation of resources. Shorter-term tactical issues are related to materials requirements planning (see MRP in Chapter 15).

Capital productivity: A partial accounting for productivity that is due to invested capital. The output divided by the input model prevails in two ways. First is units produced per dollar of capital. Second is dollar value of units produced per dollar of capital. The measures are taken over successive periods of time.

Cash flow: The amount of cash being received as revenue (input) and spent (as output) to meet business obligations over a specific period of time. Positive cash flow occurs when input is greater than output (say, in the third quarter). Negative cash flow is the reverse situation. While both occur in normal circumstances, the negative cash flow case can result in foreclosure and bankruptcy.

Cause and effect charts: Organize and illustrate what causes quality problems. All factors that impinge on quality are listed in a hierarchy of categories and subcategories. These are conveniently illustrated by the fishbone diagram developed by Ishikawa. The figure is also known by his name. The key to understanding quality achievement is developed by this taxonomical method that identifies classes and subclasses of the variables responsible for variability in the finished product or service.

CDC: Centers for Disease Control and Prevention, located in Atlanta, Georgia. CDC is an agency of the Department of Health and Human Services of the U.S. government. It is the lead federal agency for protecting the health and safety of people—at home and abroad. CDC provides credible information to enhance health decisions. CDC serves as the national focus for developing and applying disease prevention and control, environmental health, and health promotion and education activities. CDC has responsibilities that are new and not well-defined since the potential of bioterrorism has emerged as a global threat. The operational issues that CDC faces are of substantial interest to P/OM. For the latest health and safety information, consult http://www.cdc.gov.

Centroid location method: Using the mean weighted values of x and y for a set of locations, determine the best location for a central distribution point (center of mass).

Certification of suppliers: Process of grading (pass–fail) suppliers to assure conformance to standards set as necessary by P/OM. The factors required include quality assurances, delivery performance, product improvement, cost control, and reliability as a partner. See Enrichment Activity 12, page 507.

Chance causes: See **Assignable causes.**

Change management: Managing modification of the transformation process, including the inputs and the outputs, is a major challenge and opportunity in the rapidly changing environment of business. Alterations are required to maintain market status and financial well-being. Change management increases the capabilities and competencies of the firm. See **Capabilities** and **Reengineering.**

Change management projects (α): This term refers to the management of change, which requires planning, designing, building, testing, redesigning, and implementing the system. These are project management responsibilities. It is important to clarify the differences between project management and process management as to purpose and procedures. See **Control management processes (β).**

Changeovers: The steps that need to be taken to prepare equipment and people to do a new job. The term *setup* refers to the start-up of a new job. *Take down* is cleanup and put away from an old job. Taken together they create the chain of events for change-over. Refer to economies of scope and check SMED for fast changeovers.

Chasing policy: This policy, or strategy, of chasing demand is based on a total cost structure that rewards matching market demand. The firm has to be able to produce variable amounts of work so that supply can correspond to demand. Production output increases to match above-average demand. It slows down to match below-average demand. To justify the chasing strategy, the sum of costs of a variable workforce and underutilized equipment should be less than the sum of costs of reducing overstocks and eliminating backorders. The idea of chasing someone is to follow them and to catch up with them. In inventory terms, catching up may not occur. Instead, the chase is continual with the goal of getting as close as possible in matching supply and demand. Rarely will the match be exact. See **Constant production strategy.**

Classification by attributes: Units are classified as accepted or rejected, e.g., it is too heavy for the delivery system.

Classification by variables: Variables like weight can be measured on a continuous scale.

Closed-loop MRP: A system built around MRP that connects the planning functions of sales and operations. Closed-loop signifies that feedback prevails at many levels, and over time, for planning and replanning shop scheduling, supplier scheduling, capacity requirements, and sales strategies. MRP becomes more powerful with the addition of the closed-loop planning adjustment system, as it moves toward MRP II.

Coding: After parent products have had their parts explosion accomplished, coding provides a means of identifying the fact that some parts are required by more than one parent. The MRP must combine the demand of commonly shared parts. Coding captures that and other relevant information about parts, such as certified suppliers, storage locations, and acceptable substitutes. Coding of part names is the foundation for effective information systems linking components and parents together.

Compensating for defectives: More defectives are produced at start-up than later on in the production of a specific batch of units. Because of start-up defectives, to ship the ordered quantity, produce more than the order size. The compensation can be a substantial percentage of the order size if the batch size is small, job setup is complicated, and the worker's learning curve is slow to achieve the standard production rate.

Computer-aided design (CAD): Design done by software that creates drawings for any product or structure that normally requires graphic communication for implementation. CAD also provides test procedures to determine if quality and structural goals can be achieved.

Computer-aided manufacturing (CAM): Manufacturing done by software that is in communication with the CAD programming. CAD communicates the design specifications to the CAM software, which translates the specs into instructions and controls for the production machinery. CAD and CAM work together to determine the feasibility of manufacturing the new design and suggest improved design alternatives.

Computer-aided process planning (CAPP): The application of computer software to organize and evaluate the performance of a process. This includes scheduling production and determining resource requirements. Factory floor simulations allow alternatives to be tested in pursuit of continual improvement.

Concurrent engineering (CE): Parallel and simultaneous work along many project paths is supported and encouraged. CE employs more resources early in the project's evolution. CE uses a team-oriented framework. Faster completion as compared to the traditional sequential-compartmentalized, engineering method of project management. Not only are there time-based management (TBM) advantages, but there are also quality improvements arising from team contributions made at the start, before commitments are made that lead to irreversible operations. Has been called *simultaneous engineering.*

Conflict resolution: Disputes impair team performance. Until disputes can be resolved by management, interpersonal team problems will damage organizational performance. Conflict resolution, based on empirical studies, has led to the development of methodology that can be used to settle disagreements. Teams reach many decisions that can include wage determinations for members. Before wage determination by teams is used, conflict resolution skills must be developed by management.

Constant production strategy: The workforce is maintained to produce a *constant level of output,* called k. To achieve this, hiring and training are only for replacement, which occurs because employees stop working of their own accord. There is no plan to reduce the workforce. To justify the constant production strategy, the sum of costs associated with a constant workforce must be less than the sum of costs associated with a variable workforce. Spelling this out, the summed costs of carrying inventory when demand is less than k, or of lost orders and backorders when demand is more than k, should be less than the sum of costs of a variable workforce and underutilized equipment. See **Chasing policy.**

Constraints, Theory of: The theory of constraints, developed by Eliyahu Goldratt, describes a production scheduling system that optimizes overall performance (throughput) by recognizing constraints and minimizing their deleterious effects. The synchronized production system was called OPT, but theory of constraints (TOC) is now preferred terminology.

Constructive: The constructive approach (of systematic thinking) is characteristic of engineering science's creative design of systems for practical purposes.

Continuity: Related to continuous project development. Continuity refers to project teams that upon completing a project, or even during the activities of a project, begin another project. Multiple project participation, if configured properly, has the benefit of not dissipating project skills and knowledge. Traditional breakup of the project group at completion can impose penalties associated with the question, "Why reinvent the wheel?" Continuity also refers to the use of project teams in different parts of the world. Project activity progresses as it *follows the sun*; part of the team will always be awake. Transnational companies have customer support systems (24/7) that move around the globe (Southeast Asia to Europe to North America and the Far East).

Continuous improvement (CI): One of two major approaches to accomplish planned change. Continuous improvement uses constant effort to find better ways to produce a product and deliver a service. Emphasizes conversions of existing processes. Scope is local, limited to incremental change, and persistent. Continuous improvement versus reengineering (REE), the other major approach. REE's scope is global, systems-wide, and starts from scratch. Continuous improvemtent is also called *kaizen* because many firms in the United States learned continuous improvement methodology from Japanese practitioners. Visit http://www.kaizen-training.com.

Continuous processes: Produce one product continuously; or may result from the design of analytic process flows that fan out derivative products a part of a continuous stream, e.g., petroleum refineries.

Control chart: Foundation stone graphical method of statistical quality control (SQC). Chart is based on the process average for percent defectives, with upper- and lower-control limits and plotted points of successive sample means. Control limits are distanced from the process average so that the probabilities of sample means exceeding these thresholds are preselected odds (e.g., 0.001, 0.0001) if the process is stable. The distribution from which the sample means are drawn is considered to be normal. At start-up, the control chart is expected to exhibit lack of control, meaning that more sample means exceed the control limits than is statistically warranted. The process is stabilized (brought under control) by removing assignable causes. See **Control limits.**

Control limits: See **Control chart.** Upper-control limits (UCL) and lower-control limits (LCL) are developed in different ways depending upon the type of chart being used. For x-charts, the distance of the upper and lower limits from the process average are based on the range of the measured variables (R). For p-charts, the distance of the upper and lower limits from the process average ($\bar{p}$) are based on the standard deviation associated with (p). The value of p is often determined by the definition of "defective" and the use of go/no go gauges. See **p-chart.**

Control management processes (β): This term refers to the management of existing systems, which requires operating that system, controlling the inputs, the transformation process, and the outputs. Management must shield the system from external disturbances that threaten process continuity, as well as employee, customer, and vendor security and safety. The responsibility for process management belongs to P/OM. It is important to clarify the differences between process management and project management as to purpose and procedures. See **Change management projects** (α).

Core competencies: Technical, technological, and production skills possessed by a company interacting with that company's product line. For example, in the 1920s, the Ford Motor Company used sequenced assembly. No other company understood the requirements of that production system, at that time. Wal-Mart uses cross-docking to speed inventory deliveries and minimize inventory costs. No other company understood the requirements of that logistics system at the time of its inception. It is not evident that any other company has mastered the system and can emulate it. See **Capabilities.**

Correlation coefficient: This is a measure of the relationship between two variables. High positive correlation coefficients (approaching $+1$) indicate strong positive relationships between the variables. Large negative correlation coefficients (approaching -1) indicate that as one variable grows the other diminishes.

Cost benefit: Comparison of costs and benefits that applies to alternative facility configuration decisions. The comparison is difficult to make when some of the benefits are not readily stated in dollars. Not all costs are in dollars either. There are intangible costs such as foregone preferences based on closeness to family. Cost-benefit analysis can be applied to alternative suppliers, designs of products and processes, and to managers of departments.

Cost trade-off analysis: The generic trade-off model balances the improvement in one factor against the deterioration in another as a result of changing a systems variable (such as order size). For aggregate planning, the choice between a constant workforce and varying the workforce (to match demand) is based on comparison of the total costs associated with each strategy. Many different mixtures of the two pure strategies are feasible. Each blended strategy has an associated set of costs and a unique total cost, which may be less than the total costs of either pure strategy. This trade-off model examines all options.

Costs (direct and indirect): Labor cost per unit is direct; rent cost allocated to overhead is an indirect cost.

Costs (fixed and variable): Rent costs are fixed—they do not change with output volume; material costs are variable—they increase with each additional part that is made.

Costs of failure: Failure costs are most difficult to define because they include LTV (lifetime value loss of customers' revenues), word-of-mouth negative publicity, costly court and jury liability decisions, and callback costs that frequently require extensive repairs and replacements.

Costs of quality: Costs that include (1) costs of preventing defects; (2) costs of appraisal (inspecting for defects and often removing them); and (3) the costs of failures, which can comprise costs stemming from replacement warranties, costs associated with legal actions, and costs resulting from customer dissatisfaction with the company's products.

Crash time: Project managers make the comparison between *crash* times for project completion and *normal* times. Crashing an activity means spending as much as it takes to achieve *minimum* activity time. *Normal* activity time is associated with minimum spending. COST/TIME trade-off analysis is used to determine if, when, and with what activities crash time should be used. Crashing is generally used to decrease the length of the critical path. This speeds up completion, but be wary of quality deterioration. It is often wasteful of money to crash all activities. Instead, activities on the critical path are selected to be crashed. The first selected are those activities that provide the largest decrease in project time for the least amount of investment. Crashing should not be equated with rushing, which is associated with making mistakes. Crashing should not endanger the practices of safety-first and error-free performance. See **Critical path methods (CPM)** and **Normal time.**

Critical-path methods (CPM): Project management models are made up of networks of project activities designed for optimal use of resources and monitored for progress against a specific completion date. It is especially important to track the critical path, which is the longest time-path from start to finish of the project. The critical path determines completion date of the project. Called by various names including CPM and PERT, these are all network methods that are best analyzed by computer software that keeps track of the abundance of information about schedules and progress. See **PERT, Backward pass rule**, and **Forward pass rule.**

Criticality: When part behavior causes process or product failure or a marked degradation in performance, that part is considered critical, no matter what its cost. Some items are production-critical. For want of a gasket, a refinery can be shut down. Running out of a specific bolt can stop an automobile assembly line. The shuttle cannot be launched if a critical part that malfunctions cannot be replaced. It is a judgment call as to which part has A-type criticality. Probably an office running out of paper clips would call that a C-type critical event. To Office Depot, they may be an important B-type in-stock item. However, if failure to supply paper clips causes a good customer to shift permanently to a competitor, being out of stock on paper clips may be an A-type critical failure.

Cross-docking: Wal-Mart pioneered the widespread use of this method to transfer goods from incoming trucks at receiving docks to outgoing trucks at shipping docks. These docks are adjacent. Many warehousing steps are saved, but this logistic method requires excellent communication and information about what is needed and in-charge scheduling. P/OM and IT (information technology) need to coordinate the shipments from suppliers and the demands of the stores. Stock in the trucks is pipeline inventory.

Cross-training: Permits workers to enjoy job rotation between stations of the flow shop and also between areas of specialization in the job shop. Cross-training reduces worker boredom; raises self-esteem; increases flexibility for process changeovers; provides new insights about how to improve the process; and has no downside because workers seem to like it.

Custom shop: The name for the work configuration used for products or services that are made-to-order, and usually one of a kind.

Cybernetics: Study of similarities between human brains and electronic systems. Compares the way that electronic signals are generated by information in the computer system with signals transmitted between adjacent neurons across a boundary called a synapse in the body.

Cyborg: A coined word combining "cyb" from *cybernetics* with "org" from *organism*. A form of technology that assigns people and machines to work jointly to achieve results that neither could obtain by acting alone. Pacemakers are an excellent present-day example. Embedded GPS chips to locate missing persons is around the corner.

Cycle time: The interval, C, that elapses between successive units of finished work coming off the production line. For example, if every 2 1/2 minutes a completed automobile leaves the Subaru assembly line in Lafayette, Indiana, then the cycle time for that assembly line is 2.5 minutes. Productive output rate is determined by T/C. For example, if C is in minutes and T is minutes per hour, then, T/C for Subaru is 60/2.5, which equals an output rate of 24 autos per hour. Waiting time is waste in cycle time. Failure of suppliers to deliver materials needed by the flow shop will introduce delays that increase the cycle time. Good cycle-time management is diligent to see that value-adding operations are ongoing. Proper cycle-time management develops a well-balanced process for the total work content assigned to n workstations during the cycle time. See **Time-based management (TBM).**

Cycle-Time Management (CTM): Setting and controlling the interval between product completions. Management must match demand with productive capabilities and available resources.

Cycles: Repetitive patterns of sequenced values, which generally return to the same starting point. For example, alternating current (AC) follows a sinusoidal curve. Tidal cycles repeat themselves over time with variations in amplitude according to the lunar phase. High and low tides are regular, occurring monthly. This information is published in tide tables to help sailors. Long cycles such as summer high temperatures are annual. Very long economic cycles have been hypothesized. View the 54-year Kondratieff Wave at http://www.angelfire.com/or/truthfinder/index22.html. When cycles appear to exist, forecasting must take them into account in predicting future states.

Data check sheets (DCSs): Spreadsheets can be used to count and record defectives by types and times of occurrence. Organization of the data is aimed at tracking the frequency of events that relate to process qualities. For example, hotels keep track of "room not ready" complaints by time of the year and day of the week. Analysts can apply a variety of techniques to cull information from a well-prepared DCS.

Days of inventory (DOI): Total stock on-hand divided by the average demand per day gives a measure of how long it will be before the stockroom and warehouse are empty. To derive average DOI, divide average total stock on-hand by average demand per day. DOI is directly related to turnover. If the DOI indicates that the stockroom would be empty in 12 days, then the turnover is 365/12 = 30+ days, or once a month, which is 12 times a year. Purchasing times replenishment orders so that the warehouse does not run out of stock every DOI cycle.

Decision model: Elements of decision models are specific and found whenever a decision problem exists. There are strategies, states of nature, probabilities of states of nature (forecasts for these probabilities), expected values for outcomes, and strategies chosen for delivering outcomes in line with goals and objectives. In Chapter 10, breakeven models are extended using decision models as in Enrichment Activity 10.

Demand: Units of product (goods and/or services) requested for delivery within a period of time constitute demand. Many descriptions refer to types of demand such as peak, off-peak, and average demand. "Market demand" is not a tautology because "individual, regional, and national demand" exist. "Market demand" is not "actual sales" until the product is shipped and paid for by the customers. Differences between supply and demand create market forces for producers to increase or decrease production. "Variability of demand" costs can be removed or reduced by using contracts but there is a price to be paid for reduction of uncertainty. Effective forecasting reduces the costs of demand variability. Erratic (or capricious) demand patterns are the bane of forecasters.

Demand elasticity: Relationship between the quantity of goods or services demanded by customers as a function of the price charged. Elasticity measures the rate of increase in demand as prices are lowered (or vice versa). The subject is complex. Elasticity will not be the same for different demographic groups. Rates may differ for price increases and decreases of the same amount. Two consecutive, small price increases may not have the same effect as one equivalent price increase. Kinked relationships exist where a price increase results in greater demand. Effect of quality on demand volume can be significant (see quality elasticity).

Deming: Acknowledged as the Father of the Quality Movement in Japan, Dr. W. Edwards Deming became a leader in the American quality revolution after 1980. Deming's Quality Cycle of Plan-Do-Check-Act was adopted by many companies, which sought to improve product quality to levels that had been previously rejected as too costly.

Deming Prize: Prize that has been awarded since 1951 by JUSE (Japanese Union of Scientists and Engineers). Recipients can be organizations from any country, and the award criterion is to have achieved outstanding quality performance. Florida Power and Light won the prize in 1989.

Depreciation: To depreciate the value of a truck, divide the total cost by its years of use after subtracting the resale value at the end of use. That is a rough guide to a straight-line method for determining the cost per year to charge for the truck.

Design for assembly (DFA): (1) The product is designed to be put together efficiently, meaning at minimum cost and with higher quality standards. Conscious DFA is preplanning components as well as final assemblies. This not only lowers production costs and cuts cycle times, but it also allows architectural design of the assembled building blocks. It would be asking for trouble to construct a building in which the floors, walls, and façade assemblies are not rationalized as a system until the construction crew is ready to put the building in place. Another example of the need for DFA is toys that are often purchased in knocked-down format. Parents are on the spot to show their children that they can understand the instructions (manuals are often badly written) to put the toy together. Many toys are not well-designed for assembly. The same applies to furniture assembled by the customer. These examples illustrate that DFA is not a theoretical subject of interest to manufacturers alone. Also, DFA is related to the design for disassembly. (2) P/OM acts as liaison between the product designers and the assemblers on the production line. Changes are made in both design specifications and assembly procedures to simplify assembly. Many times the discussion about DFA must bridge the space between assembly and fabrication, which unites DFA with DFM and the designers. This means greater productivity and throughput as well as cost reduction and quality improvement. See **Design for disassembly (DFD)**.

Design for automation (DFAU):   Robots can decrease assembly costs and bear the brunt of difficult work such as welding and painting with toxic materials. A component of design for assembly addresses benefits of robot assemblers for precision assembly as well. The quality and speed of assembly work increases while the cost goes down. DFA and DFD are symmetric (congruent) in the planning of put-together and take-apart. Robots are able to disassemble returned units when design for automation (DFAU) has been used. See **Design for assembly (DFA)** and **Design for disassembly (DFD)**.

Design for disassembly (DFD):   The stages are design; manufacture and ship; consumer use; and postconsumption disposal. DFD innovations can be rewarding in terms of rapid disassembly, reduction in the number of parts required, reuse (rework and remanufacture), and recycle (with safe disposal when only partial reuse is possible). Advantages accrue in many ways. For example, there is a story about the expensive car that needs four hours to disassemble the door to empty the ashtray. DFD can be a consumer benefit when repair is required. Also, reuse and rework can save a great deal of money. Society benefits when rational design decreases mountains of undesirable waste. See **Greening the environment**.

Design for manufacturing (DFM):   (1) P/OM must consider the locations chosen for fabrication in the relationship between product designers and production personnel. Plant location can be related to the technology-skills mix employed in fabrication. The degree to which labor-intensive work is employed will also be a function of plant location choices. Some manufacturing facilities will not support technology-based design for manufacturing (DFM). Equipment performance evaluation is also part of the DFM procedure. Productivity of equipment must be related to the volume of work rate required. The inherent variability of the technology must be compatible with designers' tolerances. (2) P/OM acts as liaison between the product designers and the production personnel who fabricate that part, and related parts, using various manufacturing facilities. Changes are made in both design specifications and fabrication procedures to simplify operations. Many times the discussion about DFM must bridge the space between fabrication and assembly, which unites DFM with DFA and the designers. This results in greater productivity and throughput as well as cost reduction and quality improvement.

Design tolerances: Minimum and maximum dimensions for parts that fit together for proper performance. For example, the door of a car must fit within the door opening in the auto chassis. The fit must be snug. Too tight a fit makes opening the door difficult. With a fit too loose, the door rattles. Noise (and even rain) gets into the car.

Detailing: Removing the defectives so that every item in the lot conforms to the specifications. Therefore, when detailing, the inspector separates the bad from the good.

Deterministic line balancing: Line balancing (LB) is the effort to divide total work content into equal balanced parts (of the cycle time, C) at each of n workstations. Deterministic LB is based on the assumption that the total process time for making the product is exactly the same for every unit of product that is completed. To achieve that goal, all operation times are fixed and never vary. That means that statistical distributions are not applicable to the work times. Line balancing with fixed operation times is much simpler than if work times are considered to be variable. Deterministic assumptions are valid when machinery is doing all of the work. For example, all of the functions of an automated bottling plant run at the set rate because there is no human participation. Paced conveyors are an effective means of creating deterministic process results.

Dimensions of quality: There are endless numbers of ways to enumerate the dimensions of quality. Six of the eight Garvin dimensions are a good start for tangible qualities, but the intangibles are more difficult to treat. The key point is that no form of quality can be achieved until that form is defined precisely.

Disruptive innovation: A new product property or capability that overturns established product lines and restructures the marketplace. Twenty examples are charted at the Wikipedia website http://en.wikipedia.org/wiki/Disruptive_technology.

Disruptive technology: (1) Henry Ford's sequenced assembly was a disruptive process technology. Refer to the first publication of the terminology by Bower and Christensen, "Disruptive Technologies: Catching the Wave," *Harvard Business Review* (January–February 1995). (2) Technological innovation that eventually overturns presently existing dominant technology; for example, the refrigerator replaced the ice box.

Dissatisfaction: Benchmarking is the trigger for dissatisfaction with the status quo. If a benchmark shows that another person, department, or company is better than "we" are, then "us" and "them" resentment takes over. However, dissatisfaction alone will not lead to change efforts using CI or REE. The fact that dissatisfaction (D) is greater than zero is a necessary but not sufficient condition for change as hypothesized by the Gleicher model. See **Gleicher model**.

Distribution requirements planning (DRP1):   An extension to MRP, DRP1 relates to replenishing inventory at the branch warehouses. A time-phased order point approach is used to "explode" planned orders at the branch warehouse level via MRP logic. Collectively, they become *gross requirements* for suppliers. In the case of multi-level distribution networks, the explosion process continues down through the various levels of regional warehouses that are coupled to the master warehouse, factory warehouse, etc.

Distribution resource planning (DRP2):   Related to MRP II, using broad systems perspective, additional supply chain considerations are extended to warehouses and manufacturing. DRP2 is a higher order planning system than DRP1 because it also plans resource availability such as storage space in the warehouse, trucking capacity, railroad boxcar availabilities, workforce training, etc. DRP2 operates as an extension of distribution requirements planning (DRP1) by addressing what additional resources are needed in the distribution system.

Double-sampling plans: A second sample is drawn when its use lowers the cost of inspection. Double-sampling requires two acceptance numbers, c_1 and c_2 such that $c_2 > c_1$. Assume that k_1 defectives are found in a sample of n_2. Accept the lot if $k_1 \leq c_1$; reject the lot if $k_1 > c_2$; if neither, draw an additional sample of n_2.

Drift-decay quality phenomenon: Decay of product performance can occur as a result of usage or age. For example, the light output of a bulb diminishes to a point where the lumens are insufficient for reading. We expect less decay from alkaline batteries than from the traditional carbon zinc batteries. The quality issue is how fast is the rate of decay?

Due date: Sales and marketing promise delivery on a specific date (called *order promising*). From the P/OM point of view, the result of order promising shows up as a due date on the production schedule. Missing due dates is not the same as backlogging (postponed delivery at the time of order promising). Missed due dates are broken promises. P/OM schedules try to minimize the number and severity of these occurrences, i.e., how often they occur and how much delay occurs before delivery.

DVR: Digital video recorders are made by TiVo, SONY, and Scientific Atlanta.

Dynamic inventory models: The inventory models are contrasted with static inventory models. Dynamic models require a continuing stream of inventory decisions whereas static inventory models permit one decision (or at most a few decisions). Places orders repetitively over a long period of time.

Economic lot size (ELS): The ELS model focuses on how many units to make in a production run. It is designed for the intermittent flow shop, which applies sequenced operations to various products that can be made on the same production line with changeover costs. This is a smaller investment commitment than required by the continuous flow shop (e.g., auto assembly). ELS also contrasts with the economic order quantity (EOQ) model, which aims at deciding how many units to buy from a supplier at one time. This is a useful distinction that applies to the *make* versus *buy* concept faced by all manufacturers. The make versus buy model can also apply to services that consume supplies. See also **Economic order quantity (EOQ).**

Economic order quantity (EOQ): The EOQ model focuses on how many units to order when purchasing items for batch delivery. These supplies are intended for relatively continuous use as needed to support flow shop production. Another name for this model is the *optimal order quantity model.* The relatively continuous use of the ordered items is expected to continue over a long planning horizon, and the rate of use does not have to be constant, but it should be fairly stable. See also **Economic lot size (ELS).**

Economies of scale: (1) Reductions in cost per unit that can be obtained by purchasing greater quantities of goods and services. Discounts may be gotten for larger purchase orders, and investments in innovation can be increased. More training, improved methods, and new technology are cost justified. (2) Reductions in variable costs directly related to increasing volumes of production output. Scale, as used here, refers to production unit volumes.

Economies of scope: Realized when setup cost reductions allow more frequent changeovers without increasing the cost per unit of output. Smaller lots sizes provide greater variety without increasing inventories. These advantages can stem from creative engineering as well as flexible (computerized) production technology.

Efficiency frontiers: These are trade-off boundaries. For finance, where the technique originated, different amounts of risk and return are plotted as curved lines of equal expected profits. This analogy has been applied to the selection of processes for reengineering. Chosen processes should have the potential for major improvement. Process improvement that can be anticipated is denoted as IA. That process should also be important to the performance of the company. It should deliver capabilities that are significant to the well-being of the company—called *DC.* Because the chosen process can be improved a great deal, and that will help the performance of the company significantly, it will fall on a high-priority efficiency frontier. In typical management terms, this is often called *the low hanging fruit.*

Elasticity: The term used to describe the strong systems interaction between market demand and price charged. Often referred to as the price–demand elasticity, it is a rate-of-change measure expressing the degree to which demand grows or contracts in response to price decreases or increases, respectively.

Empirical testing: Testing product design characteristics is well-known in market research. It is also well-known as a check against poor design performance that might be hidden otherwise. For example, after months of use, a lightbulb might shatter at failure. Fatigue testing and simulation can speed up time and frequency of product use to provide information about a product's behavior at a distant time in the future. Empirical means that the testing is not theoretical (on paper) but it is observed as a real event with the actual product. Empirical testing is not in place of theoretical design; it is in addition to gain experiential and pragmatic knowledge. Testing can range from health of foods to safety of airplanes and protection of product from packaging.

End-of-life-of-vehicle (ELV): Standards are being set that become increasingly rigorous for disposability at ELV. Percentages are raised step-wise and eventually close to 100 percent of vehicles, computers, etc., will be returned for recycling and/or disposal by the manufacturers.

End products: Also called *parent products* are considered to have independent demand systems. Materials and components that are part of the end product are dependent on end-product demand, which can be sporadic and lumpy. MRP is the information system that details what must be done, including ordering supplies, to produce the required number of end products on schedule. The same parts can appear in various end products, and MRP manages the overlap.

Ends: Final part of the means–end chain where what appears to be an end (goal) is the means (cause) for a higher-level goal. Means and ends are part of the process planning system.

Engineering change orders (ECOs): Projects with many engineering change orders are not simple to handle. These may appear to be minor alterations in the product design or in the process used, but there are interactions that are usually unforeseen that can lead to severe systems complexities.

Enterprise Resource Planning (ERP): Company-wide integration of the information system for seamless planning across all functions.

Ergonomics: The systematic study of how people physically interact with their environment, equipment, facilities, machines, and products. (Ergo is a combining form meaning work, from Gr. érgon.) An alternate name is *human factors.* Because people differ in size and shape by age and lineage, there are significant design questions that must be decided. For example, for AT&T the Henry Dreyfuss designers created one of the first single-unit mouth and ear telephones that could be used by both grownups and children around the world. Although ergonomics starts with physical efficiency, issues of safety and comfort emerge. There are also complex psychological issues related to productivity, job turnover, absenteeism, and accident rates.

ERP: See **Enterprise Resource Planning**.

Ethics: A set of moral principles determined by culture and society. Business ethics is a subset of societal ethics, which must be congruent with social norms and moral practices. What is moral is a judgment of conformance to standards of "right" behaviors. Each culture has its own norms for what is right. Therefore, ethical standards must be established in multicultural environments that satisfy the various participants. Ethical situations are encountered with respect to such issues as how customers' complaints are treated, employee retirement plans are managed, union–management relations are administered, community members cooperate, impacts, environmental evaluations, etc. See **Greening the environment**.

Expediting: Actively following up on orders to make sure that deliveries will be on time. When delays are encountered, expediters are to assess the urgency of the situation and to initiate remedial actions that are in line with the situation. For example, if the supplier's trucking company is on strike, send a company truck to bring the items needed for production.

Experience curve: Rate of decrease in per unit costs is between 20 and 30 percent for each doubling of production output volume. The Boston Consulting Group found this result after collecting relevant data for many thousands of processes. They named this phenomenon the "Experience Curve." Volume is a surrogate for experience, learning, and discounts for higher volumes.

Expert systems: Computerized sequences or strings of intelligent inquiries with answers that are modeled on what "experts" would do to solve specific problems or to accomplish given tasks. Emulating experts takes time but has the advantage of storing more than one expert's method of approach in a software package. Expert systems learn and remember so that the departure of an expert can be an anticipated event without damaging consequences. Expert systems can compare experts' performance and activate the best expert string for a selected problem.

Explicit knowledge: The form of knowledge that describes what must be done to make things work. The character of explicit knowledge is that it can be transferred from teachers to students in words or diagrams. It is unconcealed and evident. For example, explicit knowledge includes how to replace a washer in the faucet or how to change the font of a Word document. Transfer agents can be words, pictures, equations, etc. Tacit (implicit) knowledge, which is the other form, is not transferable by word or picture. For example, how to teach a student to become intuitive may illustrate the difficulties of transferring intangible information. See **Knowledge management** and **Tacit knowledge**.

Extrapolation: The process of moving from observed data (past and present) to the projected values of future points. For example, the best guess for the next (extrapolated) value of the time series 2, 4, and 6 is 8. In this case, the linear trend is projected ahead to the future point not yet known.

Extreme quality achievement: Zero defects is called an extreme goal, but Philip Crosby showed that it is a reasonable goal. This is because the conformance to standards must be as near to perfect as possible if the standards are properly chosen. Six-sigma from Motorola, on the other hand, is extreme by present-day quality achievement levels. In this case, the product designers and process engineers must create a production system that can yield no more than 3.4 defectives per million parts. Many companies want to match the Motorola-pioneered standard of six-sigma.

Facilities planning: Four main components are geographic location, structure and specific site, equipment choice, and layout. Some of the analysis is quantitative, but a lot of it is qualitative. A major driver is the type of work configuration and process technology that will be used.

FDA: The U.S. Department of Health and Human Services includes the Food and Drug Administration (FDA) and the CDC. The FDA monitors quality integrity for food producers, warehouses, distributors, retailers, and restaurants. One of the most far-reaching FDA initiatives is HACCP, which began with the fishing industry and has now expanded to poultry and meat-processing plants. For the latest FDA developments, consult http://www.fda.gov. See **Hazard Analysis and Critical Control Point (HACCP) system**.

Ferris Wheel model: The Ferris Wheel stops and fills one of n cars with people (project team starts up). The car travels a complete cycle in time, T. Project cycle time, $C = T/n$. When a car empties, symbolically, a project has been completed. The Ferris Wheel provides a model of continuous, new product development. See **Project, Continuous development**.

FIFO: The most natural sequence for doing work is in the order that the jobs are received. That means that the first jobs into the shop get worked on first. The sequence rule: first-in, first-out is called FIFO. It can be compared to LIFO (last-in, first-out), which is the most comfortable rule on a crowded elevator. LIFO is not the supermarket manager's favorite sequencing rule for dated products, such as bread and dairy. It is the good shopper's rule as they reach behind the milk cartons out in front. People say that FIFO is fair. That is a psychological expectation. People get upset when a late arrival breaks into the waiting line and gets in front of them, or is chosen for service by the system's server. FIFO is seldom the basis for economic systems fairness. See **LIFO** and **SPT rule**.

Finite scheduling: Controlling the flow of work so that lot sizes and frequency of setups result in minimum total costs. The flow of smaller lot sizes being made more often can provide flexibility when capacity constraints prevail that create bottleneck effects. Also, process batch sizes should be variable rather than fixed for additional flexibility. See **TOC** and **OPT**.

Fixed costs (FC): Like rent, they have to be paid whether or not any units are sold. Like an insurance policy, they apply to a specific period of time. FCs are greater for flow shops than for job shops, and greatest for flexible manufacturing systems. Administrative and supervisory charges are treated as fixed costs. Overhead (fixed) costs exist before a single unit of product (goods and/or services) is delivered to customers.

Flexible manufacturing systems (FMS): (1) Machines and computers (called manufacturing cells) that work together and can be programmed to produce a menu of different products. The change-over time to move from one menu item to another is negligible because of the computer-controlled tools and transport devices. This is not limited to manufacturing. Flexible process systems (FPS) include flexible service systems (FSS) and flexible office systems (FOS). (2) Systems designed to produce a variety of outputs at low cost. Computer-controlled change-overs that are fast and inexpensive are engineered into the system. Because the method requires detailed analysis to overcome constraints imposed by each product's manufacturing requirements on the others, flexibility is limited. (3) Systems that permit rapid changeovers from one product to another on the production line. The menu of options is carefully planned beforehand. A variety of tool-changing devices, position-shifting robots, and flexible conveyors make the changeovers seem instantaneous.

Flexible office systems (FOS): Office processes are in many ways similar to manufacturing, with both job shop batch production and flow shop (or intermittent flow shop) work configurations. Computer-controlled FOS can be designed to change over from one job to another with negligible setup times. This category of flexible information systems permits searching for information and auto-preparation of documents that conform to a number of categories such as bill paying, invoicing, complaint responses, and rebates.

Flexible process system (FPS): (1) Encompasses flexible manufacturing systems (FMS) as well as flexible information systems. The latter can provide a variety of service functions. At the heart of such flexibility is the design interchangeability of the product line. Computers reconfigure the production system. An example of a flexible production system would be the palette of colors used by the artist to paint different pictures. (2) A generic name for all kinds of computer-controlled robotic and machine systems that can change over to offer a menu of products. See **Flexible manufacturing systems (FMS).**

Flexible production systems (FPS): Rapid process changeover capabilities to deliver a variety of services for information, health care, transportation, education, entertainment, and other services.

Flexible service systems (FSS): See **Flexible manufacturing systems (FMS).** In quick-service restaurants, theme parks, the U.S. Post Office, FedEx, and UPS, there are ample examples of flexible service systems.

Floor plan models: Drawings of the plant floor to achieve capacity goals, obtain balanced workloads and minimum operating costs, low levels of work in process and least storage space, and minimum travel distance for people and parts. Sketches and drawings with dollhouse-like cutouts are par for the course.

Flow shops (FS): Serialized work configurations where one unit of work is at various stages of completion at sequential workstations that are located along the line of production.

Forecasting momentum: The time series being forecast is observed to follow a course or direction that appears to be the result of an inherent force (momentum). Its movement becomes more predictable as a result of this impetus or momentum. For example, an actor's career is said to lose momentum when successive pictures are failures. Conversely, momentum can accelerate performance as a car racing down a hill has momentum assisted by gravity. However, tipping points can be reached. Suddenly the momentum evaporates. This effect keeps stock market forecasts speculative.

Forecasting: Foretelling events to come when the probabilities of these events are not known with certainty, as in a coin toss.

Forward pass rule: Also known as the forward convergence rule, it is similar and opposite to the backward pass (or convergence) rule. The forward pass rule: When two or more arrows converge at a single node, choose the arrow with the largest value of the earliest finish time. The forward pass rule enables the project managers to determine how long it will take to complete the project. It is a necessary precursor to use of the backward pass rule. Taken together with the forward pass rule, the fundamental parameters of the project can be calculated. See **Backward pass rule** and **Critical-path methods (CPM).**

Functional field approach: The functional fields are P/OM, marketing, finance, etc. The functional field approach is widely used, and it means that everyone is on her or his own. Marketing is not responsible for who makes the product, where it is made, how much it costs to make, etc. Marketing does care about consumers' perceptions of product quality. With the functional field approach, operations management is strictly tactical.

Fundamental theorem of linear programming (LP): The LP model uses a set of interdependent equations to express resource constraints that determine the solution of an optimal product mix problem. The fundamental theorem of LP states that there cannot be more active variables (i.e., products actually made) than the number of real constraints. For aggregate planning, supplies and demands (over the planning horizon) will determine the number of different active production assignments that can be made to minimize total costs (within the planning horizon).

Gantt charts: Henry L. Gantt invented a number of different charts used by P/OM. One type of chart is known as the Gantt load chart (assign actual jobs to specific departments). A load chart provides a graphic system that makes it easy to visualize how much work has been assigned to each facility. Another type of chart is the Gantt layout chart, which establishes the exact order in which jobs are to be done at each facility. It is simple to observe the progress of jobs, jobs waiting, idle facilities, load imbalances (some departments overloaded, others underutilized). Causes of problems can be noted as well.

Gantt layout charts: See Figure 16-2.

Gantt load charts: See Figure 16-1.

General-purpose equipment (GPE): Primarily used in the job shop because it is flexible machinery that can do many different kinds of jobs. For example, a lemon juicer might not be able to get juice from an orange, but a larger juicer could do grapefruit, orange, lemon, and lime.

Gleicher model (Conditions for change): Specifies the *circumstances* that are necessary for an organization to change *what* it is doing (as well as *how, where, when,* and *why*). The model built by Dr. David Gleicher hypothesizes that the product of three factors, D, V, and P, must be greater than the cost of change, C. Thus: ($D \times V \times P$) > C. If any one of these three factors is zero, no change can occur. See **Dissatisfaction**, **Practical first steps**, and **Vision.**

Greening the environment: There are many facets to this objective. Maintenance is an area where cleaning involves toxic chemicals and harmful residues. Environmentally sound maintenance may take the form of emission controls on smokestacks and water-jetting to remove coatings. Production processes may have side effects that have to be cleaned. Greening is also accomplished by design for reuse, recycling, and proper disposal when remanufacturing cannot be used. Greening is meant to connote that efforts are successful to achieve sustainable land and water resources. Vegetation thrives with proper management of the ecosystem. Visit http://www.greeningofindustry.org.

Group technology cellular manufacturing systems: An application of flexible manufacturing systems (FMS). When workstations are linked and designed to work together on common sets of projects, they are called cellular manufacturing systems. Families of parts that have many characteristics in common but vary in specific ways are said to reflect group technology (GT). Thus, small-, medium-, and large-size washers are family members if they can be made by a machine with adjustable diameters.

HACCP: Hazard Analysis monitors for causes of food contamination. Critical Control Points are set to signal that a threshold has been passed which allows spoilage to occur.

Hazard Analysis and Critical Control Point (HACCP) system: HAACP is a system designed to prevent food hazards from arising without being detected. It is a quality control system that detects the presence of defective process management. It also specifies what procedures to follow with food product that is out of control. It is one of the largest scale quality control programs in the field of P/OM. HACCP is an excellent example of total quality management. HACCP provides detailed specifications for monitoring temperatures and controlling process variables that can lead to food contamination. See **FDA**.

Hedging: Purchasing strategy that trades in futures. Hedgers neither win nor lose; they breakeven. This protects them against price fluctuations.

Heuristic line-balancing methods: Line-balancing problems are large and unwieldy. There are so many combinations for assigning work to stations that ordinary mathematical optimization solutions do not apply. This complexity has led to proposals for the use of various rules of thumb, which constitute a common sense approach to line-balancing problems. For example, Kilbridge and Wester assign a number to each operation that counts how many predecessors it has. Lowest predecessor numbers are assigned to workstations first. Many rules of thumb exist to handle complications such as ties. Linear programming methods can be used for line balancing but may not be worth the effort because heuristics are remarkably robust.

Heuristics (rules of thumb): These are methods for discovery, guides for problem-solving, and procedures for experimental learning. One of the most popular is the trial and error technique with feedback to reward steps in the right direction. "Rules-of-thumb heuristics" are based on detailing the procedures followed by successful employees, such as the scheduler who has been using reason, observation, and common sense to provide reinforcement for what works and negative feedback for what fails to work. Evaluation of results produces learning. The reason to use heuristics is that no algorithm has been developed to solve the problem.

Histograms: Relative frequency distributions of categories of events can be informative. Histograms are bar charts that illustrate the relative frequencies of a set of outcomes as a discrete probability distribution. For example, for a specific June in Orlando, Florida, spreadsheet data was recorded for daily daytime maximum temperatures. Histograms were drawn for the relative frequencies of the temperature spectrum. Because there are 30 days in June, each unique reading has a frequency of $1/30 = 0.033$. Five June days had max daily temperature of 85 degrees F. The histogram bar for 85 degrees was 0.167 in height.

HMMS: A pioneering aggregate planning model that uses nonlinear costs for its resource constraints. The acronym is from the first letter of each scientist's last name. Provides better answers but at a cost that limits use to academic understanding.

House of Quality (HOQ): A mapping and tracking system for all relevant quality dimensions for a real product. It has been used by Merrill Lynch to study in detail and depth the quality of their CMA. GE, Xerox, Ford, etc., have used the HOQ in a number of different ways. The HOQ method can be used for extreme quality achievement such as six-sigma.

I/O profit model: The input–output model captures all costs and revenues so profit can be determined. An optimal configuration of the factors can be used to improve the breakeven point and to maximize profit.

Information systems: Good information systems capture all data relevant to P/OM planning and decision making. That includes raw materials, components on hand, finished goods, work-in-process, available operators, and technology that can be utilized. It includes data about money, materials, people (in-firm and marketplace), equipment, processes, space, energy, competitors, and anything else that counts.

Input–output model: This is the basic production systems model, which assumes transformation in between inputs and outputs.

Inspection: Observation of product qualities can be made by eye or with instrumentation. Nonconformance with standards for acceptance results in a reject of the item. Inspection (appraisal) of outputs is one of the three costs of quality that must be balanced against the other two (viz., cost of failure and cost of prevention). 100 percent inspection is often inaccurate as well as costly. The key to recall: Inspectors can reduce defectives shipped but not defectives made.

Intelligent information system: Captures the management issues of *what to buy, when to buy, from whom to buy, how much to buy, how much to pay,* etc. Distinguished from a ledger that notes stock on-hand, shipments expected, sales, and withdrawals.

Interchangeable parts: A manufacturing concept that makes batches of parts (e.g., rifle barrels), any one of which will fit into the assembled products (rifles). The reason that the parts are interchangeable is that each one fits within the design tolerances.

Intermittent flow shop (IFS): Used when demand does not justify establishing a dedicated flow shop. An IFS is run for an interval of time and then shut down until it is required again.

Internal MM system: MM is materials management. The internal MM system controls production materials flowing to and through the process. Controls work in process on the plant floor and finished goods in the warehouse. The external MM system tracks shipments to distributors and retailers. Internal and external systems must be synchronized and coordinated to be effective.

Inventory: Stock on-hand for every practical reason that materials are needed to run an organization. Items can be classified as raw materials, subassemblies, outsourced components, work in process, and finished goods. In addition to repair and maintenance supplies, there are office supplies and gasoline, oil, and tires for the delivery trucks. Inventory is tying up assets at a carrying cost that is justified by the fact that when the item is needed there is a penalty to pay for not having it on hand. To make the decisions there are materials managers known as inventory managers who specialize in inventory management.

Inventory record files (IRF): One of three inputs to the MRP information system, viz., MPS, BOM, and inventory record files (IRF). Stock on-hand levels need to be up to date. Similarly, all ordering information including suppliers' prices and delivery lead times must be current. If the inventory record files are not up to date, the MRP system will produce anomalies that penalize production such as supply shortfalls and cost overruns.

Inventory turns: See **Turnover.**

ISO 14000/14001/14004/14010/14011/14012/14030/14031:   ISO stands for the International Standardization Organization. It is located in Geneva, Switzerland. The ISO 9000 series is acknowledged worldwide as the accepted set of standards for quality management. ISO 14000/14001 sets similar standards for environmental management. The methodology is the same as with ISO 9000. Both sets of standards explain what management approaches are desirable. Both do not specify details of quality such as permissible percent defectives, or acceptable emission levels. The ISO 14000 series have been widely accepted on a global basis. Such standards for conformity are sorely needed. Disparate environmental standards would make multinational and transnational firms follow different drumbeats all over the world. How bright would the world be, and how many readers of Harry Potter would exist, if every bulb manufacturer used its own socket size? Growing in importance is the ISO 17799 Toolkit. It addresses operational security.

ISO 9000 series: The International Organization for Standardization (ISO), located in Geneva, Switzerland provides quality certification for 146 national standards bodies, of which 94 are full-fledged members of countries. The ISO 9000 series relates to generic management systems standards for quality. These apply to any organization, large or small, and whatever its product—including whether its product is a service. In addition, ISO has set more than 14,000 standards for a vast variety of product attributes, which has untold benefits in removing chaos from global trade. ISO also sets generic management systems standards for environmental conditions under ISO 140000. See http://www.iso.ch.

Japanese Industrial Standard Z8101:   Standard that dates from 1981. It is the set of Japanese standards equivalent to the EURO/U.S.–ISO standards. But, Japanese standards are not precisely ISO-equivalent as can be seen from the following URL. It describes how to get Phillips head screwdrivers that properly engage with cross-head screws on R/C helicopters made by HeliProz, Inc. Cross-head screws used by HeliProz are manufactured in Japan. Western screwdrivers do not fit them. This is a good example of the need for true standardization. Matching screwdrivers to screw heads illustrates the requirement for transparency (of) and conformance to standards by cooperating partners in the global economy. See http://www. heliproz.com/jisdrivers.html.

Job evaluation: Evaluation of existing jobs permits job enrichment and improvement, and work simplification. The latter expands viewpoints to permit systems evaluation of sets of interlinked jobs. The traditional view, which is to study the individual job, lacks the scope of systems thinking.

Job shop (JS):   Used when there are many varieties of products to process in small quantities. Volume is not sufficient to justify flow shop efficiencies gained from special purpose equipment.

Just-in-case: An inventory delivery principle associated with a play-it-safe production philosophy. Fear of production interruptions leads to safety-stocking of critical parts. This is counter to the lean and agile principle of just-in-time.

Just-in-time: An inventory delivery principle associated with a lean-and-mean company philosophy. Under JIT, suppliers must provide exactly what is needed for production until the next delivery is made. The presence of defective components would stop the system, so total quality assurance is required. The interval between replenishment is kept small, which means that inventory carried is minimized. See Enrichment Activity 14, page 599.

Kanban: Any method that calls attention to a workstation's need to receive a just-in-time (JIT) delivery. An array of signaling devices for JIT delivery. In Japanese, a card sent to a prior station or upstream supplier that a need exists for a specified amount of product.

Knowledge management (KM):   Begins with managing the inventory of knowledge that exists in the company. Knowing where that knowledge resides (the directory) and being able to access it on demand are part of KM. In addition, KM assumes the ability to find, select, and absorb new knowledge to add to the prior encyclopedic storehouse. Knowledge with regard to managing change and controlling the system's behavior is vital. The inventory of explicit and tacit knowledge exists in core competencies and managerial capabilities. See **Core competencies, Explicit knowledge**, and **Tacit knowledge.**

Labor productivity: A partial accounting for productivity that is due to the use of human labor to do the job. The output divided by the input model prevails in two ways. First is units produced per dollar of labor. Second is sales dollar value of units produced per dollar of labor. Both measures are taken over successive time periods.

Lateral transferability: Operations are assigned to workstations, which form a sequential chain. When precedence diagrams permit operations to be assigned to earlier or later workstations, there is lateral flexibility. A lateral pass in football is a sideways transfer of the ball. Lateral is parallel to the line of scrimmage or away from the opponent's goal. The reason for the name in line balancing is that precedence diagrams are drawn from left to right. Switching the workstation position of an operation is a left to right (or vice versa) movement called *lateral transferability*.

Layout: (1) Plan for the arrangement of the working environment of the company's facilities. Where should machines and people be placed in the plant, office, or customer-service center? Where should power outlets be located? Where should the rest rooms be positioned? A variety of methods and criteria can be brought to bear on such questions. (2) The Gantt layout chart converts loading to specific sequencing of jobs at a facility. Loading is a *list of* jobs, in no particular order, at a facility. The Gantt layout chart arranges the list in order of processing. It does this in an optimal sequence. It is no surprise that the chart is also called a *sequencing chart*. See **Floor plan models.**

Lead time (LT):   (1) The interval that elapses between seeing the need for and placing an order and receiving the goods or services. It might even help to call it the period between *need and get*. LT is a crucial parameter for process design. Major improvements can be made by decreasing LT and/or by reducing its variability. (2) An interval of time between first knowing that there is a need to place an order for stock and when that stock is put in a specific place and logged in as available for use. A simpler definition is that lead time is the interval between order placement and order receipt (including recognized need and write up). As can be seen from the first definition, lead time can be more complex than the simple definition. This is because prior to ordering there can be delays due to a variety of problems. Also, after the delivery to the receiving dock, materials can be lost or stored incorrectly, and the computer and/or paperwork to notify users that materials are back in stock must be adequate. There is an expected lead time for any replenishment period and variability that can make delivery sooner or later than expected.

Lean accounting: Accounting under lean production conditions.

Lean production: Minimize waste and maximize value-added throughput of the value stream.

Lean production systems: Processes that have been designed to minimize their inherent wastes—of time, materials, and their surrogates (money). The methods to achieve leanness were developed during the era of new Japanese auto manufacturing (1970–1990). Lean processes do not tolerate unnecessary waiting or redoing (e.g., defectives). That makes lean firms faster in producing and delivering. By 2000, many U.S. auto firms had become lean producers. Other lean industries include computer-assembly and wireless phone manufacturers. Wal-Mart maintains its position as a lean retail and distribution center.

Learning curve: Describes how repeated practice decreases the time required to do a job. Captures the benefit of repetition and experience in quantitative terms for employees doing the same job routinely. Learning curves are based on mathematical models of learning from repetition. The learning function increases actual manufacturing capacity. Learning also alters capacity and quality in service operations; also decreases defectives, which indirectly increases useful output.

Learning organization (LO):   All organizations (for profit and not-for-profit) must adapt to change by learning what works and what fails, which leads to the realization that shared individual learning can be synergistic.

Least-squares method: Used in regression analysis, a line is placed among a series of points so as to minimize the sum of the squares of the deviations of the points from the line. When all points fall on the line, then, the least-squares sum is zero. The correlation coefficient is 1 if the line has a positive slope and -1 if the slope is negative.

Leveling factors: Used in time studies of work to convert average time (average performance) to normal time (or adjusted time). Aimed at deriving useful productivity standards, leveling reduces the output rate of faster than normal workers. It increases the output of slower than normal workers. Leveling factors are assigned by trained time study operators.

Level production: See **Constant production strategy**.

Life cycle stages: Facility decisions are a function of the life cycle stages of the items in the product line. The history of the company will explain the mixture of start-ups, mature products, products in restaging, products being retired. For each stage, products require different work configurations and floor layouts for plants. Company size will play a large role in determining optimal layouts for offices. Alternative geographical locations may be desirable for products at different stages.

Life cycle strategies: Market share and sales volume growth, maturity, and decay require different marketing and P/OM strategies. Preparation for new product introductions must be synchronized with these life cycle epochs.

Lifetime value (LTV) of customers: Customer loyalty relates to the probability of purchasing again and again from the same store (or the same brand). Lifetime value is the stream of revenue spent by each loyal customer over the lifetime of his/her relationship with the store (or brand). When a dissatisfied customer switches to another store (or brand), the stream of revenue switches from the old store to the new one. This is called the lost LTV of a customer and it can be significant. Tens of thousands of dollars are involved when a customer switches from one supermarket to another. LTV for an average customer can be segmented, e.g., average female, 18 to 25 years of age.

LIFO: This is the "last-in, first-out" rule for providing service. It sets the service priority based on arrival time. Imagine that the "take-a-number" machine in the bakery is fixed so that the latest arrival gets the smallest number. As always, the server behind the counter gives preference to holders of smallest numbers. That is the way that LIFO operates. Early arrivers might have to wait a long time for service. In the social ethic, LIFO is not fair. However, to exit from a crowded elevator, LIFO may be essential. See **FIFO** and **SPT rule**.

Line balancing (LB):   The effort to divide total work content into equal (or nearly equal) balanced parts for assignment at each of n workstations. Operations are done at the workstation during the cycle time, C. Bad design loads stations unevenly. Deterministic LB is based on no variability in operation times; stochastic LB is when variability exists in the form of statistical distributions of operation times. For example, a teller's time to complete a bank transaction could be a withdrawal, or a deposit, or both. There could be one or many checks, or withdrawal slips. Process engineers reduce uncertainty of output rates by using paced conveyors to provide fixed work time at stations.

Line efficiency (L):   Is known as capital lambda (Λ). $\Lambda = \Sigma_i t_i / nC$ where $0 \leq \Lambda \leq 1$. It is the total work content divided by the total capacity to do work. Line efficiency can be expressed as a percent, i.e., 100Λ. The relationship of balance delay and line efficiency is $d = 100(1 - \Lambda)$. See **Balance delay**.

Linear programming (LP):   Mathematical modeling technique employed by P/OM to achieve optimal use of resources. Variations include the optimal product-mix problem, production scheduling using overtime, and other capacity-sensitive situations. It is significant that often the optimal product-mix solution does not fully utilize available capacity because the LP algorithm moves toward the selection of higher total profit margin products. See **Slack** and **Fundamental theorem of linear programming (LP)**.

Linear regression: A statistical technique for determining the best straight-line $y = mx + b$ that can be fitted to a set of data $\{x, y\}$. The best fit is the line that minimizes the sum of squares of the deviations of the points from the line.

Loading: Loading decisions concern the jobs that are to be assigned to which teams or facilities. Assigning jobs on-hand is relatively risk-free. Assigning jobs that are on the books as forecasts is risky business. They may not be scheduled (loaded) because there is too high a risk of cancellation. Second level of aggregate planning is loading. Assign jobs to departments before sequencing jobs within departments. For example, a set of jobs is given to John and a different set to Mary. The order in which they do their jobs must follow loading.

Logistics: Tactics of materials management for buying, storing, and transporting materials of all kinds as required by the company's supply chain. Logistics includes product distribution through the supply chain to the customers. Original use: Branch of military science dealing with the movement, procurement, and maintenance of equipment, facilities, and personnel. Derivation from *loger*, to lodge (finding quarters for soldiers).

Lot-for-lot ordering: The planned-order receipt (materials required to fulfill end product schedule) will equal the required amounts at each point in time. In MRP language, planned-order receipts are to be equal to net requirements. In MRP notation, $PR_t = NR_t$.

Low-level coding: MRP labels the level of parts on the end product's assembly-sequence tree. Low-level coding organizes order quantity calculations for parts with combined (multi-level) demands. Parents at the treetop are labeled level zero. Parts and components one level down are called level one. The next level down is coded level two. This coding scheme shows how distant parts are (in their linkage) from their parent product. MRP record processing starts a level code zero and moves down the tree. This assures that all gross requirements are assigned to a part before its MRP record is processed. Low-level coding uses the principle that the lowest position of a part determines where the calculation of gross cumulative requirements is made. A part appearing in both level one and level three will transfer requirement at level one to level three for calculating total requirements for that part. Low-level coding is a systematic, efficient planning rule for computing material requirements.

Machine-operator chart (MOC): Provides a means for visualizing the way in which workers (can) tend machines over time. They encourage visual analysis of the interactions of operators with the equipment they run, set up, take down, changeover, and repair. MOC charts can be used to reduce changeover times.

Make or buy decision: Purchase from outside (outsource) or make it internally (self-supplier) is a complex issue. The decision is cost-oriented but not just cost minimization because there are other factors to consider such as vendor reliability, supplier creativity in improving product, lack of understanding opportunities to innovate, and reliance on outside managers. Factors can change over time, e.g., new technology can be developed that would shift buy to make or vice versa.

Make-to-order (MTO) inventory environment: In this environment, there is no finished goods inventory to meet demand. End-items are produced to customers' orders. The sales force pledges delivery dates. The pledges translate into due dates that put the production system under stress to live up to promises. Machine shops, carpenters, and plumbers live in an MTO environment. One of the advantages of holding stock is that it can buffer periods when demand is greater than supply. That benefit is lost in an MTO situation.

Make-to-stock (MTS) environment: There is latitude in what to make and the quantities to produce because various items have finished goods inventories. Production scheduling follows an aggregate plan to minimize total costs or maximize revenues (or profits). Forecasts, in conjunction with priorities and due dates, provide opportunities for optimal solutions. Because forecasts help determine the production schedule, inventory levels can be shared with marketing, which is in a position to adjust forecasts through selling strategies and pricing. Further, marketing can (to some extent) meet customers' demands by selling what is in stock.

Management of technology (MOT): Management of technology is equivalent to managing the transformation process of the P/OM input–output system. MOT requires knowing what technologies exist, their state of development, and when to shift from one format to another. Mastery of technology with regard to productivity, variety, and quality are essential. Optimal timing of adoptions is part of the job description.

Manufacturing: The processes that constitute the transformation function of the I/O model; those processes that produce goods.

Market research: Connects P/OM and marketing through information about customer evaluation of products as well as their needs and loyalty to brand names.

Mass customization: Henry Ford's sequenced assembly of (only) black Model T cars epitomized mass production (a single model in great volume). One hundred years later, using modular product designs and flexible process systems, P/OM can produce quality customized products with economies of scale associated with mass production (high volumes without increasing costs).

Master production schedule (MPS): One of three inputs to the MRP information system, viz., BOM, IRF, and MPS. Converts aggregate plans into a time-phased plan that indicates exactly when each SKU should be made and how much should be run. Responsive to customer orders on hand and forecasts. In MRP terms, the MPS calls for various amounts of parent products to be produced by a given date. Fits in the framework of the total manufacturing planning and control systems (MPCS). Used in conjunction with the BOM, it determines the items for which purchase requisitions and production orders must be released (triggering action). Helps assemble-to-order (ATO) by making sure that subassemblies are available to meet requirements within promised due dates. The MPS has to be updated regularly to incorporate new orders and to reflect other changes in existing conditions. See **Regeneration MRP.**

Material requirements planning (MRP): An information system that organizes all factors that determine production-scheduling decisions and all support functions including vendors. The MRP system includes customers' orders on-hand, forecasts of future requirements, inventory on-hand, and capacity availabilities. Applied to job shops where batch production of a variety of different items is the typical situation. A systems approach to the rational management of the entire supply chain with respect to inventory ordering and stocking. Because batch production is prevalent in the economy, MRP is used more often than its counterpart, order point policy (OPP). However, the economic order quantity (EOQ) model can play a role in determining order size.

Materials management (MM): Organizing and coordinating all management functions that are responsible for every aspect of materials movements, storage, and transformation. Organizational responsibility as a functional area with vice president for materials management being a top management representative. The cost of materials has become an increasingly dominant part of companies' cost structures. Requires management of the entire system of supply and demand, including product transportation through distribution channels.

Materials management information system (MMIS): The MMIS provides online information about stock levels for all materials and parts. This includes stock on order, lead times, supplier data, costs of materials, discount schedules, and transportation modes. All materials and parts include raw materials, components, subassemblies, work in process, and finished goods.

Materials management system (MMS): Triggered by marketplace demands (via forecasts), which deplete stocks that cause inventory managers to place replenishment orders through purchasing agents with suppliers and vendors. Contrasting terms that are consistent with original derivations: from Latin, *venditor*, to sell; from Latin, *supplere*, to fill up.

Mean flow time: Average amount of time required to complete each job in a group of *n* jobs that have been sequenced at a facility. It is the average of the "wait-to-start" plus processing time for every job in the assigned group. The equation for mean flow time is $MFT = \Sigma_i^n C_i \div n$.

Mean time between failures (MTBF): A product's expected lifetime of satisfactory utility in normal application is well-described by mean time between failures. Nonfailure (and reliability) is defined by continuity of "satisfactory utility." A competitive benchmark of MTBF is a useful guide when considered in conjunction with customer acceptance of failure.

Methods analysis: Systematic examination of all operations in every process. The objective is to search for better ways to do the jobs that the company requires. Encourages process alternatives by combining steps, eliminating operations, making work easier, and raising product quality and the quality of life for employees.

Minimum cost assignment schedule: This refers to the trade-off model for aggregate planning of the workforce. There is a need to search for the production schedule that has the minimum total cost along the scale that starts with smooth production (at one extreme) and ends with perfect matching of supply and demand (at the other).

Mixed-model systems: A family of parts or products are run on the same line, e.g., blue pens/green pens or two-door and four-door cars.

Mobile robots: Many repetitive and dangerous jobs can be assigned to machines. Fixed machines have limited abilities; mobile machines are far more useful. Mobile robots require guidance or vision capabilities, both of which are under development. Robots with mobility are especially useful for safety and security. There is growth in the application of robotics for hazardous situations including nuclear energy, bomb squads, toxic gas and fluid spills, etc. Service robots are being built smaller, smarter, more mobile, and less expensively. They can be thought of as point of contact, mobile computers. Mobile nurse and orderly robots are increasingly used in healthcare services.

Models: Attempts to image the real thing can be physical, like an airplane model or a plant layout model. Location decision models use numbers in equations for costs and preferences to maximize company performance.

Modular production (MP): The principle of modularity is to design, develop, and produce the minimum number of parts (or operations) that can be combined in the maximum number of ways to offer the greatest number of different products or services. Both modular production (MP) and group technology (GT) represent a focus on commonality of parts within product groups; for example, various sizes of motors for vacuum cleaners of different powers. Computer memories and speed are another fine example. MP increases realizable capacity of the production system by increasing the process supply capabilities as well as demand volume.

MRP II: The definitive systems plan for operating effectively at the plant level is manufacturing resource planning (called MRP II). It links P/OM and production planning with marketing goals, financial policies, R&D plans, accounting procedures, and human resource management goals. MRP II is responsive to the strategic business plan of the company, but it does not create or drive that plan as does enterprise resource planning (ERP). The subject of enterprise planning is a top management issue rather than a sole P/OM responsibility. If ERP is the scope of company planning, then MRP II will dovetail with it, because production should be a balanced component of the overall plan.

Multifactor productivity (MFP): Measured by the U.S. Labor Department, this is also called *total productivity*. It reflects the joint effects of many factors including labor and capital. It includes the impact of new technology, economies of scale, managerial skills, etc. The measure is obtained by dividing the dollar value of goods and services over time by the total dollar value of all input resources expended over the same time period.

Multiple decision makers: Quantitative scoring models can work with more than one person's evaluations of locations, suppliers, products, processes, etc. However, it is very unlikely that everyone will agree on all dimensions that are being scored. Averaging the scores of multiple decision makers reduces variability. Extreme highs cancel extreme lows. Alternatively, cluster dimensions on which there is agreement, separating them from the dimensions where there is substantial disagreement. Have the multiple decision makers (MDMs) discuss the disagreements with the goal of ascertaining the basis of differences of opinion and the goal of changing minds. Run sensitivity analyses to determine which extremes alter the selections of the scoring models. Simulations based on the data might prove valuable. The possibilities are numerous; this is still the tip of the iceberg.

Multiple project management: Managers and workers have more than one project assignment in many companies today. A variety of product development and process improvement initiatives are going on at the same time. The management of multiple projects calls on all of the skills required to manage a very complex project that has many suppliers and workers. Information control is critical. The challenges are to share resources, including management, and to compartmentalize assignments so time lines are not sacrificed on one project at the expense of another. Resource leveling can be used effectively. See **Resource leveling**.

Multiple-channel system: In queuing systems, if there are more arrivals (*n*) than servers (*M*), i.e., $n > M$, a line develops with $n - M$ waiting for service. If there is one occupied server, ($M = 1$), the next arrival must wait. If there are two busy servers, ($M = 2$), no waiting occurs until a third arrival. The effect of multiple channels (stations, servers, systems) is to provide greater systems capacity and to lower the system's utilization, ρ. See **Single-channel system.**

Multiple-sampling plans: The same procedures are followed as with double-sampling. Triple-sampling is used when doing so will lower the cost of inspection. Triple-sampling requires three acceptance numbers, c_1, c_2, and c_3, $c_3 > c_2 > c_1$.

Nanotechnology: Technology relating to products and processes that utilize very small particles. A nanometer (nm) is one billionth of a meter (m). Comparing nm to m is like comparing a marble to the earth.

Net change MRP: A fast and economical method of updating the MRP information system. The MRP files are composed of three components, viz., BOM, IRF, and MPS. If the information system is out of date, then the MRP system will fail. Therefore, updating all three files on a regular basis is crucial. Net change MRP is one of two methods widely used for updating. See **Regeneration MRP** for the other. APICS defines net change MRP: "... the materials requirements plan is continually retained in the computer. Whenever a change is needed in requirements, open order inventory status, or bill of material, a partial explosion and netting is made for only those parts affected by the change." Thus, if notified that an alteration has occurred in the situation, changes to the MRP data files are made only for the affected items. APICS is the acronym for the highly regarded American Production and Inventory Control Society.

Net present value (NPV): Method for determining the value of keeping or changing technology. NPV does this by discounting the cost of future expenditures and the value of future savings. A dollar today is worth a dollar. A dollar received or paid out a year from today is less than a dollar by the amount of interest that it would have earned during the year. NPV calculations show the time stream of values for applicable interest rates and planning horizons.

Neural networks: See **Artificial intelligence (AI)** and **Cybernetics**. The neural network model has been applied in a variety of complex situations with success. It is an adaptation of human synaptic neuron networks that provide sight, sound, smell, thinking, and reminiscing. Found to be a good basis for developing artificial intelligence and expert system capabilities.

New product development: Stages include concept selection, idea development, testing concepts, estimation and business modeling, prototype construction and testing, process specification, and pilot plant. The many stages are combinations of information collection based on R&D in the laboratories, market research regarding the opinions of people, and business modeling. If any link in the chain is weak, the system is liable to severe failure. See **Projects.**

Normal time: (1) *Normal* activity time is associated with the minimum necessary spending on project activities because there is no great stress on completing the project as soon as possible. In other words, the project budget reflects the least amount of money that has to be spent to complete the project in (what the project manager deems to be) a reasonable time. COST/TIME trade-off analysis is not required because project managers are satisfied with completion dates. See **Crash time** and **Critical path methods (CPM)**. (2) The output rate of an average worker is the expected production rate of the process. Using normal time, managers can determine how many people to employ to fill demand.

Northwest Corner (NWC) method: Transportation models are solved using linear programming methods. Alternatively, they can be solved using network algorithms that employ the Northwest Corner (NWC) method. Put the largest possible shipment in the upper-left corner and move downward and toward the right as further assignments are made. This network procedure can be speeded toward final solution by rearranging rows and columns following clever heuristics.

OEM: Original equipment manufacturer.

Olympic perspective: In a chapter dedicated to quality, the Olympic perspective deserves consideration. Problems have surfaced with the administration of the Olympics but not with the credo and goals of this international competition for excellence. Quality is a global concern, and the five rings of the Olympiad represent the union of the continents of the world. Although sporting contests abound, the Olympic ideals are sports interacting with culture and the environment. The Olympic credo is faster, higher, and stronger. It is not fastest, highest, and strongest. The idea of striving to be better is readily translated into dynamic goals of continuous improvement for management. The idea of striving to be better is also focused on ethical issues for the International Olympic Committee (IOC).

OM system: An alternative name for the P/OM system used to make goods or furnish services. OM is more service-oriented than P/OM.

Operating characteristic curves (O.C. curves): Graphics that show what happens to the probability of accepting a lot as the actual percent defective in the lot goes from zero to 100. Each O.C. curve is a unique sampling plan designed to minimize the penalties for making two kinds of errors. Buyer's risk (Type II error) is to accept lots that have too many defectives because samples indicate they are fine. Seller's risk (Type I error) is to have lots rejected by the buyer because the samples indicate they have too many defectives when in fact they are fine.

Operations management: Managing activities used to produce (and deliver) goods or furnish (and deliver) services to customers. The implication of this term is that management is professional and effective.

Opportunity costs: These are the costs of choosing options that are less than the best. The analysis of net benefits for each available option requires detailed study of all system elements. Differences between the best net benefit and other option net benefits are opportunity costs. Time needs to be considered as well because short-term net benefits are unlikely to be considered more important than long-term net benefits. Examples of situations that require opportunity cost analysis include selection of the second-best location to get the first-choice facility. The system's best choice has zero opportunity cost. See **Assignment method.**

OPT: (1) Developed by Dr. Eliyahu Goldratt to deal rationally with bottleneck-based finite production scheduling. The acronym stands for optimal production technique (also, optimized production technology). OPT controls queues by supplying the bottleneck with sufficient batches of work so that it operates at close to maximum capacity. Other features relate to the rhythm of the throughput at the bottleneck (called the *drum*). (2) Original name for a finite production scheduling technique. The lots are of finite size. OPT techniques, developed by Eli Goldratt's company, are now called *Theory of Constraints (TOC)*. Operational production scheduling remains the goal of TOC. The objective is synchronized manufacturing by making assignments so that flows are continuous, stations are balanced, and bottlenecks are fed without queues forming. See **Theory of Constraints** and **TOC.**

Order point policies (OPP): Inventory levels drop as stock is withdrawn for use by the production system. OPP are policies that define the stock level at which a new order will be placed. Lead time is a crucial factor in determining the reorder point (RP). OPP applies to both economic order quantity (EOQ) and economic lot size (ELS) type systems with a fairly stable, continuous pattern of stock withdrawals. See **(EOQ)** and **(ELS)**. OPP is used with both perpetual and periodic inventory systems. The order point for the periodic model is the order interval. (See **Perpetual inventory system** and **Periodic inventory system**).

Order promising: Sales department commitments for delivery are the basis for the assignments of the MPS. Quantities of specific models to be made at chosen times result from customer orders and forecasts of orders that are considered highly probable. Order promising is also called order dating, which answers the question "When can you ship?"

Overhead: Fixed costs associated with operating a business no matter how much revenue is being generated.

p-chart: p-charts plot successive sample measures of the percent defective for specific quality attributes. It has upper- and lower-control limits distanced from the process average (p) so that the probabilities of the sample values of p exceeding the thresholds are preselected odds (e.g., 0.001, 0.0001) if the process is stable. At start-up, the control chart is expected to exhibit lack of control, meaning that more sample values of p exceed the control limits than is statistically warranted. The process is stabilized (brought under control) by removing assignable causes. See **R-chart.**

Paced conveyor: A transporter, usually a belt, moving materials between workstations at a fixed rate of speed (station stop-time equals cycle time). The belt may stop so that workstations can be immobile.

Parent products: Parts that go into a DVR or a car are being assembled for the parent product, which is the ultimate gozinto. The parent products often have independent demand systems.

Pareto analysis: Determines the most frequent types of defects and puts them in rank order. Pareto charts graphically depict the frequency of each kind of problem, facilitating identification of frequent defects. The rank order helps assign remedial priorities. For example, complaints to the hotel manager have been put together on a spreadsheet. The most frequent one might not be the most serious one. Therefore, Pareto data have to be reinterpreted for impact on customer dissatisfaction. A Pareto frequency distribution is the best way to begin the analysis of quality problems. Pareto diagrams that use relative frequencies (sum to 100) are often preferred.

Payback period: Justification for new technology may be based on the net present value method. The payback period (PP) is an alternative calculation that requires less math and (some say) is more intuitive. PP is defined as the period of time required for an investment to produce revenues that pay back the debt. For example, a $100 investment that generates $5 per month of revenue will take 20 months (1 year and 8 months) to pay for itself. There is no discounting of the value of money with PP. Also, if the revenue of $5 per month requires $3 for materials and labor, that leaves only $2 per month for cost recovery (CR) based on profit. Fifty months (4 years and 2 months) are needed for total CR.

Peer-assist: The peer-assist process fosters learning opportunities where people at all levels in the organization communicate needs and share knowledge and ideas.

Perfect balance (pb):   See **Balance delay.**

Performance evaluation: Lauded for feedback it provides allowing employees *at all levels* to improve their performance and to provide incentives and rewards for excellence. Criticized for being inaccurate and subjective, there is mistrust on the part of those who are below average. Statisticians note that even in a random process 50 percent of the class must be below average.

Periodic inventory system: Periodic inventory systems use regular, fixed review periods (e.g., weekly or monthly) to review existing inventory levels. On consecutive, specific dates separated by the same amount of time (an interval derived to minimize total costs), each item's record is opened. An order is placed for a variable number of units. Note that for this system, the interval between orders is fixed and the order quantity is variable. The order point for the periodic model is the open-order interval. Before computers were powerful, periodic inventory systems were far more popular than their perpetual cousins. Periodic are still more appealing for certain types of inventory situations, e.g., there is one delivery per week (Thursdays) by our company to Point Barrow, Alaska. See **Order point policies (OPP)** and **Perpetual inventory system.**

Permutability of columns: Flexibility often exists within a workstation concerning the order in which operations will be done. If two operations are assigned to a workstation and either one of them can be done first, the decision about order should be made and adhered to thereafter. Random selection will defeat the advantages of systematic procedures, which often lead later to unexpected improvements in doing the job. For example, at a workstation, either open the jar or get the pickles for the jar could be done first. The manager might express a preference for getting the pickles after opening the jar because the next step is fill the jar with pickles. See **Lateral transferability.**

Perpetual inventory system: Perpetual inventory systems are most often online, real-time, computer-driven systems. They are triggered to action by the stock level dropping to the reorder point (RP). The RP is a function of the expected demand in the lead-time period. When the RP is reached, an order of fixed size (EOQ) is placed with the supplier. Note that for this system, the interval between orders is variable and the order quantity is fixed. Perpetual inventory systems exemplify management by exception (MBE) where stock withdrawals, recorded by computer, are automatically acted upon when the RP level occurs. Management action occurs when special information is received (which is the exception)—say that a design change is about to be made to the part. Then, managers will override the automatic reorder mechanism. The two-bin perpetual inventory system (before and since computers) is a physical analog that does not require record keeping. See **Economic order quantity**, **Lead time, Periodic inventory system**, and **Reorder point (RP).**

PERT: Program evaluation review technique is a project network method. Like the critical path methods (CPM), PERT identifies the longest time-path in the project. Emphasis is on estimation as the determinant of project completion time. See **Critical-path methods (CPM).**

PERT/Cost/Time: This is the trade-off between quick completion and low cost. The theory is spend more—finish faster; spend less—finish in normal time. The PERT project network method is designed to balance the project goals. See **Critical-path methods (CPM)** and **PERT.**

Pilot studies: *Scalability* is a term describing how adaptable a process is to changes in demand volume and throughput rates. Pilots are small-scale systems used to test feasibility of the process. The assumption is that if the pilot scale works, then the full-scale system will work. This assumption is not without risk. However, the alternative is so costly that there is willingness to assume that risk. It is much less expensive to build a pilot plant than the full-scale plant. If operations fail with the pilot, the losses are minor in comparison to the alternatives. *Scalability* is a term associated with IT projects where system performance may start to deteriorate as there are more users, larger databases, and increasing complexity of process requirements.

Planning horizon: First level of aggregate planning is to determine the appropriate planning horizon for forecasting demand. It cannot be less than the longest lead time for production. If the company forecasts 600 units will be required and that will take 3 months of production, then the planning horizon is set so that the 600 units can be delivered on time. Three months is the planning horizon even though all other orders can be filled in one month.

Practical first steps: Many companies have vision statements, and they may have strategies for realizing their visions. Visions are articulated goals, and strategies are specific, but undetailed plans for achieving goals. Tactics are the missing link. Tactics deal with very elementary issues that connect all of the dots. The saying that "the devil is in the details" captures the essence of practical first steps. The initial challenge is to answer the elusive query "what do we do first?" The Gleicher (conditions for) change model requires articulated goals and believable tactics for realizing initial goals. Believability that the plan can work (practical steps) is strongly dependent on documenting exactly what to do at start-up. See **Gleicher model (Conditions for change)**, **Dissatisfaction**, and **Vision**.

Precedence diagram: Goal is to design the best possible processes using precedence diagrams of serialized flow shop systems. Precedence diagrams chart all relevant operations, indicating which operations must follow others, e.g., take-off before landing. In addition to sequencing data, times for accomplishment of each operation are listed on the precedence diagram. Good engineering develops processes that save steps and allow efficient line balancing for intermittent flow shops. At Nascar races, changing a tire is done in moments because ordinary process constraints have been bypassed.

Predictive maintenance (PDM):   Maintenance based on knowledge of signs and symptoms that something is likely to go awry in the future.

Preventive maintenance (PM):   Maintenance performed before failure. Part of total productive maintenance (TPM), it is an option that is the opposite of remedial maintenance (RM), where repairs start after failure. PM works on a regular schedule based on the knowledge of mean time between failures (MTBF). Why wait for the failure to occur? Predictive maintenance (PDM) helps to determine the MTBF.

Price elasticity: See **Demand elasticity**. These terms are interchangeable. Demand as a function of price is the classical relationship. P/OM considers quality elasticity as well.

Principle of modularity: See **Modular production (MP)**. To design, develop, and produce the minimum number of parts (or service operations) that can be combined in the maximum number of ways to offer the greatest number of different products or services. One of three underlying foundations of mass customization (which are MP, GT, and FMS).

Process: At the core of P/OM. A process is a series of activities or steps required to transform materials and components into intermediates or finished goods. The service delivery process is totally qualified in the same sense.

Process analysis: The detailed study of activities required to make the product or deliver the service. After analysis comes design and redesign.

Process charts: Graphics for doing process analysis. They are also useful for doing process design and redesign.

Process steps: Stages of the process.

Product callbacks: Have costs that include labor and material rework, decreased customer loyalty, and potential litigation losses that stem from events preceding the callback. These are costs of failure that should be compared with costs of detection and correction prior to shipping product, and the costs of prevention of defectives in the first place.

Product life cycles: See **Life cycle strategies**. Note that process life cycles accompany strategic planning for product life cycles. This relationship is taken for granted and even overlooked except by P/OM, which is responsible for process management.

Production: Activities used to create (and deliver) goods or furnish (and deliver) services to customers. This term is not used with services but it is common with the manufacture of goods.

Production management: Managing activities used to produce (and deliver) goods to customers. The implication of this term is that management is professional and effective.

Production planning: The first level is aggregate planning and it is the only level that requires a forecast. See **Planning horizon**. Production planning at the second level is loading. At level three, it is sequencing. Loading for the factory is often called shop loading. Loading in service organizations is called "manpower" planning.

Production scheduling: Subject of Chapter 16, it consists of loading and sequencing. Because of combinatorial richness (there are so many ways to set up schedules) and the difficulty of optimizing such detailed complex arrays of data, the two steps of loading and sequencing are used. Assignment and transportation models can assist in the loading function. Sequencing algorithms are available for the second part of production and operations scheduling. Production scheduling is always a systems problem because jobs, people, and teams compete with each other for best facilities.

Production standards: Criteria specifying the amount of work (specific units or service times) to be accomplished in a given period of time. These standards are statements of the expected output rates from which the costs of the product can be estimated. Production standards permit supply and demand analysis to determine shortfalls or reassignment of resources.

Productivity standards: Average performance adjusted by an allowance for rest and delay. They are used to calculate expected output rates. Productivity standards allow process managers to determine how many workers will be required to meet demand.

Productivity: "Being productive" is the dictionary's general meaning of productivity. Economists define productivity as one of many ratio measures of output divided by input. Labor productivity, for example, is output per unit of labor.

Products, Continuous development: See **Continuity** and **Ferris Wheel model**.

Project management: Projects are undertakings (usually of considerable complexity) that are unique or relatively unique such as building a factory, launching a spacecraft, staging a play, starting a business, or bringing a new product to market. Project management is managing these nonrepetitive activities in a way that is both professional and effective.

Project/Cost/Time: The generic term "project" is used in place of specific project management methods such as PERT or CPM.

Projects: (1) Special work configurations designed to accomplish singular (or nearly singular) goals. Time-based endeavors that bring together skills and technology to accomplish goals such as building structures, putting on a play, writing new software, launching new products (including publishing a new book), and organizing activities (industrial, social, military, political) to bring about change. (2) A unique type of work configuration that is used for start-up purposes with major new undertakings including structures and systems. Project management is responsible for following the planned time line and being within budget.

Projects, Continuous development: See **Continuity** and **Ferris Wheel model.**

Projects, Probability of success: p_s is the probability of product success (defined as meeting specific profit goals). Given O project completions per year, p_sO is the number of successes.

Projects, Rapid completion: There is increasing pressure to cut project time significantly. For example, from scratch, design, build, and produce a car in one year, instead of three years. Many factors play a role in achieving this objective, including concurrency and continuity. See **Concurrent engineering** and **Products, Continuous development.**

Pull-production systems: Production systems that call for delivery of materials from upstream stations (including outside suppliers) are pulling materials as needed. The contrast is with upstream stations pushing finished materials on downstream stations. The advantage of pulling is that materials are delivered just-in-time or nearly so, depending upon how many units are called for by a pull signal. The disadvantage of pushing production is that production variability can create overloads on the downstream stations leading to quality problems. Upstream stations may be overproducing. Suppliers are asked to deliver small quantities (almost JIT) rather than full deliveries, which have to be put in storage with both receipt and withdrawal costs. See **Push-production systems.**

Purchasing agents (PAs): With their buying organizations, they buy supplies the company requires. This applies to every aspect of the company's needs, including supplying production and feeding the people who eat in the cafeteria, keeping the rest rooms tidy, and giving oil to the maintenance staff for the forklift trucks. Purchasing is a traditional function that has been evolving in many interesting ways, including the use of extensive online purchasing and auctions to obtain multiple bids. Purchasing agents are one of the best listening devices invented to learn about new materials and what competitors are doing.

Pure number: See **Scoring model.** Quantitative comparison of two options poses problems of combining multiple dimensions. This is often referred to as the problem of adding apples and oranges. In P/OM, it is more likely to be the problem of adding costs and qualities together. Scientists solved that problem long ago by taking ratios of the items to be compared. Scores for each dimension of every option have exponents to reflect their importance, and these are multiplied to obtain a single number. The ratios of the products of the powers yield a pure number because all dimension are canceled.

Push-production systems: Workstations pushing materials on the downstream stations are regarded as impeding productivity. Poor line balance aggravates the situation, causing uneven output. This volatility makes it difficult to trace quality problems and causes work-in-process to pile up in places. Smooth flows and balanced cycle times of pull-production systems are gradually replacing the push-production systems of earlier eras. See **Pull-production systems.**

Put-away: The end step before the next setup, make-ready cycle. It is another term for *take down* in the *changeover* cycle.

Quality: Demand is a function of price and quality. The relationship between the quantity of goods or services demanded by customers and the customers' perceived quality of the product. Price is usually an important factor, but in most cases, quality is also crucial. Quality elasticity is not primary. For example, the price charged is also included. Elasticity measures the rate of increase or decrease in demand levels as prices are raised or lowered.

Quality circles (QCs): Groups with teamwork assignments for quality achievement. Such teams are often part of a quality function deployment (QFD) initiative. Many QCs are associated with CWTQM (company-wide TQM). The deployment of quality concerns throughout the company is assisted by QCs because everyone has an opportunity to belong to one or more circles. All aspects of company activities are fair game for study.

Quality control (QC): Quality achievement is a major P/OM systems responsibility. Quality pervades every aspect of all firms' performance. Therefore, P/OM should be a partner in strategic planning. Control of quality is a tactical function. It remains the engineering prescription when a staff department audits quality. There is precedent for external policing of quality. For example, companies' best practice does not use a QC department to serve as police enforcers.

Quality function deployment (QFD): A comprehensive program with a complete agenda for extending quality throughout the firm's activities. It includes quality circles and company-wide total quality management. QFD was started in Kobe at Japanese shipyards owned by Mitsubishi. Later, it was employed by Toyota as well as other Japanese and U.S. manufacturers, including Ford Motor. QFD employs Taguchi methods as well as the philosophy and approaches of six-sigma.

Quality integrity: One of the most important ethical issues for P/OM is to ensure delivery of products and services good for the safety and health of customers. P/OM must also provide a secure and accident-free working environment for employees. Such standards are the foundation of quality integrity. Events can be thrust on a company that destroy the feeling of quality integrity. Companies may take extraordinary measures to restore the sense of integrity. For example, in 1982, using crisis management, Johnson & Johnson reacted to Tylenol tampering with effective public relations that saved the day. Perrier water was similarly successful. Corporate social responsibility (CSR) is associated with responses that are open, honest, and swift. Deviant behaviors used by some companies to defraud the community, customers, and employees are the reverse of CSR. However, every case must be judged on its own. Quality integrity is a systems property. See **Ethics.**

R-chart: Control limits are applied to the range (R) chart, which usually is a companion to the $\bar{x}$-chart. Together the two charts supply powerful diagnostics for process behavior. Range is measured for each sample of size n by $R = x_{max} - x_{min}$. The mean of the sample measures is $\bar{R}$. It is used to determine the control limits with tabled factors that are a function of n. The limits are distanced the equivalent of $k\sigma$ from the mean so that the probabilities of sample range values exceeding these thresholds are pre-selected odds (e.g., 0.001, 0.0001) if the process is stable. The range chart checks that the spread of the distribution around the mean stays constant. See $\bar{x}$-chart.

Recycling concrete: Recycling concrete from the old road to the new road is an excellent example of end-of-life (EOL) product recovery. Environmentalists generally approve of such cradle-to-the-grave recovery and reuse system. However, there has been opposition by local citizens because of on-site noise and odors. See **Remanufacturing, Reuse,** and **Reverse supply chains.**

Red Carpet system: When a single queue forms in front of multiple channel servers (such as a single waiting line for tellers in the bank), that is called a Red Carpet system. In common use, the red carpet is laid down for important visitors. In queuing it loses the connotation of royalty and Hollywood.

Redundancy: A failure prevention strategy based on having a backup unit in place in case the operating unit fails.

Reengineering (REE): (1) Given substantial dissatisfaction with things as they are and a vision of what might be, REE starts from scratch with practical first steps. Starting from scratch can be opposed by those in favor of gradual (continuous improvement) changes. There are territorial issues that may lead caretakers of the current system to fight radical changes that occur when the design process begins with a blank piece of paper. This is only one cause of REE failure. Another is to underestimate the complexity of the challenge and the commitment for success. (2) Starting from scratch to redesign the process. The goal is to make major improvements. Major means dramatic and "revolutionary" rather than "evolutionary." Reengineering is the opposite of continuous incremental changes, which Japanese production experts call "kaizen." (3) This term is used to signify that the current processes are to be completely redone so that goals can be achieved more effectively. The concept of starting from scratch means that planners are not constrained by prior system elements and structures.

Regeneration MRP: A thorough, time-demanding method of updating the MRP information system. The APICS definition is "... the master production schedule is totally reexploded down through all bills of material, to maintain valid priorities. New requirements and planned orders are completely recalculated or 'regenerated' at that time." See **Net change MRP** for the alternative method to update MRP, and the APICS reference. All three MRP input files (BOM, IRF, and MPS) take part in the recomputation of the entire data set. All MRP records are usually regenerated once a week. More frequent regeneration is used when the penalties for outdated data are severe.

Relative productivity: A measure of comparison between similar processes. These can be comparisons of productivity between two different Budweiser breweries, or between a Budweiser brewery and a competitor's brewery, or between the same breweries over time. In this case, relative productivity is used as a benchmark, and it is critical that the identical measure be used for each unit in the comparison.

Remanufacturing: The list of companies that remanufacture is impressive and always growing. Because of economic advantages, remanufacturing is not a temporary phenomenon. As companies improve their designs of renewable components, remanufacturing becomes more attractive. Continual improvements in materials and technology are also shifting market shares to enhance the value of remanufacturing. Feasible remanufacturing candidates are on the drawing boards. Main advocates include Tom's of Maine, Xerox, Panasonic, Kodak, Fuji, John Deere, Caterpillar, BMW, and Deutz in Germany (see Deutz xchange).

Remedial maintenance (RM): Maintenance after failure.

Rent: Rent, buy, or build are familiar choices for buildings, facilities, land, and equipment. Rent (lease) payments are made regularly by a tenant (lessee) to a landlord (lessor). There is a contract conveying property to another for a specified period in consideration of compensation. These are treated as fixed costs even when there are provisions for terminating the agreement with sufficient notice and payment.

Reorder point (RP): Triggers an order for more stock. This order can be placed automatically with a "trusted" supplier. There will be no managerial intervention unless an instance qualifying for MBE occurs. Then, the special situation will be brought to management's attention for review, including choice of supplier. Systems can alert management to slowdowns occurring in withdrawals (interval between RPs is statistically greater than expectation).

Resource leveling: Where slack exists, there is potential for resource trade-offs that can reduce nonvalue-adding time while decreasing the time required for completion of the project. Sometimes the resource is a person reassigned to work with a different team for a day or two. At other times, it is the transfer of equipment or facilities, such as a truck, or a place to store materials. See **Multiple project management** and **Slack.**

Reuse: There are many associations devoted to various aspects of recycling materials. Reuse is one of the recycling categories that is economically attractive because a reusable part can quickly be returned to inventory. Reusable plastics, glass, paper, and metal may require more value-adding than a nut, bolt, or gear that can be reused with just cleanup. In remanufacturing, there are combinations of new parts and reusable, repairable, reworked parts. Preplanned design decisions for reuse after disassembly can change the economics of the product, including breakeven points, margin, and return on investments. See **Design for disassembly, Recycling concrete, Remanufacturing,** and **Take-back laws.**

Reverse engineering: Intelligent disassembly that carefully notes and labels all details so that assembly can follow without any hitches. This provides maximum information about competitive products.

Reverse supply chains: Take-back momentum is increasing because end-of-product-life recovery is a social necessity as populations grow larger and life styles produce increasing amounts of disposable material. There is a reverse delivery logistic at end-of-life for both used up and damaged products. Automobile recycling commands so much attention that the acronym ELV is used for end-of-life-of-vehicle. Also on the agenda is disposal of SOC (substance of concern). Increasingly, manufacturers are held responsible for Best Practice with returned materials (intelligent ELV objectives) and for providing the means for return delivery. Saturn trucks deliver cars to dealers and return with damaged plastic doors and body parts. See **Reuse, Remanufacturing,** and **Take-back laws.**

Robots: See **Cyborgs** and **flexible process system** (FPS). Robots are evolving from mechanical devices that perform complex, repetitive, and often unpleasant, tasks into computer-controlled systems with broad sensory abilities, discernment, and forms of intelligence. Although in its infancy, robotics has transformed manufacturing technology, military and police reconnaissance, and is now beginning to provide service functions. The forces that propel increasing use of robots are miniaturization, artificial intelligence, improved sensory capabilities, and information feedback. "Robot," derived from the Czech word *robota* (compulsory labor) was first used in the play called "RUR" (Rossum's Universal Robots), written by Karel Çapek in 1926. One definition of robots includes the fact that they are made to look like people. Some service robots continue this trend.

Rough-cut capacity planning (RCCP):   At the time that the aggregate plan (AP) is being transformed into the master production schedule (MPS), RCCP is used to check that there is sufficient capacity to produce what is needed. The method uses approximation based on the bill of resources (BOR) to determine if actual capacity is adequate to match the expected capacity requirements of the MPS. Capacity requirements planning is post-MRP planning operating at the plant or enterprise level where strategic business decisions will be made about investments in additional capacity. Rough-cut capacity planning is working at the shop floor level doing the disaggregation of the aggregate plan into actual work assignments to meet real demand. RCCP can result in deferral of shipments when capacity is insufficient.

Runs: A run of numbers on any control chart is a succession of values that fall either above or below the mean line. It is like a string of heads or tails, which becomes increasingly unlikely as the streak continues. This makes runs a great telltale that something is awry with the system's behavior because normal performance is a random drawing of heads and of tails. Runs also provide diagnostic information about health of the quality system. Strings below the mean have different process interpretations than above the mean. If runs are accelerating (meaning that distances from the mean are increasing) that connotes momentum in the system's deterioration. More urgency for remedial action is indicated.

Scatter diagrams: Figures composed of data points that are thought to be associated with each other, as calories consumed (*x*) and weight (*y*). This relationship is not expected to be precisely linear, but a pattern may emerge for particular groups of people, such as those who live in a region of the world where fish is the main staple. If data for *x* and *y* are related, the relationship is likely to appear upon visual inspection. The same correlation would be difficult for most people to spot in tables of numbers.

Scientific management: The name given to the systematic approach to doing work well, developed by Frederick Winslow Taylor in the late 1800s and early 1900s. Scientific management stressed the fact that there was a best way to do work. In search of the best way, the various factors that made up the job were listed, observed, and analyzed. During the 1930s, practitioners of the approach were called *efficiency experts.* In later years, this work became the province of industrial engineering.

Scoring model: Compares quantitatively alternative options for a broad variety of situations. Various kinds of scoring models serve different purposes. Monetary analyses of costs and revenues for business options are used effectively. Business decisions often cannot rely exclusively on straight dollar comparisons. The same applies to a credit agency scoring the status of an individual's financial soundness. Scoring models using ratios can be employed with mixed dimensions because ratios produce *pure numbers.* Scoring models unify the many tangible and intangible costs and benefits that are relevant in a complex comparison. They are a means for organizing and combining personal guesses, somewhat speculative estimates, and hard numbers. Use of sensitivity analysis is recommended for exploring the effects of errors in estimations. See http://www.myfico.com for practical examples of personal credit scoring.

Sensitivity analysis: (1) By using high and low estimates, it is possible to test the sensitivity of a business model (e.g., linear programming, scoring, and transportation models) to a range of conditions. If alternative A is the preferred option under expected (average) conditions, and this remains the case when estimates are at their extreme values, then the decision is stable. However, if shifts occur, then it is important to home in on better estimates to which the solution is sensitive. (2) Whether conducted by hand, laptop spreadsheet, or full-scale computer software, sensitivity analysis allows diagnostic analysis of the effects of changing inventory costs, including purchase price (get a discount for ordering more); labor, materials, fabrication and assembly costs; carrying costs; ordering costs; setup costs; and market demands. Tests are run in response to managers' "what if" questions. When done systematically, and with innovative ideas, sensitivity analysis improves system performance.

Sequenced assembly: Henry Ford's contribution to the world of production. In 1912, he set up the continuous flow assembly line, and production was never the same again. The key was synchronization and control of the process flows, including those flows from vendors to feed the "mass production" line.

Sequencing: (1) The second part of production scheduling, sequencing follows the loading function. Job order can make a big difference in the flow time, which is the length of time it takes to process a sequence of *n* jobs. Shortest processing time (SPT) will produce the shortest flow time. See **Mean flow time, SPT rule, Total flow time.** (2) *Third* level of aggregate planning is sequencing. It provides the best ordering for jobs to be done at each department. Best can be defined in a number of different ways. A primary basis for establishing optimal sequence is to minimize the time jobs spend waiting. There are other bases too.

Sequencing chart: See **Layout chart.**

Service: P/OM needs to delineate both the differences and similarities between producing goods and providing services. The service category is complex because it includes every form of work except manufacturing of goods. That means the teaching of students, caring for patients in a healthcare facility, entertaining the guests at a theme park, cleaning the apartment, serving the food, marrying the couple, running the library, providing the concert, making the movie, and going to the theater are all classified as services.

Setup(s):   The start of the changeover cycle. It is the common term for engineering process shifts to stop making one item and start making another.

Shop floor control: Consists of tracking and communicating the status of orders in the job shop. It also requires monitoring and reporting on the productivity of workstations. Knowing what is having value-added, and what is waiting, helps to expedite jobs, decrease idle time, and increase value-adding.

Simulation: The imitative representation of the functioning of a system or process by means of the functioning of a surrogate system or process. The methodology of mechanical simulation for testing has been used for many years. For example, the device that turns a doorknob 6,000 times an hour can test the fatigue limits of the latch bolt springs in days instead of having to wait years for failure to occur. In the same empirical fashion, dropping packages permits testing durability. Growing import is placed on the results derived from crashing cars with dummies into walls. The dummies are filled with chips that communicate with computers to reveal forces on their bodies experienced during crashes. Car designers as well as buyers follow these results with interest. Simulations can now be run entirely on computers using math equations to represent special situations such as air turbulence effects on planes and large waves on ship hulls.

Single-channel system: A single server ($M = 1$) is providing service. With variable service times and variable arrival rates, a line starts to form when the number of arrivals $n > 1$, during an average service period. Simple queue equations are available to describe the behavior of the system. Single-channel systems are a special case of multiple-channel systems, for $M = 1$. See **Multiple-channel system.**

Single-minute exchange of dies (SMED): An interesting nonfiction story. Taiichi Ohno of Toyota Motor Manufacturing in Japan demanded revolutionary changes of setup times, and he asked Shigeo Shingo to cut setup times for a particular operation from four hours to three minutes. Shingo did even better. He established procedures for setups that take less than a minute. This was a sea-change in P/OM.

Six-sigma: (1) A comprehensive management system that applies every relevant tool and technique for quality assurance. (2) Goals first set by Motorola in 1986. Philip Crosby Associates had preached zero defects long before that time. However, each firm had its own approach. Crosby stated that conformance to specifications is crucial. When choosing specs that are attainable, zero defects are a reasonable goal. Motorola, on the other hand, wanted product design and production processes that could deliver near-zero defects (six-sigma is 3.4 defects per million parts). See Motorola University at http://mu.motorola.com.

SKU: The catalogue of stock-keeping units (SKU) presents every different part carried, sold, or purchased by the company. A unique identification number exists for each of the distinct parts. These ID numbers tell as much as possible about the item: suppliers, materials, sizes, colors, shapes, styles, and family tree (which model in the lineage).

Slack: (1) Free time at a project activity. This translates to allowable slippage in an activity's schedule along a slack path. The slack between activities describes the amount of time that it is safe to be late in delivering a completed activity. Project managers view activity paths with limited amounts of slack as potential problem areas because minor events can change limited slack operations into activities along the critical path. (2) Unused departmental capacity. The term means that there is room for maneuvering. It is the antonym for tightness and constraint on freedom in the system. In various LP applications, slack can apply to unused materials, people, money, and machine capacities. Linear programming optimizations of profit often occur with some unused capacity. The term is also used for projects to indicate some flexibility in the use of resources to avoid missing deadlines. Resources associated with slack paths can be traded off to critical paths (where deadlines exist) to assure completion on schedule. See **Critical path methods (CPM)** and **Multiple project management.**

Slope: Low breakeven points are preferred to high BEPs. However, the slope of the profit line before and after breakeven determines how fast loss and gain occur when demand falls below or rises above the BEP.

Smart benchmarks: An assessment of company performance can be obtained by comparison with a competitor, another division of the same organization, or with the same department over time. Benchmarking is costly and time-consuming. Therefore, a limited number of dimensions can be measured. Which dimensions are the most important to make the basis of comparison? Smart benchmarks are based on those dimensions that are most valuable for steering tactics and for redirecting strategies. For example, return on equity is increasingly popular with chief financial officers (CFOs), and inventory turns are favored by companies like Wal-Mart and Thomasville Furniture.

SME enterprise wheel: This graphic provides a "vision" of a fully integrated global manufacturing company. Links resources and responsibilities within the three sectors of product/process, manufacturing, and customer support. Organizational issues are at the core and participate with people and teamwork to satisfy the requirements of customers. Information and technology are in an outer ring that surrounds the entire complex. Minor effort is needed to recast the wheel for any nonmanufacturing system.

Special-purpose equipment (SPE): Primarily used in the flow shop. It is designed for one-, two-, or three-shift relatively continuous operation. SPE is efficient in repetitive production of the same kind of unit. In automobile assembly, several similar cars can be run through the same line with no major changeovers required to shift models.

SPT rule: Shortest processing time is a powerful heuristic rule for decreasing the time required to complete operations for n jobs. Jobs are rank-ordered in their processing times, t. The job with the smallest t goes first. The job with the next-smallest t goes second, and so forth. The SPT rule can be modified to give priority to jobs that have waited a long time in the queue. Other priority rule modifications of SPT include preference for most profitable, or loyal, customers or for due date compliance. Contrast with **FIFO** and **LIFO.**

Square root inventory model: This is the fundamental basis of order point policy (OPP) inventory models.

Stages of P/OM development: Four stages can be loosely characterized as reflecting how much management counts on P/OM for success: (1) not at all; (2) to control costs; (3) to emulate the best; (4) to set the standard for the best.

Standard units: Jobs are converted from pieces of work (order size) into standard hours required to make the pieces and fill the order on a designated machine called the standard machine. This facilitates aggregate planning for the use of production resources and the timing of events to meet expected demands (work schedules).

Static inventory models: There is only one chance to order the right amount of stock. Corrections that are allowed by dynamic inventory models do not operate in the static situation where how much to order is a one-shot decision. There is almost no second-guessing allowed when deciding how many Christmas trees to order for the three sales weeks before December 25. Sometimes the no-repetition rule is bent a bit to allow one corrective action. Thus, a mail-order catalogue preparing for the holiday season may place a first order for toys in August. Then, after observing competitors, finishing ongoing market research, and monitoring toy store sales, the decision is made to increase stock on-hand with another order placed in September. See **Dynamic inventory models.**

Static inventory problem: Classical inventory problem with some special characteristics, namely, how much to buy when there is only one purchase occasion allowed. Not usually applicable to flow shop inventories, but necessary for job shops and project management. The company that fabricates toys for Christmas may set up in August with various suppliers, each getting one order. This is also relevant to the static repair problem, where the generator is purchased with a given number of spare parts. The static problem is: Given a parts-failure distribution, how many spare parts should be bought with the generator?

Statistical process control (SPC): This set of statistical methods is part of statistical quality control (SQC). It is the control charting aspect of SQC. See **Statistical quality control (SQC).**

Statistical quality control (SQC): Statistical quality control (SQC) encompasses SPC as well as other statistical methods, including acceptance sampling. Walter Shewhart's work on SQC was published in 1930. It created a taxonomy for control of quality that led to a revolution in quality standards and capabilities throughout the world. His methodology detailed all of the factors that resulted in process variability. Shewhart explained what steps should be taken to reduce variability. He provided charts to stabilize and control a system. His work also pointed to the fact that inherent variability could only be reduced by changing the management of the process and the process itself. See **Control chart** and **Statistical process control (SPC).**

Stochastic line balancing: Stochastic line balancing occurs when variability exists in the form of statistical distributions of operation and/or transport times. It is more difficult to balance stochastic production lines because the arrival rates and the service rates at the stations are erratic and unpredictable. Line balancing has queuing elements at work. Simulation can be useful to test performances of various line-balancing strategies. Simulation is a strong method for analyzing the stochastic line-balancing system. See **Line balancing.**

Strategic business units (SBUs): SBUs are independent subdivisions of the company. They are considered to be coherent (likely self-contained) profit-making entities for the company. The management of each SBU is expected to describe clear and unambiguous strategic plans for their product lines. Generally, tactical business units are a subsidiary part of the strategic business units, which include products and processes.

Strategy: The big plan. It is directly translated into "do the right thing." Tactics is translated into "do it the right way." Strategy is the term used to describe the comprehensive and overall planning for the organization's future. In the military context, strategy must destroy the enemy capability. In the business context, strategy must be product-oriented and marketing-aware to take the customer and the competition into account. Planning military actions such as where to engage the enemy and under what circumstances is the familiar use of the term *strategy.* Derived from the Greek word *strategía,* meaning "generalship," military strategists are master planners. Their partnership with tacticians is of great importance.

Substances of concern (SOC): These include mercury, lead, cadmium, and hexavalent chromium, Cr(VI). The last chemical in this list was the subject of the Erin Brockovich movie regarding contamination of drinking water with Cr(VI), which is discussed as a suspected carcinogen. See http://www.grac.org/Chromium WhitePaper.pdf. An agreement has been reached to entirely remove Cr(VI) by Ford (July 2005), GM (August 2006), and DaimlerChrysler (January 2007).

Suggestion system: Depends upon who is speaking: Employee contributions are a great source of ideas for improvement. If no one reads the suggestions, the system is a sham. There is ample evidence that this discrepancy is a function of management's attitude and desire to employ teamwork.

Supply chain: The linkage between raw materials and finished products (goods and services) delivered into the hands of the customers. In fact, the supply chain is the fully-connected input-transformation-output (I/T/O) system. Fabrication is the one form of transformation most commonly associated with supply chains. However, transportation, entertainment, (healthcare) operations, and education are a few others. Transportation in the supply chain is crucial. Storage points occur at many locations because warehousing is essential for supply chain management. A notable point is that materials upstream (starting at the headwaters) have less investment in transformation. The investment in materials increases as they move downstream. The form of materials becomes more specific. The supply chain is replete with information of varying kinds, including the state of materials and the flow of money. The degree of finalization of all transactions (in information theory terms) is measured by its entropy. The state of the products (goods and services) transits from high entropy to low entropy as the products approach the ultimate consumer. The supply chain does not stop at retail distribution if there are any warranties and repair guarantees. What are raw materials to some are finished products to others. Thus, copper used as a raw material in auto production is a finished good from the point of view of the copper mines.

Synchronization: Flow shops are predesigned to have perfect synchronization of workstations. Job shops require major efforts to synchronize manufacturing. Synchronization requires control over the timing of flows. This includes how much is made at one time. Transfer amounts and storage amounts are determined by control rules as derived by finite scheduling methods. See **OPT** and **TOC.**

Synergy: The result of a set of agents producing a greater effect when acting together than the sum of their separate effects when acting alone as individuals. For example, if three forces can each produce a pound of pressure when acting alone, but when acting in concert they produce five pounds of pressure, there is synergy.

Synthetic or predetermined time standards: Used to make estimates for jobs that do not yet exist from a subset of common elements. Estimates influence choices in development of new designs. The process is part of design for manufacturing (DFM) and design for assembly (DFA). The time to accomplish units of work are generic (or synthetic) modules such as lift, grasp, and turn. They are also called *predetermined time standards.*

Synthetic process: Production process that starts with many ingredients. Using appropriate transformation techniques, the process combines the various materials, components, subassemblies, etc., into a single, basic product or into several similar products. For example, tires, windshields, upholstery, engines, chassis, etc., go to form the car, which requires thousands of parts.

Systematic: Analytic, synthetic, and creative systems approach that might be said to work from the inside out.

Systemic: Holistic and contemplative systems approach that might be said to work from the outside in.

Systems approach: This is contrasted with the **functional field approach.** The systems approach is the big view that includes everything that might account for what is happening. The systems approach accents connections and interactions between all functions (such as marketing and finance).

Systems utilization factor: λ is the average arrival rate and μ is the average service rate. For single-channel systems, $\rho = \lambda/\mu$. If $\lambda = 3$ and $\mu = 4$, then $\rho = 3/4 = 75$ percent. Rho is the average percent of time that the station is providing service. If that figure is close to 100 percent, then the system is overloaded. By providing M servers, the capacity problem is alleviated. For multiple-channel systems, $\rho = \lambda/M\mu$, which is the average percent of time that the M-server system is providing service. If $M = 3$, $\lambda = 3$, and $\mu = 4$, then, $\rho = 1/4$, which is an underloaded system. See **Single-channel system.**

Syzygy: The point when maximum tidal pull is exerted because the planets and the moon have lined up to support each other's gravitational forces. Generally, forces exert pulls in different directions and offset or cancel each other. Syzygy comes from the Greek word for "conjunction," and it is also the only word in the English language that has no vowels and three *y*'s. Parenthetically, *y* takes on vowel-like sounds, as in "duty."

Tacit knowledge: Significant information is transferred by tacit means such as a body language. Tacit knowledge is unstated, implicit, inferred, and unspoken. It is difficult to describe tacit knowledge because it is not evident. Because it is unclear, it is not possible to catalog it or put it into a yellow page–type directory. The only way to access tacit knowledge is to consult with people who are seen as being intuitive, instinctive, and perceptive. Such people are associated with areas of awareness that make them specialists. Project teams often operate at a distance from each other. Distance learning can be crucial to project management, and it is not effective with tacit knowledge. The classroom beats the Internet in transferring tacit knowledge. See **Explicit knowledge** and **Knowledge management.**

Tactics: Detailed procedures required to carry out strategic plans. Derived from the Greek word *taktikós,* meaning "fit for arranging," military tacticians are masters of maneuvering resources subject to strategic battle plans.

Taguchi methods: It is often said that the Western industrialized world uses goalpost standards for quality. This means that as long as the football goes between the two goal posts, it counts as a field goal score. Taguchi proposed an optimal quality point and spoke about a loss function to describe deviations from that optimal. The loss is larger as the deviation becomes greater. Using design of experiments, Taguchi advocates designing the product and the process together to deliver the minimal loss value (the closest statistical result to the optimal value). See http://kernow .curtin.edu.au/www/Taguchi/INTRO.HTM or use Google to search for Taguchi methods.

Take-back laws: Governmental rules are being invoked in Europe and in the United States (at a slightly slower rate) to ensure material reuse and/or proper disposal. Laws can force a company to take back discarded and used-up product from customers for recycling and reemployment. However, prethinking creative reuse of recycled parts can lower costs, improve quality, and satisfy new stringent laws about the percent reuse of a product.

Taxonomy: Methods of classification and categorization of phenomena usually arranged in a hierarchical structure.

Team building: Focus is on removing adversarial attitudes and replacing them with a sense of "family." Trust-building training is enhanced by a common set of goals. Trust spurs cooperative (or team) learning. Special considerations apply to cross-cultural team building.

Team learning: Also called *cooperative learning*, requires communication between members of the group and training to help each other support a common goal. Loyalty to the company "family" is cited and effective removal of adversarial relations is imperative.

Technology trap: By default, new technology is often applied to the management of old (legacy) systems. The resulting effect is to gain little improvement and to further institutionalize antiquated systems and procedures. To avoid this trap, systems studies should upgrade the way that work is done in keeping with the capabilities of new technology.

Technology: Equipment employed to accomplish the transformation that is basic to the fundamental P/OM input–output model of production. Equipment includes machines, computers, tools, and communication systems. It can include human/machine combinations known as cyborgs.

Theory of Constraints: A mind-set for determining the core problems in production scheduling, project management, and other P/OM activities. Recognition of problems leads to construction of detailed solutions, as well as means for implementing them. After OPT, Goldratt's research included additional systems factors and provided a higher level of diagnosis and prescription called Theory of Constraints (TOC). Goldratt found that optimizing production scheduling in isolation from other business variables usually does not lead to higher productivity. Using TOC, the systems viewpoint is broad. It encompasses more restricted specifics of bottleneck-based finite scheduling (called *OPT*). See **OPT.**

Time and motion study: Sampling and recording what workers do to make, finish, or pack a product. Can be used for service operations such as a serving counter at McDonalds, the back room of a bank, tellers' windows, etc. Detailed descriptions of each activity are given, including the observed times. Later study can change the workplace configuration. It can suggest alternative locations for materials as well as different tools and fixtures. Training may be recommended to improve the time required for accomplishments. Videos may be used to provide scenario repetitions for further study by team members.

Time series: A stream of numbers that represents different values over time. They are always presented in time-ordered sequence for one or more specific variables.

Time series analysis: The analysis of a stream of numbers in a time series. For example, the time series could be temperatures taken daily for a month, or barometric pressures observed every hour for a week. The values of the variables change over time because of various factors such as the multitudinous forces that create weather patterns at different times of the year. Time series analysis of business variables such as daily sales (demand) and production output (supply) can provide valuable insights even though the underlying causal factors that account for these time series are not shown or explained.

Time study: The study of how long it takes to do specific operations. Unlike work sampling, where the goal is to find out what is being done. In time study, the time required to complete specific jobs is captured. Sometimes computers are able to monitor the system. This is done, for example, for many variables in call centers. It is also standard practice for check-processing activities in the back room of the bank. In other cases, the same stopwatches that are used to time high school sprinters can be used to find out how long it takes to unload a truck or to check out customers in the supermarket.

Time-based management (TBM): An inclusive term for managers' concerns about time lines, schedules, deliveries, and project completions. The goals are to be fast-moving, rapid-responders, high velocity without quality losses. TBM includes schedule control, cycle-time management, and synchronization of production flows. The logistics of delivery and the ability to move rapidly into new markets are major elements of TBM. At the tactical level, it consists of tracking and reporting the status of orders, expediting jobs, decreasing idle time, and increasing value-adding. Elevates time to a variable of equal importance with cost, quality, and productivity. Time is a surrogate for profitability, market share, and customers' satisfaction. Time-based management is responsible for fast delivery of goods and services to customers and rapid development of new products. As such, time is both a strategic variable and a tactical factor. TBM is increasingly important as competitors excel in surpassing customer temporal expectations.

TOC: The acronym commonly used for Theory of Constraints. It is now the preferred name for finite production scheduling rules. See **Constraints, theory of** and **OPT**.

Tolerance limits: The plus and minus parts of tolerance limits (e.g., 6.00 ± 0.05) are like the goalposts described in the entry for Taguchi methods. The normal inspection process accepts products that measure within the upper and lower values of the tolerance limits. Statistical quality control (SQC) charts have equivalent upper and lower control limits. When the set of sequential sample means falls inside those "posts," the process is assumed to be stable. This is the most often used method for SQC.

Tolerance matching: Quality products must have parts that fit together properly. Windows in houses, doors on autos, CD discs in CD players, Philips head screw drivers, and Philips head screws are a few examples. Proper fitting requires careful matching of tolerances. The scenario starts with design of two parts and specification of their tolerance limits. Testing comes next, with the

parts at their limit extremes. If the fit is too loose or too tight, redesign is used until the fit is "just about right." The process that makes the parts must be able to produce them to tolerance limits. Testing by go/no go gauges (or some equivalent) should create no more defectives than the original plan specifies.

Total costs = $TC = FC + TVC$: TC are the sum of fixed costs and total variable costs. Breakeven occurs where the total cost line intersects the total revenue line.

Total flow time: The cumulative time required to complete a group of jobs. It is composed of the sum of complete-to-ship times, $C_i = W_i + t_i$. This includes waiting-to-be-done times (W_i) and job processing times (t_i). The equation for total flow time is $\Sigma_i C_i = \Sigma_i (W_i + t_i)$.

Total or cumulative lead time (LT): The time between recognition of the need for an order and the acknowledged, genuine receipt of goods. Individual components of lead time can include order preparation time, waiting-line time, transport time, computer-processing time (in-stock records of replenishment materials), and inspection time at the receiving docks. The maximum cumulative lead time for a parent product is found by looking at the longest lead-time path to obtain all of the parts that go into it as the end item. Because standard items are in stock, they have zero lead time. Special items that are not in stock participate in the computation of total or maximum lead time.

Total Productive Maintenance (TPM): A systematic program to prevent process breakdowns, failures, and stoppages. It is a rational blend of maintenance alternative.

Total productivity: See **Multifactor productivity.**

Total quality management (TQM): The result of applying systems vision to every aspect of quality in the organization. TQM assumes that what the file clerk is doing impinges on the quality output of the process. Everybody counts, all of the time, so there is a need to integrate the effects of the total supply chain with the product line and the processes used in offices as well as on the plant floor. Note that the consumer plays a crucial role. If the voice of the consumer is not being heard within the House of Quality, then there is a listening problem and quality function deployment is, at best, partial.

Total revenue = $TR = (p)V$: Total revenue is price per unit (p) multiplied by the volume (V) sold (not just made) in a period of time, T. TR applies to the same period of time, T. The emphasis is on the goods and services being sold in the marketplace because revenue creates a positive cash flow for the company only when the goods are paid for with cash and not IOUs. There have been S.E.C. problems with companies claiming sales that are still accounts receivable. Total revenue is the sum of positive cash flows from various models (SKUs) made or delivered by the same process. The same summation applies to various services delivered by the same process. The breakeven point occurs where the total revenue line intersects the total cost line.

Total variable costs = $TVC = (vc)V$: The result of multiplying the variable cost per unit (vc) by the number of units or volume (V) produced. These are also known as total direct costs. The total variable cost for 10 units is $10vc$.

Total work content (TWC): What does it take to bake a cake? Every detail must be documented and then drawn up in a precedence diagram, which shows order and time required for each operation. The sum of all operation times required to bake this specific cake is called the total work content. Another baker may do this job in a different way, which would produce a different value of TWC. It is likely to produce a different quality evaluation as well. For the equation form of TWC, see **Balance delay**.

Trade-off models: These are generic models in which raising the size of (x) brings increasing advantages of one kind (benefit) while creating larger penalties of another kind (costs). The decision maker chooses how much of x to use to balance the benefits and costs. For example, raising the order size will increase the amount of stock on-hand, which lowers the risk of going out of stock. It also decreases the number of orders that must be placed. On the other hand, it raises carrying costs and increases storage space required. Trade-off models are managers' delights because they provide opportunity for discretionary control. See **Cost trade-off analysis.**

Trade-offs: Project managers are constantly required to reach smart cost/time trade-offs. Spend more money on project resources, and finish sooner, or vice versa. See **PERT/Time/Cost** and **Slack.**

Transformation: The big T is one of the most important parts of the P/OM system. It is the transformation process capability to cut metal, polish brass, take temperatures, pack toothpaste cartons, build cars, and so forth. Transformation moves customers from one city to another. The transformation from hurting and damaged to well and repaired results from successful healthcare processes. The transformation from bad to good student is still not obvious. How are great managers fashioned? That too is still not obvious.

Transportation models: Minimize shipping costs or maximize profits where production facility location and market (shipped to) differentials exist. The data for this model include production capacities at different plants, market demand, and shipping costs per mile along each route. For example, plants exist in Dayton, Atlanta, and Denver, and each has different costs of production. Warehouses are in Seattle, Dallas, and Trenton, and the selling price in each market is different. To which warehouses should the plants ship? Solution is available by either linear programming or network methods.

Transshipment: The shipping of goods to an intermediate destination for an add-on operation or because it is a shipping hub from which the items are sent on to their final destination.

Turnover: It is the objective of supply chain managers to achieve as many inventory turns as possible. Turns are counted by the number of times per year that the warehouse is emptied and refilled. Each turn promises beneficial cash flow. Turns are measured by annual net sales divided by total average stock on-hand. Turnover can also be measured by dividing 365 days by DOI.

Turning points: The points in time when a time series changes direction. The reversal of direction is sometimes called a *tipping point.*

V-A-T: This is not your VAT tax. It is the categorization developed by Eli Goldratt's organization, and marketed as TOC, for classifying processes. V-processes are analytic. They start with a single commodity that is then refined to create dozens of by-products. A-processes are synthetic. They start with several inputs that are combined to yield a marketable product. T-processes are combinations of V and A. Bottlenecks are most likely to occur with T-processes because of conflicting patterns with aggregation (assembly through synthesis) and disaggregation (disassembly through analysis).

Value added: Raw materials have value added by the transformation process of P/OM, which makes them into parts that conform to blueprints. Assembly operations add value by combining and fastening parts to form an entity that did not exist previously (e.g., an automobile). Value added is what P/OM processes do that creates profits in the form of revenues greater than costs. When materials sit without value being added, there is a loss to the company. Flow shops are efficient cash generators. They have the advantage of adding value on continuous basis.

Value analysis (VA): (1) Adopted by materials managers since 1940, when the U.S. Navy championed the application of VA. The main ideas are to search for alternative materials as replacements for the current ones with quality gains and cost advantages. Monitor technological developments to avoid missing new materials opportunities not yet recognized. Stress creativity and innovation in the continuing effort to find better materials. Purchasing agents need management support in the value analysis quest. (2) A systematic investigation of purchased parts decisions. Applied originally to materials, the extension of VA to services is appealing. The primary questions are whether alternatives exist of superior quality and/or lower prices. Within the quality issue is reliability of delivery and the utility of supplier research to improve the product. Value analysis with its cross-boundary queries epitomizes the systems approach. The U.S. Navy developed VA methods. (3) Constant vigil must be maintained to choose the best materials for tasks since materials undergo constant improvement as well as price changes. Competitive disadvantage occurs when opportunities to shift to superior materials are missed. Cooperation with suppliers enhances innovation probabilities.

Variable costs per unit = vc: Variable costs are charges attributable to each unit of product that is made and/or delivered. They are also called *direct costs* because they are paid out only on a per unit basis. Examples are material used and labor employed to make a finished unit of product. The total variable cost for seven units is $7vc$.

Variety: The number of product alternatives (in a given product class) that are made available to the customer. The product has to satisfy a variety of customer types (called *market segments*). Variety of choice is also an important nonfunctional quality dimension. P/OM can help produce variety at a low cost by using smart methods to move from one variation of the product to another. It is known that Jello customers like to switch flavors and colors from time to time. Some processes have minimum changeover costs and times.

VARS: Value-added reseller, usually to the final consumer as a *turn-key* application. Value-adding includes special features, consulting, research, etc.

Vendor releasing: Supplier agrees to deliver small portions of the larger order on a specified schedule. The buyer obtains some of the discount benefits of large volume purchasing. The seller gets the benefits of higher certainty regarding demand for the item being sold. The buyer gets closer to just-in-time delivery with its advantages of lower storage costs, decreased carrying costs, and other benefits.

Vision: Clear and unambiguous view of what the future can become. Vision statements are articulated goals. Some companies have spent a great deal of time developing vision statements, but they lack vision-linked strategies for realizing the goals. Even when formulated strategies exist, tactics can be missing. Tactics include practical first steps for goal achievement. Vision (V) of an improved situation cannot by itself lead to change. If dissatisfaction with the current situation is not great enough, then change will not occur. $V > 0$ is a necessary but not sufficient condition for change. See **Gleicher model (Conditions for change).**

Wage determination: Based on normal time, a reasonable piecework wage can be determined by management. Because learning curve effects enable employees to produce more units after stabilization, the wage is modified so as to provide incentive for maintaining higher productivity. In general, wages are determined by job difficulty, training required, skill level needed, and value to the firm. Comparisons with other companies in the same industry and region can be helpful.

Water-jetting: High water-pressure technology that replaces toxic maintenance methods used to remove paints and coatings. Also, cuts shapes with water and abrasives. Historically, traditional surface preparation and coating renewal work has been a low-tech, labor- and time-intensive, environmentally challenging endeavor.

Work centers: Combinations of people, materials, and machines that work together on specific job assignments. Work centers can be moved around on the plant or office floor. The assignment of work centers to specific space locations on the plant or office floor should minimize costs (or times) of transport of materials, work in process, and finished goods. Multistory buildings need 3-dimensional solutions. Facility layout and work center space assignments interact.

Work configuration: Another name for a type of production process. The main categories of work configurations are custom work, job shop or batch work, flow shop and intermittent flow shop, project, and flexible process system including flexible manufacturing system. Continuous flow production systems are highly engineered flow shops.

Work in process (WIP):   It exists in the form of incomplete jobs that cannot be shipped or put into finished goods storage. WIP waits for completion of the value-added operations. In the flow shop, jobs move sequentially from workstations upstream to those downstream. At each station, further transformation is taking place and value is being added. In the job shop, batches of work are undergoing (generally) nonsequential transformations. Value added is the P/OM process contribution to raw materials and components. In the job shop, there are noticeable amounts of work that are waiting for additional value added.

Work sampling: Provides information about the percentage of time that various activities are being done during the day. Method is applicable for studying services such as office operations, R&D departments, and hospitality employees without workstations. Work sampling can be used to determine how effective training programs are in getting people to use different methods and mixes of methods to accomplish their goals. It is essential to explain to those observed that the purpose is to make the job being done easier and better.

$\bar{x}$-chart: Basic quality control chart designed for variables measured on a continuous scale such as tire pressure and particle emissions. Samples of size n are taken successively. The derived sample means are numbered to maintain their correct order. Control limits are applied to the $\bar{x}$-chart as well as its companion R-chart. The limits are distanced the equivalent of $k\sigma$ from the mean so that the probabilities of sample mean values exceeding these thresholds are preselected odds (e.g., 0.001, 0.0001) given that the process is stable. Taken together, the two charts supply powerful diagnostics for aberrant process behavior.

Zed defects (ZD):   A policy that requires eliminating any and all causes of defects. It is crucial to realize that a zero or zed defects policy is determined by what is defined to be acceptable quality. In other words, the definition of defects determines what conformance to standards is required. Quality definitions determine defect rates that will be measured. Consider extension of the application of ZD to human systems where malfunctions can lead to serious problems in such instances as surgery, air control, and piloting ships and planes.

Zero breakdowns: An option of TPM. The policy of zero breakdowns requires eliminating any and all malfunctions and failures. Machine breakdowns come to mind but should be extended to encompass other equipment such as computers and communication networks. Redundancies are used by banks, power plants, etc., to back up systems in case of failures. The next extension of the application of zero breakdowns is to human systems where malfunctions can lead to serious problems in such instances as surgery, air control, and piloting.

Zero defects: The six-sigma discussion starts out with two different approaches to zero or zed defects. It is noteworthy that when zero defects is not the standard, then some level of defects is expected. For example, some number of eggs that are in the display case of the local supermarket are cracked. Most supermarket managers accept that defective rate. Say it is 2 percent. A zero-defect manager knows that certain brands have packages that yield a significantly smaller breakage rate. Also, that manager could inspect incoming eggs to remove those that are already broken when put on display. Clear packages could help staff eliminate broken eggs. That manager may become a zed-defect person.

Zero-error mind-set: An abhorrence of defectives and determination to prevent them from occurring. This attitude is common to Japanese P/OM. It is not common among even the cognoscenti of P/OM in the Western world. "Cognoscenti" is a useful literary word (from Italian) for the people who are knowledgeable. Developing a zero-error mind-set requires culture-changing programs within the country, let alone the firm.

Zoning constraints: Technological factors exist that do not permit operations to be split between workstations. These physical restrictions can relate to the fact that a specific machine or human skill required is available at only one station, or that time is required for a chemical reaction, or a quality check at a single workstation. Although zoning is primarily a physical constraint, there are instances of psychological zoning. Often it is referred to as *territoriality*.

Company Index

Name Index

An italic *n* and number following a page number (e.g., 241*n*13) indicate information that appears in an end-of chapter note and the number of the note where the material can be found. A page number followed by an italic *n* with no note number (e.g., 241*n*) indicates an on-page note reference.

A

Abernathy, William J., 33, 182
Adams, M., 140, 276
Adler, Michael, 100*n*5
Ahmadi, Reza H., 737
Akao, Yoji, 140*n*9
Allen, Robinson, 463
Almeida, Virgilio A. F., 413
Anderson, David M., 414
Andrew, James P., 727
Angle, Colin, 862
Anupindi, Ravi, 66
Arcus, A. L., 738*n*5
Armstrong, J. Scott, 100
Arnold, Horace Lucien, 182
Arnold, J. R. Tony, 506
Ashby, W. Ross, 315
Atkeson, Christopher G., 887, 888*n*15
Attaran, M., 548
Axelrod, K., 28, 221

B

Babbage, Charles, 585–6
Baker, K. R., 640
Ball, W. W. R., 673*n*
Baloff, Nicholas, 414*n*9
Banham, Russ, 174
Barnes, Nick, 887
Barnes, Ralph M., 361
Barnett, Carole K., 836, 887
Baumol, William J., 66
Beaulieu, M., 404
Beckhard, R., 836
Bednarz, Ann, 876
Beer, Stafford, 315
Bentley, Charlotte, 351–3
Berenson, Alex, 888*n*7
Bernard, Shane K., 266
Berry, William L., 640
Bhame, C. D., 100
Birnie, D. P., 738*n*3
Birou, Laura M., 506, 598
Blackman, Sue Anne, 66, 67*n*7
Blackstone, John H., 67*n*1, 100*n*4, 182*n*1, 414, 598*n*1, 640, 641*n*3
Blasco, Sarah, xxvi
Blaxill, Mark, 724–5
Bodek, Norman, 174

Borel, Emile, 363
Bounds, G., 140, 276
Bowen, H. K., 404
Bowman, E. H., 548–9
Box, G. E. P., 100
Boyd, John R., 724–5
Bracco, Anthony, 305
Bracco, Charles, 305
Bracco, Frank, 303
Bracco, Sherril, 305
Bracco, Tracey, 305
Bramhall, D. F., 464
Brand, Stewart, 879
Bremer, Michael, 267, 276
Brett, Neil, 59
Bridges, William, 629, 888
Bridgman, Paul W., 463, 464*n*1
Brinkley, Douglas, 174
Briscoe, Dennis R., 361
Britton, Andrew, 66
Brooks, Rodney, 862
Brumberg, B., 28, 221
Buckman, Rebecca, 212–13
Buffa, Elwood S., 738*n*5
Burington, R. S., 317*n*
Burke, James, 794
Burke, R., 794
Burnham, John M., 463
Burt, D. N., 506
Buzacott, J. A., 640
Bylinsky, Gene, 888*n*2
Byrne, John A., 806, 837*n*5

C

Cahill, Gerry, 414
Caldwell, Philip, 173
Çapek, Karel, 887
Cappelli, Peter, 626, 629
Carr, D. K., 836, 837*n*21
Carson, Joseph, 212
Carter, Brent, 824
Carty, Don, 877
Cathy, S. Truett, 537–8
Cavanagh, Roland R., 140
Cedarleaf, Jay, 463
Certo, Sam, 361
Chae, H. An, 887–8
Champy, James, 836
Chapman, Stephen N., 506, 598

Chase, Richard B., 33, 182
Chow, W. M., 737
Christopher, Martin, 414
Clark, K. B., 33, 182
Clarke, Arthur C., 868
Clausing, Don, 140, 140*n*7
Cockcroft, Adrian, 414
Cockerell, Lee, 349
Cohen, Dan S., 837
Cohn, Robin, 876–7
Collins, Jim, 783, 843
Conway, Richard W., 687
Cooley, Denton, 160
Cooper, R. B., 737
Cooper, Robin, 361, 362*n*7
Corbett, Charles, 888
Correa, Henrique, xxv
Coupland, Douglas, 629
Cousteau, Jacques, 302
Cox, Jeff, 687
Crosby, Philip, 119, 122, 140, 140*n*5, 228
Crowden, D. J., 276
Crowell, Dave, 351–3
Cypress, Harold, 464

D

D'Aluisio, Faith, 888
Daniels, Lorraine, 267, 276
Dannenbring, David G., 738*n*8
Davies, R. L., 464
Da Vinci, Leonardo, 585
DeLurgio, S. A., 100
De Meyer, Arnoud, 836
Deming, W. Edwards, 126, 140, 140*n*10, 141, 173, 230, 352, 782
Deshmukh, Sudhakar D., 66
Deutschman, Alan, 806, 837*n*6
DiCamillo, Gary T., 787
Dickson, W. J., 361–2
Diesenhouse, Susan, 889*n*26
Digrius, Bonnie, 315
DiMasi, J. A., 888
Dobler, D. W., 506
Dodge, Harold F., 140, 276, 277*n*6
Donald, Jim, 587
Dougherty, K. S., 836–7
Douglas, Brinkley, 174*n*
Drucker, P., 100

Page numbers in italics identify illustrations. An italic *t* next to a page number (e.g., 241*t*) indicates information that appears in a table.

Ancient Saying...

When students are ready, teachers appear.